CASES AND MATERIALS ON
EMPLOYMENT DISCRIMINATION

ASPEN PUBLISHERS

CASES AND MATERIALS ON EMPLOYMENT DISCRIMINATION

Seventh Edition

MICHAEL J. ZIMMER
Professor of Law
Seton Hall University

CHARLES A. SULLIVAN
Professor of Law
Seton Hall University

REBECCA HANNER WHITE
Dean and
J. Alton Hosch Professor of Law
University of Georgia

AUSTIN   BOSTON   CHICAGO   NEW YORK   THE NETHERLANDS

Aspen Publishers
Attn: Permissions Department
76 Ninth Avenue, 7th Floor
New York, NY 10011-5201

To contact Customer Care, e-mail customer.care@aspenpublishers.com, call 1-800-234-1660, fax 1-800-901-9075, or mail correspondence to:

Aspen Publishers
Attn: Order Department
PO Box 990
Frederick, MD 21705

Printed in the United States of America.

1 2 3 4 5 6 7 8 9 0

ISBN 978-0-7355-7086-3

Library of Congress Cataloging-in-Publication Data

Cases and materials on employment discrimination / Michael J. Zimmer . . . [et al.]. — 7th ed.
   p.   cm.
   ISBN 0-7355-7086-8
   1. Discrimination in employment — Law and legislation — United States — Cases. I. Zimmer, Michael J.
KF3464.Z55 2008
344.7301'133 — dc22

2007051561

About Wolters Kluwer Law & Business

Wolters Kluwer Law & Business is a leading provider of research information and workflow solutions in key specialty areas. The strengths of the individual brands of Aspen Publishers, CCH, Kluwer Law International and Loislaw are aligned within Wolters Kluwer Law & Business to provide comprehensive, in-depth solutions and expert-authored content for the legal, professional and education markets.

CCH was founded in 1913 and has served more than four generations of business professionals and their clients. The CCH products in the Wolters Kluwer Law & Business group are highly regarded electronic and print resources for legal, securities, antitrust and trade regulation, government contracting, banking, pension, payroll, employment and labor, and healthcare reimbursement and compliance professionals.

Aspen Publishers is a leading information provider for attorneys, business professionals and law students. Written by preeminent authorities, Aspen products offer analytical and practical information in a range of specialty practice areas from securities law and intellectual property to mergers and acquisitions and pension/benefits. Aspen's trusted legal education resources provide professors and students with high-quality, up-to-date and effective resources for successful instruction and study in all areas of the law.

Kluwer Law International supplies the global business community with comprehensive English-language international legal information. Legal practitioners, corporate counsel and business executives around the world rely on the Kluwer Law International journals, loose-leafs, books and electronic products for authoritative information in many areas of international legal practice.

Loislaw is a premier provider of digitized legal content to small law firm practitioners of various specializations. Loislaw provides attorneys with the ability to quickly and efficiently find the necessary legal information they need, when and where they need it, by facilitating access to primary law as well as state-specific law, records, forms and treatises.

Wolters Kluwer Law & Business, a unit of Wolters Kluwer, is headquartered in New York and Riverwoods, Illinois. Wolters Kluwer is a leading multinational publisher and information services company.

To Margaret, Michael, and Lanier
M.J.Z.

To Leila, Meghan, Moira, the Marks,
and especially Jessica Leigh
C.A.S.

To Dan, Brendan, and Maren
R.H.W.

SUMMARY OF CONTENTS

CONTENTS

Chapter 2

Systemic Disparate Treatment Discrimination   115

Chapter 3

Systemic Disparate Impact Discrimination   207

Chapter 4

The Interrelation of the Three Theories of Discrimination — 293

Chapter 5

Special Problems in Applying Title VII, Section 1981, and the ADEA   317

Chapter 7

Procedures for Enforcing Antidiscrimination Laws   595

Chapter 8

Judicial Relief   653

Chapter 9

Managing Risks in Employment Discrimination Disputes   721

Chapter 10

The Policy Bases for Antidiscrimination Law   761

PREFACE

This Seventh Edition marks a dramatic change in this casebook, both in substance and in form. On the substantive side, the individual disparate treatment materials (now in Chapter 1) have been radically reordered to take into account both changes in the law and increasing social science scholarship on the nature of discrimination in the new millennium. While the changes in other chapters are less fundamental, every chapter has been reworked in significant ways. Most notable is the reconceptualization of the materials on sex discrimination in what is now Chapter 5 and the rewriting of the procedures material (now Chapter 7) to center on *Ledbetter v. Goodyear Tire & Rubber Co.* and *Dukes v. Wal-Mart*. Finally, we have added a chapter on risk management (Chapter 9) that brings together in a more coherent way materials that were scattered in prior editions.

With respect to form, the Seventh Edition reflects the return of this work to its original focus — as a casebook. Over the years, it has grown more treatise-like, and a number of our adopters have reported increasing difficulties in student engagement. Perhaps the most obvious change is size: the Sixth Edition had 1021 pages of text; this Seventh Edition only 787. It would be wrong to say that nothing has been lost in the translation, but we believe that the present effort is as sophisticated as prior editions while being far more accessible. Notes following cases are titled to provide more signposting for readers, and some material previously addressed more discursively through cases is now presented more efficiently in breakout notes. All notes have been revised and updated with an emphasis on newer cases. Despite the new format, we made a conscious (and we hope successful) effort to go beyond doctrine and retain the focus on both scholarship and practice that has always characterized our work.

The most obvious organizational changes in the Seventh Edition are the elimination or moving of the two chapters that formerly began the book. What used to be Chapter 1, Legal Approaches to the Employment Relation, has been eliminated entirely (but will appear in our Teacher's Manual with permission for adopters to reproduce it). Chapter 2, The Policy Bases for Antidiscrimination Law, has been shortened and moved to the end, where it is now Chapter 10. The remainder of the book is structured essentially as prior editions, but there is a new Chapter 9 that brings together the arbitration materials and materials on releasing antidiscrimination rights under the rubric of risk management.

Accordingly, the casebook cuts to the chase and begins with the three chapters analyzing each of the three basic theories of discrimination — individual disparate treatment, systemic disparate treatment, and disparate impact (Chapters 1, 2, and 3), followed by a chapter on the interrelation of those theories (Chapter 4). It then moves to "special problems" of discrimination law (Chapter 5), treating coverage, sex discriminaton, religion and national origin discrimination, retaliation, and age. In these five chapters, this edition continues the prior editions' merger of the treatment of the Age Discrimination in Employment Act and the Reconstruction Civil Rights Acts, primarily 42 U.S.C.A. §1981, into the Title VII discussion. Pedagogically, the casebook reflects the statutory and common law unification of discrimination analysis under all three statutes although remaining differences are noted in the relevant chapters or collected in Chapter 5 on "special problems.

As we have suggested, those who used the Sixth Edition will find substantial changes in these core chapters. Chapter 1, in particular, attempts to meld newer cases and scholarship to achieve a more sophisticated understanding of individual disparate treatment law. Needless to say, *Desert Palace* is highlighted, but the chapter also wrestles with new insights into *McDonnell Douglas*. The "adverse employment action" threshhold for suit is given renewed attention. While the systemic chapters (Chapters 2 and 3) will look familiar in structure, attention is given to new cases reviving systemic approaches and to the "new structuralism" scholarship. Chapter 4 focuses on new circuit cases which may (or may not) presage a shift in emphasis along new structuralism lines. Prior users will find Chapter 5 essentially the same in structure, with the exception of beginning the sex discrimination section with *Oncale* to focus on what constitutes "sex" under Title VII. But the chapter has been largely reworked with new principal cases in the sex, religion, national origin, and retaliation sections. The national origin material has been recast to focus on the current immigration debate by concentrating on the conflicting commands of Title VII and immigation law.

Perhaps needless to say, the ADA treatment in Chapter 6 has been revised to reflect the dramatic developments in the area. While there is no doubt that disability discrimination law is in decline, it remains an important and, for students, a confusing area. Further, there is reason to believe that, despite the lack of success of ADA claims in the courts, the statute continues to play an important role in counseling employers.

A new aspect of the Seventh Edition is our effort to draw students' attention to comparative and international materials. This field is of growing interest to employment discrimination, and we have endeavored to give the students some feeling of the approaches of other nations to the question. Our method has been to append breakout notes at the end of most of the chapters to provide an introduction to international and comparative law dealing with the problems discussed in that chapter.

Some professors who use this book have asked about coverage. None of the authors takes the same approach, and some of us vary depending on the semester. We all teach three-credit courses. While none of us tries to cover the entire book, all teach the four chapters that make up its core — Chapters 1 through 4. We also all teach most of Chapter 5 and believe that the gender and retaliation materials are essential to a comprehensive course in employment discrimination. Most of us also teach the rest of Chapter 5. We have all come increasingly to believe that Chapter 6, on the ADA, must be taught, although some of us omit more esoteric material in that chapter.

The choice of the remaining material is a matter of individual instructor preference. Chapter 10, on policy, could be taught at the beginning or the end of the course, or simply omitted on the theory that the themes there will emerge (if in a less structured fashion) from the course in any event. We have individual preferences as to Chapter 7, on procedures, Chapter 8, on remedies, and Chapter 9, on risk management.

As many of our users know, a website supports the teaching mission of the casebook. Our aim, which has been achieved within normal limits of scholarly procrastination, is to reflect recent developments no more than a month after they occur. We do not attempt to track every judicial, legislative, or administrative change since there are services that do that far better than we can. Rather, our goal is to identify the more important developments and key them to the casebook while providing a resource that faculty and student can both use in a variety of ways. The page, for example, tries to keep track of faculty websites, reproduce professors' past examinations, suggest teaching ideas and provide links to a variety of other resources. Please visit the website at http://law.shu.edu/discrimination/. The site contains a "contact" button, but we can also be reached at:

Michael J. Zimmer: zimmermi@shu.edu

Charles A. Sullivan: sullivch@shu.edu

Rebecca Hanner White: rhwhite@arches.uga.edu

A final word about our editing of excerpted material: All omissions are indicated by ellipses or brackets, except that citations (including parentheticals), footnotes, and internal cross-references are deleted with no indication. Footnotes in extract retain their original numbers, while those added by us are indicated by asterisks and daggers.

Michael J. Zimmer
Charles A. Sullivan
Rebecca Hanner White

January 2008

ACKNOWLEDGMENTS

We acknowledge the insights of the many teachers who have used the earlier editions of this work and have shared their thoughts with us. Our deepest debts are to our former co-authors, Richard F. Richards and Deborah A. Calloway. Dick was one of the original authors and continued on the book through the fifth edition. His mark continues to reverberate throughout this work. He is the master of remedies, blazed the trail when the ADA was first passed, and tried (often unsuccessfully) to control his co-authors' idiosyncracies. Deborah joined the team for the third, fourth and fifth editions. She brought new energy and insights that still profoundly influence core portions of this effort. We give both our heartfelt thanks.

Our colleagues over the years have also provided numerous useful insights. We thank especially Jake Barnes and Calvin Sharpe for reviewing portions of earlier editions of this book in order to steer us closer to the correct path. Our students have also been essential to keeping this work grounded and accessible even as the field of employment discrimination becomes increasingly complex and sophisticated. At Aspen (formerly Little, Brown), we owe a special debt to Carol McGeehan (who copyedited the first edition) and who has gently nudged us through subsequent editions in her present position as Development and Acquisition Editor of Law School Books.

Our research assistants have kept us honest and this book accurate, not to mention making the professors' lives easier in innumerable other ways. We thank the following (all of Seton Hall unless otherwise identified):

- Nathan Brown, Kaitlin Kennedy, Katherine Planer, and Tara Touloumis, class of 2009
- Christina Bae, Joseph Fanning, and Angela Kopolovich, '08
- Lauren DeWitt, '07, Wright Frank, Georgetown '07; Lindsay Leonard, Fordham '07; Merritt McAlister, Georgetown '07
- M. J. Blakely, Georgia, '06
- Lauren Walter, '05, Kira Fonteneau, Georgia, '05; Brendan Krasinzki, Georgia, '05
- Stefania DiTrolio, Sonia Middlebrooks, Mara Timourian and Dawn Woodruff, '04; Caroline Castle, Georgia, '04
- Jenny Kramer, and Amanda Dowd, '01
- Jonathan Green, Richard Kielbania, Chantal Kopp, and Shannon Philpott, '00
- Tara Schillari, '99;
- Kim Essaf, Jessica Lerner, Michael MacManus, Jason Marx and Colleen Walsh, '98;
- Victoria Melillo, '97;

- Jessica Stein and Thomas Crino, '96;
- Dena Epstein, Wendy Whitbeck, Claudine Leone, and Thomas Sarno, '95;
- Susan Farrell, '89;
- Rosanne Maraziti, Linda Biancardi, Nancy Johnson, and Julie Murray, '88;
- Laurie Fierro and Lorrie Van de Castle, '83.

To these must be added the dedicated support staff at Seton Hall, especially Latisha Porter-Vaughn, Jo Ann Maldonado, Gwen Davis, and Silvia Cardoso. Ana Santos, Seton Hall's Web Coordinator, deserves special menton for her work in creating and updating the webpage supporting this casebook. Finally, we thank Moira Sullivan for dedicated proofreading.

We gratefully acknowledge the permissions granted to reproduce the following materials:

Richard Delgado, *Words That Wound: A Tort Action for Racial Insults, Epithets, and Name Calling*, 17 HARV. CIV. RTS.-CIV. LIB. L. REV. 133 (1982). Copyright © 1982 The President and Fellows of Harvard College and the Harvard Civil Rights Civil Liberties Law Review.

John J. Donohue III, *Advocacy Versus Analysis in Assessing Employment Discrimination Law*, 44 STAN. L. REV. 1583 (1992). Copyright © 1992 by the Board of Trustees of the Leland Stanford Junior University. Reprinted by permission of Stanford Law Review and Fred B. Rothman and Company.

Jacob E. Gersen, *Markets and Discrimination*, 82 N.Y.U.L. REV. 689 (2007). Copyright © 2007 New York University Law Review. Reprinted by permission.

Michael C. Harper, *Age-Based Exit Incentives, Coercion, and the Prospective Waiver of ADEA Rights: The Failure of the Older Workers Benefit Protection Act*, 79 VA. L. REV. 1271 (1993). Copyright © 1993. Reprinted with permission of Virginia Law Review Association and Fred B. Rothman and Company.

Martin J. Katz, *Reclaiming* McDonnell Douglas, 83 NOTRE DAME L. REV. 109 (2007). Reprinted by permission. © Notre Dame Law Review, University of Notre Dame. We bear responsibility for any errors in reprinting or editing.

Douglas Laycock, *Statistical Proof and Theories of Discrimination*, 49 LAW & CONTEMP. PROBS. 97, 98-99 (Autumn 1986). Copyright © 1986, Duke University School of Law.

L. THUROW, THE ZERO SUM SOCIETY: DISTRIBUTION AND POSSIBILITIES FOR ECONOMIC CHANGE 184-187 (1980). Copyright © 1980 by Basic Books, Inc. Reprinted by permission of Basic Books, a division of Harper Collins Publishers, Inc.

PATRICIA J. WILLIAMS, THE ALCHEMY OF RACE AND RIGHTS 44-49 (1991). Reprinted by permission of the publishers from PATRICIA J. WILLIAMS, THE ALCHEMY OF RACE AND RIGHTS: DIARY OF A LAW PROFESSOR (Cambridge, MA: Harvard University Press). Copyright © 1991 by the President and Fellows of Harvard College.

NOTE TO STUDENTS

A. What You'll Be Studying

This book is devoted to employment discrimination, one of the most important areas of legal regulation of the rights and responsibilities of employers and employees. This course is concerned with the question of "discrimination" in employment and is, therefore, limited to legal doctrines that fall within the definition of that term. Indeed, much of this book is devoted to the twin questions of how "discrimination" should be defined and how it is proven in the litigation context. As you will see, employment discrimination, on both the social and the legal levels, is a complex and controversial problem, affecting the rights of all workers in one way or another.

But however important the topic of employment discrimination, it is only a subset of the more general problem of legal regulation of the employment relationship. As you will learn, "employment discrimination" is usually limited to discrimination against employees on the basis of statutorily defined characteristics. These characteristics may be immutable — such as race, gender, age, or national origin — or subject to change — such as religion, alienage, or marital status — or of either kind — such as disability discrimination, which includes mental and physical disabilities without regard to their causes.

While these categories are the traditional domain of the law of employment discrimination, employers routinely "discriminate" (perhaps we should use the word "differentiate") among employees or applicants in ways that have nothing to do with race, gender, age, or any of the other reasons prohibited by discrimination statutes. Further, employers may base their actions on rational reasons (hiring the best-qualified applicant); questionable reasons (promoting the daughter of an important customer over a better worker who lacks such "connections"); reasons that are eccentric but not necessarily legally wrong (choosing employees on the basis of astrological sign); or socially and morally unacceptable reasons (firing a "whistleblower" whose conduct had saved human lives).

The ultimate question, of course, is what, if any, limitations the law should place on the employer's power to deal with employees. The antidiscrimination laws reflect one societal answer, but the broader question is taken up in courses titled "Employment Law" or "Individual Employment Rights." *See generally* TIMOTHY P. GLYNN, RACHEL ARNOW-RICHMAN & CHARLES A. SULLIVAN, EMPLOYMENT LAW: PRIVATE ORDERING AND ITS LIMITATIONS; MARK A. ROTHSTEIN, CHARLES B. CRAVER, ELINOR P. SCHROEDER & ELAINE W. SHOBEN, EMPLOYMENT LAW (3d ed 2005). It is also treated, albeit somewhat obliquely, in labor law.

As a discipline, employment law is a sprawling area that begins with a core commitment to private ordering through contracts. In employment, as in other areas of contract law, policing the fairness of bargains is the exception, rather than the rule. Contract law purported to implement this approach to employment by adopting a general rule that prevailed in the United States for nearly a century: absent an express written contract for a specified term, the relationship between an employer and its employees was "at will." One court explained the rule and its rationale: "Generally speaking, a contract for permanent employment, for life employment, or for other terms purporting permanent employment, where the employee furnishes no consideration additional to the services incident to the employment, amounts to an indefinite general hiring terminable at the will of either party, and a discharge without cause does not constitute a breach of such contract justifying recovery of damages." *Forrer v. Sears, Roebuck & Co.*, 153 N.W.2d 587, 589 (Wis. 1967). While framed neutrally, in the sense that either party can terminate the relationship without liability to the other, the at-will doctrine in practice meant that the employer could discharge an employee "for good reason, bad reason, or no reason at all."

Because contract law provided few rights for most workers, numerous legislative interventions were designed to address deficiencies, or perceived deficiencies, of the at-will regime. The antidiscrimination statutes are a prime example, but employment law treats a huge variety of other interventions of greater or lesser legal and practical significance. On the federal level, these include:

- Leave policies: the Family and Medical Leave Act (FMLA)
- Wage and hour laws: the Fair Labor Standards Act (FLSA), 29 U.S.C. §§ 201 et seq. (2007)
- Workplace safety: the Occupational Safety and Health Act (OSHA), 29 U.S.C. § 651 et seq.
- Pension and fringe benefits: the Employee Retirement Income Security Act (ERISA), 29 U.S.C. §§ 1002 et seq. (2007)
- Privacy protection: the Employee Polygraph Protection Act (EPPA), 29 U.S.C. § 2002 (2007)
- Layoff: the Workers Adjustment and Retraining Notification Act (WARN), 29 U.S.C. § 2101 et seq.
- Whistleblower protection: Sarbanes-Oxley, 18 U.S.C.S. § 1514A (2007)

These statutes vary greatly in terms of their protection and coverage. For example, EPPA covers essentially all private-sector employers in the United States, but WARN reaches only larger employers conducting "mass layoffs." Most federal statutes have state analogs, some of which provide substantially more employee rights than do their federal counterparts. Further, some areas of employment law, such as workers' compensation, are primarily state regimes, and, of course, state tort law provides limited but important protections, most notably the "public policy tort," which has been reinforced by broad "whistleblowing" statutes in a few states. *E.g.*, N.J. Conscientious Employee Protection Act, N.J. Stat. Ann. §§ 34:191 et seq. Finally, some groups of employees have their own sources of protection — public-sector workers have constitutional rights, and civil servants and public school and college and university teachers have tenure systems.

A third group of workers with special protection consists of unionized workers under collective bargaining agreements. This regime is studied as labor law, which deals with unionization and collective bargaining. The core notion is that employees gain countervailing power vis-à-vis their employers by organizing and then bargaining collectively with their employers. While the origins of the union movement reach back well before the nineteenth century, unions did not become legal, and respectable, until relatively recently. During the Great Depression, the federal government adopted what is now known as the National Labor Relations Act (NLRA), 29 U.S.C.S. §§151 et seq. (2007), which encourages unions by declaring it an unfair labor practice for employers to discriminate against workers seeking to unionize and by requiring the employer to bargain with unions that succeed in organizing that employer's workforce. *See generally* PATRICK HARDIN ED., THE DEVELOPING LABOR LAW: THE BOARD, THE COURTS, AND THE NATIONAL LABOR RELATIONS ACT (4th ed. 2002). While wages and hours are a prime area of concern, most unions also ensure job security for workers through seniority systems and requiring just cause for discharge. This legal regime, however, scarcely proved a panacea. While many unions succeeded in raising wages, improving working conditions, and providing increased job security for those they represented, large segments of the American workforce remained unorganized. By the turn of the 21st century, the proportion of the organized workforce had shrunk to less than that when the NLRA was passed, reaching about 8.5 percent of the private workforce in 2002 (Bureau of Labor Statistics *News*, USDL 03-88, February 25, 2003). Unions are, however, stronger in the public sector.

One of the ironies of employment law and employment discrimination is that the very definition of employer and employee draws on doctrines invented for a different purpose altogether — whether an employer was liable for the torts committed by its employees (or, as it would have more typically been phrased, whether a master was liable for the torts of his servants). The answer to this question at common law was found in the law of agency and depended on whether the tortfeasor was a servant (or employee) as opposed to an "independent contractor." If the principal had sufficient "control" over the work of the agent, it was liable for the agent's torts. The principal was then called a master or an employer, and the agent became a servant or an employee. If the degree of control was insufficient, the agent was labeled an "independent contractor," and the principal was not liable for his torts.

B. The Organization of This Book

Antidiscrimination statutes have spawned complex legal theories defining discrimination and the methods used to prove it. Although the basic prohibitions enjoy broad support, the development of theories of proof and the enactment of statutory reforms expanding employer duties have generated considerable social controversy. Affirmative action, sexual harassment, discrimination on the basis of sexual orientation, and disparate impact liability are just a few of the issues that have tested the limits of discrimination theory.

This casebook undertakes a complete consideration of the federal antidiscrimination laws.

The enactment of Title VII as part of the Civil Rights Act of 1964 marked a legal watershed. Although the statute had state and federal precursors, they had proved insufficient to deal with the problem of employment discrimination. Title VII marked the first comprehensive national attack on the problem of employment discrimination.

In the wake of Title VII, a number of developments expanded the federal courts' involvement with employment problems. First, Congress passed additional statutes, most notably the Age Discrimination in Employment Act of 1967 (ADEA), prohibiting discrimination against older workers, and the Americans with

Disabilities Act of 1990 (ADA), barring discrimination against individuals with disabilities. Second, the Supreme Court resuscitated civil rights statutes passed during the Reconstruction era following the Civil War. Sections 1981 and 1983 of Title 42 of the United States Code were among the laws passed to protect the newly freed slaves in the South by implementing the Thirteenth, Fourteenth, and Fifteenth Amendments. Although these statutes had been eviscerated by the Supreme Court in the years shortly after their enactment, the Warren Court revived the early statutes, creating a wide range of statutory tools to deal with employment discrimination. While the Supreme Court thereafter restricted both the modern civil rights laws and their Reconstruction era predecessors, Congress has reacted strongly on a number of occasions to restore the effectiveness of the antidiscrimination statutes. Most notably, the Pregnancy Discrimination Act in 1978 defined pregnancy discrimination as sex discrimination after the Supreme Court had held the contrary, and the Civil Rights Act of 1991 reversed or substantially modified a number of Supreme Court decisions limiting the effectiveness of Title VII and § 1981.

This book considers all of these legislative and judicial efforts to address discrimination in employment, and it approaches the question through the lens of the three theories of liability the courts have developed — individual disparate treatment, systemic disparate treatment, and disparate impact. Some have questioned whether these understandings of discrimination adequately capture the underlying phenomenon, but they are obviously the place to start. To complicate matters, they apply somewhat differently across the four major statutes we will study — Title VII, the ADEA, 42 U.S.C. § 1981, and the ADA.

Chapter 1 takes up the most basic concept, intentional discrimination against particular applicants or employees — individual disparate treatment discrimination. Chapter 2 then extends the intentional discrimination concept to broader patterns of such practices — systemic disparate treatment. Chapter 3 considers an alternative test of discrimination, disparate impact. Then Chapter 4 attempts to synthesize the approaches previously developed into a coherent theory of discrimination. Chapter 5 takes up special problems that arise when antidiscrimination law is applied to such issues as pregnancy, sexual harassment, sexual orientation, religion, national origin, age, and retaliation.

In Chapter 6, the casebook turns to a statute that approaches the question of discrimination somewhat differently. The Americans with Disabilities Act borrows discrimination concepts from the earlier statutes but applies them in unique ways to a form of discrimination that is itself very different from those studied previously.

Chapters 7 and 8 then turn to important but second-order questions that have arisen under the antidiscrimination statutes. Thus, Chapter 7 considers procedures focusing primarily on Title VII, which is the procedural paradigm for both the ADEA and the ADA. Chapter 8 then analyzes the remedies available to redress violations of all the statutes addressed in this book.

The remaining two chapters take a somewhat different tack. The centrality of the antidiscrimination statutes to employment in the United States has led to a number of "risk management" strategies by employers, and Chapter 9 undertakes a study of a few of the most important of these — the use of arbitration as an alternative to litigation to resolve discrimination disputes and the settlement and release of potential claims.

Finally, as a coda to the book, we explore the underlying policy justifications for the statutes in Chapter 10 and speculate as to the usefulness and limitations of the antidiscrimination project at this stage in our history.

Chapter 1

Individual Disparate Treatment Discrimination

A. INTRODUCTION

In order to address the pervasive problems of employment discrimination, Congress enacted a series of statutes that deal with various aspects of the phenomenon. These laws include Title VII of the Civil Rights Act of 1964; the Civil War Reconstruction statutes, especially 42 U.S.C. §1981; the Age Discrimination in Employment Act of 1967 (ADEA); the Rehabilitation Act of 1973; and the Americans with Disabilities Act of 1990 (ADA).

The avenues of relief under the statutes differ from each other in important ways, but all are concerned with discrimination in employment. It is "discrimination" that provides the unifying theme for this casebook. That concept, however, has been developed by the courts in ways that are not always intuitively obvious. Indeed, "discrimination" is now a term of art that embraces several different theories, each with its own distinctive application.

In broad terms, three statutes adopt a unitary definition of what has been called "disparate treatment" discrimination. The term originated in cases decided under Title VII of the Civil Rights Act of 1964 and has been applied essentially unchanged in both ADEA cases and suits brought under §1981. Disparate treatment, however, has developed in two distinct ways. Individual disparate treatment is the focus of this chapter, while systemic disparate treatment is taken up in Chapter 2. In addition, Title VII jurisprudence has developed the theory of disparate impact discrimination, which is available only in a considerably diluted form under the ADEA and not available at all under §1981. The Americans with Disabilities Act, 42 U.S.C. §12101 et seq (2007), prohibits individual and systemic discrimination and also bars practices with a disparate impact; however, as developed in Chapter 6, the ADA is distinctive in many ways from the other antidiscrimination statutes.

B.   THE ELEMENTS OF AN INDIVIDUAL DISPARATE TREATMENT CASE

There are three basic elements to individual disparate treatment discrimination: (1) The employer intended to discriminate, that is, it intended to treat an individual differently than others because of her race, sex, or other prohibited ground; (2) the employer took an action that had an adverse effect on the individual's employment; and (3) the employer's action was linked to its intent to discriminate.

1.   Intent to Discriminate

In *Teamsters v. United States*, 431 U.S. 324, 335, n. 15 (1977), the seminal systemic disparate treatment case, the Court laid out a definition of disparate treatment discrimination and distinguished it from another theory of discrimination, disparate impact:

> "Disparate treatment" . . . is the most easily understood type of discrimination. The employer simply treats some people less favorably than others because of their race, religion, sex, or national origin. Proof of discriminatory motive is critical, although it can in most situations be inferred from the mere fact of differences in treatment. . . . Undoubtedly disparate treatment was the most obvious evil Congress had in mind when it enacted Title VII. . . . Claims of disparate treatment may be distinguished from claims that stress "disparate impact." The latter involve employment practices that are facially neutral in their treatment of different groups but that in fact fall more harshly on one group than another and cannot be justified by business necessity. Proof of discriminatory motive . . . is not required under a disparate-impact theory. . . . Either theory may, of course, be applied to a particular set of facts.

This definition is enigmatic because the first sentence, describing unequal treatment as discrimination, seems in tension with the second sentence requiring proof of discriminatory motive. The last clause of the second sentence — that unequal treatment is the basis for drawing the inference of intent to discriminate — suggests that unequal treatment and intent often coincide, but the "sometimes" suggests that they are not the same. Certainly, there may be unequal treatment without the requisite intent. And, of course, this passage from *Teamsters* doesn't tell us what "discriminatory motive" means, which is the core question for all the antidiscrimination statutes.

SLACK v. HAVENS
7 FEP 885 (S.D. Cal. 1973), *aff'd as modified*, 522 F.2d 1091 (9th Cir. 1975)

THOMPSON, J.: This action is brought by the plaintiffs, four black women, who allege they were discriminatorily discharged, due to their race, in violation of the Civil Rights Act of 1964, specifically 42 U.S.C. §2000e-2(a)(1). . . .

4. On January 31, 1968, plaintiffs Berrel Matthews, Emily Hampton and Isabell Slack were working in the bonding and coating department of defendant Industries' plant, engaged in preparing and assembling certain tubing components for defendant's product. A white co-worker, Sharon Murphy, was also assigned to the bonding and coating department on that day and was performing the same general work as the three plaintiffs mentioned above. The fourth plaintiff, Kathleen Hale, was working in another department on January 31st.

Near the end of the working day, plaintiffs Matthews, Hampton and Slack were called together by their immediate supervisor, Ray Pohasky, and informed that the following morning, upon reporting to work, they would suspend regular production and engage in a general cleanup of the bonding and coating department. The cleanup was to consist of washing walls and windows whose sills were approximately 12 to 15 feet above the floor, cleaning light fixtures, and scraping the floor which was caked with deposits of hardened resin. Plaintiffs Matthews, Hampton and Slack protested the assigned work, arguing that it was not within their job description, which included only light cleanup in their immediate work areas, and that it was too hard and dangerous. Mr. Pohasky agreed that it was hard work and said that he would check to see if they had to do it.

5. On the following work day, February 1, 1968, plaintiffs Matthews, Hampton, and Slack reported to the bonding and coating department along with Sharon Murphy, their white co-worker. However, Mr. Pohasky excused Sharon Murphy to another department for the day, calling in plaintiff Kathleen Hale from the winding department where she had been on loan from the bonding and coating department for about a week. Mr. Pohasky then repeated his announcement that the heavy cleaning would have to be done. The four plaintiffs joined in protest against the heavy cleanup work. They pointed out that they had not been hired to do janitorial type work, and one of the plaintiffs inquired as to why Sharon Murphy had been excused from the cleanup detail even though she had very little seniority among the ladies in the bonding and coating department. In reply, they were told by Mr. Pohasky that they would do the work, "or else." There was uncontradicted testimony that at sometime during their conversation Pohasky injected the statement that "Colored people should stay in their places," or words to that effect. Some further discussion took place between plaintiffs and Pohasky and then with Gary Helming, plaintiffs' general supervisor, but eventually each of the plaintiffs was taken to the office of Mr. Helming where she was given her final paycheck and fired. Plaintiff Matthews testified without contradiction that on the way to Mr. Helming's office Mr. Pohasky made the comment that "Colored folks are hired to clean because they clean better."

6. The general cleanup work was later performed by newly-hired male employees. Sharon Murphy was never asked to participate in this cleanup before or after the plaintiffs' termination.

7. The day following the plaintiffs' firing a conference was held between plaintiffs and defendant Glenn G. Havens, together with Mr. Helming, Mr. Pohasky and other company officials, but the dispute was not resolved as to the work plaintiffs were expected to do. Apparently, the plaintiffs were offered reinstatement if they would now agree to do the same cleanup work. They refused. . . .

B. Having concluded that defendant Industries is an "employer" under Title VII of the Civil Rights Act for the purposes of this action, we must next consider whether plaintiffs' termination amounted to unlawful discrimination against them because of their race. Defendants deny that the facts support such a conclusion, contending that plaintiffs' case amounts to nothing more than a dispute as to their job classification.

Admittedly, the majority of the discussion between plaintiffs and Industries' management on January 31 and February 1, 1968 centered around the nature of the duties which plaintiffs were ordered to perform. Plaintiffs pointed out that they had not been hired with the understanding that they would be expected to perform more than light cleanup work immediately adjacent to their work stations. They were met with an ultimatum that they do the work — or else. Additionally, no explanation was offered as to why Sharon Murphy, a white co-worker, had been transferred out of the bonding and coating department the morning that the heavy cleaning was to begin there, while plaintiff Hale was called back from the winding department, where she had been working, to the bonding and coating area, specifically for participation in the general cleanup. It is not disputed that Sharon Murphy had less seniority than all of the plaintiffs except plaintiff Hale (having been hired 8 days prior to plaintiff Hale) and no evidence of a bona fide business reason was ever educed by defendants as to why Sharon Murphy was excused from assisting the plaintiffs in the proposed cleaning project.

The only evidence that did surface at the trial regarding the motives for the decisions of the management of defendant Industries consisted of certain statements by supervisor Pohasky, who commented to plaintiff Matthews that "colored folks were hired to clean because they clean better," and "colored folks should stay in their place," or words to that effect. Defendants attempt to disown these statements with the argument that Pohasky's state of mind and arguably discriminatory conduct was immaterial and not causative of the plaintiffs' discharge.

But defendants cannot be allowed to divorce Mr. Pohasky's conduct from that of Industries so easily. First of all, 42 U.S.C. §2000e(b) expressly includes "any agent" of an employer within the definition of "employer." Secondly, there was a definite causal relation between Pohasky's apparently discriminatory conduct and the firings. Had Pohasky not discriminated against the plaintiffs by demanding they perform work he would not require of a white female employee, they would not have been faced with the unreasonable choice of having to choose between obeying his discriminatory work order and the loss of their employment. Finally, by backing up Pohasky's ultimatum the top level management of Industries ratified his discriminatory conduct and must be held liable for the consequences thereof. . . .

From all the evidence before it, this Court is compelled to find that defendant Industries, through its managers and supervisor, Mr. Pohasky, meant to require the plaintiffs to perform the admittedly heavy and possibly dangerous work of cleaning the bonding and coating department, when they would not require the same work from plaintiffs' white fellow employee. Furthermore, it meant to enforce that decision by firing the plaintiffs when they refused to perform that work. The consequence of the above was racial discrimination whatever the motivation of the management of defendant Industries may have been. Therefore, the totality of Industries' conduct amounted, in the Court's opinion, to an unlawful employment practice prohibited by the Civil Rights Act, specifically, 42 U.S.C. §2000e-2(a)(1).

NOTES

1. *At-Will Rule Modified.* The traditional common law rule of employment is that any contract not for a definite time is terminable at-will by either party — for any reason or for no reason, for good reason or for bad reason. *Slack v. Havens* clearly changes this. At the least, some "bad" reasons may not be the basis of adverse

employment actions; these include discrimination on prohibited grounds, which is the subject of this course, and causes of action like the public policy tort, which are addressed in courses in Employment Law. *See generally* TIMOTHY GLYNN, RACHEL ARNOW-RICHMAN, CHARLES A. SULLIVAN, EMPLOYMENT LAW: PRIVATE ORDERING AND ITS LIMITATIONS (Aspen 2007).

2. *The Statutory Language.* The core prohibitions of Title VII are found in §703(a), which declares it an "unlawful employment practice" for an employer —

> (1) to fail or refuse to hire or to discharge any individual, or otherwise to discriminate against any individual with respect to his compensation, terms, conditions, or privileges of employment, because of such individual's race, color, religion, sex, or national origin; or
> (2) to limit, segregate, or classify his employees or applicants for employment in any way which would deprive or tend to deprive any individual of employment opportunities or otherwise adversely affect his status as an employee, because of such individual's race, color, religion, sex, or national origin.

42 U.S.C. §2000e-2(a). Succeeding paragraphs have similar prohibitions for labor unions, and employment agencies, but employers have always been the central focus of the statute.

3. *Is Unequal Treatment Enough?* The four African American plaintiffs in *Slack* were treated differently than Sharon Murphy, a white worker. But unequal treatment, in and of itself, is not a statutory violation. The unequal treatment by Pohasky has to have been "because of" the plaintiffs' race. Such unequal treatment is evidence that the assignment was made *because of* race, but is it enough evidence? Would there be sufficient evidence in the case without the statements of Pohasky — that "colored folks are hired to clean because they clean better" — to support a fact finding that the cleaning assignment was made to plaintiffs because they were African Americans? What evidence supports the conclusion of race discrimination? Suppose you represented the defendant in *Slack*. What evidence might you look for when faced with this claim of unequal treatment; specifically, what information would you look for with respect to Sharon Murphy?

4. *Pohasky's Statements.* Whether or not the mere difference in treatment is sufficient to find causation, Pohasky's words obviously make drawing the causation conclusion easier. He essentially admitted assigning plaintiffs to the cleaning work because they were "colored." And it's pretty easy to view his views as pejorative. Even though he suggested that African Americans make better cleaners, the obvious negative implication is that they can only do menial jobs like cleaning. Given the history of assigning racial minorities to such jobs, Pohasky's views can be seen as part of a sad history of racial subordination. But does it matter whether he thought blacks inferior or superior in their ability to clean? So long as he was treating individuals unequally because of race, there would be a violation of §703(a). This distinction may not seem so important in *Slack* itself, but we will encounter cases where there is unequal treatment for more justifiable reasons. Nonetheless, the law generally treats acting on the intent to treat individuals differently on racial grounds as impermissible, regardless of whether the motive is malign, benign, or neutral.

5. *Admissions.* From an evidentiary standpoint, Pohasky was an agent of the employer acting within the scope of his agency in assigning the workers. For that reason, Havens Industry is liable for his discrimination, even if the company is otherwise not discriminatory. But Pohasky's agency has another effect: he was not only acting

within the scope of his agency in assigning the plaintiffs but he was also speaking within the scope of his agency in explaining the reason for the assignment. Such statements as "Colored folks are hired to clean because they clean better," therefore, could be introduced into evidence against the employer despite the hearsay rule and regardless of their "truth." As a practical matter, statements as unambiguous as this will almost always establish the key element in a discrimination case — that Pohasky assigned the cleaning to the plaintiffs because of their race. Suppose, however, that Pohasky had said the same words but did so a month earlier. The statements would still be admissible and still be strong evidence that his actions were influenced by his views on race, but the time difference would lessen the probability that the challenged decision was made on this ground. In other words, the statement would be admissible, but its probative force might be weakened. At what point does the probative value become so low that a reasonable jury could not find for plaintiff?

6. *Acting on Stereotypes.* Pohasky's statements reflect the phenomenon of stereotyping individual members of a group because of the characteristics (or the perceived characteristics) of the group as a whole. Obviously, stereotyping is a key problem in the employment area because much discrimination stems from employer perceptions about the abilities of various groups (racial, ethnic, or gender) in society. Stereotypes are, in a sense, just generalizations, and generalizations can be accurate or inaccurate. To the extent that an employer acts against an individual on a generalization regarding a race or gender, without pausing to consider whether that generalization is true of the individual in question, there is likely to be a violation of Title VII.

But stereotypes differ from other kinds of generalizations in that they may operate below the level of cognition; that is, the individual decision-maker may be acting without being aware of why he or she is doing so. Professor Linda Hamilton Krieger, *The Content of Our Categories: A Cognitive Bias Approach to Discrimination and Equal Employment Opportunity*, 47 STAN. L. REV. 1161 (1995), used the insights from cognitive psychology to conclude that stereotyping by race and gender is an "unintended consequence" of the necessity for humans to categorize their sensory perceptions in order to make any sense of the world:

> [The] central premise of social cognition theory [is] that cognitive structures and processes involved in categorization and information processing can in and of themselves result in stereotyping and other forms of biased intergroup judgment previously attributed to motivational processes. The social cognition approach to discrimination comprises three claims relevant to our present inquiry. The first is that stereotyping . . . is nothing special. It is simply a form of categorization [of our sensory perceptions], similar in structure and function to the categorization of natural objects. According to this view, stereotypes, like other categorical structures, are cognitive mechanisms that all people, not just "prejudiced" ones, use to simplify the task of perceiving, processing, and retaining information about people in memory. They are central, and indeed essential to normal cognitive functioning.
>
>   The second claim posited in social cognition theory is that, once in place, stereotypes bias intergroup judgment and decisionmaking. . . . [T]hey function as implicit theories, biasing in predictable ways the perception, interpretation, encoding, retention, and recall of information about other people. These biases are cognitive rather than motivational. They operate absent intent to favor or disfavor members of a particular social group. And, perhaps most significant for present purposes, they bias a decisionmaker's judgment long before the "moment of decision" [when the employment decision in question is made], as a decisionmaker attends to relevant data and interprets, encodes, stores, and retrieves it from memory. These biases "sneak up on" the

decisionmaker, distorting bit by bit the data upon which his decision is eventually based.

The third claim follows from the second. Stereotypes, when they function as implicit prototypes or schemas [by which we evaluate each other], operate beyond the reach of decisionmaker self-awareness. Empirical evidence indicates that people's access to their own cognitive processes is in fact poor. Accordingly, cognitive bias may well be both unintentional and unconscious.

Id. at 1187-88. The phenomenon that Professor Krieger identified has a number of labels, including "unconscious discrimination," "subtle discrimination," "cognitive bias," and others.

7. *The Extent of the Phenomenon.* No one seems to doubt that cognitive bias exists, but there is substantial debate about how pervasive it is and the extent to which it affects real-world decisionmaking. The most dramatic evidence is found in the Implicit Association Test (IAT), hosted at Harvard and available on the Internet. You might visit it to test your own cognitive structures. Project Implicit, https://implicit.harvard.edu/implicit. There is a large social science literature analyzing the results of literally hundreds of thousands of visits. *E.g.,* Brian A. Nosek, *Harvesting Implicit Group Attitudes and Beliefs from a Demonstration Web Site,* 6 GROUP DYNAMICS 101, 101-02 (2002) (reporting results from some 600,000 tests that confirm a much larger implicit preference among whites for whites than their explicit preferences).

Even assuming the IAT accurately identifies discriminatory attitudes, however, proof that individuals have certain attitudes is not necessarily proof that real-world decisions are influenced by them. For that, it is important to link "laboratory" proof such as the IAT to field experiments such as those reported in Marianne Bertrand & Sendhil Mullainathan, *Are Emily and Greg More Employable than Lakisha and Jamal? A Field Experiment on Labor Market Discrimination,* 94 AM. ECON. REV. 991 (2004) (reporting that, when identical resumes were sent to employers, those receiving more favorable treatment were those containing non-African American sounding names). *See also* Nilanjana Dasgupta, *Implicit Ingroup Favoritism, Outgroup Favoritism, and Their Behavioral Manifestations,* 17 SOC. JUST. RES. 143 (2004) (collecting research showing biased behavior in employment situations). Another example is the recent dispute over whether race is influencing refereeing at NBA games. *See* Joseph Price & Justin Wolfers, *Racial Discrimination Among NBA Referees,* http://ssrn.com (a paper by two researchers, who studied 13 seasons of N.B.A. games and 600,000 fouls, concluded both that white referees called fouls at a greater rate against black players than against white players and that there was a corresponding, although lower, bias for black officials and white players).

The use of the IAT to infer race discrimination in a wide range of workplaces has been challenged. *See* Gregory Mitchell & Philip E. Tetlock., *Antidiscrimination Law and the Perils of Mindreading,* 67 OHIO ST. L.J. 1023, 1023 (2006). The authors argue that

implicit prejudice research should be accepted as neither legislative authority nor litigation evidence until there is more: (1) rigorous investigation of the error rates of the new implicit measures of prejudice and of how investigators balance Type I errors of false accusations against Type II errors of failing to identify prejudice; (2) thorough analysis of how well implicit measures of prejudice predict discriminatory behavior under realistic workplace conditions; (3) open debate about the societal consequences of setting thresholds of proof for calling people prejudiced so low that the vast majority of the population qualifies as prejudiced.

But see Samuel R. Bagenstos, *Implicit Bias, Science, and Antidiscrimination Law,* HARV. L. & POL'Y REV. (forthcoming) (criticizing Mitchell & Tetlock because "to say that the concept of implicit bias lacks validity because implicit bias does not correlate empirically with explicit prejudice is therefore to assume the very conclusion that implicit bias scholars seek to disprove — that any "real" bias must be consistent with expressed attitudes").

8. *Is "Unconscious Discrimination" an Oxymoron?* Acting on the basis of stereotypes, as opposed to animus-driven conduct, can clearly violate Title VII. *Price Waterhouse v. Hopkins,* 490 U.S. 228, 251 (1989) ("we are beyond the day when an employer could evaluate employees by assuming or insisting that they matched the stereotype associated with their group, for '[i]n forbidding employers to discriminate against individuals because of their sex, Congress intended to strike at the entire spectrum of disparate treatment of men and women resulting from sex stereotypes.'") (internal quotes omitted). *See also Hazen Paper Co.* v. *Biggins,* 507 U.S. 604 (1993) (acting on the basis of the stereotype that "productivity and competence decline with old age" is "the very essence of age discrimination"). *See generally* Mary F. Radford, *Sex Stereotyping and the Promotion of Women to Positions of Power,* 41 HASTINGS L.J. 471 (1990).

Nevertheless, the opinions decrying stereotyping have involved more conscious decision-making than the implicit bias literature probes. The question then arises: *does intentional discrimination require a conscious intent to discriminate,* or is it enough to find that the plaintiff's protected class status caused the decision to occur? If a supervisor honestly believed he was acting for a nondiscriminatory reason, even if his unconscious biases in fact influenced his decision, is there liability?

This debate played out two decades ago in the constitutional law area on the issue of whether racial intent should be the basis for strict scrutiny, *e.g.,* Charles R. Lawrence III, *The Id, the Ego, and Equal Protection: Reckoning with Unconscious Racism,* 39 STAN. L. REV. 317 (1987), Barbara Flagg, *"Was Blind, But Now I See": White Race Consciousness and the Requirement of Discriminatory Intent,* 91 MICH. L. REV. 953 (1993), but, in the wake of research such as Professor Kreiger's article and the IAT, has now surfaced again with respect to what level of consciousness should be required before unequal treatment can be categorized as discriminatory under the federal statutes.

Professor Amy Wax, in *Discrimination as Accident,* 74 IND. L.J. 1129 (1999), agrees with Krieger that much discrimination may be unconscious disparate treatment, which she describes as a kind of industrial accident. She then both questions whether current law reaches this phenomenon and whether it should. Because, by definition, such discrimination is not conscious, employer efforts to reduce it will likely be unavailing, according to Wax. She further "predicts that liability for unconscious discrimination will be inefficient and will fail to compensate victims accurately." *Id.* at 1226. While not advocating an amendment to Title VII to establish that only conscious bias violates the statute, she clearly is opposed to any of the more dramatic efforts to expand Title VII liability in order to reach "discrimination as accident." *Contra* Michael Selmi *Discrimination as Accident: Old Whine, New Bottle,* 74 IND. L.J. 1234 (1999). *See also* Sheila Foster, *Causation in Antidiscrimination Law: Beyond Intent versus Impact,* 41 HOUSTON L. REV. 1469 (2005); David Benjamin Oppenheimer, *Negligent Discrimination,* 141 U. PA. L. REV. 899 (1993).

9. *Debiasing.* There are two thrusts to the work of such scholars as Professor Wax. One is normative: even if implicit bias has consequences akin to those of more conscious bias, making it actionable is problematic normatively since the law usually requires more conscious decision-making as a basis for imposing liability. A second

thrust is more pragmatic: if implicit bias is as pervasive and deep-seated as some believe, there is little that can be done about it. The two themes come together: employers should not be held liable for that which they cannot avoid or can avoid only at great cost.

A response to this argument is the emerging "debiasing" literature, which suggests that, however pervasive implicit bias may be, it is subject to change by employers who are incentivized to do so. Professor Christine Jolls, in *Is there a Glass Ceiling?*, 25 HARV. WOMEN'S L.J. 1, 3-4 (2002), describes how a symphony orchestra's musician selection was debiased by blind selection. Auditions with the performer behind a screen substantially increased the likelihood that a female candidate would advance out of the preliminary round in an orchestra's selection process. *Id.* at 4-5 (citing Claudia Goldin & Cecilia Rouse, *Orchestrating Impartiality: The Impact of "Blind" Auditions on Female Musicians*, 90 AM. ECON. REV. 715 (2000)). *See also* Christine Jolls & Cass R. Sunstein, *The Law of Implicit Bias*, 94 CAL. L. REV. 969 (2006). Depending on the cost and effectiveness of debiasing, might construing Title VII to bar unconscious discrimination be appropriate? How expensive is it for symphony orchestras to use blind auditions? Does the debiasing literature respond to the Wax's normative critique?

10. *Proving Implicit Bias.* One objection to the whole implicit bias project is that, assuming the phenomenon is real, important, and remediable, how might a plaintiff prove she was the victim of implicit bias? This is a question you will be better positioned to answer after you have more experience with Title VII proof structures.

11. *The Bad Old Days.* Whether or not the debiasing literature is persuasive, some fear that the whole debate is counterproductive because it sends the mistaken message, intended or not, that old-fashioned animus — or subordination-driven discrimination — is far less pervasive than it in fact remains. Michael Selmi, *Sex Discrimination in the Nineties, Seventies Style: Case Studies in The Preservation of Male Workplace Norms*, 9 EMPL. RTS. & EMPLOY. POL'Y J. 1 (2005).

12. *Retaliation and Labor Law Protection.* In addition to its core prohibition on discrimination, Title VII also has a very important ancillary provision that prohibits retaliation against employees who oppose discrimination. § 704(a), 42 U.S.C. § 2000e-3(a) (2007). Suppose Slack and her co-workers contended they were fired not because they were black but because they opposed what they reasonably and in good faith believed to be a discriminatory job assignment. Would they have won on that theory? Retaliation is discussed in Chapter 5, p. 460.

For students of labor law, would the protest of the black workers against being assigned the cleaning work be protected concerted activity for mutual aid and benefit that is protected by the National Labor Relations Act? *See* ROBERT A. GORDON & MATTHEW W. FINKIN, BASIC TEXT ON LABOR LAW: UNIONIZATION AND COLLECTIVE BARGAINING (2d. ed. 2004) 402-05. Would their insubordination by refusing to follow Pohasky's orders be "good cause" to discharge them under a union collective bargaining agreement? The general rule of arbitration is that workers must work now, grieve later, even if the boss's order violates the collective bargaining agreement. *See* ELKOURI & ELKOURI, HOW ARBITRATION WORKS (6th Ed., Alan Miles Ruben ed., 2003) 262-67.

HAZEN PAPER CO. v. BIGGINS
507 U.S. 604 (1993)

Justice O'CONNOR delivered the opinion of the Court.

[Hazen Paper Company manufactures coated, laminated, and printed paper and paperboard. It is owned and operated by two cousins, petitioners Robert Hazen and Thomas N. Hazen. Walter F. Biggins was hired as technical director in 1977. He was fired in 1986, when he was 62 years old. Biggins sued, claiming to have been discharged in violation of both the Age Discrimination in Employment Act and the Employee Retirement Income Security Act of 1974 (ERISA), 29 U.S.C. §1140. The company claimed that he had been fired for doing business with competitors. The case was tried to a jury, which rendered a verdict for Biggins on his ADEA claim and also found a violation of ERISA. The district court denied defendant's motion for a judgment as a matter of law and the court of appeals affirmed.]

In affirming the judgments of liability, the Court of Appeals relied heavily on the evidence that petitioners had fired respondent in order to prevent his pension benefits from vesting. That evidence, as construed most favorably to respondent by the court, showed that the Hazen Paper pension plan had a 10-year vesting period and that respondent would have reached the 10-year mark had he worked "a few more weeks" after being fired. There was also testimony that petitioners had offered to retain respondent as a consultant to Hazen Paper, in which capacity he would not have been entitled to receive pension benefits. The Court of Appeals found this evidence of pension interference to be sufficient for ERISA liability, and also gave it considerable emphasis in upholding ADEA liability. After summarizing all the testimony tending to show age discrimination, the court stated:

> Based on the foregoing evidence, the jury could reasonably have found that Thomas Hazen decided to fire [respondent] before his pension rights vested and used the confidentiality agreement [that petitioners had asked respondent to sign] as a means to that end. The jury could also have reasonably found that age was inextricably intertwined with the decision to fire [respondent]. If it were not for [his] age, sixty-two, his pension rights would not have been within a hairbreadth of vesting. [Respondent] was fifty-two years old when he was hired; his pension rights vested in ten years.

. . . The courts of appeals repeatedly have faced the question whether an employer violates the ADEA by acting on the basis of a factor, such as an employee's pension status or seniority, that is empirically correlated with age. We now clarify that there is no disparate treatment under the ADEA when the factor motivating the employer is some feature other than the employee's age. We long have distinguished between "disparate treatment" and "disparate impact" theories of employment discrimination.

. . . The disparate treatment theory is of course available under the ADEA, as the language of that statute makes clear. "It shall be unlawful for an employer . . . to fail or refuse to hire or to discharge any individual or otherwise discriminate against any individual with respect to his compensation, terms, conditions, or privileges of employment, *because of such individual's age.*" 29 U.S.C. §623(a)(1) (emphasis added). . . .

. . . In a disparate treatment case, liability depends on whether the protected trait (under the ADEA, age) actually motivated the employer's decision. The employer may have relied upon a formal, facially discriminatory policy requiring adverse treatment of employees with that trait. Or the employer may have been motivated by the protected trait on an ad hoc, informal basis. Whatever the employer's decisionmaking process, a disparate treatment claim cannot succeed unless the employee's protected trait actually played a role in that process and had a determinative influence on the outcome.

Disparate treatment, thus defined, captures the essence of what Congress sought to prohibit in the ADEA. It is the very essence of age discrimination for an older employee to be fired because the employer believes that productivity and competence decline with old age. As we explained in *EEOC v. Wyoming*, 460 U.S. 226 (1983), Congress' promulgation of the ADEA was prompted by its concern that older workers were being deprived of employment on the basis of inaccurate and stigmatizing stereotypes.

> Although age discrimination rarely was based on the sort of animus motivating some other forms of discrimination, it was based in large part on stereotypes unsupported by objective fact. . . . Moreover, the available empirical evidence demonstrated that arbitrary age lines were in fact generally unfounded and that, as an overall matter, the performance of older workers was at least as good as that of younger workers.

Thus the ADEA commands that "employers are to evaluate [older] employees . . . on their merits and not their age." *Western Air Lines, Inc. v. Criswell*, 472 U.S. 400 (1985). The employer cannot rely on age as a proxy for an employee's remaining characteristics, such as productivity, but must instead focus on those factors directly.

When the employer's decision is wholly motivated by factors other than age, the problem of inaccurate and stigmatizing stereotypes disappears. This is true even if the motivating factor is correlated with age, as pension status typically is. Pension plans typically provide that an employee's accrued benefits will become nonforfeitable, or "vested," once the employee completes a certain number of years of service with the employer. On average, an older employee has had more years in the work force than a younger employee and thus may well have accumulated more years of service with a particular employer. Yet an employee's age is analytically distinct from his years of service. An employee who is younger than 40, and therefore outside the class of older workers as defined by the ADEA, may have worked for a particular employer his entire career, while an older worker may have been newly hired. Because age and years of service are analytically distinct, an employer can take account of one while ignoring the other, and thus it is incorrect to say that a decision based on years of service is necessarily "age-based."

The instant case is illustrative. Under the Hazen Paper pension plan, as construed by the Court of Appeals, an employee's pension benefits vest after the employee completes 10 years of service with the company. Perhaps it is true that older employees of Hazen Paper are more likely to be "close to vesting" than younger employees. Yet a decision by the company to fire an older employee solely because he has nine-plus years of service and therefore is "close to vesting" would not constitute discriminatory treatment on the basis of age. The prohibited stereotype ("Older employees are likely to be ___") would not have figured in this decision, and the attendant stigma would not ensue. The decision would not be the result of an inaccurate and denigrating generalization about age, but would rather represent an accurate judgment about the employee — that he indeed is "close to vesting."

We do not mean to suggest that an employer lawfully could fire an employee in order to prevent his pension benefits from vesting. Such conduct is actionable under §510 of ERISA, as the Court of Appeals rightly found in affirming judgment for respondent under that statute. But it would not, without more, violate the ADEA. That law requires the employer to ignore an employee's age (absent a statutory exemption or defense); it does not specify further characteristics that an employer must also ignore. Although some language in our prior decisions might be read to mean that an employer violates the ADEA whenever its reason for firing an employee is improper in any respect, see *McDonnell Douglas Corp. v. Green* [reproduced at p. 50] (creating proof framework applicable to ADEA; employer must have "legitimate, nondiscriminatory reason" for action against employee), this reading is obviously incorrect. For example, it cannot be true that an employer who fires an older black worker because the worker is black thereby violates the ADEA. The employee's race is an improper reason, but it is improper under Title VII, not the ADEA.

We do not preclude the possibility that an employer who targets employees with a particular pension status on the assumption that these employees are likely to be older thereby engages in age discrimination. Pension status may be a proxy for age, not in the sense that the ADEA makes the two factors equivalent, cf. *Metz* [*v. Transit Mix Co.*, 828 F.2d 1202, 1208 (7th Cir. 1987)] (using "proxy" to mean statutory equivalence), but in the sense that the employer may suppose a correlation between the two factors and act accordingly. Nor do we rule out the possibility of dual liability under ERISA and the ADEA where the decision to fire the employee was motivated both by the employee's age and by his pension status. Finally, we do not consider the special case where an employee is about to vest in pension benefits as a result of his age, rather than years of service, and the employer fires the employee in order to prevent vesting. That case is not presented here. Our holding is simply that an employer does not violate the ADEA just by interfering with an older employee's pension benefits that would have vested by virtue of the employee's years of service.

Besides the evidence of pension interference, the Court of Appeals cited some additional evidentiary support for ADEA liability. Although there was no direct evidence of petitioners' motivation, except for two isolated comments by the Hazens, the Court of Appeals did note the following indirect evidence: Respondent was asked to sign a confidentiality agreement, even though no other employee had been required to do so, and his replacement was a younger man who was given a less onerous agreement. In the ordinary ADEA case, indirect evidence of this kind may well suffice to support liability if the plaintiff also shows that the employer's explanation for its decision — here, that respondent had been disloyal to Hazen Paper by doing business with its competitors — is "'unworthy of credence.'" But inferring age-motivation from the implausibility of the employer's explanation may be problematic in cases where other unsavory motives, such as pension interference, were present. . . . We therefore remand the case for the Court of Appeals to reconsider whether the jury had sufficient evidence to find an ADEA violation. . . .

NOTES

1. *Systemic vs. Individual Treatment. Biggins* states that "intent to discriminate" is critical to what it calls a "disparate treatment" violation. The Court cites two kinds of disparate treatment cases: (1) the employer may have "a formal, facially discriminatory policy requiring adverse treatment of employees with a protected trait" — this is "systemic disparate treatment," and it is covered in Chapter 2; or (2) the employer "may have been motivated by a protected trait on an ad hoc, informal basis." The use of "protected trait" is apparently an attempt to include the various prohibited grounds of discrimination within Title VII and the ADEA. Most of the cases cited by the Court involved race or sex discrimination, not age discrimination. It is clear, therefore, that the Court intended a unified analysis of both statutes.

2. *But-for Motivation.* The Court says that disparate treatment occurs when "the employee's protected trait played a role in [the employer's] process and had a

determinative influence on the outcome." This seems to mean that, but-for a person's age (or sex, race, etc.), she would not have been treated the way she was. The but-for standard of causation links back to the "because of" language in the ADEA and the other antidiscrimination statutes. Not only must age (or race or sex) be somehow involved in the decision, but the decision must have been reached because of that factor. Another way of saying this is that, no matter how prejudiced the employer, when the same decision would have been made for a younger employee, there is no violation. Further, it is the plaintiff's burden to prove but-for causation. That means that showing that bias was "played a role" or was "a factor" in the decision is not necessarily enough. Professor Martin Katz argues that the but-for standard is a backward-looking way of determining causation by necessity. If, say, plaintiff's discharge would not have occurred when it did without defendant's reliance on her sex, then sex is necessary to the occurrence of her being fired. Martin J. Katz, *The Fundamental Incoherence of Title VII: Making Sense of Causation in Disparate Treatment Law*, 94 GEO. L.J. 489, 496 (2006).

Is this too demanding a standard? In the law of torts, a "substantial factor" test supplements the but-for test when two or more separate causes would preclude liability under the but-for analysis. *See* RESTATEMENT (SECOND) OF TORTS § 433(2). Such causes are "overdetermined" in the sense that the "total causal influence present is more than enough to trigger the event." Katz, at 512 n.92. Would the "played a role and had a determinative influence" language be amenable to such a substantial factor test? In *Biggins* itself, plaintiff claimed two causes (pension discrimination and age discrimination), and thereby risked losing on both because neither, by itself, might have caused the decision. Whatever the problems with the but-for test, it appears to remain operative under the ADEA although we will see that it has been at least modified, and perhaps rejected, in Title VII cases, see p. 24.

3. *Mixed Motives.* One reason Biggins was discharged was to prevent his pension from vesting. That reason is illegal under ERISA but nevertheless would be a nondiscriminatory reason under the ADEA. The Court recognized the possibility that both age discrimination and pension discrimination might coexist, and presumably either could be a but-for cause in the sense that it by itself would have resulted in the same decision. Despite this logical possibility, the existence of two motives makes it harder for a jury to find that either actually caused the discharge. Recall that the placement of the burden of persuasion on plaintiff means that he bears the risk of jury equipoise. If the jury is confident that one of the two prohibited motives caused the decision, but cannot choose between them, it must find for the defendant on both counts! How often a plaintiff's case fails because of this possibility is unclear. In *Biggins* itself, plaintiff won on one ground, but the success of his ERISA claim may have doomed his ADEA claim. Note the procedural context: *Biggins* involved a motion for judgment as a matter of law to overturn a jury verdict, which meant that the only issue was whether any reasonable jury could have inferred age discrimination by a preponderance of the evidence in light of the proof offered. That means that the verdict should have been upheld if any reasonable jury could have concluded that it was slightly more likely than not that age motivated the employer's decision to discharge Biggins. Apparently, that standard was not satisfied. On remand, the ADEA claim case was re-tried, and the second jury found for the defendants. 11 F.3d 205, 208 (1st Cir. 1997).

4. *Are Motives Always Mixed?* In *Biggins* itself, both the pension-discrimination and the age-discrimination motives were illegal. If plaintiff prevailed on either, he would win a judgment (If you're wondering why the defendant took the ADEA claim

to the Supreme Court, it probably was due to the "liquidated damage" provision of the ADEA, absent from ERISA, which would double a part of his recovery. See Chapter 8, p. 700). But in other cases, the alternative motivation may not be actionable at all. So a scenario in which the employer was motivated by *both*, say, race and *any other legal consideration* raises the mixed motive question at its starkest: if race is determinative, employer loses. If it is not, employer wins.

It may be possible that particular decisions are motivated solely by bias (an employer refuses to look at a resume when it sees a woman's name), but most real-world decisions involve more complex psychological reactions. And in litigation, where employers typically have a burden to produce a nondiscriminatory reason for an action in order to rebut plaintiff's claim, employers invariably manage to find them. If that reason is found to be the only reason, there can be no liability under *Biggins.* More surprisingly, even if age discrimination also plays a role, that is to say, the employer acts from mixed motives, Biggins would still bar liability if the other reason is itself the but-for cause of the adverse decision.

5. *Age Discrimination as Acting on Stereotypes.* Whether the jury properly found age discrimination depends on what the jury was supposed to have been looking for. The Court found the answer easy: "It is the very essence of age discrimination for an older employee to be fired because the employer believes that productivity and competence decline with old age." Another stereotype is that older workers are "set in their ways," unwilling or unable to adapt to new technologies and techniques. *See EEOC v. Board of Regents of the University of Wisconsin,* 288 F.3d 296, 303 (7th Cir. 2002) (references to plaintiff as having "skills suited to the 'pre-electronic'" and having "to be brought 'up to speed' on 'new trends of advertising with electronic means" could be found to be code words for age stereotypes).

To find age discrimination in *Biggins,* must the jury believe that the Hazens fired Biggins because his increasing age led them to (incorrectly) conclude that his competence was declining? How likely is it that the Hazens incorrectly believed Biggins's competence declined? Aren't employers more likely to act on "inaccurate and stigmatizing stereotypes" regarding competence in refusing to hire older workers than in firing them? In this case, the Hazens had the opportunity to watch plaintiff perform over almost a decade. If they fired him because they believed his competence was diminishing, how could that be the result of a stereotype? Or does the implicit bias literature explain this? To prevail, would Biggins have had to show (a) that the Hazens incorrectly evaluated his competence and (b) that they attributed his perceived loss of competence to his age? What if they correctly believed Biggins's competence was dropping but also attributed it to his age as a result of implicit bias? An employer can discharge a worker for becoming less competent but not if it a worker younger than Biggins with a similar level of competence would have been retained.

6. *Statistical Discrimination.* Don't productivity and competence, in fact, decline with increasing age, at least in many jobs and at some age? This may be a stereotype that is "true." In such situations, there is little need for cognitive bias as an explanation. Ironically, the more accurate the stereotype, that is, the greater the degree to which it conforms to reality, the less need there is for either implicit bias or animus or subordination as an explanation. Everything else being equal, a "rational" employer would seek to exclude older workers if, say, their health insurance costs were substantially higher than younger workers or, say, women, if pregnancy or childcare

responsibilities made them, on average, less productive workers. *See* David A. Strauss, *The Law and Economics of Racial Discrimination in Employment: The Case for Numerical Standards*, 79 GEO. L.J. 1619, 1622 (1991) ("A rational employer will discriminate, even if no relevant actor has any discriminatory animus, if the employer concludes that race is a useful proxy for job qualifications"). See Chapter 10, p. 767. The point is not that such discrimination is legal if it's rational: it is almost always illegal, even if the employer is correct in its perceptions (and often it isn't). Rather, the point is that discrimination is a more plausible explanation when the employer's self-interest is furthered by it.

The antidiscrimination statutes strictly limit, but do not wholly prohibit, statistical discrimination. The most obvious example when it is permissible is under the bona fide occupational qualification (BFOQ) defense, which operates under the ADEA to permit age discrimination when the employer can factually demonstrate an age-linked decline and under Title VII for sex, religion, and national origin discrimination (but not for race). The employer, however, has the burden of proof as to the BFOQ. See Chapter 2, p. 171. The point of the ADEA, as *Biggins* sees it, is that employers should not presume any decline in abilities and, even where declines occur, the employer should not act on those age-based changes unless they are relevant to the job in question. Although Biggins may no longer be able to play basketball, that does not mean he is unable to be a technical director.

7. *Getting Inside the Employer's Mind to Prove Age Discrimination.* The Hazen cousins made several "stray comments" about Biggins's age, i.e., comments showing that his age was on their minds but not made in connection with his discharge. Does that support finding that age may have played a role in his discharge but not sufficiently to show that but-for his age he would not have been fired? Suppose an employer asks an older worker about her plans for retirement. Courts have been very reluctant to see bias in comments related to potential retirement. *See Cox v. Dubuque Bank & Trust Co.*, 163 F.3d 492 (8th Cir. 1998) (employer entitled to jury instruction that it had a right to make reasonable inquiries into employee's retirement plans); *Montgomery v. John Deere & Co., Inc.*, 169 F.3d 556 (8th Cir. 1999) (plaintiff's being repeatedly asked whether he was going to take retirement not sufficient to show age discrimination). *See also Rowan v. Lockheed Martin Energy Sys.*, 360 F.3d 544, 547-49 (6th Cir. 2004) (comments about the increasing average age of the plant work force did not show age bias: "Being worried about one's best workers retiring is a far cry from being motivated by 'inaccurate and stigmatizing stereotypes'").

8. *Strategic Dilemma for Plaintiffs.* Suppose a 38-year-old woman is discharged and she thinks it was because of her age and her gender. She does not have a good ADEA claim because she is not within the protected group of workers who are at least age 40. If she sues on sex discrimination, *Biggins* suggests that the employer has a complete defense by claiming she was a fired because of her age and therefore was not a victim of sex discrimination. That possibility pushes plaintiffs to sue on every possible theory to avoid what happened to Biggins. But if she adds a claim of age discrimination (which might be based on supplemental jurisdiction under a state law that bans all age discrimination) to avoid the trap set by the first part of *Biggins*, she faces the risk of the second part, that the inference of causation of any single motivation diminishes in likelihood as the number of potential motivations increases.

2. *Terms, Conditions or Privileges of Employment*

HISHON v. KING & SPALDING
467 U.S. 69 (1984)

Chief Justice BURGER wrote for the unanimous Court:

In 1972, Elizabeth Hishon became an associate of the defendant law firm, a firm of more than 50 partners and about 50 associates. She claimed that the prospect of partnership was an important factor in her initial decision to accept employment and that defendant had used that prospect as a recruiting device to induce her to join the firm. She claimed that the firm had represented that advancement to partnership after five or six years was a matter of course for associates who received satisfactory evaluations and that associates were promoted to partnership "on a fair and equal basis." Hishon sued after being considered and rejected for partnership, alleging sex discrimination.]

Petitioner alleges that respondent is an "employer" to whom Title VII is addressed. She then asserts that consideration for partnership was one of the "terms, conditions, or privileges of employment" as an associate with respondent. If this is correct, respondent could not base an adverse partnership decision on "race, color, religion, sex, or national origin."

Once a contractual relationship of employment is established, the provisions of Title VII attach and govern certain aspects of that relationship. In the context of Title VII, the contract of employment may be written or oral, formal or informal; an informal contract of employment may arise by the simple act of handing a job applicant a shovel and providing a workplace. The contractual relationship of employment triggers the provision of Title VII governing "terms, conditions, or privileges of employment." Title VII in turn forbids discrimination on the basis of "race, color, religion, sex, or national origin."

Because the underlying employment relationship is contractual, it follows that the "terms, conditions, or privileges of employment" clearly include benefits that are part of an employment contract. Here, petitioner in essence alleges that respondent made a contract to consider her for partnership.[6] Indeed, this promise was allegedly a key contractual provision which induced her to accept employment. If the evidence at trial establishes that the parties contracted to have petitioner considered for partnership, that promise clearly was a term, condition, or privilege of her employment. Title VII would then bind respondents to consider petitioner for partnership as the statute provides, i.e., without regard to petitioner's sex. The contract she alleges would lead to the same result.

Petitioner's claim that a contract was made, however, is not the only allegation that would qualify respondent's consideration of petitioner for partnership as a term, condition, or privilege of employment. An employer may provide its employees with many benefits that it is under no obligation to furnish by an express or implied contract. Such a benefit, though not a contractual right of employment, may qualify as a "privileg[e]" of employment under Title VII. A benefit that is part and parcel of

---

6. Petitioner alleges not only that respondent promised to consider her for partnership, but also that it promised to consider her on a "fair and equal basis." This latter promise is not necessary to petitioner's Title VII claim. Even if the employment contract did not afford a basis for an implied condition that the ultimate decision would be fairly made on the merits, Title VII itself would impose such a requirement. If the promised consideration for partnership is a term, condition, or privilege of employment, then the partnership decision must be without regard to "race, color, religion, sex, or national origin."

the employment relationship may not be doled out in a discriminatory fashion, even if the employer would be free under the employment contract simply not to provide the benefit at all. Those benefits that comprise the "incidents of employment," or that form "an aspect of the relationship between the employer and employees" may not be afforded in a manner contrary to Title VII.

Several allegations in petitioner's complaint would support the conclusion that the opportunity to become a partner was part and parcel of an associate's status as an employee at respondent's firm, independent of any allegation that such an opportunity was included in associates' employment contracts. Petitioner alleges that respondent's associates could regularly expect to be considered for partnership at the end of their "apprenticeships," and it appears that lawyers outside the firm were not routinely so considered. Thus, the benefit of partnership consideration was allegedly linked directly with an associate's status as an employee, and this linkage was far more than coincidental: Petitioner alleges that respondent explicitly used the prospect of ultimate partnership to induce young lawyers to join the firm. Indeed, the importance of the partnership decision to a lawyer's status as an associate is underscored by the allegation that associates' employment is terminated if they are not elected to become partners. These allegations, if proved at trial, would suffice to show that partnership consideration was a term, condition, or privilege of an associate's employment at respondent's firm, and accordingly that partnership consideration must be without regard to sex. . . .

Justice POWELL, concurring. . . .

I write to make clear my understanding that the Court's opinion should not be read as extending Title VII to the management of a law firm by its partners. The reasoning of the Court's opinion does not require that the relationship among partners be characterized as an "employment" relationship to which Title VII would apply. The relationship among law partners differs markedly from that between employer and employee — including that between the partnership and its associates.[2] The judgmental and sensitive decisions that must be made among the partners embrace a wide range of subjects.[3] The essence of the law partnership is the common conduct of a shared enterprise. The relationship among law partners contemplates that decisions important to the partnership normally will be made by common agreement . . . or consent among the partners. . . .

NOTES

1. *The Employment Relation.* While a wide variety of employment decisions may be challenged under the antidiscrimination statutes, *Hishon* suggests a limitation: Title VII's prohibition of discrimination by "employers" is limited to discrimination

---

2. Of course, an employer may not evade the strictures of Title VII simply by labeling its employees as "partners." Law partnerships usually have many of the characteristics that I describe generally here.

3. These decisions concern such matters as participation in profits and other types of compensation; work assignments; approval of commitments in bar association, civic, or political activities; questions of billing; acceptance of new clients; questions of conflicts of interest; retirement programs; and expansion policies. Such decisions may affect each partner of the firm. Divisions of partnership profits, unlike shareholders' rights to dividends, involve judgments as to each partner's contribution to the reputation and success of the firm. This is true whether the partner's participation in profits is measured in terms of points or percentages, combinations of salaries and points, salaries and bonuses, and possibly in other ways.

in the *employment* relationship. Plaintiff, as an associate with the firm, was plainly an employee. And King & Spaulding had more than enough employees (15) to be a statutory employer. See Chapter 5, p. 317. If, as plaintiff claimed, a term of her employment as associate was the opportunity to be considered for partnership, Title VII required the firm to consider her without regard to sex. Once the firm made her a partner, however, could she then be subjected to sex discrimination? At that point, she would no longer be an employee. We will see in Chapter 5 that there are many relationships in which individuals work for others that the law does not categorize as "employment" and that are, therefore, outside the reach of the antidiscrimination statutes. We will also see in that section, however, that, as Justice Powell said in his concurrence, "[a]n employer may not evade the strictures of Title VII simply by labeling its employees as 'partners.'"

2. *"Adverse Employment Actions."* Both *Slack* and *Biggins* involve what have been called "ultimate" employment actions — the decision to terminate a worker. Another "ultimate" action is the decision not to hire in the first place. For obvious reasons plaintiffs are far more likely to sue when they are fired than when not hired or even when not given promotions or raises. *Hishon* is also towards the ultimate end of the spectrum since, at least at that time, the "up or out" rule prevailed and a decision not to promote a law firm associate to partner was almost always a decision to terminate the associate's services.

But *Hishon* illustrates that a failure to promote may be actionable independent of a discharge. Recall that Title VII not only prohibits discrimination in hiring and firing but also makes it unlawful "otherwise to discriminate against any individual with respect to his compensation, terms, conditions, or privileges of employment" on the prohibited grounds or "to limit, segregate, or classify his employees or applicants for employment in any way which would deprive or tend to deprive any individual of employment opportunities or otherwise adversely affect his status as an employee." §703(a), 42 U.S.C. 2000e-2(a). Suppose the employees in *Slack* had complied with Pohasky's request and then sued for being discriminatorily assigned the work. Would they have a cause of action?

The answer isn't as clear as you might think since the lower courts have developed doctrines that preclude suit where the challenged decision is not sufficiently adverse to the plaintiff. While most denials of promotion or raises are actionable, other kinds of discriminatory conduct may not be. Dean Rebecca Hanner White in *De Minimis Discrimination*, 47 EMORY L.J. 1121, 1151 (1998), takes issue with this approach, arguing that "Congress's use of the phrase 'compensation, terms, conditions, or privileges of employment' emphasizes the employment-related nature of the prohibited discrimination. The phrase is better read as making clear that an employer who discriminates against an employee in a non-job-related context would not run afoul of Title VII, rather than as sheltering employment discrimination that does not significantly disadvantage an employee." Reconsider this argument after you read the next case.

MINOR v. CENTOCOR, INC.
457 F.3d 632 (7th Cir. 2006)

EASTERBROOK, Circuit Judge. M. Jane Minor was a sales representative for Centocor, pitching to physicians and hospitals that Centocor and its affiliates offered to treat vascular conditions. After Antonio Siciliano became her supervisor, Minor contends, she was put in an impossible situation — Siciliano required her to visit all of her accounts twice a month, and her major accounts more frequently. That led her to work 70 to 90 hours a week (much of it driving time); until then 50 to 55 hours had been enough. In August 2001, after two months of this regimen, Minor began to experience atrial fibrillation and depression. In October 2001 she stopped working. . . . She attributes here medical problems to Siciliano's demands. In this litigation Minor contends that those demands reflected both age and sex discrimination. . . .

The district court concluded, however, that Minor had not established a prima facie case . . . because Centocor did not take any "adverse employment action" against her. Minor was not fired or demoted; she is still Centocor's employee, welcome to resume work if her condition improves. The events of which she complains — not only the schedule for visiting accounts but also being bombarded by email messages from Siciliano and subject to criticism and close supervision — are the ordinary incidents of employment rather than adverse actions. . . .

Although hundreds if not thousands of decisions say that an "adverse employment action" is essential to the plaintiff's prima facie case, that term does not appear in any employment discrimination statute . . . and the Supreme Court has never adopted it as a legal requirement. The statutory term is "discrimination," and a proxy such as "adverse employment action" often may help to express the idea — which the Supreme Court *has* embraced — that it is essential to distinguish between material differences and the many day-to-day travails and disappointments that, although frustrating, are not so central to the employment relation that they amount to discriminatory terms or conditions. See, e.g., *Burlington Northern & Santa Fe Ry. v. White* [reproduced in Chapter 5 at p. 473]. . . . Helpful though a judicial gloss such as "adverse employment action" may be, that phrase must not be confused with the statute itself or allowed to displace the Supreme Court's approach, which inquires whether the difference is material.

Extra work can be a material difference in the terms and conditions of employment. Minor contends that Siciliano required her to work at least 25% longer to earn the same income as before. That is functionally the same as a 30% reduction in Minor's hourly pay, a material change by any standard. And if Centocor requires women (or older workers) to work longer hours than men (or younger workers) to obtain the same remuneration, that material difference also is discriminatory and violates federal law. [Nevertheless, summary judgment for the employer is affirmed because plaintiff failed to point to any evidence that would support drawing the inference that Centocor in fact required women or older workers to work longer hours than men or younger workers for the same pay.]

NOTES

1. *Docket Reduction and Narrowing Employers' Liability.* The court in *Minor* finds that the employer's treatment of plaintiff, if discriminatory, would be actionable because it had a substantial economic impact. Why is that an issue? In other words, why isn't discrimination related to a job necessarily actionable, whether or not there is any economic impact on the employee? In *Ferrill v. The Parker Group, Inc.*, 168 F.3d 468 (11th Cir. 1999), a §1981 case, the Eleventh Circuit struck down an employer's policy of racially segregating telemarketers aimed at getting out the vote for an election, with blacks calling blacks and whites calling whites with separate "boilerrooms" for each group to make their calls.

It is true that §1981 is not framed in language speaking of "the terms and conditions" of employment, but isn't the worksite a term or condition of employment? Even if it isn't, Title VII also bars discrimination in "privileges" of employment. Suppose an employer paints all the cubicles pink for women workers and blue for men. It seems plainly discriminatory because the choice of color reflects stereotypes about men and women and is employment-related since it involved an aspect of the job — the workspace. Might plaintiff lose a challenge to this practice because it has no immediately discernable economic effect? If so, then the courts are qualifying the plain meaning of the statutory language of Title VII. What is the value of leaving unchecked such plainly discriminatory conduct affecting the areas in which employees are assigned to work? There are two obvious possibilities. One is to reduce the number of discrimination cases before the courts. The second is to provide employers with some elbow room free of any possibility of judicial second-guessing. Is either of these reasons sufficient?

2. *Materiality.* As *Minor* suggests, the lower courts have generally required more than a mere showing that the employer discriminated in order for its conduct to be actionable. They have required an "adverse employment action," which they have usually defined to require some material effect on the terms and conditions of employment. Obviously, "ultimate employment actions" — hiring and firing — suffice, *McCoy v. City of Shreveport*, 492 F.3d 551 (5th Cir. 2007), and meaningful changes in compensation have also been held sufficient. *See Farrell v. Butler Univ.*, 421 F.3d 609, 614 (7th Cir. 2005) (while denial of bonuses is not an adverse employment action, denial of a raise can be, and the denial to plaintiff of a regularly conferred award resulting in the recipient getting a permanent increase in base salary is best characterized as a raise). When it comes to less directly economic effects on employees' lives, however, the lower courts decisions are confused. A few examples illustrate the problem in cases where the plaintiff failed to establish sufficient adversity:

- mid-range evaluation, *Primes v. Reno*, 190 F.3d 765 (6th Cir. 1999), or even negative evaluation, even if future prospects hindered, *Davis v. Town of Lake Park, Fla.*, 245 F.3d 1232, 1242-1243 (11th Cir. 2001);
- lateral transfer usually defined to mean no reduction in pay or title and any diminution in pay "indirect and minor," *Williams v. Bristol-Myers Squibb Co.*, 85 F.3d 270 (7th Cir. 1996), even though the transfer might be to a distant location, *Reynolds v. Ethicon Endo-Surgery, Inc.*, 454 F.3d 868 (8th Cir. 2006); *Vann v. Southwestern Bell Tel. Co.*, 179 Fed. Appx. 491 (10th Cir. 2006);
- investigation of plaintiff, *Mazumder v. Univ. of Mich.*, 195 Fed. Appx. 320 (6th Cir. 2006), even when plaintiff was put on paid administrative leave, *Joseph v. Leavitt*, 465 F.3d 87 (2d Cir. 2006), *cert. denied*, 127 S. Ct. 1855 (2007);
- family-oriented questions asked only of female job applicant, *Bruno v. City of Crown Point*, 950 F.2d 355 (7th Cir. 1991);
- failure to provide plaintiff with a computer, *Enowmbitang v. Seagate Tech.*, 148 F.3d 970, 973 (8th Cir. 1998).

These decisions are often fact-sensitive, and some courts see more harm in actions with little direct economic effect.

3. *Materiality = Economic Effects?* Minor might seem to be an easy case, especially for the economically-oriented panel of the Seventh Circuit, which included Judge Posner along with Judge Easterbrook. *Minor* views requiring more work for

the same pay as equivalent to a reduction in hourly pay, and appreciable decreases in pay have generally been found adverse employment actions. But the employer did not actually decrease plaintiff's compensation (she earned as much as she had before), and won't many employment actions be translatable into dollars? A transfer to a distant location might involve heavy commuting or moving expenses. As Dean White explains, the language "terms and conditions of employment" comes from the National Labor Relations Act, and unions have often focused collective bargaining on aspects of employment that do not directly implicate economic interests. *De Minimis Discrimination,* at 1190 n.367. Further, Congress seemed to intend to go even further in Title VII by adding "privileges" to the protection afforded.

4. *Adverse Employment Action Unnecessary When Discrimination Is Proven?* Dean White argued that requiring an "adverse employment action" might be appropriate when the question is whether the decision was impermissibly motivated, but she asserts there should be no such "adverse action" requirement when the discrimination is facial or proven and the action in question was employment-related. *De Minimis Discrimination* at 1173-74. *See Piercy v. Maketa,* 480 F.3d 1192 (10th Cir. 2007) (a facially discriminatory assignment policy might nevertheless not be an adverse employment action where the denied work was less arduous and stressful and the opportunity to work shifts would have increased plaintiff's chances of obtaining additional job and leave flexibility).

5. *An Unnecessary Complication?* For every decision rejecting a claim for failing to show that an adverse employment action has happened, there seems to be one going the other way. *E.g., Czekalski v. Peters,* 475 F.3d 360 (D.C. Cir. 2007) (transfer to position with significantly diminished supervisory and programmatic responsibilities could have properly been found to be an adverse employment action); *Wedow v. City of Kan. City,* 442 F.3d 661, 671-72 (8th Cir. 2006) (jury could find an adverse employment action in the lack of adequate protective clothing and private, sanitary shower and restroom facilities for a female firefighters "because these conditions jeopardize her ability to perform the core functions of her job in a safe and efficient manner"); *Keeton v. Flying J, Inc.,* 429 F.3d 259, 265 (6th Cir. 2005), *cert. denied,* 127 S. Ct. 109 (2006) (lateral transfer that increased plaintiff's commute to the extent that he considered moving was actionable); *Tart v. Ill. Power Co.,* 366 F.3d 461 (7th Cir. 2004) (reassignment without loss of pay nevertheless constituted an adverse employment action when the jobs were inferior in skill and responsibility, and had significantly harsher working conditions than the prior positions). Since people usually don't go to the effort to protest employer actions that are not important, at least to them, why not use the simpler test that plaintiff need only show the employer acted concerning the job or the conditions under which work is performed?

6. *Constructive Discharge and Contaminated Work Environment.* Some conduct by the employer may be so severe as to lead a reasonable employee to quit. Such "constructive discharges" are the equivalent of a formal discharge and are, therefore, adverse employment actions. See Chapter 5, p. 394. Similarly, some conduct may be, considered by itself, not an adverse employment action but when combined with other conduct it may contaminate the work environment and, therefore, be actionable. See Chapter 5, p. 370.

7. *Discrimination vs. Retaliation.* The issue of whether plaintiff must prove that she has suffered an adverse employment action has also been raised in retaliation cases. In *Burlington Northern & Santa Fe Ry. v. White,* reproduced in Chapter 5 at p. 473, the plaintiff claimed that, in retaliation for complaining about sexual harassment, she was taken off her job of driving a forklift and put to work doing

laborer work on the tracks. The employer argued that the reassignment was not an adverse employment action since both positions were in the same job classification. The Court rejected the test some lower courts used — that in a retaliation case, plaintiff must show she suffered an "ultimate employment action," like a discharge. It also rejected the notion that only actions concerning the terms and conditions of employment were actionable as retaliation. Instead, it allowed plaintiff to sue for any retaliation, whether or not related to employment, so long as the plaintiff can "show that a reasonable employee would have found the challenged action materially adverse." 126 S. Ct. at 2415. This objective test was important because it "separates significant from trivial harms." *Id.* Thus:

> Context matters. . . . A schedule change in an employee's work schedule may make little difference to many workers, but may matter enormously to a young mother with school age children. . . . A supervisor's refusal to invite an employee to lunch is normally trivial, a nonactionable petty slight. But to retaliate by excluding an employee from a weekly training lunch that contributes significantly to the employee's professional advancement might well deter a reasonable employee from complaining about discrimination.

Id. at 2415-15. *Minor* may have drawn its materiality test from *Burlington*, but the touchstone for retaliation is not the same for discrimination. As the quoted passage suggests, the ultimate test for materiality is whether the challenged action is likely to deter complaints about discrimination by a reasonable employer. How does that translate to a situation where an employer changes a worker's schedule because she is a woman? Shouldn't she be able to challenge that even if she would not object to the schedule change had it been made for a nondiscriminatory reason?

The Fifth Circuit, in *McCoy v. City of Shreveport*, 492 F.3d 551 (5th Cir. 2007), differentiates retaliation cases (where the court will follow *Burlington*) from discrimination cases, where it will continue to apply its "ultimate employment action" limitation on the discriminatory acts a plaintiff may challenge. In continuing its ultimate employment action rule, the Fifth Circuit emphasized that *Burlington* had limited its holding to retaliation cases and had carefully distinguished the language in the retaliation provision of Title VII, §704(a), from the discrimination provisions in §703(a). *Burlington* had written:

> There is strong reason to believe that Congress intended the differences that its language suggests, for the two provisions differ not only in language but in purpose as well. The anti-discrimination provision seeks a workplace where individuals are not discriminated against because of their racial, ethnic, religious, or gender-based status. The anti-retaliation provision seeks to secure that primary objective by preventing an employer from interfering (through retaliation) with an employee's efforts to secure or advance enforcement of the Act's basic guarantees. The substantive provision seeks to prevent injury to individuals based on who they are, i.e., their status. The anti-retaliation provision seeks to prevent harm to individuals based on what they do, i.e., their conduct. Thus, purpose reinforces what language already indicates, namely, that the anti-retaliation provision, unlike the substantive provision, is not limited to discriminatory actions that affect the terms and conditions of employment.

Id. at 2412. How does this support limiting §703(a) to "ultimate employment actions"? Isn't the *McCoy* court reading that language into §703(a) and ignoring the "terms and conditions of employment language" in that section?

8. *Academic Commentary.* In addition to Dean White's *De Minimis* article, *see* Tristin K. Green, *Discrimination in Workplace Dynamics: Toward a Structural Account of Disparate Treatment Theory*, 38 HARV. C.R.-C.L. L. REV. 98, 102 (2002) ("As hierarchies flatten, movement between institutions increases, and the employment relationship is redefined in terms of individual achievement over hierarchical advancement, employees will find it more difficult to satisfy [a material adverse action] requirement"); Ernest F. Lidge III, *The Meaning of Discrimination: Why Courts Have Erred in Requiring Employment Discrimination Plaintiffs to Prove that the Employer's Action Was Materially Adverse or Ultimate*, 47 U. KAN. L. REV. 333 (1999) (courts should look only to whether the employee's terms, conditions, or privileges of employment have been altered); Theresa M. Beiner, *Do Reindeer Games Count as Terms, Conditions or Privileges of Employment Under Title VII?*, 37 B.C. L. REV. 643 (1996) (arguing that benefits such as golf games and lunches accorded to male employees but not to females, are terms and conditions of employment; denying access to such benefits to women should be treated similarly to a hostile work environment).

3. Linking Discriminatory Intent to the Employer's Treatment of Plaintiff

Since §703(a) of Title VII and §4(a) of the Age Discrimination in Employment Act utilize the term "because of" to link the employer's conduct that the employee is complaining about to discrimination, it is not surprising that *Hazen Paper v. Biggins* described that link in traditional but-for causation language: "[A] disparate treatment claim cannot succeed unless the employee's protected trait actually played a role in that process and had a determinative influence on the outcome." Even before *Biggins*, however, there had been a crack in the "determinative factor" requirement. *Price Waterhouse v. Hopkins*, 490 U.S. 228 (1989), reproduced at p. 32, had allowed a plaintiff to prove discrimination with something less than a "determinative factor" in a narrow class of cases. While we will explore *Price Waterhouse* shortly, what is important for present purposes is that the 1991 Civil Rights Act, Pub. L. No. 102-166, 105 Stat. 1071, not only codified *Price Waterhouse* but expanded it. The two relevant sections are §703(m) and §706(g)(2)(B). Section 703(m) provides:

> Except as otherwise provided in this subchapter, an unlawful employment practice is established when the complaining party demonstrates that race, color, religion, sex, or national origin was a motivating factor for any employment practice, even though other factors also motivated the practice.

42 U.S.C §2000e-2(m). §706(g)(2)(B), in turn, amended the statute to provide a limited affirmative defense: should defendant carry a burden of persuasion that it would have reached the same decision even had the illicit "motivating factor" not been present, the plaintiff's remedies are severely restricted even though the defendant remains liable.

Both provisions had been operative for more than a decade before the Supreme Court finally construed them in *Desert Palace v. Costa*. As you read *Desert Palace*, however, remember that the 1991 CRA amended only Title VII, not the ADEA. Thus, we will revisit the *Biggins* "determinative factor" analysis in connection with age discrimination claims.

DESERT PALACE, INC. v. COSTA
539 U.S. 90 (2003)

Justice THOMAS delivered the opinion of the Court.

The question before us in this case is whether a plaintiff must present direct evidence of discrimination in order to obtain a mixed-motive instruction under Title VII of the Civil Rights Act of 1964, as amended by the Civil Rights Act of 1991. We hold that direct evidence is not required.

I

A

Since 1964, Title VII has made it an "unlawful employment practice for an employer . . . . to discriminate against any individual . . . *because of* such individual's race, color, religion, sex, or national origin." (emphasis added). In *Price Waterhouse v. Hopkins* [reproduced at p. 32], the Court considered whether an employment decision is made "because of" sex in a "mixed-motive" case, *i.e.*, where both legitimate and illegitimate reasons motivated the decision. The Court concluded that, under § 2000e-2(a)(1), an employer could "avoid a finding of liability . . . by proving that it would have made the same decision even if it had not allowed gender to play such a role." The Court was divided, however, over the predicate question of when the burden of proof may be shifted to an employer to prove the affirmative defense.

Justice Brennan, writing for a plurality of four Justices, would have held that "when a plaintiff . . . proves that her gender played a *motivating* part in an employment decision, the defendant may avoid a finding of liability only by proving by a preponderance of the evidence that it would have made the same decision even if it had not taken the plaintiff's gender into account." The plurality did not, however, "suggest a limitation on the possible ways of proving that [gender] stereotyping played a motivating role in an employment decision."

Justice White and Justice O'Connor both concurred in the judgment. Justice White would have held that the case was governed by *Mt. Healthy City Bd. of Ed. v. Doyle*, 429 U.S. 274 (1977), and would have shifted the burden to the employer only when a plaintiff "showed that the unlawful motive was a *substantial* factor in the adverse employment action." Justice O'Connor, like Justice White, would have required the plaintiff to show that an illegitimate consideration was a "substantial factor" in the employment decision. But, under Justice O'Connor's view, "the burden on the issue of causation" would shift to the employer only where "a disparate treatment plaintiff [could] show by *direct evidence* that an illegitimate criterion was a substantial factor in the decision."

Two years after *Price Waterhouse*, Congress passed the 1991 Act "in large part [as] a response to a series of decisions of this Court interpreting the Civil Rights Acts of 1866 and 1964." *Landgraf v. USI Film Products*, 511 U.S. 244 (1994). In particular, § 107 of the 1991 Act, which is at issue in this case, "responded" to *Price Waterhouse* by "setting forth standards applicable in 'mixed motive' cases" in two new statutory provisions.[1] The first establishes an alternative for proving that an "unlawful employment practice" has occurred:

---

1. This case does not require us to decide when, if ever, § 107 applies outside of the mixed-motive context.

Except as otherwise provided in this subchapter, an unlawful employment practice is established when the complaining party demonstrates that race, color, religion, sex, or national origin was a motivating factor for any employment practice, even though other factors also motivated the practice.

42 U.S.C § 2000e-2(m).

The second provides that, with respect to "a claim in which an individual proves a violation under section 2000e-2(m)," the employer has a limited affirmative defense that does not absolve it of liability, but restricts the remedies available to a plaintiff. The available remedies include only declaratory relief, certain types of injunctive relief, and attorney's fees and costs. In order to avail itself of the affirmative defense, the employer must "demonstrate that [it] would have taken the same action in the absence of the impermissible motivating factor."

Since the passage of the 1991 Act, the Courts of Appeals have divided over whether plaintiff must prove by direct evidence that an impermissible consideration was a "motivating factor" in an adverse employment action. Relying primarily on Justice O'Connor's concurrence in *Price Waterhouse*, a number of courts have held that direct evidence is required to establish liability under §2000e-2(m). In the decision below, however, the Ninth Circuit concluded otherwise.

B

Petitioner Desert Palace, Inc., dba Caesar's Palace Hotel & Casino of Las Vegas, Nevada, employed respondent Catharina Costa as a warehouse worker and heavy equipment operator. Respondent was the only woman in this job and in her local Teamsters bargaining unit.

Respondent experienced a number of problems with management and her co-workers that led to an escalating series of disciplinary sanctions, including informal rebukes, a denial of privileges, and suspension. Petitioner finally terminated respondent after she was involved in a physical altercation in a warehouse elevator with fellow Teamsters member Herbert Gerber. Petitioner disciplined both employees because the facts surrounding the incident were in dispute, but Gerber, who had a clean disciplinary record, received only a 5-day suspension. . . .

. . . At trial, respondent presented evidence that (1) she was singled out for "intense 'stalking'" by one of her supervisors, (2) she received harsher discipline than men for the same conduct, (3) she was treated less favorably than men in the assignment of overtime, and (4) supervisors repeatedly "stacked" her disciplinary record and "frequently used or tolerated" sex-based slurs against her.

Based on this evidence, the District Court denied petitioner's motion for judgment as a matter of law, and submitted the case to the jury with instructions, two of which are relevant here. First, without objection from petitioner, the District Court instructed the jury that "the plaintiff has the burden of proving . . . by a preponderance of the evidence" that she "suffered adverse work conditions" and that her sex "was a motivating factor in any such work conditions imposed upon her."

Second, the District Court gave the jury the following mixed-motive instruction:

You have heard evidence that the defendant's treatment of the plaintiff was motivated by the plaintiff's sex and also by other lawful reasons. If you find that the plaintiff's sex was a motivating factor in the defendant's treatment of the plaintiff, the plaintiff is entitled to your verdict, even if you find that the defendant's conduct was also motivated by a lawful reason.

However, if you find that the defendant's treatment of the plaintiff was motivated by both gender and lawful reasons, you must decide whether the plaintiff is entitled to damages. The plaintiff is entitled to damages unless the defendant proves by a preponderance of the evidence that the defendant would have treated plaintiff similarly even if the plaintiff's gender had played no role in the employment decision.

Petitioner unsuccessfully objected to this instruction, claiming that respondent had failed to adduce "direct evidence" that sex was a motivating factor in her dismissal or in any of the other adverse employment actions taken against her. The jury rendered a verdict for respondent, awarding backpay, compensatory damages, and punitive damages. The District Court denied petitioner's renewed motion for judgment as a matter of law. . . .

II

This case provides us with the first opportunity to consider the effects of the 1991 Act on jury instructions in mixed-motive cases. Specifically, we must decide whether a plaintiff must present direct evidence of discrimination in order to obtain a mixed-motive instruction under 42 U.S.C. §2000e-2(m). Petitioner's argument on this point proceeds in three steps: (1) Justice O'Connor's opinion is the holding of *Price Waterhouse*; (2) Justice O'Connor's *Price Waterhouse* opinion requires direct evidence of discrimination before a mixed-motive instruction can be given; and (3) the 1991 Act does nothing to abrogate that holding. Like the Court of Appeals, we see no need to address which of the opinions in *Price Waterhouse* is controlling: the third step of petitioner's argument is flawed, primarily because it is inconsistent with the text of §2000e-2(m).

Our precedents make clear that the starting point for our analysis is the statutory text. And where, as here, the words of the statute are unambiguous, the "judicial inquiry is complete." Section 2000e-2(m) unambiguously states that a plaintiff need only "demonstrate" that an employer used a forbidden consideration with respect to "any employment practice." On its face, the statute does not mention, much less require, that a plaintiff make a heightened showing through direct evidence. Indeed, petitioner concedes as much.

Moreover, Congress explicitly defined the term "'demonstrates'" in the 1991 Act, leaving little doubt that no special evidentiary showing is required. Title VII defines the term "demonstrates" as to "meet the burdens of production and persuasion." §2000e(m). If Congress intended the term "'demonstrates'" to require that the "burdens of production and persuasion" be met by direct evidence or some other heightened showing, it could have made that intent clear by including language to that effect in §2000e(m). Its failure to do so is significant, for Congress has been unequivocal when imposing heightened proof requirements in other circumstances, including in other provisions of Title 42. . . . 42 U.S.C. §5851(b)(3)(D) (providing that "relief may not be ordered" against an employer in retaliation cases involving whistleblowers under the Atomic Energy Act where the employer is able to "*demonstrate by clear and convincing evidence* that it would have taken the same unfavorable personnel action in the absence of such behavior" (emphasis added)); cf. *Price Waterhouse* ("Only rarely have we required clear and convincing proof where the action defended against seeks only conventional relief").

In addition, Title VII's silence with respect to the type of evidence required in mixed-motive cases also suggests that we should not depart from the "conventional rule of civil litigation [that] generally applies in Title VII cases." That rule requires a plaintiff to prove his case "by a preponderance of the evidence," using "direct or circumstantial evidence," *Postal Service Bd. of Governors v. Aikens*, 460 U.S. 711, 714, n. 3 (1983). We have often acknowledged the utility of circumstantial evidence in discrimination cases. For instance, in *Reeves v. Sanderson Plumbing Products, Inc.* [reproduced at p. 78], we recognized that evidence that a defendant's explanation for an employment practice is "unworthy of credence" is "one form of *circumstantial evidence* that is probative of intentional discrimination" (emphasis added). The reason for treating circumstantial and direct evidence alike is both clear and deep-rooted: "Circumstantial evidence is not only sufficient, but may also be more certain, satisfying and persuasive than direct evidence." *Rogers v. Missouri Pacific R. Co.*, 352 U.S. 500, 508, n. 17 (1957)....

Finally, the use of the term "demonstrates" in other provisions of Title VII tends to show further that § 2000e-2(m) does not incorporate a direct evidence requirement. *See, e.g.*, 42 U.S.C. §§ 2000e-2(k)(1)(A)(i), 2000e-5(g)(2)(B). For instance, § 2000e-5(g)(2)(B) requires an employer to "demonstrate that [it] would have taken the same action in the absence of the impermissible motivating factor" in order to take advantage of the partial affirmative defense. Due to the similarity in structure between that provision and § 2000e-2(m), it would be logical to assume that the term "demonstrates" would carry the same meaning with respect to both provisions. But when pressed at oral argument about whether direct evidence is required before the partial affirmative defense can be invoked, petitioner did not "agree that ... the defendant or the employer has any heightened standard" to satisfy.

Absent some congressional indication to the contrary, we decline to give the same term in the same Act a different meaning depending on whether the rights of the plaintiff or the defendant are at issue.

For the reasons stated above, we agree with the Court of Appeals that no heightened showing is required under § 2000e-2(m).

In order to obtain an instruction under § 2000e-2(m), a plaintiff need only present sufficient evidence for a reasonable jury to conclude, by a preponderance of the evidence, that "race, color, religion, sex, or national origin was a motivating factor for any employment practice." Because direct evidence of discrimination is not required in mixed-motive cases, the Court of Appeals correctly concluded that the District Court did not abuse its discretion in giving a mixed-motive instruction to the jury. Accordingly, the judgment of the Court of Appeals is affirmed....

Justice O'CONNOR, concurring.

I join the Court's opinion. In my view, prior to the Civil Rights Act of 1991, the evidentiary rule we developed to shift the burden of persuasion in mixed-motive cases was appropriately applied only where a disparate treatment plaintiff "demonstrated by direct evidence that an illegitimate factor played a substantial role" in an adverse employment decision. *Price Waterhouse v. Hopkins*, (O'Connor, J., concurring in judgment). This showing triggered "the deterrent purpose of the statute" and permitted a reasonable factfinder to conclude that "absent further explanation, the employer's discriminatory motivation 'caused' the employment decision" (O'Connor, J., concurring in judgment).

As the Court's opinion explains, in the Civil Rights Act of 1991, Congress codified a new evidentiary rule for mixed-motive cases arising under Title VII. I therefore agree with the Court that the District Court did not abuse its discretion in giving a mixed-motive instruction to the jury.

NOTES

1. *The Underlying Facts.* The Court's description of the facts is abstract and bloodless. The Ninth Circuit offered a much more robust description:

> Catharina Costa is a trailblazer. She has worked most of her life in a male-dominated environment, driving trucks and operating heavy equipment. . . . [After some time on the job,] Costa began to notice that she was being singled out because she was a woman. Her concerns not only fell on deaf ears — "my word meant nothing" — but resulted in her being treated as an "outcast."
>
> In a series of escalating events that included informal rebukes, denial of privileges accorded her male co-workers, suspension, and finally discharge. Costa's efforts to solve problems were thwarted along the way. . . . [W]hen men came in late, they were often given overtime to make up the lost time; when Costa came in late, in one case, one minute late, she was issued a written reprimand, known as a record of counseling. When men missed work for medical reasons, they were given overtime to make up the lost time; when Costa missed work for medical reasons, she was disciplined. On one occasion, a warehouse supervisor actually suspended her because she had missed work while undergoing surgery to remove a tumor; only the intervention of the director of human resources voided this action. . . .
>
> Costa presented extensive evidence that she received harsher discipline than the men. For instance, she was frequently warned and even suspended for allegedly hazardous use of equipment and for use of profanity, yet other Teamsters engaged in this conduct with impunity. . . .
>
> [W]hen Costa asked her supervisors point blank about the differential treatment of another Teamster who was favored with [more] overtime assignments, [t]he response: He "has a family to support.
>
> Costa also presented evidence that she was penalized for her failure to conform to sexual stereotypes. Although her fellow Teamsters frequently lost their tempers, swore at fellow employees, and sometimes had physical altercations, it was Costa, identified in one report as "the lady Teamster," who was called a "bitch," and told "you got more balls than the guys." . . .
>
> Supervisors frequently used or tolerated verbal slurs that were sex-based or tinged with sexual overtones. Most memorably, one co-worker called her a "fucking cunt." When she wrote a letter to management expressing her concern with this epithet . . . she received a three-day suspension in response. Although the other employee admitted using the epithet, Costa was faulted for "engaging in verbal confrontation with co-worker in the warehouse resulting in use of profane and vulgar language by other employee."

299 F.3d 838, 844-45. Ms. Costa was finally discharged after a co-worker, upset about a report that Costa had snitched on him for taking unauthorized lunch breaks, "trapped Costa in an elevator and shoved her against the wall, bruising her arm." Following an investigation that her supervisor said was inconclusive, Costa was fired and her assailant subjected to only a five day suspension.

2. *"Direct" vs. "Circumstantial" Evidence.* Costa claimed that she was subjected to unequal treatment because she was a woman. Further, it seems plausible that the treatment was not based on either conscious stereotypes or implicit bias. Rather, her male co-workers were consciously hostile to a woman's intrusion into their previously all-male enclave. We will see later that Costa might have claimed a hostile work environment even if she had never been discharged, but for the moment focus on the unequal treatment claim of discharge. Because Costa was the only woman, she might have been subjected to the treatment she challenged because she was a woman. But she might have been subjected to that treatment because she was a jerk. How did the jury conclude that the unequal treatment was because of Costa's sex?

As the *Desert Palace* Court makes clear, after *Price Waterhouse* most lower courts viewed Justice O'Connor's concurrence as stating the governing rule. *See Marks v. United States*, 430 U.S. 188 (1977) (where no majority speaks for the Court, the holding is the narrowest point upon which five justices on the prevailing side agree). As a result, if plaintiff could point to "direct" evidence that sex was "a substantial factor" in the decision, the jury could so find. Even after the 1991 Civil Rights Act substituted "a motivating factor" for Justice O'Connor's "substantial factor," the circuits still generally required "direct evidence" in order to hold the defendant liable. Absent "direct evidence," plaintiff was remitted to the but-for level of showing we saw in *Biggins*.

Direct evidence, therefore, was often outcome determinative. Where it existed, the burden of persuasion of discrimination effectively shifted: plaintiff did not have to prove but-for causation; rather, it could prove something less than that and still establish liability. The employer could avoid most damage liability (but not injunctive relief or attorneys' fees) under § 706(g)(2)(B) by proving sex was *not* the but-for cause of the action taken against the plaintiff — that's essentially what the "same decision" defense means.

While Justice O'Connor in *Price Waterhouse* did not define what evidence was "direct," the evidence in the case included admissions that gender influenced the decision to put plaintiff's candidacy on hold. In the wake of the decision, there was rampant confusion among the lower courts as to whether such admissions were needed for "direct" evidence, and, more generally, what counted as direct as opposed to "circumstantial" proof.

The classic notion of "direct" evidence is evidence that, if believed, proves the ultimate question at issue *without drawing any inferences*. Since the ultimate question in discrimination cases is the intent of the employer to discriminate, i.e., its state of mind, arguably there can never be direct evidence in that classic sense. A slightly broader, but still very narrow view would limit direct evidence to statements made by the employer revealing its state of mind to discriminate at the time it acted. For example, there would be direct evidence, if, in *Desert Palace*, the employer had handed Costa her pink slip while telling her, "We are firing you because you are a woman." *Slack v. Havens*, although decided before *Price Waterhouse*, would have been a direct evidence case. Some other courts defined "direct" evidence somewhat more broadly. For example, they might find statements by the employer not connected with the decision in question to be direct enough and some courts went so far as to include circumstantial evidence that strongly suggested the employer discriminated. Nevertheless, the direct evidence threshold to burden shifting meant that burdens rarely shifted: *Biggins*'s "determinative factor" remained the rule for both Title VII and the ADEA, with direct evidence cases providing a narrow exception. Then came *Desert Palace*.

3. *"Direct" Evidence Not a Prerequisite to Motivating Factor Proof.* The unanimous *Desert Palace* holding is a straightforward reading of § 703(m). Since the statute by its terms does not include a requirement of "direct" evidence, none is necessary: "In order to obtain an instruction under § 2000e-2(m), a plaintiff need only present sufficient evidence for a reasonable jury to conclude, by a preponderance of the evidence, that race, color, religion, sex, or national origin was a motivating factor for any employment practice." This sentence may seem pretty innocuous — after all, isn't the question in any litigation whether the plaintiff can adduce sufficient evidence to make out the violation? In reality, however, this language is potentially paradigm shifting: instead of needing direct evidence to make out a motivating factor, "sufficient evidence," however defined, will do. And a motivating factor is less than but-for causation.

Thus, in cases to which §703(m) applies, plaintiff no longer need prove that race or sex was a determinative factor in an employment decision, and whatever proof she need adduce is okay if it is "sufficient." *Biggins* no longer controls all Title VII cases although it may continue to govern under the ADEA, which was not amended to add a provision like §703(m). The status of causation under §1981 is unclear. *Compare Metoyer v. Chassman*, 2007 U.S. App. LEXIS 22750 (9th Cir. 2007) with *Mabra v. United Food & Commercial Workers Local Union No. 1996*, 176 F.3d 1357 (11th Cir. 1999).

4. *But What Is a §703(m) Case?* But to what cases does §703(m) apply? Maybe the determinative factor requirement is just cut back, not eliminated. If *Price Waterhouse* generated confusion about "direct evidence," *Desert Palace* has generated confusion about when the "motivating factor" standard applies. Although the Court's straight-forward plain meaning approach to the statute suggests that §703(m) applies to all cases, there are indications that the decision can be read narrowly. For example, footnote 1 says that the Court was not deciding the impact of this decision "outside of the mixed-motive context." What is Justice O'Connor's point in her concurrence? Is she merely announcing her acceptance of what amounts to a change Congress made in what had been her earlier view? Or is she trying to limit the scope of application of that change?

Section 703(m) obviously builds on *Price Waterhouse*, which is usually described as a mixed motives case. That is, the trial court found both stereotyping against women and legitimate concerns about plaintiff's abrasiveness. Thus, a mixed motives case involves both legitimate and prohibited factors. It is exactly in these cases that shifting from but-for causation is most significant. But why does *Costa* involve mixed-motives? Was it because plaintiff essentially conceded her conduct had played a role in the termination decision? Or is it because she was involved in a fight (although she didn't initiate it) and had a checkered record (which may have been the result, at least in part, of discrimination)? But don't all individual disparate treatment cases involve a claim of discrimination by the plaintiff and a rebuttal claim by the defendant that it acted for a reason other than discrimination? Judge Denny Chin and Jodi Golinsky in *Employment Discrimination: Beyond McDonnell Douglas: A Simplified Method for Assessing Evidence in Discrimination Cases*, 64 BROOK. L. REV. 659, 666 (1998), found that, in every reported case, plaintiff's claim of discrimination was met by defendant's putting into evidence of "a legitimate, nondiscriminatory reason" for the decision. By the way, the *McDonnell Douglas* reference in the title of Chin & Golinsky refers to a proof structure we have yet to meet but that is the main competing approach to *Desert Palace's* sufficient evidence rule. And "legitimate, nondiscriminatory reason" is an important part of that proof structure.

5. *Back to* Costa. All of this might be a little clearer by revisiting *Costa*. Asking the jury whether discrimination was "a motivating factor" in the employer's decision to fire Costa meant that liability could be established even if, as §703(m) says, "other factors also motivated the practice." Since the jury found sex to be "a motivating factor," we don't know if it concluded that other factors were also involved. But we do know that the jury did not find that the employer "would have taken the same action in the absence of the impermissible motivating factor," as the §706(g)(2)(B) affirmative defense to full remedies requires. The point is, the jury could have given the verdict it did even if it had found that Costa's involvement in a fight on the job did in part motivate the employer to discharge her. Prior *to Desert Palace*, the existence of a "legitimate, nondiscriminatory reason" that in fact motivated the

employer was typically fatal to a plaintiff's case. *Biggins* involved a claim of mixed-motive discrimination — age and pension vesting discrimination — and plaintiff lost his age claim. Rarely would a plaintiff be able to prove a prohibited reason was the determinative one when a legitimate reason also existed; in those rare cases, "direct evidence" was almost always necessary for a plaintiff to prevail.

6. *Single Motive Discrimination.* Presumably, the opposite of a mixed-motive case is a single-motive case. Plaintiff's evidence in *Desert Palace* was so strong that the jury might have found, if asked, that the sole cause of Costa's discharge was her sex. As we will see, however, sole cause is not required by any of the antidiscrimination statutes. Alternatively, the jury could have found the evidence strong enough to find linkage at the but-for level: but for her sex, Costa would not have been fired, and this could be true even had the jury decided that fighting on the job also motivated the employer. But Costa would have lost if fighting with a co-worker was the only reason for the casino's decision. Given the slap-on-the-wrist the initiator of the fight received, that would be very unlikely, but it is a logical possibility.

7. *"A Motivating Factor" Causation.* The significance of some evidence of discrimination depends on what a motivating factor means and how a plaintiff might prove it. Discrimination must play a role — or be a factor or a contributing factor — in a particular decision, but need not cause the decision to occur. *See* Kenneth Davis, *Price-Fixing: Refining the* Price Waterhouse *Standard and Individual Disparate Treatment Law,* 31 FLA. ST. U.L. REV. 859, 894 (2004) (examining legislative history of the statute that suggests that discrimination must have "actually contributed or was otherwise a factor in an employment decision or action" or "actually shown to play a role in a contested employment decision"). One author has suggested that this is best viewed as "minimal causation," which he describes as having "some tendency to influence the event in question but still not rise to the level of necessity or sufficiency." Martin J. Katz, *The Fundamental Incoherence of Title VII: Making Sense of Causation in Disparate Treatment Law,* 94 GEO. L.J. 489, 498-99 (2006). The notion of "tendency" is probabilistic; the plaintiff does not have to prove that the factor made a difference, only that it was likely to make a difference.

Now that we (sort of) know what a motivating factor is, how does a plaintiff prove it? While direct evidence is no longer necessary after *Desert Palace,* the kinds of evidence that would have been called "direct" before that case continue to be powerful in proving a motivating factor. *E.g., Jones v. Robinson Prop. Group, L.P.,* 427 F.3d 987 (5th Cir. 2005) (statements by casino managers to African American applicant for poker dealer positions that black dealers would not normally be hired because "good old white boys don't want blacks touching their cards in their face" barred summary judgment for employer). But *Desert Palace* holds that direct evidence is not required to prove a motivating factor. Circumstantial evidence may also be "sufficient" to prove "motivating factor" discrimination under §703(m).

8. *One Avenue or Two?* The possibility of using circumstantial evidence to prove discrimination creates a serious problem with another line of cases. Prior to *Desert Palace,* almost all individual disparate treatment cases (all those in which there was no direct evidence) were framed as circumstantial evidence cases under a wholly different proof structure. They were typically viewed as was *Biggins* — plaintiff had the burden of proving that a discriminatory motivation caused a particular employment decision and typically did so by a kind of burden shifting that established that the supposed non-discriminatory motivation was merely a pretext hiding the underlying bias. This is the *McDonnell Douglas* model we have referred to and will explore in detail shortly. In the vast majority of such cases, plaintiffs lost.

Has *Desert Palace* trumped *McDonnell Douglas*? Or are both available and, if so, when? We will not definitively answer this question until after studying *McDonnell Douglas* (if then!), but it is critical to individual treatment discrimination. Another way to ask the question is whether the addition of §§703(m) and 706(g)(2)(B) to Title VII by the 1991 Civil Rights Act changed all of Title VII or merely created an alternative to the "normal" analysis under §703(a), which, as we have seen, speaks in "because of" terms, which the Court has read to mean but-for causation. Under the "alternatives" view, a plaintiff could use either avenue.

But at least one employer, and a significant one, has argued a contrary reading. In *Fogg v. Gonzales*, 492 F.3d 447 (D.C. Cir. 2007), the employer was the Department of Justice. Hoping to overturn the grant of full remedies to a plaintiff who had won a jury verdict, it argued that, after the 1991 amendments, defendants in every Title VII case always have the same-decision defense to full remedies provided in §706(g)(2)(B): §703(a) "is merely the 'definition' of the employment practice, whereas §2000e-2(m) provides the standard for liability." *Id.* at 453. The court rejected that approach: "On its face Title VII provides alternative ways of establishing liability for employment practices based upon the impermissible use of race or other proscribed criteria — one in §2000e-2(a), which has been the law since 1964, and another in §2000e-2(m), which the Congress added in 1991." *Id.* In face of the canon of statutory interpretation disfavoring repeals by implication, the court concluded, "we cannot infer from the addition of §2000e-2(m) the implicit repeal of §2000e-2(a) as a standard for establishing liability in preference to the more straightforward inference that §2000e-2(m) add an additional way of establishing liability." *Id.*

This appears to leave both the "but-for" level of proof from §703(a)'s "because of" language, along with the "a motivating factor" standard in §703(m). What *Fogg* does not decide is which one applies where. If plaintiff can convince the factfinder that race or sex was the but-for cause of her treatment by the defendant, that cuts off defendant's same-decision defense of full remedies provided in §706(g)(2)(B). Is it plaintiff's choice of which standard to have applied? Or, can defendant force the plaintiff to include the "a motivating factor" standard in order to preserve defendant's potential same-decision defense to full remedies? Can the two standards be used in the alternative? *See* Note on Litigation Scorecard, p. 110.

C. PROVING THE DISCRIMINATION ELEMENT

The ultimate meaning of discrimination, while perhaps analytically distinct from methods of proving it, is nevertheless intimately bound up with proof problems. The cases that follow struggle with both the meaning of discrimination and the extent to which proof of it can be structured in manageable ways in the litigation process.

PRICE WATERHOUSE v. HOPKINS
490 U.S. 228 (1989)

Justice BRENNAN announced the judgment of the Court and delivered an opinion, in which Justice MARSHALL, Justice BLACKMUN, and Justice STEVENS join. . . .

. . . At Price Waterhouse, a nationwide professional accounting partnership, a senior manager becomes a candidate for partnership when the partners in her local office submit her name as a candidate. All of the other partners in the firm are then invited to submit written comments on each candidate — either on a "long" or a "short" form, depending on the partner's degree of exposure to the candidate. Not every partner in the firm submits comments on every candidate. After reviewing the comments and interviewing the partners who submitted them, the firm's Admissions Committee makes a recommendation to the Policy Board. This recommendation will be either that the firm accept the candidate for partnership, put her application on "hold," or deny her the promotion outright. The Policy Board then decides whether to submit the candidate's name to the entire partnership for a vote, to "hold" her candidacy, or to reject her. The recommendation of the Admissions Committee, and the decision of the Policy Board, are not controlled by fixed guidelines: a certain number of positive comments from partners will not guarantee a candidate's admission to the partnership, nor will a specific quantity of negative comments necessarily defeat her application. Price Waterhouse places no limit on the number of persons whom it will admit to the partnership in any given year.

Ann Hopkins had worked at Price Waterhouse's Office of Government Services in Washington, D.C., for five years when the partners in that office proposed her as a candidate for partnership. Of the 662 partners at the firm at that time, 7 were women. Of the 88 persons proposed for partnership that year, only 1 — Hopkins — was a woman. Forty-seven of these candidates were admitted to the partnership, 21 were rejected, and 20 — including Hopkins — were "held" for reconsideration the following year. Thirteen of the 32 partners who had submitted comments on Hopkins supported her bid for partnership. Three partners recommended that her candidacy be placed on hold, eight stated that they did not have an informed opinion about her, and eight recommended that she be denied partnership.

In a jointly prepared statement supporting her candidacy, the partners in Hopkins' office showcased her successful 2-year effort to secure a $25 million contract with the Department of State, labeling it "an outstanding performance" and one that Hopkins carried out "virtually at the partner level." Despite Price Waterhouse's attempt at trial to minimize her contribution to this project, Judge Gesell specifically found that Hopkins had "played a key role in Price Waterhouse's successful effort to win a multi-million dollar contract with the Department of State." Indeed, he went on, "[n]one of the other partnership candidates at Price Waterhouse that year had a comparable record in terms of successfully securing major contracts for the partnership."

The partners in Hopkins' office praised her character as well as her accomplishments, describing her in their joint statement as "an outstanding professional" who had a "deft touch," a "strong character, independence and integrity." Clients appear to have agreed with these assessments. At trial, one official from the State Department described her as "extremely competent, intelligent," "strong and forthright, very productive, energetic and creative." Another high-ranking official praised Hopkins' decisiveness, broadmindedness, and "intellectual clarity"; she was, in his words, "a stimulating conversationalist." Evaluations such as these led Judge Gesell to conclude that Hopkins "had no difficulty dealing with clients and her clients appear to have been very pleased with her work" and that she "was generally viewed as a highly competent project leader who worked long hours, pushed vigorously to meet deadlines and demanded much from the multidisciplinary staffs with which she worked."

On too many occasions, however, Hopkins' aggressiveness apparently spilled over into abrasiveness. Staff members seem to have borne the brunt of Hopkins' brusqueness. Long before her bid for partnership, partners evaluating her work had counseled her to improve her relations with staff members. Although later evaluations indicate an improvement, Hopkins' perceived shortcomings in this important area eventually doomed her bid for partnership. Virtually all of the partners' negative remarks about Hopkins — even those of partners supporting her — had to do with her "interpersonal skills." Both "[s]upporters and opponents of her candidacy," stressed Judge Gesell, "indicated that she was sometimes overly aggressive, unduly harsh, difficult to work with and impatient with staff."

There were clear signs, though, that some of the partners reacted negatively to Hopkins' personality because she was a woman. One partner described her as "macho"; another suggested that she "overcompensated for being a woman"; a third advised her to take "a course at charm school." Several partners criticized her use of profanity; in response, one partner suggested that those partners objected to her swearing only "because it[']s a lady using foul language." Another supporter explained that Hopkins "ha[d] matured from a tough-talking somewhat masculine hard-nosed mgr to an authoritative, formidable, but much more appealing lady ptr candidate." But it was the man who, as Judge Gesell found, bore responsibility for explaining to Hopkins the reasons for the Policy Board's decision to place her candidacy on hold who delivered the coup de grace: in order to improve her chances for partnership, Thomas Beyer advised, Hopkins should "walk more femininely, talk more femininely, dress more femininely, wear make-up, have her hair styled, and wear jewelry."

Dr. Susan Fiske, a social psychologist and Associate Professor of Psychology at Carnegie-Mellon University, testified at trial that the partnership selection process at Price Waterhouse was likely influenced by sex stereotyping. Her testimony focused not only on the overtly sex-based comments of partners but also on gender-neutral remarks, made by partners who knew Hopkins only slightly, that were intensely critical of her. One partner, for example, baldly stated that Hopkins was "universally disliked" by staff, and another described her as "consistently annoying and irritating"; yet these were people who had had very little contact with Hopkins. According to Fiske, Hopkins' uniqueness (as the only woman in the pool of candidates) and the subjectivity of the evaluations made it likely that sharply critical remarks such as these were the product of sex stereotyping — although Fiske admitted that she could not say with certainty whether any particular comment was the result of stereotyping. Fiske based her opinion on a review of the submitted comments, explaining that it was commonly accepted practice for social psychologists to reach this kind of conclusion without having met any of the people involved in the decisionmaking process.

In previous years, other female candidates for partnership also had been evaluated in sex-based terms. As a general matter, Judge Gesell concluded, "[c]andidates were viewed favorably if partners believed they maintained their femin[in]ity while becoming effective professional managers"; in this environment, "[t]o be identified as a 'women's lib[b]er' was regarded as [a] negative comment." In fact, the judge found that in previous years "[o]ne partner repeatedly commented that he could not consider any woman seriously as a partnership candidate and believed that women were not even capable of functioning as senior managers — yet the firm took no action to discourage his comments and recorded his vote in the overall summary of the evaluations."

Judge Gesell found that Price Waterhouse legitimately emphasized interpersonal skills in its partnership decisions, and also found that the firm had not fabricated its complaints about Hopkins' interpersonal skills as a pretext for discrimination. Moreover, he concluded, the firm did not give decisive emphasis to such traits only because Hopkins was a woman; although there were male candidates who lacked these skills but who were admitted to partnership, the judge found that these candidates possessed other, positive traits that Hopkins lacked.

The judge went on to decide, however, that some of the partners' remarks about Hopkins stemmed from an impermissibly cabined view of the proper behavior of women, and that Price Waterhouse had done nothing to disavow reliance on such comments. He held that Price Waterhouse had unlawfully discriminated against Hopkins on the basis of sex by consciously giving credence and effect to partners' comments that resulted from sex stereotyping. Noting that Price Waterhouse could avoid equitable relief by proving by clear and convincing evidence that it would have placed Hopkins' candidacy on hold even absent this discrimination, the judge decided that the firm had not carried this heavy burden. . . .

II . . .

In passing Title VII, Congress made the simple but momentous announcement that sex, race, religion, and national origin are not relevant to the selection, evaluation, or compensation of employees.[4] Yet, the statute does not purport to limit the other qualities and characteristics that employers may take into account in making employment decisions. The converse, therefore, of "for cause" legislation, Title VII eliminates certain bases for distinguishing among employees while otherwise preserving employers' freedom of choice. This balance between employee rights and employer prerogatives turns out to be decisive in the case before us.

Congress' intent to forbid employers to take gender into account in making employment decisions appears on the face of the statute. In now-familiar language, the statute forbids an employer to "[discriminate] *because of* such individual's . . . sex" (emphasis added). We take these words to mean that gender must be irrelevant to employment decisions. To construe the words "because of" as colloquial shorthand for "but-for causation," as does Price Waterhouse, is to misunderstand them.

But-for causation is a hypothetical construct. In determining whether a particular factor was a but-for cause of a given event, we begin by assuming that that factor was present at the time of the event, and then ask whether, even if that factor had been absent, the event nevertheless would have transpired in the same way. The present, active tense of the operative verbs of §703(a)(1) ("to fail or refuse"), in contrast, turns our attention to the actual moment of the event in question, the adverse employment decision. The critical inquiry, the one commanded by the words of §703(a)(1), is whether gender was a factor in the employment decision *at the moment it was made.* Moreover, since we know that the words "because of" do not mean "solely because of,"[7] we also know that Title VII meant to condemn even those decisions based on a mixture of legitimate and illegitimate considerations. When, therefore, an employer considers both gender and legitimate factors at the time of making a decision, that decision was "because of" sex and the other, legitimate considerations — even if we

---

4. We disregard, for purposes of this discussion, the special context of affirmative action.

7. Congress specifically rejected an amendment that would have placed the word "solely" in front of the words "because of." 110 Cong. Rec. 2728, 13837 (1964).

may say later, in the context of litigation, that the decision would have been the same if gender had not been taken into account.

To attribute this meaning to the words "because of" does not, as the dissent asserts, divest them of causal significance. A simple example illustrates the point. Suppose two physical forces act upon and move an object, and suppose that either force acting alone would have moved the object. As the dissent would have it, neither physical force was a "cause" of the motion unless we can show that but for one or both of them, the object would not have moved; to use the dissent's terminology, both forces were simply "in the air" unless we can identify at least one of them as a but-for cause of the object's movement. Events that are causally overdetermined, in other words, may not have any "cause" at all. This cannot be so.

[Congress did not intend to require a plaintiff "to identify the precise causal role played by legitimate and illegitimate motivations"; it meant only to require her "to prove that the employer relied upon sex-based considerations" in its decision.]

To say that an employer may not take gender into account is not, however, the end of the matter, for that describes only one aspect of Title VII. The other important aspect of the statute is its preservation of an employer's remaining freedom of choice. We conclude that the preservation of this freedom means that an employer shall not be liable if it can prove that, even if it had not taken gender into account, it would have come to the same decision regarding a particular person. The statute's maintenance of employer prerogatives is evident from the statute itself and from its history, both in Congress and in this Court. . . .

The central point is this: while an employer may not take gender into account in making an employment decision . . . , it is free to decide against a woman for other reasons. We think these principles require that, once a plaintiff in a Title VII case shows that gender played a motivating part in an employment decision, the defendant may avoid a finding of liability only by proving that it would have made the same decision even if it had not allowed gender to play such a role. This balance of burdens is the direct result of Title VII's balance of rights. . . . [12]

C

In saying that gender played a motivating part in an employment decision, we mean that, if we asked the employer at the moment of the decision what its reasons were and if we received a truthful response, one of those reasons would be that the applicant or employee was a woman. In the specific context of sex stereotyping, an employer who acts on the basis of a belief that a woman cannot be aggressive, or that she must not be, has acted on the basis of gender.

. . . As to the existence of sex stereotyping in this case, we are not inclined to quarrel with the District Court's conclusion that a number of the partners' comments showed sex stereotyping at work. As for the legal relevance of sex stereotyping,

---

12. Nothing in this opinion should be taken to suggest that a case must be correctly labeled as either a "pretext" case or a "mixed-motives" case from the beginning in the District Court; indeed, we expect that plaintiffs often will allege, in the alternative, that their cases are both. Discovery often will be necessary before the plaintiff can know whether both legitimate and illegitimate considerations played a part in the decision against her. At some point in the proceedings, of course, the District Court must decide whether a particular case involves mixed motives. If the plaintiff fails to satisfy the factfinder that it is more likely than not that a forbidden characteristic played a part in the employment decision, then she may prevail only if she proves . . . that the employer's stated reason for its decision is pretextual. The dissent need not worry that this evidentiary scheme, if used during a jury trial, will be so impossibly confused and complex as it imagines. Juries long have decided cases in which defendants raised affirmative defenses. . . .

we are beyond the day when an employer could evaluate employees by assuming or insisting that they matched the stereotype associated with their group. . . . An employer who objects to aggressiveness in women but whose positions require this trait places women in an intolerable and impermissible Catch-22: out of a job if they behave aggressively and out of a job if they don't. Title VII lifts women out of this bind.

Remarks at work that are based on sex stereotypes do not inevitably prove that gender played a part in a particular employment decision. The plaintiff must show that the employer actually relied on her gender in making its decision. In making this showing, stereotyped remarks can certainly be evidence that gender played a part. In any event, the stereotyping in this case did not simply consist of stray remarks. On the contrary, Hopkins proved that Price Waterhouse invited partners to submit comments; that some of the comments stemmed from sex stereotypes; that an important part of the Policy Board's decision on Hopkins was an assessment of the submitted comments; and that Price Waterhouse in no way disclaimed reliance on the sex-linked evaluations. This is not, as Price Waterhouse suggests, "discrimination in the air"; rather, it is, as Hopkins puts it, "discrimination brought to ground and visited upon" an employee. By focusing on Hopkins' specific proof, however, we do not suggest a limitation on the possible ways of proving that stereotyping played a motivating role in an employment decision, and we refrain from deciding here which specific facts, "standing alone," would or would not establish a plaintiff's case, since such a decision is unnecessary in this case.

As to the employer's proof, in most cases, the employer should be able to present some objective evidence as to its probable decision in the absence of an impermissible motive.[15] Moreover, proving "that the same decision would have been justified . . . is not the same as proving that the same decision would have been made." An employer may not, in other words, prevail in a mixed-motives case by offering a legitimate and sufficient reason for its decision if that reason did not motivate it at the time of the decision. Finally, an employer may not meet its burden in such a case by merely showing that at the time of the decision it was motivated only in part by a legitimate reason. The very premise of a mixed-motives case is that a legitimate reason was present, and indeed, in this case, Price Waterhouse already has made this showing by convincing Judge Gesell that Hopkins' interpersonal problems were a legitimate concern. The employer instead must show that its legitimate reason, standing alone, would have induced it to make the same decision.

III

The courts below held that an employer who has allowed a discriminatory impulse to play a motivating part in an employment decision must prove by clear and convincing evidence that it would have made the same decision in the absence of discrimination. We are persuaded that the better rule is that the employer must make this showing by a preponderance of the evidence. . . .

---

15. Justice White's suggestion [in his concurring opinion] that the employer's own testimony as to the probable decision in the absence of discrimination is due special credence where the court has, contrary to the employer's testimony, found that an illegitimate factor played a part in the decision, is baffling.

IV

[Price Waterhouse challenges as clearly erroneous the district court's findings both that stereotyping occurred and that it played any part in the decision to place Hopkins' candidacy on hold. The plurality disagreed.]

In finding that some of the partners' comments reflected sex stereotyping, the District Court relied in part on Dr. Fiske's expert testimony. Without directly impugning Dr. Fiske's credentials or qualifications, Price Waterhouse insinuates that a social psychologist is unable to identify sex stereotyping in evaluations without investigating whether those evaluations have a basis in reality. This argument comes too late. At trial, counsel for Price Waterhouse twice assured the court that he did not question Dr. Fiske's expertise and failed to challenge the legitimacy of her discipline. Without contradiction from Price Waterhouse, Fiske testified that she discerned sex stereotyping in the partners' evaluations of Hopkins and she further explained that it was part of her business to identify stereotyping in written documents. We are not inclined to accept petitioner's belated and unsubstantiated characterization of Dr. Fiske's testimony as "gossamer evidence" based only on "intuitive hunches" and of her detection of sex stereotyping as "intuitively divined." Nor are we disposed to adopt the dissent's dismissive attitude toward Dr. Fiske's field of study and toward her own professional integrity.

Indeed, we are tempted to say that Dr. Fiske's expert testimony was merely icing on Hopkins' cake. It takes no special training to discern sex stereotyping in a description of an aggressive female employee as requiring "a course at charm school." Nor, turning to Thomas Beyer's memorable advice to Hopkins, does it require expertise in psychology to know that, if an employee's flawed "interpersonal skills" can be corrected by a soft-hued suit or a new shade of lipstick, perhaps it is the employee's sex and not her interpersonal skills that has drawn the criticism.

Price Waterhouse also charges that Hopkins produced no evidence that sex stereotyping played a role in the decision to place her candidacy on hold. As we have stressed, however, Hopkins showed that the partnership solicited evaluations from all of the firm's partners; that it generally relied very heavily on such evaluations in making its decision; that some of the partners' comments were the product of stereotyping; and that the firm in no way disclaimed reliance on those particular comments, either in Hopkins' case or in the past. Certainly a plausible — and, one might say, inevitable — conclusion to draw from this set of circumstances is that the Policy Board in making its decision did in fact take into account all of the partners' comments, including the comments that were motivated by stereotypical notions about women's proper deportment. . . .

V

We hold that when a plaintiff in a Title VII case proves that her gender played a motivating part in an employment decision, the defendant may avoid a finding of liability only by proving by a preponderance of the evidence that it would have made the same decision even if it had not taken the plaintiff's gender into account. . . .

Justice O'CONNOR concurring in the judgment.

I agree with the plurality that on the facts presented in this case, the burden of persuasion should shift to the employer to demonstrate by a preponderance of the evidence that it would have reached the same decision concerning Ann Hopkins' candidacy absent consideration of her gender. I further agree that this burden shift is properly part of the liability phase of the litigation. I thus concur in the judgment of the Court. My disagreement stems from the plurality's conclusions concerning the substantive requirement of causation under the statute and its broad statements regarding the applicability of the allocation of the burden of proof applied in this case. . . .

I

. . . The legislative history of Title VII bears out what its plain language suggests: a substantive violation of the statute only occurs when consideration of an illegitimate criterion is the "but-for" cause of an adverse employment action. The legislative history makes it clear that Congress was attempting to eradicate discriminatory actions in the employment setting, not mere discriminatory thoughts. Critics of the bill that became Title VII labeled it a "thought control bill," and argued that it created a "punishable crime that does not require an illegal external act as a basis for judgment." Senator Case . . . responded:

> The man must do or fail to do something in regard to employment. There must be some specific external act, more than a mental act. Only if he does the act because of the grounds stated in the bill would there be any legal consequences.

Thus, I disagree with the plurality's dictum that the words "because of" do not mean "but-for" causation; manifestly they do. We should not, and need not, deviate from that policy today. . . .

The evidence of congressional intent as to which party should bear the burden of proof on the issue of causation is considerably less clear. . . . [In the area of tort liability,] the law has long recognized that in certain "civil cases" leaving the burden of persuasion on the plaintiff to prove "but-for" causation would be both unfair and destructive of the deterrent purposes embodied in the concept of duty of care. Thus, in multiple causation cases, where a breach of duty has been established, the common law of torts has long shifted the burden of proof to multiple defendants to prove that their negligent actions were not the "but-for" cause of the plaintiff's injury. See, e.g., *Summers v. Tice*, 33 Cal. 2d 80, 199 P.2d 1 (1948). The same rule has been applied where the effect of a defendant's tortious conduct combines with a force of unknown or innocent origin to produce the harm to the plaintiff. *See Kingston v. Chicago & N.W.R. Co.*, 191 Wis. 610, 616, 211 N.W. 913, 915 (1927). . . .

. . . There is no doubt that Congress considered reliance on gender or race in making employment decisions an evil in itself. . . . Reliance on such factors is exactly what the threat of Title VII liability was meant to deter. While the main concern of the statute was with employment opportunity, Congress was certainly not blind to the stigmatic harm which comes from being evaluated by a process which treats one as an inferior by reason of one's race or sex. . . . At the same time, Congress clearly conditioned legal liability on a determination that the consideration of an illegitimate factor caused a tangible employment injury of some kind.

Where an individual disparate treatment plaintiff has shown by a preponderance of the evidence that an illegitimate criterion was a *substantial* factor in an adverse employment decision, the deterrent purpose of the statute has clearly been triggered. More importantly, as an evidentiary matter, a reasonable factfinder could conclude that absent further explanation, the employer's discriminatory motivation "caused" the employment decision. The employer has not yet been shown to be a violator, but neither is it entitled to the same presumption of good faith concerning its employment decisions which is accorded employers facing only circumstantial evidence of discrimination. Both the policies behind the statute, and the evidentiary principles developed in the analogous area of causation in the law of torts, suggest that at this point the employer may be required to convince the factfinder that, despite the smoke, there is no fire. . . .

II

. . .

[T]he facts of this case, and a growing number like it decided by the Courts of Appeals, convince me that the evidentiary standard I propose is necessary to make real the promise of *McDonnell Douglas*. . . . As the Court of Appeals characterized it, Ann Hopkins proved that Price Waterhouse "permitt[ed] stereotypical attitudes towards women to play a significant, though unquantifiable, role in its decision not to invite her to become a partner."

At this point Ann Hopkins had taken her proof as far as it could go. She had proved discriminatory input into the decisional process, and had proved that participants in the process considered her failure to conform to the stereotypes credited by a number of the decisionmakers had been a substantial factor in the decision. It is as if Ann Hopkins were sitting in the hall outside the room where partnership decisions were being made. As the partners filed in to consider her candidacy, she heard several of them make sexist remarks in discussing her suitability for partnership. As the decisionmakers exited the room, she was told by one of those privy to the decisionmaking process that her gender was a major reason for the rejection of her partnership bid. [If] "presumptions shifting the burden of proof are often created to reflect judicial evaluations of probabilities and to conform with a party's superior access to the proof," one would be hard pressed to think of a situation where it would be more appropriate to require the defendant to show that its decision would have been justified by wholly legitimate concerns. . . .

[The plurality, however, goes too far by holding that the burden shifts when "a decisional process is 'tainted' by awareness of sex or race in any way."]

In my view, in order to justify shifting the burden on the issue of causation to the defendant, a disparate treatment plaintiff must show by direct evidence that an illegitimate criterion was a substantial factor in the decision. . . . Requiring that the plaintiff demonstrate that an illegitimate factor played a substantial role in the employment decision identifies those employment situations where the deterrent purpose of Title VII is most clearly implicated. As an evidentiary matter, where a plaintiff has made this type of strong showing of illicit motivation, the factfinder is entitled to presume that the employer's discriminatory animus made a difference to the outcome, absent proof to the contrary from the employer. Where a disparate treatment plaintiff has made such a showing, the burden then rests with the employer to convince the trier of fact that it is more likely than not that the decision would have been the same absent consideration of the illegitimate factor. The employer need not isolate the sole cause for the decision; rather it must demonstrate that with the illegitimate factor removed from the calculus, sufficient business reasons would have induced it to take the same employment action. . . . If the employer fails to carry this burden, the factfinder is justified in concluding that the decision was made "because of" consideration of the illegitimate factor and the substantive standard for liability under the statute is satisfied.

Thus, stray remarks in the workplace, while perhaps probative of sexual harassment, see *Meritor Savings Bank v. Vinson* [reproduced at p. 370] cannot justify requiring the employer to prove that its hiring or promotion decisions were based on legitimate criteria. Nor can statements by nondecisionmakers, or statements by decisionmakers unrelated to the decisional process itself suffice to satisfy the plaintiff's burden in this regard. In addition, in my view testimony such as Dr. Fiske's in this case, standing alone, would not justify shifting the burden of persuasion to the employer. Race and gender always "play a role" in an employment decision in the benign sense that these are human characteristics of which decisionmakers are aware and may comment on in a perfectly neutral and nondiscriminatory fashion. For example, in the context of this case, a mere reference to "a lady candidate" might show that gender "played a role" in the decision, but by no means could support a rational factfinder's inference that the decision was made "because of" sex. What is required is what Ann Hopkins showed here: direct evidence that decisionmakers placed substantial negative reliance on an illegitimate criterion in reaching their decision.

It should be obvious that the threshold standard I would adopt for shifting the burden of persuasion to the defendant differs substantially from that proposed by the plurality, the plurality's suggestion to the contrary notwithstanding. . . . Under my approach, the plaintiff must produce evidence sufficient to show that an illegitimate criterion was a substantial factor in the particular employment decision such that a reasonable factfinder could draw an inference that the decision was made "because of" the plaintiff's protected status. Only then would the burden of proof shift to the defendant to prove that the decision would have been justified by other, wholly legitimate considerations. . . .

[Justice KENNEDY, joined by Chief Justice REHNQUIST and Justice SCALIA, dissented. The dissent viewed the plurality, despite its rhetoric, as adopting a but-for standard. "Labels aside, the import of today's decision is not that Title VII liability can arise without but-for causation, but that in certain cases it is not the plaintiff who must prove the presence of causation, but the defendant who must prove its absence."

The dissent was particularly critical of Dr. Fiske: she "purported to discern stereotyping in comments that were gender neutral — e.g., 'overbearing and abrasive' — without any knowledge of the comments' basis in reality and without having met the speaker or subject." It quoted a judge below to the effect that, "[t]o an expert of Dr. Fiske's qualifications, it seems plain that no woman could be overbearing, arrogant, or abrasive: any observations to that effect would necessarily be discounted as the product of stereotyping. If analysis like this is to prevail in federal courts, no employer can base any adverse action as to a woman on such attributes."]

NOTES

1. *Causation Again.* We have omitted Justice White's opinion, but his and all of the other opinions in *Price Waterhouse* assume that but-for causation was necessary, that is, the *Biggins* determinative factor test applied to individual disparate treatment cases. The employer had a legitimate reason for not promoting Ann Hopkins — her lack of skill in dealing with her staff. But her gender was also a factor, maybe or maybe not a determinative one. *Price Waterhouse* differs from *Biggins*, however, in that six justices (the plurality and Justices White and O'Connor), would shift the burden of persuasion on causation. When plaintiff established by a preponderance of the evidence that sex was a "motivating factor" (for O'Connor and White, a "substantial factor"), the burden shifted to defendant to negate but-for causation by establishing by a preponderance of the evidence that it would have made the same decision anyway.

The six justices who took this approach would have made liability turn on whether the same decision defense was established. We've seen that the 1991 CRA altered this in an important way: not only did Congress opt for the plurality's "motivating factor" (rejecting the O'Connor/White presumably more limited "substantial factor" test), but it also provided in §703(m) that proof of a motivating factor establishes a violation — period. §706(g)(2)(B) does incorporate *Price Waterhouse's* same decision defense, but only to limit remedies — not to negate defendant's liability. And, of course, *Desert Palace* read §703(m) as rejecting Justice O'Connor's "direct evidence" requirement for proving a motivating factor.

2. A *Motivating Factor Again.* §703(m) requires proof of a motivating factor, and clearly adopted that language from the *Price Waterhouse* plurality. Justice Brennan, in turn, defined what he meant: "In saying that gender played a motivating part in an employment decision, we mean that, if we asked the employer at the moment of the decision what its reasons were and if we received a truthful response, *one of those reasons* would be that the applicant or employee was a woman" (emphasis added). A recent article unpacked this passage:

> This description reflects two "common sense" theories about the nature of discriminatory motivation. In speaking of the decision maker providing a "truthful" (as opposed to an "accurate") response, this description reflects an unstated assumption that, when disparate treatment discrimination occurs, the discriminator is consciously aware, "at the moment of decision," that he or she is discriminating. [But] the belief in transparent mental processing, and the modeling of perception and decision making as two discrete processes . . . have not withstood empirical scrutiny. Decision makers are often not aware of the impact of a target's social group membership on their judgments, and those biased judgments are often formed quite early in the social perception process, long before the moment that a decision about the target person is made.

Linda Hamilton Krieger & Susan T. Fiske, *Behavioral Realism in Employment Discrimination Law: Implicit Bias and Disparate Treatment*, 94 CAL. L. REV. 997, 1010 (2006). Further, the authors argue that intent and motive are two different things, and that the Congress's adoption of "motivating factor" suggests that it is motive that is critical:

> Although they are similar, "motive" does not mean the same thing as "intent." Black's Law Dictionary, for example, distinguishes the two concepts as follows: "Motive is what prompts a person to act, or fail to act. Intent refers only to the state of mind with which the act is done or omitted." . . . The Webster's Third New International Dictionary of the English Language, Unabridged defines the word "motive" as "something within a person (as need, idea, organic state, or emotion) that incites him to action." In other words, a "motivating factor" is an internal mental state, a category that includes cognitive structures like implicit stereotypes or other social schema that influence social perception, judgment, and action. For race, color, sex, national origin, or other protected characteristics to "motivate" an employment decision means that the characteristic served as a stimulus which, interacting with the decision maker's internal biased mental state, led the decision maker to behave toward the person differently than he otherwise would.

Id. at 1056. Krieger & Fiske argue that "it is not possible for judges to interpret what Congress meant when it used the term 'discrimination' or the phrase 'motivating factor' in Title VII without applying psychological theories about how human social perception, motivation, and judgment work — that is, psychological theories about when people are discriminating and when they are not." *Id.* at 1010.

These scholars to the contrary notwithstanding, Justice Brennan did define motivating factor in the passage the authors quote and criticize for not taking into account deeper psychological impulses. Why isn't it possible to interpret Congress as adopting Brennan's "common sense" view, even if that view would not be shared by psychologists? But he also wrote that "we are beyond the day when an employer could evaluate employees by assuming or insistent that they match the stereotype associated with their group." Was Brennan speaking only of consciously held stereotypes? In other words, what, if anything does *Price Waterhouse* and motivating factor analysis say about unconscious bias?

3. *Proving a Motivating Factor.* Does *Price Waterhouse* assist you in understanding how a motivating factor can be proven? Ann Hopkins's sex entered into the consideration of her candidacy, whether or not it had a determinative influence. Beyer's advice certainly suggested he thought that Hopkins would have more success the next year if she conformed more closely to stereotypes of the feminine, and other comments linked criticism to her sex. And then there was the partner who said that he would never vote for a woman partner — maybe that by itself shows that gender "played a role" in the decision. But all of this proof turns on statements by the decisionmakers, and most of the statements concerned the decision in question. In other words, most of the proof was what Justice O'Connor called "direct evidence." We now know from *Desert Palace* that such evidence is not needed for a §703(m) motivating factor case, but what other evidence will suffice?

4. *Mixed Motives vs. Pretext.* *Price Waterhouse* departs from discrimination cases the Court had decided previously in another fundamental way. Most of those cases could be framed as "single motive" cases — the employer had either acted from discriminatory motives or it had acted because of its asserted "legitimate, nondiscriminatory reason." But Price Waterhouse convinced the trial judge that Hopkins did in fact have serious interpersonal issues that an employer could rightly take into account in making partnership decisions. Thus, its nondiscriminatory reason was not a "pretext" for discrimination; rather, it existed together with discriminatory attitudes. While also finding that the defendant was motivated by sex, the trial judge did not determine whether discrimination or defendant's asserted reason was the but-for cause of defendant's putting Hopkins's partnership bid on hold. Instead, the trial judge found that defendant failed to prove that it would have made the same-decision even if it had not discriminated. The Court agreed, but Congress went even further by declaring that the existence of a discriminatory motivating factor was a violation, entirely apart from but-for causation.

5. *Two Distinct Proof Methods?* We have seen that Justice O'Connor's concurrence stated the narrowest grounds on which *Price Waterhouse* was decided and therefore became the holding of the case. Therefore, after *Price Waterhouse* and before *Desert Palace*, at least two separate methods of proof applied to individual disparate treatment cases. Analytically the first question for every case was whether plaintiff could point to "direct" evidence of discrimination to support her claim. If so, then the "substantial factor" showing established a violation, albeit subject to the defendant's potential same-decision affirmative defense to liability. Lacking evidence that the court would be willing to characterize as "direct," the default analysis was for the plaintiff to carry the burden of proving that discrimination was the but-for cause of defendant's action, presumably using the *McDonnell Douglas* method. That imposed on the plaintiff a higher level of proof than required by *Price Waterhouse*, but, if successful, it necessarily prevented the defendant from showing that it would have made the same-decision even absent discrimination.

The 1991 Civil Rights Act modified *Price Waterhouse* by (1) adopting the "a motivating factor" level of showing, (2) which showing established defendant's liability and, (3) providing defendants the same-decision defense to full remedies for the plaintiff, rather than a complete defense to liability. *Desert Palace* made clear, at least in so-called mixed-motive cases like *Price Waterhouse*, that there was no need for a plaintiff to point to "direct" evidence to avail herself of the "motivating factor" level of proof of liability. What is as of yet still not finally resolved is whether some types of individual disparate treatment cases are not mixed-motive cases and, therefore, are not to be analyzed using the approach established by §§ 703(m) and 706(g)(2)(B). Without getting too far ahead of ourselves, the lower courts have tended, even after *Desert Palace*, to view § 703(m) as applicable only to "mixed motive" cases, which are viewed as the exception, with single motive cases (and their requirement of "but-for" causation) as the rule. The result is that plaintiffs must still tend to disprove the defendant's asserted nondiscriminatory reason, not merely prove that discriminatory attitudes were another factor in the challenged decision.

6. *"Direct" Evidence Is Still Important.* Justice O'Connor did not really define what she meant by "direct" evidence but instead suggested some types of evidence that would *not* satisfy her — stray remarks in the workplace, statements by non-decisionmakers, or statements by decisionmakers unrelated to the decisional process that was challenged, or expert testimony that certain language, while not expressly referencing sex, nevertheless, suggested sexual stereotypes were at work. After *Desert Palace*, "direct" evidence is no longer necessary for a plaintiff to prove "a motivating factor," so presumably all of the evidence that would not have satisfied Justice O'Connor is now available to make that showing.

Nevertheless, the kind of evidence that might have been characterized as "direct" before *Desert Palace* remains very important as a way of proving discrimination under Title VII. Further, the 1991 Civil Rights Act did not amend the ADEA, which means that *Price Waterhouse* may remain controlling under that statute since the Supreme Court has generally applied precedent interpreting Title VII as it was originally passed to the ADEA, whose language was very similar. See *Smith v. City of Jackson*, reproduced at p. 223. Thus, while "direct" evidence is no longer the threshold to the "motivating factor" proof, it is worth some analysis.

7. *An Evidence Primer.* The preceding Notes suggest that employment discrimination law and evidence law intersect in potentially critical ways. The biggest evidence problem for present purposes is hearsay. When A testifies to his own motivations, there is no hearsay problem. When, however, B testifies as to what A said about A's motivations, the testimony is technically hearsay if it is introduced for its truth, that is, that A had such motivations. An example from *Price Waterhouse* is the partner who stated that no woman should ever be promoted to partner. If this statement was introduced for its truth, that is, that he believed women cannot be partners, it is hearsay. If it were introduced merely for its effects on other partners, its truth would be irrelevant, and it would not be hearsay. The law of evidence admits such statements only if defined as "nonhearsay" or pursuant to some exception to the hearsay rule. As the *Price Waterhouse* example suggests, there is a further complication: In the usual case, the employer will be a corporation or other legal entity that can only act through its agents, and the threshold question is whether the statement in question was made within the scope of the agent's employment.

The most common basis for admission of such statements in Title VII cases is admissions of a party opponent (which, of course, includes a party's agents speaking within the scope of their agency). *See* KENNETH S. BROUN, McCORMICK

ON EVIDENCE, §254, at 445 (6th ed. 2006). To the extent that the speaker was commenting about matters within the scope of his or her employment at the time of the statement, such comments would generally be admissible as nonhearsay. *See Fester v. Farmer Bros. Co.*, 49 Fed. Appx. 785, 796-97 (10th Cir. 2002) ("Henshaw, the division manager in charge of the Denver branch, led the investigation that resulted in Fester's discharge. It is also undisputed that Henshaw is the Farmer Bros. employee who notified Fester of his termination. Henshaw's statement was clearly within the scope of his employment and was nonhearsay"); *Marra v. Philadelphia Housing Auth.*, 497 F.3d 286 (3d Cir. 2007) (supervisor's statement concerning "repercussions" for employee who testified against the employer in a discrimination case was admissible because it was made within the scope of his employment); *but see Barner v. Pilkington N. Am., Inc.*, 399 F.3d 745, 750 (6th Cir. 2005) (excluded statements were not by managerial employees speaking within the scope of their duties; they were made by the employees "solely to advance their own interests" and the "scope of their employment did not include work assignments").

8. *Employer Admissions.* We have seen, p. 29, that "direct evidence" is a misnomer and that Justice O'Connor was using that term to refer to employer admissions. Assuming that to be true, such admission evidence raises four questions:

(a) *What did the agent actually say?* Students sometimes think that for an "admission" by a party to exist, the party must make the statement in court or in pleadings. While such statements are admissions, any out-of-court statement by a party to a case may also be used against it. Thus, the plaintiff's testimony of an employer's admission alone may create a jury issue of mixed-motives when it satisfies the requirement of showing an illegitimate consideration in operation. *EEOC v. Warfield-Rohr Casket Co.*, 364 F.3d 160, 163-64 (4th Cir. 2004) ("there is no requirement that an employee's testimony [of the employer's admissions] be corroborated in order to apply the mixed-motive framework"); *Horne v. Turner Construction Co.*, 136 Fed. Appx. 289 (11th Cir. 2005) (even though hearsay, testimony as to statements made by a supervisor who has a role in the decision-making process is generally admissible as admissions by a party's agent when made within the scope of the supervisor's authority).

(b) *Does the statement show illegitimate considerations?* Language is a slippery tool, and statements may be ambiguous about their racial content. In *Ash v. Tyson Foods, Inc.*, 546 U.S. 454, 456-457 (2006), the Supreme Court dealt with that issue in rejecting the crabbed approach of the lower court:

> [T]here was evidence that Tyson's plant manager, who made the disputed hiring decisions, had referred on some occasions to each of the petitioners as "boy." Petitioners argued this was evidence of discriminatory animus. The Court of Appeals disagreed, holding that "while the use of 'boy' when modified by a racial classification like 'black' or 'white' is evidence of discriminatory intent, the use of 'boy' alone is not evidence of discrimination." Although it is true the disputed word will not always be evidence of racial animus, it does not follow that the term, standing alone, is always benign. The speaker's meaning may depend on various factors including context, inflection, tone of voice, local custom, and historical usage. Insofar as the Court of Appeals held that modifiers or qualifications are necessary in all instances to render the disputed term probative of bias, the court's decision is erroneous.

On remand, the Eleventh Circuit reaffirmed its earlier decision: "the use of 'boy' by Hatley was not sufficient, either alone or with the other evidence, to provide a basis for a jury reasonably to find that Tyson's stated reasons for not promoting the plaintiffs was racial discrimination. The usages were conversational and as found by the district court were non-racial in context." 190 Fed. Appx. 924, 926 (11th Cir. 2006). Given the social history of the South, isn't a white calling an adult African American male a "boy" at least a question for the jury as to the racial significance of that usage?

Some courts, however, have found less explicit comments capable of being found racist. In *McGinest v. GTE Serv. Corp.*, 360 F.3d 1103, 1116-17 (9th Cir. 2004), the district court, although finding clear evidence of racist comments in terms of epithets such as "nigger," had viewed other harassment also as racial with respect to less explicit epithets, as when the plaintiff was called a drug dealer since that might be seen as the use of code words for race.

> [A] reasonable jury could conclude that the intent to discriminate is implicit in these comments. There are no talismanic expressions which must be invoked as a condition-precedent to the application of laws designed to protect against discrimination. The words themselves are only relevant for what they reveal — the intent of the speaker. A reasonable jury could find that statements like the ones allegedly made in this case send a clear message and carry the distinct tone of racial motivations and implications. They could be seen as conveying the message that members of a particular race are disfavored and that members of that race are, therefore, not full and equal members of the workplace.

But see Putman v. Unity Health Sys., 348 F.3d 732 (8th Cir. 2003) (comments about plaintiff not being "humble enough" and being "too prideful" not clearly linked to race). Similar issues arise in the ADEA context. *See also Skelton v. Sara Lee Corp.*, 2007 U.S. App. LEXIS 23521 (6th Cir. 2007) (statement that plaintiff had been around "since Christ was a baby" was not direct evidence when made by a supervisor with limited influence on plaintiff's termination and may not have been made near in time to the decision). *Thomas v. Sears, Roebuck & Co.*, 144 F.3d 31, 34 (1st Cir. 1998) (when plaintiff conceded that he disagreed with the company's change in business phil-osophy, "a criticism that someone is unable to change is not a coded allusion cloaking age discrimination").

(c) *Is the statement connected closely enough with the at-issue decision?* Even statements revealing bias are not necessarily admissions that constitute direct evidence as to any particular decision; Justice O'Connor and numerous circuits also required that the statement be closely enough related to the at-issue decision. In the *Ash* remand, one basis for the Eleventh Circuit's reaffirming its original decision was that, "even if somehow construed as racial, . . . the comments were ambiguous stray remarks not uttered in the context of the decisions at issue and are not sufficient circumstantial evidence of bias to provide a reasonable basis for a finding of racial discrimination in the denial of the promotions." 90 Fed. Appx. at 926. *See also Jennings v. State Dep't of Corrections*, 496 F.3d 764 (7th Cir. 2007) (no causal connection shown between discriminatory attitudes of individuals and adverse action).

Isn't the *Ash* decision on remand in tension with *Desert Palace*? If the decision-maker in question made racist statements, even if unconnected with the decision in question, isn't that evidence from which a jury could find that race "played a role"? The Eleventh Circuit referred to them as "ambiguous stray remarks," so perhaps it did not think that they even showed a racial attitude. But if the racial connotation could be found, why would it matter from a "motivating factor" perspective that the remarks were made in connection with a different decision or even a few years in the past? Even if not uttered in the context of the decision about the promotions and assuming that "boy" was used by the supervisor as a demeaning racial epithet, its use would seem strong circumstantial evidence that in the mind of the speaker the plaintiffs' race was a negative.

(d) *Did the speaker mean what he said?* Speakers joke or in other ways may not mean what they are heard to say. That does not affect admissibility, but a jury could conclude that a statement was made by the decision-maker but that he did not mean it literally. *See Goodwin v. Circuit Court*, 729 F.2d 541, 546 (8th Cir. 1984) (while the defendant claimed that his statement, "This court will never run well so long as there are women in charge" was made in jest, "the jury could well have disbelieved him or have felt that jokes like these indicate a bias against women").

9. *Expert Testimony of Stereotyping.* As to statements that did not expressly refer to sex that formed the basis of the testimony of the expert witness, Dr. Susan Fiske, the plurality in *Price Waterhouse* indicated that it might be "merely icing on the cake." Presumably, that means it was useful but not necessary. Justice O'Connor, in contrast, was more skeptical of such testimony. *See generally* Cynthia Estlund, *The Story of Price Waterhouse v. Hopkins* in EMPLOYMENT DISCRIMINATION STORIES (Joel Wm. Friedman ed. 2006) (Dr. Fiske's unprecedented testimony on stereotyping enabled the Court to recognize the "double bind" [of simultaneously being required to be and yet punished for being tough and aggressive] to which women like Ann Hopkins were subjected in traditionally male-dominated workplaces).

In contrast, Justice Kennedy's dissent was scathing: "Fiske purported to discern stereotyping in comments that were gender neutral — e.g., 'overbearing and abrasive' — without any knowledge of the comments' basis in reality and without having met the speaker or subject." Is this criticism valid? May not certain statements be susceptible of varying meanings, with expert testimony helping the factfinder in deciding whether the statements are likely to reflect stereotyping? Does the Supreme Court's decision in *Ash v. Tyson Foods, Inc.* suggest that the answer is yes? Might a social scientist enlighten the jury on the racial significance of "boy" used toward an adult black male? One state court took the exact opposite position as to expertise: sex stereotyping was so familiar to the population that juries would not be assisted by expert testimony. *Ray v. Miller Meester Adver. Inc.*, 664 N.W.2d 355, 365-66 (Minn. App. 2003) (an abuse of discretion to admit a professor's testimony on gender stereotyping because "virtually all adults in our society know about gender stereotypes").

There has recently been concern about whether various kinds of expert testimony meet the Supreme Court's heightened standards under *Daubert v. Merrell Dow Pharmaceuticals, Inc.*, 509 U.S. 579 (1993), and its progeny. *E.g., Mukhtar v. Cal. State Univ.*, 319 F.3d 1073 (2003). *See generally* Deborah Dyson Comment, *Expert Testimony and "Subtle Discrimination" in The Workplace: Do We Now Need a Weatherman to Know Which Way the Wind Blows?*, 34 GOLDEN GATE U.L. REV. 37, 72 (2004). If, instead of accepting the testimony of Dr. Fiske at trial, defendant had objected, how should the trial court have ruled as to its admissibility?

NOTE ON THE INTENT OF MULTIPLE DECISION-MAKERS

While disparate treatment is often discussed in terms of the intent of the "employer," employers typically are corporations or partnerships, sometimes involved in complicated legal relationships. One issue that arises is when the intent of one person or entity should be imputed to another. In *General Building Contractors*

Association v. Pennsylvania, 458 U.S. 375 (1982), the plaintiffs claimed discrimination in the operation of a union hiring hall. They sued not only the union, but also the employer association that bargained with the union and the employers who were bound by the resultant collective bargaining agreement to hire exclusively through the union's hiring hall. While there was discriminatory intent on the part of the union, the Court found no intent to discriminate by the employer association or the individual contractors. Accordingly, to recover from these defendants under § 1981, the intentional discrimination by the union in the operation of its hiring hall had to be imputed to the defendants who had not intentionally discriminated. The Court rejected two possible ways to do this. On the narrow issue of vicarious liability for the union's intentional discrimination, respondeat superior was held inapplicable to the relationships between the union and the three defendants. There was no fiduciary relationship, and neither the employer association nor the contractors had any control over the union. The Court also rejected the concept of a "nondelegable duty" under § 1981 that would impose a kind of strict liability on employers when their hiring methods result in the exclusion of blacks.

While *General Building Contractors* involved a number of distinct juridical entities, the problem of imputed intent also exists within a single corporation or partnership. Obviously such entities, as such, cannot have any intent at all. Thus, when we speak of a corporate entity's intent to discriminate, we are imputing to the entity the intent of the human beings who conduct its operations. For business associations, then, the intent that matters is that of the actual decision-maker. But many decisions involve not a single decision-maker but multiple deciders in a collegial, a hierarchical structure, or some combination of the two. Multiple decision-makers will be found where the decision is made collegially (as by a board or a committee) and where it is made by a hierarchical process (A recommends to B who recommends to C who "decides").

Where decision-making is collegial, the humans involved have whatever motivations may be relevant for Title VII purposes, and they may have differing motivations. *Price Waterhouse* is a good example. However, the discriminatory motivations of individuals may be attributed to the body in appropriate circumstances — most obviously, when a majority of the members have such thoughts. It should not be necessary, however, that a majority of members share a particular intent: one or more members may be so influential that they can effectively determine the result. If such "opinion leaders" act from prohibited motives, it may be fair to conclude that the decision of the body is tainted. This can be true even where the "followers" do not know of the prohibited considerations.

Another variation occurs when some members of the body cast untainted votes, but the votes of those influenced by prohibited considerations decide the outcome. If the fact-finder finds that one member acted with intent to discriminate, does that establish that discrimination was a "motivating factor" under § 703(m) or must more be shown to establish liability? In *Barbano v. Madison County*, 922 F.2d 139 (2d Cir. 1990), plaintiff was interviewed by a committee, one of whose members openly objected to hiring her because she was a woman and might become pregnant. Although the committee found all interviewees qualified, it recommended a male to the board. The court upheld a finding that the committee's tolerance of its member's discriminatory conduct, and the refusal of the other members to ask any questions not focusing on plaintiff's gender, warranted a finding that the committee as a whole discriminated. The board's subsequent decision was, therefore, also tainted by discrimination, especially because the board had been apprised of the misconduct, but did nothing about it.

As for the hierarchical model, it is clear that, if the decision-maker is the one acting with discriminatory intent, the employer is liable. But what if the decision-maker is innocent of such intent but her decision is influenced by someone who has the requisite intent? This is sometimes called the "cat's-paw" scenario, a situation where A, acting with intent to discriminate, makes recommendations to B who actually makes the employment decision but does not know of, much less share, A's intent. In *EEOC v. BCI Coca-Cola Bottling Co.*, 450 F.3d 476 (10th Cir. 2006), *cert. dismissed*, 127 S. Ct. 1931 (2007), Edgar fired Peters from the BCI Coca-Cola bottling facility in Albuquerque, N.M., but he had no idea that Peters was black. However, Peters' immediate manager had a reputation for treating blacks badly, and Edgar's decision was based on information provided by that manager. The Tenth Circuit allowed the suit to go forward, since recognizing liability in these circumstances would "encourag[e] employers to verify information and review recommendations before taking adverse employment actions against members of protected groups." *Id.* at 486. Several other circuits also recognize liability in this situation, often framing the rule in terms of B being the "cat's-paw," or dupe, of A. *E.g.*, *Tucker v. Hous. Auth.*, 229 Fed. Appx. 820 (11th Cir. 2007) (jury could have reasonably found that white plaintiff's supervisor was "cat's-paw" of biased black general counsel). Others reach the same result, but they view the question as merely one of causation, i.e., whether plaintiff can trace the adverse employment action to discrimination, rather than being concerned about whether the decisionmaker was duped. *E.g.*, *Poland v. Chertoff*, 494 F.3d 1174 (9th Cir. 2007) (if a biased subordinate sets in motion a proceeding by an independent decisionmaker, the resultant adverse employment action is still actionable if the subordinate influences the result); *Lust v. Sealy, Inc.*, 383 F.3d 580, 584 (7th Cir. 2004) ("cats paw" was "not intended to be taken literally (Sealy employs no felines), and were it taken even semi-literally it would be inconsistent with the normal analysis of causal issues in tort litigation"). Is that the approach the court in *Slack v. Havens* employed?

At least one circuit, however, has rejected this view. It requires that the decisionmaker be the person harboring the discriminatory intent: a company is liable only if the biased employee was the one who, directly or indirectly, was principally responsible for the decision. In *Hill v. Lockheed Martin Logistics Mgmt.*, 354 F.3d 277, 291 (4th Cir. 2004) (en banc) (7-4), the court rejected a construction of the antidiscrimination statutes that "would allow a biased subordinate who has no supervisory or disciplinary authority and who does not make the final or formal employment decision to become a decision-maker simply because he had a substantial influence on the ultimate decision or because he has played a role, even a significant one, in the adverse employment decision." *Hill* allows employers to immunize discharge decisions by insulating the decision-maker from knowledge of the affected workers and relying only on the paperwork submitted if it does not reveal any reason to suspect discrimination. Could Price Waterhouse have avoided suit if none of the members of the committee deciding Hopkins's partnership bid knew her personally, and all the paperwork going to the committee had been stripped of anything that might be construed to be discriminatory? What policy is served by allowing an employer to "bulletproof" itself from claims of discrimination? See pp. 168, 409.

Rebecca Hanner White & Linda Hamilton Krieger, *Whose Motive Matters?: Discrimination in Multi-Actor Employment Decision Making*, 61 LA. L. REV. 495, 534 (2001), combine doctrinal analysis with insights from cognitive psychology to advocate a causation-driven approach to intent. Rather than asking whether the ultimate decision-maker consciously intended to discriminate, they assert the question is whether there exists an unbroken chain of causation between the victim's race or sex and the decision being challenged. If so, then a disparate treatment claim should be recognized, so long as the causal link may be attributed to the employer, either directly or vicariously. The article notes that lower courts generally are following this approach in cases involving multiple decision-makers but have been less willing to embrace a causation driven approach in cases involving individual decision-makers. It analogizes decisions involving multiple decision-makers, who may be unaware of the biases of others in the decision-making chain, to decisions by individuals who are unaware of their own biases.

In the present state of the law, there is certainly substantial risk for an employer should anyone in the decision-making chain (or even someone formally outside the chain but in a position to influence decisions) harbor bias. One possible risk management response is for the employer to remove any taint in its decision-making process by ensuring that unbiased individuals make the final decision where the entire process has been sanitized to remove anything that could be the product of discrimination. *Velez v. City of Chicago*, 442 F.3d 1043, 1050 (7th Cir. 2006), concluded that any issue as to whether bias tainted a report about plaintiffs' inadequate job performance was eliminated by the employer obtaining an independent investigation into their performance, which concluded that it was unsatisfactory.

McDONNELL DOUGLAS CORP. v. GREEN
411 U.S. 792 (1973)

Justice POWELL delivered the opinion of the Court.

. . . Petitioner, McDonnell Douglas Corp., is an aerospace and aircraft manufacturer headquartered in St. Louis, Missouri, where it employs over 30,000 people. Respondent, a black citizen of St. Louis, worked for petitioner as a mechanic and laboratory technician from 1956 until August 28, 1964 when he was laid off in the course of a general reduction in petitioner's work force.

Respondent, a long-time activist in the civil rights movement, protested vigorously that his discharge and the general hiring practices of petitioner were racially motivated. As part of this protest, respondent and other members of the Congress on Racial Equality illegally stalled their cars on the main roads leading to petitioner's plant for the purpose of blocking access to it at the time of the morning shift change. The District Judge described the plan for, and respondent's participation in, the "stall-in" as follows:

> [F]ive teams, each consisting of four cars would "tie up" five main access roads into McDonnell at the time of the morning rush hour. The drivers of the cars were instructed to line up next to each other completely blocking the intersections or roads. The drivers were also instructed to stop their cars, turn off the engines, pull the emergency brake, raise all windows, lock the doors, and remain in their cars until the police arrived. The plan was to have the cars remain in position for one hour.
>
> Acting under the "stall in" plan, plaintiff [respondent in the present action] drove his car onto Brown Road, a McDonnell access road, at approximately 7:00 a.m., at the start of the morning rush hour. Plaintiff was aware of the traffic problem that would result. He stopped his car with the intent to block traffic. The police arrived shortly and requested plaintiff to move his car. He refused to move his car voluntarily. Plaintiff's car was towed away by the police, and he was arrested for obstructing traffic. Plaintiff pleaded guilty to the charge of obstructing traffic and was fined.

[O]n July 25, 1965, petitioner publicly advertised for qualified mechanics, respondent's trade, and respondent promptly applied for re-employment. Petitioner turned down respondent, basing its rejection on respondent's participation in the "stall-in." . . .

The District Court . . . found that petitioner's refusal to rehire respondent was based solely on his participation in the illegal demonstrations and not on his legitimate civil rights activities. The court concluded that nothing in Title VII or § 704 protected "such activity as employed by the plaintiff in the 'stall in' and 'lock in' demonstrations."

On appeal, the Eighth Circuit affirmed that unlawful protests were not protected activities under § 704(a),[6] but reversed the dismissal of respondent's § 703(a)(1) claim relating to racially discriminatory hiring practices. . . .

II

The critical issue before us concerns the order and allocation of proof in a private, non-class action challenging employment discrimination. The language of Title VII makes plain the purpose of Congress to assure equality of employment opportunities and to eliminate those discriminatory practices and devices which have fostered racially stratified job environments to the disadvantage of minority citizens. *Griggs v. Duke Power Co.* [reproduced at p. 207]. As noted in *Griggs,* "Congress did not intend by Title VII, however, to guarantee a job to every person regardless of qualifications. In short, the Act does not command that any person be hired simply because he was formerly the subject of discrimination, or because he is a member of a minority group. Discriminatory preference for any group, minority or majority, is precisely and only what Congress has proscribed. . . .

There are societal as well as personal interests on both sides of this equation. The broad, overriding interest, shared by employer, employee, and consumer, is efficient and trustworthy workmanship assured through fair and racially neutral employment and personnel decisions. In the implementation of such decisions, it is abundantly clear that Title VII tolerates no racial discrimination, subtle or otherwise. In this case, respondent, the complainant below, charges that he was denied employment "because of his involvement in civil rights activities" and "because of his race and color." Petitioner denied discrimination of any kind, asserting that its failure to re-employ respondent was based upon and justified by his participation in the unlawful conduct against it. Thus, the issue at the trial on remand is framed by those opposing factual contentions. . . .

The complainant in a Title VII trial must carry the initial burden under the statute of establishing a prima facie case of racial discrimination. This may be done by showing (i) that he belongs to a racial minority; (ii) that he applied and was qualified for a job for which the employer was seeking applicants; (iii) that, despite his qualifications, he was rejected; and (iv) that, after his rejection, the position remained open and the employer continued to seek applicants from persons of complainant's qualifications.[13] In the instant case, we agree with the Court of Appeals that respondent proved a prima facie case. Petitioner sought mechanics, respondent's trade, and continued to do so after respondent's rejection. Petitioner, moreover, does not

---

6. Respondent has not sought review of this issue.

13. The facts necessarily will vary in Title VII cases, and the specification above of the prima facie proof required from respondent is not necessarily applicable in every respect to differing factual situations.

dispute respondent's qualifications[14] and acknowledges that his past work performance in petitioner's employ was "satisfactory."

The burden then must shift to the employer to articulate some legitimate, nondiscriminatory reason for the employee's rejection. We need not attempt in the instant case to detail every matter which fairly could be recognized as a reasonable basis for a refusal to hire. Here petitioner has assigned respondent's participation in unlawful conduct against it as the cause for his rejection. We think that this suffices to discharge petitioner's burden of proof at this stage and to meet respondent's prima facie case of discrimination.

The Court of Appeals intimated, however, that petitioner's stated reason for refusing to rehire respondent was a "subjective" rather than objective criterion which "carr[ies] little weight in rebutting charges of discrimination." This was among the statements which caused the dissenting judge to read the opinion as taking "the position that such unlawful acts as Green committed against McDonnell would not legally entitle McDonnell to refuse to hire him, even though no racial motivation was involved. . . . " Regardless of whether this was the intended import of the opinion, we think the court below seriously underestimated the rebuttal weight to which petitioner's reasons were entitled. Respondent admittedly had taken part in a carefully planned "stall-in," designed to tie up access to and egress from petitioner's plant at a peak traffic hour.[16] Nothing in Title VII compels an employer to absolve and rehire one who has engaged in such deliberate, unlawful activity against it.[17] In upholding, under the National Labor Relations Act, the discharge of employees who had seized and forcibly retained an employer's factory buildings in an illegal sit-down strike, the Court noted pertinently: "We are unable to conclude that Congress intended to compel employers to retain persons in their employ regardless of their unlawful conduct, — to invest those who go on strike with an immunity from discharge for acts of trespass or violence against the employer's property. . . . Apart from the question of the constitutional validity of an enactment of that sort, it is enough to say that such a legislative intention should be found in some definite and unmistakable expression." *NLRB v. Fansteel Corp.*, 306 U.S. 240, 255 (1939).

Petitioner's reason for rejection thus suffices to meet the prima facie case, but the inquiry must not end here. While Title VII does not, without more, compel rehiring of respondent, neither does it permit petitioner to use respondent's conduct as a pretext for the sort of discrimination prohibited by §703(a)(1). On remand, respondent must, as the Court of Appeals recognized, be afforded a fair opportunity to show that petitioner's stated reason for respondent's rejection was in fact pretext. Especially relevant to such a showing would be evidence that white employees involved in acts against petitioner of comparable seriousness to the "stall-in" were nevertheless retained or rehired. Petitioner may justifiably refuse to rehire one who was engaged in unlawful, disruptive acts against it, but only if this criterion is applied alike to members of all races.

---

14. We note that the issue of what may properly be used to test qualifications for employment is not present in this case. Where employers have instituted employment tests and qualifications with an exclusionary effect on minority applicants, such requirements must be "shown to bear a demonstrable relationship to successful performance of the jobs" for which they were used, *Griggs v. Duke Power Co.*

16. The trial judge noted that no personal injury or property damage resulted from the "stall-in" due "solely to the fact that law enforcement officials had obtained notice in advance of plaintiff's [here respondent's] demonstration and were at the scene to remove plaintiff's car from the highway."

17. The unlawful activity in this case was directed specifically against petitioner. We need not consider or decide here whether, or under what circumstances, unlawful activity not directed against the particular employer may be a legitimate justification reason for refusal to hire.

Other evidence that may be relevant to any showing of pretext includes facts as to the petitioner's treatment of respondent during his prior term of employment; petitioner's reaction, if any, to respondent's legitimate civil rights activities; and petitioner's general policy and practice with respect to minority employment. On the latter point, statistics as to petitioner's employment policy and practice may be helpful to a determination of whether petitioner's refusal to rehire respondent in this case conformed to a general pattern of discrimination against blacks. *Jones v. Lee Way Motor Freight, Inc.*, 431 F.2d 245 (C.A. 10 1970); Blumrosen, Strangers in Paradise: *Griggs v. Duke Power Co.*, and the Concept of Employment Discrimination, 71 Mich. L. Rev. 59, 91-94 (1972).[19] In short, on the retrial respondent must be given a full and fair opportunity to demonstrate by competent evidence that the presumptively valid reasons for his rejection were in fact a coverup for a racially discriminatory decision.

The court below appeared to rely upon *Griggs v. Duke Power Co.*, in which the Court stated: "If an employment practice which operates to exclude Negroes cannot be shown to be related to job performance, the practice is prohibited." But *Griggs* differs from the instant case in important respects. It dealt with standardized testing devices which, however neutral on their face, operated to exclude many blacks who were capable of performing effectively in the desired positions. *Griggs* was rightly concerned that childhood deficiencies in the education and background of minority citizens, resulting from forces beyond their control, not be allowed to work a cumulative and invidious burden on such citizens for the remainder of their lives. Respondent, however, appears in different clothing. He had engaged in a seriously disruptive act against the very one from whom he now seeks employment. And petitioner does not seek his exclusion on the basis of a testing device which overstates what is necessary for competent performance, or through some sweeping disqualification of all those with any past record of unlawful behavior, however remote, insubstantial, or unrelated to applicant's personal qualifications as an employee. Petitioner assertedly rejected respondent for unlawful conduct against it and in the absence of proof or pretext or discriminatory application of such a reason, this cannot be thought the kind of "artificial, arbitrary, and unnecessary barriers to employment" which the Court found to be the intention of Congress to remove.[21]

III

In sum, respondent should have been allowed to pursue his claim under § 703(a)(1). If the evidence on retrial is substantially in accord with that before us in this case, we think that respondent carried his burden of establishing a prima facie case of racial discrimination and that petitioner successfully rebutted that case. But this does

---

19. The District Court may, for example, determine, after reasonable discovery that "the [racial] composition of defendant's labor force is itself reflective of restrictive or exclusionary practices." See Blumrosen, *supra*, at 92. We caution that such general determinations, while helpful, may not be in and of themselves controlling as to an individualized hiring decision, particularly in the presence of an otherwise justifiable reason for refusing to rehire. Blumrosen, *supra*, n. 19, at 93.

21. It is, of course, a predictive evaluation, resistant to empirical proof, whether "an applicant's past participation in unlawful conduct directed at his prospective employer might indicate the applicant's lack of a responsible attitude toward performing work for that employer." But, in this case, given the seriousness and harmful potential of respondent's participation in the "stall-in" and the accompanying inconvenience to other employees, it cannot be said that petitioner's refusal to employ lacked a rational and neutral business justification. As the Court has noted elsewhere: "Past conduct may well relate to present fitness; past loyalty may have a reasonable relationship to present and future trust." *Garner v. Los Angeles Board*, 341 U.S. 716, 720 (1951).

not end the matter. On retrial, respondent must be afforded a fair opportunity to demonstrate that petitioner's assigned reason for refusing to re-employ was a pretext or discriminatory in its application. . . .

NOTES

1. *The Back Story.* The "backstory" of the *McDonnell Douglas* is fascinating in its own right. As recounted by David Benjamin Oppenheimer, *The Story of* Green v. McDonnell Douglas, in EMPLOYMENT DISCRIMINATION STORIES (Joel Wm. Friedman ed. 2006), Percy Green, was an experienced civil rights activist in his home town of St. Louis, having been arrested in protests more than 100 times. In addition to the "stall in" described by the Court, Green's protests included climbing the Gateway Arch while it was under construction to underscore the lack of black workers on the project. While the Supreme Court's opinion does not explore the issue, the protests against McDonnell Douglas occurred because Green believed that his original layoff was itself discriminatory — it happened less than a month after his Arch-climbing brought him notoriety, and white workers with less seniority were retained. This led to the protests the opinion recounts, which in turn led to the denial of his application for re-employment and the subsequent suit. Professor Oppenheimer underscores that a significant, if ironic, legacy of the decision is in the language barring retaliation claims by employees who engage in unlawful civil rights demonstrations.

2. *The Mantra.* In employment discrimination law, "*McDonnell Douglas*" is more a mantra than a decision. For example, in 2006 it was cited by courts in excess of 3000 times. As the first Supreme Court decision involving what we now refer to as "individual disparate treatment," *McDonnell Douglas* appeared to establish a proof structure as a way of establishing discrimination, at least when there was no "direct evidence" (although that term would not become important until *Price Waterhouse*). *McDonnell Douglas's* most precise meaning, then, is the three step structure: (1) the plaintiff must establish a prima facie case of discrimination, which creates a "presumption" that the employer discriminated. Once the prima facie case is established, the employer, (2) has the burden of production to put into evidence a nondiscriminatory reason for the alleged discriminatory decision. Carrying that burden destroys the presumption, but (3) the plaintiff has the opportunity to prove that the supposed reason was really a pretext for an underlying discriminatory motivation. As we will see, the structure can be viewed as a process of elimination by which discrimination is proven by rejecting successive nondiscriminatory explanations.

But there are at least two other meanings of "*McDonnell Douglas.*" The shorthand is also frequently cited for the case's four pronged statement of the plaintiff's prima facie case, which, we will see shortly, is also problematic. Finally, "*McDonnell Douglas*" sometimes is invoked for the proposition that plaintiff must prove that her protected characteristic was the determinative factor — the but-for cause — of the action defendant took against her. This obviously is in tension with the "motivating factor" analysis used by the *Price Waterhouse* plurality and codified in §703(m) by the 1991 Civil Rights Act. All too often, the several usages are not clearly differentiated.

3. *The First Step: The Prima Facie Case.* Citing "*McDonnell Douglas*" to mean its four-pronged specification of the prima facie case is questionable. While the Court framed the prima facie case in terms of four specific factual showings that seemed

almost "elements" of a claim, the Court noted in footnote 13 that these specific elements could not fit every fact situation. In *Teamsters v. United States*, 431 U.S. 324, 358 n.44 (1977), the Court departed from a by-the-numbers specification to describe the rationale for the prima facie case:

> The *McDonnell Douglas* case involved an individual complainant seeking to prove one instance of unlawful discrimination. An employer's isolated decision to reject an applicant who belongs to a racial minority does not show that the rejection was racially based. Although the *McDonnell Douglas* formula does not require direct proof of discrimination, it does demand that the alleged discriminatee demonstrate at least that his rejection did not result from the two most common legitimate reasons on which an employer might rely to reject a job applicant: an absolute or relative lack of qualifications or the absence of a vacancy in the job sought. Elimination of these reasons for the refusal to hire is sufficient, absent other explanation, to create an inference that the decision was a discriminatory one.

To generalize from *Teamsters*, the *McDonnell Douglas* prima facie case proves discrimination by eliminating the most common, nondiscriminatory reasons for an employer's action, leaving for the factfinder to decide if plaintiff's claim of discrimination is the most likely reason for that action. In the case itself, a refusal to hire, the most common legitimate reasons would have been the lack of a job opening or plaintiff's lack of qualifications.

You should recognize that the *McDonnell Douglas* prima facie case, as narrowly articulated in terms of the particular four prongs, is inapplicable to the vast majority of discrimination claims. In most hiring cases, after all, the position doesn't remain open. Rather, plaintiff loses out to another applicant. In most discharge cases, the plaintiff has worked for the employer for years and is let go either for some asserted shortcoming or because of a reduction in force by the employer. What are the "elements" of the prima facie case in these instances?

(a) *Not by the Numbers.* The circuits that purport to apply the *McDonnell Douglas* prima facie case in fact adapt it in big and small ways. For example, in discharge cases, some courts have required plaintiff to prove that she was doing "satisfactory work" in order to negate an obvious reason for termination. In *Webb v. Communs., LLC*, 167 Fed. Appx. 725, 728 (10th Cir. 2006), for example, the court wrote that "a plaintiff establishes a prima facie case of age discrimination by showing that he or she was: 1) within a protected age group; 2) doing satisfactory work or qualified for the position; 3) discharged; and 4) replaced by a person outside the protected age group." Not only does this formulation require proof in a discharge case of "satisfactory work" (as opposed to qualifications in a failure to hire case) but it also requires some further evidence of discrimination in terms of the replacement by a younger worker (presumably substituting for the position continuing to remain open in the failure to hire context). *But see Berquist v. Wash. Mut. Bank*, 500 F.3d 344 (5th Cir.) (plaintiff in an individual discharge need not show he was doing satisfactory work to make out a prima facie case).

However, many age cases arise in the context of corporate reorganizations or downsizings. In such reductions in force, that is, situations where a number of employees are terminated simultaneously because the workforce is too large, the "legitimate, nondiscriminatory reason" — the need to reduce expenses — is apparent on its face. Because "positions" are being eliminated, the power of proof that the plaintiff is doing an apparently satisfactory job diminishes. Further, there is usually no "replacement" — younger or otherwise — for the plaintiff. Rather than applying the four prongs of the first step of the *McDonnell Douglas* paradigm, courts have tended to require a plaintiff to produce other evidence, such as identifying younger workers who were retained when she was discharged. *See generally* Parisis G. Filippatos & Sean Farhang, *The Rights of Employees Subjected to Reductions in Force: A Critical Evaluation*, 6 EMPLOYEE RTS. & EMP. POL'Y J. 263, 326-27 (2002).

To get a flavor of some variations on this theme, consider *Bellaver v. Quanex Corp./Nichols-Homeshield*, 200 F.3d 485, 494-495 (7th Cir. 2000):

> In a case involving a reduction in force ("RIF"), it would make no sense to require a plaintiff to show the position from which she had been terminated "remained open," as required by *McDonnell Douglas* [since no job is left after the reduction]. Rather, a prima facie case requires the employee show (in addition to the first two elements of the *McDonnell Douglas* claim) that she was discharged and that other, similarly situated employees who were not members of the plaintiff's protected class were treated more favorably. Under the *McDonnell Douglas* framework, this showing would tend to prove that the employer carried out the RIF in a discriminatory way.
>
> [But this is not a reduction in force anyway, which typically involve the layoff of many employees at once; here, the only person let go was plaintiff and her] duties were not really eliminated at all; they merely were redistributed among male employees. The prototypical RIF involves a company that perhaps once employed 100 engineers, but because of a business slowdown or change in product lines, now needs only twenty engineers. The rest of the positions are eliminated, not absorbed. There does not seem to be a serious suggestion that Quanex no longer needed someone to market the HFP line. Rather, the company asked two male employees and two telemarketers to pick up Bellaver's duties. Whether this ultimately resulted in a savings compared to Bellaver's $76,000 salary is unclear.
>
> The trial court concluded that Bellaver failed to produce evidence that similarly situated male employees were treated more favorably, but that finding is fatal only if the case is treated as a RIF. We do not believe that was the appropriate analysis here, where only one employee was terminated. Rather, we have held that the inference of discrimination arises in single-discharge cases, sometimes called "mini-RIFs," where the terminated employee's duties are absorbed by other employees not in the protected class.

Bellaver not only refuses to apply *McDonnell Douglas* literally but it lays out different prima facie cases for RIF and "mini-RIFs." You shouldn't be surprised to encounter further difference in specifications for the prima facie case for individual discharges, *Maynard v. Bd. of Regents*, 342 F.3d 1281, 1289 (11th Cir. 2003) (plaintiff "must show that: (1) he is a member of a protected class; (2) he was qualified for the position; (3) he suffered an adverse employment action; and (4) he was replaced by a person outside his protected class or was treated less favorably than a similarly-situated individual outside his protected class"); failures to hire when someone is chosen over the plaintiff, *Carter v. Smithfield's of Morehead*, 1995 U.S. App. LEXIS 19681 (4th Cir. 1995) ("In making out a prima facie case of race discrimination in the failure to hire or promote, pursuant to 42 U.S.C. § 1981, . . . the plaintiff must establish: that he is a member of a protected group; he applied for the position in question; he was qualified for the position; and he was rejected for the position in favor of someone not a member of the protected group under circumstances giving rise to an inference of unlawful discrimination"); reverse discrimination cases, see Note on "Reverse" Discrimination, p. 76, claims of discriminatory discipline, *Wheeler v. BL Dev. Corp.*, 415 F.3d 399, 406 (5th Cir. 2005) ("To establish disparate treatment, a plaintiff must demonstrate that a 'similarly situated' employee under 'nearly identical' circumstances, was treated differently"); etc.

In short, the *"McDonnell Douglas* prima facie case" is an approach, not a set of elements. Further, since the purpose of the prima facie case is to eliminate at least some common nondiscriminatory reasons, the courts have often described the plaintiff's burden as very light. Put another way, it's pretty easy to prove a prima facie case.

(b) *The Significance of the Prima Facie Case.* While it may be easy to establish a prima facie case, a plaintiff does not get much reward for his efforts. Such proof merely requires the employer to put into evidence its nondiscriminatory reason. In *Texas Department of Community Affairs v. Burdine,* 450 U.S. 248, 254 (1981), the Court described the consequences of proof of a prima facie case: "Establishment of the [*McDonnell Douglas*] prima facie case in effect creates a presumption that the employer unlawfully discriminated against the employee. If the trier of fact believes the plaintiff's evidence, and if the employer is silent in the face of the presumption, the court must enter judgment for the plaintiff because no issue of fact remains in the case." However, defendants *always* come up with some reason, and *Burdine* made clear that, when they do so, the presumption disappears. This, only when an employer flunks a basic intelligence test and fails to put into evidence some explanation, will the plaintiff get judgment if the jury believes the evidence establishing the prima facie case.

In accompanying footnote 7, *Burdine* said its use of the term "prima facie case" in *McDonnell Douglas* denoted "the establishment of a legally mandatory, rebuttable presumption," not as a description of "the plaintiff's burden of producing enough evidence to permit the trier of fact to infer the fact at issue." *Id.* Isn't it odd that evidence could create a presumption of discrimination when it might not be enough to allow a jury to find that discrimination exists? While the distinction may seem subtle, it's incredibly important: since the prima facie case does not necessarily constitute a sufficient basis for the factfinder to infer discrimination, *proof of such a case does not necessarily mean that the plaintiff goes to the jury.* If *Burdine* had held the contrary, every Title VII case would warrant a jury trial so long as the plaintiff put in enough evidence of a prima facie case; defendant's evidence of a legitimate nondiscriminatory reason would, at most, give the jury a way to hold against plaintiff. In fact, as we will see, getting to the jury turns less on the plaintiff's prima facie case then on the plaintiff's proof of pretext at the third step.

4. *The Second Step: Defendant's Easy Rebuttal.* Defendant may rebut a prima facie case by "articulat[ing] some legitimate, nondiscriminatory reason" for its action. *McDonnell Douglas* established that disloyalty is such a reason. But less rational or even illegal reasons also suffice. Suppose the court finds as a fact that Green was not rehired because he was a vegetarian? And in *Biggins,* the Court found that an *illegitimate* and *discriminatory* reason — discrimination in pension vesting that violated ERISA — sufficed as a rebuttal to plaintiff's claim of age discrimination. In short, *any* reason other than a reason made illegal by the statute in question works.

In *Purkett v. Elem,* 514 U.S. 765 (1995), a case dealing with peremptory challenges to jurors, the prosecutor tried to explain its exclusion of several blacks because of their hair length and facial hair and not their race. The Supreme Court relied on Title VII analysis to indicate that even nonsensical explanations — "implausible," "silly," "fantastic," or "superstitious" — satisfied defendant's burden of production. In *Forrester v. Rauland-Borg Corp.* 453 F.3d 416, 418 (7th Cir. 2006), Judge Posner underscored how easily a defendant may rebut plaintiff's prima facie case: "the question is never whether the employer was mistaken, cruel, unethical, out of his head, or downright irrational in taking the action for the stated reason, but simply whether the stated reason *was* his reason: not a good reason, but a true reason." So all the defendant has to do is assert a reason that cannot be challenged as illegal in the present litigation.

5. *The Requirements for Defendant's Rebuttal Case.* Indeed, there are only two meaningful requirements for defendant's rebuttal. First, defendant must be able to put the reason into evidence — it is not enough to merely argue the possibility. In *Burdine,* the Court described the consequences of the defendant carrying its rebuttal burden:

> The burden that shifts to the defendant, therefore, is to rebut the presumption of discrimination by producing evidence that the plaintiff was rejected, or someone else was preferred, for a legitimate, nondiscriminatory reason. The defendant need not persuade the court that it was actually motivated by the proffered reasons. It is sufficient if the defendant's evidence raises a genuine issue of fact as to whether it discriminated against the plaintiff. To accomplish this, the defendant must clearly set forth, through the introduction of admissible evidence, the reasons for the plaintiff's rejection. The explanation provided must be legally sufficient to justify a judgment for the defendant. If the defendant carries this burden of production, the presumption raised by the prima facie case is rebutted, and the factual inquiry proceeds to a new level of specificity.

450 U.S. at 254-55. Second, defendant must provide a sufficiently specific reason to carry its burden of production. *Alvarado v. Texas Rangers,* 492 F.3d 605 (5th Cir. 2007) (complete absence of explanation of criteria or basis for scores on interviews prevented employer from carrying its burden of production); *Iadimarco v. Runyon,* 190 F.3d 151, 166-67 (3d Cir. 1999) (an assertion that successful candidate was "the right person for the job" is "not a race-neutral explanation at all, and allowing it to suffice to rebut a prima facie case of discriminatory animus is tantamount to a judicial repeal of the very protections Congress intended under Title VII"). This specificity requirement can be drawn from footnote 8 of *Burdine,* where the Court described the purpose of the shifting burdens: "In a Title VII case, the allocation of burdens and the creation of a presumption by the establishment of a prima facie case is intended progressively to sharpen the inquiry into the elusive factual question of intentional discrimination." 450 U.S. at 256 n.8.

6. *The Third Step: Proving Pretext.* A standard dictionary definition of "pretext" is "a reason given in justification of a course of action that is not the real reason." THE NEW OXFORD AMERICAN DICTIONARY 1350 (2001). Some lower courts, however, define "pretext" even more pointedly to mean that defendant lied when it asserted its reason to rebut plaintiff's prima facie case. For example, Judge Posner in *Forrester v. Rauland-Borg Corp.,* 453 F.3d 416 (7th Cir. 2006), emphasized that evidence that the defendant's proffered reason was not true was not necessarily probative of pretext because, "A pretext, is a deliberate falsehood. . . . An honest mistake, however dumb, is not." A number of other courts have agreed with the "honest belief" rule: the question is not whether the asserted reason is true but whether the defendant be-lieved it to be true when it took the challenged action. *E.g., Johnson v. AT&T Corp.,* 422 F.3d 756, 762 (8th Cir. 2005) ("the proper inquiry is not whether AT&T was factually correct in determining that Johnson had made the bomb threats. Rather, the proper inquiry is whether AT&T honestly believed that Johnson had made the bomb threats").

Professor Katz takes this tack by saying that the *McDonnell Douglas* approach is about proof of "pretext" by proving that defendant lied when it asserted its legitimate, nondiscriminatory reason for the employment action that plaintiff challenges. But Katz argues that a lie can be found from proof that the defendant's asserted reason was not true: "This conclusion [that the employer lied to cover up some less benign fact] might be based on the fact that the employer's reason was mistaken . . . or from the fact of mistake in addition to other facts which might suggest that the employer knew [the reason it asserted] was wrong." Martin J. Katz, *Reclaiming* McDonnell Douglas, 83 NOTRE DAME L. REV. 109, 122 n. 56 (2007). This seems correct and suggests that Posner is both right and wrong: a finding by the jury that the defendant's reason is not the real reason does not automatically justify a finding of pretext but would often (usually?) at least permit the inference that the defendant was lying by asserting it. Posner is wrong if he is insisting there must be evidence, separate from the evidence that defendant's reason was not true, that defendant lied about it being the reason. As we will soon see, this would resurrect in new language the "pretext-plus" rule repudiated in *Reeves v. Sanderson Plumbing Products, Inc.*, reproduced at p. 78.

Linda Hamilton Krieger & Susan T. Fiske, *Behavioral Realism in Employment Discrimination Law: Implicit Bias and Disparate Treatment*, 94 CAL. L. REV. 997, 1036 (2006), take a dramatically different approach to the whole truth-or-lie question. They criticize the "honest belief rule" as "plainly inconsistent with what empirical social psychologists have learned over the past twenty years about the manner in which stereotypes, functioning not as consciously held beliefs but as implicit expectancies, can cause a decision-maker to discriminate against members of a stereotyped group." Thus, if acting on unconscious bias is nevertheless intentional discrimination, then the fact that the defendant acted on its "honest belief" is not determinative of whether there is discrimination.

7. *Pretext for Discrimination.* If *McDonnell Douglas* is truly a process of elimination, as suggested in *Teamsters*, then showing that defendant's asserted reason is not the real reason for its action undermines that assertion, leaving plaintiff's claim of discrimination as a more likely explanation for what motivated the employer. But what about the possibility that defendant lied, but not to conceal its discrimination? The notion that the *McDonnell Douglas* proof structure was designed to progressively sharpen the inquiry would seem to require that a decision by the factfinder that the defendant lied mandates judgment for plaintiff. Another way to say the same thing is that, with no nondiscriminatory explanations remaining, the only possible motivation is a discriminatory one.

Despite that reasoning, the Supreme Court has held to the contrary. Proof of pretext, that is proof that defendant's asserted reason is not the real reason for the action, is *not necessarily* sufficient to find for plaintiff. Rather, the factfinder has to find both (1) defendant's reason to be pretextual and (2) the pretext to be a cover-up for an underlying discriminatory motive, In *St. Mary's Honor Center v. Hicks*, 509 U.S. 502, 511 (1993), Justice Scalia, for the Court, described a finding of pretext as requiring more than proof that the employer's reason was not the true motivation:

> The factfinder's disbelief of the reasons put forward by the defendant (particularly if disbelief is accompanied by a suspicion of mendacity) may, together with the elements of the prima facie case, suffice to show intentional discrimination. Thus, rejection of the defendant's proffered reasons will *permit* the trier of fact to infer the ultimate fact of intentional discrimination, and the Court of Appeals was correct when it noted that, upon such rejection, "no additional proof of discrimination is *required*" (emphasis added).

As we will see, later cases make clear that it will usually be permissible to infer from a finding that the defendant's asserted reason was not true the further conclusion that it was a pretext for discrimination. But after *Hicks* that is a permissible, not a required, inference.

8. *A Process of Elimination?* Professor Zimmer, drawing from *Teamsters*, has described *McDonnell Douglas* as a process of elimination: the plaintiff eliminates the most common legitimate nondiscriminatory reasons in proving its prima facie and then eliminates the defendant's asserted legitimate, nondiscriminatory reason. Since employers can be assumed to act for some reason, elimination of these reasons allows the factfinder to infer that discrimination as the remaining reason for its action. Michael J. Zimmer, *The New Discrimination Law: Price Waterhouse Is Dead, Whither McDonnell Douglas?*, 53 EMORY L.J. 1887. 1893-95 (2004).

Professor Martin Katz, disagrees, arguing that *McDonnell Douglas* is not a process of elimination because it does not depend on eliminating every reason other than discrimination. Rather, it is a process of proving causation by a chain of inferences. Defendant's nondiscriminatory reason is a target, which gives plaintiff a chance to win if she can convince the factfinder that, whether or not all possible nondiscriminatory reasons are eliminated, that "(1) the proffered reason was factually erroneous, (2) the error was a lie [not a mistake], (3) the lie was a cover-up, and (4) the cover-up was designed to conceal discrimination [not to conceal a benign or an embarrassing reason such as nepotism]." This is how Professor Katz maps out his understanding of the process:

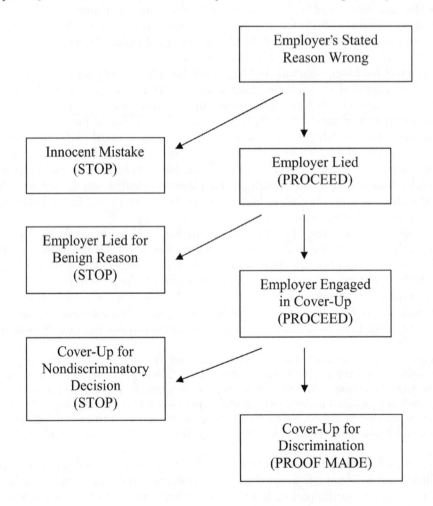

Reclaiming McDonnell Douglas, 83 NOTRE DAME L. REV. at 129. Are the Zimmer and Katz positions so far apart? While it is logically possible that a non-discriminatory motive explains the employer's action even if the "most common" reasons are eliminated, including the employer's supposed reason, isn't it far less likely?

9. *The Quixotic Nature of* McDonnell Douglas. In *Reclaiming* McDonnell Douglas, Professor Katz argues that the *McDonnell Douglas* framework "is innocent of most of the charges leveled at it by its critics. In fact, it should be seen as a gift to disparate treatment law." However, in another article he suggests that it should be replaced with a uniform approach based on §703(m). Martin Katz, *Unifying Disparate Treatment (Really)*, 59 HASTINGS L.J. (forthcoming 2008) (the *Price Waterhouse* and *McDonnell Douglas* frameworks have significant normative flaws, which can be avoided by unifying disparate treatment law under the 1991 Act framework). Recon-ciling these two positions, Professor Katz argues in the Notre Dame piece for *McDonnell Douglas* as a method of proving individual disparate treatment discrimination; while most commentators see it as required, but-for causation, Katz believes that a motivating factor test would suffice. In the Hastings article, he suggests that the "motivating factor" standard should be used uniformly.

10. *A Mixed-Motive Case?* Green did not contest that he had engaged in the sit-in protesting defendant's discrimination, and McDonnell Douglas claimed that was the reason for not rehiring him. That seems to establish one motivation of the employer beyond much doubt. Or could a jury find it a complete lie by the employer? The question was whether, given Green's participation in the protest (a legitimate non-discriminatory reason), Green's race was a factor in the defendant's not rehiring him. Even were the factfinder to find that Green's race motivated the employer's decision in part, the question would still remain, under *Biggins's* determinative factor standard, whether race was the but-for reason for the defendant's action. Such a finding would not be precluded by the fact that Green's protest activities also motivated defendant, but it might be difficult to make given the strong non-racial motivation that obviously existed.

After *Desert Palace*, would liability be established under §703(m) if the factfinder concluded only that Green's race was *a motivating factor* in defendant's decision, even though his participation in the protest activities was the *but-for* reason? Under this view, Green's participation in the protest activities would be irrelevant for liability, once the finding was made that his race did play a role. The extent that his protest activities influenced the result, however, would be relevant to whether defendant could carry its burden under the same-decision defense to full remedies in §706(g)(2)(B).

11. *Retaliation.* Although *McDonnell Douglas* focuses on §703(a), the Court also noted that plaintiff asserted a cause of action under §704(a), Title VII's anti-retaliation provision. Didn't the defendant admit to discriminating against Green on the basis of his "opposition" conduct by asserting that the reason for not rehiring him was his participation in activities protesting its discrimination? We will examine that provision in Chapter 5, p. 467.

PATTERSON v. McLEAN CREDIT UNION
491 U.S. 164 (1989)

Justice KENNEDY delivered the opinion of the Court. . . .

I

[Brenda Patterson, a black woman, was employed by McLean Credit Union as a teller and a file coordinator from 1972 until 1982, when she was laid off. She sued, claiming that McLean had violated §1981 by harassing her, failing to promote her to an intermediate accounting clerk position, and then discharging her because of her race. The jury found for defendant on the claims for discharge and the failure to promote. In a portion of the opinion since overturned by the Civil Rights Act of 1991, the Supreme Court held that §1981 did not reach racial harassment. The new statute also overruled the portion of the Court's opinion limiting promotion claims under §1981 to those in which "the nature of the change in position was such that it involved the opportunity to enter into a new contract with the employer." These portions of the opinion are not reproduced below. For present purposes, the critical question was plaintiff's challenge to the district court's jury instructions that, in order to prevail as to her promotion, she had to show that she was better qualified than her successful white competitor. Because defendant had not argued that the promotion claim was outside of §1981, the Court had to decide whether the instruction to the jury on proving pretext was correct.]

This brings us to the question of the District Court's jury instructions on petitioner's promotion claim. We think the District Court erred when it instructed the jury that petitioner had to prove that she was better qualified than the white employee who allegedly received the promotion. In order to prevail under §1981, a plaintiff must prove purposeful discrimination. *General Building Contractors Assn., Inc. v. Pennsylvania*, 458 U.S. 375, 391 (1982). We have developed, in analogous areas of civil rights law, a carefully designed framework of proof to determine, in the context of disparate treatment, the ultimate issue whether the defendant intentionally discriminated against the plaintiff. See *Texas Dept. of Community Affairs v. Burdine*; *McDonnell Douglas Corp. v. Green*. We agree with the Court of Appeals that this scheme of proof, structured as a "sensible, orderly way to evaluate the evidence in light of common experience as it bears on the critical question of discrimination," should apply to claims of racial discrimination under §1981.

Although the Court of Appeals recognized that the *McDonnell Douglas/Burdine* scheme of proof should apply in §1981 cases such as this one, it erred in describing petitioner's burden. Under our well-established framework, the plaintiff has the initial burden of proving, by a preponderance of the evidence, a prima facie case of discrimination. *Burdine*. The burden is not onerous. Here, petitioner need only prove by a preponderance of the evidence that she applied for and was qualified for an available position, that she was rejected, and that after she was rejected respondent either continued to seek applicants for the position, or, as is alleged here, filled the position with a white employee. *McDonnell Douglas*.[7]

---

7. Here, respondent argues that petitioner cannot make out a prima facie case on her promotion claim because she did not prove either that respondent was seeking applicants for the intermediate accounting clerk position or that the white employee named to fill that position in fact received a "promotion" from her prior job. Although we express no opinion on the merits of these claims, we do emphasize that in order to prove that she was denied the same right to make and enforce contracts as white citizens, petitioner must show, inter alia, that she was in fact denied an available position.

Once the plaintiff establishes a prima facie case, an inference of discrimination arises. See *Burdine*. In order to rebut this inference, the employer must present evidence that the plaintiff was rejected, or the other applicant was chosen, for a legitimate nondiscriminatory reason. Here, respondent presented evidence that it gave the job to the white applicant because she was better qualified for the position, and therefore rebutted any presumption of discrimination that petitioner may have established. At this point, as our prior cases make clear, petitioner retains the final burden of persuading the jury of intentional discrimination.

Although petitioner retains the ultimate burden of persuasion, our cases make clear that she must also have the opportunity to demonstrate that respondent's proffered reasons for its decision were not its true reasons. In doing so, petitioner is not limited to presenting evidence of a certain type. This is where the District Court erred. The evidence which petitioner can present in an attempt to establish that respondent's stated reasons are pretextual may take a variety of forms. *McDonnell Douglas*. Indeed, she might seek to demonstrate that respondent's claim to have promoted a better qualified applicant was pretextual by showing that she was in fact better qualified than the person chosen for the position. The District Court erred, however, in instructing the jury that in order to succeed petitioner was required to make such a showing. There are certainly other ways in which petitioner could seek to prove that respondent's reasons were pretextual. Thus, for example, petitioner could seek to persuade the jury that respondent had not offered the true reason for its promotion decision by presenting evidence of respondent's past treatment of petitioner, including the instances of the racial harassment which she alleges and respondent's failure to train her for an accounting position. While we do not intend to say this evidence necessarily would be sufficient to carry the day, it cannot be denied that it is one of the various ways in which petitioner might seek to prove intentional discrimination on the part of respondent. She may not be forced to pursue any particular means of demonstrating that respondent's stated reasons are pretextual. It was, therefore, error for the District Court to instruct the jury that petitioner could carry her burden of persuasion only by showing that she was in fact better qualified than the white applicant who got the job.

ASH v. TYSON FOODS, INC.
546 U.S. 454 (2006)

[In a per curiam opinion, the Court reversed the lower court grant of summary judgment for the defendant. The] Court of Appeals erred in articulating the standard for determining whether the asserted nondiscriminatory reasons for Tyson's hiring decisions were pretextual. Petitioners had introduced evidence that their qualifications were superior to those of the two successful applicants. . . . The Court of Appeals, in finding petitioners' evidence insufficient, cited one of its earlier precedents and stated: "Pretext can be established through comparing qualifications only when 'the disparity in qualifications is so apparent as virtually to jump off the page and slap you in the face.'"

Under this Court's decisions, qualifications evidence may suffice, at least in some circumstances, to show pretext. See *Patterson v. McLean Credit Union* (indicating a plaintiff "might seek to demonstrate that respondent's claim to have promoted a better qualified applicant was pretextual by showing that she was in fact better qualified than the person chosen for the position"); *Texas Dep't of Community*

Affairs v. Burdine ("The fact that a court may think that the employer misjudged the qualifications of the applicants does not in itself expose him to Title VII liability, although this may be probative of whether the employer's reasons are pretexts for discrimination").

The visual image of words jumping off the page to slap you (presumably a court) in the face is unhelpful and imprecise as an elaboration of the standard for inferring pretext from superior qualifications. Federal courts, including the Court of Appeals for the Eleventh Circuit in a decision it cited here, have articulated various other standards, see, e.g., *Cooper [v. Southern Co.*, 390 F.3d 695, 732 (CA11 2004)] (noting that "disparities in qualifications must be of such weight and significance that no reasonable person, in the exercise of impartial judgment, could have chosen the candidate selected over the plaintiff for the job in question") (internal quotation marks omitted)); *Raad v. Fairbanks North Star Borough School Dist.*, 323 F.3d 1185, 1194 (CA9 2003) (holding that qualifications evidence standing alone may establish pretext where the plaintiff's qualifications are " 'clearly superior' " to those of the selected job applicant); *Aka v. Washington Hospital Center*, 156 F.3d 1284, 1294 (CADC 1998) (en banc) (concluding the factfinder may infer pretext if "a reasonable employer would have found the plaintiff to be significantly better qualified for the job"), and in this case the Court of Appeals qualified its statement by suggesting that superior qualifications may be probative of pretext when combined with other evidence This is not the occasion to define more precisely what standard should govern pretext claims based on superior qualifications. Today's decision, furthermore, should not be read to hold that petitioners' evidence necessarily showed pretext. The District Court concluded otherwise. It suffices to say here that some formulation other than the test the Court of Appeals articulated in this case would better ensure that trial courts reach consistent results.

NOTES

1. *Comparators as Proof of Pretext.* In *Patterson*, the defendant's asserted reason for not promoting plaintiff was that the person promoted in her stead was more qualified. In *Ash*, plaintiffs' claimed discrimination because less qualified whites were promoted instead of them. In both situations, evidence of the qualifications of those promoted as compared to the plaintiffs' qualifications was important, perhaps critical: If defendant in fact promoted those with lesser qualifications than plaintiffs, a trier of fact could conclude that discrimination motivated the choice of less qualified whites. Indeed, proof of plaintiff's superior qualifications, standing alone, may be sufficient evidence of pretext to go to a jury. *E.g., Raad v. Fairbanks North Star Borough Sch. Dist.*, 323 F.3d 1185 (9th Cir. 2003). *See also Wilson v. B/E Aero., Inc.*, 376 F.3d 1079, 1091 (11th Cir. 2004) (evidence of decision-maker's admissions that she was more qualified than the male selected, together with decision-maker's statement — "women aren't typically in that type of position" — sufficient to allow jury to infer discrimination).

2. *Ash as an Equal Treatment Case.* Both *Patterson* and *Ash* were argued as *McDonnell Douglas* cases. That is, the question of comparative qualifications entered in the pretext part of the analysis. But is there any need for the three-step mantra here? In other words, suppose plaintiffs in *Ash* simply posed a straightforward unequal treatment claim: they were treated less favorably than comparable whites, leading to the inference that they would have been promoted had they been white.

Under this approach, plaintiffs would bear the burden of proving that they were as or more qualified than those who were promoted. The "slap in the face" rule would not make any sense in that setting, unless the court decided that the risk of finding an innocent employer to have discriminated vastly exceeded the risk of failing to find discrimination when it existed. The preponderance of evidence standard treats those risks of error to be of nearly the same significance: Finding an innocent defendant guilty is only slightly worse than finding a guilty defendant innocent. The preponderance test is simply a tiebreaker when the evidence is at equipoise.

3. *Role of Qualifications in* McDonnell Douglas *Cases.* Even assuming *McDonnell Douglas* applied, the issue of qualifications can appear in both the prima facie case — plaintiff must prove she met the minimum qualifications for the job at issue — and at the pretext stage — an employer's choice of someone less qualified than plaintiff to promote may support the inference that discrimination was the real reason for the decision. As the Court in *Patterson* recognizes, evidence that plaintiff was *more* qualified would be potent evidence in terms of proving pretext — that defendant's asserted reason for not promoting plaintiff was not true. On the issue of pretext, does the lower court's "slap in the face" rule in *Ash* make any more sense than in the context of a claim of pure unequal treatment? The Court does not dig deeply into the issue, simply rejecting the "slap in the face" rule. But we saw in *Hicks*, see Note 7 on p. 59, that plaintiff must prove more than that the defendant's asserted reason was not true. To be pretextual the reason must be both inaccurate and conceal a discriminatory motive. Was the lower court in *Ash* suggesting that no reasonable person could find the defendant's asserted reason to be other than the actual explanation for its decision? Or merely that the marginal superiority of the plaintiff in qualifications would not support a finding of pretext for discrimination?

Brooks v. County Comm'n, 446 F.3d 1160, 1163 (11th Cir. 2006), decided in the wake of *Ash*, reaffirmed the *Cooper* standard referred to in *Ash*: "A plaintiff must show that the disparities between the successful applicant's and her own qualifications were 'of such weight and significance that no reasonable person, in the exercise of impartial judgment, could have chosen the candidate selected over the plaintiff.'" Is *Brooks* still too narrow a view? Wouldn't it be better to frame the question as whether it is more likely than not that a reasonable person would not have chosen the successful candidate over the plaintiff absent discrimination?

Can plaintiff win even if she cannot prove that she was more qualified, or even if she admits that she is less qualified than those who were promoted? *Patterson* seems to say yes. In *Dominguez-Curry v. Nevada Transportation Dept.*, 424 F.3d 1027 (9th Cir. 2005), the court found that plaintiff could claim discrimination in promotions even though she conceded that the person defendant promoted instead of her was more qualified. In that case, however, there were employer admissions.

A more general problem with qualifications is that the term is susceptible to much manipulation. Professor Anne Lawton, *The Meritocracy Myth and the Illusion of Equal Employment Opportunity*, 85 MINN. L. REV. 587, 645 (2000), argues that "Employers normally hire and promote on the basis of multiple criteria. As a result, an employer can always point to at least one criterion, which it claims is critical to the position, on which the plaintiff is weaker than the candidate selected." Of course, plaintiffs can often undercut such claims by pointing to other situations in which the employer itself did not view the supposed critical qualification as important.

4. *Methods of Proving Pretext.* In *Patterson*, the Court rejected the notion that proof of pretext in a promotion case was limited to evidence that plaintiff was more qualified than the person defendant had promoted.

(a) *Prior Treatment of Plaintiff.* One possibility was defendant's earlier treatment of the plaintiff in *Patterson.* Why would that help to prove that defendant's asserted reason for not promoting her was a pretext for discrimination? Would earlier unfavorable treatment of her establish that the employer was discriminating against Brenda Patterson because she was black or merely because it did not like her? Recall *Desert Palace* where Catharina Costa was subjected to a pattern of adverse treatment. It might have been easy to infer gender discrimination there because Costa was the only woman in a traditionally male job. Was Patterson the only African American at the bank?

(b) *Defendant's Stats.* The partial dissent of Justices Brennan and Stevens in *Patterson* argued that the jury instruction below was "much too restrictive," and it stressed that, "We suggested in *McDonnell Douglas,* for example, that a black plaintiff might be able to prove pretext . . . by proving the employer's 'general policy and practice with respect to minority employment.'" 491 U.S. at 217. Why would statistical evidence of the representation of women and minority men in the various jobs of the employer be relevant to whether the employer discriminated in a particular instance? Is an employer with "good stats" less likely to discriminate in any particular employment decision than one with "bad stats?" Was the trailblazer status of Costa in *Desert Palace* significant to the finding of discrimination? In Chapter 8, the Remedies chapter, you will discover that, when a plaintiff establishes liability under a systemic theory of discrimination (which you will learn more about in Chapters 2 and 3), then the burden of persuasion shifts to the defendant to prove that members of the class adversely affected by defendant's systemic policy or practice of discrimination in fact were not victims of discrimination. But are bad stats sufficient to establish pretext? See p. 294.

(c) *Failure to Follow Procedures.* Can defects in the employer's approach to an employment decision be probative of intent to discriminate? In *Carter v. Three Springs Res. Treatment,* 132 F.3d 635 (11th Cir. 1998), the court reversed summary judgment for the employer in a failure-to-promote case. "Carter proved that Three Springs had a policy of posting job vacancies, not adhered to in this case. We have held that the failure to promulgate hiring and promotion policies can be circumstantial evidence of discrimination. . . . Certainly, it is even more suspicious where it is alleged that established rules were bent or broken to give a non-minority applicant an edge in the hiring process." *Id.* at 644. Isn't this another example of discrimination as unequal treatment? If the employer can't explain why it failed to do what it normally does in the same situation and that works to the disadvantage of the plaintiff, doesn't that unequal treatment support drawing the inference of discrimination?

Some say no. In *Walker v. Abbott Laboratories,* 416 F.3d 641, 643-44 (7th Cir. 2005), Judge Posner denies that there is any probative value to such evidence:

> This [evidence] makes it seem that Abbott complies with its personnel rules only when it wants to. Indeed so. And there is nothing wrong with that. Unless a rule is part of the company's contract with its employees, the company is free to create exceptions to it at will. . . . A well-managed company will not make exceptions to its personnel rules promiscuously because that will generate ill will among the employees; they will feel they're being subjected to arbitrary treatment, which nobody likes. . . . But neither will a well-managed company adhere to its personnel rules with a rigidity blind to circumstances that may make the rule occasionally wholly inapt. People in supervisory positions are not doing their best for the company if they are content to administer rules. Fairness, consistency, and demonstrated interest in employee problems are the

> backbone of supervisory morale building. . . . No set of written policies should become
> a straitjacket on management thinking.

This is a variation of the argument that the employer is free to act on any ground
other than a prohibited one. That may be true, but isn't the unexplained failure to
follow the normal procedures fishy? And might fishiness hide discrimination, not
creative administration à la Posner?

5. *Several Nondiscriminatory Reasons.* When defendant has more than one supposed legitimate nondiscriminatory reason, some courts have required the plaintiff to
put in evidence of the pretextual nature of all the reasons. *See Crawford v. City of
Fairburn*, 482 F.3d 1305, 1308 (plaintiff must rebut each reason proffered by defendant); *Kautz v. Met-Pro Corp.*, 412 F.3d 463 (3d Cir. 2005) (summary judgment
against employee who could not show that all of employer's non-discriminatory
reasons were pretextual). Other courts believe that proof that any reason is pretextual
will usually permit the jury to infer that the pretext conceals a discriminatory motive.
E.g., Tomasso v. Boeing Co., 445 F.3d 702, 704 (3d Cir. 2006) (plaintiff sufficiently
challenged the defendant's "primary rationales" for the layoff and "a rational
factfinder could dismiss the secondary reasons as pretextual, not because they
played no role in Tomasso's layoff but because they cannot explain the layoff
sufficiently"); *Jaramillo v. Colo. Judicial Dep't.*, 427 F.3d 1303, 1310 (10th
Cir. 2005) ("Something less than total failure of the employer's defense is sufficient
to create a genuine issue of fact when (1) the reasons are so intertwined that a
showing of pretext as to one raises a genuine question whether the remaining
reason is valid, (2) the pretextual character of one explanation is 'so fishy and suspicious,' that a jury could 'find that the employer (or its decisionmaker) lacks all
credibility,' (3) the employer offers a plethora of reasons, and the plaintiff raises
substantial doubt about a number of them, (4) the plaintiff discredits each of the
employer's objective explanations, leaving only subjective reasons to justify its decision, or (5) the employer has changed its explanation under circumstances that
suggest dishonesty or bad faith.") *See generally* Lawrence D. Rosenthal, *Motions
for Summary Judgment When Employers Offer Multiple Justifications for Adverse
Employment Actions: Why the Exceptions Should Swallow the Rule*, 2002 UTAH L.
REV. 335.

Of course, sometimes an employer's multiple reasons will conflict, thus providing
another basis to infer pretext. *See Juarez v. AGS Gov't Solution Group*, 314 F.3d 1243
(10th Cir. 2003) (proof that manager's evaluation contained fraudulent data and the
employer's conflicting reasons for discharge is sufficient to establish pretext in a race
discrimination case). Along these lines, a change in defendant's rebuttal over time
can be fatal to it. *See Zaccagnini v. Chas. Levy Circulating Co.*, 338 F.3d 672 (7th
Cir. 2003) (jury could reasonably refuse to credit employer's explanation for not
rehiring employee due to lack of reference by union since that explanation differed
from its original stated reason that he was not rehired because of company policy of
not rehiring laid off employees).

6. *Patterson* formally adopts the *McDonnell Douglas/Burdine* litigation structure
for §1981 cases. The Supreme Court has several times employed this structure in
ADEA cases, although, oddly enough, it has explicitly assumed the application
rather than held it to apply. *E.g., Reeves v. Sanderson Plumbing Products, Inc.*,
reproduced at p. 78. Nevertheless, the lower courts generally apply this structure to
ADEA cases, and it seems likely that there is a unified approach to cases of individual
disparate treatment under Title VII, §1981, and the ADEA.

McDONALD v. SANTA FE TRAIL
TRANSPORTATION CO.
427 U.S. 273 (1976)

Justice MARSHALL delivered the opinion of the Court.

. . . On September 26, 1970, petitioners, both white, and Charles Jackson, a Negro employee of Santa Fe, were jointly and severally charged with misappropriating 60 one-gallon cans of antifreeze which was part of a shipment Santa Fe was carrying for one of its customers. Six days later, petitioners were fired by Santa Fe, while Jackson was retained. . . .

[The plaintiffs sued their employer under both Title VII and § 1981 for discrimination in the discharge and their union for discrimination in not properly pursuing their grievances. The district court dismissed the complaint because "the dismissal of white employees charged with misappropriating company property while not dismissing a similarly charged Negro employee" violated neither Title VII nor § 1981.]

II

Title VII of the Civil Rights Act of 1964 prohibits the discharge of "any individual" because of "such individual's race." Its terms are not limited to discrimination against members of any particular race. Thus, although we were not there confronted with racial discrimination against whites, we described the Act in *Griggs v. Duke Power Co.* [reproduced at p. 207], as prohibiting "[d]iscriminatory preference for *any* [racial] group, *minority* or *majority*" (emphasis added).[6] Similarly the Equal Employment Opportunity Commission (EEOC), whose interpretations are entitled to great deference, has consistently interpreted Title VII to proscribe racial discrimination in private employment against whites on the same terms as racial discrimination against nonwhites. . . . EEOC Decision No. 74-31, 7 FEP 1326, 1328, CCH EEOC Decisions ¶6404, p. 4084 (1973). This conclusion is in accord with uncontradicted legislative history to the effect that Title VII was intended to "cover white men and white women and all Americans," 110 Cong. Rec. 2578 (1964) (remarks of Rep. Celler), and create an "obligation not to discriminate against whites," id., at 7218 (memorandum of Sen. Clark); id., at 8912 (remarks of Sen. Williams). We therefore hold today that Title VII prohibits racial discrimination against the white petitioners in this case upon the same standards as would be applicable were they Negroes and Jackson white. . . .[8]

Respondents contend that, even though generally applicable to white persons, Title VII affords petitioners no protection in this case, because their dismissal was based upon their commission of a serious criminal offense against their employer. We think this argument is foreclosed by our decision in *McDonnell Douglas Corp. v. Green.* [The Court quoted that case and elaborated on the "pretext" phrasing:

6. Our discussion in *McDonnell Douglas Corp. v. Green* of the means by which a Title VII litigant might make out a prima facie case of racial discrimination is not contrary. . . . As we particularly noted, however, this "specification . . . of the prima facie proof required . . . is not necessarily applicable in every respect to differing factual situations." Requirement (i) of this sample pattern of proof was set out only to demonstrate how the racial character of the discrimination could be established in the most common sort of case, and not as an indication of any substantive limitation of Title VII's prohibition of racial discrimination.

8. . . . Santa Fe disclaims that the actions challenged here were any part of an affirmative action program, and we emphasize that we do not consider here the permissibility of such a program, whether judicially required or otherwise prompted.

The use of the term "pretext" in this context does not mean, of course, that the Title VII plaintiff must show that he would have in any event been rejected or discharged solely on the basis of his race, without regard to the alleged deficiencies; . . . no more is required to be shown than that race was a "but-for" cause.]

We find this case indistinguishable from *McDonnell Douglas*. Fairly read, the complaint asserted that petitioners were discharged for their alleged participation in a misappropriation of cargo entrusted to Santa Fe, but that a fellow employee, likewise implicated, was not so disciplined, and that the reason for the discrepancy in discipline was that the favored employee is Negro while petitioners are white.[11] While Santa Fe may decide that participation in a theft of cargo may render an employee unqualified for employment, this criterion must be "applied, alike to members of all races," and Title VII is violated if, as petitioners alleged, it was not.

We cannot accept respondents' argument that the principles of *McDonnell Douglas* are inapplicable where the discharge was based, as petitioners' complaint admitted, on participation in serious misconduct or crime directed against the employer. The Act prohibits all racial discrimination in employment, without exception for any group of particular employees, and while crime or other misconduct may be a legitimate basis for discharge, it is hardly one for racial discrimination. Indeed, the Title VII plaintiff in *McDonnell Douglas* had been convicted for a nontrivial offense against his former employer. It may be that theft of property entrusted to an employer for carriage is a more compelling basis for discharge than obstruction of an employer's traffic arteries, but this does not diminish the illogic in retaining guilty employees of one color while discharging those of another color. . . .

III

. . . We have previously held, where discrimination against Negroes was in question, that § 1981 affords a federal remedy against discrimination in private employment on the basis of race, and respondents do not contend otherwise. *Johnson v. Railway Express Agency*, 421 U.S. 454 (1975). The question here is whether § 1981 prohibits racial discrimination in private employment against whites as well as nonwhites.

While neither of the courts below elaborated its reasons for not applying § 1981 to racial discrimination against white persons, respondents suggest two lines of argument to support that judgment. First, they argue that by operation of the phrase "as is enjoyed by white citizens," § 1981 unambiguously limits itself to the protection of nonwhite persons against racial discrimination. Second, they contend that such a reading is consistent with the legislative history of the provision, which derives its operative language from § 1 of the Civil Rights Act of 1866. The 1866 statute, they assert, was concerned predominantly with assuring specified civil rights to the former Negro slaves freed by virtue of the Thirteenth Amendment, and not at all with protecting the corresponding civil rights of white persons.

---

11. Santa Fe contends that petitioners were required to plead with "particularity" the degree of similarity between their culpability in the alleged theft and the involvement of the favored coemployee, Jackson. [But] precise equivalence in culpability between employees is not the ultimate question: as we indicated in *McDonnell Douglas*, an allegation that other "employees involved in acts against [the employer] of *comparable seriousness* . . . were nevertheless retained . . ." is adequate to plead an inferential case that the employer's reliance on his discharged employee's misconduct as grounds for terminating him was merely a pretext (emphasis added).

We find neither argument persuasive. Rather, our examination of the language and history of § 1981 convinces us that § 1981 is applicable to racial discrimination in private employment against white persons.

First, we cannot accept the view that the terms of § 1981 exclude its application to racial discrimination against white persons. On the contrary, the statute explicitly applies to "*all* persons" (emphasis added), including white persons. While a mechanical reading of the phrase "as is enjoyed by white citizens" would seem to lend support to respondents' reading of the statute, we have previously described this phrase simply as emphasizing "the racial character of the rights being protected." *Georgia v. Rachel*, 384 U.S. 780, 791 (1966). In any event, whatever ambiguity there may be in the language of § 1981 is clarified by an examination of the legislative history of § 1981's language as it was originally forged in the Civil Rights Act of 1866. It is to this subject that we now turn.

The bill ultimately enacted as the Civil Rights Act of 1866 was introduced by Senator Trumbull of Illinois as a "bill . . . to protect *all* persons in the United States in their civil rights . . . " (emphasis added), and was initially described by him as applying to "every race and color." Cong. Globe, 39th Cong., 1st Sess., 211 (1866) (hereinafter Cong. Globe). Consistent with the views of its draftsmen, and the prevailing view in the Congress as to the reach of its powers under the enforcement section of the Thirteenth Amendment, the terms of the bill prohibited any racial discrimination in the making and enforcement of contracts against whites as well as nonwhites. . . .

While it is, of course, true that the immediate impetus for the bill was the necessity for further relief of the constitutionally emancipated former Negro slaves, the general discussion of the scope of the bill did not circumscribe its broad language to that limited goal. On the contrary, the bill was routinely viewed, by its opponents and supporters alike, as applying to the civil rights of whites as well as nonwhites. . . .

It is clear, thus, that the bill, as it passed the Senate, was not limited in scope to discrimination against nonwhites. Accordingly, respondents pitch their legislative history argument largely upon the House's amendment of the Senate bill to add the "as is enjoyed by white citizens" phrase. But the statutory history is equally clear that that phrase was not intended to have the effect of eliminating from the bill the prohibition of racial discrimination against whites. . . .

This cumulative evidence of congressional intent makes clear, we think, that the 1866 statute, designed to protect the "same right . . . to make and enforce contracts" of "citizens of every race and color" was not understood or intended to be reduced by Representative Wilson's amendment, or any other provision, to the protection solely of nonwhites. Rather, the Act was meant, by its broad terms, to proscribe discrimination in the making or enforcement of contracts against, or in favor of, any race. Unlikely as it might have appeared in 1866 that white citizens would encounter substantial racial discrimination of the sort proscribed under the Act, the statutory structure and legislative history persuade us that the 39th Congress was intent upon establishing in the federal law a broader principle than would have been necessary simply to meet the particular and immediate plight of the newly freed Negro slaves. And while the statutory language has been somewhat streamlined in re-enactment and codification, there is no indication that § 1981 is intended to provide any less than the Congress enacted in 1866 regarding racial discrimination against white persons. Thus, we conclude that the District Court erred in dismissing petitioners' claims under § 1981 on the ground that the protections of that provision are unavailable to white persons.

NOTES

1. *Good Cause vs. At-Will.* After *Santa Fe,* it is clear that whites are protected against race discrimination under both Title VII and §1981. It is equally clear that men are protected against sex discrimination in employment under Title VII. *Slack, Desert Palace, Price Waterhouse, McDonnell Douglas,* and *Santa Fe* all mean that *any* racial or gender motivation that results in an adverse employment action is unlawful, just as age motivation resulting in a discharge was critical in *Biggins.* Doctrinally, that is quite a bit more limited than a general good cause standard.

But from a risk management perspective, isn't it still a good idea for an employer to have a defensible reason for any significant employment action? After all, majority and minority men and all women are protected against discrimination, and beginning at 40, all workers are protected against age discrimination. Isn't the absence of a good reason risky because every employee can sue?

2. *Legitimate Nondiscriminatory Reason?* Surely Santa Fe had a legitimate non-discriminatory reason for firing plaintiffs. The plaintiffs admitted participating in the thefts that the defendant claimed to be the basis for their discharge, yet the Court finds the case "indistinguishable from *McDonnell Douglas.*" Is that because there was a good reason for discharge in both cases? Given their admitted theft, how could the defendant's acting on that be a "pretext" for discrimination? Is *Santa Fe* really a mixed motives case, with good reason and bad reasons intertwined? On remand, how will the plaintiffs prove their discharge was actionable?

A more straightforward way to describe *Santa Fe* is as an unequal treatment case. "It may be that theft of property entrusted to an employer for carriage is a . . . compelling basis for discharge . . . but this does not diminish the illogic in retaining guilty employees of one color while discharging those of another color." Thus, as in *Slack* and *Desert Palace,* the unequal treatment is powerful evidence to establish liability and may get the plaintiff past summary judgment even if the defendant provides a non-racial explanation. Or, if viewed through the lens of *McDonnell Douglas,* would plaintiff then have to adduce evidence proof, independent of the proof of unequal treatment, that defendant's explanation is not the real reason?

If you represented the defendant, what evidence would you look for to rebut plaintiffs' prima facie case? The best would be evidence that the black co-worker had not been involved in the theft. Then the decision is a guilt/innocence one, not a black/white one. Even if the black co-worker participated in the theft, maybe another non-racial difference might be past records: if the plaintiffs' had long records of disciplinary actions against them but this was the black worker's first offense, the racial motivation might be undercut. Does this all take us back to *McDonnell Douglas*'s three-part approach: the apparent unequal treatment gives rise to a presumption of discrimination, which can be rebutted by a non-racial explanation, which, in turn, can be proven to be pretext?

3. *"Comparator" Cases.* It is possible to cast *Santa Fe* in the *McDonnell Douglas* mold, but to do so one has to say that the prima facie case is established not by any of the usual multi-element steps but rather by unequal treatment of people who are alike but for their race (or other prohibited classification). Another way to view cases like *Santa Fe* is as literal "disparate treatment" cases: plaintiff prevails by proving that she was treated differently than a "comparator" (a similarly situated person of the other sex or a different race). And that difference in treatment supports the inference that the different treatment was because of race. Most lower courts try to frame the analysis in *McDonnell Douglas* terms rather than as mere literal disparate treatment.

In any event, the problem is less the label than how close a comparator must be in order to count. Some lower courts seem to require the comparator to be "nearly identical" to the plaintiff, which is strange if the point of the inquiry is to infer a racial motivation from a difference in treatment. For example, in *Roland v. United States Postal Serv.*, 200 Fed. Appx. 868, 872 (11th Cir. 2006), plaintiff, claiming that whites engaged in similar conduct to her conduct were not discharged, was found not "nearly identical" to a comparator. The differences included that the whites "worked in a different facility [and] reported to a different supervisor." Further, plaintiff's conduct was more egregious than the white comparator because she "engaged in Mary Kay sales and marketing in the postal facility and while in a position of authority. Grier [the comparator], on the other hand, delivered his wife's Avon products outside of the postal facility and did not involve subordinates in his Avon activities." Nor is *Roland* a mere outlier, as other circuits have imposed a "nearly identical" standard. *E.g., Johnson v. Ready Mixed Concrete Co.*, 424 F.3d 806 (8th Cir. 2005) (black truck driver who was discharged for lying in report about damage to his truck was not similarly situated to undisciplined white truck drivers who had not voluntarily reported similar damage to their trucks but did not make misrepresentations in a report); *Ramon v. Cont'l Airlines Inc.*, 153 Fed. Appx. 257 (5th Cir. 2005) (fired plaintiff was not similarly situated to more senior worker, who was allowed to work until he was eligible for retirement precisely because of their different retirement-eligibility).

However, *Crawford v. Ind. Harbor Belt R.R. Co.*, 461 F.3d 844, 846 (7th Cir. 2006), disapproved of a trend "to require closer and closer comparability between the plaintiff and the members of the comparison group." It explained:

> The requirement is a natural response to cherry-picking by plaintiffs. . . . If a plaintiff can make a prima facie case by finding just one or two male or nonminority workers who were treated worse than she, she should have to show that they really are comparable to her in every respect.
>
> But if as we believe cherry-picking is improper, the plaintiff should have to show only that the members of the comparison group are sufficiently comparable to her to suggest that she was singled out for worse treatment. Otherwise plaintiffs will be in a box: if they pick just members of the comparison group who are comparable in every respect, they will be accused of cherry-picking; but if they look for a representative sample, they will unavoidably include some who were not comparable in every respect, but merely broadly comparable. The cases that say that the members of the comparison group must be comparable to the plaintiff in all material respects get this right.

Nevertheless, the cases that require the same supervisor may make more sense than others precisely because they focus on the intent of the individual decisionmaker. The argument is that supervisor A's intent can't be inferred from what Supervisor B did. So if A thinks tardiness is a firing offense for an African American, the fact that B allows her white workers to be tardy does not prove that A had any discriminatory intent. This issue is treated in more detail in Note on Special Issues of Proof at p. 107. Putting the same supervisor issue aside, however, the better view of the comparator question is that the case should go to the jury unless no reasonable factfinder could find unequal treatment. That a jury might find in *Roland* that the differential treatment was explained by reasons other than race does not mean that the situations of the two workers were not alike enough to find a violation based on the inequality of treatment. *See generally* Ernest F. Lidge III, *The Courts' Misuse of the Similarly Situated Concept in Employment Discrimination Law*, 67 MO. L. REV. 831 (2002).

4. *§ 1981. Santa Fe* introduces us in more detail to 42 U.S.C. § 1981 (2007). That statute originated in the Reconstruction era, but was revived in the wake of Title VII. *Johnson v. Railway Express Agency*, 421 U.S. 454 (1975), held that private race discrimination against blacks is prohibited by the statute, and *Santa Fe* confirms that, despite the "as is enjoyed by white citizens" language, whites are also protected from racial discrimination. Thus, § 1981 is at once both broader and narrower than Title VII. While coverage questions are discussed in more detail in Chapter 5, § 1981 is broader not only in covering all employment contracts, even those of small employers, but also in reaching beyond the employment relation to all contracts. It is narrower in that it is limited to race (and probably alienage discrimination, see p. 441) discrimination, while Title VII includes sex, religion, and national origin.

Because discrimination must be "racial" to fall within § 1981, gender discrimination obviously is not covered. *E.g., Bobo v. ITT, Continental Banking Co.*, 662 F.2d 340 (5th Cir. 1981). *See also Runyon v. McCrary*, 427 U.S. 160, 167 (1976). But other kinds of discrimination are less clear. For example, is anti-Semitism racial or religious bias? Is discrimination against Mexican-Americans based on their race or their national origin? *See Ugalde v. W. A. McKenzie Asphalt Co.*, 990 F.2d 239 (5th Cir. 1993) (Title VII) (employer discharging plaintiff while calling her a "wetback" made her claim racial, not national origin). *Cf. Salas v. Wisconsin Dep't of Corrections*, 483 F.3d 913 (7th Cir. 2007) (looking to EEOC regulations to conclude that "Hispanics" are a national origin). Under Title VII, such questions are rarely important because the statute bars race, religion, and national origin discrimination (although religion and national origin discrimination can both be justified by a bona fide occupational qualification, while race discrimination cannot). Under § 1981, however, recovery depends on the charged conduct being race-based.

Does § 1981 require mere racial motivation or actual racial animus? A number of Supreme Court cases, *e.g., Saint Francis College v. Al-Khazraji*, 481 U.S. 604 (1987), have used the latter term, while others, such as *Santa Fe*, seem to focus on the racial nature of the motivation. *See also General Building Contractors Assn. v. Pennsylvania*, 458 U.S. 375 (1982) (using "racial animus" interchangeably with "purposeful discrimination" and "racially motivated" discrimination). Generally, speaking, however, the courts have read the substantive prohibitions of § 1981 and Title VII to be identical. *See Patterson v. McLean Credit Union*, reproduced at p. 62 (applying the *McDonnell Douglas* approach in a § 1981 case).

5. *What Is "Race"?* In may seem odd to wait until this point in the course to ask what we mean by race, but it turns out that, however intuitive the meaning of the word, it has generated complications, especially under § 1981 where the discrimination must be race-based to be actionable. The Supreme Court addressed the question of what "race" means in *Saint Francis College v. Al-Khazraji*, 481 U.S. 604 (1987), a suit by a United States citizen who had been born in Iraq and claimed that he was denied tenure at the college based on his Arab ancestry. The district court rejected his § 1981 claim because Arabs are generally considered Caucasians. The Supreme Court reversed; it held Arabs to be a race, at least for purposes of § 1981:

> There is a common popular understanding that there are three major human races — Caucasoid, Mongoloid, and Negroid. Many modern biologists and anthropologists, however, criticize racial classifications as arbitrary and of little use in understanding the variability of human beings. It is said that genetically homogeneous populations do not exist and traits are not discontinuous between populations; therefore, a population can only be described in terms of relative frequencies of various

traits. Clear-cut categories do not exist. The particular traits which have generally been chosen to characterize races have been criticized as having little biological significance. It has been found that differences between individuals of the same race are often greater than the differences between the "average" individuals of different races. These observations and others led some, but not all, scientists to conclude that racial classifications are for the most part sociopolitical, rather than biological, in nature. S. Molnar, Human Variation (2d ed. 1983); S. Gould, The Mismeasure of Man (1981); M. Banton & J. Harwood, The Race Concept (1975); A. Montagu, Man's Most Dangerous Myth (1974).

Id. at 610 n.4. Current scientific thinking on race, however, was ultimately irrelevant to the Court. Even if Arabs are now considered Caucasians, that was not the understanding in the nineteenth century when § 1981 was enacted:

[Dictionaries commonly referred to race as a "continued series of descendants from a parent who is called the *stock*," "[t]he lineage of a family," or "descendants of a common ancestor."] The 1887 edition of Webster's expanded the definition somewhat: "The descendants of a common ancestor; a family, tribe, people or nation, believed or presumed to be-long to the same stock." It was not until the 20th century that dictionaries began referring to the Caucasian, Mongolian and Negro races, or to race as involving divisions of mankind based upon different physical characteristics. Even so, modern dictionaries still include among the definitions of race as being "a family, tribe, people, or nation belonging to the same stock." Webster's Third New International Dictionary 1870 (1971); Webster's Ninth New Collegiate Dictionary 969 (Springfield, Mass. 1986).

Encyclopedias of the 19th century also described race in terms of ethnic groups, which is a narrower concept of race than petitioners urge. Encyclopedia Americana in 1858, for example, referred in 1854 to various races such as Finns, gypsies, Basques, and Hebrews. . . . These dictionary and encyclopedic sources are somewhat diverse, but it is clear that they do not support the claim that for the purposes of § 1981, Arabs, Englishmen, Germans, and certain other ethnic groups are to be considered a single race. We would expect the legislative history of § 1981, which the Court held in Runyon v. McCrary had its source in the Civil Rights Act of 1866, as well as the Voting Rights Acts of 1870, to reflect this common understanding, which it surely does.

Id. at 611-12. The Court noted references to "race" for Scandinavians, Chinese, Spanish, Anglo-Saxons, blacks, Mongolians, and gypsies. In this light, it concluded:

Congress intended to protect from discrimination identifiable classes of persons who are subjected to intentional discrimination solely because of their ancestry or ethnic characteristics. Such discrimination is racial discrimination that Congress intended § 1981 to forbid, whether or not it would be classified as racial in terms of modern scientific theory. The Court of Appeals was thus quite right in holding that § 1981, "at a minimum," reaches discrimination against an individual "because he or she is genetically part of an ethnically and physiognomically distinctive sub-grouping of homo sapiens." It is clear from our holding, however, that a distinctive physiognomy is not essential to qualify for § 1981 protection.

Id. at 613. *See also Shaare Tefila Congregation v. Cobb*, 481 U.S. 615, 617 (1987) (§ 1982 suit by a synagogue for defacement of its walls with anti-Semitic slogans permissible because, when § 1982 was adopted, "Jews and Arabs were among the people then considered to be distinct races and hence within the protection of the statute").

Title VII, however, was enacted nearly a century after § 1981. By 1964, "race" had acquired more or less its present meaning. Does that mean that discrimination against Arabs is not actionable under Title VII as race discrimination? If discrimination against Arabs is not racial discrimination, is it national origin discrimination, even though Arabs do not come from one political entity, but rather from a number of states in the Mideast? Similarly, with respect to Jews, is anti-Semitism actionable as race, religion, or national origin discrimination under Title VII? Before you answer that question too quickly, remember that much anti-Semitism, including the ultimate discrimination manifested in the Holocaust, made no distinctions between religious and non-religious Jews, but rather defined its victims in terms of race-like characteristics. *See Sinai v. New England Telephone & Telegraph Co.*, 3 F.3d 471, 474 (1st Cir. 1993) (derogatory comments about Israel, plaintiff's birthplace, could be the basis for inferring race discrimination).

6. *Colorism.* The question of what is "race" triggers a related inquiry: what is discrimination because of "color"? § 1981, which is framed in terms of equal treatment with "whites," certainly implicates that question, and Title VII explicitly bars discrimination on account of color. § 703(a). In many cases, color and race are perceived as the same, but there have been cases, often involving what might be called intra-race discrimination, where the claim is that darker skin is the basis of the disparate treatment. *See* Cynthia E. Nance, *The Continuing Significance of Color under Title VII Forty Years after Its Passage*, 26 BERKELEY J. EMP. & LAB. L. 435, 473 (2005) (colorism and its detrimental personal and economic effects remain an issue in this country [that] is not isolated to any particular community but is found within all racial groups and notably within groups towards members of the same group); Taunya Lovell Banks, *Colorism: A Darker Shade of Pale*, 47 UCLA L. REV. 1705, 1710-11 (2000) (arguing that "courts rigidly adhere to the commonly accepted notion that a person with any known African ancestry is raced as black" although the overwhelming majority of such people in the United States "have mixed ancestry and vary widely both in skin tone and phenotypical characteristics"); Trina Jones, *Shades of Brown: The Law of Skin Color*, 49 DUKE L. J. 1487 (2000) (colorism occurs in both the white and black communities, and will assume increasing significance in the future). *See also* Tanya Katerí Hernández, *Latino Inter-Ethnic Employment Discrimination and the "Diversity" Defense*, HARV. C.R-C.L. L. REV. 259 (2007) (exploring discrimination by some Latinos against others, whether on racial or national origin grounds).

7. *Discrimination by Mistake.* Suppose a white applicant for employment is discriminated against because she is mistakenly perceived to be African American. Does she have a claim under Title VII? *See* Angela Onwuachi-Willig & Mario L. Barnes, *By Any Other Name?: On Being "Regarded As" Black, and Why Title VII Should Apply Even if Lakisha and Jamal Are White*, 2005 WISC. L. REV. 1283 (borrowing from the disability framework, the authors argue for race discrimination claims where an individual is "'regarded as' black, with all of its 'collective negative imaging'").

8. *Relationship-Based Discrimination.* In *Deffenbaugh-Williams v. Wal-Mart Stores*, Inc., 156 F.3d 581, 589 (5th Cir. 1998), the employer argued that a white plaintiff, claiming discrimination because of her interracial personal relationship, failed to show that she was a member of a class protected by Title VII. Finding that Title VII prohibits discrimination premised on an interracial relationship, the court rejected Wal-Mart's argument. "[A] reasonable juror could find that Deffenbaugh

was discriminated against because of her race (white), if that discrimination was premised on the fact that she, a white person, had a relationship with a black person."

NOTE ON "REVERSE" DISCRIMINATION

Santa Fe makes clear that "reverse" discrimination is cognizable under both Title VII and § 1981, although the affirmative action plan question, reserved in footnote 8 in *Santa Fe*, was resolved in favor of the voluntary use of some racial and gender preferences. See *Johnson v. Transportation Agency of Santa Clara County*, reproduced at p. 184. Thus, some racial preferences are permissible and some are not under those statutes. How does a white or male plaintiff make out a prima facie case? Where white plaintiffs were "minorities" in the institution or occupation where they sought work, *McDonnell Douglas* applies with little adjustment. See *Lincoln v. Board of Regents*, 697 F.2d 928 (11th Cir. 1983) (affirming judgment against a predominately black university in an action brought by a white faculty member). Similarly, the fact that African Americans are the decisionmakers may be an important factor in making out a prima facie case by a white plaintiff. See *Hague v. Thompson Distrib. Co.*, 436 F.3d 816, 822 (7th Cir. 2006) (white plaintiffs' proof that their black boss fired them and replaced them with blacks or left the position open was sufficient). Might one also expect that employers will discriminate against males when they attempt to perform traditionally female jobs? See *Martinez v. El Paso County*, 710 F.2d 1102 (5th Cir. 1983), affirming a finding of sex discrimination against a male secretary.

But when a predominately white institution discharges a white worker and there is no evidence of unequal treatment, no admissions against interest or proof that actions were taken on racial stereotypes, is *McDonnell Douglas* available, and how can plaintiff establish a prima facie case? Where a white plaintiff challenges an employment decision against the typical white-dominated employer, it is difficult to draw the inference that the employer acted because of discrimination against whites, even where the most common, legitimate reasons for the decision are negated. This reality has led a number of courts to require that such a plaintiff show something more than a minority plaintiff or a woman would need to prove. A typical formulation is that, to establish a prima facie case, a reverse discrimination plaintiff must "present evidence of background circumstances that establish that the defendant is that unusual employer who discriminates against the majority.'" *Parker v. Balt. & Ohio R.R. Co.*, 652 F.2d 1012, 1017 (D.C. Cir. 1981). Most circuits continue to use the "background circumstances" label, but a wide range of circumstances seems to qualify. *E.g.*, *Mastro v. Potomac Elec. Power Co.*, 447 F.3d 843, 852-53 (D.C. Cir. 2006) (a "nominally expired" consent decree was a background circumstance such that, when coupled with evidence that the employer was reluctant to discipline black workers, even for serious offenses, plaintiff stated a prima facie case); *Myers v. Cuyahoga County*, 182 Fed. Appx. 510, 517 (6th Cir. 2006) (white employee established prima facie case of reverse discrimination where she presented testimony that Hispanic supervisors were trying to create "a basically Hispanic welfare office to meet the needs of the Hispanic community," and she was replaced by a Hispanic employee); *Rudin v. Lincoln Land Cmty. College*, 420 F.3d 712, 722 (7th Cir. 2005) ("evidence of LLCC's practice of inserting minorities into the interview pool plus an affirmative action plan sufficed); *Sutherland v. Michigan Dep't of Treasury*, 344 F.3d 603 (6th Cir. 2003) (requisite "background circumstances" found where statistical evidence of promotion and hiring patterns reflected racial and gender preferences against majority over a period of twenty years). *But see Mlynczak v. Bodman,* 442 F.3d 1050, 1058 (7th Cir. 2006) (neither the existence of an affirmative action policy nor ultimate decisionmaker being philosophically inclined toward hiring minorities was sufficient evidence of reverse discrimination).

Other courts have rejected the background circumstances test, although it is not clear whether they are really applying an undiluted *McDonnell Douglas* approach. In *Iadimarco v. Runyon,* 190 F.3d 151, 158 (3d Cir. 1999), the Third Circuit held that a prima facie case of "reverse" discrimination requires that the plaintiff present sufficient evidence to allow a fact finder to conclude that the employer is treating some people less favorably than others based upon a trait that is protected under Title VII. But the court then held that this test was not satisfied by showing that the managers who made the decision plaintiff challenged were African American. Other circumstances, however, were sufficient to raise "material issues of fact as to whether the proffered explanation for not hiring him was a pretext for illegal discrimination." *Id.* at 167. Even in the Third Circuit, is it still harder for a white plaintiff than for an African American to make out a prima facie case?

Does the existence of an affirmative action plan make it easier for a white or a male plaintiff to establish discrimination, even if the employer may be able to justify it? In *Bass v. Board of County Commissioners,* 256 F.3d 1095 (11th Cir. 2001), plaintiff, a white male, challenged his layoff when the fire department was reorganized. He claimed that he was not appointed to a newly created position because of his race. The employer responded that he was not chosen because he had not scored as well on his interview as the successful candidates. While there was an affirmative action plan in place, the defendant did not rely on it; instead, plaintiff claimed the defendant had relied on the plan, which, he argued, was invalid. The court noted that, in "a typical Title VII case involving an affirmative action plan," it is the employer who puts the plan in issue, with the plaintiff then being required to prove that the plan is invalid. In this case, however, "the County has sought no cover from its affirmative action plans" Rather, it was plaintiff who pointed to the plans in order to support his claim that he was discriminated against. In such a case,

> [t]he first step in ascertaining whether the County can be held liable for discrimination as a result of its affirmative action plans is a determination of whether there is sufficient evidence that it acted pursuant to those plans. . . . [Second], the existence of an affirmative action plan, when combined with evidence that the plan was followed in an employment decision, is sufficient to constitute direct evidence of unlawful discrimination unless the plan is valid.

Id. at 1009-10. The court concluded: "[W]e hold that where there is an invalid affirmative action plan in effect relating to the employer's allegedly discriminatory actions, that plan constitutes direct evidence of discrimination if there is sufficient circumstantial evidence to permit a jury reasonably to conclude the employer acted pursuant to the plan when it took the employment actions in question." *Id.* at 1111. *See generally* Charles A. Sullivan, *Circling Back to the Obvious: The Convergence of Traditional and Reverse Discrimination in Title VII Proof,* 46 WM. & MARY L. REV. 1031 (2004). Revisit this question after you have studied affirmative action plans in Chapter 2.

NOTE ON PREFERENCES FOR OLDER WORKERS

"Affirmative action" is a term not often used in the ADEA context, but occasionally plaintiffs who were younger workers but still protected class members claimed to have been treated less favorably than older workers. The issue was unresolved until the Supreme Court's decision in *General Dynamics Land Systems, Inc. v. Cline*, 540 U.S. 581 (2004). There, the employer and its union agreed to "grandparent" incumbent workers over age 50 from the elimination of health benefits for workers once they retired. Plaintiffs, workers between 40 and 50 and not given grandparent status, claimed age discrimination. Reviewing the legislative history of the ADEA, the Court in a 6 to 3 decision concluded "that the ADEA was concerned to protect a relatively old worker from discrimination that works to the advantage of the relatively young." Therefore, the "word 'age' takes on a definite meaning from being in the phrase 'discrimination . . . because of such individual's age,' occurring as that phrase does in a statute structured and manifestly intended to protect the older from arbitrary favor for the younger. . . . " *See* D. Aaron Lacy, *You Are Not Quite as Old as You Think: Making the Case for Reverse Age Discrimination under the ADEA*, 26 BERKELEY J. EMP. & LAB. L. 363 (2005) (critiquing *Cline* as incorrect). The effect of *Cline* is to eliminate any ADEA claim when the preferences challenged are for older workers, and there is nothing in the decision that would prevent more dramatic employment actions than the curtailing of benefits from also being permissible. For example, if the employer chose to lay off younger workers rather than older workers, the Court's reading of the statute would bar any suit by the younger workers, even if these younger workers were over age 40. See Note on "Affirmative Action" under the ADEA at p. 200.

NOTE COMPARING SECTION 1981 AND TITLE VII

As compared to Title VII, § 1981 has procedural advantages which are explored in Chapter 7, including a generally longer statute of limitations and the absence of any requirement to file a charge with the EEOC. Section 1981 remedies also are broader than those available under Title VII, mostly due to the absence of a statutory cap on damages. See Chapter 8, p. 684. A third advantage of § 1981 is that, unlike Title VII, its coverage is not expressly limited to employment, which means that discrimination against independent contractors is actionable. See Chapter 5B, p. 317.

In *Johnson v. Railway Express Agency, Inc.*, 421 U.S. 454, 461 (1975), the Supreme Court wrote: "the remedies available under Title VII and under § 1981, although related, and although directed to most of the same ends, are separate, distinct, and independent." This means that, where both statutes apply, both may be invoked against the same conduct, and the failure of a plaintiff to meet the procedural requirements of Title VII does not affect a § 1981 suit. As a result of this independence, however, a filing with the EEOC under Title VII does not toll the § 1981 statute of limitations, *id.*, although neither is there is any requirement of exhaustion of state remedies prior to a § 1981 action. *Patsy v. Board of Regents*, 457 U.S. 496 (1982) (§ 1983).

REEVES v. SANDERSON PLUMBING
PRODUCTS, INC.
530 U.S. 133 (2000)

Justice O'CONNOR delivered the opinion of the Court.

This case concerns the kind and amount of evidence necessary to sustain a jury's verdict that an employer unlawfully discriminated on the basis of age. Specifically, we must resolve whether a defendant is entitled to judgment as a matter of law when the plaintiff's case consists exclusively of a prima facie case of discrimination and sufficient evidence for the trier of fact to disbelieve the defendant's legitimate, nondiscriminatory explanation for its action. We must also decide whether the employer was entitled to judgment as a matter of law under the particular circumstances presented here.

I

In October 1995, petitioner Roger Reeves was 57 years old and had spent 40 years in the employ of respondent, Sanderson Plumbing Products, Inc., a manufacturer of toilet seats and covers. Petitioner worked in a department known as the "Hinge Room," where he supervised the "regular line." Joe Oswalt, in his mid-thirties, supervised the Hinge Room's "special line," and Russell Caldwell, the manager of the Hinge Room and age 45, supervised both petitioner and Oswalt. Petitioner's responsibilities included recording the attendance and hours of those under his supervision, and reviewing a weekly report that listed the hours worked by each employee.

In the summer of 1995, Caldwell informed Powe Chesnut, the director of manufacturing and the husband of company president Sandra Sanderson, that "production was down" in the Hinge Room because employees were often absent and were "coming in late and leaving early." Because the monthly attendance reports did not indicate a problem, Chesnut ordered an audit of the Hinge Room's timesheets for July, August, and September of that year. According to Chesnut's testimony, that investigation revealed "numerous timekeeping errors and misrepresentations on the part of Caldwell, Reeves, and Oswalt." Following the audit, Chesnut, along with Dana Jester, vice president of human resources, and Tom Whitaker, vice president of operations, recommended to company president Sanderson that petitioner and Caldwell be fired. In October 1995, Sanderson followed the recommendation and discharged both petitioner and Caldwell.

At trial, respondent contended that it had fired petitioner due to his failure to maintain accurate attendance records, while petitioner attempted to demonstrate that respondent's explanation was pretext for age discrimination. Petitioner introduced evidence that he had accurately recorded the attendance and hours of the employees under his supervision, and that Chesnut, whom Oswalt described as wielding "absolute power" within the company had demonstrated age-based animus in his dealings with petitioner.

[The jury returned a verdict in favor of petitioner of $35,000 in compensatory damages, which the judge doubled as liquidated damages pursuant to the jury's finding that the employer's age discrimination was "willful." The judge also awarded plaintiff $28,490.80 in front pay for two years' lost income.]

The Court of Appeals for the Fifth Circuit reversed, holding that petitioner had not introduced sufficient evidence to sustain the jury's finding of unlawful discrimination. After noting respondent's proffered justification for petitioner's discharge, the court acknowledged that petitioner "very well may" have offered sufficient evidence for "a reasonable jury [to] have found that [respondent's] explanation for its employment decision was pretextual." The court explained, however, that this was "not dispositive" of the ultimate issue — namely, "whether Reeves presented sufficient evidence that his age motivated [respondent's] employment decision." Addressing this question, the court weighed petitioner's additional evidence of discrimination against other circumstances surrounding his discharge. Specifically, the court noted that Chesnut's age-based comments "were not made in the direct context of Reeves's termination"; there was no allegation that the two other individuals who had recommended that petitioner be fired (Jester and Whitaker) were motivated by age; two of the decision makers involved in petitioner's discharge (Jester and Sanderson) were over the age of 50; all three of the Hinge Room supervisors were accused of inaccurate record keeping; and several of respondent's management positions were filled by persons over age 50 when petitioner was fired. On this basis, the court concluded that petitioner had not introduced sufficient evidence for a rational jury to conclude that he had been discharged because of his age. . . .

II . . . .

When a plaintiff alleges disparate treatment, "liability depends on whether the protected trait (under the ADEA, age) actually motivated the employer's decision." *Hazen Paper Co. v. Biggins.* That is, the plaintiff's age must have "actually played a role in [the employer's decision making] process and had a determinative influence on the outcome." Recognizing that "the question facing triers of fact in discrimination cases is both sensitive and difficult," and that "there will seldom be 'eyewitness' testimony as to the employer's mental processes," *Postal Service Bd. of Governors v. Aikens,* 460 U.S. 711 (1983), the Courts of Appeals, including the Fifth Circuit in this case, have employed some variant of the framework articulated in *McDonnell Douglas* to analyze ADEA claims that are based principally on circumstantial evidence. . . . This Court has not squarely addressed whether the *McDonnell Douglas* framework, developed to assess claims brought under §703(a)(1) of Title VII of the Civil Rights Act of 1964, also applies to ADEA actions. Because the parties do not dispute the issue, we shall assume, arguendo, that the *McDonnell Douglas* framework is fully applicable here.

[Under this framework, petitioner established a prima facie case and respondent rebutted it.] Although intermediate evidentiary burdens shift back and forth under this framework, "the ultimate burden of persuading the trier of fact that the defendant intentionally discriminated against the plaintiff remains at all times with the plaintiff." And in attempting to satisfy this burden, the plaintiff — once the employer produces sufficient evidence to support a nondiscriminatory explanation for its decision — must be afforded the "opportunity to prove by a preponderance of the evidence that the legitimate reasons offered by the defendant were not its true reasons, but were a pretext for discrimination." That is, the plaintiff may attempt to establish that he was the victim of intentional discrimination "by showing that the employer's proffered explanation is unworthy of credence." Moreover, although the presumption of discrimination "drops out of the picture" once the defendant meets its burden of production, the trier of fact may still consider the evidence establishing the plaintiff's prima facie case "and inferences properly drawn therefrom . . . on the issue of whether the defendant's explanation is pretextual."

In this case, the evidence supporting respondent's explanation for petitioner's discharge consisted primarily of testimony by Chesnut and Sanderson and documentation of petitioner's alleged "shoddy record keeping." Chesnut testified that a 1993 audit of Hinge Room operations revealed "a very lax assembly line" where employees were not adhering to general work rules. As a result of that audit, petitioner was placed on 90 days' probation for unsatisfactory performance. In 1995,

Chesnut ordered another investigation of the Hinge Room, which, according to his testimony, revealed that petitioner was not correctly recording the absences and hours of employees. Respondent introduced summaries of that investigation documenting several attendance violations by 12 employees under petitioner's supervision, and noting that each should have been disciplined in some manner. Chesnut testified that this failure to discipline absent and late employees is "extremely important when you are dealing with a union" because uneven enforcement across departments would keep the company "in grievance and arbitration cases, which are costly, all the time." He and Sanderson also stated that petitioner's errors, by failing to adjust for hours not worked, cost the company overpaid wages. Sanderson testified that she accepted the recommendation to discharge petitioner because he had "intentionally falsified company pay records."

Petitioner, however, made a substantial showing that respondent's explanation was false. First, petitioner offered evidence that he had properly maintained the attendance records. Most of the timekeeping errors cited by respondent involved employees who were not marked late but who were recorded as having arrived at the plant at 7 A.M. for the 7 A.M. shift. Respondent contended that employees arriving at 7 A.M. could not have been at their workstations by 7 A.M., and therefore must have been late. But both petitioner and Oswalt testified that the company's automated timeclock often failed to scan employees' timecards, so that the timesheets would not record any time of arrival. On these occasions, petitioner and Oswalt would visually check the workstations and record whether the employees were present at the start of the shift. They stated that if an employee arrived promptly but the timesheet contained no time of arrival, they would reconcile the two by marking "7 A.M." as the employee's arrival time, even if the employee actually arrived at the plant earlier. On cross-examination, Chesnut acknowledged that the timeclock sometimes malfunctioned, and that if "people were there at their work stations" at the start of the shift, the supervisor "would write in seven o'clock." Petitioner also testified that when employees arrived before or stayed after their shifts, he would assign them additional work so they would not be overpaid.

Petitioner similarly cast doubt on whether he was responsible for any failure to discipline late and absent employees. Petitioner testified that his job only included reviewing the daily and weekly attendance reports, and that disciplinary write-ups were based on the monthly reports, which were reviewed by Caldwell. Sanderson admitted that Caldwell, and not petitioner, was responsible for citing employees for violations of the company's attendance policy. Further, Chesnut conceded that there had never been a union grievance or employee complaint arising from petitioner's record keeping, and that the company had never calculated the amount of overpayments allegedly attributable to petitioner's errors. Petitioner also testified that, on the day he was fired, Chesnut said that his discharge was due to his failure to report as absent one employee, Gina Mae Coley, on two days in September 1995. But petitioner explained that he had spent those days in the hospital, and that Caldwell was therefore responsible for any overpayment of Coley. Finally, petitioner stated that on previous occasions that employees were paid for hours they had not worked, the company had simply adjusted those employees' next paychecks to correct the errors.

Based on this evidence, the Court of Appeals concluded that petitioner "very well may be correct" that "a reasonable jury could have found that [respondent's] explanation for its employment decision was pretextual." Nonetheless, the court held that this showing, standing alone, was insufficient to sustain the jury's finding of liability: "We must, as an essential final step, determine whether Reeves presented sufficient evidence that his age motivated [respondent's] employment decision." And in making this determination, the Court of Appeals ignored the evidence supporting petitioner's prima facie case and challenging respondent's explanation for its decision. The court confined its review of evidence favoring petitioner to that evidence showing that Chesnut had directed derogatory, age-based comments at petitioner, and that Chesnut had singled out petitioner for harsher treatment than younger employees. It is therefore apparent that the court believed that only this additional evidence of discrimination was relevant to whether the jury's verdict should stand. That is, the Court of Appeals proceeded from the assumption that a prima facie case of discrimination, combined with sufficient evidence for the trier of fact to disbelieve the defendant's legitimate, nondiscriminatory reason for its decision, is insufficient as a matter of law to sustain a jury's finding of intentional discrimination.

In so reasoning, the Court of Appeals misconceived the evidentiary burden borne by plaintiffs who attempt to prove intentional discrimination through indirect evidence. This much is evident from our decision in *St. Mary's Honor Center* [*v. Hicks*, 509 U.S. 502 (1993)]. There we held that the factfinder's rejection of the employer's legitimate, nondiscriminatory reason for its action does not compel judgment for the plaintiff. The ultimate question is whether the employer intentionally discriminated, and proof that "the employer's proffered reason is unpersuasive, or even obviously contrived, does not necessarily establish that the plaintiff's proffered reason . . . is correct." In other words, "it is not enough . . . to disbelieve the employer; the factfinder must believe the plaintiff's explanation of intentional discrimination."

In reaching this conclusion, however, we reasoned that it is permissible for the trier of fact to infer the ultimate fact of discrimination from the falsity of the employer's explanation. Specifically, we stated:

> The factfinder's disbelief of the reasons put forward by the defendant (particularly if disbelief is accompanied by a suspicion of mendacity) may, together with the elements of the prima facie case, suffice to show intentional discrimination. Thus, rejection of the defendant's proffered reasons will permit the trier of fact to infer the ultimate fact of intentional discrimination.

Proof that the defendant's explanation is unworthy of credence is simply one form of circumstantial evidence that is probative of intentional discrimination, and it may be quite persuasive. [*St. Mary's Honor Center.*] ("Proving the employer's reason false becomes part of (and often considerably assists) the greater enterprise of proving that the real reason was intentional discrimination"). In appropriate circumstances, the trier of fact can reasonably infer from the falsity of the explanation that the employer is dissembling to cover up a discriminatory purpose. Such an inference is consistent with the general principle of evidence law that the factfinder is entitled to consider a party's dishonesty about a material fact as "affirmative evidence of guilt." *Wright v. West*, 505 U.S. 277 (1992); 2 J. Wigmore, Evidence §278(2), p. 133 (J. Chadbourn rev. ed. 1979). Moreover, once the employer's justification has been eliminated, discrimination may well be the most likely alternative explanation, especially since the employer is in the best position to put forth the actual reason for its decision. Cf. *Furnco Constr. Corp. v. Waters*, 438 U.S. 567, 577 (1978) ("When all legitimate reasons for rejecting an applicant have been eliminated as possible reasons for the employer's actions, it is more likely than not the employer, who we generally assume acts with some reason, based his decision on an impermissible consideration").

Thus, a plaintiff's prima facie case, combined with sufficient evidence to find that the employer's asserted justification is false, may permit the trier of fact to conclude that the employer unlawfully discriminated.

This is not to say that such a showing by the plaintiff will always be adequate to sustain a jury's finding of liability. Certainly there will be instances where, although the plaintiff has established a prima facie case and set forth sufficient evidence to reject the defendant's explanation, no rational factfinder could conclude that the action was discriminatory. For instance, an employer would be entitled to judgment as a matter of law if the record conclusively revealed some other, nondiscriminatory reason for the employer's decision, or if the plaintiff created only a weak issue of fact as to whether the employer's reason was untrue and there was abundant and uncontroverted independent evidence that no discrimination had occurred. See *Fisher v. Vassar College*, 114 F.3d 1332, 1338 (2d Cir. 1997) ("If the circumstances show that the defendant gave the false explanation to conceal something other than discrimination, the inference of discrimination will be weak or nonexistent"). To hold otherwise would be effectively to insulate an entire category of employment discrimination cases from review under Rule 50, and we have reiterated that trial courts should not "'treat discrimination differently from other ultimate questions of fact.'" *St. Mary's Honor Center*.

Whether judgment as a matter of law is appropriate in any particular case will depend on a number of factors. Those include the strength of the plaintiff's prima facie case, the probative value of the proof that the employer's explanation is false, and any other evidence that supports the employer's case and that properly may be considered on a motion for judgment as a matter of law. For purposes of this case, we need not — and could not — resolve all of the circumstances in which such factors would entitle an employer to judgment as a matter of law. It suffices to say that, because a prima facie case and sufficient evidence to reject the employer's explanation may permit a finding of liability, the Court of Appeals erred in proceeding from the premise that a plaintiff must always introduce additional, independent evidence of discrimination.

III

A

The remaining question is whether, despite the Court of Appeals' misconception of petitioner's evidentiary burden, respondent was nonetheless entitled to judgment as a matter of law. Under Rule 50, a court should render judgment as a matter of law when "a party has been fully heard on an issue and there is no legally sufficient evidentiary basis for a reasonable jury to find for that party on that issue." . . .

[I]n entertaining a motion for judgment as a matter of law, the court should review all of the evidence in the record.] In doing so, however, the court must draw all reasonable inferences in favor of the nonmoving party, and it may not make credibility determinations or weigh the evidence. *Lytle v. Household Mfg., Inc.*, 494 U.S. 545, 554-55 (1990). "Credibility determinations, the weighing of the evidence, and the drawing of legitimate inferences from the facts are jury functions, not those of a judge." [*Anderson v. Liberty Lobby*, 477 U.S. 242 (1986).] Thus, although the court should review the record as a whole, it must disregard all evidence favorable to the moving party that the jury is not required to believe. See Wright & Miller 299. That is, the court should give credence to the evidence favoring the non-movant as well as that "evidence supporting the moving party that is uncontradicted and unimpeached, at least to the extent that that evidence comes from disinterested witnesses."

B

Applying this standard here, it is apparent that respondent was not entitled to judgment as a matter of law. In this case, in addition to establishing a prima facie case of discrimination and creating a jury issue as to the falsity of the employer's explanation, petitioner introduced additional evidence that Chesnut was motivated by age-based animus and was principally responsible for petitioner's firing. Petitioner testified that Chesnut had told him that he "was so old [he] must have come over on the Mayflower" and, on one occasion when petitioner was having difficulty starting a machine, that he "was too damn old to do [his] job." According to petitioner, Chesnut would regularly "cuss at me and shake his finger in my face." Oswalt, roughly 24 years younger than petitioner, corroborated that there was an "obvious difference" in how Chesnut treated them. He stated that, although he and Chesnut "had [their] differences," "it was nothing compared to the way [Chesnut] treated Roger." Oswalt explained that Chesnut "tolerated quite a bit" from him even though he "defied" Chesnut "quite often," but that Chesnut treated petitioner "in a manner, as you would . . . treat . . . a child when . . . you're angry with [him]." Petitioner also demonstrated that, according to company records, he and Oswalt had nearly identical rates of productivity in 1993. Yet respondent conducted an efficiency study of only the regular line, supervised by petitioner, and placed only petitioner on probation. Chesnut conducted that efficiency study and, after having testified to the contrary on direct examination, acknowledged on cross-examination that he had recommended that petitioner be placed on probation following the study.

Further, petitioner introduced evidence that Chesnut was the actual decisionmaker behind his firing. Chesnut was married to Sanderson, who made the formal decision to discharge petitioner. Although Sanderson testified that she fired petitioner because he had "intentionally falsified company pay records," respondent only introduced evidence concerning the inaccuracy of the records, not their falsification. A 1994 letter authored by Chesnut indicated that he berated other company directors, who were supposedly his co-equals, about how to do their jobs. Moreover, Oswalt testified that all of respondent's employees feared Chesnut, and that Chesnut had exercised "absolute power" within the company for "as long as [he] can remember."

In holding that the record contained insufficient evidence to sustain the jury's verdict, the Court of Appeals misapplied the standard of review dictated by Rule 50. Again, the court disregarded critical evidence favorable to petitioner — namely, the evidence supporting petitioner's prima facie case and undermining respondent's nondiscriminatory explanation. The court also failed to draw all reasonable inferences in favor of petitioner. For instance, while acknowledging "the potentially damning nature" of Chesnut's age-related comments, the court discounted them on the ground that they "were not made in the direct context of Reeves's termination." And the court discredited petitioner's evidence that Chesnut was the actual decision maker by giving weight to the fact that there was "no evidence to suggest that any of the other decision makers were motivated by age." Moreover, the other evidence on which the court relied — that Caldwell and Oswalt were also cited for poor record keeping, and that respondent employed many managers over age 50 — although relevant, is certainly not dispositive. In concluding that these circumstances so overwhelmed the evidence favoring petitioner that no rational trier of fact could have found that petitioner was fired because of his age, the Court of Appeals impermissibly substituted its judgment concerning the weight of the evidence for the jury's.

The ultimate question in every employment discrimination case involving a claim of disparate treatment is whether the plaintiff was the victim of intentional discrimination. Given the evidence in the record supporting petitioner, we see no reason to subject the parties to an additional round of litigation before the Court of Appeals rather than to resolve the matter here. The District Court plainly informed the jury that petitioner was required to show "by a preponderance of the evidence that his age was a determining and motivating factor in the decision of [respondent] to terminate him." The court instructed the jury that, to show that respondent's explanation was a pretext for discrimination, petitioner had to demonstrate "1, that the stated reasons were not the real reasons for [petitioner's] discharge; and 2, that age discrimination was the real reason for [petitioner's] discharge." Given that petitioner established a prima facie case of discrimination, introduced enough evidence for the jury to reject respondent's explanation, and produced additional evidence of age-based animus, there was sufficient evidence for the jury to find that respondent had intentionally discriminated. The District Court was therefore correct to submit the case to the jury, and the Court of Appeals erred in overturning its verdict.

Justice GINSBURG, concurring.

The Court today holds that an employment discrimination plaintiff may survive judgment as a matter of law by submitting two categories of evidence: first, evidence establishing a "prima facie case," as that term is used in *McDonnell Douglas Corp. v. Green*, and second, evidence from which a rational factfinder could conclude that the employer's proffered explanation for its actions was false. Because the Court of Appeals in this case plainly, and erroneously, required the plaintiff to offer some evidence beyond those two categories, no broader holding is necessary to support reversal.

I write separately to note that it may be incumbent on the Court, in an appropriate case, to define more precisely the circumstances in which plaintiffs will be required to submit evidence beyond these two categories in order to survive a motion for judgment as a matter of law. I anticipate that such circumstances will be uncommon. As the Court notes, it is a principle of evidence law that the jury is entitled to treat a party's dishonesty about a material fact as evidence of culpability. Under this commonsense principle, evidence suggesting that a defendant accused of illegal discrimination has chosen to give a false explanation for its actions gives rise to a rational inference that the defendant could be masking its actual, illegal motivation. Whether the defendant was in fact motivated by discrimination is of course for the finder of fact to decide; that is the lesson of *St. Mary's Honor Center v. Hicks*. But the inference remains — unless it is conclusively demonstrated, by evidence the district court is required to credit on a motion for judgment as a matter of law, that discrimination could not have been the defendant's true motivation. If such conclusive demonstrations are (as I suspect) atypical, it follows that the ultimate question of liability ordinarily should not be taken from the jury once the plaintiff has introduced the two categories of evidence described above. Because the Court's opinion leaves room for such further elaboration in an appropriate case, I join it in full.

NOTES

1. *The Significance of* Reeves. It is hard to overestimate the significance of *Reeves*, which makes three important points. First, the Supreme Court rejected the so-called

"pretext plus" rule in *McDonnell Douglas* cases that had originated in *St. Mary's Honor Center v. Hicks*, 509 U.S. 502 (1993), and that had derailed many plausible suits. Second, the Court instructed the lower courts to take a more holistic review of the record evidence and reminded them to draw all inferences in favor of the party opposing summary judgment or judgment as a matter of law, typically the plaintiff in discrimination cases. The Court accepted any evidence indicating discrimination as relevant and probative of the ultimate question of discrimination and made clear that cases were not confined to any particular theory or claim of discrimination. Third, as part of that broadened viewpoint, the Court held that ageist comments that did not qualify as "direct" evidence of discrimination nevertheless were circumstantial evidence that could support drawing the inference of discrimination.

2. *Rejecting the "Pretext-Plus" Rule.* In *St. Mary's Honor Center v. Hicks*, the Court held that a plaintiff was not entitled to judgment as a matter of law merely because the factfinder determined that the defendant's asserted nondiscriminatory reason was false. Rather, plaintiff could prevail only if the trier of fact made the further finding on the ultimate question that defendant discriminated against the plaintiff. In *Hicks*, plaintiff, an African American supervisor at a correctional facility, was discharged some time after a new management team took over running the facility. At the rebuttal stage of *McDonnell Douglas*, defendant asserted that Hicks had been discharged because of the severity and the accumulation of rules violations he had committed. The trial judge, sitting as factfinder, found that these reasons were *not* the real reasons for Hicks' discharge; but the judge also found that plaintiff failed to prove that race was the determining factor in his discharge: "[A]lthough plaintiff has proven a crusade to terminate him, he has not proven that the crusade was racially rather than personally motivated." In short, the judge found that personal animosity, not race, motivated the supervisor.

What was disconcerting about the trial judge's approach was that the only evidence relating to personal hostility between plaintiff and his new supervisor was the *denial* by the supervisor that he had any personal hostility toward the plaintiff. From a doctrinal perspective, the litigation process had not narrowed the dispute to a question of whether defendant's asserted reason or discrimination motivated the defendant's action; rather, the trier of fact found for the defendant based on its belief, not supported, and even controverted, by the evidence in the record, that the defendant was motivated by personal hostility and therefore not by race.

The court of appeals, concluding that asserting reasons that were not true was the equivalent of not offering any reason at all (which, under *McDonnell Douglas* would require a judgment for plaintiff), held that plaintiff was entitled to judgment as a matter of law. The Supreme Court reversed, reinstating the trial judge's dismissal, holding that a judgment for plaintiff must rest on an affirmative finding of discrimination:

> If . . . the defendant has succeeded in carrying its burden of production [of evidence of its nondiscriminatory reason], the *McDonnell Douglas* framework — with its presumptions and burdens — is no longer relevant. . . . The defendant's "production" (whatever its persuasive effect) having been made, the trier of fact proceeds to decide the ultimate question: whether plaintiff has proven "that the defendant intentionally discriminated against [him] because of his race. The factfinder's disbelief of the reasons put forward by the defendant (particularly if disbelief is accompanied by a suspicion of mendacity) may, together with the elements of the prima facie case, suffice to show intentional discrimination. Thus, rejection of defendant's proffered reasons, will permit the trier of fact to infer the ultimate fact of intentional discrimination, and the Court of

Appeals was correct when it noted that, upon such rejection, "no additional proof of discrimination is *required*." (emphasis added). But the Court of Appeals' holding that rejection of the defendant's proffered reasons compels judgment for the plaintiff disregards the fundamental principle of [Federal Rule of Evidence] 301 that a presumption does not shift the burden of proof, and ignores our repeated admonition that the Title VII plaintiff at all times bears the "ultimate burden of persuasion."

Id. at 511. Although this language requires a finding of discrimination, not merely a finding of pretext in the sense that the defendant's reason was untrue, it seemed very clearly to allow the factfinder to infer discrimination based on finding the defendant's asserted reason to be false. Put another way, the *Hicks* Court would have affirmed the district court if it had come out the other way, because both inferences (false reason as a pretext for discrimination or false reason as a pretext for some other motive) were possible. Despite that, some courts read *Hicks* as adopting a "pretext-plus" rule, which required plaintiff to introduce *additional* evidence of discrimination, even if she had established a prima facie case and shown that defendant's reason was not true. Most courts, however, adopted a "pretext only" rule, which *Reeves* confirmed. Thus, plaintiff has the burden of proving a prima facie case and the burden of proving defendant's asserted reason to be a pretext for discrimination, but, as the Court says, "a plaintiff's prima facie case, combined with sufficient evidence to find that the employer's asserted justification is false, may permit the trier of fact to conclude that the employer unlawfully discriminated."

While the *Reeves* Court rejected the "pretext-plus" rule, it stopped short of saying that, when plaintiff proves a *McDonnell Douglas* prima facie case and adduces sufficient evidence for a jury to find defendant's reasons not to be true, judgment as a matter of law for defendant is never appropriate. In what situations might the defendant still be entitled to judgment as a matter of law even though plaintiff proved a prima facie case and pretext? When would a reasonable factfinder have to find for the defendant? Justice O'Connor cites *Fisher v. Vassar College* for the proposition that judgment as a matter of law was appropriate where defendant asserted a false reason in order to avoid articulating an embarrassing reason that was nondiscriminatory. Shouldn't that go to the jury to decide unless the evidence was so powerful that no reasonable jury could find discrimination? What does Justice Ginsburg add?

3. A *Civil Procedure Refresher*. Part III of *Reeves* applied traditional rules concerning how courts are to review the record to decide motions for judgment as a matter of law. Based on F.R.C.P. 50, the review should decide whether there is "no legally sufficient evidentiary basis for a reasonable jury to find for" the party opposing the motion. In reviewing all the evidence in the record, "the court must draw all reasonable inferences in favor of the nonmoving party, and it may not make credibility determinations or weigh the evidence. . . . [I]t must disregard all evidence favorable to the moving party that the jury is not required to believe."

Normally, when the Court rules that the lower court erred on the law, as the lower court did in *Reeves* in adopting the "pretext-plus" rule, the Court reverses and remands to the lower court to get it right. In *Reeves*, however, the Court felt it necessary to show how the lower court had failed to apply this settled law to the facts of the case. And then the Court ordered the jury verdict for the plaintiff to be reinstated. Was the Court sending a message to the lower courts by doing this? If so, what was that message?

Reeves did not set forth a new conceptual structure for analyzing individual disparate treatment cases. But it did say, "The ultimate question in every employment discrimination case involving a claim of disparate treatment is whether the plaintiff was the victim of intentional discrimination." And, further, "In this case, in addition to establishing a prima facie case of discrimination and creating a jury issue as to the falsity of the employer's explanation, petitioner introduced additional evidence that Chesnut was motivated by age-based animus and was principally responsible for petitioner's firing." This seems a step away from the traditional and rigid *McDonnell Douglas* proof structure and toward the more holistic "sufficient evidence" approach in *Desert Palace*. If so, it is possible that there is not as much difference between mixed motive and single motive cases as sometimes is believed. Thus, even under *McDonnell Douglas*, in deciding whether defendant discriminated, it is necessary to look at all the evidence, regardless of under what step in the analysis it arrived.

Justice O'Connor assumed in *Reeves* that plaintiff had both established the *McDonnell Douglas* prima facie case and successfully rebutted the defendant's non-discriminatory reason. To that extent, she is true to the traditional proof structure. But after that, she described the ageist comments as evidence of discriminatory motive in a way that evokes *Price Waterhouse*, both in its sense of admissions and acting on age stereotypes. There was also testimony that Chesnut changed his tune when his original reason for terminating Reeves proved untenable: Reeves had been in the hospital and not at work when his alleged infractions occurred. Finally, the Court discusses the testimony of Reeve's co-worker, Oswalt, as supporting an unequal treatment claim as well as showing that Chesnut was out to get Reeves. All of this can be shoehorned into the *McDonnell Douglas* proof structure under an expansive view of pretext, but it could alternatively be seen as simply finding there was sufficient evidence to support the ultimate finding of intentional discrimination.

4. *Rejecting the Lower Court's "Direct" Evidence Rule.* The lower court had not only used a narrow definition of "direct" evidence to escape applying the *Price Waterhouse* burden-shifting approach but had also denied the statements it found not to be direct evidence any probative effect at all. The Court did not address the lower court's definition of "direct" evidence, but it did reject the view that non-direct evidence has no impact. Instead of having no probative force, the evidence of these ageist remarks by Chesnut was found to be probative circumstantial evidence supporting drawing the inference of discrimination. Thus, even evidence that a court would treat as "stray remarks" — what might be referred to as "direct-lite" evidence — constitutes circumstantial evidence of discrimination. Its probative strength varies along several axes, including whether it was said by the decisionmaker, how close to the decision it was uttered, and how clearly it evinces bias.

5. *Inferring Discrimination from Direct, Direct-Lite, and Circumstantial Evidence.* The Court in *Reeves* contemplates that all evidence — direct or circumstantial, or somewhere in between — that is probative of discrimination can be relied on by a reasonable factfinder in developing a chain of inferences leading to the ultimate inference that the defendant discriminated. Even before *Reeves*, the Court used this broad, inference-drawing approach. In *O'Connor v. Consolidated Coin Caterers Corp.,* 517 U.S. 308, 311-12 (1996), the lower court had found that a 56-year-old plaintiff had not made out a prima facie case of age discrimination because the person who replaced plaintiff was over age 40 and thus in the same protected group as plaintiff. The Court rejected this formalistic approach in favor of one that connected the ultimate question to the reasonableness of any inferences drawn from the evidence:

> As the very name "prima facie case" suggests, there must be at least a logical connection between each element of the prima facie case and the illegal discrimination for which

it establishes a "legally mandatory, rebuttable presumption." The element of replacement by someone under 40 fails this requirement. The discrimination prohibited by the ADEA is discrimination "because of [an] individual's age," though the prohibition is "limited to individuals who are at least 40 years of age." This language does not ban discrimination because they are aged 40 or over; it bans discrimination against employees because of their age, but limits the protected class to those who are 40 or older. The fact that one person in the protected class has lost out to another person in the protected class is thus irrelevant, so long as he has lost out because of his age. Or to put the point more concretely, there can be no greater inference of age discrimination (as opposed to "40 or over" discrimination) when a 40 year-old is replaced by a 39 year-old than when a 56 year-old is replaced by a 40 year-old.

The Court went on to deal with the hypothetical situations of a 68-year-old replaced by a 65-year-old and a 40-year-old replaced by a 39-year-old and indicated that it would not be proper to draw an inference of discrimination in either case. An inference of age discrimination "can not be drawn from the replacement of one worker with another worker insignificantly younger. Because the ADEA prohibits discrimination on the basis of age and not class membership, the fact that a replacement is substantially younger than the plaintiff is a far more reliable indicator of age discrimination than is the fact that the plaintiff was replaced by someone outside the protected class." 517 U.S. at 313. Presumably, as the difference in ages between the two workers increases, so does the reasonableness of drawing the inference that age was a factor in the decisionmaking.

Consolidated Coin is, of course, limited in its holding to the age context, but its broader message is that evidence must be capable of supporting an inference of discrimination. For example, when an employer acts at variance with its own policies to the disadvantage of a woman, it would seem possible to infer sex discrimination. Whether that inference would be sufficiently plausible to permit the case to go to the jury might well depend on other evidence, which itself will be inferential.

6. *The Plausibility of Alternative Explanations.* The response of the lower courts to *Reeves* to date is mixed. While no courts continue to formally use the "pretext-plus" rule, *see Ratliff v. City of Gainesville, Tex.*, 256 F.3d 355, 361 (5th Cir. 2001) (acknowledging *Reeves*'s disapproval of pretext plus in favor of a "permissive pretext only" standard), there is still resistance to the broader implications of that case. For example, the Seventh Circuit has adopted a pretext-as-a-lie rule. In *Millbrook v. IBP, Inc.*, 280 F.3d 1169 (7th Cir. 2002) (2-1), the court wrote:

> Pretext means a lie, specifically a phony reason for some action. The question is not whether the employer properly evaluated the competing applicants, but whether the employer's reason for choosing one candidate over the other was honest. Pretext for discrimination means more than an unusual act; it means something worse than a business error; pretext means deceit used to cover one's tracks. Thus, even if IBP's reason for selecting Harris over Millbrook were mistaken, ill considered or foolish, so long as [the employer] honestly believed those reasons, pretext has not been shown.

While a showing that a reason is "mistaken, ill considered or foolish" is not per se proof of discrimination, it certainly raises the possibility, and therefore permits the inference, that discrimination is at work. Another way to say this is that a jury confronted with a choice between the possibility of defendant acting on some irrational (but nondiscriminatory) basis and its acting discriminatorily might be permitted to find the former but certainly should normally be allowed to find the latter.

Employers, after all, should not be viewed as likely to act irrationally. The same should be true when the employer claims to have made a mistake. Again, that would be, as a matter of law, a good defense to a charge of discrimination but, as a matter of fact, the jury should be permitted to determine whether an employer indeed made a mistake or discriminated. And the less reasonable the mistake, the more likely the inference of discrimination.

But what about motivations that do not appear to advance the employer's business interests at all yet are all too common human motivations? In *Hicks* the trial court found the adverse decision to be based on personal animosity, presumably an animosity the court believed to be totally unconnected with race. *See* Chad Derum & Karen Engle, *The Rise of the Personal Animosity Presumption in Title VII and the Return to "No Cause" Employment*, 81 TEX. L. REV. 1177, 1182 (2003) (courts increasingly view interpersonal problems as a result of the personal animosity which "bespeaks both a judicial inability, or at least refusal, to attend to unconscious bias and an ideological commitment to employment at will"). Other courts have found decisions to be the result of converse, favoritism, again presumably unconnected to race. *See* Ann C. McGinley, *The Emerging Cronyism Defense and Affirmative Action: A Critical Perspective on the Distinction Between Color-Blind and Race Conscious Decision Making Under Title VII*, 39 ARIZ. L. REV. 1003 (1997) (arguing that recent Supreme Court cases have unreasonably narrowed the intent requirement in Title VII law, permitting the emergence of the cronyism defense; the cronyism defense exalts the employer's liberty interest over an employee's right to equality in hiring). Are these motivations common enough to be more likely explanation of decisions than discrimination?

7. *Or Is It the Relative Plausibility of Alternative Explanations?* It may be that results such as the ones canvassed in the previous note are founded less on a belief in the pervasiveness of nonrational (or at least, not merit-based) reasons for employer actions than in a belief that bias is no longer as significant a problem as it once was. In an early decision, *Furnco Constr. Corp. v. Waters*, 438 U.S. 567, 577 (1978), the Court wrote:

> A prima facie case under *McDonnell Douglas* raises an inference of discrimination only because we presume these acts, if otherwise unexplained, are more likely than not based on the consideration of impermissible factors. See *Teamsters v. United States*. And we are willing to presume this largely because we know from our experience that more often than not people do not act in a totally arbitrary manner, without any underlying reasons, especially in a business setting. Thus, when all legitimate reasons for rejecting an applicant have been eliminated as possible reasons for the employer's actions, it is more likely than not the employer, who we generally assume acts only with some reason, based his decision on an impermissible consideration such as race.

In short, whether *Desert Palace* and *Reeves* will make a difference may depend on whether the courts still share this background assumption about how common discrimination is.

In commenting on *Hicks*, Professor Deborah A. Calloway, in St. Mary's Honor Center v. Hicks: *Questioning the Basic Assumption*, 26 CONN. L. REV. 997, 1008-09 (1995), argued that the Supreme Court had revised its underlying assumption about the pervasiveness of the discrimination:

> *Hicks* is significant, not for its narrow legal holding, but for the attitude underlying that holding. . . . [T]his case is about what evidence is sufficient to meet the plaintiff's

burden of persuasion on discriminatory intent. What evidence makes it "more likely than not" that the defendant discriminated? The answer to this question depends on one's beliefs about the prevalence of discrimination. Whether a reasonable person (or judge) will be convinced that discrimination has been shown depends on whether he believes that discrimination is a logical inference in the absence of some other explanation for adverse conduct. The district court and the majority of the Supreme Court in *Hicks* reached their result, not because it was required by any formal legal rules, but rather because they just plain do not believe in that basic assumption.

If this is true, we can expect the courts to give more weight to evidence that this particular employer does not share the equality norm which courts believe generally prevails. The importance of "direct evidence" was one indication, but, consistent with *Reeves*, the circuits appear to be finding that "stray comment" evidence, i.e., evidence that fails to satisfy the circuit's test for direct evidence of discrimination, is, nevertheless, circumstantial evidence that the factfinder may find shows the employer acted with an intent to discriminate. *E.g., Gorence v. Eagle Food Ctrs., Inc.,* 242 F.3d 759, 763 (7th Cir. 2001) ("evidence of inappropriate remarks not shown to be directly related to the employment decision may not support a direct-method-of-proof case, but, in connection with other evidence, might support a case under *McDonnell Douglas*"); *Santiago-Ramos v. Centennial P.R. Wireless Corp.,* 217 F.3d 46, 55 (1st Cir. 2000) (jury could rely on a remarks by several persons at the employer and its parent company concerning the company's treatment of female employees with children, together with evidence such as comments by decision-makers, to find the employer's explanations pretextual); *Fisher v. Pharmacia & Upjohn,* 225 F.3d 915, 922 (8th Cir. 2000) ("Stray remarks therefore constitute circumstantial evidence of age discrimination"). *But see Stone v. Autoliv Asp., Inc.,* 210 F.3d 1132, 1136 (10th Cir. 2000) ("Age-related comments referring directly to the plaintiff can support an inference of age discrimination, but 'isolated or ambiguous comments' may be, as here, too abstract to support such an inference").

8. *Litigating Individual Disparate Treatment Cases.* The cases we have seen thus far have been a mixture of reviews of judge findings or jury verdicts, summary judgment motions, dismissals or motions for judgment as a matter of law. However, there are other methods of resolving disputes, ranging from motions to dismiss for failure to state a claim based on plaintiff's complaint to judgment as a matter of law after plaintiff puts in her evidence. While the vast majority of nonconsensual dispositions under the antidiscrimination statutes are by summary judgment, it might be helpful to reconsider the *Desert Palace* and *McDonnell Douglas/Reeves* models in connection with the procedural steps in litigation:

(a) *Motions to Dismiss.* In response to plaintiff's complaint, defendant may move under Rule 12(b)(6) of the Federal Rules of Civil Procedure to dismiss for "failure to state a claim upon which relief can be granted." In *Swierkiewicz v. Sorema N.A.* 534 U.S. 506 (2002), a unanimous Supreme Court held that the notice pleading standard of F.R.C.P. Rule 8(a) required reversal of the dismissal of plaintiff's complaint for failing to plead facts establishing the four prongs of a prima facie case under *McDonnell Douglas*: "the prima facie case relates to the employee's burden of presenting evidence that raises an inference of discrimination" and does not "apply to the pleading standard that plaintiffs must satisfy in order to survive a motion to dismiss." *Id.* at 511. Plaintiff satisfied Rule 8(a)(2)'s requirement that a complaint must include only "a short and plain statement of the claim showing that the pleader is entitled to relief," by alleging that he had been terminated on account of his national origin in violation of Title VII and on account of his age in violation of the ADEA. His complaint detailed the events leading to his termination, provided relevant dates, and included the ages and nationalities of at least some of the relevant persons involved with his termination. These allegations gave respondent fair notice of petitioner's claims and the grounds upon which they rest and state claims upon which relief could be granted under both statutes. *See also Maduka v. Sunrise Hosp.*, 375 F.3d 909 (9th Cir. 2004) (error to require § 1981 plaintiff to plead facts showing he was treated worse than a white doctor). Thus, defendants will generally be forced to file an answer and move to the discovery phase when a discrimination complaint is filed. *But see Raytheon Co. v. Hernandez*, 540 U.S. 44 (2003) (failure to plead systemic disparate impact claim means that an employer rule that it did not rehire former employees terminated for workplace misconduct was only analyzed as potential individual disparate treatment case, so that business necessity was irrelevant); *Bell Atl. Corp. v. Twombly*, 127 S. Ct. 1955 (2007) (requiring more detailed pleading regarding conspiracy in an antitrust case).

(b) *Summary Judgment Motions.* Under Rule 56(b) of the Federal Rules, the defendant can, usually after discovery, move for summary judgment. The "trilogy" allows summary judgment relatively freely. *Matsushita Elec. Indus. Corp. v. Zenith Radio Corp.*, 475 U.S. 574 (1986); *Anderson v. Liberty Lobby*, 477 U.S. 242 (1986); *Celotex Corp. v. Catrett*, 477 U.S. 317 (1986). Because many discrimination cases depend on drawing inferences, courts often grant summary judgment against plaintiffs on the ground that a reasonable jury could not infer discrimination from the facts that plaintiff is able to put into evidence. Courts grant summary judgment to employers very freely in discrimination cases. *See generally* Henry L. Chambers, Jr., *Recapturing Summary Adjudication Principles in Disparate Treatment Cases*, 58 SMU L. REV. 103 (2005); Ann C. McGinley, *Credulous Courts and the Tortured Trilogy: The Improper Use of Summary Judgment in Title VII and ADEA Cases*, 34 B.C. L. REV. 203, 210 (1993); Note on Litigation Scorecard at p. 110.

(c) *Judgment as Matter of Law: Case in Chief.* If the defendant's motion for summary judgment is denied, the case proceeds to trial. At the close of plaintiff's case in chief, the defendant may, pursuant to Rule 50(a), move for judgment as a matter of law if "there is no legally sufficient evidentiary basis for a reasonable jury to find for" the plaintiff. In order to understand how this works, however, it is important to realize that the three stages of the *McDonnell Douglas* case are an analytic device, not the actual order of proof in how the case is tried. *See St. Mary's Honor Ctr. v. Hicks*, 509 U.S. 502, 533 n.9 (1993) (Souter, J. dissenting) ("The foregoing analysis of burdens describes who wins on various combinations of evidence and proof. It may or may not also describe the actual sequence of events at trial. In a bench trial, for example, the parties may be limited in their presentation of evidence until the court has decided whether the plaintiff has made his prima facie showing. But the court also may allow in all the evidence at once.") Thus, at the end of the plaintiff's case, she will typically not only have put in her prima facie case but will have also anticipated defendant's nondiscriminatory reason (which she will have identified in discovery) and put in her evidence of pretext. Presumably, the court will then decide if a reasonable jury could find for plaintiff; if not, there is no need for defendant to put on its case. If so, the defendant loses its motion for judgment as a matter of law and proceeds to introduce its own case.

(d) *Judgment as Matter of Law: Close of Evidence.* At the close of all the evidence, another motion by the defendant for a judgment as a matter of law is appropriate. At that stage, however, the issue of plaintiff's proof of a prima facie case can no longer be raised.

[W]hen the defendant fails to persuade the district court to dismiss the action for lack of a prima facie case, and responds to plaintiff's proof by offering evidence of the reason for the plaintiff's rejection, the factfinder must then decide whether the rejection was discriminatory within the meaning of Title VII. . . . Where the defendant has done everything that would be required of him if the plaintiff had properly made out a prima facie case, whether he did so is no longer relevant. The district court has before it all the evidence it needs to decide whether "the defendant intentionally discriminated against the plaintiff."

United States Postal Service Bd. of Governors v. Aikens, 460 U.S. 711, 715 (1983).

(e) *Judge as Factfinder.* In a bench trial, the district judge is the finder of fact. Under the federal rules, her determinations are entitled to great deference. In *Anderson v. City of Bessemer City,* 470 U.S. 564 (1985), the trial court found that plaintiff had been denied an appointment because of her gender, but the Fourth Circuit reversed. Under Rule 52 of the Federal Rules of Civil Procedure, an appellate court may reverse on factual grounds only if the district judge's findings are "clearly erroneous." The Supreme Court found that the appellate court had overstepped its bounds:

In detecting clear error in the District Court's finding that petitioner was better qualified than Mr. Kincaid [the male who was offered the job], the Fourth Circuit improperly conducted what amounted to a de novo weighing of the evidence in the record. . . .

Based on our own reading of the record, we cannot say that either interpretation of the facts is illogical or implausible. Each has support in inferences that may be drawn from the facts in the record; and if either interpretation had been drawn by a district court on the record before us, we would not be inclined to find it clearly erroneous. The question we must answer, however, is not whether the Fourth Circuit's interpretation of the facts was clearly erroneous, but whether the District Court's finding was clearly erroneous. . . .

470 U.S. at 577. Even greater deference should be given to findings of fact based on credibility determinations: "[W]hen a trial judge's finding is based on his decision to credit the testimony of one of two or more witnesses, each of whom has told a coherent and facially plausible story that is not contradicted by extrinsic evidence, that finding, if not internally inconsistent, can virtually never be clear error." *Id.* at 575.

(f) *Jury Trials.* While Title VII bench trials will continue when the parties so agree, the 1991 Civil Rights Act for the first time made jury trials available under Title VII. Jury trials were already available under §1981 and the ADEA. If the judge has properly instructed the jury, the resulting verdict will rarely be overturned, although even at this stage judgment as a matter of law can be granted if no reasonable jury could reach that result. That is what happened in *Reeves.* Alternatively, a new trial can be ordered if the verdict is found to be against the weight of the evidence.

Increased use of jury trials introduced another complication for discrimination suits: What instructions should be given to the jury to decide the case? Having worked your way through the complexities of this chapter, you will probably not be surprised to learn that juries are not typically instructed in the exact *McDonnell Douglas* methodology. E.g., *Whittington v. Nordam Group Inc.,* 429 F.3d 986, 998 (10th Cir. 2005) (the concern with a *McDonnell Douglas* instruction "is not that it favors one party over another. It is that it unnecessarily complicates the jury's job, and unnecessary complexity increases the opportunity for error"). But how are juries to be instructed?

In *Reeves*, the Court quoted the instructions, which required plaintiff

> to show "by a preponderance of the evidence that his age was a determining and motivating factor in the decision of [respondent] to terminate him." The court instructed the jury that, to show that respondent's explanation was a pretext for discrimination, petitioner had to demonstrate "1, that the stated reasons were not the real reasons for [petitioner's] discharge; and 2, that age discrimination was the real reason for [petitioner's] discharge." Given that petitioner established a prima facie case of discrimination, introduced enough evidence for the jury to reject respondent's explanation, and produced additional evidence of age-based animus, there was sufficient evidence for the jury to find that respondent had intentionally discriminated.

Since the plaintiff won, he had no need to challenge the jury instruction, but do you think that it is adequate in the wake of *Reeves*? For example, it didn't tell the jury how to take account of the "additional evidence of age-based animus."

Alternatively, could Reeves have asked for a mixed motive instruction based on the "a motivating factor" standard of §703(m) in order to avoid the burden of proving that age was "a determining and motivating factor"? Today, would Reeves be entitled to an instruction advising the jury that they were entitled to draw an inference of discrimination, even though they were not required to draw it, from the defendant's proffering of a false reason for the discharge? In *Desert Palace*, the Court appeared to approve the mixed-motive instruction given by the trial judge:

> You have heard evidence that the defendant's treatment of the plaintiff was motivated by the plaintiff's sex and also by other lawful reasons. If [, based on the preponderance of the evidence,] you find that the plaintiff's sex was a motivating factor in the defendant's treatment of the plaintiff, the plaintiff is entitled to your verdict, even if you find that the defendant's conduct was also motivated by a lawful reason.
>
> However, if you find that the defendant's treatment of the plaintiff was motivated by both gender and lawful reasons, you must decide whether the plaintiff is entitled to damages. The plaintiff is entitled to damages unless the defendant proves by a preponderance of the evidence that the defendant would have treated plaintiff similarly even if the plaintiff's gender had played no role in the employment decision.

This is the broadest, most generic instruction based on the level of proof — the "motivating factor" standard. This clearly can be given once the judge determines that the case is a mixed motive case. But can the plaintiff claiming single motive in a *McDonnell Douglas* case ask for it? Would it be error not to give it?

Whatever instruction is given, should trial judges fill in the instruction with more specific references to particular evidence and the parties' claims why that evidence either supports a finding of discrimination or supports finding that intent to discriminate was not proved? Or, does this broad instruction suffice, assuming the parties' final arguments to the jury will develop the claims that there was or wasn't discrimination?

D. IMPLEMENTING *DESERT PALACE* AND *REEVES*

RACHID v. JACK IN THE BOX, INC.
376 F.3d 305 (5th Cir. 2004)

CLEMENT, Circuit Judge:

Ahmed P. Rachid ("Rachid") filed an age discrimination claim under the Age Discrimination in Employment Act ("ADEA"), alleging that he was terminated from his managerial position at Jack In The Box, Inc. ("JIB"). Because Rachid established a prima facie case and because issues of material fact concerning JIB's proffered reason for terminating Rachid are disputed, summary judgment was improper. . . .

Rachid was employed by JIB from October 1995 to February 2001. Patrick Powers ("Powers") became Rachid's supervisor in September 1999. Rachid managed two restaurants, and shared managerial duties at one of the restaurants with Khalil Haidar ("Haidar"). Powers repeatedly criticized Rachid, and, according to both Rachid and Haidar, made disparaging comments about Rachid's age. Rachid, who was 52 years old, reported these comments to JIB's human resources department, and even requested a transfer because he feared that Powers sought to fire him because of his age. A transfer was never approved and Rachid was fired, according to JIB, for failing to follow policies related to recording employee time.

The parties sharply join issue over whether Rachid violated company policy. On June 15, 2000, Powers sent the following email to managers of JIB restaurants:

> Each week I down load [sic] the "punch changes" at each store for the prior week. I am concerned about the increased number of "punch changes" that are related to BREAKS. Let me make clear if anyone alters an employee's hours to save labor, THEY [sic] ARE BREAKING THE LAW! This is the type of offense that I have no ability to help an individual. Employees must punch out for breaks on there [sic] own, M[anagers-In-Charge] need to verify that each employee punched out at the clock. If an employee fails to punch out at the clock they [sic] are to be written up on a P108 [disciplinary form]. NO MANAGER IS TO GO BACK AND DO A PUNCH CHANGE WITHOUT A SIGNED P108 FOR PROOF! The P108 needs to be kept in the employee file. If the employee contests their [sic] hours and there are punch changes without a P108 for back-up documentation, the manager is putting their [sic] job at risk. It becomes a case of "he said/she said" and the manager has no proof that they [sic] didn't "illegally alter" the time clock. The P108 is the only protection you have against this kind of allegation. Remember: "very few people have ever been fired for missing a number, but all that get caught reporting a false number will always be fired!" I cannot help you out of this kind of problem.

The parties disputed whether this email sent by Powers represents JIB's company policy.[1] One of JIB's human resources employees, Kellie Teal-Guess ("Teal-Guess"), investigated several "punch changes" entered for employees at restaurants that Rachid managed. Though Rachid disputes whether this investigation revealed any

---

1. JIB's Employee Handbook directs employees in the following manner: "To make sure there is agreement on what hours you worked, your Manager will post an Hours Report at the end of each pay period for employees to check. If you don't agree with your hours on the report, let your Manager know immediately."

time-card alterations made by Rachid,[2] he concedes in his deposition that he occasionally changed time-cards when employees took breaks, and that he did not fill out P108 forms for all of those changes. Without further investigation, Powers terminated Rachid immediately upon learning that he had altered time-cards without completing P108 forms. Rachid's replacement was 47 years old. . . .

III. DISCUSSION

A. PROPER LEGAL STANDARD FOR AN ADEA CLAIM.

It appears that the district court applied the *McDonnell Douglas* approach in analyzing Rachid's claim. The district court's opinion states that Rachid did not establish a prima facie case, and later notes that "nothing in the record suggests that J[IB]'s basis for terminating Rachid was a pretext." The term "pretext" strongly suggests that the district court engaged in a *McDonnell Douglas* burden shifting analysis. It is disputed, however, whether this is the proper legal framework.

(1) Age Discrimination Under the ADEA Pre-Desert Palace. . . .

"When a plaintiff alleges disparate treatment, liability depends on whether the protected trait (under the ADEA, age) actually motivated the employer's decision." *Reeves* citing *Hazen Paper.* To demonstrate age discrimination a "plaintiff must show that '(1) he was discharged; (2) he was qualified for the position; (3) he was within the protected class at the time of discharge; and (4) he was either i) replaced by someone outside the protected class, ii) replaced by someone younger, or iii) otherwise discharged because of his age.'" That is, regardless of how much younger his replacement is, a plaintiff in the protected class may still establish a prima facie case by producing evidence that he was "discharged because of his age." ADEA coverage extends to "[i]ndividuals at least 40 years of age." A plaintiff can demonstrate age discrimination in two ways, either through:

> direct evidence or by an indirect or inferential method of proof. Discrimination can be shown indirectly by following the "pretext" method of proof set out in *McDonnell Douglas.* If, however, plaintiff produces direct evidence of discrimination, the *McDonnell Douglas* test is "inapplicable." The *Price Waterhouse* mixed-motives theory of discrimination comes into play where direct evidence of discrimination is presented, but the employer asserts that the same adverse employment decision would have been made regardless of discrimination. Although *Price Waterhouse* can be characterized as a method to prove discrimination, the mixed-motives theory is probably best viewed as a defense for an employer. *See Price Waterhouse* ("[T]he employer's burden is most appropriately deemed an affirmative defense: the plaintiff must persuade the factfinder on one point, and the employer, if it wishes to prevail, must persuade it on another.").
>
> Unlike *McDonnell Douglas*, which simply involves a shifting of the burden of *production*, *Price Waterhouse* involves a shift of the burden of *persuasion* to the defendant. In other words, under *Price Waterhouse*, once a plaintiff presents direct evidence of discrimination, the burden of proof shifts to the employer to show that the

---

2. Three of those employees reported alterations in their time-cards. Apparently, none of the employees alleged that Rachid himself (as opposed to another manager) altered his time-card during the period under investigation by Teal-Guess. Teal-Guess informed Powers that certain employees in restaurants where Rachid was a manager had improper deletions of time. Teal-Guess noted that it was Powers's responsibility to determine whether Rachid (or another manager) had made the improper changes.

same adverse employment decision would have been made regardless of discriminatory animus. If the employer fails to carry this burden, plaintiff prevails. . . .

In summary, *Price Waterhouse* and *McDonnell Douglas* are alternative methodologies for proving discrimination.

Mooney v. Aramco Serv. Co., 54 F.3d 1207, 1216-17 & n. 11 (5th Cir. 1995). . . . The parties contest whether *Desert Palace* alters the analysis by allowing a plaintiff to proceed with a mixed-motives approach in a case where there is not direct evidence[6] of discrimination.

(2) Mixed-Motives Analysis is Available for ADEA Claims.

Rachid argues that this case should be analyzed under the mixed-motives analysis described in *Price Waterhouse* and, more recently, in *Desert Palace*. JIB maintains that the mixed-motives analysis is relevant only where there is *direct* evidence of discrimination, and that because there is no direct evidence here, the *McDonnell Douglas* approach governs.

In *Desert Palace*, the Supreme Court unanimously held that in the context of Title VII, as amended by Congress in 1991, "direct evidence of discrimination is not required in mixed-motive[s] cases. As the district court in *Louis v. E. Baton Rouge Parish Sch. Bd.*, 303 F. Supp. 2d 799 (M.D. La. 2003), observed, "[b]ecause the direct evidence requirement has been removed from mixed-motive[s] cases, it is now harder to draw a distinction between *McDonnell Douglas* and mixed-motive[s] cases." This Court has not yet addressed whether *Desert Palace* alters the *Price Waterhouse* and *McDonnell Douglas* analyses.

We must first decide whether the mixed-motives analysis discussed in *Desert Palace* in the context of a Title VII claim is equally applicable in the ADEA context. "[T]he starting point for our analysis is the statutory text." *Desert Palace*. The ADEA states that "[i]t shall be unlawful for an employer . . . to discharge any individual or otherwise discriminate against any individual with respect to his compensation, terms, conditions, or privileges of employment, *because of* such individual's age." Title VII similarly prohibits discrimination "because of" a protected characteristic. In *Desert Palace* the Supreme Court applied the mixed-motives analysis because, "[o]n its face, [Title VII] does not mention, much less require, that a plaintiff make a heightened showing through direct evidence." *Desert Palace*.

Given that the language of the relevant provision of the ADEA is similarly silent as to the heightened direct evidence standard,[8] and the presence of heightened

---

6. "Direct evidence is evidence that, if believed, proves the fact of discriminatory animus without inference or presumption." *Sandstad v. CB Richard Ellis, Inc.*, 309 F.3d 893, 897 (5th Cir. 2002). Although some of the evidence in the case *sub judice* might qualify as direct evidence, Rachid does *not* argue that there was direct evidence of discrimination.

8. In response to *Price Waterhouse*, Title VII was amended in 1991 specifically "to eliminate the employer's ability to escape liability in Title VII mixed-motive[s] cases by proving that it would have made the same decision in the absence of the discriminatory motivation." *Hill v. Lockheed Martin Logistics Mgmt., Inc.*, 354 F.3d 277, 284 (4th Cir. 2004); *see* 42 U.S.C. § 2000e-2(m). The ADEA was not similarly amended, and Title VII's amendment was noted by the Supreme Court in *Desert Palace*. One circuit court assumed in dictum, without so holding, that this difference in statutory text is significant. *See Hill* (assuming in dictum, without deciding, that *Desert Palace* does not apply to ADEA claims, given the absence from that statute of an explicit mixed-motives provision like the one found in Title VII). Unlike Title VII which explicitly permits mixed-motives cases, the ADEA neither countenances nor prohibits the mixed-motives analysis. Because we base our holding on the absence of a heightened direct evidence requirement in the ADEA, we do not find the statute's silence on the mixed-motives analysis to be dispositive.

pleading requirements in other statutes, we hold that direct evidence of discrimination is not necessary to receive a mixed-motives analysis for an ADEA claim. *Accord Estades-Negroni v. Assoc. Corp. of N. Am.*, 345 F.3d 25, 31 (1st Cir. 2003) (holding that after *Desert Palace* the mixed-motives analysis applies in ADEA cases even without direct evidence of discrimination). . . .

Our holding today that the mixed-motives analysis used in Title VII cases post-*Desert Palace* is equally applicable in ADEA represents a merging of the *McDonnell Douglas* and *Price Waterhouse* approaches. Under this integrated approach, called, for simplicity, the modified *McDonnell Douglas* approach: the plaintiff must still demonstrate a prima facie case of discrimination; the defendant then must articulate a legitimate, non-discriminatory reason for its decision to terminate the plaintiff; and, if the defendant meets its burden of production, "the plaintiff must then offer sufficient evidence to create a genuine issue of material fact 'either (1) that the defendant's reason is not true, but is instead a pretext for discrimination (pretext alternative); or (2) that the defendant's reason, while true, is only one of the reasons for its conduct, and another "motivating factor" is the plaintiff's protected characteristic (mixed-motive[s] alternative)." . . . If a plaintiff demonstrates that age was a motivating factor in the employment decision, it then falls to the defendant to prove "that the same adverse employment decision would have been made regardless of discriminatory animus. If the employer fails to carry this burden, plaintiff prevails." . . .

B. RACHID'S CLAIM.

We now turn to whether Rachid's claim survives summary judgment under the modified *McDonnell Douglas* approach detailed above.

(1) Rachid Established a Prima Facie Case.

JIB essentially concedes that Rachid satisfies the first three factors necessary for a prima facie case. Rachid argues that he demonstrated the fourth factor by showing that: (1) his replacement was five years younger; (2) he long suspected that Powers was going to fire him because of his age and he voiced these concerns to human resources; and (3) Powers made ageist comments to and about Rachid.

The parties spend considerable effort contesting whether an age difference of five years is "significant" or "substantial" under *O'Connor* [v. *Consolidated Coin Caterers Corp.*, 517 U.S. 308 (1996)] (holding that merely being replaced by someone outside the protected class is not sufficient to establish a prima facie case; rather, an employee demonstrates an inference of age discrimination when he is replaced by an employee "significantly" younger). While this is a close question, we need not reach it because Rachid's other evidence easily establishes a prima facie case.

Evidence in the record demonstrates that Powers repeatedly made ageist comments to and about Rachid. In his deposition Rachid notes that, prior to his termination, he reported to human resources that Powers was harassing him about his age. Haidar testified that Powers suggested that Rachid's absence from a meeting was due to the fact that "he's probably in bed or he's sleeping by [now] because of his age. . . . " Such evidence of discrimination easily establishes a prime facie case that Rachid was "discharged because of his age."

(2) Material Issues of Fact are Disputed, Making Summary Judgment Inappropriate.

JIB argues that it had a non-discriminatory reason for firing Rachid — i.e., Rachid's failure to follow company policy regarding altering subordinates' time-sheets without documentation. JIB notes that "since 1999, the Company has terminated at least 11 other employees [including some of whom were substantially younger than Rachid] in the same region for violating the Company's time[-]sheet policy."

While violating a non-discriminatory company policy is adequate grounds for termination, two fact issues remain: (1) Rachid claims that Powers's email did not reflect JIB's company policy; and (2) he claims that, based on his understanding of the policy, he did not violate the policy. Rachid also argues that JIB's assertion that other employees were terminated for violating the policy is inapposite here because none of those employees were fired by Powers, nor were any of those employees fired for violating the specific time-card policy stated in Powers's email.

(a) Company policy concerning time-card alterations is unclear.

Rachid claims that "Company Policy said nothing about the Manager signing a P108 Discipline Slip." Though JIB argues that a company policy was violated, it cites to nothing other than Powers's email. Rachid notes that the Employee Handbook only requires that if an employee "do[esn't] agree with [his] hours on the [report at the end of each pay period, he must let his] Manager know immediately."

JIB's argument that other employees were fired for violating a time-card policy does not resolve this issue. JIB issued separation notices to employees discharged for "employees' hours deletions," but none of those notices references failure to complete P108 forms. Additionally, all of those notices assume that employee hours were unlawfully deleted. In the instant case, Rachid claims that he only made lawful deletions (i.e., deletions when employees failed to punch out for breaks). The basis of Rachid's termination by Powers seems to have had less to do with whether the deletions were accurate than with whether Rachid had completed P108 forms when he made the deletions.[13] The fact that some employees were terminated for "employees' hours deletions" does suggest that JIB had a policy on this matter, but it does not address the contours of that policy.

Furthermore, the other employees were terminated by other managers, mitigating the relevance of their terminations to the question of whether Powers unlawfully discriminated against Rachid. "This court and others have held that testimony from former employees who had different supervisors than the plaintiff, who worked in different parts of the employer's company, or whose terminations were removed in time from the plaintiff's termination cannot be probative of whether age was a determinative factor in the plaintiff's discharge." *Wyvill v. United Cos. Life Ins. Co.*, 212 F.3d 296, 302 (5th Cir. 2000). JIB does not appear to have produced *any* evidence that other managers were fired by Powers (or by anyone else) merely for failing to complete P108 forms in situations where: (1) those managers altered employee hours; and (2) the employees did not — as required by the Employee

---

13. Powers fired Rachid immediately after Rachid admitted to making some alterations without completing P108 forms. Powers did not make any investigation to determine whether those deletions were accurate.

Handbook — contest the alterations. Therefore, a genuine issue of material fact exists whether Powers's email describes JIB's company policy.

(b)   It is uncertain whether Rachid violated the policy stated in Powers's email.

Rachid argues that his and Haidar's understanding of Powers's email "was that, if the 'employee contests their [sic] hours' after the Manager made the change, the Manager was to write a P108 form." Haidar testified that he did not think a P108 form was necessary unless an employee disputed changes made to the time-card. According to Rachid's and Haidar's interpretation, a P108 was necessary only if, after an employee was notified of an alteration to his hours, he were still to contest it. Therefore, according to Rachid, he never violated the directive as stated in Powers's email. Of course, whether Rachid violated JIB's policy is a question of fact.

Even if JIB did have a policy (which seems likely), and even if that policy required P108 forms to be filled out in certain circumstances (which is uncertain), a factual question remains as to whether Rachid violated that policy by only completing P108s when an employee contested the alteration.

(c)   Summary judgment was improper.

Because issues of material fact are disputed, summary judgment in favor of JIB was unwarranted. This Court's decision in *Bienkowski v. American Airlines, Inc.*, 851 F.2d 1503, 1506-07 (5th Cir. 1988), informs the analysis of whether summary judgment was appropriate at this stage. In *Bienkowski*, this Court faced a similar situation: the parties contested the quality of plaintiff's performance, and the plaintiff alleged that his supervisors made ageist comments. Bienkowski alleged that his managers commented that he look "'sharp' if he was [sic] going to look for another job . . . [and] commented on his inability or willingness to 'adapt' to new systems in the department." This Court reversed the district court's grant of summary judgment in favor of the defendant, noting:

> Unlike the district court, we are unwilling to assume that indirect comments about his age and adaptability are not possibly probative of an unlawful discriminatory intent, given the parties' sharp disagreements over the operative facts of [plaintiff]'s performance. Moreover, live testimony will assist the necessary credibility choices in this case more effectively than printed affidavits.

Comments to look "sharp" and comments concerning an employee's willingness to "adapt" to new systems are rather nebulous, but they allowed Bienkowski to avoid summary judgment. The alleged ageist comments in the instant case are substantially more egregious. . . .

In the case *sub judice*, Rachid presents far more evidence of age discrimination than was presented in *Bienkowski*. Rachid testified that Powers made numerous ageist comments-including one situation where Powers allegedly said: "[A]nd don't forget it, [Rachid], you're too old, too" — and Haidar supported Rachid's assertions that Powers continually made such comments. Rachid even spoke with human resources prior to his termination to express his fear that Powers would try to fire him because of his age. Despite JIB's focus on Teal-Guess's investigation and company policy, it was Powers who terminated Rachid, and it was Powers who repeatedly made ageist comments to and about Rachid. Such comments preclude summary judgment because a rational finder of fact could conclude that age played a role in Powers's decision to terminate Rachid. . . .

NOTES

1. Desert Palace *Applies to ADEA Claims.* The court in *Rachid* adopts a uniform approach across Title VII and the ADEA (and, presumably, 42 U.S.C. §1981) that emphasizes a single view of what constitutes discrimination and applies the "motivating factor" standard to ADEA claims. But *Desert Palace* is based on the 1991 Civil Rights Act amendment to Title VII; the ADEA was not amended to add a provision like §703(m). Had *Rachid* focused more on this aspect, it might have found the ADEA different than Title VII. But this would not make the court's entire analysis irrelevant. Presumably, an unamended ADEA would at least incorporate the *Price Waterhouse* burden-shifting approach. Thus, a plaintiff who could prove that age was a "substantial factor" in an adverse action by the use of "direct evidence" would shift the burden to defendant to prove the "same decision anyway," which would (if established) be a defense to liability not merely a limitation of damages.

Arguably, however, using the *McDonnell Douglas/Price Waterhouse* approach rather than *Desert Palace* would have resulted in affirming the district court in *Rachid* — the evidence may not have been "direct" enough to shift any burden. An alternative is that *Rachid* came out correctly even if viewed as a pure *McDonnell Douglas* case, as interpreted by *Reeves*.

But *Rachid's* overarching theme is that there ought to be a unified approach to all discrimination cases. One advantage of this would be simplifying your studying for the final examination! Beyond that, however, is the court justified in ignoring differences in the statutory language of the two enactments? While some Supreme Court cases under the ADEA seem to track Title VII without much fuss, others have focused on language differences between the two statutes to create different rules. Revisit this question after you have encountered *Smith v. City of Jackson*, reproduced at p. 223 in Chapter 3. Are you satisfied with *Rachid's* explanation? While both statutes use the language "because of," only Title VII has the "motivating factor" language of §703(m). Further, should the ADEA be read to include the same-decision defense that §706(g)(2)(B) applies to "motivating factor" cases under Title VII? *Rachid* says that, if the defendant fails to carry its same-decision affirmative defense, plaintiff wins. But it doesn't say what happens if the defendant is successful. Under *Price Waterhouse*, defendant wins. Under §703(m), plaintiff still wins but doesn't get full relief,

2. *Modified* McDonnell Douglas *Approach.* How does the court modify *McDonnell Douglas* in light of *Desert Palace*? The requirement of "direct" evidence is eliminated and plaintiff, as an alternative to showing defendant's reason not to be true (i.e., a pretext), can prove "that the defendant's reason, while true, is only one of the reasons for its conduct, and that another 'motivating factor' is the plaintiff's protected characteristic." Does this merely replace the but-for level of proof with the "a motivating factor" standard for liability? What happens to claims, like those in *Desert Palace*, *Price Waterhouse*, and *McDonald*, that are arguably not based on *McDonnell Douglas*? Must all such plaintiffs now prove a *McDonnell Douglas* prima facie case as a threshold to other proof, such as admissions, acting on stereotypes, or unequal treatment? Or might such proof itself satisfy the *McDonnell Douglas* prima facie case?

Establishing a *McDonnell Douglas* prima facie case sets a fairly low bar that can be easily satisfied, *see Machinchick v. PB Powers, Inc.*, 398 F.3d 345 (5th Cir. 2005) (ageist statements in email satisfy fourth prong of *McDonnell Douglas* prima facie case even where the plaintiff's replacement was not much younger than he), but at

least some plaintiffs will not be able to establish a prima facie case as it has traditionally been conceived. Remember that in *Price Waterhouse* the Court appeared to
assume that *McDonnell Douglas* did not apply because the employer did in fact act
on the basis of the plaintiff' interpersonal relationship deficiencies and so its assertion
of that reason was true, and was not a pretext for discrimination. Again, in *McDonald v.
Santa Fe Trail Transportation*, there was no question that plaintiffs had engaged in
theft, the reason advanced by the defendant for discharging them.

Judge Moore in her concurring opinion in *Wright v. Murray Guard, Inc.*, 455
F.3d 702 (6th Cir. 2006), criticized *Rachid* because it did "not accurately screen for
unlawful employment practices as Congress defined them in the 1991 Civil Rights
Act." *Rachid* did not go far enough because requiring a *McDonnell Douglas* prima
facie case as a threshold to proving all individual disparate treatment claims could
defeat too many claims because they in fact involved mixed-motives that should be
judged by the "a motivating factor" standard.

> Making the showing of a prima facie case a predicate to proceeding on a mixed-motive
> claim would therefore improperly allow summary judgment to defeat claims when one
> or more of "the most common nondiscriminatory reasons" played some role in
> the adverse decision, but when a discriminatory reason also played some role. In these
> circumstances, the plaintiff might not be able to maintain a prima facie case, but might
> be able to present evidence that a discriminatory reason was a motivating factor in the
> adverse employment decision. In such cases, the plaintiff would have a cognizable
> mixed-motive claim under [703(m)], but her claim would otherwise be barred under
> "the modified *McDonnell Douglas* approach."

405 F.3d at 717. In *Keelan v. Majesco Softward, Inc.*, 407 F.3d 332 (5th Cir. 2005),
summary judgment for defendant was upheld because plaintiff failed to establish a
McDonnell Douglas prima facie case despite evidence that the employer's high
officials admitted that they were making the company "all Indian." Is *Keelan* an
example of the problem Judge Moore raises?

3. *Other Courts' Approaches.* Other circuits have taken a variety of approaches to
dealing with *Desert Palace*. So far, no approach seems to have gained ascendance.

(a) *Avoidance.* One court has simply limited *Desert Palace* to its facts and denied it
has any impact beyond those facts. *Cooper v. Southern Co.*, 390 F.2d 695, 725 n. 17
(11th Cir. 2004), *rev'd in part on other grounds, Ash v. Tyson Foods*, 546 U.S. 454
(2006), responded in a footnote to an argument by plaintiff that *Desert Palace* had
"radically revised" *McDonnell Douglas*. It stated that *Desert Palace* was "expressly
limited to mixed-motive cases" and that the Court "did not decide whether its
analysis applied in other contexts" and "did not even mention *McDonnell Douglas*."

The Eighth Circuit has held that *Desert Palace* does not apply to *McDonnell
Douglas* cases at the summary judgment stage because *Desert Palace* arose in the
context of a challenge to the appropriateness of jury instructions that echoed §§ 703(m)
and 706(g)(2)(B). In *Griffith v. City of Des Moines*, 387 F.3d 733 (8th Cir. 2004),
the plaintiff argued that, at the pretext stage of analysis for a summary judgment
motion, *McDonnell Douglas* should be modified to simply ask whether plaintiff introduced sufficient evidence "to meet his or her 'ultimate burden' to prove intentional
discrimination, rather than in terms of whether the plaintiff can prove 'pretext.'" The
court disagreed because "*Desert Palace*, a decision in which the Supreme Court
decided only a mixed-motive jury instruction issue, is an inherently unreliable basis for
district courts to begin ignoring this Circuit's [prior and still] controlling
summary judgment precedents." *See* Carolyn Shapiro, *The Limits of the Olympian*

Court: Common Law Judging versus Error Correction in the Supreme Court, 63
WASH. & LEE L. REV. 271 (2006).

Without directly addressing the issues raised by *Desert Palace*, Judge Posner implicitly limited its impact on *McDonnell Douglas* cases. In *Forrester v. Rauland-Borg
Corp.*, 453 F.3d 416 (7th Cir. 2006), he cited "persistent dictum to the effect that
pretext can be shown not only by proof that the employer's stated reason was not the
honest reason for his action but also by proof that the stated reason was 'insufficient
to motivate' the action." For him it was "time the dictum is laid to rest." He analyzed
some of the possible meanings that could be given to the "insufficient to motivate"
language:

> If the stated reason for the challenged action did not motivate the action, then it was
> indeed pretextual. If it was *insufficient* to motivate the action, either this means that it
> didn't motivate it, or that it shouldn't have motivated it. If the first is the intended sense,
> the dictum is just a murky way of saying that the stated reason was not the real reason. If
> the second sense is the one intended, then the dictum is wrong because the question is
> never whether the employer was mistaken, cruel, unethical, out of his head, or
> downright irrational in taking the action for the stated reason, but simply whether the
> stated reason *was* his reason: not a good reason, but a true reason.

Id. at 417-18. Posner also contemplated whether the "insufficient to motivate" language really meant that the defendant's asserted reasons "were factors that the employer considered but that did not have enough weight in his thinking to induce him
to take the action complained of." For him, using the language "insufficient to
motivate" masks that this is simply another way of saying that the reason, though on
the mind of the employer, was a pretext because it "wasn't what induced him to take
the challenged employment action."

But Posner failed to address another sense suggested by the "insufficient to motivate" language: one reason may be insufficient to motivate a decision because it was
only one of a number of reasons that together motivated the employer's action. In
other words, the reason played a role but didn't cause the decision. Under § 703(m),
that should suffice for liability. By trying to put the "insufficient to motivate" dictum
to rest, is Judge Posner attempting to foreclose the § 703(m) standard for *McDonnell
Douglas* cases where the evidence would support a factfinder concluding that both
defendant's asserted reason and discrimination were motivating factors for the decision the plaintiff challenges? Dean Steven J. Kaminshine in *Disparate Treatment
as a Theory of Discrimination: The Need for a Restatement, Not a Revolution*, 2 STAN.
J. OF CIV. RTS. & CIV. LIB. 1 (2006), argues that successful proof of pretext means
plaintiff has proven that defendant's asserted reason played no role in defendant's
decision. Plaintiff has to knock out defendant's reason completely. He would reject a
"partial pretext" approach and would, apparently, agree with Judge Posner.

(b) *Denial* The Fourth Circuit, in *Hill v. Lockheed Martin Logistics Management,
Inc.*, 354 F.3d 277 (4th Cir. 2004), appeared at first to take account of *Desert Palace*,
but then it reverted to the determinative influence standard for *McDonnell Douglas*
cases that originated in *Biggins* and was reiterated in *Reeves*:

> *Regardless of the type of evidence offered by a plaintiff* as support for her discrimination
> claim (direct, circumstantial, or evidence of pretext), or whether she proceeds under a
> mixed-motive or single-motive theory, "[t]he ultimate question in every employment
> discrimination case involving a claim of disparate treatment is whether the plaintiff
> was the victim of intentional discrimination." To demonstrate such an intent to

discriminate on the part of the employer, an individual alleging disparate treatment based upon a protected trait must produce sufficient evidence upon which one could find that "the protected trait . . . actually motivated the employer's decision." *The protected trait "must have actually played a role in the employer's decisionmaking process and had a determinative influence on the outcome."*

Id. at 286 (emphasis added). What happened to the "a motivating factor" standard of § 703(m)?

(c) *Acceptance?* The Ninth Circuit's approach to the question in the decision ultimately affirmed by the Supreme Court in *Desert Palace* may have sketched out a unitary approach to the problem. It would essentially allow *McDonnell Douglas*, along with all the other theories that can be applied, with all pointing toward the ultimate question of liability for discrimination to be determined by § 703(m)'s "motivating factor" test. In other words, the single-motive approach of *McDonnell Douglas* is merged into the mixed-motive approach of § 703(m) along with all other claims of disparate treatment.

In *Dominguez-Curry v. Nevada Transportation Dept.*, 424 F.3d 1027 (9th Cir. 2005), plaintiff brought claims of hostile work environment sex discrimination and failure to promote. The court reversed summary judgment for defendant on both claims. The record included a great deal of evidence of sexist language and treatment aimed at plaintiff, particularly by plaintiff's supervisor. That evidence supported plaintiff's hostile environment claim but, more important for present purposes, it was also useful to establish her failure to promote claim. Plaintiff relied on *McDonnell Douglas* to establish her prima facie case, and defendant asserted that it had not promoted plaintiff because the person it had promoted was much more qualified than she. While plaintiff had admitted that her successful competitor was the more qualified, she still maintained that discrimination was "a motivating factor" in the promotion incident because her biased supervisor was one of two managers who interviewed the candidates and made the promotion decision. Under the "motivating factor" test, the fact that the person promoted was more qualified does not justify granting summary judgment for the defendant. "Even if it were uncontested that Andrews' qualifications were superior, this would not preclude a finding of discrimination. An employer may be held liable under Title VII even if it had a legitimate reason for its employment decision, as long as an illegitimate reason was a motivating factor in the decision." In essence, this case is similar to *Patterson v. McLean Credit Union*, reproduced at p. 62, which involves proof of pretext, but here the standard is "motivating factor" rather than the determinative influence standard used at that time in *McDonnell Douglas* cases.

(d) *Or Just a Grab-bag?* The D.C. Circuit took a first step into this area by suggesting that "single-motive" or "mixed-motive" approaches were both viable. It held that the 1991 amendments, adding §§ 703(m) and 706(g)(2)(B), did not repeal the "because of" standard set forth in original § 703(a). In *Fogg v. Gonzales*, 492 F.3d 447 (D.C. Cir. 2007), the court wrote: "On its face Title VII provides alternative ways of establishing liability for employment practices based upon the impermissible use of race or other proscribed criteria — one in § 2000e-2(a), which has been the law since 1964, and another in § 2000e-2(m), which the Congress added in 1991." *Id.* at 453. The court went on, "we cannot infer from the addition of § 2000e-2(m) the implicit repeal of § 2000e-2(a) as a standard for establishing liability in preference to the more straightforward inference that § 2000e-2(m) adds an additional way of establishing liability." *Id.* The court characterized the two standards that link defendant's actions to its intent to discriminate as involving "single" and "mixed" motives. It further held that the trial judge did not abuse her discretion in deciding that the case had been tried as a single-motive case to which the same-decision defense to full remedies did not apply. The court did not go further to suggest how what it called "single" and "mixed" motive cases would be treated if the parties had not litigated the case as a single-motive case.

(e) *Serial But-For/Pretext, A Motivating Factor/Mixed-Motive Analysis.* Dean Steven J. Kaminshine in *Disparate Treatment as a Theory of Discrimination: The Need for a Restatement, Not a Revolution*, 2 STAN. J. OF CIV. RTS. & CIV. LIB. 1, 7 (2006), argues for retaining a distinction between pretext and mixed motive cases. For him, "*McDonnell Douglas* is not dead, just wounded." He therefore argues for a serial approach: each individual disparate treatment case should first be analyzed as a pretext case and then as a mixed-motive case.

For Dean Kaminshine, proving pretext means knocking out defendant's asserted reason completely; this means the *McDonnell Douglas* process of elimination is successful only if plaintiff can prove defendant's reason played no part in the decision plaintiff challenges. That showing then leaves only discrimination as a reason in the record. Such a finding would establish discrimination at the but-for level. In making the determination of the pretext method, a court (and, presumably, the jury) would review only the evidence (direct and circumstantial) regarding defendant's asserted reason and whether plaintiff proved it played no part in defendant's decision. If plaintiff introduced evidence, again direct or circumstantial, probative of discrimination but not attempting to negate defendant's asserted reason, that evidence would be evaluated under the "motivating factor" standard, with the potential for the defendant to limit plaintiff's full remedies if it could prove it would have made the same decision even if it had not discriminated.

Dean Kaminshine's textual analysis turns largely on defining the reach of §703(m) in terms of §706(g)2)(B), concluding that §703(m) governs only in the mixed motives context. Thus, he defends his approach by arguing, "It would be odd, to say the least, if an employer whose explanation is exposed as a pretext for discrimination was then afforded a defense [under §706(g)2)(B)] to show that it would have reach [sic] the same decision on the basis of this discredited explanation." *Id.* at 45. While Kaminshine's structure is logically coherent, why maintain the distinction between proving pretext and proving discrimination by other means? Is it to maintain separate roles for the "motivating factor" standard of §703(m) and the "because of" standard in §703(a)? What policy is served by doing that? Finally, how would jury instructions work under this system?

(f) *A Comprehensive and Uniform Approach.* Individual disparate treatment cases involve proof of three independent elements — (1) defendant's intent to discriminate, (2) an adverse employment action against the plaintiff, (3) which action was the result of the intent to discriminate.

(1) *Intent.* Intent can be proved to a factfinder by relying on a wide array of evidence that can be argued to reveal such intent. This includes failure to treat like cases alike on the merits; violations of employer procedures; admissions by the employer that race or sex played a role; actions most easily explainable as based on discriminatory stereotypes; eliminating the most likely nondiscriminatory reasons for the action, leaving discrimination as the most likely explanation; and proving an

asserted nondiscriminatory explanation to be false or a lie. After *Reeves*, a holistic approach would seem to embrace a wide array of arguments that could convince a reasonable jury that the defendant's act was motivated by discrimination. That leaves to the creativity of lawyers representing the parties to develop new and imaginative ways of arguing that discrimination has, or has not, occurred.

(2) *Adverse Employment Action.* While generally people do not go to the trouble of bringing a law suit unless they feel seriously wronged, the courts have been struggling to find the right test when the action challenged is too insubstantial to justify a law suit. The materiality test of *Minor v. Centocur* is the latest step in the evolution of the instincts of courts to not let plaintiff's desire for vindication of a perceived wrong be the sole test. A plain meaning approach to the statutory language would be broader still and would allow plaintiffs to challenge any actions that involved employment versus some non-employment issue.

(3) *Linking the Intent to the Action.* Underlying the debate over the continuing viability of *McDonnell Douglas*, the level of linkage that must be shown between defendant's discriminatory intent and its action harming plaintiff to establish liability and to justify full recovery of damages. "Determinative factor" and "motivating factor" are the two competing tests, and there remains a fundamental question as to when they apply. If either is available in any particular case, then the question of who gets to choose becomes important — at least by those who believe that these different tests influence the findings of triers of fact. Presumptively, a risk-averse plaintiff will ask for the "a motivating factor" standard making it easier to find liability, but thereby opening her case to the risk that a jury would deny full remedies under the "same-decision" affirmative defense. A risk preferring plaintiff, perceiving her case as strong, can ask for a determinative influence test in order to diminish the chance of a jury splitting the difference by finding liability under the "a motivating factor" test but finding for the defendant on the "same-decision" defense to remedies. These possibilities raise the question whether the defendant can force the plaintiff to also ask for the "a motivating factor" test in order to preserve its chance to win on the limitation of remedies defense. And overarching parties' preferences is the "right" instruction for any given court facing any given case.

4. *Academic Response to* Desert Palace. Several commentators read *Desert Palace* as destroying *McDonnell Douglas*. *See* Michael J. Zimmer, *The New Discrimination Law:* Price Waterhouse *is Dead, Whither* McDonnell Douglas?, 53 EMORY L.J. 1887 (2004); William R. Corbett, McDonnell Douglas, *1973-2003: May You Rest in Peace?*, 6 U. PA. J. LAB. & EMP. L. 199, 212-13 (2003); William R. Corbett, *An Allegory of the Cave and the* Desert Palace, 41 HOUS. L. REV. 1549, 1576 (2005); Henry L. Chambers, Jr., *The Effect of Eliminating Distinctions Among Title VII Disparate Treatment Cases*, 57 SMU REV. 83, 102-03 (2004; Kenneth R. Davis, Price-*Fixing: Refining the* Price Waterhouse *Standard and Individual Disparate Treatment Law*, 31 FLA. ST. U.L. REV. 859, 861(2004); Jeffrey A. Van Detta , *"Le Roi Est Mort; Vive Le Roi!": An Essay on the Quiet Demise of* McDonnell Douglas *and the Transformation of Every Title VII Case after* Desert Palace, Inc. v. Costa *into a "Mixed-Motives" Case*, 52 DRAKE L. REV. 71, 79 (2003). *See also* Marcia L. McCormick, *The Allure and Danger of Practicing Law as Taxonomy*, 58 ARK. L. REV. 159, 161; Melissa Hart, *Subjective Decisionmaking and Unconscious Discrimination*, 56 ALA. L. REV. 741, 790-91 (2005).

NOTE ON SPECIAL ISSUES OF PROOF

Although the bases to infer, or not to infer, discrimination are potentially limitless, there are some areas of special interest because they have generated a number of lower court decisions. These include the "same actor" and the "same supervisor" questions which, despite their similar labels, reflect very different concerns, and the question of how large an age difference is necessary in ADEA cases to infer discrimination, and, more generally, whether replacements in race or sex cases by members of plaintiff's class prevent an inference of discrimination.

"Same Actor" Rule vs. Inference. Courts have sometimes dismissed a plaintiff's discrimination case when the person who hired the plaintiff was also the person who discharged him relatively soon after the hiring decision. The rationale is that, had the employer held stereotypical views, he would not have hired the plaintiff in the first place. This principle emerged first under the ADEA, *e.g., Brown v. CSC Logic, Inc.* 82 F.3d 651 (5th Cir. 1996); *Lowe v. J. B. Hunt Transport, Inc.,* 963 F.2d 173 (8th Cir. 1992), but it has been applied under other antidiscrimination statutes. *E.g., Bradley v. Harcourt, Brace & Co.,* 104 F.3d 267 (9th Cir. 1996) (sex discrimination); *Jaques v. Clean-Up Group, Inc.,* 96 F.3d 506 (1st Cir. 1996) (disability discrimination). *See generally* Anna Laurie Bryant & Richard A. Bales, *Using the Same Actor "Inference" in Employment Discrimination Cases,* 1999 UTAH L. REV. 225; Ross B. Goldman, Note, *Overrating Sameness: A New Perspective on the Same-Actor Inference in Employment Discrimination Cases,* 93 VA. L. REV. 1533 (2007).

While some courts have described "same actor" as a "presumption," it is more accurately viewed as an inference, that is, as a basis for making it less likely that a given situation involves intent to discriminate. *Waldron v. SL Industries, Inc.,* 56 F.3d 491 (3d Cir. 1995) (that hirer and firer are the same and discharge occurred shortly after hiring is simply evidence like any other and should not be accorded any presumptive value). This means that the factfinder can enter this factor into its calculus when making the ultimate determination. But should the same actor inference play much of a role in deciding whether a reasonable jury could find discrimination in circumstances that would otherwise raise a jury question?

One court thought that would not often be appropriate. *Johnson v. Zema Systems Corp.,* 170 F.3d 734, 745 (7th Cir. 1999), explained that the inference was unlikely to make a difference in many cases:

> The psychological assumption underlying the same-actor inference [that it does not make sense to hire workers from a group one dislikes] may not hold true on the facts of the particular case. For example, a manager might hire a person of a certain race expecting them not to rise to a position in the company where daily contact with the manager would be necessary. Or an employer might hire an employee of a certain gender expecting that person to act, or dress, or talk in a way that employer deems acceptable for that gender and then fire that employee if she fails to comply with the employer's gender stereotypes. Similarly, if an employee were the first African-American hired, an employer might be unaware of his own stereotypical views of African-Americans at the time of hiring.

See also Wexler v. White's Fine Furniture, 317 F.3d 564, 573-74 (6th Cir. 2003) (en banc) ("We therefore specifically hold that where, as in this case, the factfinder decides to draw the same-actor inference, it is insufficient to warrant summary judgment for the defendant if the employee has otherwise raised a genuine issue of material fact.") *But see Coghlan v. American Seafoods Co. LLC,* 413 F.3d 1090 (9th

Cir. 2005) (stronger evidence of discrimination is needed to defeat summary judgment when alleged discriminatory actor previously selected claimant for favorable treatment).

Consistent with the Seventh Circuit's view that it really isn't "common sense" that someone who hires a protected class member is unlikely to harbor bias against that group, Linda Hamilton Krieger & Susan T. Fiske, *Behavioral Realism in Employment Discrimination Law: Implicit Bias and Disparate Treatment*, 94 CAL. L. REV. 997, 1048 (2006), argue that "empirical research suggests that "dispositionism," the common-sense model of behavioral consistency on which the same actor inference is based, is deeply flawed, and that human behavior is far less consistent across situations than lay people tend to believe."

Same Supervisor. A second recurring situation arises when plaintiff attempts to bolster her case by adducing evidence of discrimination against other members of her class. While there is no doubt that such evidence is often admissible, and may be very probative, there has been considerable resistance to its use when the alleged discrimination was by a different supervisor than the one accused of discrimination against plaintiff. In *Mendelsohn v. Sprint/United Management Co.*, 466 F.3d 1223 (10th Cir. 2006), *cert. granted*, 127 S. Ct. 2937 (2007), a reduction in force case, plaintiff wanted to call as witnesses five other older workers who claimed that they, too, were discriminated against because of their age in the downsizing. Defendant objected because none of the other potential witnesses worked under the same supervisor as the plaintiff. The trial court excluded the testimony, and the jury found for the defendant. The court of appeals reversed: "We have previously recognized the testimony of employees, other than the plaintiff, concerning how the employer treated them as relevant to the employer's discriminatory intent." *Id.* at 1226.

It distinguished an earlier case, *Aramburu v. The Boeing Co.*, 112 F.3d 1398, 1404 (10th Cir. 1997), that limited testimony to employees working for the same supervisor where plaintiff sought to introduce evidence that the supervisors of other employees enforced company rules less strictly:

> *Aramburu* has no application where, as here, plaintiff claims to be a victim of a *company-wide* discriminatory RIF. Applying *Aramburu's* "same supervisor" rule in the context of an alleged discriminatory company-wide RIF would, in many circumstances, make it significantly difficult, if not impossible, for a plaintiff to prove a case of discrimination based on circumstantial evidence. Conceivably, a plaintiff might be the only employee selected for a RIF supervised by a particular supervisor. Meanwhile, scores of other employees within the protected group also selected for the RIF might work for different supervisors. In such cases, the constraints of *Aramburu* would preclude a plaintiff from introducing testimony from those other employees.

Id. at 1228. If plaintiff is assuming the RIF policy is neutral as to age, what is the relevance of the testimony that she sought to introduce of how other older workers were treated by their supervisors? One possibility is that such proof shows that the RIF policy, though age neutral on its face and, perhaps, in its intent, allowed for age discrimination in its application. The supervisors making the decisions had broad discretion and, in using that discretion, could discriminate because of age, either consciously or unconsciously.

That might be true, but doesn't the question remain whether plaintiff's supervisor discriminated? If A, B, and C are each separate decision-makers, how could the fact that B discriminated show that A did? Even if there is some umbrella policy that allowed each of them freedom to make decisions? *See Mattenson v. Baxter*

Healthcare Corp., 438 F.3d 763, 770-71 (7th Cir. 2006) (in a division of 7,000 employees with hundreds of executives, the fact that some may dislike old workers and even fire old workers because of their age is weak evidence that a particular older employee was fired because of his age; absent proof of a pervasive culture of prejudice, such evidence may be excluded under Rule 403, although it is not reversible error to admit it). And what about C? Can the employer put in evidence that C (and maybe D and E) did *not* discriminate?

Is the real problem in *Mendelsohn* the "same supervisor" rule in *Aramburu?* While unexplained unequal treatment by the same supervisor is a strong basis to draw the inference of discrimination, is evidence that different supervisors enforced the same employer rule more leniently as to other workers without *any* probative value for plaintiff? Couldn't one argue that, when institutional norms cut one way (for example, tolerating tardiness), the fact that a single supervisor violates those norms with respect to a protected class member is at least some evidence of bias? After *Reeves*, should that evidence be admissible unless no jury could reasonably rely on it to build a chain of inferences leading to a finding of discrimination?

In any event, this question can cut both ways. Recall that *Rachid* rejected evidence supporting the defendant's explanation when it consisted of actions by other supervisors.

Age Difference in ADEA Cases. We saw in *O'Connor v. Consolidated Coin Caterers* Corp., 517 U.S. 308 (1996), that it is the age difference that matters when a plaintiff claims to have been replaced by a younger worker, not whether that worker is within the protected class. "Because the ADEA prohibits discrimination on the basis of age and not class membership, the fact that a replacement is substantially younger than the plaintiff is a far more reliable indicator of age discrimination than is the fact that the plaintiff was replaced by someone outside the protected class." 517 U.S. at 313. Building on this theme some lower courts have required that replacements be significantly younger than the plaintiff before age discrimination can be inferred. In *Barber v. CSX Distribution Servs.*, 68 F.3d 694, 699 (3d Cir. 1995), the court, acknowledging there "is no magical formula to measure a particular age gap and determine if it is sufficiently wide to give rise to an inference of discrimination," found that an eight-year difference between the plaintiff and the beneficiary of the discrimination could support a finding that the beneficiary was "sufficiently younger" than the plaintiff to permit an inference of age discrimination. In contrast, in the absence of other evidence, a seven-year age difference was not enough to establish a prima facie case in *Richter v. Hook-SupeRx, Inc.*, 142 F.3d 1024 (7th Cir. 1998). Neither was a six-year difference in *Grosjean v. First Energy Corp.*, 349 F.3d 332 (6th Cir. 2003). While the Seventh Circuit generally requires that plaintiff be replaced by persons at least 10 years younger, that rule is "not so bright as to exclude cases where the gap is smaller but evidence nevertheless reveals the employer's decision to be motivated by plaintiff's age." *EEOC v. Board of Regents of the University of Wisconsin System*, 288 F.3d 296, 302 (7th Cir. 2002). *See also Whittington v. Nordam Group Inc.*, 429 F.3d 986, 996 (10th Cir. 2005) (when comparing a laid-off to a retained worker in a reduction in force, rejecting any requirement of at least five years' difference in age because such a difference may be more significant when older employee is close to retirement age, or the "employer may simply wish to rid itself of its older workers, beginning with oldest").

Replacement by a Member of the Same Race or Sex. A similar problem can arise in race or sex cases. Most courts of appeals have held that, in a termination case, the plaintiff need not prove as part of the prima facie case that she was replaced by someone outside the relevant class. *E.g., Stella v. Mineta*, 284 F.3d 135, 146 (D.C. Cir. 2002) ("plaintiff in a discrimination case need not demonstrate that she was replaced by a person outside her protected class in order to establish a prima facie case under *McDonnell Douglas*"); *Pivirotto v. Innovative Systems, Inc.*, 191 F.3d 344 (3d Cir. 1999). One court requires a plaintiff in a sex discrimination case to prove she was replaced by a man. *Brown v. McLean*, 159 F.3d 898, 905 (4th Cir. 1998). *See also Miles v. Dell, Inc.*, 429 F.3d 480 (4th Cir. 2005) (while generally plaintiff must show replacement by someone outside protected class, this is not necessary when the discharge and hiring decisions were made by different decisionmakers). The *Pivirotto* court explained:

> An employer's failure to hire someone of a different class from the plaintiff, after the plaintiff's discharge, could be explained in many ways. . . . [A]n employer may treat women less favorably than men, but still be willing to hire a woman to fill a position left vacant by the firing of a discriminated-against woman. Or an employer may act on gender-based stereotypes, firing women it perceives as not feminine enough (or as too feminine), or discharging women who are too aggressive while not doing the same to male employees. Such an employer would not necessarily replace a discriminated-against female employee with a man. Indeed, some employers, anticipating litigation, may hire a woman solely to attempt to defeat a sex discrimination claim.

191 F.3d at 355. While that may be true, the replacement by a member of the plaintiff's class is not without probative value on the ultimate issue of discrimination. *See Walker v. St. Anthony's Med. Ctr.*, 881 F.2d 554, 558 (8th Cir. 1989) (while there is no per se requirement of replacement by an individual from outside the protected class, "this fact is relevant in evaluating the employer's motive"). More generally, some courts have allowed testimony of employer's good acts, such as favoring older workers, to rebut the inference of age discrimination that plaintiff is attempting to have the jury draw. *Ansell v. Green Acres Contr. Co.* 347 F.3d 515 (3d Cir. 2003).

NOTE ON LITIGATION SCORECARD

There is a large literature documenting the low success rates of plaintiffs in employment discrimination suits, although the results are not as dire as some would claim. For example, David Benjamin Oppenheimer, *Verdicts Matter: An Empirical Study of California Employment Discrimination and Wrongful Discharge Jury Verdicts Reveals Low Success Rates for Women and Minorities*, 37 U.C. DAVIS L. REV. 511, 516-17 (2003), looks at California cases and finds employment discrimination suits very hard to win. Not only are plaintiffs' success rates somewhat lower than with common law discharge cases, but, when sexual harassment cases were excluded, plaintiffs' success in statutory cases dropped significantly. "[T]he data demonstrate that discrimination cases are hardest to win when brought by non-whites (and particularly black women) alleging race discrimination, women alleging sex discrimination (except for sexual harassment), and women over forty alleging age discrimination." Professor Oppenheimer believes that the most likely explanation is judicial and juror bias. *See also* Michael Selmi, *Why Are Employment Discrimination Cases So Hard to Win?*, 61 LA. L. REV. 555 (2001) (insurance defendants are far more likely to lose than employers in federal employment discrimination suits); Kevin M. Clermont, Theodore Eisenberg & Stewart J. Schwab, *How Employment Discrimination Plaintiffs Fare in the Federal Courts of Appeals*, 7 EMPLOYEE RTS. & EMP. POL'Y J. 551-52 (2004) ("appellate courts reverse plaintiffs' wins below far more often than defendants' wins"); Wendy Parker, *Lessons in Losing: Race and National Origin Employment Discrimination Litigation in Federal District Court*, 81 NOTRE DAME L. REV. 889 (2006) ("race and national origin cases are even harder for plaintiffs to win in federal district court than other types of employment discrimination claims").

If it is true that plaintiffs have a very hard time winning discrimination cases, why do you think that is? One possible explanation is that the really strong plaintiffs' cases settle early and so never get to trial or, maybe, even into the courts. *See* Minna J. Kotkin, *Outing Outcomes: An Empirical Study of Confidential Employment Discrimination Settlements*, 64 WASH. & LEE L. REV. 111 (2007) (employment discrimination litigation results in a mean recovery of $54,651, far more than nuisance value). Another possible explanation is that many discrimination cases are brought by the plaintiff pro se, so the failure to have professional representation may take its toll. A third explanation may be that plaintiffs' cases are weak, at least in light of the difficulty posed in litigating them successfully. Might that be because, in the world of at-will employment, claiming discrimination is one of the few hooks employees have when they feel that they have been mistreated by their employers? Are there other reasons you can think of for the low success rate?

Will the developing jurisprudence based on *Reeves* and *Desert Palace* make any difference? Professor Charles Sullivan predicts that the litigation scorecard will not change because judges and jurors underestimate the amount of discrimination that continues to occur and are, therefore, reluctant to find defendants discriminated, no matter how the case is presented to them. *See* Charles A. Sullivan, *Disparate Impact: Looking Past the* Desert Palace *Mirage*, 47 WM. & MARY L. REV. 911 (2006).

PROBLEM 1.1

In response to a help-wanted ad, Jane Armstrong, a 38-year-old woman, applies for a job as a cab driver at the Hacker Cab Company. She has a valid driver's license and has driven extensively, but not for pay, for 20 years. She is a vegetarian and a Capricorn. After a brief interview, at which all these facts emerge, she is rejected by "Tip" O'Neill, Hacker's president. Armstrong comes to you for legal counsel. You do some investigation. The first call you make is to O'Neill, who admits that the job is still open but explains that he rejected Armstrong because "Capricorns make lousy drivers; besides she's too old to adjust to the rigors of cab driving, especially since she doesn't eat meat." When asked whether Armstrong's gender played a part in the decision, O'Neill replied, "Hell no. Some of my best friends are women. I don't care if my brother marries one. Har, har." A "windshield survey" of the Hacker Cab Company at shift-changing times reveals an almost total absence of women drivers. It is common knowledge that there is a heavy turnover in the cab-driving business.

How would you analyze this case based on the law of individual disparate treatment discrimination as you understand it?

NOTE ON INTERNATIONAL AND COMPARATIVE ANTIDISCRIMINATION LAW

One of the enduring questions of labor and employment law as viewed from a global perspective is whether national laws dealing with labor and employment are converging, diverging or some of both. As you read the notes on international and comparative antidiscrimination law in this and subsequent chapters, keep that question in mind. For a general treatise on international and comparative law, *see* INTERNATIONAL LABOR AND EMPLOYMENT LAWS (William L. Keller & Timothy J. Darby, 2d ed. 2003), a two-volume set with relatively frequent updates published by the ABA Section on Labor and Employment Law. For a casebook, *see* ROGER BLAN-PAIN, SUSAN BISOM-RAPP, WILLIAM R. CORBETT, HILARY K. JOSEPHS & MICHAEL J. ZIMMER, THE GLOBAL WORKPLACE: INTERNATIONAL AND COMPARATIVE EMPLOY-MENT LAW — *CASES AND MATERIALS* (2007) ("BLANPAIN, THE GLOBAL WORKPLACE").

1. *Background Norms.* Just as employment discrimination in the United States must be understood in the context of the background at-will norm for most employees, so also must the application of international and national antidiscrimination principles be understood in the light of the fundamentally different approach to employment of many other countries. While Canada has a modified at-will rule of job security requiring the employer to provide a reasonable notice period before terminating an employee, the member states of the EU and Mexico provide job security so that employers have to have very good reasons to terminate employees. The difference between a regime of at-will employment and for-cause employment fundamentally alters when antidiscrimination claims are brought. Rather than having to prove the employer discriminated against her because of her sex, a worker in such countries is protected unless the employer can prove it has a legally justified reason for its action. Thus, unlike the U.S., discrimination claims in these other countries tend to arise not in the discharge context but rather for failure to hire or promote. *See generally* Joseph Slater, *The American Rule That Swallows the Exceptions*, http://papers/ssrn.com.

2. *International Antidiscrimination Law.* The International Labor Organization, originally part of the League of Nations, became an arm of the United Nations following World War II. ILO member nations each send a three-person delegation to the ILO representing the government, its employers and its workers, and the ILO promulgates international standards — generally by Conventions — for implementation by its member nations.

As to discrimination, the ILO's Philadelphia Declaration of 1944 included in its statement of its aims and purposes that "all human beings, irrespective of race, creed or sex, have the right to pursue both their material well-being and their spiritual development in conditions of freedom and dignity, of economic security and equal opportunity." Declaration Concerning the Aims and Purposes of the International Labour Organization, ILO Constitution, *as amended*, Oct 9, 1946, Annex, 62 *Stat.* 3485, 15 U.N.T.S. 35. In response to the decision of the World Trade Organization that labor standards were not within its jurisdiction, the ILO issued a new Declaration in 1998 focusing on four fundamental principles, including "the elimination of discrimination in respect of employment and occupation." ILO Declaration on Fundamental Principles and Rights at Work, adopted June 18, 1998, 37 I.L.M. 1233 (1998).

Convention 100, adopted in 1953, establishes an equal pay for equal work standard: "Each Member shall, by means appropriate to the methods in operation for determining rates of remuneration, promote and, in so far as is consistent with such methods, ensure the application to all workers of the principle of equal remuneration for men and women workers for work of equal value." Convention 111, adopted in 1958, expands that obligation: "to declare and pursue a national policy designed to promote, by methods appropriate to national conditions and practice, equality of opportunity and treatment in respect of employment and occupation, with a view to eliminating any discrimination in respect thereof." Discrimination is defined in Article 1 to include:

(a) any distinction, exclusion or preference made on the basis of race, colour, sex, religion, political opinion, national extraction or social origin, which has the effect of nullifying or impairing equality of opportunity or treatment in employment or occupation;

(b) such other distinction, exclusion or preference which has the effect of nullifying or impairing equality of opportunity or treatment in employment or occupation as may be determined by the Member concerned after consultation with representative employers' and workers' organisations, where such exist, and with other appropriate bodies.

2. Any distinction, exclusion or preference in respect of a particular job based on the inherent requirements thereof shall not be deemed to be discrimination.

While the United States has enacted the equal pay for equal work requirement in the Equal Pay Act, 29 U.S.C. § 206 (2007), and has generally proscribed discrimination by Title VII and other statutes, it has not ratified these basic conventions. However, the 1998 Declaration provides that "all Members, even if they have not ratified the Conventions in question, have an obligation arising from the very fact of membership in the Organization, to respect, to promote and to realize, [the fundamental principles] in good faith and in accordance with the Constitution."

Another international approach to discrimination is found in the labor-side accord to NAFTA, the North American Agreement on Labor Cooperation (NAALC), which commits the three North American countries — Canada, Mexico and the U.S. — to enforce their respective national laws regarding eleven different labor principles. Principle 7 deals with employment discrimination: "Elimination of employment discrimination on such grounds as race, religion, age, sex or other grounds, subject to certain reasonable exceptions, such as, where applicable *bona fide* occupational requirements or qualifications and established practices or rules governing retirement ages, and special measures of protection or assistance for particular groups designed to take into account the effects of discrimination." Principle 8 provides for, "Equal wages for women and men by applying the principle of equal pay for equal work in the same establishment."

3. *The European Union.* The EU has been the driving force for its now 27 member nations to expand worker protection against discrimination. It began with the protection of equal rights for women in Article 119 of the original Treaty. Article 13, added by the 1997 Amsterdam Treaty, empowers the EU to "take appropriate action to combat discrimination based on sex, racial or ethnic origin, religion or belief, disability, age or sexual orientation." Based on that new authority, the EU has issued several Directives, which require each member state to harmonize its national laws with the requirements of the Directives.

Directive 2002/73/EC defines sex discrimination broadly to include harassment and sexual harassment as well as "direct" and "indirect" discrimination. Direct discrimination is framed like U.S. law disparate treatment: "where one person is treated less favourably on grounds of sex than another is, has been or would be treated in a comparable situation" Indirect discrimination is what we call disparate impact discrimination: "where an apparently neutral provision, criterion or practice would put persons of one sex at a particular disadvantage compared with persons of the other sex, unless that provision, criterion or practice is objectively justified by a legitimate aim, and the means of achieving that aim are appropriate and necessary." When the plaintiff makes out a prima facie case of direct or indirect discrimination, the burden of proof shifts to the defendant to prove that it did not discriminate. Directive 2000/43/EC requires the member nations to prohibit direct or indirect discrimination "based on racial or ethnic origin." Directive 2000/78/EC, creating a

General Equal Treatment Directive, expands the scope of antidiscrimination to include "religion or belief, disability, age or sexual orientation." BLANPAIN, THE GLOBAL WORKPLACE, at 321.

4. *Some National Antidiscrimination Laws.* In Canada, most employment regulation is by the different provinces, but federal law and the law of all the provinces "prohibit[s] discrimination on grounds of race, color, national or ethnic origin, place of origin, age, sex, marital status, physical disability, religion or creed, and mental disability." *Id.* at 186. Sexual orientation discrimination has also been banned, with the federal government and almost all the provinces having done so by statute. The Canadian Supreme Court, in interpreting the Canadian Charter of Rights and Freedoms, held that the failure of Alberta to prohibit sexual orientation discrimination was impermissibly underinclusive in light of the similarity of the problem to the other bases for prohibiting discrimination; thus, Alberta failure violated the fundamental rights of its citizens. *Vriend v. Alberta*, [1998] 1. S.C.R. 493.

The 1917 Mexican Constitution, which as amended is still in effect, established the equal pay for equal work principle: "Equal wages shall be paid for equal work, regardless of sex or nationality." The 1931 Federal Labor Law, which applies to all employment in Mexico, prohibits discrimination more broadly: "No distinction shall be established among the workers by reason of race, sex, age, religious creed, political doctrine or social condition." In 2003, federal legislation expanded the prohibition to include national or ethnic origin, disability, economic condition, health conditions, pregnancy, language, opinions and sexual preference. BLANPAIN, THE GLOBAL WORKPLACE, at 247. The laws of Mexico make it a high labor standard country. However, well over half of the workforce is estimated not to be included in the formal economy subject to the protection of those standards. *Id.* at 210. The problem of an informal economy seems to be increasing worldwide, but it is especially troublesome in the less developed countries.

India, as a developing country, still faces significant issues of discrimination based on its cultural history as well as its poverty. While the Indian Constitution provides that the "State shall not discriminate against any citizen on grounds only of race, caste, sex, place of birth or any of them" and abolishes "untouchability," BLANPAIN, THE GLOBAL WORKPLACE, at 578, the problem of the Dalits remains serious. In 2005, the ILO's Committee of Experts on the Application of Conventions and Recommendations, dealt with the failure of India to end the practice by an estimated 1 million Dalits, who are untouchables, of making their bare subsistence living by manual scavenging of public and private latrines. The ILO called for the Indian government to "step up its efforts to ensure the prompt elimination of this practice and the access of the persons involved to other, more decent, jobs." In 1984, the Indian Supreme Court challenged the practice of bonded labor in the quarrying of stone. *See Bandhua Mukti Moracha v. Union of India (The Bonded Labour Case)*, 1984 AIR 802, 1984 SCC(3) 161.

Chapter 2

Systemic Disparate Treatment Discrimination

A. INTRODUCTION

In Chapter 1, individuals challenged adverse employment decisions, requiring the courts to focus on how plaintiffs had been individually treated by defendants. Plaintiffs can also challenge employment policies or practices that sweep more broadly. Thus, an employer's policy to hire only men, to fire older workers, or to separate employees by race, gender, or age raises systemic issues. This chapter will develop systemic disparate treatment, one of the two concepts of systemic discrimination presently governing Title VII actions. 42 U.S.C.S. §§ 2000e to 2000e-17 (2007). This theory is also available under the Age Discrimination in Employment Act ("ADEA"), 29 U.S.C.S. §§ 631-634 (2007), and under 42 U.S.C.S. § 1981 (2007), *Anderson v. Fulton County, Ga.*, 207 F.3d 1303 (11th Cir. 2000). The other systemic concept, disparate impact will be considered in Chapter 3.

Systemic disparate treatment can be proven in two ways. First, the plaintiff may simply demonstrate that the employer has an announced, formal policy of discrimination. Second, the plaintiff who fails to prove a formal policy may nevertheless establish that the employer's pattern of employment decisions reveals that a practice of disparate treatment operates. Although these two methods parallel the direct and inferential proof of individual disparate treatment examined in Chapter 3, there are significant differences between the individual and systemic theories.

B. FORMAL POLICIES OF DISCRIMINATION

The employer in *Slack v. Havens*, reproduced at p. 2, violated Title VII by requiring employees to perform a cleaning job because they were black. If such a requirement is part of a policy that regularly segregates black workers into unfavorable jobs, a systemic claim of discrimination could be established. Historically, formal systems excluding women and minority group members or segregating them into inferior jobs were common. An example was the sign that appeared in a Boston window in the nineteenth century, "Irish need not apply." During much of the twentieth century, many employers, particularly in the South, segregated jobs by race, with blacks typically consigned to lower-paying, less attractive jobs. We will see, for example, in *Griggs v. Duke Power Co.*, reproduced at p. 207, that the employer formally restricted African Americans to the lowest level positions prior to the passage of Title VII. Most employers also segregated many jobs by gender, again with lower-level jobs assigned to female workers. With the passage of Title VII in 1964, most formal discriminatory policies of race or sex discrimination ended. Similarly, prior to the enactment of the Age Discrimination in Employment Act, employers frequently had formal policies explicitly discriminating on account of age. For example, policies mandating retirement at age 65 were common. In the wake of the antidiscrimination statutes, most such formal discriminatory policies have disappeared. Nevertheless, not all formal policies were rescinded without court intervention.

LOS ANGELES DEPARTMENT OF WATER & POWER v. MANHART
435 U.S. 702 (1978)

Justice STEVENS delivered the opinion of the Court.

As a class, women live longer than men. For this reason, the Los Angeles Department of Water and Power required its female employees to make larger contributions to its pension fund than its male employees. We granted certiorari to decide whether this practice discriminated against individual female employees because of their sex in violation of §703(a)(1) of the Civil Rights Act of 1964, as amended.

For many years the Department had administered retirement, disability, and death-benefit programs for its employees. Upon retirement each employee is eligible for a monthly retirement benefit computed as a fraction of his or her salary multiplied by years of service. The monthly benefits of men and women of the same age, seniority and salary are equal. Benefits are funded entirely by contributions from the employees and the Department, augmented by the income earned on those contributions. No private insurance company is involved in the administration or payment of benefits.

Based on a study of mortality tables and its own experience, the Department determined that its 2,000 female employees, on the average, will live a few years longer than its 10,000 male employees. The cost of a pension for the average retired female is greater than for the average male retiree because more monthly payments must be made to the average woman. The Department therefore required female employees to make monthly contributions to the fund which were 14.84% higher than the contributions required of comparable male employees. Because employee contributions were withheld from paychecks, a female employee took home less pay than a male employee earning the same salary.[5] . . .

I

There are both real and fictional differences between women and men. It is true that the average man is taller than the average woman; it is not true that the average woman driver is more accident prone than the average man. Before the Civil Rights Act of 1964 was enacted, an employer could fashion his personnel policies on the basis of assumptions about the differences between men and women, whether or not the assumptions were valid.

It is now well recognized that employment decisions cannot be predicated on mere "stereotyped" impressions about the characteristics of males or females. Myths and purely habitual assumptions about a woman's inability to perform certain kinds of work are no longer acceptable reasons for refusing to employ qualified individuals, or for paying them less. This case does not, however, involve a fictional difference between men and women. It involves a generalization that the parties accept as unquestionably true: Women, as a class, do live longer than men. The Department treated its women employees differently from its men employees because the two classes are in fact different. It is equally true, however, that all individuals in the respective classes do not share the characteristic that differentiates the average class representatives. Many women do not live as long as the average man and many men outlive the average woman. The question, therefore, is whether the existence or nonexistence of "discrimination" is to be determined by comparison of class characteristics or individual characteristics. A "stereotyped" answer to that question may not be the same as the answer that the language and purpose of the statute command.

The statute makes it unlawful "to discriminate against any *individual* with respect to his compensation, terms, conditions, or privileges of employment, because of such *individual's* race, color, religion, sex, or national origin (emphasis added). The statute's focus on the individual is unambiguous. It precludes treatment of individuals as simply components of a racial, religious, sexual, or national class. If height is required for a job, a tall woman may not be refused employment merely because, on the average, women are too short. Even a true generalization about the class is an insufficient reason for disqualifying an individual to whom the generalization does not apply.

That proposition is of critical importance in this case because there is no assurance that any individual woman working for the Department will actually fit the generalization on which the Department's policy is based. Many of those individuals will not live as long as the average man. While they were working, those individuals received smaller paychecks because of their sex, but they will receive no compensating advantage when they retire.

It is true, of course, that while contributions are being collected from the employees, the Department cannot know which individuals will predecease the average woman. Therefore, unless women as a class are assessed an extra charge, they will be

---

5. The significance of the disparity is illustrated by the record of one woman whose contributions to the fund (including interest on the amount withheld each month) amounted to $18,171.40; a similarly situated male would have contributed only $12,843.53.

subsidized, to some extent, by the class of male employees.[14] It follows, according to the Department, that fairness to its class of male employees justifies the extra assessment against all of its female employees.

But the question of fairness to various classes affected by the statute is essentially a matter of policy for the legislature to address. Congress has decided that classifications based on sex, like those based on national origin or race, are unlawful. Actuarial studies could unquestionably identify differences in life expectancy based on race or national origin, as well as sex.[15] But a statute that was designed to make race irrelevant in the employment market could not reasonably be construed to permit a take-home-pay differential based on a racial classification.

Even if the statutory language were less clear, the basic policy of the statute requires that we focus on fairness to individuals rather than fairness to classes. Practices that classify employees in terms of religion, race, or sex tend to preserve traditional assumptions about groups rather than thoughtful scrutiny of individuals. The generalization involved in this case illustrates the point. Separate mortality tables are easily interpreted as reflecting innate differences between the sexes; but a significant part of the longevity differential may be explained by the social fact that men are heavier smokers than women.

Finally, there is no reason to believe that Congress intended a special definition of discrimination in the context of employee group insurance coverage. It is true that insurance is concerned with events that are individually unpredictable, but that is characteristic of many employment decisions. Individual risks, like individual performance, may not be predicted by resort to classifications proscribed by Title VII. Indeed, the fact that this case involves a group insurance program highlights a basic flaw in the Department's fairness argument. For when insurance risks are grouped, the better risks always subsidize the poorer risks. Healthy persons subsidize medical benefits for the less healthy; unmarried workers subsidize the pensions of married workers;[18] persons who eat, drink, or smoke to excess may subsidize pension benefits for persons whose habits are more temperate. Treating different classes of risks as though they were the same for purposes of group insurance is a common practice that has never been considered inherently unfair. To insure the flabby and the fit as though they were equivalent risks may be more common than treating men and women alike;[19] but nothing more than habit makes one "subsidy" seem less fair than the other.[20]

14. The size of the subsidy involved in this case is open to doubt, because the Department's plan provides for survivor's benefits. Since female spouses of male employees are likely to have greater life expectancies than the male spouses of female employees, whatever benefits men lose in "primary" coverage for themselves, they may regain in "secondary" coverage for their wives.

15. For example, the life expectancy of a white baby in 1973 was 72.2 years; a nonwhite baby could expect to live 65.9 years, a difference of 6.3 years. See Public Health Service, IIA Vital Statistics of the United States 1973, Table 5-3.

18. A study of life expectancy in the United States for 1949-1951 showed that 20-year-old men could expect to live to 60.6 years of age if they were divorced. If married, they could expect to reach 70.9 years of age, a difference of more than 10 years. Id., at 93.

19. The record indicates, however, that the Department has funded its death-benefit plan by equal contributions from male and female employees. A death benefit — unlike a pension benefit — has less value for persons with longer life expectancies. Under the Department's concept of fairness, then, this neutral funding of death benefits is unfair to women as a class.

20. A variation on the Department's fairness theme is the suggestion that a gender-neutral pension plan would itself violate Title VII because of its disproportionately heavy impact on male employees. Cf. *Griggs v. Duke Power Co.* This suggestion has no force in the sex discrimination context because each retiree's total pension benefits are ultimately determined by his actual life span; any differential in benefits paid to men and women in the aggregate is thus "based on [a] factor other than sex," and

An employment practice that requires 2,000 individuals to contribute more money into a fund than 10,000 other employees simply because each of them is a woman, rather than a man, is in direct conflict with both the language and the policy of the Act. Such a practice does not pass the simple test of whether the evidence shows "treatment of a person in a manner which but for that person's sex would be different." It constitutes discrimination and is unlawful unless exempted by the Equal Pay Act of 1963 or some other affirmative justification.

III . . .

[T]he Department argues that the absence of a discriminatory effect on women as a class justifies an employment practice which, on its face, discriminated against individual employees because of their sex. But even if the Department's actuarial evidence is sufficient to prevent plaintiffs from establishing a prima facie case on the theory that the effect of the practice on women as a class was discriminatory, that evidence does not defeat the claim that the practice, on its face, discriminated against every individual woman employed by the Department.[30]

In essence, the Department is arguing that the prima facie showing of discrimination based on evidence of different contributions for the respective sexes is rebutted by its demonstration that there is a like difference in the cost of providing benefits for the respective classes. That argument might prevail if Title VII contained a cost-justification defense comparable to the affirmative defense available in a price discrimination suit. But neither Congress nor the courts have recognized such a defense under Title VII.

Although we conclude that the Department's practice violated Title VII, we do not suggest that the statute was intended to revolutionize the insurance and pension industries. All that is at issue today is a requirement that men and women make unequal contributions to an employer-operated pension fund. Nothing in our holding implies that it would be unlawful for an employer to set aside equal retirement contributions for each employee and let each retiree purchase the largest benefit which his or her accumulated contributions could command in the open market.[33] Nor does it call into question the insurance industry practice of

---

consequently immune from challenge under the Equal Pay Act, 29 U.S.C. § 206(d). Even under Title VII itself — assuming disparate-impact analysis applies to fringe benefits, cf. *Nashville Gas Co. v. Satty*, 434 U.S. 136, 144-145 — the male employees would not prevail. Even a completely neutral practice will inevitably have some disproportionate impact on one group or another. *Griggs* does not imply, and this Court has never held, that discrimination must always be inferred from such consequences.

30. Some amici suggest that the Department's discrimination is justified by business necessity. They argue that, if no gender distinction is drawn, many male employees will withdraw from the plan, or even the Department, because they can get a better pension plan in the private market. But the Department has long required equal contributions to its death-benefit plan, and since 1975 it has required equal contributions to its pension plan. Yet the Department points to no "adverse selection" by the affected employees, presumably because an employee who wants to leave the plan must also leave his job, and few workers will quit because one of their fringe benefits could theoretically be obtained at a marginally lower price on the open market. In short, there has been no showing that sex distinctions are reasonably necessary to the normal operation of the Department's retirement plan.

33. Title VII and the Equal Pay Act primarily govern relations between employees and their employer, not between employees and third parties. We do not suggest, of course, that an employer can avoid its responsibilities by delegating discriminatory programs to corporate shells. Title VII applies to "any agent" of a covered employer, 42 U.S.C. § 2000e(b), and the Equal Pay Act applies to "any person acting directly or indirectly in the interest of an employer in relation to an employee." 29 U.S.C. § 206(d). In this case, for example, the Department could not deny that the administrative board was its agent after it successfully argued that the two were so inseparable that both shared the city's immunity from suit under 42 U.S.C. § 1983.

considering the composition of an employer's work force in determining the probable cost of a retirement or death benefit plan.[34] Finally, we recognize that in a case of this kind it may be necessary to take special care in fashioning appropriate relief. . . .

NOTES

1. *"Facial Discrimination."* The employer's plan in *Manhart* did not explicitly say that women with the same salary as men would receive a lower take-home pay. The policy of discrimination becomes clear, however, by comparing the different contribution rates for men and women. There was probably a document reflecting that decision. Is that showing the equivalent of admissions in individual disparate treatment cases, such as in *Slack* and *Price Waterhouse?*

2. *Why Did the City Discriminate?* Why would the city adopt a facially discriminatory plan? First, it may have believed that, although the plan technically discriminated on gender grounds, no court would find it to be sex discrimination. Second, whether or not it is sex discrimination, the city may have believed that it fit within a statutory exception. Third, the plan may predate Title VII and the city may have never reviewed it once Title VII became effective.

3. *Is Sex Discrimination Always Actionable?* The first possibility is not as far-fetched as one might think. Sex distinctions in employer dress and grooming codes generally have been held not to constitute illegal sex discrimination under Title VII when they treat male and female employees separately, but equally. See p. 347. We also will encounter racial and gender preferences that sometimes are permissible under Title VII as part of valid affirmative action plans. See p. 183.

Why might the city have thought that the gender distinction would not be viewed as discriminatory? While it seems unfair to women to receive less take-home pay than men paid the same salary, women, as a group, will receive more months of retirement pay because, as a group, they live longer than men. In group terms, lower monthly salary is offset by more months of coverage. But an individual female may get the short end of the stick: if she does not live as long as predicted, she will receive less pay each month she works but will not be compensated by more months of coverage when retired. While insurance risks are, individually, unpredictable, this woman's disadvantage results solely from her sex. This might have led the city to have hoped that the courts would accept what the Court termed a "cost justification" defense. While such a defense is not written into the statute, is it so unlikely that the courts would recognize one judicially, at least in extreme cases? Should the courts recognize a cost justification defense? We will see that, where age is concerned, the ADEA has a kind of cost justification for fringe benefits. See p. 483.

4. *A BFOQ?* Even if the conduct was sex discrimination and otherwise actionable, we have seen that Title VII offers a statutory defense, the bona fide occupational qualification ("BFOQ"). Because the employer concededly used gender to classify pension contributions, why couldn't it claim a BFOQ defense? In *Trans World*

---

34. Title VII bans discrimination against an "individual" because of "such individual's" sex, 42 U.S.C. § 2000e-2(a)(1). The Equal Pay Act prohibits discrimination "within any establishment," and discrimination is defined as "paying wages to employees . . . at a rate less than the rate at which [the employer] pays wages to employees of the opposite sex" for equal work. 29 U.S.C. § 206(d)(1). Neither of these provisions makes it unlawful to determine the funding requirements for an establishment's benefit plan by considering the composition of the entire force.

Airlines, Inc. v. Thurston, 469 U.S. 111 (1985), plaintiffs challenged a rule that discriminated on the basis of age for transfer from pilot to flight engineer jobs: Pilots forced to retire by the FAA age 60 rule could not "bump" down into the flight engineer job, while those disqualified for any other reason could bump and continue as flight engineers past age 60. The Court held that the BFOQ in the ADEA did not apply: "TWA's discriminatory transfer policy is not permissible under §4(f)(1) because age is not a BFOQ for the 'particular' position of flight engineer." *Id.* at 122. Similarly, all women workers in *Manhart* were the victims of the sex discrimination, without regard to the particular jobs they performed or their abilities. See p. 171.

5. *Does Discrimination Require Animus or Stereotype?* Perhaps the city thought it could not be guilty of sex discrimination because it was motivated neither by animus nor by a desire to disadvantage women. The city merely used gender as a proxy for longevity. That might be called a stereotype, but, if so, it's one of those "true" stereotypes — one that's accurate across the genders although not true of every woman. Is that disparate treatment? *Manhart* tells us the answer is yes. While that decision about intent makes the city's actual motivation irrelevant, perhaps the city did "intend" to disadvantage women. The city did not use sex-segregated life expectancy tables to set contribution levels for life insurance. Because women live longer than men, sex-based tables would have resulted in lower premiums for women. If it truly wanted to treat the sexes equally, why wasn't the employer consistent? Perhaps the city viewed its male employees as the norm, both for pensions and life insurance. A number of commentators have noted the existence of male norms and white norms — the white male is unconsciously viewed as the baseline, with departures having to be justified. See p. 458.

6. *Disparate Treatment to Avoid Disparate Impact?* The city might also have hoped to convince the courts that its conduct was not discriminatory by arguing that it was damned if it did and damned if it didn't: (a) by requiring females to make larger contributions than males, disparate treatment discrimination is established; (b) if equal contributions were collected from all employees, retired women as a group would collect more than retired men as a group, thereby creating an adverse impact on males. How did the Court avoid this dilemma? Does footnote 20 help? This question is further discussed in Chapter 4 at pp. 315-16.

7. *The Equal Pay Act and the Bennett Amendment.* Title VII is not the only federal statute dealing with sex discrimination in employment. A much narrower enactment, the Equal Pay Act of 1963, 29 U.S.C.S. §206(d) (2007), bars discrimination in pay on account of sex where members of each gender are doing "equal work." The Bennett Amendment to Title VII makes discrimination authorized by the Equal Pay Act legal under Title VII. The city might have hoped to bring its plan within the EPA provision allowing differentials based on a factor "other than sex." But how can something that is sex discrimination under Title VII be "other than sex" within the EPA?

8. *"Bullet-Proofing" Employers' Policies.* Well-represented employers should no longer have express policies that discriminate because all of their policies should be regularly reviewed by counsel. Any that involve explicit classifications based on race, sex, age, etc., should be reviewed carefully to determine if they are nevertheless legal. That sometimes may be a bit tricky to establish. In *Thurston*, the age classifier came into the picture because the FAA requires that pilots, but not flight engineers, retire at age 60. The airline allowed pilots, who became disqualified for that job for any reason other than the age 60 rule, to bump down into the flight engineer job, which

had no FAA-mandated age cap. Only once the interaction of these different rules became clear, did the age discrimination also become clear.

9. *Partial Remedy Only. Manhart* established that gender-explicit classifications in pension *contributions* violate Title VII. Some of the questions left unanswered by *Manhart* were resolved in *Arizona Governing Committee v. Norris*, 463 U.S. 1073 (1983), holding that Title VII was violated by offering women lower monthly retirement *benefits* than men who contributed the same amount. The *Norris* Court first applied *Manhart*: "We conclude that it is just as much discrimination 'because of . . . sex' to pay a woman lower benefits when she has made the same contributions as a man as it is to make her pay larger contributions to obtain the same benefits." *Id.* at 1086. A different majority decided that only retirement benefits attributed to contributions made after the date of the decision had to be calculated without regard to the gender of the beneficiary. That limitation of remedies insulated all of the earlier unlawful pay discrimination. Why should the victims of defendant's discrimination be made only partially whole? See p. 656.

10. *Effect on Insurance Annuities.* A twist in *Norris* was the defendant's argument that it was not responsible for the discrimination: the employer collected employee contributions, but the plan was administered and all benefits paid by private insurance companies. The employer argued that it acted within the language in *Manhart* suggesting that an employer would not be liable if it set aside contributions and paid them in a lump sum upon retirement. The defendant also stressed that all the available annuities sold by insurance companies used sex-segregated life expectancy tables. The Court rejected those arguments:

> Under these circumstances there can be no serious question that petitioners are legally responsible for the discriminatory terms on which annuities are offered by the companies chosen to participate in the plan. Having created a plan whereby employees can obtain the advantages of using deferred compensation to purchase an annuity only if they invest in one of the companies specifically selected by the State, the State cannot disclaim responsibility for the discriminatory features of the insurers' options.

463 U.S. at 1088-89.

11. *The Rise of the 401(k) and the Demise of Sex Neutrality.* The principle animating *Manhart* — that differentiating on the basis of a prohibited characteristic is impermissible unless within a statutory exception — remains robust. However, the actual holding of the case has diminished in importance. When *Manhart* was decided, "defined benefit" retirement plans were the norm, and, as the name suggests, such plans require employers to provide a specified level of benefits. The Department was thus faced with the damned if you do/damned if you don't problem discussed in Note 6. While such plans continue to operate to some extent, mostly in the public sector, they have largely disappeared in the private sector. Instead, employers offer "defined contribution" plans, of which the "401(k)" is the most common. Such plans in essence create individual retirement accounts for each worker, with the workers getting what has accumulated in their accounts once they retire. Employers can make equal contributions for all workers, usually a percentage of income. Will women seeking to buy an annuity with their accumulated contributions face sex-segregated mortality labels? The answer seems clearly yes. Accordingly, the plaintiffs in *Manhart* won the battle but may have lost the war as to retirement benefits. However, women at least have the individual choice to take an annuity. And the *Manhart* decision may deter employers who might have offered other benefits — such as health insurance — on a gender-differentiated basis.

C. PATTERNS AND PRACTICES OF DISCRIMINATION

TEAMSTERS v. UNITED STATES
431 U.S. 324 (1977)

Justice STEWART delivered the opinion of the Court.

. . . I

[The United States brought two actions, which were consolidated for trial. The first was against T.I.M.E.-D.C., charging discriminatory hiring, assignment, and promotion policies against Negroes at its Nashville terminal in violation of §707(a). The second action against the company charged a pattern and practice of employment discrimination against Negroes and Spanish-surnamed persons throughout the company's transportation system. The International Brotherhood of Teamsters union was also named a defendant.]

The central claim in both lawsuits was that the company had engaged in a pattern or practice of discriminating against minorities in hiring so-called line drivers. Those Negroes and Spanish-surnamed persons who had been hired, the Government alleged, were given lower paying, less desirable jobs as servicemen or local city drivers, and were thereafter discriminated against with respect to promotions and transfers.[3] . . .

II . . .

A

Consideration of the question whether the company engaged in a pattern or practice of discriminatory hiring practices involves controlling legal principles that are relatively clear. The Government's theory of discrimination was simply that the company, in violation of §703(a) of Title VII, regularly and purposefully treated Negroes and Spanish-surnamed Americans less favorably than white persons. The disparity in treatment allegedly involved the refusal to recruit, hire, transfer, or promote minority group members on an equal basis with white people, particularly with respect to line-driving positions. The ultimate factual issues are thus simply whether there was a pattern or practice of such disparate treatment and, if so, whether the differences were "racially premised." *McDonnell Douglas Corp. v. Green.*[15]

---

3. Line drivers, also known as over-the-road drivers, engage in long-distance hauling between company terminals. They compose a separate bargaining unit at the company. Other distinct bargaining units include servicemen, who service trucks, unhook tractors and trailers, and perform similar tasks; and city operations, composed of dockmen, hostlers, and city drivers who pick up and deliver freight within the immediate area of a particular terminal. . . .

15. "Disparate treatment" such as is alleged in the present case is the most easily understood type of discrimination. The employer simply treats some people less favorably than others because of their race, color, religion, sex, or national origin. Proof of discriminatory motive is critical, although it can in some situations be inferred from the mere fact of differences in treatment. See, e.g., *Arlington Heights v. Metropolitan Housing Dev. Corp.*, 429 U.S. 252, 265-266. Undoubtedly disparate treatment was the most obvious evil Congress had in mind when it enacted Title VII. See, e.g., 110 Cong. Rec. 13088 (1964) (remarks of Sen. Humphrey) ("What the bill does . . . is simply to make it an illegal practice to use race as a factor in denying employment. It provides that men and women shall be employed on the basis of

As the plaintiff, the Government bore the initial burden of making out a prima facie case of discrimination. *Albemarle Paper Co. v. Moody*, 422 U.S. 405, 425; *McDonnell Douglas Corp. v. Green*. And, because it alleged a systemwide pattern or practice of resistance to the full enjoyment of Title VII rights, the Government ultimately had to prove more than the mere occurrence of isolated or "accidental" or sporadic discriminatory acts. It had to establish by a preponderance of the evidence that racial discrimination was the Company's standard operating procedure — the regular rather than the unusual practice.[16]

We agree with the District Court and the Court of Appeals that the Government carried its burden of proof. As of March 31, 1971, shortly after the Government filed its complaint alleging systemwide discrimination, the company had 6,472 employees. Of these, 314 (5%) were Negroes and 257 (4%) were Spanish-surnamed Americans. Of the 1,828 line drivers, however, there were only 8 (0.4%) Negroes and 5 (0.3%) Spanish-surnamed persons, and all of the Negroes had been hired after the litigation had commenced. With one exception — a man who worked as a line driver at the Chicago terminal from 1950 to 1959 — the company and its predecessors did not employ a Negro on a regular basis as a line driver until 1969. And, as the Government showed, even in 1971 there were terminals in areas of substantial Negro population where all of the Company's line drivers were white.[17] A great majority of the Negroes (83%) and Spanish-surnamed Americans (78%) who did work for the company held the lower paying city operations and serviceman jobs,[18] whereas only 39% of the nonminority employees held jobs in those categories.

The Government bolstered its statistical evidence with the testimony of individuals who recounted over 40 specific instances of discrimination. Upon the basis of his testimony the District Court found that "[n]umerous qualified black and Spanish-surnamed American applicants who sought line driving jobs at the company over the years had either their requests ignored, were given false or misleading information about requirements, opportunities, and application procedures, or were not considered and hired on the same basis that whites were considered and hired."

their qualifications, not as Catholic citizens, not as Protestant citizens, not as Jewish citizens, not as colored citizens, but as citizens of the United States.").

Claims of disparate treatment may be distinguished from claims that stress "disparate impact." The latter involve employment practices that are facially neutral in their treatment of different groups but that in fact fall more harshly on one group than another and cannot be justified by business necessity. Proof of discriminatory motive, we have held, is not required under a disparate-impact theory. Compare, e.g., *Griggs v. Duke Power Co.*, with *McDonnell Douglas Corp. v. Green*. See generally B. Schlei & P. Grossman, Employment Discrimination Law 1-12 (1976); Blumrosen, Strangers in Paradise: Griggs v. Duke Power Co. and the Concept of Employment Discrimination, 71 Mich. L. Rev. 59 (1972). Either theory may, of course, be applied to a particular set of facts.

16. The "pattern or practice" language in § 707(a) of Title VII was not intended as a term of art, and the words reflect only their usual meaning. . . .

17. In Atlanta, for instance, Negroes composed 22.35% of the population in the surrounding metropolitan area and 51.3% of the population in the city proper. The company's Atlanta terminal employed 57 line drivers. All were white. In Los Angeles, 10.84% of the greater metropolitan population and 17.88% of the city population were Negro. But at the company's two Los Angeles terminals there was not a single Negro among the 374 line drivers. The proof showed similar disparities in San Francisco, Denver, Nashville, Chicago, Dallas, and at several other terminals.

18. Although line-driver jobs pay more than other jobs, and the District Court found them to be "considered the most desirable of the driving jobs," it is by no means clear that all employees, even driver employees, would prefer to be line drivers. Of course, Title VII provides for equal opportunity to compete for any job, whether it is thought better or worse than another.

Minority employees who wanted to transfer to line-driver jobs met with similar difficulties.[19]

The company's principal response to this evidence is that statistics can never in and of themselves prove the existence of a pattern or practice of discrimination, or even establish a prima facie case shifting to the employer the burden of rebutting the inference raised by the figures. But, as even our brief summary of the evidence shows, this was not a case in which the Government relied on "statistics alone." The individuals who testified about their personal experiences with the company brought the cold numbers convincingly to life.

In any event, our cases make it unmistakably clear that "[s]tatistical analyses have served and will continue to serve an important role" in cases in which the existence of discrimination is a disputed issue. *Mayor of Philadelphia v. Educational Equality League*, 415 U.S. 605, 620. See also *McDonnell Douglas Corp. v. Green*. Cf. *Washington v. Davis*, 426 U.S. 229, 241-242. We have repeatedly approved the use of statistical proof, where it reached proportions comparable to those in this case, to establish a prima facie case of racial discrimination in jury selection cases, see, e.g., *Turner v. Fouche*, 396 U.S. 346; *Hernandez v. Texas*, 347 U.S. 475; *Norris v. Alabama*, 294 U.S. 587. Statistics are equally competent in proving employment discrimination.[20] We caution only that statistics are not irrefutable; they come in

---

19. Two examples are illustrative: George Taylor, a Negro, worked for the company as a city driver in Los Angeles, beginning late in 1966. In 1968, after hearing that a white city driver had transferred to a line-driver job, he told the terminal manager that he also would like to consider line driving. The manager replied that there would be "a lot of problems on the road . . . with different people, Caucasian, et cetera," and stated: "I don't feel that the company is ready for this right now. . . . Give us a little time. It will come around, you know." Mr. Taylor made similar requests some months later and got similar responses. He was never offered a line-driving job or an application. Feliberto Trujillo worked as a dockman at the company's Denver terminal. When he applied for a line-driver job in 1967, he was told by a personnel officer that he had one strike against him. He asked what that was and was told: "You're a Chicano, and as far as we know, there isn't a Chicano driver in the system."

20. Petitioners argue that statistics, at least those comparing the racial composition of an employer's work force to the composition of the population at large, should never be given decisive weight in a Title VII case because to do so would conflict with §703(j) of the Act. That section provides:

> Nothing contained in this subchapter shall be interpreted to require any employer . . . to grant preferential treatment to any individual or to any group because of the race . . . or national origin of such individual or group on account of an imbalance which may exist with respect to the total number or percentage of persons of any race . . . or national origin employed by any employer . . . in comparison with the total number or percentage of persons of such race . . . or national origin in any community, State, section, or other area, or in the available work force in any community, State, section, or other area.

The argument fails in this case because the statistical evidence was not offered or used to support an erroneous theory that Title VII requires an employer's work force to be racially balanced. Statistics showing racial or ethnic imbalance are probative in a case such as this one only because such imbalance is often a telltale sign of purposeful discrimination; absent explanation, it is ordinarily to be expected that nondiscriminatory hiring practices will in time result in a work force more or less representative of the racial and ethnic composition of the population in the community from which employees are hired. Evidence of longlasting and gross disparity between the composition of a work force and that of the general population thus may be significant even though §703(j) makes clear that Title VII imposes no requirement that a work force mirror the general population. See, e.g., *United States v. Sheet Metal Workers Local 36*, 416 F.2d 123, 127 n.7 (C.A. 8). Considerations such as small sample size may, of course, detract from the value of such evidence, see, e.g., *Mayor of Philadelphia v. Educational Equality League*, 415 U.S. 605, 620-621, and evidence showing that the figures for the general population might not accurately reflect that pool of qualified job applicants would also be relevant. Ibid. See generally Schlei & Grossman, supra, n.15, at 1161-1193.

"Since the passage of the Civil Rights Act of 1964, the courts have frequently relied upon statistical evidence to prove a violation. . . . In many cases the only available avenue of proof is the use of racial statistics to uncover clandestine and covert discrimination by the employer or union involved." *United States v. Ironworkers Local 86*, 443 F.2d, at 551.

infinite variety and, like any other kind of evidence, they may be rebutted. In short, their usefulness depends on all of the surrounding facts and circumstances.

In addition to its general protest against the use of statistics in Title VII cases, the company claims that in this case the statistics revealing racial imbalance are misleading because they fail to take into account the company's particular business situation as of the effective date of Title VII. The company concedes that its line drivers were virtually all white in July 1965, but it claims that thereafter business conditions were such that its work force dropped. Its argument is that low personnel turnover, rather than post-Act discrimination, accounts for more recent statistical disparities. It points to substantial minority hiring in later years, especially after 1971, as showing that any pre-Act patterns of discrimination were broken.

The argument would be a forceful one if this were an employer who, at the time of suit, had done virtually no new hiring since the effective date of Title VII. But it is not. Although the company's total number of employees apparently dropped somewhat during the late 1960s, the record shows that many line drivers continued to be hired throughout this period, and that almost all of them were white.[21] To be sure, there were improvements in the company's hiring practices. The Court of Appeals commented that "T.I.M.E.-D.C.'s recent minority hiring progress stands as a laudable good faith effort to eradicate the effects of past discrimination in the area of hiring and initial assignment."[22]

But the District Court and the Court of Appeals found upon substantial evidence that the Company had engaged in a course of discrimination that continued well after the effective date of Title VII. The company's later changes in its hiring and promotion policies could be of little comfort to the victims of the earlier post-Act discrimination, and could not erase its previous illegal conduct or its obligation to afford relief to those who suffered because of it.[23]

The District Court and the Court of Appeals, on the basis of substantial evidence, held that the Government had proved a prima facie case of systematic and purposeful employment discrimination, continuing well beyond the effective date of

21. Between July 2, 1965, and January 1, 1969, hundreds of line drivers were hired systemwide, either from the outside or from the ranks of employees filling other jobs within the company. None was a Negro.

22. For example, in 1971 the company hired 116 new line drivers, of whom 16% were Negro or Spanish-surnamed Americans. Minority employees composed 7.1% of the company's systemwide work force in 1967 and 10.5% in 1972. Minority hiring increased greatly in 1972 and 1973, presumably due at least in part to the existence of the consent decree.

23. The company's narrower attacks upon the statistical evidence — that there was no precise delineation of the areas referred to in the general population statistics, that the Government did not demonstrate that minority populations were located closer to terminals or that transportation was available, that the statistics failed to show what portion of the minority population was suited by age, health, or other qualifications to hold trucking jobs, etc — are equally lacking in force. At best, these attacks go only to the accuracy of the comparison between the composition of the company's work force at various terminals and the general population of the surrounding communities. They detract little from the Government's further showing that Negroes and Spanish-surnamed Americans who were hired were overwhelmingly excluded from line-driver jobs. Such employees were willing to work, had access to the terminal, were healthy and of working age, and often were at least sufficiently qualified to hold city-driver jobs. Yet they became line drivers with far less frequency than whites. (Of 2,919 whites who held driving jobs in 1971, 1,802 (62%) were line drivers and 1,117 (38%) were city drivers; of 180 Negroes and Spanish-surnamed Americans who held driving jobs, 13 (7%) were line drivers and 167 (93%) were city drivers.) In any event, fine tuning of the statistics could not have obscured the glaring absence of minority line drivers. As the Court of Appeals remarked, the company's inability to rebut the inference of discrimination came not from a misuse of statistics but from "the inexorable zero."

Title VII. The company's attempts to rebut that conclusion were held to be inadequate.[24] For the reasons we have summarized, there is no warrant for this Court to disturb the findings of the District Court and the Court of Appeals on this basic issue. . . .

NOTES

1. *Proving a Pattern or Practice Case.* The Department of Justice, which at the time had authority now vested in the EEOC to bring "pattern or practice" cases, used a "snapshot" of the defendant's employment statistics as of one particular day, March 31, 1971. Evidence of "over 40 specific instances of discrimination" was also relied upon. Assuming that evidence was believed and defendant did not introduce any rebuttal evidence, why does that establish that "racial discrimination was the Company's standard operating procedure — the regular rather than the unusual practice?" Why does statistical evidence prove discriminatory intent? If a plaintiff's evidence simply proved that over 99% of underground coal miners were men, would that establish a prima facie case? Look at footnotes 20 and 23 for the rationale for the use of comparative statistics.

Probability theory drives the use of statistics to prove systemic disparate treatment. Plaintiff proves systemic disparate treatment by showing that members of a particular group, such as African Americans, Latinos, or women are underrepresented in the employer's workforce. "Underrepresentation," in turn, means that there are fewer of such individuals than we would expect if the employer chose his workers without regard to race, national origin, or sex. Underrepresentation is a meaningless concept unless plaintiff establishes the percentage of such individuals who would be employed absent such discrimination. If the plaintiff does that, however, the inference is that the employer is excluding such groups. Even then, to be guilty of disparate treatment discrimination, the employer must be doing so intentionally. A final question, then, is whether hiring results like those in *Teamsters* also show the intent required.

What role does the anecdotal evidence described in footnote 19 play? Coupled with the statistical data, it certainly suggests that discrimination is the explanation for underrepresentation. But is such evidence necessary to establish systemic disparate treatment or is it simply confirmatory of what the statistical evidence shows?

2. *Defendant's Rebuttal.* While rejecting defendant's broad attack on the use of statistical evidence, the Court appears to accept the possibility that defendant could rebut the government's prima facie case of systemic disparate treatment with evidence that it had not done any hiring of line drivers since Title VII became effective.

---

24. The company's evidence, apart from the showing of recent changes in hiring and promotion policies, consisted mainly of general statements that it hired only the best qualified applicants. But "affirmations of good faith in making individual selections are insufficient to dispel a prima facie case of systematic exclusion." *Alexander v. Louisiana*, 405 U.S. 625, 632.

The company also attempted to show that all of the witnesses who testified to specific instances of discrimination either were not discriminated against or suffered no injury. The Court of Appeals correctly ruled that the trial judge was not bound to accept this testimony and that it committed no error by relying instead on the other overpowering evidence in the case. The Court of Appeals was also correct in the view that individual proof concerning each class member's specific injury was appropriately left to proceedings to determine individual relief. In a suit brought by the Government under § 707(a) of the Act, the District Court's initial concern is in deciding whether the Government has proved that the defendant has engaged in a pattern or practice of discriminatory conduct.

The Court held that defendant failed to make such a showing, but suppose it had. The defendant would not have shown that it did not discriminate; rather, it would have shown that it did not discriminate after July 2, 1965, the date Title VII became effective!

How else can the defendant rebut a systemic case? The Court, in footnote 24, rejected defendant's claim that it hired "only the best qualified applicants," as an affirmation of "good faith" that would not rebut the prima facie case. The defendant also tried to introduce evidence that the workers who testified that they had been discriminated against were not in fact victims of discrimination. The Court upheld the trial court's rejection of that evidence at this stage in the case. Doesn't that mean that a defendant cannot adduce evidence that it did not discriminate against any African American or Latino applicants after the effective date of Title VII? Note, however, that, as Chapter 8, Remedies, discusses, defendants found liable for systemic disparate treatment discrimination can limit individualized relief by proving that each member of the class allegedly the victim of discrimination in fact was not discriminated against.

3. *Shifting Burdens*. This litigation structure seems very strange to one familiar with the *McDonnell Douglas* proof structure. Other than rebutting plaintiff's proof, defendant seems to have no defense. It can, at the remedies stage, try to establish that a particular individual was not the victim of discrimination, but this seems much like the "same decision anyway" defense for individual cases — defendant is guilty of discrimination, but its intent didn't harm this particular person. We will see, however, that the defendant can argue something akin to the "legitimate nondiscriminatory reason" in *McDonnell Douglas* cases: it can offer an explanation as to how the underrepresentation could have occurred if the employer were not discriminating in its hiring. Can you think of what kinds of explanation T.I.M.E.-D.C. could have offered that was more than a protestation of good faith? Note also that this is not, strictly speaking, a defense: the plaintiff bears the burden of proof of intent to discriminate, and the employer's nondiscriminatory explanation is a way to challenge the inference of intent that might otherwise be drawn from plaintiff's statistical proof.

4. *Individual vs. Systemic Cases*. *Teamsters* differs from *Manhart* in not requiring proof of a facially discriminatory policy. Is *Teamsters* to *McDonnell Douglas* as *Manhart* is to *Price Waterhouse*? The systemic theory is usually asserted either in a government enforcement action (as in *Teamsters*) or in a private class action. Given the advantages of the systemic theory, may a plaintiff bring an individual disparate treatment case but employ the systemic disparate treatment theory to obtain the advantage of the shift in burdens? See Note 3, p. 298, Chapter 4. Recall that *McDonnell Douglas* stated that systemic evidence can be used by the plaintiff in an individual disparate case to show pretext

5. *Justification for Different Approaches*. What justification is there for treating systemic cases more permissively than individual ones? Is it that we are more confident of our conclusions as to the existence of discriminatory intent when a cluster of employment decisions is involved? Put simply, one might with greater reason suspect the fairness of a coin that yielded 60 "heads" in 100 tosses than one that comes up "heads" 6 times out of 10. But perhaps even with larger numbers, the inference of intentional discrimination is not always as strong as may first appear.

6. *Easy vs. Harder Cases*. In part because discrimination in the unionized trucking industry was so notorious and pervasive, *Teamsters* presented a relatively easy statistical case of discrimination because the statistics were so stark: Virtually no

minority group members were assigned line-driver positions anywhere in the industry. What must a plaintiff do to establish a statistical case of systemic disparate treatment discrimination when the numbers are not so stark and the discriminatory reputation of the defendants not so clear?

HAZELWOOD SCHOOL DISTRICT v. UNITED STATES
433 U.S. 299 (1977)

Justice STEWART delivered the opinion of the Court.

[Hazelwood School District is in the northern part of St. Louis County, Missouri. The Attorney General sued Hazelwood, alleging a "pattern or practice" of employment discrimination in violation of Title VII.]

Hazelwood was formed from 13 rural school districts between 1949 and 1951 by a process of annexation. By the 1967-1968 school year, 17,550 students were enrolled in the district, of whom only 59 were Negro; the number of Negro pupils increased to 576 of 25,166 in 1972-1973, a total of just over 2%.

From the beginning, Hazelwood followed relatively unstructured procedures in hiring its teachers. Every person requesting an application for a teaching position was sent one, and completed applications were submitted to a central personnel office, where they were kept on file. During the early 1960s the personnel office notified all applicants whenever a teaching position became available, but as the number of applications on file increased in the late 1960s and early 1970s, this practice was no longer considered feasible. The personnel office thus began the practice of selecting anywhere from 3 to 10 applicants for interviews at the school where the vacancy existed. The personnel office did not substantively screen the applicants in determining which of them to send for interviews, other than to ascertain that each applicant, if selected, would be eligible for state certification by the time he began the job. Generally, those who had most recently submitted applications were most likely to be chosen for interviews.

Interviews were conducted by a department chairman, program coordinator, or the principal at the school where the teaching vacancy existed. Although those conducting the interviews did fill out forms rating the applicants in a number of respects, it is undisputed that each school principal possessed virtually unlimited discretion in hiring teachers for his school. The only general guidance given to the principals was to hire the "most competent" person available, and such intangibles as "personality, disposition, appearance, poise, voice, articulation, and ability to deal with people" counted heavily. The principal's choice was routinely honored by Hazelwood's Superintendent and the Board of Education.

In the early 1960s Hazelwood found it necessary to recruit new teachers, and for that purpose members of its staff visited a number of colleges and universities in Missouri and bordering States. All the institutions visited were predominantly white, and Hazelwood did not seriously recruit at either of the two predominantly Negro four-year colleges in Missouri. As a buyer's market began to develop for public school teachers, Hazelwood curtailed its recruiting efforts. For the 1971-1972 school year, 3,127 persons applied for only 234 teaching vacancies; for the 1972-1973 school year, there were 2,373 applications for 282 vacancies. A number of the applicants who were not hired were Negroes.

Hazelwood hired its first Negro teacher in 1969. The number of Negro faculty members gradually increased in successive years: 6 of 957 in the 1970 school year; 16 of 1,107 by the end of the 1972 school year; 22 of 1,231 in the 1973 school year. By comparison, according to 1970 census figures, of more than 19,000 teachers employed in that year in the St. Louis area, 15.4% were Negro. That percentage figure included the St. Louis City School District, which in recent years has followed a policy of attempting to maintain a 50% Negro teaching staff. Apart from that school district, 5.7% of the teachers in the county were Negro in 1970.

Drawing upon these historic facts, the Government mounted its "pattern or practice" attack in the District Court upon four different fronts. It adduced evidence of (1) a history of alleged racially discriminatory practices, (2) statistical disparities in hiring, (3) the standardless and largely subjective hiring procedures, and (4) specific instances of alleged discrimination against 55 unsuccessful Negro applicants for teaching jobs. Hazelwood offered virtually no additional evidence in response, relying instead on evidence introduced by the Government, perceived deficiencies in the Government's case, and its own officially promulgated policy "to hire all teachers on the basis of training, preparation and recommendations, regardless of race, color or creed."

The District Court ruled that the Government had failed to establish a pattern or practice of discrimination. The court was unpersuaded by the alleged history of discrimination, noting that no dual school system had ever existed in Hazelwood. The statistics showing that relatively small numbers of Negroes were employed as teachers were found nonprobative, on the ground that the percentage of Negro pupils in Hazelwood was similarly small. The court found nothing illegal or suspect in the teacher-hiring procedures that Hazelwood had followed. Finally, the court reviewed the evidence in the 55 cases of alleged individual discrimination, and after stating that the burden of proving intentional discrimination was on the Government, it found that this burden had not been sustained in a single instance. Hence, the court entered judgment for the defendants.

The Court of Appeals for the Eighth Circuit reversed. After suggesting that the District Court had assigned inadequate weight to evidence of discriminatory conduct on the part of Hazelwood before [March 24, 1972] the effective date of Title VII [for public employment], the Court of Appeals rejected the trial court's analysis of the statistical data as resting on an irrelevant comparison of Negro teachers to Negro pupils in Hazelwood. The proper comparison, in the appellate court's view, was one between Negro teachers in Hazelwood and Negro teachers in the relevant labor market area. Selecting St. Louis County and St. Louis City as the relevant area,[8] the Court of Appeals compared the 1970 census figures, showing that 15.4% of teachers in that area were Negro, to the racial composition of Hazelwood's teaching staff. In the 1972-1973 and 1973-1974 school years, only 1.4% and 1.8%, respectively, of Hazelwood's teachers were Negroes. This statistical disparity, particularly when viewed against the background of the teacher-hiring procedures that Hazelwood had followed, was held to constitute a prima facie case of a pattern or practice of racial discrimination.

In addition, the Court of Appeals reasoned that the trial court had erred in failing to measure the 55 instances in which Negro applicants were denied jobs against the four-part standard for establishing a prima facie case of individual discrimination set out in this Court's opinion in *McDonnell Douglas Corp. v. Green*. Applying that

---

8. The city of St. Louis is surrounded by, but not included in, St. Louis County.

standard, the appellate court found 16 cases of individual discrimination, which "buttressed" the statistical proof. Because Hazelwood had not rebutted the Government's prima facie case of a pattern or practice of racial discrimination, the Court of Appeals directed judgment for the Government. . . .

The petitioners primarily attack the judgment of the Court of Appeals for its reliance on "undifferentiated work force statistics to find an unrebutted prima facie case of employment discrimination." The question they raise, in short, is whether a basic component in the Court of Appeals' finding of a pattern or practice of discrimination — the comparatively small percentage of Negro employees on Hazelwood's teaching staff — was lacking in probative force.

This Court's recent consideration in *Teamsters v. United States* of the role of statistics in pattern-or-practice suits under Title VII provides substantial guidance in evaluating the arguments advanced by the petitioners. In that case we stated that it is the Government's burden to "establish by a preponderance of the evidence that racial discrimination was the [employer's] standard operating procedure — the regular rather than the unusual practice." We also noted that statistics can be an important source of proof in employment discrimination cases, since "absent explanation, it is ordinarily to be expected that nondiscriminatory hiring practices will in time result in a work force more or less representative of the racial and ethnic composition of the population in the community from which employees are hired. Evidence of long lasting and gross disparity between the composition of a work force and that of the general population thus may be significant even though §703(j) makes clear that Title VII imposes no requirement that a work force mirror the general population." Where gross statistical disparities can be shown, they alone may in a proper case constitute prima facie proof of a pattern or practice of discrimination. *Teamsters.*

There can be no doubt, in light of the *Teamsters* case, that the District Court's comparison of Hazelwood's teacher work force to its student population fundamentally misconceived the role of statistics in employment discrimination cases. The Court of Appeals was correct in the view that a proper comparison was between the racial composition of Hazelwood's teaching staff and the racial composition of the qualified public school teacher population in the relevant labor market.[13] See *Teamsters.* The percentage of Negroes on Hazelwood's teaching staff in 1972-1973 was 1.4%, and in 1973-1974 it was 1.8%. By contrast, the percentage of qualified

13. In *Teamsters*, the comparison between the percentage of Negroes on the employer's work force and the percentage in the general areawide population was highly probative, because the job skill there involved — the ability to drive a truck — is one that many persons possess or can fairly readily acquire. When special qualifications are required to fill particular jobs, comparisons to the general population (rather than to the smaller group of individuals who possess the necessary qualifications) may have little probative value. The comparative statistics introduced by the Government in the District Court, however, were properly limited to public school teachers, and therefore this is not a case like *Mayor v. Educational Equality League*, 415 U.S. 605 (1974), in which the racial-composition comparisons failed to take into account special qualifications for the position in question.

Although the petitioners concede as a general matter the probative force of the comparative work-force statistics, they object to the Court of Appeals' heavy reliance on these data on the ground that applicant-flow data, showing the actual percentage of white and Negro applicants for teaching positions at Hazelwood, would be firmer proof. . . . [T]here was no clear evidence of such statistics. We leave it to the District Court on remand to determine whether competent proof of those data can be adduced. If so, it would, of course, be very relevant. *Cf. Dothard v. Rawlinson* [reproduced at p. 246].

Negro teachers in the area was, according to the 1970 census, at least 5.7%.[14] Although these differences were on their face substantial, the Court of Appeals erred in substituting its judgment for that of the District Court and holding that the Government had conclusively proved its "pattern or practice" lawsuit.

The Court of Appeals totally disregarded the possibility that this prima facie statistical proof in the record might at the trial court level be rebutted by statistics dealing with Hazelwood's hiring after it became subject to Title VII. Racial discrimination by public employers was not made illegal under Title VII until March 24, 1972. A public employer who from that date forward made all its employment decisions in a wholly nondiscriminatory way would not violate Title VII even if it had formerly maintained an all-white work force by purposefully excluding Negroes. For this reason, the Court cautioned in the *Teamsters* opinion that once a prima facie case has been established by statistical work force disparities, the employer must be given an opportunity to show that "the claimed discriminatory pattern is a product of pre-Act hiring rather than unlawful post-Act discriminations."

The record in this case showed that for the 1972-1973 school year, Hazelwood hired 282 new teachers, 10 of whom (3.5%) were Negroes; for the following school year it hired 123 new teachers, 5 of whom (4.1%) were Negroes. Over the two-year period, Negroes constituted a total of 15 of the 405 new teachers hired (3.7%). Although the Court of Appeals briefly mentioned these data in reciting the facts, it wholly ignored them in discussing whether the Government had shown a pattern or practice of discrimination. And it gave no consideration at all to the possibility that post-Act data as to the number of Negroes hired compared to the total number of Negro applicants might tell a totally different story.

What the hiring figures prove obviously depends upon the figures to which they are compared. The Court of Appeals accepted the Government's argument that the relevant comparison was to the labor market area of St. Louis County and the city of St. Louis, in which, according to the 1970 census, 15.4% of all teachers were Negro. The propriety of that comparison was vigorously disputed by the petitioners, who urged that because the city of St. Louis has made special attempts to maintain a 50% Negro teaching staff, inclusion of that school district in the relevant market area distorts the comparison. Were that argument accepted, the percentage of Negro teachers in the relevant labor market area (St. Louis County alone) as shown in the 1970 census would be 5.7% rather than 15.4%.

The difference between these figures may well be important; the disparity between 3.7% (the percentage of Negro teachers hired by Hazelwood in 1972-1973 and 1973-1974) and 5.7% may be sufficiently small to weaken the Government's other proof, while the disparity between 3.7% and 15.4% may be sufficiently large to

---

14. As is discussed below, the Government contends that a comparative figure of 15.4%, rather than 5.7%, is the appropriate one. But even assuming, arguendo, that the 5.7% figure urged by the petitioners is correct, the disparity between that figure and the percentage of Negroes on Hazelwood's teaching staff would be more than fourfold for the 1972-1973 school year, and threefold for the 1973-1974 school year. A precise method of measuring the significance of such statistical disparities was explained in *Castaneda v. Partida*, 430 U.S. 482, 496-497, n.17. It involves calculation of the "standard deviation" as a measure of predicted fluctuations from the expected value of a sample. Using the 5.7% figure as the basis for calculating the expected value, the expected number of Negroes on the Hazelwood teaching staff would be roughly 63 in 1972-1973 and 70 in 1973-1974. The observed number in those years was 16 and 22, respectively. The difference between the observed and expected values was more than six standard deviations in 1972-1973 and more than five standard deviations in 1973-1974. The Court in *Castaneda* noted that "[a]s a general rule for such large samples, if the difference between the expected value and the observed number is greater than two or three standard deviations," then the hypothesis that teachers were hired without regard to race would be suspect. 430 U.S., at 497 n.17.

reinforce it.[17] In determining which of the two figures — or, very possibly, what intermediate figure — provides the most accurate basis for comparison to the hiring figures at Hazelwood, it will be necessary to evaluate such considerations as (i) whether the racially based hiring policies of the St. Louis City School District were in effect as far back as 1970, the year in which the census figures were taken; (ii) to what extent those policies have changed the racial composition of that district's teaching staff from what it would otherwise have been; (iii) to what extent St. Louis' recruitment policies have diverted to the city, teachers who might otherwise have applied to Hazelwood; (iv) to what extent Negro teachers employed by the city would prefer employment in other districts such as Hazelwood; and (v) what the experience in other school districts in St. Louis County indicates about the validity of excluding the City School District from the relevant labor market. . . .

We hold, therefore, that the Court of Appeals erred in disregarding the post-Act hiring statistics in the record, and that it should have remanded the case to the District Court for further findings as to the relevant labor market area and for an ultimate determination of whether Hazelwood engaged in a pattern or practice of employment discrimination after March 24, 1972.[21] . . .

Justice WHITE, concurring.

I join the Court's opinion . . . but with reservations with respect to the relative neglect of applicant pool data in finding a prima facie case of employment discrimination and heavy reliance on the disparity between the areawide percentage of black public school teachers and the percentage of blacks on Hazelwood's teaching staff. Since the issue is whether Hazelwood discriminated against blacks in hiring after Title VII became applicable to it in 1972, perhaps the Government should have looked initially to Hazelwood's hiring practices in the 1972-1973 and 1973-1974 academic years with respect to the applicant pool, rather than to history and to comparative work-force statistics from other school districts. [A]rguably the United States should have been required to adduce evidence as to the applicant pool before it was entitled to its prima facie presumption. At least it might have been required to present some

17. Indeed, under the statistical methodology explained in *Castaneda v. Partida*, supra, at 496-497, n.17, involving the calculation of the standard deviation as a measure of predicted fluctuations, the difference between using 15.4% and 5.7% as the areawide figure would be significant. If the 15.4% figure is taken as the basis for comparison, the expected number of Negro teachers hired by Hazelwood in 1972-1973 would be 43 (rather than the actual figure of 10) of a total of 282, a difference of more than five standard deviations; the expected number in 1973-1974 would be 19 (rather than the actual figure 5) of a total of 123, a difference of more than three standard deviations. For the two years combined, the difference between the observed number of 15 Negro teachers hired (of a total of 405) would vary from the expected number of 62 by more than six standard deviations. Because a fluctuation of more than two or three standard deviations would undercut the hypothesis that decisions were being made randomly with respect to race, 430 U.S., at 497 n.17, each of these statistical comparisons would reinforce rather than rebut the Government's other proof. If, however, the 5.7% areawide figure is used, the expected number of Negro teachers hired in 1972-1973 would be roughly 16, less than two standard deviations from the observed number of 10; for 1973-1974, the expected value would be roughly seven, less than one standard deviation from the observed value of 5; and for the two years combined, the expected value of 23 would be less than two standard deviations from the observed total of 15. A more precise method of analyzing these statistics confirms the results of the standard deviation analysis. See F. Mosteller, R. Rourke, & G. Thomas, Probability with Statistical Applications 494 (2d ed. 1970).

These observations are not intended to suggest that precise calculations of statistical significance are necessary in employing statistical proof, but merely to highlight the importance of the choice of the relevant labor market area.

21. It will also be open to the District Court on remand to determine whether sufficiently reliable applicant-flow data are available to permit consideration of the petitioner's argument that those data may undercut a statistical analysis dependent upon hirings alone.

defensible ground for believing that the racial composition of Hazelwood's applicant pool was roughly the same as that for the school districts in the general area, before relying on comparative work-force data to establish its prima facie case. . . .

Justice STEVENS, dissenting. . . .

I

The first question [whether the government established a prima facie case], is clearly answered by the Government's statistical evidence, its historical evidence, and its evidence relating to specific acts of discrimination.

One-third of the teachers hired by Hazelwood resided in the city of St. Louis at the time of their initial employment. As Mr. Justice Clark explained in his opinion for the Court of Appeals, it was therefore appropriate to treat the city, as well as the county, as part of the relevant labor market. In that market, 15% of the teachers were black. In the Hazelwood District at the time of trial less than 2% of the teachers were black. An even more telling statistic is that after Title VII became applicable to it, only 3.7% of the new teachers hired by Hazelwood were black. Proof of these gross disparities was in itself sufficient to make out a prima facie case of discrimination. See *Teamsters v. United States; Castaneda v. Partida.*

As a matter of history, Hazelwood employed no black teachers until 1969. Both before and after the 1972 amendment making the statute applicable to public school districts, Hazelwood used a standardless and largely subjective hiring procedure. Since "relevant aspects of the decisionmaking process had undergone little change," it is proper to infer that the pre-Act policy of preferring white teachers continued to influence Hazelwood's hiring practices.

The inference of discrimination was corroborated by post-Act evidence that Hazelwood had refused to hire 16 qualified black applicants for racial reasons. Taking the Government's evidence as a whole, there can be no doubt about the sufficiency of its prima facie case.

II

Hazelwood "offered virtually no additional evidence in response." It challenges the Government's statistical analysis by claiming that the city of St. Louis should be excluded from the relevant market and pointing out that only 5.7% of the teachers in the county (excluding the city) were black. It further argues that the city's policy of trying to maintain a 50% black teaching staff diverted teachers from the county to the city. There are two separate reasons why these arguments are insufficient: they are not supported by the evidence; even if true, they do not overcome the Government's case.

The petitioners offered no evidence concerning wage differentials, commuting problems, or the relative advantages of teaching in an inner-city school as opposed to a suburban school. Without any such evidence in the record, it is difficult to understand why the simple fact that the city was the source of a third of Hazelwood's faculty should not be sufficient to demonstrate that it is a part of the relevant market. The city's policy of attempting to maintain a 50/50 ratio clearly does not undermine that conclusion, particularly when the record reveals no shortage of qualified black applicants in either Hazelwood or other suburban school districts. Surely not all of the 2,000 black teachers employed by the city were unavailable for employment in Hazelwood at the time of their initial hire.

But even if it were proper to exclude the city of St. Louis from the market, the statistical evidence would still tend to prove discrimination. With the city excluded, 5.7% of the teachers in the remaining market were black. On the basis of a random selection, one would therefore expect 5.7% of the 405 teachers hired by Hazelwood in the 1972-1973 and 1973-1974 school years to have been black. But instead of 23 black teachers, Hazelwood hired only 15, less than two-thirds of the expected number. Without the benefit of expert testimony, I would hesitate to infer that the disparity between 23 and 15 is great enough, in itself, to prove discrimination.[5] It is perfectly clear, however, that whatever probative force this disparity has, it tends to prove discrimination and does absolutely nothing in the way of carrying Hazelwood's burden of overcoming the Government's prima facie case.

Absolute precision in the analysis of market data is too much to expect. We may fairly assume that a nondiscriminatory selection process would have resulted in the hiring of somewhere between the 15% suggested by the Government and the 5.7% suggested by petitioners, or perhaps 30 or 40 black teachers, instead of the 15 actually hired.[6] On that assumption, the Court of Appeals' determination that there were 16 individual cases of discriminatory refusal to hire black applicants in the post-1972 period seems remarkably accurate.

In sum, the Government is entitled to prevail on the present record. It proved a prima facie case, which Hazelwood failed to rebut. Why, then, should we burden a busy federal court with another trial? . . .

NOTES

1. *The Backstory.* "Lawyers hate statistics." So begins an article by Stewart J. Schwab & Steven L. Willborn, *The Story of Hazelwood: Employment Discrimination by the Numbers* in EMPLOYMENT DISCRIMINATION STORIES (Joel Wm. Friedman ed. 2006), describing the history of *Hazelwood*. Perhaps the most remarkable aspect of the opinion is the introduction of sophisticated statistical analysis to employment discrimination law. *Teamsters* had spoken of "the inexorable zero," but *Hazelwood* was a much closer case (at least for hiring after Title VII's effective date). The Court looked for, and received, guidance from statistics. Looking behind the Court's opinion into intra-chambers correspondence between the Justices, the authors explain why, despite the absence of a word in the briefs or the record about statistical analysis, the opinion has become a landmark in statistical application. As they recount it, a law clerk with a Ph.D. in applied physics played a pivotal role in convincing members of the Court to embrace these statistical concepts and to formulate a statistical model for establishing the existence of systemic discrimination.

2. *Refining Teamsters.* *Hazelwood* confirms the statistical approach in *Teamsters* but refines it. Without either the notorious history of discrimination in the trucking industry or the "inexorable zero," plaintiff had an uphill battle. Start simple: do you understand why the district court was wrong in comparing the ratio of black teachers to the ratio of black students in the school district? The right approach is to compare

---

5. After I had drafted this opinion, one of my law clerks advised me that, given the size of the two-year sample, there is only about a 5% likelihood that a disparity this large would be produced by a random selection from the labor pool. If his calculation (which was made using the method described in H. Blalock, Social Statistics 151-173 (1972)) is correct, it is easy to understand why Hazelwood offered no expert testimony.

6. Some of the other school districts in the county have a 10% ratio of blacks on their faculties.

the representation of African Americans in the employer's workforce with the percentage of African Americans available to be hired by the employer. How much disparity must be shown to establish that it is "gross?" The "inexorable zero" in *Teamsters* suffices simply by "eyeballing" the numbers, but what if the comparison is not that stark? Look at footnotes 14 and 17 for the Court's discussion of more sophisticated statistical techniques. Must there be expert testimony showing that the difference based on race is "statistically significant"? And do you understand what that means?

3. *Defining Underrepresentation.* In order to determine whether blacks are underrepresented at an employer such as Hazelwood, we must compare the "observed" (i.e., the percentage now employed) with the "expected" (the percentage who would be employed absent discrimination). Another way to say that is that we must ascertain the racial composition of the labor market from which the employer draws its workforce. This comparison must be considered in three dimensions — time, geography, and skill.

(a) *Post-Act Hiring.* From a time perspective, the extension of Title VII to public employers, like the defendant, required comparing Hazelwood's hiring of blacks since 1972, not the overall percentage of blacks in the school system. This makes what was implicit in *Teamsters* explicit. Where plaintiff uses a "snapshot" of the employer's workforce composition on any particular day as the basis for comparison with the relevant labor market, any resulting discriminatory pattern may be a product of pre-Act hiring, rather than unlawful post-Act discrimination. Thus, "flow" statistics, or movements in and out of jobs over time, are relevant to show whether the snapshot statistics incorporate pre-Act conduct. However, it has now been decades since the last major expansion of Title VII coverage; accordingly, it is unlikely that the temporal dimension of defining the labor market will be of consequence. Defining the labor market geographically and by skills, however, continues to be critical, as it was in *Hazelwood*.

(b) *Applicant Pool.* One way to avoid having to construct a relevant labor market is to look at the actual applicants. In *Teamsters,* the company had hired African Americans and Latinos but had segregated them out of the line driver jobs. Since the actual work was quite similar — truck driving is truck driving — the comparison of racial representation of the city drivers and the line drivers was especially powerful comparative evidence. The applicants for city jobs weren't actual applicants for line driver jobs (indeed, a part of the opinion not reproduced refused to assume that all city drivers wanted to be line drivers), but they constituted a pretty good proxy pool.

Hazelwood involved the absence of minority teachers, not their segregation. Thus, to find an appropriate comparison, it was necessary to look beyond the incumbent workforce of the defendant. Justice White is surely correct when he suggests that applicant flow data can be very useful for a comparison. Looking only at actual applicants for the job in question eliminates many problems: it is unlikely that persons lacking minimal skills will apply, and, by definition, those who apply are interested in the work and willing to consider the location. *See Paige v. California,* 291 F.3d 1141 (9th Cir. 2002) (the actual pool of promotional applicants is the correct comparison group for plaintiffs' claim of systemic disparate treatment in the promotion process). But employers such as Hazelwood do not always keep applications, and Hazelwood's haphazard method of dealing with applications might make such data suspect. Further, what if the employer keeps all application forms but has no record of the race or gender of any of the applicants? Gender is sometimes ascertainable by first name, but race is much less so.

(c) *Qualified Labor Pool: Skills and Interest.* Looking beyond either the incumbent workforce or applicant flow, *Hazelwood* looks at African Americans and Latinos available to work in the local labor market. In *EEOC v. Joe's Stone Crab, Inc.*, 220 F.3d 1263 (11th Cir. 2000), the at-issue jobs were wait staff positions at a popular Miami Beach restaurant. The number of women hired approximated their representation in the applicant pool, those who showed up for a "roll call." But the court rejected this actual applicant pool as the appropriate comparison because there was reason to believe that women were deterred from applying by Joe's reputation for hiring only male wait staff. What labor pool should be used instead? Rather than looking to the 44.1 percent representation of women among food servers in Miami Beach, the district court "refined" the relevant labor pool to include only "servers who lived or worked in Miami Beach and earned between $25,000 and $50,000 . . . thereby using past earnings as a proxy for experience, and by extension, experience as a proxy for qualification." *Id.* at 1272. The resulting pool was 31.1 percent female, which the court concluded resulted in a disparity that "bordered on statistical significance" and did support a prima facie case. Why discount the pool by income? Wouldn't lower income food servers be exactly the people you would expect to apply for higher paying jobs, such as at Joe's Stone Crab? Should experience and qualifications matter for determining the appropriate labor pool? For wait staff jobs, shouldn't general population statistics be used — can't most everyone learn that job? Other cases have also struggled with defining the relevant labor pool when actual applicants are not used. *Bennett v. Roberts*, 295 F.3d 687, 697 (7th Cir. 2002), held plaintiff's statistical evidence unreliable because the expert underestimated potential applicants' interest in working in the school district and inaccurately assumed that the district would hire only in-state applicants.

In *Teamsters*, the Court also accepted general population statistics as a basis for comparison rather than either actual applicants or a "refined" labor pool. Why did the Court in *Hazelwood* distinguish its facts from *Teamsters*? How long does it take for a member of the general population to be trained to be a truck driver versus a school teacher? Is that the basis for distinguishing the two cases, or is the point that many fewer members of the general population could ever qualify to teach while many more could drive a truck? What if the job in question is completely unskilled? Can plaintiff argue for the use of the pool of unskilled laborers, rather than general population figures, because the pool of unskilled workers has a higher minority or female component than the general population?

(d) *Qualified Labor Pool: Geography.* Defining the geographic labor market was the turning point in *Hazelwood*. Should teachers in the city of St. Louis be included? Justice Stevens stressed that the high number of actual Hazelwood teachers who resided in the city mandated the inclusion of the city as part of the appropriate labor pool. The defendant, however, claimed that St. Louis City hired to meet a goal of 50 percent black teachers. What is the significance of such a hiring pattern? Two possibilities might be raised: (1) St. Louis pays more; therefore, Hazelwood cannot attract St. Louis teachers into its system. Factually, one would have expected Hazelwood to have made this argument the first time if that had been true. Analytically, is it a reason to exclude the whole St. Louis pool or merely to discount it somewhat? Might not some teachers prefer teaching jobs in the suburbs, even at lower pay? (2) St. Louis hires unqualified persons for affirmative action purposes. In that case, the pool of qualified teachers may not be as large as it first appears. But is that true? Second, even if some less-qualified persons were hired, should the St. Louis pool be discounted, or eliminated?

How should the geographic area of the labor pool be established? Is it the geographic area from which the employer recruits employees? In most areas of the United States, substantial housing segregation exists. *See NAACP v. Town of Harrison*, 940 F.2d 792 (3d Cir. 1991) (resident-only hiring rule of town struck down as disparate impact discrimination because of housing segregation). How would you state a fair standard for establishing the geographic area?

In many jobs, recruitment is national or even global. Should the geographic scope of recruitment be used for comparison in those jobs? Thus, for law school professors, should the geographic pool be national since most law schools participate in a national recruitment system run by the Association of American Law Schools? How should the labor market be determined if a school recruits nationally but ends up mostly hiring locally? Perhaps the statistics should be weighted to take account of different rates of representation in the local versus the national market.

4. *Statistical Techniques*. The *Hazelwood* Court uses binomial distribution as a way of determining whether the defendant acted with the intent to discriminate: Be clear what this means: if a certain result is "statistically significant," it is unlikely to be the result of chance. Actually, we will see that there are different levels of significance but all of them rule out chance as an explanation for certain results. But what does it mean to say a result is "significant"? Again, we will study this in more detail shortly. All a statistician can conclude is that race (or sex) is related to a particular situation. If the results in *Hazelwood* were statistically significant, that would mean that there was something about being black that correlated with not being employed by the school district. That "something" might, of course, be intent by the employer to discriminate against blacks. The finder of fact is permitted to infer that defendant's "standard operating procedure — the regular rather than the unusual practice" — was to discriminate.

In *Bazemore v. Friday*, 478 U.S. 385 (1986), the Court approved another statistical technique, multiple regression, to prove systemic disparate treatment discrimination. Multiple regression is a technique to measure the influence of many variables; by holding other variables constant, it can determine whether the variable of interest — race, for example — has a statistically significant influence. *Bazemore* involved a claim of salary discrimination where many different factors might influence the salary of the workers. The Court upheld the probative value of plaintiff's expert statistical study, even in face of defendant's claims that the study failed to include all possible variables on salary.

5. *Case Study of Statistical Proof*. In *Hemmings v. Tidyman's Inc.*, 285 F.3d 1174 (9th Cir. 2002), plaintiffs claimed the defendant discriminated against them because of their sex by failing to pay them equally with their male counterparts and by failing to promote them. With respect to pay, the court described the statistics offered:

> Women in management at Tidyman's earn an average of $12,000 less than men in management. The mean starting salary for women in management at Tidyman's was $26,400, while the mean starting salary for men was $38,400. Dr. Polissar also testified that he analyzed the progression of wages of women and men over time as a method of controlling for factors other than gender — such as experience — that might explain the initial wage differential. Dr. Polissar used regression analysis to control for differences in experience, and reached the same conclusion — that gender predicted a statistically significant wage differential. Dr. Polissar also performed a "step analysis," which compared the number of women to the number of men within each rank of Tidyman's' management hierarchy. Dr. Polissar explained that some of the step levels had no women employees, which made comparison impossible for those levels. Where

comparisons were possible, Dr. Polissar testified that the step analysis revealed wage differentials between men and women for most of the ranks. For example, at the "step four" level, the average salary for female workers was $29,400, while the average salary for male workers was $40,800.

Id. at 1183-84. With respect to promotions, the expert analyzed the distribution of men and women in different job categories at Tidyman's and concluded that it reflected a pattern of segregation of men and women that was unlikely to be due to chance.

The court rejected a number of defendant's attacks on this statistical evidence. First, it was appropriate to include lower management positions in the labor pool for upper level positions because Tidyman's filled higher management by internal promotions. "Therefore, the potential applicant pool — and thus the appropriate comparison pool — for promotions to upper and middle management jobs at Tidyman's is comprised of the current employees in lower management positions." *Id.* at 1185-86. Second, including store management with corporate management positions was not an error, even though plaintiffs were not qualified to be store managers, because "store management may be a career path to corporate management for some employees." *Id.* at 1186. Finally, based on *Bazemore*, the court rejected defendant's argument that the statistical analysis should have been excluded because it did not eliminate all possible nondiscriminatory factors, including the employee's qualifications, level of education, and preferences, that might explain apparent sex differences. "[T]he law does not require the near-impossible standard of eliminating all possible nondiscriminatory factors. . . . Vigorous cross-examination of a study's inadequacies allows the jury to appropriately weigh the alleged defects and reduces the possibility of prejudice." *Id.* at 1188. Further, Tidyman's could have introduced its own studies controlling for such nondiscriminatory factors to show that sex was not an explanatory variable or at least offered testimony that such factors were central in promotions.

6. *Systemic Age Cases.* Systemic disparate treatment cases can also be litigated under the ADEA, typically in the context of large-scale reductions in force. In *Adams v. Ameritech Servs., Inc.,* 231 F.3d 414 (7th Cir. 2000), the employer substantially reduced its personnel, eliminating some 2500 of 21,000 management employees "either by persuasion or by force." Plaintiffs' evidence of age discrimination included statistical analysis of the outcomes, the manner of the layoffs, the use of a combination of age and pension status in the employer's plans "which the plaintiffs assert created a strong financial incentive to terminate people below the chronological age thresholds set by the Plan," and certain statements allegedly showing age bias. The Seventh Circuit reaffirmed the admissibility of statistical evidence in systemic discrimination cases, found the statistical evidence plaintiffs had proffered admissible, and held that this evidence, together with plaintiffs' other evidence, precluded summary judgment against them. As the court summarized the evidence against one of the defendants: "ASI selected for termination 12.63% of those aged 40-44, 16.71% of those aged 45-49, 24.58% of those aged 50-54, and 29.19% of those aged 55 and older." *Id.* at 419-20. Plaintiff's statistician found that, within each 10-year age cohort, older workers were more likely to be terminated that younger ones, and these findings were statistically significant. *Adams* thus clearly illustrates how a large-scale reduction in force can become a textbook exercise in the application of statistical analysis to prove a correlation between age and layoff in order to make out a prima facie case of systemic disparate treatment.

By contrast, in *EEOC v. McDonnell Douglas Corp.*, 191 F.3d 948 (8th Cir. 1999), the court found that a statistical showing that employees 55 years of age or older were more than twice as likely to be laid off as younger workers was not sufficient to preclude summary judgment for defendant. The court noted that individuals aged 55 or older comprised 13.6 percent of the workforce after the layoffs and only 14.7 percent before. Why is this not probative of age discrimination? Summary judgment was granted even though the EEOC proffered admissions by managers that "retirement eligibility" was a factor in deciding who to lay off. Under *Biggins*, this did not constitute age discrimination. Such evidence, even coupled with evidence that some managers manipulated performance evaluations to favor younger workers, was held insufficient to create a question whether there was a pattern or practice of age discrimination.

7. *EEOC Systemic Disparate Treatment Initiative.* In 2006, the EEOC voted to shift focus from individual cases to systemic discrimination cases. This followed the report of its Systemic Discrimination Task Force that bluntly criticized the EEOC's recent performance, which showed that systemic cases had "evaporated." Although the Report did not cite the work of Professors Alfred W. Blumrosen and Ruth G. Blumrosen, it may well have been a response to their articles *The Reality of Intentional Discrimination in Metropolitan America — 1999* (2002) (available at www.eeo1.com), and *Intentional Job Discrimination — New Tools for Our Oldest Problem*, 37 U. MICH. J.L. REF. 681 (2004).

The Blumrosens analyzed data that employers with over 50 employees are required to submit annually to the EEOC on EEO-1 Forms. While the study reported many advances in equal employment opportunity, some disturbing facts were revealed. First, one third of the employers who were legally obligated to file EEO-1 Forms failed to do so. For those employers who did file, the authors found considerable evidence of discrimination by looking at other employers within the same metropolitan areas and comparing the representation of women and minority men through the binomial distribution technique approved in *Hazelwood*:

> For 1999, 75,793 — or 37% — of establishments discriminated against Minorities in at least one occupational category. This discrimination affected 1,361,083 Minorities who were qualified and available to work in the labor markets, industries and occupations of those who discriminated. These Minorities were 57% Black, 27% Hispanic, 9% Asian and .2% Native American.
>
> For 1999, 60,425 — or 29% — of establishments discriminated against Women in at least one occupational category. This discrimination affected 952,130 Women who were qualified and available to work in the labor markets, industries and occupations of those who discriminated. Women were 69% White, 17% Black, 9% Hispanic, 5% Asian and 1% Native American.
>
> A "hard core" of 22,369 establishments appear to have discriminated over a nine-year period against Minorities, and 13,173 establishments appear to have done so against Women. This "hard core" is responsible for roughly half of the intentional discrimination we have identified.

Reality, at 74. Although, as the authors admit, these findings are very rough-grained, and may or may not be admissible in court, they do seem to offer a useful tool for enforcement agencies to identify potential systemic violators. And there may be even more reason to focus on many employers who simply fail to file EEO-1 Forms, who may be likely to be among the worst offenders. The EEOC Task Force did recommend more robust use of EEO-1 data and linking that data to charge filings.

*NOTE ON SOPHISTICATED STATISTICAL TECHNIQUES**

Application of Statistical Analysis to Discrimination Litigation. The basis for the use of statistical evidence in employment discrimination litigation is, as the Court said in *Teamsters*, probability theory.

> [A]bsent explanation, it is ordinarily to be expected that non-discriminatory hiring practices will in time result in a work force more or less representative of the racial and ethnic composition of the population in the community from which employees are hired.

The converse of this is that a substantial departure from what is to be expected, absent discrimination, is so improbable that the trier of fact should conclude, at least prima facie, that discrimination explains the disparity.

This assumption has been controverted. Professor Kingsley R. Browne, in *Statistical Proof of Discrimination: Beyond "Damned Lies,"* 68 WASH. L. REV. 477 (1993), questions what he calls the "Central Assumption" of statistical proof in employment discrimination: that different racial and ethnic groups and both genders have the same interests and abilities. Browne argues that this is at odds with the real world and inconsistent with the conceptual underpinnings of disparate impact theory, which assumes people have different interests and abilities related to ethnic, racial, and gender differences.

Professor Browne does recognize that, to some extent, these differences are taken into account in formulating the relevant labor market: the percentage of African-American teachers in the labor market in *Hazelwood* was undoubtedly less than the percentage of African Americans in the general population. The comparison, therefore, filtered out — at least in gross terms — those whose abilities and interests were very different. But Browne doubts that abilities and interests are randomly distributed by race or sex even within the relevant labor market. Professor Browne also recognizes that the Central Assumption is only a tool for the plaintiff's prima facie case and that the defendant can, theoretically at least, rebut the inference of discrimination by showing factors other than the employer's discriminatory selection process that produce the nonrepresentative result. Nevertheless, he argues that the Central Assumption imposes an unfair burden on employers, a burden that is heightened by the tendency of some courts to require a strong rebuttal showing to defeat a systemic case. Reconsider this argument after you have read *EEOC v. Sears, Roebuck & Co.*, 839 F.2d 302 (7th Cir. 1988), reproduced at p. 157. The Supreme Court has, however, endorsed the Central Assumption, and the courts have refined it by looking increasingly to sophisticated statistical proofs.[†]

(a) *Probability Theory.* Probability is the basis of the science of statistics. As reflected in employment discrimination cases, probability theory starts with a

---

* For a general study on the use of statistics in litigation, see DAVID W. BARNES, STATISTICS AS PROOF: FUNDAMENTALS OF QUANTITATIVE EVIDENCE (1983). Professor Barnes has also been kind enough to review this section, and make some suggestions for improvement.

† Some of Professor Browne's objections can be met by the defendant's introduction of its own statistical proof. For example, Browne criticizes defining the relevant labor market in terms of those with minimal qualifications. If, however, the employer hires only (or disproportionately) persons with higher qualifications, a statistical study could show that it is qualifications, not race, that explain the makeup of the workforce. Similarly, the defendant can proffer studies using other variables not reflected in plaintiff's analysis. It is true, however, that some factors — "subjective or otherwise unquantifiable" — will be hard to account for in this way.

comparison between the "observed" racial (or gender or age) distribution in the employer's workforce and the "expected," that is, the racial distribution one would anticipate if race were not a factor in the selection of employees.

(b) *The Null Hypothesis.* To use probability theory to prove discrimination, a statistician would construct an assumption, called the null hypothesis, which would then be tested and either accepted or rejected. The null hypothesis, which states the opposite of what the plaintiff hopes to prove, is based on two assumptions: first, that there is no difference between the observed and the expected, that is, that the difference is null; second, that if there is any difference between the observed (the sample we are examining) and the expected, that difference is the result of chance. The classic example is determining whether a coin is fair. A statistician would start with an assumption, the null hypothesis, that flipping a coin would result in no difference between the number of heads and the number of tails, and that, if there is a difference, it is due to chance.

In the employment context, this first means that the null hypothesis is that the employer does not discriminate, so that there will be no significant difference between the observed number of minorities employed and the expected number if hiring continued in the present way indefinitely. Second, if there is a difference between the observed sample we are looking at (the employer's workforce) and the expected, that difference is due to chance. The plaintiff obviously wants to rule out the null hypothesis — that is, to show that there is difference and that difference is unlikely to be due to chance. The employer would prefer to confirm the null hypothesis — that is, to show that any difference is due to chance.

The statistician's job is to determine the probability that chance explains the difference. With a coin, the statistician could test the null hypothesis by counting the number of "heads" and "tails" when the coin is flipped. Suppose the statistician flips the coin 100 times, resulting in 49 heads and 51 tails. That outcome would be so close to what would be expected if the coin were fair (50 percent "heads," 50 percent "tails") that the statistician could accept the null hypothesis. Based on reason and logic, but not statistics, the statistician would take the next step and conclude that, because it cannot be shown that the coin is unfair, it may be concluded that the coin is fair.

An example more attuned to the discrimination context is selection of marbles from a fishbowl. Suppose the statistician knows the racial composition of the relevant universe, that is, the percentages of white marbles and black marbles in the fishbowl — say, 80 percent white and 20 percent black. She can then make some probability judgments about the "fairness" of a drawing of a sample from the fishbowl that obtains 100 white marbles and no black ones.

Indeed, it should be apparent that the *Teamsters* decision is simply a commonsense conclusion that the employer's draw of a sample (i.e., its workforce of line drivers) from the fishbowl (i.e., the relevant labor market of city drivers) is so obviously unfair as to at least require an explanation. Further, the *Hazelwood* use of standard deviation analysis is merely a way of quantifying the commonsense judgment by stating how unlikely it is that the draw of 100 white marbles could occur if being white were totally unconnected with the selection.

In short, a statistician can inform the court how probable it is that a certain pattern of selections would have occurred if color were not somehow influencing the selection decision.

(c) *Rejecting the Null Hypothesis.* Accepting or rejecting a null hypothesis, like making any decision, always entails a risk of being mistaken. Two possible errors may result from a decision based on sample information: a party who should not be found liable may be found liable (a "false inculpation"), and a party who should be found liable may be found not liable (a "false exculpation"). Statisticians have labeled false inculpations as "Type I error" and false exculpations as "Type II error." *See* Neil B. Cohen, *Confidence in Probability: Burdens of Persuasion in a World of Imperfect Knowledge*, 60 N.Y.U. L. REV. 385, 410 (1985). In law, a jury that finds a defendant guilty of a crime when he is innocent commits what statisticians would call a Type I error, false inculpation. Juries in criminal cases are instructed to test the evidence under the "beyond a reasonable doubt" standard. Thus, unless the jury is convinced of the defendant's guilt beyond all reasonable doubt, the jury must acquit. This reflects the legal policy decision that it is much worse to convict an innocent person, a Type I false inculpation error, than it is to commit a Type II false exculpation error by letting a guilty person go free. In terms of probability theory, the criminal law sets the test of proof so that, if error is made, it is more likely to be a Type II error, freeing the guilty, than a Type I error, convicting the innocent. This is a deliberate policy decision that Type I errors are worse than Type II errors: many guilty people should go free, rather than one innocent person be convicted.

Statisticians address the probability of error in rejecting a null hypothesis based on a particular observation in terms of "significance level" or "p-value," terms which are used interchangeably. The threshold or critical significance level specifies the degree of risk of error the decision-maker is willing to accept. The higher the p-value, therefore, the greater the risk of error. Once the level of significance is set, the null hypothesis will be rejected only if the calculated significance level (or p-value) is less than the threshold level.

By setting the level of confidence before a probability estimate is accepted, statisticians are directly deciding the risk of Type I error. The level is set by hundredths from zero to one. If it is very important to avoid Type I errors, that is, to avoid incorrectly finding an innocent employer guilty of discrimination, statisticians would set the level of statistical significance very high. Setting the level of significance at 0.05 means that a Type I error is made in only 5 percent of the cases, that is, 5 in 100 times.[*] As we will see, the 0.05 level is the one typically chosen for discrimination litigation.

In *Statistical Proof of Discrimination: Beyond "Damned Lies,"* 68 WASH. L. REV. 477 (1993), Professor Kingsley R. Browne argues that courts and commentators have erred by confusing one particular employer's workforce statistics with the overall probabilities. Professor Browne illustrates his point by an experiment in which each of 100 persons flips a coin 100 times. Prior to the coin toss, one would predict that, even if the coin is fair, five of the subjects would obtain a split of 60/40 or greater. Thus, with respect to any one subject chosen at random, there is a prior probability of 5 percent of obtaining such a split. What is the likelihood that a particular subject who got a 60/40 split when flipping a coin used a fair coin? Those who equate the significance level with the likelihood of a random result would conclude that there is only a 5 percent chance that the subject obtained that result by chance and therefore

[*] The risk to innocent defendants is actually somewhat higher than 5 percent. Statistics only suggest a connection between race and employment decisions. They do not determine whether that connection is intentional discrimination. Statistical significance set at .05 means that in 5 percent of the cases statistics will find a correlation between race and employment decisions when there is, in fact, no relationship (e.g., the defendant is innocent). Even if there is a relationship, however, that relationship could result from some reason other than intentional discrimination. Thus, some defendants will be innocent even though statistics have accurately identified a relationship. In order to simplify the discussion of Type I and Type II errors, however, we will assume that, whenever there is a relationship between race and employment decisions, this relationship results from intentional discrimination.

a 95 percent chance that there was a nonrandom cause. However, in reaching that conclusion they confuse the probability of a particular result given the null hypothesis with the probability of the null hypothesis given the observed result.

This analysis can be applied to the employment setting. By hypothesis, one knows that 1 out of 20 employers will have a statistically significant disparity, so in an economy with, say, 200,000 nondiscriminating employers, there will be 10,000 employers who in fact do not discriminate but whose workforce statistics will suggest that they did discriminate. This is the thrust of Professor Browne's claim. However, without knowing how many discriminating employers there actually are, it is not possible to estimate the likelihood that a given statistical imbalance was caused by chance, by discrimination, or by some other nonrandom factor. For example, suppose the "base rate" of systemic discrimination is 1 percent. Then, based on statistical evidence, 6 out of 100 employers will be found liable, but only 1 of those 6 employers will actually be guilty of discrimination. Therefore, the likelihood that the employer discriminated is less than 17 percent. According to Professor Browne, this flawed statistical logic leads courts faced with a statistically significant disparity to reason, "I'm faced with a disparity that is very unlikely to have occurred by chance; this rare result is suspicious, and the employer ought to explain it," when it should be thinking, "The plaintiff has described statistics that would be true for thousands of nondiscriminating employers; if the plaintiff wants me to suspect discrimination, he'd better give me a lot more than that." *Id.* at 490.

The problem is a "base rate" one, and the standard illustration of base rate is testing for diseases. Suppose a test is developed which is 99 percent accurate in testing positive, that is, 99 percent of the positive test results correctly identify the presence of the disease and only 1 percent of the tests yield a Type I false positive, that is, incorrectly indicate the presence of a disease that the patient does not have. While the test is in some sense highly accurate, its use could result in far more false positives than true positives if the base rate of the disease is very low. The population of the United States is about 300 million, so that a disease so rare that only one person in a million suffers from it, would result in the number of afflicted persons in the United States being 300. But if the test is to be administered to the entire population of this country, its 99 percent accuracy rate would result in about 3,000,000 positives, of which all but 300 would be false.

Professor Browne argues that a similar problem exists with the use of the 5 percent level in employment discrimination. While he is theoretically correct, Professor Browne fails to demonstrate why the legal system should conclude that base rate discrimination is especially rare. If 10 percent of employers discriminate, two true positives will be reported for every false positive. If 20 percent discriminate, there will be four true positives for every Type I false inculpation. Does the Blumrosens' study (see p. 140) suggest that the base rate is much higher than Professor Browne believes? Or is Browne's analysis a powerful critique of the Blumrosen study? Further, Professor Browne's analysis does not take sufficiently into account the role of the statistical proof in discrimination litigation. Such proof never does more than establish plaintiff's prima facie case, leaving defendant the opportunity to rebut by offering proof that it does not discriminate. Sufficiently strong testimony might convince the jury that it was chance that explained the disparity.

In sum, probability theory suggests a basis for the use of statistical evidence in disparate treatment discrimination cases. Within probability theory, there are numerous statistical techniques available to analyze whether a null hypothesis should be accepted or rejected. When any one of these techniques is used to conclude that the null hypothesis (that discrimination is not involved because any difference between the observed and the expected is the result of chance) should be rejected, the next step, based on reason and logic, should be to draw the inference that systemic disparate treatment discrimination has occurred. While the employer will have an opportunity to rebut that conclusion, the prima facie case will be established.

Binomial Distribution and the Two- or Three-Standard Deviations Test. The Supreme Court decided two cases in 1977 that used binomial distribution. The first, *Castaneda v. Partida*, 430 U.S. 482, 496 n.17 (1977), involved the exclusion of Mexican Americans from juries. The null hypothesis was that the juries are randomly drawn, without regard to whether a person picked was Mexican American. The probability, or expected outcome given random selection, was based on the percentage of Mexican Americans in the population, which was 79.1 percent. Among the 870 persons picked for juries over an 11-year period, on average 79.1 percent, or 688, are expected to be Mexican American. Over that period, only 339 of the persons selected were Mexican Americans. While in a random selection process it is unlikely that each jury panel drawn would approximate 79.1 percent Mexican Americans, the probability assumption is that the observed outcomes should be bunched close to that expected figure. Figure 2.1 shows the expected outcome.

Each X plots the Mexican American representation in one jury panel. As the percentage of Mexican American representation in the panels departs from the expected outcome of 79.1 percent, fewer panels are represented. The "range" of the distribution is the spread of observed outcomes from highest to lowest. If samples are randomly drawn, some values will be higher and some lower than the expected value, so the range will include the expected value. In this example of an expected outcome, the range is between 66 and 92 percent, but in some other samples of jury panel selections, the range could be greater or smaller. For example, some juries may have no Mexican Americans, and others would be 100 percent Mexican American. In such a sample, the range would be from zero to 100 percent. To use the coin-flipping example, in some experimental runs the results will be bunched closer together than in other samples. In one sample, few, if any, outcomes of 100 flips will be more than 3 or 4 percent apart — say, 48 to 52 percent "heads" — while, in others, the variance might be much greater; some sample flips will be, say, 40 "heads" to 60 "tails."

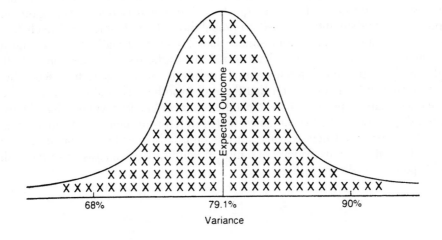

Figure 2.1

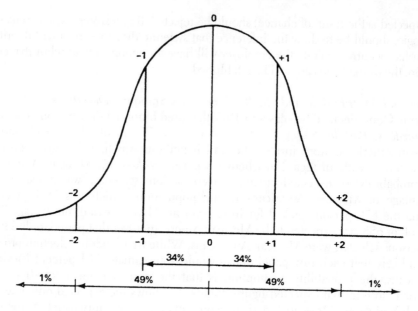

Figure 2.2

Statisticians need some way of determining what kind of deviations from the expected value are possible, and how much deviation from the expected value can be viewed as due to chance. It is here that the concept of "standard deviation" is used. Standard deviation may be thought of as "normal" or "typical" or "average" deviation. Without regard to the exact variance along any baseline, 68 percent of all outcomes will fall between 1 and 2 "standard deviations" of the expected outcome. Only 2 percent of the outcomes will fall beyond 1 and 2 standard deviations from the expected outcome. Figure 2.2 illustrates this use of the standard deviation.

By characterizing data in terms of the number of standard deviations, it is possible to use standard deviation as a way of deciding whether to reject the null hypothesis. The test normally used is to reject the null hypothesis when an outcome falls more than 2 standard deviations from the expected value. The reason for rejecting the null hypothesis in this situation is based on probability. The outcome is not likely to be the result of chance when a result is more than 2 standard deviations from the norm; in such a case, there are only 4 chances in 100 that the result is consistent with the null hypothesis, that the differences are the result of chance. As we have seen, there is a general statistical convention that the null hypothesis should be rejected when there is less than a 5 percent chance that the result could occur without there being a relationship between the two variables. Stated in terms of standard deviations, the 5 percent (or .05) level occurs when an outcome falls outside plus or minus 1.96 standard deviations. This .05 level of statistical significance as a basis for rejecting the null hypothesis is shown in Figure 2.3.

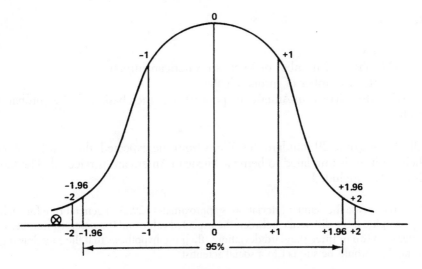

Figure 2.3

The outcome X casts doubt on the null hypothesis because that outcome could be consistent with the hypothesis less than 5 percent of the time if chance were the explanation. Rejecting the null hypothesis means that it is much more likely than not (though not certain) that the null hypothesis is incorrect. In the coin-flipping example, an outcome so far from the expected, as X is in Figure 2.3, is so unlikely if the coin is fair that it is a better judgment to reject the idea that the coin is fair.

So far, standard deviation has been described verbally and graphically, but it can also be performed mathematically. To calculate the probability of a Type I error in cases like *Castaneda*, statisticians start by calculating a "Z score." A Z score is simply the number of standard deviations between the observed and the expected. In mathematical terms, the Z score is

$$Z = \frac{O - NP}{\sqrt{NP(1 - P)}}$$

where

    Z = number of standard deviations
    O = observed number of minority group members in the sample
    N = size of the sample
    P = minority percentage of the underlying population.

N × P, therefore, is the expected number of minorities in the sample.

In this formula, the top (or numerator) is the difference between the observed and the expected. The bottom (or denominator) is the formula for one standard deviation. The facts of *Castaneda* can be plugged into the formula as follows:

$$Z = \frac{339 - (870 \times .79)}{\sqrt{(870 \times .79)(1 - .79)}} = \frac{339 - 687}{\sqrt{687 \times .21}} = \frac{-348}{\sqrt{144}} = \frac{-348}{12}$$

$$Z = -29$$

where

Z = unknown
O = 339 (observed number of Mexican-American jurors)
N = 870 (total number of jurors selected)
P = .79 (the Mexican-American population, the basis of the probability assumption)

With the outcome 29 standard deviations from the expected, the null hypothesis, that being a juror is unrelated to being a Mexican American, is rejected. The Court in *Castaneda* concluded:

> Thus, in this case the standard deviation is approximately 29. As a general rule for such large samples, if the difference between the expected value and the observed number is greater than two or three standard deviations, then the hypothesis that the jury drawing was random would be suspect to a social scientist.

Id. The calculations for this formula are quite simple.

The result in *Castaneda* is shown graphically in Figure 2.4. The outcome X is -29 standard deviations from the expected result. The figure is a negative one because Mexican-American representation on juries fell far short of the expected outcome. (Only if the representation of Mexican Americans exceeded the expected would a positive standard deviation figure be involved.) The chance that this outcome could occur with the null hypothesis being true, that is, that being Mexican American is unconnected with the chance of being selected for jury service, is infinitesimal.

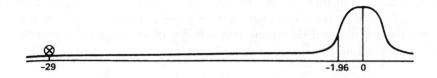

Figure 2.4

The two- or three-standard deviation rule was accepted by the Supreme Court in *Hazelwood*. Surprisingly, the technique was not used by the Court in *Teamsters*, the case that set forth the probability assumptions underpinning the use of sophisticated statistical techniques such as binomial distribution. The almost total exclusion of minority group members from line-driver jobs, only 13 of 1,828, made statistical techniques unnecessary to show discrimination. But it is possible to work the analysis in terms of the facts given in the case for defendant's employment in several cities where it operated. For employment at defendant's Atlanta terminal, the number of standard deviations, the Z score, is calculated as follows:

$$Z = \frac{O - NP}{\sqrt{NP(1 - P)}} = \frac{0 - (57 \times .22)}{\sqrt{(57 \times .22)(1 - .22)}} = \frac{-12.54}{\sqrt{9.78}} = \frac{-12.54}{3.13}$$

$$Z = -4.01$$

where

> Z = unknown
> O = zero (no minority line drivers)
> N = 57 (number of Atlanta line drivers)
> P = .22 (using metropolitan minority population figures)

In Atlanta, the null hypothesis is rejected: the outcome of four standard deviations far exceeds the two or three standard deviations guideline. But note also that the probability was determined by metropolitan area. Had only city population been used, the showing would have been even more dramatic. If the minority population of the city of Atlanta, which was 51.31 percent, is used to establish the probability, the observed outcome is 7.76 standard deviations from the expected.

In these examples, the Z score (the number of standard deviations) is negative because the observed outcome of minority representation falls short of the expected outcome. Where the possibility that the statistical showing would be favorable to women or minority men (thereby producing a positive Z score) can be ruled out as defying logic, then the necessary conclusion that there is underrepresentation may be the basis for use of a "one-tailed" test of statistical significance. The one-tailed test means that the entire 5 percent chance of randomness all lies in the negative "tail," that is, the left side, of the bell-shaped curve of normal distribution. If the one-tailed test is appropriate, the Z score that justifies rejecting the null hypothesis is reduced to 1.65 standard deviations. *Palmer v. Schultz (Kissinger)*, 815 F.2d 84 (D.C. Cir. 1987), rejected a one-tailed test: while women were clearly underrepresented in some Foreign Service jobs, they were overrepresented in others, so it could not be concluded that a positive Z score defied logic.

The Supreme Court decision in *Hazelwood* added two refinements in the use of statistics that are of continuing significance. First, it distinguished between the use of general population statistics and the use of more limited labor pools reflecting the special qualifications needed for the job. In *Teamsters*, the general population was appropriate for comparison with the employer's workforce because "the job skill there involved — the ability to drive a truck — is one that many persons possess or can fairly readily acquire." *Hazelwood*. In contrast, the jobs in *Hazelwood* were teaching positions. "When special qualifications are required to fill particular jobs, comparisons to the general population (rather than to the smaller group of individuals who possess the necessary qualifications) may have little probative value." Thus, the Court used the pool of qualified teachers as the basis for comparison with defendant's workforce.

The second refinement in *Hazelwood* concerned the geographic area of concentration, the city of St. Louis. Plaintiff sought to use the entire metropolitan area. The Court remanded for a decision on what area was appropriate because the difference could determine the outcome. Assuming that post-Act hiring is the focus and further assuming that a pool of qualified teachers including those in the city of St. Louis is used as the basis for comparison, the expected percentage of minority group hires in 1972-1973 would be 15.4 percent. The Z score formula would yield a result of 5.6 standard deviations.

If the city of St. Louis is carved out of the geographic area, the qualified labor pool drops to 5.7 percent minority representation. With the new probability or expectancy of 5.7 percent, the result is a Z score of 1.5 standard deviations, which is less than the 1.96 cutoff showing statistical significance at the .05, or 1-chance-in-20, level. The 1.5 standard deviation figure means that there is a 14 percent chance that an outcome with this large a difference between the observed and the expected outcomes occurred randomly. The result is graphically shown in Figure 2.5, where X marks the observed outcome.

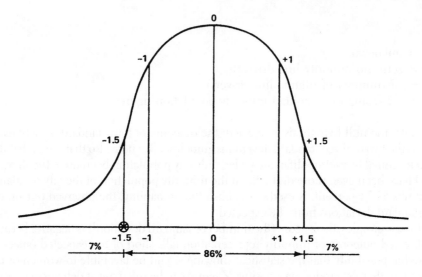

Figure 2.5

Statistical convention would have it that this showing is *not* sufficient to reject the null hypothesis. It could be accepted that race and teacher hiring were unrelated in the hiring by the Hazelwood district in 1972-1973. However, the Court did not decide whether that statistical convention must be followed in Title VII litigation. The *Hazelwood* Court, after working through the above examples, noted: "These observations are not intended to suggest that precise calculations of statistical significance are necessary in employing statistical proof. . . . "

Subsequent cases have tended not to be much more definitive as to the level of statistical significance needed. The Supreme Court has recognized that, in relying on statistical evidence, courts are not bound by scientific tests of significance. In *Bazemore v. Friday*, 478 U.S. 385, 400 (1986), the Court said, "A plaintiff in a Title VII suit need not prove discrimination with scientific certainty; rather, his or her burden is to prove discrimination by a preponderance of evidence." The lower courts are in agreement that a showing of statistical significance at the 1.96 level will, at least in the normal case, suffice. *See Anderson v. Zubieta*, 180 F.3d 329 (D.C. Cir. 1999) (disparities exceeding 1.96 standard deviations under a two-tailed test of statistical significance, are "sufficient to establish a prima facie case of both disparate treatment and disparate impact."); *Paige v. California*, 233 Fed. Appx. 646 (9th Cir. 2007) (error for the district court to reject plaintiffs' statistical results showing a disparity of greater than 1.96 standard deviations, although district court was not clearly erroneous in according plaintiff's expert little weight because of methodological and data deficiencies).

But it is not clear whether that level of significance is required. Statistical significance, in the sense that statisticians use that term, is not necessary to the theories. *Teamsters*, the seminal systemic disparate treatment case, did not rely on expert testimony of statistical significance; the "inexorable zero" may have made that unnecessary. And *Kadas v. MCI Systemhouse Corp.* found "The 5 percent test is arbitrary. . . . [T]he question whether a study is responsible and therefore admissible under the *Daubert* standard is different from the weight to be accorded to the significance of a particular correlation found by the study. It is for the judge to say, on the basis of the evidence of a trained statistician, whether a particular significance level, in the context of a particular study in a particular case, is too low to make the study worth the consideration of judge or jury." 255 F.3d 359, 362-63 (7th Cir. 2001). The reference was to *Daubert v. Merrell Dow Pharmaceuticals, Inc.*, 509 U.S. 579 (1993), dealing with the standards for admissibility of scientific evidence.

Binomial distribution focuses on the relationship between two factors, the race or gender composition of the available labor pool versus that of the employer's workforce. While powerful where applicable, this technique is limited because it cannot take account of added variables sometimes involved in employment issues. For example, in *Hazelwood*, the Court used binomial distribution as a way of comparing the employer's workforce with the pool of qualified teachers. While useful once the pool of those who were qualified is defined, binomial distribution cannot define what factors were considered in determining the qualifications relied on in hiring teachers.

Multiple Regression.   Multiple regression is a technique used to study the influence of any number of factors, or variables. Its use in discrimination litigation was first approved by the Supreme Court in *Bazemore v. Friday*, a case involving race discrimination in salary. Like the other techniques, multiple regression cannot show what qualifications are actually needed to do a job, but it can be useful in finding what factors an employer relied on in a particular employment setting and the weight given to each factor.

The core notion of multiple regression is an extension of the notion of matching pairs. Suppose two employees are so similarly situated in education, experience in the industry, seniority, job title, and work performed that they are a matched pair. It would be odd if these two employees do not receive the same pay. If they are of different races or genders and the pay difference is not otherwise explained, there would be a prima facie case of employment discrimination.

Multiple regression expands that notion so it is possible to compare the influence of many variables among a large group of employees. Once it is decided what variables are thought to bear on the employment situation, multiple regression makes it possible to hold these factors constant and then determine whether sex or race is also a statistically significant factor in setting salary.

Multiple regression is beyond simple graphical or mathematical statement, but the following may help to develop the concept. Assume someone suggests that the relevant factor in determining salary for an employer is education: the more education, the higher the pay. Graphically, each person's pay and years of education would look like the scattergram in Figure 2.6, with each X representing a particular person plotted on the graph by years of education and salary.

Notice that there appears to be some relationship between salary and years of education, but no straight-line relationship exists. To say it another way, there is no automatic rule that causes salary to go up a set amount of dollars for each increase of a year in education for every employee. But statistically it is possible to draw a "regression line" that is the "best fit" straight line to describe all the individual cases. Figure 2.7 illustrates such a linear regression. The notion is to balance out all the employees above the line with those below the line. In Figure 2.7, employee 1 has higher pay for the same education as employee 2, but those differences balance out if each is "regressed" to line A-B, the regression line, sometimes called the line of best fit.

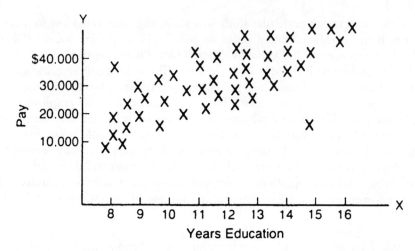

Figure 2.6

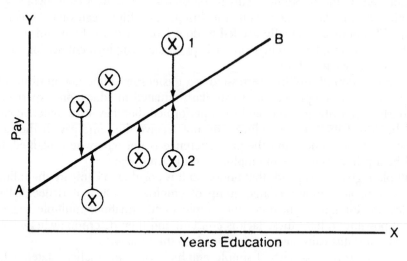

Figure 2.7

When another variable — say, seniority — is suggested as being relevant in determining salary, the graphic description requires three dimensions, as shown in Figure 2.8.

Notice that, instead of a regression line, there is a three-dimensional plane that is the "best fit" description of the contribution of education and seniority to the determination of salary. Graphic demonstration stops at three dimensions, so it is not useful when more than two variables are to be taken into account in describing salary. Multiple regression is a statistical technique that can demonstrate how any number of independent variables affect a continuous variable like salary. In short, multiple regression is "a method used to extract a systematic signal from the noise prescribed by the data." Franklin M. Fisher, *Multiple Regression in Legal Proceedings*, 80 COLUM. L. REV. 702, 706 (1980). Further, the result is quantifiable:

The relationship between the dependent variable and the independent variable (race or sex) is then estimated by extracting the effects of the other major variables. When this has been done, one has the best available substitute for controlled experimentation. The results of multiple regression can be read as showing the effects of each variable on the dependent variable, holding the others constant. Moreover, those results allow one to make statements about the probability that the effect described has merely been observed as a result of chance fluctuation.

Multiple regression generates an equation that explains the relationship between the dependent variable (e.g., salary) and the independent variables (e.g., the factors used by the employer to determine salary). Note that the information used to generate the equation is drawn from the employer's own salary scheme. The resulting equation looks like this:

$$Y = a + b_1x_1 + b_2x_2 + b_3x_3 + b_4x_4 \ldots b_kx_k$$

In this equation, "Y" equals salary, "a" equals a constant dollar amount, "b_1" and "b_2" are dollar amounts, and "x_1" and "x_2" are factors relevant to the salary determination. For example, in an academic setting, "x_1" may equal number of years of seniority, while "x_2" equals number of years of education past undergraduate school, "x_3" equals number of articles written, and "x_4" equals number of committee chairs held. Each factor has a dollar value. Any individual faculty member's salary can be determined (approximately) by inserting that faculty member's characteristics into the equation. The factors and the dollar amounts associated with the factors are based on a study of the employer's salary system. If the factor "white" or "male" has a dollar value, we might suspect discrimination. An alternative approach is to generate two different equations — for example, one for women and another for men. Assuming an adequate p-value, if the factors have substantially different dollar values and/or the constant is different in the two different equations, we might again suspect discrimination.

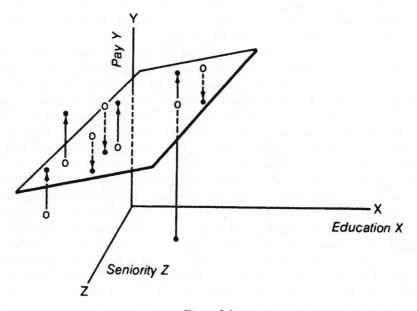

Figure 2.8

One question that has emerged is whether a multiple regression analysis is probative of discrimination even though a variable that might influence salary is not included in the study. In *Bazemore*, the Court found that the absence of a variable does not necessarily destroy the probative value of a multiple regression. The multiple regression in the case used four variables that might influence salary — race, education, tenure, and job title. Though the study showed a statistically significant relationship between race and the dependent variable of salary, the lower courts rejected the study because it did not include all the possible variables that might have influenced salary. The unanimous Supreme Court rejected that view, holding that statistical evidence is to be evaluated as is all other evidence.

> While the omission of variables from a regression analysis may render the analysis less probative than it otherwise might be, it can hardly be said, absent some other infirmity, that an analysis which accounts for the major factors "must be considered unacceptable as evidence of discrimination." . . . Normally, failure to include variables will affect the analysis' probativeness, not its admissibility.
>
> Importantly, it is clear that a regression analysis that includes less than "all measurable variables" may serve to prove a plaintiff's case. A plaintiff in a Title VII suit need not prove discrimination with scientific certainty; rather, his or her burden is to prove discrimination by a preponderance of the evidence. . . . Whether, in fact, such a regression analysis does carry the plaintiffs' ultimate burden will depend in a given case on the factual context of each case in light of all the evidence presented by both the plaintiff and the defendant.

The *Bazemore* Court did note that a multiple regression analysis could be so incomplete as to be inadmissible. Presumably, the question would be whether the analysis was so incomplete that no reasonable trier of fact could credit it. Suppose, in *Bazemore*, that the plaintiff's statistical analysis controlled only for race and education, omitting "tenure" and "job title." Should it nevertheless have been admitted into evidence? Professor Barnes has pointed out that the omission of a variable that does affect salary will make no difference unless the omitted variable is also correlated with race; only in that case would it tend to negate race as the explanation for the disparity shown. *See* DAVID W. BARNES & JOHN M. CONLEY, STATISTICAL EVIDENCE IN LITIGATION, §8.16, and 1989 Supp. pp. 70-71.

From a statistician's perspective, the issue of the best regression analysis is characterized as one of "goodness of fit." Professor Thomas J. Campbell has suggested that the law use a statistical test of goodness of fit, the "R statistic." R expresses, as a percentage, the part of the total variance explained by the factors used in the study. He would set a minimum R score of .50. Thomas J. Campbell, *Regression Analysis in Title VII Cases: Minimum Standards, Comparable Worth, and Other Issues Where Law and Statistics Meet*, 36 STAN. L. REV. 1299 (1984). Is that consistent with the preponderance of evidence standard emphasized in *Bazemore*?

A final point concerns what statisticians call practical (as opposed to statistical) significance. It is possible that a statistical study will show a statistically significant relationship between gender and salary, but one at such a low level that it may not be cognizable. For example suppose the regression showed that, in a workforce of thousands, women were underpaid relative to men by $5 a year. No matter how robust the statistical proof, it is questionable whether a finding of discrimination ought to follow because the difference is so small. *See Rudebusch v. Hughes*, 313 F.3d 506, 515 (9th Cir. 2002) (expressing "concern about inferring discrimination from a study in which the highest single pay disparity for ethnic minorities fell 2.0

standard deviations away from predicted salary — but produced a lowest statistically unexplainable difference of $87 between ethnic minorities and their Anglo counterparts"). In the disparate impact chapter, we address a similar question in discussing quantum of impact. See p. 252.

D. DEFENSES TO DISPARATE TREATMENT CASES

There are three approaches to defending against a systemic disparate treatment case. The first is to challenge the factual basis on which plaintiff's case is predicated. Thus, the employer could deny that a formal policy exists or could challenge the facts on which plaintiff's case is based. Where plaintiff demonstrates a systemic practice-based case using statistics, the best defense would be statistical studies that counter plaintiff's statistical studies. *Bazemore* was such a case. The second line of defense is to challenge not the statistics plaintiff uses, but the inference of discriminatory intent the statistics raise. The third and final line of defense is to admit the discrimination but to assert a recognized defense. The second and third possibilities are explored in the next two sections.

1. *Rebutting the Inference of Discriminatory Intent*

PERSONNEL ADMINISTRATOR v. FEENEY
442 U.S. 256 (1979)

[The Court was faced with an equal protection challenge to a Massachusetts law granting military veterans absolute preference for state jobs. Because at that time 98 percent of the veterans were male, few women could realistically compete for jobs desired by veterans. The lower court found the consequences for women too inevitable to have been "unintended." The Supreme Court, per Justice Stewart, reversed the finding of unconstitutionality.]

The appellee's ultimate argument rests upon the presumption, common to the criminal and civil law, that a person intends the natural and foreseeable consequences of his voluntary actions. Her position was well stated in the concurring opinion in the District Court: "Conceding . . . that the goal here was to benefit the veteran, there is no reason to absolve the legislature from awareness that the means chosen to achieve this goal would freeze women out of all those state jobs actively sought by men. To be sure, the legislature did not wish to harm women. But the cutting-off of women's opportunities was an inevitable concomitant of the chosen scheme — as inevitable as the proposition that if tails is up, heads must be down. Where a law's consequences are that inevitable, can they meaningfully be described as unintended?"

This rhetorical question implies that a negative answer is obvious, but it is not. The decision to grant a preference to veterans was of course "intentional." So, necessarily, did an adverse impact upon nonveterans follow from that decision. And it cannot seriously be argued that the legislature of Massachusetts could have been unaware that most veterans are men. It would thus be disingenuous to say that the adverse consequences of this legislation for women were unintended, in the sense that they were not volitional or in the sense that they were not foreseeable.

"Discriminatory purpose," however, implies more than intent as volition or intent as awareness of consequences.[24] It implies that the decisionmaker, in this case a state legislature, selected or reaffirmed a particular course of action at least in part "because of," not merely "in spite of," its adverse effects upon an identifiable group.[25] Yet, nothing in the record demonstrates that this preference for veterans was originally devised or subsequently re-enacted because it would accomplish the collateral goal of keeping women in a stereotypic and predefined place in the Massachusetts Civil Service.

To the contrary, the statutory history shows that the benefit of the preference was consistently offered to "any person" who was a veteran. That benefit has been extended to women under a very broad statutory definition of the term veteran. The preference formula itself, which is the focal point of this challenge, was first adopted — so it appears from this record — out of a perceived need to help a small group of older Civil War veterans. It has since been reaffirmed and extended only to cover new veterans. When the totality of legislative actions establishing and extending the Massachusetts veterans' preference are considered, see *Washington v. Davis*, the law remains what it purports to be: a preference for veterans of either sex over non-veterans of either sex, not for men over women.

NOTES

1. *Equal Protection vs. Title VII. Feeney* could not have been brought under Title VII because §712 explicitly excepts veterans' preference laws from attack under the statute. *Feeney* is consistent with *Washington v. Davis*, 426 U.S. 229 (1976), where plaintiffs mounted an equal protection attack on a test used for selecting recruits for police training in Washington, D.C. In rejecting the use of a disparate impact theory under equal protection, the Court held that liability under the equal protection clause depended on proving what would, in Title VII terms, be called disparate treatment. But this does not mean that the effect or impact of an employer's actions is irrelevant to a disparate treatment case.

> This is not to say that the necessary discriminatory racial purpose must be express or appear on the face of the statute or that a law's disproportionate impact is irrelevant in cases involving Constitution-based claims of racial discrimination. A statute, otherwise neutral on its face, must not be applied so as invidiously to discriminate on the basis of race. . . .

---

24. Proof of discriminatory intent must necessarily usually rely on objective factors, several of which were outlined in *Arlington Heights v. Metropolitan Housing Development Corp.*, 429 U.S. 252, 266. The inquiry is practical. What a legislature or any official entity is "up to" may be plain from the results its actions achieve, or the results they avoid. Often it is made clear from what has been called, in a different context, "the give and take of the situation."

25. This is not to say that the inevitability or foreseeability of consequences of a neutral rule has no bearing upon the existence of discriminatory intent. Certainly, when the adverse consequences of a law upon an identifiable group are as inevitable as the gender-based consequences of [the veterans' preference] a strong inference that the adverse effects were desired can reasonably be drawn. But in this inquiry — made as it is under the Constitution — an inference is a working tool, not a synonym for proof. When, as here, the impact is essentially an unavoidable consequence of a legislative policy that has in itself always been deemed to be legitimate, and when, as here, the statutory history and all of the available evidence affirmatively demonstrate the opposite, the inference simply fails to ripen into proof.

Necessarily, an invidious discriminatory purpose may often be inferred from the totality of the relevant facts, including the fact, if it is true, that the law bears more heavily on one race than another. It is also not infrequently true that the discriminatory impact . . . may for all practical purposes demonstrate unconstitutionality because in various circumstances the discrimination is very difficult to explain on nonracial grounds. . . . Disproportionate impact is not irrelevant, but it is not the sole touchstone of an invidious racial discrimination forbidden by the Constitution.

426 U.S. at 241-42. In a concurring opinion in *Washington v. Davis,* Justice Stevens described a rationale for using impact data to show intent to discriminate:

Frequently the most probative evidence of intent will be objective evidence of what actually happened rather than evidence describing the subjective state of mind of the actor. For normally the actor is presumed to have intended the natural consequences of his deeds. This is particularly true in the case of governmental action which is frequently the product of compromise, of collective decision-making, and of mixed motivation. It is unrealistic, on the one hand, to require the victim of alleged discrimination to uncover the actual subjective intent of the decision-maker or, conversely, to invalidate otherwise legitimate action simply because an improper motive affected the deliberation of a participant in the decisional process. A law conscripting clerics should not be invalidated because an atheist voted for it.

429 U.S. at 253. Thus, where disparate treatment is concerned, the statutory and constitutional approaches are similar, and underrepresentation is relevant but only to the extent it casts light on the intent underlying policies or practices.

2. *No Intent to Discriminate Shown?* Did the Court in *Feeney* reject the natural and probable consequences test of intent? Or did Massachusetts successfully rebut a prima facie case of intent inferred from the natural and probable consequences approach? Or was the Court simply convinced that, whatever the impact, gender discrimination was the last thing the legislature intended when it enacted the veterans' preference? Cf. footnote 24 in *Teamsters* on p. 127. Consider that, if Massachusetts today has the same rule absolutely preferring veterans for public jobs, its impact on women now would be far lower because women are better represented in the armed services.

Can you imagine anything that might rebut the inference of discriminatory intent (without necessarily challenging the underlying statistics) in *Teamsters* or *Hazelwood?* In *Hazelwood,* for example, suppose the defendant claimed that residents of the school district were given preference as teachers so that it was Hazelwood's mostly white population that explained the scarcity of black teachers.

EEOC v. SEARS, ROEBUCK & CO.
839 F.2d 302 (7th Cir. 1988)

H. WOOD, JR., Circuit Judge.

[The EEOC challenged Sears' hiring, promotion, and compensation practices as systemic disparate treatment on the basis of gender, with the principal issue being the concentration of men in higher-paying sales jobs compensated by commissions and the concentration of women in lower-paying sales jobs paid by the hour. Sears won in the trial court. The Seventh Circuit first held that the burden of persuasion on the issue of intent to discriminate remains at all times on the plaintiff. Second, the court reviewed the trial court's findings on that issue, using a clearly erroneous standard of review.]

The EEOC presented, almost exclusively, statistical evidence in the form of regression analyses based on information from employment applications of rejected sales applicants and Sears' computerized payroll records from 1973 through 1980. The EEOC based other regression analyses on information from Applicant Interview Guides Sears had administered at various times from 1978 through 1980 at two Sears stores in its Southwestern Territory. The EEOC attempted to bolster this statistical evidence through nonstatistical evidence regarding the subjective nature of Sears' selection process and allegedly discriminatory aspects of Sears' testing practices.

Sears did not respond with like regression analyses based on employment application and payroll records. Instead, most of Sears' evidence was directed at undermining two assumptions Sears claimed were faulty and fatal to the validity of the EEOC's statistical analysis — the assumptions of equal interests and qualifications of applicants for commission sales positions. This evidence consisted of testimony by Sears store managers, personnel managers, and other store officials, a study based on interviews of women in nontraditional jobs at Sears, national surveys and polls regarding the changing status of women in American society, morale surveys of Sears employees and 1976 and 1982 job interest surveys of Sears employees, national labor force data, and an analysis of the Applicant Interview Guides that attempts to measure differences in interest among men and women. Sears also presented evidence regarding its hiring figures, general evidence regarding the characteristics of commission salespersons including a case study of all commission sales hires in all stores, based on information in personnel files of applicants who were hired and sales performance data, evidence regarding the employment milieu at Sears, especially relating to commission selling and the structure of Sears, and evidence regarding its affirmative action efforts. . . .

The EEOC argues that Sears' "generalized interest evidence" is inadequate as a matter of law to refute the EEOC's statistical presentation. . . . The EEOC implies that Sears had the burden of responding with a more probative statistical analysis. The Supreme Court in *Teamsters* specifically stated, however, that "we do not . . . suggest that there are any particular limits on the type of evidence an employer may use." An employer may attempt to show that plaintiffs' proof is "either inaccurate or insignificant," or the [employer] may attempt to provide a "nondiscriminatory explanation for the apparently discriminatory result." Then-Justice, now Chief Justice Rehnquist, concurring in *Dothard v. Rawlinson* [reproduced at p. 246], stated that defendants in a discrimination case "may endeavor [in rebuttal] to impeach the reliability of the statistical evidence, they may offer rebutting evidence, or they may disparage in arguments or in briefs the probative weight which the Plaintiffs' evidence should be accorded." See also *Catlett v. Missouri Highway & Transportation Commission*, 828 F.2d 1260, 1266 (8th Cir. 1987) (defendant may introduce evidence that a lesser interest in certain jobs on part of female applicants explains statistical disparity). . . . The cases cited by the EEOC to support its argument that Sears had the burden of rebutting its statistical analysis with more "refined, accurate and valid" statistical evidence did not state that the defendant must produce such evidence to succeed in rebutting the plaintiffs' case. Instead, those cases indicated that a defendant could or "was entitled to" use such a means of rebuttal. These cases involve disparate impact claims — without deciding whether these principles are applicable in a disparate treatment case, we can say that EEOC misconstrues the principles. These cases suggest, and the cases we have cited above confirm, that statistical evidence is only one method of rebutting a statistical case. We therefore reject the EEOC's contention that Sears' interest evidence, consisting of testimony of Sears' store witnesses, external labor force data, national survey data, and data from surveys of Sears' employees, is insufficient as a matter of law to undermine the EEOC's statistical evidence. . . .

The district judge found a plethora of problems in the statistical analyses that the EEOC had offered to support the claim that Sears discriminated against women in hiring into commission sales positions from 1973 to 1980. Before addressing the EEOC's specific challenges to the district court's criticisms of its statistical evidence, it is helpful to discuss three key findings made by the district court, which we believe are not clearly erroneous. Those findings are that during the period at issue in this case (1973-1980): (1) commission selling was significantly different from non-commission selling at Sears; (2) women were not as interested in commission selling as were men; and (3) women were not as qualified for commission selling as were men.

The finding that colors the district court's entire treatment of the EEOC's hiring as well as its promotion claims is that selling on commission at Sears is a very different job from "regular," or noncommission selling at Sears. We cannot say that finding is clearly erroneous. The court's description of commission and non-commission selling at Sears indicates that the two forms of selling differed in the type of merchandise sold, the risk involved, which was reflected in the manner of compensation, and the technical knowledge, expertise, and motivation involved. The district court describes the differences at length, thus we need only mention major differences. As the district court found, commission selling at Sears usually involved selling "big ticket" items, which are high-cost merchandise such as major appliances, furnaces, roofing, and sewing machines. Merchandise sold on a noncommission basis understandably was generally low-cost and included apparel, paint, and cosmetics. Commission selling involved some risk, especially before 1977. During that period commission salespersons generally received a commission ranging from 6% to 9% percent [sic] plus a "draw" each week. The draw usually did not exceed 70% of average or estimated earnings, but was subject to reduction if the employee's commission did not equal the amount of the draw. There was always a risk that the employee could lose some of the draw if the commissions did not equal the amount of the draw. After 1977, commission salespersons no longer faced deficits. In what the court noted was an effort "to reduce the financial risk of selling on commission in an effort to attract more women to commission sales," Sears paid commission salespersons a nominal salary plus a 3% commission. Noncommission salespersons were paid on a straight hourly rate, and full-time salespersons received 1% commission on all sales until January 1979 when the practice was discontinued. The district court found that commission selling often required salespersons to be available after the normal working hours of 8:00 a.m. to 5:00 p.m., sometimes required that they sell in people's homes, might require a license depending on the products sold, and required qualities usually not as necessary in regular selling, including a high degree of technical knowledge, expertise, and motivation.

The court's next two major findings, that there were different interests and qualifications among men and women for commission selling, were grounded in part on the court's recognition of differences between noncommission and commission selling at Sears. The court based these findings on the large amount of evidence presented by Sears on these issues. The court extensively discusses this evidence. Again, we cannot say that these findings are clearly erroneous.

Regarding the question of differing interests in general among men and women in commission selling, [the district] court found that "[t]he most credible and convincing evidence offered at trial regarding women's interest in commission sales at Sears was the detailed, uncontradicted testimony of numerous men and women who were Sears store managers, personnel managers and other officials, regarding their efforts to recruit women into commission sales." These witnesses testified to their only limited success in affirmative action efforts to persuade women to sell on commission, and testified that women were generally more interested in product lines like clothing, jewelry, and cosmetics that were usually sold on a noncommission basis, than they were in product lines involving commission selling like automotives, roofing, and furnaces. The contrary applied to men. Women were also less interested in outside sales which often required night calls on customers than were men, with the exception of selling custom draperies. Various reasons for women's lack of interest in commission selling included a fear or dislike of what they perceived as cut-throat competition, and increased pressure and risk associated with commission sales. Noncommission selling, on the other hand, was associated with more social contact and friendship, less pressure and less risk. This evidence was confirmed by a study of national surveys and polls from the mid-1930's through 1983 regarding the changing status of women in American society, from which a Sears expert made conclusions regarding women's interest in commission selling; morale surveys of Sears employees, which the court found "demonstrate[d] that noncommission saleswomen were generally happier with their present jobs at Sears, and were much less likely than their male counterparts to be interested in other positions, such as commission sales"; a job interest survey taken at Sears in 1976; a survey taken in 1982 of commission and noncommission salespeople at Sears regarding their attitudes, interests, and the personal beliefs and lifestyles of the employees, which the court concluded showed that noncommission salesmen were "far more interested" in commission sales than were noncommission saleswomen, and national labor force data.

The court recognized the EEOC's expert witness testimony regarding women's general interests in employment, which essentially was that there were no significant differences between women and men regarding interests and career aspirations. We cannot determine the district court clearly erred in finding the evidence not credible, persuasive or probative. These expert witnesses used small samples of women who had taken traditional jobs when opportunities arose. Larger samples would have been more persuasive. In addition as the court found, "[n]one of these witnesses had any specific knowledge of Sears." The court found Sears' evidence clearly more persuasive on the issue of different interest in commission selling between men and women. The court also found significant Sears' evidence that women became increasingly willing to accept commission sales positions between 1970 and 1980 due to, among other things, changes in commission sales positions from mostly full-time to largely part-time (more women preferred part-time), change in compensation to salary plus commission (which eliminated a lot of risk), increased availability of day care, and a group of successful saleswomen who served as role models. . . .

In short, we hold that the district court did not clearly err in finding that women were not as interested in commission sales positions as were men.

We similarly find that the district court did not clearly err in concluding that women applicants had different qualifications than did men applicants. The court noted that the EEOC's Commission Sales Report indicated that "on average, female applicants in the 'sales' pool were younger, less educated, less likely to have commission sales experience, and less likely than male applicants to have prior work experience with the products sold on commission at Sears." The EEOC does not challenge this finding.

All three of the court's findings discussed above — that commission selling is significantly different from noncommission selling, that women were not equally interested with men in commission selling at Sears, and that women applicants were not equally qualified with men for commission selling at Sears — form the bases for the court's criticisms of the EEOC's statistics regarding hiring at Sears. . . .

CUDAHY, Circuit Judge, concurring in part and dissenting in part. . . .

Perhaps the most questionable aspect of the majority opinion is its acceptance of women's alleged low interest and qualifications for commission selling as a complete explanation for the huge statistical disparities favoring men. The adoption by the district court and by the majority of Sears' analysis of these arguments strikes me as extremely uncritical. Sears has indeed presented varied evidence that these gender-based differences exist, both in our society as a whole and in its particular labor pool. But it remains a virtually insuperable task to overcome the weight of the statistical evidence marshalled by the EEOC or the skepticism that courts ought to show toward defenses to Title VII actions that rely on unquantifiable traits ascribed to protected groups.

[T]he majority's more benign view tends to minimize the significance of Sears' contentions that women lack the interest and qualifications to sell on commission. Women, as described by Sears, the district court and the majority, exhibit the very same stereotypical qualities for which they have been assigned low-status positions throughout history. . . .

These conclusions, it seems to me, are of a piece with the proposition that women are by nature happier cooking, doing the laundry and chauffeuring the children to softball games than arguing appeals or selling stocks. The stereotype of women as less greedy and daring than men is one that the sex discrimination laws were intended to address. It is disturbing that this sort of thinking is accepted so uncritically by the district court and by the majority. Perhaps they have forgotten that women have been hugely successful in such fields as residential real estate, and door-to-door and other direct outside merchandising. There are abundant indications that women lack neither the desire to compete strenuously for financial gain nor the capacity to take risks.

Sears, the district court and the majority hang much of their refutation of the EEOC's hiring and promotion claims on the putative difference between men's and women's interest in undertaking commission sales. Huge statistical disparities in participation in various commission selling jobs are ascribed to differences in interest. Yet there is scarcely any recognition of the employer's role in shaping the interests of applicants. Even the majority is willing to concede that lack of opportunity may drive lack of interest, but dismisses the matter as a "chicken-egg" problem. . . .

NOTES

1. *A Prima Facie Case?* The record in *Sears* revealed that, across the entire company and over a period of many years, women constituted 61 percent of the *applicants* for full-time sales jobs at Sears, but only 27 percent of the newly hired commission salespeople. Women made up seventy-five percent of the non-commission sales force.

Median hourly wages were about twice as high for commission as non-commission salespeople. *See* Vicki Schultz, *Telling Stories About Women and Work: Judicial Interpretation of Sex Segregation in the Workplace in Title VII Cases Raising the Lack of Interest Argument*, 103 HARV. L. REV. 1749, 1752 nn. 5-6 (1990). Using the applicant pool meant that all in the pool had expressed an interest in the jobs and likely thought they met the minimal job qualifications. Would these figures by themselves, without the use of any sophisticated statistical studies, show a gross enough disparity to establish a prima facie case? In other words, is this a *Teamsters* case? In any event, a binomial distribution study would no doubt have established that sex was a statistically significant factor in whether an applicant was hired at all and whether those hired were assigned to commission or noncommission sales jobs. Thus, *Hazelwood* would also be satisfied.

If the trial court found that no prima facie case was established, was that because the EEOC failed to bring those cold statistics to life with anecdotal evidence of women applicants who were not hired at all or who, if hired, were channeled into noncommission sales jobs? The Government in both *Teamsters* and *Hazelwood* deployed evidence of individual instances of discrimination, and plaintiffs have learned from the EEOC's debacle in *Sears* and have bulwarked statistical evidence with other proof. Nevertheless, it remains possible that a prima facie case could be established solely on the basis of statistical evidence. *See Kadas v. MCI Systemhouse*, 255 F.3d 359, 363 (7th Cir. 2001) ("If 100 employees in a department of 1,000 employees were riffed and every one of the 100 was 40 years old or older and every one of the 900 retained was under 40, that would, we should think, be enough evidence of age discrimination (the probability of its occurring by chance being inconceivably minute) to place on the employer a burden of explaining, which is all that making out a prima facie case means").

2. *Defense or Rebuttal*? Sears failed to introduce its own studies to contradict the EEOC's, surely a remarkable strategy if such studies would have undercut the inference of discrimination. Does Sears' failure to do so mean that it conceded the prima facie showing of intent to discriminate? What seems clear is that Sears escaped liability by offering a non-discriminatory explanation for the gender correlation that the EEOC apparently had established. Sears' offered testimony describing how women had different interests than men, that commission selling was different from noncommission selling, and, based on the difference between men and women, women were not as qualified for nor as interested in commission sales jobs as were men.

How is this rationalized? Did Sears win because it carried a burden of production or one of persuasion? In other words, having offered a nondiscriminatory explanation for the apparently damning data, perhaps Sears won because the EEOC failed to disprove that explanation. Alternatively, Sears might have prevailed because it persuaded the district court by a preponderance of evidence that the underrepresentation was the result of women's lack of interest, not Sears' actions? In *St. Mary's Honor Center v. Hicks*, 509 U.S. 502 (1993), see p. 59, the trial court held that plaintiff had proved that defendant's asserted reason for its action was not true; it nevertheless found for the defendant because it believed that the action was based on a personality conflict and not on discrimination. Is *Sears* another example where the trial court simply did not believe that the cause of the dramatic shortfall of women in commission jobs was the result of defendant's intent to discriminate? Or did the court accept a claim of good faith as a defense, a defense not accepted in *Teamsters*?

3. *Feminist Theory in Litigation Context.* One of the more controversial aspects of the case was Sears' success in using feminist theory to defend itself from liability. The case involved two different themes in feminist thought, with Sears splitting the seam between the two:

(a) *Difference Theory.* Sears' relied on one school of feminist thinking that stresses the differences between men and women. The divergent life experiences of men and women lead them to develop different perspectives and attitudes. Carol Gilligan, IN A DIFFERENT VOICE (1982), is the most prominent spokesperson for this view. Sears called Dr. Rosalind Rosenberg, a feminist historian at Barnard College, to make the point. In an offer of proof to the court, she wrote:

> Women's role in American society and in the American family unit has fostered the development of "feminine" values that have been internalized by women themselves and reinforced by society, through its customs, its culture, and its laws. . . . Throughout American history women have been trained from earliest childhood to develop the humane and nurturing values expected of the American mother. Thus trained, women have assumed primary responsibility for maintaining family relationships. . . . Women's participation in the labor force is affected by the values they have internalized. For example:
>
> a) Women tend to be more relationship centered and men tend to be more work centered. Although both men and women find satisfaction and a sense of self-worth in their jobs, men are more likely than women to derive their self-image from their work. Most employed women continue to derive their self-image from their role as wife and mother. Women tend to be more interested than men in the cooperative, social aspects of the work situation.
>
> b) Women are trained from earliest childhood to develop different expectations from men about what aspirations are socially acceptable. Women who challenged those expectations by choosing jobs typically pursued by men often experience doubts about their ability to do well. . . .
>
> c) Women are seen by themselves and society as less competitive than men and more concerned with protecting personal relationships.
>
> d) Men's more extensive experience in competitive sports prepares them for the competitiveness, aggressiveness, teamwork, and leadership required for many jobs.

Should this testimony rebut the inference of intent to discriminate in a systemic disparate treatment case? Would this evidence alone be sufficient to explain away the statistical evidence presented by the EEOC? Or would there have to be some quantification of the male/female differences? This raises, again, the question whether Sears carried a burden of persuasion or only one of production.

Dr. Rosenberg did not contend that the male/female differences she identified were based on genetic differences between men and women. Rosenberg did not treat gender roles as caused by "women's choices alone, and she was careful to present differences of interest as a matter of statistical distributions, not inherent features of gender. She freely allowed that the current allocation of roles is 'reinforced externally through social pressures and governmental action' as well as 'internally through the internalization of norms.'"

A related issue arose recently with regard to the remarks of the then-president of Harvard, Lawrence Summers, regarding the relative paucity of women in the academic sciences. Although most of the resultant outcry focused on his suggesting that there might be a biological basis for the underrepresentation of women, *see* Owen D. Jones, *The Causation Equation: Summers on Science*, 11 CARDOZO WOMEN'S L.J. 577 (2005), Dr. Summers also referred to cultural differences that Dr. Rosenberg had identified, and which many feminists have also noted. *See generally* Ellen M. Bublick, *Summers' Personal as Political: Reasoning Without Effort from Stereotypes,* 11 CARDOZO WOMEN'S L.J. 529 (2005) (faulting Summers for too easily attributing differences to biology rather than either socialization or discrimination).

Does Sears' argument amount to little more than blaming the victim? But if women are the victims, who is the victimizer? If society has socialized women in certain ways, why is that Sears' fault? Does Title VII impose an affirmative duty on employers to re-socialize women or to alter job requirements to meet women's needs?

(b) *Equality Theory.* The EEOC countered with its own historian, Dr. Alice Kessler-Harris, who represents the equality vision of feminism, i.e., that for purposes of employment women and men are basically alike. In her written testimony to the court, she responded to Dr. Rosenberg:

> [N]ew historical information calls into question the idea that women can "choose" not to work in certain areas, and insists that choice can be understood only within the framework of available opportunity. It flatly contradicts the notion that biology, culture, or socialization enables us to make statements about "all" women or about women generally. In particular, it provides the basis for refuting testimony that attributes to most women, and especially to those women who did work for wages, perceptions and attitudes that influenced the lives of relatively few. . . .
>
> A more accurate interpretation of the history of women's work in the U.S. would take the following form. The structure of the labor force is the product of a complex interaction between labor force needs and a socialization process that reinforces desirable roles. Women's "interests" as well as their expectations are thus a consequence of life experiences that are reinforced or discouraged by the larger society. In an industrial society, a major part of the cycle of reinforcement is played by employers whose hiring policies significantly influence women's self-perception, their assessment of reasonable aspirations, and their announced goals. What appear to be women's choices, and what are characterized as women's "interests" are, in fact, heavily influenced by the opportunities for work made available to them. In the past, opportunities offered to women have been conditioned by society's perceptions of women and assumptions about them. Thus, women have been hired into limited numbers of jobs, and discriminated against in the work force generally. The resulting profile of "women's work" has been then perceived to be what the women "chose."

See also Schultz, *supra* Note 1 at 1851.

Professor Scott A. Moss, *Women Choosing Diverse Workplaces: A Rational Preference with Disturbing Implications for Both Occupational Segregation and Economic Analysis of Law,* 27 HARV. WOMEN'S L.J. 1, 5 (2004), argues that a gender segregated workplace begets more segregation, without the need for employer discrimination. "In economic terms, women rationally use the level of diversity as a proxy for discrimination, which is more difficult to observe. In this light, women's preference for diversity is 'rational discrimination' by employees against employers — a generalization that, though imperfect, is logical given employees' imperfect information about which employers discriminate." Should the employer be legally responsible for the continuing momentum of job segregation or must it be up to trailblazers, like Catharina Costa from *Desert Palace,* to push their way into segregated workplaces?

4. *Lack of Interest.* The EEOC factored into its regression analyses the fact that women as a group had less interest in commission sales jobs than did men as a group. The studies still found a statistically significant relationship between gender and

commission sales jobs. In other words, the parties were not disputing that women are less interested, but only how much less interested they were. The EEOC acknowledged that women were less interested, but presented statistical evidence of discrimination that quantified and took into consideration that lower level of interest. If Sears agreed that women are less interested, but failed to quantify the impact of that lack of interest, how does this undermine the EEOC's case? How could the court possibly find in favor of Sears on this evidence?

Professor Vicki Schultz, in *Telling Stories, supra* Note 1, and with Stephen Petterson, in *Race, Gender, and Choice: An Empirical Study of the Lack of Interest Defense in Title VII Cases Challenging Job Segregation*, 59 U. CHI. L. REV. 1073 (1992), shows that the lack of interest defense was not born with the *Sears* decision. The conclusion of Schultz's study is that judges have become increasingly more receptive to employer claims than in early race discrimination cases. She attributes this shift "among judges of all political affiliations" in recent decades as resulting from federal judges beginning "to share the general public's belief that employment discrimination against minorities had been largely eradicated." *Id.* at 1180-81.

5. *Less Qualified.* The *Sears* court found it significant that "on average, female applicants in the 'sales' pool were younger, less educated, less likely to have commission sales experience, and less likely than male applicants to have prior work experience with the products sold on commission at Sears." Even assuming that is true, does that rebut a strong prima facie case based on statistics? Wouldn't Sears be expected to take the data it used as a basis for that testimony and show how, in light of that data, the statistical study presented by the EEOC had lost its probative value?

6. *Failure to Redress as Intentional Discrimination.* Taking Dr. Rosenberg's approach, what aspects of work culture would prove that Sears intended to keep women out of commission-paying sales jobs? What about job descriptions or application forms stressing that commission sales is competitive and requires aggressive tactics? Would evidence that competitive sales contests were used to motivate the workers be enough for a finding that Sears intended to discriminate on the basis of gender? Is it intentional discrimination to fail to alter the work culture for commission sales jobs to make it more compatible with the interests and values of women? Perhaps Sears convinced the trial judge that it did all that could be expected to recruit women for commission sales jobs and so the failure to be successful could not be considered intentional discrimination on the employer's part.

Chapter 3 deals with disparate impact discrimination, which is a way to attack employer's practices that have an adverse effect on women or minority men and that are not job related and necessary for business. Intent to discriminate is not an element. Should the EEOC have used the disparate impact theory to attack these practices that had the effect of making the jobs much less attractive to women than to men? Disparate impact theory requires the employer to take account of differences among workers to the extent that its practices weigh more heavily on one group or another. Would Dr. Rosenberg's testimony have helped the EEOC in a disparate impact case?

7. *Questioning the Basic Assumption?* Sears won by attacking the basic underlying assumption of antidiscrimination laws: that underrepresentation of protected-class individuals is based on untrue stereotypes about those groups, rather than on real differences between those groups and the dominant culture. But did Congress decide in passing antidiscrimination laws that, even if protected groups have been socialized or deprived in ways that impair their ability to compete, employers cannot rely on those differences to further oppress these groups by depriving them of

employment? If so, is this better pursued under a disparate impact than a disparate treatment theory?

NOTE ON THE NEW STRUCTURALISM

Sears has been read by many as the turning point in the use of systemic disparate treatment, at least as conceived in *Teamsters* and *Hazelwood*. It was a major defeat not only for the EEOC but also for the entire civil rights community. Nevertheless, rumors of the theory's demise may be exaggerated, especially in light of *Dukes v. Wal-Mart*, reproduced at p. 632, which certified a class action of 1.5 million women against an even bigger retailer than Sears. Plaintiffs claim that Wal-Mart allowed workplace managers to use unstructured discretion in evaluating employees and its use across the entire company produced a dramatic difference in promotion for men and women and much lower salaries for women than men. The claim is that according this discretion allowed the conscious, but especially the unconscious, bias of the supervisors to produce the statistical differences in promotion and pay. *Dukes* may indicate that a smarter case, brought in a more sympathetic court, can implement the *Teamsters/Hazelwood* theory without major modifications. Further, the EEOC's avowed new interest in systemic disparate treatment, see Note 7 on p. 140, augurs well for such a revival, especially since EEOC actions do not pose the procedural problems of class actions which are the threshold barriers to cases like *Dukes*.

But *Dukes* might also reflect the emergence of a "new structuralist" approach to discrimination law. Two major proponents of this approach are Professors Susan Sturm and Tristin Green. The new structuralists draw from the older approaches a concern about underrepresentation resulting from employer policies and practices. But they have a dramatically different view of the causes of such underrepresentation and the solutions for it. *Hazelwood* and especially *Teamsters* seemed to be predicated on the belief that old-fashioned animus against African Americans largely drove the employers to refuse to hire them. *Sears*, of course, locates the cause of underrepresentation entirely away from the employer and places the responsibility on women who either do not acquire the qualifications for promotion or do not want to incur the costs of working in a higher stress environment.

The new structuralists, however, see the problem of discrimination today as much more complicated than any of these cases. They believe that underrepresentation is caused to a large extent by a combination of more subtle discrimination (the unconscious bias we discussed in Chapter 1) and changing workplace dynamics that enable such bias to operate more freely than in the past. For example, Sears' policies that may have contributed to the shortfall of women doing commission sales work were neutral on their face. But the real underlying problem may have been that those policies were administered by Sears' managers with unstructured discretion that allowed intentional and unconscious bias of those managers to influence how the policies were implemented. In *Second Generation Employment Discrimination: A Structural Approach*, 101 COLUM. L. REV. 458, 485-90 (2001), Professor Sturm writes:

> For a variety of reasons, decisions requiring the exercise of individual or collective judgment that are highly unstructured tend to reflect, express, or produce biased outcomes. This bias has been linked to patterns of underrepresentation or exclusion of members of nondominant groups. . . . [Those outcomes reflect] the failure of the employer's decisionmaking system to minimize the expression of bias. . . .

Professor Sturm mentions disparate impact, and you will reconsider the possibility that that theory offers a solution to this problem when you reach Chapter 3. But the larger problem is that new structuralism does not fit comfortably within either of the systemic theories currently recognized. Thus, Professor Tristin Green agrees with Sturm that the employer's harmful action in these circumstances is its failure to minimize discriminatory bias in individual decision-making:

> An independent conceptualization of a form of discrimination in terms of workplace dynamics tells a certain and important causal story about how discrimination continues to operate in the modern workplace. Significantly, it recognizes the role that discriminatory bias, even in individuals who subscribe to an egalitarian ideal, continues to play in the allocation of opportunity and perpetuation of stratification. This story tells individual employees that they do not stand as innocent bystanders to inequity and discrimination simply because they believe that all employees should be judged equally on merit rather than race- or sex-based characteristics. But it also recognizes that discrimination today rarely operates in isolated states of mind; rather, it is often influenced, enabled, even encouraged by the structures, practices, and opportunities of the organizations within which groups and individuals work

Discrimination in Workplace Dynamics: Toward a Structural Account of Disparate Treatment Theory, 38 HARV. C.R.-C.L. L. REV. 91, 128 (2002). *See also* Tristin Green, *Work Culture and Discrimination*, 93 CAL. L. REV. 623 (2005) (discussing work culture as a source of discrimination and considering legal pressure on employers to devise meaningful programs for reform). But Professor Green doubts that either systemic disparate treatment or disparate impact, at least as traditionally deployed, will solve the problem, in part because she doubts the ability of statistical analysis to uncover underrepresentation in many workplaces. *Workplace Dynamics*, at 120-21.

The new structuralist solution seems to be mostly procedural. One alternative described by Professor Sturm approves the law's encouragement of voluntary employer initiatives aimed at achieving workplace equality. She examines structures put into place at several large private employers that treat discrimination and harassment as but a subset of workplace problems that need to be resolved, a problem-solving approach that may be more effective than litigation at rooting out the subconscious bias that characterizes much of today's discrimination. 101 COLUM. L. REV. at 462-63. *See also* Melissa Hart, *The Possibility of Avoiding Discrimination: Considering Compliance and Liability*, 39 CONN. L. REV. 1623, 1639 (2007) (possible approaches include "neutral and well-advertised posting of management positions and training opportunities; written standards of both expectation and evaluation; monitoring and appraisal of workplace statistics; and antidiscrimination policies and training."); Susan Sturm & Howard Gadlin, *Conflict Resoluton and Systemic Change*, 2007 J. DISP. RES. No. 1 (2007). Professor Green also favors encouraging employers to examine their practices to reduce the operation of discriminatory bias. While Professor Green approves some recent class action lawsuits targeting organizational context as a source of discrimination in individual decision, Tristin K. Green, *Targeting Workplace Context: Title VII as a Tool for Institutional Reform*, 72 FORDHAM L. REV. 659 (2003), neither scholar is very clear about what forces would impel such an examination. To the extent that neither of the systemic theories raises a realistic threat of liability, one might be justifiably skeptical of far-reaching change.

A frontal assault on the new structuralism was launched by Professor Samuel R. Bagenstos, *The Structural Turn and the Limits of Antidiscrimination Law*, 94 CAL. L. REV. 1, 2-3 (2006). While Bagenstos agrees with some of the diagnoses, he argues that the failure of current doctrines cautions against optimism. Some structural theories "seek to sidestep that history, but they do so largely by urging judicial deference to professional communities — such as those of human relations professionals and lawyers — that are as likely to subvert as to promote norms of workplace equality." The dubiousness of reliance on such communities is underscored by the work of Professor Susan Bisom-Rapp whose research raises serious questions about the effectiveness of current corporate efforts to deal with even blatant forms of discrimination and harassment. Her theme is that such efforts are more effective in limiting employer liability than in eliminating discrimination. *See* Susan Bisom-Rapp, *An Ounce of Prevention Is a Poor Substitute for a Pound of Cure: Confronting the Developing Jurisprudence of Education and Prevention in Employment Discrimination Law*, 22 BERKELEY J. EMP. & LAB. L. 1 (2001); Susan Bisom-Rapp, *Fixing Watches with Sledgehammers: The Questionable Embrace of Employee Sexual Harassment Training by the Legal Profession*, 24 U. ARK. LITTLE ROCK L. REV. 147 (2001). These organizational responses to claims of discrimination tend to work only when the employer's managers are evaluated by the actual success they have in meeting equal employment opportunity goals. Susan Bisom-Rapp, *How Well Do Internal EEO Alternative Dispute Resolution and Litigation Prevention Measures Advance the Traditional Goal of Anti-Discrimination Law?*, 11 EMPLOYEE RTS. & EMP. POL'Y J. 139 (2007). Even Professor Green, in *Targeting Workplace Context: Title VII as a Tool for Institutional Reform*, 72 FORDHAM L. REV. 659 (2003), warns more generally against unqualified acceptance of employer-initiated efforts at institutional reform.

Professor Bagenstos includes in his critique not only new structuralists who build on systemic disparate treatment but those who build on systemic disparate impact. See Note 4 on p. 235. The underlying thrust of Professor Bagenstos's attack on all the structuralist approaches is that these theorists have failed to support their prescriptions with a strong normative foundation. We have seen this argument before: as discriminatory intent moved away from animus and more towards unconscious bias, the need (much less the ability) to eliminate it seems attenuated. See Note 6 on p. 6. Professor Green responded to Professor Bagenstos in *A Structural Approach as Antidiscrimination Mandate: Locating Employer Wrong*, 60 VAND. L. REV. 849 (2007) (pessimism over the political viability of a structural approach stems from the mistaken assumption that it aims to impose costs on employers for societal barriers to employment; in fact a structural approach ties costs to employers' wrongs against individuals).

NOTE ON NATURE VERSUS NATURE

The question whether differences among the races and between the sexes is inherent or genetic is always explosive, in part because claimed differences have all too frequently been used justify denying full equality. The concurring opinion of Justice Bradley in the 1871 decision in *Bradwell v. Illinois*, 83 U.S. (16 Wall.) 130, 141, justified the exclusion of women from the practice of law, because the "paramount destiny and mission of women are to fulfill the noble and benign offices of wife and mother. This is the law of the creator." There is the long, ugly history of eugenics, typified by *Buck v. Bell*, 274 U.S 200, 202 (1927), in which Justice Oliver Wendell

Holmes made the stunning statement justifying sterilizations on the ground that, "Three generations of imbeciles are enough." More recently, the President of Harvard, Lawrence Summers, began his fall from power by suggesting that the shortfall of women in the sciences might be based on biology. *See* Remarks at NBER Conference on Diversifying the Science & Engineering Workforce, Lawrence H. Summers, January 14, 2005.

Originating around the turn of the twentieth century, efforts to differentiate the races were characterized by attempts to demonstrate the racial inferiority of non-white groups. *See generally* STEPHEN JAY GOULD, THE MISMEASURE OF MAN (1981). Such efforts were cast into disrepute by a variety of scientific developments capped by charges of fraud leveled at Sir Cyril Burt, who had published a study of twins separated early in life purporting to show that 80 percent of IQ is inherited. In the 1970s, doubts about the validity of the study led the British Psychological Society to find that Burt had been guilty of fraud. While Burt continues to have his defenders and detractors, *see* Peter Lennon, *Mind Games — IQ*, The Guardian, July 18, 1992, at 4, other research has continued the underlying controversy. Arthur Jensen, in *How Much Can We Boost IQ and Scholastic Achievement?*, 39 HARV. EDUC. REV. 1, 82 (1969), concluded that the average difference between IQ scores of blacks as a group and whites as a group can be explained only by genetic differences between the two racial groups. Similarly, William Shockley, in *Dysgenics, Geneticity and Raceology: A Challenge to the Intellectual Responsibility of Educators*, 72 PHI DELTA KAPPAN 297 (1972), attributed differences in black-white IQ to biological causes. Such studies have been questioned on a variety of grounds, including their source of funding. Lennon, supra. *See generally* Richard Delgado et al., *Can Science Be Inopportune? Constitutional Validity of Governmental Restrictions on Race-IQ Research*, 31 UCLA L. REV. 128 (1983). Other studies have found that the so-called persistent IQ gap between blacks and whites is not persistent at all. Daniel Goleman, *An Emerging Theory on Blacks' I.Q. Scores*, N.Y. Times, Apr. 10, 1988, at 12-22. That article concludes on an ironic note:

> There is one aspect of IQ research which American researchers have singularly failed to take to its logical conclusion. In the United States, orientals (Japanese and Chinese) always score higher than whites. But while heredity scientists feel continually obliged, with a Walrus and Carpenter air of regret, to make the point that blacks are inferior to whites there is a notable reluctance to highlight the fact that whites should, by the same tests, be judged inferior to orientals.

The debate over genetic racial differences in intelligence broke out anew with the publication in 1994 of THE BELL CURVE: INTELLIGENCE AND CLASS STRUCTURE IN AMERICAN LIFE by Richard Herrnstein and Charles Murray. This book's central thesis is that social ills can largely be traced to low intelligence and that intelligence is largely inherited. Because blacks consistently score lower than whites on standard intelligence tests and other criteria, the book also argues that blacks as a race are significantly less intelligent than whites as a race. Needless to say, THE BELL CURVE prompted an enormous amount of criticism of its methods and conclusions. *E.g.,* Stephen J. Gould, THE MISMEASURE OF MAN (rev. ed. 1996) at 367. While the genetic link of "intelligence" has been less studied recently, the stunning advances in DNA research resulting in the mapping of the human genome has led to an increasing scientific focus on racial differences for medical research and treatments. *See generally* Erik Lillquist & Charles A. Sullivan, *The Law and Genetics of Racial Profiling in Medicine*, 39 HARV. C.R.-C.L. L. REV. 391 (2004).

There is more scientific basis for sex-linked differences beyond those obviously related to reproduction. *See generally* Cynthia Fuchs Epstein, *Deceptive Distinctions: Sex, Gender, and the Social Order* (1988); CAROL TARVIS, THE MISMEASURE OF WOMAN (1992). Scientific research, often conducted by women, has sought to identify such differences. Doreen Kimura, in Sex Differences in the Brain, *Scientific American*, Sept. 1992, at 118, 119, writes:

> Women and men differ not only in physical attributes and reproductive function but also in the way in which they solve intellectual problems. It has been fashionable to insist that these differences are minimal, the consequence of variations in experience during development. The bulk of the evidence suggests, however, that the effects of sex hormones on brain organization occur so early in life that from the start the environment is acting on differently wired brains in girls and boys. Such differences make it almost impossible to evaluate the effects of experience independent of physiological predisposition.

She goes on to conclude that sex differences "in intellectual function seem to lie in patterns of ability rather than in overall level of intelligence (IQ)." *Id.* Thus,

> [m]en, on average, perform better than women on certain spatial tasks. In particular, men have an advantage in tests that require the subject to imagine rotating an object or manipulating it in some other way. They outperform women in mathematical reasoning tests and in navigating their way through a route. Further, men are more accurate in tests of target-directed motorskills — that is, in guiding or intercepting projectiles.
>
>   Women tend to be better than men at rapidly identifying matching items, a skill called perceptual speed. They have greater verbal fluency, including the ability to find words that begin with a specific letter or fulfill some other constraint. Women also outperform men in arithmetic calculation and in recalling landmarks from a route. Moreover, women are faster at certain precision manual tasks, such as placing pegs in designated holes on a board.

Id. Based on Kimura's research, some differences are slight, but others are large. Less significant than the observation of such differences, however, is the conclusion that "[d]iffering patterns of ability between men and women most probably reflect different hormonal influences on their developing brains." *Id.* at 120. Much of the data relied on to reach this conclusion is from animal studies, but some is drawn from studies of humans, including studies of girls exposed to excess androgens in the prenatal or neonatal stage, which can occur because of a genetic defect called congenital adrenal hyperplasia. Professor Kimura speculates that sex-role specialization during evolution explains the differences she observes. She concludes: "The finding of consistent and, in some cases, quite substantial sex differences suggests that men and women may have different occupational interests and capabilities, independent of societal influences." *Id.* at 125. *See also* DOREEN KIMURA, SEX AND COGNITION (1999). If *Dukes v. Wal-Mart* goes to trial, can you see Wal-Mart calling Professor Kimura to the stand, much as Sears used Professor Rosenberg?

  Dr. Summers' controversial remarks suggested a biological cause for the lower representation of women in elite science positions because of what he described as the gender variability of male intelligence compared to females. That is, the male curve has longer tails on both ends of the spectrum. Males have more geniuses but also more low scoring individuals. Lawrence H. Summers, President, Harvard University, Remarks at NBER Conference on Diversifying the Science & Engineering Workforce

(Jan. 14, 2005). In the wake of Dr. Summers' questioning whether the absence of women in the sciences was genetic, the whole issue again reached national prominence. *E.g.*, Doriane Lambelet Coleman *The Alchemy of a Moral Discourse About the Biology of Gender: Historical Sensitivity, Genetic Literacy, and the Will to Imagine a Different Equality* 11 CARDOZO WOMEN'S L.J. 543 (2005). *See also* Julie A. Seaman, *Form and (Dys)Function in Sexual Harassment Law: Biology, Culture, and the Spandrels of Title VII*, 37 ARIZ. ST. L.J. 321 (2005).

While many feminists and others resist biological explanations for race or sex differences, some advocates of gay rights seem to welcome them. Professor Kimura also noted intriguing studies suggesting that "sexual behavior may reflect further anatomic differences," including a smaller brain region (an interstitial nucleus of the anterior hypothalamus) in homosexual than in heterosexual men. Kimura, *supra* at 125. A 1993 study published in 261 SCIENCE 321 noted a disproportionately high number of gay men found among the relatives on the mothers' side of gay males being studied. Dean H. Hamer, Stella Hu, Victoria L. Magnuson, Nan Hu & Angela Pattatucci, *A Linkage Between DNA Markers on the X Chromosome and Male Sexual Orientation*, 261 SCIENCE 321-27. The researchers then analyzed the X chromosome received from the mother in 40 pairs of homosexual brothers, finding that 33 brother pairs shared a similar pattern of genetic material in a particular area on the X chromosomes. This was unusual because these chromosomes normally vary greatly in brothers. The researchers, therefore, suspect a genetic origin for homosexuality. *But see* Alan P. Medinger, *Study of Twins Has Important Implications*, http://www.messiah.edu/hpages/facstaff/chase/h/articles/regenera/twins.htm (last visited Dec. 6, 2002). If further research confirms this tendency, some legal scholars think that laws regulating homosexual behavior will be undermined as unconstitutional. Presumably, that is because it is unfair to punish individuals for an immutable characteristic, much as race or sex. *But see* Janet E. Halley, *Sexual Orientation and the Politics of Biology: A Critique of the Argument from Immutability*, 46 STAN. L. REV. 503 (1994). Are you persuaded? There are, of course, other possible uses for such information — attempts to biologically engineer sexual orientation or abort homosexual fetuses.

PROBLEM 2.1

Reread Problem 1.1, p. 111. Can Jane Armstrong recover in a systemic disparate treatment case?

2.   *Bona Fide Occupational Qualifications*

Section 703(e) of Title VII provides:

> Notwithstanding any other provision of this title . . . it shall not be an unlawful employment practice for an employer to hire and employ employees . . . on the basis of religion, sex, or national origin in those certain instances where religion, sex, or national origin is a bona fide occupational qualification reasonably necessary to the normal operation of that particular business or enterprise.

Although the bona fide occupational qualification (BFOQ) defense does not reach race discrimination, it constitutes a potentially large loophole in Title VII's general prohibition of employment discrimination on the other three grounds. The Age Discrimination in Employment Act also provides a BFOQ defense in language identical to Title VII.

The Court's first meaningful treatment of the BFOQ was in *Dothard v. Rawlinson*, 433 U.S. 321 (1977). Although the Court's language was restrictive, indicating that the BFOQ is "an extremely narrow exception to the general prohibition of discrimination on the basis of sex," *id.* at 334, it nevertheless upheld a rule requiring prison guards in "contact" positions to be of the same gender as the inmates they guarded. The majority stressed that Alabama's penitentiaries had been held unconstitutional because of their dangerous and inhumane conditions. Since there was no attempt to segregate inmates according to dangerousness, the 20 percent of male prisoners who were sex offenders were scattered throughout the dormitories. "In this environment of violence and disorganization, it would be an over-simplification to characterize [the rule against women] as an exercise in Romantic paternalism." *Id.* at 335. While Title VII normally allows individual women to decide for themselves whether jobs are too dangerous for them, in the Alabama prisons it was likely that women could not perform the essence of the correctional counselor's job — to maintain security:

> A woman's relative ability to maintain order in a male, maximum-security, unclassified penitentiary of the type Alabama now runs could be directly reduced by her womanhood. There is a basis in fact for expecting that sex offenders who have criminally assaulted women in the past would be moved to do so again if access to women were established within the prison. There would also be a real risk that other inmates, deprived of a normal heterosexual environment, would assault women guards because they were women.

Id. at 336. Thus, an "employee's very womanhood" would undermine her ability to do the job. The dissent of Justice Marshall protested this analysis as justifying discrimination because of the barbaric state of the prisons. Those conditions violate the Constitution and, therefore, cannot constitute "the normal operation of that particular business or enterprise" required by the BFOQ defense. The notion that "the employee's very womanhood" makes assaults more likely

> regrettably perpetuates one of the most insidious of the old myths about women — that women, wittingly or not, are seductive sexual objects. The effect of the decision, made I am sure with the best of intentions, is to punish women because their very presence might provoke sexual assaults. It is women who are made to pay the price in lost job opportunities for the threat of depraved conduct by prison inmates. Once again, "[t]he pedestal upon which women have been placed has . . . , upon closer inspection, been revealed as a cage." It is particularly ironic that the cage is erected here in response to feared misbehavior by imprisoned criminals.

Id. at 345.

The Supreme Court's next encounter with the BFOQ defense was not in a Title VII case challenging gender discrimination but in a suit under the Age Discrimination in Employment Act. In *Western Air Lines v. Criswell*, 472 U.S. 400 (1985), the Court made clear that it was adopting a uniform analysis applicable to both statutes. As originally enacted, the ADEA barred discrimination on account of age against those between the ages of 40 and 65. The upper limit was first extended to 70 and then removed entirely. The statute, however, has always permitted discrimination where age is "a bona fide occupational qualification." In *Criswell*, the Court was construing the ADEA during the period when the protected age bracket was 40 to 70. *Criswell* involved the question whether age 60 was a BFOQ for flight engineers, the third "pilot" who monitored side-facing instrument panels in larger commercial aircraft of that era. An FAA regulation banned individuals over age 60 from the other two pilot jobs — captain and first officer — but did not set any standard for flight engineers.

Defendant's evidence focused on the possibility that flight engineers would suffer a heart attack, the risks of which generally increased with age. Plaintiff's evidence focused on the fact that physiological deterioration was individualized and could be discovered through physical examinations that the FAA required for all flight engineers. Other airlines allowed flight engineers over age 60 to continue to fly without any apparent reduced safety records.

The jury was instructed that the "BFOQ defense is available only if it is reasonably necessary to the normal operation or essence of defendant's business." Having been informed that "the essence of Western's business is the safe transportation of their passengers," the jury was also instructed:

> One method by which defendant Western may establish a BFOQ in this case is to prove:
>   (1) That in 1978, when these plaintiffs were retired, it was highly impractical for Western to deal with each second officer over age 60 on an individualized basis to determine his particular ability to perform his job safely; and
>   (2) That some second officers over age 60 possess traits of a physiological, psychological or other nature which preclude safe and efficient job performance that cannot be ascertained by means other than knowing their age.

This jury instruction, upon which a verdict for the plaintiff was reached, was based on authority developed in the lower courts, and the Supreme Court approved it:

> Every Court of Appeals that has confronted a BFOQ defense based on safety considerations has analyzed the problem consistently with [this] standard. An EEOC regulation embraces the same criteria. Considering the narrow language of the BFOQ exception, the parallel treatment of such questions under Title VII, and the uniform applications of the standard by the federal courts, the EEOC and Congress, we conclude that this two-part inquiry properly identifies the relevant considerations for resolving a BFOQ defense to an age-based qualification purportedly justified by considerations of safety.

Id. at 416. Another prong of the text, relatively rarely used, would also approve of a BFOQ if "all or substantially all" persons in the disfavored group "would be unable to perform safely and efficiently the duties of the job involved." *Id.* at 414.

Colleges and universities cannot now retire tenured faculty at a given age unless they can establish a BFOQ. Do you think that a college with a mandatory retirement policy could prevail in an ADEA suit? At what age?

INTERNATIONAL UNION, UAW v.
JOHNSON CONTROLS, INC.
499 U.S. 187 (1991)

Justice BLACKMUN delivered the opinion of the Court. . . .

I

Respondent Johnson Controls, Inc., manufactures batteries. In the manufacturing process, the element lead is a primary ingredient. Occupational exposure to lead entails health risks, including the risk of harm to any fetus carried by a female employee.

Before the Civil Rights Act of 1964 became law, Johnson Controls did not employ any woman in a battery-manufacturing job. [By June 1977, its first official policy discouraged women for taking jobs with lead exposure but left the decision to the employees. In 1982, however] Johnson Controls shifted from a policy of warning to a policy of exclusion. Between 1979 and 1983, eight employees became pregnant while maintaining blood lead levels in excess of 30 micrograms per deciliter. This appeared to be the critical level noted by the Occupational Safety and Health Administration (OSHA) for a worker who was planning to have a family. See 29 C.F.R. § 1910.1025 (1989). The company responded by announcing a broad exclusion of women from jobs that exposed them to lead:

> [I]t is [Johnson Controls'] policy that women who are pregnant or who are capable of bearing children will not be placed into jobs involving lead exposure or which could expose them to lead through the exercise of job bidding, bumping, transfer or pro-motion rights.

The policy defined "women . . . capable of bearing children" as "all women except those whose inability to bear children is medically documented." It further stated that an unacceptable work station was one where, "over the past year," an employee had recorded a blood lead level of more than 30 micrograms per deciliter or the work site had yielded an air sample containing a lead level in excess of 30 micrograms per cubic meter.

II

[Plaintiffs filed a Title VII class action challenging the fetal-protection policy.] Among the individual plaintiffs were petitioners Mary Craig, who had chosen to be sterilized in order to avoid losing her job; Elsie Nason, a 50-year-old divorcee, who had suffered a loss in compensation when she was transferred out of a job where she was exposed to lead; and Donald Penney, who had been denied a request for a leave of absence for the purpose of lowering his lead level because he intended to become a father. . . .

[The district court granted summary judgment for defendant. The Seventh Circuit, en banc, affirmed by a 7-to-4 vote. The majority relied on the defense of business necessity, while all the dissenters thought that only the BFOQ defense applied when a systemic policy of discrimination was proven. Two dissenters thought that the defendant would not be able to prove the BFOQ defense because concern for the health of the unborn was irrelevant to Johnson Control's business.]

III

The bias in Johnson Controls' policy is obvious. Fertile men, but not fertile women, are given a choice as to whether they wish to risk their reproductive health for a particular job. Section 703(a) prohibits sex-based classifications in terms and conditions of employment, in hiring and discharging decisions, and in other employment decisions that adversely affect an employee's status. Respondent's fetal-protection policy explicitly discriminates against women on the basis of their sex. The policy excludes women with childbearing capacity from lead-exposed jobs and so creates a facial classification based on gender. Respondent assumes as much in its brief before this Court.

Nevertheless, the Court of Appeals assumed, as did the two appellate courts who already had confronted the issue, that sex-specific fetal-protection policies do not involve facial discrimination. These courts analyzed the policies as though they were facially neutral, and had only a discriminatory effect upon the employment opportunities of women. Consequently, the courts looked to see if each employer in question had established that its policy was justified as a business necessity. The business necessity standard is more lenient for the employer than the statutory BFOQ defense. The Court of Appeals . . . assumed that because the asserted reason for the sex-based exclusion (protecting women's unconceived offspring) was ostensibly benign, the policy was not sex-based discrimination. That assumption, however, was incorrect.

First, Johnson Controls' policy classifies on the basis of gender and childbearing capacity, rather than fertility alone. Respondent does not seek to protect the unconceived children of all its employees. Despite evidence in the record about the debilitating effect of lead exposure on the male reproductive system, Johnson Controls is concerned only with the harms that may befall the unborn offspring of its female employees. . . . This Court faced a conceptually similar situation in *Phillips v. Martin Marietta Corp.*, 400 U.S. 542 (1971), and found sex discrimination because the policy established "one hiring policy for women and another for men — each having pre-school-age children." Johnson Controls' policy is facially discriminatory because it requires only a female employee to produce proof that she is not capable of reproducing.

Our conclusion is bolstered by the Pregnancy Discrimination Act of 1978 (PDA) in which Congress explicitly provided that, for purposes of Title VII, discrimination "on the basis of sex" includes discrimination "because of or on the basis of pregnancy, childbirth, or related medical conditions." "The Pregnancy Discrimination Act has now made clear that, for all Title VII purposes, discrimination based on a woman's pregnancy is, on its face, discrimination because of her sex." *Newport News Shipbuilding & Dry Dock Co. v. EEOC*, 462 U.S. 669, 684 (1983). In its use of the words "capable of bearing children" in the 1982 policy statement as the criterion for exclusion, Johnson Controls explicitly classifies on the basis of potential for pregnancy. Under the PDA, such a classification must be regarded, for Title VII purposes, in the same light as explicit sex discrimination. Respondent has chosen to treat all its female employees as potentially pregnant; that choice evinces discrimination on the basis of sex.

We concluded above that Johnson Controls' policy is not neutral because it does not apply to the reproductive capacity of the company's male employees in the same way as it applies to that of the females. Moreover, the absence of a malevolent motive does not convert a facially discriminatory policy into a neutral policy with a discriminatory effect. Whether an employment practice involves disparate treatment through explicit facial discrimination does not depend on why the employer discriminates but rather on the explicit terms of the discrimination. In *Martin Marietta*, the motives underlying the employers' express exclusion of women did not alter the intentionally discriminatory character of the policy. Nor did the arguably benign motives lead to consideration of a business necessity defense. The question in that case was whether the discrimination in question could be justified under §703(e) as a BFOQ. The beneficence of an employer's purpose does not undermine the conclusion that an explicit gender-based policy is sex discrimination under §703(a) and thus may be defended only as a BFOQ. . . .

In sum, Johnson Controls' policy "does not pass the simple test of whether the evidence shows 'treatment of a person in a manner which but for that person's sex would be different.'" *Los Angeles Dept. of Water & Power v. Manhart*. We hold that Johnson Controls' fetal-protection policy is sex discrimination forbidden under Title VII unless respondent can establish that sex is a "bona fide occupational qualification."

IV . . .

The BFOQ defense is written narrowly, and this Court has read it narrowly. See, e.g., *Dothard v. Rawlinson; Trans World Airlines, Inc. v. Thurston*, 469 U.S. 111 (1985). We have read the BFOQ language of §4(f) of the Age Discrimination in Employment Act of 1967 (ADEA), which tracks the BFOQ provision in Title VII, just as narrowly. See *Western Air Lines, Inc. v. Criswell*. Our emphasis on the restrictive scope of the BFOQ defense is grounded on both the language and the legislative history of §703.

The wording of the BFOQ defense contains several terms of restriction that indicate that the exception reaches only special situations. The statute thus limits the situations in which discrimination is permissible to "certain instances" where sex discrimination is "reasonably necessary" to the "normal operation" of the "particular" business. Each one of these terms — certain, normal, particular — prevents the use of general subjective standards and favors an objective, verifiable requirement. But the most telling term is "occupational"; this indicates that these objective, verifiable requirements must concern job-related skills and aptitudes.

The concurrence defines "occupational" as meaning related to a job. According to the concurrence, any discriminatory requirement imposed by an employer is "job-related" simply because the employer has chosen to make the requirement a condition of employment. In effect, the concurrence argues that sterility may be an occupational qualification for women because Johnson Controls has chosen to require it. This reading of "occupational" renders the word mere surplusage. "Qualification" by itself would encompass an employer's idiosyncratic requirements. By modifying "qualification" with "occupational," Congress narrowed the term to qualifications that affect an employee's ability to do the job.

Johnson Controls argues that its fetal-protection policy falls within the so-called safety exception to the BFOQ. Our cases have stressed that discrimination on the basis of sex because of safety concerns is allowed only in narrow circumstances. In *Dothard v. Rawlinson*, this Court indicated that danger to a woman herself does not justify discrimination. We there allowed the employer to hire only male guards in contact areas of maximum-security male penitentiaries only because more was at stake than the "individual woman's decision to weigh and accept the risks of employment." We found sex to be a BFOQ inasmuch as the employment of a female guard would create real risks of safety to others if violence broke out because the guard was a woman. Sex discrimination was tolerated because sex was related to the guard's ability to do the job — maintaining prison security. We also required in *Dothard* a high correlation between sex and ability to perform job functions and refused to allow employers to use sex as a proxy for strength although it might be a fairly accurate one.

Similarly, some courts have approved airlines' layoffs of pregnant flight attendants at different points during the first five months of pregnancy on the ground that the employer's policy was necessary to ensure the safety of passengers. See [, e.g.,] *Harriss v. Pan American World Airways, Inc.*, 649 F.2d 670 (CA9 1980). In these cases, the courts pointedly indicated that fetal, as opposed to passenger, safety was best left to the mother.

We considered safety to third parties in *Western Airlines, Inc. v. Criswell* in the context of the ADEA. We focused upon "the nature of the flight engineer's tasks," and the "actual capabilities of persons over age 60" in relation to those tasks. Our safety concerns were not independent of the individual's ability to perform the assigned tasks, but rather involved the possibility that, because of age-connected debility, a flight engineer might not properly assist the pilot, and might thereby cause a safety emergency. Furthermore, although we considered the safety of third parties in *Dothard* and *Criswell*, those third parties were indispensable to the particular business at issue. In *Dothard*, the third parties were the inmates; in *Criswell*, the third parties were the passengers on the plane. We stressed that in order to qualify as a BFOQ, a job qualification must relate to the "essence," or to the "central mission of the employer's business."

The concurrence ignores the "essence of the business" test and so concludes that "the safety to fetuses in carrying out the duties of battery manufacturing is as much a legitimate concern as is safety to third parties in guarding prisons (*Dothard*) or flying airplanes (*Criswell*)." By limiting its discussion to cost and safety concerns and rejecting the "essence of the business" test that our case law has established, the concurrence seeks to expand what is now the narrow BFOQ defense. Third-party safety considerations properly entered into the BFOQ analysis in *Dothard* and *Criswell* because they went to the core of the employee's job performance. Moreover, that performance involved the central purpose of the enterprise. . . . The concurrence attempts to transform this case into one of customer safety. The unconceived fetuses of Johnson Controls' female employees, however, are neither customers nor third parties whose safety is essential to the business of battery manufacturing. No one can disregard the possibility of injury to future children; the BFOQ, however, is not so broad that it transforms this deep social concern into an essential aspect of batterymaking.

Our case law, therefore, makes clear that the safety exception is limited to instances in which sex or pregnancy actually interferes with the employee's ability to perform the job. This approach is consistent with the language of the BFOQ provision itself, for it suggests that permissible distinctions based on sex must relate to ability to perform the duties of the job. Johnson Controls suggests, however, that we expand the exception to allow fetal-protection policies that mandate particular standards for pregnant or fertile women. We decline to do so. Such an expansion contradicts not only the language of the BFOQ and the narrowness of its exception but the plain language and history of the Pregnancy Discrimination Act.

The PDA's amendment to Title VII contains a BFOQ standard of its own: unless pregnant employees differ from others "in their ability or inability to work," they must be "treated the same" as other employees "for all employment-related purposes." This language clearly sets forth Congress' remedy for discrimination on the basis of pregnancy and potential pregnancy. Women who are either pregnant or potentially pregnant must be treated like others "similar in their ability . . . to work." In other words, women as capable of doing their jobs as their male counterparts may not be forced to choose between having a child and having a job. . . .

We conclude that the language of both the BFOQ provision and the PDA which amended it, as well as the legislative history and the case law, prohibit an employer from discriminating against a woman because of her capacity to become pregnant unless her reproductive potential prevents her from performing the duties of her job. We reiterate our holdings in *Criswell* and *Dothard* that an employer must direct its concerns about a woman's ability to perform her job safely and efficiently to those aspects of the woman's job-related activities that fall within the "essence" of the particular business.[4]

V

We have no difficulty concluding that Johnson Controls cannot establish a BFOQ. Fertile women, as far as appears in the record, participate in the manufacture of batteries as efficiently as anyone else. Johnson Controls' professed moral and ethical concerns about the welfare of the next generation do not suffice to establish a BFOQ of female sterility. Decisions about the welfare of future children must be left to the parents who conceive, bear, support, and raise them rather than to the employers who hire those parents. Congress has mandated this choice through Title VII, as amended by the Pregnancy Discrimination Act. Johnson Controls has attempted to exclude women because of their reproductive capacity. Title VII and the PDA simply do not allow a woman's dismissal because of her failure to submit to sterilization.

Nor can concerns about the welfare of the next generation be considered a part of the "essence" of Johnson Controls' business. Judge Easterbrook in this case pertinently observed: "It is word play to say that 'the job' at Johnson [Controls] is to make batteries without risk to fetuses in the same way 'the job' at Western Air Lines is to fly planes without crashing."

Johnson Controls argues that it must exclude all fertile women because it is impossible to tell which women will become pregnant while working with lead. This argument is somewhat academic in light of our conclusion that the company may not exclude fertile women at all; it perhaps is worth noting, however, that Johnson Controls has shown no "factual basis for believing that all or substantially all women would be unable to perform safely and efficiently the duties of the job involved." Even on this sparse record, it is apparent that Johnson Controls is concerned about only a small minority of women. Of the eight pregnancies reported among the female employees, it has not been shown that any of the babies have birth defects or other abnormalities. The record does not reveal the birth rate for Johnson Controls' female workers but national statistics show that approximately nine percent of all fertile women become pregnant each year. The birthrate drops to two percent for blue collar workers over age 30. Johnson Controls' fear of prenatal injury, no matter how sincere, does not begin to show that substantially all of its fertile women employees are incapable of doing their jobs.

---

4. The concurrence predicts that our reaffirmation of the narrowness of the BFOQ defense will preclude considerations of privacy as a basis for sex-based discrimination. We have never addressed privacy-based sex discrimination and shall not do so here because the sex-based discrimination at issue today does not involve the privacy interests of Johnson Controls' customers. Nothing in our discussion of the "essence of the business test," however, suggests that sex could not constitute a BFOQ when privacy interests are implicated. See, e.g., *Backus v. Baptist Medical Center*, 510 F. Supp. 1191 (E.D. Ark. 1981), *vacated as moot*, 671 F.2d 1100 (CA8 1982) (essence of obstetrics nurse's business is to provide sensitive care for patient's intimate and private concerns).

VI

A word about tort liability and the increased cost of fertile women in the workplace is perhaps necessary. [At the Seventh Circuit, Judge Posner] expressed concern about an employer's tort liability and concluded that liability for a potential injury to a fetus is a social cost that Title VII does not require a company to ignore. It is correct to say that Title VII does not prevent the employer from having a conscience. The statute, however, does prevent sex-specific fetal-protection policies. These two aspects of Title VII do not conflict.

[The majority recognized that more than 40 states currently recognized a right to recover for a prenatal injury based either on negligence or on wrongful death. But Johnson Controls purportedly complied with OSHA lead standards and also warned its female employees about the damaging effects of lead. This would seem to preclude negligence, and "[w]ithout negligence, it would be difficult for a court to find liability on the part of the employer." Further, while the Court stressed that "the issue is not before us," it also suggested that, should tort liability "punish employers for complying with Title VII's clear command," federal law would preempt state tort law. Nevertheless, because] Johnson Controls has not argued that it faces any costs from tort liability, not to mention crippling ones, the pre-emption question is not before us. We therefore say no more than that the concurrence's speculation appears unfounded as well as premature.

The tort-liability argument reduces to two equally unpersuasive propositions. First, Johnson Controls attempts to solve the problem of reproductive health hazards by resorting to an exclusionary policy. Title VII plainly forbids illegal sex discrimination as a method of diverting attention from an employer's obligation to police the workplace. Second, the spectre of an award of damages reflects a fear that hiring fertile women will cost more. The extra cost of employing members of one sex, however, does not provide an affirmative Title VII defense for a discriminatory refusal to hire members of that gender. See *Manhart*. Indeed, in passing the PDA, Congress considered at length the considerable cost of providing equal treatment of pregnancy and related conditions, but made the "decision to forbid special treatment of pregnancy despite the social costs associated therewith."

We, of course, are not presented with, nor do we decide, a case in which costs would be so prohibitive as to threaten the survival of the employer's business. We merely reiterate our prior holdings that the incremental cost of hiring women cannot justify discriminating against them. . . .

Justice WHITE, with whom The Chief Justice and Justice KENNEDY join, concurring in part and concurring in the judgment.

The Court properly holds that Johnson Controls' fetal protection policy overtly discriminates against women, and thus is prohibited by Title VII unless it falls within the bona fide occupational qualification (BFOQ) exception. . . . The Court erroneously holds, however, that the BFOQ defense is so narrow that it could never justify a sex-specific fetal protection policy. I nevertheless concur in the judgment of reversal because on the record before us summary judgment in favor of Johnson Controls was improper. . . .

[A] fetal protection policy would be justified under the terms of the statute if, for example, an employer could show that exclusion of women from certain jobs was reasonably necessary to avoid substantial tort liability. . . .

Dothard and *Criswell* also confirm that costs are relevant in determining whether a discriminatory policy is reasonably necessary for the normal operation of a business.

In *Dothard*, the safety problem that justified exclusion of women from the prison guard positions was largely a result of inadequate staff and facilities. If the cost of employing women could not be considered, the employer there should have been required to hire more staff and restructure the prison environment rather than exclude women. Similarly, in *Criswell* the airline could have been required to hire more pilots and install expensive monitoring devices rather than discriminate against older employees. The BFOQ statute, however, reflects "Congress' unwillingness to require employers to change the very nature of their operations." Price Waterhouse v. Hopkins (plurality opinion). . . .

Justice SCALIA, concurring in the judgment.

I generally agree with the Court's analysis, but have some reservations, several of which bear mention.

First, I think it irrelevant that there was "evidence in the record about the debilitating effect of lead exposure on the male reproductive system." Even without such evidence, treating women differently "on the basis of pregnancy" constitutes discrimination "on the basis of sex," because Congress has unequivocally said so. Pregnancy Discrimination Act of 1978.

Second, the Court points out that "Johnson Controls has shown no factual basis for believing that all or substantially all women would be unable to perform safely . . . the duties of the job involved." In my view, this is not only "somewhat academic in light of our conclusion that the company may not exclude fertile women at all"; it is entirely irrelevant. By reason of the Pregnancy Discrimination Act, it would not matter if all pregnant women placed their children at risk in taking these jobs, just as it does not matter if no men do so.

Third, [as to possible liability under state tort law,] all that need be said in the present case is that Johnson has not demonstrated a substantial risk of tort liability — which is alone enough to defeat a tort-based assertion of the BFOQ exception.

Last, the Court goes far afield, it seems to me, in suggesting that increased cost alone — short of "costs . . . so prohibitive as to threaten survival of the employer's business" — cannot support a BFOQ defense. I agree with Justice White's concurrence that nothing in our prior cases suggests this, and in my view it is wrong. I think, for example, that a shipping company may refuse to hire pregnant women as crew members on long voyages because the on-board facilities for foreseeable emergencies, though quite feasible, would be inordinately expensive. In the present case, however, Johnson has not asserted a cost-based BFOQ. . . .

NOTES

1. *A Policy of Sex Discrimination.* While not all women were prevented from working in the lead exposure jobs, the Court found the employer's rule to be a policy that discriminated because of sex. That is because all those excluded from working in the at-issue jobs were women, even though the exclusion did not apply to sterile women. The rule did not apply to exclude any men, fertile or not. As you will see in Chapter 5 dealing with sex discrimination, this clear understanding eluded a majority of the Court when it first considered whether pregnancy discrimination was sex discrimination. The Pregnancy Discrimination Act cleared up that problem. Here the challenged rule is sex discrimination, even without the need to consider the PDA, but that statute reinforces the Court's analysis. *Johnson Controls* is also

important for its holding that disparate treatment analysis (and, therefore, the BFOQ defense) applies whenever an employer facially discriminates or acts on the basis of gender, regardless of whether it is motivated by animus.

2. *The BFOQ Defense. Johnson Controls* rejected an attempt to sidestep the rigors of the BFOQ as developed in *Dothard* and *Criswell* by employing the more lenient business necessity test. This defense is available in disparate impact cases, see Chapter 3, and several courts had applied it to fetal-protection policies by treating them as impact cases. *Johnson Controls* is significant for reasserting that business necessity applies *only* to disparate impact cases. The Civil Rights Act of 1991 codified *Johnson Controls* in this respect by adding subsection (k)(2) to §703 of Title VII: "A demonstration that an employment practice is required by business necessity may not be used as a defense against a claim of intentional discrimination under this title."

Is *Johnson Controls* consistent with *Dothard?* In both cases, third parties (fetuses or other prison guards and prisoners) could be affected by a woman's decision to perform a certain job. Is the difference that the third parties affected in *Dothard* are the essence of the business? Who defines that? The "essence" of a business test originated in *Diaz v. Pan American Airways, Inc.*, 442 F.2d 385 (5th Cir. 1971). There the district court had, surprisingly by present standards, found that stewardesses were superior to male stewards by being sexually attractive to male passengers and comforting to female passengers. The court of appeals avoided this fact finding by saying that only superiority in aspects of the job that went to the essence of the business counted; the supposed female superiority was in aspects of the job peripheral to the airline's essential concern with safe transportation.

Despite the stringent standard, some cases have found BFOQs established. In *Healey v. Southwood Psychiatric Hospital*, 78 F.3d 128 (3d Cir. 1996), plaintiff challenged a gender-specific rule for assigning child care specialists at a hospital for emotionally disturbed children and adolescents, some of whom had been sexually abused. The court upheld summary judgment for the employer based on the BFOQ defense:

> The "essence" of Southwood's business is to treat emotionally disturbed and sexually abused adolescents and children. Southwood has presented expert testimony that staffing both males and females on all shifts is necessary to provide therapeutic care. "Role modeling," including parental role modeling, is an important element of the staff's job, and a male is better able to serve as a male role model than a female and vice versa. A balanced staff is also necessary because children who have been sexually abused will disclose their problems more easily to a member of a certain sex, depending on their sex and the sex of the abuser. If members of both sexes are not on a shift, Southwood's inability to provide basic therapeutic care would hinder the "normal operation" of its "particular business." Therefore, it is reasonably necessary to the normal operation of Southwood to have at least one member of each sex available to the patients at all times.

Id. at 132-33. If you agree with *Diaz*, do you also agree with *Healey?*

3. *Customer Preference as a BFOQ.* When, if ever, is "customer preference" a basis for establishing a BFOQ? When framed this broadly, the court have tended to answer this question no. For example, the Ninth Circuit rejected a BFOQ claim in *Fernandez v. Wynn Oil Co.*, 653 F.2d 1273 (9th Cir. 1981), where the defendant argued that the plaintiff could not be made vice-president of international operations because Latin American clients would react negatively to a woman in such a position. Although finding the defense not factually supported, the Ninth Circuit also

held the defense inadequate as a matter of law because customer preference cannot justify gender discrimination. But if the question is framed more in terms of job performance, customer reaction to the employee seems to be an acceptable basis. *See EEOC v. Univ. of Texas Health Science Ctr.*, 710 F.2d 1091, 1095 (5th Cir. 1983) (age-45 limitation on initial hiring of campus police was a BFOQ in part because of testimony that "younger officers are better able to handle frequent confrontational episodes on campus because of their ability to relate to youthful offenders"). Indeed, *Healey* could be described as an extreme case of customer preference. *See also* Ernest F. Lidge III, *Law Firm Employment Discrimination in Case Assignments at the Client's Insistence: A Bona Fide Occupational Qualification?*, 38 Conn. L. Rev. 159 (2005) (arguing for broad use of BFOQs where the individual client's trust in the lawyer is at stake).

A continuing customer preference issue arises in sexualized businesses. For example, the Hooters chain of restaurants hires only women to serve food to customers; the "Hooter Girls" dress in revealing outfits. The company defended its practice by arguing that, "A lot of places serve good burgers. The Hooters' Girls, with their charm and All-American sex appeal, are what our customers come for." N.Y. Times, Nov. 16, 1995, at A20, col. 5. The EEOC dropped its investigation against Hooters after the company launched a massive public relations campaign against the Commission. A private action was then settled, under terms which allowed Hooters to continue to hire only women as waitstaff. The men who were discriminated against by this company policy did, however, receive monetary compensation. Hooters to Pay $3.75 Million in Sex Suit, USA Today, Oct. 1, 1997, at 1A. Isn't Hooters just buying lawsuits by men claiming they want wait staff jobs? Is selling sex appeal a BFOQ? Or, is Hooters merely arguing customer preference under another name? *See generally* Kimberly A. Yuracko, *Private Nurses and Playboy Bunnies: Explaining Permissible Sex Discrimination*, 92 Cal. L. Rev. 147, 151-52 (2004) (courts "are far more permissive of sex discrimination on behalf of privacy concerns than they are of discrimination on behalf of sexual-titillation desires"). *See also* Ann C. McGinley, *Harassing "Girls" at the Hard Rock: Masculinities In Sexualized Environments*, 2007 U. Ill. L. Rev. 1229 (BFOQ defense should not expand to defend an employer's failure to protect women employees from harassing behavior in a highly sexualized workplace). See Chapter 5.

4. *BFOQ Based on Privacy.* Can personal privacy concerns of patients, clients, or inmates justify a BFOQ defense? Justice White's concurrence feared the majority's opinion would do away with privacy BFOQs. The majority denied this, but the Court has never upheld a privacy BFOQ, and the lower courts have reached mixed results. There are only a scattering of cases outside the prison context, *see generally* Emily Gold Waldman, The *Case of the Male OB-GYN: A Proposal for Expansion of the Privacy BFOQ in the Healthcare Context*, 6 U. Pa. J. Lab. & Emp. L. 357 (2004), but the courts have been sympathetic to rules restricting prison guard jobs to members of the same sex as the inmate, especially when female inmates are involved, although one might have thought that inmate privacy was not a very compelling basis for restricting employment opportunities by sex. *E.g., Everson v. Mich. Dep't of Corr.*, 391 F.3d 737, 751 (6th Cir. 2004) (being female was a BFOQ for positions in housing units at female prisons in large part because the exclusion of males would decrease the likelihood of sexual abuse of women prisoners and protect their privacy rights); *Robino v. Iranon*, 145 F.3d 1109, 1109 (9th Cir. 1998) (upholding a BFOQ for six of 41 positions because "a person's interest in not being viewed unclothed by members of the opposite sex survives incarceration," and the

prison could justifiably take into account "security, rehabilitation, and morale"); *Reed v. County of Casey*, 184 F.3d 597 (6th Cir. 1999) (transfer of female guard to midnight shift was a BFOQ when justified by need to supervise female prisoners and there were no satisfactory alternatives). *See generally* Kim Shayo Buchanan, *Beyond Modesty: Privacy in Prison and the Risk of Sexual Abuse*, 88 MARQ. L. REV. 751, (2005) ("when women prisoners are sexually exploited by guards, they are victims of sexual aggression; feminists do them no favor by pretending that they are not").

5. *BFOQ for Race?* Title VII contains no BFOQ for race, and there is no doubt that the omission was intentional. The Seventh Circuit, however, adopted what amounts to a narrow, judicially crafted racial BFOQ in *Wittner v. Peters*, 87 F.3d 916 (7th Cir. 1996), for a black lieutenant at a prison run like a boot camp. But *Wittner* was an equal protection, not a Title VII, case, and even that principle has been read stringently. *See Patrolmen's Benevolent Assn. v. City of New York*, 310 F.3d 43 (2d Cir. 2002) (upholding jury verdict under the Equal Protection Clause finding city had not demonstrated that transferring minority police officers to a racially troubled precinct was narrowly tailored to the justification for doing so). In *Ferrill v. The Parker Group, Inc.*, 168 F.3d 468 (11th Cir. 1999), a § 1981 case, the Eleventh Circuit rejected a BFOQ for racially segregating telemarketers aimed at getting out the vote for an election, with blacks calling blacks and whites calling whites. Given that Congress did not extend the BFOQ defense to include race, does that mean courts should interpret § 1981 as not including a BFOQ for race? Is authenticity a compelling justification for a race BFOQ in the entertainment industry? Could the First Amendment concerns sometimes limit Title VII's prescription? *See* Russell K. Robinson, *Casting and Caste-ing: Reconciling Artistic Freedom and Antidiscrimination Norms*, 95 CAL. L. REV. 1 (2007) (first amendment would justify limited use of race/sex classifications).

6. *No Adverse Employment Action?* We saw in Chapter 1 that the circuits have differing standards with respect to what constitutes an adverse employment action. For many, a "lateral transfer," that is, one that does not result in loss of pay or a demotion, is not actionable. In jurisdictions with stringent definitions of adverse employment action, an employer may be able to assign individuals by sex, age, or even race without having to establish a BFOQ. *See Tipler v. Douglas County*, 482 F.3d 1023, 1025 (8th Cir. 2007 ("a bona fide occupational qualification analysis is unnecessary if (1) the policy requiring female-only supervision of female inmates is reasonable, and (2) such a policy imposes only a "minimal restriction" on the employee"); *but see Piercy v. Maketa*, 480 F.3d 1192 (10th Cir. 2007) (facial discrimination might be actionable when it was not clear that assignments were purely lateral).

3. Voluntary Affirmative Action

In *United Steelworkers of America v. Weber*, 443 U.S. 193 (1979), a 5-2 majority upheld the employer's use of a voluntary affirmative action plan negotiated with the union representing its workers to create a training program for incumbent unskilled workers to fill skilled job categories. Until this plan was adopted, craft positions were filled by people with craft experience, typically learned through the apprentice system of craft unions in the area that historically excluded blacks from membership. Hiring craft skilled craft workers to work in the employer's plant meant that these job categories were all white. In order to address this problem, the plan reserved for black employees 50 percent of the openings in these newly created in-plant training programs until the percentage of black skilled craftworkers approximated the percentage of blacks in the local labor force. Brian Weber, an unskilled white worker in the plant, sued because some black workers with less plant seniority were accepted into the craft training program.

After holding that Title VII's prohibition against racial discrimination does not condemn all private, voluntary, race-conscious affirmative action plans, the Court upheld the particular plan:

> We need not today define in detail the line of demarcation between permissible and impermissible affirmative action plans. It suffices to hold that the challenged Kaiser-USWA affirmative action plan falls on the permissible side of the line. The purposes of the plan mirror those of the statute. Both were designed to break down old patterns of racial segregation and hierarchy. Both were structured to "open unemployment opportunities for Negroes in occupations which have been traditionally closed to them."
>
> At the same time, the plan does not unnecessarily trammel the interests of the white employees. The plan does not require the discharge of white workers and their replacement with new black hirees. . . . Nor does the plan create an absolute bar to the advancement of white employees; half of those trained in the program will be white. Moreover, the plan is a temporary measure; it is not intended to maintain racial balance, but simply to eliminate a manifest racial imbalance.

Id. at 208.

Justice REHNQUIST, joined by then-Chief Justice BURGER, dissented.

> The operative sections of Title VII prohibit racial discrimination in employment *simpliciter.* Taken in its normal meaning, and as understood by all Members of Congress who spoke to the issue during the legislative debates, this language prohibits a covered employer from considering race when making an employment decision, whether the race be black or white. . . . We have never wavered in our understanding that Title VII "prohibits all racial discrimination in employment, without exception for any group of particular employees." . . .
>
> Thus, by a tour de force reminiscent not of jurists such as Hale, Holmes, and Hughes, but of escape artists such as Houdini, the Court eludes clear statutory language, "uncontradicted" legislative history, and uniform precedent in concluding that employers are, after all, permitted to consider race in making employment decisions.

Id. at 220-22. *See generally* Deborah C. Malamud, *The Story of United Steelworkers v. Weber* in EMPLOYMENT DISCRIMINATION STORIES (Joel Wm. Friedman ed. 2006) (exploring the role played by unions generally, and the United Steelworkers of America in particular, in the adoption of affirmative action programs in an attempt to preserve seniority systems).

JOHNSON v. TRANSPORTATION AGENCY OF SANTA CLARA COUNTY
480 U.S. 616 (1987)

Justice BRENNAN delivered the opinion of the Court.

Respondent, Transportation Agency of Santa Clara County, California, unilaterally promulgated an Affirmative Action Plan applicable, inter alia, to promotions of employees. In selecting applicants for the promotional position of road dispatcher, the Agency, pursuant to the Plan, passed over petitioner Paul Johnson, a male employee, and promoted a female employee applicant, Diane Joyce. The question for decision is whether in making the promotion the Agency impermissibly took into account the sex of the applicants in violation of Title VII of the Civil Rights Act of 1964. . . .

I

A

In December 1978, the Santa Clara County Transit District Board of Supervisors adopted an Affirmative Action Plan (Plan) for the County Transportation Agency. The Plan implemented a County Affirmative Action Plan, which had been adopted, declared the County, because "mere prohibition of discriminatory practices is not enough to remedy the effects of past practices and to permit attainment of an equitable representation of minorities, women and handicapped persons." Relevant to this case, the Agency Plan provides that, in making promotions to positions within a traditionally segregated job classification in which women have been significantly underrepresented, the Agency is authorized to consider as one factor the sex of a qualified applicant.

In reviewing the composition of its work force, the Agency noted in its Plan that women were represented in numbers far less than their proportion of the County labor force in both the Agency as a whole and in five of seven job categories. Specifically, while women constituted 36.4% of the area labor market, they composed only 22.4% of Agency employees. Furthermore, women working at the Agency were concentrated largely in EEOC job categories traditionally held by women: women made up 76% of Office and Clerical Workers, but only 7.1% of Agency Officials and Administrators, 8.6% of Professionals, 9.7% of Technicians, and 22% of Service and Maintenance Workers. As for the job classification relevant to this case, none of the 238 Skilled Craft Worker positions was held by a woman. The Plan noted that this underrepresentation of women in part reflected the fact that women had not traditionally been employed in these positions, and that they had not been strongly motivated to seek training or employment in them "because of the limited opportunities that have existed in the past for them to work in such classifications." . . .

The Agency stated that its Plan was intended to achieve "a statistically measurable yearly improvement in hiring, training and promotion of minorities and women throughout the Agency in all major job classifications where they are under-represented." As a benchmark by which to evaluate progress, the Agency stated that its long-term goal was to attain a work force whose composition reflected the proportion of minorities and women in the area labor force. Thus, for the Skilled Craft category in which the road dispatcher position at issue here was classified, the Agency's aspiration was that eventually about 36% of the jobs would be occupied by women.

The Plan acknowledged that a number of factors might make it unrealistic to rely on the Agency's long-term goals in evaluating the Agency's progress in expanding job opportunities for minorities and women. Among the factors identified were low turnover rates in some classifications, the fact that some jobs involved heavy labor, the small number of positions within some job categories, the limited number of entry positions leading to the Technical and Skilled Craft classifications, and the limited number of minorities and women qualified for positions requiring special-ized training and experience. As a result, the Plan counseled that short-range goals be established and annually adjusted to serve as the most realistic guide for actual employment decisions. . . .

The Agency's Plan thus set aside no specific number of positions for minorities or women, but authorized the consideration of ethnicity or sex as a factor when evaluating qualified candidates for jobs in which members of such groups were poorly represented. One such job was the road dispatcher position that is the subject of the dispute in this case.

B

[In 1979, the Agency announced a vacancy for dispatcher in the Roads Division. Dispatchers assign road crews, equipment, and materials and maintain records. The position required a minimum of four years' experience with Santa Clara County. Twelve county employees applied, including Joyce and Johnson.] Joyce had worked for the County since 1970, serving as an account clerk until 1975. She had applied for a road dispatcher position in 1974, but was deemed ineligible because she had not served as a road maintenance worker. In 1975, Joyce transferred from a senior account clerk position to a road maintenance worker position, becoming the first woman to fill such a job. During her four years in that position, she occasionally worked out of class as a road dispatcher.

Petitioner Johnson began with the County in 1967 as a road yard clerk, after private employment that included working as a supervisor and dispatcher. He had also unsuccessfully applied for the road dispatcher opening in 1974. In 1977, his clerical position was downgraded, and he sought and received a transfer to the position of road maintenance worker. He also occasionally worked out of class as a dispatcher while performing that job.

Nine of the applicants, including Joyce and Johnson, were deemed qualified for the job, and were interviewed by a two-person board. Seven of the applicants scored above 70 on this interview, which meant that they were certified as eligible for selection by the appointing authority. The scores awarded ranged from 70 to 80. Johnson was tied for second with a score of 75, while Joyce ranked next with a score of 73. A second interview was conducted by three Agency supervisors, who ultimately recommended that Johnson be promoted. Prior to the second interview, Joyce had contacted the County's Affirmative Action Office because she feared that her application might not receive disinterested review.[5] The Office in turn contacted the Agency's Affirmative Action Coordinator, whom the Agency's Plan makes responsible for, inter alia, keeping the Director informed of opportunities for the Agency to accomplish its objectives under the Plan. At the time, the Agency employed no

5. Joyce testified that she had had disagreements with two of the three members of the second interview panel. One had been her first supervisor when she began work as a road maintenance worker. In performing arduous work in this job, she had not been issued coveralls, although her male co-workers had received them. After ruining her pants, she complained to her supervisor, to no avail. After three other similar incidents, ruining clothes on each occasion, she filed a grievance, and was issued four pairs of coveralls the next day. Joyce had dealt with a second member of the panel for a year and a half in her capacity as chair of the Roads Operations Safety Committee, where she and he "had several differences of opinion on how safety should be implemented." In addition, Joyce testified that she had informed the person responsible for arranging her second interview that she had a disaster preparedness class on a certain day the following week. By this time about 10 days had passed since she had notified this person of her availability, and no date had yet been set for the interview. Within a day or two after this conversation, however, she received a notice setting her interview at a time directly in the middle of her disaster preparedness class. This same panel member had earlier described Joyce as a "rebel-rousing, skirt-wearing person."

women in any Skilled Craft position, and had never employed a woman as a road dispatcher. The Coordinator recommended to the Director of the Agency, James Graebner, that Joyce be promoted.

Graebner, authorized to choose any of the seven persons deemed eligible, thus had the benefit of suggestions by the second interview panel and by the Agency Coordinator in arriving at his decision. After deliberation, Graebner concluded that the promotion should be given to Joyce. As he testified: "I tried to look at the whole picture, the combination of her qualifications and Mr. Johnson's qualifications, their test scores, their expertise, their background, affirmative action matters, things like that. . . . I believe it was a combination of all those."

The certification for naming Joyce as the person promoted to the dispatcher position stated that both she and Johnson were rated as well qualified for the job. The evaluation of Joyce read: "Well qualified by virtue of 18 years of past clerical experience including 3 1/2 years at West Yard plus almost 5 years as a [road maintenance worker]." The evaluation of Johnson was as follows: "Well qualified applicant; two years of [road maintenance worker] experience plus 11 years of Road Yard Clerk. Has had previous outside Dispatch experience but was 13 years ago." Graebner testified that he did not regard as significant the fact that Johnson scored 75 and Joyce 73. . . .

. . . The District Court found that Johnson was more qualified for the dispatcher position than Joyce, and that the sex of Joyce was the *"determining factor* in her selection." The court acknowledged that, since the Agency justified its decision on the basis of its Affirmative Action Plan, the criteria announced in *Steelworkers v. Weber* should be applied in evaluating the validity of the Plan. It then found the Agency's Plan invalid on the ground that the evidence did not satisfy *Weber's* criterion that the Plan be temporary. . . .

II

As a preliminary matter, we note that petitioner bears the burden of establishing the invalidity of the Agency's Plan. [This case] fits readily within the analytical framework set forth in McDonnell Douglas Corp. v. Green. Once a plaintiff establishes a prima facie case that race or sex has been taken into account in an employer's employment decision, the burden shifts to the employer to articulate a nondiscriminatory rationale for its decision. The existence of an affirmative action plan provides such a rationale. If such a plan is articulated as the basis for the employer's decision, the burden shifts to the plaintiff to prove that the employer's justification is pretextual and the plan is invalid. As a practical matter, of course, an employer will generally seek to avoid a charge of pretext by presenting evidence in support of its plan. That does not mean, however, as petitioner suggests, that reliance on an affirmative action plan is to be treated as an affirmative defense requiring the employer to carry the burden of proving the validity of the plan. The burden of proving its invalidity remains on the plaintiff.

The assessment of the legality of the Agency Plan must be guided by our decision in *Weber.*[6] In that case, the Court addressed the question whether the employer

6. [The majority rejected Justice Scalia's argument in dissent that Title VII standards should be identical to those of the Constitution for public employers. Justice Scalia reasoned that Title VI embodies the same constraints as the Constitution and Title VI and Title VII have the thrust. The majority rejected] equating Title VI with Title VII. As noted in *Weber,* "Title VI was an exercise of federal power 'over a matter in which the Federal Government was already directly involved,'" since

violated Title VII by adopting a voluntary affirmative action plan designed to "eliminate manifest racial imbalances in traditionally segregated job categories." The respondent employee in that case challenged the employer's denial of his application for a position in a newly established craft training program, contending that the employer's selection process impermissibly took into account the race of the applicants. The selection process was guided by an affirmative action plan, which provided that 50% of the new trainees were to be black until the percentage of black skilled craftworkers in the employer's plant approximated the percentage of blacks in the local labor force. Adoption of the plan had been prompted by the fact that only 5 of 273, or 1.83%, of skilled craftworkers at the plant were black, even though the work force in the area was approximately 39% black. Because of the historical exclusion of blacks from craft positions, the employer regarded its former policy of hiring trained outsiders as inadequate to redress the imbalance in its work force.

We upheld the employer's decision to select less senior black applicants over the white respondent, for we found that taking race into account was consistent with Title VII's objective of "[breaking] down old patterns of racial segregation and hierarchy." As we stated:

> It would be ironic indeed if a law triggered by a Nation's concern over centuries of racial injustice and intended to improve the lot of those who had "been excluded from the American dream for so long" constituted the first legislative prohibition of all voluntary, private, race-conscious efforts to abolish traditional patterns of racial segregation and hierarchy.[7]

We noted that the plan did not "unnecessarily trammel the interests of the white employees," since it did not require "the discharge of white workers and their replacement with new black hirees." Nor did the plan create "an absolute bar to the advancement of white employees," since half of those trained in the new program were to be white. Finally, we observed that the plan was a temporary measure, not designed to maintain racial balance, but to "eliminate a manifest racial imbalance." As Justice Blackmun's concurrence made clear, *Weber* held that an employer seeking to justify the adoption of a plan need not point to its own prior discriminatory practices, nor even to evidence of an "arguable violation" on its part. Rather, it need point only to a "conspicuous . . . imbalance in traditionally segregated job categories." Our decision was grounded in the recognition that voluntary employer action can play a crucial role in furthering Title VII's purpose of eliminating the effects of

---

Congress 'was legislating to assure federal funds would not be used in an improper manner.'" In contrast, Title VII "was enacted pursuant to the commerce power to regulate purely private decisionmaking" and not intended to incorporate constitutional commands.

7. Justice Scalia's dissent maintains that *Weber*'s conclusion that Title VII does not prohibit voluntary affirmative action programs "rewrote the statute it purported to construe." [But not only was that decision sound, but Justice Blackmun's concurrence invited Congress to correct the result if Weber was wrongly decided. There have been no such amendments even proposed], and we therefore may assume that our interpretation was correct.

Justice Scalia's dissent faults the fact that we take note of the absence of congressional efforts to amend the statute to nullify *Weber*. It suggests that congressional inaction cannot be regarded as acquiescence under all circumstances, but then draws from that unexceptional point the conclusion that any reliance on congressional failure to act is necessarily a "canard." The fact that inaction may not always provide crystalline revelation, however, should not obscure the fact that it may be probative to varying degrees. *Weber*, for instance, was a widely publicized decision that addressed a prominent issue of public debate. Legislative inattention thus is not a plausible explanation for congressional inaction. . . .

discrimination in the workplace, and that Title VII should not be read to thwart such efforts.[8]

. . . The first issue is therefore whether consideration of the sex of applicants for Skilled Craft jobs was justified by the existence of a "manifest imbalance" that reflected underrepresentation of women in "traditionally segregated job categories." In determining whether an imbalance exists that would justify taking sex or race into account, a comparison of the percentage of minorities or women in the employer's work force with the percentage in the area labor market or general population is appropriate in analyzing jobs that require no special expertise, [citing *Teamsters v. United States* and *Weber*]. Where a job requires special training, however, the comparison should be with those in the labor force who possess the relevant qualifications [citing *Hazelwood School Dist. v. U.S.*]. The requirement that the "manifest imbalance" relate to a "traditionally segregated job category" provides assurance both that sex or race will be taken into account in a manner consistent with Title VII's purpose of eliminating the effects of employment discrimination, and that the interests of those employees not benefiting from the plan will not be unduly infringed.

A manifest imbalance need not be such that it would support a prima facie case against the employer, as suggested in Justice O'Connor's concurrence, since we do not regard as identical the constraints of Title VII and the Federal Constitution on voluntarily adopted affirmative action plans. Application of the "prima facie" standard in Title VII cases would be inconsistent with *Weber*'s focus on statistical imbalance,[10] and could inappropriately create a significant disincentive for employers to adopt an affirmative action plan. A corporation concerned with maximizing return on investment, for instance, is hardly likely to adopt a plan if in order to do so it must compile evidence that could be used to subject it to a colorable Title VII suit.[11]

---

8. Justice Scalia's suggestion that an affirmative action program may be adopted only to redress an employer's past discrimination was rejected in *Steelworkers v. Weber* because the prospect of liability created by such an admission would create a significant disincentive for voluntary action. As Justice Blackmun's concurrence in that case pointed out, such a standard would "[place] voluntary compliance with Title VII in profound jeopardy. The only way for the employer and the union to keep their footing on the 'tightrope' it creates would be to eschew all forms of voluntary affirmative action." . . .

10. The difference between the "manifest imbalance" and "prima facie" standards is illuminated by *Weber*. Had the Court in that case been concerned with past discrimination by the employer, it would have focused on discrimination in hiring skilled, not unskilled, workers, since only the scarcity of the former in Kaiser's work force would have made it vulnerable to a Title VII suit. In order to make out a prima facie case on such a claim, a plaintiff would be required to compare the percentage of black skilled workers in the Kaiser work force with the percentage of black skilled craft workers in the area labor market.

Weber obviously did not make such a comparison. Instead, it focused on the disparity between the percentage of black skilled craft workers in Kaiser's ranks and the percentage of blacks in the area labor force. Such an approach reflected a recognition that the proportion of black craft workers in the local labor force was likely as miniscule as the proportion in Kaiser's work force. The Court realized that the lack of imbalance between these figures would mean that employers in precisely those industries in which discrimination has been most effective would be precluded from adopting training programs to increase the percentage of qualified minorities. Thus, in cases such as *Weber*, where the employment decision at issue involves the selection of unskilled persons for a training program, the "manifest imbalance" standard permits comparison with the general labor force. By contrast, the "prima facie" standard would require comparison with the percentage of minorities or women qualified for the job for which the trainees are being trained, a standard that would have invalidated the plan in *Weber* itself.

11. In some cases, of course, the manifest imbalance may be sufficiently egregious to establish a prima facie case. However, as long as there is a manifest imbalance, an employer may adopt a plan even where the disparity is not so striking, without being required to introduce the nonstatistical evidence of past discrimination that would be demanded by the "prima facie" standard. See, e.g., *Teamsters* (statistics in pattern and practice case supplemented by testimony regarding employment practices). Of course, when there is sufficient evidence to meet the more stringent "prima facie" standard, be it statistical, nonstatistical, or a combination of the two, the employer is free to adopt an affirmative action plan.

It is clear that the decision to hire Joyce was made pursuant to an Agency Plan that directed that sex or race be taken into account for the purpose of remedying underrepresentation. . . .

As an initial matter, the Agency adopted as a benchmark for measuring progress in eliminating underrepresentation the long-term goal of a work force that mirrored in its major job classifications the percentage of women in the area labor market.[13] Even as it did so, however, the Agency acknowledged that such a figure could not by itself necessarily justify taking into account the sex of applicants for positions in all job categories. For positions requiring specialized training and experience, the Plan observed that the number of minorities and women "who possess the qualifications required for entry into such job classifications is limited." The Plan therefore directed that annual short-term goals be formulated that would provide a more realistic indication of the degree to which sex should be taken into account in filling particular positions. The Plan stressed that such goals "should not be construed as 'quotas' that must be met," but as reasonable aspirations in correcting the imbalance in the Agency's work force. . . . From the outset, therefore, the Plan sought annually to develop even more refined measures of the underrepresentation in each job category that required attention.

[When Joyce was selected for the road dispatcher position, the Agency was still in the process of refining its short-term goals for Skilled Craft Workers in accordance with the Plan.]

We reject petitioner's argument that, since only the long-term goal was in place for Skilled Craft positions at the time of Joyce's promotion, it was inappropriate for the Director to take into account affirmative action considerations in filling the road dispatcher position. The Agency's Plan emphasized that the long-term goals were not to be taken as guides for actual hiring decisions, but that supervisors were to consider a host of practical factors in seeking to meet affirmative action objectives, including the fact that in some job categories women were not qualified in numbers comparable to their representation in the labor force.

By contrast, had the Plan simply calculated imbalances in all categories according to the proportion of women in the area labor pool, and then directed that hiring be governed solely by those figures, its validity fairly could be called into question. This is because analysis of a more specialized labor pool normally is necessary in determining underrepresentation in some positions. If a plan failed to take distinctions in qualifications into account in providing guidance for actual employment decisions, it would dictate mere blind hiring by the numbers. . . .

The Agency's Plan emphatically did *not* authorize such blind hiring. . . .

Furthermore, in considering the candidates for the road dispatcher position in 1980, the Agency hardly needed to rely on a refined short-term goal to realize that it had a significant problem of underrepresentation that required attention. Given the obvious imbalance in the Skilled Craft category, and given the Agency's commitment to eliminating such imbalances, it was plainly not unreasonable for the Agency to determine that it was appropriate to consider as one factor the sex of Ms. Joyce in

---

13. Because of the employment decision at issue in this case, our discussion henceforth refers primarily to the Plan's provisions to remedy the underrepresentation of women. Our analysis could apply as well, however, to the provisions of the Plan pertaining to minorities.

making its decision.[14] The promotion of Joyce thus satisfies the first requirement enunciated in *Weber*, since it was undertaken to further an affirmative action plan designed to eliminate Agency work force imbalances in traditionally segregated job categories.

We next consider whether the Agency Plan unnecessarily trammeled the rights of male employees or created an absolute bar to their advancement. In contrast to the plan in *Weber*, which provided that 50% of the positions in the craft training program were exclusively for blacks . . . , the Plan sets aside no positions for women. The Plan expressly states that "[the] 'goals' established for each Division should not be construed as 'quotas' that must be met." Rather, the Plan merely authorizes that consideration be given to affirmative action concerns when evaluating qualified applicants. As the Agency Director testified, the sex of Joyce was but one of numerous factors he took into account in arriving at his decision. . . . [T]he Agency Plan requires women to compete with all other qualified applicants. No persons are automatically excluded from consideration; all are able to have their qualifications weighed against those of other applicants.

In addition, petitioner had no absolute entitlement to the road dispatcher position. Seven of the applicants were classified as qualified and eligible, and the Agency Director was authorized to promote any of the seven. Thus, denial of the promotion unsettled no legitimate, firmly rooted expectation on the part of petitioner. Furthermore, while petitioner in this case was denied a promotion, he retained his employment with the Agency, at the same salary and with the same seniority, and remained eligible for other promotions.

[Finally, the Plan was intended to *attain* a balanced work force, not to maintain one, despite the absence of an explicit end date.]

III

. . . The Agency in the case before us has undertaken such a voluntary effort, and has done so in full recognition of both the difficulties and the potential for intrusion on males and nonminorities. The Agency has identified a conspicuous imbalance in job categories traditionally segregated by race and sex. It has made clear from the outset, however, that employment decisions may not be justified solely by reference to this imbalance, but must rest on a multitude of practical, realistic factors. It has therefore committed itself to annual adjustment of goals so as to provide a reasonable guide for actual hiring and promotion decisions. The Agency earmarks no positions for anyone; sex is but one of several factors that may be taken into account in evaluating qualified applicants for a position.[17] As both the Plan's language and its

14. In addition, the Agency was mindful of the importance of finally hiring a woman in a job category that had formerly been all male. The Director testified that, while the promotion of Joyce "made a small dent, for sure, in the numbers," nonetheless "philosophically it made a larger impact in that it probably has encouraged other females and minorities to look at the possibility of so-called 'non-traditional' jobs as areas where they and the agency both have samples of a success story."

17. Justice Scalia's dissent predicts that today's decision will loose a flood of "less qualified" minorities and women upon the work force, as employers seek to forestall possible Title VII liability. . . .

A . . . more fundamental problem with Justice Scalia's speculation is that he ignores the fact that [i]t is a standard tenet of personnel administration that there is rarely a single, "best qualified" person for a job. An effective personnel system will bring before the selecting official several fully-qualified candidates who each may possess different attributes which recommend them for selection. Especially where the job is an unexceptional, middle-level craft position, without the need for unique work experience or educational attainment and for which several well-qualified

manner of operation attest, the Agency has no intention of establishing a work force whose permanent composition is dictated by rigid numerical standards.

We therefore hold that the Agency appropriately took into account as one factor the sex of Diane Joyce in determining that she should be promoted to the road dispatcher position. Accordingly, the judgment of the Court of Appeals is Affirmed.

[Justice STEVENS concurred, essentially on the grounds of stare decisis. In light of "the authoritative construction" of *Bakke* and *Weber*, he was compelled to accept this view even if he thought it "at odds with [his] understanding of the actual intent of the authors of the legislation."]

Justice O'CONNOR, concurring in the judgment. . . .

In my view, the proper initial inquiry in evaluating the legality of an affirmative action plan by a public employer under Title VII is no different from that required by the Equal Protection Clause. In either case, consistent with the congressional intent to provide some measure of protection to the interests of the employer's nonminority employees, the employer must have had a firm basis for believing that remedial action was required. An employer would have such a firm basis if it can point to a statistical disparity sufficient to support a prima facie claim under Title VII by the employee beneficiaries of the affirmative action plan of a pattern or practice claim of discrimination.

In *Weber*, this Court balanced two conflicting concerns in construing §703(d): Congress' intent to root out invidious discrimination against any person on the basis of race or gender, and its goal of eliminating the lasting effects of discrimination against minorities. Given these conflicting concerns, the Court concluded that it would be inconsistent with the background and purpose of Title VII to prohibit affirmative action in all cases. As I read *Weber*, however, the Court also determined that Congress had balanced these two competing concerns by permitting affirmative action only as a remedial device to eliminate actual or apparent discrimination or the lingering effects of this discrimination. . . .

The *Weber* view of Congress' resolution of the conflicting concerns of minority and nonminority workers in Title VII appears substantially similar to this Court's resolution of these same concerns in *Wygant* [*v. Jackson Bd. of Ed.*, 476 U.S. 267 (1986)] which involved the claim that an affirmative action plan by a public employer violated the Equal Protection Clause. In *Wygant*, the Court was in agreement that remedying past or present racial discrimination by a state actor is a sufficiently weighty interest to warrant the remedial use of a carefully constructed affirmative action plan. The Court also concluded, however, that "[societal] discrimination, without more, is too amorphous a basis for imposing a racially classified remedy." Instead, we determined that affirmative action was valid if it was crafted to remedy past or present discrimination by the employer. Although the employer need not point to any contemporaneous findings of actual discrimination, I concluded in *Wygant* that the employer must point to evidence sufficient to establish a firm basis for believing that remedial action is required, and that a

---

candidates are available, final determinations as to which candidate is "best qualified" are at best subjective.

Brief for the American Society for Personnel Administration as *Amicus Curiae* 9.

This case provides an example of precisely this point. Any differences in qualifications between Johnson and Joyce were minimal, to say the least. The selection of Joyce thus belies Justice Scalia's contention that the beneficiaries of affirmative action programs will be those employees who are merely not "utterly unqualified."

statistical imbalance sufficient for a Title VII prima facie case against the employer would satisfy this firm basis requirement. . . .

The *Wygant* analysis is entirely consistent with *Weber*. In *Weber*, the affirmative action plan involved a training program for unskilled production workers. There was little doubt that the absence of black craftworkers was the result of the exclusion of blacks from craft unions. *Weber* ("Judicial findings of exclusion from crafts on racial grounds are so numerous as to make such exclusion a proper subject for judicial notice"). The employer in *Weber* had previously hired as craftworkers only persons with prior craft experience, and craft unions provided the sole avenue for obtaining this experience. Because the discrimination occurred at entry into the craft union, the "manifest racial imbalance" was powerful evidence of prior race discrimination. Under our case law, the relevant comparison for a Title VII prima facie case in those circumstances — discrimination in admission to entry-level positions such as membership in craft unions — is to the total percentage of blacks in the labor force. See *Teamsters*, cf. [Local 28 of] *Sheet Metal Workers' [Int'l Ass'n v. EEOC*, 478 U.S. 421 (1986)] (observing that lower courts had relied on comparison to general labor force in finding Title VII violation by union). Here, however, the evidence of past discrimination is more complex. The number of women with the qualifications for entry into the relevant job classification was quite small. A statistical imbalance between the percentage of women in the work force generally and the percentage of women in the particular specialized job classification, therefore, does not suggest past discrimination for purposes of proving a Title VII prima facie case.

Unfortunately, the Court today gives little guidance for what statistical imbalance is sufficient to support an affirmative action plan. Although the Court denies that the statistical imbalance need be sufficient to make out a prima facie case of discrimination against women, the Court fails to suggest an alternative standard. Because both *Wygant* and *Weber* attempt to reconcile the same competing concerns, I see little justification for the adoption of different standards for affirmative action under Title VII and the Equal Protection Clause.

While employers must have a firm basis for concluding that remedial action is necessary, neither *Wygant* nor *Weber* places a burden on employers to prove that they actually discriminated against women or minorities. Employers are "trapped between the competing hazards of liability to minorities if affirmative action is not taken to remedy apparent employment discrimination and liability to nonminorities if affirmative action is taken." *Wygant* (O'Connor, J., concurring in part and concurring in judgment). Moreover, this Court has long emphasized the importance of voluntary efforts to eliminate discrimination. Thus, I concluded in *Wygant* that a contemporaneous finding of discrimination should not be required because it would discourage voluntary efforts to remedy apparent discrimination. A requirement that an employer actually prove that it had discriminated in the past would also unduly discourage voluntary efforts to remedy apparent discrimination. As I emphasized in *Wygant*, a challenge to an affirmative action plan "does not automatically impose upon the public employer the burden of convincing the court of its liability for prior unlawful discrimination; nor does it mean that the court must make an actual finding of prior discrimination based on the employer's proof before the employer's affirmative action plan will be upheld." Evidence sufficient for a prima facie Title VII pattern or practice claim against the employer itself suggests that the absence of women or minorities in a work force cannot be explained by general societal discrimination alone and that remedial action is appropriate. . . .

The long-term goal of the plan was "to attain a work force whose composition in all job levels and major job classifications approximates the distribution of women . . . in the Santa Clara County work force." If this long-term goal had been applied to the hiring decisions made by the Agency, in my view, the affirmative action plan would violate Title VII. "[I]t is completely unrealistic to assume that individuals of each [sex] will gravitate with mathematical exactitude to each employer . . . absent unlawful discrimination." *Sheet Metal Workers* (O'Connor, J., concurring in part and dissenting in part). Thus, a goal that makes such an assumption, and simplistically focuses on the proportion of women and minorities in the work force without more, is not remedial. Only a goal that takes into account the number of women and minorities qualified for the relevant position could satisfy the requirement that an affirmative action plan be remedial. This long-range goal, however, was never used as a guide for actual hiring decisions. Instead, the goal was merely a statement of aspiration wholly without operational significance. The affirmative action plan itself recognized the host of reasons why this goal was extremely unrealistic and as I read the record, the long-term goal was not applied in the promotion decision challenged in this case. Instead, the plan provided for the development of short-term goals, which alone were to guide the respondents, and the plan cautioned that even these goals "should not be construed as 'quotas' that must be met." . . .

At the time of the promotion at issue in this case, the short-term goals had not been fully developed. Nevertheless, the Agency had already recognized that the long-range goal was unrealistic, and had determined that the progress of the Agency should be judged by a comparison to the qualified women in the area work force. As I view the record, the promotion decision in this case was entirely consistent with the philosophy underlying the development of the short-term goals. . . .

The ultimate decision to promote Joyce rather than petitioner was made by James Graebner, the Director of the Agency. As Justice Scalia views the record in this case, the Agency Director made the decision to promote Joyce rather than petitioner solely on the basis of sex and with indifference to the relative merits of the two applicants. In my view, however, the record simply fails to substantiate the picture painted by Justice Scalia. The Agency Director testified that he "tried to look at the whole picture, the combination of [Joyce's] qualifications and Mr. Johnson's qualifications, their test scores, their experience, their background, affirmative action matters, things like that." Contrary to Justice Scalia's suggestion, the Agency Director knew far more than merely the sex of the candidates and that they appeared on a list of candidates eligible for the job. The Director had spoken to individuals familiar with the qualifications of both applicants for the promotion, and was aware that their scores were rather close. Moreover, he testified that over a period of weeks he had spent several hours making the promotion decision, suggesting that Joyce was not selected solely on the basis of her sex. Additionally, the Director stated that had Joyce's experience been less than that of petitioner by a larger margin, petitioner might have received the promotion. As the Director summarized his decision to promote Joyce, the underrepresentation of women in skilled craft positions was only one element of a number of considerations that led to the promotion of Ms. Joyce. While I agree with Justice Scalia's dissent that an affirmative action program that automatically and blindly promotes those marginally qualified candidates falling within a preferred race or gender category, or that can be equated with a permanent plan of "proportionate representation by race and sex," would violate Title VII, I cannot agree that this is such a case. Rather, as the Court demonstrates, Joyce's sex was simply used as a "plus" factor.

Justice SCALIA, with whom The Chief Justice joins, and with whom Justice WHITE joins in Parts I and II, dissenting.

... The Court today completes the process of converting [Title VII] from a guarantee that race or sex will not be the basis for employment determinations, to a guarantee that it often will. Ever so subtly, without even alluding to the last obstacles preserved by earlier opinions that we now push out of our path, we effectively replace the goal of a discrimination-free society with the quite incompatible goal of proportionate representation by race and by sex in the workplace.

I . . .

Several salient features of the plan should be noted. Most importantly, the plan's purpose was assuredly not to remedy prior sex discrimination by the Agency. It could not have been, because there was no prior sex discrimination to remedy. The majority, in cataloging the Agency's alleged misdeeds, neglects to mention the District Court's finding that the Agency "has not discriminated in the past, and does not discriminate in the present against women in regard to employment opportunities in general and promotions in particular." This finding was not disturbed by the Ninth Circuit.

Not only was the plan not directed at the results of past sex discrimination by the Agency, but its objective was not to achieve the state of affairs that this Court has dubiously assumed would result from an absence of discrimination — an overall work force "more or less representative of the racial and ethnic composition of the population in the community." *Teamsters.* Rather, the oft-stated goal was to mirror the racial and sexual composition of the entire county labor force, not merely in the Agency work force as a whole, but in each and every individual job category at the Agency. In a discrimination-free world, it would obviously be a statistical oddity for every job category to match the racial and sexual composition of even that portion of the county work force qualified for that job; it would be utterly miraculous for each of them to match, as the plan expected, the composition of the entire work force. Quite obviously, the plan did not seek to replicate what a lack of discrimination would produce, but rather imposed racial and sexual tailoring that would, in defiance of normal expectations and laws of probability, give each protected racial and sexual group a governmentally determined "proper" proportion of each job category. . . .

The fact of discrimination against Johnson is much clearer, and its degree more shocking, than the majority and Justice O'Connor's concurrence would suggest — largely because neither of them recites a single one of the District Court findings that govern this appeal, relying instead upon portions of the transcript which those findings implicitly rejected, and even upon a document (favorably comparing Joyce to Johnson) that was prepared after Joyce was selected. Worth mentioning, for example, is the trier of fact's determination that, if the Affirmative Action Coordinator had not intervened, "the decision as to whom to promote . . . would have been made by [the Road Operations Division Director]," who had recommended that Johnson be appointed to the position. Likewise, the even more extraordinary findings that James Graebner, the Agency Director who made the appointment, "did not inspect the applications and related examination records of either [Paul Johnson] or Diane Joyce before making his decision," and indeed "did little or nothing to inquire into the results of the interview process and conclusions which [were] described as of critical importance to the selection process." In light of these determinations, it is impossible to believe (or to think that the District Court believed) Graebner's self-serving statements relied upon by the majority and Justice O'Connor's concurrence, such as the assertion that he "tried to look at the whole picture, the combination of [Joyce's] qualifications and Mr. Johnson's qualifications, their test scores, their expertise, their background, affirmative action matters, things like that," (O'Connor, J., concurring in judgment). It was evidently enough for Graebner to know that both candidates (in the words of Johnson's counsel, to which Graebner assented) "met the M. Q.'s, the minimum. Both were minimally qualified." When asked whether he had "any basis," for determining whether one of the candidates was more qualified than the other, Graebner candidly answered, "No. . . . As I've said, they both appeared, and my conversations with people tended to corroborate, that they were both capable of performing the work."

After a 2-day trial, the District Court concluded that Diane Joyce's gender was "the determining factor," in her selection for the position. . . .

II

The most significant proposition of law established by today's decision is that racial or sexual discrimination is permitted under Title VII when it is intended to over-come the effect, not of the employer's own discrimination, but of societal attitudes that have limited the entry of certain races, or of a particular sex, into certain jobs. Even if the societal attitudes in question consisted exclusively of conscious discrimination by other employers, this holding would contradict a decision of this Court rendered only last Term. *Wygant v. Jackson Board of Education* held that the objective of remedying societal discrimination cannot prevent remedial affirmative action from violating the Equal Protection Clause. While Mr. Johnson does not advance a constitutional claim here, it is most unlikely that Title VII was intended to place a lesser restraint on discrimination by public actors than is established by the Constitution.[4] . . .

[T]oday's decision goes well beyond merely allowing racial or sexual discrimination in order to eliminate the effects of prior societal discrimination. The majority opinion often uses the phrase "traditionally segregated job category" to describe the evil against which the plan is legitimately (according to the majority) directed. As originally used in *Weber* that phrase described skilled jobs from which employers and unions had systematically and intentionally excluded black workers — traditionally segregated jobs, that is, in the sense of conscious, exclusionary discrimination. But that is assuredly not the sense in which the phrase is used here. It is

4. Justice O'Connor's concurrence at least makes an attempt to bring this Term into accord with last. Under her reading of Title VII, an employer may discriminate affirmatively, so to speak, if he has a "firm basis" for believing that he might be guilty of (nonaffirmative) discrimination under the Act, and if his action is designed to remedy that suspected prior discrimination. This is something of a halfway house between leaving employers scot-free to discriminate against disfavored groups, as the majority opinion does, and prohibiting discrimination, as do the words of Title VII. In the present case, although the District Court found that in fact no sex discrimination existed, Justice O'Connor would find a "firm basis" for the agency's belief that sex discrimination existed in the "inexorable zero": the complete absence, prior to Diane Joyce, of any women in the Agency's skilled positions. There are two problems with this: First, even positing a "firm basis" for the Agency's belief in prior discrimination, as I have discussed above, the plan was patently not designed to remedy that prior discrimination, but rather to establish a sexually representative work force. Second, even an absolute zero is not "inexorable." While it may inexorably provide "firm basis" for belief in the mind of an outside observer, it cannot conclusively establish such a belief on the employer's part, since he may be aware of the particular reasons that account for the zero. That is quite likely to be the case here, given the nature of the jobs we are talking about, and the list of "Factors Hindering Goal Attainment" recited by the Agency plan. The question is in any event one of fact, which, if it were indeed relevant to the outcome, would require a remand to the District Court rather than an affirmance.

absurd to think that the nationwide failure of road maintenance crews, for example, to achieve the Agency's ambition of 36.4% female representation is attributable primarily, if even substantially, to systematic exclusion of women eager to shoulder pick and shovel. It is a "traditionally segregated job category" not in the *Weber* sense, but in the sense that, because of longstanding social attitudes, it has not been regarded by women themselves as desirable work. . . . There are, of course, those who believe that the social attitudes which cause women themselves to avoid certain jobs and to favor others are as nefarious as conscious, exclusionary discrimination. Whether or not that is so (and there is assuredly no consensus on the point equivalent to our national consensus against intentional discrimination), the two phenomena are certainly distinct. And it is the alteration of social attitudes, rather than the elimination of discrimination, which today's decision approves as justification for state-enforced discrimination. This is an enormous expansion, undertaken without the slightest justification or analysis.

III

[Justice Scalia noted that *Weber* did not involve a public employers, and the damage that case did could be limited by Title VII not to permit discrimination by public actors that the Constitution forbids. But he also stressed that the language of Title VII "draws no distinction between private and public employers," and the better approach would be to use "the Fourteenth Amendment ramifications which *Weber* did not address and which are implicated for the first time here — as the occasion for reconsidering and overruling it. It is well to keep in mind just how thoroughly *Weber* rewrote the statute it purported to construe."] In effect, *Weber* held that the legality of intentional discrimination by private employers against certain disfavored groups or individuals is to be judged not by Title VII but by a judicially crafted code of conduct, the contours of which are determined by no discernible standard, aside from (as the dissent convincingly demonstrated) the divination of congressional "purposes" belied by the face of the statute and by its legislative history. We have been recasting that self-promulgated code of conduct ever since — and what it has led us to today adds to the reasons for abandoning it.

NOTES

1. *Extending* Weber *to Sex*. Since the Court decided in *Weber* that voluntary affirmative action based on race, within prescribed limits, did not violate Title VII, it was hard not to extend that approach to affirmative action on the basis of sex. Indeed, given the "inexorable zero" of women in the at-issue jobs, the employer in *Johnson* might have been able to justify its affirmative action plan as a way of curing its own past discrimination. Or does *Sears* make that problematic, absent some showing that women were interested in these jobs?

2. *Litigation Structure*. Prior to *Johnson*, many had viewed the litigation structure of "reverse discrimination" cases as follows: the plaintiff must prove that a minority group member or female was preferred over him. The employer could then defend such a preference by showing, as an affirmative defense, that the preference was pursuant to a valid affirmative action plan. Of course, the plaintiff and the defendant would frequently concede the racial or gender nature of the preference (as in *Weber* itself, where the plan was expressly intended to benefit blacks) and move immediately on to

the validity of the plan. After *Johnson*, it is clear that this structure is inaccurate. The Court states that the plaintiff has the burden of showing that an affirmative action plan is invalid. *See* Cynthia L. Estlund, *Putting* Grutter *to Work: Diversity, Integration, and Affirmative Action in the Workplace*, 26 BERKELEY J. EMP. & LAB. L. 1, 35 (2005) ("The existence of a valid affirmative action plan operates not as an affirmative defense along the lines of 'business necessity' or a 'bona fide occupational qualification'; it is treated as a legitimate, non-discriminatory basis for the challenged employment decision. *Johnson* thus makes room in the statute for affirmative action not by creating an affirmative defense but by narrowing the scope of what courts view as 'intentional discrimination' ").

But not all "reverse discrimination" results from affirmative action plans. As we saw in Chapter 1, it is impermissible to discriminate against any race or either sex in individual disparate treatment cases. There have even been systemic disparate treatment cases finding discrimination against whites. *E.g.*, *Decorte v. Jordan*, 497 F.3d 433 (5th Cir. 2007) (elected official's restructuring staff to move from 77 whites and 56 blacks to 27 whites and 130 blacks established discrimination against whites). There thus seem to be alternative structures for such cases: the plaintiff may prove (1) he was the victim of an ad hoc racial or gender preference that was intentional discrimination or (2) he was the victim of a systematic racial or gender preference where no affirmative action plan is involved; and (3) he was a victim of a preference pursuant to an affirmative action plan, which the plaintiff proves is invalid. The first two theories require only proof of the employer's discrimination; the latter requires proof that the plaintiff was disadvantaged and that the affirmative action plan was invalid.

If this analysis is correct, why would a plaintiff ever try to show that the preference he was challenging was pursuant to an affirmative action plan? If the employer's decision is simply challenged as ad hoc, won't the defendant have at least the burden of pleading and entering into evidence the fact that the challenged decision was the result of an affirmative action plan? Isn't this now a "legitimate, nondiscriminatory reason"?

Does *Price Waterhouse* or the 1991 Civil Rights Act alter the proof scheme *Johnson* established? Recall that the plurality in *Price Waterhouse* reserved the application of its holding to the affirmative action context. But Justice O'Connor and the three dissenters believed the *Price Waterhouse* approach should be fully applicable to reverse discrimination cases. The actual decision in *Johnson* to name Joyce was made by Graebner. Under *Price Waterhouse* analysis, does his quoted testimony show "direct evidence" of discrimination in favor of Joyce because she is a woman? If so, presumably one way that the county could limit remedies is to persuade the trier of fact that Joyce would have been hired in any event. But another way is to show that favoring Joyce was pursuant to a valid affirmative action plan. As to the latter, does the burden of persuasion still rest on the plaintiff in accordance with *Johnson*?

3. *§1981*. As might be expected, courts have applied affirmative action concepts developed under Title VII to §1981 claims alleging reverse discrimination. Thus, according to *Schurr v. Resorts International Hotel, Inc.*, 196 F.3d 486 (3d Cir. 1999), if an affirmative action plan is valid under Title VII, then actions based upon it will not violate §1981; however, a plan that is invalid under Title VII will not excuse racially motivated decisions challenged under §1981.

4. *Will* Weber *and* Johnson *Survive?* Both cases generated heated dissents. How would the presently constituted Supreme Court, with Chief Justice Roberts and Justice Alito now on the Court, decide these cases on statutory grounds? Since *Johnson*, the Civil Rights Act of 1991 amended Title VII. Would a decision by

Graebner to name Joyce "for affirmative action reasons" establish a "motivating factor"? Before you answer, the 1991 Amendments, however, added a new section to Title VII:

> Nothing in the amendments made by this title shall be construed to affect court-ordered remedies, affirmative action, or conciliation agreements, that are in accordance with the law.

§ 166, 105 Stat. 1071, 1079. Does this amendment affect your analysis? Michael J. Zimmer, Taxman: *Affirmative Action Dodges Five Bullets*, 1 U. PA. J. LAB. & EMP. L. 229, 235 (1998), concludes that § 116, if anything, reinforces the law of voluntary affirmative action. "Congress has gone beyond the mere 'silent or passive assent' connoted by the word 'acquiescence.' Whether or not § 116 amounts to a full reenactment of *Weber/Johnson*, it is a statement recognizing the law in those cases. Thus, under any view, § 116 bolsters *Weber/Johnson* and the stare decisis effect that the courts should give to that law."

Nevertheless, the lower courts have been hostile to affirmative action under Title VII. Perhaps influenced by the Equal Protection cases, discussed in Note on Affirmative Action and the Constitution, p. 201, they have purported to apply *Weber/Johnson's* more relaxed standards and nevertheless found the plan in question invalid. Perhaps most surprising, they have continued to do so even after *Grutter v. Bollinger*, 539 U.S. 306 (2003), upholding the limited use of race in the University of Michigan Law School's admissions process, relaxed the constitutional standard. One blog summarized these developments:

> After *Grutter*, the United States Courts of Appeals for the Third, Fifth, Seventh and Eighth Circuits sustained Title VII challenges to race-conscious diversity programs used by the cities of Milwaukee, Newark, Shreveport, Chicago, and Omaha, as well as at least one major private employer, Xerox Corporation. And, perhaps surprisingly, the courts cited *Grutter* as compelling the conclusion that the challenged diversity programs violated Title VII. *See Alexander v. City of Milwaukee*, 474 F.3d 437 (7th Cir. 2007); *Lomack v. City of Newark*, 463 F.3d 303 (3d Cir. 2006); *Kohlbek v. City of Omaha*, 447 F.3d 552 (8th Cir. 2006); *Dean v. City of Shreveport*, 438 F.3d 448 (5th Cir. 2006); *Biondo v. City of Chicago*, 382 F.3d 680 (7th Cir. 2004); *Frank v. Xerox Corp.*, 347 F.3d 130, 133, 137 (5th Cir. 2003).

Eric Dreiband, What the Schools Cases Mean for the Workplace, http://www .scotusblog.com/movabletype/archives/2007/07/what_the_school_1.html. This posting was triggered by the Court's most recent word on the subject, *Parents Involved in Community Schools v. Seattle School Dist. No. 1*, 127 S. Ct. 2738 (2007), discussed at p. 201, which took a far more restrictive approach than *Grutter*.

If the Court were to cut back on *Weber/Johnson* without overruling them, it might take the path established by the Third Circuit some years ago. In *United States v. Board of Educ. of the Township of Piscataway*, 91 F.3d 1547 (3d Cir. 1996) (en banc), the school board decided to lay off one teacher from its high school's business education department. According to its collective bargaining agreement with the union, the board was required to lay off by seniority. Two teachers, Sharon Taxman, a white, and Debra Williams, a black, were tied in terms of seniority. They were also found to be equally qualified. Pursuant to an affirmative action plan and because Williams was the only African American in the business department, the school board retained Williams to maintain diversity among its teachers. Taxman was laid off. The Third Circuit, with 8 of 12 judges joining in the majority, found this violated Title VII both because the board's purpose of maintaining diversity in the workforce was not one of the remediation purposes for affirmative action approved in *Weber* and *Johnson* and because the plan unnecessarily trammeled the interests of nonminority employees:

> The Board admits that it did not act to remedy the effects of past employment discrimination. The parties have stipulated that neither the Board's adoption of its affirmative action policy nor its subsequent decision to apply it in choosing between Taxman and Williams was intended to remedy the results of any prior discrimination or identified underrepresentation of Blacks within the Piscataway School District's teacher workforce as a whole. . . . Even though the Board's race-conscious action was taken to avoid what could have been an all-White faculty within the Business Department, the Board concedes that Blacks are not underrepresented in its teaching workforce as a whole or even in the Piscataway High School.

91 F.3d at 1563. Further, the affirmative action plan of the employer lacked the necessary definition and structure to ensure that it did not wrongly trammel the interests of nonminority employees. "[T]he Board's policy, devoid of goals and standards, is governed entirely by the Board's whim, leaving the Board free, if it so chooses, to grant racial preferences that do not promote even the policy's claimed purpose." *Id.* at 1564. The Supreme Court granted certiorari in *Taxman*, but the parties settled the dispute prior to its being argued. Accordingly, the Court dismissed the case, 522 U.S. 1010 (1997).

5. *Joyce as Victim of Discrimination.* Obviously, Johnson believed that Joyce received a preference because she was a woman. Is that so clear? Read footnote 10 concerning the second interview panel. Might not the hiring of Joyce have reflected merely an effort to remove disadvantages imposed on Joyce because she was a woman? If so, that would not be "affirmative action," but only nondiscrimination. Justice O'Connor concludes that Joyce's sex was a "plus factor" in her hiring. Is she saying that sex discrimination did not occur? It would certainly violate Title VII for a man's sex to be "a plus factor," at least if it affected the decision and probably even were it a motivating factor under *Desert Palace.* Is that Justice Scalia's point? The actual decision to name Joyce was made by Graebner. Does his quoted testimony amount to an admission of discrimination in favor of Joyce because she was a woman?

"AFFIRMATIVE ACTION" UNDER THE ADEA

While not normally denominated "affirmative action" when the Age Discrimination in Employment Act is concerned, a lingering question persisted about whether older workers could be favored over younger workers. Of course, when the younger workers were outside the protected class, i.e., younger than 40, there was no problem. When, however, an employer favored some workers within the protected group (say, those over 60) over some other protected group members (say, those between 40 and 50), there was a question as to whether the conduct was permissible. In *General Dynamics Land Systems, Inc. v. Cline,* 540 U.S. 581 (2004), the Court resolved this question definitively, holding that the statute simply did not make such discrimination illegal. There was, therefore, no need to engage in any affirmative action analysis.

Cline involved a collective-bargaining agreement between General Dynamics and the United Auto Workers, which "eliminated the company's obligation to provide health benefits to subsequently retired employees, except as to then-current workers at least 50 years old." The plaintiffs were then at least 40, and therefore protected by the Act, but under 50 and thus were denied benefits. The Court, in a 6-3 decision, found that "The Age Discrimination in Employment Act of 1967 forbids discriminatory preference for the young over the old. The question in this case is whether it also prohibits favoring the old over the young. We hold it does not." *Id.* at 584. To reach its result, the Court had to read "age discrimination" not to mean discrimination on account of age but rather discrimination on account of old age. It also had to ignore an EEOC regulations and some legislative history.

Since discriminating in favor of the old is simply not barred by the statute, the Court did not have to engage in the *Weber/Johnson* analysis as to when preferences were permissible and when they were not. Although the plan in question did not "unnecessarily trammel" the rights of the plaintiffs (they did not lose their jobs, just a future benefit), it might have been difficult to justify had something like the "traditionally segregated" prong of *Weber/Johnson* been applied.

Justice Thomas dissented: "The plain language of the ADEA clearly allows for suits brought by the relatively young when discriminated against in favor of the relatively old. The phrase 'discriminate . . . because of such individual's age,' 29 U.S.C. § 623(a)(1), is not restricted to discrimination because of relatively older age. If an employer fired a worker for the sole reason that the worker was under 45, it would be entirely natural to say that the worker had been discriminated against because of his age. I struggle to think of what other phrase I would use to describe such behavior. . . . " 540 U.S. at 603.

One way to look at *Cline* is to compare it with the Supreme Court's decision in *McDonald v. Santa Fe Trail Transp. Co.*, reproduced at p. 68, where the Court held that Title VII barred all race discrimination, not merely discrimination against racial minorities. Had *Santa Fe* come out the other way, there would be no need to consider the limits on affirmative action. One major difference between the Title VII and ADEA contexts, however, is that Title VII itself would have been subject to constitutional challenge had it been so construed: it would then have accorded a benefit on the basis of race. *See* Charles A. Sullivan, *The World Turned Upside Down?: Disparate Impact Claims by White Males*, 98 Nw. U.L. Rev. 1505 (2004) (serious constitutional questions would be raised by interpreting Title VII to foreclose disparate impact challenges by white and males); *but see* Richard A. Primus, *Equal Protection and Disparate Impact: Round Three*, 117 Harv. L. Rev. 493 (2003) (arguing that such a conclusion need not be viewed as a racial classification subject to strict scrutiny). But age discrimination is not subject to any kind of heightened scrutiny. Rather, age classifications by the government are judged under the rational relationship test, *e.g.*, *Kimel v. Fla. Bd. of Regents*, 528 U.S. 62, 83 (2000) ("age is not a suspect classification under the Equal Protection Clause"). *Cline*, therefore, does not raise any serious constitutional issues in its construction of the statute to favor older workers over younger workers.

NOTE ON AFFIRMATIVE ACTION AND THE CONSTITUTION

In *Parents Involved in Community Schools v. Seattle School Dist. No. 1*, 127 S. Ct. 2738 (2007), the Supreme Court rendered its latest decision in a long line of cases involving the "benign" use of race by state actors, resuming the hostile approach that had been briefly interrupted by the University of Michigan admissions cases.

Parents Involved addressed the use of race by two school districts in determining assignments of pupils to elementary and secondary schools. Both the Seattle and Louisville school districts were based on student choice. For example, in Seattle, rising ninth graders were allowed to choose which of the district's ten regular high schools to attend by ranking them in order of preference. Most students got their choice. But several schools were more popular than others and were oversubscribed. In that situation, "tiebreakers" were used, with the first being whether a sibling attended the first choice school. The second tiebreaker was based on race and was designed to prevent any school from becoming all white or all minority. If a school was not within 10% of the school district's overall white/nonwhite racial balance, this tiebreaker was used.

Chief Justice Roberts wrote an opinion for a plurality including Justices Scalia, Thomas and Alito, which struck down this use of race. Justice Breyer wrote a dissent which was joined by Justices Stevens, Souter and Ginsburg. That meant that Justice Kennedy's opinion was decisive, and he voted to invalidate the race-based assignment but in a less sweeping fashion than would have the Roberts opinion. Justices Thomas and Stevens also wrote separate opinions, although they respectively joined the plurality and the Breyer dissent..

Chief Justice Robert's plurality opinion drew an analogy between the white plaintiffs in these cases and the African-American plaintiffs in *Brown v. Board of Education.*

> Before *Brown*, school children were told where they could and could not go to school based on the color of their skin. The school districts in these cases have not carried the heavy burden of demonstrating that we should allow this once again — even for very different reasons. . . . [T]he way "to achieve a system of determining admission the public schools on a nonracial basis" *Brown II* . . . is to stop assigning students on a racial basis. The way to stop discrimination on the basis of race is to stop discriminating on the basis of race.

Id. at 2768. Applying traditional analysis, the plurality noted that only two interests had been recognized "as compelling in the school context," remedying past intentional discrimination (but not de facto segregation) and "diversity in higher education." *Id.* at 2793. Neither applied to the cases before the Court. Although challenged in a suit that was settled by adoption of a desegregation plan, the Seattle school district had never been found to have engaged in de jure segregation. While the Louisville school district had engaged in de jure segregation, its desegregation order had been dissolved after the school district had shown that that segregation had been remediated. Thus, the first compelling state interest was unavailable to either of the defendants.

> As for diversity, unlike *Grutter v. Bollinger*, 539 U.S. 306 (2003), race was not considered as part of a broader effort to achieve "exposure to widely diverse people, cultures, ideas, and viewpoints." . . . [Race] is not simply one factor weighed with others in reaching a decision, as in *Grutter*, it is *the* factor. Like the University of Michigan undergraduate plan struck down in *Gratz* [*v. Bollinger*, 539 U.S. 244 (2003)], the plans here "do not provide for a meaningful individualized review of applicants" but instead rely on racial classifications in a "nonindividualized, mechanical" way.

Id. at 1254-55.

Chief Justice Roberts rejected the arguments of the school districts that their use of race was justified by, "educational and broader socialization benefits [that] flow from a racially diverse learning environment;" for the plurality, the plans were "directed only to racial balance, pure and simple" and were not narrowly tailored to achieve the asserted educational and social benefits. "Racial balancing is not transformed from 'patently unconstitutional' to a compelling state interest simply by relabeling it 'racial diversity.' . . . " *Id.* at 2759. Without actually using the words, the Chief Justice appears to view equal protection as demanding a color-blind test that basically does not differentiate between uses of race invidiously and to aid those members of groups in society that historically have been victims of race discrimination.

Since Justice Kennedy did not join this part of the plurality opinion and since his concurrence is necessary to support the judgment, his decision is the applicable law to be followed. *See Marks v. United States*, 430 U.S. 188, 192 (1977). In response to what he described as the "all-too-unyielding insistence that race cannot be a factor" approach of the plurality opinion, Justice Kennedy left some room for taking race into account in decision-making by differentiating hope from reality: "The enduring hope is that race should not matter; the reality is that too often it does." *Id.* at 2791. He wrote:

> School districts can seek to reach *Brown's* objective of equal opportunity. The plurality opinion is at least open to the interpretation that the Constitution requires school districts to ignore the problems of *de facto* resegregation in schooling. I cannot endorse that conclusion. To the extent the plurality opinion suggests the Constitution mandates that state and local school authorities must accept the status quo of racial isolation in schools, it is, in my view, profoundly mistaken.

Id. at 2792. For Justice Kennedy, what the school districts did wrong was to assign "to each student a personal designation according to a crude system of individual racial classifications." *Id.* But what a school district can do is to take account of race as one component in its decision-making process because avoiding racial isolation is a compelling governmental interest.

> This Nation has a moral and ethical obligation to fulfill its historic commitment to creating an integrated society that ensures equal opportunity for all of its children. A compelling interest exists in avoiding racial isolation, an interest that a school district, in its discretion and expertise, may choose to pursue. Likewise, a district may consider it a compelling interest to achieve a diverse student population.

Id. at 2797. Instead of pupil assignment based on race, even as a second level tiebreaker in a general system of letting students choose their schools, Justice Kennedy said that other factors must be involved:

> Race may be one component of that diversity, but other demographic factors, plus special talents and needs, should also be considered. What the government is not permitted to do, absent a showing of necessity not made here, is to classify every student on the basis of race and to assign each of them to schools based on that classification. Crude measures of this sort threaten to reduce children to racial chits valued and traded according to one school's supply and another's demand.

Id. In the school assignment setting, it appears that a school board could use race in a number of ways to avoid resegregation and be in compliance with Justice Kennedy's approach, an approach that in many ways echoes the concurring opinion of Justice Powell in *Regents of the Univ. of Cal. v. Bakke*, 438 U.S. 265 (1978), which governed affirmative action analyses for many years.

One way would be to replace the hierarchical system of school assignment by choice followed by tiebreakers, with a system that looked at all the same factors — choice, sibling assignment, geographic distance from the schools, and race — at one time when making school assignment decisions. This multifactored decision might reduce the effect of student choice but it would seem to satisfy Justice Kennedy. Alternatively, school boards probably could adopt a two step process — student choice is the first step, but, if that would produce an overcrowded school, then look at the other factors, such as sibling school assignment, distance from the school, and race, as the second step.

What does *Parents Involved* say about affirmative action plans enacted by public employers? It would seem that the tiebreaker approach of the Piscataway School District, in *Taxman* referred to above, would not be permissible. But, would a public employer in making an employment decision be acting constitutionally if it considered race as long as it made the decision in the context of looking at additional factors that might be relevant to the job? After *Grutter* and before *Parents Involved*, some circuits approved of public employer affirmative action plans. See *Petit v. City of Chicago*, 352 F.3d 1111 (7th Cir. 2003) (the city had a compelling operational need for a diverse police department given the size of the police force and its charge to protect a racially and ethnically divided major city in light of evidence that minority supervision of police officers reduced fears that the police department was hostile to the minority community). *But see Lomack v. City of Newark*, 463 F.3d 303, 309 (3d Cir. 2006) (fire department affirmative action plan resulting in involuntary transfers after all fire companies were integrated does not serve compelling state interest where single-race fire companies resulted not from discrimination but from allowing employees to work where they chose: "While *Grutter* established that educational benefits are compelling *in a law school context*, we do not find its holding applicable in the firefighting context.") (emphasis in original)). *See generally* Rebecca Hanner White, *Affirmative Action in the Workplace: The Significance of Grutter?* 92 KY. L.J. 263 (2003). *See also* Michael J. Yelnosky, *The Prevention Justification for Affirmative Action*, 64 OHIO ST. L.J. 1385, 1387 (2003).

Parents Involved considered race, what about sex? The employer in *Johnson* was a public employer. If *Johnson* returned to the Supreme Court, but as a case raising the constitutional question of affirmative action based on sex, what standard would apply? The starting point of *Parents Involved* and its predecessors is that all racial classifications by the government are subject to strict scrutiny. E.g., *Adarand Constructors v. Pena*, 515 U.S. 200 (1995); *Wygant v. Jackson Bd. of Ed.*, 476 U.S. 267 (1986). But the use of sex classifications by the government is judged using intermediate scrutiny, *United States v. Virginia*, 518 U.S. 515 (1996). Would a public employer be able to use the sex of an individual, by itself, to make an employment decision pursuant to an affirmative action plan, such as the one approved as to Title VII in *Johnson?*

What does *Parents Involved* mean for affirmative action as to race, sex and age in the private sector? Will *Weber* and *Johnson* be decided differently today in light of *Parents Involved?*

NOTE ON INTERNATIONAL AND COMPARATIVE ANTIDISCRIMINATION LAW

The antidiscrimination laws of the major trading partners of the United States do not distinguish between individual and systemic cases, with the focus instead on whether the case involves direct or indirect discrimination. See p. 111. Direct discrimination includes what in the U.S. is defined as individual and systemic disparate treatment, and, as we have seen, the intent of the defendant to discriminate is a key element of proof.

The courts of some countries find systemic direct discrimination based on statistics, even absent proof of defendant's intent to discriminate. For example, in *Canada (Canadian Human Rights Commission) v. Canadian National Railway ("Action Travail des Femmes")*, [1987] 1 S.C.R. 1114, the massive underrepresentation of women in unskilled blue-collar jobs on the railway sufficed to establish direct discrimination, even in the absence of any proof of specific discriminatory incidents or an intent to discriminate. Similarly in *4 AZ R 30/92*, September 23, 1992, the German Federal Labor Court found discrimination based on evidence that women were paid less for performing substantially the same work as men. Discrimination was found even though men, but not women, sometimes drove forklift trucks and even though there was no finding that defendant acted with intent to discriminate. "[A] substantially greater number of members of one sex among those who are disadvantaged serves as an indicator of discrimination on the ground of sex. In such case, the court should presume the existence of discrimination unless the employer demonstrates that there were objective reasons unrelated to sex for the difference. In the present case, with a total number of 28 men and women employed in the warehouse, the random distribution of the sexes between wage groups is unlikely to be so uneven."

The EU's General Equal Treatment Directive, Directive 2000/78/EC, created a defense in Article 4(1) available to discrimination on all of the proscribed bases:

> Notwithstanding Article 2(1) and (2), Member States may provide that a difference of treatment which is based on a characteristic related to any of the grounds referred to in Article 1 shall not constitute discrimination where, by reason of the nature of the particular occupational activities concerned or of the context in which they are carried out, such a characteristic constitutes a genuine and determining occupational requirement, provided that the objective is legitimate and the requirement is proportionate.

How does this compare to the BFOQ defense in Title VII? How would *Johnson Controls* be decided if the issue arose pursuant to the national law of an EU member state that conformed to the Directive?

Article 7 of the EU equal treatment directive allows member states to take "positive action" to aid victims of discrimination by "specific measures to prevent or compensate for disadvantages linked to any of the grounds referred to in Article 1." Textually, this seems a broader exception than Title VII accords voluntary affirmative action plans.

Chapter 3

Systemic Disparate Impact
Discrimination

While disparate treatment discrimination is the purposeful exclusion of protected class members from jobs, disparate impact discrimination exists when employment policies, regardless of intent, adversely affect one group more than another and cannot be adequately justified. This chapter presents the structure of disparate impact analysis, the policies subject to disparate impact analysis, and defenses to a disparate impact case.

As we will see, the disparate impact theory clearly applies under Title VII of the Civil Rights Act of 1964 and the Americans with Disabilities Act (ADA). It also operates, albeit in a considerably diluted form, under the Age Discrimination in Employment Act (ADEA), but it is *not* available under 42 U.S.C.S. § 1981 (2007), *General Bldg. Contractors Assn. v. Pennsylvania*, 458 U.S. 375 (2002), or under 42 U.S.C.S. § 1983 (2007) in suits enforcing the equal protection clause of the United States Constitution, *e.g.*, *Washington v. Davis*, 426 U.S. 229 (U.S. 1976)

A. THE CONCEPT OF DISPARATE IMPACT DISCRIMINATION

GRIGGS v. DUKE POWER CO.
401 U.S. 424 (1971)

Chief Justice BURGER delivered the opinion of the Court.

We granted the writ in this case to resolve the question whether an employer is prohibited by the Civil Rights Act of 1964, Title VII, from requiring a high school education or passing of a standardized general intelligence test as a condition of employment in or transfer to jobs when (a) neither standard is shown to be significantly related to successful job performance, (b) both requirements operate to disqualify Negroes at a substantially higher rate than white applicants, and (c) the jobs in question formerly had been filled only by white employees as part of a long-standing practice of giving preference to whites. . . .

All the petitioners are employed at the Company's Dan River Steam Station, a power generating facility located at Draper, North Carolina. At the time this action was instituted, the Company had 95 employees at the Dan River Station, 14 of whom were Negroes; 13 of these are petitioners here.

The District Court found that prior to July 2, 1965, the effective date of the Civil Rights Act of 1964, the company openly discriminated on the basis of race in the hiring and assigning of employees at its Dan River plant. The plant was organized into five operating departments: (1) Labor, (2) Coal Handling, (3) Operations, (4) Maintenance, and (5) Laboratory and Test. Negroes were employed only in the Labor Department where the highest paying jobs paid less than the lowest paying jobs in the other four "operating" departments in which only whites were employed.[2] Promotions were normally made within each department on the basis of job seniority. Transferees into a department usually began in the lowest position.

In 1955 the Company instituted a policy of requiring a high school education for initial assignment to any department except Labor, and for transfer from the Coal Handling to any "inside" department (Operations, Maintenance, or Laboratory). When the Company abandoned its policy of restricting Negroes to the Labor Department in 1965, completion of high school also was made a prerequisite to transfer from Labor to any other department. From the time the high school requirement was instituted to the time of trial, however, white employees hired before the time of the high school education requirement continued to perform satisfactorily and achieve promotions in the "operating" departments. Findings on this score are not challenged.

The Company added a further requirement for new employees on July 2, 1965, the date on which Title VII became effective. To qualify for placement in any but the Labor Department it became necessary to register satisfactory scores on two professionally prepared aptitude tests, as well as to have a high school education. Completion of high school alone continued to render employees eligible for transfer to the four desirable departments from which Negroes had been excluded if the incumbent had been employed prior to the time of the new requirement. In September 1965 the Company began to permit incumbent employees who lacked a high school education to qualify for transfer from Labor or Coal Handling to an "inside" job by passing two tests — the Wonderlic Personnel Test, which purports to measure general intelligence, and the Bennett Mechanical Comprehension Test. Neither was directed or intended to measure the ability to learn to perform a particular job or category of jobs. The requisite scores used for both initial hiring and transfer approximated the national median for high school graduates.[3]

---

2. A Negro was first assigned to a job in an operating department in August 1966, five months after charges had been filed with the Equal Employment Opportunity Commission. The employee, a high school graduate who had begun in the Labor Department in 1953, was promoted to a job in the Coal Handling Department.

3. The test standards are thus more stringent than the high school requirement, since they would screen out approximately half of all high school graduates.

The District Court had found that while the Company previously followed a policy of overt racial discrimination in a period prior to the Act, such conduct had ceased. . . .

The Court of Appeals noted . . . that the District Court was correct in its conclusion that there was no showing of a racial purpose or invidious intent in the adoption of the high school diploma requirement or general intelligence test and that these standards had been applied fairly to whites and Negroes alike. It held that, in the absence of a discriminatory purpose, use of such requirements was permitted by the Act. In so doing, the Court of Appeals rejected the claim that because these two requirements operated to render ineligible a markedly disproportionate number of Negroes, they were unlawful under Title VII unless shown to be job related. . . .

The objective of Congress in the enactment of Title VII is plain from the language of the statute. It was to achieve equality of employment opportunities and remove barriers that have operated in the past to favor an identifiable group of white employees over other employees. Under the Act, practices, procedures, or tests neutral on their face, and even neutral in terms of intent, cannot be maintained if they operate to "freeze" the status quo of prior discriminatory employment practices.

The Court of Appeals' [judges] agreed that, on the record in the present case, "whites register far better on the Company's alternative requirements" than Negroes.[6] This consequence would appear to be directly traceable to race. Basic intelligence must have the means of articulation to manifest itself fairly in a testing process. Because they are Negroes, petitioners have long received inferior education in segregated schools and this Court expressly recognized these differences in Gaston County v. United States, 395 U.S. 285 (1969). There, because of the inferior education received by Negroes in North Carolina, this Court barred the institution of a literacy test for voter registration on the ground that the test would abridge the right to vote indirectly on account of race. Congress did not intend by Title VII, however, to guarantee a job to every person regardless of qualifications. In short, the Act does not command that any person be hired simply because he was formerly the subject of discrimination, or because he is a member of a minority group. Discriminatory preference for any group, minority or majority, is precisely and only what Congress has proscribed. What is required by Congress is the removal of artificial, arbitrary, and unnecessary barriers to employment when the barriers operate invidiously to discriminate on the basis of a racial or other impermissible classification.

Congress has now provided that tests or criteria for employment or promotion may not provide equality of opportunity merely in the sense of the fabled offer of milk to the stork and the fox. On the contrary, Congress has now required that the posture and condition of the job-seeker be taken into account. It has — to resort again to the fable — provided that the vessel in which the milk is proffered be one all seekers can use. The Act proscribes not only overt discrimination but also practices that are fair in form, but discriminatory in operation. The touchstone is business necessity. If an employment practice which operates to exclude Negroes cannot be shown to be related to job performance, the practice is prohibited.

---

6. In North Carolina, 1960 census statistics show that, while 34% of white males had completed high school, only 12% of Negro males had done so. U.S. Bureau of the Census, U.S. Census of Population: 1960, Vol. 1, Characteristics of the Population, pt. 35, Table 47. Similarly, with respect to standardized tests, the EEOC in one case found that use of a battery of tests, including the Wonderlic and Bennett tests used by the Company in the instant case, resulted in 58% of whites passing the tests as compared with only 6% of the blacks. Decision of EEOC, CCH Empl. Prac. Guide, ¶17,304.53 (Dec. 2, 1966). See also Decision of EEOC 70-552, CCH Empl. Prac. Guide, ¶6139 (Feb. 19, 1970).

On the record before us, neither the high school completion requirement nor the general intelligence test is shown to bear a demonstrable relationship to successful performance of the jobs for which it was used. Both were adopted, as the Court of Appeals noted, without meaningful study of their relationship to job-performance ability. Rather, a vice president of the Company testified, the requirements were instituted on the Company's judgment that they generally would improve the overall quality of the work force.

The evidence, however, shows that employees who have not completed high school or taken the tests have continued to perform satisfactorily and make progress in departments for which the high school and test criteria are now used. The promotion record of present employees who would not be able to meet the new criteria thus suggests the possibility that the requirements may not be needed even for the limited purpose of preserving the avowed policy of advancement within the Company. In the context of this case, it is unnecessary to reach the question whether testing requirements that take into account capability for the next succeeding position or related future promotion might be utilized upon a showing that such long-range requirements fulfill a genuine business need. In the present case the Company has made no such showing.

The Court of Appeals held that the Company had adopted the diploma and test requirements without any "intention to discriminate against Negro employees." We do not suggest that either the District Court or the Court of Appeals erred in examining the employer's intent; but good intent or absence of discriminatory intent does not redeem employment procedures or testing mechanisms that operate as "built-in headwinds" for minority groups and are unrelated to measuring job capability.

The Company's lack of discriminatory intent is suggested by special efforts to help the undereducated employees through Company financing of two-thirds the cost of tuition for high school training. But Congress directed the thrust of the Act to the *consequences* of employment practices, not simply the motivation. More than that, Congress has placed on the employer the burden of showing that any given requirement must have a manifest relationship to the employment in question.

The facts of this case demonstrate the inadequacy of broad and general testing devices as well as the infirmity of using diplomas or degrees as fixed measures of capability. History is filled with examples of men and women who rendered highly effective performance without the conventional badges of accomplishment in terms of certificates, diplomas, or degrees. Diplomas and tests are useful servants, but Congress has mandated the common sense proposition that they are not to become masters of reality.

The Company contends that its general intelligence tests are specifically permitted by § 703(h) of the Act.[8] That section authorizes the use of "any professionally developed ability test" that is not "designed, intended or *used* to discriminate because of race. . . ." (Emphasis added.)

The Equal Employment Opportunity Commission, having enforcement responsibility, has issued guidelines interpreting Section 703(h) to permit only the use of

---

8. Section 703(h) applies only to tests. It has no applicability to the high school diploma requirement.

job-related tests.[9] The administrative interpretation of the Act by the enforcing agency is entitled to great deference. Since the Act and its legislative history support the Commission's construction, this affords good reason to treat the guidelines as expressing the will of Congress.

Section 703(h) was not contained in the House version of the Civil Rights Act but was added in the Senate during extended debate. For a period, debate revolved around claims that the bill as proposed would prohibit all testing and force employers to hire unqualified persons simply because they were part of a group formerly subject to job discrimination. Proponents of Title VII sought throughout the debate to assure the critics that the Act would have no effect on job-related tests. Senators Case of New Jersey and Clark of Pennsylvania, co-managers of the bill on the Senate floor, issued a memorandum explaining that the proposed Title VII "expressly protects the employer's right to insist that any prospective applicant, Negro or white, *must meet the applicable job qualifications*. Indeed, the very purpose of Title VII is to promote hiring on the basis of job qualifications, rather than on the basis of race or color." 110 Cong. Rec. 7247.[11] (Emphasis added.) Despite these assurances, Senator Tower of Texas introduced an amendment authorizing "professionally developed ability tests." Proponents of Title VII opposed the amendment because, as written, it would permit an employer to give any test, "whether it was a good test or not, so long as it was professionally designed. Discrimination could actually exist under the guise of compliance with the statute." 110 Cong. Rec. 13504 (remarks of Sen. Case).

The amendment was defeated and two days later Senator Tower offered a substitute amendment which was adopted verbatim and is now the testing provision of §703(h). Speaking for the supporters of Title VII, Senator Humphrey, who had vigorously opposed the first amendment, endorsed the substitute amendment, stating: "Senators on both sides of the aisle who were deeply interested in Title VII have examined the text of this amendment and have found it to be in accord with the intent and purpose of that title." 110 Cong. Rec. 13724. The amendment was then

---

9. EEOC Guidelines on Employment Testing Procedures, issued August 24, 1966, provide:

The Commission accordingly interprets "professionally developed ability test" to mean a test which fairly measures the knowledge or skills required by the particular job or class of jobs which the applicant seeks, or which fairly affords the employer a chance to measure the applicant's ability to perform a particular job or class of jobs. The fact that a test was prepared by an individual or organization claiming expertise in test preparation does not, without more, justify its use within the meaning of Title VII.

The EEOC position has been elaborated in the new Guidelines on Employee Selection Procedures, 29 C.F.R. §1607, 35 Fed. Reg. 12333 (Aug. 1, 1970). These guidelines demand that employers using tests have available "data demonstrating that the test is predictive of or significantly correlated with important elements of work behavior which comprise or are relevant to the job or jobs for which candidates are being evaluated." Id., at §1607.4(c).

11. The Court of Appeals majority, in finding no requirement in Title VII that employment tests be job related, relied in part on a quotation from an earlier Clark-Case interpretive memorandum addressed to the question of the constitutionality of Title VII. The Senators said in that memorandum:

There is no requirement in Title VII that employers abandon bona fide qualifications tests where, because of differences in background and education, members of some groups are able to perform better on these tests than members of other groups. An employer may set his qualifications as high as he likes, he may test to determine which applicants have these qualifications, and he may hire, assign, and promote on the basis of test performance. [110 Cong. Rec. 7213.]

However, nothing there stated conflicts with the later memorandum dealing specifically with the debate over employer testing, 110 Cong. Rec. 7247 (quoted from in the text above), in which Senators Clark and Case explained that tests which measure "applicable job qualifications" are permissible under Title VII. In the earlier memorandum Clark and Case assured the Senate that employers were not to be prohibited from using tests that determine *qualifications*. Certainly a reasonable interpretation of what the Senators meant, in light of the subsequent memorandum directed specifically at employer testing, was that nothing in the Act prevents employers from requiring that applicants be fit for the job.

adopted. From the sum of the legislative history relevant in this case, the conclusion is inescapable that the EEOC's construction of §703(h) to require that employment tests be job related comports with congressional intent.

Nothing in the Act precludes the use of testing or measuring procedures; obviously they are useful. What Congress has forbidden is giving these devices and mechanisms controlling force unless they are demonstrably a reasonable measure of job performance. Congress has not commanded that the less qualified be preferred over the better qualified simply because of minority origins. Far from disparaging job qualifications as such, Congress has made such qualifications the controlling factor, so that race, religion, nationality, and sex become irrelevant. What Congress has commanded is that any tests used must measure the person for the job and not the person in the abstract. . . .

NOTES

1. *The Backstory.* The *Griggs* opinion was authored by Chief Justice Burger, and stands out in stark contrast to his more conservative approach to most other questions of statutory or constitutional interpretation. Professor Samuel Estricher, *The Story of Griggs v. Duke Power Co.* in EMPLOYMENT DISCRIMINATION STORIES (Joel William Friedman ed. 2006), explores the surprising departure of Chief Justice Burger from a text-bound mode of statutory interpretation in favor of a more contextual or purposive construction of the statute. Professor Estreicher offers two alternative explanations for the Court's expansive ruling: first, the Nixon Administration's forceful advocacy of that approach (itself perhaps surprisingly to some) and, second, a perception that rejecting disparate impact claims would encourage employers to rely on facially neutral criteria as a more subtle mechanism for producing the discriminatory results that had previously been achieved by more overt bias. *Griggs* was, after all, decided at a time when the success of the entire antidiscrimination project was in doubt.

2. *The* Griggs *"Structure."* The Court's approach to the structure of a disparate impact case (as opposed to more complicated proof structures that would emerge later in individual disparate treatment cases) seems reasonably clear. If the use of a particular selection device — in *Griggs*, the high school diploma credential and passing two standardized tests, the Wonderlic Personnel Test and the Bennett Mechanical Comprehension Test — has a greater adverse impact on African American workers than on whites, see footnote 6, they are presumptively impermissible. At that point, however, the defendant can prevail by showing that these selection devices were justified, although in *Griggs* itself Duke Power had not shown that the requirements measured the ability to perform any of the jobs, and thus their use violated Title VII: "The Act proscribes not only overt discrimination but also practices that are fair in form, but discriminatory in operation. The touchstone is business necessity. If an employment practice which operates to exclude Negroes cannot be shown to be related to job performance, the practice is prohibited."

3. *"Tests" vs. Other Employer Practices.* The diploma requirement is, presumably, subject to this straightforward analysis. The Wonderlic and Bennett tests, however, introduce a twist because of an exception to liability in §703(h) for any "professionally developed ability test" that is not "designed, intended or *used* to discriminate because of race." Look at the EEOC test guidelines in footnote 9. Do they make the use of tests even more at risk from a disparate impact attack than other practices, such as the high school diploma requirement? See p. 275.

4. *The Role of the EEOC.* The *Griggs* Court states that "The administrative interpretation of the Act by the enforcing agency [the Equal Opportunity Commission] is entitled to great deference." What does this mean? How much deference is the Court paying to the EEOC's interpretation of the statute? How much should it pay? *Griggs* was the Court's first encounter with the EEOC and its interpretation of Title VII. For further discussion of the question of deference to the Commission, see Note on Deference to the EEOC, Chapter 6 at p. 520.

5. *The Scope of Practices Subject to the Disparate Impact Theory.* In 1988, in *Watson v. Fort Worth Bank & Trust*, 487 U.S. 977, 988 (1988), Justice O'Connor, writing for the Court, described the disparate impact cases the Supreme Court had decided up until that time as all involving "standardized employment tests or criteria," such as written tests, height and weight requirements, and a rule against employing drug addicts. In contrast, *Watson* involved subjective employment practices, which had generated considerable confusion in the lower courts to the applicability of disparate impact. *See generally*, Julia Lamber, *Alternatives to Challenged Selection Criteria: The Significance of Nonstatistical Evidence in Disparate Impact Cases Under Title VII*, 1985 WIS. L. REV. 1. The issue before the Court was whether such practices were subject to the disparate impact theory. After being denied promotion a number of times by the small bank in which she worked, plaintiff challenged the practice of her employer to have all-white supervisors use their subjective judgments to decide whom to promote. All of their promotions went to whites. The Court held it was "persuaded that our decisions in *Griggs* and succeeding cases could largely be nullified if disparate impact analysis were applied only to standardized selection practices . . . [w]e conclude, accordingly, that subjective or discretionary employment practices may be analyzed under the disparate impact approach in appropriate cases." *Id.* at 989.

Watson seemed to be a high-water mark for disparate impact since the range of the theory had been expanded to cover all employment practices. However, in a part of her opinion that was joined only by a plurality, Justice O'Connor tempered her expansion of the application of the theory by recasting *Griggs* in a manner that substantially weakened its usefulness. A majority of the Court adopted that approach the next year.

WARDS COVE PACKING CO. v. ATONIO
490 U.S. 642 (1989)

Justice WHITE delivered the opinion of the Court.

. . . I

The claims before us are disparate-impact claims, involving the employment practices of petitioners, two companies that operate salmon canneries in remote and widely separated areas of Alaska. The canneries operate only during the salmon runs in the summer months. They are inoperative and vacant for the rest of the year. In May or June of each year, a few weeks before the salmon runs begin, workers arrive and prepare the equipment and facilities for the canning operation. Most of these workers possess a variety of skills. When salmon runs are about to begin, the workers who will operate the cannery lines arrive, remain as long as there are fish to can, and then depart. The canneries are then closed down, winterized, and left vacant until the next spring. During the off-season, the companies employ only a small number of individuals at their headquarters in Seattle and Astoria, Oregon, plus some employees at the winter shipyard in Seattle. . . .

Jobs at the canneries are of two general types: "cannery jobs" on the cannery line, which are unskilled positions; and "noncannery jobs," which fall into a variety of classifications. Most noncannery jobs are classified as skilled positions.[3] Cannery jobs are filled predominantly by nonwhites: Filipinos and Alaska Natives. The Filipinos are hired through, and dispatched by, Local 37 of the International Longshoremen's and Warehousemen's Union pursuant to a hiring hall agreement with the local. The Alaska Natives primarily reside in villages near the remote cannery locations. Noncannery jobs are filled with predominantly white workers, who are hired during the winter months from the companies' offices in Washington and Oregon. Virtually all of the noncannery jobs pay more than cannery positions. The predominantly white noncannery workers and the predominantly nonwhite cannery employees live in separate dormitories and eat in separate mess halls.

In 1974, respondents, a class of nonwhite cannery workers who were (or had been) employed at the canneries, brought this Title VII action against petitioners. Respondents alleged that a variety of petitioners' hiring/promotion practices — e.g., nepotism, a rehire preference, a lack of objective hiring criteria, separate hiring channels, a practice of not promoting from within — were responsible for the racial stratification of the work force and had denied them and other nonwhites employment as noncannery workers on the basis of race. Respondents also complained of petitioners' racially segregated housing and dining facilities. . . .

II

In holding that respondents had made out a prima facie case of disparate impact, the Court of Appeals relied solely on respondents' statistics showing a high percentage of nonwhite workers in the cannery jobs and a low percentage of such workers in the noncannery positions. Although statistical proof can alone make out a prima facie case, the Court of Appeals' ruling here misapprehends our precedents and the purposes of Title VII, and we therefore reverse.

"There can be no doubt," as there was when a similar mistaken analysis had been undertaken by the courts below in *Hazelwood*, "that the . . . comparison . . . fundamentally misconceived the role of statistics in employment discrimination cases." The "proper comparison [is] between the racial composition of [the at-issue jobs] and the racial composition of the qualified . . . population in the relevant labor market." It is such a comparison — between the racial composition of the qualified persons in the labor market and the persons holding at-issue jobs — that generally forms the proper basis for the initial inquiry in a disparate impact case. Alternatively, in cases where such labor market statistics will be difficult if not impossible to ascertain, we have recognized that certain other statistics — such as measures indicating the racial composition of "otherwise-qualified applicants" for at-issue

---

3. The noncannery jobs were described as follows by the Court of Appeals: "Machinists and engineers are hired to maintain the smooth and continuous operation of the canning equipment. Quality control personnel conduct the FDA-required inspections and record keeping. Tenders are staffed with a crew necessary to operate the vessel. A variety of support personnel are employed to operate the entire cannery community, including, for example, cooks, carpenters, store-keepers, bookkeepers, beach gangs for dock yard labor and construction, etc."

jobs — are equally probative for this purpose. See, e.g., *New York City Transit Authority v. Beazer*, 440 U.S. 568 (1979).[6]

It is clear to us that the Court of Appeals' acceptance of the comparison between the racial composition of the cannery work force and that of the noncannery work force, as probative of a prima facie case of disparate impact in the selection of the latter group of workers, was flawed for several reasons. Most obviously, with respect to the skilled noncannery jobs at issue here, the cannery work force in no way reflected "the pool of *qualified* job applicants" or the "*qualified* population in the labor force." Measuring alleged discrimination in the selection of accountants, managers, boat captains, electricians, doctors, and engineers — and the long list of other "skilled" noncannery positions found to exist by the District Court, by comparing the number of nonwhites occupying these jobs to the number of nonwhites filling cannery worker positions is nonsensical. If the absence of minorities holding such skilled positions is due to a dearth of qualified nonwhite applicants (for reasons that are not petitioners' fault), petitioners' selection methods or employment practices cannot be said to have had a "disparate impact" on nonwhites.

One example illustrates why this must be so. Respondents' own statistics concerning the noncannery work force at one of the canneries at issue here indicate that approximately 17% of the new hires for medical jobs, and 15% of the new hires for officer worker positions, were nonwhite. If it were the case that less than 15 to 17% of the applicants for these jobs were nonwhite and that nonwhites made up a lower percentage of the relevant qualified labor market, it is hard to see how respondents, without more, would have made out a prima facie case of disparate impact. Yet, under the Court of Appeals' theory, simply because nonwhites comprise 52% of the cannery workers at the cannery in question respondents would be successful in establishing a prima facie case of racial discrimination under Title VII.

Such a result cannot be squared with our cases or with the goals behind the statute. The Court of Appeals' theory, at the very least, would mean that any employer who had a segment of his work force that was — for some reason — racially imbalanced, could be haled into court and forced to engage in the expensive and time-consuming task of defending the "business necessity" of the methods used to select the other members of his work force. The only practicable option for many employers would be to adopt racial quotas, insuring that no portion of their work forces deviated in racial composition from the other portions thereof; this is a result that Congress expressly rejected in drafting Title VII. See 42 U.S.C. § 2000e-2(j). . . . The Court of Appeals' theory would "leave the employer little choice . . . but to engage in a subjective quota system of employment selection. This, of course, is far from the intent of Title VII." *Albemarle Paper Co. v. Moody*, 422 U.S. 405, 449 (1975) (Blackmun, J., concurring in judgment).

The Court of Appeals also erred with respect to the unskilled noncannery positions. Racial imbalance in one segment of an employer's work force does not, without more, establish a prima facie case of disparate impact with respect to the selection of workers for the employer's other positions, even where workers for the different positions may have somewhat fungible skills (as is arguably the case for cannery and unskilled noncannery workers). As long as there are no barriers or practices deterring qualified nonwhites from applying for noncannery positions, if

---

6. In fact, where "figures for the general population might . . . accurately reflect the pool of qualified job applicants," we have even permitted plaintiffs to rest their prima facie cases on such statistics as well. See, e.g., *Dothard v. Rawlinson*.

the percentage of selected applicants who are nonwhite is not significantly less than the percentage of qualified applicants who are nonwhite, the employer's selection mechanism probably does not operate with a disparate impact on minorities.[8] Where this is the case, the percentage of nonwhite workers found in other positions in the employer's labor force is irrelevant to the question of a prima facie statistical case of disparate impact. As noted above, a contrary ruling on this point would almost inexorably lead to the use of numerical quotas in the workplace, a result that Congress and this Court have rejected repeatedly in the past.

Moreover, isolating the cannery workers as the potential "labor force" for unskilled noncannery positions is at once both too broad and too narrow in its focus. It is too broad because the vast majority of these cannery workers did not seek jobs in unskilled noncannery positions; there is no showing that many of them would have done so even if none of the arguably "deterring" practices existed. Thus, the pool of cannery workers cannot be used as a surrogate for the class of qualified job applicants because it contains many persons who have not (and would not) be noncannery job applicants. Conversely, if respondents propose to use the cannery workers for comparison purposes because they represent the "qualified labor population" generally, the group is too narrow because there are obviously many qualified persons in the labor market for noncannery jobs who are not cannery workers. . . .

Consequently, we reverse the Court of Appeals' ruling that a comparison between the percentage of cannery workers who are nonwhite and the percentage of noncannery workers who are nonwhite makes out a prima facie case of disparate impact. . . .

III

Since the statistical disparity relied on by the Court of Appeals did not suffice to make out a prima facie case, any inquiry by us into whether the specific challenged employment practices of petitioners caused that disparity is pretermitted, as is any inquiry into whether the disparate impact that any employment practice may have had was justified by business considerations.[9] Because we remand for further proceedings, however, on whether a prima facie case of disparate impact has been made in defensible fashion in this case, we address two other challenges petitioners have made to the decision of the Court of Appeals.

8. We qualify this conclusion — observing that it is only "probable" that there has been no disparate impact on minorities in such circumstances — because bottom-line racial balance is not a defense under Title VII. See *Connecticut v. Teal.* Thus, even if petitioners could show that the percentage of selected applicants who are nonwhite is not significantly less than the percentage of qualified applicants who are nonwhite, respondents would still have a case under Title VII, if they could prove that some particular hiring practice has a disparate impact on minorities, notwithstanding the bottom-line racial balance in petitioners' work force.

9. As we understand the opinions below, the specific employment practices were challenged only insofar as they were claimed to have been responsible for the overall disparity between the number of minority cannery and noncannery workers. The Court of Appeals did not purport to hold that any specified employment practice produced its own disparate impact that was actionable under Title VII. This is not to say that a specific practice, such as nepotism, if it were proved to exist, could not itself be subject to challenge if it had a disparate impact on minorities. Nor is it to say that segregated dormitories and eating facilities in the workplace may not be challenged under 42 U.S.C. § 2000e-2(a)(2) without showing a disparate impact on hiring or promotion.

A

First is the question of causation in a disparate-impact case. The law in this respect was correctly stated by Justice O'Connor's opinion last Term in *Watson v. Fort Worth Bank & Trust*:

> [W]e note that the plaintiff's burden in establishing a prima facie case goes beyond the need to show that there are statistical disparities in the employer's work force. The plaintiff must begin by identifying the specific employment practice that is challenged. . . . Especially in cases where an employer combines subjective criteria with the use of more rigid standardized rules or tests, the plaintiff is in our view responsible for isolating and identifying the specific employment practices that are allegedly responsible for any observed statistical disparities.

. . . Our disparate-impact cases have always focused on the impact of *particular* hiring practices on employment opportunities for minorities. Just as an employer cannot escape liability under Title VII by demonstrating that, "at the bottom line," his work force is racially balanced (where particular hiring practices may operate to deprive minorities of employment opportunities), see *Connecticut v. Teal*, 457 U.S. [440, 450 (1980) reproduced at p. 237], a Title VII plaintiff does not make out a case of disparate impact simply by showing that, "at the bottom line," there is racial imbalance in the work force. As a general matter, a plaintiff must demonstrate that it is the application of a specific or particular employment practice that has created the disparate impact under attack. Such a showing is an integral part of the plaintiff's prima facie case in a disparate-impact suit under Title VII.

Here, respondents have alleged that several "objective" employment practices (e.g., nepotism, separate hiring channels, rehire preferences), as well as the use of "subjective decision making" to select noncannery workers, have had a disparate impact on nonwhites. Respondents base this claim on statistics that allegedly show a disproportionately low percentage of nonwhites in the at-issue positions. However, even if on remand respondents can show that nonwhites are underrepresented in the at-issue jobs in a manner that is acceptable under the standards set forth above, this alone will not suffice to make out a prima facie case of disparate impact. Respondents will also have to demonstrate that the disparity they complain of is the result of one or more of the employment practices that they are attacking here, specifically showing that each challenged practice has a significantly disparate impact on employment opportunities for whites and nonwhites. To hold otherwise would result in employers being potentially liable for "the myriad of innocent causes that may lead to statistical imbalances in the composition of their work forces." *Watson*. . . .

B

If, on remand, respondents meet the proof burdens outlined above, and establish a prima facie case of disparate impact with respect to any of petitioners' employment practices, the case will shift to any business justification petitioners offer for their use of these practices. This phase of the disparate-impact case contains two components: first, a consideration of the justifications an employer offers for his use of these practices; and second, the availability of alternative practices to achieve the same business ends, with less racial impact. See, e.g., *Albemarle Paper Co. v. Moody*. We consider these two components in turn.

(1)

Though we have phrased the query differently in different cases, it is generally well established that at the justification stage of such a disparate-impact case, the dispositive issue is whether a challenged practice serves, in a significant way, the legitimate employment goals of the employer. The touchstone of this inquiry is a reasoned review of the employer's justification for his use of the challenged practice. A mere insubstantial justification in this regard will not suffice, because such a low standard of review would permit discrimination to be practiced through the use of spurious, seemingly neutral employment practices. At the same time, though, there is no requirement that the challenged practice be "essential" or "indispensable" to the employer's business for it to pass muster: this degree of scrutiny would be almost impossible for most employers to meet, and would result in a host of evils we have identified above.

. . . We acknowledge that some of our earlier decisions can be read as suggesting otherwise. But to the extent that those cases speak of an employers' "burden of proof" with respect to a legitimate business justification defense, they should have been understood to mean an employer's production — but not persuasion — burden. The persuasion burden here must remain with the plaintiff, for it is he who must prove that it was "because of such individual's race, color," etc., that he was denied a desired employment opportunity. See 42 U.S.C. § 2000e-2(a).

(2)

Finally, if on remand the case reaches this point, and respondents cannot persuade the trier of fact on the question of petitioners' business necessity defense, respondents may still be able to prevail. To do so, respondents will have to persuade the factfinder that "other tests or selection devices, without a similarly undesirable racial effect, would also serve the employer's legitimate [hiring] interest[s]"; by so demonstrating, respondents would prove that "[petitioners were] using [their] tests merely as a 'pretext' for discrimination." *Albemarle Paper Co.*; see also *Watson*. If respondents, having established a prima facie case, come forward with alternatives to petitioners' hiring practices that reduce the racially disparate impact of practices currently being used, and petitioners refuse to adopt these alternatives, such a refusal would belie a claim by petitioners that their incumbent practices are being employed for nondiscriminatory reasons.

Of course, any alternative practices which respondents offer up in this respect must be equally effective as petitioners' chosen hiring procedures in achieving petitioners' legitimate employment goals. Moreover, "[f]actors such as the cost or other burdens of proposed alternative selection devices are relevant in determining whether they would be equally as effective as the challenged practice in serving the employer's legitimate business goals." *Watson.* "Courts are generally less competent than employers to structure business practices," *Furnco Construction Corp. v. Waters*, 438 U.S. 567 (1978); consequently, the judiciary should proceed with care before mandating that an employer must adopt a plaintiff's alternative selection or hiring practice in response to a Title VII suit. . . .

Justice STEVENS, with whom Justice BRENNAN, Justice MARSHALL, and Justice BLACKMUN join, dissenting.

Fully 18 years ago, this Court unanimously held that Title VII of the Civil Rights Act of 1964 prohibits employment practices that have discriminatory effects as well as those that are intended to discriminate. *Griggs*. Federal courts and agencies consistently have enforced that interpretation, thus promoting our national goal of eliminating barriers that define economic opportunity not by aptitude and ability but by race, color, national origin, and other traits that are easily identified but utterly irrelevant to one's qualification for a particular job. Regrettably, the Court retreats from these efforts in its review of an interlocutory judgment respecting the "peculiar facts" of this lawsuit. Turning a blind eye to the meaning and purpose of Title VII, the majority's opinion perfunctorily rejects a longstanding rule of law and under-estimates the probative value of evidence of a racially stratified work force.[4] I cannot join this latest sojourn into judicial activism. . . .

Decisions of this Court and other federal courts repeatedly have recognized that while the employer's burden in a disparate-treatment case is simply one of coming forward with evidence of legitimate business purpose, its burden in a disparate-impact case is proof of an affirmative defense of business necessity. . . .

In a disparate-treatment case there is no "discrimination" within the meaning of Title VII unless the employer intentionally treated the employee unfairly because of race. Therefore, the employee retains the burden of proving the existence of intent at all times. . . .

In contrast, intent plays no role in the disparate-impact inquiry. The question, rather, is whether an employment practice has a significant, adverse effect on an identifiable class of workers — regardless of the cause or motive for the practice. The employer may attempt to contradict the factual basis for this effect; that is, to prevent the employee from establishing a prima facie case. But when an employer is faced with sufficient proof of disparate impact, its only recourse is to justify the practice by explaining why it is necessary to the operation of business. Such a justification is a classic example of an affirmative defense.

[The dissent quoted prior cases, including *Griggs*, which stressed "business ne-cessity."] I am thus astonished to read that the "touchstone of this inquiry is a reasoned review of the employer's justification for his use of the challenged prac-tice. . . . [T]here is no requirement that the challenged practice be . . . 'essential.'" This casual — almost summary — rejection of the statutory construction that devel-oped in the wake of *Griggs* is most disturbing. I have always believed that the *Griggs* opinion correctly reflected the intent of the Congress that enacted Title VII. Even if I were not so persuaded, I could not join a rejection of a consistent interpretation of a federal statute. Congress frequently revisits this statutory scheme and can readily correct our mistakes if we misread its meaning. . . .

---

4. [Plaintiff's suit alleged] that petitioners engage in hiring, job assignment, housing, and messing practices that segregate nonwhites from whites in violation of Title VII. Evidence included this response in 1971 by a foreman to a college student's inquiry about cannery employment:

> We are not in a position to take many young fellows to our Bristol Bay canneries as they do not have the background for our type of employees. Our cannery labor is either Eskimo or Filipino and we do not have the facilities to mix others with these groups.

Some characteristics of the Alaska salmon industry described in this litigation — in particular, the segregation of housing and dining facilities and the stratification of jobs along racial and ethnic lines — bear an unsettling resemblance to aspects of a plantation economy. See generally Plantation, Town, and County, Essays on the Local History of American Slave Society 163-334 (E. Miller & E. Genovese eds. 1974). Indeed the maintenance of inferior, segregated facilities for housing and feeding nonwhite employees, strikes me as a form of discrimination that, although it does not necessarily fit neatly into a disparate-impact or disparate-treatment mold, nonetheless violates Title VII. Respondents, however, do not press this theory before us.

NOTES

1. Wards Cove *Remakes* Griggs. The *Wards Cove* majority remodeled disparate impact law (1) by requiring a highly focused showing that *particular* employment practices caused a disparate impact; (2) by reducing the employer's rebuttal obligations from a showing of job-relatedness and business necessity to "a reasoned review of the employer's justification"; and (3) by redefining the rebuttal stage to involve a burden of production, not of persuasion. It also reformulated an element added in *Albemarle Paper Co. v. Moody* — a final "pretext" surrebuttal step that allows plaintiffs to win if they can show an "alternative practice" to the one challenged. After *Wards Cove*, disparate impact law looked more like individual disparate treatment law as set forth in *McDonnell Douglas v. Green*, though still without an intent to discriminate element.

2. *The Underlying Rationale for the Disparate Impact Theory*. The *Wards Cove* Court's remaking of disparate impact law in the image of disparate treatment law may have been driven by the view of the majority that disparate impact was justified only to the extent that it allowed attack on intentional discrimination that could not be proven, the problem of the "discreet discriminator" we have encountered earlier. The plurality in *Watson* had described disparate impact as "functionally equivalent to intentional discrimination." 487 U.S. at 987. And numerous commentators have pointed out that *Griggs* itself can be viewed as precisely such a case: despite the district court's finding of no intent to discriminate, the new selection criteria may have been adopted to continue, in effect if not form, the prior formal exclusion of blacks for the better jobs.

Alternatively, disparate impact could be used to address the problems of unconscious bias. Justice O'Connor in *Watson* had noted that "even if one assumed that any such discrimination can be adequately policed through disparate treatment analysis, the problem of subconscious stereotypes and prejudices would remain." 487 U.S. at 990. *See generally* Charles A. Sullivan, *Disparate Impact: Looking Past the Desert Palace Mirage*, 47 WM. & MARY L. REV. 911 (2005) (arguing that the difficulties of dealing with cognitive biases do not change by describing them as problems of disparate treatment or disparate impact, and disparate impact offers an opportunity to explicitly weigh the necessity of current practices that are shown to enable bias).

But these are not the only possible rationales for disparate impact. Another, far more limited, rationale emerges from the *Griggs* Court's reference to racial segregation in North Carolina, where Duke Power was located. Such a view would justify and possibly limit disparate impact to those settings where prior de jure discrimination made it unfair to use a particular criterion. Although this seems like a particularly compelling justification for the theory, other cases applied disparate impact to the gender context, e.g., *Dothard v. Rawlinson*, 433 U.S. 321 (1977) (height and weight minimum subject to disparate impact attack by women), thus establishing that the theory was neither confined to de jure segregation nor limited to racial discrimination.

These cases, however, suggest a more expansive justification that would look not to de jure discrimination that hampered the disfavored group from satisfying the particular criterion at issue, as in *Griggs*, but to a history of discrimination and subordination of the group in question. Thus, in *Dothard v. Rawlinson*, no reason existed to believe that women's shorter stature and lower weight as compared to men were the result of de jure or even de facto societal discrimination. Nevertheless, women had a long history of legal and societal subordination in this country, which might justify removing unnecessary barriers to their advancement. *See* Julia Lamber, *Discretionary Decisionmaking: The Application of Title VII's Disparate Impact Theory*, 1985 U. ILL. L. REV. 869, 903 (Congress imposed a responsibility on employers to heed disproportionate outcomes for blacks and women, even when caused by equal treatment, based on a recognition that historical, social, and structural barriers can impede the achievement of minority group members). *See also* Julie Chi-hye Suk, *Antidiscrimination Law in the Administrative State*, 2006 U. ILL. L. REV. 405, 412-35 (2006) (viewing disparate impact as involving distributive justice).

Professor Stacy E. Seicshnaydre, *Is the Road to Disparate Impact Paved with Good Intentions? — Stuck on State of Mind in Antidiscrimination Law*, 42 WAKE FOREST L. REV. 1141 (2007), makes a powerful normative claim justifying disparate impact law that is completely freed from concerns about defendant's intent or state of mind. Based on Hurricane Katrina and the work of SUSAN NIEMAN, EVIL ON MODERN THOUGHT: AN ALTERNATIVE HISTORY OF PHILOSOPHY (2002), Seicshnaydre argues that evil results happen, e.g., that poor blacks were most devastated and least helped in the Katrina crisis, not because of anyone's evil intent; however, that does not mean that their plight does not deserve remediation. Failing to keep separate and distinct disparate impact theory, not based on intent to discriminate, from disparate treatment, based on intent, tends to weaken both to the end that the antidiscrimination laws are further underenforced.

Other justifications are more utilitarian. Professor Paulette Caldwell believes that one purpose of Title VII is to increase productive efficiency by allowing individuals to achieve their full economic potential. *Reaffirming the Disproportionate Effects Standard of Liability in Title VII Litigation*, 46 U. PITT. L. REV. 555 (1985). Caldwell's point is that, in the long run, efficiency will be improved if the pool of potential workers is increased by adding persons whose full potential would never be developed if denied entry-level positions. Is this what Chief Justice Burger meant when he wrote in *Griggs* that "[h]istory is filled with examples of men and women who rendered highly effective performance without the conventional badges of accomplishment in terms of certificates, diplomas, and degrees"? While increasing productivity is a good idea, does it have much to do with why Title VII was enacted?

3. *Losing Its Normative Way?* While all these approaches provide justifications for disparate impact, they progressively depart from the strong normative force underlying Title VII. As "discrimination" moves along a spectrum from animus to conscious intent to unconscious intent to antisubordination to expanding labor pools, its moral force becomes progressively weaker. While it is still possible to justify the statute even if the discrimination is simply a form of negligence, *see* David Benjamin Oppenheimer, *Negligent Discrimination*, 141 U. PA. L. REV. 899 (1993), some have argued that the attenuated way in which such theories define discrimination undercuts Title VII's legitimacy. See Note on the New Structuralism, p. 166.

4. *Systemic Disparate Treatment or Disparate Impact?* Plaintiffs in *Wards Cove* used statistics comparing the racial composition of the cannery and noncannery jobs. The disparity would have to be considered gross and longlasting if systemic disparate treatment theory applied here. Why didn't it? If viewed as a disparate treatment case, it would have to be considered a *Hazelwood* case, not a *Teamsters* case. Because the cannery jobs were unskilled and most of the noncannery jobs required a wide array of different kinds of skills, the cannery jobs were not the qualified labor pool for most noncannery jobs. Nevertheless, there were other aspects of the case that suggested intent to discriminate, including the segregated housing and eating areas that Justice Stevens referred to in footnote 4.

5. *Clash Between Disparate Treatment and Disparate Impact.* Whatever the underlying justifications of impact liability, is the disparate impact theory at odds with the basic premise of antidiscrimination legislation: because members of protected groups are indistinguishable from similarly situated members of the majority, they ought not be treated differently in the workplace? Skin color does not make a worker less effective, nor does advancing age necessarily make her less efficient. While group differences may exist, disparate treatment ignores those differences and focuses instead on members of the protected group who are similarly situated to other individuals.

In contrast, impact analysis not only acknowledges, but also focuses on, differences between and among the groups. Individuals will be entitled to a remedy precisely because they are members of a group that is different. The impact approach, however, does not abandon the equality principle that similarly situated individuals should be treated equally. The business necessity defense is designed to permit the employer to rely on differences between employees when those differences are relevant to the job. Employers are prohibited from considering only differences that are not related to job performance. Thus, for purposes of qualifying for work, the underlying premise remains true: protected group members should be treated equally when their work qualifications are the same

6. *Identifying the Practice That Produces the Impact.* Looking for a specific employment practice that produced the impact, the *Wards Cove* Court lists some practices that plaintiffs were challenging: "nepotism, a rehire preference, a lack of objective hiring criteria, separate hiring channels, a practice of not promoting from within." All but the last two did not seem to produce the radical difference in the racial composition of the cannery and noncannery jobs. The employer's practices of using separate hiring channels, segregating the workers hired in the separate channels and not promoting from cannery to noncannery jobs produced the impact. Therefore, the actual employment practice that should have been the focus of the challenge was failing to recruit for the unskilled noncannery jobs from the same sources — the union hiring hall and the local areas close to the canneries — that the defendants used to hire for the unskilled cannery jobs. While both the majority and dissent acknowledge that some noncannery jobs were unskilled, see footnote 3, neither opinion quantifies how many of the noncannery jobs were unskilled. That percentage, whatever it was, would be the appropriate focus of a disparate impact attack on the employer's recruiting practices. In other words, if a substantial number of noncannery jobs were unskilled, then a court could find that the failure to recruit from the heavily minority sources for the cannery jobs was a specific employment practice that had a disparate impact.

7. *Disparate Impact and the "Q" Word. Wards Cove* generated a national controversy about the continued viability of the disparate impact theory that was ultimately resolved by the enactment of the Civil Rights Act of 1991. While that statute also addresses other Supreme Court decisions issued that same term that Congress viewed as cutting back on civil rights protection, the focus of the debate was on "quotas," *Wards Cove,* and the appropriate structure of the disparate impact theory. During the debates, proponents argued that a strong impact theory was needed to open up job opportunities to minorities and women. Opponents vociferously claimed that disparate impact would result in quotas by encouraging employers to hire minorities and women, without regard to qualifications, merely to avoid potential liability. Recall the majority opinion's defense of its dilution of the litigation structure: "The only practicable option for many employers would be to adopt

racial quotas, insuring that no portion of their work forces deviated in racial composition from the other portions thereof." What do you think of the argument? Did *Griggs* encourage quota hiring?

Ian Ayres & Peter Siegelman, *The Q-Word as Red Herring: Why Disparate Impact Liability Does Not Induce Hiring Quotas*, 74 TEX. L. REV. 1487 (1996), challenge the quota claim. They note a tension between protecting applicants against discrimination in hiring and protecting workers from discriminatory firing after they have been hired. Antidiscrimination law forbids both kinds of conduct, but they argue the two prohibitions are inherently at odds. "By making it harder to fire certain workers, employment discrimination law tends to make these workers less attractive prospects at the hiring stage. An employer would prefer to hire someone who can be easily fired (should that prove necessary) than an otherwise identical applicant whose firing would be subject to legal scrutiny." *Id.* at 1488-89. Ayres & Siegelman then argue that, "far from producing hiring quotas that induce employers to discriminate in favor of minorities, disparate impact liability may actually induce hiring discrimination against minorities (and other protected groups)." *Id.* at 1489. By making it harder to fire protected workers, the authors argue that disparate impact liability discourages probationary employment generally and might even lead employers to discriminate deliberately against protected workers at the hiring stage. *Id.* at 1491. Does this suggest that both proponents and opponents of the 1991 Amendments were wrong in their assessments? *See also* Paul E. Oyer & Scott Schaeffer, *The Unintended Consequences of the '91 Civil Rights Act*, 26 REGULATION 42 (2003) (the opponents' quota-based hiring fears were unfounded, but the bill also appears not to have improved minority employment in traditionally exclusionary industries and may have even reversed improving minority employment trends in those industries); Paul Oyer & Scott Schaefer, *Sorting, Quotas, and the Civil Rights Act of 1991: Who Hires When It's Hard to Fire?*, 45 J.L. & ECON. 41 (2002) (data suggest firms more susceptible to litigation substitute away from protected workers but no evidence that firms with fewer protected workers substitute toward this group).

SMITH v. CITY OF JACKSON
544 U.S. 228 (2005)

Justice STEVENS announced the judgment of the Court and delivered the opinion of the Court with respect to Parts I, II, and IV, and an opinion with respect to Part III, in which Justice SOUTER, Justice GINSBURG, and Justice BREYER join.

Petitioners, police and public safety officers employed by the city of Jackson, Mississippi (hereinafter City), contend that salary increases received in 1999 violated the Age Discrimination in Employment Act of 1967 (ADEA) because they were less generous to officers over the age of 40 than to younger officers. Their suit raises the question whether the "disparate-impact" theory of recovery announced in *Griggs* for cases brought under Title VII of the Civil Rights Act of 1964, is cognizable under the ADEA. Despite the age of the ADEA, it is a question that we have not yet addressed.

I

On October 1, 1998, the City adopted a pay plan granting raises to all City employees. The stated purpose of the plan was to "attract and retain qualified people, provide incentive for performance, maintain competitiveness with other public sector agencies and ensure equitable compensation to all employees regardless of age, sex, race and/or disability." On May 1, 1999, a revision of the plan, which was motivated, at least in part, by the City's desire to bring the starting salaries of police officers up to the regional average, granted raises to all police officers and police dispatchers. Those who had less than five years of tenure received proportionately greater raises when compared to their former pay than those with more seniority. Although some officers over the age of 40 had less than five years of service, most of the older officers had more. . . .

We . . . hold that the ADEA does authorize recovery in "disparate-impact" cases comparable to *Griggs*. Because, however, we conclude that petitioners have not set forth a valid disparate-impact claim, we affirm. . . .

III

In determining whether the ADEA authorizes disparate-impact claims, we begin with the premise that when Congress uses the same language in two statutes having similar purposes, particularly when one is enacted shortly after the other, it is appropriate to presume that Congress intended that text to have the same meaning in both statutes. We have consistently applied that presumption to language in the ADEA that was "derived *in haec verba* from Title VII." *Lorillard v. Pons*, 434 U.S. 575, 584 (1978). Our unanimous interpretation of §703(a)(2) of the Title VII in *Griggs* is therefore a precedent of compelling importance. . . .

. . . Neither §703(a)(2) nor the comparable language in the ADEA simply prohibits actions that "limit, segregate, or classify" persons; rather the language prohibits such actions that "deprive any individual of employment opportunities or *otherwise adversely affect* his status as an employee, because of such individual's" race or age. *Watson* [*v. Fort Worth Bank & Trust*, 487 U.S. 977 (1988)] (explaining that in disparate-impact cases, "the employer's practices may be said to 'adversely affect [an individual's status] as an employee'" (alteration in original) (quoting 42 U.S.C. §2000e-2(a)(2)). Thus the text focuses on the *effects* of the action on the employee rather than the motivation for the action of the employer. *Griggs*, which interpreted the identical text at issue here, thus strongly suggests that a disparate-impact theory should be cognizable under the ADEA. . . .

[The ADEA has a provision without any parallel in Title VII.] The RFOA provision provides that it shall not be unlawful for an employer "to take any action otherwise prohibited under subsection (a) . . . where the differentiation is based on reasonable factors other than age discrimination. . . ." In most disparate-treatment cases, if an employer in fact acted on a factor other than age, the action would not be prohibited under subsection (a) in the first place. See *Hazen Paper* [*v. Biggins*] ("There is no disparate treatment under the ADEA when the factor motivating the employer is some feature other than the employee's age.") In those disparate-treatment cases, such as in *Hazen Paper* itself, the RFOA provision is simply unnecessary to avoid liability under the ADEA, since there was no prohibited action in the first place. The RFOA provision is not, as Justice O'Connor suggests, a "safe harbor from liability," (emphasis deleted), since there would be no liability under §4(a). See *Texas Dep't of Community Affairs v. Burdine*, 450 U.S. 248, 254 (1981) (noting, in a Title VII case, that an employer can defeat liability by showing that the employee was rejected for "a legitimate, nondiscriminatory reason" without reference to an RFOA provision).

In disparate-impact cases, however, the allegedly "otherwise prohibited" activity is not based on age. Ibid. ("'Claims that stress disparate impact [by contrast] involve employment practices that are facially neutral in their treatment of different groups but that in fact fall more harshly on one group than another . . . '") (quoting Teamsters v. United States). It is, accordingly, in cases involving disparate-impact claims that the RFOA provision plays its principal role by precluding liability if the adverse impact was attributable to a nonage factor that was "reasonable." Rather than support an argument that disparate impact is unavailable under the ADEA, the RFOA provision actually supports the contrary conclusion.

Finally, we note that both the Department of Labor, which initially drafted the legislation, and the EEOC, which is the agency charged by Congress with responsibility for implementing the statute, have consistently interpreted the ADEA to authorize relief on a disparate-impact theory. . . .

The text of the statute, as interpreted in *Griggs*, the RFOA provision, and the EEOC regulations all support petitioners' view. We therefore conclude that it was error for the Court of Appeals to hold that the disparate-impact theory of liability is categorically unavailable under the ADEA.

IV

Two textual differences between the ADEA and Title VII make it clear that even though both statutes authorize recovery on a disparate-impact theory, the scope of disparate-impact liability under ADEA is narrower than under Title VII. The first is the RFOA provision, which we have already identified. The second is the amendment to Title VII contained in the Civil Rights Act of 1991. One of the purposes of that amendment was to modify the Court's holding in *Wards Cove*, a case in which we narrowly construed the employer's exposure to liability on a disparate-impact theory. While the relevant 1991 amendments expanded the coverage of Title VII, they did not amend the ADEA or speak to the subject of age discrimination. Hence, *Wards Cove*'s pre-1991 interpretation of Title VII's identical language remains applicable to the ADEA. Congress' decision to limit the coverage of the ADEA by including the RFOA provision is consistent with the fact that age, unlike race or other classifications protected by Title VII, not uncommonly has relevance to an individual's capacity to engage in certain types of employment. To be sure, Congress recognized that this is not always the case, and that society may perceive those differences to be larger or more consequential than they are in fact. However, as Secretary Wirtz noted in his report [that Congress relied on in enacting the ADEA], "certain circumstances . . . unquestionably affect older workers more strongly, as a group, than they do younger workers." Thus, it is not surprising that certain employment criteria that are routinely used may be reasonable despite their adverse impact on older workers as a group. Moreover, intentional discrimination on the basis of age has not occurred at the same levels as discrimination against those protected by Title VII. While the ADEA reflects Congress' intent to give older workers employment opportunities whenever possible, the RFOA provision reflects this historical difference.

Turning to the case before us, we initially note that petitioners have done little more than point out that the pay plan at issue is relatively less generous to older workers than to younger workers. They have not identified any specific test, requirement, or practice within the pay plan that has an adverse impact on older workers. As we held in *Wards Cove*, it is not enough to simply allege that there is a disparate impact on workers, or point to a generalized policy that leads to such an impact. Rather, the employee is "'responsible for isolating and identifying the *specific* employment practices that are allegedly responsible for any observed statistical dis-parities.'" (emphasis added) (quoting *Watson*). Petitioners have failed to do so. Their failure to identify the specific practice being challenged is the sort of omission that could "result in employers being potentially liable for 'the myriad of innocent causes that may lead to statistical imbalances. . . .'" In this case not only did petitioners thus err by failing to identify the relevant practice, but it is also clear from the record that the City's plan was based on reasonable factors other than age.

The plan divided each of five basic positions — police officer, master police of-ficer, police sergeant, police lieutenant, and deputy police chief — into a series of steps and half-steps. The wage for each range was based on a survey of comparable communities in the Southeast. Employees were then assigned a step (or half-step) within their position that corresponded to the lowest step that would still give the individual a 2% raise. Most of the officers were in the three lowest ranks; in each of those ranks there were officers under age 40 and officers over 40. In none did their age affect their compensation. The few officers in the two highest ranks are all over 40. Their raises, though higher in dollar amount than the raises given to junior officers, represented a smaller percentage of their salaries, which of course are higher than the salaries paid to their juniors. They are members of the class complaining of the "disparate impact" of the award.

Petitioners' evidence established two principal facts: First, almost two-thirds (66.2%) of the officers under 40 received raises of more than 10% while less than half (45.3%) of those over 40 did. Second, the average percentage increase for the entire class of officers with less than five years of tenure was somewhat higher than the percentage for those with more seniority. Because older officers tended to occupy more senior positions, on average they received smaller increases when measured as a percentage of their salary. The basic explanation for the differential was the City's perceived need to raise the salaries of junior officers to make them competitive with comparable positions in the market.

Thus, the disparate impact is attributable to the City's decision to give raises based on seniority and position. Reliance on seniority and rank is unquestionably rea-sonable given the City's goal of raising employees' salaries to match those in sur-rounding communities. In sum, we hold that the City's decision to grant a larger raise to lower echelon employees for the purpose of bringing salaries in line with that of surrounding police forces was a decision based on a "reasonable factor other than age" that responded to the City's legitimate goal of retaining police officers.

While there may have been other reasonable ways for the City to achieve its goals, the one selected was not unreasonable. Unlike the business necessity test, which asks whether there are other ways for the employer to achieve its goals that do not result in a disparate impact on a protected class, the reasonableness inquiry includes no such requirement. . . .

Justice SCALIA, concurring in part and concurring in the judgment. . . .

This is an absolutely classic case for deference to agency interpretation. The Age Discrimination in Employment Act of 1967 (ADEA) confers upon the EEOC au-thority to issue "such rules and regulations as it may consider necessary or appro-priate for carrying out the" ADEA. §628. Pursuant to this authority, the EEOC promulgated, after notice-and-comment rulemaking, see 46 Fed. Reg. 47724, 47727 (1981), a regulation that reads as follows:

> When an employment practice, including a test, is claimed as a basis for different treatment of employees or applicants for employment on the grounds that it is a 'factor

other than' age, and such a practice has an adverse impact on individuals within the protected age group, it can only be justified as a business necessity.

29 CFR § 1625.7(d) (2004). . . .

As this text makes clear, the RFOA defense is relevant *only* as a response to employer actions "otherwise prohibited" by the ADEA. Hence, the unavoidable meaning of the regulation at issue is that the ADEA prohibits employer actions that have an "adverse impact on individuals within the protected age group." 29 CFR § 1625.7(d) (2004). And, of course, the only provision of the ADEA that could conceivably be interpreted to effect such a prohibition is § 4(a)(2) . . .

The EEOC has express authority to promulgate rules and regulations interpreting the ADEA. It has exercised that authority to recognize disparate-impact claims. And, for the reasons given by the plurality opinion, its position is eminently reasonable. In my view, that is sufficient to resolve this case.

Justice O'CONNOR, with whom Justice KENNEDY and Justice THOMAS join, concurring in the judgment. . . .

I would . . . affirm the judgment below on the ground that disparate impact claims are not cognizable under the ADEA. The ADEA's text, legislative history, and purposes together make clear that Congress did not intend the statute to authorize such claims. Moreover, the significant differences between the ADEA and Title VII of the Civil Rights Act of 1964 counsel against transposing to the former our construction of the latter in *Griggs*. Finally, the agencies charged with administering the ADEA have never authoritatively construed the statute's prohibitory language to impose disparate impact liability. Thus, on the precise question of statutory interpretation now before us, there is no reasoned agency reading of the text to which we might defer.

I

A. . . .

[The dissent read both § 4(a)((1) and (2) as requiring intent to discriminate, essentially because both used the term "because of . . . age" in "precisely the same manner." At no point, however, did Justice O'Connor explain why this construction of the ADEA led to a finding that intent to discriminate was always essential for age discrimination when essentially identical language in Title VII in *Griggs*, and even *Wards Cove*, authorized the disparate impact theory under that statute.]

B

While § 4(a)(2) of the ADEA makes it unlawful to intentionally discriminate because of age, § 4(f)(1) clarifies that "it shall not be unlawful for an employer . . . to take any action otherwise prohibited under subsections (a), (b), (c), or (e) of this section . . . where the differentiation is based on reasonable factors other than age. . . ." 29 U.S.C. § 623(f)(1). This "reasonable factors other than age" (RFOA) provision "insures that employers [are] permitted to use neutral criteria" other than age, *EEOC v. Wyoming*, 460 U.S. 226, 232-33 (1983), even if this results in a disparate adverse impact on older workers. The provision therefore expresses Congress' clear intention that employers *not* be subject to liability absent proof of intentional age-based discrimination. That policy, in my view, cannot easily be reconciled with the plurality's expansive reading of § 4(a)(2).

The plurality however, reasons that the RFOA provision's language instead confirms that §4(a) authorizes disparate impact claims. If §4(a) prohibited only intentional discrimination, the argument goes, then the RFOA provision would have no effect because any action based on a factor other than age would not be "'otherwise prohibited'" under §4(a). Moreover, the plurality says, the RFOA provision applies only to employer actions based on *reasonable* factors other than age — so employers may still be held liable for actions based on *un*reasonable nonage factors.

This argument misconstrues the purpose and effect of the RFOA provision. Discriminatory intent *is* required under §4(a). . . . The role of the RFOA provision is to afford employers an independent *safe harbor* from liability. It provides that, where a plaintiff has made out a prima facie case of intentional age discrimination under §4(a) — thus "creating a presumption that the employer unlawfully discriminated against the employee," *Texas Dep't of Community Affairs v. Burdine* — the employer can rebut this case by producing evidence that its action was based on a reasonable nonage factor. Thus, the RFOA provision codifies a safe harbor analogous to the "legitimate, nondiscriminatory reason" (LNR) justification later recognized in Title VII suits. Ibid.; *McDonnell Douglas.* . . .

NOTES

1. *Rehashing an Old Title VII Debate.* Prior to the Civil Rights Act of 1991, there was a continuing challenge to the disparate impact theory as a matter of statutory construction. *Griggs* itself had not focused on the statutory language (as opposed to the general policy), which raised questions about the textual basis for the decision. *See* RICHARD A. EPSTEIN, FORBIDDEN GROUNDS: THE CASE AGAINST EMPLOYMENT DISCRIMINATION LAWS 197 (1992); Michael E. Gold, Griggs' *Folly: An Essay on the Theory, Problems, and Origin of the Adverse Impact Definition of Employment Discrimination and a Recommendation for Reform,* 7 INDUS. REL. L.J. 429 (1985). To the extent the *Griggs* principle can be found in the provisions of §703, it is in the language of paragraph (a)(2), which declares it an unlawful employment practice "to limit, segregate, or classify his employees or applicants for employment in any way which would deprive *or tend to deprive* any individual of employment opportunities. . . ." (Emphasis added.) The argument is that practices with a disparate impact tend to deprive individuals of employment opportunities. To the extent that is the textual basis of the *Griggs*, it would be important to distinguish between (a)(1) claims, which could be based only on disparate treatment, and (a)(2) claims, which could be also based on disparate impact. While there was some indication in the earlier cases that such a distinction might be drawn, *Nashville Gas Co. v. Satty*, 434 U.S. 136, 142 (1977), the issue became moot under Title VII with the passage of the 1991 Amendments.

But prior to *City of Jackson*, the Supreme Court had never decided whether the ADEA barred disparate impact discrimination and the 1991 Civil Rights Act had not amended the ADEA. The Court, therefore, had to revisit the issue it had avoided under Title VII. The majority continued to avoid any deep textual analysis, reasoning mainly syllogistically: Title VII barred disparate impact; the ADEA tracked Title VII's language; ergo, the ADEA bars disparate impact. Justice O'Connor's opinion undertakes a more sophisticated textual analysis, which is largely omitted, but she never explains why her analysis of the ADEA would not also mean that *Griggs* was wrongly decided.

2. *Winning the Battle But Losing the War?* The *City of Jackson* opinion was trumpeted by some as a victory for plaintiffs and as creating serious problems for employers. But the Court applied the *Wards Cove* version of disparate impact to the ADEA, and *Wards Cove* was pretty unanimously viewed as a defeat for plaintiffs, freeing employers from many of the strictures of *Griggs*. As you work through these Notes, ask yourself what role disparate impact will play in the age context in the future.

3. *What Policy Produced the Impact?* The employer policy at issue in *City of Jackson* was designed to create salary "parity" with other public employers in comparable communities the Southeast. To do that, defendant set up salary comparison groups among its employees and then compared the salaries of its workers in those groups with the salaries of comparable employees of other employers. Salaries were then raised to bring Jackson in line with the comparison groups. The result was that most workers under age 40 received wage increases over 10% while fewer than half of those over age 40 did. But, given that the older workers typically earned more, the older workers may well have received larger dollar increases than younger workers, even though the percentage was less.

In this scenario, isn't the Court wrong to say that the plaintiffs did not identify a specific employment policy here? While the ultimate source of the age impact is in the pay structures of other employers, modeling pay on the pay of those other employers seems like a specific practice. How could the plaintiffs have been more specific?

One possibility is compensation and benefits are simply not the kind of employment practice that should be subject to disparate impact attack. In *Finnegan v. Trans World Air Lines, Inc.*, 967 F.2d 1161 (7th Cir. 1992), the court found that changes in fringe benefits were not subject to attack even though they caused an adverse impact on older workers. After all, any percentage reduction/increase in compensation or certain types of fringe benefits, such as the vacation pay in *Finnegan*, will necessarily have an impact. Is the employer required to use equal percentage wage increases to avoid causing disparate impact on older workers? While doing that would cause an adverse impact on younger workers, they are not protected against by the ADEA if they are younger than age 40. Further, after *Gen. Dynamics Land Sys. v. Cline*, 540 U.S. 581 (2004), workers over age 40 are not protected if the benefit flows to workers older than them.

4. *Employer Justification.* Another explanation for both *City of Jackson* and *Finnegan* is that both reflect a kind of quick-look business necessity defense. *City of Jackson* presumably adopts the *Wards Cove* approach to the defendant's burden — it is only one of production, not persuasion, and "the dispositive issue is whether a challenged practice serves, in a significant way, the legitimate employment goals of the employer." The RFOA defense would seem, if anything, to make this test even more permissive. The Court says that "reliance on seniority and rank" are reasonable factors other than age. But the practice to be justified was not its own seniority and rank but, instead, the defendant's reliance on the salary structures of other employers. Such reliance is neutral on its face, but that just establishes that the factor is "other than age." What else is necessary to make it "reasonable"? Is it a kind of industry practices approach — if many employers do some variation of the practice, it is reasonable? Or, is it unreasonable unless explained, here by the desire to meet competition?

In any event, with such a minimal standard, it is not surprising that the Court found the employer's desire to be competitive with other police departments sufficient justification, even absent any showing that compensation was needed to attain or retain sufficient qualified workers. *Finnegan* involved benefit cuts backs by an airline in financial distress; the justification, again, was clear on its face — or at least it would be under the *City of Jackson* approach.

Another, more pessimistic view for the advocates of disparate impact is that *City of Jackson* just articulates what the courts are now doing in applying disparate impact law, even in Title VII cases and despite the changes made to it in the 1991 Civil Rights Act. If an employer puts forward a "reasonable" explanation for its challenged practice, is it likely to win a disparate impact case, notwithstanding the statutory provision requiring that it prove the practice is "job related and consistent with business necessity"? We'll revisit this question shortly.

5. *Is Causation Irrelevant?* Ramona L. Paetzold & Steven L. Willborn, in *Deconstructing Disparate Impact: A View of the Model Through New Lenses*, 74 N.C. L. Rev. 325, 356 (1995), argue that the plaintiff in a disparate impact case need not prove actual causation:

> [D]isparate impact cases . . . [do] not require that the plaintiff prove that the employer's criterion has actually produced a disparate impact in the workplace. In *Griggs*, for example, the same disparate impact on blacks may have occurred even if the employer had not utilized the high school diploma requirement. Employees applying for the jobs at issue in *Griggs* also had to attain a certain score on a general "intelligence" test that approximated the national median score for high school graduates. Blacks as a class may have suffered from the same (or even a greater) disparate impact as a result of the test requirement. The disparate impact model as applied in *Griggs*, then, did not require any proof that the criterion at issue actually produced a disparate impact; it merely required proof that the criterion at issue would have screened out protected class members disproportionately if applied independently of any other factors at play in the selection process.

Did *City of Jackson* fail to come to grips with this problem? Was that the reason it did not understand what practice caused the impact? Benchmarking salaries with the salaries of comparable employers incorporates into the employer's salary structure whatever adverse affect exists in the structures of these other employers. But, for disparate impact theory, that should not make a difference, just as the impact of the segregated schools did not make a difference in *Griggs*.

6. *The Future of Disparate Impact under the ADEA.* In *Biggins*, p. 9, plaintiff lost his disparate treatment claim because his evidence that increasing age correlated with pension vesting status was not sufficient to show that the employer was motivated by age. After *City of Jackson* would a disparate impact case be available to challenge a practice, such as pension vesting, if it correlated with age?

Perhaps the best test case is *Meacham v. Knolls Atomic Power Lab.*, 381 F.3d 56, 74 (2d Cir. 2004), *vacated on other grounds*, 544 U.S. 957 (2005), which was decided prior to *City of Jackson*, and found that plaintiffs had met their burden of isolating specific employment practices causing a RIF's lopsided age outcome. The practices at issue involved the use of matrices, which disproportionately selected older employees for layoff. The matrices relied heavily on managers' judgments about workers' "flexibility and criticality," and left this decision largely to the unguided and unaudited "subjective decision making" of the managers. As to justification, the Second Circuit was unpersuaded that a system with "more safeguards against subjectivity" was not possible. The Supreme Court vacated *Meacham* for reconsideration in light of *City of Jackson* and, on remand, the Second Circuit found that plaintiffs had not established the unreasonableness of the challenged practices. 461 F.3d 134 (2d Cir. 2006), *cert. granted*, 2008 WL 161475 (2008).

Pippin v. Burlington Res. Oil & Gas Co., 440 F.3d 1186 (10th Cir. 2006), is perhaps even more remarkable. The court found the employer's decision to make layoff decisions based on prior job performance and skill sets not unreasonable, which is not surprising; but it also found the employer's decision to honor commitments to hire several new employees fresh out of college to protect its hiring reputation at involved schools to be reasonable. The latter amounts to preferring young workers to older ones. If it is "reasonable," does disparate impact theory under the ADEA mean anything? *See* Judith J. Johnson, *Rehabilitate the Age Discrimination in Employment Act: Resuscitate the "Reasonable Factors Other Than Age" Defense and the Disparate Impact Theory*, 55 HASTINGS L.J. 1399 1402-03 (2004).

7. *The Role of the EEOC.* Refusing to join Part III of the opinion, Justice Scalia criticizes Justice Stevens for independently analyzing the statute rather than simply deferring to the EEOC's interpretation that disparate impact analysis is available under the ADEA. But he then joins Justice Stevens in rejecting the "business necessity" test endorsed by the agency. Do you understand why he didn't defer to the agency on that point as well?

8. *Age Subgroups.* One problem peculiar to disparate impact under the ADEA is whether the plaintiff must show an impact on the entire over-40 group or whether it is sufficient to demonstrate that a particular subgroup, say, employees over 60. The courts thus far have rejected subgroup analysis. *See EEOC v. McDonnell Douglas Corp.*, 191 F.3d 948 (8th Cir. 1999); *Lowe v. Commack Union Sch. Dist.*, 886 F.2d 1364 (2d Cir. 1990). *See generally* Sandra F. Sperino, *The Sky Remains Intact: Why Allowing Subgroup Evidence Is Consistent with the Age Discrimination in Employment Act*, 90 MARQ. L. REV. 227 (2006).

9. *Different Analyses under Different Statutes.* We have seen that *Wards Cove* was superseded in part by the 1991 Civil Rights Act. You may have wondered why we made you read the case. One answer should now be apparent: *Wards Cove* lives on under the ADEA. This is another exception to the uniform treatment of discrimination under the various federal statutes. We've already seen a couple of other major differences between Title VII and the ADEA: the absence of anything comparable to §703(m) in the age context and the permissibility of discrimination in favor of older workers within the protected group. But *Wards Cove* provides another instance. It remains viable under the ADEA but has been significantly changed by the 1991 amendments to Title VII.

B.   THE STRUCTURE OF DISPARATE IMPACT LAW AFTER THE 1991 CIVIL RIGHTS ACT

Section 703(k) was added to Title VII to provide a statutory basis for disparate impact law. It is a complex provision which legislatively overrules much of *Wards Cove* but also codifies some of the *Wards Cove* analysis.

Section 703(k)(1) sets forth the new statutory action for disparate impact discrimination:

(A) An unlawful employment practice based on disparate impact is established under this title only if —
(i) a complaining party demonstrates that a respondent uses a particular employment practice that causes a disparate impact on the basis of race, color,

religion, sex, or national origin and the respondent fails to demonstrate that the challenged practice is job related for the position in question and consistent with business necessity; or

(ii) the complaining party makes the demonstration described in subparagraph (C) with respect to an alternative employment practice and the respondent refuses to adopt such alternative employment practice.

(B)(i) With respect to demonstrating that a particular employment practice causes a disparate impact as described in subparagraph (A)(i), the complaining party shall demonstrate that each particular challenged employment practice causes a disparate impact, except that if the complaining party can demonstrate to the court that the elements of a respondent's decisionmaking process are not capable of separation for analysis, the decisionmaking process may be analyzed as one employment practice.

(ii) If the respondent demonstrates that a specific employment practice does not cause the disparate impact, the respondent shall not be required to demonstrate that such practice is required by business necessity.

As was discussed in Chapter 1, §701(m) defines "demonstrates" as carrying the burden of production and persuasion.

1. Plaintiff's Proof of a Prima Facie Case

a. A Particular Employment Practice

Section 703(k)(1)(A)(i) states the general rule for a disparate impact case by accepting part of *Wards Cove*: plaintiff carries the burden of persuasion that the employer "uses a particular employment practice that causes disparate impact on the basis of race, color, religion, sex, or national origin." This embraces two questions that arose before the 1991 Amendments: (1) is every employment-related action of an employer a qualifying "employment practice"; and (2) how does a plaintiff establish that a disparate impact resulted from a "particular" practice as opposed to a congeries of causes? The former question was addressed by the next principal case, and the latter by *Wards Cove*.

WATSON v. FORT WORTH BANK & TRUST
487 U.S. 977 (1988)

Justice O'CONNOR announced the judgment of the Court [and delivered its opinion with respect to the portions reproduced below]:

. . . I

Petitioner Clara Watson, who is black, was hired by respondent Fort Worth Bank and Trust (the Bank) as a proof operator in August 1973. In January 1976, Watson was promoted to a position as teller in the Bank's drive-in facility. In February 1980, she sought to become supervisor of the tellers in the main lobby; a white male, however, was selected for this job. Watson then sought a position as supervisor of the drive-in bank, but this position was given to a white female. In February 1981, after Watson had served for about a year as a commercial teller in the Bank's main lobby, and informally as assistant to the supervisor of tellers, the man holding that position was promoted. Watson applied for the vacancy, but the white female who was the supervisor of the drive-in bank was selected instead. Watson then applied for the vacancy created at the drive-in; a white male was selected for that job. The Bank, which has about 80 employees, had not developed precise and formal criteria for evaluating candidates for the positions for which Watson unsuccessfully applied. It relied instead on the subjective judgment of supervisors who were acquainted with the candidates and with the nature of the jobs to be filled. All the supervisors involved in denying Watson the four promotions at issue were white. . . .

II

A

. . . The distinguishing features of the factual issues that typically dominate in disparate impact cases do not imply that the ultimate legal issue is different than in cases where disparate treatment analysis is used. Nor do we think it is appropriate to hold a defendant liable for unintentional discrimination on the basis of less evidence than is required to prove intentional discrimination. Rather, the necessary premise of the disparate impact approach is that some employment practices, adopted without a deliberately discriminatory motive, may in operation be functionally equivalent to intentional discrimination. . . .

This Court has repeatedly reaffirmed the principle that some facially neutral employment practices may violate Title VII even in the absence of a demonstrated discriminatory intent. We have not limited this principle to cases in which the challenged practice served to perpetuate the effects of pre-Act intentional discrimination. Each of our subsequent decisions, however, like *Griggs* itself, involved standardized employment tests or criteria. See, e.g., *Albemarle Paper Co. v. Moody*, 422 U.S. 405 (1975) (written aptitude tests); *Washington v. Davis* (written test of verbal skills); *Dothard v. Rawlinson* (height and weight requirements); *New York City Transit Authority v. Beazer* (rule against employing drug addicts); *Connecticut v. Teal* (written examination). In contrast, we have consistently used conventional disparate treatment theory, in which proof of intent to discriminate is required, to review hiring and promotion decisions that were based on the exercise of personal judgment or the application of inherently subjective criteria. See, e.g., *McDonnell Douglas Corp. v. Green* (discretionary decision not to rehire individual who engaged in criminal acts against employer while laid off). . . .

Our decisions have not addressed the question whether disparate impact analysis may be applied to cases in which subjective criteria are used to make employment decisions. . . .

B

The parties present us with stark and uninviting alternatives. Petitioner contends that subjective selection methods are at least as likely to have discriminatory effects as are the kind of objective tests at issue in *Griggs* and our other disparate impact cases. Furthermore, she argues, if disparate impact analysis is confined to objective tests, employers will be able to substitute subjective criteria having substantially identical effects, and *Griggs* will become a dead letter. Respondent and the United States (appearing as amicus curiae) argue that conventional disparate treatment analysis is adequate to accomplish Congress' purpose in enacting Title VII.

They also argue that subjective selection practices would be so impossibly difficult to defend under disparate impact analysis that employers would be forced to adopt numerical quotas in order to avoid liability.

We are persuaded that our decisions in *Griggs* and succeeding cases could largely be nullified if disparate impact analysis were applied only to standardized selection practices. . . .

We are also persuaded that disparate impact analysis is in principle no less applicable to subjective employment criteria than to objective or standardized tests. In either case, a facially neutral practice, adopted without discriminatory intent, may have effects that are indistinguishable from intentionally discriminatory practices. It is true, to be sure, that an employer's policy of leaving promotion decisions to the unchecked discretion of lower level supervisors should itself raise no inference of discriminatory conduct. Especially in relatively small businesses like respondent's, it may be customary and quite reasonable simply to delegate employment decisions to those employees who are most familiar with the jobs to be filled and with the candidates for those jobs. It does not follow, however, that the particular supervisors to whom this discretion is delegated always act without discriminatory intent. Furthermore, even if one assumed that any such discrimination can be adequately policed through disparate treatment analysis, the problem of subconscious stereotypes and prejudices would remain. In this case, for example, petitioner was apparently told at one point that the teller position was a big responsibility with "a lot of money . . . for blacks to have to count." Such remarks may not prove discriminatory intent, but they do suggest a lingering form of the problem that Title VII was enacted to combat. If an employer's undisciplined system of subjective decision-making has precisely the same effects as a system pervaded by impermissible intentional discrimination, it is difficult to see why Title VII's proscription against discriminatory actions should not apply. In both circumstances, the employer's practices may be said to "adversely affect [an individual's] status as an employee, because of such individual's race, color, religion, sex, or national origin." 42 U.S.C. § 2000e-2(a)(2). We conclude, accordingly, that subjective or discretionary employment practices may be analyzed under the disparate impact approach in appropriate cases.

[Since the lower court had not evaluated the statistical evidence to determine if a prima facie disparate impact case was made out, the case was remanded with the caution that "[i]t may be that the relevant data base is too small to permit any meaningful statistical analysis. . . ."]

NOTES

1. *Employer Practices Subject to Disparate Impact.* Section 703(k) apparently codifies *Watson's* extension of disparate impact to both objective and subjective practices insofar as it applies to "a particular employment practice" without qualification as to the practice's objective or subjective characteristics. However, *Wards Cove* required that plaintiff show a causal connection between the particular or specific employment policy identified and the racial imbalance shown, and the amended statute codifies that requirement. *See also Cooper v. Southern Co.*, 390 F.3d 695, 726 (11th Cir. 2004) (the plaintiffs "failed to demonstrate a causal nexus between any statistical disparities in the defendants' workforce and the practice of using partially subjective hiring criteria by some managers in some of the defendants' facilities").

2. *Affirmative vs. Negative Practices.* In *EEOC v. Chicago Miniature Lamp Works*, 947 F.2d 292 (7th Cir. 1991), the employer relied on "word-of-mouth" recruitment by incumbent workers to fill job openings. Citing *Wards Cove*, the court reversed the finding of disparate impact liability.

> The EEOC does not allege that Miniature affirmatively engaged in word-of-mouth recruitment of the kind where it told or encouraged its employees to refer applicants for entry-level jobs. Instead, it is uncontested that Miniature passively waited for applicants who typically learned of opportunities from current Miniature employees. The court erred in considering passive reliance on employee word-of-mouth recruiting as a particular employment practice for the purposes of disparate impact. The practices here are undertaken solely by employees. Therefore, disparate impact liability against Miniature must be reversed.

Is *Chicago Miniature Lamps* still good law under §703(k)? Perhaps the Seventh Circuit has reconsidered. In *DeClue v. Central Ill. Light Co.*, 223 F.3d 434 (7th Cir. 2000), the employer's failure to provide restroom facilities for its employees was found to have a disparate impact on women. Would that have fallen within the "passivity" exception?

3. *Subjective Employment Practices.* In a portion of her opinion in *Watson* joined by only a plurality of the Court, Justice O'Connor expressed concern that "validating" subjective employment criteria could prove to be nearly impossible:

> Some qualities — for example, common sense, good judgment, originality, ambition, loyalty, and tact — cannot be measured accurately through standardized testing techniques. Moreover, success at many jobs in which such qualities are crucial cannot itself be measured directly. Opinions often differ when managers and supervisors are evaluated, and the same can be said for many jobs that involve close cooperation with one's co-workers or complex and subtle tasks like the provision of professional services or personal counseling. Because of these difficulties, we are told, employers will find it impossible to eliminate subjective selection criteria and impossibly expensive to defend such practices in litigation.

487 U.S. at 991-92. For O'Connor, this was not fatal to applying disparate impact because she would have simultaneously diluted the business necessity defense, as a majority later did in *Wards Cove*. After §703(k), however, this problem clearly exits. Do you think that that explains the reluctance of the lower courts to apply disparate impact that we saw in Notes 1 and 2? *See also Morgan v. UPS of Am., Inc.*, 380 F.3d 459, 465 n.2 (8th Cir. 2004) ("It is difficult to understand this claim as one of disparate impact. Plaintiffs' claim as to the subjective decision-making process is not that this facially race-neutral process has an adverse impact on blacks and the process cannot be justified by business necessity. Rather, Plaintiffs claim the subjective decision-making resulted in blacks remaining in center-manager positions longer than whites before they were promoted to the division-manager level. We read Plaintiffs' argument as alleging disparate treatment through the subjective decision-making process").

4. *New Structuralism and Debiasing Subjectivity.* Assume that on remand in *Watson*, the court found the practice of relying on subjective supervisor evaluations had a disparate impact on African Americans. How could the employer go about proving that the practice was job related and consistent with business necessity? Must it prove that the employer had put in place a way to structure the exercise of that subjective decision making that minimized the possibility that discrimination, either

conscious or unconscious, could enter the system? Professor Susan Sturm, *Second Generation Employment Discrimination: A Structural Approach*, 101 COLUM. L. REV. 458, 485-90 (2001), writes:

> If subjective employment practices produce a disparate impact on women or people of color, this disparity operates as a signal of the possibility that the system is contributing to the production or expression of bias. [Some lower courts have started to assess] the subjective decisionmaking process to determine whether it provided adequate steps to minimize or eliminate the expression of bias. The emphasis is on whether the degree of unaccountable or unstructured exercise of discretion is warranted. To make this determination, courts will look at the available alternatives. Are there systems of decisionmaking that will permit the exercise of discretion, but will institute standards and processes that minimize the expression of bias?

Does Professor's Sturm's view reinvigorate disparate impact as a means of rooting out unintended discrimination, even if such impact is the result of unconscious prejudices? Consistent with this approach, in *Malave v. Potter*, 320 F.3d 321 (2d Cir. 2003), plaintiff successfully relied on the disparate impact theory to attack the employer's subjective promotion practices as contaminated with favoritism, friendship, and ethnic loyalty.

Professor Tristin Green, although agreeing with Professor Sturm that the employer's harmful action in these circumstances is its failure to minimize discriminatory bias in individual decision-making, doubts that disparate impact theory is capable of supporting the inquiry needed for change. She argues that the problem is not the use of identifiable subjective criteria per se, such as "friendliness" or "leadership ability," which, may indeed be job related and justified by business necessity, but rather with the application of such criteria: "Rather than requiring the elimination of the practice itself, we need to begin exploring the ways in which employers can be held accountable for managing diversity within modern structures and practices to minimize the operation of discriminatory bias." *Discrimination in Workplace Dynamics: Toward a Structural Account of Disparate Treatment Theory*, 38 HARV. C.R.-C.L. L. REV. 91, 142-43 (2002). As we saw in Chapter 2's Note on the New Structuralism, p. 166, these theories may fit better into the systemic disparate treatment paradigm than into disparate impact, although they can perhaps best be described as urging a new conceptualization of discrimination rather than being shoehorned into any existing paradigm.

5. *Volitional Exception?* Some cases seem to recognize a "personal preference" or volitional exception to disparate impact discrimination, sometimes formulated as an employee duty to make reasonable efforts to qualify. *See generally* Peter Siegelman, *Contributory Disparate Impacts in Employment Law*, ssrn; Sandi Farrell, *Toward Getting Beyond the Blame Game: A Critique of the Ideology of Voluntarism in Title VII Jurisprudence*, 92 KY. L.J. 483 (2003/2004); Laya Sleiman, Note, *A Duty to Make Reasonable Efforts and a Defense of the Disparate Impact Doctrine in Employment Discrimination Law*, 72 FORDHAM L. REV. 2677, 2682 (2004). The core notion is that some employer requirements ought not to be subject to disparate impact analysis because employees or prospective employees can, more or less easily, conform their conduct to the requirement. The classic example is *Garcia v. Spun Steak Co.*, 998 F.2d 1480, 1483 (9th Cir. 1993), in which the employer required its bilingual employees to speak only English on the job. Although the rule fell more harshly on employees of Mexican origin than others, the Ninth Circuit found it immune from disparate impact attack. Bilingual employees could comply with the rule and thus could avoid

discipline. A volitional exception is more or less problematic depending on what conduct is defined as volitional, but it is scarcely well established. *Spun Steak's* authority is limited because it was not governed by the 1991 Amendments, but a post-Act decision, *Lanning v. SEPTA*, 308 F.3d 286 (3d Cir. 2002), revived the notion. In that case, employment as a transit police officer was dependent upon each candidate running 1.5 miles within twelve minutes. Although the requirement had a disparate impact on female applicants, the Third Circuit upheld the policy, in part because nearly all women would be able to pass after only a moderate amount of training. The court did not think it unreasonable to expect women to train prior to applying; doing so, the court said, would demonstrate their commitment to the job. Obviously, this suggests some version of a volitional exception to disparate impact analysis.

6. *Disparate Impact and Hostile Environment.* In *Maldonado v. City of Altus*, 433 F.3d 1294, 1304-05 (10th Cir. 2006), the court faced a challenge by Hispanic workers to an English-only rule. In contrast to *Spun Steak*, see Note 5, the focus of this attack on an English-only policy was predicated on the hostile work environment that the policy allegedly generated. See Chapter 5 for a full discussion of hostile environment law. The court reversed summary judgment for the defendant on both disparate treatment and disparate impact grounds. As to the latter,

> [t]he policy itself, and not just the effect of the policy in evoking hostility by co-workers [of which plaintiffs had produced evidence], may create or contribute to the hostility of the work environment. A policy requiring each employee to wear a badge noting his or her religion, for example, might well engender extreme discomfort in a reasonable employee who belongs to a minority religion, even if no co-worker utters a word on the matter. Here, the very fact that the City would forbid Hispanics from using their preferred language could reasonably be construed as an expression of hostility to Hispanics. At least that could be a reasonable inference if there was no apparent legitimate purpose for the restrictions. . . . The less the apparent justification for mandating English, the more reasonable it is to infer hostility toward employees whose ethnic group or nationality favors another language. For example, Plaintiffs presented evidence that the English-only policy extended beyond its written terms to include lunch hours, breaks, and even private telephone conversations, if non-Spanish-speaking co-workers were nearby. Absent a legitimate reason for such a restriction, the inference of hostility may be reasonable.

Is the point that this is a disparate impact case because, although the policy makers had no intent to discriminate, adverse consequences would follow, at least if other workers were reasonable (if wrong) in inferring hostility by those in charge?

CONNECTICUT v. TEAL
457 U.S. 440 (1982)

Justice BRENNAN delivered the opinion of the Court.

We consider here whether an employer sued for violation of Title VII of the Civil Rights Act of 1964 may assert a "bottom line" theory of defense. Under that theory, as asserted in this case, an employer's acts of racial discrimination in promotions — effected by an examination having disparate impact — would not render the employer liable for the racial discrimination suffered by employees barred from promotion if the "bottom line" result of the promotional process was an appropriate racial balance. We hold that the "bottom line" does not preclude respondent-employees from establishing a prima facie case, nor does it provide petitioner-employer with a defense to such a case.

Four of the respondents, Winnie Teal, Rose Walker, Edith Latney, and Grace Clark, are black employees of the Department of Income Maintenance of the State of Connecticut. Each was promoted provisionally to the position of Welfare Eligibility Supervisor and served in that capacity for almost two years. To attain permanent status as supervisors, however, respondents had to participate in a selection process that required, as the first step, a passing score on a written examination. This written test was administered on December 2, 1978, to 329 candidates. Of these candidates, 48 identified themselves as black and 259 identified themselves as white. The results of the examination were announced in March 1979. With the passing score set at 65,[3] 54.17 percent of the identified black candidates passed. This was approximately 68 percent of the passing rate for the identified white candidates.[4] The four respondents were among the blacks who failed the examination, and they were thus excluded from further consideration for permanent supervisory positions. . . .

More than a year after this action was instituted, and approximately one month before trial, petitioners made promotions from the eligibility list generated by the written examination. In choosing persons from that list, petitioners considered past work performance, recommendations of the candidates' supervisors and, to a lesser extent, seniority. Petitioners then applied what the Court of Appeals characterized as an affirmative action program in order to ensure a significant number of minority supervisors. Forty-six persons were promoted to permanent supervisory positions, 11 of whom were black and 35 of whom were white. The overall result of the selection process was that, of the 48 identified black candidates who participated in the selection process, 22.9 percent were promoted and of the 259 identified white candidates, 13.5 percent were promoted. It is this "bottom-line" result, more favorable to blacks than to whites, that petitioners urge should be adjudged to be a complete defense to respondents' suit. . . .

II

A . . .

Petitioners' examination, which barred promotion and had a discriminatory impact on black employees, clearly falls within the literal language of §703(a)(2), as interpreted by *Griggs*. The statute speaks, not in terms of jobs and promotions, but in terms of *limitations* and *classifications* that would deprive any individual of employment *opportunities*. A disparate impact claim reflects the language of §703(a)(2) and Congress' basic objectives in enacting that statute: "to achieve equality of employment *opportunities* and remove barriers that have operated in the past to favor an identifiable group of white employees over other employees." (Emphasis added.) When an employer uses a non-job-related barrier in order to deny a minority or woman applicant employment or promotion, and that barrier has a significant adverse effect on minorities or women, then the applicant has been deprived of an employment *opportunity* "because of . . . race, color, religion, sex, or national origin." In other words,

3. The mean score on the examination was 70.4 percent. However, because the black candidates had a mean score 6.7 percentage points lower than the white candidates, the passing score was set at 65, apparently in an attempt to lessen the disparate impact of the examination.

4. . . . Petitioners do not contest the District Court's implicit finding that the examination itself resulted in disparate impact under the "eighty percent rule" of the Uniform Guidelines on Employee Selection Procedures adopted by the Equal Employment Opportunity Commission. Those guidelines provide that a selection rate that "is less than [80 percent] of the rate for the group with the highest rate will generally be regarded . . . as evidence of adverse impact." 29 C.F.R. §1607.4D (1981).

§ 703(a)(2) prohibits discriminatory "artificial, arbitrary, and unnecessary barriers to employment" that "limit . . . or classify . . . applicants for employment . . . in any way which would deprive or tend to deprive any individual of employment *opportunities*." . . . (Emphasis added.)

In short, the District Court's dismissal of respondents' claim cannot be supported on the basis that respondents failed to establish a prima facie case of employment discrimination under the terms of § 703(a)(2). The suggestion that disparate impact should be measured only at the bottom line ignores the fact that Title VII guarantees these individual respondents the *opportunity* to compete equally with white workers on the basis of job-related criteria. Title VII strives to achieve equality of opportunity by rooting out "artificial, arbitrary and unnecessary" employer-created barriers to professional development that have a discriminatory impact upon individuals. Therefore, respondents' rights under § 703(a)(2) have been violated, unless petitioners can demonstrate that the examination given was not an artificial, arbitrary, or unnecessary barrier, because it measured skills related to effective performance in the role of Welfare Eligibility Supervisor. . . .

III

Having determined that respondents' claim comes within the terms of Title VII, we must address the suggestion of petitioners and some *amici curiae* that we recognize an exception, either in the nature of an additional burden on plaintiffs seeking to establish a prima facie case or in the nature of an affirmative defense, for cases in which an employer has compensated for a discriminatory pass-fail barrier by hiring or promoting a sufficient number of black employees to reach a nondiscriminatory "bottom line." We reject this suggestion, which is in essence nothing more than a request that we redefine the protections guaranteed by Title VII.

Section 703(a)(2) prohibits practices that would deprive or tend to deprive "*any individual* of employment opportunities." The principal focus of the statute is the protection of the individual employee, rather than the protection of the minority group as a whole. Indeed, the entire statute and its legislative history are replete with references to protection for the individual employee. See, e.g., §§ 703(a)(1), (b), (c), 704(a), as amended; 110 Cong. Rec. 7213 (1964) (interpretive memorandum of Sens. Clark and Case) ("discrimination is prohibited as to any individual"); 110 Cong. Rec. 8921 (remarks of Sen. Williams) ("Every man must be judged according to his ability. In that respect, all men are to have an equal opportunity to be considered for a particular job.").

In suggesting that the "bottom line" may be a defense to a claim of discrimination against an individual employee, petitioners and *amici* appear to confuse unlawful discrimination with discriminatory intent. The Court has stated that a nondiscriminatory "bottom line" and an employer's good faith efforts to achieve a nondiscriminatory work force, might in some cases assist an employer in rebutting the inference that particular action had been intentionally discriminatory: "Proof that [a] work force was racially balanced or that it contained a disproportionately high percentage of minority employees is not wholly irrelevant on the issue of intent when that issue is yet to be decided." *Furnco Construction Corp. v. Waters*. See also *Teamsters v. United States*, n.20. But resolution of the factual question of intent is not what is at issue in this case. Rather, petitioners seek simply to justify discrimination against respondents, on the basis of their favorable treatment of other members of respondents' racial group. Under Title VII, "A racially balanced work force cannot immunize an employer from liability for specific acts of discrimination." *Furnco Construction Corp. v. Waters.* . . .

It is clear that Congress never intended to give an employer license to discriminate against some employees on the basis of race or sex merely because he favorably treats other members of the employees' group. We recognized in *Los Angeles Dept. of Water & Power v. Manhart* [reproduced at p. 116], that fairness to the class of women employees as a whole could not justify unfairness to the individual female employee because the "statute's focus on the individual is unambiguous." Similarly, in *Phillips v. Martin Marietta Corp.*, 400 U.S. 542 (1971) (per curiam), we recognized that a rule barring employment of all married *women* with preschool children, if not a bona fide occupational qualification under §703(e), violated Title VII, even though female applicants without preschool children were hired in sufficient numbers that they constituted 75 to 80 percent of the persons employed in the position plaintiff sought.

Petitioners point out that *Furnco, Manhart,* and *Phillips* involved facially discriminatory policies, while the claim in the instant case is one of discrimination from a facially neutral policy. The fact remains, however, that irrespective of the form taken by the discriminatory practice, an employer's treatment of other members of the plaintiffs' group can be "of little comfort to the victims of . . . discrimination." *Teamsters v. United States.* Title VII does not permit the victim of a facially discriminatory policy to be told that he has not been wronged because other persons of his or her race or sex were hired. That answer is no more satisfactory when it is given to victims of a policy that is facially neutral but practically discriminatory. Every *individual* employee is protected against both discriminatory treatment and against "practices that are fair in form, but discriminatory in operation." *Griggs.* Requirements and tests that have a discriminatory impact are merely some of the more subtle, but also the more pervasive, of the "practices and devices which have fostered racially stratified job environments to the disadvantage of minority citizens." *McDonnell Douglas Corp..* . . .

Justice POWELL, with whom the Chief Justice, Justice REHNQUIST, and Justice O'CONNOR join, dissenting.

. . . Although [the language of §703(a)(2)] suggests that discrimination occurs only on an individual basis, . . . our disparate impact cases consistently have considered whether the result of an employer's *total selection process* had an adverse impact upon the protected group. If this case were decided by reference to the total process — as our cases suggest that it should be — the result would be clear. Here 22.9 percent of the blacks who entered the selection process were ultimately promoted, compared with only 13.5 percent of the whites. To say that this selection process had an unfavorable "disparate impact" on blacks is to ignore reality.

The Court, disregarding the distinction drawn by our cases, repeatedly asserts that Title VII was designed to protect individual, not group, rights. It emphasizes that some individual blacks were eliminated by the disparate impact of the preliminary test. But this argument confuses the *aim* of Title VII with the legal theories through which its aims were intended to be vindicated. It is true that the aim of Title VII is to protect individuals, not groups. But in advancing this commendable objective, Title VII jurisprudence has recognized two distinct methods of proof. In one set of cases — those involving direct proof of discriminatory intent — the plaintiff seeks to establish direct, intentional discrimination against him. In that type case, the individual is at the forefront throughout the entire presentation of evidence. In disparate impact cases, by contrast, the plaintiff seeks to carry his burden of proof by way of *inference* — by showing that an employer's selection process results in the rejection of a disproportionate number of members of a protected group to which he belongs. From such a showing a fair inference then may be drawn that the rejected applicant, as a member of that disproportionately excluded group, was himself a victim of that process's "built-in headwinds." *Griggs.* But this method of proof — which actually *defines* disparate impact theory under Title VII — invites the plaintiff to prove discrimination by reference to the group rather than to the allegedly affected individual. There can be no violation of Title VII on the basis of disparate impact in the absence of disparate impact on a *group.*

In this case the plaintiff seeks to benefit from a conflation of "discriminatory treatment" and "disparate impact" theories. But he cannot have it both ways. Having undertaken to prove discrimination by reference to one set of group figures (used at a preliminary point in the selection process), the plaintiff then claims that *nondis-crimination* cannot be proved by viewing the impact of the entire process on the group as a whole. The fallacy of this reasoning — accepted by the Court — is transparent. It is to confuse the individualistic *aim* of Title VII with the methods of proof by which Title VII rights may be vindicated. The respondent, as an individual, is entitled to the full personal protection of Title VII. But, having undertaken to prove a violation of his rights by reference to group figures, respondent cannot deny petitioner the opportunity to rebut his evidence by introducing figures of the same kind. Having pleaded a disparate impact case, the plaintiff cannot deny the defendant the opportunity to show that there was no disparate impact. . . .

Where, under a facially neutral employment process, there has been no adverse effect on the group — and certainly there has been none here — Title VII has not been infringed. . . .

III

Today's decision takes a long and unhappy step in the direction of confusion. Title VII does not require that employers adopt merit hiring or the procedures most likely to permit the greatest number of minority members to be considered for or to qualify for jobs and promotions. See *Texas Dept. of Community Affairs v. Burdine; Furnco.* Employers need not develop tests that accurately reflect the skills of every individual candidate; there are few if any tests that do so. Yet the Court seems unaware of this practical reality, and perhaps oblivious to the likely consequences of its decision. By its holding today, the Court may force employers either to eliminate tests or rely on expensive, job-related, testing procedures, the validity of which may or may not be sustained if challenged. For state and local governmental employers with limited funds, the practical effect of today's decision may well be the adoption of simple quota hiring.[8] This arbitrary method of employment is itself unfair to individual applicants, whether or not they are members of minority groups. And it is not likely to produce a competent workforce. Moreover, the Court's decision actually may

---

8. Another possibility is that employers may integrate consideration of test results into one overall hiring decision based on that "factor" *and* additional factors. Such a process would not, even under the Court's reasoning, result in a finding of discrimination on the basis of disparate impact unless the actual hiring decisions had a disparate impact on the minority group. But if employers integrate test results into a single-step decision, they will be free to select *only* the number of minority candidates proportional to their representation in the workforce. If petitioner had used this approach, it would have been able to hire substantially fewer blacks without liability on the basis of disparate impact. The Court hardly could have intended to encourage this.

result in employers employing *fewer* minority members [by discouraging voluntary affirmative action plans].

NOTES

1. *The Employment Practice Plaintiffs' Challenged.* The plaintiffs here had successfully performed the job that they sought. They lost their positions when they failed a civil service test used to fill the job permanently. Since the test knocked them out of further consideration in the selection process, its use was the practice that plaintiffs challenged. The data on the racial impact of the test was clear. In a sense, this is simply a *Griggs* case; the twist is that the test used here was part of a multistep selection process. The only question was whether the fact that, at the end of the process, African Americans did not experience any negative impact was significant, though that fact would be small comfort to the plaintiffs who lost their jobs. *Teal* permits an attack on any practice with an identifiable impact and, just as importantly, renders a nondiscriminatory bottom line no defense to the impact of a particular practice.

2. *Hoist with Their Own Petard? Teal* was a victory for the plaintiffs, and the "liberal" wing of the Court was in the majority. But in *Wards Cove*, the plaintiffs lost because they focused on the bottom line and could not identify a particular practice that caused the impact. The "conservative" wing was in the ascendancy. How could the same principle cut so severely both ways? The explanation is simple: the underlying assumption of the majority in *Teal* seemed to be that plaintiffs could have their cake and eat in too; that is, they could focus on any stage in the selection process or the bottom line, wherever there was an impact. After *Wards Cove*, however, plaintiffs could only challenge the effects of a particular employment practice. Bottom line results were, presumably, subject to attack only under systemic disparate treatment. As we will see in more detail, §703(k) split the difference: it follows *Wards Cove* by normally requiring plaintiff to identify the practice causing the impact but also creates an exception for the use of bottom line statistics.

3. *Choice of Labor Market as a Particular Practice.* Is an employer's use of a particular labor market to recruit workers a particular employment practice within the general rule of §703(k)(1)(A)(i)? Recall that *Wards Cove* restricted that application of disparate impact law, but plaintiffs failed to focus on the defendant's choice of place of recruitment as the employment practice at issue; they instead lumped that practice in with a number of other practices, such as nepotism. Also, does the failure of the Court in *Smith v. City of Jackson* to understand the practice at issue there suggest that making such a case would be difficult? Nevertheless, lower courts have found similar practices to be subject to disparate impact attack. In *NAACP, Newark Branch v. Town of Harrison*, 940 F.2d 792 (3d Cir. 1991), the town's residents-only rule had a disparate impact because Harrison was almost exclusively white, while nearby areas, such as Newark, were predominately black. In short, Harrison had defined a geographic labor market, but the plaintiff challenged that very definition as creating an adverse impact. Why is Newark the relevant comparison in *Harrison? See also United States v. City of Warren, Michigan*, 138 F.3d 1083, 1093 (6th Cir. 1998) (city's residents-only rule and its refusal to advertise outside of predominantly white Macomb County, a suburb of Detroit, could both be challenged).

4. *Multicomponent Selection Processes under §703(k).* The 1991 Amendments struck a compromise between the extremes marked out by *Teal* and *Wards Cove*.

The "plain meaning" of the term "particular employment practice" in §703(k) suggests an intent to separate out multicomponent selection processes into their individual parts if that is possible. But what is also clear is that it allows a disparate impact attack to the "bottom line" result of the process if the data is not available to analyze the separate parts of the process. Thus, §703(k)(1)(B) normally requires the plaintiff to show that "each particular challenged employment practice" causes an impact. However, it creates an exception when "the complaining party can demonstrate to the court that the elements of [an employer's] decisionmaking process cannot be separated for analysis"; in that event, "the decisionmaking process may be analyzed as one employment practice." Thus, plaintiffs in *Teal* could use the general rule of new §703(k) because the data concerning the racial impact of the test was available. If that data were unavailable and if there was no disparate impact on blacks at the end of the selection process, then these plaintiffs would be out of luck on the disparate impact theory. But, if, at the end of the process, there was impact, even though the source of that impact could not be identified, plaintiff would then have a "bottom line" case — that is, plaintiff could establish liability by showing that the proportion of women or minority men who were successful getting through the selection process was lower than for white males.

5. *The Truncated Legislative History of the '91 Act.* Resorting to the legislative history of the Civil Rights Act in general would confirm the approach described in Note 4 to multicomponent systems. However, the Act itself has a provision limiting judicial use of legislative history. Section 105(b) of the Act says, "No statements other than [a specified] interpretive memorandum shall be considered legislative history of, or relied upon in any way as legislative history in construing or applying, any provision of this Act that relates to *Wards Cove* — business necessity/cumulation/alternative employment practice." Presumably, the "particular employment practice" question is within this limitation, perhaps due to the "cumulation" language. Resort to the referenced Interpretative Memorandum of October 25, 1991, on this point does seem helpful:

> When a decision-making process includes particular, functionally-integrated practices which are components of the same criterion, standard, method of administration, or test, such as the height and weight requirements designed to measure strength in Dothard v. Rawlinson [involving a challenge to minimum height and weight prerequisites to being a prison guard], the particular functionally-integrated practices may be analyzed as one employment practice.

Clearly, an entire multiple-choice exam is one employment practice under this definition. But why are the height and weight requirements in *Dothard*, which are in some ways quite different, nevertheless viewed as one practice? Does *Teal* provide the answer?

The employer in *Teal* used a sequential, multistep procedure: passing the test was a condition for being considered at the next level. In the last footnote of his dissent, Justice Powell suggested that the decision could be avoided by integrating the test into a single, but multifactored, decision. Under his view, the bottom line would then become the only focus. Is that what the new statute envisions? If so, the interpretive memorandum's citation to *Dothard* would be wrong because the height requirement and the weight requirement were separate: an applicant could satisfy one and fail the other. Perhaps the point, however, is that the requirements can be passed and failed. They are not, like Justice Powell's hypothetical, just factors to be weighed. A person who is too short will not be employed, regardless of his or her weight or strength in other regards. But what would happen if the employer multiplied applicant's weight by their height to get a composite "size" score? Would reliance on the size score to choose among the applicants be a single practice, or would plaintiff have to "backout" the numbers to ascertain the separate influences of weight and height?

6. *Incapable of Separation for Analysis.* Contrary to *Wards Cove*, new § 703(k)(1)(B) provides that "bottom line" statistics can sometimes be used to prove disparate impact discrimination:

> With respect to demonstrating that a particular employment practice causes a disparate impact as described in subparagraph (A)(i), the complaining party shall demonstrate that each particular challenged employment practice causes a disparate impact, except that if the complaining party can demonstrate to the court that the elements of a respondent's decisionmaking process are not capable of separation for analysis, the decisionmaking process may be analyzed as one employment practice.

As a practical matter, all of the data concerning the selection process will be maintained by the employer, and whether all that data is turned over in discovery will be the first question. An employer who resists discovery may well provide the plaintiff with "incapable of being separated for analysis" on a silver platter. This also should be true if the employer simply doesn't preserve the data. But if full information is turned over, the question of "separation for analysis" is likely to turn on plaintiff's experts' testimony. Recall Justice Powell's *Teal* hypothetical, where the employer considers many factors, whether those factors are objective, subjective, or mixed, but does not "score" any of them. Presumably § 703(k)(1)(B)(i) would apply, enabling plaintiff to establish a prima facie case based on the bottom-line statistics of those hired or promoted by the entire process compared to those considered in the process. *See Phillips v. Cohen*, 400 F.3d 388 (6th Cir. 2004) (2-1) (focusing on entire promotion decision process).

7. *Employer Defenses to Bottom Line Proof.* Whenever a plaintiff makes out a case of disparate impact, the defendant may defend by carrying the burden of persuasion that (1) that the practices that do cause an impact are justified as job related and consistent with business necessity; or (2) that those practices fall within the § 703(h) defenses. Assuming however, that plaintiff can make out a prima facie case based on the bottom line exception to the general requirement that plaintiff identify a particular employment practice causing the impact, the defendant has another defense under § 703(k)(1)(B)(ii): "If the respondent demonstrates that a specific employment practice does not cause the disparate impact, the respondent shall not be required to demonstrate that such practice is required by business necessity." There is an obvious, and unresolved, tension between the statute placing on the employee the burden of persuasion that a selection process is not capable of being separated for analysis while also placing on the employer the burden of proof that a particular component does not cause an impact. See p. 251.

8. *Impact on a Protected Group.* The statistics in *Teal* show that, at the end of the selection process — the "bottom line" — the overall selection process had an adverse impact on whites: 22.9 percent of blacks who applied were promoted while only 13.5 percent of whites were. It is possible, of course, that disappointed white applicants could claim intentional discrimination in favor of blacks during the latter part of the process, especially given the majority's reference to "an affirmative action program."

But what if whites argued disparate impact against their race? Such impact clearly existed, right?

Title VII protects all persons against employment discrimination because of race, color, sex, religion, and national origin. *McDonald v. Santa Fe Trail Transp. Co.*, reproduced at p. 68. That protection extends to disparate treatment discrimination but it is not clear that disparate impact theory is available to whites or males. All of the disparate impact cases decided by the Supreme Court under Title VII involved claims by women or minority men. *Griggs* emphasized that Title VII was "to achieve equality of employment opportunities and remove barriers that have operated in the past to favor an identifiable group of white employees over other employees." 401 U.S. at 429-30 (1971). The strong suggestion is that whites and males could not utilize the theory.

City of Los Angeles v. Manhart, 435 U.S. 702, 710 n.20 (1978), came closer to so stating. That case dealt with the argument that equalizing both pension benefits and contributions for men and women to eliminate the use of an illegal gender classification would produce a disparate impact on men, who as a group do not live as long as women. The Court suggested that men would not be able to use the disparate impact theory. "Even a completely neutral practice will inevitably have some disproportionate impact on one group or another. *Griggs* does not imply, and this Court has never held, that discrimination must always be inferred from such consequences." Some lower courts have also encountered the question. In *Foss v. Thompson*, 242 F.3d 1131 (9th Cir. 2001), a male plaintiff lost his job when he was not allowed to bump into another position during a reduction in force because he lacked a nursing degree. He claimed the preference for such a degree had a disparate impact on men since nurses were overwhelmingly female. The court dismissed his claim, holding that "the proper analysis turns on the percentage of men and women who are otherwise qualified but lack a nursing degree." *Id.* at 1134. The dissent argued that the practice at issue was the requirement of a nursing degree, which clearly had an adverse impact on men: under that "requirement, nine out of ten people who can fill the job are limited to one sex. And 100% of the people who got the position in the Portland Area Office were of one sex. Without it, the sex distribution of those filing the job is pretty evenly balanced." *Id.* at 1137. There was no discussion of whether disparate impact was available to a male plaintiff. Do you think, nevertheless, that was on the mind of the majority?

The answer to the question of whether whites (and males) can use disparate impact could depend on the language of the statute, the rationale underlying the theory, and the constitutionality of providing a cause of action to minorities and not to whites. *See generally* Charles A. Sullivan, *The World Turned Upside Down?: Disparate Impact Claims by White Males*, 98 Nw. U. L. Rev. 1505 (2004) (applying disparate impact beyond minorities and women is profoundly ahistorical and inconsistent with the theoretic underpinnings of the theory; nevertheless, limiting the theory to minorities and women cannot survive equal protection analysis. Accordingly, Title VII should be read to avoid the constitutional question by interpreting disparate impact as available to all races and both sexes).

9. *Exception for Drug Use Rules.* The 1991 Civil Rights Act created a specific exception to the application of disparate impact discrimination for employment practices dealing with illegal drug use. Section 703(k)(3) provides that "a rule barring the employment of an individual who currently and knowingly uses or possesses a controlled substance . . . other than the use or possession of a drug taken under the supervision of a licensed health care professional, . . . shall be considered an

unlawful employment practice under this title only if such rule is adopted or applied with an intent to discriminate because of race, color, sex, or national origin." This appears to resolve the tension within disparate impact doctrine resulting from *New York City Transit Auth. v. Beazer*, 440 U.S. 568 (1979), which involved a disparate impact challenge to an employer rule prohibiting employment of individuals on methadone maintenance. In upholding the employer's rule, the Court imposed a very high threshold showing of impact to make out a prima facie case and then, in dicta, suggested a low burden on the employer to justify the rule under the business necessity defense. The Court did this without suggesting it was applying special rules because a drug rule was involved. But §703(k) now specifically bars disparate impact analysis for employer rules dealing with the illegal use of drugs. Ironically, §703(k)(3) would not exempt the rule in *Beazer* since that rule involved the legal use of drugs. Presumably, if *Beazer* arose again today, it would be subject to normal disparate treatment analysis under §703(k)(1).

PROBLEM 3.1

Fogey.com is an e-commerce business that is growing rapidly. Alice Aortop is in charge of hiring, and she says that she interviews every applicant and subjectively evaluates each one looking for "creativity, decisiveness, ambition, loyalty and ability to create buzz!" Assuming that comparatively few of the African-American and Latino applicants are hired, can the "bottom-line" number of minority group members be used to make out a prima facie case of disparate impact discrimination since the subjective evaluation system is a particular employment practice? Or since factors such as creativity, decisiveness, etc., are relied upon, must the plaintiff first convince the judge that these elements are not capable of separation for analysis because he is using bottom-line statistics to prove disparate impact?

b. The Employer Uses the Practice

Section 703(k)(1)(A)(i) requires that plaintiff prove that the employer "*uses* a particular employment practice that causes a disparate impact."

DOTHARD v. RAWLINSON
433 U.S. 321 (1977)

Justice STEWART delivered the opinion of the Court. . . .

. . . I

At the time she applied for a position as correctional counselor trainee, Rawlinson was a 22-year-old college graduate whose major course of study had been correctional psychology. She was refused employment because she failed to meet the minimum 120-pound weight requirement established by an Alabama statute. The statute also establishes a height minimum of 5 feet 2 inches. . . .

Like most correctional facilities in the United States, Alabama's prisons are segregated on the basis of sex. Currently the Alabama Board of Corrections operates four major all-male penitentiaries. . . . The Board also operates the Julia Tutwiler Prison for Women, the Frank Lee Youth Center, the Number Four Honor Camp, the State Cattle Ranch, and nine Work Release Centers, one of which is for women. The Julia Tutwiler Prison for Women and the four male penitentiaries are maximum-security institutions. Their inmate living quarters are for the most part large dormitories, with communal showers and toilets that are open to the dormitories and hallways. The Draper and Fountain penitentiaries carry on extensive farming operations, making necessary a large number of strip searches for contraband when prisoners re-enter the prison buildings.

A correctional counselor's primary duty within these institutions is to maintain security and control of the inmates by continually supervising and observing their activities. To be eligible for consideration as a correctional counselor, an applicant must possess a valid Alabama driver's license, have a high school education or its equivalent, be free from physical defects, be between the ages of 20 1/2 years and 45 years at the time of appointment, and fall between the minimum height and weight requirements of 5 feet 2 inches, and 120 pounds, and the maximum of 6 feet 10 inches, and 300 pounds. Appointment is by merit, with a grade assigned each applicant based on experience and education. No written examination is given. . . .

II . . .

A

The gist of the claim that the statutory height and weight requirements discriminate against women does not involve an assertion of purposeful discriminatory motive. It is asserted, rather, that these facially neutral qualification standards work in fact disproportionately to exclude women from eligibility for employment by the Alabama Board of Corrections. We dealt in *Griggs* and *Albemarle Paper* with similar allegations that facially neutral employment standards disproportionately excluded Negroes from employment, and those cases guide our approach here.

Those cases make clear that to establish a prima facie case of discrimination, a plaintiff need only show that the facially neutral standards in question select applicants for hire in a significantly discriminatory pattern. Once it is thus shown that the employment standards are discriminatory in effect, the employer must meet "the burden of showing that any given requirement [has] . . . a manifest relationship to the employment in question." *Griggs*. If the employer proves that the challenged requirements are job related, the plaintiff may then show that other selection devices without a similar discriminatory effect would also "serve the employer's legitimate interest in 'efficient and trustworthy workmanship.'" *Albemarle Paper*, quoting *McDonnell Douglas*.

Although women 14 years of age or older compose 52.75% of the Alabama population and 36.89% of its total labor force, they hold only 12.9% of its correctional counselor positions. In considering the effect of the minimum height and weight standards on this disparity in rate of hiring between the sexes, the District Court found that the 5'2" requirement would operate to exclude 33.29% of the women in the United States between the ages of 18-79, while excluding only 1.28% of men between the same ages. The 120-pound weight restriction would exclude 22.29% of the women and 2.35% of the men in this age group. When the height and weight restrictions are combined, Alabama's statutory standards would exclude 41.13% of the female population while excluding less than 1% of the male population.[12] Accordingly, the District Court found that Rawlinson had made out a prima facie case of unlawful sex discrimination.

The appellants argue that a showing of disproportionate impact on women based on generalized national statistics should not suffice to establish a prima facie case. They point in particular to Rawlinson's failure to adduce comparative statistics concerning actual applicants for correctional counselor positions in Alabama. There is no requirement, however, that a statistical showing of disproportionate impact must always be based on analysis of the characteristics of actual applicants. *See Griggs v. Duke Power Co.* The application process itself might not adequately reflect the actual potential applicant pool, since otherwise qualified people might be discouraged from applying because of a self-recognized inability to meet the very standards challenged as being discriminatory. *See Teamsters v. United States.* A potential applicant could easily determine her height and weight and conclude that to make an application would be futile. Moreover, reliance on general population demographic data was not misplaced where there was no reason to suppose that physical height and weight characteristics of Alabama men and women differ markedly from those of the national population.

For these reasons, we cannot say that the District Court was wrong in holding that the statutory height and weight standards had a discriminatory impact on women applicants. The plaintiffs in a case such as this are not required to exhaust every possible source of evidence, if the evidence actually presented on its face conspicuously demonstrates a job requirement's grossly discriminatory impact. If the employer discerns fallacies or deficiencies in the data offered by the plaintiff, he is free to adduce countervailing evidence of his own. In this case no such effort was made.

B

We turn, therefore, to the appellants' argument that they have rebutted the prima facie case of discrimination by showing that the height and weight requirements are job related. These requirements, they say, have a relationship to strength, a sufficient but unspecified amount of which is essential to effective job performance as a correctional counselor. In the District Court, however, the appellants produced no evidence correlating the height and weight requirements with the requisite amount of strength thought essential to good job performance. Indeed, they failed to offer evidence of any kind in specific justification of the statutory standards.[14]

If the job-related quality that the appellants identify is bona fide, their purpose could be achieved by adopting and validating a test for applicants that measures strength directly. Such a test, fairly administered, would fully satisfy the standards of

---

12. Affirmatively stated, approximately 99.76% of the men and 58.87% of the women meet both these physical qualifications. From the separate statistics on height and weight of males it would appear that after adding the two together and allowing for some overlap the result would be to exclude between 2.35% and 3.63% of males from meeting Alabama's statutory height and weight minima. None of the parties has challenged the accuracy of the District Court's computations on this score, however, and the discrepancy is in any event insignificant in light of the gross disparity between the female and male exclusions. Even under revised computations the disparity would greatly exceed the 34% to 12% disparity that served to invalidate the high school diploma requirement in the *Griggs* case.

14. [T]he appellants contend that the establishment of the minimum height and weight standards by statute requires that they be given greater deference than is typically given private employer-established job qualifications. The relevant legislative history of the 1972 amendments extending Title VII to the States as employers does not, however, support such a result. Instead, Congress expressly indicated the intent that the same Title VII principles be applied to governmental and private employers alike. See H.R. Rep. No. 92-238, p. 17 (1971); S. Rep. No. 92-415, p. 10 (1971). . . .

Title VII because it would be one that "measure[s] the person for the job and not the person in the abstract." *Griggs.* But nothing in the present record even approaches such a measurement. . . .

[Justice REHNQUIST, joined by the Chief Justice and Justice BLACKMUN, filed a concurring opinion.]

Justice WHITE, dissenting.
. . . I have . . . trouble agreeing that a prima facie case of sex discrimination was made out by statistics showing that the Alabama height and weight requirements would exclude a larger percentage of women in the United States than of men. As in *Hazelwood,* the issue is whether there was discrimination in dealing with actual or potential applicants; but in *Hazelwood* there was at least a colorable argument that the racial composition of the area-wide teacher work force was a reasonable proxy for the composition of the relevant applicant pool and hence that a large divergence between the percentage of blacks on the teaching staff and the percentage in the teacher work force raised a fair inference of racial discrimination in dealing with the applicant pool. In *Dothard,* however, I am unwilling to believe that the percentage of women applying or interested in applying for jobs as prison guards in Alabama approximates the percentage of women either in the national or state population. A plaintiff could, of course, show that the composition of the applicant pool was distorted by the exclusion of nonapplicants who did not apply because of the allegedly discriminatory job requirement. But no such showing was made or even attempted here; and although I do not know what the actual fact is, I am not now convinced that a large percentage of the actual women applicants, or of those who are seriously interested in applying, for prison guard positions would fail to satisfy the height and weight requirements. . . .

NOTES

1. *The Employer "Used" the Challenged Practices.* It was simple in *Dothard* to show that the employer had "used" height and weight thresholds in selecting prison guards because it was a written employment policy. Were the same facts to arise today, the question would be whether plaintiff's proof of national height and weight statistics satisfied $703(k)(1)(A)(i)$'s requirement that plaintiff prove that the practice the employer "uses" in fact produces the impact. Justice White's dissent would require the plaintiff to prove that the employer's use caused the impact by showing, for example, what impact it had on those who applied. Should the disparate impact theory be available to challenge, at least at a prima facie level, employment practices that, if used by employers generally, would cause a disparate impact? Justice White's point may be that only taller, heavier women are interested in prison guard positions in the first place, so that there is no actual (as opposed to theoretic) impact by the employer's policy. Given that people who know of the rule and do not meet it would be unlikely to apply, it seems unlikely that looking at actual applicants would measure the impact. But is the Court correct in deciding that the national statistics suffice? The assumption seems to be that a cross-section of the population will apply for this job. Presumably, the employer could prove the contrary, but does this assumption effectively shift the burden of proof to defendant?

2. *Back to General Population Statistics. Dothard* approves general population statistics, as opposed to applicant flow, but the Court has not been consistent as to

the use of general population statistics. In *New York City Transit Auth. v. Beazer*, 440 U.S. 568 (1979), plaintiffs invoked Title VII to challenge an employer rule disqualifying people taking methadone, a drug used in the treatment of heroin addiction. Plaintiffs showed that 81 percent of all Transit Authority (TA) employees suspected of drug use were black or Hispanic and, less certainly, that between 62 percent and 65 percent of all methadone-maintained people in New York City were black or Hispanic. The Supreme Court rejected that challenge in part because of the inadequate showing of impact.

> [R]espondents have only challenged the rule to the extent that it is construed to apply to methadone users, and [the statistics about overall drug use tell] us nothing about the racial composition of the employees suspected of using methadone. Nor does the record give us any information about the number of black, Hispanic, or white persons who were dismissed for using methadone. . . . We do not know . . . how many of these persons [in methadone maintenance programs] ever worked or sought to work for TA. This statistic therefore reveals little if anything about the racial composition of the class of TA job applicants and employees receiving methadone treatment.

Id. at 585. Was the majority unduly severe in its statistical analysis of the showing of impact? Could an inference be drawn that these statistics indicated a racial impact for the methadone rule? The lesson seems to be that plaintiffs must introduce data that focus more directly on the effect of defendant's use of the challenged rule. The Court suggests that the relevant group for deriving impact statistics is the Transit Authority's applicant pool. But, as in *Dothard*, wouldn't individuals on methadone who are aware of the TA's methadone restriction not bother to apply?

3. *The Problem of Small Numbers.* We saw in *Watson*, see p. 232, that only some 80 employees worked at the bank, and Justice O'Connor suggested that the numbers might be too small to support a finding of impact at the bank. The "small numbers" difficulty can be a serious obstacle to the proof of disparate impact, but it is not always fatal. In *Pietras v. Board of Fire Commrs.*, 180 F.3d 468 (2d Cir. 1999), plaintiff challenged a physical agility test used by a fire department, the most difficult part of which was the "charged hose drag," which involved dragging a 280-pound, water-filled hose over a distance of 150 feet in four minutes. Of the candidates, 63 out of 66 males passed (95%), but only 4 out of 7 females (57%). Acknowledging the small numbers, the court nevertheless upheld a finding of disparate impact based on expert testimony "of the practices of other fire departments." Liability then attached because of no evidence that the physical ability test was job-related. *See also EEOC v. Steamship Clerks Union, Local 1066*, 48 F.3d 594, 605 (1st Cir. 1995) ("the sample, though small, is telling. Given the unique factual mosaic from which the statistical scaffolding hangs, and the logical force of the conclusion that the numbers suggest, it would blink reality to conclude that a serious 'sample size' problem lurks here").

As you may have guessed, the "small numbers" problem is a statistical one. There was no doubt in *Petras* (or probably in *Watson*), that the challenged practices had a disparate impact on the groups of employees in question: the 95% to 57% established that. But it was not so clear that, applied over all applicants, those percentages would hold up. Statistically, the probability that these results could have happened by chance was too high. But *Petras* holds that other evidence can reinforce a statistical showing and establish disparate impact.

4. *Defendant's Rebuttal of, or Defense Against, Impact Showing.* In *Espinoza v. Farah Mfg. Co.*, 414 U.S. 86, 93 (1973), the Court allowed the employer to rebut plaintiff's showing that a rule requiring American citizenship had a disparate impact

on those born outside the United States by presenting statistics that the rule did not have that effect at its plant:

> [P]ersons of Mexican ancestry make up more than 96% of the employees at the company's San Antonio division, and 97% of those doing the work for which Mrs. Espinoza applied. While statistics such as these do not automatically shield an employer from a charge of unlawful discrimination, the plain fact of the matter is that Farah does not discriminate against persons of Mexican national origin with respect to employment in the job Mrs. Espinoza sought.

See also Newark Branch, NAACP v. City of Bayonne, 134 F.3d 113 (3d Cir. 1998) (no error in refusing to enjoin residency requirement when statistics showed that, during the years when the rule was suspended, representation of minorities had decreased rather than increased).

Section 703(k)(1)(B)(ii) now provides that, if the employer "demonstrates that a specific employment practice does not cause the disparate impact, the [employer] shall not be required to demonstrate that such practice is required by business necessity." This subsection (ii) follows subsection (i), which creates the bottom-line exception to the general rule of §703(k)(1)(A)(i) that plaintiffs must point to a particular employment practice that the employer uses that causes a disparate impact. Thus, it is clear that subsection (ii) creates an affirmative defense to a prima facie case based on bottom line statistics pursuant to subsection (i).

The broader question is whether subsection (ii) also creates an affirmative defense the general rule of §703(k)(1)(A)(i), that is, where the plaintiff identifies a particular employment practice used by the employer that causes a disparate impact, can the employer prevail by demonstrating that the practice does not cause the impact? The argument against applying the subsection (ii) affirmative defense to this is that the burden of persuasion on the same point — whether the challenged practice causes a disparate impact — would then be on both parties. A response is that these two provisions, when read together, first require the plaintiff to carry the burden of persuasion that the employer used a practice that causes a disparate impact, which burden can be satisfied with national statistics as in *Dothard* and *Griggs*. Once the plaintiff satisfies that burden, the employer may prevail by proving the affirmative defense created by §703(k)(1)(B)(ii), as the employer did in *Espinoza*, that its own use of the practice did not cause a disparate impact. Note, however, that, even if such employer proof is not an affirmative defense, it clearly can operate as a rebuttal to the plaintiff's case of disparate impact.

PROBLEM 3.2

The Naperville police department chief wants to replace the traditional police revolver used as standard equipment with the much more powerful Smith & Wesson Model 59 service revolver. The Model 59 is very powerful and is quite large, with a wide hand grip. National data show that over 50 percent of all women and about 10 percent of all men would be unable to handle the gun because of the size of the hand grip. Assume the police chief asks you if there would be any legal problem with the department adopting the Model 59. What more facts would you like to know before you render an opinion? Could you recommend that the department take any steps before requiring that the Model 59 be used by all department officers that might help insulate the department from disparate impact liability?

c.   The Quantum of Impact

Section 703(k)(1)(A)(i) requires plaintiff to prove that the practice she challenges "causes a disparate impact," but it does not define "disparate" in terms of the quantum of impact that suffices. Obviously, to show impact, it is necessary to compare the impact on the protected group with the impact on others. Thus, in *Peace v. Wellington*, 211 Fed. Appx. 352 (6th Cir. 2006), the fact that 3 of 4 African-American police corporals who took a test for promotion to sergeant flunked does not make out disparate impact without showing data about the performance of the whites who took the test. But what if the plaintiffs in *Peace* had shown that whites passed at 90%? Would the comparison between 75% and 90% carry the plaintiff's burden? *See also Smith v. Xerox Corp.*, 196 F.3d 358, 369 (2d Cir. 1999) ("In some workforces, a disparate impact might well be actionable if older workers were retained at 88.79% of the rate for younger workers, but not if the comparison were 96.69%"). One effort to quantify this is the EEOC's 80% (or four/fifths) rule treated below.

This question actually involves two issues. The first is the "small numbers" problem we encountered in Note 3. Some circuits require statistical significance to make out a prima facie case. In *Mems v. City of St. Paul*, 224 F.3d 735 (8th Cir. 2000), the court found that the sample size ranging from 3 to 7 was too small to be statistically significant. While this can be a serious problem, other courts have been willing to find other proof sufficient when too few employees were directly affected. See Note 3. And we saw in Chapter 2 on Systemic Disparate Treatment that statistical significance, while probative, is not necessary. See p. 150. Or are different rules appropriate for the two theories because systemic treatment cases can bolster statistical proof by other evidence of intentional discrimination while the sole question in disparate impact is the impact?

Another question, however, goes not to whether there is an impact but rather the *amount* of impact. The Uniform Guidelines on Employee Selection Procedures, 29 C.F.R. § 1607.4D (2007), adopted by federal civil rights enforcement agencies, including the EEOC, create a standard of the impact necessary to trigger enforcement efforts:

> A selection rate for any race, sex, or ethnic group which is less than four-fifths (4/5) (or eighty percent) of the rate for the group with the highest rate will generally be regarded by the Federal enforcement agencies as evidence of adverse impact, while a greater than four-fifths rate will generally not be regarded by Federal enforcement agencies as evidence of adverse impact.

In other words, the agencies will not challenge an impact that is not substantial. *See Watson v. Ft. Worth Bank & Trust*, 487 U.S. 977, 995 n. 3 (1988) (these Guidelines have adopted an enforcement rule under which adverse impact will not ordinarily be inferred unless the members of a particular race, sex, or ethnic group are selected at a rate that is less than four-fifths of the rate at which the group with the highest rate is selected. 29 CFR § 1607.4(D) (1987) . . . , and it has not provided more than a rule of thumb for the courts). *Isabel v. City of Memphis*, 404 F.3d 404, 412 (6th Cir. 2005) rejected the claim that compliance with the four-fifths rule is a safe harbor from a disparate impact claim. And *Bew v. City of Chicago*, 252 F.3d 891 (7th Cir. 2001), found impact even though 98.24% of the African-American test takers passed compared with 99.96% of the whites, meaning that the four-fifths rule was not violated. The challenged test had a disparate impact because a statistically significant correlation existed between race and test failure. The fact that the difference in magnitude between the pass rates was so small was not relevant because the difference was statistically significant.

To understand the concern, suppose the difference is real but quite small. Test A yields two curves of performance, one for men and one for women. There is obviously a gender impact, the female median being 20 points lower than the male median. If a passing score is set at the male median, 75, half the men would be qualified, but a much smaller percentage of the women would be. The curves in Figure 3.1 might reflect something like the situation in *Dothard*.*

Suppose, however, that Test B yields disparate gender impact, but with a much smaller margin, such as that shown in Figure 3.2. Given the fact that the whole universe is represented, there is no doubt as to the gender correlation, but the impact adverse to women is slight. If a passing score is set at the male median — so that 50 percent of males are hired — 49 percent of females will also qualify; the impact is very real but the difference is so small as to not justify treating it as sufficiently disparate to count.

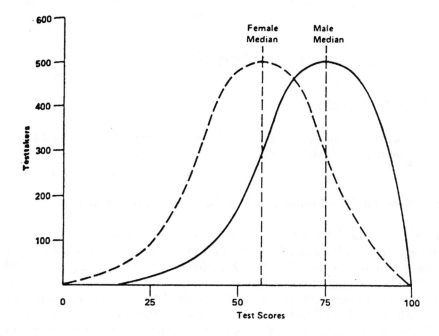

Figure 3.1

---

* The curves have been drawn to reflect equal numbers of test-takers for purposes of clarity of presentation. This is likely to be true in a significant number of sex discrimination cases. In the typical race case, however, the universe of blacks is smaller than the universe of whites. Thus, the black curve will be smaller than the white curve.

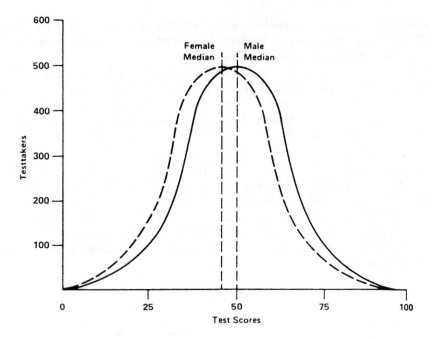

Figure 3.2

2. Defendant's Options

There are five rebuttal possibilities available to the employer to respond to a case of disparate impact discrimination.

a. Rebuttal: The Employer's Use Does Not Cause Impact

Even before the 1991 Act, the employer could try to undermine the plaintiff's showing of a prima facie case by introducing evidence that the data plaintiff relied on was flawed. In *Council 31, AFSCME v. Doherty*, 169 F.3d 1068 (7th Cir. 1999), the plaintiff presented evidence that an employer's layoff criteria had a disparate impact on black employees. The court allowed the defendant to rebut the impact by showing that the plaintiff had not accounted for all persons who were subject to the challenged practice, and, when all persons were accounted for, no disparate impact existed. This rebuttal possibility does not change the basic rule that the plaintiff has the burden of persuasion to prove a prima facie case. Section 703(k)(1)(A)(i) states the general rule that "a complaining party demonstrates that a respondent uses a particular employment practice that causes a disparate impact," with "demonstrate" being separately defined in §701(m) as "meets the burdens of production and persuasion."

Section 703(k)(1)(B)(ii), however, appears to create an affirmative defense that imposes on the employer the burden of persuasion in one situation: when the plaintiff uses bottom line data under the "incapable of separation for analysis" heading, the defendant may seek to prove that "a specific employment practice does not cause the disparate impact."

Since the burden of persuasion cannot be on both the plaintiff and the defendant on the same issue, the apparent tension between the two requirements must be resolved by differentiating the types of proof used by plaintiff to establish the prima facie case. If the plaintiff makes out a prima facie case based on data showing the experience of the employer's use of the challenged practice, the employer may rebut such a showing by challenging the accuracy of the evidence that plaintiff relied upon. The defendant, presumably, does not carry the burden of persuasion when it merely undermines the evidence the plaintiff uses to establish a prima facie case. However, if the plaintiff establishes disparate impact by national data or with the experience of other employers, §701(k)(1)(B)(ii) then accords the employer an affirmative defense (as to which it has the burden of persuasion) that its *own* use of the practice does not have a disparate impact.

b. Business Necessity and Job Relatedness

EL v. SOUTHEASTERN PENNSYLVANIA
TRANSPORTATION AUTHORITY
479 F.3d 232 (3d Cir. 2007)

AMBRO, Circuit Judge.

This appeal arises out of a Title VII action alleging employment discrimination based on race. Plaintiff Douglas El claims that the Southeastern Pennsylvania Transportation Authority (SEPTA) unnecessarily disqualifies applicants because of prior criminal convictions — a policy that he argues has a disparate impact on minority applicants because they are more likely than white applicants to have convictions on their records.

The Court granted summary judgment, however, in favor of SEPTA, concluding that it had borne the burden of proving that its policy is consistent with business necessity. Though we have reservations about such a policy in the abstract, we affirm here because El did not present any evidence to rebut SEPTA's expert testimony.

I. FACTUAL BACKGROUND AND PROCEDURAL HISTORY

In January 2000, King Paratransit Services, Inc. conditionally hired El to drive paratransit buses. The position involves providing door-to-door and curb-to-curb transportation service for people with mental and physical disabilities. King subcontracted with SEPTA to provide paratransit services on SEPTA's behalf. King's subcontract with SEPTA disallowed hiring anyone with, among other things, a violent criminal conviction. Accordingly, among the conditions stipulated in El's offer was successful completion of a criminal background check. Within the first few weeks of El's employment, King discovered that El had a 40-year-old conviction for second-degree murder.[2] Following the terms of King's subcontract with SEPTA and El's employment offer, King terminated his employment. According to King personnel, the murder conviction was their sole reason.

As the background check revealed, El was convicted of second-degree murder in 1960. According to his testimony, the murder took place in the context of a

---

2. El actually had disclosed the conviction on his application, but King personnel apparently did not notice it until they examined the criminal background report.

gang-related fight in which the victim was shot and died. El was 15 years old at the time, and the victim was 16. El claims not to have been the triggerman, and, indeed, he was not the only person convicted of the murder, but no objective report of the circumstances appears in the record before us. Following his conviction, El served three-and-a-half years for his crime. This now 47-year-old conviction is El's only violent offense.

According to the contract in place between King and SEPTA in 2000, King was required to ensure that anyone in SEPTA service as a driver or attendant have:

> e. no record of driving under [the] influence (DUI) of alcohol or drugs, and no record of any felony or misdemeanor conviction for any crime of moral turpitude or of violence against any person(s);
> f. have no record of any conviction within the last seven (7) years for any other felony or any other misdemeanor in any category referenced below (see section F.2.10.C) [listing specific offenses], and not be on probation or parole for any such crime, no matter how long ago the conviction for such crime may be. . . .

[After being terminated, El filed a complaint with the EEOC and then sued, arguing that the policy has a disparate impact because African Americans and Hispanics were more likely to have a criminal record and thus be excluded by the policy. Because SEPTA sought and was granted summary judgment on its affirmative defense of business necessity, on which it would bear the burden of proof at trial, it had to show that it had produced enough evidence that a reasonable factfinder would be compelled to find for it.] Specious objections will not, of course, defeat a motion for summary judgment, but real questions about credibility, gaps in the evidence, and doubts as to the sufficiency of the movant's proof, will. . . .

III. DISCUSSION

A. THE BUSINESS NECESSITY DEFENSE . . .

[After *Griggs*, the] Supreme Court further developed the business necessity defense over a series of cases. In *Griggs*, it dealt with aptitude tests administered by an employer in making hiring decisions. The Court held that discriminatory employment tests must "bear a demonstrable relationship to successful performance of the jobs for which it was used." It further held that "any given requirement must have a manifest relationship to the employment in question." In *Albemarle Paper Co.*, it elaborated on the use of discriminatory tests by adopting the EEOC's determination that test results must predict or correlate with "important elements of work behavior which comprise or are relevant to the job or jobs for which candidates are being evaluated." In *Dothard*, the Court rejected height and weight criteria for hiring prison guards, holding that discriminatory requirements must "be shown to be necessary to safe and efficient job performance." The employer in that case argued that strength was an essential quality and that the height and weight criteria served as a proxy for strength. The Court rejected this argument, holding that while strength may have been an essential quality, the employer had not specified the amount of strength necessary or demonstrated any correlation between these height and weight criteria and the necessary amount thereof. In *Teal*, it held that an employer may not justify using a discriminatory test for determining promotion eligibility by also using an affirmative action system after the fact to achieve an appropriate racial balance. As the Court noted, Title VII operates not primarily to the benefit of racial or minority groups, but to ensure that individual applicants receive the consideration they are due and are not screened out by arbitrary policies or devices.

For our purposes, two aspects of these cases are noteworthy. First, the Court refused to accept bare or "common-sense"-based assertions of business necessity and instead required some level of empirical proof that challenged hiring criteria accurately predicted job performance. *Dothard* is particularly noteworthy because the Court rejected an employer's common-sense argument that prison guards must be relatively strong to justify criteria that roughly measured strength. The lesson is that employers cannot rely on rough-cut measures of employment-related qualities; rather they must tailor their criteria to measure those qualities accurately and directly for each applicant.

Second, the Court did not allow employers to rely on "more is better"-style reasoning to justify their policies. In *Griggs*, *Albemarle*, and *Dothard*, the employers argued that the challenged criteria were justified by the fact that one would naturally prefer smarter or stronger employees to less intelligent or weaker ones, and so it was of no moment that the criteria might be set a bit higher than strictly necessary. The Court held, however, that some abstract notion that more of a given quality is better is insufficient to justify a discriminatory policy under Title VII; rather, the employer must present real evidence that the challenged criteria " 'measure[s] the person for the job and not the person in the abstract.' " *Dothard* (quoting *Griggs*). . . .

Unfortunately, as numerous courts and commentators have noted, *Griggs* and its progeny did not provide a precise definition of business necessity. *See, e.g., Lanning v. Southeastern Pa. Transp. Auth.*, 181 F.3d 478, 488 (3d Cir. 1999) (*Lanning I*) (noting that the Act was so unclear that both proponents and opponents of a strict business necessity standard claimed victory); Susan S. Grover, *The Business Necessity Defense in Disparate Impact Discrimination Cases*, 30 GA. L. REV. 387, 391-93 (1996); Andrew C. Spiropoulos, *Defining the Business Necessity Defense to the Disparate Impact Cause of Action: Finding the Golden Mean*, 74 N.C. L. REV. 1479, 1520 (1996). Normally, we would look to additional legislative history to determine if it clarifies what Congress meant by business necessity. However, Congress stipulated that courts may not consider any document other than [an interpretive memorandum] as the Act's legislative history. Civil Rights Act of 1991, § 105(b) (stating that nothing other than a specified interpretive memorandum should be considered legislative history and thereby used to construe the Act). In *Lanning I and II*, we heeded Congress's instruction and looked no further than the memorandum.

While some may be skeptical of Congress's power to instruct courts what legislative history they may take into account when interpreting a statute, we need not consider anything beyond the interpretive memorandum because doing so would be unhelpful in this case.[10] Members of Congress simply could not agree on a precise

---

10. Even if we did review additional legislative history, it would not clarify the issue. In floor debate, then-Minority Leader Senator Robert Dole stated that the Act's definition of business necessity is less strict than those articulated in the initial versions of the Senate bill that eventually became the Act and the parallel House bill. 137 Cong. Rec. S 15, 472-01 (daily ed. Oct. 30, 1991) (statement of Sen. Dole). In the initial version of the Senate bill, business necessity was defined as "bear[ing] a manifest relationship" to "the performance of actual work activities required by the employer for a job or class of jobs" or "any behavior that is important to the job, but may not comprise actual work activities." S. 1745, 102d Cong. § 7 (Sep. 26, 1991). In the initial version of the House bill, business necessity was defined as "bear[ing] a significant relationship to successful performance of the job." H.R. 1, 102d Cong. § 3 (Jan. 6, 1991). A confusing aspect of the House bill is that, while it purports to overrule *Wards Cove*, the language is strikingly similar to that used in the case.

definition of business necessity; all they could agree upon was overruling *Wards Cove* and reinstating the Supreme Court's somewhat conflicting post-*Griggs* and pre-*Wards Cove* jurisprudence. Thus, our task is to be as faithful to that intent as possible.

Attempting to implement the *Griggs* standard, we have held that hiring criteria must effectively measure the "minimum qualifications for successful performance of the job in question." See *Lanning I.* This holding reflects the *Griggs/Albemarle/Dothard* rejection of criteria that are overbroad or merely general, unsophisticated measures of a legitimate job-related quality. It is also consistent with the fact that Congress continues to call the test "business necessity," not "business convenience" or some other weaker term.

However, hiring policies need not be perfectly tailored to be consistent with business necessity. As we held in *Lanning II*, employers need not set the bar so low that they consider an applicant with some, but unreasonably low, probability of successful performance. *Lanning II* ("It would clearly be unreasonable to require SEPTA applicants to score so highly on the run test that their predicted rate of [job] success be 100%. It is perfectly reasonable, however, to demand a chance of success that is better than 5% to 20%."). After all, the Supreme Court has held that Title VII never forces an employer to accept an unqualified-or even less qualified-applicant in the name of non-discrimination. *Griggs* ("Congress has not commanded that the less qualified be preferred over the better qualified simply because of minority origins."). Moreover, the Supreme Court has noted that bright-line criteria, such as aptitude tests, are legitimate and useful hiring tools so long as they accurately measure a person's qualifications. *Id.*

Putting these standards together, then, we require that employers show that a discriminatory hiring policy accurately — but not perfectly — ascertains an applicant's ability to perform successfully the job in question. In addition, Title VII allows the employer to hire the applicant most likely to perform the job successfully over others less likely to do so.

2. Applying the Defense to Criminal Conviction Policies

Prior decisions on business necessity do not directly control here. The standards set out in *Griggs* and its progeny (including the standards noted by our Court in *Lanning I* and *II*) do not parallel the facts of this case. In the cases cited above, the hiring policies at issue were tests designed or used — at least allegedly — to measure an employee's ability to perform the relevant jobs. Here, however, the hiring policy has nothing to do with the applicant's ability to drive a paratransit bus; rather, it seeks to exclude applicants who, while able to drive a bus, pose too much of a risk of potential harm to the passengers to be trusted with the job. Thus, our standard of "minimum qualifications necessary for successful performance of the job in question" is appropriate in test-score cases, but awkward here because "successful performance of the job" in the usual sense is not at issue. SEPTA could argue that successful performance of the job includes not attacking a passenger and, therefore, that the standard is still appropriate. However, the standard is worded to address ability, not risk. Yet, the issue before us is the risk that the employee will harm a passenger, and the phrase "minimum qualification" simply does not fit, as it is hard to articulate the minimum qualification for posing a low risk of attacking someone.

The only reported appellate level case to address squarely the issue of exclusions from eligibility on the basis of prior convictions is *Green v. Missouri Pac. R.R. Co.,*

523 F.2d 1290 (8th Cir. 1975). There the employer refused to hire anyone for any position who had been convicted of any offense other than a minor traffic violation. Green had applied for an office job, and he was not considered because of a previous conviction for refusing to answer the draft (after failing to qualify as a conscientious objector). The Court held that the employer's policy was too broad to be justified by business necessity.

Green, however, presented materially different facts than those before us in two respects. First, the job in Green was an office job at a corporate headquarters; it did not require the employee to be alone with and in close proximity to vulnerable members of society. The public safety concern is of more moment in our case. Second, the hiring policy in Green prevented hiring a person with any criminal conviction, "no matter how remote, insubstantial, or unrelated to [the] applicant's personal qualifications as an employee." Here, SEPTA's policy only prevents consideration of people with certain types of convictions — those that it argues have the highest and most unpredictable rates of recidivism and thus present the greatest danger to its passengers. In this context, Green was an easier case insofar as the Supreme Court has held firmly that an employer with an extremely broad exclusionary policy that fails to offer any empirical justification for it is unable to make out a successful business necessity defense, Dothard, whereas SEPTA has a narrower policy for a position in which criminal convictions are more job-related.

The EEOC has spoken to the issue in its Compliance Manual, which states that an applicant may be disqualified from a job on the basis of a previous conviction only if the employer takes into account:

> 1. The nature and gravity of the offense or offenses;
> 2. The time that has passed since the conviction and/or completion of the sentence; and
> 3. The nature of the job held or sought.

Equal Empl. Opp. Comm. Compliance Manual §605 App. The EEOC clarifies that "nature and gravity of the offense" means for employers to consider the circumstances of that offense. The EEOC's Guidelines, however, do not speak to whether an employer can take these factors into account when crafting a bright-line policy, nor do they speak to whether an employer justifiably can decide that certain offenses are serious enough to warrant a lifetime ban. SEPTA's policy arguably takes into account the sensitive nature of the job and sorts applicants by type of offense. For some offenses, it considers the time since the conviction; for others, it does not.

[The court found the EEOC's Guidelines entitled only to Skidmore deference, Skidmore v. Swift & Co., 323 U.S. 134, 140 (1944), that is whatever deference is due in light of "the thoroughness of its research and the persuasiveness of its reasoning"; the policy in question "does not substantively analyze the statute."]

Considering the dearth of authority directly on point, we believe that our standards from Lanning I and II — namely that discriminatory hiring policies accurately but not perfectly distinguish between applicants' ability to perform successfully the job in question — can be adapted to fit the context of criminal conviction policies. In a broad sense, hiring policies, such as the one at issue here, ultimately concern the management of risk. In Lanning I & II, we dealt with how employers manage the risk that applicants will be unable to perform the job in question. Here we deal with the risk that an applicant will endanger the employer's patrons. In both cases, it is impossible to measure the risk perfectly,[12] and in both cases Title VII does not ask the impossible. It does, however, as in the case of performance-related policies, require that the policy under review accurately distinguish between applicants that pose an unacceptable level of risk and those that do not.[13]

El urges us to go further and hold that Title VII prohibits any bright-line policy with regard to criminal convictions; he argues, rather, that Title VII requires that each applicant's circumstances be considered individually without reference to any bright-line rules. We decline to go so far. If a bright-line policy can distinguish between individual applicants that do and do not pose an unacceptable level of risk, then such a policy is consistent with business necessity. Whether a policy can do so is most often a question of fact that the district courts-and juries-must resolve in specific cases.[14]

3. Could a Reasonable Juror Find that SEPTA's Policy Is Not Consistent with Business Necessity?

In arguing that its policy is consistent with business necessity, SEPTA claims that it has presented evidence such that a reasonable juror must find that: (1) the job of a paratransit driver requires that the driver be in very close contact with passengers, (2) the job requires that the driver often be alone with passengers, (3) paratransit passengers are vulnerable because they typically have physical and/or mental disabilities, (4) disabled people are disproportionately targeted by sexual and violent criminals, (5) violent criminals recidivate at a high rate, (6) it is impossible to predict with a reasonable degree of accuracy which criminals will recidivate, (7) someone with a conviction for a violent crime is more likely than someone without one to commit a future violent crime irrespective of how remote in time the conviction is, and (8) SEPTA's policy is the most accurate way to screen out applicants who present an unacceptable risk.

As an initial matter, we agree with SEPTA that these facts, if proved, would be sufficient to show that its policy is consistent with business necessity, at least as it applies to a person with a violent criminal conviction like El.[15] If someone with a violent conviction presents a materially higher risk than someone without one, no matter which other factors an employer considers, then SEPTA is justified in not

---

12. As SEPTA discovered in the tragic case of paratransit driver David deSouza, even applicants with clean criminal records sometimes endanger passengers. At the time of his hire by King, deSouza had no prior criminal convictions. Nevertheless, he attacked and raped a passenger while serving as a SEPTA driver.

13. It may seem odd to speak of an acceptable level of risk in this context, given the horrors that drivers can inflict on disabled passengers, but, as the deSouza case demonstrates, some level of risk is inevitable, see *supra* note 12. SEPTA may minimize that risk to the extent reasonably possible, but whatever criteria it uses must distinguish with sufficient accuracy between those who pose that minimal level of risk and those who pose a higher level.

14. In this case, we have no occasion to hold that bright-line policies in the criminal conviction context are per se invalid. Indeed, we have upheld policies in other Title VII contexts that effectively bar an applicant from employment on the basis of a single, bright-line test result, but whatever criteria it uses must distinguish with sufficient accuracy between those who pose that minimal level of risk and those who do not. *Lanning II* (affirming SEPTA's use of a bright-line aerobic capacity test to bar applicants from employment as transit police officers).

15. It is worth noting that SEPTA also perpetually bans from paratransit employment people with convictions for crimes of moral turpitude. Because the evidence submitted has focused on violent convictions like El's, we have no occasion to determine whether SEPTA's policy may be justified as to those convicted of non-violent crimes of moral turpitude.

considering people with those convictions.[16] For example, SEPTA may be able to show that a policy excluding all violent offenders is justified by business necessity because other factors — such as age at conviction, the number of violent convictions, and/or the remoteness of that conviction — are unreliable or otherwise fail to reduce the risk to an acceptable level.

In support of its summary judgment motion, SEPTA submitted the reports of three experts. All three rely heavily on data from the Department of Justice that tracked recidivism of prisoners within three years of their release from prison. Indeed, those data show relatively high rates of recidivism in those first three years. But what about someone who has been released from prison and violence-free for 40 years? The DOJ statistics do not demonstrate that someone in this position — or anything like it — is likely to recidivate.

One of SEPTA's experts was Dr. Alfred Blumstein, a noted authority on recidivism. He stated:

> It is also the case that an individual's propensity to commit a future violent crime decreases as that individual's crime-free duration increases. That is, an individual with a prior violent conviction who has been crime-free in the community for twenty years is less likely to commit a future crime than one who has been crime-free in the community for only ten years. But neither of these individuals can be judged to be less or equally likely to commit a future violent act than comparable individuals who have no prior violent history. It is possible that those differences might be small, but making such predictions of comparable low-probability events is extremely difficult, and the criminological discipline provides no good basis for making such predictions with any assurance that they will be correct.

This statement bridges, as best it can, the gap between the three-year statistics and El's 40 year-old conviction. Because Dr. Blumstein is a duly qualified professional criminologist and because nothing in the record rebuts his statement, we must take him at his word that former violent criminals who have been crime free for many years are at least somewhat more likely than members of the general population to commit a future violent act. He notes that the difference between the probability that someone with a remote conviction and someone with no conviction will commit a future violent crime "might be small," but given the marked sensitivity of the paratransit position at issue, a small but extant difference is sufficient. It is also noteworthy that Dr. Blumstein reports that the criminological discipline is incapable of distinguishing accurately between violent criminals who are and are not likely to commit future violent crimes. In other words, he believes that SEPTA's policy distinguishes as accurately as the criminological discipline allows. Again, because we see nothing in the record rebutting this statement, we must take Dr. Blumstein at his word.

SEPTA also submitted the report of Dr. Dick Sobsey, an education psychologist. Dr. Sobsey reported that disabled people are proportionately more likely than others to be the victims of violent or sexual crimes. He further reported that employees of

16. SEPTA too heavily emphasizes the sixth alleged fact: that it is impossible to predict which criminal will recidivate. This fact, if proved, is of little use because it is also impossible to predict which non-criminal will commit a crime. What matters is the risk that the individual presents, taking into account whatever aspects of the person's criminal history are relevant. Thus, if screening out applicants with very old violent criminal convictions accurately distinguishes between those who present an unacceptable risk, then reliance on this factor is appropriate; if the criterion is inaccurate or overbroad in the case of very old convictions, then it is inappropriate for Title VII purposes.

transportation providers commit a disproportionate share of those crimes against disabled people. Like Dr. Blumstein, Dr. Sobsey claims that the strength of violent criminal activity as a predictor of future criminal activity "moderates over time but remains regardless of how much time passes." Dr. Sobsey's report, therefore, provides evidence for SEPTA's argument that paratransit positions are extraordinarily sensitive, and that screening out individuals with violent convictions — no matter how remote — is appropriate.

Thus, on this record, we have little choice but to conclude that a reasonable juror would necessarily find that SEPTA's policy is consistent with business necessity. This is not to say that we are convinced that SEPTA's expert reports are ironclad in the abstract. But El chose neither to hire an expert to rebut SEPTA's experts on the issue of business necessity nor even to depose SEPTA's experts. These choices are fatal to his claim [since there is nothing that a reasonable jury could rely on to find against SEPTA].

Had El produced evidence rebutting SEPTA's experts, this would be a different case. Had he, for example, hired an expert who testified that there is time at which a former criminal is no longer any more likely to recidivate than the average person, then there would be a factual question for the jury to resolve. Similarly, had El deposed SEPTA's experts and thereby produced legitimate reasons to doubt their credibility, there would be a factual question for the jury to resolve. Here, however, he did neither, and he suffers pre-trial judgment for it.

This inability is particularly striking given that the policy SEPTA claims it applied makes distinctions among crimes, setting apart some crimes for a lifetime ban from SEPTA employment and applying a seven-year ban to others. If the policy were developed with anything approaching the level of care that *Griggs*, *Albemarle*, and *Dothard* seem to contemplate, then we would expect that someone at SEPTA would be able to explain how it decided which crimes to place into each category, how the seven-year number was selected, and why SEPTA thought a lifetime ban was appropriate for a crime like simple assault. Almost all of El's relevant questions about the policy were met with silence from SEPTA personnel, suggesting the reasonable inference that SEPTA has no real basis for asserting that its policy accurately distinguishes between applicants that do and do not present an unacceptable level of risk.

Title VII, however, does not measure care in formulating hiring policies; rather, it requires that an employer be able to show that its policy is consistent with business necessity when challenged. Granted, the two will typically go hand-in-hand. Here, however, for all of SEPTA's apparent loose manner in formulating and defending its policy, it produced credible expert testimony that its policy accurately screened out applicants too likely to commit acts of violence against paratransit passengers. . . .

Taking all of the record evidence into account, there is no substantive evidence on which a reasonable juror could find that SEPTA's policy is inconsistent with business necessity. Summary judgment in SEPTA's favor was, therefore, appropriate. . . .

NOTES

1. *The Burden of Proof of Business Necessity.* The court in *El* defined "business necessity" as requiring "that employers show that a discriminatory hiring policy accurately — but not perfectly — ascertains an applicant's ability to perform successfully the job in question." This statement has two thrusts: one is the burden of

proof, and the other is the substantive standard. Imposing the burden of persuasion on the defendant to prove business necessity is consistent with the 1991 Amendments, but, despite the burden shift, the court upholds summary judgment for defendant.

2. *The Definition of Business Necessity.* Burdens of proof aside, *El* articulates a standard for business necessity that links the practice at issue to the accuracy of its prediction of job-related performance. If you recall from Chapter 2's discussion of the BFOQ defense to disparate treatment, *Johnson Controls* made clear the BFOQ defense is narrower, harder for a defendant to establish, than *El*'s version of business necessity.

3. *The Business Necessity Standard and* Lanning I. The court in *El* refers to two earlier decisions that also involved SEPTA. *Lanning I — Lanning v. Southeastern Pennsylvania Transportation Authority*, 181 F.3d 478 (3d Cir. 1999), involved a physical exertion test for candidates to become SEPTA transit police officers; it required them to be able to run 1.5 miles in 12 minutes. The test had a drastic impact on women: in two years, 6.7% and 12% of women passed it as compared to between 60% and 55.6% of male applicants. The court reviewed the development of the business necessity standard from *Griggs* through *Wards Cove* and then concluded that Congress had intended to reject the *Wards Cove* approach in favor of a return to *Griggs*. "[B]ecause the Act clearly chooses *Griggs* over *Wards Cove*, the Court's interpretation of the business necessity standard in *Wards Cove* does not survive the Act." 181 F.3d at 488. Looking to *Griggs* and other pre-*Wards Cove* cases, *Lanning I* summarized what the defense required in the case before it: "a discriminatory cutoff score [must] be shown to measure the minimum qualifications necessary for the successful performance of the job in question in order to survive a disparate impact challenge." It remanded to the district court for the application of that standard. If *Lanning I* is correct as to the standard, is *El* consistent with it? Is a "minimum qualification" for a paratransit driver that he or she pose *no* risk to passengers? Or perhaps that the driver pose no unavoidable risk?

4. *The Business Necessity Standard and* Lanning II. SEPTA transit police did not in fact undertake 1.5 mile runs in the performance of their jobs; in fact, the jobs rarely required any running at all. The prescribed run, however, was conceded to measure a certain level of aerobic capacity, and SEPTA's argument was that this capacity was necessary for the job. That, too, seemed doubtful since SEPTA required only new officers to meet this level; incumbent officers were encouraged, but not required, to do so. Quite literally, it was not necessary to have that aerobic capacity to work as a transit police officer. Nevertheless, SEPTA introduced further testimony on remand comparing the performance of transit police based on their times running the 1.5 miles. In *Lanning II*, 308 F.3d 286, 290 (3d Cir. 2002), the court upheld the test. "The study found that individuals who passed the run test had a success rate on the job standard ranging from 70% to 90%. The success rate of individuals who failed the run test ranged from 5% to 20%." Given that SEPTA wanted to improve the fitness and "crime fighting ability" of its police and that "the business necessity standard takes public safety into consideration," the test satisfied the business necessity standard, especially since women applicants could undertake aerobic training that would significantly improve their chances of passing it. *See also IBEW v. Miss. Power & Light Co.*, 442 F.3d 313 (5th Cir. 2006) (increasing a cut-off score was a business necessity in light of evidence that a passing applicant had a 50% chance of developing into an above-average worker, as compared with 39% chance for passing applicants under the prior cut-off). *Lanning II* seems to hold that a selection device

that measurably and substantially increases the likelihood of job success is a business necessity. But, accepting SEPTA's numbers, the increased success rate was very substantial. *El*, in contrast, does not quantify, or even suggest ranges, for the increased likelihood of violence at issue.

5. *Applying the Synthesis in* El. We have seen that synthesis that the *El* court finds between *Lanning I* and *II* is that the challenged test "accurately — but not perfectly — ascertains an applicant's ability to perform successfully." Assuming that is a fair synthesis, does the court in *El* apply it correctly? The chance that any paratransit driver will attack a passenger is very remote, without regard to the driver's criminal record. Even assuming some (slightly?) increased risk of a driver with a criminal record engaging in such an unlikely occurrence, does business necessity mean much if such a rule is valid?

6. *More is Better?* There has been recurrent debate about whether "more is better" in business necessity determinations. In other words, the question has been not merely whether some increase in performance (or, in *El*, some decrease in risk) is sufficient or whether some requirement of quantitative substantiality is required. *See Lanning v. SEPTA*, 308 F.3d 286, 292 (3d Cir. 2002) ("We are not saying . . . that 'more is better.' While, of course, a higher aerobic capacity will translate into better field performance — at least as to many job tasks which entail physical capability — to set an unnecessarily high cutoff score would contravene *Griggs*."). Isn't *El* saying exactly that — more (safety) is better? Why does setting an unnecessarily rigorous criterion for hiring not also contravene *Griggs*?

7. *Business Necessity and SEPTA's Public Image.* Footnote 12 in *El* refers to the rape and murder by a paratransit driver of an 80 pound passenger who suffered from cerebral palsy. That driver had no prior criminal record. Shouldn't that support denying rather than granting summary judgment to SEPTA? Or does the murder of a patron by one of its bus drivers support SEPTA doing something, even though this rule would not have prevented deSouza, the murderer, from being hired? SEPTA's rule at least makes it appear to be taking patron safety seriously. In *New York City Transit Auth. v. Beazer*, 440 U.S. 568 (1979), the Court appeared to strain disparate impact theory in order to uphold a rule prohibiting hiring workers who were on methadone maintenance during a period in which the Court was otherwise applying the theory robustly. Is "safety" a hot button issue such that its invocation is likely to skew judicial analysis?

8. *Summary Judgment for Defendant.* The evidence of SEPTA's experts does appear to support a finding that someone convicted of a violent crime is more likely than someone who was never convicted of a violent crime to attack a paratransit passenger. But to grant summary judgment to the defendant on that basis, when the defendant bears the burden of persuasion on that issue, requires that showing to be so clear that no reasonable factfinder could find against defendant. Remember *St. Mary's Honor Center v. Hicks* from Chapter 1, p. 59, where the factfinder concluded that personal animosity, not discrimination and not plaintiff's rule violations, motivated plaintiff's discharge. Yet the only evidence in the record was that there was no personal animosity between plaintiff and his supervisor. In *El*, however, the court says the jury would have to believe defendant's evidence because plaintiff did not counter it. Either *El* or *Hicks* is wrong. The general rule is that a factfinder is not required to accept as fact evidence just because it is not contested. *E.g.*, *Blodgett v. Comm'r*, 394 F.3d 1030, 1036 (8th Cir. 2005) (noting that, "A fact finder may choose to disbelieve evidence on its face even without evidence to the contrary"). Is the

court here still applying the view of the majority in *Wards Cove* that defendant does not carry the burden of persuasion on business necessity?

9. *Judge Trial.* Maybe the explanation for summary judgment in *El* is simpler. Although the 1991 Civil Rights Act amended Title VII to provide a right to a jury trial in disparate treatment cases, it did not do so for disparate impact cases, which means that juries are either not used at all or are "advisory." See Chapter 7. So do not be confused by the recurrent references in *El* to the "reasonable jury." But, given that this would be a judge trial, why does the court talk of the reasonable juror here? Is it that the standard for deciding whether material issues of fact exist is the same whether the case would ultimately be decided by a judge or by a jury? In any event, could *El* be explained as a kind of judicial short-cut: the trial judge (i.e., the individual who would act as fact finder were this case to be tried) granted summary judgment to SEPTA. That's a pretty good indication of what would have happened if the case had been tried, which perhaps means that the arguments in Note 7 are of more theoretical than practical interest.

10. *No Battle of the Experts.* Plaintiff lost his case because of the experts — his failure to call any experts for his side and his failure even to depose SEPTA's experts. An expert on one side almost always begets an expert witness on the other. Why didn't plaintiff hire experts to counter defendant's experts? The answer may be the economics of practice: plaintiffs could not afford to hire experts. But why did the plaintiffs' lawyers not depose defendant's witnesses? Plaintiff need not have its own experts in order to depose the other party's experts. What questions could be asked of the experts to help plaintiffs keep a material issue of fact alive in order to avoid summary judgment?

Dr. Blumstein, the key witness, said in his report that "neither of these individuals [those with a history of violent crime] can be judged to be less or equally likely to commit a future violent act than comparable individuals who have no prior violent history." This is a pretty cautious statement. In any event what supports that opinion? The court indicates that none of the data backing up the experts' opinions bore on that question. Is it just a hunch or is it based on broader background information known to professional criminologist? The court says that "Dr. Blumstein reports that the criminological discipline is incapable of distinguishing accurately between violent criminals who are and are not likely to commit future violent crimes." Doesn't this undermine the conclusion that criminology supports any conclusion about recidivism many years after a conviction?

11. *Defects in Process Irrelevant.* Plaintiffs did depose SEPTA management employees, and they all testified that they did not know why SEPTA had adopted the bright line rule challenged in the case. Do you agree that the lack of procedural regularity is irrelevant to the ultimate determination of business necessity? In *Albemarle Paper Co. v. Moody,* 422 U.S. 405, 411 (1975), the Court critiqued what it described as an "eve of trial" effort to validate a test that had not been validated on adoption; nevertheless, the Court did not indicate that a failure to validate before adopting a selection device would be fatal.

12. *Arrest Records and Discrimination.* There is some reason to believe that employer policies regarding conviction records do not have the adverse effects on black employment that one might expect from *El.* For example, Harry J. Holzer & Steven Raphael, *Perceived Criminality, Criminal Background Checks, and the Racial Hiring Practices of Employers,* 49 J. LAW & ECON. 451, 473 (2006), find that employers who

perform criminal background checks are more likely to hire black applicants than employers that do not. They believe that the potential adverse consequence of such checks in terms of the likelihood of hiring African Americans are more than offset by the positive effect of eliminating "statistical discrimination." Even if this is true, it does not alter the fact that some individuals, like El, are excluded by the policy. And *Teal* would allow El to attack this screening device, even if the bottom line is that blacks are proportionately represented among SEPTA paratransit drivers.

13. *"Job Related and Consistent with Business Necessity."* The Supreme Court jurisprudence on the affirmative defenses to disparate impact discrimination had used both the concept of "job related" and "business necessity." They are not necessarily identical and, until the enactment of § 703(k), it was unclear whether defendant had to establish both in order to prevail. The plain meaning of the new statute conjoins them, suggesting that defendant must prove that its challenged practice is both job related and consistent with "business necessity." The *El* opinion seems to blend them: the policy is a business necessity since it sufficiently predicts job performance on at least one axis — reducing the risk of driver attacks on passengers. Passenger safety goes to the essence of the job (to borrow a phrase from BFOQ law), but perhaps not all job requirements are so obviously important. Perhaps the business necessity standard requires not only that the criterion in question be job related but that job requirements be defined in terms of "important business goals." *See* Linda Lye, Comment, *Title VII, Tangled Tale: The Erosion and Confusion of Disparate Impact and the Business Necessity Defense*, 19 BERKELEY J. EMP. & LAB. L. 315, 355-56 (1998).

14. *Who was the Employer?* You may have noticed that Mr. El was not formally employed by SEPTA but rather by a subcontractor, King Limousine, that was required to enforce SEPTA's policy. King was clearly El's employer, and its contract with SEPTA would not excuse it from a violation if the policy were illegal. But the court treats SEPTA as El's employer. Reconsider this scenario when you reach Chapter 5A, Coverage.

PROBLEM 3.3

Rath Packing had a rule prohibiting the employment of spouses of current employees. The plaintiff has succeeded in establishing that the no-spouse rule has a disparate impact on the employment of women. Rath asserts that the rule is necessary to promote optimum production and employee performance because spousal relationships in the workplace create situations that are problematic for the employer and employees — problems of efficiency, productivity, and ease of management. Rath says that its no-spouse rule is directed at problems that occurred in the past when married couples worked at Rath. The problems include dual absenteeism, vacation scheduling, supervision, and pressure to hire spouses. During a three-year period for which information on absenteeism is available, employees with spouses working at Rath exhibited a lower absentee rate than did those without spouses working there. Rath was able to point to one incident of habitual dual absenteeism, which was perceived by Rath management as having a significant disruptive effect on plant operations. Vacation scheduling for spouses impacted on the efficiency of Rath's production until Rath instituted a policy allowing employees to trade vacation time. Since the new policy went into effect, actual scheduling problems have been reduced significantly, but spouses remain dissatisfied with the procedure, and disgruntled fellow workers often apply for vacation times sought by less senior spousal employees in order to prevent couples from securing a joint vacation. Rath cites one instance where spousal supervision resulted in complaints of favoritism to and harassment of the supervised spouse. Is the no-spouse rule justified by business necessity? *See EEOC v. Rath Packing Co.*, 787 F.2d 318 (8th Cir. 1986).

3. Alternative Employment Practices

Early disparate impact cases, particularly *Albemarle Paper Co. v. Moody*, 422 U.S. 405, 425 (1975), described the litigation structure of a disparate impact case as including a plaintiff's surrebuttal, even if the employer proves the challenged practice is justified as job-related and consistent with business necessity:

> If an employer does then meet the burden of proving that its tests are "job related," it remains open to the complaining party to show that other tests or selection devices, without a similarly undesirable racial effect, would also serve the employer's legitimate interest in "efficient and trustworthy workmanship." Such a showing would be evidence that the employer was using its tests merely as a "pretext" for discrimination.

It was not clear whether "pretext" was used as a state-of-mind concept, as in *McDonnell Douglas*, or merely as a kind of shorthand for a "less restrictive alternative" analysis, but. the Civil Rights Act of 1991 resolved this problem. While a plaintiff presumably can always prevail by establishing intent to discriminate, "pretext" is not a formal part of disparate impact analysis.

Rather, the new statute adds §703(k)(1)(A) to Title VII. We have already discussed the first prong of that analysis when plaintiff proves the employer uses a particular employment practice with a disparate impact, and the employer fails to establish job relation and business necessity. §703(k)(1)(A)(i). But a disparate impact violation also exists when, despite the employer's successful proof of job relation and business necessity, the plaintiff "makes the demonstration described in subparagraph C with respect to an alternative employment practice and the [employer] refuses to adopt such alternative employment practice." §703(k)(1)(A)(ii). Subparagraph (C), in turn, defines the plaintiff's surrebutal burden as in "accordance with the law as it existed on June 4, 1989, with respect to the concept of 'alternative employment practice.'" The Court's decision in *Wards Cove* was issued on June 5, 1989, suggesting that Congress meant "alternative employment practice" to embrace the law prior to *Wards Cove*, as it had explicitly provided with respect to business necessity and job relatedness.

So far, so good, but it was *Wards Cove* that first spoke of "alternative business practices" with a less discriminatory impact. Further, that case viewed the failure to adopt such alternatives as raising doubts about the employer's intent. On June 4, 1989, that is, prior to *Wards Cove*, the closest phrase to "alternative employment practices" was Justice O'Connor's plurality opinion in *Watson v. Fort Worth Bank & Trust*, 487 U.S. 977 (1988), which had permitted the plaintiff to demonstrate less discriminatory "alternative selection devices" in response to the defendant's business necessity showing. Justice O'Connor went on to note that "[f]actors such as the cost or other burdens of proposed alternative selection devices are relevant in determining whether they would be equally as effective as the challenged practice in serving the employer's legitimate business goals." *Id.* at 998.

ADAMS v. CITY OF CHICAGO
469 F.3d. 609 (7th Cir. 2006)

MANION, Circuit Judge

. . . I.

Chicago employs approximately 10,000 sworn law enforcement officials, including 8,000 police officers and 1,200 sergeants. Sergeants supervise the officers, and lieutenants, in turn, supervise the sergeants. Chicago's methods for promoting officers up these ranks has proven to be a contentious issue that has spawned litigation over the past several decades.

Responding to the continuing controversy over promotions, Chicago's mayor appointed a panel in 1990 to make recommendations concerning future promotions. Based on those recommendations, Chicago hired an outside consultant to create a promotional examination. In the present suit, black and Hispanic officers challenge the resulting 1994 examination used to promote officers to sergeants and the promotions made based on the examination scores. . . . The parties agree that this examination and ranking had a disparate impact on minorities. Chicago made promotions to sergeant based on this ranking in August 1994, March 1996, and, relevant here, on February 22, 1997, before retiring the promotional list. . . .

As the litigation continued, the mayor appointed a task force to make recommendations for the promotional process. The task force issued its report on January 16, 1997, which included a recommendation that, in the future, thirty percent of promotions to sergeant be based upon merit, with the promotional tests used to assure "a minimum level of competence." Merit refers to the officers' on-the-job performance, as rated by their supervisors. Merit does not necessarily correlate with performance on the examination. Chicago did not follow this recommendation in making its February 22, 1997 promotions just over one month later.

Chicago administered its first written examination for police officers over a century ago in 1894. It did not make promotions from officer to sergeant based on merit until after the task force's recommendations in 1998. Nonetheless, the officers submit that Chicago could have and should have instituted a merit component for promoting officers to sergeants. The officers point out that, beginning in 1989, the City used merit to fill twenty percent of D-2 positions. D-2 positions retain the rank of police officers, but function as detectives, youth officers, and gang crimes specialists. Furthermore, the officers note that pursuant to the task force's recommendations, Chicago made thirty percent of its promotions from officer to sergeant and from sergeant to lieutenant based on merit beginning in 1998. Since Chicago considered merit in appointing D-2 positions and lieutenants, and since the panel recommended merit considerations for prospective sergeant promotions, the officers argue that Chicago could have used merit in making thirty percent of the promotions to sergeants in 1997. They claim that this consideration would have been an equally valid, less discriminatory method of promotion and that Chicago's failure to consider merit therefore violated Title VII. . . .

II. . . .

At the outset, we address the district court's exclusion of evidence of the 1998 promotions, which provided that thirty percent of the promotions be based on merit.

Since "decisions regarding the admission and exclusion of evidence are peculiarly within the competence of the district court," we review the district court's "rulings on motions in limine for an abuse of discretion." As noted, the district court reasoned that the later promotions to a different rank were irrelevant to determining the available methods for sergeant promotions in 1994, and also analogized the changes in promotional methods to subsequent remedial measures that should be excluded under Federal Rule of Evidence 407. The officers contest these rulings on appeal.

Rule 407 provides that "[w]hen, after an injury or harm allegedly caused by an event, measures are taken that, if taken previously, would have made the injury or harm less likely to occur, evidence of the subsequent measures is not admissible to prove negligence, culpable conduct, a defect in a product, a defect in a product's design, or a need for a warning or instruction." We have previously noted that "[t]he purpose of Rule 407 is to promote safety by removing the disincentive to take post-accident safety measures that would exist if the accident victim could introduce evidence of these measures on the issue of the defendant's liability." *Probus v. K-Mart Inc.*, 794 F.2d 1207, 1210 (7th Cir. 1986). The plain language of this rule does not readily apply to disparate impact claims, which are not naturally described as "an injury or harm allegedly caused by an event." Even if we were to apply Rule 407, our analysis of this disparate impact claim requires us to address the availability of an alternative promotional method, as will be discussed below. A subsequently enacted method bears on the availability of the alternative method at an earlier time. Because we must discuss the availability of an alternative method, this situation falls within the ambit of the exception contained in Rule 407, which explicitly "does not require the exclusion of evidence of subsequent remedial measures when offered for another purpose, such as proving . . . feasibility of precautionary measures." Since another purpose is at issue here, Rule 407 is an improper basis for the exclusion of the 1998 promotional method.

The district court also excluded this evidence based on relevancy, concluding that "evidence of [the City's] promotion practices well after the promotions at issue is irrelevant to the issue of what information/alternatives were available when the disputed promotions were made." In addressing hiring practices, the Sixth Circuit has explained that "in proving the existence of a viable alternative hiring procedure, the court should consider evidence that the plaintiff might introduce on a variety of factors. Certainly any subsequent practices adopted by the company would be relevant." *Chrisner v. Complete Auto Trans., Inc.*, 645 F.2d 1251, 1263 (6th Cir. 1981). We agree that evidence of subsequent procedures may be relevant to proving the availability of a procedure at an earlier time. Consequently, the district court abused its discretion in excluding this evidence. Even considering this evidence, however, the officers fail to show that Chicago had an opportunity to adopt an alternative available method for evaluating the merit of officers seeking promotion to sergeants before the promotions were made in 1997. . . .

Chicago concedes that the 1994 promotional examination, the employment practice at issue, had a disparate impact on minority officers. Having established the disparate impact, "the burden shifts to the City to demonstrate that the promotion process is 'job related' and 'consistent with business necessity.'" The officers concede that the examination was job related and consistent with business necessity in the wake of *Bryant v. City of Chicago*, 200 F.3d 1092 (7th Cir. 2000), which validated a similarly constructed examination for promotions from sergeant to lieutenant. Thus, "the burden shifts back to the plaintiff to prove that there was another available method of evaluation which was equally valid and less discriminatory that the employer refused to use."

We therefore consider whether the officers meet this burden. The officers propose as an alternative that Chicago could have made thirty percent of the 1997 promotions based on merit. To succeed with this claim, this alternative "must be available, equally valid and less discriminatory." *Allen* [*v. City of Chicago*, 351 F.3d 306, 312 (7th Cir. 2003)] (citing *Bryant*). Thus, to prevail, the officers must show that making the thirty percent of the promotions to sergeant based on merit "would be of substantially equal validity" as promotions based solely on the 1994 sergeant examination, and that including such merit promotions "would be less discriminatory than" use of the examination alone. In other words, "the officers effectively bear the burden of establishing that the last officer promoted [in the proposed] merit-based selection process would be roughly as qualified as the officer with the [ ] lowest score on the" 1994 examination who was slated to be promoted. Most critical to this case, "the statutory scheme requires plaintiffs to demonstrate a viable alternative and give the employer an opportunity to adopt it." Disparate impact, then, requires the officers to demonstrate that Chicago "refuse[d] to adopt such alternative employment practice." 42 U.S.C. § 2000e-2(k)(1)(A)(ii).

In subsequent litigation related to the 1998 promotional examination, Chicago agreed "that merit-based promotions at the thirty percent level are of substantial equal validity as assessment-based promotions." *Allen*. Even if we were to apply this concession in this case, the officers have not shown that a process for evaluating officers on their merit for promotions to sergeant was available in 1997 or that Chicago refused to adopt this alternative earlier.[2] Without an available method for Chicago to adopt, the officers' claims fail. We will explain.

No procedure for evaluating the merit of potential sergeants existed at the time of the contested 1997 promotions.[3] In fact, when the consultant created the 1994 examination, on which the 1997 promotions were based, Chicago had never considered merit for promotions to sergeant in the 100 years after written exams were instituted for the police officers. The parties also agreed that as of February 22, 1997, the date of the contested promotions, "the City had never developed, and had never had developed for it, a mechanism or procedure for merit promotions to the rank of police sergeant that had ever been validated." The lack of a validated procedure is significant, since, as the expert who created the examination testified, it is difficult to obtain objective, reliable merit ratings from supervisors in a litigious climate where "they may be accused of favoritism, bias, perhaps even discrimination" based on the ratings.

The subsequent January 16, 1997, task force report did recommend the use of merit in future promotions to sergeant, perhaps in part due to the undisputed disparate impact of the 1994 examination. This recommendation, however, was

---

2. We agree with Judge Williams' statement that "[a] reasonable alternative is not unavailable simply because the defendant has not completed its own inquiry into the viability of the alternative." As the remainder of this opinion explains, however, after a thorough search, we find the record to be devoid of evidence that the City could have feasibly developed and applied a valid merit selection method for promotions to sergeant during the month between the recommendation of merit selection and the promotions at issue. This remains plaintiffs' burden to demonstrate.

3. The vice chairman of the mayor's 1990 panel testified that, before the creation of the 1994 examination at issue, the minority police officer organizations expressed "a great distrust of any subjective components of test processes, including any reliance on performance evaluations." In accordance with this submission, the panel recommended the creation of an examination by outside consultants over a defined set of materials, without merit consideration.

prospective, noting that "the criteria for merit promotions should be developed by the Superintendent and broadly distributed." After receiving the recommendation, Chicago hired another expert to develop a new promotional examination and an appropriate merit selection procedure. The expert spent months performing a job analysis of the sergeant position and developed criteria for merit selection based on an analysis of the skills necessary to the position. The resulting merit selection process involved the training of select nominators, who were then held accountable for the accuracy of their nominations, and the further review of the nominees by the Academic Selection Board and the Superintendent of the Chicago Police Department. This process, from recommendation through implementation, spanned about nineteen months. Merit was then used in making the August 1998 sergeant promotions. To demonstrate that merit should have been used in the 1997 sergeant promotions, the officers bear the burden of demonstrating that a valid merit selection process was available on February 22, 1997, only one month after the task force recommended considering merit and before the development of appropriate criteria and process, and that Chicago refused to adopt it.

To meet this burden, the officers submit that merit evaluations could have been implemented sooner, since merit was already used in selecting the D-2 positions. The task force did suggest in January 1997 using "the existing merit selection process for detectives as a model" for sergeant promotions. Nothing in the record, however, indicates that the D-2 process could be adopted in toto for sergeants. Both the D-2 and sergeant positions were filled by police officers. Unlike the D-2 positions, however, the sergeant positions were supervisory. Thus, the merit selection process needed to discern and evaluate supervisory attributes in the non-supervisory rank of officers. Although the D-2 merit promotion process existed in 1997, it does not follow that Chicago had an available, equally valid method for promoting officers to sergeants at that time based on the D-2 procedure. There was no method for promoting sergeants that Chicago "refuse[d] to adopt" and apply in 1997. 42 U.S.C. §2000e-2(k)(1)(A)(ii).

The officers' next point to certain promotions from sergeant to lieutenant, which incorporated merit in 1995. Again, the merit promotion process for lieutenants does not demonstrate that a process would be available for sergeants or that Chicago refused to adopt an available alternative method. First of all, unlike evaluating non-supervisory officers for a promotion to a supervisory position, both the sergeant and lieutenant positions are supervisory. Thus, evaluations of sergeants' performance already encompassed the supervisory aspects. The officers have not shown the availability of a merit evaluation process of officers that would evaluate attributes for the sergeant position. Furthermore, the pool of sergeants seeking promotion to lieutenant is significantly smaller than the pool of officers seeking promotion to sergeant. For example, in 1994, 765 sergeants sought promotion to lieutenant, while 4,700 officers sought promotion to sergeant. The officers have not shown that a valid evaluation method was available on this large scale. See *Allen* (addressing limitations in merit evaluation when number of candidates for promotion increase). Furthermore, the 1995 promotions to lieutenant were, unsurprisingly, challenged in federal court. *Brown v. City of Chicago*, 19 F.Supp.2d 890 (N.D. Ill. 1998). In that case, the district court noted that the "criteria and procedures put in place" for making the 1995 merit promotions (which were based on past job performance) "were abbreviated and, as the parties agree, inferior" to the merit evaluations subsequently used in 1998. The plaintiffs here do not present evidence that evaluation of officers' past performance or an alternative evaluation method was available or sufficient for ascertaining the merit of potential sergeants, let alone demonstrate that such an inferior method would be equally valid to the rankings from the 1994 examination alone.[4] Thus, the officers have not demonstrated that Chicago refused to adopt an available method for considering merit in making sergeant promotions in 1997. 42 U.S.C. §2000e-2(k)(1)(A)(ii).

In sum, while the officers assert that thirty percent of the promotions to sergeant should be made based on merit, a proposition subsequently adopted by Chicago, the officers have not demonstrated that this method was available in February 1997 or that Chicago refused to adopt an alternative method. As we explained above, "the statutory scheme requires plaintiffs to demonstrate a viable alternative and give the employer an opportunity to adopt it." . . .

WILLIAMS, Circuit Judge, dissenting . . .

The majority opinion seems to conclude that the plaintiffs have not met their burden of demonstrating availability because the plaintiffs never presented the City with a proposal validated under the methods that were ultimately employed by the city. Nothing in the statute, the applicable regulations, or in our caselaw, however, indicates that, under 42 U.S.C. §2000e-2(k)(1)(A)(ii), for an alternative to be available it must have been validated in this manner. At bottom, the relevant question is simply whether there is evidence in the record from which a reasonable jury could conclude that at the time of the contested promotions, the City could have used the 30% merit promotions proposal. The answer to this question is "yes." Regardless of whether the process of formulating a promotional process for sergeants was more complex than that for either D-2 or lieutenant promotions, the fact that the City had successfully implemented essentially the same system for these ranks is powerful evidence that the alternative was available for sergeant promotions and the City refused to adopt it.

At the very least, a question of material fact remains as to whether the pace and nature of the City's investigation into the possibility of using 30% merit promotions for sergeants was reasonable. This is underscored by the timeline of this case — as the majority opinion describes, the City's Task Force recommended the use of the 30% merit promotions proposal more than one month before the promotions in question. In contrast, it took the City only eight days to move from the Task Force's recommendation to implementation when the City examined its system for promoting lieutenants. There is a logical disconnect between the idea that the City's own task force had recommended use of this system and the majority's conclusion that this alternative was unavailable more than one month later. The explanation for this disconnect is that the majority has unnecessarily complicated the question of availability. An alternative is unavailable when, for verifiable reasons, the defendant cannot adopt it. A reasonable alternative is not unavailable simply because the defendant has not completed its own inquiry into the viability of the alternative.

A true situation of no viable alternative being available can be found in the Eleventh Circuit's decision in *Fitzpatrick v. City of Atlanta*, 2 F.3d 1112 (11th Cir.

---

4. Judge Williams emphasizes in her dissent the eight-day period during which the City implemented merit promotions from sergeant to lieutenant (between February 28, 1995 and March 8, 1995). We note that the lieutenant merit promotions were almost immediately enjoined by the Illinois courts for violating state law. The injunction was invalidated by federal litigation, but notably not until July 6, 1998, more than 16 months after the promotions to sergeant at issue in this case. Of course, a state court injunction is no excuse for violating federal law, but it does indicate that the City did not "refuse[ ] to adopt" an available alternative. 42 U.S.C. §2000e-2(k)(1)(A)(ii). Regardless, the size and scale of the applicant pool and the officers' lack of supervisory experience distinguish the available methods used for promotions to sergeant from the promotions to lieutenant.

1993). In *Fitzpatrick*, black firefighters challenged an Atlanta Fire Department rule that required them to be clean shaven because of the racially discriminatory impact of this rule. ("The twelve plaintiff-appellant firefighters in this case are all African-American men who suffer from pseudofolliculitis barbae ('PFB'), a bacterial disorder which causes men's faces to become infected if they shave them. It is generally recognized that PFB disproportionately afflicts African-American men."). The firefighters proposed that "shadow beards" would constitute a less-discriminatory alternative with equal safety value, but the Eleventh Circuit concluded that the firefighter plaintiffs had failed to introduce sufficient evidence to raise an issue of material fact where the City had submitted voluminous evidence of the safety-necessity of its no-beard policy. This case is not like *Fitzpatrick*, where a less-discriminatory alternative *literally* did not exist for scientifically verifiable reasons.

An alternative was available here. There is a question of material fact as to whether the City took proper steps in assessing its viability and in promptly implementing it. While the City's timing may have been perfectly reasonable in this case, this was a question for trial. By deferring to the defendant's calculation of the time needed to implement an equally valid alternative, our decision invites abuse by defendants acting in bad faith. I therefore respectfully dissent from the majority's affirmance of the grant of summary judgment.

NOTES

1. *Proposing an Alternative Employment Practice.* Since all employers presumably know about the possibility of using merit determinations and most prefer to have the unfettered discretion to rely on their merit determinations in employment decision making, in what sense did the majority find that the use of merit was not available here? Was it that the plaintiffs failed to present an actual merit proposal to the employer before it decided to promote based on test scores? Does that make the alternative employment practice surrebuttal stage simply, at the first step, a question of fact: Was an alternative presented to the defendant before it undertook the action that was challenged and defendant refused to adopt it? How would Judge Williams deal with the issue? In *IBEW v. Miss. Power & Light Co.*, 442 F.3d 313 (5th Cir. 2006), plaintiffs failed to carry their alternative employment practices burden because their expert's vague description of a process requiring applicants to perform sample tasks, perhaps during the interview, was too tenuous to be considered an "alternative" to the testing practices that MP&L had justified as business necessity.

2. *Proving the Adequacy of the Proposed Alternative.* If the first step is satisfied, the second step would seem to be to determine whether the proposed alternative was a true alternative. Presumably, plaintiff must demonstrate that the proposed alternative would have had a lesser impact than the use of the practice that defendant planned to use. If so, must plaintiff also show, to use the words of Justice O'Connor in *Watson*, that the alternative was "equally as effective"? The majority never reaches that question because, for it, the alternative was not available. How would Judge Williams view the effectiveness issue? For her, *Fitzpatrick* is the paradigm: no alternative was available because of the overwhelming evidence that nothing worked as well to protect firefighters as being clean shaven when using the face masks to protect the health of the firefighters. That means that nothing is "equally as effective." Suppose, however, shadow beards were pretty effective but not quite as effective as having no beard at all. Are they a viable alternative?

3. *The Alternative Employment Practice in* El v. SEPTA. In a portion of *El v. SEPTA* not reproduced, the court, as an alternative holding, affirmed the district court's grant of summary judgment because plaintiff did not point to evidence of an alternative employment practice. Didn't the employer concede an alternative by providing in its rule that for some lesser offenses the bar lasted only seven years? How about the EEOC Guideline that requires an individualized review where an applicant had a record of criminal convictions? Given how thin the support was for finding that a permanent bright-line rule for convictions for violent crimes justified as job related and consistent with business necessity, should there have been a trial on the question of how effective an alternative system of case-by-case review would be? Presumably, the costs of implementing an individualized inquiry would be relevant but, as a threshold question, would there have to be evidence about how many applicants for paratransit driver jobs had convictions for violent crimes?

4. *Reasonable Procedures Again.* Judge Williams's dissent focuses on "the pace and nature of the City's investigation into the possibility of using 30% merit promotions for sergeants"; she finds a material issue of fact as to whether the City's procedure was reasonable. In contrast, *El* found SEPTA's procedure in establishing its standards irrelevant to their business necessity. Are these positions reconcilable? In other words, is their something about alternative employment practices that justifies focusing on process rather than result?

5. *Individual Disparate Impact.* All of the Supreme Court cases dealing with systemic disparate impact focus on employment practices used by the employer rather than on claims by individual employees challenging their treatment. But is §703(k) necessarily limited to systemic cases or does it create a new right of action, independent of the basic §703(k)(1)(A)(i) group disparate impact action? *See* Michael J. Zimmer, *Individual Disparate Impact Law: On the Plain Meaning of the 1991 Civil Rights Act,* 30 LOY. U. CHI. L.J 473 (1998). Professor Zimmer argues that §703 (k)(1)(A) expressly recognizes two ways of establishing a disparate impact claim. Paragraph (i) more or less codifies the traditional notion that a generally applicable employment practice is subject to disparate impact attack if it has an unjustified impact on race, gender or other protected groups. But, because it is phrased in the disjunctive "or," paragraph (ii) appears to expressly create another method of establishing a violation that does not include any requirement of proof of disparity of impact on a group: "An unlawful employment practice based on disparate impact is established under this title if . . .

> (ii) the complaining party makes the demonstration described in subparagraph (c) with respect to an alternative employment practice and the respondent refuses to adopt such alternative employment practice."

This reading would have the odd result of Congress labeling liability as based on "disparate impact" but without any requirement of proving that any group suffered disparate impact. But reading a showing of group disparate impact into (ii) would contravene the plain meaning of the text.

If this view is taken, §703(k)(1)(A)(ii) would create an entirely new "individual disparate impact" action. An individual protected by Title VII would be able to establish a disparate impact claim under §703(k)(1)(A)(ii) simply by proving (1) that the employer took adverse action based on an "employment practice," (2) that an alternative practice exists that serves the employer's interests yet would not adversely affect the plaintiff, and (3) that the employer refused to adopt the better alternative.

Contrary to pre-existing Title VII law, this new cause of action neither includes an intent to discriminate or pretext element nor requires any showing of group impact.

Consider how this "individual disparate impact" cause of action would work in *El.* (1) The employer discharged El, clearly an adverse action, based on its rule not to employ workers with prior convictions involving a violent crime. That rule is clearly an "employment practice." (2) Can plaintiff point to an alternative practice that serves the employer's interests yet would not adversely affect the plaintiff? The employer's own rule for dealing with convictions other than for violent crimes would be one alternative that was known to and, presumably, used by the employer already. Since the employer clearly refused to apply the alternative when it decided to fire El, element (3) would be satisfied. The entire case would turn on whether the alternative sufficiently served the employer's interests. The answer to that might depend on the prior experience of SEPTA under its rule. If the only patron ever attacked by a paratransit driver was deSouza, and he had no prior criminal record, plaintiff's preferred alternative might satisfy defendant's interests.

An advantage of joining an individual disparate impact action with one for individual disparate treatment is the interaction of the two: to the extent the employer characterizes its action as not being based on an employment practice, the adverse action will then appear to be ad hoc, perhaps subjective, and therefore more likely to be found the product of intent to discriminate. To the extent the employer claims the non-discriminatory basis for its adverse action against plaintiff is merely the application of a neutral employment policy or practice, it may be conceding the first part of the §703(k)(1)(A)(ii) action. That still requires plaintiff to prove that an alternative exists that satisfies the employer's legitimate interests and that the employer refused to adopt it. See Chapter 4.

If faced with deciding which of the two theories to employ, plaintiffs would prefer the individual disparate treatment action since it provides for the possibility of compensatory and punitive damages as well as a right to trial by jury, rights that are not available in the individual disparate impact action. If it had to choose, which theory would the employer prefer?

C. SECTION 703(H) EXCEPTIONS

In addition to undermining plaintiff's showing of impact or showing the job relatedness/business necessity defense, Title VII offers three other statutory defenses in disparate impact cases. Section 703(h) creates exceptions for professionally developed employment tests, for bona fide seniority systems, and for bona fide merit systems.

1. *Professionally Developed Tests*

Section 703(h) provides that, "notwithstanding any other provision of Title VII, it shall not be an unlawful employment practice for an employer to give and to act upon the results of any professionally developed ability test provided that such test, its administration or action upon the results is not designed, intended or used to discriminate because of race, color, religion, sex or national origin."

Griggs accepted the EEOC's position that, where there was a disparate impact, §703(h) incorporated the strict validation standards that industrial psychologists established for themselves for any test or selection device. With that holding, §703(h) operates less as an exception than as a fundamental part of the broad interpretation given Title VII at that time.

ALBEMARLE PAPER CO. v. MOODY
422 U.S. 405 (1975)

Justice STEWART delivered the opinion of the Court.

. . . Like the employer in *Griggs*, Albemarle uses two general ability tests, the Beta Examination, to test nonverbal intelligence, and the Wonderlic Test (Forms A and B), the purported measure of general verbal facility which was also involved in the *Griggs* case. Applicants for hire into various skilled lines of progression at the plant are required to score 100 on the Beta Exam and 18 on one of the Wonderlic Test's two alternative forms.

The question of job relatedness must be viewed in the context of the plant's operation and the history of the testing program. The plant, which now employs about 650 persons, converts raw wood into paper products. It is organized into a number of functional departments, each with one or more distinct lines of progression, the theory being that workers can move up the line as they acquire the necessary skills. The number and structure of the lines have varied greatly over time. For many years, certain lines were themselves more skilled and paid higher wages than others, and until 1964 these skilled lines were expressly reserved for white workers. In 1968, many of the unskilled "Negro" lines were "end-tailed" onto skilled "white" lines, but it apparently remains true that at least the top jobs in certain lines require greater skills than the top jobs in other lines. In this sense, at least, it is still possible to speak of relatively skilled and relatively unskilled lines.

In the 1950's while the plant was being modernized with new and more sophisticated equipment, the Company introduced a high school diploma requirement for entry into the skilled lines. Though the Company soon concluded that this requirement did not improve the quality of the labor force, the requirement was continued until the District Court enjoined its use. In the late 1950's the Company began using the Beta Examination and the Bennett Mechanical Comprehension Test (also involved in the *Griggs* case) to screen applicants for entry into the skilled lines. The Bennett Test was dropped several years later, but use of the Beta Test continued.

The Company added the Wonderlic Tests in 1963, for the skilled lines, on the theory that a certain verbal intelligence was called for by the increasing sophistication of the plant's operations. The Company made no attempt to validate the test for job relatedness, and simply adopted the national "norm" score of 18 as a cut-off point for new job applicants. After 1964, when it discontinued overt segregation in the lines of progression, the Company allowed Negro workers to transfer to the skilled lines if they could pass the Beta and Wonderlic Tests, but few succeeded in doing so. Incumbents in the skilled lines, some of whom had been hired before adoption of the tests, were not required to pass them to retain their jobs or their promotion rights. The record shows that a number of white incumbents in high-ranking job groups could not pass the tests. . . .

Four months before this case went to trial, Albemarle engaged an expert in industrial psychology to "validate" the job relatedness of its testing program. He spent a half day at the plant and devised a "concurrent validation" study, which was conducted by plant officials, without his supervision. The expert then subjected the results to statistical analysis. The study dealt with 10 job groupings, selected from near the top of nine of the lines of progression. Jobs were grouped together solely by their proximity in the line of progression; no attempt was made to analyze jobs in terms of the particular skills they might require. All, or nearly all, employees in the selected groups participated in the study — 105 employees in all, but only four Negroes. Within each job grouping, the study compared the test scores of each employee with an independent "ranking" of the employee, relative to each of his coworkers, made by two of the employee's supervisors. . . .

For each job grouping, the expert computed the "Phi coefficient" of statistical correlation between the test scores and an average of the two supervisorial rankings. Consonant with professional conventions, the expert regarded as "statistically significant" any correlation that could have occurred by chance only five times, or fewer, in 100 trials. On the basis of these results, the District Court found that "[t]he personnel tests administered at the plant have undergone validation studies and have been proven to be job related." Like the Court of Appeals, we are constrained to disagree.

The EEOC has issued "Guidelines" for employers seeking to determine, through professional validation studies, whether their employment tests are job related. 29 C.F.R. pt. 1607. These Guidelines draw upon and make reference to professional standards of test validation established by the American Psychological Association.[29] The EEOC Guidelines are not administrative "regulations" promulgated pursuant to formal procedures established by the Congress. But, as this Court has heretofore noted, they do constitute "[t]he administrative interpretation of the Act by the enforcing agency," and consequently they are "entitled to great deference."

The message of these Guidelines is the same as that of the *Griggs* case — that discriminatory tests are impermissible unless shown, by professionally acceptable methods, to be "predictive of or significantly correlated with important elements of work behavior which comprise or are relevant to the job or jobs for which candidates are being evaluated." 29 C.F.R. § 1607.4(c).

Measured against the Guidelines, Albemarle's validation study is materially defective in several respects:

(1) Even if it had been otherwise adequate, the study would not have "validated" the Beta and Wonderlic test battery for all of the skilled lines of progression for which the two tests are, apparently, now required. The study showed significant correlations for the Beta Exam in only three of the eight lines. Though the Wonderlic Test's Form A and Form B are in theory identical and interchangeable measures of verbal facility, significant correlations for one form but not for the other were obtained in four job groupings. In two job groupings neither form showed a significant correlation. Within some of the lines of progression, one form was found acceptable for some job groupings but not for others. Even if the study were otherwise reliable, this odd patchwork of results would not entitle Albemarle to impose its testing program under the Guidelines. A test may be used in jobs other than those for which it has

---

29. American Psychological Association, Standards for Educational and Psychological Tests and Manuals (1966) (hereafter APA Standards). A volume of the same title, containing modifications, was issued in 1974 . . .

been professionally validated only if there are "no significant differences" between
the studied and unstudied jobs. 29 C.F.R. §1607.4(c)(2). The study in this case
involved no analysis of the attributes of, or the particular skills needed in, the studied
job groups. There is accordingly no basis for concluding that "no significant differences" exist among the lines of progression, or among distinct job groupings
within the studied lines of progression. Indeed, the study's checkered results appear
to compel the opposite conclusion.

(2) The study compared test scores with subjective supervisorial rankings. While
they allow the use of supervisorial rankings in test validation, the Guidelines quite
plainly contemplate that the rankings will be elicited with far more care than was
demonstrated here. Albemarle's supervisors were asked to rank employees by a
"standard" that was extremely vague and fatally open to divergent interpretations. As
previously noted, each "job grouping" contained a number of different jobs, and the
supervisors were asked, in each grouping, to "determine which [employees] they felt
irrespective of the job that they were actually doing, but in their respective jobs, did a
better job than the person they were rating against. . . . " There is no way of knowing
precisely what criteria of job performance the supervisors were considering, whether
each of the supervisors was considering the same criteria or whether, indeed, any of
the supervisors actually applied a focused and stable body of criteria of any kind.[32]
There is, in short, simply no way to determine whether the criteria *actually* considered were sufficiently related to the Company's legitimate interest in job-specific
ability to justify a testing system with a racially discriminatory impact.

(3) The Company's study focused, in most cases, on job groups near the top of the
various lines of progression. In Griggs v. Duke Power Co., the Court left open "the
question whether testing requirements that take into account capability for the next
succeeding position or related future promotion might be utilized upon a showing
that such long-range requirements fulfill a genuine business need." The Guidelines
take a sensible approach to this issue, and we now endorse it:

> If job progression structures and seniority provisions are so established that new
> employees will probably, within a reasonable period of time and in a great majority of
> cases, progress to a higher level, it may be considered that candidates are being eval-
> uated for jobs at that higher level. However, where job progression is not so nearly
> automatic, or the time span is such that higher level jobs or employees' potential may
> be expected to change in significant ways, it shall be considered that candidates are
> being evaluated for a job at or near the entry level. 29 C.F.R. §1607.4(c)(1).

The fact that the best of those employees working near the top of a line of
progression score well on a test does not necessarily mean that that test, or some
particular cutoff score on the test, is a permissible measure of the minimal qualifications of new workers entering lower level jobs. In drawing any such conclusion,
detailed consideration must be given to the normal speed of promotion, to the
efficacy of on-the-job training in the scheme of promotion, and to the possible use of
testing as a promotion device, rather than as a screen for entry into low-level jobs.
The District Court made no findings on these issues. The issues take on special
importance in a case, such as this one, where incumbent employees are permitted to

---

32. It cannot escape notice that Albemarle's study was conducted by plant officials, without neutral,
on-the-scene oversight, at a time when this litigation was about to come to trial. Studies so closely
controlled by an interested party in litigation must be examined with great care.

work at even high-level jobs without passing the company's test battery. *See* 29 C.F.R. § 1607.11. . . .

[T]he respondents were consequently not entitled to equitable relief. . . .

NOTES

1. *What is a "Test" Subject to Validation?* According to § 703(h), the statutory exception applies to "any professionally developed ability test." Because of *Griggs* and *Albemarle Paper*, the use of a test moves the affirmative defense in a disparate impact case from the general job related/business necessity defense of § 703(k) to the professional test validation standards. If "tests" are subject to more stringent proof of job relatedness by virtue of § 703(h), then it becomes necessary to distinguish employment tests from other neutral criteria used by employers to make employment-related decisions. What is a test? Beyond "intelligence" tests such as those used in *Griggs* and *Albemarle*, employers often use "honesty" or "integrity" tests as pre-employment screening devices. In *Lanning*, the test was a physical fitness exercise, but the court looked to test validation standards. In short, most "tests" require validation. Is it wise to discourage, through § 703(h), the use of neutral or objective testing, given that an employer may opt instead for far more subjective criteria? After *Watson*, subjective practices are also subject to disparate impact attack but are they "tests"?

2. *Albemarle's Dicta.* Most of the discussion of test validation in *Albemarle Paper* is dicta because the flaw in the attempted validation was so basic: As a matter of testing theory, the fundamental flaw of the validation study in *Albemarle* was the failure of the test expert to perform a job analysis of any of the jobs for which the tests were used. Absent such an analysis, it would be impossible to correlate job performance with test performance, at least across any jobs other than the exact ones rated.

3. *Evolution of the Guidelines. Albemarle's* close comparison of the employer's validation study to the EEOC Uniform Guidelines provoked strong criticism from the testing community as "professionally unrealistic and effectively unattainable," and few employment tests had ever been used that would satisfy the rigorous requirements of the EEOC's original Guidelines. *See* Dean Booth & James L. Mackay, *Legal Constraints on Employment Testing and Evolving Trends in the Law,* 29 EMORY L.J. 121, 125 (1980). Those Guidelines, however, reflected the extant standards of industrial psychologists, which meant that test experts were opposed to applying their own best practices.

In response to these kinds of criticisms, new Uniform Guidelines on Employee Selection Procedures, 29 CFR § 1607.1 *et seq.* (2007), were promulgated. They still looked to the standards the industrial psychologists set for themselves, but the test professionals had by then relaxed their own professional standards. See Division 14, American Psychological Association (Industrial-Organizational Psychology), PRINCIPLES FOR THE VALIDATION AND USE OF PERSONNEL SELECTION PROCEDURES (1979). The Uniform Guidelines now provide that any one of the three generally accepted validation strategies is acceptable where appropriate: criterion, content, or construct. However, while the presumption of the EEOC guidelines for criterion validation has been eliminated, the same presumption still exists in the professional standards of industrial psychology. So, while the test expert should decide what type of validation strategy to use based on the skills, functions, and traits revealed in the job analysis, criterion validation is preferred because it is based on a statistical comparison of two sets of data — test scores and job performance scores — that results in a number, the correlation coefficient, which is a mathematical expression of the relationship between test scores and job performance. In contrast, content validation starts with one empirical basis — job analysis data — and requires the test expert to argue that the test is, in fact, a sample of critical job behaviors shown in the analysis.

4. *Three Approved Validation Strategies*. There are three ways by which a study may be validated: criterion-related validation, construct-related validation, and content validation. In criterion-related validation, the general criterion selected is some aspect of performance on the job. For example, if a job analysis reveals that good job performance requires good vision, good hearing, or motor dexterity, the employer can devise tests for those skills, and validate them by comparing test performance to job performance. In a predictive criterion-related validation, the employer tests individuals, but then hires them without regard to their performance on the tests to see if good test performance really predicts good job performance.

A variation of this technique is "concurrent validation," such as that attempted in *Albemarle*. As compared to criterion validation, the basic difference is that the current employees are tested, and the tests are validated by comparing the test results to job performance ratings. In theory, concurrent validation is less reliable since the employees tested may not resemble the individuals who will be given the tests in the future.

A second form of validation is construct validation. This requires a testing expert to analyze the job and construct a test that she thinks will measure traits necessary for success on the job. Construct validation is appropriate for traits more abstract than those subject to criterion-related validation. Thus, traits such as intelligence, mechanical comprehension, and verbal fluency are subject to construct validation. The Uniform Guidelines do not permit construct validation unless there has been a criterion validation, either for the job in question or for a similar job. 29 CFR § 1607.14 (D)(4).

Perhaps most intuitively appealing is the third kind of validation, content validation, which, at its simplest, uses a sample of the work done on the job as the test. If the sample is really representative of the job, success on the test necessarily implies success on the job. Rather than developing a statistical study correlating test and job performance, the test expert using the content validation technique simply testifies why the test is, in fact, a good sample of the actual job for which the test is used.

That any job requires skills appropriate for only one type of validation technique is debatable. Take a job that includes typing as a major function. Obviously, a typing test can be validated by content validation if the test reflects the kind of typing the job requires. Criterion-related validation can be used if a motor function, such as finger dexterity, is viewed as the skill shared by people who could likely learn to become good typists. Even construct validation can be used if the predominate mental trait of good typists is the ability to withstand boredom.

Guardians Assn. v. Civil Service Comm., 630 F.2d 79, 92 (2d Cir. 1980), described the legal significance of choosing among the different test validation strategies. After first noting that construct validation could be used only if empirically validated, the court wrote:

> This content-construct distinction has a significance beyond just selecting the proper technique for validating the exam; it frequently determines who wins the lawsuit. Content validation is generally feasible while construct validation is frequently

impossible. Even the Guidelines acknowledge that construct validation requires "an extensive and arduous effort." The principal difficulty with construct validation is that it requires a technique that includes a criterion-related study. Developing such data is difficult, and tests for which it is required have frequently been declared invalid. As a result, a conclusion that construct validation is required would often decide a case against a test-maker, once a disparate racial impact has been demonstrated.

5. *Differential Validation.* In a portion of the opinion not reproduced, *Albemarle* referred to EEOC guidelines requiring differential validation by race, thus suggesting that different scores could predict different levels of performance for blacks and whites. This technique may have been invalidated by the Civil Rights Act of 1991, which changed the law of employment testing by prohibiting "race norming." Section 703(l) now provides:

> It shall be an unlawful employment practice for a respondent, in connection with the selection or referral of applicants or candidates for employment or promotion, to adjust the scores of, use different cutoff scores for, or otherwise alter the results of, employment related tests on the basis of race, color, religion, sex, or national origin.

While this provision does not specifically bar differential validation in testing, what would be the use of such validation if lower-scoring African Americans or Latinos could not be hired on the basis that they were likely to perform as well as higher-scoring whites? Or does the phrasing of the statute permit an employer to hire lower-scoring individuals so long as their scores are not adjusted and different cutoff scores are not used? In *Billish v. City of Chicago*, 989 F.2d 890 (7th Cir. 1993), the court upheld a challenge by white firefighters where the city had raised minority candidates' scores sufficiently to avoid having a racial impact under the EEOC guidelines. The court found this would have violated the new §703(l). Would it be race norming for an employer, pursuant to an affirmative action plan, to promote a minority group member with a lower test score than a white?

BRYANT v. CITY OF CHICAGO
200 F.3d 1092 (7th Cir. 2000)

H. WOOD, JR., Circuit Judge.

Plaintiffs are forty-four African-American or Latino present or former sergeants of the Chicago Police Department. Plaintiffs failed to be promoted to lieutenant after taking the 1994 police lieutenant examination. Seven hundred sixty-five police sergeants took the examination of which 184 (24%) were African-American and 55 (7%) were Hispanic. The Police Department made 108 rank-order promotions based on the 1994 examination, granting promotions to those officers who obtained the highest 108 scores on the examination. Of the 108 officers promoted, five were African-American and one was Hispanic. Minority promotions, therefore, represented slightly less than 6% of the total number of promotions granted. It is undisputed that the 1994 examination had a disparate impact on minority candidates, and the parties have stipulated that this statistical evidence constitutes a prima facie case of discrimination. . . .

In a Title VII disparate impact case, the plaintiff bears the initial burden of establishing a prima facie case by showing that the promotional method in question had an adverse impact on minorities. If the plaintiff makes this required initial showing, the burden then shifts to the employer who must prove that the evaluation method is valid by showing that it is "job related" and "consistent with business necessity." The evaluation method may be shown to be job related under any one of three tests: criterion related, content validity, or construct validity. Uniform Guidelines on Employee Selections Procedures, 29 C.F.R. § 1607.5(B). If the employer succeeds in validating the evaluation method, the burden shifts back to the plaintiff to prove that there was another available method of evaluation which was equally valid and less discriminatory that the employer refused to use. . . .

I. BACKGROUND . . .

Following [the recommendations of a "Blue Ribbon Committee" appointed by the mayor], the City retained Barrett & Associates, Inc., of Akron, Ohio, described as a "Human Resource Consulting Firm" specializing in employee matters including promotion testing. The firm is headed by Dr. Gerald B. Barrett who holds a Ph.D. in psychology, as well as a law degree. He teaches testing and measurement, personnel selection, performance evaluation, and personnel psychology as well as law at the University of Akron. Dr. Barrett developed and administered the lieutenant examination challenged in this suit. Dr. Barrett and his firm had previously developed more than fifty examinations for police and fire departments including examinations for the cities of Cleveland and Akron, Ohio. . . .

Dr. Barrett was no stranger to the Chicago Police Department. In 1993, Dr. Barrett had developed an examination for promotion to Chicago Police Sergeant. In preparing that examination, Dr. Barrett conducted a job analysis of the sergeant position by interviewing approximately ninety Chicago sergeants along with twenty-eight lieutenants about their duties and responsibilities. For the lieutenant examination now in question, Dr. Barrett, following that same course, interviewed additional lieutenants, captains, and sergeants, including minorities. Dr. Barrett also toured the police districts, rode along with lieutenants on duty, observed the work of lieutenants, and reviewed applicable police documents, reports, and orders. Based on the data he gathered from his preliminary work, Dr. Barrett prepared a "Master Job Description" for the Chicago Police Lieutenant position. The Master Job Description identified what are referred to as "major work behaviors," including the associated tasks and responsibilities of lieutenants. In creating the Master Job Description, Dr. Barrett measured the importance and frequency of a lieutenant's tasks and responsibilities. Dr. Barrett also consulted certain source materials which contained information with which a lieutenant was expected to be familiar. These materials included Police Department policies and directives, certain sections of the Illinois Statutes and the Chicago Municipal Code, the collective bargaining agreement of the Union, and the Department's community policing strategy. A list of those source materials was made available to the candidates prior to the examination.

The examination developed by Dr. Barrett had three components. The first was a written job-knowledge test consisting of 150 multiple choice questions derived from the source materials. It was first pilot tested and then further refined before being given. The next component of the examination was referred to as the "In-Basket Exercise." This exercise was based on a hypothetical situation which a candidate might face in an emergency where he or she would have to assume the duties of a lieutenant who had become ill or incapacitated. In this exercise, the lieutenant candidates were each presented with a packet of information simulating a lieutenant's in-basket. The candidates were allowed two and one-half hours to study the materials before being given ninety minutes to answer sixty multiple choice questions. The answers to these sixty questions were contained in the materials provided to the candidates, and the candidates were allowed to refer to these materials during the examination. The in-basket materials had first been reviewed by Chicago Police Department subject matter experts, and the exercise was also pilot tested prior to implementation. The purpose of the in-basket exercise was to measure necessary skills and abilities of possible lieutenants, not to test job-knowledge as was intended by the first component. Those responsibilities, for instance, required knowledge of reports, personnel actions, and the assignment of tasks.

The third component of the examination was an oral briefing exercise intended to demonstrate a candidate's analytical abilities and oral communication skills. This exercise simulated a Chicago Police Lieutenant's responsibilities at roll call. Each candidate was given materials about Chicago gang activity and related Department directives. The candidates were allowed twenty-five minutes to review those materials and then they were required to give an oral briefing on the issue not to exceed ten minutes. During their oral presentations, candidates were allowed to refer to the materials and their own study notes. The oral presentations were recorded on audio tape for later review. A monitor sat in the room during the oral presentations, but was not permitted to communicate with the candidate. The oral presentation reviewers evaluated the recorded presentations without knowing the identity of the candidates. Three trained raters independently scored each presentation on an objective check list and then reached a conclusion about each of the candidates. This component had also been reviewed by Chicago Police Department subject matter experts and pilot tested.

II. CONSIDERATION OF THE ISSUES

Plaintiffs raise a number of arguments on appeal, but the core argument is that the district court committed reversible error when it accepted Dr. Barrett's testimony that the examination was content valid as sufficient evidence to rebut the plaintiffs' prima facie showing of disparate impact. Plaintiffs argue first that Dr. Barrett's testimony is inadmissible under *Daubert v. Merrell Dow Pharmaceuticals, Inc.*, 509 U.S. 579 (1993), and, secondly, that, even if admissible, Dr. Barrett's testimony is insufficient to justify the examination on which minorities fared so poorly. We address each of these arguments in turn.

A. DR. BARRETT'S TESTIMONY

Citing *Daubert*, plaintiffs characterize Dr. Barrett's testimony that the examination was content valid and that the final test scores could be used for rank-order promotions as nothing more than inadmissible conjecture, arguing that the testimony lacks "scientific validity." *Daubert* involved expert testimony in a personal injury suit involving a prescription drug taken by an expectant mother. The drug was alleged to have caused birth defects in plaintiff's children. The district court granted summary judgment in behalf of the drug company finding petitioner's scientific evidence and the principle upon which it was based were not "sufficiently established to have general acceptance in the field to which it belongs." Likewise, plaintiffs in the present case claim that Dr. Barrett's opinions are unsubstantiated and lack "scientific validity." His opinions, it is argued, were nevertheless admitted by the district court because of Dr. Barrett's "expertise." Appellants contend that the district court's decision was erroneous.

Under *Daubert*, the testimony of a scientific expert is admissible only if it is both relevant and reliable. *Kumho Tire Co., Ltd. v. Carmichael*, 526 U.S. 137 (1999). In the present case, appellants challenge only the reliability of the admitted expert testimony. A district court enjoys broad latitude both in deciding how to determine reliability and in making the ultimate reliability determination. . . . Appellants contend that Dr. Barrett's testimony fails to meet the reliability prong of *Daubert* because there was no showing that his opinions were scientifically valid.

We review the district court's reliability determination for abuse of discretion and affirm. The *Daubert* inquiry is "a flexible one" and is not designed to serve as a "definitive checklist or test but rather to ensure "that an expert, whether basing testimony upon professional studies or personal experience, employs in the courtroom the same level of intellectual rigor that characterizes the practice of an expert in the relevant field. In the present case, it is clear that Dr. Barrett's testimony had "'a reliable basis in the knowledge and experience of [the relevant] discipline.'" Dr. Barrett has extensive academic and practical experience in designing employment evaluations. Furthermore, it is not accurate to claim that the district judge declined to conduct an inquiry into the scientific validity of Dr. Barrett's opinion. As the district court noted, Dr. Barrett based his opinions, at least in part, on the job analysis that Barrett & Associates meticulously formulated which detailed a relationship between the skills measured in the examination and an individual's effectiveness as a lieutenant. Furthermore, while plaintiffs contend that the "general scientific literature" in the area consists of a single unpublished study, it is undisputed that Dr. Barrett himself has authored approximately fifty articles dealing with employee selection and promotion testing for peer-reviewed journals. This is not a case in which the expert failed to conduct any studies or analysis to substantiate his opinion. Given these facts, it is clear that the district judge's decision to admit Dr. Barrett's testimony was not manifestly erroneous.

B. TEST VALIDITY

Plaintiffs argue in the alternative that Dr. Barrett's testimony, if properly admitted, was insufficient to support a finding that the examination was job related. They contend that the 1994 test was not job related because it did not approximate the work situation. Plaintiffs cite *Griggs*, in which the Court held that, under Title VII, employment tests are forbidden which produce a disparate impact "unless they are demonstrably a reasonable measure of job performance." Additionally, plaintiffs note that, in 1972, Congress realized that equal employment had been thwarted when employment was based on "criteria unrelated to job performance and on discriminatory supervisory ratings," citing *Teal*. From these two cases it can be seen that, if a facially neutral employment practice has a significant discriminatory impact, the employer bears the burden of demonstrating that any requirement of employment imposed has a manifest relationship to the particular employment. *Griggs* makes clear, however, that even employment tests with a disparate impact are acceptable if "they are demonstrably a reasonable measure of job performance." It would be unrealistic to require more than a reasonable measure of job performance. It therefore is a matter of reasonableness, except in cases in which the plaintiff can show that the employer was using the practice as a mere pretext for discrimination. There is no claim, however, of employer pretext in the present case.

As previously noted, an evaluation method may be shown to be job related under any one of three tests: criterion related, content validity, or construct validity. *Gillespie v. State of Wisconsin*, 771 F.2d 1035, 1040 (7th Cir. 1985). In the present case, the district court found that the test was content valid. In evaluating content validity, a court must consider

> (1) the degree to which the nature of the examination procedure approximates the job conditions; (2) whether the test measures abstract or concrete qualities; and (3) the combination of these factors, i.e. [sic] whether the test attempts to measure an abstract trait with a test that fails to closely approximate the working situation.

Id. In the present case, the district court recognized the correct standard for determining content validity. After considering all of the evidence, the court determined that the 1994 examination measured a significant portion of the knowledge, skills, and abilities necessary for a police lieutenant and, therefore, was content valid. Because this is a factual finding, we will affirm the decision of the district court unless it is clearly erroneous.

The factual details we have already related about the development of the lieutenant test are enough to refute plaintiffs' arguments. The record shows not only the knowledge, expertise, and experience of those involved in the test development, but also the preliminary use of peer review and pilot testing of each of its three parts. Officers of various police ranks and experience, including minorities, were consulted during the development of the process. It would be totally unjustified to fail to take note of those preliminary efforts and, considering our standard of review, to reverse the trial judge who had carefully considered and weighed all the evidence before coming to the conclusion of test validity. The standard to be applied is not simply whether minorities do well or not on a test. That is only the beginning. It is obviously not impossible to develop a useful and nondiscriminatory test.

C. VALIDITY OF THE SCORING SYSTEM

Plaintiffs also raise an issue about the City's use of the examination scores to make promotions in rank order for the proposition that the use of rank-ordering must be independently justified when the scoring system results in a disparate impact. In *Gillespie*, this court relied on the Second Circuit's decision in *Guardians Ass'n of New York City v. Civil Service Commission*, 630 F.2d 79 (2d Cir. 1980). The *Guardians* court recognized that an employer who wants to use rank-order scores for hiring decisions must demonstrate that rank-ordering is sufficiently justified. That "task is by no means impossible," even without resort to a criterion related study of the issue. Under *Guardians*, rank-order promotions can be validated by a substantial showing that (1) the test is job related and representative and (2) the test maker achieved "an adequate degree of reliability."

As previously discussed, the 1994 lieutenant examination was based on a detailed job analysis and was constructed in adherence to the Uniform Guidelines. The City has made a substantial showing of job relatedness sufficient to satisfy the first prong of the *Guardians* test. The reliability prong is also met. Barrett & Associates used a number of methods, including pre-testing, to ensure the reliability of the 1994 examination. Furthermore, we agree with the Second Circuit's holding that when an examination measures ability with sufficient differentiating power to justify rank-ordering, it is permissible for the City to set a cut-off score at the point where the rank-ordering provides the number of promotions necessary to fill the City's available openings. In the present case, the City's use of rank-ordering is valid, and the City was justified in setting a cut-off score which resulted in the necessary number of promotions. . . .

NOTES

1. *Doing the Job Analysis.* In *Griggs*, Duke Power adopted the challenged tests allegedly because it thought that their use would generally upgrade its workforce. In essence, the test companies convinced the employer to buy their tests as a way to select among applicants when there were more applicants than jobs. *Albemarle Paper* involved an attempted validation study, but only on the eve of trial. Again, the test had been adopted without any effort to validate. Since each employer had to retrospectively defend the use that it had made of the tests, its expert could not do a job analysis. Had the employers in the two cases done so, the first question would have been whether any test is useful for the jobs in question and, if so, second, what sort of test it should be. Since *Griggs* and *Albemarle Paper*, many employers, particularly in the public sector, have learned the importance of a job analysis prior to attempting to validate a test. The City of Chicago hired Dr. Barrett to do that, which may have been its best decision. An employer may well win a challenge to its use of a test as long as it conducts a job analysis. If that is so, *Griggs* may be invalidating fewer tests because it has changed the ground rules for the use of tests. In other words, cases like *Bryant* may be proof of the success of the disparate impact theory in rationalizing employment testing.

2. *Developing the Test.* If the testing expert decides that some sort of testing is appropriate for the job, he or she then develops or chooses the test that seems appropriate for selecting good workers. Here, Dr. Barrett developed a three-part test, with the first two parts being pencil-and-paper tests involving multiple-choice questions about knowledge that he had found necessary for the job and an "In-Basket" problem that he had determined would involve issues like those that would arise on the job. The third part involved an oral presentation that tried to mimic the presentation a lieutenant would have to make at a roll call at the start of a shift.

3. *Choosing Validation Strategies.* Once the test is prepared, the next question is what validation strategy should be used. The oral presentation appeared to be close to a sample of part of the job a police lieutenant would perform regularly — running a roll call of police officers at the start of a shift. Thus, content validation would appear appropriate, with the test expert testifying descriptively about how close the simulation matched an actual roll call. But, what about the other two elements of the test?

Answering multiple choice questions is unlikely to be part of a lieutenant's job, so content validation would appear inappropriate. Does the fact that the questions asked dealt with job-relevant information make the test susceptible to content validation? Not according to the professional test standards. But the courts have stretched content validation to apply to multiple-choice tests for a variety of positions. In *Guardians Assn. v. Civil Service Comm.*, 630 F.2d 79, 92 (2d Cir. 1980), another police test case, the court noted: "Content validation is generally feasible while construct [or criterion] validation is frequently impossible." It then approved use of this validation strategy. However, the statistical studies correlating good performance on the elements found in the job analysis with high test scores did not end up with a high enough correlation to justify the use of the test. In *Association of Mexican-American Educators v. State of California*, 183 F.3d 1055 (9th Cir. 1999), the court held that the California teaching credential exam did not violate Title VII because the state was not acting as an employer in using it. Nevertheless, in dicta, the court said the test was content valid because the skills the test addressed were necessary for teachers, even though there was no showing that the test was in any way a sample of the job of teaching. Similarly, in *Williams v. Ford Motor Co.*, 187 F.3d 533 (6th Cir. 1999), the court upheld a paper-and-pencil test used for unskilled labor positions in an automobile plant because the job analysis was well done; again, there was no showing that the test was in any way a sample of the jobs for which it was used. *See also Firefighters Inst. for Racial Equality v. City of St. Louis*, 220 F.3d 898 (8th Cir. 2000) (multiple-choice exam for fire chiefs content valid).

4. *Employers Expand the Use of Tests.* Most of the tests we have seen so far have been in the civil service context, although a few have been in the private sector. The tests have also been more-or-less traditional efforts to ascertain skills or knowledge, as opposed to more amorphous constructs like "intelligence" or "good judgment." However, there is an increasing use of "honesty" or "personality" tests by a wide range of employers. Various studies show different rates of test usage, but all substantial. For example, a 2003 study by Management Recruiters International revealed that 30% of responding companies used personality tests. The 2001 American Management Ass'n, Survey of Workplace Testing found that only 13.1% use personality tests while 29% used psychological tests. *See generally* David C. Yamada, *The Regulation of Pre-Employment Honesty Testing: Striking a Temporary (?) Balance Between Self-Regulation and Prohibition*, 39 WAYNE L. REV. 1549 (1993); Sujata S. Menjoge, Comment, *Testing the Limits of Anti-discrimination Law: How Employers' Use of Pre-employment Psychological and Personality Tests Can Circumvent Title VII and the ADA*, 82 N.C.L. REV. 326 (2003). There have been few reported Title VII challenges to such tests. Is that because they do not have a race or gender impact? *See Reynolds v. Arizona*, 1993 U.S. App. LEXIS 9915 (9th Cir. Nov. 4, 1993) (plaintiff failed to prove disparate impact of psychological tests, but survived summary judgment on her disparate treatment claim in the use of such tests).

However, the Americans with Disabilities Act has recently been employed to successfully challenge an employer's use of the Minnesota Multiphasic Personality Inventory (MMPI) as a medical examination. *Karraker v. Rent-A-Center, Inc.*, 411 F.3d 831, 833-34 (7th Cir. 2005). The MMPI "considers where an applicant falls on scales measuring traits such as depression, hypochondriasis, hysteria, paranoia, and mania. In fact, elevated scores on certain scales of the MMPI can be used in diagnoses of certain psychiatric disorders." There is reason to believe that the MMPI is valid for such uses — at least for those who can read and understand the questions. If such persons cannot figure out what the testmaker considers the "correct" answer, they are probably suffering from a clinical disorder. However, the ADA bars the use of "medical examinations" prior to an offer of employment, see Chapter 6, p. 583, so there was no question as to validity. The mere giving of the test was a violation. Suppose the employer made an offer of employment and then administered the test and withdrew the offer based on the results. Under the ADA, the question would then be whether the test was valid, and, if so, whether the trait identified was job-related.

2. *Bona Fide Seniority Systems*

Section 703(h) also provides an exception to Title VII liability for seniority systems:

> [I]t shall not be an unlawful employment practice for an employer to apply different standards of compensation, or different terms, conditions, or privileges of employment pursuant to a bona fide seniority or merit system . . . provided that such differences are not the result of an intention to discriminate because of race, color, religion, sex, or national origin.

Seniority systems tend to reify the status quo by preferring more senior workers to ones hired more recently. Where racial or gender discrimination had been common in the past, seniority systems tended to freeze that status quo.

LESTER C. THUROW, THE ZERO SUM SOCIETY
188-189 (1980)

Imagine a race with two groups of runners of equal ability. Individuals differ in their running ability, but the average speed of the two groups is identical. Imagine that a handicapper gives each individual in one of the groups a heavy weight to carry. Some of those with weights would still run faster than some of those without weights, but on average, the handicapped group would fall farther and farther behind the group without the handicap.

Now suppose that someone waves a magic wand and all of the weights vanish. Equal opportunity has been created. If the two groups are equal in their running ability, the gap between those who never carried weights and those who used to carry weights will cease to expand, but those who suffered the earlier discrimination will never catch up. If the economic baton can be handed on from generation to generation, the current effects of past discrimination can linger forever.

If a fair race is one where everyone has an equal chance to win, the race is not fair even though it is now run with fair rules. To have a fair race, it is necessary to (1) stop the race and start over, (2) force those who did not have to carry weights to carry them until the race has equalized, or (3) provide extra aid to those who were handicapped in the past until they catch up.

While these are the only three choices, none of them is a consensus choice in a democracy. Stopping the race and starting over would involve a wholesale redistribution of physical and human wealth. This only happens in real revolution, if ever. This leaves us with the choice of handicapping those who benefited from the previous handicaps or giving special privileges to those who were previously handicapped. Discrimination against someone unfortunately always means discrimination in favor of someone else. The person gaining from discrimination may not be the discriminator, but she or he will have to pay part of the price of eliminating discrimination. This is true regardless of which technique is chosen to eliminate the current effects of past discrimination.

An individualistic ethic is acceptable if society has never violated this individualistic ethic in the past, but it is unacceptable if society has not, in fact, lived up to its individualistic ethic in the past. To shift from a system of group discrimination to a system of individual performance is to perpetuate the effects of past discrimination into the present and the future. The need to practice discrimination (positive or negative) to eliminate the effects of past discrimination is one of the unfortunate costs of past discrimination. To end discrimination is not to create "equal opportunity."

* * *

In *Quarles v. Philip Morris*, 279 F. Supp. 505 (E.D. Va. 1968), the departmental seniority system established in a collective bargaining agreement with a union continued after formal race segregation among different departments ended. Blacks, wishing to transfer to formerly white departments, would lose their seniority once they transferred. Declaring that "Congress did not intend to freeze an entire generation of Negro employees into discriminatory patterns that existed before the act," the court created the "present effects of past discrimination" concept of liability. "[T]he present differences in departmental seniority of Negroes and whites that result from the company's intentional, racially discriminatory hiring policy before January 1, 1965 [the effective date of Title VII] are not validated by the proviso of §703(h)." In other words, just as the use of a professionally developed test did not really shelter a test from disparate impact attack after *Griggs*, so, too, §703(h) did not shelter the operation of seniority systems from attack relying on the disparate impact theory. *Quarles* would not really have started the race over for all the competitors, but it would have equalized the race for those workers who had seniority in different departments.

The Supreme Court disavowed this approach in *International Brotherhood of Teamsters v. United States*, 431 U.S. 324 (1977). In a portion of *Teamsters* we have not encountered before, the Court considered a collective bargaining agreement that created separate seniority lines for city driver jobs and line driver jobs. Blacks had been confined to the city driver jobs and excluded from the better line driver positions. To move to the better jobs, minority drivers would have to surrender their city driver seniority. The Supreme Court held that the mere perpetuation of earlier discrimination does not make a seniority provision in a collective bargaining agreement illegal. "[A]n otherwise neutral, legitimate seniority system does not become unlawful under Title VII simply because it may perpetuate pre-Act discrimination." Because of §703(h), Title VII does not invalidate a seniority system even where, owing to discrimination that occurred before Title VII became effective, women and minority males were handicapped in their present ability to compete for jobs. "[T]hat conclusion is inescapable even in a case, such as this one, where the pre-Act discriminatees are incumbent employees who accumulated seniority in other bargaining units."

The Court turned *Quarles* on its head: by including §703(h), Congress did intend to freeze an entire generation of employees in the discriminatory patterns that existed before Title VII was enacted: The use of a seniority system was no longer the basis for liability under the "present effects of past discrimination" concept of discrimination.

Just as important, the *Teamsters* Court also treated §703(h) as creating a defense to disparate impact claims for actions taken pursuant to a bona fide seniority system. "Were it not for §703(h), the seniority system in this case would seem to fall under the *Griggs* rationale." Thus, whenever the plaintiff establishes a prima facie case of disparate impact discrimination, one possible defense is that the barrier to employment opportunity that plaintiff has shown is really the product of a bona fide seniority system.

All of the early cases involving seniority involved collective bargaining systems. But more recently the Supreme Court recognized a seniority defense even where no collective bargaining agreement was involved In *USAirways, Inc. v. Barnett*, 535 U.S. 391 (2002), an ADA case, defendant had unilaterally promulgated a seniority system. Plaintiff requested accommodation of his disability by allowing him to continue doing his light duty job, even though the seniority system would have allowed employees with greater seniority to "bump" him. Although, unlike Title VII, the ADA has no explicit seniority exception, the Court held that, "in the run of cases," a requested accommodation that would conflict with the rules of a seniority system is not reasonable. Whether or not a seniority system is the product of collective bargaining, such systems generally create expectations by employees of fair treatment and encourage employee loyalty. Those values would be undermined were an employer required to demonstrate, on a case-by-case basis, special circumstances that would permit it to adhere to the system in the face of a requested accommodation. Such case-by-case analysis "might well undermine the employees' expectations of consistent, uniform treatment — expectations upon which the seniority system's benefits depend." *Id.* at 404.

While seniority connotes length of service, the Supreme Court has rejected any bright-line test of what is sheltered by §703(h) in favor of a broader test set by commonly accepted notions of what constitutes a seniority system. In *California Brewers Assn. v. Bryant*, 444 U.S. 598 (1980), plaintiffs challenged a clause in a collective bargaining agreement in the state's brewing industry that required a temporary employee to work at least 45 weeks in a single calendar year in order to become a permanent employee. Permanent employees were entitled to greater benefits than temporary employees, and no black had ever attained permanent-employee status because of the operation of the 45-week rule. While the court of appeals had found that the 45-week rule was not a protected by §703(h) because it had no connection to either total time worked or overall length of service, the Supreme Court reversed. "'[S]eniority' is a term that connotes length of employment. A 'seniority system' is a scheme that, alone or in tandem with non-'seniority' criteria, allots to employees ever improving employment rights and benefits as their relative lengths of pertinent employment increase." *Id.* at 605-6. Since §703(h) by its terms protects seniority *systems* and since Title VII was passed against a backdrop of labor policy favoring unregulated bargaining between labor and management, even those parts of a seniority system that do not turn on length of service are sheltered from disparate impact liability.

Since §703(h) is an exception from liability for disparate impact discrimination, the seniority system issue is an affirmative defense with the burden of proof and persuasion on the defendant. If the employer carries its burden of establishing its affirmative defense, then the plaintiff has a surrebuttal of proving that the system was itself the product of intentional discrimination. In *Pullman-Standard v. Swint*, 456 U.S. 273 (1982), the Court treated a challenge to the bona fides of a department seniority system having a disparate impact on black workers; they were required to forfeit their departmental seniority in order to transfer to a different department, including departments that had been restricted to whites before passage of Title VII. The Supreme Court held the court of appeals had violated F.R.C.P. Rule 52, which requires that findings of fact not be set aside unless clearly erroneous. Given the broad protection of §703(h), a seniority system can be overturned only if it was put in place to intentionally discriminate. That is a question of fact, not of law.

In light of the extreme deference given by the courts to seniority, few seniority cases are brought. It is possible that the 1991 Amendments to Title VII changed the ground rules somewhat by applying the alternative employment practice surrebuttal step of disparate impact analysis to cases involving seniority. At least in the context of unionization, employers abjure the use of seniority and, absent a disparate impact case, generally proclaim that many alternative practices are much more effective than is seniority. However, given the broad reading given §703(h) and the anemic reading so far accorded to alternative employment practices, much movement along this front seems unlikely.

As a final note, the Court has treated seniority as largely sacrosanct, presumably because of the embedded expectations of other workers. Nevertheless, the significance of seniority depends ultimately not on whether workers rely on it but rather whether employers (alone or in collective bargaining agreements with unions) adopt such systems. Should employers choose to reject seniority, there is unlikely to be a problem. This was illustrated recently, in *Smith v. City of Jackson*, reproduced at p. 223, an ADEA case, involving "reverse seniority"; in other words, the more senior the worker the lower percentage his pay raise. The Court had no difficulty in upholding this policy against disparate impact attack as a "reasonable factor other than age."

3. Bona Fide Merit and Piecework Systems

Section 703(h) sets forth an exception to disparate impact liability for bona fide merit and piecework systems:

> [I]t shall not be an unlawful employment practice for an employer to apply different standards of compensation, or different terms, conditions, or privileges of employment pursuant to a bona fide . . . merit system, or a system which measures earnings by quantity or quality of production . . . provided that such differences are not the result of an intention to discriminate.

Systems that measure compensation by quantity of production are piecework systems: the more a worker produces, the more he or she is paid. Since quantity of production obviously is a factor in determining a quality of a worker, piecework systems (sometimes called incentive systems) are one type of merit system. A system that measures compensation by quality of production may also be part of a piecework system in the sense that rejects do not count for pay. A quality-of-production system might be broader, however, in that it involves the evaluation of the quality-of-worker performance. In that sense the quality-of-production notion is really just another name for a merit system. The general concept of this exception is that better job performance is rewarded. There are few cases interpreting these exceptions.

NOTE ON LITIGATION SCORECARD

The Supreme Court's decision in 1989 in *Wards* Cove provoked general outrage at the Court's diminution of the disparate impact theory. While other anti-civil rights decisions in that same term also generated resistance, overturning *Wards Cove* was the driving force for what became the Civil Rights Act of 1991. What is ironic is that disparate impact is rarely used despite the pro-plaintiff provisions of §703(k). Elaine W. Shoben, *Disparate Impact Theory in Employment Discrimination: What's Griggs Still Good For? What Not?*, 42 BRANDEIS L.J. 597, 598-99 (2004), details possible reasons for this underutilization:

First, it is a less desirable claim for plaintiffs than intent-based claims because there are no compensatory or punitive damages available for disparate impact claims. . . . Second, the theory is underutilized because it is inherently a class-based theory and class actions are difficult, if not impossible, for private plaintiffs to undertake unless they involve the possibility of very large damage awards. . . . Third, the world has changed in the last thirty-two years and employers now know the rules. . . . Fourth, disparate impact theory is under attack in some judicial quarters," [notably under the ADEA].

Professor Charles A. Sullivan, however, has recently called for a revival of disparate impact theory in substantial part because intentional discrimination has become so hard to prove. *See* Charles A. Sullivan, *Disparate Impact: Looking Past the* Desert Palace *Mirage*, 47 WILL. & MARY L. REV. 911 (2006). In contrast, Professor Michael L. Selmi, in *Was the Disparate Impact Theory a Mistake?*, 53 UCLA L. REV. 701, 701 (2006), argues that it was disparate impact that caused the problem: "by pushing an expansive theory of impact we were left with a truncated theory of intentional discrimination, one that continues to turn on animus and motive." After studying this chapter, is it likely that plaintiff's disparate impact cases will have any better chance of success than disparate treatment cases?

NOTE ON INTERNATIONAL AND COMPARATIVE ANTIDISCRIMINATION LAW

The EU has now established a uniform structure for dealing with what it calls indirect discrimination in three directives dealing with sex, Directive 1997/80/EC, racial or ethnic origin, Directive 2000/43/EC, and religion, disability, age and sexual orientation, Directive 2000/78/EC. Article 1 of the latter provides as follows:

> (b) indirect discrimination shall be taken to occur where an apparently neutral provision, criterion or practice would put persons having a particular religion or belief, a particular disability, a particular age, or a particular sexual orientation at a particular disadvantage compared with other persons unless:
> (i) that provision, criterion or practice is objectively justified by a legitimate aim and the means of achieving that aim are appropriate and necessary . . .

Article 10(1) requires the national laws of each member state to shift the burden of proof to the defendant once plaintiff establishes a prima facie case. The employer must "prove that there has been no breach of the principle of equal treatment." How different is this than the provision in Title VII's § 703(k) requiring the defendant to prove that a challenged employment practice is "job related and consistent with business necessity?"

Chapter 4

The Interrelation of the Three Theories
of Discrimination

The individual disparate treatment, systemic disparate treatment, and disparate impact approaches to discrimination have each developed separately. The courts have yet to synthesize these approaches into a coherent field theory of employment discrimination law. This chapter will attempt to lay the groundwork for that synthesis.

PROBLEM 4.1

You are an attorney who has been visited by a potential client, Ann Abalos, who claims she was denied a promotion because she is Latina. The employer, Shuffled Papers Inc., hires many people for entry-level clerical jobs. In a metropolitan area with an 18 percent Latino population, the entry level is made up of 16 percent Latinos — 160 of the 1,000 clericals. Persons promoted to supervisor come from the pool of clericals; other than promoting from within, no announced policy describes the promotion process. Openings are not posted, and people apparently are simply picked for promotion by the managers, who are predominately white and male. Only 2 of the 50 supervisors are Latinos.

Abalos asked her supervisor, Bernie Baker, if she could be promoted. He told her that he thought she was well qualified and that he would suggest her name to his manager. After several other people were promoted, Abalos asked Baker why she had not been chosen. He told her that she was "in the running" but had to wait until her turn came.

In your initial discussions with the lawyer for Shuffled Papers, you were told that, to be considered for promotion to supervisor, a clerical employee must have two years of college and three years of experience. All of the supervisors satisfy those prerequisites, but some clericals, including Abalos, also satisfy them. Twenty percent of the white clerical workers meet these minimum requirements, while only 10 percent of the Latino clerical workers have both three years of experience and two years of college.

Evaluate Abalos's case in light of all three general theories of discrimination.

As you read through the following material, reconsider what theories of liability are available to you on behalf of Abalos and what defenses Shuffled Papers can assert in response to each theory of liability.

A.   THE INTERRELATIONSHIP OF INDIVIDUAL AND SYSTEMIC DISPARATE TREATMENT

Perhaps the easiest interrelationship question is that between individual and systemic disparate treatment. A plaintiff can, of course, claim individual disparate treatment, focusing on only his own situation without bringing in evidence of other actions against other members of his protected group. At the opposite extreme, a plaintiff might try to make out what is essentially a systemic case of discrimination in order to put his treatment into context. Typically, however, this evidence will be introduced not to make out a systemic theory but rather to enable the trier of fact to place the claims of intentional individual discrimination in the proper context as part of the plaintiff's proof of pretext.

In *McDonnell Douglas Corp. v. Green*, reproduced at p. 50, the Supreme Court invited such proof: "Other evidence that may be relevant to any showing of pretext includes facts as to . . . the [employer's] general policy and practice with respect to minority employment. On the latter point, statistics as to petitioner's employment policy and practice may be helpful to a determination of whether petitioner's refusal to rehire respondent in this case conformed to a general pattern of discrimination against blacks." But the Court simultaneously dropped a footnote warning against giving this proof too much weight:

> The District Court may, for example, determine, after reasonable discovery that "the [racial] composition of defendant's labor force is itself reflective of restrictive or exclusionary practices." We caution that such general determinations, while helpful, may not be in and of themselves controlling as to an individualized hiring decision, particularly in the presence of an otherwise justifiable reason for refusing to rehire.

411 U.S. at 806 n. 19. *See also Cornish v. City of Los Angeles, Dep't of Water & Power*, 1994 U.S. App. LEXIS 8405 (9th Cir. 1994) (statistics "raise disturbing questions with respect to DWP's historical treatment and promotion of African-Americans. However, such evidence of a racially unbalanced workforce cannot in and of itself be conclusive proof of discriminatory intent in a specific disparate treatment case").

BAYLIE v. FRB
476 F.3d 522 (7th Cir. 2007)

EASTERBROOK, Chief Judge.

This appeal presents the tail end of a class action in which employees accused the Federal Reserve Bank of Chicago of race, sex, and age discrimination. Four years ago the district court decertified the class and allowed employees to pursue individual claims. Only two remain for resolution on this appeal. The district judge concluded that these two had not established even a *prima facie* case of discrimination and granted summary judgment to the Bank.

Although only two employees' claims remain for decision, their brief proceeds largely as if a class continued to seek systemic relief. Plaintiffs rely heavily on the report of an expert who concluded that black employees were less likely to be promoted than white employees. They maintain that this report is enough by itself to require a trial. Going to the opposite extreme, the Bank contends that statistical evidence is never relevant outside a class action or a suit by a public agency on behalf of employees as a group. Both of these positions misunderstand the role of statistical inference.

Most contentions in litigation are empirical rather than axiomatic. Propositions of fact are arrived at by inductive rather than deductive means. All inferences are statistical — whether implicitly or explicitly does not matter. A plaintiff who accuses Supervisor X of discrimination because he never has promoted a black person, and often says disparaging things about black workers, is drawing a statistical inference: that if X has been indifferent to race, then selections from the pool of employees eligible for promotion would have included some black workers, and in particular would have included the plaintiff. Likewise the proposition "9 of 10 people exposed to sarin die within 20 minutes, so sarin is deadly" is a statistical inference, one so obvious that no expert is needed to show causation. But the inference often may be elusive, and then someone trained in the analysis of numbers will help.

Professional statistics is a rigorous means to analyze large numbers of events and inquire whether what appear to be patterns really are the result of chance (and, if not, which variables are associated with which outcomes). Suppose we know that 20,000 of 100,000 persons exposed to high dosage x-rays eventually develop cancer, and that 19,500 of 100,000 persons not so exposed develop cancer. Should we attribute the apparent excess risk of 500 cancers to the x-ray, or might it have some other cause? Is this excess risk real or an illusion caused by errors in measurement and analysis, the sort of variance that may occur by chance? A statistical analysis may be able to answer these questions — and, if the answer is yes, the knowledge that high-dosage x-rays increase the risk of cancer may inform a decision whether the benefits of the procedure are worth the extra risk. But it will not tell us whether a given person who develops cancer did so because of the x-ray; only 2.5% of cancers can be attributed to the radiation, so 97.5% of all cancers, even among persons exposed to high-dosage x-rays, have other causes. This is the sense in which statistics are more helpful in a pattern-or-practice case, where a judge will be asked to direct the employer to change how it makes hiring or promotion decisions.

In individual cases, studies of probabilities are less helpful. Suppose 1,000 employees apply for 100 promotions; 150 of the workers are black and 850 white. If all are equally qualified and the employer ignores race, then 85 white workers and 15 black workers will be promoted, plus or minus some variation that can be chalked up to chance. Suppose only 10 black workers are promoted. Is that the result of discrimination or chance? Econometric analysis (an application of statistical techniques) may suggest the answer by taking into account both other potentially explanatory variables and the rate of random variance. *See Mister v. Illinois Central Gulf R.R.*, 832 F.2d 1427 (7th Cir. 1987); Federal Judicial Center, *Reference Manual on Scientific Evidence* 83-227 (2d ed. 2000); Paul Meier, Jerome Sacks & Sandy L. Zabell, *What Happened in Hazelwood: Statistics, Employment Discrimination, and the 80% Rule*, 1984 Am. Bar Foundation Research J. 139, 158-70; Thomas J. Campbell, *Regression Analysis in Title VII Cases*, 36 Stan. L. Rev. 1299 (1984).

When the answer is positive (discrimination occurred; the conclusion is statistically significant) it cannot reveal with certainty whether any given person suffered. In this example, 150 black workers applied for promotion; 10 were promoted and the other 140 were not. But for discrimination, 15 would have been promoted and 135 not. Which of the 140 non-promoted employees would have received the other 5 promotions? The statistical analysis does not tell us — and in civil litigation, where the plaintiff's burden is to show more likely than not that he was harmed by a legal wrong, data of this kind will not get a worker over that threshold.

Statistical analysis is relevant in the technical sense that it "has a tendency to make the existence of [a material] fact . . . more probable or less probable than it would be without the evidence." Fed. R. Evid. 401. But data showing a small increase in the probability of discrimination cannot by itself get a plaintiff over the more-likely-than-not threshold; it must be coupled with other evidence, which does most of the work. A disappointed worker could ask for damages measured by the lost opportunity: each of the 140 disappointed workers might receive as damages 5/140 of the extra income enjoyed by those who received promotions. That's the loss-of-a-chance measure of damages. *See Doll v. Brown*, 75 F.3d 1200 (7th Cir. 1996). But it is more suited to classwide litigation, and our two plaintiffs have not requested this remedy.

What statistics did these plaintiffs offer — the kind that permit a sound inference in an individual case (our examples of Supervisor X and exposure to sarin) or the kind that may support class-wide equitable relief but are only marginally relevant when an individual plaintiff seeks an award of damages? Plaintiffs' expert analyzed all non-managerial workers at the Bank between 1995 and 2000. Workers as a whole enjoyed a probability of about 0.25 of being promoted to a higher pay grade each year (stated otherwise, the average worker was promoted once every four years). Coefficients in an econometric regression implied that black workers had about a 0.20 probability and white workers about a 0.27 probability, and after controlling for other variables the expert concluded that 5/7 of this difference (or a 0.05 chance of promotion each year) was unaccounted for by any hypothesis other than race. In other words, the average white worker received an extra promotion every 20th year compared with the average black worker, holding constant factors (such as education) other than race. The Bank's experts questioned whether this result is statistically significant (that is, whether the difference is a result of chance rather than race) and whether it is meaningful for most of the workers. It turns out that the most frequent "promotion" is from temporary to full-time work. If the analysis is limited to persons (such as plaintiffs) already working at the Bank full time, then black workers are slightly more likely than white workers to be promoted in any given year.

Given the consequence of restricting the data set to full-time workers, this econometric analysis offers our two plaintiffs no support. Even presented as plaintiffs' expert did, rolling the temporary-to-full-time promotions into the data, the study doesn't provide plaintiffs with much assistance. These two plaintiffs applied for several promotions annually. If race affects one promotion every 20 years, and workers seek three promotional opportunities a year, then there is one chance in 60 that a given application would have been successful if the applicant were white rather than black. Over many years and many employees this effect could be substantial — which is why such analysis is helpful in class actions — but in a single employee's case it does very little to get the claim over the more-likely-than-not threshold. A worker can't say simply: "I've been here 20 years, so I'm entitled to one extra promotion." All of that time except the most recent 300 days falls outside Title VII's statute of limitations. *See National Railroad Passenger Corp. v. Morgan*, 536 U.S. 101 (2002). Analysis thus must proceed vacancy-by-vacancy in an individual case, not career-by-career.

If a plaintiff had evidence suggesting that the probability that race accounted for a given turn-down was (say) 49.8%, then the addition of the statistical analysis would push the probability past 50%. In other words, the expert's conclusion in this litigation could serve as a tie-breaker. But first there would have to *be* a tie — and plaintiffs' evidence does not come close to making this case a tossup that statistics might decide in their favor. Cf. *Sun v. University of Illinois*, 473 F.3d 799 (7th Cir. Jan. 16, 2007) (considering statistical evidence in an individual case but finding that the data did not create a material dispute).

NOTES

1. *The Role of Statistics in Individual Disparate Treatment Cases.* Judge Easterbrook does not rule out the use of statistics in individual disparate treatment cases, but he assigns it a very limited role. Unless the plaintiff's case is otherwise very close to establishing intent to discriminate by a preponderance of the evidence, it will not tip the balance and thus summary judgment against plaintiff is still appropriate. Statistical evidence is, at most, a tie-breaker. If the plaintiff's case goes to the jury without considering the statistics, however, Judge Easterbrook's opinion suggests that the evidence is probative (even if of slight value), which should mean it is admissible. *See also Obrey v. Johnson*, 400 F.3d 691 (9th Cir. 2005) (while statistical evidence could not prove that a particular employee had been discriminated against, it should have been admitted for whatever probative value it had). While of slight value to Judge Easterbrook, might such evidence make a big difference with the jury? If it would likely make a big difference, however, maybe that's a basis to exclude it under FRE 403 since its potential for prejudice would exceed its probative value.

2. *What if This Were a Systemic Case?* The litigation in *Baylie* started as a class action. While we will not discuss the requirements of class actions until Chapter 7, had the case continued as a class action, plaintiff's statistical proof would have played an entirely different role. We encountered this in *Teamsters* and *Hazelwood*, but it most clearly emerges in *Franks v. Bowman Transp. Co.*, 424 U.S. 747 (1976), which established the relationship between systemic disparate treatment and individual disparate treatment where liability is established on the systemic claim. Essentially, *Franks* held that demonstrating a systemic pattern of intentional discrimination creates a presumption that the individual members of the racial group in question had themselves been discriminated against on account of race. Thus, the employer can avoid granting relief to individual members of the class only if it can carry the burden of persuasion that each individual was *not* a victim of discrimination. As

applied to *Baylie, Franks* means that, had the class action continued and the statistics sufficed to prove systemic disparate treatment, the two individual plaintiffs would have been presumed to have been victims. It would then have been the Federal Reserve Board's burden to prove that they would not have been promoted in any event. In a portion of the opinion that has been omitted, Judge Easterbrook found that neither plaintiff carried her burden, but there would have been no burden to carry in a systemic case.

3. *Why Isn't* Baylie *a Systemic Case?* The Seventh Circuit does not explicitly address the issue, but *Baylie* implicitly suggests that systemic disparate treatment can be invoked only in the context of a class action or a government enforcement action. These are, in fact, the two situations in which the theory has been applied by the Supreme Court in *Teamsters/Hazelwood* and *Franks.* Some courts have explicitly held that systemic disparate treatment is limited to these settings. *E.g., Celestine v. Petroleos de Venezuella SA*, 266 F.3d 343, 355-56 (5th Cir. 2001) (not error for district court to not apply the theory); *Gilty v. Oak Park*, 919 F.2d 1247, 1251 (7th Cir, 1991) (pattern and practice evidence can only be "collateral" to individual case). The rationale appears to be that systemic treatment is a class concept and therefore applicable only in class actions. Some older cases, however, hold that a burden shift is appropriate even in an individual case where plaintiff can prove a pattern or practice of discrimination. *Cox v. Am. Cast Iron Pipe Co.*, 784 F.2d 1546, 1559 (11th Cir. 1986). *See also Davis v. Califano*, 613 F.2d 957 224 (D.C. Cir. 1979). In the present era, there is certainly judicial skepticism towards class actions of any kind. Are the courts also limiting class-based theories of liability? What policy is served by truncating the use of class approaches in litigation?

4. *Loss of Chance.* Is the individual/systemic question related to "the loss-of-a-chance measure of damages"? *Baylie* suggests that, in the hypothetical of 140 disappointed workers, each "might receive as damages 5/140 of the extra income enjoyed by those who received promotions." The opinion goes on to say that this measure "is more suited to class-wide litigation, and our two plaintiffs have not requested this remedy." Is that a sufficient reason to deny them a remedy that would otherwise be appropriate? Suppose they had asked for loss-of-chance damages? Why shouldn't it be awarded, assuming sufficient reason to find discrimination against the group? We will revisit this measure in Chapter 8 at p. 669.

5. *Non-statistical Systemic Proof.* The logic of *Baylie* is that "non-statistical" proof of other discriminatory decisions is admissible but may lack the power of statistical proof. Another way to say the same thing is that proof that four out of five whites were promoted while only one of five blacks were is probative of discrimination. Such proof is not "statistical" in the sense that the numbers are too small to yield statistical significance, and no expert is needed; but the proof is admissible and may be a factor in plaintiff's establishing his case by a preponderance of the evidence. *See Sun v. Bd. of Trs.*, 473 F.2d 700, 813 (7th Cir. 2007) ("Although the sample size is insufficient to provide statistically reliable evidence, the PTC's voting pattern [against Asians and in favor of Caucasians] has some probative value regarding discriminatory employment practices").

6. *Same Decision Maker?* Judge Easterbrook fails to address whether the same decision-maker was responsible for all the decisions that the statistical proof addressed, but it seems unlikely. Some courts in individual disparate treatment cases have required that any proof of other instances of discrimination be limited to actions by the person responsible for the at-issue employment action. This is very common where the claim is discriminatory discipline, but it also operates in other

settings. *See Mendelsohn v. Sprint/United Mgmt. Co.*, 466 F.3d 1223 (10th Cir. 2006), *cert granted*, 127 S. Ct. 2937 (2007) (where a company-wide policy is at issue, such as a reduction in force, it is error to limit testimony to those employees who worked for the same supervisor as plaintiff; the "same supervisor rule" is limited to challenges to discriminatory discipline). See p. 108. In systemic cases, of course, there is no such limitation.

NOTE ON THE RELATION BETWEEN INDIVIDUAL CASES AND UNSUCCESSFUL CLASS ACTIONS

We have seen that individuals in successful class actions have the advantage of being presumptively found to have suffered from discrimination. In *Baylie*, the class action was decertified before any class-wide decision was made; thus the individual plaintiffs were neither helped nor hurt. But what about a class action in which the defendant prevails? *Cooper v. Federal Reserve Bank of Richmond*, 467 U.S. 867 (1984), held that failure of the systemic claims in a class action does not cut off the right of individuals making up the class to advance claims of individual disparate treatment:

> The crucial difference between an individual's claim of discrimination and a class action alleging a general pattern or practice of discrimination is manifest. The inquiry regarding an individual's claim is the reason for a particular employment decision, while "at the liability stage of a pattern-or-practice trial the focus often will not be on individual hiring decisions, but on a pattern of discriminatory decisionmaking."

Id. at 876. The members of the class are barred by res judicata from bringing another class action against the employer alleging systemic disparate treatment discrimination for the time period. But because the claims of individual disparate treatment made by individual class members have never been litigated, individual claims (other than those of the named plaintiff) are not precluded merely because the systemic claim has been litigated.

B. THE RELATIONSHIP BETWEEN INDIVIDUAL DISPARATE TREATMENT AND DISPARATE IMPACT

Although litigants often try to use both theories, see Stacy Seicshnaydre, *Is the Road to Disparate Impact Paved with Good Intentions? — Stuck on State of Mind in Antidiscrimination Law*, 42 WAKE FOREST L. REV. ___ (2008), disparate impact analysis is neither necessary nor relevant in a pure disparate treatment case. The point is obvious with respect to individual disparate treatment: a plaintiff typically will present her case by focusing on facts relevant to her situation; there will be no need to develop broader theories. Similarly, the employer will not seek to justify, in business necessity terms, an individual employment decision. Under individual disparate treatment analysis, the employer's usual strategy will be to show a "legitimate, nondiscriminatory reason" for its actions. Because this is far easier to establish than "business necessity," employers will not try to shoulder the heavier burden.

This was confirmed by *Raytheon Co. v. Hernandez*, 540 U.S. 44 (2003), where the Court held that, absent pleading a disparate impact claim, an individual disparate treatment case focuses on whether the defendant's explanation was a "legitimate, nondiscriminatory reason," which makes the business necessity defense irrelevant. Had Hernandez also pled a disparate impact claim and made out a prima facie case, then the business necessity defense would be appropriate. In *Raytheon*, the employer's asserted reason for not rehiring plaintiff was that he had been terminated for violation of personal conduct rules, which the employer claimed to be its policy. Since misconduct was broader than drug or alcohol-related disability, such a rule was disability-neutral in intent terms. While neutrality would not itself make such a rule job related or necessary for business, that's unimportant in a disparate treatment case.

It is true that a plaintiff bringing an individual case of disparate treatment might try to establish that the employer's "legitimate, nondiscriminatory reason" has a disparate impact. Such a case, however, will then become a garden-variety disparate impact case. The only difference is that, by asserting the reason as the basis for its decision to take an adverse employment action, the employer will have eliminated the potential argument that the policy in issue was not what caused the adverse employment action for plaintiff.

C. THE RELATIONSHIP BETWEEN SYSTEMIC DISPARATE TREATMENT AND DISPARATE IMPACT

1. Disparate Impact Analysis Inapplicable to Systemic Disparate Treatment Cases

Disparate impact analysis should not be applied to systemic disparate treatment claims. With respect to formal systems of disparate treatment, the Supreme Court has several times spoken directly, most definitively in *International Union, UAW v. Johnson Controls, Inc.*, reproduced at p. 173, where the Court was confronted with several circuit court decisions upholding fetal-protection policies on the grounds they were a "business necessity." It rejected this approach: such policies facially discriminate on the basis of gender and pregnancy, and business necessity is not a defense to intentional discrimination. Rather, it can be employed only to defend a disparate impact attack. See also *Los Angeles Dept. of Water & Power v. Manhart*, reproduced at p. 116 ("treatment of a person in a manner which but for that person's sex would be different" violates Title VII even if there is no disparate impact on women); *Trans World Airlines, Inc. v. Thurston*, 469 U.S. 111 (1985) (the absence of adverse effects on older workers as a group does not bar suit challenging a formal discriminatory policy under the ADEA).

The Court's position in *Johnson Controls* was codified by the Civil Rights Act of 1991, which added §703(k)(2), to Title VII: "A demonstration that an employment practice is required by business necessity may not be used as a defense against a claim of intentional discrimination under this title." This amendment also resolved a question not formally raised by the earlier cases: the appropriate analysis when the plaintiff, unable to show formal systemic disparate treatment, seeks to establish disparate treatment by showing a pattern or practice of conduct that gives rise to an inference of intentional discrimination. The seminal case, of course, is *Teamsters v. United States*, reproduced at p. 123. The language of §703(k)(2) makes clear that the employer in such a case may not prevail by proving business necessity. Rather, as we have seen, it may prevail only by disproving the pattern or by offering an alternative explanation for the inference of discriminatory intent the plaintiff seeks to draw. It should be noted, however, that — while business necessity is not a formal defense in this setting — the more reasonable and necessary are an employer's discriminatory reasons for acting in a certain way, the more likely they will be, as a practical matter, to rebut an inference of discriminatory intent that would otherwise be drawn from statistics or other circumstances.

2.   Intent to Discriminate: The Dividing Line Between the Two Systemic Theories

The lower courts have repeatedly confused systemic disparate treatment and disparate impact. The Court in *Johnson Controls*, for example, rejected an attempt by the lower courts to import the business necessity defense from disparate impact law into a systemic disparate treatment case. As the Supreme Court made clear, the intentional use of a prohibited characteristic (in that case, sex) by the employer is disparate treatment, and thus the employer had engaged in unlawful discrimination unless it could prove it had a BFOQ.

More recently, in the context of the Americans with Disabilities Act, the Court again rejected an effort to blend the two analyses. *Raytheon Co. v. Hernandez*, 540 U.S. 44 (2003), involved a claim by a former employee that he had been discriminatorily denied re-employment by Raytheon because he was "regarded as" or had "a record of" being disabled. Plaintiff had resigned, in lieu of being fired, for drug use. When he applied for reemployment two years later, his application was rejected. According to the company, the rejection was pursuant to its policy not to rehire employees who left the company for violating personal conduct rules. While we will study the ADA in more detail in Chapter 6, it is impermissible to discriminate against qualified individuals with a disability on the basis of their addiction or record of addiction, but it is legal to discriminate on the basis of their current illegal use of drugs. Thus, the original discharge was legal but a refusal to rehire because Hernandez was, or was believed to be, a recovering addict would not have been. See p. 300.

In *Raytheon* itself, however, the employer claimed that the person in its Labor Relations Department who reviewed Hernandez's application and rejected him did not know that he was a former drug addict when she made the decision to turn him down. She knew only that he had been discharged for violating "personal conduct" rules, and she rejected him because of that in accordance with Raytheon's (admittedly unwritten) policy to that effect. The Ninth Circuit reversed summary judgment in favor of the employer on the plaintiff's disparate treatment claim. In doing so, it found that the "no rehire rule," at least as applied to former drug addicts, was not a legitimate, nondiscriminatory reason because it would create a disparate effect by screening out those with a record of drug addiction.

The Supreme Court reversed because the lower court had "improperly applied a disparate-impact analysis in a disparate-treatment case." *Id.* at 55. The appeals court had admitted that a no-rehire for misconduct rule was facially lawful, but nonetheless held it to be unlawful as applied to individuals like the plaintiff who were terminated for reasons connected to their addiction. The Supreme Court found that such a conclusion could be reached only by erroneously applying impact analysis to a treatment case:

> [W]hile ostensibly evaluating whether petitioner had proffered a legitimate, nondiscriminatory reason for failing to rehire respondent sufficient to rebut respondent's prima facie showing of disparate treatment, the Court of Appeals held that a neutral no-rehire policy could never suffice in a case where the employee was terminated for illegal drug use, because such a policy has a disparate impact on recovering drug addicts. In so holding, the Court of Appeals erred by conflating the analytical framework for disparate-impact and disparate-treatment claims. Had the Court of Appeals correctly applied the disparate-treatment framework, it would have been obliged to conclude that a neutral no-rehire policy is, by definition, a legitimate, nondiscriminatory reason under the ADA. And thus the only remaining question would be whether respondent could produce sufficient evidence from which a jury could conclude that "petitioner's stated reason for respondent's rejection was in fact pretext."

Id. at 51-52. It cautioned that "Because 'the factual issues, and therefore the character of the evidence presented, differ when the plaintiff claims that a facially neutral employment policy has a discriminatory impact on protected classes,' courts must be careful to distinguish between these theories." *Id.* at 53. The defendant's putting into evidence its neutral no-rehire policy satisfied its burden under *McDonnell Douglas*; indeed, the "no-rehire policy is a quintessential legitimate, nondiscriminatory reason for refusing to rehire an employee who was terminated for violating workplace conduct rules." *Id.* at 45. The only appropriate inquiry at that stage, therefore, was whether that reason was a pretext for discrimination. The Court suggested that the policy could have been challenged as having a disparate impact on disability grounds, but plaintiff had not asserted that theory in a timely fashion. *But see* Elizabeth Roseman, *A Phoenix from the Ashes? Heightened Pleading Requirements in Disparate Impact Cases*, 36 SETON HALL L. REV. 1043 (2005) (arguing that the disparate impact claim had in fact been properly pled); see p. 91.

Raytheon reinforces the intent notion and sets out a litmus test: An employer cannot intentionally discriminate on the basis of a particular trait if it does not know of the trait. Obviously, the absence of knowledge is more likely where disability is concerned than race or sex, but *Raytheon* has application even in such cases (as where a higher level manager makes a decision without knowing the races of those affected) and can certainly apply to areas of Title VII such as discrimination on account of religion, see Section 5D, p. 421, and perhaps even national origin.

3. Applying the Two Systemic Theories in One Case

Pleading aside, it's easy to see how, in a case like *Raytheon Co. v. Hernandez*, a plaintiff could deploy both individual disparate treatment and disparate impact in one case. Mr. Hernandez could have claimed that the supposed nondiscriminatory reason was pretext because the Raytheon decision maker in fact knew of his record of disability and acted on that basis; in fact, on remand, the Ninth Circuit required a trial on just this theory. *Hernandez v. Hughes Missile Sys. Co.*, 362 F.3d 564, 566 (9th Cir. 2004). Simultaneously, the plaintiff could have asserted that, if the no-hire policy was, in reality, the basis for the decision, it had a disparate impact on disability grounds (or that the ADA's duty of reasonable accommodation would require a modification of the no-rehire rule in a case where the misconduct was a product of the disability).

More common, however, is the situation where there is no formal policy at issue. In *Raytheon* itself, the supposed policy was unwritten, which means that perhaps it is better described as a practice. Suppose plaintiff proved that a large number of former addicts were denied employment by Raytheon; indeed, suppose he proved that addicts were disproportionately denied employment. Is such proof systemic disparate treatment, disparate impact, or both? Bismarck is reputed to have said, "Laws are like sausages, it is better not to see them being made." The next principal case offers a unique opportunity for students to answer this question while seeing laws and sausages being made simultaneously.

EEOC v. DIAL CORPORATION
469 F.3d 735 (8th Cir. 2006)

MURPHY, Circuit Judge.

The Equal Employment Opportunity Commission (EEOC) brought this sex discrimination action against The Dial Corporation under Title VII of the Civil Rights Act of 1964 on behalf of a number of women who had applied for work but were not hired. A jury found that Dial had engaged in a pattern or practice of intentional discrimination against women and awarded compensatory damages, and the district court concluded that Dial's use of a preemployment strength test had an unlawful disparate impact on female applicants and awarded back pay and benefits. . . .

Dial is an international company with a plant located in Fort Madison, Iowa that produces canned meats. Entry level employees at the plant are assigned to the sausage packing area where workers daily lift and carry up to 18,000 pounds of sausage, walking the equivalent of four miles in the process. They are required to carry approximately 35 pounds of sausage at a time and must lift and load the sausage to heights between 30 and 60 inches above the floor. Employees who worked in the sausage packing area experienced a disproportionate number of injuries as compared to the rest of the workers in the plant.

Dial implemented several measures to reduce the injury rate starting in late 1996. These included an ergonomic job rotation, institution of a team approach, lowering the height of machines to decrease lifting pressure for the employees, and conducting periodic safety audits. In 2000 Dial also instituted a strength test used to evaluate potential employees, called the Work Tolerance Screen (WTS). In this test job applicants were asked to carry a 35 pound bar between two frames, approximately 30 and 60 inches off the floor, and to lift and load the bar onto these frames. The applicants were told to work at their "own pace" for seven minutes. An occupational therapist watched the process, documented how many lifts each applicant completed, and recorded her own comments about each candidate's performance. Starting in 2001, the plant nurse, Martha Lutenegger, also watched and documented the process. From the inception of the test, Lutenegger reviewed the test forms and had the ultimate hiring authority.

For many years women and men had worked together in the sausage packing area doing the same job. Forty six percent of the new hires were women in the three years before the WTS was introduced, but the number of women hires dropped to fifteen percent after the test was implemented. During this time period the test was the only change in the company's hiring practices. The percentage of women who passed the test decreased almost each year the test was given, with only eight percent of the women applicants passing in 2002. The overall percentage of women who passed was thirty eight percent while the men's passage rate was ninety seven percent. While overall injuries and strength related injuries among sausage workers declined consistently after 2000 when the test was implemented, the downward trend in injuries had begun in 1998 after the company had instituted measures to reduce injuries.

[The EEOC brought this action on behalf of a charging party and 53 other women who had been denied employment after taking the WTS; 24 of these applicants had been unable to complete the test.]

A jury trial was held in August 2004, and EEOC and Dial offered testimony by competing experts. EEOC presented an expert on industrial organization who testified that the WTS was significantly more difficult than the actual job workers performed at the plant. He explained that although workers did 1.25 lifts per minute on average and rested between lifts, applicants who took the WTS performed 6 lifts per minute on average, usually without any breaks. He also testified that in two of the three years before Dial had implemented the WTS, the women's injury rate had been lower than that of the male workers. EEOC's expert also analyzed the company's written evaluations of the applicants and testified that more men than women were given offers of employment even when they had received similar comments about their performance. EEOC also introduced evidence that the occupational nurse marked some women as failing despite their having completed the full seven minute test.

Dial presented an expert in work physiology, who testified that in his opinion the WTS effectively tested skills which were representative of the actual job, and an industrial and organizational psychologist, who testified that the WTS measured the requirements of the job and that the decrease in injuries could be attributed to the test. Dial also called plant nurse Martha Lutenegger who testified that although she and other Dial managers knew the WTS was screening out more women than men, the decrease in injuries warranted its continued use.

[The jury found that Dial had engaged in a pattern or practice of intentional discrimination. The trial judge then found that "the WTS had had a discriminatory impact, that Dial had not demonstrated that the WTS was a business necessity or shown either content or criterion validity, and that Dial had not effectively controlled for other variables which may have caused the decline in injuries, including other safety measures that Dial had implemented." The judge assessed backpay for individual applicants ranging from $120,236 to $920 and health benefits ranging from $30,385 to $882.]

On appeal Dial challenges the district court's denial of its motion for judgment as a matter of law, arguing there was insufficient evidence for a jury to find intentional discrimination. Dial also attacks the district court's findings of disparate impact and claims it proved that the WTS was a business necessity because it drastically decreased the number of injuries in the sausage production area of the plant. . . .

A pattern or practice of intentional sex discrimination must be shown by proving "regular and purposeful" discrimination by a preponderance of the evidence, *Int'l Brotherhood of Teamsters v. United States*. EEOC must show that more than an isolated act of discrimination occurred and that "discrimination was the company's standard operating procedure," but statistics combined with anecdotal examples of discrimination may establish a pattern or practice of regular, purposeful discrimination.

Morgan v. United Parcel Service of America, Inc., 380 F.3d 459, 463-64 (8th Cir. 2004). Moreover, discriminatory intent can be inferred from the mere fact of differences in treatment, *Teamsters*.

Statistical disparities are significant if the difference between the expected number and the observed number is greater than two or three standard deviations. *Hazelwood Sch. Dist. v. U.S.* Here, the disparity between hiring of men and women showed nearly ten standard deviations. The percentage of women who passed the WTS declined with each implementation of the test. Despite knowing about the statistical difference, Dial continued to use the WTS. Dial argues that EEOC's statistics are inapplicable because men and women are not similarly situated and have profound physiological differences. There was evidence, however, that women and men worked the same job together for many years before the WTS was instituted. There was also evidence of women and men receiving similar comments on their test forms, but only the males receiving offers of employment.

. . . A reasonable jury could discredit Lutenegger's testimony that the decrease in injuries was the company's motivation for continuing to use the WTS. A reasonable jury could also have found that the differing treatment of males and females supported an inference of intentional discrimination. We conclude that the evidence was sufficient for a reasonable jury to find that there was a pattern and practice of intentional discrimination against women and that the district court did not err by denying Dial's motion for judgment as a matter of law.

Dial objects to the district court's findings of disparate impact and its conclusion that the company failed to prove the WTS was necessary to establish effective and safe job performance. We review the district court's factual findings regarding disparate impact for clear error and its legal findings de novo. Fed. R. Civ. P. 52(a). In a disparate impact case, once the plaintiff establishes a prima facie case the employer must show the practice at issue is "related to safe and efficient job performance and is consistent with business necessity." *Firefighters' Inst. for Racial Equality v. City of St. Louis*, 220 F.3d 898, 904 (8th Cir. 2000). An employer using the business necessity defense must prove that the practice was related to the specific job and the required skills and physical requirements of the position. *Belk v. Southwestern Bell Telephone Co.*, 194 F.3d 946, 951 (8th Cir. 1999). Although a validity study of an employment test can be sufficient to prove business necessity, it is not necessary if the employer demonstrates the procedure is sufficiently related to safe and efficient job performance. *Hawkins v. Anheuser-Busch, Inc.*, 697 F.2d 810, 815-16 (8th Cir. 1983). If the employer demonstrates business necessity, the plaintiff can still prevail by showing there is a less discriminatory alternative. *Firefighters*.

Dial contends the WTS was shown by its experts to have both content and criterion validity. Under EEOC guidelines, "A content validity study should consist of data showing that the content of the selection procedure is representative of important aspects of performance on the job for which the candidates are to be evaluated." 29 C.F.R. § 1607.5(B). Dial's physiology expert testified that the WTS was highly representative of the actions required by the job, and Dial claims that his testimony was not rebutted by EEOC which had no physiology witness. The district court was persuaded by EEOC's expert in industrial organization and his testimony "that a crucial aspect of the WTS is more difficult than the sausage making jobs themselves" and that the average applicant had to perform four times as many lifts as current employees and had no rest breaks. There was also evidence that in a testing environment where hiring is contingent upon test performance, applicants tend to work as fast as possible during the test in order to outperform the competition.

Dial argues the WTS was criterion valid because both overall injuries and strength related injuries decreased dramatically following the implementation of the WTS. The EEOC guidelines establish that criterion validity can be shown by "empirical data demonstrating that the selection procedure is predictive of or significantly correlated with important elements of job performance." 29 C.F.R. § 1607.5(B). Although Dial claims that the decrease in injuries shows that the WTS enabled it to predict which applicants could safely handle the strenuous nature of the work, the sausage plant injuries started decreasing before the WTS was implemented. Moreover, the injury rate for women employees was lower than that for men in two of the three years before Dial implemented the WTS. The evidence did not require the district court to find that the decrease in injuries resulted from the implementation of the WTS instead of the other safety mechanisms Dial started to put in place in 1996.

Dial contends finally that the district court improperly gave it the burden to establish that there was no less discriminatory alternative to the WTS. Dial claims the burden should have been allocated to EEOC as part of the burden shifting framework in disparate impact cases, *Firefighters*. Since Dial failed to demonstrate that the WTS was a business necessity, however, EEOC never was required to show the absence of a nondiscriminatory alternative. . . .

NOTES

1. *Systemic Proof and the Overlap of the Two Theories.* The *Dial* opinion starts its analysis by noting the statistical significance of "the disparity between hiring of men and women" of nearly ten standard deviations. But the disparity was not in overall hiring practices — it was the effects of the administration of the WTS. In other words, the court begins its systemic disparate treatment analysis with proof that would satisfy the disparate impact theory: a showing that a particular employment practice (here, the WTS) has a disparate impact on a protected group (here women).

This shouldn't seem so unusual. The common thread to both systemic theories, disparate treatment and disparate impact, is finding discrimination from the effects of an employer's decisions. In disparate treatment, of course, the effects create an inference of discriminatory intent; in disparate impact, the effects by themselves establish a violation unless the defendant can show business necessity. Both theories, therefore, begin with disparate effects: when a particular group is affected by a selection device or a congeries of selection practices, it might be that the explanation is intent to exclude that group (as in *Teamsters* and *Hazelwood*) or unintentional exclusion attributable to the employer (as in *Griggs*). It might also be that the disadvantage does not stem from the practices at issue at all, but rather from some other factor (as in *Sears*).

2. Dial *as a Systemic Disparate Treatment Case.* It is no accident that, immediately after reporting the statistical proof of disparate effects, the *Dial* court stresses the declining success of women and Dial's knowledge of this fact. But didn't we see in *Personnel Administrator v. Feeney*, p. 155, that knowledge that a particular policy (in that case, a veterans' preference) has an adverse impact doesn't necessarily prove the policy was adopted "because of, not despite" that impact? In *Feeney*, the cause of the impact was the exclusion of women from the U.S. military, and the Court believed that the state was merely rewarding veterans for their service. Is *Dial* different? Presumably, the employer acted to reduce accident rates, but there are other factors that make that motive questionable. Here the test seems to be the only cause for the

decline in women's employment, so would a jury be reasonable in drawing the inference of discrimination in this case when it would not be in *Feeney*? Is the issue of intent made easier here by the (1) "evidence of women and men receiving similar comments on their test forms, but only the males receiving offers of employment," and (2) women often having had lower accident rates than men for two of the three years prior to the institution of the challenged test? Put together with the impact/ knowledge evidence, is that a sufficient basis for a jury to find that the test was adopted (or at least continued) in order to exclude women?

Another example where disparate impact is used to infer disparate treatment is *Fisher v. Transco Services-Milwaukee, Inc.*, 979 F.2d 1239 (7th Cir. 1992), in which the defendant instituted a "Measured Day Work Program" to track performance of its warehouse workers. The result was 11 of 52 selectors being fired, of whom 10 were age 40 or older. For the court, this disproportionate effect was not enough to establish disparate treatment, but, coupled with "errors" in the implementation of the Program prejudicing older workers, it found a jury question as to whether the Program was a pretext for age discrimination.

3. Dial *as a Disparate Impact Case.* Given the statistical evidence of the test's impact, there could be no serious question that the EEOC made out its case of disparate impact discrimination. But the real question was whether the WTS was a business necessity. The answer seems to depend on a single, albeit crucial, aspect of test validation: the test was harder than the job. While the district court so found, and probably could have done so in a pure disparate impact case, do you think the additional evidence that the test itself was misused to exclude women may have influenced the court's decision?

4. *Judge and Jury Roles.* As we have seen, Title VII accords a jury trial right to disparate treatment claims but not to disparate impact claims. Since both were involved in *Dial*, both the jury and the judge were involved in factfinding. Further, although we will not discuss the issue in detail until Chapter 8, there is a division of functions with respect to remedies. The jury decides damages — compensatory and punitive; the judge decides "backpay" and also orders other equitable relief such as instatement or reinstatement. These issues all played out in *Dial*, although you might be surprised to discover that the jury's award for damages was only a small fraction of the judge's award for backpay. But don't be confused: the judge, presumably, would have awarded the same amount of backpay even if there were not a disparate impact claim. That's part of the judicial role in Title VII remedies. Presumably, the jurors were instructed that the judge would take care of the backpay, and they needed to worry only about other damages.

There is, however, a twist when juries and judges are both factfinders. The Supreme Court has held that, in such situations, any findings of fact by the jury bind the judge. *Lytle v. Household Mfg., Inc.*, 494 U.S. 545 (1990) (when judge-tried and jury-tried claims are both involved in a suit, the jury should decide its issue first, which finding will bind the judge on all facts so found).

5. *Another Two-Front Case.* In *Maldonado v. City of Altus*, 433 F.3d 1294 (10th Cir. 2006), plaintiffs challenged an English-only policy. The Tenth Circuit found the policy subject to disparate impact analysis on the basis that it had created a hostile work environment for Hispanic workers. While we will see in Chapter 5 that hostile work environment claims are commonly disparate treatment claims requiring proof of discriminatory intent, "[p]laintiffs here bring such a disparate-treatment claim as well as this discriminatory-impact claim. But there is no reason to prohibit discriminatory-impact claims predicated on a hostile work environment." *Id.* at 1304. The plaintiffs

argued that the English-only policy had led to taunting by Anglo city workers, but the court went further:

> The policy itself, and not just the effect of the policy in evoking hostility by co-workers, may create or contribute to the hostility of the work environment. A policy requiring each employee to wear a badge noting his or her religion, for example, might well engender extreme discomfort in a reasonable employee who belongs to a minority religion, even if no co-worker utters a word on the matter. Here, the very fact that the City would forbid Hispanics from using their preferred language could reasonably be construed as an expression of hostility to Hispanics. At least that could be a reasonable inference if there was no apparent legitimate purpose for the restrictions. It would be unreasonable to take offense at a requirement that all pilots flying into an airport speak English in communications with the tower or between planes; but hostility would be a reasonable inference to draw from a requirement that an employee calling home during a work break speak only in English. The less the apparent justification for mandating English, the more reasonable it is to infer hostility toward employees whose ethnic group or nationality favors another language.

Id. at 1304-05. This court seems to be separating out the employer from the harassing co-workers. Presumably, their conduct is intentional, but under rules we will study in Section 5C, see p. 370, the employer is not necessarily liable for their conduct. When, however, the employer adopts a policy that is likely to result in such action, it can be viewed as having a disparate impact, even if the employer does not wish for such consequences to follow.

As for disparate treatment, there was obviously a hostile environment claim for the taunting, but *Maldonado* went further to hold that the policy itself could be attacked under that theory. The policy was not facially discriminatory (all workers were required to speak English only, regardless of whether they were Anglo, Hispanics, or of some other national origin). Thus, the issue "is whether those who established the English-only policy did so with the intent to create a hostile work environment." As to that, the court acknowledged that "the disparate impact of the English-only rule (creation of a hostile work environment) is in itself evidence of intent." *Id.* at 1308. But there was other proof, including evidence that management realized that the policy was likely to lead to taunting Hispanic employees. And "a jury could find that there were no substantial work-related reasons for the policy (particularly if it believed Plaintiffs' evidence that the policy extended to nonwork periods), suggesting that the true reason was illegitimate." *Id.*

6. *The Limits of the Two Theories.* Both *Dial* and *Maldonado* are cases in which the two systemic theories were deployed successfully, with the courts finding the evidence sufficient to support liability on either or both grounds. Do they make sense to you? Do they fit better under one theory than the other? Another case which struggled with the intersection of the two theories ultimately rejected disparate impact in favor of systemic disparate treatment, but it may be no more satisfactory. *EEOC v. Joe's Stone Crab, Inc.*, 220 F.3d 1263 (11th Cir. 2000), described by the court as "the paradigmatic 'hard' case," was an appeal from a judgment in favor of the EEOC. Joe's Stone Crab is "a landmark Miami Beach seafood restaurant" which, in one period, hired 108 male food servers and zero female food servers. After the EEOC filed its discrimination charge, Joe's hired another 88 food servers, nineteen of whom, 21.7%, were female. The district court found no intentional discrimination but held Joe's liable under the disparate impact theory. The appeals court vacated the judgment because the EEOC had failed to identify "a particular

employment practice" as the predicate for disparate impact; however, it remanded to the district court for reconsideration of the systemic treatment claim, and the district court promptly found intentional discrimination.

The circumstances were highly suspicious: given the large number of female wait staff in the Miami area and the "inexorable zero" before the EEOC charge, it seemed likely that discrimination was at play. Further, the apparent cause was Joe's " 'Old World' European tradition, in which the highest level of food service is performed by [tuxedo-clad] men, in order to create an ambience of 'fine dining' for its customers." *Id.* at 1270. Joe's had traditionally hired at a "roll call" at which the number of female applicants was miniscule, resulting in no underrepresentation in Joe's staff as compared to the applicant pool prior to the EEOC charge. The publicity surrounding the charge generated more female applicants, which Joe's hired in numbers roughly proportion to their representation at the roll-call. Thus, there was no evidence of discrimination if selection from applicants was the measure. However, unlike *EEOC v. Sears*, reproduced at p. 157, the record reflected reason to believe any lack of interest by women was due to Joe's business model: its Old World atmosphere discouraged women from applying since that atmosphere had historically excluded women. The district court, therefore, constructed a qualified female labor pool of 31.9%, which "included all female servers who lived or worked on Miami Beach and earned between $25,000 and $50,000 — thereby 'using past earning capacity as a proxy for experience, and by extension, experience as a proxy for qualification.' " Compared to this pool, of course, Joe's had a problem.

Conceptually, however, this scenario did not fit either of the systemic theories well. As for disparate impact, and even assuming that the correct comparison group was the labor market the district court had constructed, there was no facially-neutral employment practice causally connected to this disparity. The EEOC argued that Joe's word of mouth recruiting and its subjective "roll call" hiring were the practices, but area wait staff knew about the roll-call and still didn't apply in proportionate numbers. The real problem was Joe's *reputation* as a discriminator against women, but "reputation itself is neither a specific act or a practice. It is far more amorphous." *Id.* at 1280. Further, "where Joe's neutral hiring and recruiting practices did not cause its reputation, we think it is wholly inappropriate to use reputation as the causal bridge connecting neutral practices to a statistical disparity for the purposes of establishing Joe's disparate impact liability." *Id.* at 1281. Why was Joe's "Old World atmosphere" not cognizable as particular employment practice? Is it because it wasn't an *employment* practice, whatever its impact?

Nevertheless, the Eleventh Circuit found sufficient evidence of systemic disparate treatment to justify a remand:

> [I]n light of the district court's findings that "Joe's management acquiesced in and gave silent approbation to the notion that male food servers were preferable to female food servers," and that "what prevailed at Joe's, albeit not mandated by written policy or verbal direction, was the ethos that female food servers were not to be hired," we also emphasize that under our controlling case law, either under a disparate treatment or a pattern or practice theory, Plaintiff need not show that hiring decisions were made pursuant to an *express* policy or directive from Joe's owners. It is enough to show in a disparate treatment case that a particular employment decision was made because of sex and in a pattern or practice case that employment decisions were generally made deliberately because of sex, regardless of whether in either context a *formal* or *express* policy of discrimination existed from the employer. *See Teamsters.*

Id. at 1285. On remand, the district court found that Joe's had "engaged in intentional disparate treatment sex discrimination." 136 F. Supp. 2d 1311, 1313 (S.D. Fla. 2001).

There is reason to believe that upper crust restaurants tend to favor male wait staff. Christine Jolls, in *Is There a Glass Ceiling?* 25 HARV. WOMEN'S L.J. 1, 5-7 (2002), described a restaurant audit study of discrimination in wait staff selection, David Neumark, *Sex Discrimination in Restaurant Hiring: An Audit Study*, 111 Q.J. ECON. 915 (1996). The study used fictional resumes with male or female names, and Jolls summarizes:

> Neumark's results are striking. Resumes with male names led to interviews in sixty-one percent of cases at high-price restaurants (where pay is higher than at middle- and low-price restaurants), whereas female resumes led to interviews in only twenty-six percent of cases at such restaurants. Clearly, high-price restaurants exhibited a strong preference for waiters over waitresses with on-average-identical resumes. . . .

Further, using live testers, Neumark found that male candidates who interviewed received offers in 48% of cases, while females received offers in only 9% of cases. This is, of course, consistent with other empirical evidence we have seen. See p. 7. Such evidence would support disparate treatment liability in general, but what is its application to *Joe's?* Contrary to the Neumark tester study, women were selected in proportion to their representation in the applicant pool.

4. The Relationship of the Systemic Theories

a. When Can the Theories Be Deployed?

Dial and *Maldonado* both suggest that the two systemic theories can work together. Most obviously, proof of disparate impact can not only make out the plaintiff's disparate impact case (thus shifting to the defendant the burden of persuasion) but also be evidence in plaintiff's systemic disparate treatment case. With regard to the latter, it will rarely by itself be sufficient to create a jury question of intentional discrimination, at least when the impact is attributable to a particular employment practice, as must occur for an impact claim. After all, once the disparity is tied to a neutral practice, then the impact alone is not enough; there must be a finding the employer acted for the purpose of, that is intentionally, to achieve the impact. It is possible that impact will be so extreme as to warrant a finding of intent, but in most cases there will have to be additional evidence. In *Dial* the additional evidence included: the declining injury rate before the institution of the test; the employer's knowledge of its dramatic impact on women; the fact that women had had lower injury rates than men; and the test not being evenhandedly administered. In *Maldonado*, it was evidence that the city expected the taunting that resulted and that it had no good business reasons for the policy.

Of course, whether the evidence of disparity in impact is sufficient to satisfy the relevant theory is another issue. We have seen that the disparate impact theory reaches all employment practices, objective or subjective. However, the plaintiff is normally required to "demonstrate that each particular challenged employment practice causes a disparate impact." In contrast, the systemic disparate treatment theory can focus on the employer's "bottom line."

This would seem to create a sharp distinction between the two systemic models: a plaintiff can use the impact theory to challenge any employment practice, whether "objective" or "subjective," but only so long as she can identify the practice and show that it (as distinguished from other components of the process) has a disparate impact. A plaintiff may, however, utilize bottom-line or "snapshot" statistics to make out a disparate treatment case.

The sharpness of any such distinction, however, is blunted by two further considerations. First, we have seen that, even in a disparate impact case, bottom line results can be used "if the complaining party can demonstrate to the court that the elements of a respondent's decisionmaking process are not capable of separation for analysis." See p. 244. Second, as *Dial* and *Maldonado* hold, the disparate effects of a particular employment practices can be relevant to proving disparate treatment. It was the disparate impact of the particular employment practice that the EEOC successfully deployed in *Dial* as part of its proof of systemic disparate treatment. Thus, the requisites of each theory must be met, but both have potentially broad application.

b. Out of the Disparate Treatment Pan into the Disparate Impact Fire?

There is, however, one other relationship between the two systemic theories that may not be immediately apparent. *Segar v. Smith*, 738 F.2d 1249 (D.C. Cir. 1984), raises some possibilities regarding the way the two theories work in tandem. Chief Judge J. Skelly Wright wrote the opinion for the court in this suit against the Drug Enforcement Agency in which the plaintiffs used both systemic theories. He stressed that both theories can rest on the same proof:

> Though allocations of proof differ [for each theory], an important point of convergence exists in class actions like the present case. Both pattern or practice disparate treatment claims and disparate impact claims are attacks on the systemic results of employment practices. The pattern or practice claim amounts to an allegation that an observed disparity is the systemic result of an employer's intentionally discriminatory practices. The disparate impact claim amounts to an allegation that an observed disparity is the systemic result of a specific employment practice that cannot be justified as necessary to the employer's business. *Consequently the proof of each claim will involve a showing of disparity between the minority and majority groups in an employer's work force.*

Id. at 1267 (emphasis added). *See also Allison v. Citgo Petroleum Corp.*, 151 F.3d 402, 424 (5th Cir. 1998) (stressing the overlap of proof when disparate impact and systemic disparate treatment claims are both asserted in the same suit). If the plaintiff makes out a prima facie case of systemic disparate treatment by "providing evidence — often in statistical form — of a disparity in the position of members of the plaintiff class and *comparably qualified* whites," *id.* (emphasis in original), the defendant must respond, either by refuting the claim that a disparity exists or by "offer[ing] an explanatory defense; such a defense amounts to a claim that an observed disparity has not resulted from illegal discrimination." *Segar*, at *id.*

The "explanatory defense" has further implications:

> To rebut a disparate treatment challenge the employer can argue that the observed disparity between the plaintiff class and the majority group does not support an inference

of intentional discrimination because there is a legitimate, nondiscriminatory explanation for the disparity. For example, the defendant might come forward with some additional job qualification — not sufficiently perceptible to plaintiffs to have permitted them to account for it in their initial proof — that the plaintiff class lacks, thus explaining the disparity. . . .

[T]he employer's effort to rebut the pattern or practice claim by articulating a legitimate nondiscriminatory explanation may have the effect of putting before the court all elements of a traditional disparate impact case. By its explanation of an observed disparity the employer will typically pinpoint an employment practice (or practices) having a disparate impact on a protected class. And to rebut plaintiffs' case the employer will typically be required to introduce evidence showing that the employment practice in fact caused the observed disparity. In this situation, between the plaintiffs' prima facie showing of disparity and the defendant's rebuttal explanation of the disparity, the essential elements of a disparate impact case will have been placed before the trier of fact. Such a case is ripe for resolution using disparate impact analysis. Though the plaintiffs in a disparate treatment case bear the burden of persuasion as to the existence of a disparity, the defendant bears the burden of proving the business necessity of the practices causing the disparity. Thus when an employer defends a disparate treatment challenge by claiming that a specific employment practice causes the observed disparity, and this defense sufficiently rebuts the plaintiffs' initial case of disparate treatment, the defendant should at this point face a burden of proving the business necessity of the practice.

The only difference between this situation and the traditional disparate impact case is that in the latter the plaintiff articulates the employment practice causing the adverse impact and forces the employer to defend it, while in the former the employer articulates the employment practice and must then go on to defend it.

Id. at 1268-70.

To appreciate this, consider a simple hypothetical. Plaintiff launches a disparate treatment attack, showing that the employer's workforce, which consists of non-skilled workers, is 99 percent white in a geographic labor market that is 23 percent minority. Her statistician finds the correlation between race and employment statistically significant. Defendant responds by arguing that it does not intentionally discriminate in hiring; rather, it employs only workers who reside in the town in which it is located, and the town happens to be 99 percent white. *See NAACP, Newark Branch v. Town of Harrison*, 940 F.2d 792 (3d Cir. 1991).

In statistical terms, defendant is showing a co-variable — residence — that is related to race and is arguing that residence, not race, explains its actions. Of course, the employer might have chosen to employ only town residents precisely because this policy would exclude blacks. This was the EEOC's theory in *Dial*. But even if we accept the employer's explanation as nondiscriminatory in motivation, the effect of its proof is to make out a disparate impact case. In other words, defendant's rebuttal of the inference of discrimination raised by plaintiff's statistics turns entirely on whether the employer utilizes an intent-neutral practice that happens to have a disparate impact on blacks. Proof of that, as *Segar v. Smith* suggests, may mean that defendant can avoid disparate treatment liability, but only by, in effect, conceding a prima facie case of disparate impact liability — although it can avoid both if it also shows that the policy producing the impact is justified by business necessity. *See also Powers v. Alabama Dept. of Educ.*, 854 F.2d 1285 (11th Cir. 1988).

Segar is a relatively straightforward meshing of the two theories. Indeed, it is difficult to avoid the conclusion that, no matter who proves the various elements of a

disparate impact claim, once it is shown, the employer can defend only by establishing business necessity. Further, *Segar* stressed that its analysis is not as radical as
it might first appear:

> An employer will face the justificatory burden only after a plaintiff class has shown
> a disparity in the positions of members of the class and the majority group who appear
> to be comparably qualified; if plaintiffs fail to make their prima facie case, the employer
> never faces this justificatory burden. But if the plaintiffs have made their prima facie
> case, the employer, to avoid liability under the disparate treatment theory, will have to
> advance some nondiscriminatory explanation for the disparity. An employer's claim
> that it cannot isolate the cause of the disparity will be unlikely to deflect the force of the
> inference of discrimination from plaintiffs' proof. The defendant will in all likelihood
> point to a specific job qualification or performance/evaluation rating as the explanation
> for the observed disparity. Thus application of disparate impact in this situation will
> not . . . place on the employer any additional burden of articulation; to rebut the
> disparate treatment claim the employer will have had to articulate which employment
> practices cause an observed disparity. Nor will the employer be forced to justify all of its
> employment practices. The employer will be required to show the job relatedness of
> only the practice or practices identified as the cause of the disparity.

738 F.2d at 1271.

Segar preceded the Civil Rights Act of 1991, and that statute's restriction of
disparate impact to "a particular employment practice" narrows the occasions when
plaintiffs may use a statistical showing of the defendant's overall employment picture
to support a disparate impact challenge. Such a claim is allowed only when the
plaintiff can also show that the individual components of the whole process are not
capable of separation.

But the new statute does not bar the plaintiff from using such proof to make out a
systemic disparate treatment case, which is the main thrust of *Segar*. The statute does
contain a no-cause defense — "If the respondent demonstrates that a specific
employment practice does not cause the disparate impact, the respondent shall not
be required to demonstrate that such practice is required by business necessity,"
§703(k)(1)(B)(ii), but it is by its terms inapposite to a systemic disparate treatment
challenge. Presumably, then, the defendant is left under the new statute basically
where it was when *Segar v. Smith* was decided: to avoid a finding of disparate
treatment, it can prove a practice giving rise to disparate impact. This is, in fact, the
converse of §703(k)(1)(B)(ii).

If this is correct, why would an employer come forth with a "neutral" reason for a
statistical disparity? Remember that the only defense to disparate treatment is the
BFOQ, which is difficult to establish. And in race cases, the statute theoretically
provides no defense at all except for affirmative action. Thus, it may be important for
the defendant to shift the analysis from disparate treatment to disparate impact,
where it has at least the defense of business necessity.

Plaintiff's incentives are the reverse: disparate treatment attacks will typically be
preferred because prevailing on this issue effectively wins the case (except where a
bona fide occupational qualification or affirmative action is involved), while proof of
disparate impact leaves the defendant able to prevail by showing business necessity.
Further, plaintiff has a right to a jury trial and compensatory and punitive damages
for disparate treatment; nevertheless, disparate impact may be a fall-back theory, and
Dial shows that the recoveries can be largely the same under either theory.

D. RECONCILING THE TENSION BETWEEN DISPARATE TREATMENT AND DISPARATE IMPACT

Professor Douglas Laycock, in *Statistical Proof and Theories of Discrimination*, 49 LAW & CONTEMP. PROBS. 97, 98-99 (1986), argues that there is a fundamental inconsistency between the statistical showings for the two systemic theories:

> The [*Teamsters*] Court explicitly assumes that but for discrimination, the employer's work force would in the long run mirror the racial composition of the labor force from which it was hired. That conclusion requires the further implicit assumption that the black and white populations are substantially the same in all relevant ways, so that any differences in result are attributable to discrimination.
>
> Some variation of that assumption is critical to all statistical evidence of disparate treatment. It is a powerful and implausible assumption: the two populations are assumed to be substantially the same in their distribution of skills, aptitudes, and job preferences. Two hundred and fifty years of slavery, nearly a century of Jim Crow, and a generation of less virulent discrimination are assumed to have had no effect: the black and white populations are assumed to be substantially the same. All the differential socialization of little girls that feminists justifiably complain about is assumed to have had no effect; the male and female populations are assumed to be substantially the same.
>
> This assumption, which is so critical to statistical disparate treatment cases, is fundamentally inconsistent with the policy premise of disparate impact theory. The explicit premise of disparate impact theory is that women and minorities have suffered from discrimination. Measures of skill and merit are suspect because discrimination has left many minorities with fewer and less developed skills. *Griggs*, the seminal disparate impact case, relies explicitly on the history of segregated and inferior education for blacks in North Carolina schools. So disparate impact theory insists that employers require only those skills essential to the job. To require skills unnecessarily is to exclude minorities unnecessarily.
>
> It should now be clear what is wrong with the one-two punch of turning all disparate treatment defenses into disparate impact claims: the two theories are inconsistent. The disparate treatment half of the strategy assumes that the black and white populations, or the male and female populations, are identical. The disparate impact half simultaneously assumes that they are greatly different. This pair of inconsistent assumptions lets the plaintiff "prove" discrimination, but the proof is invalid.

Are you persuaded by Professor Laycock's argument?

Certainly, his predicates are correct: disparate treatment involves treating people differently despite the fact they are alike; disparate impact assumes people from different groups are different. If applicant A is, in fact, different from applicant B in some way other than his race, the employer can rely on that difference to treat the two differently with impunity — so far as disparate treatment is concerned. And that is true regardless of whether the employer's reasons are based on job relation or business necessity — or are even rational. An employer could prefer a white Aries to a black Capricorn so long as the decision was truly based on zodiacal considerations.

But disparate impact liability focuses on the reasons an employer gives. While reliance on employees' astrological signs would not have a disparate impact, use of other factors might. If a private employer used service in the armed forces as a basis for hiring, it certainly would tend to exclude women. This requirement might or might not be justified as a business necessity.

The point is relatively simple: employers may not intentionally use prohibited factors; employers may use any other criteria unless they have a disparate impact, in which case they may be used only if justified.

Suppose plaintiff shows snapshot statistics revealing that an employer has promoted men almost exclusively from a pool that includes many women workers. Not many years ago, this would have been a good description of school systems in the United States, particularly elementary schools. Even today, men are disproportionately represented as principals in elementary schools compared to their numbers in the teacher workforce. Suppose that, in response to the disparate treatment claim, the employer explains that it has a policy of promoting the tallest person among those eligible applicants. As a result, while tall women occasionally were promoted over short men, most of the promotions went to men. If the finder of fact believes the company's story that it was height and not gender that caused the almost total exclusion of women from promotions, that would exonerate the company of disparate treatment liability. But given the disparity of impact, the employer has still acted illegally if height is not job related.

Isn't the simple answer to Professor Laycock's criticism that Title VII presumes that the relevant groups (blacks and whites or males and females) are the same unless the employer demonstrates that they are *different in ways that are relevant to the employer's business*? Statistically, women are shorter than men, and statistically, blacks are less well educated than whites. Nevertheless, the employer must treat the two groups as the same unless it can show that height or educational requirements are necessary to the job in question.

At this point, the law of employment discrimination might be summed up as follows: disparate treatment is not allowed because discriminatory intent is not a permissible basis for denying employment opportunities to individuals in our society; but even a nondiscriminatory motivation will not save practices that are not justified by business necessity and that have the effect of falling more harshly on a protected group. So stated, disparate treatment and disparate impact principles seem to work in conjunction to achieve the basic goals of Title VII.

But are the principles always consistent? May they come into conflict? As indicated previously, in *Los Angeles Dept. of Water & Power v. Manhart*, reproduced at p. 116, the Supreme Court held that the lack of disparate impact on one gender (or racial group) does not justify disparate treatment of that group. But what of the other side of that coin? Doesn't the absence of disparate impact on, say, women who are being treated disparately mean that, if women were treated equally with men, there would be a disparate impact on men?

In *Manhart*, had the employer collected equal pension contributions from men and women and paid out equal monthly retirement benefits, women as the longer-lived class would collect more total benefits than would the class of men. That would seem to show an adverse impact on males. Footnote 20 of *Manhart* tries to resolve this tension:

> A variation on the Department's fairness theme is the suggestion that a gender-neutral pension plan would itself violate Title VII because of its disproportionately heavy impact on male employees. Cf. *Griggs v. Duke Power Co.* This suggestion has no force in the sex discrimination context because each retiree's total pension benefits are ultimately determined by his actual life span; any differential in benefits paid to men and women in the aggregate is thus "based on [a] factor other than sex," and consequently immune from challenge under the Equal Pay Act, 29 U.S.C. § 206(d). Even under Title VII itself — assuming disparate-impact analysis applies to fringe benefits, cf.

Nashville Gas Co. v. Satty, 434 U.S. 136, 144-45 — the male employees would not prevail. Even a completely neutral practice will inevitably have some disproportionate impact on one group or another. *Griggs* does not imply, and this Court has never held, that discrimination must always be inferred from such consequences.

Id. at 710 n. 20. The meaning of this passage is far from clear. Indeed, the Court seems to make three points. First, it states that the determination of total benefits is based on each individual's actual life span and is thus immune under the "factor other than sex" exception in the Equal Pay Act. This might suggest that the disparate impact theory does not exist under that statute. Beyond this possibility, the Court does not explain why a disparity of impact against men resulting from benefits paid over the lives of all employees is not a violation.

Second, the reference to *Nashville Gas Co. v. Satty*, although tentative in its phrasing, invokes the possibility that impact analysis applies not to cases brought under § 703(a)(1) (which bars discrimination), but only to cases brought under § 703(a)(2) (which bars classifications that "tend to deprive" individuals of employment opportunities). However, the Supreme Court never squarely held that a different mode of analysis applies to the two subsections of § 703(a), and, whatever the status of this theory when *Manhart* was decided, it does not survive the Civil Rights Act of 1991.

Third, footnote 20 in *Manhart* may imply that there is no tension between the two theories because disparate impact is not available to men (and, by implication, whites). We have explored this issue in Chapter 3 at p. 245, and the answer is unclear. Were the theory available to both races, the disparate impact theory would create a dilemma. Imagine a new employer who is considering what employee selection procedure to adopt., and suppose further that using a written test will result in 90 percent white employees and 10 percent black employees. In contrast, a structured interview will result in 70 percent whites and 30 percent blacks. Isn't it clear that whether the employer picks the test or the structured interview, there will be a disparate impact on some group? Does that mean that, except for devices that are neutral along all axes, every selection device must be job related and a business necessity?

PROBLEM 4.2

Assume you hang out your shingle to practice law and you are open to taking plaintiff's employment discrimination cases. If a potential client came through the door, what approach would you take to make sure that you did not miss any possible theories of recovery? What information would you try to find out that might support what theories? Starting at the broadest theory, what information would you want to have to support a systemic disparate treatment claim? While that information is also relevant to a disparate impact claim and to an individual disparate treatment claim, what information would you want to know that might support a claim based on the disparate impact theory? What information about possible defenses to all three theories would be desirable?

Assume you represent employers in employment discrimination cases. How would you go about creating a strategy that would successfully defend your clients as to each theory, taking into account the interrelationships among the three main theories?

In approaching these questions from either side, reconsider the facts of Problem 4.1.

Chapter 5

Special Problems in Applying Title VII, Section 1981, and the ADEA

A. INTRODUCTION

The broad theories developed in Chapters 1 through 4 generally control any Title VII suit. Distinctive problems, however, have arisen in applying these concepts to different types of discrimination.

This chapter considers the following topics. Section B treats the threshold question of coverage of Title VII, § 1981, and the Age Discrimination in Employment Act (ADEA). The next five sections deal with distinctive problems under Title VII. Thus, Section C addresses several issues concerning gender discrimination, including pregnancy, sexual harassment, grooming and dress codes, and sexual orientation. Section D focuses on discrimination on the basis of religion, including the duty to accommodate. Section E examines national origin discrimination and alienage restrictions. Section F considers questions of union liability. In Section G, we turn to a topic common to Title VII and the ADEA: retaliation for resisting discrimination. Finally, Section H treats distinctive problems that arise under the ADEA.

B. COVERAGE OF TITLE VII, SECTION 1981, AND THE ADEA

The prohibitions of both Title VII and the ADEA are directed at "employers," "employment agencies," and "labor organizations." § 703(a)-(c), 42 U.S.C. § 2000e-2(a)-(c)

(2007); ADEA, 29 U.S.C. §623(a)-(c) (2007). It is these entities that are prohibited from engaging in discrimination, and entities that do not qualify as one of these do not violate the statute, no matter their effect on employment. *See Coleman v. New Orleans & Baton Rouge S.S. Pilots' Ass'n*, 437 F.3d 471, 482 (5th Cir. 2006) (pilot associations, which refused to certify pilot applicants over age 40, do not employ the pilots, even though they play almost monopolistic gate-keeper role in who works as a pilot). Neither employment agencies nor labor organizations have caused much interpretive difficulty, but the questions of who is a statutory "employer" and whether discrimination occurs in the "employment" relationship have generated much confusion.

The starting point is the statutory language: an "employer" under Title VII means "a person engaged in an industry affecting commerce who has fifteen or more employees for each working day in each of twenty or more calendar weeks in the current or preceding calendar year, and any agent of such person." §701(b), 42 U.S.C. §2000e(b). The ADEA is phrased identically, except that an employer must have 20 or more employees. 29 U.S.C. §630(b). However, these definitions are circular. An "employer" must have "employees," but the statutes define "employee" as "an individual employed by an employer." §701(f); 29 U.S.C. §630(f). The critical concept for these statutes, then, is what constitutes "employment." (The ADA, as we will see in Chapter 6, prohibits discrimination by a "covered entity" but that term also embraces "employers" as defined in the other statutes.) That term, however, is not defined by either Title VII or the ADEA, leaving courts to struggle with where "employment" begins and other legal relationships end.

LEROHL v. FRIENDS OF MINNESOTA SINFONIA
322 F.3d 486 (8th Cir. 2003)

LOKEN, J.

[Tricia Lerohl and Shelley Hanson commenced separate actions against the Friends of the Minnesota Sinfonia, a nonprofit corporation that governs the Sinfonia. They alleged that they were terminated as regular members of the Sinfonia in violation of, respectively, Title VII and the ADA. Both complaints were dismissed on summary judgment on the basis that neither statute applied to the plaintiffs because they were independent contractors, not employees of either the Sinfonia or its conductor, defendant Jay Fishman.]

I. BACKGROUND

The Sinfonia was formed in 1989 by Fishman and other former members of the Minneapolis Chamber Symphony Orchestra. Its mission is to perform free classical music concerts in inner-city public schools and other locations accessible to inner-city youth, families with young children, and people of limited means. In its first decade of operation, the Sinfonia grew from thirty-two to seventy concerts per year. Fishman conducts the Sinfonia and acts as its executive and artistic director. Sinfonia concerts are performed by twenty-five to thirty professional musicians. Fishman and all Sinfonia players are members of Local 30-73 of the American Federation of Musicians. The Sinfonia advertises that its musicians are "the best of the area's freelance pool."

After scheduling a series of Sinfonia concerts, Fishman prepares a list of musicians eligible to play for that series. The schedule is mailed to eligible "regular" or "first call" players who then advise the Sinfonia whether they agree to play that series. The Sinfonia's free-lance musicians also perform for other organizations and as solo performers. They may even opt out of Sinfonia concerts they have agreed to play, so long as they give two weeks notice and arrange for an eligible substitute to perform. However, to remain a Sinfonia "regular," which ensures being invited to play in most if not all Sinfonia concerts, Fishman's policy is that a musician must "accept the vast majority of the work."

All Sinfonia players, and Fishman as conductor, are paid on a per-concert basis at the union scale. The Sinfonia does not withhold income or FICA taxes on these payments, instead documenting the payments for tax purposes on an IRS Form 1099. The Sinfonia does not provide musicians annual leave, health or life insurance, worker's compensation coverage, or other fringe benefits except that it does contribute an agreed percentage of the union scale payments to the musicians union pension fund. The parties dispute whether Fishman was required to agree to these contributions to remain in good standing as a union member. The Sinfonia also pays Fishman lump sums for his work as executive and artistic director. For tax and other purposes, he is treated as an employee with respect to these payments.

From 1990 to 1999, Lerohl and Hanson were "regular" players at Sinfonia concerts. Lerohl plays the French horn and Hanson plays the clarinet. In mid-1999, the Sinfonia stopped offering work to Lerohl and Hanson. Lerohl alleges the Sinfonia and Fishman violated Title VII by terminating her in retaliation for complaining about sexual harassment by Fishman. Hanson alleges defendants violated the ADA by ending her long-standing working relationship when she sought to resume playing after being absent several months while recovering from injuries sustained during a Sinfonia rehearsal. Both statutes protect "employees" but not independent contractors. See *Birchem* [*v. Knights of Columbus*, 116 F.3d 310 (8th Cir. 1997)] (ADA); *Wilde v. County of Kandiyohi*, 15 F.3d 103 (8th Cir. 1994) (Title VII).

II. THE RELEVANT LEGAL STANDARD

The issue whether a person is an employee or an independent contractor arises in many legal contexts. When the issue concerns the scope of a federal statute, we must first examine the relevant statutory language. In both Title VII and the ADA, Congress adopted a circular definition of "employee" — an employee is an "individual employed by an employer." See 42 U.S.C. §§ 2000e(f), 12111(4). In such cases, the Supreme Court applies the general common law of agency to determine whether a hired party is an employee or an independent contractor. See *Nationwide Mut. Ins. Co. v. Darden*, 503 U.S. 318 (1992) (ERISA), followed in *Birchem* (ADA), and in *Wilde* (Title VII). In applying this test, the Court has instructed us to consider a nonexhaustive list of factors derived primarily from the Restatement (Second) of Agency § 220(2) (1958):

> In determining whether a hired party is an employee under the general common law of agency, we consider the hiring party's right to control the manner and means by which the product is accomplished. Among the other factors relevant to this inquiry are the skill required; the source of the instrumentalities and tools; the location of the work; the duration of the relationship between the parties; whether the hiring party has the right to assign additional projects to the hired party; the extent of the hired party's discretion

over when and how long to work; the method of payment; the hired party's role in hiring and paying assistants; whether the work is part of the regular business of the hiring party; whether the hiring party is in business; the provision of employee benefits; and the tax treatment of the hired party. . . . No one of these factors is determinative.

Cmty. for Creative Non-Violence v. Reid, 490 U.S. 730 (footnotes omitted). In weighing these factors, "all of the incidents of the relationship must be assessed and weighed with no one factor being decisive." *Darden* (quotation omitted). The district court may properly consider economic aspects of the parties' relationship. See *Wilde.* "Our inquiry . . . requires more than simply tallying factors on each side and selecting the winner on the basis of a point score." *Schwieger v. Farm Bureau Ins. Co. of Neb.,* 207 F.3d 480, 487 (8th Cir. 2000).

On appeal, Lerohl, Hanson, and the EEOC primarily argue that, in the EEOC's words, "it is critical that 'control' be given primary consideration." They then state the control issue in terms of individual Sinfonia concerts and conclude, not surprisingly, that Fishman as conductor "controlled" the rehearsals and concerts, and therefore all Sinfonia musicians are employees. We emphatically reject that approach. First, it is contrary to the Supreme Court's repeated admonition that no factor is determinative and all aspects of the parties' relationship must be considered. See *Darden,* (expressly rejecting a similar contention by the United States as amicus curiae); *Reid.*

Second, on a more practical level, the notion that musicians are always employees when they perform in a conducted band or orchestra flies in the face of both common sense and undisputed facts in this record, such as plaintiff Hanson's affidavit reciting that she is not an employer when she hires musicians to play while she records a musical composition. Work by independent contractors is often, if not typically, performed to the exacting specifications of the hiring party. In *Reid,* for example, the Supreme Court determined that a sculptor was an independent contractor for the purposes of the Copyright Act of 1976 even though the nonprofit association that hired him defined the scene to be sculpted and specified most of the details of the sculpture's appearance, including its scale and the materials to be used. Thus, although one relevant factor was Fishman's undisputed control in selecting the music to be played, scheduling Sinfonia rehearsals and concerts, and determining the manner in which the concert music was collectively played, that factor is not determinative of the common-law agency issue.

III. Prior Musician Case Law

There are surprisingly few cases addressing whether musicians who played in a band or orchestra were employees of either the entity that engaged the performance, or the musicians' band leader or orchestra conductor. *Hilton Int'l Co. v. NLRB,* 690 F.2d 318 (2d Cir. 1982), a National Labor Relations Act case, held that the members of "steady engagement" bands were not employees of the casino hotels that engaged them. The decision confirms that the question is thorny, but it is not particularly relevant because the musicians were admittedly employees of someone (their independent band leaders), as were the musicians in *Associated Musicians of Greater Newark, Local 16,* 206 N.L.R.B. 581 (1973), *aff'd per curiam,* 512 F.2d 991 (D.C. Cir. 1975). Here, on the other hand, the issue is whether the musicians were freelance independent contractors, or were employees of either Fishman, the orchestra conductor, *or* his employer, the Sinfonia.

A more relevant labor law case is *Seattle Opera v. NLRB*, 292 F.3d 757 (D.C. Cir. 2002), where a divided panel upheld the NLRB's determination that the Seattle Opera's auxiliary choristers were employees of the Opera. But the majority relied heavily on the deference due the NLRB's decision, consistent with *NLRB v. Town & Country Elec., Inc.* 516 U.S. 85 (1995). On the control theory urged by Lerohl, Hanson, and the EEOC, we find Judge Randolph's dissent more persuasive:

> The Board and the majority find it significant in determining whether the auxiliary choristers are employees rather than volunteers that the Opera "has the power or right to control and direct the person in the material details of how such work is to be performed." This is outright silly. Are we to suppose that volunteer firefighters or volunteer rescue workers become "employees" because the fire chief or the head of the rescue squad directs them? . . . Auxiliary choristers join other singers to perform musical works. . . . Rehearsal cannot be done independently. Choir members need to know not only the notes and the words, but they must also blend their voices together into a single sound.

. . . IV.   ANALYSIS

Like the sculptor in *Reid*, Sinfonia musicians such as Lerohl and Hanson are highly skilled professionals who own their own instruments and need no on-the-job training other than rehearsals to perform in a variety of musical settings. Obviously, professional musicians have the option of becoming employees of a particular band or orchestra. The record in this case suggests that is true of the musicians who play for the Minnesota Orchestra, the St. Paul Chamber Orchestra, and the Minnesota Opera. But other musicians may prefer to remain "free-lance," committing themselves fully to no client and retaining the discretion to pick and choose among available engagements, much like lawyers, accountants, and business consultants who choose private practice instead of "in-house" employment.

Our cases applying the common-law agency test have recognized this freedom-of-choice principle in determining whether a skilled professional was an employee or an independent contractor in a particular case. In our view, this is the relevant control issue, not whether Fishman could tell Lerohl and Hanson where to sit and when to play during a concert or a rehearsal. Thus, the "key distinction" is whether Sinfonia musicians retained the discretion to decline particular Sinfonia concerts and play elsewhere. *Berger Transfer & Storage v. Cent. States, S.E. & S.W. Areas Pension Fund*, 85 F.3d 1374, 1380 (8th Cir. 1996) (truck owner-operators who drove for more than one company were independent contractors); accord *Kirk v. Harter*, 188 F.3d 1005, 1008-09 (8th Cir. 1999) (computer programmer); *Wilde* ("self-employed business owner").

Here, it is undisputed that Lerohl, Hanson, and the other "regular" Sinfonia musicians retained the discretion to perform elsewhere and to accept or reject playing in a particular concert series. Indeed, they were permitted to back out of specific performances after agreeing to perform in a series if they arranged for suitable substitutes. Though the Sinfonia understandably offered inducements to preferred performers, such as "regular" status, the musicians retained control over the extent to which they committed their available professional time to the Sinfonia.

It is also highly significant that the Sinfonia withheld no income or FICA taxes, documented musician payments on an IRS Form 1099, and provided no employee benefits other than contributions to an independent union pension fund. "Every case since *Reid* that has applied the [common-law] test has found the hired party to be an independent contractor where the hiring party failed to extend benefits or pay social security taxes." *Kirk*; see *Birchem*. A recent exception is *Eisenberg v. Advance Relocation & Storage, Inc.*, 237 F.3d 111, 118 (2d Cir. 2000), but *Eisenberg* is readily distinguishable because it involved an hourly full-time warehouse worker, not a consultant or free-lance professional. Here, the Sinfonia's professional musicians retained the discretion to perform elsewhere and accepted payments structured in a manner that confirmed their independent contractor status. In such a case, we are loath to destroy the parties' freedom to choose that form of relationship by deciding, after the fact, that they were required to contract as employer and employees, particularly when Congress remains free to extend Title VII and the ADA to this kind of independent contractor relationship if it determines that to be in the public interest.

[Thus,] the undisputed facts in this case establish that Lerohl and Hanson were independent contractors as a matter of law, and the disputed facts, viewed most favorably to Lerohl and Hanson, do not affect that conclusion.

Finally, Lerohl and Hanson object that the district courts improperly dismissed Fishman as a separate defendant sua sponte, citing cases in which independent band leaders have been found to be employers. . . . Here, Fishman was not an independent orchestra conductor; he was an employee of the Sinfonia. If Lerohl and Hanson were employees of Fishman, they were employees of the Sinfonia. Thus, when the district courts concluded that Lerohl and Hanson were *not* employees, despite Fishman's control over their musical performances, that determination necessarily encompassed any separate claim against Fishman, whose relevant actions were taken on behalf of his employer. In these circumstances, the courts properly granted summary judgment in favor of Fishman as well as the Sinfonia.

NOTES

1. *Employment vs. Other Relationships.* The principal case makes clear that working for someone does not mean you are that person's employee. This may seem counterintuitive, at least when a long term relationship is involved, but stop and think for a moment about all the individuals who perform some kind of work for you. Is the attorney who drafts a will, the doctor who removes an appendix, or the accountant who prepares a tax return an employee of the person for whom she performs services? And, in this context, the absence of control seems pretty clear: you retain a professional precisely because she has skills that you lack; you have neither the interest nor the ability to "control" her work in any meaningful sense. In the nonprofessional setting, is the painter who paints your house or the plumber who fixes your pipes or the gardener who mows your lawn your employee? Here your ability to control might be greater, but you will probably have little interest in overseeing the work — you hire the individual to avoid the need to devote the time to the task of supervising.

Note that all of these individuals may be *someone's* employee: you may contract with a law firm or a plumbing firm, which would make the person who does the work the employee of that firm — but not of you. But even if you contract directly with an individual to perform services for you, the person may or may not be your employee. As *Lerohl* indicates, she may be an independent contractor instead, in which case you are free to discriminate under Title VII and the ADEA. The ADA is somewhat different because it also reaches public accommodations, see *Bragdon v. Abbott*, reproduced at p. 492, but as far as employment discrimination is concerned, it tracks the other statutes. *Lerohl* focuses on one kind of "non-employee," the independent contractors. We will also see other relationships, most notably partners and other owners of businesses, who work for a firm but may not be employees of that firm.

2. *Independent Contractors.* The Supreme Court has recognized that the definitional terms in most employment-related statutes are "completely circular and explain[] nothing", *e.g., Clackamas Gastroenterology Assocs., P.C. v. Wells*, 538 U.S. 440, 444 (2003) (ADA); *Nationwide Mut. Ins. Co. v. Darden*, 503 U.S. 318, 322 (1992) (ERISA). As a result, the Court views Congress as having meant by "employment" what it described in *Community for Creative Non-Violence v. Reid*, 490 U.S. 730, 740 (1989), as "the conventional master-servant relationship as understood by common-law agency doctrine." Master-servant law, however, was designed largely to determine when a master would be liable to a third party for the torts of his servants; it is not surprising that it focuses on the right of a master to "control" the actions of his servant, which would thereby justify holding the master responsible since he could have avoided the tort by virtue of better supervision. Nevertheless, *Reid's* statement of the common law principles has come to dominate all subsequent discussions of the issue of when an individual is an employee as opposed to an independent contractor. The passage *Lerohl* quoted from *Reid* bears repeating, but with perhaps a different emphasis:

> *In determining whether a hired party is an employee under the general common law of agency, we consider the hiring party's right to control the manner and means by which the product is accomplished.* Among the other factors relevant to this inquiry are [1] the skill required; [2] the source of the instrumentalities and tools; [3] the location of the work; [4] the duration of the relationship between the parties; [5] whether the hiring party has the right to assign additional projects to the hired party; [6] the extent of the hired party's discretion over when and how long to work; [7] the method of payment; [8] the hired party's role in hiring and paying assistants; [9] whether the work is part of the regular business of the hiring party; [10] whether the hiring party is in business; [11] the provision of employee benefits; and [12] the tax treatment of the hired party. . . . No one of these factors is determinative.

(Emphasis added.) The italicized sentence seems to state that "control" is what is being assessed, with the twelve "factors" being ways, among others, to ascertain "control."

Under this reading, which the EEOC urged, the two plaintiffs in *Lerohl* were clearly employees because their work was very closely controlled — a conductor not only dictates when and where a orchestra members plays, but also how he or she plays, what she wears, and even her facial expressions. The alternative approach, the one used by the *Lerohl* court, is to assess the factors and, using some undefined weighting scheme, conclude whether or not the individual is an employee. Under this view, which seems to be the more common, the question is less "control" in the abstract than adding and subtracting factors. *E.g., Alberty-Velez v. Corporacion de P.R. para la Difusion Publica*, 361 F.3d 1, 7-9 (1st Cir. 2004) (female co-host of a television show was an independent contractor); *Weary v. Cochran*, 377 F.3d 522, 526 (6th Cir. 2004) (2-1) (plaintiff insurance agent was an independent contractor); *Wojewski v. Rapid City Reg'l Hosp., Inc.*, 450 F.3d 338, 343 (8th Cir. 2006) (doctor was an independent contractor, despite hospital's control over him for patient safety reasons). Does either approach make sense in terms of the aims of the antidiscrimination laws? Remember, the Court views these laws as simply adopting common law concepts, concepts developed mostly for purposes of liability to third parties.

Did Sinfonia structure its relationships with its musicians to avoid being covered by antidiscrimination and other laws? The "independent contractor" category offers an escape hatch from laws regulating employment, and some companies have radically restructured their operations by converting "employees" to "independent contractors." See Joseph B. Treaster, *Federal Agency Sues Allstate, Claiming Age Discrimination*, N.Y. TIMES, Oct. 8, 2004, at C5. There have been challenges to such conversions as disparate treatment. *See Isbell v. Allstate Ins. Co.*, 418 F.3d 788, 795 (7th Cir. 2005) (Allstate did not violate the ADEA when it eliminated employee-agent positions; "every employee in that position lost his job, *regardless* of age," and every employee was offered a new position, although not necessarily as an employee) (emphasis in original). *See generally* Richard R. Carlson, *Why the Law Still Can't Tell an Employee When It Sees One and How It Ought to Stop Trying*, 22 BERKELEY J. EMP. & LAB. L. 295 (2001); Lewis L. Maltby & David C. Yamada, *Beyond "Economic Realities": The Case for Amending Federal Employment Discrimination Laws to Include Independent Contractors*, 38 B.C. L. REV. 239 (1997).

3. *Owners as Employees.* A recurrent question is whether individuals who are owners of a business entity can also be employees. Of course, ownership can be completely separate from employment, as in the case of a stock ownership in a publicly traded company. But owners of the entity can also work for it, whether they are denominated "partners" or, in the case of professional corporations, "shareholders." This issue is important not only for the individuals in question but also for individuals who are true employees. For example, in *EEOC v. Sidley Austin Brown & Wood*, 315 F.3d 696 (7th Cir. 2002), the law firm was clearly a statutory employer since it had far more than fifteen employees, but it was not clear whether individuals denominated "partners" were true partners or merely employees of the firm. If the latter, Sidley's mandatory retirement policy would be illegal. But the question is also important for smaller firms who may not be covered by the statute at all unless the owners are included in the count of employees.

A case in point is *Clackamas Gastroenterology Assocs., P.C. v. Wells*, 538 U.S. 440 (2003), where the professional corporation, a medical clinic, had fourteen employees and four physician-owners who also worked for the firm. When the plaintiff sued under the ADA, the question was whether the statute applied: only if one or more of the owners was also an employee would the ADA's minimum of 15 employees be satisfied.

Although the doctors were formally employees, apparently in order to qualify for tax benefits under ERISA, and the entity form at issue — a professional corporation — was relatively new to the law, the Court nevertheless reiterated its position that common law principles guide the inquiry. Looking to the *Restatement (Second) of Agency* §2(2) (1958), the Court concluded that "the common-law element of control is the principal guidepost that should be followed in this case." This was also the position taken by the EEOC in its *Compliance Manual* §§605:0008-605:0010 (2000), which asked courts to "examine 'whether shareholder-directors operate independently and manage the business or instead are subject to the firm's control.' According to the EEOC's view, 'if the shareholder-directors operate independently and manage the business, they are proprietors and not employees; if they are subject to the firm's control, they are employees.'" 539 U.S. at. 448.

More specifically, as to when partners, members of boards of directors, and major shareholders qualify as employees, the issue is "'whether the individual acts independently and participates in managing the organization, or whether the individual is subject to the organization's control.'" *Id. quoting* §605:0009. To answer this question, the Compliance Manual suggests six factors:

> Whether the organization can hire or fire the individual or set the rules and reg-
> ulations of the individual's work
> Whether and, if so, to what extent the organization supervises the individual's work
> Whether the individual reports to someone higher in the organization
> Whether and, if so, to what extent the individual is able to influence the organization
> Whether the parties intended that the individual be an employee, as expressed in
> written agreements or contracts
> Whether the individual shares in the profits, losses, and liabilities of the organization.

Id. at 449. Job titles are not critical, nor is the existence of an "employment" contract between the firm and the putative employee. Since the Court remanded the case for application of this law to the facts of the case, *Clackamas* does not provide as much guidance as might be desired, but it is clear that professional corporations and other business entities may structure relationships as "employment" without that decision being outcome-determinative for purposes of the antidiscrimination laws.

As different entities multiply, the question of whether particular individuals are employees will become increasingly important, both in terms of whether they are protected by the statute and in terms of whether the entity is itself a statutory employer of non-owners. While the cases preceded *Clackamas*, there is increasing reason to believe that "partners" or "shareholders" in large, modern law and accounting firms are often employees. *E.g., EEOC v. Sidley Austin Brown & Wood*, 315 F.3d 696 (7th Cir. 2002); *Simpson v. Ernst & Young*, 100 F.3d 436 (6th Cir. 1996). *See generally* Ann C. McGinley, *Functionality or Formalism? Partners and Shareholders as "Employees" Under the Anti-Discrimination Laws*, 57 SMU L. REV. 3, 6 (2004) (lower courts should find employee status when "the individual wields insufficient power within the organization — economic, social, and/or political — to avoid discrimination [and] is sufficiently connected to the organization to suffer the economic and dignitary harms resulting from discrimination"); Leonard Bierman & Rafael Gely, *So, You Want To Be a Partner at Sidley & Austin?*, 40 HOUS. L. REV. 969, 991 (2003) ("Only where the partner label carries with it real authority that allows the named partner to take effective action against others in the firm should the court find the individual to be an employer," and thus outside statutory coverage).

4. *Ownership as a Perk of Employment.* The fact that a partner (or other owner) might not be an employee of the partnership does not mean that true employees — such as associates in a law firm — can be discriminated against in being selected for partnership. In *Hishon v. King & Spalding*, 467 U.S. 69 (1984), reproduced at p. 16, the Court held that an associate in a law firm could bring a Title VII sex discrimination claim for being denied partnership. The holding was not that partners were employees but rather that Title VII would be violated if sex discrimination prevented advancement to partnership, one of the "privileges" of employment as an associate: "A benefit that is part and parcel of the employment relationship may not be doled out in a discriminatory fashion, even if the employer would be free under the employment contract simply not to provide the benefit at all." *Id.* at 75. *Hishon* creates the paradox of requiring firms to advance employees to ownership status without discrimination but leaving such persons unprotected once they become partners or shareholders. Thus, it remains quite common for large law firms to have mandatory retirement policies for partners, policies that would quite certainly be illegal were the ADEA to apply to partners. Similarly, a firm acquiring partners by "lateral entry," that is, by inviting into the partnership persons not previously affiliated with the firm, is unlikely to be subject to the antidiscrimination laws.

5. *Bitter with the Sweet.* The dissent in *Clackamas* of Justices Ginsburg and Breyer saw no reason why an owner could not also be an employee under the statutes, and argued that the fact that the physicians sought the benefits of employee status under laws such as ERISA was a strong, if not decisive, factor cutting in favor of holding them to the burdens of such status under other laws. For these two justices, the choice of the corporate form seems decisive. Is this a fair interpretation of "employee" in the antidiscrimination statutes, or is there some other policy at work here? Note that *Clackamas* opens the door to a wide variety of private ordering allowing individuals and firms to avoid the strictures of some employment regulations while taking advantage of other regulatory schemes.

6. *The Numbers Game.* As *Clackamas* indicates, even assuming an employment relationship and that the plaintiff is an employee, the antidiscrimination statutes do not apply unless the employer is a statutory employer, that is, unless it has the requisite number of employees (15 for Title VII and the ADA and 20 for the ADEA) for the requisite time ("each working day in each of twenty or more calendar weeks in the current or preceding calendar year"). The employer must also be "engaged in an industry affecting commerce," but this has rarely posed a separate obstacle. There are issues about how to compute the requisite numbers. For example, hourly, part-time, and on-leave employees count, *Walters v. Metropolitan Educ. Enters.*, 519 U.S. 202 (1997). However, the requirement of a minimum number of employees is not "jurisdictional" under the antidiscrimination statutes. *Arbaugh v. Y & H Corp.*, 546 U.S. 500, 516 (2006) (the numerical "threshold is an element of a plaintiff's claim for relief, not a jurisdictional issue"). This ruling not only preserves verdicts from subsequent attack on "jurisdictional" grounds, as in *Arbaugh* itself, but also ensures that the jury, rather than the judge, decides fact issues related to coverage. *See* Stefania A. Di Trolio, Comment, *Undermining and Unentwining: The Right to a Jury Trial and Rule 12(b)(1)*, 33 SETON HALL L. REV. 1247 (2003).

7. *Integrated Enterprises and Joint Employers.* It is sometimes possible to aggregate two or more entities into a statutory employer. The "integrated enterprise" or "single employer" doctrine views two or more formally distinct legal entities as being in reality a single employer, thus allowing all of the employees of all to be aggregated to make the required minimum number. *See Arculeo v. On-Site Sales & Mktg., L.L.C.*, 425 F.3d 193, 199 (2d Cir. 2005) ("although nominally and technically distinct, several entities [may] properly seen as a single integrated entity"). While there is dispute as to what constitutes an integrated enterprise, something more than corporate affiliation is required. *See Iverson v. Ingersoll-Rand Co.*, 125 Fed. Appx. 73 (8th Cir. 2004) (more than a normal parent-subsidiary relationship before a parent corporation is deemed the employer of a subsidiary's employee; the parent must control day-to-day employment decisions). One court suggested three situations in which a company and its affiliates are a single employer:

(1) a company splits itself into entities with less than fifteen employees intending to evade Title VII's reach;

(2) a parent company has directed the subsidiary's discriminatory act of which the plaintiff is complaining;

(3) as in bankruptcy law, when "two or more entities' affairs are so interconnected that they collectively caused the alleged discriminatory employment practice. More colloquially, the question is whether the 'eggs' — consisting of the ostensibly separate companies — are so scrambled that we decline to unscramble them. We note, however, that substantive consolidation is an equitable remedy and is difficult to achieve."

Nesbit v. Gears Unlimited, Inc., 347 F.3d 72, 85-86 (3d Cir. 2003). *See generally* Richard R. Carlson, *The Small Firm Exemption and the Single Employer Doctrine in Employment Discrimination Law*, 80 ST. JOHN'S L. REV. 1197 (2006) (arguing that the single employer doctrine is not only consistent with the purpose of the small firm exemption but is also necessary to fully achieve that exemption's purpose).

Distinct from the single employer/integrated enterprise doctrine is the "joint employment" doctrine under which an employee of one entity may hold another entity liable; the premise is not the two entities are one but rather that "they co-determine the essential terms and conditions of employment." *Bristol v. Bd. of County Comm'rs*, 312 F.3d 1213, 1218 (10th Cir. 2002). One of the entities may, of course, be too small to be a statutory employer, which may make joint employment critical to liability for anyone. But joint employment also expands the number of entities that may be held liable for a particular violation, which can be important should one of the entities be in financial difficulty.

8. *Interns and Volunteers.* In *Lerohl*, the court quotes approvingly an earlier case finding "silly" the claim that volunteer firefighters or volunteer rescue workers are employees "because the fire chief or the head of the rescue squad directs them." It may in fact be silly, but perhaps because "employment" entails both control and compensation. In other words, the firefighters are not employees because they are unpaid, even assuming their work is controlled by the putative employer. The courts have generally required compensation as one condition of employment, *see York v. Ass'n of the Bar*, 286 F.3d 122 (2d Cir. 2002) (attorney volunteering at the association was not an "employee" under Title VII). *Cf. United States v. City of New York*, 359 F.3d 83, 92 (2d Cir. 2004) ("workfare" participants were employees when their work was completely controlled by the various agencies, and they had to work to receive their grant). This means, for example, that many student interns lack statutory protection. *See generally* David C. Yamada, *The Employment Law Rights of Student Interns*, 35 CONN. L. REV. 215 (2002). By contrast, a graduate student assistant may be an employee. *Cuddeback v. Fla. Bd. of Educ.*, 381 F.3d 1230, 1234 (11th Cir. 2004).

9. *State and Local Government.* Title VII, the ADEA and the ADA generally reach state and local governmental employers, although the Eleventh Amendment poses problems for private suits under the ADEA and the ADA. See p. 648. But both Title VII and the ADEA exempt from their definitions of "employee" elected officers and "any person chosen by such officer to be on such officer's personal staff, or an appointee on the policy-making level or an immediate adviser with respect to the exercise of the constitutional or legal powers of the office." 42 U.S.C. § 2000e(f); 29 U.S.C. § 630(f). *E.g., Crumpacker v. Kansas*, 474 F.3d 747 (10th Cir. 2007) (person not appointed by an elected official was not within the exception). *See also Gregory v. Ashcroft*, 501 U.S. 452 (1991) (ADEA did not provide a sufficient clear statement to justify applying it to state judges). Such persons, however, may have protection under a related statute. *E.g., Brazoria County v. EEOC*, 391 F.3d 685, 689 (5th Cir. 2004). See pp. 650-51.

10. *Federal Government.* Almost all federal civilian employment is also covered by Title VII and the ADEA through separate provisions in each law. §717, 42 U.S.C. § 2000e-16; 29 U.S.C. § 633(a). The remaining federal civilian employees are protected either by the Civil Rights Act of 1991 or the Congressional Accountability Act of 1995, Pub. L. No. 104-1, 109 Stat. 3. The military is, however, beyond the reach of Title VII and the other antidiscrimination statutes, although sometimes hybrid cases arise. *See Overton v. New York State Div. of Military & Naval Affairs*, 373 F.3d 83 (2d Cir. 2004) (technician who served as both a civilian employee and service-member

had his civilian and military roles so intertwined that his Title suit would intrude too much into his military relationship with the supervisor even though he claimed that the focus of the suit was on conduct related to his civilian duties).

11. *Extraterritorial Effect.* As originally enacted, Title VII did not extend to the employment of Americans outside the United States. *EEOC v. Arabian Am. Oil Co.*, 499 U.S. 244 (1991). The Civil Rights Act of 1991 prospectively overruled this decision by revising the definition of "employee" to include American citizens employed in a foreign country. §701(f), 42 U.S.C. §2000e(f). *But see Shekoyan v. Sibley Int'l.*, 409 F.3d 414 (D.C. Cir. 2005) (Title VII does not protect lawful permanent resident of the United States working in foreign country). Congress, however, simultaneously added §702(b), which allows discrimination "with respect to an employee . . . in a foreign country if compliance [with Title VII] would cause such employer . . . to violate the law of the foreign country in which such workplace is located." Thus, if foreign law excluded women from certain occupations, the exemption would immunize discrimination against American women applicants for those positions. These provisions closely parallel those Congress had earlier added to the ADEA. 29 U.S.C. §623(h). *See Mahoney v. RFE/RL, Inc.*, 47 F.3d 447 (D.C. Cir. 1995) (exemption applied when application of the ADEA would require violating a collective bargaining agreement in a country where such departures are illegal without approval by government-established "works councils"). Although U.S. citizens abroad are now "employees," the statute expressly excludes foreign companies acting abroad from coverage in §702(c)(2). In short, Americans working abroad are covered, but only when working for American corporations, although §702(c)(1) extends Title VII to foreign corporations that are "controlled" by American corporations.

12. *Creative Applications.* Some courts expand Title VII's reach in ways that are not obvious. In *Sibley Meml. Hosp. v. Wilson*, 488 F.2d 1338 (D.C. Cir. 1973), a male private-duty nurse challenged the defendant hospital's refusal to assign him to care for female patients. The hospital responded that neither the plaintiff nor the hospital contemplated an employment relationship between them; rather, the employment relationship was between the nurse and his patients. The hospital contended, therefore, that it was not an "employer." The court held that Title VII prohibits an "employer" from discriminating against any "individual" (not merely against "employees") with regard to employment; therefore, the hospital's discriminatory referral practices were actionable because they "interfer[ed] with an individual's employment opportunities with another employer." *Id.* at 1341. *Accord Association of Mexican-Am. Educators v. California*, 231 F.3d 572 (9th Cir. 2000) (en banc) (Title VII applied to a state credentialing agency in light of the power such agency exerted over employment as a teacher); *but see Shah v. Deaconess Hosp.*, 355 F.3d 496, 500 (6th Cir. 2004) (doctor with hospital admitting privileges not protected); *Gulino v. N.Y. State Educ. Dep't*, 460 F.3d 361, 375 (2d Cir. 2006) (discussing *Sibley* interference test but ruling that, even under that test, the defendants were not employers because the relationship between New York and its local school districts differed from that in *Association of Mexican-American Educators*); *Camacho v. P.R. Ports Auth.*, 369 F.3d 570 (1st Cir. 2004) (agency that licenses and regulated pilots was not their de facto employer).

13. *Exemptions.* There are several explicit exemptions in the antidiscrimination statutes. Title VII, for example, exempts a "bona fide private membership club." §701(b)(2), 42 U.S.C. §2000e(b)(2), and also exempts Indian tribes. §701(b), 42 U.S.C. §2000e(b) (2007). While this exception is not expressly included in the ADEA,

it has been read into the statute. *E.g., Thomas v. Choctaw Management/Services Enter.*, 313 F.3d 910 (5th Cir. 2002) (business owned entirely by the Choctaw Nation did not constitute an "employer" under Title VII). *See generally* Vicki J. Limas, *Application of Federal Labor and Employment Statutes to Native American Tribes: Respecting Sovereignty and Achieving Consistency*, 26 ARIZ. ST. L.J. 681 (1994). While not a formal exemption, the denial of a security clearance may also effectively preclude Title VII suit, even if the plaintiff claims that this is merely a pretext for a decision taken for discriminatory reasons. *See Bennett v. Chertoff*, 425 F.3d 999, 1003-04 (D.C. Cir. 2005) (court cannot adjudicate whether revocation of clearance is pretextual since that would require the trier of fact to evaluate the validity of the agency's security determination).

Other exceptions from the antidiscrimination statutes may be found in other federal laws. For example, in *Sumitomo Shoji, America, Inc. v. Avagliano*, 457 U.S. 176 (1982), the Supreme Court considered a claim that, by virtue of the Friendship, Commerce, and Navigation Treaty between the United States and Japan, the defendant was immune for discrimination against non-Japanese in filling certain positions. The Court rejected the defense on the ground that the defendant, a New York-incorporated subsidiary of a Japanese corporation, did not qualify as a "company of Japan," but it indicated that a true "company of Japan" can invoke this defense. *See also Papaila v. Uniden Am. Corp.*, 51 F.3d 54 (5th Cir. 1995) (U.S. subsidiary can invoke treaty where discrimination dictated by parent); *MacNamara v. Korean Air Lines*, 863 F.2d 1135 (3d Cir. 1988) (reading the treaty to allow citizenship discrimination but to prohibit a beneficiary of the treaty from intentionally discriminating, even in its executive positions, on the basis of age, sex, religion, or race).

NOTE ON COVERAGE OF §1981

Questions of "employment" as such do not arise under §1981 since that statute reaches all "contract" relations, not merely employment. *See Runyon v. McCrary*, 427 U.S. 160 (1976). Thus, §1981 embraces relationships that do not constitute "employment" under Title VII, such as partnership or independent contractor status. *E.g., Wortham v. Am. Family Ins. Group*, 385 F.3d 1139 (8th Cir. 2004) (while Title VII suit was barred because plaintiff was an independent "contractor," he was protected by §1981). The statute has been held applicable to at-will employment, despite that argument that, in some states, such employment is not contractual under state law. *Walker v. Abbott Labs.*, 340 F.3d 471 (7th Cir. 2003) (Seventh Circuit joined five other circuits in allowing an at-will employee to state a claim under §1981).

Further, §1981 reaches all employers except the federal government, *Brown v. General Serv. Admin.*, 425 U.S. 820, 825 (1976) (Title VII exclusive discrimination remedy for federal employment within its scope), thus covering employers exempt from Title VII. Section 1981 also reaches the contractual relationships of state and local governmental employers. Any doubt as to this was resolved by the 1991 Civil Rights Act's addition of paragraph (c), providing that "[t]he rights protected by this section are protected against impairment by nongovernmental discrimination and impairment under color of State law." However, the recovery of punitive damages from a governmental entity may be subject to several limitations, see p. 698, and there may also be Eleventh Amendment questions about private suits against state entities. See p. 648. While its coverage is broad, § 1981 bars only racial and alienage discrimination.

NOTE ON CONSTITUTIONAL LIMITATIONS ON THE REACH OF THE ANTIDISCRIMINATION LAWS

A number of efforts have been made to limit the reach of antidiscrimination laws by invoking various constitutional provisions. We will examine in more detail a narrow, but well established limitation on these statutes, the "ministerial exception," which is predicated on the religion clauses of the First Amendment. See p. 459. Until relatively recently, however, more general attempts to invoke the constitution to immunize certain activities from attack have failed. Freedom of association claims, for example, were rejected in *Roberts v. United States Jaycees*, 468 U.S. 609 (1984) (upholding decision that Jaycees had to admit women). *See also New York State Club Assn. v. City of New York*, 487 U.S. 1 (1988) (upholding constitutionality of amendment to New York City Human Rights Law substantially narrowing its "private club" exemption); *Runyon v. McCrary*, 427 U.S. 160, (1976) (no constitutional right for a private school to exclude black children in violation of § 1981). And *Hishon v. King & Spalding*, reproduced at p. 16, rejected a freedom of association defense by King & Spalding: "[i]nvidious private discrimination may be characterized as a form of exercising freedom of association protected by the First Amendment, but it has never been accorded affirmative constitutional protections." 467 U.S. at 78 (quoting *Norwood v. Harrison*, 413 U.S. 455, 470 (1973)).

More recently, however, the right of expressive association has been revived to somewhat limit the antidiscrimination laws. *Boy Scouts of America v. Dale*, 530 U.S. 640 (2000), over vigorous dissents by Justices Stevens, Souter, Breyer and Ginsburg, held that the First Amendment right of expressive association insulated the Boy Scouts of America from New Jersey's ban on discrimination on the basis of sexual orientation in public accommodations. At issue was whether, "a private, not-for-profit organization engaged in instilling its system of values in young people," *id.* at 644, could be required to accept a gay scoutmaster. The Court held no: the BSA persuaded it both that homosexual conduct was inconsistent with scouting values and that having "an avowed homosexual and gay rights activist," *id.*, would impair the BSA's ability to impart those values.

While *Dale* could be read broadly, it is unlikely to create any sweeping exception to the antidiscrimination laws. Although the Court stressed that First Amendment protection expressive association is not limited to advocacy groups, "a group must engage in some form of expression, whether it be public or private" to be protected. *Id.* at 648. Some have argued that it will be rare for a profit-making enterprise to be viewed as an expressive association, and, in any event, to be protected from the antidiscrimination laws, the entity must, in essence, support discrimination. While the *Dale* majority found that the Boy Scouts disapproved of homosexuality, a hotly contested front in the discrimination debate, even that disapproval was not so clear, and few organizations in modern times are likely to advocate racial or sexual discrimination.

Further, even those organizations that have a particular expressive purpose at odds with the antidiscrimination laws are protected from them only if complying "would significantly affect [their] ability to advocate public or private viewpoints." *Id.* at 648. While the *Dale* Court found such an effect in the case before it, it distinguished earlier decisions, such as *Roberts* as not only involving a compelling interest in eliminating discrimination against women but also as concluding that "the enforcement of these statutes would not materially interfere with the ideas that the organization sought to express." *Id.* at 650.

The Supreme Court's only expressive association decision after *Dale* confirms that *Dale* will have relatively little impact on the discrimination laws. In an attempt to deploy the "sauce for the goose is sauce for the gander" principle, a group of law schools and law professors invoked *Dale* to resist the "Solomon Amendment," which requires educational institutions receiving financial aid to allow access to military recruiters. Accreditation standards require law schools to close their facilities to employers who discriminate on a variety of grounds, including sexual orientation. Given the United States military's position on gays, this led large numbers of law schools to exclude JAG from their campuses. The Solomon Amendment was Congress's effort to counter this by threatening loss of federal funding.

Although there was no doubt that the law schools were expressive associations and that the values they imparted included nondiscrimination, *Rumsfeld v. Forum for Academic & Institutional Rights, Inc.*, 547 U.S. 47, 69 (2006), rejected several First Amendment challenges to the Solomon Amendment:

> To comply with the statute, law schools must allow military recruiters on campus and assist them in whatever way the school chooses to assist other employers. Law schools therefore "associate" with military recruiters in the sense that they interact with them. But recruiters are not part of the law school. Recruiters are, by definition, outsiders who come onto campus for the limited purpose of trying to hire students — not to become members of the school's expressive association. This distinction is critical. Unlike the public accommodations law in *Dale*, the Solomon Amendment does not force a law school "to accept members it does not desire."

Prior to *FAIR*, *Dale* triggered an enormous outpouring of scholarship. Both the right and the left read the case to have enormous potential implications. *Compare* Richard A. Epstein, *The Constitutional Perils of Moderation: The Case of the Boy Scouts*, 74 S. CAL. L. REV. 119, 139 (2000) (all private associations that are not monopolists have expressive association rights, even though that "calls for the constitutional invalidation of much of the Civil Rights Act, including Title VII insofar as it relates to employment") *with* Andrew Koppelman, *Signs of the Times:* Dale v. Boy Scouts of America *and the Changing Meaning of Nondiscrimination*, 23 CARDOZO L. REV. 1819, 1819-20 (2002) ("All antidiscrimination laws are unconstitutional in all their applications. Citizens are allowed to disobey laws whenever obedience would be perceived as endorsing some message. Both of these propositions are absurd. However, [*Dale*] stands for at least one of them, and perhaps both"). *See also* Jed Rubenfeld, *The Anti-Antidiscrimination Agenda*, 111 YALE L.J. 1141 (2002); Dale Carpenter, *Expressive Association and Anti-Discrimination Law After* Dale: A *Tripartite Approach*, 85 MINN. L. REV. 1515 (2001).

C. SEX DISCRIMINATION

In prior chapters, we've explored what is meant by "discrimination," as well as the proof structures involved in determining whether discrimination occurred. We now turn to what is or is not encompassed within the various protected classifications under Title VII. Sex discrimination claims, in particular, have raised a series of difficult problems, problems that flow from what it means to discriminate "because of sex" under Title VII. Simply put, what is "sex" for purposes of Title VII?

This section begins by exploring that topic in Part 1. Is discrimination on the basis of sexual orientation or transgender discrimination actionable? What about claims of sex stereotyping? Is giving preferential treatment on the job to one's paramour actionable under Title VII? And what about the separate dress and grooming codes for men and women that are ubiquitous in the working world? How can those be squared with Title VII's antidiscrimination mandate? Finally, is discrimination because of "pregnancy, childbirth or related medical conditions" sex discrimination? Each of these questions is explored below.

Part 2 then turns to sexual harassment, which has raised difficult interpretive issues for the courts. Because most of the law dealing with racial and other discriminatory harassment originated with sexual harassment cases, these topics are also treated in this part.

1. Discrimination "Because of Sex"

ONCALE v. SUNDOWNER OFFSHORE SERVICES, INC.
523 U.S. 75 (1998)

Justice SCALIA delivered the opinion of the Court.

This case presents the question whether workplace harassment can violate Title VII's prohibition against "discrimination . . . because of . . . sex," when the harasser and the harassed employee are of the same sex.

I

The District Court having granted summary judgment for respondent, we must assume the facts to be as alleged by petitioner Joseph Oncale. The precise details are irrelevant to the legal point we must decide, and in the interest of both brevity and dignity we shall describe them only generally. In late October 1991, Oncale was working for respondent Sundowner Offshore Services on a Chevron U.S.A., Inc., oil platform in the Gulf of Mexico. He was employed as a roustabout on an eight-man crew which included respondents John Lyons, Danny Pippen, and Brandon Johnson. Lyons, the crane operator, and Pippen, the driller, had supervisory authority. On several occasions, Oncale was forcibly subjected to sex-related, humiliating actions against him by Lyons, Pippen and Johnson in the presence of the rest of the crew. Pippen and Lyons also physically assaulted Oncale in a sexual manner, and Lyons threatened him with rape.

Oncale's complaints to supervisory personnel produced no remedial action; in fact, the company's Safety Compliance Clerk, Valent Hohen, told Oncale that Lyons and Pippen "picked [on] him all the time too," and called him a name suggesting homosexuality. Oncale eventually quit — asking that his pink slip reflect that he "voluntarily left due to sexual harassment and verbal abuse." When asked at his deposition why he left Sundowner, Oncale stated "I felt that if I didn't leave my job, that I would be raped or forced to have sex."

[The district court held that "Mr. Oncale, a male, has no cause of action under Title VII for harassment by male co-workers." The Fifth Circuit affirmed.]

II

Title VII of the Civil Rights Act of 1964 provides, in relevant part, that "it shall be an unlawful employment practice for an employer . . . to discriminate against any individual with respect to his compensation, terms, conditions, or privileges of employment, because of such individual's race, color, religion, sex, or national origin." . . .

Title VII's prohibition of discrimination "because of . . . sex" protects men as well as women, *Newport News* [*Shipbuilding & Dry Dock Co. v. EEOC*, 462 U.S. 669 (1983)], and in the related context of racial discrimination in the workplace we have rejected any conclusive presumption that an employer will not discriminate against members of his own race. "Because of the many facets of human motivation, it would be unwise to presume as a matter of law that human beings of one definable group will not discriminate against other members of that group." *Castaneda v. Partida*, 430 U.S. 482 (1977). In *Johnson v. Transportation Agency, Santa Clara County* [reproduced at p. 184], a male employee claimed that his employer discriminated against him because of his sex when it preferred a female employee for promotion. Although we ultimately rejected the claim on other grounds, we did not consider it significant that the supervisor who made that decision was also a man. If our precedents leave any doubt on the question, we hold today that nothing in Title VII necessarily bars a claim of discrimination "because of . . . sex" merely because the plaintiff and the defendant (or the person charged with acting on behalf of the defendant) are of the same sex.

Courts have had little trouble with that principle in cases like *Johnson*, where an employee claims to have been passed over for a job or promotion. But when the issue arises in the context of a "hostile environment" sexual harassment claim, the state and federal courts have taken a bewildering variety of stances. Some, like the Fifth Circuit in this case, have held that same-sex sexual harassment claims are never cognizable under Title VII. Other decisions say that such claims are actionable only if the plaintiff can prove that the harasser is homosexual (and thus presumably motivated by sexual desire). Compare *McWilliams v. Fairfax County Board of Supervisors*, 72 F.3d 1191 (4th Cir. 1996), with *Wrightson v. Pizza Hut of America*, 99 F.3d 138 (4th Cir. 1996). Still others suggest that workplace harassment that is sexual in content is always actionable, regardless of the harasser's sex, sexual orientation, or motivations. See *Doe v. Belleville*, 119 F.3d 563 (7th Cir. 1997).

We see no justification in the statutory language or our precedents for a categorical rule excluding same-sex harassment claims from the coverage of Title VII. As some courts have observed, male-on-male sexual harassment in the workplace was assuredly not the principal evil Congress was concerned with when it enacted Title VII. But statutory prohibitions often go beyond the principal evil to cover reasonably comparable evils, and it is ultimately the provisions of our laws rather than the principal concerns of our legislators by which we are governed. Title VII prohibits "discrimination . . . because of . . . sex" in the "terms" or "conditions" of employment. Our holding that this includes sexual harassment must extend to sexual harassment of any kind that meets the statutory requirements.

Respondents and their amici contend that recognizing liability for same-sex harassment will transform Title VII into a general civility code for the American workplace. But that risk is no greater for same-sex than for opposite-sex harassment, and is adequately met by careful attention to the requirements of the statute. Title VII does not prohibit all verbal or physical harassment in the workplace; it is directed only at "discrimination . . . because of . . . sex." We have never held that workplace harassment, even harassment between men and women, is automatically discrimination because of sex merely because the words used have sexual content or connotations. "The critical issue, Title VII's text indicates, is whether members of one sex are exposed to disadvantageous terms or conditions of employment to which members of the other sex are not exposed." *Harris v. Forklift Systems, Inc.*, 510 U.S. 17 (1993) [reproduced at p. 376].

Courts and juries have found the inference of discrimination easy to draw in most male-female sexual harassment situations, because the challenged conduct typically involves explicit or implicit proposals of sexual activity; it is reasonable to assume those proposals would not have been made to someone of the same sex. The same chain of inference would be available to a plaintiff alleging same-sex harassment, if there were credible evidence that the harasser was homosexual. But harassing conduct need not be motivated by sexual desire to support an inference of discrimination on the basis of sex. A trier of fact might reasonably find such discrimination, for example, if a female victim is harassed in such sex-specific and derogatory terms by another woman as to make it clear that the harasser is motivated by general hostility to the presence of women in the workplace. A same-sex harassment plaintiff may also, of course, offer direct comparative evidence about how the alleged harasser treated members of both sexes in a mixed-sex workplace. Whatever evidentiary route the plaintiff chooses to follow, he or she must always prove that the conduct at issue was not merely tinged with offensive sexual connotations, but actually constituted "discrimination . . . because of . . . sex."

And there is another requirement that prevents Title VII from expanding into a general civility code: As we emphasized in *Meritor* [*Sav. Bank, FSB v. Vinson*, 477 U.S. 57 (1986), reproduced at p. 370] and *Harris*, the statute does not reach genuine but innocuous differences in the ways men and women routinely interact with members of the same sex and of the opposite sex. The prohibition of harassment on the basis of sex requires neither asexuality nor androgyny in the workplace; it forbids only behavior so objectively offensive as to alter the "conditions" of the victim's employment. "Conduct that is not severe or pervasive enough to create an objectively hostile or abusive work environment — an environment that a reasonable person would find hostile or abusive — is beyond Title VII's purview." *Harris*. We have always regarded that requirement as crucial, and as sufficient to ensure that courts and juries do not mistake ordinary socializing in the workplace — such as male-on-male horseplay or intersexual flirtation — for discriminatory "conditions of employment."

We have emphasized, moreover, that the objective severity of harassment should be judged from the perspective of a reasonable person in the plaintiff's position, considering "all the circumstances." *Harris*. In same-sex (as in all) harassment cases, that inquiry requires careful consideration of the social context in which particular behavior occurs and is experienced by its target. A professional football player's working environment is not severely or pervasively abusive, for example, if the coach smacks him on the buttocks as he heads onto the field — even if the same behavior would reasonably be experienced as abusive by the coach's secretary (male or female) back at the office. The real social impact of workplace behavior often depends on a constellation of surrounding circumstances, expectations, and relationships which are not fully captured by a simple recitation of the words used or the physical acts performed. Common sense, and an appropriate sensitivity to social context, will enable courts and juries to distinguish between simple teasing or roughhousing among members of the same sex, and conduct which a reasonable person in the plaintiff's position would find severely hostile or abusive. . . .

NOTES

1. *Same Sex Discrimination Is Actionable.* We will consider claims of sexual harassment later in this chapter, but for present purposes it is sufficient to understand that the Supreme Court previously had recognized that hostile work environment claims could be actionable under Title VII as sex discrimination. The cases previously before the Supreme Court, however, had all involved claims by women accusing their male supervisors of harassment, and the Fifth Circuit in *Oncale* concluded that, when the allegations involved male-on-male harassment, no claim could be brought. *Oncale* makes clear that, regardless of the genders of the harasser and victim, the central issue for purposes of establishing liability under Title VII is whether the terms and conditions of the victim's employment were altered because of, or on the basis of, sex.

2. *Harassment Need Not Be "Sexual" to Be Actionable.* Justice Scalia's opinion in *Oncale* states that harassment not based on sexual desire whatsoever can be actionable under Title VII *if* the victim has been targeted because of her sex. It seems unlikely that the harassment in *Oncale* was predicated on a desire of the harassers to have sex with their victim. And a number of cases have found nonsexual harassment to be discriminatory when it is directed only at female employees. *E.g., Boumehdi v. Plastag Holdings LLC*, 489 F.3d. 781, 788 (7th Cir. 2007) ("Although most of Vega's alleged comments were sexist rather than sexual, our precedent does not limit hostile environment claims to situations in which the harassment was based on sexual desire"); *EEOC v. Nat'l Educ. Ass'n, Alaska*, 422 F.3d 840, 842 (9th Cir. 2005) ("offensive conduct that is not facially sex-specific nonetheless may violate Title VII if there is sufficient circumstantial evidence of qualitative and quantitative differences in the harassment suffered by female and male employees"); *Gorski v. New Hampshire Dept. of Corr.*, 290 F.3d 466 (1st Cir. 2002) (remarks and conduct directed toward plaintiff's pregnancy or because of her pregnancy stated a claim based on a hostile work environment).

3. *Proving the Harassment Was "Because of Sex."* Although *Oncale* establishes that same-sex harassment is actionable under Title VII, the question remains, how can a fact finder determine whether the harassment is because of or on the basis of sex? The Court confirms prior opinions in which an inference of sex-based discrimination was based on sexual advances made by a heterosexual toward a victim of the opposite sex. Consistent with this logic, the Court indicates that sexual advances by a homosexual toward an individual of the same sex also may give rise to the inference that such action is "because of sex." Moreover, that the harassment is sexual in nature is powerful evidence the harassment is because of sex, but, as *Oncale* demonstrates, the sexual form of the harassment is not conclusive.

On remand, what evidence would you present to establish that Oncale's co-workers were harassing him *because of* his sex? What evidence would you present for the employer to prove an alternative motivation such as jealousy or dislike or, as we will see below, suspicions of sexual orientation? *Shepherd v. Slater Steel Corp.*,

168 F.3d 998 (7th Cir. 1999), read *Oncale* to establish two prongs by which same-sex harassment may be gender discrimination:

> (1) credible evidence that the harasser is gay or lesbian — in which case it is reasonable to assume that the harasser would not harass members of the other sex (or at least not with "explicit or implicit proposals of sexual activity"); and (2) proof that the plaintiff was harassed in "such sex-specific and derogatory terms" as to reveal an antipathy to persons of plaintiff's gender.

Id. at 1009. In the case before it, the *Shepherd* court found sufficient evidence that defendant's harassment was "borne of sexual attraction" to infer that plaintiff was harassed because he was male. It distinguished other cases in which "sexual references were essentially incidental to what was otherwise run-of-the-mill horseplay and vulgarity." *Id.* at 1010. Might that be the employer's defense in *Oncale* on remand? *Shepherd* found more difficult the evidence that a woman had been harassed as well. While recognizing that a fact-finder could find defendant's harassment to be "bisexual and therefore beyond the reach of Title VII," *id.* at 1011, it recognized that a contrary inference was also supportable.

4. *The "Equal Opportunity" Harasser.* As *Shepherd* suggests, a test case is the "equal opportunity harasser," the person who directs offensive conduct and remarks against both men and women. At least under the "equality" approach, such a person is not guilty of sex discrimination under Title VII. Charles R. Calleros, *The Meaning of "Sex": Homosexual and Bisexual Harassment under Title VII*, 20 VT. L. REV. 55, 70-78 (1995). *See also* Martin J. Katz, *Reconsidering Attraction in Sexual Harassment*, 79 Ind. L.J. 101, 125-39 (2004) (discussing the "Bisexuality Gap" and examining approaches to causation in sexual harassment cases where the harasser is — or claims to be — bisexual); Ronald Turner, *Title VII and the Inequality-Enhancing Effects of the Bisexual and Equal Opportunity Harasser Defenses*, 7 U. PA. J. LAB. & EMP. L. 341, 342, 345 (2005) (arguing that "incidents of bisexual and equal opportunity harassment should be and are actionable"). This is not merely a law school hypothetical. *See Holman v. Indiana*, 211 F.3d 399 (7th Cir. 2000) (complaint of an "equal opportunity harasser" failed to state a claim of sex discrimination); *Venezia v. Gottlieb Mem'l Hosp., Inc.*, 421 F.3d 468 (7th Cir. 2005) (husband and wife could join in sexual harassment action against their employer when they pled sufficiently distinct discrimination such that they were not essentially claiming that one supervisor was an "equal opportunity harasser").

5. *Retaliation as Evidence of Sex Discrimination?* In *Jensen v. Potter*, 435 F.3d 444, 454 (3d Cir. 2006), in an opinion by then-Judge Alito, the Third Circuit held that, when a woman who complains of sexual harassment is thereafter harassed because of the complaint, the harassment can support not only a retaliation claim but a sex discrimination claim. "In such a situation, the evidence will almost always be sufficient to give rise to a reasonable inference that the harassment would not have occurred if the person making the complaint were a man." Do you agree? *See also Jackson v. Birmingham Bd. of Educ.*, 544 U.S. 167 (U.S. 2005) (Title IX case holding that retaliation for complaining about sex discrimination was because of sex).

6. *Academic Commentary.* For additional academic commentary on *Oncale* and the issues it raises, *see* David S. Schwartz, *When Is Sex Because of Sex? The Causation Problem in Sexual Harassment Law*, 150 U. PA. L. REV. 1697 (2002); Camille Hébert, *Sexual Harassment as Discrimination "Because of . . . Sex": Have We Come Full Cir-*

cle?, 27 OHIO N.U. L. REV. 439 (2001); Henry L. Chambers, Jr., *A Unifying Theory of Sex Discrimination*, 34 GA. L. REV. 1591, 1594 (2000); Catherine J. Lanctot, *The Plain Meaning of* Oncale, 7 WM. & MARY BILL RTS. J. 913, 926 (1999); Rebecca Hanner White, *There's Nothing Special About Sex: The Supreme Court Mainstreams Sexual Harassment*, 7 WM. & MARY BILL RTS. J. 725, 734 (1999); Steven Wilborn, *Taking Discrimination Seriously:* Oncale *and the Fate of Exceptionalism in Sexual Harassment Law*, 7 WM. & MARY BILL RTS. J. 677 (1999); Vicki Schultz, *Reconceptualizing Sexual Harassment*, 107 YALE L.J. 1683, 1686-87, 1689 (1998).

a. Discrimination on the Basis of Sexual Orientation

Oncale holds that discrimination against a man because he is male is actionable under Title VII, even if the discrimination occurs at the hands of other men. Standing alone, that is an unremarkable position. However, the lower courts have consistently held that discrimination on the basis of sexual orientation is not actionable. And, as *Oncale* suggests and the following case illustrates, it can be difficult to determine when an individual has been discriminated against because of sex, as opposed to sexual orientation.

VICKERS v. FAIRFIELD MEDICAL CENTER
453 F.3d 757 (6th Cir. 2006)

Julia S. GIBBONS

Christopher Vickers brought a claim against Fairfield Medical Center (FMC), three co-workers, and a co-worker's spouse alleging sex discrimination, sexual harassment and retaliation in violation of Title VII. . . . The district court granted defendants' motion for judgment on the pleadings pursuant to *Federal Rule of Civil Procedure 12(c)*, finding that Vickers could not prevail on any of his federal claims as a matter of law. . . .

For the following reasons, we affirm the decision of the district court.

I

Vickers was employed as a private police officer by Fairfield Medical Center in Lancaster, Ohio. Kory Dixon and John Mueller were also police officers at FMC and often worked with Vickers. Steve Anderson was Police Chief of FMC's police department and was Vickers' supervisor.

Vickers' seventy-one page complaint is extremely detailed. It gives a virtually day-by-day account of Vickers' allegations of harassment. According to the complaint, Vickers befriended a male homosexual doctor at FMC and assisted him in an investigation regarding sexual misconduct that had allegedly occurred against the doctor. Once his co-workers found out about the friendship, Vickers contends that Dixon and Mueller "began making sexually based slurs and discriminating remarks and comments about Vickers, alleging that Vickers was 'gay' or homosexual, and questioning his masculinity." Vickers asserts that following a vacation in April 2002 to Florida with a male friend, Dixon's and Mueller's harassing comments and behavior increased. Vickers asserts that Anderson witnessed the harassing behavior but took no action to stop it and frequently joined in the harassment. Vickers asserts that he has never discussed his sexuality with any of his co-workers.

Vickers contends that he was subject to daily instances of harassment at the hands of his co-workers from May 2002 through March 2003. The allegations of harassment include impressing the word "FAG" on the second page of Vickers' report forms, frequent derogatory comments regarding Vickers' sexual preferences and activities, frequently calling Vickers a "fag," "gay," and other derogatory names, playing tape-recorded conversations in the office during which Vickers was ridiculed for being homosexual, subjecting Vickers to vulgar gestures, placing irritants and chemicals in Vickers' food and other personal property, using the nickname "Kiss" for Vickers, and making lewd remarks suggesting that Vickers provide them with sexual favors.

Vickers also asserts that on several occasions, he was physically harassed by his co-workers. According to his complaint, on October 20, 2002, Vickers and Mueller were conducting handcuff training. Dixon handcuffed Vickers and then simulated sex with Vickers while Anderson photographed this incident. Vickers downloaded the digital picture and placed it in his mailbox, intending to take it home later, but it was removed from his mailbox. Vickers contends that a few days later, Dixon's wife, a nurse at Grant Medical Center, faxed the picture to FMC's Registration Center, where several people saw it. Vickers further contends that the picture was hanging up in a window at FMC on January 15, 2003, where FMC officers, staff and visitors could see it. On other occasions, Vickers' co-workers repeatedly touched his crotch with a tape measure, grabbed Vickers' chest while making derogatory comments, tried to shove a sanitary napkin in Vickers' face, and simulated sex with a stuffed animal and then tried to push the stuffed animal into Vickers' crotch. . . .

[Vickers sued, alleging sex discrimination and sexual harassment under Title VII. The trial court granted defendants' motion for judgment on the pleadings, reasoning "that Title VII does not protect individuals from discrimination based on sexual orientation and that Supreme Court and Sixth Circuit case law do not recognize Vickers' claims of harassment based on being perceived as homosexual."]

II . . .

Vickers argues on appeal that the district court erred in finding that he cannot prevail on his Title VII claims as a matter of law. Vickers contends that while some of the facts alleged in the complaint establish, as the district court found, that the discrimination Vickers experienced was motivated by Vickers' perceived homosexuality, more of the facts suggest that Vickers' harassers were motivated by Vickers' gender non-conformity. As a result, Vickers argues, his claim is covered under the sex stereotyping theory of liability embraced by the Supreme Court in *Price Waterhouse v. Hopkins*, [reproduced at p. 32]. . . .

Title VII of the Civil Rights Act of 1964 prohibits an employer from discriminating against an individual "with respect to his compensation, terms, conditions, or privileges of employment, because of such individual's race, color, religion, sex, or national origin." 42 U.S.C. §2000e-2(a)(1). As is evident from the above-quoted language, sexual orientation is not a prohibited basis for discriminatory acts under Title VII. However, the Supreme Court has held that same-sex harassment is actionable under Title VII under certain circumstances. *See Oncale; see also Rene v. MGM Grand Hotel, Inc.*, 305 F.3d 1061, 1063 (9th Cir. 2002) (en banc) ("[S]exual orientation is irrelevant for purposes of Title VII. It neither provides nor precludes a cause of action for sexual harassment"). Likewise, individuals who are perceived as or who identify as homosexuals are not barred from bringing a claim for sex discrimination under Title VII. . . .

Vickers relies on the theory of sex stereotyping adopted by the Supreme Court in *Price Waterhouse* to support both his sex discrimination and sexual harassment claims. In *Price Waterhouse*, the plaintiff, a senior manager in an accounting firm, was passed over for partnership in part because she was too " 'macho' " and " 'overcompensated for being a woman.' " The plaintiff was told that in order to improve her chances for partnership, she should " 'walk more femininely, talk more femininely, dress more femininely, wear make-up, have her hair styled, and wear jewelry.' " The Supreme Court held that making employment decisions based on sex stereotyping, i.e., the degree to which an individual conforms to traditional notions of what is appropriate for one's gender, is actionable discrimination under Title VII. ("In the specific context of sex stereotyping, an employer who acts on the basis of a belief that a woman cannot be aggressive, or that she must not be, has acted on the basis of gender.")

Vickers contends that this theory of sex stereotyping supports his claim, and thus, the district court should be reversed. Vickers argues in his brief that he was discriminated against because his harassers objected to "those aspects of homosexual behavior in which a male participant assumes what Appellees perceive as a traditionally female-or less masculine-role." In other words, Vickers contends that in the eyes of his co-workers, his sexual practices, whether real or perceived, did not conform to the traditionally masculine role. Rather, in his supposed sexual practices, he behaved more like a woman.

We conclude that the theory of sex stereotyping under *Price Waterhouse* is not broad enough to encompass such a theory. The Supreme Court in *Price Waterhouse* focused principally on characteristics that were readily demonstrable in the workplace, such as the plaintiff's manner of walking and talking at work, as well as her work attire and her hairstyle. Later cases applying *Price Waterhouse* have interpreted it as applying where gender non-conformance is demonstrable through the plaintiff's appearance or behavior. . . . By contrast, the gender non-conforming behavior which Vickers claims supports his theory of sex stereotyping is not behavior observed at work or affecting his job performance. Vickers has made no argument that his appearance or mannerisms on the job were perceived as gender non-conforming in some way and provided the basis for the harassment he experienced. Rather, the harassment of which Vickers complains is more properly viewed as harassment based on Vickers' perceived homosexuality, rather than based on gender non-conformity.

In considering Vickers' sex stereotyping argument, the Second Circuit's recent opinion in *Dawson v. Bumble & Bumble*, 398 F.3d [211 (2d Cir. 2005)], is instructive. In *Dawson*, a female former employee of a hair salon and self-described lesbian attempted to bring a sex discrimination claim against her employer after she was terminated based on alleged gender stereotyping. The plaintiff in that case complained that the discrimination she suffered was based on her non-conforming appearance. The Second Circuit noted the faulty logic in viewing what is, in reality, a claim of discrimination based on sexual orientation as a claim of sex stereotyping:

> When utilized by an avowedly homosexual plaintiff, . . . gender stereotyping claims can easily present problems for an adjudicator. This is for the simple reason that stereotypical notions about how men and women should behave will often necessarily blur into ideas about heterosexuality and homosexuality. Like other courts, we have

therefore recognized that a gender stereotyping claim should not be used to bootstrap protection for sexual orientation into Title VII.

(Internal quotation marks, citations, and alteration omitted.) Although Vickers has declined to reveal whether or not he is, in fact, homosexual, the claim he presents displays precisely the kind of bootstrapping that the *Dawson* court warned against.

This court's opinion in *Smith v. City of Salem*, 378 F.3d [566 (6th Cir. 2004)] does not alter this conclusion. The plaintiff in *Smith*, a lieutenant in the Salem Fire Department, was a transsexual undergoing a physical transformation from male to female. The treatment resulted in a display of "'a more feminine appearance on a full-time basis.'" The plaintiff was suspended based, at least in part, on co-workers' expressed concerns that "his appearance and mannerisms were not 'masculine enough.'" In *Smith*, the court made explicit that a plaintiff cannot be denied coverage under Title VII for sex discrimination merely based on a classification with a group that is not entitled to coverage. ("Sex stereotyping based on a person's gender non-conforming behavior is impermissible discrimination, irrespective of the cause of that behavior; a label, such as 'transsexual,' is not fatal to a sex discrimination claim where the victim has suffered discrimination because of his or her gender non-conformity."). The point is well-taken; we do not suggest that Vickers' claim fails merely because he has been classified by his co-workers and supervisor, rightly or wrongly, as a homosexual. Rather, his claim fails because Vickers has failed to allege that he did not conform to traditional gender stereotypes in any observable way at work. Thus, he does not allege a claim of sex stereotyping. The *Smith* opinion does nothing to lessen the requirement that a plaintiff hoping to succeed on a claim of sex stereotyping show that he "fails to act and/or identify with his or her gender." *Id. See also Barnes v. City of Cincinnati*, 401 F.3d 729, 738 (6th Cir. 2005) (affirming district court's denial of defendant's motion for judgment as a matter of law on discrimination claim where pre-operative male-to-female transsexual was demoted based on his "ambiguous sexuality and his practice of dressing as a woman" and his co-workers' assertions that he was "not sufficiently masculine").

Ultimately, recognition of Vickers' claim would have the effect of *de facto* amending Title VII to encompass sexual orientation as a prohibited basis for discrimination. In all likelihood, any discrimination based on sexual orientation would be actionable under a sex stereotyping theory if this claim is allowed to stand, as all homosexuals, by definition, fail to conform to traditional gender norms in their sexual practices. Indeed, this may be Vickers' intent; he argues in his brief that the unique nature of homosexuality entitles it to protection under Title VII sex discrimination law. . . . While the harassment alleged by Vickers reflects conduct that is socially unacceptable and repugnant to workplace standards of proper treatment and civility, Vickers claim does not fit within the prohibitions of the law. *See Bibby v. Phila. Coca-Cola Bottling Co.*, 260 F.3d 257, 265 (3d Cir. 2001) ("Harassment on the basis of sexual orientation has no place in our society. Congress has not yet seen fit, however, to provide protection against such harassment.") (internal citations omitted).

David M. Lawson, District Judge, dissenting.

As the majority correctly states, in *Price Waterhouse v. Hopkins*, the Supreme Court held that "making employment decisions based on sex stereotyping, i.e., the degree to which an individual conforms to traditional notions of what is appropriate for one's gender, is actionable under Title VII." Because I believe that the plaintiff in this case has pleaded exactly that, I conclude that he has stated a cognizable claim in his complaint that should have survived dismissal under the standard of review that applies to motions under Federal Rule of Civil Procedure 12(c). Since the majority has concluded otherwise, I must respectfully dissent.

I

It is beyond debate that Title VII does not prohibit workplace discrimination or harassment based on sexual preference, sexual orientation, or homosexuality. It is equally clear that employment decisions or workplace harassment that are based on the perception that the employee is not masculine enough or feminine enough — that is, he or she fails "to conform to [gender] stereotypes," *Price Waterhouse v. Hopkins* (O'Connor, J. concurring), violates Title VII's declaration that "[i]t shall be an unlawful employment practice for an employer ... to discriminate against any individual ... because of ... sex." 42 U.S.C. § 2000e-2(a)(1) ...

The majority apparently believes that *Price Waterhouse* extends only to behavior and appearances that manifest themselves in the workplace, and not to private sexual conduct, beliefs, or practices that an employee might adopt or display elsewhere. It concludes, therefore, that Vickers's tormentors were motivated by Vickers's perceived homosexuality rather than an outward workplace manifestation of less-than-masculine gender characteristics.

However, I believe that such a reading of the complaint in this case is too narrow. . . .

I have no quarrel with the proposition that a careful distinction must be drawn between cases of gender stereotyping, which are actionable, and cases denominated as such that in reality seek protection for sexual-orientation discrimination, which are not. Nor do I believe that gender stereotyping is actionable *per se* under Title VII, although certainly it may constitute evidence of discrimination on the basis of sex. As Judge Posner of the Seventh Circuit pointed out:

> [T]here is a difference that subsequent cases have ignored between, on the one hand, using evidence of the plaintiff's failure to wear nail polish (or, if the plaintiff is a man, his using nail polish) to show that her sex played a role in the adverse employment action of which she complains, and, on the other hand, creating a subtype of sexual discrimination called "sex stereotyping," as if there were a federally protected right for male workers to wear nail polish and dresses and speak in falsetto and mince about in high heels, or for female ditchdiggers to strip to the waist in hot weather.

Hamm v. Weyauwega Milk Products, Inc., 332 F.3d 1058, 1067 (7th Cir. 2003) (Posner, J. concurring). However, these distinctions can be complicated, and where, as here, the plaintiff has pleaded facts from which a fact finder could infer that sex (and not simply homosexuality) played a role in the employment decision and contributed to the hostility of the work environment, drawing the line should not occur at the pleading stage of the lawsuit. . . .

II

Looking at the allegations in this case, I cannot conclude that no set of facts could be proved that would entitle the plaintiff to relief. The allegations permit the conclusion that the defendants were hostile to the plaintiff because he was not masculine enough, justifying an inference that a female — or a man with female characteristics — would not be tolerated in the job of private police officer at the Fairfield Medical Center (FMC). . . .

These allegations, in my view, provide a basis for the inference that the plaintiff was perceived as effeminate and therefore unworthy to be considered "a real officer." The permissible conclusion that emerges is that the plaintiff was not tolerated — and the defendants made the workplace environment hostile — because the job required only "manly men," not woman-like ones or women themselves. The complaint need only contain "direct *or inferential* allegations respecting all the material elements to sustain a recovery under some viable legal theory." *Johnson v. City of Detroit*, 446 F.3d 614, 618 (6th Cir. 2006) (emphasis added). Certainly, the complaint is replete with allegations that the plaintiff also was harassed because of his perceived homosexuality. But as homosexuality is not a qualifying classification for relief under Title VII, neither is it disqualifying. That point has been made clear by this court's precedents. In *Smith v. City of Salem*, 378 F.3d 566 (6th Cir. 2004), the court reversed a judgment on the pleadings for the defendant in a claim brought by a transsexual male fireman under Title VII. "Sex stereotyping based on a person's gender non-conforming behavior is impermissible discrimination, irrespective of the cause of that behavior; a label, such as 'transsexual,' is not fatal to a sex discrimination claim where the victim has suffered discrimination because of his or her gender non-conformity." *Smith*.

As in *Smith*, I believe that the plaintiff in this case has "alleged that his failure to conform to sex stereotypes concerning how a man should look and behave was the driving force behind Defendants' actions." Following *Smith*, this court has held that "[s]ex stereotyping based on a person's gender non-conforming behavior is impermissible discrimination, irrespective of the cause of that behavior." *Barnes v. City of Cincinnati*, 401 F.3d 729, 737 (6th Cir. 2005) (citations omitted). Allegations that a plaintiff's "failure to conform to sex stereotypes concerning how a man should look and behave was the driving force behind defendant's actions" has been deemed sufficient to "state[] a claim for relief pursuant to Title VII's prohibition of sex discrimination." Therefore, I must conclude that Vickers "has sufficiently pleaded claims of sex stereotyping and gender discrimination." *Smith*.

NOTES

1. *Sexual Orientation ≠ "Sex" under Title VII.* The *Vickers* court spends no time debating whether discrimination on the basis of sexual orientation is within the reach of Title VII, asserting simply that it is not. That is in line with the rulings of other lower courts to address the issue. *See, e.g., DeSantis v. Pacific Telephone & Telgraph Co.*, 608 F.2d 327 (1979). In *Vickers*, the court points to the language of the statute, saying "sexual orientation" is not included in the statute's protected classifications. Are you so sure that "sex" cannot be construed to include sexual orientation?

Moreover, why isn't a simple disparate treatment theory applicable? In *DeSantis*, the plaintiff argued that he was discriminated against for engaging in conduct (sexual relations with males) that would not be held against him were he a female. Why isn't that a persuasive argument? A long line of cases has held that whites who are discriminated against because of interracial associations, including marriage, are the victims of race discrimination. *Tomczyk v. Jocks & Jills Rests., LLC*, 198 Fed. Appx. 804, 808-09 (11th Cir. 2006) (harassment of white based on race when it was based on the race of the African American man with whom she was romantically involved). *See also Loving v. Virginia,* 388 U.S. 1 (1967) (striking down state law banning interracial marriages, although Virginia argued that it did not discriminate against either race). If the race of a spouse can establish racial discrimination, why can't the gender of a sex partner establish sex discrimination?

2. *Distinguishing Sexual Orientation from Sex Stereotyping.* Although the lower courts have rejected claims based on sexual orientation per se, claims based on a failure to conform to sex stereotypes have been upheld, with courts relying on *Price Waterhouse. See Nichols v. Azteca Restaurant Enterprises, Inc.,* 256 F.3d 864 (9th Cir. 2001). Even though the *Vickers* court rejected plaintiff's discrimination claim, it agreed that a sex stereotyping claim could be actionable in theory. Do you find convincing the majority's explanation for why Vickers had no claim for sex stereotyping? Was Vickers the victim of the egregious harassment he suffered because he was believed to be homosexual? And if so, was he believed to be gay because he failed to conform to masculine stereotypes? The *Vickers* majority observed that recognizing Vickers' sex stereotyping claim would make any discrimination based on sexual orientation actionable. Do you agree? And if so, was that a legitimate basis for denying the claim? *See Medina v. Income Support Division,* 413 F.3d 1131 (10th Cir. 2005) (woman claiming harassment for failure to conform to what she termed "lesbian stereotypes" had no claim; being harassed because of heterosexuality not prohibited by Title VII).

3. *"Sex Stereotyping" Claims by Transsexuals.* The Sixth Circuit had seemed more receptive to some kinds of GLBT claims before *Vickers.* In *Smith v. City of Salem,* 378 F.3d 566, 572 (6th Cir. 2004), discussed by the *Vickers* court, a transsexual stated a Title VII claim by alleging that he was a victim of discrimination because his conduct and mannerisms "did not conform with his employers' and co-workers' sex stereotypes of how a man should look and behave." The comments about him not being sufficiently masculine culminated in his supervisors seeking to compel his resignation "by forcing him to undergo multiple psychological evaluations of his gender non-conforming behavior." The district court's reliance on pre-*Price Waterhouse* cases such as *Ulane v. Eastern Airlines, Inc.,* 742 F.2d 1081, 1085, 1086 (7th Cir. 1984), holding that transsexuals are not protected under Title VII, was error. *Smith* wrote:

> After *Price Waterhouse,* an employer who discriminates against women because, for instance, they do not wear dresses or makeup, is engaging in sex discrimination because the discrimination would not occur but for the victim's sex. It follows that employers who discriminate against men because they do wear dresses and makeup, or otherwise act femininely, are also engaging in sex discrimination, because the discrimination would not occur but for the victim's sex. . . .
>
> Yet some courts have held that this latter form of discrimination is of a different and somehow more permissible kind. For instance, the man who acts in ways typically associated with women is not described as engaging in the same activity as a woman who acts in ways typically associated with women, but is instead described as engaging in the different activity of being a transsexual (or in some instances, a homosexual or transvestite). Discrimination against the transsexual is then found not to be discrimination "because of . . . sex," but rather, discrimination against the plaintiff's unprotected status or mode of self-identification. In other words, these courts superimpose classifications such as "transsexual" on a plaintiff, and then legitimize discrimination based on the plaintiff's gender non-conformity by formalizing the non-conformity into an ostensibly unprotected classification. . . .

Such analyses cannot be reconciled with *Price Waterhouse*, which does not make Title VII protection against sex stereotyping conditional or provide any reason to exclude Title VII coverage for non sex-stereotypical behavior simply because the person is a transsexual.

An earlier version of the opinion contained the following paragraph, which was removed from the final version:

Even if Smith had alleged discrimination based only on his self-identification as a transsexual — as opposed to his specific appearance and behavior — this claim too is actionable pursuant to Title VII. By definition, transsexuals are individuals who fail to conform to stereotypes about how those assigned a particular sex at birth should act, dress, and self-identify. Ergo, identification as a transsexual is the statement or admission that one wishes to be the opposite sex or does not relate to one's birth sex. Such an admission — for instance the admission by a man that he self-identifies as a woman and/or that he wishes to be a woman — itself violates the prevalent sex stereotype that a man should perceive himself as a man. Discrimination based on transsexualism is rooted in the insistence that sex (organs) and gender (social classification of a person as belonging to one sex or the other) coincide. This is the very essence of sex stereotyping. Accordingly, to the extent that Smith also alleges discrimination based solely on his identification as a transsexual, he has alleged a claim of sex stereotyping pursuant to Title VII. As noted above, Smith's birth sex is male and this is the basis for his protected class status under Title VII even under this formulation of his claim.

369 F.3d 912, 921-22. Vickers had attempted to rely on this paragraph to argue that an individual who identifies with a gender non-conforming group would necessarily have a successful sex stereotyping claim, but the *Vickers* court stated, "the decision to omit the language from the *Smith* opinion strongly indicates that the law simply does not embrace his claim." However blurred the line, current Title VII jurisprudence permits discrimination against gays and lesbians so long as that discrimination isn't predicated on failure to conform to gender stereotypes; similarly, bisexuals and transsexuals are also outside of Title VII's protection unless gender nonconformity is the basis for a decision. Does that suggest that transvestites are necessarily protected because gender nonconformity is the essence of the conduct? Whatever the logic of these distinctions, do they make any sense?

4. *Protection Outside Title VII.* The absence of a federal statute prohibiting discrimination on the basis of sexual orientation has led to a number of other legal theories attacking such conduct. In public employment, discrimination against gays has been challenged on the basis of the right of privacy, due process, free speech, and equal protection.

Development of expansive protection based on the right of privacy was originally rejected by *Bowers v. Hardwick*, 478 U.S. 186 (1986), in which the Supreme Court rejected a privacy attack on a Georgia criminal statute used to prosecute consensual homosexual conduct. But in *Lawrence v. Texas*, 539 U.S. 558 (2003), the Supreme Court overruled *Bowers*. *Lawrence* involved the prosecution of two men under a Texas statute that criminalized persons of the same sex engaging in certain sexual conduct, including sodomy. The men had been arrested after police discovered them engaged in a sexual act in the privacy of an apartment. The defendants challenged their convictions, contending that the Texas law violated their rights of equal protection and due process. The Supreme Court, in an opinion by Justice Kennedy, agreed. The due process clause of the 14th amendment, said the Court, protected the rights of gays to choose to enter into personal relationships and to engage in intimate conduct in their homes "without being punished as criminals." As the Court stated:

> The case does involve two adults who, with full and mutual consent from each other, engaged in sexual practices common to a homosexual lifestyle. The petitioners are entitled to respect for their private lives. The State cannot demean their existence or control their destiny by making their private sexual conduct a crime. Their right to liberty under the Due Process Clause gives them the full right to engage in their conduct without intervention of the government.

539 U.S. 558, 578 (2003). The Court declined to resolve the case on narrower grounds under the Equal Protection Clause. The Texas statute, unlike the Georgia statute before the Court in *Bowers*, punished only same-sex sodomy, not sodomy per se. The Court, therefore, could have struck down the statute as not rationally related to legitimate state interests; Justice O'Connor's concurrence followed this route. Instead, the Court overruled *Bowers*, a decision it described as "demean[ing] the lives of homosexual persons." *Bowers*, the Court ruled, "was not correct when it was decided, and it is not correct today. It ought not to remain binding precedent." *Id.* at 562. *See, e.g.,* Paul M. Secunda, *The (Neglected) Importance of Being* Lawrence: *The Constitutionalization of Public Employee Rights to Decisional Non-Interference in Private Affairs,* 40 U.C. DAVIS L. REV. 85 (2006).

Some challenges based on state constitutions have also been successful. On the same day and in the same city where *DeSantis* was handed down rejecting protection of gays under Title VII, the Supreme Court of California decided *Gay Law Students Assn. v. Pacific Telephone & Telegraph Co.,* 595 P.2d 592 (Cal. 1979), holding that gays could sue a public utility for employment discrimination under the equal protection clause of the California constitution. Some other state constitutions have been held to bar discrimination on the basis of sexual orientation although usually in connection with marriage, not employment. *E.g., Goodridge v. Dep't of Pub. Health,* 798 N.E.2d 941 (Mass. 2003); *Lewis v. Harris,* 908 A.2d 196 (N.J. 2006).

In response to the current lack of statutory protection for gays under federal law, a number of states have enacted their own civil rights legislation expressly covering sexual orientation. *See* Ian Ayres & Jennifer Gerarda Brown, *Mark(et)Ing Nondiscrimination: Privatizing ENDA With A Certification Mark,* 104 MICH. L. REV. 1639, 1712 n. 98 (2006) ("47% of the U.S. population lives in jurisdictions that have adopted nondiscrimination laws. This includes 38% who live in states with such laws; another 9% are covered by city or county law"). Such statutes typically protect against discrimination on the basis of sexual orientation, normally defined as including heterosexuality, bisexuality, and homosexuality. And some states are adding gender identity bias to the list of protected classifications.

The Americans with Disabilities Act states explicitly that "homosexuality and bisexuality are not impairments and as such are not disabilities." It separately states that "transvestism, transsexualism, pedophilia, voyeurism, gender identity disorders not resulting from physical impairments, or other sexual behavior disorders" are not disabilities. 42 U.S.C. § 12211 (2007); *see also* 42 U.S.C. § 12208.

Federal legislation to provide protection against discrimination based on sexual orientation passed the House of Representatives in November 2007. The bill originally also had provided protection for transgendered employees, but that provision was removed from the bill before it was passed by the House. David M. Herszenhorn, *House Approves Broad Protection for Gay Workers,* NY Times, Nov. 8, 2007.

b. "Reverse Discrimination" and "Personal Relationships"

What happens when an employee uses his or her sexual attractiveness or a sexual relationship to obtain an advantage relative to other employees? Is this actionable under Title VII? Does it matter if the disfavored employees and the favored employee are of the opposite sex?

This form of "reverse discrimination" was litigated in *DeCintio v. Westchester County Medical Center*, 807 F.2d 304 (2d Cir. 1986). Male respiratory therapists complained that their department head discriminated against them by adopting promotion standards designed to disqualify them and to favor a female applicant with whom he was romantically involved. The court found no Title VII violation:

> Ryan's conduct, although unfair, simply did not violate Title VII. Appellees were not prejudiced because of their status as males; rather, they were discriminated against because Ryan preferred his paramour. Appellees faced exactly the same predicament as that faced by any woman applicant for the promotion: No one but Guagenti could be considered for the appointment because of Guagenti's special relationship to Ryan. That relationship forms the basis of appellees' sex discrimination claims. Appellees' proffered interpretation of Title VII prohibitions against sex discrimination would involve the EEOC and federal courts in the policing of intimate relationships. Such a course, founded on a distortion of the meaning of the word "sex" in the context of Title VII, is both impracticable and unwarranted.

Id. at 308. The court emphasized that Title VII protects individuals from discrimination on the basis of status, "not on his or her sexual affiliations." *Id.* at 306-07. As we will see later in this section, this is essentially the reasoning that led to early Title VII decisions in which courts declined to find liability for quid pro quo sexual harassment. That, of course, is no longer true for such harassment.

The court in *DeCintio* distinguished sexual harassment claims because the issue there is "the coercive nature of the employer's acts, rather than the fact of the relationship itself." *Id.* at 307. But doesn't *Oncale* confirm that the basis of sexual harassment liability is the notion that, "but for" an individual's sex, he or she would not be subjected to harassment? Didn't the plaintiffs in *DeCintio* lose a job opportunity that, "but for" their gender, they would have had? However problematic the analysis, *DeCintio* continues to control. *E.g., Preston v. Wis. Health Fund*, 397 F.3d 539 (7th Cir. 2005) (replacement of male by female with whom supervisor was rumored to be having an affair not actionable since male executive's romantically-motivated favoritism toward female subordinate is not sex discrimination inasmuch as such favoritism is not based on belief that women are better workers, or otherwise deserve to be treated better, than men).

Did the plaintiffs in *DeCintio* lose because the court was unwilling to recognize a Title VII discrimination claim for an employee because he was *not* a victim of sexual harassment? Is that result justified because a woman who was similarly passed over could not sue? Or could a female plaintiff have complained about Ryan's actions? *Compare King v. Palmer*, 778 F.2d 878 (D.C. Cir. 1985) (employer liable when a male supervisor passed over a qualified woman in favor of a female with whom he was having a sexual relationship), with *Taken v. Oklahoma Corp. Comm.*, 125 F.3d 1366 (10th Cir. 1997) (promotion of girlfriend over two other female candidates does not violate Title VII). *See also Tenge v. Phillips Modern AG Co.*, 446 F.3d 903 (8th Cir. 2006) (plaintiff's consensual and sexually provocative behavior toward her boss, which caused the boss's wife to have her fired, was not sex discrimination within the meaning of Title VII). *Cf. Miller v. Dept. of Corrections*, 115 P.3d 77, 80 (Cal. 2005) ("although an isolated instance of favoritism on the part of a supervisor toward a female employee with whom the supervisor is conducting a consensual sexual affair ordinarily would not constitute sexual harassment, when such sexual favoritism in a workplace is sufficiently widespread it may create an actionable hostile work environment in which the demeaning message is conveyed to female employees that they are viewed by management as 'sexual playthings' or that the way required for women to get ahead in the workplace is by engaging in sexual conduct with their supervisors or the management").

Suppose Guagenti, after being hired by Ryan, refused to continue their romantic relationship and Ryan discharged her. Would she have a discrimination claim? In *Green v. Administrators of Tulane Educational Fund*, 284 F. 3d 642 (5th Cir. 2002), the court rejected Tulane's argument that harassment triggered by the ending of a consensual relationship was merely "personal animosity" and not actionable. The court found the harassing behavior was causally related to plaintiff's gender; plaintiff was harassed because she refused to continue to have a "casual" sexual relationship after the breakup. What if there had been no demand for sex after the breakup? Would harassing her simply because she was once a consensual sexual partner be actionable? *Cf. Pipkins v. City of Temple Terrace*, 267 F.3d 1197 (11th Cir. 2001) (disappointment in failed relationship not because of sex); *Succar v. Dade County Sch. Bd.*, 229 F.3d 1343 (11th Cir. 2000) (co-worker harassment not based on gender but result of anger over plaintiff's termination of relationship). If, in a race discrimination case, the court concludes that an employer treated an individual differently because of personal dislike unconnected with race, the employer will prevail. Should that same reasoning control in a sex discrimination case? Was Ryan's attraction to Guagenti unrelated to her sex?

c. Grooming and Dress Codes

JESPERSEN v. HARRAH'S OPERATING COMPANY, INC.
444 F.3d 1104 (9th Cir. 2006) (en banc)

SCHROEDER, Chief Judge. . . .

I. BACKGROUND

Plaintiff Darlene Jespersen worked successfully as a bartender at Harrah's for twenty years and compiled what by all accounts was an exemplary record. During Jespersen's entire tenure with Harrah's, the company maintained a policy encouraging female beverage servers to wear makeup. The parties agree, however, that the policy was not enforced until 2000. In February 2000, Harrah's implemented a "Beverage Department Image Transformation" program at twenty Harrah's locations, including its casino in Reno. Part of the program consisted of new grooming and appearance standards, called the "Personal Best" program. The program contained certain appearance standards that applied equally to both sexes, including a standard uniform of black pants, white shirt, black vest, and black bow tie. Jespersen has never objected to any of these policies. The program also contained some sex-differentiated appearance requirements as to hair, nails, and makeup.

In April 2000, Harrah's amended that policy to require that women wear makeup. Jepersen's only objection here is to the makeup requirement. . . .

II.   UNEQUAL BURDENS . . .

In this case, Jespersen argues that the makeup requirement itself establishes a prima facie case of discriminatory intent and must be justified by Harrah's as a bona fide occupational qualification. Our settled law in this circuit, however, does not support Jespersen's position that a sex-based difference in appearance standards alone, without any further showing of disparate effects, creates a prima facie case.

In *Gerdom v. Cont'l Airlines, Inc.*, 692 F.2d 602 (9th Cir. 1982), we considered the Continental Airlines policy that imposed strict weight restrictions on female flight attendants, and held it constituted a violation of Title VII. We did so because the airline imposed no weight restriction whatsoever on a class of male employees who performed the same or similar functions as the flight attendants. Indeed, the policy was touted by the airline as intended to "create the public image of an airline which offered passengers service by thin, attractive women, whom executives referred to as Continental's 'girls.'" In fact, Continental specifically argued that its policy was justified by its "desire to compete [with other airlines] by featuring attractive female cabin attendants[,]" a justification which this court recognized as "discriminatory on its face." The weight restriction was part of an overall program to create a sexual image for the airline.

In contrast, this case involves an appearance policy that applied to both male and female bartenders, and was aimed at creating a professional and very similar look for all of them. All bartenders wore the same uniform. The policy only differentiated as to grooming standards.

In *Frank v. United Airlines, Inc.*, 216 F.3d 845 (9th Cir. 2000), we dealt with a weight policy that applied different standards to men and women in a facially un-equal way. The women were forced to meet the requirements of a medium body frame standard while men were required to meet only the more generous require-ments of a large body frame standard. In that case, we recognized that "an appear-ance standard that imposes different but essentially equal burdens on men and women is not disparate treatment." The United weight policy, however, did not impose equal burdens. On its face, the policy embodied a requirement that categorically "'applied less favorably to one gender[,]'" and the burdens imposed upon that gender were obvious from the policy itself. (quoting *Gerdom*) (alteration omitted).

This case stands in marked contrast, for here we deal with requirements that, on their face, are not more onerous for one gender than the other. Rather, Harrah's "Personal Best" policy contains sex-differentiated requirements regarding each employee's hair, hands, and face. While those individual requirements differ according to gender, none on its face places a greater burden on one gender than the other. Grooming standards that appropriately differentiate between the genders are not facially discriminatory.

We have long recognized that companies may differentiate between men and women in appearance and grooming policies, and so have other circuits. *See, e.g., Fountain v. Safeway Stores, Inc.*, 555 F.2d 753, 755 (9th Cir. 1977); *Barker v. Taft Broad. Co.*, 549 F.2d 400, 401 (6th Cir. 1977); *Earwood v. Cont'l Southeastern Lines, Inc.*, 539 F.2d 1349, 1350 (4th Cir. 1976). The material issue under our settled law is not whether the policies are different, but whether the policy imposed on the plaintiff creates an "unequal burden" for the plaintiff's gender. *See Frank; Gerdom; see also Fountain.*

Not every differentiation between the sexes in a grooming and appearance policy creates a "significantly greater burden of compliance[.]" *Gerdom.* For example, in *Fountain*, this court upheld Safeway's enforcement of its sex-differentiated appearance standard, including its requirement that male employees wear ties, because the company's actions in enforcing the regulations were not "overly burdensome to its employees[.]" *See also Baker.* Similarly, as the Eighth Circuit has recognized, "where, as here, such [grooming and appearance] policies are reasonable and are imposed in an evenhanded manner on all employees, slight differences in the appearance requirements for males and females have only a negligible effect on employment opportunities." *Knott* [*v. Missouri P. R. Co.*, 527 F.2d 1249, 1252 (8th Cir. 1975)]. Under established equal burdens analysis, when an employer's grooming and appearance policy does not unreasonably burden one gender more than the other, that policy will not violate Title VII.

Jespersen asks us to take judicial notice of the fact that it costs more money and takes more time for a woman to comply with the makeup requirement than it takes for a man to comply with the requirement that he keep his hair short, but these are not matters appropriate for judicial notice. Judicial notice is reserved for matters "generally known within the territorial jurisdiction of the trial court" or "capable of accurate and ready determination by resort to sources whose accuracy cannot reasonably be questioned." Fed. R. Evid. 201. The time and cost of makeup and haircuts is in neither category. . . .

Having failed to create a record establishing that the "Personal Best" policies are more burdensome for women than for men, Jespersen did not present any triable issue of fact. The district court correctly granted summary judgment on the record before it with respect to Jespersen's claim that the makeup policy created an unequal burden for women.

III. SEX STEREOTYPING

[Plaintiff claimed that the makeup requirement constituted unlawful sex stereotyping under *Price Waterhouse*. The en banc court rejected this argument as well].

The stereotyping in *Price Waterhouse* interfered with Hopkins' ability to perform her work; the advice that she should take "a course at charm school" was intended to discourage her use of the forceful and aggressive techniques that made her successful in the first place. Impermissible sex stereotyping was clear because the very traits that she was asked to hide were the same traits considered praiseworthy in men.

Harrah's "Personal Best" policy is very different. The policy does not single out Jespersen. It applies to all of the bartenders, male and female. It requires all of the bartenders to wear exactly the same uniforms while interacting with the public in the context of the entertainment industry. It is for the most part unisex, from the black tie to the non-skid shoes. There is no evidence in this record to indicate that the policy was adopted to make women bartenders conform to a commonly-accepted stereotypical image of what women should wear. The record contains nothing to suggest the grooming standards would objectively inhibit a woman's ability to do the job. The only evidence in the record to support the stereotyping claim is Jespersen's own subjective reaction to the makeup requirement.

Judge Pregerson's dissent improperly divides the grooming policy into separate categories of hair, hands, and face, and then focuses exclusively on the makeup requirement to conclude that the policy constitutes sex stereotyping. This parsing, however, conflicts with established grooming standards analysis. *See, e.g., Knott* ("Defendant's hair length requirement for male employees is *part of a comprehensive personal grooming code* applicable to all employees.") (Emphasis added). The requirements must be viewed in the context of the overall policy. The dissent's conclusion that the unequal burdens analysis allows impermissible sex stereotyping to persist if imposed equally on both sexes is wrong because it ignores the protections of *Price Waterhouse* our decision preserves. If a grooming standard imposed on either sex amounts to impermissible stereotyping, something this record does not establish, a plaintiff of either sex may challenge that requirement under *Price Waterhouse*.

We respect Jespersen's resolve to be true to herself and to the image that she wishes to project to the world. We cannot agree, however, that her objection to the makeup requirement, without more, can give rise to a claim of sex stereotyping under Title VII. If we were to do so, we would come perilously close to holding that every grooming, apparel, or appearance requirement that an individual finds personally offensive, or in conflict with his or her own self-image, can create a triable issue of sex discrimination.

This is not a case where the dress or appearance requirement is intended to be sexually provocative, and tending to stereotype women as sex objects. *See, e.g., EEOC v. Sage Realty Corp.*, 507 F. Supp. 599 (S.D.N.Y. 1981). In *Sage Realty*, the plaintiff was a lobby attendant in a hotel that employed only female lobby attendants and required a mandatory uniform. The uniform was an octagon designed with an opening for the attendant's head, to be worn as a poncho, with snaps at the wrists and a tack on each side of the poncho, which was otherwise open. The attendants wore blue dancer pants as part of the uniform but were prohibited from wearing a shirt, blouse, or skirt under the outfit. There, the plaintiff was required to wear a uniform that was "short and revealing on both sides [such that her] thighs and portions of her buttocks were exposed." Jespersen, in contrast, was asked only to wear a unisex uniform that covered her entire body and was designed for men and women. The "Personal Best" policy does not, on its face, indicate any discriminatory or sexually stereotypical intent on the part of Harrah's. . . .

We emphasize that we do not preclude, as a matter of law, a claim of sex-stereotyping on the basis of dress or appearance codes. Others may well be filed, and any bases for such claims refined as law in this area evolves. This record, however, is devoid of any basis for permitting this particular claim to go forward, as it is limited to the subjective reaction of a single employee, and there is no evidence of a stereotypical motivation on the part of the employer. This case is essentially a challenge to one small part of what is an overall apparel, appearance, and grooming policy that applies largely the same requirements to both men and women. As we said in *Nichols* in commenting on grooming standards, the touchstone is reasonableness. A makeup requirement must be seen in the context of the overall standards imposed on employees in a given workplace.

[Dissenting opinions omitted.]

NOTES

1. *Separate but Equal.* Perhaps the most blatant remaining form of gender discrimination in employment is employer dress and grooming codes, which frequently

have disparate standards for males and females. The *Jespersen* court correctly observed that different grooming codes or appearance standards for men and women have routinely been upheld by the courts, despite being facially discriminatory. Why? In *Willingham v. Macon Telegraph Publishing Co.*, 507 F.2d 1084, 1091-92 (5th Cir. 1975) (en banc), the Fifth Circuit denied a man's challenge to an employer's rule prohibiting male (but not female) employees from having hair longer than shoulder length:

> Equal employment *opportunity* may be secured only when employers are barred from discriminating against employees on the basis of immutable characteristics, such as race and national origin. Similarly, an employer cannot have one hiring policy for men and another for women *if* the distinction is based on some fundamental right. But a hiring policy that distinguishes on some other ground, such as grooming codes or length of hair, is related more closely to the employer's choice of how to run his business than to equality of employment opportunity. In [*Phillips v. Martin Marietta*, 400 U.S. 532 (1971),] the Supreme Court condemned a hiring distinction based on having pre-school age children, an existing condition not subject to change. In *Sprogis v. United Air Lines*[, 444 F.2d 1194 (7th Cir. 1971)], the Seventh Circuit reached a similar result with respect to marital status. We have no difficulty with the result reached in those cases; but nevertheless perceive that a line must be drawn between distinctions grounded on such fundamental rights as the right to have children or to marry and those interfering with the manner in which an employer exercises his judgment as to the way to operate a business. Hair length is not immutable and in the situation of employer vis à vis employee enjoys no constitutional protection. If the employee objects to the grooming code he has the right to reject it by looking elsewhere for employment, or alternatively he may choose to subordinate his preference by accepting the code along with the job. . . .
>
> We adopt the view, therefore, that distinctions in employment practices between men and women on the basis of something other than immutable or protected characteristics do not inhibit employment *opportunity* in violation of Sec. 703(a). Congress sought only to give all persons equal access to the job market, not to limit an employer's right to exercise his informed judgment as to how best to run his shop.
>
> We are in accord also with the alternative ground. . . . "From all that appears, equal job opportunities are available to both sexes. It does not appear that defendant fails to impose grooming standards for female employees; thus in this respect each sex is treated equally."

Willingham's holding that the mere fact of gender-specific differences in dress and grooming codes does not violate Title VII is the accepted view, as the *Jespersen* court notes.

No one seems to doubt that permitting female, but not male, employees to have shoulder-length hair is sex discrimination in an analytic sense. What, then, is the justification for permitting it? Does *Willingham* establish a de minimis test: if the sex distinctions in question are too trivial, they do not warrant federal court intervention? That would explain the court's distinction between cases involving hair length and cases involving "fundamental rights," a concept that seems to have been borrowed from equal protection doctrine. Remember, also, as we saw in Chapter 1, that courts have required different treatment to have material adverse effects in order to constitute discrimination, and *Jespersen* is consistent with that view: the only job requirement she challenged was not a material difference in the terms and conditions of her employment. Moreover, declining protection because the different treatment is considered trivial is consistent with the Supreme Court's treatment of sexual harassment that is not sufficiently serious or pervasive to create a hostile environment, as we shall see in the next section. But sexual harassment becomes actionable when job benefits are contingent on acceptance of the discriminatory remarks or conduct, and here Jespersen lost her job over her refusal to conform to the casino's grooming code. How can this be viewed as trivial?

Many commentators look on grooming cases as sui generis. But don't these cases reflect stereotypes so ingrained that they are not even recognized as such? *See* Karl E. Klare, *Power/Dressing: Regulation of Employee Appearance*, 26 NEW ENG. L. REV. 1395 (1992); Robert Post, *Prejudicial Appearances: The Logic of American Antidiscrimination Law*, 88 CAL. L. REV. 1, 30-34 (2000). Why is it that an employer can legally prohibit males from wearing dresses or eye shadow? Is it because there is something wrong with males assuming "female" roles? Is a man wrong to assume such roles in turn because females are inferior and a man demeans himself by appropriating them? Is it merely coincidence that society looks more favorably on women who appropriate "male" attire (e.g., the pants suit) than the other way around? Perhaps the courts are simply applying what they perceive as legislative intent: whatever Congress *said*, it did not *mean* to bar this kind of employer rule. Isn't it clear that Congress did not intend Title VII to require a unisex dress code? But, as Justice Scalia noted in *Oncale*, neither did Congress intend to bar same-sex harassment when it enacted the statute.

2. *Separate but Unequal.* While "separate but equal" grooming codes have not been considered illegal, "separate but unequal" requirements have been. As *Jespersen* noted, "The material issue under our settled law is not whether the policies are different, but whether the policy imposed on the plaintiff creates an 'unequal burden' for the plaintiff's gender." Do you agree that a grooming code that requires women, but not men, to wear makeup imposes equal burdens on men and women?

In *Carroll v. Talman Federal Savings & Loan Assn.*, 604 F.2d 1028, 1033 (7th Cir. 1979), the court struck down a policy allowing males to wear "customary business attire," but requiring women to wear uniforms. In doing so, the court stated: "[W]e do not view the recognition of different dress norms for males and females to be offensive or illegal stereotyping. What is offensive is the compulsion to wear employer-identified uniforms and the assumption on which the employer openly admits that rule is based: that women cannot be expected to exercise good judgment in choosing business apparel, whereas men can." And in *Frank v. United Air Lines*, 216 F.3d 845 (9th Cir. 2000), distinguished by the *Jespersen* court, the Ninth Circuit struck down an airline's weight standards for flight attendants as facially discriminatory. United based men's weight limits on large body frames, while women's weight limits were based on medium body frames. Because the standards imposed unequal burdens on men and women, they were unlawful. The court declined to decide whether different weight limits for men and women in and of themselves would be unlawful. While acknowledging that separate but equal dress and grooming codes for men and women have been upheld, it questioned whether weight limits should receive similar treatment.

Do you think Jespersen's "unequal burden" claim failed because the court believed the differences in the grooming standards for men and women were really not that significant or because Jespersen failed to introduce evidence of the cost and time involved in applying makeup? Should she have been required to present such evidence? Judge Kozinski's dissenting opinion would have upheld Jespersen's "unequal burden" claim, finding that "Harrah's overall grooming policy is substantially more burdensome for women than for men. . . . The requirement that women spend time and money applying full facial makeup has no corresponding requirement for men, making the 'overall policy' more burdensome for the former than for the latter."

3. *Grooming Codes as "Sex Stereotyping."* In addition to her claim that the makeup requirement was facially discriminatory, Jespersen also argued sex stereotyping, relying on *Price Waterhouse.* Why did that claim fail? After all, the casino was requiring its employees to adhere to a stereotypical view of masculine and feminine appearances. Women must wear makeup, and men must not. Judge Pregerson's dissenting opinion found that plaintiff "articulated a classic case of *Price Waterhouse* discrimination"; as he observed, "The inescapable message is that women's undoctored faces compare unfavorably to men's, not because of a physical difference between men's and women's faces, but because of a cultural assumption — and gender-based stereotype — that women's faces are incomplete, unattractive or unprofessional without full makeup."

Jespersen has triggered considerable discussion in the literature concerning grooming codes and sex discrimination. *See* Devon Carbado, Mitu Gulati, & Gowri Ramachandran, *The Story of* Jesperson v. Harrah's: *Makeup and Women at Work in* EMPLOYMENT DISCRIMINATION STORIES (Joel Wm. Friedman ed. 2006); Michael Selmi, *The Many Faces of Darlene Jespersen,* 14 DUKE J. GENDER L. & POL'Y 467 (2007); Dianne Avery & Marion Crain, *Branded: Corporate Image, Sexual Stereotyping, and the New Face of Capitalism,* 14 DUKE J. GENDER L. & POL'Y 13 (2007); Gowri Ramachandran, *Intersectionality as "Catch 22": Why Identity Performance Demands Are Neither Harmless Nor Reasonable,* 69 ALB. L. REV. 299, 303 (2005); Kimberly A. Yuracko, *Trait Discrimination as Race Discrimination: An Argument About Assimilation,* 74 GEO. WASH. L. REV. 365, 434 (2006). There is also scholarship favoring at least a limited right of personal autonomy in dress and grooming apart from any concerns with discrimination. Catherine L. Fisk, *Privacy, Power, and Humiliation at Work: Re-Examining Appearance Regulation as an Invasion of Privacy,* 66 LA. L. REV. 1111 (2006) (arguing for autonomy privacy to supplement discrimination analysis for challenges to workplace appearance requirements); Gowri Ramachandran, *Freedom of Dress: State and Private Regulation of Clothing, Hairstyle, Jewelry, Makeup, Tattoos, and Piercing,* 66 MD. L. REV. 11 (2006) (urging a right of free dress, which derives not from the first amendment or equal protection but from "the personal (as an exercise of control over the physical self) and the political and cultural (as the performance of social identity)."). For other articles discussing grooming codes, *see* Katherine Bartlett, *Only Girls Wear Barrettes: Dress and Appearance Standards, Community Norms, and Workplace Equality,* 92 MICH. L. REV. 2541, 2543-46 (1994); Kimberly A. Yuracko, *Trait Discrimination as Sex Discrimination: An Argument Against Neutrality,* 83 TEX. L. REV. 167, 172 (2004).

4. *Other Sources of Protection.* Litigants with complaints regarding grooming and dress codes should also explore the possibility of a claim under state or local antidiscrimination provisions. The District of Columbia Human Rights Act, for example, prohibits discrimination based on personal appearance. D.C. Code Ann. §2-140211.

d.   Discrimination Because of Pregnancy

The central theme of employment discrimination law is the notion that similarly situated individuals should receive equal treatment by employers. In previous chapters, we have seen courts struggle to remain true to this theme even though the groups protected by antidiscrimination laws are not, in fact, always similarly situated.

First, the statutes have been interpreted to permit (but not require) employers to engage in affirmative action because courts recognize that some of the groups protected by the antidiscrimination laws are not similarly situated as a result of past discrimination. Second, differences among groups sometimes cause neutral work rules to have a disparate impact on the employment opportunities of different groups. Even though these neutral rules treat similarly situated employees equally, employers cannot use them unless they are job related and consistent with business necessity. Impact analysis, however, remains true to the equality principle by allowing job-related differences to justify group-based differences. Third, we will see later in this chapter that Title VII requires employers to accommodate religious differences, a candid recognition that some religious practices distinguish religious employees from secular society.

These exceptions to the equality principle reflect an alternative theme for employment discrimination law: *equalizing employment opportunity* even for groups who are different in some respects. Title VII's prohibition against discrimination on the basis of pregnancy highlights the tension between equal treatment and equal opportunity inherent in the antidiscrimination laws. Pregnancy, childbirth, and related medical conditions affect a woman's ability to work. Most women who carry a child to term will require at least six to eight weeks of leave to deliver the child and physically recover from childbirth. Women who work in jobs that require physical exertion also may be impaired during the latter months of their pregnancy. Given these differences, what constitutes discrimination on the basis of pregnancy? What is *equal* treatment? Is equal treatment sufficient to provide pregnant women with equal employment opportunities?

This section will first explore Title VII's response to discrimination on the basis of pregnancy and will then consider whether Title VII adequately addresses the problems faced by fertile women in the workplace. In this latter regard, we will examine the most recent statute addressing this and similar problems, the Family and Medical Leave Act of 1993 (FMLA).

The Supreme Court's first encounter with the question of pregnancy discrimination was not auspicious. In *General Electric Co. v. Gilbert*, 429 U.S. 125 (1976), the Court concluded that discrimination on the basis of pregnancy was *not* discrimination on the basis of sex within the meaning of Title VII. *Gilbert* involved an employer-sponsored disability insurance plan that excluded pregnancy from coverage. The Court followed Fourteenth Amendment equal protection precedent established in *Geduldig v. Aiello*, 417 U.S. 484 (1974), holding that pregnancy classifications are not gender classifications. In reaching its result, the *Gilbert* Court quoted from a footnote in *Geduldig*:

> The lack of identity between the excluded disability [pregnancy] and gender as such . . . becomes clear upon the most cursory analysis. The program divides potential recipients into two groups — pregnant women and nonpregnant persons. While the first group is exclusively female, the second includes members of both sexes.

429 U.S. at 135.

Congress soon overruled *Gilbert* by passing the Pregnancy Discrimination Act of 1978 (PDA), Pub. L. No. 95-555, 92 Stat. 2076 (Oct. 31, 1978), which amended Title VII to include a new §701(k):

> The terms "because of sex" or "on the basis of sex" include, but are not limited to, because of or on the basis of pregnancy, childbirth, or related medical conditions; and women affected by pregnancy, childbirth, or related medical conditions shall be treated the same for all employment-related purposes, including receipt of benefits under

fringe benefit programs, as other persons not so affected but similar in their ability or inability to work, and nothing in section 703(h) of this title shall be interpreted to permit otherwise. . . .

The Supreme Court's first decision considering pregnancy discrimination after the PDA was, ironically, a case brought by men. In *Newport News Shipbuilding & Dry Dock Co. v. EEOC*, 462 U.S. 669 (1983), the Court confronted an employer-sponsored medical plan that provided the same hospitalization coverage for male and female employees but differentiated between female employees and spouses of male employees by imposing a cap on the pregnancy-related hospital benefits for spouses of male workers. The Court held that the employer's plan failed the "simple test of Title VII discrimination that we enunciated in *Los Angeles Department of Water & Power v. Manhart* [reproduced at p. 116], for it would treat a male employee with dependents 'in a manner which but for that person's sex would be different.'" While a female employee's spouse had hospitalization coverage for all conditions, a male employee's spouse was covered for all conditions except pregnancy. As the *Newport* News Court stated,

> The 1978 Act makes clear that it is discriminatory to treat pregnancy-related conditions less favorably than other medical conditions. Thus, petitioner's plan unlawfully gives married male employees a benefit package for their dependents that is less inclusive than the dependency coverage provided to married female employees.

Id. at. 684. However, the Court stressed that the issue was not pregnancy coverage per se: there is no requirement that an employer provide any medical insurance at all. If an employer fails to insure its workers, it is treating them all equally, and there can be no violation of Title VII.

***

After the PDA, and the Court's decision in *Newport News*, it is clear that discrimination because of pregnancy, childbirth and related medical conditions *is* discrimination because of sex under Title VII. And it is clear that an employer may not single out pregnancy for unfavorable treatment. But beyond that, what does it mean to discriminate on the basis of pregnancy? Under what circumstances, if any, is it permissible for an employer to take an employee's pregnancy into account in making employment decisions? Is there any duty on the part of the employer to accommodate an employee's pregnancy? These questions are explored in the case and notes below.

MALDONADO v. U.S. BANK AND MANUFACTURERS BANK
186 F.3d 759 (7th Cir. 1999)

CUDAHY, Circuit Judge.

From what we can tell, this case goes to the core of the Pregnancy Discrimination Act (PDA), 42 U.S.C. § 2000e(k): an employer cannot discriminate against a pregnant employee simply because it believes pregnancy *might* prevent the employee from doing her job. U.S. Bank fired Jessica Maldonado the day after she announced to her supervisor, Amalia Gonzalez, that she was pregnant. Maldonado sued, alleging sex discrimination in violation of the PDA. The district court granted the defendant's motion for summary judgment. Maldonado now appeals that decision. . . . For the reasons which follow, we reverse the district court's order granting summary judgment in favor of the bank. . . .

I . . .

Title VII makes it "an unlawful employment practice for an employer to fail or refuse to hire or to discharge any individual, or otherwise to discriminate against any individual with respect to his compensation, terms, conditions, or privileges of employment, because of such individual's . . . sex. . . . " 42 U.S.C. §2000e-2(a). Congress amended Title VII in 1978 to explicitly extend protection to pregnant women: "women affected by pregnancy, childbirth or related medical conditions shall be treated the same for all employment-related purposes . . . as other persons not so affected but similar in their ability or inability to work. . . . " 42 U.S.C. §2000e(k). It designed the PDA specifically to address the stereotype that "women are less desirable employees because they are liable to become pregnant," *Sheehan v. Donlen Corp.*, 173 F.3d 1039 (7th Cir. 1999), and to insure that the decision whether to work while pregnant "was reserved for each individual woman to make for herself." *International Union, United Auto. Workers v. Johnson Controls, Inc.*, [reproduced at p. 173]; see also 29 C.F.R. §§1604.10(b) and 1604 App. (Intro.). Nonetheless, under the PDA, employers are not required to give pregnant women special treatment; they must only treat them the same as all other employees.

To prevail on a pregnancy discrimination claim, a plaintiff "must show that she was treated differently because of her pregnancy." *Geier v. Medtronic, Inc.*, 99 F.3d 238, 241 (7th Cir. 1996); *see also Marshall v. American Hosp. Ass'n*, 157 F.3d 520, 525 (7th Cir. 1998) (on summary judgment, the court "must determine whether [the employee] presented a question of fact as to whether [the employer] treated her less favorably because of her pregnancy"). Put another way, "an unlawful employment practice occurs whenever pregnancy is a motivating factor for an adverse employment decision." *Hunt-Golliday v. Metropolitan Water Reclamation Dist. of Greater Chicago*, 104 F.3d 1004, 1010 (7th Cir. 1997). . . .

The broader factual framework is not in dispute. Sometime in late January or early February 1997, Maldonado filled out a job application at the bank. Gonzalez later contacted Maldonado and arranged to interview her for a part-time teller position. On February 10, Gonzalez interviewed Maldonado and told her that part-time tellers had the same duties as full-time tellers (helping customers, counting money, etc.) and were required to be available six days a week to substitute for absent full-time tellers. Maldonado understood that Gonzalez had a particular need for part-timers during the peak summer vacation months. Three days later, Maldonado learned that she was pregnant and that the baby was due in July. Maldonado began her two-to-three weeks of teller training at the bank on February 20. As part of that training, she received an employee manual, which made it clear that she was a "provisional" employee for her first three months and that she must have at least one year of service to be eligible for pregnancy leave. On either Thursday, February 27, or Friday, February 28, Maldonado told at least one of her colleagues that she was pregnant. The following Monday, March 3, while still in training, Maldonado informed Gonzalez that she was pregnant. Gonzalez fired Maldonado the next day. . . .

Maldonado testified that on March 3, 1997 she told Gonzalez that she was pregnant: "I told Amalia I just found out I'm pregnant, and then she told me okay. She told me she was going to have to talk to someone else at another bank, and that she'd get back to me." The next day, Gonzalez fired her. Maldonado recounted the March 4 termination:

> I went over to [Gonzalez's] desk, and she told me *due to your condition*, we're going to have to let you go because you're not going to be able to work the whole summer how we're going to need you. And then I told her that my physician had said it was okay that I was able to work up until the day I delivered my son because my pregnancy was going okay. And she told me, no, that she was going to have to find someone else. Because of my condition I wasn't going to be able to work how she wanted me to work. . . .

Viewing the evidence in the light most favorable to Maldonado, as we must on summary judgment, Maldonado has presented evidence which suggests that her termination was motivated at least in part by her pregnancy. Maldonado testified that Gonzalez told her she was being fired "due to her condition." This statement could be interpreted as an "acknowledgment of discriminatory intent by the [bank]." The comment was contemporaneous with her termination; it concerned the particular employment action at issue here; and it was uttered by the person with decision-making authority. The inference of impermissible motivation flows directly from Gonzalez's statement.

The bank does not dispute that it fired Maldonado because she was pregnant. Instead, it argues that it discharged her because her pregnancy would make her unavailable during the summer months; it is impossible to separate Maldonado's job performance from her medical condition, the bank asserts. The bank is correct that an employer can dismiss an employee for excessive absenteeism, even if the absences were a direct result of the employee's pregnancy. *See, e.g., Troupe* [*v. May Department Store Co*, 20 F.3d 734, 738 (7th Cir. 1994).] This case raises a different issue, however, because there is no evidence that Maldonado had an attendance problem; the bank simply assumed that, because of her pregnancy, Maldonado would be absent from work for an indeterminate period sometime in the future.[7] The question, then, is under what circumstances, if any, the bank's assumption would be justified.

---

7. Thus, the bank's (and the district court's) reliance on *Marshall v. American Hosp. Ass'n*, 157 F.3d 520 (1998), is misplaced. In that case, when the American Hospital Association (AHA) hired Marshall, she was pregnant and due in June. She understood that one of her most important duties was to organize an AHA conference in September. Immediately after starting work, Marshall informed her bosses that she was pregnant and planned to take eight weeks leave after delivering her baby. The AHA fired her several weeks later. This Court upheld the district court's grant of summary judgment in favor of the AHA because, in part, Marshall had produced no direct evidence and only in substantial [sic] circumstantial evidence that the "AHA terminated her because of her pregnancy rather than because she was planning an extended absence during the busiest time of her first year" on the job. In this case, there is a dispute about whether Maldonado was planning on an extended absence: Maldonado never testified that she asked for one; Gonzalez claimed that Maldonado did make such a request, but also testified that she (Gonzalez) simply anticipated an absence. We must credit Maldonado's evidence. So, in short, whereas Marshall asked for special treatment, Maldonado did not. (Or, at the very least, there is a dispute about this material fact, and summary judgment must be denied on that ground.) Further, unlike Marshall, Maldonado has produced direct evidence that her termination was motivated by her pregnancy. *Marshall* does not support the bank's position.

There might be some limited circumstances in which an employer could be justified in taking anticipatory adverse action against a pregnant employee. Although the PDA was designed to allow individual women to make independent choices about whether to continue to work while pregnant, it was not designed to handcuff employers by forcing them to wait until an employee's pregnancy causes a special economic disadvantage. The PDA does not create such an artificial divide between pregnancy, childbirth and related medical conditions and the secondary effects of a pregnancy which might affect job performance. Pregnancy causes normal inconveniences that might "interrupt the workplace's daily routines," including, for example, the need to take more frequent snack and restroom breaks and the need to take some time off, at the very least, to give birth. Judith G. Greenberg, *The Pregnancy Discrimination Act: Legitimating Discrimination Against Pregnant Women in the Workforce*, 50 Me. L. Rev. 225, 250 (1998); *see also In re Carnegie Center Associates*, 129 F.3d 290, 306 (3rd Cir. 1997) (McKee, J., dissenting) (describing "the absence [from work] endemic to pregnancy"). An employer may, under narrow circumstances that we are not convinced are present here, project the normal inconveniences of pregnancy and their secondary effects into the future and take actions in accordance with and in proportion to those predictions. Of course, it will rarely be one hundred percent demonstrable that a pregnant woman will be unable to meet a BFOQ sometime in the future. Cases such as *Marshall*, in which an employee announces that she will be unavailable to work in the future and thus explicitly requests special treatment, are exceptional. It is not merely a question whether the pregnant employee asks for special treatment, however; other evidence might also be probative of the employee's ability to continue to meet the employer's legitimate job expectations. But an employer cannot take anticipatory action unless it has a good faith basis, supported by sufficiently strong evidence, that the normal inconveniences of an employee's pregnancy will require special treatment.

In this case, assuming summer availability is a BFOQ (something that Maldonado does not contest with respect to her particular job), did the bank have a good faith basis in the spring to believe, supported by sufficiently strong evidence, that Maldonado's pregnancy would result in her unavailability during the summer? Probably not. By all accounts, the discussion between Gonzalez and Maldonado about Maldonado's ability to work through her pregnancy was brief and took place only after Gonzalez had announced the firing. Gonzalez declared in her affidavit that she merely "anticipated" that Maldonado would take leave and be unable to cover for vacationing full-time tellers. The factual basis for this assumption is hotly contested. Maldonado apparently did not ask for leave; nor did she request any other kind of special treatment. To the contrary, she indicated that she planned to work until she delivered and even intimated that she might not carry the fetus to term. Gonzalez, of course, testified that she believed that Maldonado would take pregnancy leave. Whether Gonzalez or Maldonado provided a more credible version of events is a judgment for a factfinder to make. On summary judgment, though, we must resolve this dispute in favor of Maldonado. Thus, the bank did not have sufficient specific evidence (apart from general assumptions about pregnancy) that Maldonado would require special treatment. Absent such evidence, the bank cannot terminate Maldonado simply because it "anticipated" that she would be unable to fulfill its job expectations. This is the exact sort of employment action that the PDA was designed to prevent. Because there is a genuine issue of material fact about the reason the bank fired Maldonado, summary judgment was inappropriate.

NOTES

1. *Is the PDA's Protection Only Status Protection?* Does the PDA flatly bar discrimination because of pregnancy? Surprisingly, but as *Maldonado* suggests, failing to hire a woman because she is pregnant does not necessarily violate Title VII. In *Marafino v. St. Louis County Circuit Court,* 707 F.2d 1005 (8th Cir. 1983), a court's failure to hire a pregnant woman as a judicial law clerk who would require a leave of absence soon after starting work was held to be lawful because the employer would not have hired *anyone* who required a leave of absence shortly after beginning work. But in *Maldonado,* the Seventh Circuit reversed summary judgment in favor of the employer when it fired a pregnant employee because it believed she would require a leave of absence. Is the only difference between the cases that Maldonado had not asked for any leave of absence? If she had said she would need six weeks off in the summer, could the bank have fired her or refused to hire her? Is *Maldonado* then an outlier case, since most women will ask for, or at least acknowledge, the need for a leave of absence? If Maldonado had missed work in the summer due to the birth of her child, could the bank have fired her then? If so, what is the protection the PDA provides Maldonado?

Or would the Seventh Circuit have permitted the firing only if being at work during the summer were a "BFOQ"? *Marafino* did not mention the bona fide occupational qualification defense: it was enough for the court that the plaintiff was treated equally, i.e., as would any worker in a time-limited job who asked for leave. But *Maldonado* seems to require a BFOQ analysis. Can you state the likely difference in practice between these two approaches?

Assuming equal treatment is all that is required, how would a plaintiff show that she was treated unequally? In *Marafino,* there was no male comparator who was fired because he sought leave; rather, the court credited the employer's claim that that is how a nonpregnant person would have been treated. But there are limits to such deference. In *Byrd v. Lakeshore Hospital,* 30 F.3d 1380 (11th Cir. 1994), plaintiff missed ten days of work within two months due to pregnancy-related medical complications. In compliance with Lakeshore's sick leave policy, Byrd applied accrued sick leave to her absences, giving her supervisors sufficient notice on each occasion. Nevertheless, Lakeshore fired her for unsatisfactory performance. The court of appeals specifically rejected the defendant's claim that Byrd must show that other employees used the guaranteed sick leave benefits without being discharged. *Id.* at 1383. According to the court,

> the only logical inference to be drawn in this case is that the Lakeshore policy customarily was followed. A contrary result would amount to a presumption . . . that Lakeshore Hospital commonly discharges employees for taking their allotted sick leave time. If such is the case, then the burden was on Lakeshore to prove this unusual scenario. The effect of our decision today is simple: it is a violation of the PDA for an employer to deny a pregnant employee the benefits commonly afforded temporarily disabled workers in similar positions, or to discharge a pregnant employee for using those benefits.

Id. at 1383-84.

2. *The Two Clauses of the PDA.* One analysis of the PDA offers two different meanings of the statute based on the two clauses in the law:

> One reading . . . suggests that the second clause [women affected by pregnancy . . . shall be treated the same as other persons not so affected but similar in their ability or inability

to work] gives substance to the first [the terms "because of sex" or "on the basis of sex" include, but are not limited to, because of or on the basis of pregnancy . . .], which is viewed as primarily definitional. Thus the prohibition of differential treatment means that pregnant women shall not be singled out because of their disability, but rather shall be treated the same as any other employees, based on their ability to work. . . . An alternative reading places greater emphasis on the fact that Congress specifically amended Title VII to remedy problems of pregnancy discrimination. [It focuses on the first clause of the amendments.]

. . . Following this [alternative] reading, Title VII . . . prohibits, for example, an employer from discharging an employee because she is pregnant, regardless of the treatment of a similarly disabled but non-pregnant employee — because the employee would not be fired but for her pregnancy.

Andrew Weissmann, Note, *Sexual Equality Under the Pregnancy Discrimination Act*, 83 COLUM. L. REV. 690, 694-96 (1983). *See also* Wendy W. Williams, *Equality's Riddle: Pregnancy and the Equal Treatment/Special Treatment Debate*, 13 N.Y.U. REV. L. & SOC. CHANGE 325 (1985). Which of these two readings does *Maldonado* embrace?

To appreciate the difference between the two approaches, suppose an employer has a policy of no leave for everyone. Does Title VII require that employer to provide leave to pregnant women? *Stout v. Baxter Healthcare Corp.*, 282 F.3d 856, 861 (5th Cir. 2002) (although a "no leave" policy would affect all or substantially all pregnant women, no treatment or impact claim was stated; "To hold otherwise would be to transform the PDA into a guarantee of medical leave for pregnant employees, something we have specifically held that the PDA does not do").

3. *Proving Discrimination.* Sometimes, a policy will facially discriminate on the basis of pregnancy and will be struck down on that basis. *See EEOC v. W & O Inc.*, 213 F.3d 600 (11th Cir. 2000) (restaurant's policy prohibiting pregnant waitresses from serving tables after their fifth month was discriminatory on its face). *But see Fjelsta v. Zogg Dermatology, PLC*, 488 F.3d 804 (6th Cir. 2007) (office manager's comment that an employee "better take precautions" so that both of a clinic's full time nurses wouldn't "end up pregnant" and "be gone at the same time" was not direct evidence of discrimination). However, as *Maldonado* suggests, pregnancy discrimination, like other sex discrimination, can be justified if "not being pregnant" is a BFOQ. If the discrimination is not facial, the employer has a choice between simply denying that pregnancy had anything to do with the adverse employment decision or admitting that pregnancy was the basis for the decision and asserting a BFOQ. Litigating cases in which the employer denies acting on the basis of pregnancy is nearly indistinguishable from litigating other individual disparate treatment claims. The issue is whether pregnancy was the basis of the employer's decision. *Maldonado* was an easy case, largely because of Ms. Gonzalez's statements. Other cases may be harder, and to prevail there must be evidence the defendant knew plaintiff was pregnant. *See Prebilich-Holland v. Gaylord Entm't Co.*, 297 F.3d 438 (6th Cir. 2002) (summary judgment granted to employer on pregnancy discrimination claim because employee failed to present evidence that her supervisor knew of her pregnancy at the time he decided to discharge her); *DeBoer v. Musashi Auto Parts, Inc.*, 124 Fed. Appx. 387, 391 (6th Cir. 2005) ("the temporal proximity between DeBoer's announcement of her pregnancy, her filing for FMLA leave, and her demotion satisfies the 'nexus' requirement").

But is there a middle ground? Can the employer admit that the employee's pregnancy was relevant to the challenged employment decision but nevertheless win without establishing a BFOQ? *Marafino*, 707 F.2d at 1006 n. 2, indicates that the answer is yes. Would the *Maldonado* court agree, so long as the decision was not made anticipatorily but in response to actual absences? In *EEOC v. Detroit-Macomb Hosp. Ctr.*, 1992 U.S. App. LEXIS 647 (6th Cir. 1992), a nurse's aide who was medically restricted from entering isolation rooms to protect her unborn child was placed on involuntary leave until after the birth. Although the medical restriction was necessitated by Jancowicz's pregnancy and was the basis of the decision to place her on leave, the court found no violation of the PDA because "non-pregnant workers with temporary disabilities and medical restrictions have been placed on disability leave similar to Jancowicz's." *Id.* at **3-4.

Are these individual disparate treatment claims based on the first clause, the second clause, or both clauses of the PDA? The cases denying causes of action seem inconsistent with the first clause of the PDA, but perhaps they are consistent with the second clause. The second clause can be viewed as defining "legitimate, nondiscriminatory reason" to include reasons that relate to pregnancy, but that apply to other disabilities as well. Alternatively, is it a defense — decisions based on pregnancy are permitted if similarly disabled individuals are treated in the same way? Or maybe just a "quick look" BFOQ?

4. *The "Immorality" Defense.* Suppose an employer fires an unmarried pregnant woman. May it escape liability under the first clause of §701(k) by claiming that it discriminated not because of pregnancy, but because of "immorality"? The courts seem to believe that it is permissible to discharge pregnant women as part of a policy against sexual immorality so long as the employer does (or would) also discharge men who engaged in premarital sex. *E.g., Cline v. Catholic Diocese*, 206 F.3d 651, 658 (6th Cir. 1999) ("The central question in this case, therefore, is whether St. Paul's nonrenewal of Cline's contract constituted discrimination based on her pregnancy as opposed to a gender-neutral enforcement of the school's premarital sex policy. While the former violates Title VII, the latter does not"). *See also Griffin v. Sisters of St. Francis, Inc.*, 489 F.3d 838 (7th Cir. 2007) (male who claimed he was fired because of his fiancée's pregnancy had no PDA claim; he was not fired because of his sex, and statute does not offer protection of male reproductive rights).

5. *The Question of Accommodation.* Is an employee whose pregnancy precludes heavy duty work entitled to a light duty assignment? Not necessarily. Several courts have upheld employer policies that offer light duty work only to accommodate a work-related injury and thus have upheld employer refusals to provide light duty work to pregnant employees. *See Reeves v. Swift Transp. Co.*, 446 F.3d 637 (6th Cir. 2006); *Urbano v. Continental Airlines*, 138 F.3d 204, 208 (5th Cir. 1998).

Is it pregnancy discrimination for an employer to refuse to accommodate an employee's need to pump breast milk? *See Martinez v. NBC, Inc.*, 49 F. Supp. 2d 305 (S.D.N.Y. 1999) (no); *see also* Elissa Aaronson Goodman, Note, *Breastfeeding or Bust: The Need for Legislation to Protect a Mother's Right to Express Milk at Work*, 10 CARDOZO WOMEN'S L.J. 146 (2003) (discussing unsuccessful attempts under federal law to require accommodation for women to express breast milk at work and cataloguing legislative solutions by the states; six states had laws requiring such accommodation). Could it be argued that the PDA, by rejecting the analysis in *Gilbert*, established that discrimination based on *any* characteristic that is exclusive to women constitutes sex discrimination? Is breastfeeding "a related medical condition"?

6. *Contraceptives and Other Health Plan Coverage Issues.* Is it sex discrimination for an employer's prescription drug plan to exclude coverage for contraceptives? One circuit has held no. *See Standridge v. Union Pac. R.R. Co.*, 479 F.3d 936 (8th Cir. 2007)

(holding that the PDA does not apply to contraception and that it is not gender discrimination for health plan to exclude coverage of prescription contraceptive). Addressing a related benefits issue, *Saks v. Franklin Covey Co.*, 316 F.3d 337 (2d Cir. 2003), rejected a claim that denial of coverage for fertility treatments violated Title VII. The court viewed the proper test for reviewing a sex discrimination challenge to a health benefits plan as "whether sex-specific conditions exist, and if so, whether exclusion of benefits for those conditions results in a plan that provides inferior coverage to one sex." *Id.* at 344. "[B]ecause the exclusion of surgical impregnation procedures disadvantages infertile male and female employees equally, Saks's claim does not fall within the purview of the PDA." *Id.* at 346. Further, while the particular procedure plaintiff sought was performed on women, there was no sex discrimination in denying coverage since "the need for the procedures may be traced to male, female, or couple infertility with equal frequency. Thus, surgical impregnation procedures may be recommended regardless of the gender of the ill patient." *Id.* at 347. *But see Erickson v. Bartell Drug Co.*, 141 F. Supp. 2d 1266 (W.D. Wash. 2001) (exclusion of contraceptive coverage violates Title VII). What if a plan excludes coverage for Viagra? Is that sex discrimination? *See generally* Brietta R. Clark, Erickson v. Bartell Drug Co.: *A Roadmap for Gender Equality in Reproductive Health Care or an Empty Promise?*, 23 J.L. & INEQUALITY 299 (2005) (Title VII challenges to prescription contraception are more likely to be successful than challenges to infertility benefits even though both exclusions reflect gender stereotyping based on pervasive notions of motherhood and sexual freedom and both exclusions have significant adverse health effects on women); Ernest F. Lidge III , *An Employer's Exclusion of Coverage for Contraceptive Drugs Is Not Per Se Sex Discrimination*, 76 TEMPLE L. REV. 533 (2003). *See also* Melissa Cole, *Beyond Sex Discrimination: Why Employers Discriminate Against Women with Disabilities When Their Employee Health Plans Exclude Contraceptives from Prescription Coverage*, 43 ARIZ. L. REV. 501 (2001) (exclusion of contraceptives from prescription coverage may violate the ADA).

***

In the Supreme Court's second encounter with the PDA, an employer challenged a California statute that mandated benefits for pregnant employees on the ground that it was preempted by Title VII.

CALIFORNIA FEDERAL SAVINGS & LOAN
ASSOCIATION v. GUERRA
479 U.S. 272 (1987)

Justice MARSHALL delivered the opinion of the Court.

The question presented is whether Title VII of the Civil Rights Act of 1964, as amended by the Pregnancy Discrimination Act of 1978, pre-empts a state statute that requires employers to provide leave and reinstatement to employees disabled by pregnancy.

I

California's Fair Employment and Housing Act (FEHA) . . . prohibits discrimination in employment and housing. In September 1978, California amended the

FEHA to proscribe certain forms of employment discrimination on the basis of pregnancy. . . . It requires these employers to provide female employees an unpaid pregnancy disability leave of up to four months. Respondent Fair Employment and Housing Commission, the state agency authorized to interpret the FEHA, has construed §12945(b)(2) to require California employers to reinstate an employee returning from such pregnancy leave to the job she previously held, unless it is no longer available due to business necessity. In the latter case, the employer must make a reasonable, good faith effort to place the employee in a substantially similar job. The statute does not compel employers to provide *paid* leave to pregnant employees. Accordingly, the only benefit pregnant workers actually derive from §12945(b)(2) is a qualified right to reinstatement.

II . . .

Lillian Garland was employed by Cal Fed as a receptionist for several years. In January 1982, she took a pregnancy disability leave. When she was able to return to work in April of that year, Garland notified Cal Fed, but was informed that her job had been filled and that there were no receptionist or similar positions available.

III

A

In determining whether a state statute is pre-empted by federal law and therefore invalid under the Supremacy Clause of the Constitution, our sole task is to ascertain the intent of Congress. See *Shaw v. Delta Air Lines, Inc.*, 463 U.S. 85, 95 (1983). Federal law may supersede state law in several different ways. First, when acting within constitutional limits, Congress is empowered to pre-empt state law by so stating in express terms. Second, congressional intent to pre-empt state law in a particular area may be inferred where the scheme of federal regulation is sufficiently comprehensive to make reasonable the inference that Congress "left no room" for supplementary state regulation. *Rice v. Santa Fe Elevator Corp.*, 331 U.S. 218, 230 (1947). Neither of these bases for pre-emption exists in this case. Congress has explicitly disclaimed any intent categorically to pre-empt state law or to "occupy the field" of employment discrimination law.

As a third alternative, in those areas where Congress has not completely displaced state regulation, federal law may nonetheless pre-empt state law to the extent it actually conflicts with federal law. Such a conflict occurs either because "compliance with both federal and state regulations is a physical impossibility," *Florida Lime & Avocado Growers, Inc. v. Paul*, 373 U.S. 132 (1963), or because the state law stands "as an obstacle to the accomplishment and execution of the full purposes and objectives of Congress." *Hines v. Davidowitz*, 312 U.S. 52, 67 (1941). Nevertheless, pre-emption is not to be lightly presumed.

This third basis for pre-emption is at issue in this case. In two sections of the 1964 Civil Rights Act, §§708 and 1104, Congress has indicated that state laws will be pre-empted only if they actually conflict with federal law. Section 708 of Title VII provides:

> Nothing in this title shall be deemed to exempt or relieve any person from any liability, duty, penalty, or punishment provided by any present or future law of any State or political subdivision of a State, other than any such law which purports to require or

permit the doing of any act which would be an unlawful employment practice under this title. § 2000e-7.

Section 1104 of Title XI, applicable to all titles of the Civil Rights Act, establishes the following standard for pre-emption:

> Nothing contained in any title of this Act shall be construed as indicating an intent on the part of Congress to occupy the field in which any such title operates to the exclusion of State laws on the same subject matter, nor shall any provision of this Act be construed as invalidating any provision of State law unless such provision is inconsistent with any of the purposes of this Act, or any provision thereof. § 2000h-4.

Accordingly, there is no need to infer congressional intent to pre-empt state laws from the substantive provisions of Title VII; these two sections provide a "reliable indicium of congressional intent with respect to state authority" to regulate employment practice.

Sections 708 and 1104 severely limit Title VII's pre-emptive effect. Instead of pre-empting state fair employment laws, § 708 "'simply left them where they were before the enactment of title VII.'" *Shaw.* Similarly, § 1104 was intended primarily to "assert the intention of Congress to preserve existing civil rights laws." 110 Cong. Rec. 2788 (1964) (remarks of Rep. Meader). The narrow scope of preemption available under §§ 708 and 1104 reflects the importance Congress attached to state antidiscrimination laws in achieving Title VII's goal of equal employment opportunity. The legislative history of the PDA also supports a narrow interpretation of these provisions, as does our opinion in *Shaw.*

In order to decide whether the California statute requires or permits employers to violate Title VII, as amended by the PDA, or is inconsistent with the purposes of the statute, we must determine whether the PDA prohibits the States from requiring employers to provide reinstatement to pregnant workers, regardless of their policy for disabled workers generally.

B

Petitioners argue that the language of the federal statute itself unambiguously rejects California's "special treatment" approach to pregnancy discrimination, thus rendering any resort to the legislative history unnecessary. They contend that the second clause of the PDA forbids an employer to treat pregnant employees any differently than other disabled employees. Because "[t]he purpose of Congress is the ultimate touchstone" of the pre-emption inquiry, however, we must examine the PDA's language against the background of its legislative history and historical context. As to the language of the PDA, "[i]t is a 'familiar rule, that a thing may be within the letter of the statute and yet not within the statute, because not within its spirit, nor within the intention of its makers.'" *Steelworkers v. Weber*, 443 U.S. 193 (1979). . . .

It is well established that the PDA was passed in reaction to this Court's decision in *General Electric Co. v. Gilbert*, 429 U.S. 125 (1976). "When Congress amended Title VII in 1978, it unambiguously expressed its disapproval of both the holding and the reasoning of the Court in the *Gilbert* decision." *Newport News Shipbuilding & Dry Dock Co. v. EEOC*, 462 U.S. 669 (1983). By adding pregnancy to the definition of sex discrimination prohibited by Title VII, the first clause of the PDA reflects Congress' disapproval of the reasoning in *Gilbert*. Rather than imposing a limitation on the remedial purpose of the PDA, we believe that the second clause was intended to overrule the holding in *Gilbert* and to illustrate how discrimination against pregnancy is to be remedied. . . . Accordingly, subject to certain limitations, we agree with the Court of Appeals' conclusion that Congress intended the PDA to be "a floor beneath which pregnancy disability benefits may not drop — not a ceiling above which they may not rise."

The context in which Congress considered the issue of pregnancy discrimination supports this view of the PDA. Congress had before it extensive evidence of discrimination *against* pregnancy, particularly in disability and health insurance programs like those challenged in *Gilbert*. The reports, debates, and hearings make abundantly clear that Congress intended the PDA to provide relief for working women and to end discrimination against pregnant workers. In contrast to the thorough account of discrimination against pregnant workers, the legislative history is devoid of any discussion of preferential treatment of pregnancy, beyond acknowledgments of the existence of state statutes providing for such preferential treatment. Opposition to the PDA came from those concerned with the cost of including pregnancy in health and disability benefit plans and the application of the bill to abortion, not from those who favored special accommodation of pregnancy.

In support of their argument that the PDA prohibits employment practices that favor pregnant women, petitioners and several amici cite statements in the legislative history to the effect that the PDA does not *require* employers to extend any benefits to pregnant women that they do not already provide to other disabled employees. . . . We do not interpret these references to support petitioners' construction of the statute. On the contrary, if Congress had intended to *prohibit* preferential treatment, it would have been the height of understatement to say only that the legislation would not *require* such conduct. It is hardly conceivable that Congress would have extensively discussed only its intent not to require preferential treatment if in fact it had intended to prohibit such treatment.

We also find it significant that Congress was aware of state laws similar to California's but apparently did not consider them inconsistent with the PDA. . . .

Title VII, as amended by the PDA, and California's pregnancy disability leave statute share a common goal. The purpose of Title VII is "to achieve equality of employment opportunities and remove barriers that have operated in the past to favor an identifiable group of . . . employees over other employees." *Griggs*. Rather than limiting existing Title VII principles and objectives, the PDA extends them to cover pregnancy. As Senator Williams, a sponsor of the Act, stated: "The entire thrust . . . behind this legislation is to guarantee women the basic right to participate fully and equally in the workforce, without denying them the fundamental right to full participation in family life." 123 Cong. Rec. 29658 (1977).

Section 12945(b)(2) also promotes equal employment opportunity. By requiring employers to reinstate women after a reasonable pregnancy disability leave, § 12945(b)(2) ensures that they will not lose their jobs on account of pregnancy disability. . . .

We emphasize the limited nature of the benefits § 12945(b)(2) provides. The statute is narrowly drawn to cover only the period of *actual physical disability* on account of pregnancy, childbirth, or related medical conditions. Accordingly, unlike the protective labor legislation prevalent earlier in this century, § 12945(b)(2) does not reflect archaic or stereotypical notions about pregnancy and the abilities of pregnant workers. A statute based on such stereotypical assumptions would, of course, be inconsistent with Title VII's goal of equal employment opportunity.

C

Moreover, even if we agreed with petitioners' construction of the PDA, we would nonetheless reject their argument that the California statute requires employers to violate Title VII. Section 12945(b)(2) does not prevent employers from complying with both the federal law (as petitioners construe it) and the state law. This is not a case where "compliance with both federal and state regulations is a physical impossibility," or where there is an "inevitable collision between the two schemes of regulation." Section 12945(b)(2) does not compel California employers to treat pregnant workers better than other disabled employees; it merely establishes benefits that employers must, at a minimum, provide to pregnant workers. Employers are free to give comparable benefits to other disabled employees, thereby treating "women affected by pregnancy" no better than "other persons not so affected but similar in their ability or inability to work." Indeed, at oral argument, petitioners conceded that compliance with both statutes "is theoretically possible." . . .

IV

Thus, petitioners' facial challenge to §12945(b)(2) fails. The statute is not preempted by Title VII, as amended by the PDA, because it is not inconsistent with the purposes of the federal statute, nor does it require the doing of an act which is unlawful under Title VII.

NOTES

1. *A Floor, Not a Ceiling.* In *Guerra,* the Court indicated that the second clause of the PDA provides "a floor beneath which pregnancy disability benefits may not drop — not a ceiling above which they may not rise." As we have seen previously, lower courts have not read the statute as imposing on employers a duty to accommodate pregnant women with maternity leave, light duty, or modified work assignments when they do not provide such accommodations for other similarly disabling conditions. *Guerra* seems to agree.

2. *When Is Preferential Treatment Permitted?* The Court in *Guerra* concluded that preferential treatment of pregnancy, as compared with other disabilities, is *permitted* under the PDA, though not required. How did the Court reach this conclusion? Is it consistent with the language of the amendment? Is this the result Congress would have wanted had it addressed the issue when it was considering the Pregnancy Discrimination Act?

In his concurrence, Justice Stevens characterized the preferential treatment permitted by the majority as analogous to voluntary affirmative action permitted in *United Steelworkers of America v. Weber,* 443 U.S. 193 (1979). But *Weber* and subsequent affirmative action cases impose limits on affirmative action plans in order to protect the rights of other employees. What limits does *Guerra* place on an employer's right to voluntarily provide preferential treatment to pregnant women as compared with similarly disabled individuals? The *Guerra* Court noted that California's statute "is narrowly drawn to cover only the period of actual physical disability" related to pregnancy. Does preferential treatment for pregnant women that is not so limited violate the PDA or Title VII's general prohibition against sex discrimination? Does the Court provide any other limitations for voluntary preferential treatment?

In *Johnson v. Univ. of Iowa*, 431 F.3d 325, 328-29 (8th Cir. 2005), plaintiff challenged his employer's policy that provided leave to birth mothers and adoptive parents. While the court agreed it would be impermissible to provide biological mothers, but not biological fathers with "time to care for, and bond with, a newborn," it viewed the leave accorded mothers as related only to the "the physical trauma they sustain giving birth, . . . a valid reason wholly separate from gender." The challenged policy "does not allow mothers to use accrued sick leave after their period of disability has ended. Thus, the period away from work constitutes disability leave, even though mothers are likely caring for their newborns during this period." According mothers leave comparable to that provided workers with disabilities "is not only permissible, but is required by the Pregnancy Discrimination Act of 1978."

What if an employer provided disability leave for pregnant women but no leave at all for other workers? Would such a policy violate Title VII? What if an employer provided "light duty" for pregnant employees but not for other employees similarly disabled? Does it matter that both men and women suffer from nonpregnancy-related disabilities? Are these situations examples of permissible "preferential treatment" or prohibited discrimination? Could such preferential treatment be justified on the ground that neutral leave provisions, light-duty provisions, and medical restriction provisions may have a disparate impact on pregnant workers?

Some civil rights groups aligned themselves with the employer in *Guerra*. One possible reason was ideological: "protective" laws have traditionally "protected" women right out of job opportunities, and it is better to resist such statutes, no matter how well intended. Another possibility was practical: the expenses incident to compliance provide an incentive to employers not to hire women. How does the majority deal with the problem of "protective" legislation that operates to restrict the employment opportunities of women? What is the impact of the FMLA on this issue? See p. 369.

3. *The PDA and the BFOQ Defense.* Recall the Supreme Court's decision in *International Union UAW v. Johnson Controls, Inc.*, reproduced at p. 173. *Johnson Controls* described the PDA as containing "a BFOQ of its own" in the second clause, providing that pregnant women must be treated the same as other persons "similar in their ability or inability to work." The concurrence, in contrast, quoted *Guerra*: "[T]he purpose of the PDA was simply to make the treatment of pregnancy consistent with general Title VII principles." Does the second clause of the PDA define pregnancy discrimination or does it provide a statutory defense to pregnancy discrimination? Who bears the burden of proof on the question whether the employer has treated pregnant women the same as other similarly situated individuals? Is there any difference between the second clause of the PDA and the BFOQ defense? Would *Johnson Controls* have come out differently without the PDA?

4. *Disparate Impact Theory.* Is disparate impact a viable theory under the PDA? The *Guerra* Court noted the issue but did not address it. In his dissent, however, Justice White wrote that "[w]hatever remedies Title VII would otherwise provide for victims of disparate impact, Congress expressly ordered pregnancy to be treated in the same manner as other disabilities." 479 U.S. at 297 n. 1. Was Justice White saying that the second clause of the PDA bars the application of the disparate impact theory? If so, does the codification of the disparate impact theory in the Civil Rights Act of 1991 alter that conclusion?

Certainly it would seem that if a practice disproportionately disadvantaged women, even if it were because of pregnancy, disparate impact theory would be available. But would a disparate impact claim be stated if the practice disproportionately disadvantaged *pregnant* women, as opposed to women as a whole? *See Garcia v. Woman's Hosp. of Tex.*, 97 F.3d 810 (5th Cir. 1996) (permitting a disparate impact claim if proof of impact on pregnant women was shown). *But see Stout v. Baxter Healthcare Corp.*, 282 F.3d 856, 861 (5th Cir. 2002) ("we are unwilling to extend the *Garcia* rule to those disparate impact claims, such as this one, in which the plaintiff's only challenge is that the amount of sick leave granted to employees is insufficient to accommodate the time off required in a typical pregnancy. To hold otherwise would be to transform the PDA into a guarantee of medical leave for pregnant employees, something we have specifically held that the PDA does not do").

NOTE ON ACCOMMODATING PREGNANCY UNDER THE AMERICANS WITH DISABILITIES ACT

The Americans with Disabilities Act (ADA) requires employers to provide reasonable accommodations to qualified employees with disabilities unless such accommodation would impose an undue hardship on the employer. 42 U.S.C. § 12112(b)(5)(A) (2007). In order to be qualified, an individual must be able to perform the essential functions of the job in question, with or without reasonable accommodation. See Chapter 6. The EEOC's interpretive guidance concludes that, because pregnancy is not an impairment, it is not a disability. Pregnant women, therefore, are not entitled to the ADA's protection. 29 C.F.R. pt. 1630 app. § 1630.2(h), (j). Although normal pregnancies are not covered under the ADA, complications or conditions arising out of pregnancy may be covered.

Even if the ADA does not directly protect pregnant women, however, the ADA may indirectly accord pregnant women rights to accommodation under the PDA. Pregnancy is at least a temporarily disabling condition. Pregnant employees viewing their situation as comparable to those of individuals with disabilities may attempt to claim the same accommodations to which disabled employees are entitled under the ADA. Deborah Calloway, *Accommodating Pregnancy in the Workplace*, 25 Stetson L. Rev. 1, 29-30 (1995). Individuals covered by the ADA may, like pregnant women, require flexible work rules or medical leave or relief from tasks such as climbing stairs and lifting heavy weights. If an employer, in compliance with the ADA's reasonable accommodation requirement, grants leave, provides flexible work rules, or assigns a disabled employee to light duty, would the PDA require that employer to provide the same accommodations to pregnant employees who have similar needs? They are, after all, similar in their ability or inability to work.

NOTE ON CHILDREARING LEAVE

Suppose medical testimony establishes that a pregnant woman is unable to work for only six weeks. If she asks for more time, isn't she seeking leave not for *childbearing,* but for *childrearing?* Does Title VII require employers to grant such leave? Can childrearing be considered "pregnancy, childbirth, or related medical conditions"? *See Fisher v. Vassar Coll.*, 70 F.3d 1420 (2d Cir. 1995) (choice to remain home for an extended period following birth of a child is not the inevitable consequence of pregnancy or a medical condition related to pregnancy as required by the PDA); *but see Kocak v. Cmty. Health Ptnrs. of Ohio, Inc.*, 400 F.3d 466 (6th Cir. 2005) (employer failure to rehire an applicant because of scheduling complications caused by her prior pregnancy impermissible because Title VII prohibits discrimination because of a woman's capacity to become pregnant, and potential pregnancy is sex-related medical condition).

In May 2007, the EEOC issued an Enforcement Guidance on "Unlawful Disparate Treatment of Workers with Caregiving Responsibilities" (www.eeoc.gov/policy/docs/caregiving.html). Recognizing that caregivers are not per se within the protected class under Title VII, the guidance is aimed at explaining when discrimination against caregivers might constitute unlawful disparate treatment under Title VII or the Americans with Disabilities Act.

NOTE ON THE FAMILY AND MEDICAL LEAVE ACT

Some of the problems faced by pregnant women and parents of small children are addressed by the Family and Medical Leave Act of 1993 (FMLA), 29 U.S.C. §2601 (2007), which ensures up to 12 weeks of unpaid leave for a variety of purposes, including the birth or adoption of a child. *See* Family & Medical Leave Act, 58 Fed. Reg. 31,794 (1993) (DOL's Interim Final Rule). The Department of Labor (DOL) recognizes that "[c]ircumstances may require that leave for the birth of a child, or for placement for adoption or foster care, be taken prior to the actual birth or placement." *Id.* at 31,798 (summary and discussion of §825.112). The DOL has indicated, however, that "[a]n employee's entitlement to FMLA leave for birth or placement of a child expires 12 months after the birth or placement." *Id.* at 31,801 (summary and discussion of §825.201).

The FMLA reduces, but by no means eliminates, the importance of the PDA for pregnant workers. The FMLA applies only to employers with 50 or more employees. Further:

> To be "eligible," an employee must have worked for the employer: (1) For at least 12 months and (2) for at least 1,250 hours during the year preceding the start of the leave, and (3) be employed at a worksite where the employer employs at least 50 employees within a 75-mile radius. . . .

Id. at 31,798 (summary and discussion of §§825.110 and 825.111). Thus, part-time employees, first-year employees, and employees who work for small employers are not entitled to leave under the FMLA. Even for employers covered by the FMLA, there have been questions raised as to the statute's effectiveness. *See generally* Stacy A. Hickox, *The Elusive Right to Reinstatement Under the Family Medical Leave Act,* 91 Ky. L.J. 477 (2002/2003). Further, the FMLA does not resolve disputes regarding pregnancy accommodations other than unpaid leave. The FMLA is also discussed on p. 591.

PROBLEM 5.1

Charlene works in a company mail room. Her duties include helping to unload bags of mail from the mail trucks. She also sorts mail and works at the front counter serving customers. Charlene is in her sixth month of pregnancy and has been advised by her doctor not to lift the heavy mailbags at work. When she asked her employer to permit her to limit her work to sorting mail and working at the counter for the remaining period of her pregnancy, the employer refused and put her on leave without pay, promising to return her to her job after the baby was delivered and she became well enough to perform all of the duties of her job. Charlene's employer has no pregnancy leave policy and no long-term disability policy. The employer permits employees to take two weeks of sick leave each year. Employees who require more than two weeks of sick leave are discharged. Charlene filed suit under the PDA, alleging discrimination on the basis of her pregnancy. A male employee, who recently suffered injuries in a car accident also has filed suit, complaining that, rather than receiving leave without pay and a promise of reinstatement, he was discharged after using up his allotted two weeks of sick leave. What rights and remedies (if any) do these employees have?

2.   *Sexual and Other Discriminatory Harassment*

In this section, we consider employees' rights to a workplace free from sexual and other discriminatory harassment. Under Title VII, employees have a cause of action for harassment when it discriminates on the basis of membership in a protected group. Sexual harassment imposes different conditions of employment on women because of their gender. Harassment also is actionable when aimed at racial, religious, or ethnic groups or at older or disabled workers. Sexual harassment is unique, however, for a variety or reasons. First, unlike other discriminatory behavior, sexual harassment involves much conduct that, in other times and settings, is perfectly appropriate. Second, unlike other statutory violations, for which an adverse employment action usually requires some tangible change in compensation or position, harassment can violate Title VII even if the victim suffers no adverse employment decision or economic impact as a result. Third, harassment frequently is practiced in violation of, rather than in compliance with, company policy, and harassers typically are satisfying their own personal interests, rather than seeking to further their employer's interests. This attribute of discriminatory harassment has generated an additional question: what is the employer's liability for discrimination or harassment by supervisors and co-workers in violation of company policy? Finally, because controlling discriminatory harassment in the workplace by disciplining harassing employees may relieve an employer of liability, harassment raises questions about the rights of employees who perpetrate this form of discrimination.

MERITOR SAVINGS BANK v. VINSON
477 U.S. 57 (1986)

Justice REHNQUIST delivered the opinion of the Court.

I

[In 1974, Michelle Vinson met Sidney Taylor, a vice president of Meritor Savings Bank and manager of one of its branch offices. Taylor hired her and became her supervisor. Vinson started as a trainee, but ultimately was promoted to assistant branch manager, working at the same branch until her discharge in 1978. "[I]t is undisputed that her advancement there was based on merit alone." In late 1978, Vinson took sick leave and finally was discharged for excessive use of that leave.

Vinson sued both Taylor and the bank, claiming that she had "constantly been subjected to sexual harassment" by Taylor during her four years of employment.]

At . . . trial, the parties presented conflicting testimony about Taylor's behavior during respondent's employment. Respondent testified that during her probationary period as a teller-trainee, Taylor treated her in a fatherly way and made no sexual advances. Shortly thereafter, however, he invited her out to dinner and, during the course of the meal, suggested that they go to a motel to have sexual relations. At first she refused, but out of what she described as fear of losing her job she eventually agreed. According to respondent, Taylor thereafter made repeated demands upon her for sexual favors, usually at the branch, both during and after business hours; she estimated that over the next several years she had intercourse with him some 40 or 50 times. In addition, respondent testified that Taylor fondled her in front of other employees, followed her into the women's restroom when she went there alone, exposed himself to her, and even forcibly raped her on several occasions. These activities ceased after 1977, respondent stated, when she started going with a steady boyfriend.

Respondent also testified that Taylor touched and fondled other women employees of the bank, and she attempted to call witnesses to support this charge. But while some supporting testimony apparently was admitted without objection, the District Court did not allow her "to present wholesale evidence of a pattern and practice relating to sexual advances to other female employees in her case in chief, but advised her that she might well be able to present such evidence in rebuttal to the defendants' cases." Respondent did not offer such evidence in rebuttal. Finally, respondent testified that because she was afraid of Taylor she never reported his harassment to any of his supervisors and never attempted to use the bank's complaint procedure.

Taylor denied respondent's allegations of sexual activity, testifying that he never fondled her, never made suggestive remarks to her, never engaged in sexual intercourse with her, and never asked her to do so. He contended instead that respondent made her accusations in response to a business-related dispute. The bank also denied respondent's allegations and asserted that any sexual harassment by Taylor was unknown to the bank and engaged in without its consent or approval.

The District Court denied relief, but did not resolve the conflicting testimony about the existence of a sexual relationship between respondent and Taylor. It found instead that:

> [i]f [respondent] and Taylor did engage in an intimate or sexual relationship during the time of [respondent's] employment with [the bank], that relationship was a voluntary one having nothing to do with her continued employment at [the bank] or her advancement or promotions at that institution.

The court ultimately found that respondent "was not the victim of sexual harassment and was not the victim of sexual discrimination" while employed at the bank. . . .

II . . .

Respondent argues, and the Court of Appeals held, that unwelcome sexual advances that create an offensive or hostile working environment violate Title VII. Without question, when a supervisor sexually harasses a subordinate because of the subordinate's sex, that supervisor "discriminate[s]" on the basis of sex. Petitioner apparently does not challenge this proposition. It contends instead that in prohibiting discrimination with respect to "compensation, terms, conditions, or privileges" of employment, Congress was concerned with what petitioner describes as "tangible loss" of "an economic character," not "purely psychological aspects of the work-place environment." In support of this claim petitioner observes that in both the legislative history of Title VII and this Court's Title VII decisions, the focus has been on tangible, economic barriers erected by discrimination.

We reject petitioner's view. First, the language of Title VII is not limited to "economic" or "tangible" discrimination. The phrase "terms, conditions, or privi-leges of employment" evinces a congressional intent " 'to strike at the entire spec-trum [of] disparate treatment of men and women' " in employment. *Los Angeles Dept. of Water and Power v. Manhart.* Petitioner has pointed to nothing in the Act to suggest that Congress contemplated the limitation urged here.

Second, in 1980 the EEOC issued Guidelines specifying that "sexual harassment," as there defined, is a form of sex discrimination prohibited by Title VII. As an "administrative interpretation of the Act by the enforcing agency," *Griggs v. Duke Power Co.,* these guidelines, " 'while not controlling upon the courts by reason of their authority, do constitute a body of experience and informed judgment to which courts and litigants may properly resort for guidance.' " *General Electric v. Gilbert* (quoting *Skidmore v. Swift & Co.,* 323 U.S. 134, 140 (1944)). The EEOC Guidelines fully support the view that harassment leading to noneconomic injury can violate Title VII.

In defining "sexual harassment," the Guidelines first describe the kinds of work-place conduct that may be actionable under Title VII. These include "[u]nwelcome sexual advances, requests for sexual favors, and other verbal or physical conduct of a sexual nature." 29 C.F.R. § 1604.11(a) (1985). Relevant to the charges at issue in this case, the Guidelines provide that such sexual misconduct constitutes prohibited "sexual harassment," whether or not it is directly linked to the grant or denial of an economic quid pro quo, where "such conduct has the purpose or effect of unrea-sonably interfering with an individual's work performance or creating an intimi-dating, hostile, or offensive working environment." § 1604.11(a)(3).

In concluding that so-called "hostile environment" (i.e., non quid pro quo) ha-rassment violates Title VII, the EEOC drew upon a substantial body of judicial decisions and EEOC precedent holding that Title VII affords employees the right to work in an environment free from discriminatory intimidation, ridicule, and insult. *Rogers v. EEOC,* 454 F.2d 234 (5th Cir. 1971), was apparently the first case to recognize a cause of action based upon a discriminatory work environment.

In *Rogers,* the Court of Appeals for the Fifth Circuit held that a Hispanic com-plainant could establish a Title VII violation by demonstrating that her employer created an offensive work environment for employees by giving discriminatory ser-vice to its Hispanic clientele. The court explained that an employee's protections under Title VII extend beyond the economic aspects of employment:

> [T]he phrase "terms, conditions or privileges of employment" in [Title VII] is an expansive concept which sweeps within its protective ambit the practice of creating a working envi-ronment heavily charged with ethnic or racial discrimination. . . . One can readily envision working environments so heavily polluted with discrimination as to destroy completely the emotional and psychological stability of minority group workers. . . .

Courts applied this principle to harassment based on race, religion, and national origin. Nothing in Title VII suggests that a hostile environment based on discrimi-natory sexual harassment should not be likewise prohibited. The Guidelines thus appropriately drew from, and were fully consistent with, the existing case law.

Since the Guidelines were issued, courts have uniformly held, and we agree, that a plaintiff may establish a violation of Title VII by proving that discrimination based on sex has created a hostile or abusive work environment. As the Court of Appeals for the Eleventh Circuit wrote in *Henson v. Dundee*, 682 F.2d 897, 902 (1982):

> Sexual harassment which creates a hostile or offensive environment for members of one sex is every bit the arbitrary barrier to sexual equality at the workplace that racial harassment is to racial equality. Surely, a requirement that a man or woman run a gauntlet of sexual abuse in return for the privilege of being allowed to work and make a living can be as demeaning and disconcerting as the harshest of racial epithets.

Of course, as the courts in both *Rogers* and *Henson* recognized, not all workplace conduct that may be described as "harassment" affects a "term, condition, or privilege" of employment within the meaning of Title VII. For sexual harassment to be actionable, it must be sufficiently severe or pervasive "to alter the conditions of [the victim's] employment and create an abusive working environment." Respondent's allegations in this case — which include not only pervasive harassment but also criminal conduct of the most serious nature — are plainly sufficient to state a claim for "hostile environment" sexual harassment.

The question remains, however, whether the District Court's ultimate finding that respondent "was not the victim of sexual harassment" effectively disposed of respondent's claim. The Court of Appeals recognized, we think correctly, that this ultimate finding was likely based on one or both of two erroneous views of the law. First, the District Court apparently believed that a claim for sexual harassment will not lie absent an economic effect on the complainant's employment. . . . Since it appears that the District Court made its findings without ever considering the "hostile environment" theory of sexual harassment, the Court of Appeals' decision to remand was correct.

Second, the District Court's conclusion that no actionable harassment occurred might have rested on its earlier "finding" that "[i]f [respondent] and Taylor did engage in an intimate or sexual relationship . . . , that relationship was a voluntary one." But the fact that sex-related conduct was "voluntary," in the sense that the complainant was not forced to participate against her will, is not a defense to a sexual harassment suit brought under Title VII. The gravamen of any sexual harassment claim is that the alleged sexual advances were "unwelcome." 29 C.F.R. § 1604.11(a) (1985). While the question whether particular conduct was indeed unwelcome presents difficult problems of proof and turns largely on credibility determinations committed to the trier of fact, the District Court in this case erroneously focused on the "voluntariness" of respondent's participation in the claimed sexual episodes. The correct inquiry is whether respondent by her conduct indicated that the alleged sexual advances were unwelcome, not whether her actual participation in sexual intercourse was voluntary.

Petitioner contends that even if this case must be remanded to the District Court, the Court of Appeals erred in one of the terms of its remand. Specifically, the Court of Appeals stated that testimony about respondent's "dress and personal fantasies," which the District Court apparently admitted into evidence, "had no place in this litigation." The apparent ground for this conclusion was that respondent's voluntariness vel non in submitting to Taylor's advances was immaterial to her sexual harassment claim. While "voluntariness" in the sense of consent is not a defense to such a claim, it does not follow that a complainant's sexually provocative speech or dress is irrelevant as a matter of law in determining whether he or she found particular sexual advances unwelcome. To the contrary, such evidence is obviously relevant. The EEOC Guidelines emphasize that the trier of fact must determine the existence of sexual harassment in light of "the record as a whole" and "the totality of circumstances, such as the nature of the sexual advances and the context in which the alleged incidents occurred." 29 C.F.R. § 1604.11(b) (1985). Respondent's claim that any marginal relevance of the evidence in question was outweighed by the potential for unfair prejudice is the sort of argument properly addressed to the District Court. In this case the District Court concluded that the evidence should be admitted, and the Court of Appeals' contrary conclusion was based upon the erroneous, categorical view that testimony about provocative dress and publicly expressed sexual fantasies "had no place in this litigation." While the District Court must carefully weigh the applicable considerations in deciding whether to admit evidence of this kind, there is no per se rule against its admissibility.

NOTES

1. *What Constitutes Harassment?* Because the alleged conduct by Taylor was so egregious, it may not be clear from *Meritor* that one central theoretical problem with the sexual harassment cause of action is deciding what constitutes harassment. At one extreme, a violation will be established if accepting sexual advances is an explicit or implicit quid pro quo for obtaining, retaining, or advancing in a job. The Court in *Meritor* clearly prohibits less egregious conduct than this, holding that a contaminated work environment also is prohibited. At the other extreme, however, defining harassment becomes problematic. As the Court emphasized in *Oncale*, Title VII is not a "civility code." Is every "pass" a Title VII violation? Every pass by a supervisor? Does harassment by co-workers (or even subordinates) violate Title VII? Is mere exposure to raw language harassment? What about compliments or criticisms regarding an employee's appearance? These questions will be explored in the cases following. But although the line between harassment and acceptable social behavior is sometimes unclear, many cases concern behavior that any reasonable person, male or female, would recognize as harassment.

2. *F.R.E. 412.* The *Meritor* Court admitted evidence of Vinson's dress and sexual fantasies. In rape cases, defendants commonly seek to make the moral character of the victim an issue. Might such a defense be raised in a sexual harassment case? What is the appropriate judicial response? Consider the relevance of dress or past conduct to the question whether sexual advances were unwelcome. Rule 412 of the Federal Rules of Evidence regulates the admissibility of evidence of past sexual conduct. In trials relating to sexual misconduct, it makes inadmissible

> evidence offered to prove that any alleged victim engaged in other sexual behavior . . . [or] . . . to prove any alleged victim's sexual predisposition . . . [unless] its probative value substantially outweighs the danger of harm to any victim and of unfair prejudice to any party. Evidence of an alleged victim's reputation is admissible only if it has been placed in controversy by the alleged victim.

What effect is this rule of evidence likely to have on sexual harassment litigation? *See Rodriguez-Hernandez v. Miranda-Valez*, 132 F.3d 848 (1st Cir. 1998) (sexual history of plaintiff properly excluded under Rule 412). *But see Wilson v. City of Des Moines*,

442 F.3d 637 (8th Cir. 2006) (admission of testimony of plaintiff's workplace behavior and sexually charged comments was not abuse of discretion, despite the trial court failing to hold a required hearing under Fed. R. Evid. 412, where testimony was highly probative of question of whether alleged harassment was unwelcome and plaintiff's behavior was public). *See generally* Theresa M. Beiner, *Sexy Dressing Revisited: Does Target Dress Play a Part in Sexual Harassment Cases?*, 14 DUKE J. GENDER L. & POL'Y 125, 127 (2007) (finding very few cases where the target's dress was relevant and even fewer where it was used to argue that the target welcomed the sexually harassing behavior); Andrea A. Curcio, *Rule 412 Laid Bare: A Procedural Rule That Cannot Adequately Protect Sexual Harassment Plaintiffs from Embarrassing Exposure*, 67 U. CIN. L. REV. 125 (1998) (contending that Rule 412 has not fully achieved its purpose of protecting plaintiffs from exploration of their consensual sexual activities).

Why wouldn't the district court allow plaintiff to introduce evidence of Taylor's harassment of other employees as part of her case in chief? Doesn't that evidence make Taylor's denial that he harassed Vinson less credible? Why didn't plaintiff produce such evidence in rebuttal when she apparently was permitted to?

3. *Remedial Issues.* The 1991 Civil Rights Act expanded the remedies available in Title VII cases to include compensatory and punitive damages and damages for emotional distress. This was largely due to the controversy generated by Anita Hill's accusations of harassment during the Clarence Thomas confirmation hearings. The debate exposed the fact that Title VII as originally enacted provided only equitable remedies, which were largely ineffective in hostile environment cases because plaintiffs could secure only attorneys' fees and injunctive relief against further violations. By providing emotional distress and punitive damages, the 1991 Act reinvigorated Title VII's prohibition of harassment. The amount of damages available is limited, however, depending on the size of the plaintiff's employer. See Chapter 8. Further, courts may hold, as they have in tort suits, that a plaintiff seeking damages for mental and emotional distress places her mental state in controversy, justifying an order to undergo psychiatric examination.

NOTE ON OTHER DISCRIMINATORY HARASSMENT

Sexual harassment claims have predominated among the hostile environment cases under Title VII, but, as the Court noted in *Meritor*, the first case to recognize hostile environment as a basis for liability under Title VII concerned an employer who "created an offensive work environment for employees by giving discriminatory service to its Hispanic clientele."

While racial and other discriminatory harassment claims have never been as common as those asserting sexual harassment, courts have granted relief in a number of instances. *See, e.g., El-Hakem v. BJY, Inc.*, 415 F.3d 1068 (9th Cir. 2005) (racially hostile environment claim under §1981); *Reedy v. Quebecor Printing Eagle, Inc.*, 333 F.3d 906 (8th Cir. 2003) (summary judgment for defendant denied in §1981 racial harassment case involving physically threatening graffiti directed at plaintiff which were allowed to remain on wall); *Jackson v. Flint Ink N. Am. Corp.*, 382 F.3d 869 (8th Cir. 2004) (trial warranted when plaintiff's "name was written in a shower at his workplace and that there was an arrow connecting his name with a burning cross and a KKK sign [since] an objective observer would regard this combination of figures as a threat of serious bodily harm if not death"); *Kassner v. 2nd Ave. Delicatessen, Inc.*, 496 F.3d 229 (2007) (age-based harassment actionable under ADEA).

While any harassment claim under Title VII must allege harassment based on membership in a statutorily protected group, complaints of discriminatory harassment involve many of the same issues discussed in this subsection concerning sexual harassment. As we will see, the core question is frequently whether the conduct in question was "severe or pervasive" enough to contaminate the work environment, and that issue is as important for other discriminatory harassment. *E.g., Bourini v. Bridgestone/Firestone N. Am. Tire, L.L.C.*, 136 Fed. Appx. 747, 751 (6th Cir. 2005) (eight incidents spread out over a period of five years were too infrequent and isolated to constitute discriminatory changes in the terms and conditions of employment, even though several of the incidents were offensive and highly inappropriate). Although recognizing the benefits of analogizing race and sexual harassment, one commentator, however, has cautioned of the dangers:

> The use of the standard developed in the context of sexual harassment requiring that conduct be "severe or pervasive" in order to be actionable has led the courts to conclude that even quite damaging and serious racially motivated behavior, including references to lynching or racially motivated assault, is insufficient to state a cause of action for racial harassment. . . . Analogies between race and sex may also lead courts to conclude that even racially explicit conduct is not racially motivated, similar to the conclusions drawn by some courts that sexually explicit conduct is not motivated by gender.

L. Camille Hébert, *Analogizing Race and Sex in Workplace Harassment Claims*, 58 OHIO ST. L.J. 819, 878-79 (1997). *See also* Pat K. Chew, *Freeing Racial Harassment from the Sexual Harassment Model*, 85 OR. L. REV. 615 (2006). In *National Railroad Passenger Corp. v. Morgan*, 536 U.S. 101, 116 n. 10 (2002), however, the Court asserted that "[h]ostile work environment claims based on racial harassment are reviewed under the same standard as those based on sexual harassment." Issues unique to other discriminatory harassment will be noted throughout this section.

a. Severe or Pervasive Harassment

HARRIS v. FORKLIFT SYSTEMS, INC.
510 U.S. 17 (1993)

O'CONNOR, J., delivered the opinion for a unanimous Court. . . .

I

Teresa Harris worked as a manager at Forklift Systems, Inc., an equipment rental company, from April 1985 until October 1987. Charles Hardy was Forklift's president.

The Magistrate found that, throughout Harris' time at Forklift, Hardy often insulted her because of her gender and often made her the target of unwanted sexual innuendos. Hardy told Harris on several occasions, in the presence of other employees, "You're a woman, what do you know" and "We need a man as the rental manager"; at least once, he told her she was "a dumb ass woman." Again in front of others, he suggested that the two of them "go to the Holiday Inn to negotiate [Harris'] raise." Hardy occasionally asked Harris and other female employees to get coins from his front pants pocket. He threw objects on the ground in front of Harris and other women, and asked them to pick the objects up. He made sexual innuendos about Harris' and other women's clothing.

In mid-August 1987, Harris complained to Hardy about his conduct. Hardy said he was surprised that Harris was offended, claimed he was only joking, and apologized. He also promised he would stop, and based on this assurance Harris stayed on the job. But in early September, Hardy began anew: While Harris was arranging a deal with one of Forklift's customers, he asked her, again in front of other employees, "What did you do, promise the guy . . . some [sex] Saturday night?" On October 1, Harris collected her paycheck and quit.

Harris then sued Forklift, claiming that Hardy's conduct had created an abusive work environment for her because of her gender. The [district court] found this to be "a close case," but held that Hardy's conduct did not create an abusive environment. The court found that some of Hardy's comments "offended [Harris], and would offend the reasonable woman," but that they were not "so severe as to be expected to seriously affect [Harris'] psychological well-being." A reasonable woman manager under like circumstances would have been offended by Hardy, but his conduct would not have risen to the level of interfering with that person's work performance.

> Neither do I believe that [Harris] was subjectively so offended that she suffered injury. . . . Although Hardy may at times have genuinely offended [Harris], I do not believe that he created a working environment so poisoned as to be intimidating or abusive to [Harris].

. . . We granted certiorari to resolve a conflict among the Circuits on whether conduct, to be actionable as "abusive work environment" harassment (no quid pro quo harassment issue is present here), must "seriously affect [an employee's] psychological well-being" or lead the plaintiff to "suffer injury." . . .

II

Title VII of the Civil Rights Act of 1964 makes it "an unlawful employment practice for an employer . . . to discriminate against any individual with respect to his compensation, terms, conditions, or privileges of employment, because of such individual's race, color, religion, sex, or national origin." As we made clear in *Meritor*, this language "is not limited to 'economic' or 'tangible' discrimination. The phrase 'terms, conditions, or privileges of employment' evinces a congressional intent 'to strike at the entire spectrum of disparate treatment of men and women' in employment," which includes requiring people to work in a discriminatorily hostile or abusive environment. When the workplace is permeated with "discriminatory intimidation, ridicule, and insult," that is "sufficiently severe or pervasive to alter the conditions of the victim's employment and create an abusive working environment," Title VII is violated.

This standard, which we reaffirm today, takes a middle path between making actionable any conduct that is merely offensive and requiring the conduct to cause a tangible psychological injury. As we pointed out in *Meritor*, "mere utterance of an . . . epithet which engenders offensive feelings in an employee," does not sufficiently affect the conditions of employment to implicate Title VII. Conduct that is not severe or pervasive enough to create an objectively hostile or abusive work environment — an environment that a reasonable person would find hostile or abusive — is beyond Title VII's purview. Likewise, if the victim does not subjectively perceive the environment to be abusive, the conduct has not actually altered the conditions of the victim's employment, and there is no Title VII violation.

But Title VII comes into play before the harassing conduct leads to a nervous breakdown. A discriminatorily abusive work environment, even one that does not seriously affect employees' psychological well-being, can and often will detract from employees' job performance, discourage employees from remaining on the job, or keep them from advancing in their careers. Moreover, even without regard to these tangible effects, the very fact that the discriminatory conduct was so severe or pervasive that it created a work environment abusive to employees because of their race, gender, religion, or national origin offends Title VII's broad rule of workplace equality. The appalling conduct alleged in *Meritor*, and the reference in that case to environments "'so heavily polluted with discrimination as to destroy completely the emotional and psychological stability of minority group workers,'" quoting *Rogers v. EEOC*, merely present some especially egregious examples of harassment. They do not mark the boundary of what is actionable.

We therefore believe the District Court erred in relying on whether the conduct "seriously affected plaintiff's psychological well-being" or led her to "suffer injury." Such an inquiry may needlessly focus the factfinder's attention on concrete psychological harm, an element Title VII does not require. Certainly Title VII bars conduct that would seriously affect a reasonable person's psychological well-being, but the statute is not limited to such conduct. So long as the environment would reasonably be perceived, and is perceived, as hostile or abusive, there is no need for it also to be psychologically injurious.

This is not, and by its nature cannot be, a mathematically precise test. We need not answer today all the potential questions it raises, nor specifically address the EEOC's new regulations on this subject, see 58 Fed. Reg. 51266 (1993) (proposed 29 C.F.R. §§ 1609.1, 1609.2); see also 29 C.F.R. § 1604.11 (1993). But we can say that whether an environment is "hostile" or "abusive" can be determined only by looking at all the circumstances. These may include the frequency of the discriminatory conduct; its severity; whether it is physically threatening or humiliating, or a mere offensive utterance; and whether it unreasonably interferes with an employee's work performance. The effect on the employee's psychological well-being is, of course, relevant to determining whether the plaintiff actually found the environment abusive. But while psychological harm, like any other relevant factor, may be taken into account, no single factor is required.

III

[The Court reversed because the district court's legal error regarding psychological harm] may well have influenced its ultimate conclusion, especially given that the court found this to be a "close case." ...

NOTES

1. *How Bad Is Bad Enough? Harris* reaffirms the *Meritor* standard, which requires that, "[f]or sexual harassment to be actionable, it must be sufficiently severe or pervasive 'to alter the conditions of [the victim's] employment and create an abusive working environment.'" What does this standard reveal about drawing the line between acceptable social behavior and actionable sexual harassment? Does *Harris*

make the standard any clearer than it was after *Meritor*? Justice Scalia wrote a concurrence that stressed the vagueness of the standard, leaving "virtually unguided juries [to] decide whether sex-related conduct engaged in (or permitted by) an employer is egregious enough to warrant an award of damages." However, because "I know of no test more faithful to the inherently vague statutory language than the one the Court today adopts," he joined the Court's opinion. What should the district court find on remand? Was Hardy's conduct "severe" or "pervasive" or both? If the harassment in this case was not severe, when did it become pervasive enough to be actionable?

More than a decade after *Harris*, courts are struggling to apply its standard, evaluating whether the conduct was sufficiently severe or pervasive. *See McKinnis v. Crescent Guardian, Inc.*, 189 Fed. Appx. 307, 310 (5th Cir. 2006) (touching intimate areas on a number of occasions actionable); *Schiano v. Quality Payroll Sys. Inc.*, 445 F.3d 597, 608 (2d Cir. 2006) (given the frequency of the conduct, "the nature of the words exchanged, the context in which they were uttered, the physical nature of some of acts complained of, the response of the harasser to the steps Schiano took to repel the unwanted advances, and the effect of it all on Schiano's ability to do her job," a reasonable jury could find a violation); *Harvill v. Westward Communs., L.L.C.*, 433 F.3d 428 (5th Cir. 2005) (reaffirming that harassment can result from conduct that is either severe *or* pervasive, the court held that fondling by a male co-worker, numerous times, over seven-month period sufficed).

Some decisions find very questionable conduct not to qualify. In *Henthorn v. Capitol Communs., Inc.*, 359 F.3d 1021, 1027-28 (8th Cir. 2004), the court viewed the harasser's behavior as "inappropriate, immature, and unprofessional," but ruled it did not cross "the high threshold" for sexual harassment:

> Parker's requests that Henthorn go out with him were repetitive and annoying, but they were not lewd or threatening. Parker did not touch Henthorn inappropriately, nor did he make sexual comments about her in her presence. His two late-night/early morning calls urged her to accept his social invitations and expressed his interest in her, but they did not contain sexual propositions. Although Henthorn was made uncomfortable by Parker's conduct, she was able to continue to perform her assignments, and Parker's actions did not result in a change of her probationary status.

See also LeGrand v. Area Res. for Cmty. & Human Servs., 394 F.3d 1098 (8th Cir. 2005) (viewing LeGrand's claim in light of the "demanding standard" required, "Father Nutt's behavior did not rise to the level of actionable hostile work environment sexual harassment. None of the incidents was physically violent or overtly threatening. [T]hree isolated incidents, which occurred over a nine-month period, were not so severe or pervasive as to poison LeGrand's work environment"). For a study of sexual harassment cases in the federal courts, concluding that a successful claim is most likely to involve sexualized conduct directed toward an individual, see Ann Juliano & Stewart Schwab, *The Sweep of Sexual Harassment Cases*, 86 CORNELL L. REV. 548 (2001).

2. *Severe or Pervasive.* Since conduct need be either severe *or* pervasive, doesn't that mean that in appropriate circumstances, a single incident will be enough to constitute actionable harassment? Some courts have been willing to find serious single incidents of harassment sufficient to establish liability under Title VII, especially if the complaint involves physical contact. *See, e.g., Little v. Windermere Relocation, Inc.*, 301 F.3d 958 (9th Cir. 2002) (rape by client and employer's subsequent reinforcement of

the harassment was sufficient to satisfy severity requirement); *Ferris v. Delta Air Lines, Inc.*, 277 F.3d 128 (2d Cir. 2001) (single incident of rape satisfies severity prong). In particularly egregious cases, even a single instance of *verbal* harassment can be enough. *See, e.g., Howley v. Town of Stratford*, 217 F.3d 141 (2d Cir. 2000) (references to plaintiff as a "fucking whining cunt" who received her job because she performed oral sex were enough to send the case to a jury).

3. *Summary Judgment or a Jury Question?* The Second Circuit has held that judges should be cautious in granting summary judgment in sexual harassment cases because juries are better qualified to evaluate appropriate behavior in the workplace:

> Today, while gender relations in the workplace are rapidly evolving, and views of what is appropriate behavior are diverse and shifting, a jury made up of a cross-section of our heterogenous communities provides the appropriate institution for deciding whether borderline situations should be characterized as sexual harassment.

Gallagher v. Delaney, 139 F.3d 338, 342 (2d Cir. 1998). *See* Theresa M. Beiner, *Let the Jury Decide: The Gap Between What Judges and Reasonable People Believe Is Sexually Harassing*, 75 S. CAL. L. REV. 791 (2002) (cautioning against summary judgment because "reasonable people believe that conduct is sexually harassing in situations that courts fail to acknowledge"). Despite these cautions, summary judgment for defendants is common, and some have warned that even cases that get to the jury may be decided by a group used to an "American popular culture [that] can, on occasion, be highly sexist and offensive. What *is*, is not always what is right, and reasonable people can take justifiable offense at comments that the vulgar among us, even if they are a majority, would consider acceptable." *Torres v. Pisano*, 116 F.3d 625, 633 n. 7 (2d Cir. 1997). Should expert witness testimony be admitted on what constitutes sexual harassment? *See* Donna Shestowsky, Note, *Where Is the Common Knowledge? Empirical Support for Requiring Expert Testimony in Sexual Harassment Trials*, 51 STAN. L. REV. 357 (1999).

4. *Non-Targeted Harassment.* Whether the conduct is targeted at the plaintiff may be relevant to whether it is viewed as sufficiently severe or pervasive. For an analysis of whether non-targeted workplace sexual conduct should amount to a Title VII violation and the potential ramifications if permitted, *see* Kelly Cahill Timmons, *Sexual Harassment and Disparate Impact: Should Non-Targeted Workplace Sexual Conduct be Actionable Under Title VII?*, 81 NEB. L. REV. 1152, 1155 (2003) (concluding "that non-targeted sexual conduct in the workplace should be actionable only if the conduct's disproportionate impact on women is great").

5. *Pervasiveness and Timeliness.* Contaminated workplace sexual harassment is often "pervasive" precisely because a number of incidents — no one of which may suffice — occur over a period of time and collectively alter the plaintiff's terms and conditions of employment. Title VII, however, has a very short period in which to file a charge with EEOC — 180 or 300 days from a violation. This raises a question of whether events occurring before that period can be the basis of a sexual harassment claim. In *National R.R. Passenger Corp. v. Morgan*, 536 U.S. 101 (2002), the Supreme Court held that "the entire scope of a hostile work environment claim, including behavior alleged outside the statutory time period, is permissible for the purposes of assessing liability, so long as any act contributing to that hostile environment takes place within the statutory time period." 536 U.S. at 117. See p. 598.

6. *Does Context Matter?* In discussing the requirement that conduct be severe or pervasive to be actionable, the *Oncale* Court states, "in same-sex (as in all) harassment cases, that inquiry requires careful consideration of the social context in which particular behavior occurs and is experienced by its target." What does that mean? Does the nature of the workplace matter? In *Williams v. General Motors*, 187 F.3d 553 (6th Cir. 1999), the court held that the standard for establishing sexual harassment does not vary with the work environment. The same standard applies, therefore, whether the complaint is asserted in a coarse blue-collar environment or in a more refined professional environment. Is this holding consistent with *Oncale?* Consider the following:

> It is true that the severity of alleged harassment must be assessed in light of the social mores of American workers and workplace culture, see *Oncale*, but nothing in *Oncale* even hints at the idea that prevailing culture can excuse discriminatory actions. Employers who tolerate workplaces marred by exclusionary practices and bigoted attitudes cannot use their discriminatory pasts to shield them from the present-day mandate of Title VII.

Smith v. Sheahan, 189 F.3d 529 (7th Cir. 1999). *See generally* Michael J. Frank, *The Social Context Variable in Hostile Environment Litigation*, 77 NOTRE DAME L. REV. 437 (2002); Rebecca K. Lee, *Pink, White, and Blue: Class Assumptions in the Judicial Interpretations of Title VII Hostile Environment Sex Harassment*, 70 BROOKLYN L. REV. 677 (2005). *See also* Melissa Hart, *Why* Jensen v. Eveleth *Didn't Change Sexual Harassment Law, But Still Has a Story Worth Telling*, 18 BERKELEY WOMEN'S L.J. 282 (2003) (reviewing Clara Bingham & Laura Leedy Gansler, CLASS ACTION: THE STORY OF LOIS JENSON AND THE LANDMARK CASE THAT CHANGED SEXUAL HARASSMENT LAW (2002)).

7. *Harassment BFOQ?* Is conduct that would otherwise constitute harassment ever permissible because of the necessities of the employment at question? In *Lyle v. Warner Brothers Television Productions*, 132 P.3d 211 (Cal. 2006), the California Supreme Court upheld summary judgment in favor of the employer, finding that in the context of the television show on which plaintiff was working (*Friends*), the language used by the writers could not reasonably be viewed as harassment of the plaintiff. If such conduct is justifiable, is it because sexualized activity is a BFOQ in such settings? *Lyle* analogized the argument to the "business necessity" defense in disparate impact cases. Was that an appropriate analogy? *See generally* Ann C. McGinley, *Harassment of Sex(y) Workers: Applying Title VII to Sexualized Industries*, 18 YALE J.L. & FEMINISM 65 (2006) (arguing for a contextual approach to harassment in sexualized environments that would look both to whether the employer "has explicitly or implicitly communicated to its employees that certain customer behavior and environmental conditions are necessary to the job performed and relate to the essence of the business, and the employees agree" and to whether a worker welcomes even behaviors not expected by the employer).

These issues often arise in institutions whose inmates harass their guards or keepers. Even in such settings, employers may be held liable if they do not take reasonable steps to protect their employees. *See Freitag v. Ayers*, 468 F.3d 528, 539 (9th Cir. 2006) (upholding jury harassment verdict for prison guard because "prison officials may [not] ignore sexually hostile conduct and refrain from taking corrective actions that would safeguard the rights of the victims, whether they be guards or inmates"); *Randolph v. Ohio Dep't of Youth Servs.*, 453 F.3d 724, 732 (6th Cir. 2006) (plaintiff's "allegations are so serious that they satisfy the hostile work environment prong despite the mitigating consideration of the prison work environment"). *But see Vajdl v. Mesabi Acad. of Kidspeace, Inc.*, 484 F.3d 546 (8th Cir. 2007) ("By choosing to work in a prison, corrections personnel have acknowledged and accepted the probability that they will face inappropriate and socially deviant behavior); *EEOC v. Nexion Health at Broadway, Inc.*, 199 Fed. Appx. 351, 354 (5th Cir. 2006) (since plaintiff worked in a nursing home "where most of the people around him were often unable to control" themselves, it was objectively unreasonable for him "to perceive a racially hostile work environment based solely on statements made by those who are mentally impaired").

b.   The "Reasonable Person" Requirement

Harris judges harassment in part by an objective standard. Thus, the fact that the victim feels harassed is not sufficient: the conduct must *reasonably* be perceived as hostile. But reasonably be perceived by whom? Presumably, by a reasonable person in the victim's shoes.

However, studies have shown that men and women may react differently to harassing conduct. Does that suggest that, if the victim is a woman, the conduct should be evaluated from the perspective of a reasonable woman? Prior to *Harris*, the Ninth Circuit adopted such an approach. In *Ellison v. Brady*, 924 F.2d 872 (9th Cir. 1991), the court stated:

> If we only examined whether a reasonable person would engage in allegedly harassing conduct, we would run the risk of reinforcing the prevailing level of discrimination. . . . We therefore prefer to analyze harassment from the victim's perspective. A complete understanding of the victim's view requires, among other things, an analysis of the different perspectives of men and women. Conduct that many men consider unobjectionable may offend many women.

Id. at 878. The Ninth Circuit's analysis in *Ellison* found support in Professor Kathryn Abrams' article, *Gender Discrimination and the Transformation of Workplace Norms*, 42 VAND. L. REV. 1183, 1203 (1989), in which she noted that the characteristically male view depicts sexual harassment as comparatively harmless amusement and stated that:

> While many women hold positive attitudes about uncoerced sex, their greater physical and social vulnerability to sexual coercion can make women wary of sexual encounters. Moreover, American women have been raised in a society where rape and sex-related violence have reached unprecedented levels, and a vast pornography industry creates continuous images of sexual coercion, objectification and violence. Finally, women as a group tend to hold more restrictive views of both the situation and type of relationship in which sexual conduct is appropriate. Because of the inequality and coercion with which it is so frequently associated in the minds of women, the appearance of sexuality in an unexpected context or a setting of ostensible equality can be an anguishing experience.

Id. at 1205.

After *Harris*, the Ninth Circuit modified its standard for evaluating sexual harassment in an attempt to reconcile *Ellison* with the standard applied in *Harris*: "[w]hether the workplace is objectively hostile must be determined from the perspective of a reasonable person with the same fundamental characteristics." *Fuller v. City of Oakland*, 47 F.3d 1522, 1527 (9th Cir. 1995). But in *McGinest v. GTE Service Corp.*, 360 F.3d 1103, 1115 (9th Cir. 2004), a racially hostile work environment case, the Ninth Circuit adopted the *Ellison* holding, saying when "evaluating the significance of the statements in question, [the court considers] the hostility of the workplace from the perspective of the . . . reasonable person belonging to the racial or ethnic group of the plaintiff." The court did note that other courts have read *Harris* to reject a "reasonable person standard based on the perspective of a person sharing the characteristics of the plaintiff." Which is the better reading of *Harris?*

c. "Unwelcome" Conduct

Harris also made clear that it is not enough for the conduct to reasonably be perceived as hostile or abusive; the victim herself must *subjectively* perceive the conduct to be abusive for a Title VII violation to exist. For example, the Eighth Circuit recently held that no sexual harassment claim could exist if a plaintiff were unaware she was being watched by her supervisor through a peephole into the restroom. *Cottrell v. MFA Inc.*, 443 F.3d 629 (8th Cir. 2006). If she did not know the conduct was occurring, the conduct could not have altered her work environment, reasoned the court. Do you agree that is a correct reading of *Meritor* and *Harris?*

Meritor had required that harassment be "unwelcome" to be actionable. *Harris* did not mention "welcomeness" but spoke of the victim's subjective perception that the conduct be abusive. Are the two standards simply different ways of saying the same thing? In most cases, it should be sufficient for this prong for a plaintiff to simply testify she found the conduct unwelcome or offensive. Occasionally, however, defendants have attempted to rebut the allegation that the conduct was unwelcome by introducing evidence of the plaintiff's behavior, language or appearance. Recall that in *Meritor* the Court stated that Vinson's style of dress was "obviously relevant" to the question whether she welcomed Taylor's sexual advances. Does this mean that an employee who dresses in a sexually provocative manner can lose her right to be free of sexual harassment? Surely not. And the Seventh Circuit recently rejected a "welcoming" argument by defendant when the girl in question was underage when the harassment occurred, *Doe v. Oberweis Dairy*, 456 F.3d 704, 714 (7th Cir. 2006), and thus legally precluded from welcoming it.

But might a woman's conduct somehow permit conduct that would otherwise be impermissible? Might "welcoming" refer not to her subjective feelings but what a reasonable man might perceive she welcomed? Is that why *Meritor* felt Ms. Vinson's conduct was obviously relevant? Suppose a woman uses foul language or tells off-color jokes at work. Does her behavior preclude her from successfully claiming she was offended when supervisors or co-workers engage in similar conduct? In determining whether a victim's behavior precludes recovery because she welcomed sexually charged comments or behavior, courts seem to weigh the victim's conduct against that of the alleged perpetrators. *Compare Carr v. Allison Gas Turbine Div.*, 32 F.3d 1007 (7th Cir. 1994) (plaintiff's bawdy behavior and use of foul language did not constitute welcoming behavior justifying four years of extensive harassment that included derogatory sexual comments, foul names, sex-related pranks, and sexual graffiti and pictures), *with Horney v. Westfield Gage Co.*, 77 Fed. Appx. 24, 28-30 n. 1 (1st Cir. 2003) (defendants could proffer evidence that plaintiff bared her breasts while working at a previous job to show that vulgar sexual remarks made to her by her supervisor at a later place of employment were not unwelcome).

Plaintiffs have been understood to bear the burden of proving they subjectively perceived the conduct to be sufficiently offensive, a burden placement that has been criticized. *See* Mary F. Radford, *By Invitation Only: The Proof of Welcomeness in Sexual Harassment Cases*, 72 N.C. L. REV. 499 (1994) (arguing that defendants should bear the burden of proving welcomeness). After all, in harassment cases not involving sex, the question of "welcomeness" is rarely at issue or discussed.

However, in the wake of the next principal case, the burden of proof on the question of whether the victim subjectively viewed the conduct as hostile and offensive may, in many cases, have been shifted to the defendant as a practical matter. As you read it, ask yourself whether the affirmative defense makes the "welcomeness" inquiry unnecessary in most sexual harassment cases. *See* Henry L. Chambers, Jr., *(Un)Welcome Conduct and the Sexually Hostile Work Environment*, 53 ALA. L. REV. 733 (2002).

d. Vicarious Liability

BURLINGTON INDUSTRIES, INC. v. ELLERTH
524 U.S. 742 (1998)

Justice KENNEDY delivered the opinion of the Court.

We decide whether, under Title VII of the Civil Rights Act of 1964, an employee who refuses the unwelcome and threatening sexual advances of a supervisor, yet suffers no adverse, tangible job consequences, can recover against the employer without showing the employer is negligent or otherwise at fault for the supervisor's actions.

I

Summary judgment was granted for the employer, so we must take the facts alleged by the employee to be true. The employer is Burlington Industries, the petitioner. The employee is Kimberly Ellerth, the respondent. From March 1993 until May 1994, Ellerth worked as a salesperson in one of Burlington's divisions in Chicago, Illinois. During her employment, she alleges, she was subjected to constant sexual harassment by her supervisor, one Ted Slowik.

In the hierarchy of Burlington's management structure, Slowik was a mid-level manager. . . . He had authority to make hiring and promotion decisions subject to the approval of his supervisor, who signed the paperwork. According to Slowik's supervisor, his position was "not considered an upper-level management position," and he was "not amongst the decision-making or policy-making hierarchy." Slowik was not Ellerth's immediate supervisor. Ellerth worked in a two-person office in Chicago, and she answered to her office colleague, who in turn answered to Slowik in New York.

Against a background of repeated boorish and offensive remarks and gestures which Slowik allegedly made, Ellerth places particular emphasis on three alleged incidents where Slowik's comments could be construed as threats to deny her tangible job benefits. In the summer of 1993, while on a business trip, Slowik invited Ellerth to the hotel lounge, an invitation Ellerth felt compelled to accept because

Slowik was her boss. When Ellerth gave no encouragement to remarks Slowik made about her breasts, he told her to "loosen up" and warned, "[y]ou know, Kim, I could make your life very hard or very easy at Burlington."

In March 1994, when Ellerth was being considered for a promotion, Slowik expressed reservations during the promotion interview because she was not "loose enough." The comment was followed by his reaching over and rubbing her knee. Ellerth did receive the promotion; but when Slowik called to announce it, he told Ellerth, "you're gonna be out there with men who work in factories, and they certainly like women with pretty butts/legs."

In May 1994, Ellerth called Slowik, asking permission to insert a customer's logo into a fabric sample. Slowik responded, "I don't have time for you right now, Kim — unless you want to tell me what you're wearing." Ellerth told Slowik she had to go and ended the call. A day or two later, Ellerth called Slowik to ask permission again. This time he denied her request, but added something along the lines of, "are you wearing shorter skirts yet, Kim, because it would make your job a whole heck of a lot easier."

A short time later, Ellerth's immediate supervisor cautioned her about returning telephone calls to customers in a prompt fashion. In response, Ellerth quit. She faxed a letter giving reasons unrelated to the alleged sexual harassment we have described. About three weeks later, however, she sent a letter explaining she quit because of Slowik's behavior.

During her tenure at Burlington, Ellerth did not inform anyone in authority about Slowik's conduct, despite knowing Burlington had a policy against sexual harassment. In fact, she chose not to inform her immediate supervisor (not Slowik) because " 'it would be his duty as my supervisor to report any incidents of sexual harassment.' " On one occasion, she told Slowik a comment he made was inappropriate.

. . . The District Court granted summary judgment to Burlington. The Court found Slowik's behavior, as described by Ellerth, severe and pervasive enough to create a hostile work environment, but found Burlington neither knew nor should have known about the conduct. . . .

The Court of Appeals en banc reversed in a decision which produced eight separate opinions and no consensus for a controlling rationale. . . .

II

At the outset, we assume an important proposition yet to be established before a trier of fact. It is a premise assumed as well, in explicit or implicit terms, in the various opinions by the judges of the Court of Appeals. The premise is: a trier of fact could find in Slowik's remarks numerous threats to retaliate against Ellerth if she denied some sexual liberties. The threats, however, were not carried out or fulfilled. Cases based on threats which are carried out are referred to often as *quid pro quo* cases, as distinct from bothersome attentions or sexual remarks that are sufficiently severe or pervasive to create a hostile work environment. The terms *quid pro quo* and hostile work environment are helpful, perhaps, in making a rough demarcation between cases in which threats are carried out and those where they are not or are absent altogether, but beyond this are of limited utility.

Section 703(a) of Title VII forbids "an employer" —

(1) to fail or refuse to hire or to discharge any individual, or otherwise to discriminate against any individual with respect to his compensation, terms, conditions or privileges of employment, because of such individual's . . . sex.

"*Quid pro quo*" and "hostile work environment" do not appear in the statutory text. The terms appeared first in the academic literature, found their way into decisions of the Courts of Appeals, and were mentioned in this Court's decision in *Meritor*.

In *Meritor*, the terms served a specific and limited purpose. There we considered whether the conduct in question constituted discrimination in the terms or conditions of employment in violation of Title VII. We assumed, and with adequate reason, that if an employer demanded sexual favors from an employee in return for a job benefit, discrimination with respect to terms or conditions of employment was explicit. Less obvious was whether an employer's sexually demeaning behavior altered terms or conditions of employment in violation of Title VII. We distinguished between *quid pro quo* claims and hostile environment claims, and said both were cognizable under Title VII, though the latter requires harassment that is severe or pervasive. The principal significance of the distinction is to instruct that Title VII is violated by either explicit or constructive alterations in the terms or conditions of employment and to explain the latter must be severe or pervasive. The distinction was not discussed for its bearing upon an employer's liability for an employee's discrimination. On this question *Meritor* held, with no further specifics, that agency principles controlled.

Nevertheless, as use of the terms grew in the wake of *Meritor*, they acquired their own significance. The standard of employer responsibility turned on which type of harassment occurred. If the plaintiff established a quid pro quo claim, the Courts of Appeals held, the employer was subject to vicarious liability. The rule encouraged Title VII plaintiffs to state their claims as quid pro quo claims, which in turn put expansive pressure on the definition. The equivalence of the quid pro quo label and vicarious liability is illustrated by this case. The question presented on certiorari is whether Ellerth can state a claim of quid pro quo harassment, but the issue of real concern to the parties is whether Burlington has vicarious liability for Slowik's alleged misconduct, rather than liability limited to its own negligence. . . .

We do not suggest the terms *quid pro quo* and hostile work environment are irrelevant to Title VII litigation. To the extent they illustrate the distinction between cases involving a threat which is carried out and offensive conduct in general, the terms are relevant when there is a threshold question whether a plaintiff can prove discrimination in violation of Title VII. When a plaintiff proves that a tangible employment action resulted from a refusal to submit to a supervisor's sexual demands, he or she establishes that the employment decision itself constitutes a change in the terms and conditions of employment that is actionable under Title VII. For any sexual harassment preceding the employment decision to be actionable, however, the conduct must be severe or pervasive. Because Ellerth's claim involves only unfulfilled threats, it should be categorized as a hostile work environment claim which requires a showing of severe or pervasive conduct. For purposes of this case, we accept the District Court's finding that the alleged conduct was severe or pervasive. The case before us involves numerous alleged threats, and we express no opinion as to whether a single unfulfilled threat is sufficient to constitute discrimination in the terms or conditions of employment.

When we assume discrimination can be proved, however, the factors we discuss below, and not the categories *quid pro quo* and hostile work environment, will be controlling on the issue of vicarious liability. That is the question we must resolve.

III

We must decide, then, whether an employer has vicarious liability when a supervisor creates a hostile work environment by making explicit threats to alter a subordinate's terms or conditions of employment, based on sex, but does not fulfill the threat. We turn to principles of agency law, for the term "employer" is defined under Title VII to include "agents." . . .

As *Meritor* acknowledged, the Restatement (Second) of Agency (1957) (hereinafter Restatement), is a useful beginning point for a discussion of general agency principles. . . .

A

Section 219(1) of the Restatement sets out a central principle of agency law:

> A master is subject to liability for the torts of his servants committed while acting in the scope of their employment.

An employer may be liable for both negligent and intentional torts committed by an employee within the scope of his or her employment. Sexual harassment under Title VII presupposes intentional conduct. While early decisions absolved employers of liability for the intentional torts of their employees, the law now imposes liability where the employee's "purpose, however misguided, is wholly or in part to further the master's business." W. Keeton, D. Dobbs, R. Keeton & D. Owen, Prosser and Keeton on Law of Torts § 70, p. 505 (5th ed. 1984) (hereinafter Prosser and Keeton on Torts). In applying scope of employment principles to intentional torts, however, it is accepted that "it is less likely that a willful tort will properly be held to be in the course of employment and that the liability of the master for such torts will naturally be more limited." F. Mechem, Outlines of the Law of Agency § 394, p. 266 (P. Mechem 4th ed., 1952). The Restatement defines conduct, including an intentional tort, to be within the scope of employment when "actuated, at least in part, by a purpose to serve the [employer]," even if it is forbidden by the employer. Restatement §§ 228(1)(c), 230.

As Courts of Appeals have recognized, a supervisor acting out of gender-based animus or a desire to fulfill sexual urges may not be actuated by a purpose to serve the employer. The harassing supervisor often acts for personal motives, motives unrelated and even antithetical to the objectives of the employer. There are instances, of course, where a supervisor engages in unlawful discrimination with the purpose, mistaken or otherwise, to serve the employer.

The general rule is that sexual harassment by a supervisor is not conduct within the scope of employment.

B

Scope of employment does not define the only basis for employer liability under agency principles. In limited circumstances, agency principles impose liability on employers even where employees commit torts outside the scope of employment. The principles are set forth in the much-cited § 219(2) of the Restatement:

> (2) A master is not subject to liability for the torts of his servants acting outside the scope of their employment, unless:
> (a) the master intended the conduct or the consequences, or
> (b) the master was negligent or reckless, or
> (c) the conduct violated a non-delegable duty of the master, or
> (d) the servant purported to act or to speak on behalf of the principal and there was reliance upon apparent authority, or he was aided in accomplishing the tort by the existence of the agency relation.

Subsection (a) addresses direct liability, where the employer acts with tortious intent, and indirect liability, where the agent's high rank in the company makes him or her the employer's alter ego. None of the parties contend Slowik's rank imputes liability under this principle. There is no contention, furthermore, that a non-delegable duty is involved. See § 219(2)(c). So, for our purposes here, subsections (a) and (c) can be put aside.

Subsections (b) and (d) are possible grounds for imposing employer liability on account of a supervisor's acts and must be considered. Under subsection (b), an employer is liable when the tort is attributable to the employer's own negligence. Thus, although a supervisor's sexual harassment is outside the scope of employment because the conduct was for personal motives, an employer can be liable, nonetheless, where its own negligence is a cause of the harassment. An employer is negligent with respect to sexual harassment if it knew or should have known about the conduct and failed to stop it. Negligence sets a minimum standard for employer liability under Title VII; but Ellerth seeks to invoke the more stringent standard of vicarious liability.

Subsection 219(2)(d) concerns vicarious liability for intentional torts committed by an employee when the employee uses apparent authority (the apparent authority standard), or when the employee "was aided in accomplishing the tort by the existence of the agency relation" (the aided in the agency relation standard). As other federal decisions have done in discussing vicarious liability for supervisor harassment, we begin with § 219(2)(d).

C

As a general rule, apparent authority is relevant where the agent purports to exercise a power which he or she does not have, as distinct from where the agent threatens to misuse actual power. In the usual case, a supervisor's harassment involves misuse of actual power, not the false impression of its existence. Apparent authority analysis therefore is inappropriate in this context. If, in the unusual case, it is alleged there is a false impression that the actor was a supervisor, when he in fact was not, the victim's mistaken conclusion must be a reasonable one. When a party seeks to impose vicarious liability based on an agent's misuse of delegated authority, the Restatement's aided in the agency relation rule, rather than the apparent authority rule, appears to be the appropriate form of analysis.

D

We turn to the aided in the agency relation standard. In a sense, most workplace tortfeasors are aided in accomplishing their tortious objective by the existence of the agency relation: Proximity and regular contact may afford a captive pool of potential victims. Were this to satisfy the aided in the agency relation standard, an employer would be subject to vicarious liability not only for all supervisor harassment, but also for all co-worker harassment, a result enforced by neither the EEOC nor any court of appeals to have considered the issue. The aided in the agency relation standard, therefore, requires the existence of something more than the employment relation itself.

At the outset, we can identify a class of cases where, beyond question, more than the mere existence of the employment relation aids in commission of the harassment: when a supervisor takes a tangible employment action against the subordinate.

Every Federal Court of Appeals to have considered the question has found vicarious liability when a discriminatory act results in a tangible employment action. In *Meritor*, we acknowledged this consensus . . . Although few courts have elaborated how agency principles support this rule, we think it reflects a correct application of the aided in the agency relation standard.

In the context of this case, a tangible employment action would have taken the form of a denial of a raise or a promotion. The concept of a tangible employment action appears in numerous cases in the Courts of Appeals discussing claims involving race, age, and national origin discrimination, as well as sex discrimination. Without endorsing the specific results of those decisions, we think it prudent to import the concept of a tangible employment action for resolution of the vicarious liability issue we consider here. A tangible employment action constitutes a significant change in employment status, such as hiring, firing, failing to promote, reassignment with significantly different responsibilities, or a decision causing a significant change in benefits. Compare *Crady v. Liberty Nat. Bank & Trust Co. of Ind.*, 993 F.2d 132, 136 (7th Cir. 1993) ("A materially adverse change might be indicated by a termination of employment, a demotion evidenced by a decrease in wage or salary, a less distinguished title, a material loss of benefits, significantly diminished material responsibilities, or other indices that might be unique to a particular situation"), with *Flaherty v. Gas Research Institute*, 31 F.3d 451, 456 (7th Cir. 1994) (a "bruised ego" is not enough); *Kocsis v. Multi-Care Management, Inc.*, 97 F.3d 876, 887 (6th Cir. 1996) (demotion without change in pay, benefits, duties, or prestige insufficient); and *Harlston v. McDonnell Douglas Corp.*, 37 F.3d 379, 382 (8th Cir. 1994) (reassignment to more inconvenient job insufficient).

When a supervisor makes a tangible employment decision, there is assurance the injury could not have been inflicted absent the agency relation. A tangible employment action in most cases inflicts direct economic harm. As a general proposition, only a supervisor, or other person acting with the authority of the company, can cause this sort of injury. A co-worker can break a co-worker's arm as easily as a supervisor, and anyone who has regular contact with an employee can inflict psychological injuries by his or her offensive conduct. But one co-worker (absent some elaborate scheme) cannot dock another's pay, nor can one co-worker demote another. Tangible employment actions fall within the special province of the supervisor. The supervisor has been empowered by the company as a distinct class of agent to make economic decisions affecting other employees under his or her control.

Tangible employment actions are the means by which the supervisor brings the official power of the enterprise to bear on subordinates. A tangible employment decision requires an official act of the enterprise, a company act. The decision in most cases is documented in official company records, and may be subject to review by higher level supervisors. The supervisor often must obtain the imprimatur of the enterprise and use its internal processes.

For these reasons, a tangible employment action taken by the supervisor becomes for Title VII purposes the act of the employer. Whatever the exact contours of the aided in the agency relation standard, its requirements will always be met when a supervisor takes a tangible employment action against a subordinate. In that instance, it would be implausible to interpret agency principles to allow an employer to escape liability, as *Meritor* itself appeared to acknowledge.

Whether the agency relation aids in commission of supervisor harassment which does not culminate in a tangible employment action is less obvious. Application of the standard is made difficult by its malleable terminology, which can be read to either expand or limit liability in the context of supervisor harassment. On the one hand, a supervisor's power and authority invests his or her harassing conduct with a particular threatening character, and in this sense, a supervisor always is aided by the agency relation. See *Meritor.* (Marshall, J., concurring in judgment) ("It is precisely because the supervisor is understood to be clothed with the employer's authority that he is able to impose unwelcome sexual conduct on subordinates"). On the other hand, there are acts of harassment a supervisor might commit which might be the same acts a co-employee would commit, and there may be some circumstances where the supervisor's status makes little difference.

It is this tension which, we think, has caused so much confusion among the Courts of Appeals which have sought to apply the aided in the agency relation standard to Title VII cases. The aided in the agency relation standard, however, is a developing feature of agency law, and we hesitate to render a definitive explanation of our understanding of the standard in an area where other important considerations must affect our judgment. In particular, we are bound by our holding in *Meritor* that agency principles constrain the imposition of vicarious liability in cases of supervisory harassment. See *Meritor* ("Congress' decision to define 'employer' to include any 'agent' of an employer, 42 U.S.C. § 2000e(b), surely evinces an intent to place some limits on the acts of employees for which employers under Title VII are to be held responsible"). Congress has not altered *Meritor*'s rule even though it has made significant amendments to Title VII in the interim. Although *Meritor* suggested the limitation on employer liability stemmed from agency principles, the Court acknowledged other considerations might be relevant as well. For example, Title VII is designed to encourage the creation of antiharassment policies and effective grievance mechanisms. Were employer liability to depend in part on an employer's effort to create such procedures, it would effect Congress' intention to promote conciliation rather than litigation in the Title VII context and the EEOC's policy of encouraging the development of grievance procedures. See 29 CFR § 1604.11(f) (1997); EEOC Policy Guidance on Sexual Harassment, 8 BNA FEP Manual 405:6699 (Mar. 19, 1990). To the extent limiting employer liability could encourage employees to report harassing conduct before it becomes severe or pervasive, it would also serve Title VII's deterrent purpose. As we have observed, Title VII borrows from tort law the avoidable consequences doctrine, and the considerations which animate that doctrine would also support the limitation of employer liability in certain circumstances.

In order to accommodate the agency principles of vicarious liability for harm caused by misuse of supervisory authority, as well as Title VII's equally basic policies of encouraging forethought by employers and saving action by objecting employees, we adopt the following holding in this case and in *Faragher v. Boca Raton*, also decided today. An employer is subject to vicarious liability to a victimized employee for an actionable hostile environment created by a supervisor with immediate (or successively higher) authority over the employee. When no tangible employment action is taken, a defending employer may raise an affirmative defense to liability or damages, subject to proof by a preponderance of the evidence. The defense comprises two necessary elements: (a) that the employer exercised reasonable care to prevent and correct promptly any sexually harassing behavior, and (b) that the plaintiff employee unreasonably failed to take advantage of any preventive or corrective opportunities provided by the employer or to avoid harm otherwise. While proof that an employer had promulgated an anti-harassment policy with complaint procedure is not necessary in every instance as a matter of law, the need for a stated policy suitable to the employment circumstances may appropriately be addressed in any case when litigating the first element of the defense. And while proof that an employee failed to fulfill the corresponding obligation of reasonable care to avoid harm is not limited to showing any unreasonable failure to use any complaint procedure provided by the employer, a demonstration of such failure will normally suffice to satisfy the employer's burden under the second element of the defense. No affirmative defense is available, however, when the supervisor's harassment culminates in a tangible employment action, such as discharge, demotion, or undesirable reassignment.

[The Court remanded so Ms. Ellerth would have an adequate opportunity to prove she has a claim for which Burlington is liable and so Burlington would have an opportunity to prove its affirmative defense.]

NOTES

1. *Employer Liability and Harassment Claims.* In a part of *Meritor* not reproduced previously, the Court addressed, but did not fully resolve one of the major issues in sexual harassment cases — under what circumstances is the *employer* liable for harassment in the workplace? The *Meritor* Court did not impose liability automatically:

> ... Congress' decision to define "employer" to include any "agent" of an employer, 42 U.S.C. §2000e(b), surely evinces an intent to place some limits on the acts of employees for which employers under Title VII are to be held responsible. For this reason, we hold that the Court of Appeals erred in concluding that employers are always automatically liable for sexual harassment by their supervisors. For the same reason, absence of notice to an employer does not necessarily insulate that employer from liability.
>
> ... [W]e reject petitioner's view that the mere existence of a grievance procedure and a policy against discrimination, coupled with respondent's failure to invoke that procedure, must insulate petitioner from liability. While those facts are plainly relevant, the situation before us demonstrates why they are not necessarily dispositive. Petitioner's general nondiscrimination policy did not address sexual harassment in particular, and thus did not alert employees to their employer's interest in correcting that form of discrimination. Moreover, the bank's grievance procedure apparently required an employee to complain first to her supervisor, in this case Taylor. Since Taylor was the alleged perpetrator, it is not altogether surprising that respondent failed to invoke the procedure and report her grievance to him. Petitioner's contention that respondent's failure should insulate it from liability might be substantially stronger if its procedures were better calculated to encourage victims of harassment to come forward.

Meritor Savings Bank v. Vinson, 477 U.S. 57, 72-73 (1986).

Resolving the issue of employer liability is particularly important because, although Title VII defines "employer" to include "any agent" of an employer, courts have generally refused to hold individual employees personally liable for their discriminatory conduct. See Chapter 8 at p. 699. If employers are not liable for their supervisors' conduct, there will typically be no liability for admittedly harassing conduct. *Ellerth,* and *Faragher v. City of Boca Raton,* 524 U.S. 775 (1998), a companion case to *Ellerth,* attempted to resolve the issues *Meritor* left open. *Faragher* adopted the same holding as in *Ellerth. See id.* at 802-08. Did the Court in *Ellerth* and *Faragher* create a rule of employer liability that is fair to plaintiffs? Is this rule fair to defendants?

2. *The Use of Agency Principles.* Prior to *Ellerth,* courts held that, if the harasser is himself in a high enough position in the employer's hierarchy, the actions and knowledge of the harasser are imputed to the employer, what *Ellerth* referred to as "alter ego" liability. In *Faragher,* the Court addressed imputed liability:

> [It was not] exceptional that standards for binding the employer were not in issue in *Harris.* In that case of discrimination by hostile environment, the individual charged with creating the abusive atmosphere was the president of the corporate employer, who was indisputably within that class of an employer organization's officials who may be treated as the organization's proxy.

524 U.S. at 790. *Ellerth* also notes the possibility of "direct liability, where the employer acts with tortious intent, and indirect liability, where the agent's high rank in the company makes him or her the employer's alter ego." 524 U.S. at 758. Is the defense created in *Ellerth* and *Faragher* available in cases in which the harasser's actions are imputed to the employer under the "alter ego" or "proxy" approach? *See Ackel v. Nat'l Communications, Inc.,* 339 F.3d 376, 383-84 (5th Cir. 2003) (interpreting *Faragher* and *Ellerth* to mean that an employer is vicariously liable for its employees' activities and the affirmative defense is not available if the harassing employee is a proxy for the employer).

3. *Who Is a Supervisor?* In the more usual situation, the threshold question will be whether the harasser is a supervisor or not. Supervisors are capable of taking "tangible employment actions" and thus incurring employer liability automatically. They are also capable of other kinds of harassment for which the employer is presumptively liable, although the employer is able to assert the affirmative defense. Is any individual with supervisory status necessarily a supervisor for purposes of imposing vicarious liability under *Ellerth* and *Faragher?* The analysis of the two cases suggests the answer is no. *See Swinton v. Potomac Corp.,* 270 F.3d 794 (9th Cir. 2001) (actions of supervisor who had no supervisory authority over the plaintiff could not subject employer to vicarious liability); *Merritt v. Albemarle Corp.,* 496 F.3d 880 (8th Cir. 2007) (individual who could not take a tangible job action against the plaintiff was not a supervisor).

Some cases have been grudging over who counts as a "supervisor" even when the harasser supervises the plaintiff's work. *E.g., Rhodes v. Ill. Dep't of Transp.,* 359 F.3d 498, 506 (7th Cir. 2004) (although harassers "managed plaintiff's work assignments, investigated complaints and disputes, and made recommendations concerning sanctions for rule violations," neither had authority to affect the terms and conditions of Rhodes' employment); *Weyers v. Lear Operations Corp.,* 359 F.3d 1049, 1057-58 (8th Cir. 2004) ("Although Brosius had the authority as team leader to assign employees to particular tasks, he could not reassign them to significantly different duties. While it is true that Brosius signed at least three of Weyers's initial performance evaluations and that Tony Mendez acknowledged that he had based his decision to terminate Weyers at least in part on Weyers's job evaluation scores, Brosius himself did not have the authority to take tangible employment action against Weyers"). *Cf. Valentine v. City of Chi.,* 452 F.3d 670, 678 (7th Cir. 2006) (there was a material question of fact as to whether an individual was plaintiff's supervisor since a supervisor is one who has "the power to hire, fire, demote, promote, transfer, or discipline an employee," and the person in question had at least the power to transfer employees between lots).

4. *Tangible Employment Actions.* A key issue in the wake of *Ellerth* and *Faragher* is what constitutes a tangible employment action. "Determining whether the complaining employee has suffered a tangible employment action is the indispensable

first step in every supervisor sexual harassment/vicarious liability case under Title VII." *Casiano v. AT&T Corp.*, 213 F.3d 278, 284 (5th Cir. 2000) (*see also* "Supervisor Sexual Harassment Roadmap" at app., 213 F.3d at 288). Deciding whether a tangible employment action has occurred is often outcome determinative since the employer may not assert the affirmative defense if a supervisor's discrimination results in a tangible employment action. But courts have yet to agree on what constitutes a tangible employment action. Is a lateral transfer a tangible employment action if an employee's pay is not affected? Is being assigned different tasks? Being denied perks such as travel to conferences? *See Roebuck v. Washington*, 408 F.3d 790 (D.C. Cir. 2005) (changing door locks, ordering a transfer and then rescinding it, and a lateral transfer of plaintiff were not tangible employment actions; it is not the official nature of the act that matters but whether it has a significant effect on the plaintiff's employment status).

One commentator, Rebecca Hanner White, *De Minimis Discrimination*, 47 EMORY L.J. 1121, 1158 (1998), asserts that the best way to determine whether an action is tangible within the meaning of *Ellerth* and *Faragher* is to look to the agency theory relied on in those cases and thus to examine whether the action is one the supervisor's authority *as supervisor* enabled him to take. If so, it should be deemed a tangible employment action:

> Only a supervisor can transfer, reassign, or negatively evaluate a worker, but supervisors and co-workers alike may use racial epithets, may hurt an employee's feelings, or smack an employee on the rear. When the supervisor "brings the official power of the enterprise to bear on subordinates" — a "decision in most cases . . . documented in official company records and . . . subject to review by higher level supervisors" — such action, if discriminatorily motivated, will be attributed to the employer. . . . Accordingly, it is not the economic or materially adverse nature of the discrimination that makes [the employer vicariously liable] but the fact that it involves an action only supervisors can inflict on their subordinates.

In *Jin v. Metropolitan Life Insurance Co.*, 310 F.3d 84 (2d Cir. 2002), the court employed a similar analysis to find that a supervisor's insistence that an employee engage in sex acts or be fired was a tangible employment action when the employee submitted to the demands. Even if the employee suffered no economic harm, it was the supervisor's position of power to terminate or retain plaintiff and to require her to report to his private office where the abuse occurred that enabled him to take the actions. *Accord Holly D. v. Cal. Inst. of Tech.*, 339 F.3d 1158 (9th Cir. 2003) (an employee who consents to her supervisor's sexual demands in order to avoid threatened termination has suffered a "tangible employment action"). *But see* Heather S. Murr, *The Continuing Expansive Pressure to Hold Employers Strictly Liable for Supervisory Sexual Extortion: An Alternative Approach Based on Reasonableness*, 39 U.C. DAVIS L. REV. 529 (2006) (imposing strict liability in supervisory sexual extortion cases is inconsistent both with the Court's jurisprudence regarding tangible employment actions and with congressional intent regarding Title VII's goals of preventing and deterring harassment).

Professor White's approach to "tangible employment actions" is broader than that followed by numerous lower courts. Is it too broad? Professor Michael Harper suggests a somewhat different analysis. He asserts that a tangible employment action should be viewed as any supervisory action that is recorded or reported, as it would be "readily available for review." Michael C. Harper, *Employer Liability for Harassment Under Title VII: A Functional Rationale for* Faragher *and* Ellerth, 36

SAN DIEGO L. REV. 41 (1999). For an article analyzing the lower courts' approaches to "tangible employment actions" and criticizing these approaches, *see* Susan Grover, *After* Ellerth: *The Tangible Employment Action in Sexual Harassment Analysis*, 35 U. MICH. J.L. REFORM 809 (2002).

5. *Scope of Employment.* After *Ellerth*, can sexual harassment by a supervisor be "within the scope of employment" of the supervisor? Suppose a supervisor, in order to boost sales, requires female employees to wear revealing attire that generates severe and pervasive responses by customers? *See EEOC v. Sage Realty Co.*, 507 F. Supp. 599 (S.D.N.Y. 1981). If employer liability can be based on harassment being "within the scope of employment" of a supervisor, is the defense created in *Ellerth* available, or is the defense available only when "agency" is based on the "aided in the agency relation" approach and no "tangible employment actions" are involved?

PENNSYLVANIA STATE POLICE v. SUDERS
542 U.S. 129 (2004)

GINSBURG, J.

Plaintiff-respondent Nancy Drew Suders alleged sexually harassing conduct by her supervisors, officers of the Pennsylvania State Police (PSP), of such severity she was forced to resign. The question presented concerns the proof burdens parties bear when a sexual harassment/constructive discharge claim of that character is asserted under Title VII of the Civil Rights Act of 1964.

To establish hostile work environment, plaintiffs like Suders must show harassing behavior "sufficiently severe or pervasive to alter the conditions of [their] employment." [citing *Meritor* and *Harris*]. Beyond that, we hold, to establish "constructive discharge," the plaintiff must make a further showing: She must show that the abusive working environment became so intolerable that her resignation qualified as a fitting response. An employer may defend against such a claim by showing both (1) that it had installed a readily accessible and effective policy for reporting and resolving complaints of sexual harassment, and (2) that the plaintiff unreasonably failed to avail herself of that employer-provided preventive or remedial apparatus. This affirmative defense will not be available to the employer, however, if the plaintiff quits in reasonable response to an employer-sanctioned adverse action officially changing her employment status or situation, for example, a humiliating demotion, extreme cut in pay, or transfer to a position in which she would face unbearable working conditions. In so ruling today, we follow the path marked by our 1998 decisions in *Burlington Industries, Inc. v. Ellerth*, and *Faragher v. Boca Raton*.

I . . .

In March 1998, the PSP hired Suders as a police communications operator for the McConnellsburg barracks. Suders' supervisors were Sergeant Eric D. Easton, Station Commander at the McConnellsburg barracks, Patrol Corporal William D. Baker, and Corporal Eric B. Prendergast. Those three supervisors subjected Suders to a continuous barrage of sexual harassment that ceased only when she resigned from the force.

Easton "would bring up [the subject of] people having sex with animals" each time Suders entered his office. He told Prendergast, in front of Suders, that young girls should be given instruction in how to gratify men with oral sex. Easton also would sit down near Suders, wearing spandex shorts, and spread his legs apart. Apparently imitating a move popularized by television wrestling, Baker repeatedly made an obscene gesture in Suders' presence by grabbing his genitals and shouting out a vulgar comment inviting oral sex. Baker made this gesture as many as five-to-ten times per night throughout Suders' employment at the barracks. Suders once told Baker she "didn't think [he] should be doing this"; Baker responded by jumping on a chair and again performing the gesture, with the accompanying vulgarity. Further, Baker would "rub his rear end in front of her and remark 'I have a nice ass, don't I?' " Prendergast told Suders " 'the village idiot could do her job' "; wearing black gloves, he would pound on furniture to intimidate her.[2]

In June 1998, Prendergast accused Suders of taking a missing accident file home with her. After that incident, Suders approached the PSP's Equal Employment Opportunity Officer, Virginia Smith-Elliott, and told her she "might need some help." Smith-Elliott gave Suders her telephone number, but neither woman followed up on the conversation. On August 18, 1998, Suders contacted Smith-Elliott again, this time stating that she was being harassed and was afraid. Smith-Elliott told Suders to file a complaint, but did not tell her how to obtain the necessary form. Smith-Elliott's response and the manner in which it was conveyed appeared to Suders insensitive and unhelpful.

Two days later, Suders' supervisors arrested her for theft, and Suders resigned from the force. The theft arrest occurred in the following circumstances. Suders had several times taken a computer-skills exam to satisfy a PSP job requirement. Each time, Suders' supervisors told her that she had failed. Suders one day came upon her exams in a set of drawers in the women's locker room. She concluded that her supervisors had never forwarded the tests for grading and that their reports of her failures were false. Regarding the tests as her property, Suders removed them from the locker room. Upon finding that the exams had been removed, Suders' supervisors devised a plan to arrest her for theft. The officers dusted the drawer in which the exams had been stored with a theft-detection powder that turns hands blue when touched. As anticipated by Easton, Baker, and Prendergast, Suders attempted to return the tests to the drawer, whereupon her hands turned telltale blue. The supervisors then apprehended and handcuffed her, photographed her blue hands, and commenced to question her. Suders had previously prepared a written resignation, which she tendered soon after the supervisors detained her. Nevertheless, the supervisors initially refused to release her. Instead, they brought her to an interrogation room, gave her warnings under *Miranda v. Arizona* and continued to question her. Suders reiterated that she wanted to resign, and Easton then let her leave. The PSP never brought theft charges against her.

[The District Court granted the PSP's motion for summary judgment. While a trier of fact could conclude that the supervisors had created a hostile work environment, the PSP was not vicariously liable for their conduct.]

In so concluding, the District Court referred to our 1998 decision in *Faragher*. In *Faragher*, along with *Ellerth*, decided the same day, the Court distinguished between supervisor harassment unaccompanied by an adverse official act and supervisor harassment attended by "a tangible employment action." Both decisions hold that an employer is strictly liable for supervisor harassment that "culminates in a tangible

---

2. In addition, the supervisors made derogatory remarks about Suders' age, e.g., stating " 'a 25-year-old could catch on faster' " than she could, and calling her " 'momma.' " They further harassed her for having political influence. Suders' age and political-affiliation discrimination claims are not before us.

employment action, such as discharge, demotion, or undesirable reassignment." *Ellerth.* But when no tangible employment action is taken, both decisions also hold, the employer may raise an affirmative defense to liability, subject to proof by a preponderance of the evidence: "The defense comprises two necessary elements: (a) that the employer exercised reasonable care to prevent and correct promptly any sexually harassing behavior, and (b) that the plaintiff employee unreasonably failed to take advantage of any preventive or corrective opportunities provided by the employer or to avoid harm otherwise." *Ellerth.*

Suders' hostile work environment claim was untenable as a matter of law, the District Court stated, because she "unreasonably failed to avail herself of the PSP's internal procedures for reporting any harassment." Resigning just two days after she first mentioned anything about harassment to Equal Employment Opportunity Officer Smith-Elliott, the court noted, Suders had "never given [the PSP] the opportunity to respond to [her] complaints." The District Court did not address Suders' constructive discharge claim.

[The Third Circuit reversed.] It disagreed with the District Court in two fundamental respects. First, assuming the PSP could assert the affirmative defense genuine issues of material fact existed concerning the effectiveness of the PSP's sexual harassment program. Second, Suders had stated a claim of constructive discharge due to the hostile work environment.

A plaintiff alleging constructive discharge in violation of Title VII, the Court of Appeals stated, must establish:

> (1) he or she suffered harassment or discrimination so intolerable that a reasonable person in the same position would have felt compelled to resign . . . ; and (2) the employee's reaction to the workplace situation — that is, his or her decision to resign — was reasonable given the totality of circumstances. . . .

Viewing the complaint in that context, the court determined that Suders had raised genuine issues of material fact relating to her claim of constructive discharge.

The Court of Appeals then made the ruling challenged here: It held that "a constructive discharge, when proved, constitutes a tangible employment action." Under *Ellerth* and *Faragher*, the court observed, such an action renders an employer strictly liable and precludes employer recourse to the affirmative defense announced in those decisions. . . .

We conclude that an employer does not have recourse to the *Ellerth/Faragher* affirmative defense when a supervisor's official act precipitates the constructive discharge; absent such a "tangible employment action," however, the defense is available to the employer whose supervisors are charged with harassment. We therefore vacate the Third Circuit's judgment and remand the case for further proceedings.

II

A

Under the constructive discharge doctrine, an employee's reasonable decision to resign because of unendurable working conditions is assimilated to a formal discharge for remedial purposes. See 1 B. Lindemann & P. Grossman, Employment Discrimination Law 838-39 (3d ed. 1996) (hereinafter Lindemann & Grossman). The inquiry is objective: Did working conditions become so intolerable that a reasonable person in the employee's position would have felt compelled to resign? See C. Weirich et al., 2002 Cumulative Supplement to Lindemann & Grossman 651-52, and n. 1 (collecting cases) (hereinafter Weirich). . . .

Although this Court has not had occasion earlier to hold that a claim for constructive discharge lies under Title VII, we have recognized constructive discharge in the labor-law context, see *Sure-Tan, Inc. v. NLRB*, 467 U.S. 883, 894 (1984) (NLRB may find employer engaged in unfair labor practice "when, for the purpose of discouraging union activity, . . . [the employer] creates working conditions so intolerable that the employee has no option but to resign — a so-called 'constructive discharge.'"). Furthermore, we have stated that "Title VII is violated by either explicit or constructive alterations in the terms or conditions of employment." *Ellerth*. See also *Meritor Savings Bank* ("The phrase 'terms, conditions, or privileges of employment' [in Title VII] evinces a congressional intent to strike at the entire spectrum of disparate treatment of men and women in employment." (some internal quotation marks omitted)). We agree with the lower courts and the EEOC that Title VII encompasses employer liability for a constructive discharge.

B

This case concerns an employer's liability for one subset of Title VII constructive discharge claims: constructive discharge resulting from sexual harassment, or "hostile work environment," attributable to a supervisor. Our starting point is the framework *Ellerth* and *Faragher* established to govern employer liability for sexual harassment by supervisors.[6] As earlier noted, those decisions delineate two categories of hostile work environment claims: (1) harassment that "culminates in a tangible employment action," for which employers are strictly liable, *Ellerth*, and (2) harassment that takes place in the absence of a tangible employment action, to which employers may assert an affirmative defense, *Ellerth*. With the background set out above in mind, we turn to the key issues here at stake: Into which *Ellerth/Faragher* category do hostile-environment constructive discharge claims fall — and what proof burdens do the parties bear in such cases.

[In *Ellerth* and *Faragher* we] then identified "a class of cases where, beyond question, more than the mere existence of the employment relation aids in commission of the harassment: when a supervisor takes a tangible employment action against the subordinate." *Ellerth*. A tangible employment action, the Court explained, "constitutes a significant change in employment status, such as hiring, firing, failing to promote, reassignment with significantly different responsibilities, or a decision causing a significant change in benefits." Unlike injuries that could equally be inflicted by a co-worker, we stated, tangible employment actions "fall within the special province of the supervisor," who "has been empowered by the company as . . . [an] agent to make economic decisions affecting other employees under his or her control." The tangible employment action, the Court elaborated, is, in essential character, "an official act of the enterprise, a company act." It is "the means by which the supervisor brings the official power of the enterprise to bear on subordinates." Often, the supervisor will "use [the company's] internal processes" and thereby "obtain the imprimatur of the enterprise."

---

6. *Ellerth* and *Faragher* expressed no view on the employer liability standard for co-worker harassment. Nor do we.

Ordinarily, the tangible employment decision "is documented in official company records, and may be subject to review by higher level supervisors." In sum, we stated, "when a supervisor takes a tangible employment action against a subordinate[,] . . . it would be implausible to interpret agency principles to allow an employer to escape liability."

When a supervisor's harassment of a subordinate does not culminate in a tangible employment action, the Court next explained, it is "less obvious" that the agency relation is the driving force. We acknowledged that a supervisor's "power and authority invests his or her harassing conduct with a particular threatening character, and in this sense, a supervisor always is aided by the agency relation." But we also recognized that "there are acts of harassment a supervisor might commit which might be the same acts a co-employee would commit, and there may be some circumstances where the supervisor's status [would] make little difference."

An "aided-by-the-agency-relation" standard, the Court suggested, was insufficiently developed to press into service as the standard governing cases in which no tangible employment action is in the picture. Looking elsewhere for guidance, we focused on Title VII's design "to encourage the creation of anti-harassment policies and effective grievance mechanisms." The Court reasoned that tying the liability standard to an employer's effort to install effective grievance procedures would advance Congress' purpose "to promote conciliation rather than litigation" of Title VII controversies. At the same time, such linkage of liability limitation to effective preventive and corrective measures could serve Title VII's deterrent purpose by "encouraging employees to report harassing conduct before it becomes severe or pervasive." Accordingly, we held that when no tangible employment action is taken, the employer may defeat vicarious liability for supervisor harassment by establishing, as an affirmative defense, both that "the employer exercised reasonable care to prevent and correct promptly any sexually harassing behavior," and that "the plaintiff employee unreasonably failed to take advantage of any preventive or corrective opportunities provided by the employer or to avoid harm otherwise."

Ellerth and *Faragher* also clarified the parties' respective proof burdens in hostile environment cases. Title VII, the Court noted, "borrows from tort law the avoidable consequences doctrine," *Ellerth*, under which victims have "a duty 'to use such means as are reasonable under the circumstances to avoid or minimize the damages' that result from violations of the statute," *Faragher*. The *Ellerth/Faragher* affirmative defense accommodates that doctrine by requiring plaintiffs reasonably to stave off avoidable harm. But both decisions place the burden squarely on the defendant to prove that the plaintiff unreasonably failed to avoid or reduce harm. *Ellerth*; accord *Faragher*.[7]

1

The constructive discharge here at issue stems from, and can be regarded as an aggravated case of, sexual harassment or hostile work environment. For an atmosphere of sexual harassment or hostility to be actionable, we reiterate the offending behavior "must be sufficiently severe or pervasive to alter the conditions of the victim's employment and create an abusive working environment." *Meritor*. A

---

7. The employer is in the best position to know what remedial procedures it offers to employees and how those procedures operate. See 9 J. Wigmore, Evidence § 2486, p 290 (J. Chadbourn rev. ed. 1981) ("[T]he burden of proving a fact is said to be put on the party who presumably has peculiar means of knowledge enabling him to prove its falsity if it is false." (emphasis deleted)).

hostile-environment constructive discharge claim entails something more: A plaintiff who advances such a compound claim must show working conditions so intolerable that a reasonable person would have felt compelled to resign.[8]

Suders' claim is of the same genre as the hostile work environment claims the Court analyzed in *Ellerth* and *Faragher*. Essentially, Suders presents a "worse case" harassment scenario, harassment ratcheted up to the breaking point. Like the harassment considered in our pathmarking decisions, harassment so intolerable as to cause a resignation may be effected through co-worker conduct, unofficial supervisory conduct, or official company acts. Unlike an actual termination, which is always effected through an official act of the company, a constructive discharge need not be. A constructive discharge involves both an employee's decision to leave and precipitating conduct: The former involves no official action; the latter, like a harassment claim without any constructive discharge assertion, may or may not involve official action.

To be sure, a constructive discharge is functionally the same as an actual termination in damages-enhancing respects. As the Third Circuit observed, both "end the employer-employee relationship," and both "inflict . . . direct economic harm." But when an official act does not underlie the constructive discharge, the *Ellerth* and *Faragher* analysis, we here hold, calls for extension of the affirmative defense to the employer. As those leading decisions indicate, official directions and declarations are the acts most likely to be brought home to the employer, the measures over which the employer can exercise greatest control. Absent "an official act of the enterprise," as the last straw, the employer ordinarily would have no particular reason to suspect that a resignation is not the typical kind daily occurring in the work force. And as *Ellerth* and *Faragher* further point out, an official act reflected in company records — a demotion or a reduction in compensation, for example — shows "beyond question" that the supervisor has used his managerial or controlling position to the employee's disadvantage. Absent such an official act, the extent to which the supervisor's misconduct has been aided by the agency relation . . . is less certain. That uncertainty, our precedent establishes, justifies affording the employer the chance to establish, through the *Ellerth/Faragher* affirmative defense, that it should not be held vicariously liable.

The Third Circuit drew the line differently. Under its formulation, the affirmative defense would be eliminated in all hostile-environment constructive discharge cases, but retained, as *Ellerth* and *Faragher* require, in "ordinary" hostile work environment cases, i.e., cases involving no tangible employment action. That placement of the line, anomalously, would make the graver claim of hostile-environment constructive discharge easier to prove than its lesser included component, hostile work environment. Moreover, the Third Circuit's formulation, that court itself recognized, would make matters complex, indeed, more than a little confusing to jurors. . . .

We note, finally, two recent Court of Appeals decisions that indicate how the "official act" (or "tangible employment action") criterion should play out when constructive discharge is alleged. Both decisions advance the untangled approach we

---

8. As earlier noted, a prevailing constructive discharge plaintiff is entitled to all damages available for formal discharge. The plaintiff may recover postresignation damages, including both backpay and, in fitting circumstances, frontpay, see 1 Lindemann & Grossman 838; Weirich 651, as well as the compensatory and punitive damages now provided for Title VII claims generally, see 42 U.S.C. § 1981a(a)(1); *Pollard v. E. I. du Pont de Nemours & Co.*, 532 U.S. 843, 848 (2001) (noting expanded remedies under Civil Rights Act of 1991).

approve in this opinion. In *Reed v. MBNA Marketing Systems, Inc.*, 333 F.3d 27 (CA1 2003), the plaintiff claimed a constructive discharge based on her supervisor's repeated sexual comments and an incident in which he sexually assaulted her. The First Circuit held that the alleged wrongdoing did not preclude the employer from asserting the *Ellerth/Faragher* affirmative defense. As the court explained in *Reed*, the supervisor's behavior involved no official actions. Unlike, "e.g., an extremely dangerous job assignment to retaliate for spurned advances," the supervisor's conduct in *Reed* "was exceedingly unofficial and involved no direct exercise of company authority"; indeed, it was "exactly the kind of wholly unauthorized conduct for which the affirmative defense was designed." In contrast, in *Robinson v. Sappington*, 351 F.3d 317 (CA7 2003), after the plaintiff complained that she was sexually harassed by the judge for whom she worked, the presiding judge decided to transfer her to another judge, but told her that "her first six months [in the new post] probably would be 'hell,'" and that it was in her "'best interest to resign.'" The Seventh Circuit held that the employer was precluded from asserting the affirmative defense to the plaintiff's constructive discharge claim. The *Robinson* plaintiff's decision to resign, the court explained, "resulted, at least in part, from [the presiding judge's] official action in transferring" her to a judge who resisted placing her on his staff. The courts in *Reed* and *Robinson* properly recognized that *Ellerth* and *Faragher*, which divided the universe of supervisor-harassment claims according to the presence or absence of an official act, mark the path constructive discharge claims based on harassing conduct must follow.

2

[Unlike the Third Circuit, the Court saw no reason to leave the district courts unguided as to burdens of persuasion]. Following *Ellerth* and *Faragher*, the plaintiff who alleges no tangible employment action has the duty to mitigate harm, but the defendant bears the burden to allege and prove that the plaintiff failed in that regard. The plaintiff might elect to allege facts relevant to mitigation in her pleading or to present those facts in her case in chief, but she would do so in anticipation of the employer's affirmative defense, not as a legal requirement.

We agree with the Third Circuit that the case, in its current posture, presents genuine issues of material fact concerning Suders' hostile work environment and constructive discharge claims.[11] We hold, however, that the Court of Appeals erred in declaring the affirmative defense described in *Ellerth* and *Faragher* never available in constructive discharge cases. Accordingly, we vacate the Third Circuit's judgment and remand the case for further proceedings consistent with this opinion.

Justice THOMAS, dissenting.

As the Court explains, the National Labor Relations Board (NLRB) developed the concept of constructive discharge to address situations in which employers coerced employees into resigning because of the employees' involvement in union activities. In light of this specific focus, the NLRB requires employees to establish two elements to prove a constructive discharge. First, the employer must impose burdens upon the employee that "cause, and [are] intended to cause, a change in his working conditions so difficult or unpleasant as to force him to resign. Second, it must be shown

---

11. Although most of the discriminatory behavior Suders alleged involved unofficial conduct, the events surrounding her computer-skills exams were less obviously unofficial.

that those burdens were imposed because of the employee's union activities." *Crystal Princeton Refining Co.*, 222 N. L. R. B. 1068, 1069 (1976).

When the constructive discharge concept was first imported into Title VII of the Civil Rights Act of 1964, some courts imposed similar requirements. Moreover, because the Court had not yet recognized the hostile work environment cause of action, the first successful Title VII constructive discharge claims typically involved adverse employment actions. If, in order to establish a constructive discharge, an employee must prove that his employer subjected him to an adverse employment action with the specific intent of forcing the employee to quit, it makes sense to attach the same legal consequences to a constructive discharge as to an actual discharge.

The Court has now adopted a definition of constructive discharge, however, that does not in the least resemble actual discharge. The Court holds that to establish "constructive discharge," a plaintiff must "show that the abusive working environment became so intolerable that [the employee's] resignation qualified as a fitting response." Under this rule, it is possible to allege a constructive discharge absent any adverse employment action. Moreover, a majority of Courts of Appeals have declined to impose a specific intent or reasonable foreseeability requirement. Thus, as it is currently conceived, a "constructive" discharge does not require a "company act[ ] that can be performed only by the exercise of specific authority granted by the employer," *Burlington Industries, Inc. v. Ellerth* (Thomas, J., dissenting) (i.e., an adverse employment action), nor does it require that the act be undertaken with the same purpose as an actual discharge. Under these circumstances, it no longer makes sense to view a constructive discharge as equivalent to an actual discharge. Instead, as the Court points out, a constructive discharge is more akin to "an aggravated case of . . . sexual harassment or hostile work environment." And under this "hostile work environment plus" framework, the proper standard for determining employer liability is the same standard for hostile work environment claims that I articulated in *Ellerth*. "An employer should be liable if, and only if, the plaintiff proves that the employer was negligent in permitting the supervisor's conduct to occur." If a supervisor takes an adverse employment action because of sex that directly results in the constructive discharge, the employer is vicariously liable. But, where the alleged constructive discharge results only from a hostile work environment, an employer is liable if negligent. Because respondent has not adduced sufficient evidence of an adverse employment action taken because of her sex, nor has she proffered any evidence that petitioner knew or should have known of the alleged harassment, I would reverse the judgment of the Court of Appeals.

NOTES

1. *Applying* Ellerth. *Suders* upholds constructive discharge as a viable theory under Title VII, a not surprising result, and it agrees that, for remedial purposes, a constructive discharge should be viewed as the functional equivalent of a termination. The Third Circuit had held, categorically, that a constructive discharge resulting from a hostile work environment created by supervisory harassment was a tangible employment action, rendering the *Ellerth/Faragher* affirmative defense unavailable. It reasoned that, because termination was unquestionably a tangible employment action, a constructive termination, carrying the same economic consequences, should be similarly viewed. In rejecting that approach, the Supreme

Court looked to the agency theory underlying *Ellerth* and *Faragher*. Do you understand why the Court would accept that a constructive discharge is equivalent remedially to a termination and yet would view *Ellerth* and *Faragher* as incompatible with the Third Circuit's categorical approach equating constructive discharge to a tangible employment action?

2. *Rejecting a "Bright Line" Test.* In rejecting the Third Circuit's categorical approach, the *Suders* Court held the affirmative defense unavailable only if the constructive discharge is in response to a tangible employment action. The affirmative defense remains available when the employee quits in response to a hostile work environment created by a supervisor and no tangible job action is present. Thus, defining the parameters of a "tangible employment action" continues to be of utmost importance. *Suders*, however, adds to the notion of what constitutes a "tangible" action the phrase "official action." One of the actions it cites, the *Robinson* case involving a transfer, adds little to the notion of a tangible employment action. But does footnote 11 assist you? What was there about the events surrounding the test that was "official" — the failure to forward the tests for grading, the set-up of Suders, or the questioning complete with *Miranda* warning? Couldn't all of those acts have been done by co-workers?

There's also the question of whether any official act must be "the last straw" to preclude assertion of the affirmative defense. What if it a tangible job action, coupled with prior and subsequent supervisory harassment, creates an intolerable work environment? Finally, what if a plaintiff alleges that discriminatory harassment culminated in a tangible employment action but also asserts a hostile work environment claim? Does the existence of the tangible employment action preclude assertion of the affirmative defense for the hostile work environment claim? *See Ogden v. Wax Works, Inc.*, 214 F.3d 999 (8th Cir. 2000) (raising, but not resolving, this question).

3. *Quitting Is Not Always a Reasonable Response.* The *Suders* Court did not find that every hostile work environment, even one created by a supervisor, will support a constructive discharge claim. Instead, the plaintiff must establish an additional element: "She must show that the abusive working environment became so intolerable that her resignation qualified as a fitting response." Accordingly, do you agree that the Third Circuit's ruling eliminating the affirmative defense in constructive discharge cases in fact would have made it "easier" for the plaintiff to prove a hostile work environment constructive discharge claim?

That aside, *Suders* raises an interesting question about burdens of proof. It is the employer's burden to prove both prongs of the affirmative defense, including a showing that the plaintiff unreasonably failed to use the employer's remedial routes or to otherwise avoid harm. Yet *Suders* places on the plaintiff in a constructive discharge case the burden of showing that her resignation was a fitting response to the harassment. Is that a burden of production or a burden of proof? Does the Court's discussion toward the end of its opinion resolve this issue to your satisfaction?

4. *No Intent to Force the Plaintiff Out.* Justice Thomas is correct that a number of lower courts had required that the employer subjectively intend for the employee to quit in order for a constructive discharge. Although several circuits had rejected this limitation, does the majority definitively, if implicitly, also reject it? Stephen F. Befort & Sarah J. Gorajski critique *Suders* in *When Quitting is Fitting: The Need for a Reformulated Sexual Harassment/Constructive Discharge Standard in the Wake of Pennsylvania State Police v. Suders*, 67 OHIO ST. L.J. 595 (2006), for, inter alia, not clarifying that the "fitting response" standard rejects case law requiring that the

employer have the specific intent that the employee quit before a constructive discharge is found.

***

When no tangible employment action has occurred, *Ellerth* permits the employer to assert an affirmative defense. What facts must a defendant prove to establish this defense?

MATVIA v. BALD HEAD ISLAND
MANAGEMENT, INC.
259 F.3d 261 (4th Cir. 2001)

TRAXLER, Circuit Judge.

Christina Matvia appeals from the grant of summary judgment in favor of Bald Head Island Management ("BHIM") on her claims of sexual harassment. . . . We affirm.

I

On June 16, 1997, BHIM hired Matvia as a housekeeper. One month later, BHIM transferred Matvia to the position of Maintenance Worker I in the Contractor Service Village ("CSV"). Her supervisor at the CSV was Richard Terbush. Beginning in September 1997, Matvia became the recipient of unwanted attentions from Terbush:

- Terbush approached Matvia, said he needed a hug, and proceeded to hug her;
- Terbush told Matvia, who had just dyed her hair brown, that he would have to fantasize about a brunette rather than a blond;
- Terbush informed Matvia that he no longer had sexual relations with his wife;
- Terbush placed a pornographic picture on Matvia's desk;
- Terbush told Matvia she looked good enough to eat;
- Terbush frequently placed his arm around Matvia when they were riding in a golf cart and massaged her shoulder;
- Terbush repeatedly told Matvia that he loved her and had a crush on her;
- Terbush, on December 10, 1997, told Matvia that he had a dream that she sued him for sexual harassment and warned her that if she did bring suit she would be in big trouble; and
- Terbush, five days after recounting his dream, pulled Matvia close to him in the golf cart, tried to kiss her, and struggled with Matvia until she was able to escape.

Matvia became physically ill after the attempted kiss and went home early. The next day Terbush told BHIM officials what had happened in the cart and was suspended pending an investigation. Matvia participated in the investigation and also pressed criminal charges against Terbush. On December 31, BHIM fired Terbush for sexually harassing Matvia.

While the harassment was ongoing, BHIM had in place a policy against sexual harassment. The policy is printed in the employee handbook which Matvia signed for at her orientation. The policy defines sexual harassment as "unwelcome or unwanted conduct of a sexual nature, whether verbal or physical." Examples of sexual harassment are given, and employees are encouraged to report improper behavior to their supervisor, the personnel department, or the chief operating officer.

According to Matvia, after Terbush's termination co-workers and managers at BHIM altered their behavior towards her. Co-workers would move away if she sat near them on BHIM's buses or ferries; the bus drivers, who were often at the CSV, would stop talking among themselves when Matvia entered the room; the bus drivers traduced [sic. Ed.: While the word is used in obsolete construction to mean "calumniously blame," its most common meaning is "to convey from one place to another." OED (2d ed. 1989)] Matvia while on their routes; and members of management stopped saying "hello" to Matvia while waiting for the ferry. . . .

II . . .

To prevail on a Title VII hostile work environment claim, Matvia must establish four elements: (1) unwelcome conduct, (2) based on Matvia's gender, (3) sufficiently pervasive or severe to alter the conditions of employment and to create a hostile work environment, and (4) some basis for imputing liability to BHIM. The district court assumed the first three elements had been established, but granted summary judgment on the fourth element in light of the affirmative defense outlined in *Faragher v. City of Boca Raton*, and *Burlington Industries, Inc. v. Ellerth*.

The affirmative defense of *Faragher* and *Ellerth* allows an employer to avoid strict liability for a supervisor's sexual harassment of an employee if no tangible employment action was taken against the employee. Examples of tangible employment action include "discharge, demotion, or undesirable reassignment." If entitled to raise the affirmative defense, the employer must establish: "(a) that the employer exercised reasonable care to prevent and correct promptly any sexually harassing behavior, and (b) that the plaintiff employee unreasonably failed to take advantage of any preventative or corrective opportunities provided by the employer or to avoid harm otherwise."

A. TANGIBLE EMPLOYMENT ACTION

Matvia contends that the affirmative defense is not available because there was tangible employment action. However, Matvia was not discharged, demoted, or reassigned — in fact, during her tenure at BHIM she received a raise, promotion, and good evaluations. She claims that these positive events happened because she silently suffered Terbush's advances and therefore there was tangible employment action. See *Brown v. Perry*, 184 F.3d 388, 395 (4th Cir. 1999) (implying that receipt of a promotion can be a tangible employment action under *Faragher* and *Ellerth*).

However, in the present case there is no evidence that Matvia received benefits in exchange for acquiescing in Terbush's advances. Regarding Matvia's promotion from Maintenance Worker I to Maintenance Worker II and the accompanying increase in pay, Matvia testified that she and a co-worker received this status change because "we took on a lot more responsibilities" when the CSV began fuel sales. Terbush, according to Matvia's testimony, "thought that me and the other worker should receive more because we were doing more work." Indeed, in requesting that his subordinates be reclassified to the category of Maintenance Worker II, Terbush observed that "these employees are woefully underpaid" in light of their additional responsibilities. Clearly, the promotion and raise were not unique to Matvia — the other worker Terbush supervised received the same benefit. Moreover, Matvia never alleged that Terbush offered her the promotion and pay increase in exchange for sexual favors. Matvia's own testimony indicates that these benefits were conferred because she and her colleague acquired additional responsibilities. Hence, the raise and promotion do not amount to tangible employment action.

Similarly, the evaluations indicating that Matvia was performing at a "satisfactory" level and that her employment should be continued do not amount to tangible employment actions. There are no allegations that Terbush promised Matvia a satisfactory evaluation in exchange for sexual favors, or that Matvia was performing at an unsatisfactory level but received a satisfactory rating in exchange for her tolerance of Terbush's unwelcome conduct. The evaluations were routine matters and cannot operate to prevent BHIM from raising the affirmative defense.

In sum, there was no tangible employment action in this case. While Matvia is entitled to all reasonable inferences from the evidence, her theory of "silent sufferance" would transform any ordinary employment action into tangible employment action. For example, under her theory, so long as sexual harassment is present, an upgrade in equipment used by the employee, a grant of sick leave, or any other mundane, non-adverse action would constitute tangible employment action and thus deprive the employer of the affirmative defense. *Faragher* and *Ellerth* simply do not lend themselves to a result that would make a grant of summary judgment in favor of the employer an impossibility. Of course, this does not mean that the affirmative defense is available when supervisors guilty of sexual harassment do bestow benefits in exchange for an employee's silence. However, in the present case there is no evidence that Matvia received her pay increase, promotion, or satisfactory evaluations in exchange for refraining from reporting the unwelcome conduct. Accordingly, BHIM is entitled to raise the affirmative defense outlined in *Faragher* and *Ellerth*.

B.   PREVENTION AND CORRECTION OF IMPROPER BEHAVIOR

Matvia argues that BHIM did not take reasonable care to prevent and correct sexually harassing behavior because BHIM's antiharassment policy was not an effective preventative program. Our cases have held that dissemination of "an effective anti-harassment policy provides compelling proof" that an employer has exercised reasonable care to prevent and correct sexual harassment. Evidence showing that the employer implemented the policy in bad faith or was deficient in enforcing the policy will rebut this proof.

Matvia does not allege that the policy was implemented in bad faith, but rather argues that it was deficient because BHIM employees did not understand it. Tellingly, Matvia points to no language in the policy rendering it ambiguous or difficult to follow. Nor does she suggest how the policy against sexual harassment could have been made any clearer. Her only evidence of the alleged deficiency is deposition testimony in which BHIM employees had trouble recalling the details of their orientation briefings. . . .

The failure to recollect the details of an orientation session does not mean that the employee does not understand the sexual harassment policy. . . . The record also contains numerous affidavits from BHIM employees indicating an awareness of the policy against sexual harassment and the company officials to whom harassment could be reported. In the face of a policy that clearly defines sexual harassment and to whom harassment should be reported, Matvia cannot survive summary judgment by claiming that employees failed to recall their orientation briefings. Hence, Matvia's contention that BHIM lacked an effective preventative program must fail.

As for correction of sexually harassing behavior, BHIM suspended Terbush without pay four days after he attempted to kiss Matvia. Twelve days later, after completing an investigation, BHIM terminated Terbush. As this sequence of events indicates, shortly after it learned of Terbush's improper conduct, BHIM took prompt corrective action as required by *Faragher* and *Ellerth*.

Questioning the adequacy of BHIM's corrective action, Matvia focuses her arguments not on BHIM's suspension and termination of Terbush, but on the ostracism she suffered at the hands of the bus drivers and others. The first prong of the affirmative defense, however, focuses on the employer's exercise of "reasonable care to prevent and correct promptly any sexually harassing behavior." *Faragher*; *Ellerth*. Matvia alleges no sexually harassing behavior occurring after the date of the attempted kiss. Though co-workers were often uncivil towards Matvia, they did not sexually harass her. Accordingly, BHIM's response to the ostracism and vilification of Matvia, which was bereft of a sexual component, is irrelevant to the first prong of the affirmative defense.

C.   FAILURE TO TAKE ADVANTAGE OF PREVENTATIVE OR CORRECTIVE OPPORTUNITIES

Matvia argues that her reluctance to report Terbush's conduct was not unreasonable. According to circuit precedent, "evidence that the plaintiff failed to utilize the company's complaint procedure will normally suffice to satisfy [the company's] burden under the second element of the defense." *Barrett v. Applied Radiant Energy Corp.*, 240 F.3d 262, 267 (4th Cir. 2001). If Title VII's prohibitions against sexual harassment are to be effective, employees must report improper behavior to company officials. See *Faragher*, (observing "that a victim [of sexual harassment] has a duty to use such means as are reasonable under the circumstances to avoid or minimize the damages that result from violations of the statute"); *Parkins v. Civil Constructors, Inc.*, 163 F.3d 1027, 1038 (7th Cir. 1998) (observing that "the law against sexual harassment is not self-enforcing and an employer cannot be expected to correct harassment unless the employee makes a concerted effort to inform the employer that a problem exists"). Otherwise, the harasser's conduct would continue, perhaps leading other employees to infer that such behavior is acceptable in the workplace.

Matvia contends that she needed time to collect evidence against Terbush so company officials would believe her. But *Faragher* and *Ellerth* command that a victim of sexual harassment report the misconduct, not investigate, gather evidence, and then approach company officials. Sexual harassment cases often involve the word of the harasser versus the word of the harassed employee, but this is no different from any other case where the outcome depends on the credibility of the parties' testimony. Though we understand why Matvia would want tangible evidence to buttress her version of events, this cannot excuse her failure to report Terbush's unwelcome conduct.

Matvia also argues that it was proper to refrain from reporting Terbush so she could determine whether he was a "predator" or merely an "interested man" who could be politely rebuffed. According to Matvia, she discovered that Terbush was a predator just days before the attempted kiss in the golf cart and consequently she should not be penalized for failing to take preventative or corrective action. We disagree. As an initial matter, our case law makes no distinction between "predators" and "interested men." So long as the conduct is unwelcome, based on the employee's gender, and sufficiently pervasive or severe to alter the conditions of employment, the label given to the harasser is immaterial. Moreover, even if we were to use Matvia's proffered nomenclature, the gravity and numerosity of the incidents make clear that Terbush was not merely an interested man who could be politely rebuffed. Matvia informed Terbush that her husband would not appreciate his conduct and she often turned her back to him and left the room when Terbush's actions or comments made her feel uncomfortable. Nonetheless, Terbush persisted in harassing her. In light of this long-term and persistent harassment, Matvia cannot be excused from failing to report Terbush to BHIM officials.

Next, Matvia points to the actions of the bus drivers and argues that she reasonably feared retaliation from co-employees. Without question, the reporting of sexual harassment can place "the harassed employee in an awkward and uncomfortable situation." *Barrett.* Not only is it embarrassing to discuss such matters with company officials, but after the harassed employee overcomes this hurdle she may have to deal with a negative reaction from coworkers. While such events might cause an employee stress, the unpleasantness cannot override the duty to report sexual harassment. The reporting requirement is so essential to the law of sexual harassment that we "have refused to recognize a nebulous fear of retaliation as a basis for remaining silent." *Barrett.* The bringing of a retaliation claim rather than failing to report sexual harassment, is the proper method for dealing with retaliatory acts. Consequently, Matvia's fear that her co-workers would react negatively is insufficient to deprive BHIM of the affirmative defense.

Finally, Matvia argues that the attempted kiss alone should be considered in assessing the hostility of her work environment, and because she contacted BHIM soon after the incident, BHIM cannot as a matter of law establish that Matvia unreasonably failed to invoke the company's anti-harassment policy. From the filing of her complaint, Matvia has characterized the inappropriate behavior as beginning "after Terbush became Plaintiff's supervisor." In an effort to avoid the affirmative defense set forth in *Faragher* and *Ellerth*, Matvia now asks this court to ignore the numerous incidents of sexual harassment enumerated in her complaint and discussed in her deposition testimony, and to instead focus only on the final indignity she suffered. This we cannot do. The evidence reveals a pattern of behavior beginning in September 1997 and ending December 15. The only way we can assess whether Matvia "failed to take advantage of any preventative or corrective opportunities provided by the employer," is to examine Matvia's actions from the time the unwelcome conduct began. Matvia's pick-and-choose method would make a mockery of this inquiry and would violate the basic tenets of fairness.

In short, though Terbush's advances began in September 1997 and ended on December 15, BHIM did not learn of the harassment until December 16. BHIM had an effective anti-harassment policy in place that Matvia failed to utilize. Hence, BHIM has established the second prong of the affirmative defense. . . .

NOTES

1. *Silence or Acquiescence and the Tangible Job Action Requirement.* Matvia contended that, because she silently suffered Terbush's advances, she was rewarded with a raise, a promotion, and good evaluations and that a tangible employment action thus was present. The Fourth Circuit appears to agree that job benefits bestowed in exchange for an employee's silence about ongoing harassment would preclude the affirmative defense but finds Matvia did not prove the actions occurred because of her forbearance. If the facts supported her, would her theory be correct? Is a raise or promotion received because an employee does not report a supervisor's

sexual advance a tangible employment action within the meaning of *Ellerth* and *Faragher*? *See Jin v. Metropolitan Life Ins.*, 310 F.3d 84 (2d Cir. 2002) (economic harm not required to hold an employer liable where the victim submits to the harasser's sexual advances); *see also Lutkewitte v. Gonzalez*, 436 F.3d 248 (D.C. Cir.), *cert. denied*, 127 S. Ct. 846 (2006) (receiving a car not a tangible employment action related to submission to sexual advances when employee already had a car).

2. *Prong 1(a): Reasonable Care to Prevent Harassment.* In *Matvia*, the employer had promulgated and disseminated an antiharassment policy that defined sexual harassment and identified multiple reporting channels. The court finds this to be "compelling proof" that the employer has exercised reasonable care to prevent and correct harassment, leaving it to the employee to rebut with evidence the policy was implemented in bad faith or not effectively enforced. Is this approach consistent with placing on the defendant the burden of proving the affirmative defense? Should a policy that looks good on paper be sufficient prima facie proof that the employer has met this prong of the defense? *See* Anne Lawton, *Operating in an Empirical Vacuum: The* Ellerth *and* Faragher *Affirmative Defense*, 13 COLUM. J. GENDER & L. 197, 266-67 (2004) (federal courts "should require employers to produce evidence of the following: (1) complaint records; (2) a system of post-complaint follow-up; (3) employees' evaluations of the employer's policy and procedure; and (4) a system for evaluating managers on their compliance with the firm's anti-harassment policy and procedure").

However, that harassment has occurred, despite the employer's efforts, does not mean the employer did not exercise reasonable care to prevent harassment. As noted by the Seventh Circuit, "the law does not require success — it only requires that an employer act reasonably to prevent harassment." In *Shaw v. Autozone, Inc.*, 180 F.3d 806 (7th Cir. 1999), the employer was found to have acted reasonably because it distributed to every employee a policy clearly stating that the employer would not tolerate sexual harassment, provided multiple mechanisms for reporting and resolving complaints, and regularly conducted training sessions. What if the employer conducts training sessions but does not ensure that they are attended and understood by all employees, particularly supervisory employees? *See Loughman v. Malnati Org., Inc.*, 395 F.3d 404, 407 (7th Cir. 2005) (although the employer responded to plaintiff's complaints of serious physical violations, "a reasonable jury could determine that simply talking to the people involved in the first two aggressive incidents was not a sufficient response," especially since a "consistent stream of verbal harassment suggests that Malnati's policy was actually not very effective at all").

3. *Drafting an Effective Policy.* Although the Supreme Court stated that an employer need not necessarily have promulgated an antiharassment policy to satisfy its duty of reasonable care, it is unusual for an employer to prevail absent such a policy. Although courts have been reluctant to lay down a rigid list of requirements that an antiharassment policy must meet to be considered effective, it is helpful to the employer if the policy not only prohibits sexual harassment but also gives some explanation or description of what is meant by sexual harassment. *See Molnar v. Booth*, 229 F.3d 593 (7th Cir. 2000). Particularly important are alternative avenues for reporting harassment; often it is the immediate supervisor who is engaging in the harassment, and thus, a requirement that an employee report harassment to her supervisor will likely render the policy ineffective. *See Madray v. Publix Supermarkets, Inc.*, 208 F.3d 1290 (11th Cir. 2000). Moreover, clear identification of to whom within the organization complaints are to be made is important. *See Gentry v. Export Packing Co.*, 238 F.3d 842 (7th Cir. 2001). Some employers have adopted an "open door" program, which enables an employee "to speak with any other member

of management," which may suffice for the first prong but also results in an employee's very informal complaints satisfying her reporting obligation. *Olson v. Lowe's Home Centers Inc.*, 130 Fed. Appx. 380, 390 (11th Cir. 2005). The policy's assurance against retaliation for reporting has been important to some courts. *See, e.g., Barrett v. ARECO*, 240 F.3d 262 (4th Cir. 2000). For a description of features an antiharassment policy should contain, *see* Paul Buchanan & Courtney W. Wisall, *The Evolving Understanding of Workplace Harassment and Employer Liability: Implications of Recent Supreme Court Decisions Under Title VII*, 34 WAKE FOREST L. REV. 55 (1999). One court required policies to be crafted for the understanding of the average teenager when a large number of such persons were in its workforce. *EEOC v. V&J Foods, Inc.*, 507 F.3d 575 (7th Cir. 2007).

4. *Bullet-Proofing or Real Structural Change?* Professor Susan Sturm, in *Second Generation Employment Discrimination: A Structural Approach*, 101 COLUM. L. REV. 458 (2001), approves the law's encouragement of employer initiatives aimed at achieving workplace equality. She examines structures put into place at several large employers that treat discrimination and harassment as but a subset of workplace problems that need to be resolved, a problem-solving approach that may be more effective than litigation at rooting out the subconscious bias that characterizes much of today's discrimination. However, other commentators have questioned the Court's willingness to allow training programs to ground an affirmative defense, suggesting that the effectiveness of these programs in deterring harassing behavior (as opposed to limiting employer liability) has yet to be shown. *See* Susan Bisom-Rapp, *An Ounce of Prevention Is a Poor Substitute for a Pound of Cure: Confronting the Developing Jurisprudence of Education and Prevention in Employment Discrimination Law*, 22 BERKELEY J. EMP. & LAB. L. 1 (2001); Susan Bisom-Rapp, *Fixing Watches with Sledgehammers: The Questionable Embrace of Employee Sexual Harassment Training by the Legal Profession*, 24 U. ARK. LITTLE ROCK L. REV. 147 (2001). *See also* Anne Lawton, *The Bad Apple Theory in Sexual Harassment Law*, 13 GEORGE MASON L. REV. 817 (2005) (reporting that the lower courts are allowing employers to create what are in effect statutes of limitations for sexual harassment claims via their affirmative defense policies); Joanna L. Grossman, *The Culture of Compliance: The Final Triumph of Form over Substance in Sexual Harassment Law*, 26 HARV. WOMEN'S L.J. 3 (2003). Taking another tack, Tristin K. Green, in *Targeting Workplace Context: Title VII as a Tool for Institutional Reform*, 72 FORDHAM L. REV. 659 (2003), warns more generally against unqualified acceptance of employer-initiated efforts at institutional reform. She argues that, as the lingering problem of workplace discrimination becomes more complex, involving the influence of organizational context on individual decision making, remedial measures become more difficult to devise and to implement, which in turn widens the opportunity for employers to shape change in ways that may undermine the law's substantive impact.

5. *Prong 1(b): Reasonable Steps to Correct Harassment.* In addition to taking reasonable care to prevent harassment, the employer also must establish that it took reasonable steps to *correct* harassment when it is reported. Matvia's employer suspended Terbush and then terminated him following the investigation. But the court finds the company's response to the "ostracism and vilification of Matvia" irrelevant to this prong of the affirmative defense because the conduct lacked a sexual component. Is this correct? Can an employer that tolerates misconduct directed toward an employee because she has complained of sexual harassment be acting reasonably to correct the harassment? *Cf. Wyatt v. Hunt Plywood Co.*, 297 F.3d 405 (5th Cir. 2002) (co-worker shunning of plaintiff for complaining about harassment does not implicate sexual harassment law).

An employer may act reasonably if it is unable to corroborate a woman's complaint of harassment and thus takes no action against the accused. *See Baldwin v. Blue Cross/Blue Shield of Ala.*, 480 F.3d 1287, 1303 (11th Cir. 2007 ("The requirement of a reasonable investigation does not include a requirement that the employer credit uncorroborated statements the complainant makes if they are disputed by the alleged harasser"). How aggressive and professional does the employer's response have to be? *See Williams v. Waste Mgmt. of Ill., Inc.*, 361 F.3d 1021, 1030 (7th Cir. 2004) (remedial actions had the purpose and effect of eliminating further race-based harassment even though "the investigation was by no means textbook in its execution"); *Benefield v. Fulton Co., Ga*, 130 Fed. Appx. 308, 312 (11th Cir. 2005) (focusing on "substantive measures" by the employer not "the process under which those measures are adopted"). *But see Engel v. Rapid City Sch. Dist.*, 506 F.3d 1118 (8th Cir. 2007) (while initial steps may have appeared reasonable, employer should have responded more aggressively when the harassment resumed).

Promptly firing the harasser will certainly suffice as reasonable corrective action. *Green v. Franklin Nat'l Bank*, 459 F.3d 903, 912 (8th Cir. 2006) (firing harasser within a month was sufficiently prompt remedial action to avoid liability). But is termination of the harasser always a necessary or proper course of action? Employers who discipline harassers in order to avoid liability under Title VII must be careful to avoid liability to the harassing employee. Employees who have individual employment contracts, civil service rights, or academic tenure, or who work under the protection of a policy manual or a collective bargaining agreement may be protected against discharge without just cause.

Employers who have disciplined harassers have been sued for violating the rights of the harassing employees, although usually unsuccessfully. *See, e.g., Duffy v. Leading Edge Prods. Inc.*, 44 F.3d 308 (5th Cir. 1995) (unsuccessful defamation suit); *Chalmers v. Quaker Oats Co.*, 61 F.3d 1340 (7th Cir. 1995) (unsuccessful ERISA suit); *Scherer v. Rockwell Intl. Corp.*, 975 F.2d 356 (7th Cir. 1992) (unsuccessful breach of contract claim). In *Pierce v. Commonwealth Life Ins. Co.*, 40 F.3d 796 (6th Cir. 1994), a supervisor demoted for violating the employer's sexual harassment policy asserted that, because the victim, who was a willing participant, was not disciplined, he was a victim of reverse sex discrimination. *Id.* at 799. The court ruled, however, that his status as a supervisor was a legitimate, nondiscriminatory reason justifying different treatment. *Id.* at 803-04. *See also Wright v. Murray Guard, Inc.*, 455 F.3d 702 (6th Cir. 2006) (where black male's alleged sexual harassment was substantially greater than female co-worker's alleged misconduct, there was no showing of discrimination in his discharge despite failure of decisionmaker to independently investigate). *But see Russell v. City of Kansas City*, 414 F.3d 863, 868 (8th Cir. 2005) (white female supervisor demoted for allegedly fostering racially harassing workplace may have been the victim of discrimination when black and white males were given only a "slap on the wrist").

6. *Requests for Confidentiality.* What if the employee who complains about harassment asks the employer to keep her complaint confidential? In *Torres v. Pisano*, 116 F.3d 625 (2d Cir. 1997), the Second Circuit ruled that an employee's confidentiality request insulated the employer from liability for its failure to act. *Id.* at 627. The court emphasized that some complaints, such as those alleging harassment of other employees, may require the employer to breach the trust of an employee who has requested confidentiality but found that this was not such a case. *Id.* at 639. *See also Hardage v. CBS Broad. Inc.*, 436 F.3d 1050 (9th Cir.), *cert. denied*, 127 S. Ct. 55

(2006) (plaintiff's statement to employer that he preferred to handle the matter himself meant that the defendant's failure to investigate was not unreasonable even though its policy required investigation); *Nurse "Be" v. Columbia Palms W. Hosp. Ltd. P'ship*, 490 F.3d 1302 (11th Cir. 2007) (employee did not sufficiently put employer on notice when she reported to her supervisor that she received a few "harassing" phone calls from a fellow employee but requested that her supervisor not report the incident). Are *Torres* and *Hardage* consistent with *Ellerth* and *Faragher?* Could there be a difference between liability to the employee who asks that no action be taken and liability to later victims of harassment if the complaining person's request is honored and no action is taken? *See* Martha S. West, *Preventing Sexual Harassment: The Federal Courts' Wake-Up Call*, 68 BROOKLYN. L. REV. 457, 497 (2002).

7. *Prong 2: Did the Employee Act Unreasonably?* Even if the employer took reasonable preventive and corrective action, the affirmative defense will still fail unless the employer also proves that the employee unreasonably failed to take advantage of preventive or corrective opportunities. Matvia waited until the final incident to complain, arguing it was sufficiently severe that it should be the focus of her "duty" to complain. The court disagrees, reasoning that her actions throughout the period of harassment must be assessed. Is this correct? Must a victim complain at the earliest opportunity to preserve her claim? Was Matvia acting reasonably when she waited to determine whether Terbush was an interested man or a predator?

In *Watts v. Kroger Co.*, 170 F.3d 505, 510 (5th Cir. 1999), the Fifth Circuit reversed summary judgment on the ground that the employer could not, as a matter of law, establish that Watts "unreasonably failed to take advantage of any preventive or corrective opportunities provided by the employer." Although Watts alleged that her supervisor had harassed her for nearly a year, she did not complain until the harassment intensified. The court believed that a jury might find it "not unreasonable" to hold off complaining under these circumstances. And in *Craig v. M&O Agencies, Inc.*, 496 F.3d 1047 (9th Cir. 2007), the court found a 19-day delay in reporting supervisory harassment was not unreasonable, reasoning the employee may have hoped the situation would resolve itself without a complaint being filed. However, in *Wyatt v. Hunt Plywood Co.*, 297 F.3d 405 (5th Cir. 2002), the court held that plaintiff's failure to report harassment by her boss and his supervisor was unreasonable, precluding her from recovering for a four-month period of harassment that culminated in her supervisor's pulling her pants down in view of other employees. When plaintiff then complained, both her supervisor and his boss were fired, and no further acts of sexual harassment occurred. Is there some absolute rule that a victim must report the first act of harassment, or is the test whether a reasonable person would report at a particular point in time?

8. *Fears of Retaliation.* As was true in *Matvia*, courts generally have not been sympathetic to plaintiffs' claims that they delayed reporting because they feared retaliation. In *Matvia*, however, retaliatory acts in fact occurred, and yet summary judgment for the employer was granted because the employee had no evidence, but only a suspicion, that she would be retaliated against, at the time she delayed reporting. Why isn't the fact that retaliatory behavior occurred sufficient at least to create a fact question on the reasonableness of the plaintiff's fear of retaliation?

9. *Law Changing Norms?* It is pretty clear that women are reluctant to report harassment, which makes the second prong of the employer's defense often easy to establish. *See* L. Camille Hébert, *Why Don't "Reasonable Women" Complain about*

Sexual Harassment?, 82 INDIANA L.J. 711 (2007) (explaining why women reasonably fail to immediately file formal complaints concerning harassing conduct, thus often satisfying the second prong of the *Ellerth* affirmative defense); Theresa M. Beiner, *Sex, Science and Social Knowledge: The Implications of Social Science Research on Imputing Liability to Employers for Sexual Harassment*, 7 WM. & MARY J. WOMEN & L. 273 (2001); Joanna L. Grossman, *The First Bite Is Free: Employer Liability for Sexual Harassment*, 61 U. PITT. L. REV. 671 (2000); Theresa M. Beiner, *Using Evidence of Women's Stories in Sexual Harassment Cases*, 24 U. ARK. LITTLE ROCK L. REV. 117 (2001); Linda Hamilton Krieger, *Employer Liability for Sexual Harassment — Normative, Descriptive, and Doctrinal Interactions: A Reply to Professors Beiner and Bisom-Rapp*, 24 U. ARK. L. REV. 169 (2001). Heather S. Murr, *The Continuing Expansive Pressure to Hold Employers Strictly Liable for Supervisory Sexual Extortion: An Alternative Approach Based on Reasonableness*, 39 U.C. DAVIS L. REV. 529 (2006).

Assuming that the research is correct as a descriptive matter that women are reluctant to report harassment until it becomes extreme, does this answer the normative question of whether their rights should depend on speedy reporting? The Supreme Court clearly intended to change employers' conduct through the affirmative defense; perhaps it also intended to change the conduct of women workers. The requirement of speedy reporting is often treated as a kind of mitigation of damages approach: there is no "duty" to report but a victim cannot recover for harm that would have been avoided had she acted "reasonably" and reported.

Even under this approach, however, the lower courts' requirement that plaintiffs speak up at the earliest opportunity is in some tension with the Supreme Court's decision in *Clark County v. Breeden*, reproduced at p. 461, holding that complaint of sexual conduct that obviously was not severe or pervasive enough to state a claim for a hostile work environment was not protected from retaliation. Is the reconciliation that a woman is protected so long as she is reasonable in reporting harassment the first time it occurs? For discussion of the interaction between the antiretaliation provisions of Title VII and the use of internal complaint procedures, *see* Edward Marshall, *Excluding Participation in Internal Complaint Mechanisms From Absolute Retaliation Protection: Why Everyone, Including the Employer, Loses*, 5 EMP. RTS. & EMPLOY. POL'Y J. 549 (2001). *See also* Elinor P. Schroeder, *Handbooks, Disclaimers, and Harassment Policies: Another Look at* Clark County School District v. Breeden, 42 BRANDEIS L.J. 581 (2004). In finding the affirmative defense met, the *Matvia* court stated that plaintiff's recourse for retaliatory acts was to bring a retaliation claim. Matvia, however, did bring a retaliation claim, but that action was dismissed for want of an adverse action. See Retaliation section beginning on p. 460.

10. *Both Prongs of the Affirmative Defense Must Be Satisfied.* What happens if a supervisor commits a severe act of harassment, such as a rape or attempted rape, and the employee immediately reports the harassment to her employer? If the employer has a strong antiharassment policy in place and engages in prompt and effective corrective action, can the employer still be vicariously liable for the hostile work environment? Since it is the employer's burden to establish *both* prongs of the affirmative defense, the answer should be yes. The employer would be unable to establish the second prong of the defense because the employee has acted reasonably. See *Frederick v. Sprint/United Mgt. Co.*, 246 F.3d 1305 (11th Cir. 2001); *Harrison v. Eddy Potash Inc.*, 248 F.3d 1014 (10th Cir. 2001); *Johnson v. West*, 218 F.3d 725 (7th Cir. 2000). However, some courts are answering the question in the negative. *See McCurdy v. Arkansas State Police*, 375 F.3d 762, 771 (8th Cir. 2004)

("Strict adherence to the Supreme Court's two-prong affirmative defense in this case is like trying to fit a square peg into a round hole. . . . Instead, we critically ask whether Title VII envisions strict employer liability for a supervisor's single incident of sexual harassment when the employer takes swift and effective action to insulate the complaining employee from further harassment the moment the employer learns about the harassing conduct, answering the question no").

In light of *Ellerth* and the availability of damages under the 1991 Act, how would you advise employers? Is there any way for an employer to avoid liability short of taking aggressive and serious steps to ensure that no supervisory harassment occurs? How should an employer respond if it has reason to believe that a supervisor has been harassing employees, but the victims are unwilling to make a formal complaint? Are restrictions of socio-sexual activity among employees an appropriate response? What about "dating waivers," i.e., documents executed by employees "desiring to undertake and pursue a mutually consensual social and/or amorous relationship"?

NOTE ON EMPLOYER LIABILITY FOR HARASSMENT BY CO-WORKERS AND CUSTOMERS

Before *Ellerth*, courts generally agreed that the employer is liable for the harassing conduct of coworkers only if the employer knew or should have known of the harassment and failed to take adequate corrective action. Did *Ellerth* change this rule? Who bears the burden of establishing that the employer knew or should have known about co-worker harassment? The lower courts continue to hold employers liable for harassment by co-workers only if the employer knew or should have known of the harassment and failed to take corrective measures. As one circuit has observed, the difference between employer liability for supervisory harassment as opposed to co-worker harassment essentially comes down to which party bears the burden of proof. The factors examined in determining whether the affirmative defense has been satisfied are very similar to those looked at in employer liability for co-worker harassment. However, when it is a supervisor's harassment that is at issue, it is the employer that bears the burden of proving the affirmative defense. In co-worker harassment cases, it is the plaintiff's burden to prove the employer's negligence. *Swinton v. Potomac Corp.*, 270 F.3d 794 (9th Cir. 2001).

Even in cases of co-worker harassment, the issue of who the "employer" is and when the employer "knows" about the harassment can arise. *See Bombaci v. Journal Cmty. Publ'g Group, Inc.*, 482 F.3d 979 (7th Cir. 2007) (employee offered no evidence that her belief that a certain individual was a "supervisor" was reasonable, and none of that individual's duties suggested that she could effect the terms of another person's employment in a way that could remedy sexual harassment). Does *Ellerth* indicate how to resolve the issue of who the "employer" is for purposes of receiving complaints about harassment by co-workers? Is it sufficient that the worker inform his or her supervisor of harassment by a co-worker if the employer's harassment policy assigns the task of taking complaints to the human resources department? After *Ellerth*, who bears the burden of establishing that an appropriate agent of the employer knew or should have known of co-worker harassment? *See Williamson v. City of Houston*, 148 F.3d 462 (5th Cir. 1998) (employer's policy directing employees to report harassment to supervisors establishes that supervisor's knowledge of harassment is imputed to the employer).

In deciding whether an individual's knowledge may be imputed to the employer under the "knew or should have known standard," the Ninth Circuit held that one who has authority over either the harasser or the harassee's terms or conditions of employment *or* who has an official or de facto duty to serve as a conduit of information will have his knowledge imputed to the employer. *Swinton v. Potomac Corp.*, 270 F.3d 794 (9th Cir. 2001). Because the employment manual directed employees to report harassing conduct to their supervisors, a supervisor's knowledge that a subordinate was being harassed was imputed to the employer. The court further held the manual's directive to report harassing conduct to supervisors made those supervisors managerial employees within the meaning of the standard for punitive damages. See Chapter 8. Is this the correct test for imputing knowledge? For assessing punitive damages?

What happens when it is the supervisor who is being harassed by her subordinates? For discussion of this issue and collecting cases, *see* Ann Juliano, *Harassing Women with Power: The Case for Including Contra-Power Harassment Within Title VII*, 87 B.U.L. Rev. 491 (2007).

Must the employer have knowledge that the plaintiff herself had been the victim of harassment, or will knowledge of harassment of other co-workers by the perpetrator be sufficient to establish liability? *See Ferris v. Delta Air Lines, Inc.*, 277 F.3d 128 (2d Cir.) (employer knowledge that worker had raped other co-workers sufficient basis for imputing liability). What if it is common knowledge throughout a department that an employee is being sexually harassed by a co-worker? What if the whole department is aware that a supervisor is harassing an employee, but the human resources officer who handles harassment complaints is unaware? In *Faragher*, the Court commented on situations where knowledge of harassing behavior is widespread:

> There have . . . been myriad cases [that] have held employers liable on account of actual knowledge by the employer, or high-echelon officials of an employer organization, of sufficiently harassing action by subordinates, which the employer or its informed officers have done nothing to stop. In such instances, the combined knowledge and inaction may be seen as demonstrable negligence, or as the employer's adoption of the offending conduct and its results, quite as if they had been authorized affirmatively as the employer's policy.

Faragher at 788. Is the *Ellerth* defense available when employer liability is based on negligent failure to take action to stop known harassing conduct? If the defense is available, could such an employer meet its requirements?

Additionally, there is the question of employer liability for sexual harassment by customers. Suppose a sales representative must regularly deal with a customer's purchasing agent who harasses her. Does her employer have a duty to protect her? How far does this duty reach? Must it cease doing business with the harasser's firm if other methods fail? *Quinn v. Green Tree Credit Corp.*, 159 F.3d 759, 766 (2d Cir. 1998), held that an employer's duty with respect to controlling harassment by customers is the same as its duty with respect to co-worker harassment — the employer is responsible for sexual harassment if it knows or should have known of it unless it can demonstrate immediate and appropriate corrective action. This is the approach taken in *Dunn v. Wash. County Hosp.*, 429 F.3d 689 (7th Cir. 2005), where the harasser was a doctor with admitting privileges at the hospital but who was not an employee. The court found the relationship of the harasser to the employer irrelevant:

Because liability is direct rather than derivative, it makes no difference whether the person whose acts are complained of is an employee, an independent contractor, or for that matter a customer. Ability to "control" the actor plays no role. Employees are not puppets on strings; employers have an arsenal of incentives and sanctions (including discharge) that can be applied to affect conduct. It is the use (or failure to use) these options that makes an employer responsible — and in this respect independent contractors are no different from employees. Indeed, it makes no difference whether the actor is human. Suppose a patient kept a macaw in his room, that the bird bit and scratched women but not men, and that the Hospital did nothing. The Hospital would be responsible for the decision to expose women to the working conditions affected by the macaw, even though the bird (a) was not an employee, and (b) could not be controlled by reasoning or sanctions. It would be the Hospital's responsibility to protect its female employees by excluding the offending bird from its premises. This is, by the way, the norm of direct liability in private law as well. . . .

Id. at 691. But in *Vajdl v. Mesabi Acad. of Kidspeace, Inc.*, 484 F.3d 546 (8th Cir. 2007), the court refused to hold the employer responsible for behavior by detainees.

Once an employer has notice that a co-worker, customer, or client is harassing an employee, what constitutes an adequate response, and to what extent is adequacy different when supervisor harassment is concerned? The Tenth Circuit has ruled that responses that are "reasonably calculated to end the harassment" are adequate to insulate the employer from liability even if new incidents of harassment occur. *See Adler v. Wal-Mart Stores, Inc.*, 144 F.3d 664, 676 (10th Cir. 1998). Other courts also have been sympathetic to employers' attempts to control harassment by co-workers, customers, clients, and anonymous harassers. *See, e.g., Folkerson v. Circus Circus Enterprises*, 107 F.3d 754 (9th Cir. 1997) (casino not liable for customer's harassment of professional mime because casino warned offensive patrons and assigned a large male employee to follow her and notify security of problems); *Hirras v. National R.R. Passenger Corp.*, 95 F.3d 396 (5th Cir. 1996) (by taking complaints seriously, conducting prompt and thorough investigation, and referring complaints to law enforcement, railroad responded adequately to complaints about anonymous harassing calls, notes, and graffiti even though harasser was never identified).

In *Swenson v. Potter*, 271 F.3d 1184 (9th Cir. 2001), the court addressed the employer's obligation to take steps reasonably calculated to end the harassment in a case involving co-worker harassment. The inquiry has two steps. First, what were the temporary steps taken while the matter was under investigation? The court said an employer must, at a minimum, attempt to eliminate contact between the accuser and accused that is not business related. Second, what are the permanent remedial steps that have been taken? A harasser need not necessarily be punished if there is insufficient evidence to support discipline.

NOTE ON THE FIRST AMENDMENT IMPLICATIONS OF SEXUAL HARASSMENT LIABILITY

The First Amendment implications of regulating sexual harassment in the workplace are broad-reaching and complex. This note provides no more than a brief introduction to the issue. One source of further information is Professor Eugene Volokh's website on free speech and workplace harassment, which is located at http://www.law.ucla.edu/faculty/volokh/harass.

Before considering the First Amendment implications of prohibiting harassing speech, it is necessary to clarify the issue. Evidence of sexist or racist speech in the workplace is relevant in employment discrimination litigation for a variety of reasons. Most obviously, sex or race stereotyping or expressions of bias and prejudice may provide evidence that an employer made decisions on the basis of sex or race, rather than for nondiscriminatory reasons. See *Price Waterhouse v. Hopkins*, reproduced at p. 32. The government, through Title VII, imposes liability in such cases not because of what was said but because of the discriminatory *actions* taken. The speech merely provides evidence of motive and does not, therefore, create First Amendment problems of restricting speech. Similarly, sexual propositions may be evidence of quid pro quo sexual harassment. The employer may inform a female employee, for example, that she will not receive an employment benefit unless she cooperates by providing him with sexual favors. If she rejects the advance and suffers an adverse action, the proposition evidences the Title VII violation in the same way an offer to sell a controlled substance may be criminalized. In contrast to these uses of speech in discrimination litigation, sexist or racist speech may provide the basis for claiming that the employer is maintaining a hostile environment in violation of Title VII. The speech is *not merely evidence* of discriminatory conduct. It is prohibited because it is offensive enough to contaminate the work setting for women or minorities. The *speech itself* forms the basis of liability. Hostile environment cases that rely primarily on speech, rather than on actual or proposed conduct, most clearly implicate First Amendment rights.

The First Amendment implications of sexual harassment liability are minimal when *private* employers voluntarily choose to regulate the speech absent any government coercion. In such cases, the actions of the private employer do not implicate the Constitution because no government action is involved. Of course, government employers who control the speech of their own employees are subject to some First Amendment restrictions. Moreover, when courts impose Title VII liability on private employers on the basis of their speech or their agents' speech, First Amendment concerns are implicated. Just as common law defamation is subject to First Amendment restrictions, *New York Times v. Sullivan*, 376 U.S. 254 (1964), so, too, is Title VII harassment law.

The Supreme Court has recognized categories of speech that the government may prohibit or restrict in some circumstances without violating the First Amendment. Several of these categories, including fighting words, offensive speech, and obscenity, are potentially analogous to speech that creates a discriminatory, hostile environment. While some speech at issue in sexual harassment cases readily fits within these categories, other speech does not.

Not only is classifying sexually harassing speech as an unprotected category of speech difficult, but prohibiting discriminatory harassing speech raises further First Amendment problems. Viewpoint restrictions have nearly always been considered violations of the First Amendment, and the Court specifically held that prohibiting discriminatory fighting words *because* they express a particular point of view violates the First Amendment. See *R.A.V. v. City of St. Paul, Minnesota*, 505 U.S. 377 (1992) (successful challenge to a statute on which a cross-burning prosecution was based; the statute prohibited symbols known to arouse "anger, alarm, or resentment in others on the basis of race, color, creed, religion, or gender"). Nevertheless, *R.A.V.* suggested that Title VII's prohibition of sexual harassment is distinguishable from the St. Paul statute:

[S]ince words can in some circumstances violate laws directed not against speech but against conduct (a law against treason, for example, is violated by telling the enemy the nation's defense secrets), a particular content-based subcategory of a proscribable class of speech can be swept up incidentally within the reach of a statute directed at conduct rather than speech. Thus, for example, sexually derogatory "fighting words," among other words, may produce a violation of Title VII's general prohibition against sexual discrimination in employment practices, 42 U.S.C. §2000e-2; 29 C.F.R. §1604.11 (1991). See also 18 U.S.C. §242; 42 U.S.C. §§1981, 1982. Where the government does not target conduct on the basis of its expressive content, acts are not shielded from regulation merely because they express a discriminatory idea or philosophy.

505 U.S. at 389. *See also Virginia v. Black*, 538 U.S. 343 (2003) (upholding conviction for cross-burning). Does the Court's distinction apply to all hostile environment cases or only those based on "fighting words"? What does the Court mean by "'fighting words' among other words" in the context of sexual harassment? What about obscene and indecent speech? Could a court find that artwork depicting naked women creates a discriminatory environment without violating the First Amendment? What about statements like "there's nothing worse than having to work around women"? Does the Court's attempt to distinguish sexual harassment cases extend to other discriminatory hostile environment cases involving communicative "conduct"? Note that the *R.A.V.* Court's attempt to distinguish hostile environment liability clearly was dicta.

Since *R.A.V.*, the Court decided *Harris v. Forklift Systems Inc.* [reproduced at p. 376]. The sexually harassing behavior in that case was primarily evidenced by offensive remarks. Although the constitutionality of imposing liability on the employer for those remarks was raised in briefs submitted in that case, the Court did not address the issue in its opinion. Are the remarks in *Harris* fighting words? Does the Court's dicta in *R.A.V.* explain why Hardy's statements are not protected by the First Amendment?

In the public sector, the Supreme Court has, outside of the harassment context, developed First Amendment doctrine to accommodate both government employees' free speech rights and government employers' interest in controlling the behavior of their own employees in the workplace. In this context, the Court has ruled that public employees may not be disciplined or discharged for engaging in speech on a matter of public concern unless the government can assert some interest in restricting that speech, such as disruption of the workplace, that outweighs the employees' interest in speaking. *Connick v. Meyers*, 461 U.S. 138 (1983); *Pickering v. Board of Educ.*, 391 U.S. 563 (1968). A major limitation is that, to be protected, the employee's speech must not be part of his job. *Garcetti v. Ceballos*, 126 S. Ct. 1951 (2006). *See generally* Cynthia Estlund, *Free Speech Rights That Work at Work: From the First Amendment to Due Process*, 54 UCLA L. REV. 1463 (2007). Does this suggest that a harasser who spoke in the workplace could not raise a First Amendment defense? Or maybe it suggests the opposite — such speech is never part of the job because it is prohibited by employer policies.

NOTE ON ALTERNATIVE REMEDIES FOR HARASSMENT

Title VII is not the only source of remedies for sexual and other harassment in the employment setting. Harassment also can be attacked under state employment discrimination statutes, and state employees may assert a violation of their constitutional right to equal protection. Resort to state tort claims, such as intentional infliction of emotional distress and assault, may also be desirable in order to improve on Title VII remedies. *See generally* Martha Chamallas, *Discrimination and Outrage: The Migration from Civil Rights to Tort Law*, 48 WM. & MARY L. REV. 2115

(2007). Although the Civil Rights Act of 1991 amended Title VII to provide for punitive and compensatory damages, § 102 limits the amount of damages that can be awarded. See Chapter 8.

In addition, such remedies may be critical should the harassment not be severe or pervasive enough to be actionable under Title VII or to hold an individual tortfeasor liable when the employer has a viable affirmative defense. In some jurisdictions, however, workers' compensation statutes may provide the exclusive remedy for intentional infliction of mental distress on the job. *See* Jane B. Korn, *The Fungible Woman and Other Myths of Sexual Harassment,* 67 TUL. L. REV. 1363 (1993). Note, also, that state law claims that cannot be resolved without interpreting a collective bargaining agreement may be preempted by federal law.

D. DISCRIMINATION ON ACCOUNT OF RELIGION

Title VII prohibits discrimination because of religion. The statute's definition of religion, however, introduces a kind of discrimination we have not encountered before — the failure to reasonably accommodate religious practices and observances. Further, the statute permits religious discrimination by certain religious employers and also permits such discrimination when religion is a bona fide occupational qualification. Overarching all of these statutory provisions is the First Amendment. In some cases, employees resort to the free exercise clause to supplement Title VII's statutory protections, and in other cases churches and other religious institutions invoke the free exercise clause to limit the intrusion of Title VII and other antidiscrimination statutes into their operations. Finally, the establishment clause plays a part in this complicated mix, limiting the extent to which the state can favor religion by its enactments in this area.

Religious discrimination cases often proceed on the same general theories of discrimination as race and gender cases. Thus, there are cases in which the plaintiff claims that the defendant admitted its religious motivation, *e.g., Mandell v. County of Suffolk,* 316 F.3d 368 (2d Cir. 2003) (comments by police chief could permit reasonable jury to infer that he viewed Christianity "as a necessary part of a good police officer's make-up"), and others in which the courts must infer an impermissible purpose from more circumstantial evidence, *e.g., Goldmeier v. Allstate Ins. Co.,* 337 F.3d 629 (6th Cir. 2003) (prima facie case where Orthodox Jewish husband and wife were only licensed insurance agents in office and resigned after company announced plans to require offices to stay open on Friday evenings and Saturday mornings). But religious discrimination is different from other kinds of discrimination in a variety of ways, including Title VII's imposition of an affirmative duty of employers to reasonably accommodate the religious beliefs and practices of employees.

REED v. GREAT LAKES COS.
330 F.3d 931 (7th Cir. 2003)

POSNER, Circuit Judge.

[Melvin Reed appealed from the grant of summary judgment to his former employer, Great Lakes. Reed] was hired to be the executive housekeeper of a newly opened Holiday Inn that Great Lakes operates in Milwaukee. One of his duties was to see to it that a copy of the Bible, supplied free of charge to the hotel by the Gideons, was placed in every room. It is customary for representatives of management to meet with the Gideons when they deliver Bibles to a newly opened hotel. Reed had been working for Great Lakes for less than a month when the Gideons showed up to deliver the Bibles. A few days before their scheduled arrival, the manager of the Holiday Inn had told Reed in a joking manner that they were going to "pray with the Gideons," which Reed understood to mean that, given his responsibility for the distribution of the Bibles to the rooms, he was to accompany the manager to the meeting at which they would receive the Bibles from the Gideons. Reed did not object to attending the meeting. But, to the manager's surprise, at the meeting the Gideons, besides delivering Bibles, did some Bible reading and some praying. Reed was offended by the religious character of the meeting and left in the middle, to the manager's chagrin. Later in the day, the manager ran into Reed and told him: "Don't do that again, you embarrassed me." Reed riposted: "You can't compel me to a religious event," to which the manager replied that Reed would do what he was told to do. Reed responded, "Oh, hell no, you won't, not when it comes to my spirituality," whereupon the manager fired him for insubordination.

Oddly, Reed at his deposition refused to indicate what if any religious affiliation or beliefs (or nonbeliefs) he has; refused even to deny that he might be a Gideon! His position was that Title VII forbids an employer to require an employee to attend a religious meeting, period.

Title VII does forbid an employer, unless it is a religious organization, which Great Lakes is not, to discriminate against an employee on the basis of the employee's religion. 42 U.S.C. § 2000e-2(a)(1). And for these purposes, as assumed by the parties, as strongly intimated in *EEOC v. Townley Engineering & Mfg. Co.*, 859 F.2d 610, 613-14 n. 5 (9th Cir. 1988), and *Young v. Southwestern Savings & Loan Ass'n*, 509 F.2d 140, 142 (5th Cir. 1975), and as supported by analogy to cases under the free-exercise clause of the First Amendment, *County of Allegheny v. American Civil Liberties Union*, 492 U.S. 573 (1989); *Wallace v. Jaffree*, 472 U.S. 38 (1985) — cases which hold that religious freedom includes the freedom to reject religion — "religion" includes antipathy to religion. And so an atheist (which Reed may or may not be) cannot be fired because his employer dislikes atheists. If we think of religion as taking a position on divinity, then atheism is indeed a form of religion.

But there is no indication that Reed was fired because of his religious beliefs, identity, or observances or because of his aversion to religion, to Christianity, or to the Gideons, whatever the case may be (remember that we don't know anything about his religion or lack of religion). Great Lakes accepts Bibles from the Gideons because the Bibles are free, not because any of Great Lakes' owners or managers, including the manager of the Holiday Inn who fired Reed, is a Gideon. So far as appears, none is. The manager's joking reference to "praying with the Gideons" makes it pretty clear that he is not one of them; anyway there is no contention that he is. For that matter, there is no evidence that he expected to encounter prayers and Bible reading at the meeting with them. At previous such meetings the Gideons had handed over the Bibles and the manager had thanked them, and that was that. The religious service was a surprise. It is apparent that the manager fired Reed because Reed's sudden departure from the meeting was embarrassing to the manager, who would be in trouble with his superiors if the Gideons became huffy and cut off the supply of free Bibles to Great Lakes hotels, and also because Reed's refusal to see the manager's point of view indicated that he was unlikely to be a cooperative employee.

The manager *must* have been indifferent to Reed's religious views, because Reed never expressed them to the manager; to this day we do not know what his religion is, as he refused to say at his deposition. It is difficult to see how an employer can be charged with discrimination on the basis of an employee's religion when he doesn't know the employee's religion (or lack thereof, which, as we have noted, is in the eyes of the law a form of religion), *O'Connor v. Northshore Int'l Ins. Services*, 325 F.3d 73, 74 (1st Cir. 2003) (per curiam); *Lubetsky v. Applied Card System, Inc.*, 296 F.3d 1301 (11th Cir. 2002), though the employee can survive summary judgment if, while declining to specify his religious beliefs, he attests that they differ from his employer's and that that is why he was fired. *Venters v. City of Delphi*, 123 F.3d 956, 972 (7th Cir. 1997); *Shapolia v. Los Alamos Nat'l Laboratory*, 992 F.2d 1033, 1037 (10th Cir. 1993).

Reed has utterly failed to make a prima facie case of intentional religious discrimination. But he has another string to his bow. Besides forbidding intentional discrimination, Title VII requires an employer to try to accommodate the religious needs of its employees, that is, to try to adjust the requirements of the job so that the employee can remain employed without giving up the practice of his religion, provided the adjustment would not work an undue hardship on the employer. 42 U.S.C. § 2000e(j); *Ansonia Board of Education v. Philbrook*, 479 U.S. 60, 70 (1986). And again for these purposes hostility to religion counts as a form of religion. So if attending a meeting at which Gideons might pray or read from the Bible would offend Reed's religious or antireligious sensibilities, he might be entitled to an accommodation.

We say "might be" rather than "would be" for two reasons. First, the duty to accommodate is not absolute; the cost to the employer must be considered. *Ansonia Board of Education v. Philbrook*. Second, an employee is not permitted to redefine a purely personal preference or aversion as a religious belief. *EEOC v. Union Independiente de la Autoridad de Acueductos y Alcantarillados de Puerto Rico*, 279 F.3d 49 (1st Cir. 2002); *Seshadri v. Kasraian*, 130 F.3d 798 (7th Cir. 1997) (belief in the deeply spiritual effects of eating Kozy Kitten People/Cat Food); *Vetter v. Farmland Industries, Inc.*, 120 F.3d 749 (8th Cir. 1997). Otherwise he could announce without warning that white walls or venetian blinds offended his "spirituality," and the employer would have to scramble to see whether it was feasible to accommodate him by repainting the walls or substituting curtains for venetian blinds. This case is not so extreme, because compelled attendance at sectarian religious services is the sort of thing that is likely to offend someone who does not belong to the sect in question, though we repeat that for all we know Reed is a Gideon and his claim for accommodation therefore completely spurious.

But putting that possibility to one side, and assuming that it would have been no sort of hardship for Great Lakes to have excused Reed from attendance at meetings with the Gideons, who are hardly likely to ask, "Why isn't the executive housekeeper here?" we think the district court was right to grant summary judgment for Great Lakes with respect to this claim as well as the disparate-treatment claim. There is a line, indistinct but important, between an employee who seeks an accommodation to his religious faith and an employee who asserts as Reed did an unqualified right to disobey orders that he deems inconsistent with his faith though he refuses to indicate at what points that faith intersects the requirements of his job. Today he storms out of a meeting with the Gideons; tomorrow he may refuse to place their Bibles in the rooms; the day after that he may announce that he will not come to work on the day when the Gideons visit. Reed failed to give any indication of what future occurrences at the Holiday Inn would impel him to make a scene embarrassing to the manager and potentially injurious to the employer. Title VII imposes a duty on the employer but also a reciprocal duty on the employee to give fair warning of the employment practices that will interfere with his religion and that he therefore wants waived or adjusted. *EEOC v. United Parcel Service*, 94 F.3d 314 (7th Cir. 1996). A person's religion is not like his sex or race — something obvious at a glance. Even if he wears a religious symbol, such as a cross or a yarmulka, this may not pinpoint his particular beliefs and observances; and anyway employers are not charged with detailed knowledge of the beliefs and observances associated with particular sects. Suppose the employee is an Orthodox Jew and believes that it is deeply sinful to work past sundown on Friday. He does not tell his employer, the owner of a hardware store that is open from 9 a.m. to 6 p.m. on Fridays, who leaves the employee in sole charge of the store one Friday afternoon in mid-winter, and at 4 p.m. the employee leaves the store. The employer could fire him without being thought guilty of failing to accommodate his religious needs. This case is similar.

[The district judge had imposed sanctions on Reed for filing a frivolous claim, and the Seventh Circuit agreed that his claim of having been intentionally discriminated against on account of his religion was frivolous. But Reed's accommodation claim, though unsuccessful, was not frivolous, and the district judge had based the sanction on the fact that in the last 15 years Reed had worked for 25 different employers and had filed 13 federal employment discrimination suits with almost no success. The district court judge thought this represented attempts at extortion, but the Seventh Circuit, noting Reed's lack of success, viewed it as "more likely that he has a psychological problem than that he has been committing extortion for the last 15 years with nothing to show for it." In any event, none of the prior suits had been adjudged to be frivolous, which barred using them as a basis for sanctions in the present case. Judge Ripple, concurring, agreed that Reed had failed to prove any claim, but he disagreed that either of his allegations was be frivolous.]

NOTES

1. *Differences in Discrimination on Account of Religion.* The principal case introduces us to a number of ways in which religious discrimination differs from other kinds of discrimination. Most obviously, *Reed* turns on the fact that, unlike race, sex, and age, an individual's religious beliefs are often not apparent, which requires the employer to know of such beliefs before it can violate the statute. Second, an employer may violate the statute not only by discriminating but also by failing to accommodate the employer's religion. Still another way in which this kind of discrimination departs from the varieties we have encountered before is that the core notion of religion itself can be contested. For example, Judge Posner assumes atheists are protected even though it's not so obvious how an atheist qualifies as one who has a "religious" belief. Posner is not alone in this view. The following Notes explore these and other aspects of Title VII's prohibition of discrimination on account of religion

2. *Knowledge.* We have seen in other contexts that disparate treatment requires proof that the employer knew of the protected characteristic. The most authoritative statement of this requirement emerges from *Raytheon Co. v. Hernandez*, 540 U.S. 44 (2003), discussed at pp. 301-02, where the Court held that, absent proof of knowledge of the protected trait (in that case, a disability), an employer could be liable only for disparate impact discrimination. Given that religious beliefs may be purely

internal, this has barred plaintiff's recovery in cases such as *Reed. Accord Lubetsky v. Applied Card Sys.*, 296 F.3d 1301 (11th Cir. 2002) (plaintiff had to adduce evidence that decision-maker knew of his religion to establish prima facie case). Of course, even if employer knowledge is necessary, the religion of certain employees may be easily ascertainable. *E.g., Rosen v. Thornburgh*, 928 F.2d 528, 534 (2d Cir. 1991) ("a trier of fact might reasonably conclude that Rosen's religion was apparent from his surname as well as from the vocal anti-semitism engendered by his presence. . . . ").

The court never knew Mr. Reed's religion, which is more than a little odd but ultimately irrelevant: plaintiff's claim failed because his *employer* did not know of Reed's religion at the time of the Gideons incident or when Reed was discharged for insubordination. *See also Storey v. Burns Int'l Sec. Servs.*, 390 F.3d 760, 764-65 (3d Cir. 2004) (even assuming the Confederate flag was a religious symbol for plaintiff, the employer was not aware of the religious symbolism he attached to it). But the employer knew Reed had religious (or at least "spiritual") objections to being present during religious-infused events. And he fired Reed for refusing to attend such events in the future. Why isn't that discrimination on account of religion or at least failure to accommodate religious beliefs?

Posner does state that a plaintiff may avoid summary judgment "if, while declining to specify his religious beliefs, he attests that they are different from his employers and that that is why he was fired." But isn't that a fair description of the case before the court? *See Ollis v. Hearthstone Homes, Inc.*, 495 F.3d 570, 575 (8th Cir. 2007) (upholding jury verdict for an employee who testified that he was required to attend sessions to "cleanse negative energy," which involved affirming the belief in past lives, participating in ritual-like activities, and reading Hindu and Buddhist literature that conflicted with his sincere Christian religious beliefs). Or is the point that there was no discrimination — the manager was treating Reed exactly as he would have treated any other employee? It was Reed who was seeking to be treated differently, i.e., to be accommodated by being excused from normal work duties, and to do so, he needed to explain his religious beliefs. *See Moranski v. GMC*, 433 F.3d 537, 542 (7th Cir. 2005) (GM treated employees identically with respect to religion: "any employee with any religious position may join any of the recognized Affinity Groups, but the company will not recognize as an Affinity Group a group organized on the basis of a religious position"). *See generally* Laura S. Underkuffler, *"Discrimination" on the Basis of Religion: An Examination of Attempted Value Neutrality in Employment*, 30 WM. & MARY L. REV. 581, 589 (1989) (arguing in favor of employer religious practices unless they preclude other employees from equal opportunity; however, those who object to exposure to a religious work environment should be accommodated).

3. *"Knowledge Plus" for the Prima Facie Case?* Judge Posner cites approvingly *Shapolia v. Los Alamos National Laboratory*, 992 F.2d 1033, 1033 (10th Cir. 1993), which focused on tension between the employer's religion and that of the employee, suggesting that perhaps another requirement of the prima facie case is that proof that the employee "fail[ed] to hold or follow his or her employer's religious beliefs." This doesn't mean that a Baptist cannot discriminate on account of religion against another Baptist but merely underscores that there has to be some additional basis to conclude that religion is the basis of the discrimination. Given the recurrent history of theological disputes, not only between religions but within what is otherwise viewed as a single religion, this is certainly possible.

The point, however, can be generalized to ask how likely it is that an adherent of Faith X would discriminate against an adherent of Faith Y on the basis of religion. So framed, the question is not susceptible of an answer. Americans practice hundreds of different religions. See the Religious Movements Homepage at the University of Virginia, www .religiousmovements.org, and they take them more or less seriously. Some religions are inclusive and some exclusive. Some are viewed sympathetically by most Americans while some are viewed with suspicion by many Americans. *See* Rebecca French, *Shopping for Religion: The Change in Everyday Religious Practice and its Importance to the Law,* 51 BUFFALO L. REV. 127 (2003). In this setting, something akin to the "background circumstances" or "additional evidence" tests for reverse discrimination claims, see p. 76, may be required for a prima facie case. That is, plaintiff might have to adduce evidence why this employer would be hostile to a person of plaintiff's religion. Another way to say this is that perhaps it is more likely that an individual will be fired for being a Wiccan than, say, for being a Methodist, *see Van Koten v. Family Health Mgmt.,* 955 F. Supp. 898 (N.D. Ill. 1997), or for being a Muslim than a Catholic. In *Reed* itself, and supposing Reed were Jewish, would a showing that the Gideons stressed the New Testament and Jesus as God be sufficient evidence to infer discrimination?

Perhaps for this reason, most successful religion cases turn on some statements by the employer implicating religious bias, even if circumstantial evidence also played a role. *E.g., Campos v. City of Blue Springs, Mo.,* 289 F.3d 546 (8th Cir. 2002) (city youth outreach counselor who observed tenets of Native American spirituality was constructively discharged because she was not Christian); *EEOC v. Univ. of Chi. Hosps.,* 276 F.3d 326 (7th Cir. 2002) (hospital recruiter's constructive discharge could be found to be religious discrimination when her supervisor repeatedly asked her to tone down her religious expression).

4. *What's a "Religion"?* Judge Posner did not have to explore the meaning of religion in *Reed,* and the concept is neither self-defining nor in any meaningful way defined by the statute — although the statute does tell us that, whatever counts as religion, "includes all aspects of religious observance and practice, as well as belief, unless an employer demonstrates that he is unable to reasonably accommodate to an employee's or prospective employee's religious observance or practice without undue hardship on the conduct of the employer's business." Courts have considered, for example, whether the vegan belief system is a religion. *Friedman v. Southern Cal. Permanente Medical Group,* 125 Cal. Rptr. 2d 663 (Cal. App. 2002), applied state law to hold that a person who was not hired because he had refused to be inoculated with a mumps vaccine grown in chicken embryos was not a victim of religious discrimination; the vegan belief system is a secular philosophy and not a religion. Put another way, if Posner's hypothetical employee demanded white walls and no Venetian blinds, and if he were to explain the basis of that desire, how does the law distinguish between personal preferences, moral or philosophical beliefs, and personal preferences?

The short answer is, not very well. The most authoritative cases are those concerning conscientious objector status. The relevant statute exempted from service in the armed forces anyone who, "by reason of religious training and belief, is conscientiously opposed to participation in war in any form." Construing that statute, the Supreme Court first formulated a definition of a religious-based belief as a "sincere and meaningful belief which occupies in the life of its possessor a place parallel to that filled by the God of those admittedly qualifying for the exemption." *United States v. Seeger,* 380 U.S. 163, 176 (1965). Later, it expanded the definition to include moral and ethical beliefs that assumed the function of a religion in the registrant's life. Only if the belief "rests solely upon considerations of policy, pragmatism, or expediency" does it fail to qualify. *Welsh v. United States,* 398 U.S. 333, 342-43 (1970). This expansive approach to the meaning of religion under the Selective Service statute may well have been driven by constitutional concerns of not overly favoring religion and thereby violating the Establishment Clause, but those concerns seem applicable to Title VII. The EEOC has adopted an expansive definition in accordance with *Seeger/Welsh:*

> [T]he Commission will define religious practices to include moral or ethical beliefs as to what is right and wrong which are sincerely held with the strength of traditional religious views. . . . The fact that no religious group espouses such beliefs or the fact that the religious group to which the individual professes to belong may not accept such belief will not determine whether the belief is a religious belief of the employee or prospective employee.

29 CFR § 1605.1 (2007). *See generally* Kent Greenawalt, *Title VII and Religious Liberty*, 33 LOY. U. CHI. L.J. 1, 32-35 (2001) (critiquing this definition). Perhaps because of the breath of this definition, few cases find claimed belief system not to be religious, even in relatively extreme situations such as the Church of Body Modification, which celebrates piercings, *Cloutier v. Costco Wholesale Corp.*, 390 F.3d 126 (1st Cir. 2004), and the "World Church of the Creator," which preaches white supremacy. *Peterson v. Wilmur Communs., Inc.*, 205 F. Supp. 2d 1014, 1015 (E.D. Wis. 2002).

5. *Sincerity.* The expansive definition of religion raises questions about whether a particular employee might falsely use "religion" to avoid job burdens or obtain job benefits. Indeed, the district court judge in *Reed* clearly believed that plaintiff was not in good faith in claiming that his spirituality was violated, and Judge Posner's hypothetical white wall worshipper is also concerned with this possibility. It is well-established that, while there can be no inquiry into the rationality of a particular belief, a court can determine whether the asserted belief is sincerely held. Relevant to that determination is whether the employee's conduct is consistent with the professed belief. *See EEOC v. Union Independiente De La Autoridad De Acueductos y Alcantarillados de P.R.*, 279 F.3d 49, 56-57 (1st Cir. 2002) (summary judgment denied where the sincerity of a claimed Seventh Day Adventist was challenged by specific evidence of his conduct contrary to the tenets of his professed religious belief, including lying on an employment application, being divorced, and taking an oath). Nevertheless, just as there are relatively few cases holding a particular belief is not religious, there are very few cases successfully challenging an employee's sincerity.

6. *Linking Religion to a Practice.* While we will review this question in more detail after the next principal case, the 1972 expansion of the statutory protection of "religion" to embrace religious "observances and practices" means that there will be far more opportunities for discrimination or failure to accommodate than would be true if the statute merely prohibited discriminating against those who hold particular belief systems.

7. *Justifying Religious Discrimination.* Suppose the defendant discriminated against plaintiff on the basis of his religion. Is that ever permissible?

(a) Normal "mixed motives" analysis applies: while it is a violation of the statute for religion to be a motivating factor in an employment decision, an employer may limit the plaintiff's remedies by demonstrating that it would have taken the same action for nondiscriminatory reasons. In *Cowan v. Strafford R-VI Sch. Dist.*, 140 F.3d 1153 (8th Cir. 1998), a teacher was fired in part because of parents' reaction to the plaintiff sending home with her second graders a "magic rock" which would allow them to do anything they set their mind to. While the exercise might have seemed inoffensive esteem-building to some, relatives, including a local pastor, objected to her "teaching New Ageism." *Id.* at 1156. At the end of that school year, Cowan's contract was not renewed. Applying *Price Waterhouse,* a jury found for Cowan, which was affirmed on appeal. The Eighth Circuit, however, stressed that the defendant could have avoided paying damages had it carried its burden of showing that "it would have made the same decision even in the absence of the illegal criteria." *Id.* at 1158. *See also Brown v. Polk County, Iowa,* 61 F.3d 650 (8th Cir. 1995) (en banc) (finding no reasonable factfinder could determine that plaintiff would have been fired but for his religious activities).

(b) Title VII contains exemptions permitting discrimination on account of religion. One permits certain religious organizations to discriminate on account of religion (but not on the basis of race, sex, or other prohibited ground). See p. 435. A second exemption is the bona fide occupational qualification. The exemption of religious institutions obviates the application of the BFOQ in the most likely cases when it might apply, but it is also available to secular employers in appropriate cases. See p. 436.

(c) Religious restrictions have also been upheld when necessary to avoid Establishment Clause problems. This defense, which has arisen in response to constitutional challenges to public employer restrictions on employees' religious expression, would analytically be a BFOQ in a Title VII suit. *See Berry v. Dep't of Soc. Servs.,* 447 F.3d 642 (9th Cir. 2006) (neither the constitution nor Title VII violated by the employer's ban on plaintiff discussing religion with the employer's clients or displaying religious items in his cubicle because of the risk of Establishment Clause violations); *Helland v. South Bend Community Sch. Corp.,* 93 F.3d 327 (7th Cir. 1996) (upholding discharge of a public school teacher for reading the Bible aloud to a fifth-grade class because of a compelling government interest against teaching religion in public schools). *But see Wigg v. Sioux Falls Sch. Dist. 49-5,* 382 F.3d 807, 815 (8th Cir. 2004) (Establishment Clause concerns did not justify school district's flat prohibition of teachers participating in religious-based programs held on school grounds when no reasonable observer would perceive such participation as state endorsement of religion); *Tucker v. Cal. Dept. of Educ.,* 97 F.3d 1204 (9th Cir. 1996) (invalidating state employer's policy barring religious artifacts outside of the owners' "closed offices or defined cubicles" and also barring religious advocacy during work hours or in the workplace).

8. Title VII makes clear that an employer may not discriminate on the basis of practices or observances (in addition to beliefs), but also, as *Reed* notes, imposes an affirmative duty on employers who must not only avoid discrimination but also "reasonably accommodate" an employee's religious observance unless to do so would be "an undue hardship on the conduct of the employer's business."

THE DUTY OF REASONABLE ACCOMMODATION

Reed's accommodation claim failed for the same reason his discrimination claim failed — the employer did not know what religion it might accommodate. The two duties, however, are distinct, and it is plausible to require more knowledge about the employee's religion before the accommodation duty kicks in than would be true of the duty not to discriminate. Accommodation requires treating the employee differently than other workers, and the employer may well need to understand the employee's observances and practices to develop a reasonable accommodation.

Accommodating religious practices reflected a congressional concern with the problems of those whose religions forbid work on their Sabbath or other holy day. For example, both Seventh Day Adventists and Orthodox Jews have strict limitations on the kinds of work they can perform on their Sabbaths, and Jews are also limited with respect to such high holy days as Yom Kippur. In fact, the vast majority of "accommodation" cases involve refusals by employers to adjust work schedules to the religious observances of particular employees. But the language of the statute is not limited to excusing employees from work when their religion forbids labor (or demands religious practices). It reaches a broad spectrum of other activities, which may range from wearing distinctive clothes to not shaving to displaying religious icons.

The broad formulation of the reasonable accommodation provision suggests that religious observances are privileged as opposed to secular practice. But the law on reasonable accommodation of religion has evolved in a much less stringent fashion than the statute's language might suggest, and much less stringently than has the similar reasonable accommodation requirement under the Americans with Disabilities Act. See Chapter 6. Despite its broad language, the Supreme Court has read §701(j) provision quite narrowly.

The first question is what accommodation is "reasonable." This inquiry focuses on the relationship between the employee's religious needs and the employer's offered accommodation. In *Ansonia Bd. of Educ. v. Philbrook*, 479 U.S. 60 (1986), the Court held that the fit did not have to be very tight. In that case, a teacher needed six days off to attend required religious services and asked the employer to accommodate him by allowing him to use three of his paid personal days for this purpose. The employer refused because the collective bargaining agreement allowed three paid days for religious observances. The Supreme Court found that the agreement offered a reasonable accommodation of religion because it provided time for religious observance, even though it did not completely satisfy plaintiff's religious-based needs. Once an employer has made a reasonable accommodation, the employer has fully satisfied its duty under §701(j). The Court declared:

> We find no basis in either the statute or its legislative history for requiring an employer to choose any particular reasonable accommodation. By its very terms the statute directs that any reasonable accommodation by the employer is sufficient to meet its accommodation obligation. . . . Thus, where the employer has already reasonably accommodated the employee's religious needs, the statutory inquiry is at an end. The employer need not further show that each of the employee's alternative accommodations would result in undue hardship. As [*Trans World Airlines v.*] *Hardison* illustrates, the extent of undue hardship on the employer's business is at issue only where the employer claims that it is unable to offer any reasonable accommodation without such hardship. Once the Court of Appeals assumed that the school board had offered to Philbrook a reasonable alternative, it erred by requiring the board to nonetheless demonstrate the hardship of Philbrook's alternatives.
>
> . . . Under the approach articulated by the Court of Appeals, however, the employee is given every incentive to hold out for the most beneficial accommodation, despite the fact that an employer offers a reasonable resolution of the conflict. This approach, we think, conflicts with both the language of the statute and the views that led to its enactment. We accordingly hold that an employer has met its obligation under §701(j) when it demonstrates that it has offered a reasonable accommodation to the employee.

Id. at 68-69. Note, however, that Philbrook was essentially asking to be paid for time not worked. "Accommodating" this may be viewed as quite different than ensuring no adverse job consequences for religious practice of observance. *See Tepper v. Potter*, 505 F.3d 508 (6th Cir. 2007) (discontinuing a ten-year practice of exempting a Jewish letter carrier from Saturday work was not a failure to accommodate when the employee could use unpaid leave to avoid any conflict with his religious belief). Examples of cases where an accommodation was found sufficient include *Morrisette-Brown v. Mobile Infirmary Med. Ctr.*, 506 F.3d 1317 (11th Cir. 2007) (transfer to flex time position a reasonable accommodation for a sabbatarian); *Cosme v. Henderson*, 287 F.2d 152 (2d Cir. 2002) (offer to transfer a reasonable accommodation although it entailed a small loss of seniority); *Dachman v. Shalala*, 2001 U.S. App. LEXIS 9888 (4th Cir. 2001) (accommodation reasonable when Jewish employee who was permitted to leave work early enough to be home for her Sabbath but not early enough to do certain preparations for it). How can an accommodation be "reasonable" if it does not accommodate the religious observance at issue? *See Baker v. Home Depot*, 445 F.3d 541, 547 (2d Cir. 2006) (a shift trade that would allow plaintiff to attend church services was not a reasonable accommodation when it completely ignored plaintiff's religious need not to work on that day); *EEOC v. Robert Bosch Corp.*, 169 Fed. Appx. 942 (6th Cir. 2006) (granting permission to find volunteers to swap shifts is not necessarily a sufficient accommodation, as where the employee believes that it was a sin to ask another to work for him).

If the employer fails to offer any reasonable accommodation, the second issue, whether a requested accommodation poses an undue hardship for the employer, becomes relevant. In *Trans World Airlines, Inc. v. Hardison*, 432 U.S. 63 (1977), referred to in *Philbrook*, the Court defined undue hardship quite narrowly in a case in which a Saturday Sabbatarian asked that a shift schedule requiring Saturday work be modified for him. He proposed a number of alternatives, but the Court found each to involve an "undue hardship" under a remarkably deferential definition: "To require TWA to bear more than a de minimis cost in order to give Hardison Saturdays off is an undue hardship." *Id.* at 84. Hardship would flow either from TWA paying other employees premium rates to do Hardison's work or from TWA allocating days off on a religious basis: if Hardison were given Saturdays off for religious reasons, other employees would lose their opportunity to have Saturdays off. The Court concluded:

> . . . Title VII does not contemplate such unequal treatment. The repeated, unequivocal emphasis of both the language and the legislative history of Title VII is on eliminating discrimination in employment, and such discrimination is proscribed when it is directed against majorities as well as minorities. Indeed, the foundation of Hardison's claim is that TWA and IAM engaged in religious discrimination in violation of § 703(a)(1) when they failed to arrange for him to have Saturdays off. It would be anomalous to conclude that by "reasonable accommodation" Congress meant that an employer must deny the shift and job preference of some employees, as well as deprive them of their contractual rights, in order to accommodate or prefer the religious needs of others, and we conclude that Title VII does not require an employer to go that far.
>
> . . . Like abandonment of the seniority system, to require TWA to bear additional costs when no such costs are incurred to give other employees the days off that they want would involve unequal treatment of employees on the basis of their religion. By suggesting that TWA should incur certain costs in order to give Hardison Saturdays off the Court of Appeals would in effect require TWA to finance an additional Saturday off and then to choose the employee who will enjoy it on the basis of his religious beliefs. While incurring extra costs to secure a replacement for Hardison might remove the necessity of compelling another employee to work involuntarily in Hardison's place, it

would not change the fact that the privilege of having Saturdays off would be allocated according to religious beliefs.

As we have seen, the paramount concern of Congress in enacting Title VII was the elimination of discrimination in employment. In the absence of clear statutory language or legislative history to the contrary, we will not readily construe the statute to require an employer to discriminate against some employees in order to enable others to observe their Sabbath.

Id. at 80-85. De minimis cost entails not only monetary costs but also less tangible impact on the employer's business. *See Aron v. Quest Diagnostics Inc.*, 174 Fed. Appx. 82, 84 (3d Cir. 2006) (undue hardship established by showing that accommodating plaintiff's religious need not to work on Saturday "would result in unequal treatment of the other employees and negatively affect employee morale"). While the mere existence of a seniority system does not necessarily preclude reasonable accommodation, because some practices may be accommodated without violating the system, *see Balint v. Carson City, Nev.*, 180 F.3d 1047 (9th Cir. 1999), violating a collective bargaining agreement has been frequently held to be an undue hardship. *E.g., Virts v. Consolidated Freightways Corp. of Del.*, 285 F.3d 508 (6th Cir. 2002) (undue hardship for trucking company to accommodate a Christian truck driver who refused to make overnight runs with female drivers because it would require violating a collective bargaining agreement under which drivers are dispatched in the order of seniority).

Even if there is no contrary collective bargaining agreement, courts have refused to find as "reasonable" (or have found an "undue hardship") accommodations that significantly impact other workers. *E.g., Weber v. Roadway Exp., Inc.*, 199 F.3d 270 (5th Cir. 2000) (accommodating driver's religious objections to being partnered with female driver would unduly burden other workers); *Broff v. North Miss. Health Serv., Inc.*, 244 F.3d 495 (5th Cir. 2001) (undue hardship to accommodate counselor's religious beliefs by not assigning her patients who wished help involving homosexual or extramarital relations). *See also Phillips v. Collings*, 256 F.3d 843 (8th Cir. 2001) (not undue hardship to excuse social worker from placing foster children in homosexual parents' homes when few homosexual couples applied).

Nor is an accommodation reasonable where it would require the employer to violate federal laws. Thus, an employee's religious-based refusal to provide an employer with his Social Security number was a valid basis for refusing to hire him because federal immigration and tax laws required that the employer obtain this information. *Sutton v. Providence St. Joseph Medical Ctr.*, 192 F.3d 826 (9th Cir. 1999).

Despite the overall guidance provided by the Supreme Court in *Philbrook* and *Hardison*, the lower courts have had to wrestle with a number of issues at the intersection of nondiscrimination and reasonable accommodation.

WILSON v. U.S. WEST COMMUNICATIONS
58 F.3d 1337 (8th Cir. 1995)

GIBSON, Senior Circuit Judge. . . .

[Christine L.] Wilson worked for U.S. West for nearly 20 years before U.S. West transferred her to another location as an information specialist, assisting U.S. West engineers in making and keeping records of the location of telephone cables. This facility had no dress code. In late July 1990, Wilson, a Roman Catholic, made a religious vow that she would wear an anti-abortion button "until there was an end to abortion or until [she] could no longer fight the fight." The button was two inches in diameter and showed a color photograph of an eighteen to twenty-week old fetus. The button also contained the phrases "Stop Abortion," and "They're Forgetting Someone." Wilson chose this particular button because she wanted to be an instrument of God like the Virgin Mary. She believed that the Virgin Mary would have chosen this particular button. She wore the button at all times, unless she was sleeping or bathing. She believed that if she took off the button she would compromise her vow and lose her soul.

Wilson began wearing the button to work in August 1990. Another information specialist asked Wilson not to wear the button to a class she was teaching. Wilson explained her religious vow and refused to stop wearing the button.

The button caused disruptions at work. Employees gathered to talk about the button. U.S. West identified Wilson's wearing of the button as a "time robbing" problem. Wilson acknowledged that the button caused a great deal of disruption. A union representative told Wilson's supervisor, Mary Jo Jensen, that some employees threatened to walk off their jobs because of the button. Wilson's co-workers testified that they found the button offensive and disturbing for "very personal reasons," such as infertility problems, miscarriage, and death of a premature infant, unrelated to any stance on abortion or religion.

In early August 1990, Wilson met with her supervisors, Jensen and Gail Klein, five times. Jensen and Klein are also Roman Catholics against abortion. Jensen and Klein told Wilson of co-workers' complaints about the button and anti-abortion T-shirt Wilson wore which also depicted a fetus. Jensen and Klein told Wilson that her co-workers were uncomfortable and upset and that some were refusing to do their work. Klein noted a 40 percent decline in the productivity of the information specialists since Wilson began wearing the button.

Wilson told her supervisors that she should not be singled out for wearing the button because the company had no dress code. She explained that she "just wanted to do [her] job," and suggested that co-workers offended by the button should be asked not to look at it. Klein and Jensen offered Wilson three options: (1) wear the button only in her work cubicle, leaving the button in the cubicle when she moved around the office; (2) cover the button while at work; or (3) wear a different button with the same message but without the photograph. Wilson responded that she could neither cover nor remove the button because it would break her promise to God to wear the button and be a "living witness." She suggested that management tell the other information specialists to "sit at their desk[s] and do the job U.S. West was paying them to do."

[For a time, Wilson took personal and vacation days off, but she] returned to work on September 18, 1990, and disruptions resumed. Information specialists refused to go to group meetings with Wilson present. The employees complained that the button made them uneasy. Two employees led grievances based on Wilson's button. Employees accused Jensen of harassment for not resolving the button issue to their satisfaction. Eventually, U.S. West told Wilson not to report to work wearing anything depicting a fetus, including the button or the T-shirt. U.S. West told Wilson again that she could cover or replace the button or wear it only in her cubicle. U.S. West sent Wilson home when she returned to work wearing the button and fired her for missing work unexcused for three consecutive days. Wilson sued U.S. West, claiming that her firing constituted religious discrimination.

An employee establishes a prima facie case of religious discrimination by showing that: (1) the employee has a bona fide religious belief that conflicts with an employment requirement; (2) the employee informed the employer of this belief;

(3) the employee was disciplined for failing to comply with the conflicting employment requirement. *Bhatia v. Chevron U.S.A., Inc.*, 734 F.2d 1382, 1383 (9th Cir. 1984). The parties stipulated that Wilson's "religious beliefs were sincerely held," and the district court ruled that Wilson made a prima facie case of religious discrimination. The court then considered whether U.S. West could defeat Wilson's claim by demonstrating that it offered Wilson a reasonable accommodation. An employer is required to "reasonably accommodate" the religious beliefs or practices of their employees unless doing so would cause the employer undue hardship. 42 U.S.C. § 2000e(j); *Ansonia Board of Education v. Philbrook*.

The court considered the three offered accommodations and concluded that requiring Wilson to leave the button in her cubicle or to replace the button were not accommodations of Wilson's sincerely held religious beliefs because: (1) removing the button at work violated Wilson's vow to wear the button at all times; and (2) replacing the button prohibited Wilson from wearing the particular button encompassed by her vow. However, the court concluded that requiring Wilson to cover the button while at work was a reasonable accommodation. The court based this determination on its factual finding that Wilson's vow did not require her to be a living witness. The court reasoned that covering the button while at work complied with Wilson's vow but also reduced office turmoil. The court also concluded that, even if Wilson's vow required her to be a living witness, U.S. West could not reasonably accommodate Wilson's religious beliefs without undue hardship. The court entered judgment for U.S. West, and Wilson appeals. . . .

I . . .

The district court's finding that Wilson's vow did not require her to be a living witness is supported by the record. First, the stipulation that Wilson's religious beliefs were sincerely held does not cover the details of her religious vow. Second, there is evidence that Wilson's vow did not always include the requirement that she be a living witness. Indeed, the evidence suggests that Wilson first mentioned the living witness requirement only after her supervisor suggested that she cover the button. Wilson's answer to an interrogatory asking her to explain her vow did not mention any living witness requirement, but explained that her vow was "to acknowledge the sanctity of the unborn by wearing the pro-life button until the days [sic] that abortions were no longer performed." Although Wilson testified at trial that wearing the button would allow her to be a "living witness to the truth," on cross-examination, she admitted that, in an interview given in August 1990 to a reporter for *The Catholic Voice*, she said nothing about being a living witness. Klein testified that he never heard Wilson use the word witness in explaining her vow, but rather, that he understood Wilson's vow was to "wear the button until abortions were ended." Accordingly, the district court's finding is supported by the evidence and is not clearly erroneous.

II

We next consider Wilson's argument that the district court erred as a matter of law in concluding that U.S. West offered to reasonably accommodate Wilson's religious views. Wilson argues that her religious beliefs did not require her or any other employee to miss or rearrange work schedules, as typically causes a reasonable accommodation dispute. She argues that it was her co-workers' response to her beliefs that caused the workplace disruption, not her wearing the button. Wilson contends that U.S. West should have focused its attention on her co-workers, not her. Wilson's brief states: "Quite frankly, . . . Klein and Jensen should have simply instructed the troublesome co-workers to ignore the button and get back to work."

The district court, however, succinctly answered Wilson's argument: Klein was unable to persuade the co-workers to ignore the button. Although Wilson's religious beliefs did not create scheduling conflicts or violate dress code or safety rules, Wilson's position would require U.S. West to allow Wilson to impose her beliefs as she chooses. Wilson concedes the button caused substantial disruption at work. To simply instruct Wilson's co-workers that they must accept Wilson's insistence on wearing a particular depiction of a fetus as part of her religious beliefs is antithetical to the concept of reasonable accommodation.

Moreover, U.S. West did not oppose Wilson's religious beliefs, but rather, was concerned with the photograph. The record demonstrates that U.S. West did not object to various other religious articles that Wilson had in her work cubicle or to another employee's anti-abortion button. It was the color photograph of the fetus that offended Wilson's co-workers, many of whom were reminded of circumstances un-related to abortion. Indeed, many employees who opposed Wilson's button shared Wilson's religion and view on abortion.

Wilson also argues that requiring her to cover the button is not a reasonable accommodation. . . . [S]he argues that the accommodation offered required her to abandon her religious beliefs, and therefore, that the accommodation was no accommodation at all. Having affirmed the finding that Wilson's religious vow did not require her to be a living witness, we summarily reject this argument. U.S. West's proposal allowed Wilson to comply with her vow to wear the button and respected the desire of co-workers not to look at the button. Hence, the district court did not err in holding that U.S. West reasonably accommodated Wilson's religious beliefs.

III

Finally, Wilson argues that the district court erred in concluding that her suggested proposals would be an undue hardship for U.S. West.

In *Ansonia Board of Education*, the Supreme Court held that an employer is not required to select the employee's proposal of reasonable accommodation and that any reasonable accommodation by the employer is sufficient to comply with the statute. "The employer violates the statute unless it 'demonstrates that [it] is unable to rea-sonably accommodate . . . an employee's . . . religious observance or practice without undue hardship on the conduct of the employer's business.'" When the employer reasonably accommodates the employee's religious beliefs, the statutory inquiry ends. The employer need not show that the employee's proposed accommodations would cause an undue hardship. Undue hardship is at issue "only where the employer claims that it is unable to offer any reasonable accommodation without such hardship."

Because we hold that U.S. West offered Wilson a reasonable accommodation, our inquiry ends, and we need not consider Wilson's argument that her suggested accommodations would not cause undue hardship.

NOTES

1. *Central to Religion or Merely Religious?* Did the *Wilson* court inquire too closely into the nature of plaintiff's religious beliefs in its findings about whether she

was a "living witness"? There was no question that Wilson's beliefs were sincere, and they would seem to have been religious. *Cf. Altman v. Minn. Dept. of Corr.*, 251 F.3d 1199 (8th Cir. 2001) (reprimand for reading Bible during sensitivity training on gay and lesbian issues raised triable issue of religious discrimination). Did the court mean that the Catholic Church did not require such conduct? Is that the same as saying that plaintiff's conduct was not "religious"?

A number of courts have rejected claims because the employee did not allege or prove that her religious beliefs *required* certain conduct, even if they admittedly motivated it. *Chalmers v. Tulon Co.*, 101 F.3d 1012 (4th Cir. 1996) (religious beliefs did not require plaintiff to send letters to co-workers criticizing their lives); *Tiano v. Dillard Dept. Store*, 139 F.3d 679 (9th Cir. 1998) (no need to give an employee time off from work for a religious pilgrimage since she did not prove that her beliefs required her to go on the pilgrimage during peak season). Where does the statute say that a religious practice or observance must be required to be accommodated? In fact, the whole notion of "required" religious observances seems to reflect a very Western, even Christian, view of religion since many religions are less Commandment-oriented.

Other courts have rejected any requirement that the observance or practice be required or central. *See Anderson v. U.S.F. Logistics (IMC), Inc.*, 274 F.3d 470 (7th Cir. 2001) (district court would "probably" have erred if it viewed plaintiff's desire to use "have a blessed day" with customers as subject to a lesser requirement of accommodation because it was not required by her religion); *Heller v. EBB Auto Co.*, 8 F.3d 1433, 1438 (9th Cir. 1993) (upholding a claim for failure to accommodate an employee's attendance at his wife's conversion ceremony; a court should not inquire whether a particular practice is mandated or prohibited by a religion because that would involve deciding religious questions); *Peterson v. Minidoka*, 1997 U.S. App. LEXIS 36357, *13 (9th Cir. 1997) ("Francis of Assisi was exercising his religion when he gave his costly clothes to the poor; if a government had tried to prevent the gesture it would have violated his free exercise although he acted from no binding precept"). At least one state has amended its fair employment practices law to protect sincerely held religious beliefs "without regard to whether such beliefs are approved, espoused, prescribed or required by an established church or other religious institution or organization." Mass. Gen. L. ch. 151 B, §4(1A) (2007).

2. *Knowledge Again.* In the typical case, an employer will learn of the employee's religious needs because the employee will approach a supervisor seeking an accommodation. But *Wilson* illustrates that the accommodation issue may arise defensively, i.e., when the employer seeks to get the employer to conform to some workplace rule. *Brown v. Polk County, Iowa*, 61 F.3d 650, 654 (8th Cir. 1995) (en banc), rejected the argument that a defendant could not violate the duty to accommodate unless the employee explicitly requested an accommodation for his religious activities. *See also Heller v. EBB Auto Co.*, 8 F.3d 1433, 1439 (9th Cir. 1993) (employer need have "only enough information about an employee's religious needs to permit the employer to understand the existence of a conflict between the employee's religious practices and the employer's job requirements"). *But see Chalmers v. Tulon Co.*, 101 F.3d 1012, 1020 (4th Cir. 1996) ("Knowledge that an employee has strong religious beliefs does not place an employer on notice that she might engage in any religious activity, no matter how unusual").

3. *Three-Step Approach or Merely Balancing?* The duty of reasonable accommodation can be seen as a three-step analysis: plaintiff's proof that a neutral practice burdens his religious observance or practice; and that he sought some kind of accommodation; at that point defendant must prove either that it offered a reasonable

accommodation or that any accommodation would be an undue hardship. *EEOC v. United Parcel Service*, 94 F.3d 314 (7th Cir. 1996). Courts like *Wilson* that have narrowed the definition of what counts as a religious practice have necessarily radically cut back on the need to pursue the last two steps. However, another way to view the cases is not as proceeding down an analytic framework but rather as engaging in an ad hoc balancing of the plaintiff's religious needs and defendant's interests. This explains why the court could denigrate the religious nature of Wilson's protest. Would a broader approach to Title VII put too large a burden on employers, requiring them to accommodate any act based on a worker's religious motivation?

4. *Accommodation or Discrimination?* Why is *Wilson* an accommodation case? Would plaintiff have been better off eschewing any accommodation claim and, instead, arguing that she was simply discharged because of her religion? Reread the statute. While "undue hardship" is a defense to a reasonable accommodation claim, it is not a defense to a charge of disparate treatment religious discrimination. It is true that BFOQ might be a defense in theory, but did U.S. West establish the elements of a BFOQ?

Or is the employer entitled to raise the accommodation issue — that it could not reasonably accommodate plaintiff's religious beliefs without undue hardship — as a defense to an individual disparate treatment case? In *Brown v. Polk County, Iowa*, 61 F.3d 650 (8th Cir. 1995) (en banc) the plaintiff made a straightforward claim that he was terminated because of his religion. The employer then raised accommodation as a defense: it argued that, because plaintiff never explicitly asked for accommodation of his religious activities, he could not claim the protections of Title VII. The court seemed to accept this approach. While it held against the defendant on the facts, it did suggest that the employer could prevail if it could show that any accommodation of the plaintiff's religious expression was an undue hardship. *Id.* at 655. How could that be? Is "undue hardship" another name for BFOQ in this setting? *See generally* Robert Corrada, *The Interrelation of Accommodation and Discrimination in Title VII Religion Cases*, http://ssrn.com/sol3/papers.cfm?abstract_id=960171.

5. *Religious Harassment.* Was Wilson "harassed" because of her religious beliefs or merely because she wore something, admittedly for religious reasons, that offended others for reasons having nothing to do with religion? Courts have been careful to distinguish situations where observant individuals were offended by conduct that was not motivated by religion. *See Rivera v. P.R. Aqueduct & Sewers Auth.*, 331 F.3d 183, 190 (1st Cir. 2003) (there "is a conceptual gap between an environment that is offensive to a person of strong religious sensibilities and an environment that is offensive because of hostility to the religion guiding those sensibilities"). Or was Wilson "harassing" others because of her religious beliefs? *See Powell v. Yellow Book USA, Inc.*, 445 F.3d 1074, 1078 (8th Cir. 2006) (employers have no obligation to suppress religious expression merely because it annoys a single employee). We examined sexual and other kinds of harassment in the preceding section, but religious harassment raises some distinctive issues. Indeed, the EEOC has attempted to formulate guidelines for religious harassment with little success. *See generally* Kent Greenawalt, *Title VII and Religious Liberty*, 33 LOY. U. CHI. L.J. 1 (2001); Eugene Volokh, *Freedom of Speech, Religious Harassment Law, and Religious Accommodation Law*, 33 LOY. U. CHI. L.J. 57 (2001); David L. Gregory, *Religious Harassment in the Workplace: An Analysis of the EEOC's Proposed Guidelines*, 56 MONT. L. REV. 119 (1995).

The problem, of course, is that one person's harassment is another person's free exercise of religion. In this regard, Title VII poses a problem within itself: both the person expressing herself religiously and the person who is offended by that expression may seek the protection of the statute. Further, the Constitution can come into play. To the extent that the statute curbs religious expression, it implicates free exercise notions. *Cf.* Note on the First Amendment Implications of Sexual Harassment Liability, p. 415. *See* Thomas C. Berg, *Religious Speech in the Workplace: Harassment or Protected Speech?*, 22 HARV. L.J. & PUB. POL'Y 954, 959 (1999).

6. *Free Exercise Protection.* Title VII bars religious discrimination, and will typically be the only federal statute implicated when religious discrimination by a private employer is concerned. However, where the employer is a governmental agency, the First Amendment also comes into play. It is generally thought "that in the governmental employment context, the first amendment [free exercise clause] protects at least as much religious activity as Title VII does." *Brown v. Polk County, Iowa*, 61 F.3d 650, 654 (8th Cir. 1995) (en banc). The *Brown* court went on to state that "if a governmental employer has violated Title VII, it has also violated the guarantees of the first amendment." *Id.* at 654. This formulation makes it possible that the First Amendment may prohibit conduct that Title VII would permit. However, the courts have upheld bans on religious displays for public employees. *See Daniels v. City of Arlington*, 246 F.3d 500 (5th Cir. 2001) (city could bar display of cross as part of "no pin" policy for uniformed officers); *United States v. Bd. of Educ.*, 911 F.2d 882, 890 (3d Cir. 1990) (upholding Pennsylvania's Garb Statute for public school teachers). These cases involved local government employees as to whom the First Amendment was the governing federal source of protection. However, where federal workers are concerned, some version of the Equal Protection Clause's compelling state interest test seems like to apply under the Religious Freedom Restoration Act. See p. 438.

7. *Co-Worker Backlash Trumps Religion?* In *Wilson*, the response of co-workers to the religious practices of the plaintiff was critical to determining whether the employer attempted to reasonably accommodate plaintiff and whether the accommodations plaintiff desired were an undue hardship. If co-worker reactions against having a female or an African-American supervisor or customer hostility to women or minority employees is not a justification for an employer's race or gender discrimination, why is co-worker backlash relevant in a religious discrimination case? Would co-worker hostility to an employee wearing a crucifix or a Star of David justify asking the wearer to remove or cover it? *See generally* Theresa M. Beiner & John M.A. DiPappa, *Hostile Environments and the Religious Employee*, 19 U. ARK. LITTLE ROCK L.J. 577 (1997).

8. *Too Extreme to Accommodate?* Perhaps some religious practices cannot be reasonably accommodated or are inherently an undue hardship. We've seen compliance with the Establishment Clause as a justification for suppressing some religious expression, see Note 7(c) on p. 425. Another example is *Chalmers v. Tulon Co.*, 101 F.3d 1012, 1020 (4th Cir. 1996), where the plaintiff was fired for sending letters to co-workers criticizing their personal lives. "Chalmers' conduct is not the type that an employer can possibly accommodate, even with notice. If Tulon had the power to authorize Chalmers to write such letters, and if Tulon had granted Chalmers' request to write the letters, the company would subject itself to possible suits from [co-workers] claiming that Chalmers' conduct violated their religious freedoms or constituted religious harassment." *Id.* at 1021. *Accord Peterson v. Hewlett-Packard Co.*, 358 F.3d 599, 606-07 (9th Cir. 2004) (the employer could not accommodate plaintiff's religiously-based desire to post anti-gay scriptural passages; it would be an undue hardship to either permit posting of messages intended to demean his co-workers or to exclude sexual orientation from the employer's workplace diversity program).

Similarly, in *Rodriguez v. City of Chicago*, 156 F.3d 771 (7th Cir. 1998), plaintiff police officer alleged that the city discriminated against him by refusing to exempt him from an assignment to guard an abortion clinic. The court held that the city had satisfied "its duty to accommodate Officer Rodriguez by providing him the opportunity, through the [collective bargaining agreement], to transfer to a district that did not have an abortion clinic with no reduction in his level of pay or benefits." This was a "paradigm" of reasonable accommodation, *Accord Shelton v. Univ. Med. & Dentistry of N.J.*, 223 F.3d 220 (3d Cir. 2000) (moving labor/delivery nurse to another department was reasonable accommodation of her beliefs concerning abortion). But neither *Rodriguez* nor *Sheldon* held that a right to transfer was required: they simply held that that was a sufficient accommodation.

However, courts have also found undue hardship in more equivocal settings. *E.g., Cloutier v. Costco Wholesale Corp.*, 390 F.3d 126 (1st Cir. 2004) (undue hardship to defendant's public image for it accommodate plaintiff's religious beliefs as a member of the Church of Body Modification by allowing her to wear her facial jewelry, even though there were no complaints and other employees' piercings went unnoticed). *See* Karen Engle, *The Persistence of Neutrality: The Failure of the Religious Accommodation Provision to Redeem Title VII*, 76 TEX. L. REV. 317, 321 (1997) (courts have been unable to break out of the "neutrality paradigm" and adopt a accommodationist approach). There are, however, a number of situations where accommodation has been required, often when the effects on the employer would be truly minimal and the centrality of observance has been plain. *E.g., EEOC v. Ilona of Hungary*, 108 F.3d 1569 (7th Cir. 1997) (violation to refuse unpaid leave to two Jewish employees for Yom Kippur).

9. *Tortured Statutory Language*. The structure of accommodation law for religious beliefs and practices is quite strict and does not seem consistent with the plain meaning of §701(j) or its legislative history. Senator Randolph, the sponsor of the current version of §701(j), argued that it would protect employees who were members of religious sects that "believe there should be steadfast observance of the Sabbath and require that the observance of the day of worship, the day of the Sabbath, be other than on Sunday. On this day of worship work is prohibited where the day should fall on Friday, or Saturday, or Sunday." 118 Cong. Rec. 705 (1972). Why has the Supreme Court decided to underenforce §701(j)? Might it be a concern that full enforcement would violate the establishment clause of the First Amendment? See Note on the Establishment Clause, p. 436.

NOTE ON RELIGIOUS INSTITUTIONS' EXEMPTION FROM THE PROHIBITION OF RELIGIOUS DISCRIMINATION

Religious entities are exempted from Title VII's prohibition of discrimination on the basis of religion. *See Corporation of the Presiding Bishop v. Amos*, 483 U.S. 327 (1987). Even religious employers, however, are barred from discriminating on the other grounds prohibited by Title VII. *E.g., Bollard v. California Province of Socy. of Jesus*, 196 F.3d 940 (9th Cir. 1999) (a valid Title VII sexual harassment claim was stated against a religious order). This structure raises several questions, two of which frequently arise in tandem: is an employer "religious," and, if so, is the discrimination it practices "religious" in nature?

With regard to those exempted, Title VII has several provisions that exempt religious discrimination by religious institutions. Section 702(a), 42 U.S.C. § 2000e-1(a) (2007), provides that "This title shall not apply . . . to a religious corporation, association, educational institution, or society with respect to the employment of individuals of a particular religion to perform work connected with carrying on" the activities of such an entity. *See Killinger v. Samford Univ.*, 113 F.3d 196 (11th Cir. 1997). Section 2000e-1(e) has a similar exemption for "educational institutions" employing individuals "of a particular religion." The latter exemption has been construed not to include a school which is merely nominally religious. *EEOC v. Kamehameha Schs./Bishop Estate*, 990 F.2d 458 (9th Cir. 1993).

While these exemptions allow such institutions to employ "individuals of a particular religion," this has been read not merely to permit religious institutions to prefer members of their own faiths but also to allow such institutions to exclude individuals who, while claiming to be of the same faith of the institution, have violated some of its tenets. *See Little v. Wuerl*, 929 F.2d 944, 951 (3d Cir. 1991) (statutory "permission to employ persons 'of a particular religion' includes permission to employ only persons whose beliefs and conduct are consistent with the employer's religious precepts"). While scholars have challenged the wholesale exemption of religious institutions from the statute's prohibition of religious discrimination, *see, e.g.,* Jane Rutherford, *Equality as the Primary Constitutional Value: The Case for Applying Employment Discrimination Laws to Religion*, 81 CORNELL L. REV. 1049, 1126-28 (1996), there seems no serious effort to cut back on the statutory immunity for religions. *See also* Executive Order 13279, 62 Fed. Reg. 241, Dec. 12, 2002 (exempting "faith-based organizations" from Executive Order 11246's prohibition of religious discrimination in employment by government contractors).

NOTE ON BFOQ DEFENSE TO RELIGIOUS DISCRIMINATION

Because of the exemptions for religious institutions, church-related organizations rarely need to rely on the BFOQ defense. In some cases, however, institutions that were not within the exemption, but were nevertheless religiously oriented, have used the defense. For example, *Pime v. Loyola University*, 803 F.2d 351 (7th Cir. 1986), found a BFOQ established for tenured lines reserved for Jesuits in Loyola's philosophy department, although it did not find Loyola to be a religious employer. *Pime* was decided before *International Union, UAW v. Johnson Controls*, reproduced at p. 173, which narrowed the BFOQ exemption. Is *Pime* still good law?

EEOC v. Kamehameha Schs./Bishop Estate, 990 F.2d 458, 466 (9th Cir. 1993), rejected a BFOQ for hiring Protestants to teach in the Kamehameha school, and in the process distinguished *Pime*:

> Even if *Pime* were an accurate statement of the law in light of *Johnson Controls*, however, it could not bear the weight the Schools would have it carry. *Pime* approved a Jesuit "presence" of four positions in the Philosophy Department of Loyola University, a school with "a long Jesuit tradition" and a largely Catholic student body. The court focused on the tradition and character of the school and the desire of administrators "'that students would *occasionally* encounter a Jesuit.'" (Emphasis added.) The court stated it was "wholly reasonable to believe that the educational experience at Loyola would be different if a Jesuit presence were not maintained." In this case, the [Kamehameha] Schools will have a Protestant "presence" equal to or greater than the Jesuit "presence" at Loyola even if the proportion of Protestants on the faculty falls well below one hundred percent, and there is no indication the educational experience at the Schools will be any different if some of the teachers are not Protestants. Moreover, the Schools seek to retain a wholly Protestant faculty at a school whose student body has a majority of non-Protestant students and whose tradition and character is rooted more in Hawaiian history and culture than in specific principles of Protestantism.

All of these employers had some religious connection. Is it possible for a purely secular employer to establish a BFOQ? *See Kern v. Dynalection Corp.*, 577 F. Supp. 1196 (N.D. Tex. 1983) (Saudi Arabian law forbidding non-Muslims from flying over certain holy areas justified Muslim faith as a BFOQ for the position of helicopter pilot). Professor Steven D. Jamar argues that Title VII is underprotective of religion by failing to take account of what he calls religious secular employers, that is, employers who view religious beliefs and practices as key to their otherwise secular businesses. *Accommodating Religion at Work: A Principled Approach to Title VII and Religious Freedom*, 40 N.Y.L. L. Rev. 719, 788-89 (1996).

NOTE ON THE ESTABLISHMENT CLAUSE

Constitutional challenges to Title VII's treatment of religion have not been well received. The Supreme Court rejected a challenge to the exemption of religious institutions from the statute's prohibition on religious discrimination. *Corporation of the Presiding Bishop v. Amos*, 483 U.S. 327 (1987), involved the Deseret Gymnasium in Salt Lake City, Utah, a nonprofit facility, open to the public, but operated by two religious corporations, both associated with The Church of Jesus Christ of Latter-day Saints, sometimes called the Mormon Church. A building engineer sued when he was discharged because he failed to qualify for "a temple recommend, that is, a certificate that he is a member of the Church and eligible to attend its temples." *Id.* at 330. When the defendants moved to dismiss on the basis that §702 shielded them from liability, plaintiff contended that §702 would violate the Establishment Clause if it were construed to allow religious employers to discriminate in hiring for non-religious jobs. The Supreme Court upheld the §702 exemption:

> "This Court has long recognized that the government may (and sometimes must) accommodate religious practices and that it may do so without violating the Establishment Clause." It is well established, too, that "[t]he limits of permissible state accommodation to religion are by no means co-extensive with the noninterference mandated by the Free Exercise Clause." There is ample room under the Establishment Clause for "benevolent neutrality which will permit religious exercise to exist without sponsorship and without interference." At some point, accommodation may devolve into "an unlawful fostering of religion," but this is not such a case, in our view.

Id. at 334 (citations omitted). The Court found no occasion to re-examine the much-criticized three-pronged test for Establishment Clause validity of *Lemon v. Kurtzman*, 403 U.S. 602 (1971), since "the exemption involved here is in no way questionable under *Lemon*." 483 U.S. at 327. Section 702 had a "secular legislative purpose" of alleviating governmental interference with a religious organization's ability to define and carry out its religious missions. Second, its primary effect was neither to advance nor inhibit religion because the section merely allows churches themselves to advance religion; the government's activities are not doing so. As for the third prong, the exemption did not impermissibly entangle church and state; indeed it effectuated "a more complete separation of the two and avoids the kind of intrusive inquiry into religious belief" than might be required of a less complete exemption. *Id.* at 339.

A second constitutional challenge on establishment clause grounds has been to the whole notion of reasonable accommodation. An unqualified duty to accommodate employees' religious beliefs may go too far. In *Estate of Thornton v. Caldor, Inc.*, 472 U.S. 703 (1985), the Court struck down a Connecticut statute which prohibited employers from requiring an employee to work on his Sabbath. That statute was not limited to "reasonable" accommodation, but required accommodation by the employer, regardless of the burden imposed. *Amos* described the statute struck down in *Thornton* as effectively having given "the force of law to an employee's designation of his sabbath day and required accommodation by the employer regardless of the burden that constituted for the employer or other employees." *Amos*, 483 U.S. at 337-38, n. 15.

Title VII, which provides only for "reasonable" accommodation and provides employer protection for undue hardship, would seem to be distinguishable, *see Protos v. Volkswagen of America, Inc.*, 797 F.2d 129 (3d Cir. 1986) ("Unlike the Connecticut statute, Title VII does not require absolute deference to the religious practices of the employee, allows for consideration of the hardship to other employees and to the company, and permits an evaluation of whether the employer has attempted to accommodate the employee"), a conclusion recently reinforced by *Cutter v. Wilkinson*, 544 U.S. 709 (2005). In *Cutter*, the Court took a more permissive view of legislation imposing duties of accommodations, upholding the Religious Land Use and Institutionalized Persons Act as applied to state prisons. Refusing to read RLUIPA to "elevate accommodation of religious observances over an institution's need to maintain order and safety," the Court rejected the lower court's invalidation of RLUIPA as impermissibly advancing religion.

These kinds of Establishment Clause concerns may have led the Supreme Court to so narrowly construe the duty of reasonable accommodation in both *Hardison* and *Philbrook*. Certainly, the Court's reading is far narrower than the literal language would suggest, and far narrower than the similarly phrased duty of reasonable accommodation under the Americans with Disabilities Act. See Chapter 6. And the Supreme Court has a history of reading statutes to avoid having to face constitutional questions under the religion clauses of the First Amendment. *E.g., NLRB v. Catholic Bishop*, 440 U.S. 490 (1979) (interpreting National Labor Relations Act not to reach religiously affiliated schools in order to avoid free exercise problems). However, the constitutional landscape may have changed. Would the Court that decided *Cutter* strike down a literal interpretation of Title VII's duty of reasonable accommodation?

NOTE ON THE FREE EXERCISE CLAUSE

The free exercise clause can be viewed as having two major beneficiaries — individuals who wish to worship as they choose and the religious institutions in which those individuals worship. Title VII's prohibition of religious discrimination and its requirement of reasonable accommodation tend to further the individual's interest by limiting the ability of covered employers to infringe upon the individual's liberty to both to believe and to practice her religion. We have seen some sharp limitations on the duty to accommodate which reduce the scope of this protection, but it remains a major thrust of the statute.

Religious institutions have also been protected by Title VII, most notably in permitting them to discriminate on account of religion and therefore further their religious missions. See Note on Religious Institutions' Exemption from the Prohibition of Religious Discrimination, p. 435. This exemption essentially allows religious institutions' interests to trump individual interests when they conflict. Mr. Amos's interests, for example, were subordinated to the interests of the Church of Latter-day Saints. *See generally* David Gregory, *Government Regulation of Religion through Labor and Employment Discrimination Laws*, 22 STET. L. REV. 27, 28 (1992) (the law today as insufficiently protective of religious individuals and excessively protective of traditional religious institutions).

But Title VII does not exempt religious institutions from its other prohibitions. Thus, a church or religious educational institution is barred from discriminating on the grounds of race, sex, and national origin by Title VII; it is also barred from discrimination on account of age or disability by the ADEA and the ADA. In a number of cases, religious employers have claimed a Free Exercise right to do exactly what these statutes proscribe.

Prior to 1990, the issue would have been framed as whether the Free Exercise Clause was violated by the antidiscrimination statutes to the extent they imposed a "substantial burden" on the church and could not be justified by a "compelling state interest." That analysis was rejected in *Employment Div., Dept. of Human Resources v. Smith*, 494 U.S. 872 (1990), which announced a new approach to free exercise-mandated exceptions to statutes of general application. Plaintiffs in *Smith* challenged the state's denial of unemployment compensation benefits after they had been fired from their private-sector jobs because of their sacramental use of the drug peyote. Writing for the Court, Justice Scalia found no support in the Court's precedents for the proposition that an individual's religious practices might relieve her from the duty to comply with a criminal law of general application. *Id.* at 878-79. Further, he rejected using the compelling governmental interest test in these cases. *Id.* at 886-87. For the free exercise clause to be implicated, the law in question presumably would have to be aimed at religious practices. *Cf. Church of Lukumi Babalu Aye v. Hialeah*, 508 U.S. 520 (1993) (ordinance prohibiting ritual animal sacrifice targets religion and violates the First Amendment because it is not narrowly tailored to serve the asserted government interests).

Smith would seem to have ended the debate: the antidiscrimination statutes are clearly laws of general application only incidentally affecting religious institutions. Thus, sex discrimination by a church could be challenged. But in fact *Smith* merely triggered a more confusing era whose resolution is only now beginning to emerge clearly.

The most dramatic response to *Smith* was the Religious Freedom Restoration Act (RFRA), 42 U.S.C. §2000bb (2007), whose stated purpose was to overturn *Smith*, and which essentially reinstated the substantial burden/compelling governmental interest analysis as a matter of statutory protection, not constitutional law. In *City of Boerne v. Flores*, 521 U.S. 507 (1997), however, the Supreme Court found RFRA unconstitutional as applied to the states. This, in turn, led to a number of states passing "little RFRAs." More important for our purposes, *City of Boerne* seemed to imply that RFRA remained valid as applied to the federal government, a position which the Court recently confirmed in *Gonzales v. O Centro Espirita Beneficente Uniao do Vegetal*, 546 U.S. 418 (2006) (upholding preliminary injunction against federal government enforcement of the Controlled Substances Act when the sacramental use of hoasca was thereby burdened). *But see Francis v. Mineta*, 505 F.3d 266 (3d Cir. 2007) (RFRA abuses by federal employees must be vindicated in a Title VII suit).

This obviously means that federal employees have potential RFRA protections, which could be read to be broader than the crabbed interpretation the courts have accorded Title VII's duty of accommodation. More intriguingly for present purposes, does RFRA limit what would otherwise be the reach of federal statutes such as Title VII wherever a religious institution would be burdened? Another way to frame the question is to ask whether RFRA pro tanto amends Title VII, the ADA, and the ADEA. *See generally* Gregory P. Magarian, *How to Apply the Religious Freedom Restoration Act to Federal Law without Violating the Constitution*, 99 MICH. L. REV. 1903 (2001). The answer is unclear. Some courts have suggested that RFRA is applicable only when the United States is seeking to enforce a federal statute, *Tomic v. Catholic Diocese of Peoria*, 442 F.3d 1036, 1042 (7th Cir.), *cert. denied* 127 S. Ct. 190 (2006) ("RFRA is applicable only to suits to which the government is a party"), but others have held that RFRA limits the application of other federal laws even in private suits, *Hankins v. Lyght*, 441 F.3d 96 (2d Cir. 2006) (2-1, Judge Sotomayor dissenting on the ground that RFRA does not apply to disputes between private parties), which seems the better view. *See also Francis v. Mineta*, 505 F.3d 266 (3d Cir. 2007) (federal employee could not challenge his discharge under RFRA since Title VII was exclusive avenue of redress).

Entirely apart from RFRA, a line of cases has recognized a "ministerial exception" to the antidiscrimination statutes. These cases are in some tension with *Smith* because they create an exception to a law of general application precisely because of the significant burden on a central function of the religion. The ministerial exception actually predates *Smith*, e.g., *McClure v. Salvation Army*, 460 F.2d 553, 560 (5th Cir. 1972), and rested in part on a consistent line of Supreme Court cases that placed the internal affairs of churches beyond government control. *E.g.*, *Gonzalez v. Roman Catholic Archbishop of Manila*, 280 U.S. 1 (1929); *Kedroff v. St. Nicholas Cathedral*, 344 U.S. 94 (1952). In the wake of *Smith*, however, every circuit to have considered the question has reaffirmed the ministerial exception. As one court said, "*Smith*, which concerned individual free exercise, did not purport to overturn a century of precedent protecting the church against governmental interference in selecting its ministers." *Combs v. Central Texas Annual Conference of the United Methodist Church*, 173 F.3d 343, 349 (5th Cir. 1999); *Accord Petruska v. Gannon Univ.*, 462 F.3d 294 (3d Cir. 2006) (ministerial exception barred suit against religious institution challenging its right to select who will perform spiritual functions, such as the chaplaincy at issue); *Werft v. Desert Southwest Annual Conf.*, 377 F.3d 1099 (9th Cir. 2004) (minister's claims of church's failure to accommodate his disabilities barred because otherwise the court would have to pass on a religious justification for the failure to accommodate).

Further, the exception is broader than its title might suggest. While ministers and priests have been barred from suing, other individuals whose jobs are less clearly "ministerial" have also been precluded. For example, *Alicea-Hernandez v. Catholic Bishop*, 320 F.3d 698, 704 (7th Cir. 2003), held that plaintiff's duties as press secretary for the diocese, "responsible for conveying the message of an organization to the public as a whole," fell within the ministerial exception). *Accord Starkman v. Evans*, 198 F.3d 173 (5th Cir. 1999) (choir director qualifies as "minister" for purposes of the ministerial exception because she "participated in religious rituals and had numerous religious duties"). *See also Curay-Cramer v. Ursuline Acad. of Wilmington, Del., Inc.*, 450 F.3d 130 (3d Cir. 2006) (Congress had not spoken clearly enough to justify applying Title VII to a decision by a religious school to dismiss teacher for pro-choice actions when assessment of whether her conduct was comparable to that of a male would require assessment of the degree to which Catholic teachings were implicated by their respective actions).

While the exemption seems to be predicated at least in part on a judicial desire to avoid passing on theological questions, some courts have explicitly rejected any such limitation. As *Combs*, phrased it:

> [T]he First Amendment concerns are two-fold. The first concern is that secular authorities would be involved in evaluating or interpreting religious doctrine. The second quite independent concern is that in investigating employment discrimination claims by ministers against their church, secular authorities would necessarily intrude into church governance in a manner that would be inherently coercive, even if the alleged discrimination were purely nondoctrinal.

173 F.3d. at 350. *See generally* Caroline Mala Corbin, *Above The Law? The Constitutionality of the Ministerial Exemption from Antidiscrimination Law*, 75 FORDHAM L. REV. 1965 (2007).

Despite this approach to the ministerial exception, the antidiscrimination statutes may apply to some church actions. *See Bollard v. Cal. Socy. of Jesus*, 196 F.3d 940 (9th Cir. 1999) (Title VII sexual harassment suit stated a claim where the challenged conduct neither involved a church selecting its ministers nor was religious in nature). *Cf. Elvig v. Calvin Presbyterian Church*, 375 F.3d 951, 964 (9th Cir. 2004) (inquiry into a church's decision to terminate plaintiff's ministry foreclosed, but plaintiff's hostile environment claims may be pursued subject to the *Ellerth/Faragher* affirmative defense since this inquiry "does not require interpretations of religious doctrine or scrutiny of the Defendants' ministerial choices").

The interaction of RFRA with the ministerial exception is unclear. One argument is that RFRA in effect statutorily amended Title VII to incorporate some version of the ministerial exception. At least one court, however, viewed RFRA as completely displacing the exception. *Hankins v. Lyght*, 441 F.3d 96, 102 (2d Cir. 2006), held that, rather than employing the judicially-created ministerial exception, "RFRA must be deemed the full expression of Congress's intent with regard to the religion-related issues . . . . and displace earlier judge-made doctrines that might have been used to ameliorate the ADEA's impact on religious organizations and activities." *Contra Tomic v. Catholic Diocese of Peoria*, 442 F.3d 1036 (7th Cir.), *cert. denied* 127 S. Ct. 190 (2006) (rejecting *Hankins* as "unsound" to the extent that decision would "invalidate the many decisions in this and other circuits recognizing the ministerial exception to federal employment discrimination law"). Might RFRA in fact operate to expand the exception beyond the scope accorded it by the earlier cases? Or might Title VII be nevertheless applied as written — there is a compelling governmental interest in eliminating discrimination? Does *Boy Scouts of Am. v. Dale*, see Note on Constitutional Limitations on the Reach of the Antidiscrimination Laws, p. 330, help answer the question?

Smith did not overrule all prior cases that seemed to subject laws of general application to strict scrutiny. For example, *Fraternal Order of Police Newark Lodge No. 12 v. City of Newark*, 170 F.3d 359 (3d Cir. 1999), written by then-Judge Alito, held that a city's refusal to accommodate officers whose religion required them to wear beards violated the free exercise clause, at least where the city permitted officers with medical conditions that limited shaving to wear beards. Although the no-beard rule seemed a rule of general application within the meaning of *Smith*, Judge Alito found *Smith* inapplicable since the city already made an exception for medical conditions. Does this distinction make sense to you? Applying heightened scrutiny, the court found no sufficient justification for the policy as applied to religious observers.

A final note on this complicated subject. It has been argued that *Boy Scouts of American v. Dale* might have plugged the constitutional hole created by *Smith*, at least as far as religious institutions (as opposed to individual believers) are concerned.

This is an especially intriguing possibility since both opinions were authored by Justice Scalia. The argument is, essentially, that churches should have a right of expressive association that will immunize them from antidiscrimination and other laws that might adversely affect the message they seek to convery. *See generally* Mark Tushnet, *The Redundant Free Exercise Clause?*, 33 LOY. U. CHI. L.J. 71 (2001); Daniel O. Conkle *The Free Exercise Clause: How Redundant, and Why?*, 33 LOY. U. CHI. L.J. 95 (2001).

E. NATIONAL ORIGIN AND ALIENAGE DISCRIMINATION

Americans have long had a complex love-hate relationship with immigrants to this country, which is reflected in our laws. Title VII, of course, bars national origin discrimination but has been held to permit discrimination on account of alienage. The Immigration Reform and Control Act of 1986 (IRCA), Pub. L. No. 99-603, 100 Stat. 3359 (1986), also proscribes national origin discrimination, but it both prohibits alienage discrimination (against those aliens authorized to work by our immigration laws) and requires alienage discrimination (against those aliens who are not permitted to work). Further, § 1981 prohibits discrimination on account of alienage. The resulting legal regime creates a complicated obstacle course for both employers and employees. Current efforts to amend the laws to deal more harshly with those not legally in the United States may compound the problem.

ZAMORA v. ELITE LOGISTICS, INC.
478 F.3d 1160 (10th Cir. 2007) (en banc)

EBEL, Circuit Judge.

[Plaintiff Ramon Zamora sued his former employer, Elite Logistics, Inc., under Title VII alleging Elite discriminated against him] because of his race and national origin 1) by suspending Zamora from work until he presented documentation establishing his right to work in the United States; and 2) then, after reinstating Zamora, firing him after he requested an apology. The district court granted Elite summary judgment on both claims. A divided panel of this court reversed that decision. After rehearing this appeal en banc, this court VACATES the panel's decision. As to Zamora's first claim involving Zamora's suspension, because the en banc court is evenly divided, we simply AFFIRM the district court's decision granting Elite summary judgment. As to the second claim involving Zamora's termination, a majority of this court AFFIRMS summary judgment in Elite's favor.

I. BACKGROUND

Viewing the evidence in the light most favorable to Zamora, the evidence in the record established the following: Elite operates a grocery warehouse in Kansas City, Kansas. In June 2000, Elite needed to hire an additional 300 workers in just a few weeks' time. In doing so, Elite failed to verify that all of its new employees were authorized to work in the United States.

A year later, in August 2001, Elite hired Zamora. At that time, Zamora was a Mexican citizen who had been a permanent legal resident of the United States since 1987. As part of the hiring process and in compliance with the Immigration Reform and Control Act of 1986 ("IRCA"), Zamora showed Elite his social security card, which he had had since 1980 or 1981, and his alien registration card. Zamora also filled out an I-9 form truthfully indicating that he was a Mexican citizen and a lawful permanent resident of the United States.

Four months after hiring Zamora, in December 2001, Elite received a tip that the Immigration and Naturalization Service (INS)[3] was going to investigate warehouses in the area. Elite was particularly concerned about such an investigation in light of its earlier hiring practices in June 2000. Elite, therefore, hired two independent contractors to check the social security numbers of all 650 Elite employees. This investigation indicated that someone other than Zamora had been using the same social security number that he was using. The investigation turned up similar problems with thirty-five other employees' social security numbers.

On May 10, 2002, therefore, Elite's human resources manager, Larry Tucker, met specifically with Zamora and gave him an "Important Memorandum," written in Spanish and English, giving him ten days to produce adequate documentation of his right to work in the United States. Tucker followed this same procedure with the other thirty-five employees whose social security numbers raised concerns.[5] The memorandum Tucker gave Zamora and the other affected workers read:

> It is required by federal law that all employees produce documents, which establish their identity and/or employment eligibility to legally work in the United States when they are hired. This eligibility can be established with a US Passport, a Certificate of Citizenship or Naturalization; or with a combination of other documents, such as a state's driver's license, state or federal ID card, US Social Security card and/or a certified copy of a birth certificate, issued by a state of the United States.
>
> It has come to our attention that the documents you provided us previously are questionable. Therefore, we are asking that you obtain proper documentation, or you may not be permitted to continue working here. Please bring proper evidence of your identity and employment eligibility no later than 5:00 p.m. on Monday, May 20, 2002, to the Department of Human Resources, or you may be terminated.
>
> Thank you.

At the bottom of this memorandum there was a place where Zamora indicated that

> I understand and agree that until and if I provide documents, which establish my identity and/or employment eligibility to legally work in the United States, Elite Logistics may not be able to continue permitting me to work. I also understand and agree that I have until 5:00 p.m. on Monday, May 20, 2002, to produce this documentation.

Zamora signed and dated that section of the memorandum. Zamora testified in his deposition that he understood at that time that he needed to bring in a valid social security card and documents establishing that he had a right to work in the United States. Zamora continued working during this ten-day period.

---

3. The INS no longer exists. In March 2003, its duties were transferred to the Department of Homeland Security.

5. Most of these thirty-five employees, when asked for this documentation, just quit. Only Zamora eventually provided paperwork verifying his right to work in the United States.

Zamora did not present Elite with any of the requested documents by May 20, 2002. Therefore, Tucker again met with Zamora[6] and, according to Zamora, Tucker told him that he could not "come to work anymore until you got a different Social Security number." Zamora left Tucker's office and returned that same day with a document from the Social Security Administration showing wage earnings for the years 1978-85 for an "R. Zamora" under Zamora's social security number. This document had been mailed to an address in Washington, which Zamora had scratched out and replaced with his then-current Missouri address. More problematic, however, was that the date of birth for R. Zamora on this earnings statement was different than the date of birth Ramon Zamora had given Elite at the time Elite hired him. After reviewing the earnings statement, Tucker became concerned that yet a third individual had been using Zamora's social security number. Therefore, Tucker informed Zamora that this earnings statement was not "acceptable." Neither was an INS document Zamora showed Tucker that indicated that Zamora had previously applied to become a United States citizen.

At some point, Zamora also showed Tucker his naturalization certificate, indicating that Zamora had in fact become a naturalized citizen of the United States. But Tucker rejected that document as well.

The next day, May 23, Zamora brought Tucker a statement from the Social Security Administration indicating that the social security number Zamora had given Elite was in fact his number. Tucker then told Zamora that "[w]e will check this out ourselves. And if it checks out, you can come back to work." Tucker's assistant verified this document's authenticity and then called Zamora, asking him to return to work on May 29.

On May 29, however, instead of returning to work, Zamora went to Tucker's office and handed him a letter stating that "[b]efore I could consider going back to work I need from you two things: 1) an apology in writing, and 2) a complete explanation of why I was terminated. Please send a response to my home." Tucker refused to apologize. Tucker may then have told Zamora to get out of Tucker's office or the building, or to "[j]ust get the hell out." According to Zamora, Tucker also told him he was fired. . . .

III.   DISCUSSION

In alleging that Elite discriminated against him on the basis of his race and national origin, Zamora challenges two separate incidents: 1) Elite's suspending Zamora from work until he was able to produce documentation establishing his right to work in the United States; and 2) after Elite reinstated him, Elite's decision to fire Zamora after he requested an explanation and an apology.

A.   SUSPENSION

[The district court granted Elite summary judgment on the suspension claim after applying *McDonnell Douglas's* burden-shifting analysis because Zamora had failed to create a triable issue of fact as to whether Elite's proffered justification was merely a pretext for discrimination. The en banc court was evenly divided on this issue, and therefore affirmed the district court.]

---

6. Union steward Ray Puentes was at this meeting between Tucker and Zamora and acted as a translator between the two.

B.   TERMINATION

[As to the claim that Elite discriminated on the basis of race and national origin when it fired Zamora when he requested an apology, the majority assumed that Zamora had established a prima facie discrimination claim and Zamora conceded that] Elite asserted a legitimate, nondiscriminatory reason for firing Zamora — its human resources manager, Tucker, believed that Zamora would not return to work unless Tucker apologized, and Tucker refused to apologize. Elite's proffered justi-fication was sufficient for Elite to meet its "exceedingly light" burden under *McDonnell Douglas* and shift the burden back to Zamora to show that Elite's proffered justification was merely a pretext for race and national origin discrimi-nation.

Zamora argues that Elite's proffered reason for terminating Zamora was not worthy of belief because Tucker could not have reasonably believed that Zamora had actually conditioned his return to work on Zamora apologizing. "In determining whether the proffered reason for a decision was pretextual, we examine the facts as they appear to the person making the decision." *Watts v. City of Norman*, 270 F.3d 1288, 1295 (10th Cir. 2001) (emphasis added; quotations omitted). And the undisputed evidence in this case establishes that, although Elite informed Zamora he could return to work on May 29, Zamora did not return to work but instead went to Tucker's office and gave him the letter. And that letter specifically stated that "[b]efore I could consider going back to work I need from you two things: 1) an *apology in writing*, and 2) a complete explanation of why I was terminated. Please send a response to my home." (Emphasis added). Further, because Zamora had asked that Tucker's written apology be sent to his home, Tucker could have reasonably believed that Zamora was not going to return to work on May 29, as Elite had requested. Based upon these undisputed facts known to Tucker, he could reasonably have believed that Zamora was not going to return to work unless Tucker apologized.[10]

Zamora argues that Tucker's strong reaction to Zamora's request for a written apology and explanation indicates that his proffered reason for terminating Zamora was a pretext for his true discriminatory motive. Zamora testified that when he gave Tucker the letter requesting a written explanation and apology, Tucker grabbed it out of Zamora's hand and told Zamora he was fired "because [Tucker] was not apologizing to anybody." But there is simply no evidence in the record indicating that Tucker's reaction was because Zamora was a Mexican-born Hispanic. In fact, the evidence indicates just the opposite. Once Zamora provided Elite with docu-mentation indicating that he was eligible to work in the United States, and that the social security number he was using was his, Tucker offered Zamora his job back. If Tucker was discriminating against Zamora based upon his race or national origin, Tucker would not have reinstated him. There is nothing in the record to suggest that Tucker was not going to permit Zamora to return to work on May 29; in fact, the undisputed evidence indicates that Zamora could have returned to work that day. Under the facts of this case, then, Tucker's suspending Zamora and his later decision to terminate Zamora's employment must be viewed as discrete, separate events. Tucker did not terminate Zamora until Zamora requested a written explanation and apology as a condition for his returning to work. And even Zamora concedes that

10. At various places in the record, Zamora asserts that he would, and that he would not, have returned to work even without Tucker's apology. But Zamora's subjective intent is not relevant to the question of how the facts objectively appeared to Tucker, as the decisionmaker. . . .

Elite had no legal obligation to apologize. We agree with that. Nor is there any suggestion that Tucker had ever treated similarly situated employees who were not Hispanic or Mexican-born any differently. Because Zamora failed to present sufficient evidence establishing a genuinely disputed issue of fact as to whether or not Elite's proffered reason for firing Zamora was a pretext for discrimination, summary judgment for Elite was warranted on this claim. . . .

[Two separate concurring opinions are omitted.]

[McCONNELL, concurring, joined in whole or part by five other judges.]

. . . Elite claims that its reason for demanding additional documentation from Mr. Zamora was a good faith — even if flawed — attempt to comply with the Immigration Reform and Control Act of 1986. IRCA is relevant here in two respects. First, the statute prohibits the knowing employment of unauthorized aliens and places affirmative burdens on employers to verify the identity and employment eligibility of employees, at the hiring stage, by examining certain documents specified by statute and regulation. See 8 U.S.C. §§ 1324a(a)(1)(A)-(B), 1324a(b); 8 C.F.R. § 274a.2(b)(1)(ii) & (v). The statute provides that, at the time of initial hiring, compliance "in good faith with the[se] requirements . . . with respect to the hiring . . . for employment of an alien in the United States . . . establish[es] an affirmative defense that [the employer] has not violated" the above provisions. 8 U.S.C. § 1324a(a)(3). IRCA also makes it unlawful for an employer "to continue to employ [an] alien in the United States knowing the alien is (or has become) an unauthorized alien with respect to such employment." Id. § 1324a(a)(2). It is this latter obligation — combined with the range of civil and criminal penalties that await employers who violate IRCA, see id. § 1324a(e)-(f) — that Elite claims prompted its actions in this case.

Second, IRCA has created employer incentives to protect against the significant disruption that may occur when immigration enforcement agents inspect a workplace and find workers out of compliance. As the then-Acting Deputy Director of United States Citizenship and Immigration Services ("USCIS") explained in recent congressional testimony:

> [O]ne of the primary reasons for a human resources manager to push participation in [a voluntary program for employee verification] was to avoid that moment when the INS would come in and raid the place and take away half the workers, and make it impossible to make any kind of production. That's the kind of event that gets the human resources manager fired, and that's the kind of event that they would try to plan against.[6]

Immigrant Employment Verification and Small Business: Hearing Before the Subcomm. on Workforce, Empowerment, & Gov't Programs of the H. Comm. on Small Business, 109th Cong. (2006) [hereinafter *Verification Hearing*] (statement of Robert

---

6. Indeed, Mr. Tucker enunciated a concern very similar to this in explaining why he staggered distribution of the memoranda alerting employees of their reported SSN discrepancies:

> [W]e knew that once we started calling these people in, not only they but others that may have had social security numbers that checked out would leave the work force and that if we had a large group of warehouse employees leave at one time, it would have been disruptive. So we set up — originally I was going to call five individuals in each week. But the first week, the first five I called in, they and about five other guys just disappeared the next day. So we slowed the process down to where we were doing like two to three every other week or so.

Divine, Acting Deputy Director, USCIS, Department of Homeland Security). As recent events around the country illustrate, this is not an obligation that employers can afford to take lightly.[7]

One of the principal methods of ensuring employee eligibility is verification of Social Security numbers. Indeed, this is the key feature of the federal government's Basic Pilot Program — a voluntary employment eligibility verification system created by Congress in 1997. Employers who participate in Basic Pilot electronically submit information from a newly hired employee's I-9 form — name, date of birth, SSN, citizenship status (if provided) — for comparison with information on the SSA's primary database, irrespective of the facially compliant documents provided by the employee to satisfy I-9 requirements. [If the submitted information matches SSA data, the employer is so notified. If not, the federal government continues to research and, if there is still a problem, issues a "tentative nonconfirmation," which the employer must provide to the employee. Employees then may try to resolve the problem. If they are unsuccessful a "final nonconfirmation" is issued, and the employer may terminate the employee. An employer who chooses not to terminate after a final nonconfirmation must notify the government or face penalties.]

Compliance efforts have shifted to Social Security number verification because of the easy availability of forged documents and the prevalence of identity theft, which make other forms of documentation less reliable. . . .

In his dissenting opinion, Judge Lucero writes at length about the anti-discrimination requirements contained within IRCA, 8 U.S.C. §1324b(a), despite the fact that Mr. Zamora has not alleged a violation of those provisions. Citing the text, legislative history, and implementing regulations of the IRCA provisions, the dissent seems to imply that our interpretation of Title VII ought to be guided by these provisions. That suggestion is unfounded because — as the dissent acknowledges — the IRCA anti-discrimination provisions were intended to " 'broaden[] the Title VII protections against national origin discrimination, while not broadening other Title VII protections.'" (emphasis removed) (quoting H.R. Conf. Rep. No. 99-1000 (1986), *reprinted in* 1986 U.S.C.C.A.N. 5840, 5842). This case arises under Title VII — not IRCA's anti-discrimination provisions — and the principles we interpret will apply across the board to all Title VII claims. It would be contrary to congressional intent for us to "broaden" Title VII by interpreting it to coincide with the IRCA anti-discrimination provisions. To confine our analysis to Title VII does not "go far in insulating employers from national origin discrimination claims," as the dissent charges. It simply respects the different reach of the two different statutes.

IV

Turning first to Mr. Zamora's suspension claim, I am at a loss to see how a reasonable factfinder could construe the sequence of events detailed above as discriminatory. [Elite examined the Social Security numbers of all of its employees, without regard to their race or national origin, and it treated all of those for whom their were discrepancies the same. While Mr. Zamora's argued that his production of his naturalization certificate should have absolved Elite of any liability under IRCA,

---

7. On December 12, 2006, Department of Homeland Security officials raided six meatpacking plants across the nation in search of illegally employed immigrants. The action resulted in the arrest of 1,282 workers — nearly ten percent of the targeted company's workforce. *See* Rachel L. Swarns, *Illegal Immigrants at Center of New ID Theft Crackdown*, N.Y. Times, Dec. 14, 2006, at A38 . . .

and that therefore, further requests for documentation belied the employer's stated rationale and thus evidence of pretext, the concurrence disagreed. The naturalization certificate by itself might have sufficed, but plaintiff also presented Tucker with a Social Security document that displayed a birth date different from the one he had previously reported to Elite, which "understandably heightened Mr. Tucker's suspicion regarding whether the SSN used by Mr. Zamora was legitimately his."]

It may have been wrong, but it was not unreasonable for Mr. Tucker to believe that, under these circumstances, examination of the naturalization certificate would fail to bring the company into compliance with IRCA. IRCA makes it "unlawful for [an employer], after hiring an alien for employment in accordance with [IRCA's hiring procedures] to continue to employ the alien in the United States knowing the alien is (or has become) an unauthorized alien with respect to such employment." 8 U.S.C. § 1324a(a)(2). Thus, Mr. Tucker may have reasonably believed that while examination of a facially valid naturalization certificate would satisfy Elite's statutory duties at the *hiring stage, see* 8 U.S.C. § 1324a(a)(3), once the company was confronted with a *specific* question about a worker's documentation, it was under a duty to investigate and resolve that specific concern.

Indeed, case law interpreting IRCA supports Elite in this view. The Ninth Circuit has held that 8 U.S.C. § 1324a(a)(2) adopts a "constructive knowledge standard," whereby "a deliberate failure to investigate suspicious circumstances imputes knowledge" to an employer. *New El Rey Sausage Co. v. INS*, 925 F.2d 1153 (9th Cir. 1991) (citing *Mester Mfg. Co. v. INS*, 879 F.2d 561 (9th Cir. 1989)). As that court explained, employers share "part of [the] burden" of "proving or disproving that a person is unauthorized to work." Initial verification at the hiring stage is done through document inspection, but "[n]otice that these documents are incorrect places the employer in the position it would have been if the alien had failed to produce documents in the first place: it has failed to adequately ensure that the alien is authorized." . . .

Whether or not this Court ultimately agrees with the Ninth Circuit's interpretation — which we need not decide in this case — *New El Ray Sausage* demonstrates that Mr. Tucker's diligence in seeking resolution of all reported SSN discrepancies was within the bounds of reasonableness and, therefore, that his continued focus on resolving Mr. Zamora's SSN problem does not constitute strong evidence of pretext.

Mr. Zamora's position appears to be that whenever an employer has "good" documents on file — that is, documents that facially comply with IRCA and for which questions have not been raised — the employer is barred from pursuing any suspicious circumstances that arise concerning other documents on file. As *New El Ray Sausage* demonstrates, IRCA does not necessarily read that way, and I do not believe an employer should be held to have discriminated under Title VII for failing to adopt this somewhat surprising reading of its responsibilities. Indeed, if any action beyond facial examination of eligibility documents is discriminatory, then the entire Basic Pilot Program — which is designed to curb the growing problems of document fraud and identity theft — might be called into question, since it is premised on the examination of data discrepancies rather than documents. . . .

[LUCERO, J., joined by four judges, dissenting.]

Although half of the members of this court agree that Zamora presented sufficient evidence of pretext as to his continued suspension, the majority opinion concludes that the record contains no evidence that Tucker terminated Zamora because Zamora was a "Mexican-born Hispanic." This ignores the events surrounding Zamora's suspension, which had ended a mere four days before. I fail to understand how we can be evenly divided over whether Tucker was motivated by racial bias against Mexican-Americans on May 25, and yet issue a majority opinion concluding that Tucker had no racial motivations as a matter of law on May 29. . . .

III

[This case turns on the third stage of *McDonnell Douglas*, in which Zamora must offer evidence showing that the proffered reason is pretextual.]

A

Because Tucker effectively conceded that his actions were not driven by IRCA — he admitted he no longer had concerns about Zamora's right to work in this country as of May 22, 2002 — I see little merit in providing an in-depth discussion of the statute. Nevertheless, because I differ greatly from the concurrence in my view of IRCA's requirements and restrictions, I briefly outline my thoughts on this matter.

IRCA was designed to curb the influx of undocumented immigrants by creating a regime of sanctions against employers that hire them. Toward this end, the Act requires employers to verify the identity and eligibility of employees at the time of hiring by examining certain documents. 8 U.S.C. § 1324a(a)(1)(B), (b). Well-meaning employers are provided with significant legal protection at the hiring stage because they are allowed to assert "good faith" compliance with IRCA as an affirmative defense to liability. Id. § 1324a(a)(3). IRCA also declares that requesting "more or additional documents" at hiring than those specifically identified in the Act "shall be treated as an unfair immigration-related employment practice." Id. § 1324b(a)(6). After the employment relationship is established, IRCA makes it unlawful to "continue to employ [an] alien in the United States knowing the alien is (or has become) an unauthorized alien with respect to such employment." Id. § 1324a(a)(2).

Employer sanctions, however, represent only one side of the IRCA coin. When IRCA was initially debated, advocates and members of Congress voiced widespread concerns that the Act would become a tool of invidious discrimination against Hispanic-Americans and other minorities. Although the original bill introducing IRCA did not contain strong anti-discrimination measures, the full House voted to include a significant anti-discrimination amendment. See H.R. Rep. No. 99-682(II) (1986), pt. 2, at 12 (1986), reprinted in 1986 U.S.C.C.A.N. 5757, 5761. Explaining its support for this amendment, the House Committee on Education and Labor stated:

> The [committee] strongly endorses [the anti-discrimination amendment] and . . . has consistently expressed its fear that the imposition of employer sanctions will give rise to employment discrimination against Hispanic Americans and other minority group members. It is the committee's view that if there is to be sanctions enforcement and liability there must be an equally strong and readily available remedy if resulting employment discrimination occurs.

In adopting the House amendment to the bill, the Joint Senate and House Conference Committee ("Conference Committee") agreed "[t]he antidiscrimination provisions of this bill are a complement to the sanctions provisions, and must be considered in this context." H.R. Conf. Rep. No. 99-1000 (1986), reprinted in 1986 U.S.C.C.A.N. 5840, 5842. It went on to explain that the provisions "broaden[] the

Title VII protections against national origin discrimination, while not broadening the other Title VII protections, because of the concern of some Members that people of 'foreign' appearance *might be made more vulnerable* by the imposition of sanctions." Id. (Emphasis added.)

[The Conference Committee added a clause to the statute providing, "[t]he antidiscrimination provisions would . . . be repealed in the event of a joint resolution approving a [General Accounting Office] finding that the sanctions had resulted in no significant discrimination." Id. at 5843; see 8 U.S.C. §1324b(k)(2)). But a 1990, GAO report to Congress found] IRCA had indeed resulted in a "serious pattern" of national origin discrimination. GAO, Employer Sanctions and the Question of Discrimination 5 (1990) ("GAO estimates that 461,000 (or 10 percent) of the 4.6 million employers in the survey population nationwide began one or more practices that represent national origin discrimination."). Thus, IRCA — as enacted, and as it stands today — declares that "[i]t is an unfair immigration-related employment practice for a person or other entity to discriminate against any individual . . . with respect to the hiring, or recruitment or referral for a fee, of the individual for employment or the discharging of the individual from employment . . . because of such individual's national origin."[8] 8 U.S.C. §1324b(a)(1)(A).[9]

The concurrence would go far in insulating employers from national origin discrimination claims. It suggests that because employers face sanctions for knowingly continuing to employ unauthorized aliens, employers should be given a virtual safe-harbor against Title VII claims for investigating an employee, so long as they cite IRCA to defend their actions. Assuredly, employers should undertake meaningful investigation if an employee's lawful work status is legitimately called into question. However, fear of sanction for "knowing" employment of unauthorized aliens cannot justify discriminatory precautionary measures. Indeed, regulations implementing IRCA expressly warn employers:

> Knowledge that an employee is unauthorized may not be inferred from an employee's foreign appearance or accent. Nothing in [the definition of knowing] should be interpreted as permitting an employer to request more or different documents than are required under section 274A(b) of the Act or to refuse to honor documents tendered that on their face reasonably appear to be genuine and to relate to the individual.

8 C.F.R. §274a.1(1)(2).[10]

---

8. Although the concurrence looks to numerous external sources, including the New York Times, to illuminate the purposes and effects of IRCA, it neglects to carefully consider the anti-discrimination provisions of IRCA itself. It maintains that because "Zamora has not pursued" the administrative procedures set forth in §1324b, "[t]hese provisions are thus not at issue in this case.") IRCA expressly provides that these procedures apply only to claims that cannot be brought under Title VII. 8 U.S.C. §1324b(a)(2)(B). Although I agree that the anti-discrimination provisions have not been directly placed at issue in this case, these provisions are indispensable in any serious discussion of the Act.

9. I do not suggest that IRCA's anti-discrimination provisions necessarily guide our analysis. This dissent merely points out that allowing employers to cite IRCA concerns as a shield against Title VII claims is not contemplated by IRCA itself.

10. As the concurrence notes, some courts have held that employers violate §1324a(a)(2) when they have "constructive knowledge" of an employee's unauthorized work status and yet continue to employ that individual. See, e.g., *New El Rey Sausage Co., v. INS*, 925 F.2d 1153, 1157-58 (9th Cir. 1991). However, no court has held that a credit check revealing only that an employee's SSN was used by another person constitutes "constructive knowledge" of a person's unauthorized work status. Nor do the government's actions under IRCA support this broader view of "constructive knowledge." The concurrence suggests that the government's adoption of social security verification in its Basic Pilot Program supports Elite's actions. To the contrary, this argument ignores significant differences between the

Adopting the concurrence's approach would undoubtedly narrow the scope of recovery for national origin discrimination claims. This result thwarts Congress's clear intent in passing IRCA to "broaden[] the Title VII protections against national origin discrimination" and to prescribe a "strong and readily available remedy" for such discrimination. H.R. Conf. Rep. No. 99-1000 (1986), reprinted in 1986 U.S.C.C.A.N. 5840, 5842; H.R. Rep. No. 99-682(II) (1986), pt. 2, at 12 (1986), reprinted in 1986 U.S.C.C.A.N. 5757, 5761. Due consideration of IRCA does not and should not preclude examination of whether Zamora presented evidence sufficient to reach a jury on his Title VII claims.

B

[The dissent found sufficient evidence of pretext from several sources. First, there was evidence that Elite's proffered reason for his suspension — a desire to verify Zamora's right to work in the United States — was false, including what it characterized as Tucker's own admission that concern over Zamora's right to work did not underlie his decision to continue Zamora's suspension. Second, there was Elite's violation of its own May 10, 2002 written memorandum procedures by not accepting Zamora's naturalization certificate as sufficient. Third, although Zamora could have as easily been a victim as a perpetrator of identity theft, he testified that Tucker accused him of stealing someone else's SSN. Finally,] Zamora has shown that Elite has acted contrary to its alleged good-faith attempt to comply with IRCA, even during the period of his suspension. After Zamora vigorously asserted that his original social security number was correct and true, Tucker instructed Zamora to return to him with a different SSN. Together this evidence demonstrates "weaknesses, implausibilities, inconsistencies, incoherencies, or contradictions" in Elite's proffered reason of IRCA compliance, such that a reasonable factfinder could find that reason "unworthy of credence." . . .

NOTES

1. *The Facts.* The principal case elicited five separate opinions from a deeply divided court, all stemming out of a relatively simple set of circumstances. Two concurrences have been omitted, and even the portions of the opinions reproduced above have been heavily edited. The conflicting legal analyses of relatively straightforward facts suggests both the difficulties of inferring national origin under Title VII and the complexities introduced into that analysis by IRCA. The core question seems to be when, if ever, demand for proof of authorization to work equates with national origin discrimination, given that proof was demanded of someone of foreign national origin.

2. *National Origin under Title VII.* If Mr. Zamora had been suspended because he was of Mexican birth, Elite would have violated Title VII. The same would be true had

---

government's Basic Pilot Program, which requires employers to verify employee SSNs with the federal government, and the ad hoc approach used by Elite. At no point before Zamora's suspension did Elite or anyone else attempt to verify Zamora's SSN by contacting the Social Security Administration ("SSA"). Instead, Elite hired independent contractors to run checks on his SSN information. Only the SSA can conclusively identify the proper holder of a given SSN — recognizing this, the independent contractor employed by Elite instructed the company to verify the number with the SSA and provided a telephone number for the agency.

the discrimination been because Mr. Zamora's parents (or more remote ancestors) been from Mexico even had he been a native-born citizen. National origin discrimination may have a racial aspect to it — recall *St. Francis College v. Al-Khazraji*, p. 73, which held that groups now considered to be more ethnic than racial should be considered races for purposes of § 1981. *See generally* Gary A. Greenfield & Don B. Kates, Jr., *Mexican Americans, Racial Discrimination, and the Civil Rights Act of 1866*, 63 CAL. L. REV. 662, 730-31 (1975). But national origin discrimination can occur apart from race as a result of world events that trigger hostility toward persons associated with particular nations or regions. Most obviously, in the wake of September 11th, discrimination has intensified against Arabs and, more generally, Muslims. *But see* Leti Volpp, *The Citizen and the Terrorist*, 49 UCLA L. REV. 1575, 1576 (2002) ("September 11 facilitated the consolidation of a new identity category that groups together persons who appear 'Middle Eastern, Arab, or Muslim.' This consolidation reflects a racialization wherein members of this group are identified as terrorists, and are disidentified as citizens"). And national origin discrimination might occur if employers treated individuals differently based on their perception that, say, those who spoke Spanish were more likely to be unauthorized than those who speak English.

3. *Alienage under Title VII.* Perhaps surprisingly, Title VII has been held not to bar alienage discrimination, despite its close connection with national origin. In *Espinoza v. Farah Mfg. Co.*, 414 U.S. 86 (1973), the employer refused to hire a lawfully admitted resident alien, a citizen of Mexico, because she was not a citizen of the United States. The Court rejected her suit. Since "national origin" refers to the country from which a person or her ancestors came, it does not refer to a person's citizenship status. Further, there was no reason to believe that the employer discriminated against Mexican national origin from either a disparate treatment or disparate impact perspective because individuals of Mexican ancestry made up 97% of the workers in the job Ms. Espinosa sought.

4. *Enter IRCA. Espinosa* was decided before the enactment of the Immigration Reform and Control Act of 1986. To understand IRCA, it is important to appreciate that it is a compromise resolving an earlier iteration of the immigration "crisis." The statute provided amnesty for most individuals then in the country illegally, 8 U.S.C. § 1255a (2007), but simultaneously, and for the first time in American history, prohibited private employers from hiring undocumented aliens. 8 U.S.C. § 1324a. The idea was that the immigration problem would be solved humanely by legalizing those presently in the country while removing any incentive for future illegal immigration by cutting off prospects for employment. *See generally* Natalie Prescott, *Immigration Reform Fuels Employment Discrimination*, 55 DRAKE L. REV. 1 (2006).

However, precisely because employers would be sanctioned for hiring unauthorized aliens, Congress counterbalanced the resulting incentives to discriminate on the basis of national origin. It defined the kinds of documents that could be required by the employer, § 1324a(b)(1)(B), and limited employers' right to ask for "more or different documents" or "refusing to honor documents tendered that on their face reasonably appear to be genuine." It did so by declaring that such actions are unfair immigration-related employment practices "if made for the purpose or with the intent of discriminating against an individual on the basis of either national origin or because of a lawfully admitted individual's citizenship status." § 1324b(a)(6). Had IRCA been in force at the time, Farah would have violated it since Ms. Espinosa was "a lawfully admitted resident alien," married to a United States citizen. Presumably, she had a "green card," which meant she was permitted to work.

5. *Interrelation of Title VII and IRCA.* As the various opinions in *Zamora* suggest, many believe that IRCA has failed in its goals. With respect to immigration, there is a consensus that the numbers of unauthorized aliens in the United States have increased since 1986, generating calls for new legislation and enhanced border protection. *See* Sheila Jackson Lee, *Why Immigration Reform Requires a Comprehensive Approach that Includes Both Legalization Programs and Provisions to Secure the Border*, 43 HARV. J. ON LEGIS. 267 (2006) (advocating legislation to secure the border that would provide 15,000 new border agents and extensive new equipment). The failure of IRCA in this regard explains the hostility of those seeking more effective exclusionary policies to any form of immigrant amnesty. Simultaneously, there is no confidence that the provisions of IRCA intended to bar national origin discrimination have been effective. Judge Lucero's dissent in *Elite* cites a 1990 GAO report finding widespread national origin discrimination, and the situation has, if anything, worsened. *See Immigration Reform: Employer Sanctions and the Question of Discrimination*, GAO/T-GGD-90-31, p. 5 (Mar. 30, 1990). While IRCA has its own prohibition against such discrimination, §1324b, that provision explicitly excludes from its coverage any national origin discrimination prohibited by Title VII. It's not clear exactly what this means, but it may explain why Mr. Zamora chose to sue under Title VII rather than IRCA. Another reason, however, may be IRCA's remedial mechanism, which establishes an administrative enforcement scheme that culminates in civil penalties, backpay, reinstatement, and attorneys' fees, but not the compensatory and punitive damages available under Title VII for disparate treatment.

6. *Damned If You Do and Damned If You Don't.* It should be easy to see how the interaction of Title VII and IRCA put employers in a bind. One way to avoid hiring individuals variously described as "illegal" or "undocumented" is to simply refuse to hire anybody who doesn't speak English, has an accent, or looks "foreign." But that would violate Title VII's prohibition on national origin discrimination. Alternatively, the employer could hire only United States citizens. While that would be legal under Title VII according to *Espinosa*, it would violate IRCA's prohibition of discrimination against resident aliens. You should at this point be able to appreciate the problem confronting Elite: it wanted to employ only United States citizens or green card holders, without discriminating based upon factors such as language against individuals whom it might have suspected (but not known) were working illegally. Mr. Zamora apparently spoke so little English he needed a translator.

7. *Did Elite Get It Right?* The fact that Elite was walking a legal tightrope doesn't mean it got it right. The dramatic split in the en banc court revealed serious divisions about when compliance with IRCA turns into national origin discrimination. A bright line would find a violation of Title VII when an employer did anything more than IRCA requires employers to do. Under that view, cases such as *New El Rey Sausage Co. v. INS*, 925 F.2d 1153, 1157-58 (9th Cir. 1991), would be wrong. The downside of this approach is obvious — by refusing to allow employers to question documents or discrepancies, IRCA's mandate to stop employment of unauthorized immigrants would be undercut. But isn't the converse also true? That is, by encouraging employers to act when discrepancies arise, such as in *Zamora* itself, doesn't IRCA create a perverse incentive for employers to discriminate on the basis of national origin? Is there much question that Elite pressed the issue with Mr. Zamora at least in part because his name and lack of English language skills, both tied to his Mexican national origin, suggested he was an alien? Why did a majority of the court privilege IRCA over Title VII?

Although *El Rey* is out of the Ninth Circuit, another Ninth Circuit case decided that same year recognized the problem of competing incentives. *Collins Foods Intl., Inc. v. INS*, 948 F.2d 549 (9th Cir. 1991), reversed a finding that the employer had constructive knowledge of a person's status as an unauthorized alien from facts such as the employer's failing to compare the employee's Social Security card with the sample in the INS Service Manual. *Collins* stressed that not only did Congress not intend the statute to force employers to become experts in employment authorization documents but also that expanding liability by the constructive knowledge doctrine would cause employers to discriminate against people on national origin or citizenship grounds. Recently, the Bush Administration announced the employers would be fired if they continued to employ workers whose social security numbers did not match government's records. This initiative was preliminarily enjoined in *Am. Fedn. of Labor v. Chertoff*, 2007 U.S. Dist. LEXIS 75233, *14 (N.D. Cal. 2007), in part because the Social Security Administration records were error-ridden and the no-match directive would, accordingly, "result in the termination of employment to lawfully employed workers."

8. *Immigrants Doing Jobs No One Else Wants?* Another view of *Zamora* is that it involved an employer who wanted to use workers such as Mr. Zamora and, indeed, would have been happy to employ "illegals" if it wasn't against the law. Elite sought to "staff up" low wage operation and could hardly do so without relying on groups with few other alternatives. That would cut against national origin discrimination. Or would it? Did Mr. Zamora's demand for an apology separate him out from the subservient workers Elite wished to hire? *See generally* Leticia M. Saucedo, *The Employer Preference for the Subservient Worker and the Making of the Brown Collar Workplace*, 67 OHIO ST. L. REV. 961 (2006).

9. *Outsourcing to Avoid the Problem.* Large employers often seek to avoid the complications of labor and employment statutes by outsourcing work to other entities that then become the "employer" for purposes of the law. While this strategy is limited by some of the doctrines we examined in the Coverage section, see Note 7 on p. 327, it remains an effective technique to shift responsibility to other entities. Where the work is typically performed by immigrants — whether citizens, green card holders, or unauthorized workers — this is an especially common tactic. *See* John A. Pearce II, *The Dangerous Intersection of Independent Contractor Law and the Immigration Reform and Control Act: The Impact of the Wal-Mart Settlement*, 10 LEWIS & CLARK L. REV. 597 (2006)

10. *Protecting American Citizens.* Both Title VII and IRCA can be read to protect American citizens from discrimination, Title VII because of American national origin and IRCA because of American citizenship. *But see Chaiffetz v. Robertson Research Holding, Ltd.*, 798 F.2d 731, 735 (5th Cir. 1986) (§1981 does not protect United States citizens from citizenship discrimination"). However, the most likely employers to discriminate against Americans in the United States are foreign-owed firms, which are also the employers likely to be protected by treaties in preferring their nationals. See Note 13 on pp. 328-29.

NOTE ON LANGUAGE AND NATIONAL ORIGIN DISCRIMINATION

While national origin discrimination is distinctive from other kinds of discrimination in its interaction with alienage, it is also distinctive with respect to language.

Recall that in *Zamora* the plaintiff could apparently not speak English and needed his union representative to translate. Elite also provided its notice in both English and Spanish versions.

Had Elite chosen not to employ any workers unless they were fluent in English, such a policy would probably have been permissible under Title VII. *See Garcia v. Rush-Presbyterian-St. Luke's Med. Ctr.*, 660 F.2d 1217, 1222 (7th Cir. 1981) (finding no disparate treatment or disparate impact in a hospital's requirement that employees speak and read English, but also suggesting that such a requirement would be a BFOQ where most patients and staff of the hospital speak English). Requiring advanced facility in English also seems a permissible basis of decision. *See De la Cruz v. New York City Human Res. Admin. Dep't. Social Servs.*, 82 F.3d 16 (2d Cir. 1996) (lawful to replace bilingual Puerto Rican who had difficulty writing English with better writer when job requires good writing skills). A requirement that employees speak a foreign language is also legal. *Church v. Kare Distrib.*, 211 Fed. Appx. 278 (5th Cir. 2006).

While requiring English facility is generally permitted, there have been more questions about discrimination on account of a foreign accent. Such discrimination does not necessarily single out persons with particular national origins, and many people with a foreign national origin do not have a foreign accent. Nevertheless, the rule seems to be that such discrimination is impermissible, *e.g., Gold v. Fed Ex Freight East, Inc.*, 487 F.3d 1001 (6th Cir. 2007) (comments about accent were direct evidence of national origin discrimination); *Hasham v. Cal. State Bd. of Equalization*, 200 F.3d 1035 (7th Cir. 2000) (comment that foreign accent cannot be understood supports inference of national origin discrimination); *see also Griffis v. City of Norman*, 2000 U.S. App. LEXIS 25947 (10th Cir. 2000) (reliance on plaintiff Griffis' black "accent" as a reason not to promote may create an inference of intentional discrimination), unless the accent is sufficiently "thick" to impede communication important to the job. *See Fragante v. City & County of Honolulu*, 888 F.2d 591 (9th Cir. 1989) (holding it permissible to reject an individual whose accent would have hindered his performance of a position requiring interaction with the public). Professor Mari J. Matsuda, in *Voices of America: Accent, Antidiscrimination Law, and a Jurisprudence for the Last Reconstruction*, 100 YALE L.J. 1329, 1384-1385 (1991), questions both *Fragante's* result and whether its distinction is likely to be applied correctly.

These cases, however, are often confusing as to their rationale. In *Fragante*, for example, the Ninth Circuit's opinion indicates that foreign accent discrimination constitutes national origin discrimination but then intermixes the BFOQ defense and *McDonnell Douglas* analysis, concluding that the plaintiff had failed to prove that the employer's job-related reason was a pretext. In the court's view, the defendant's claim that "the deleterious effect his Filipino accent had upon his ability to communicate orally, not merely because he had such an accent" was a legitimate, nondiscriminatory reason for his non-selection. *See also Tippie v. Spacelabs Med., Inc.*, 180 Fed. Appx. 51, 53-54 (11th Cir. 2006) (the phrase "not native" described plaintiff's Spanish language abilities, not her national origin and in any event was not blatant enough to indicate an intent to discriminate); *Jiminez v. Mary Washington Coll.*, 57 F.3d 369 (4th Cir. 1995) (in the context of a college teaching position, consideration of a foreign accent is equivocal evidence of an intent to discriminate on the basis of national origin).

We have seen that an employer can require employees to be able to speak English. Can employer rules requiring that that English be the *only* language spoken in the workplace survive Title VII? *Garcia v. Gloor*, 618 F.2d 264, 270 (5th Cir. 1980), upheld a rule requiring bilingual sales personnel to speak only English on the job:

> [T]he language a person who is multi-lingual elects to speak at a particular time is by definition a matter of choice. . . . In some circumstances, the ability to speak or the speaking of a language other than English might be equated with national origin, but this case concerns only a requirement that persons capable of speaking English do so while on duty.

In fact, the employees were required to speak English to English-speaking customers and Spanish to Spanish-speaking customers, but to speak only English with co-workers. Although the *Gloor* court believed that which language bilingual persons speak is volitional, socio-linguistic scholarship suggests that such individuals often "code switch," that is, speak a combination of languages without always being conscious of which language(s) they are using. *See generally* Mark Colon, Note, *Line Drawing, Code Switching, and Spanish as Second-Hand Smoke: English-Only Workplace Rules and Bilingual Employees*, 20 YALE L. & POL'Y. REV. 227, 251 (2002).

Regardless, *Gloor* is not the only case permitting English-only rules for bilingual employees. *Garcia v. Spun Steak Co.*, 998 F.2d 1480 (9th Cir. 1993), rejected a disparate impact challenge to such a rule on the ground that Title VII requires a significant impact, not just inconvenience. It also rejected a hostile environment claim since an English-only rule does not by itself create a hostile environment, although it might if imposed in the context of an environment of discrimination or if enforced in a draconian and harassing manner. *See* David Ruiz Cameron, *How the Garcia Cousins Lost Their Accents: Understanding the Language of Title VII Decisions Approving English-Only Rules as the Product of Racial Dualism, Latino Invisibility, and Legal Indeterminacy*, 10 LA RAZA L.J. 261 (1998).

Although its guidelines in this area have not been given much deference, the EEOC stakes out a contrary position, presuming English-only rules to be invalid (though rules that require English at certain times are acceptable if justified by business necessity). Such rules, according to the EEOC, "create an atmosphere of inferiority, isolation and intimidation based on national origin which could result in a discriminatory working environment." 29 C.F.R. §1606.7 (2007). *See generally* Cristina Rodriguez, *Language Diversity in the Workplace*, 100 Nw. U. L. REV. 1689 (2006) (English-only rules interfere with profound associational interests held by workers, both in the workplace and in social life more generally). Recently, the Tenth Circuit has departed from the holdings of *Gloor* and *Spun Steak* by finding that an English-only rule could be challenged as both disparate treatment and disparate impact violations. *Maldonado v. City of Altus*, 433 F.3d 1294 (10th Cir. 2006). See pp. 307-08.

The continuing debate about English-only in the workplace is only a subset of recurring disputes about the extent to which the nation should encourage or discourage other languages. *See generally* Cristina M. Rodriguez, *Accommodating Linguistic Difference: Toward a Comprehensive Theory of Language Rights in the United States*, 36 HARV. C.R.-C.L. L. REV. 133 (2001).

NOTE ON TRAIT DISCRIMINATION

We have encountered trait discrimination before, i.e., discrimination on the basis of some trait highly associated with a protected class but not co-extensive with it. If cornrows are associated with blacks, for example, does Title VII prohibit limiting expression of that trait at work? *Rogers v. American Airlines*, 527 F. Supp. 229 (S.D.N.Y. 1981) (holding no). As suggested by the previous notes, trait discrimination is highly relevant to national origin since there are numerous traits — including, but not limited to, language — that characterize particular national origin groups.

The notion of cultural manifestations of identity has received new attention in the literature recently. One influential article, focusing on discrimination against gays, addressed the failure of courts construing the constitution and antidiscrimination statutes to protect aspects that are highly correlated with the protected class, although not the class itself. Kenji Yoshino, *Covering*, 111 YALE L.J. 769 (2002). Yoshino describes this as an "assimilationist bias" and argues that this bias tends to require groups protected by the statutes to engage in compulsory assimilation. Professor Perea makes a related argument in connection with the refusal of the courts to invoke Title VII's national origin branch to protect language and accent. Juan F. Perea, *Buscando America: Why Integration and Equal Protection Fail to Protect Latinos*, 117 HARV. L. REV. 1420 (2004) (language or accent discrimination often functions like race discrimination and ought to be redressable in the same way).

Of course, the practice at issue may be more or less critical to the group involved. Professor Perea explored foreign language and accent as traits that may be both functionally immutable for many individuals and highly constitutive of national origin identity. For gays, Professor Yoshiro considers the distinction between homosexuality and such acts as sodomy — highly correlated but not the same. The more highly correlated the more likely a court will view discrimination on the basis of that trait as being the same as discrimination on the protected basis with which it is correlated. But Justice O'Connor's opinion in *Biggins*, see p. 9, distinguishing between age discrimination and discrimination to avoid pension vesting, indicates that courts draw distinctions even between highly correlated factors. Further, courts, such as *Garcia v. Spun Steak Co.*, 998 F.2d 1480 (9th Cir. 1993), use the supposed "volitional" nature of some characteristics, no mater how constitutive of identity, to justify allowing employers to discriminate against certain traits. See pp. 455-56.

There is, however, an argument that giving more traits legal protection is also dangerous. An interesting Note in the Stanford Law Review argues:

> Yoshino's regime of cultural rights calls upon the courts to engage in the essentialist endeavor of tracing the metes and bounds of a given identity group in order to determine which cultural traits are deserving of legal protection. Even if a court could resolve the conflicting claims over which traits are essential to a group's identity — and even if a court could separate the empowering narratives of identity from those that are repressive — recognizing cultural rights would nonetheless solidify one version of the group's identity over others and bolster the notion that groups have essences. And once the "truth" of each identity group is codified into the law, it would come to subtly shape the lives, both within and outside the group, of those persons the law purported to describe. . . .

Roberto J. González, Note, *Cultural Rights and the Immutability Requirement in Disparate Impact Doctrine*, 55 STAN. L. REV. 2195, 2198-99 (2003). He cites, inter alia, *Richard T. Ford, Beyond "Difference": A Reluctant Critique of Legal Identity Politics* in LEFT LEGALISM/LEFT CRITIQUE 38 (Wendy Brown & Janet E. Halley eds., 2002). Yoshino himself has backed off of the more radical implications of his position. *See* KENJI YOSHINO, COVERING: THE HIDDEN ASSAULT ON OUR CIVIL RIGHTS (2006).

Mr. Gonzalez, however, suggests that Title VII can navigate between the risks of assimilationist bias and the antiessentialist critique by deploying the disparate impact theory to protect groups who are characterized, although not defined, by certain traits or practices; however, he suggests "a dramatically reduced threshold for establishing 'adversity.' A plaintiff's showing of minimal adversity should be sufficient." *Id.* at 2222-23. *See also* Tristin Green, *Discomfort at Work: Workplace Assimilation Demands, Social Equality, and the Contact Hypothesis,* 86 N. Car. L. REV. (forthcoming 2008); Kim Yuracko, *Trait Discrimination as Race Discrimination: An Argument About Assimilation,* 74 GEO. WASH. L. REV. 265 (2006) (employees should not be allowed to use invalid trait proxies at all and to use valid ones only if there is no disparate impact); Kim Yuracko, *Trait Discrimination as Sex Discrimination: An Argument Against Neutrality,* 83 TEX. L. REV. 167 (2004) (trait discrimination should be actionable sex discrimination "only when it stems from gender norms and scripts that are themselves incompatible with sex equality in the workplace"); Camille Gear Rich, *Performing Racial and Ethnic Identity: Discrimination by Proxy and the Future of Title VII,* 79 N.Y.U. L. REV. 1134, 1239 (2004) (downplaying the risk that courts will recognize employees' race or ethnicity performance only when it "comports with stereotypical negative representations of minority communities").

NOTE ON SECTION 1981'S APPLICATION TO NATIONAL ORIGIN AND ALIENAGE DISCRIMINATION

We have seen that §1981 prohibits much of what we would now call national origin discrimination as "racial" discrimination because, when the statute was first passed, "race" had a broader meaning than it does today. See p. 73. Nevertheless, other national origin discrimination would seem beyond the reach of that statute. Oddly, however, §1981 has been held to prohibit alienage discrimination, even though Title VII does not.

As we have seen, §1981 accords "all persons within the jurisdiction of the United States" the same right to make and enforce contracts "as is enjoyed by white citizens," and this language and the statute's legislative history have led courts to hold that §1981 prohibits alienage discrimination in both state and private employment. *Anderson v. Conboy,* 156 F.3d 167 (2d Cir. 1998) (§1981 prohibits discrimination based on race, including ancestry and ethnic characteristics, in the making and enforcement of contracts, and that prohibition extends to private as well as public actors). *See also Duane v. GEICO,* 37 F.3d 1036 (4th Cir. 1994) (§1981 prohibits alienage discrimination in the making of private insurance contracts). While one decision held that §1981 prohibited alienage discrimination in state employment, but not private employment, *Bhandari v. First Natl. Bank of Commerce,* 887 F.2d 609 (5th Cir. 1989), that distinction probably disappeared with the 1991 Amendments to the statute. *See generally* Angela M. Ford, Note, *Private Alienage Discrimination and the Reconstruction Amendments: The Constitutionality of 42 U.S.C. §1981,* 49 U. KAN. L. REV. 457 (2001). Assuming §1981 does generally bar alienage discrimination, it is likely that the statute will not require employment of individuals not authorized to work by IRCA. *See Anderson v. Conboy* (reconciling §1981 and the IRCA by stating that an unauthorized alien who was denied employment because of his unauthorized status has not experienced alienage discrimination).

LIMITING THE RIGHTS OF UNAUTHORIZED ALIENS

Espinosa v. Farah, 414 U.S. 86 (1973), while holding that alienage discrimination is not within Title VII's prohibition of national origin discrimination, nevertheless stressed that aliens remain protected by Title VII from discrimination for race, sex, national origin or religion. Subsequent developments, however, have cast doubt on that statement. It remains true that aliens who are authorized to work by the immigration laws are fully protected by the statute. However, IRCA may provide the employer with a defense in an employment discrimination action by an unauthorized alien.

In *Egbuna v. Time-Life Libraries, Inc.*, 153 F.3d 184 (4th Cir. 1998) (en banc), an unauthorized alien filed a Title VII action alleging that he had been denied employment in retaliation for his testimony in connection with an EEOC charge. The court affirmed summary judgment for the defendant, holding that IRCA rendered the plaintiff ineligible for employment. Because the court did not indicate that the employer had acted on the basis of the applicant's unauthorized status, the opinion must mean that the applicant was simply beyond the protection of Title VII. Strangely, the court did not think it necessary to distinguish *Espinoza*. There is language in *Egbuna*, however, suggesting a different result if the unauthorized alien had been hired and then subjected to discrimination.

In the same vein but not exactly to the same effect, the Supreme Court has held that, even when a violation of federal law can be made out, the fact that the plaintiff is unauthorized may sharply limit the remedies available. In *Hoffman Plastic Compounds, Inc. v. NLRB*, 535 U.S. 137 (2002), decided under the National Labor Relations Act, the majority set aside a NLRB backpay award to an unauthorized alien who had fraudulently obtained employment, but who then had been unlawfully discharged due to his union activity:

> We therefore conclude that allowing the Board to award backpay to illegal aliens would unduly trench upon explicit statutory prohibitions critical to federal immigration policy, as expressed in IRCA. It would encourage the successful evasion of apprehension by immigration authorities, condone prior violations of the immigration laws, and encourage future violations. However broad the Board's discretion to fashion remedies when dealing only with the NLRA, it is not so unbounded as to authorize this sort of an award.

Id. at 151. The Court, however, indicated that Hoffman would not get off scot-free because of the other significant sanctions the Board had imposed. Does *Hoffman* carry over to the antidiscrimination statutes? Should an unauthorized alien be allowed to obtain a prohibitory injunction and attorneys' fees, but no other relief, in a Title VII or § 1981 action? The answer is not yet clear. *Rivera v. NIBCO, Inc.*, 364 F.3d 1057, 1068-69 (9th Cir. 2004) (doubting that *Hoffman* applies because of the overriding national policy against discrimination). *See generally* Lori Nessel, *Undocumented Immigrants in the Workplace: The Fallacy of Labor Protection and the Need for Reform*, 36 HARV. C.R.-C.L. L. REV. 345 (2001).

F. UNION LIABILITY

In 1935, Congress passed the Wagner Act, which, as amended and now called the National Labor Relations Act (NLRA), 29 U.S.C. §§ 151 et seq. (2007), established the legal structure for the relationship between unions and employers. The act made no provisions for the problems of race or gender discrimination and, as originally passed, did not include any direct control of the activities of unions.

Despite the absence of statutory language, one of the first theories of federal law available to attack employment discrimination was the duty of fair representation. In *Steele v. Louisville & Nashville R.R.*, 323 U.S. 192 (1944), the Court created a federal cause of action on behalf of black railroad employees who claimed that the union that was legally charged with representing them was bargaining with the employer to have them replaced. While the statute did not give these black workers the right to become members of the union that represented them, the Court found that a union granted exclusive bargaining representative status over some workers under the NLRA had the duty to represent them fairly. "While the majority of the craft chooses the bargaining representative, when chosen it represents, as the Act by its terms makes plain, the craft or class, and not the majority. The fair interpretation of the statutory language is that the organization chosen to represent a craft is to represent all its members, the majority as well as the minority, and it is to act for and not against those whom it represents." *Id.* at 202.

In 1964, in Title VII's §703, Congress directly barred discrimination by unions. Section 703(c)(1) prohibits a union from discriminating in union membership, "or otherwise to discriminate"; subsection (2) prohibits a union from limiting, segregating, or classifying members or applicants "in any way which would deprive or tend to deprive any individual of employment opportunities"; and subsection (3) prohibits a union from causing an employer to discriminate against an individual.

In *Goodman v. Lukens Steel Co.*, 482 U.S. 656 (1987), the Supreme Court construed §703(c). The lower court had found that the union had failed to challenge the employer's discriminatory discharge of black probationary employees, had failed to assert race discrimination as a ground for grievances, and had tolerated the employer's racial harassment. The union argued that it could be liable for an employer's action if, under §703(c)(3), the union had caused the employer to discriminate. The Court rejected that narrow reading of Title VII and referred to §703(c)(1), which made it an unlawful practice for a union to "exclude or to expel from its membership, or *otherwise to discriminate against*" any individual (emphasis added). *See also Beck v. UFCW Local 99*, 506 F.3d 874 (9th Cir. 2007) (holding union liable under both the duty of fair representation and Title VII for not pursuing grievances on behalf of former employee).

In contrast to the broad approach of the majority, which would prohibit discrimination by unions in their representation of workers, Justice Powell, joined by Justices Scalia and O'Connor, would have construed §703(c) more narrowly. "§703(c)(1) prohibits direct discrimination by a union against its members; it does not impose upon a union an obligation to remedy discrimination by the employer. Moreover, §703(c)(3) specifically addresses the union's interaction with the employer by outlawing efforts by the union to 'cause or attempt to cause an employer to discriminate against an individual in violation of this section.'" *Id.* at 688. *See also Thorn v. Amalgamated Transit Union*, 305 F.3d 826 (8th Cir. 2002) (no affirmative duty for union to investigate and take steps to remedy employer discrimination); *EEOC v. Pipefitters Ass'n Local Union* 597, 334 F.3d 656 (7th Cir. 2003) (employer, not union, responsible for removal of graffiti from the workplace and therefore union could not be liable for harassment).

Neither the majority nor the dissent in *Goodman* referred to §703(c)(2), which prohibits a union from classifying any individual "in any way which would deprive or tend to deprive any individual of employment opportunities." Under §703(c)(2), it would appear that a union would be liable for classifying individuals by race in failing to assert grievances because of the race of the grievants, since that failure

would tend to deprive those individuals of the employment opportunity of participating in the grievance process.

G. RETALIATION

In addition to prohibiting discrimination on the grounds of race, sex, religion, national origin, and age, Title VII, § 1981, and the ADEA create a remedy for certain
retaliatory conduct. Retaliation is also prohibited by the Americans with Disabilities
Act as treated in Chapter 6. Section 704(a) of Title VII, 42 U.S.C. § 2000e-3(a)
(2007), provides:

> It shall be an unlawful employment practice for an employer to discriminate against
> any of his employees or applicants for employment . . . because he has opposed any
> practice made an unlawful employment practice by this title, or because he has made a
> charge, testified, assisted, or participated in any manner in an investigation, proceeding,
> or hearing under this title.

The ADEA prohibits retaliation in substantially identical language. 29 U.S.C. § 623(d)
(2007).

Section 1981 does not expressly prohibit retaliation, although recent appellate
decisions have interpreted the statute as doing so. *E.g., Foley v. University of Houston
Sys.*, 355 F. 3d 333, 338-39 (5th Cir. 2003); *Hawkins v. 1115 Legal Serv. Care*, 163 F.3d
684 (2d Cir. 1998). The Supreme Court has taken a case to decide this issue:
Humphries v. CBOCS West, Inc., 474 F.3d 387 (7th Cir.), *cert. granted*, 128 S. Ct. 30
(2007).

This section will focus on retaliation decisions under Title VII and the ADEA.
The relevant provision in each statute consists of two separate clauses that present
distinct legal questions. The first bars retaliation for "oppos[ing] . . . any practice
made an unlawful employment practice." This "opposition clause" encompasses
more types of conduct than the second clause, the "free access" or "participation"
clause, which proscribes retaliation "because [an employee or applicant] has made a
charge, testified, assisted, or participated . . . in an investigation, proceeding, or
hearing" under the relevant statute.

CLARK COUNTY SCHOOL DISTRICT v. BREEDEN
532 U.S. 268 (2001)

PER CURIAM.
Under Title VII of the Civil Rights Act of 1964, 42 U.S.C. § 2000e-3(a), it is
unlawful "for an employer to discriminate against any of his employees . . . because
[the employee] has opposed any practice made an unlawful employment practice by
[Title VII], or because [the employee] has made a charge, testified, assisted, or
participated in any manner in an investigation, proceeding, or hearing under [Title
VII]." In 1997, respondent filed a § 2000e-3(a) retaliation claim against petitioner
Clark County School District. The claim as eventually amended alleged that petitioner had taken two separate adverse employment actions against her in response to
two different protected activities in which she had engaged. . . .

On October 21, 1994, respondent's male supervisor met with respondent and another male employee to review the psychological evaluation reports of four job applicants. The report for one of the applicants disclosed that the applicant had once commented to a co-worker, "I hear making love to you is like making love to the Grand Canyon." At the meeting respondent's supervisor read the comment aloud, looked at respondent and stated, "I don't know what that means." The other employee then said, "Well, I'll tell you later," and both men chuckled. Respondent later complained about the comment to the offending employee, to Assistant Superintendent George Ann Rice, the employee's supervisor, and to another assistant superintendent of petitioner. Her first claim of retaliation asserts that she was punished for these complaints.

The Court of Appeals for the Ninth Circuit has applied § 2000e-3(a) to protect employee "opposition" not just to practices that are actually "made . . . unlawful" by Title VII, but also to practices that the employee could reasonably believe were unlawful. We have no occasion to rule on the propriety of this interpretation, because even assuming it is correct, no one could reasonably believe that the incident recounted above violated Title VII.

Title VII forbids actions taken on the basis of sex that "discriminate against any individual with respect to his compensation, terms, conditions, or privileges of employment." 42 U.S.C. § 2000e-2(a)(1). Just three Terms ago, we reiterated, what was plain from our previous decisions, that sexual harassment is actionable under Title VII only if it is "so 'severe or pervasive' as to 'alter the conditions of [the victim's] employment and create an abusive working environment.'" *Faragher v. Boca Raton*, 524 U.S. 775, 786 (1998) (quoting *Meritor Savings Bank, FSB v. Vinson* [reproduced at p. 370] (some internal quotation marks omitted)). *See also Burlington Industries, Inc. v. Ellerth* [reproduced at p. 384] (only harassing conduct that is "severe or pervasive" can produce a "constructive alteration in the terms or conditions of employment"); *Oncale v. Sundowner Offshore Services, Inc.* [reproduced at p. 332] (Title VII "forbids only behavior so objectively offensive as to alter the 'conditions' of the victim's employment"). Workplace conduct is not measured in isolation; instead, "whether an environment is sufficiently hostile or abusive" must be judged "by 'looking at all the circumstances,' including the 'frequency of the discriminatory conduct; its severity; whether it is physically threatening or humiliating, or a mere offensive utterance; and whether it unreasonably interferes with an employee's work performance.'" *Faragher v. Boca Raton* (quoting *Harris v. Forklift Systems, Inc.* [reproduced at p. 377]). Hence, "[a] recurring point in [our] opinions is that simple teasing, offhand comments, and isolated incidents (unless extremely serious) will not amount to discriminatory changes in the 'terms and conditions of employment.'" *Faragher v. Boca Raton*.

No reasonable person could have believed that the single incident recounted above violated Title VII's standard. The ordinary terms and conditions of respondent's job required her to review the sexually explicit statement in the course of screening job applicants. Her co-workers who participated in the hiring process were subject to the same requirement, and indeed, in the District Court respondent "conceded that it did not bother or upset her" to read the statement in the file. Her supervisor's comment, made at a meeting to review the application, that he did not know what the statement meant; her co-worker's responding comment; and the chuckling of both are at worst an "isolated incident" that cannot remotely be considered "extremely serious," as our cases require, *Faragher v. Boca Raton*. The holding of the Court of Appeals to the contrary must be reversed.

Besides claiming that she was punished for complaining to petitioner's personnel about the alleged sexual harassment, respondent also claimed that she was punished for filing charges against petitioner with the Nevada Equal Rights Commission and the Equal Employment Opportunity Commission (EEOC) and for filing the present suit. Respondent filed her lawsuit on April 1, 1997; on April 10, 1997, respondent's supervisor, Assistant Superintendent Rice, "mentioned to Allin Chandler, Executive Director of plaintiff's union, that she was contemplating transferring plaintiff to the position of Director of Professional Development Education,"; and this transfer was "carried through" in May. In order to show, as her defense against summary judgment required, the existence of a causal connection between her protected activities and the transfer, respondent "relied wholly on the temporal proximity of the filing of her complaint on April 1, 1997 and Rice's statement to plaintiff's union representative on April 10, 1997 that she was considering transferring plaintiff to the [new] position." The District Court, however, found that respondent did not serve petitioner with the summons and complaint until April 11, 1997, one day after Rice had made the statement, and Rice filed an affidavit stating that she did not become aware of the lawsuit until after April 11, a claim that respondent did not challenge. Hence, the court concluded, respondent "had not shown that any causal connection exists between her protected activities and the adverse employment decision."

The Court of Appeals reversed, relying on two facts: The EEOC had issued a right-to-sue letter to respondent three months before Rice announced she was contemplating the transfer, and the actual transfer occurred one month after Rice learned of respondent's suit. The latter fact is immaterial in light of the fact that petitioner concededly was contemplating the transfer before it learned of the suit. Employers need not suspend previously planned transfers upon discovering that a Title VII suit has been filed, and their proceeding along lines previously contemplated, though not yet definitively determined, is no evidence whatever of causality.

As for the right-to-sue letter: Respondent did not rely on that letter in the District Court and did not mention it in her opening brief on appeal. Her demonstration of causality all along had rested upon the connection between the transfer and the filing of her lawsuit — to which connection the letter was irrelevant. When, however, petitioner's answering brief in the Court of Appeals demonstrated conclusively the lack of causation between the filing of respondent's lawsuit and Rice's decision, respondent mentioned the letter for the first time in her reply brief. The Ninth Circuit's opinion . . . suggests that the letter provided petitioner with its first notice of respondent's charge before the EEOC, and hence allowed the inference that the transfer proposal made three months later was petitioner's reaction to the charge. This will not do.

First, there is no indication that Rice even knew about the right-to-sue letter when she proposed transferring respondent. And second, if one presumes she knew about it, one must also presume that she (or her predecessor) knew *almost two years earlier* about the protected action (filing of the EEOC complaint) that the letter supposedly disclosed. . . . The cases that accept mere temporal proximity between an employer's knowledge of protected activity and an adverse employment action as sufficient evidence of causality to establish a prima facie case uniformly hold that the temporal proximity must be "very close," *Neal v. Ferguson Constr. Co.*, 237 F.3d 1248, 1253 (CA10 2001). See e.g., *Richmond v. Oneok, Inc.*, 120 F.3d 205, 209 (CA10 1997) (3-month period insufficient); *Hughes v. Derwinski*, 967 F.2d 1168, 1174-1175 (CA7 1992) (4-month period insufficient). Action taken (as here) 20 months later suggests, by itself, no causality at all.

In short, neither the grounds that respondent presented to the District Court, nor the ground she added on appeal, nor even the ground the Court of Appeals developed on its own, sufficed to establish a dispute substantial enough to withstand the motion for summary judgment. The District Court's granting of that motion was correct. The judgment of the Court of Appeals is reversed.

NOTES

1. *Broader Protection Under the Participation Clause.* Shirley Breeden presented two distinct claims of retaliation. One was for opposition conduct (her internal complaints), while the other was for participation conduct (her filing of charges to the state agency and the EEOC). Many courts and commentators have perceived a sharp distinction between the protections of the "opposition" clause and the "participation" clause. While a plaintiff invoking the opposition clause must demonstrate a reasonable, good faith belief that the conduct complained of is unlawful, the protections of the participation clause have been almost absolute. One of the first "participation" cases, *Pettway v. American Cast Iron Pipe Co.*, 411 F.2d 998 (5th Cir. 1969), set the tone for these decisions by finding actionable retaliation when a worker was fired for filing an allegedly false and malicious charge with the EEOC — namely, that the employer had bought off an EEOC investigator. The court wrote:

> There can be no doubt about the purpose of § 704(a). In unmistakable language it is to protect the employee who utilizes the tools provided by Congress to protect his rights. The Act will be frustrated if the employer may unilaterally determine the truth or falsity of charges and take independent action.

Id. at 1004-05. *See also Glover v. S.C. Law Enf.*, 170 F.3d 411 (4th Cir. 1999) (unreasonable deposition testimony protected by participation clause); *Clover v. Total Sys. Serv., Inc.*, 176 F.3d 1346 (11th Cir. 1999) (reasonable belief not needed for participation clause protections to be triggered). *But see Mattson v. Caterpillar, Inc.*, 359 F.3d 885, 889-90 (7th Cir. 2004) (sexual harassment charge was unprotected because it was "both objectively and subjectively unreasonable, as well as made with the bad faith purpose of retaliating against his female supervisor . . . "; "this Court has consistently stated that utterly baseless claims do not receive protection under Title VII"); *Johnson v. ITT Aerospace*, 272 F.3d 498 (7th Cir. 2001) (filing frivolous charges against employer not protected); *Barnes v. Small*, 840 F.2d 972 (D.C. Cir. 1988) (although plaintiff's letters to the agency head were sufficiently related to race discrimination proceedings to be protected, discharge was permissible because the letters were both false and malicious). However, the employee must properly invoke the EEOC's powers to be protected under the participation clause. *Slagle v. County of Clarion*, 435 F.3d 262, 268 (3d Cir. 2006) (to be protected, an employee must do more than charge vague "civil rights" violations with the EEOC; an invalid charge did not trigger antiretaliation protections).

After the *Breeden* Court disposed of the plaintiff's "opposition clause" claim by deciding that no reasonable person could believe that she had been sexually harassed, it went on to consider the causation issue on her "participation" clause claim. Doesn't *Breeden* thus establish that the participation clause prohibits retaliation even where the underlying discrimination claim lacks a reasonable basis? Why should that be so? Bad faith law suits can be sanctioned by attorneys fees. What if the plaintiff's charge and suit had been filed in bad faith? *Cf. Christiansburg Garment Co. v. EEOC*, reproduced at p. 703 (Supreme Court holding that employer can be awarded attorneys' fees for Title VII action that was "frivolous, unreasonable, or groundless" or in bad faith). Is there a reason to allow courts to decide the bad faith of claims while precluding employers from doing so by taking adverse employment actions?

2. *Distinguishing Participation Conduct from Opposition Conduct.* Because the protections afforded by these two clauses differ, perhaps dramatically, what is the line between participation, as opposed to opposition, conduct? Internal complaints of discrimination, it appears from *Breeden*, are opposition, not participation, conduct. On the other hand, participation includes not only filing a charge or lawsuit but testifying in court or at deposition. What about answering questions in an employer's investigation of a complaint, perhaps one that appears to be conducted to provide the employer its affirmative defense? *See Deravin v. Kerik*, 335 F.3d 195 (2d Cir. 2003) (an employee defending himself against a charge of sexual harassment is engaged in protected activity under the participation clause).

3. *Retaliation and the* Ellerth *Affirmative Defense.* Is *Breeden's* classification of internal complaints as opposition, not participation, conduct consistent with the affirmative defense set forth in *Ellerth*, reproduced at p. 384? If the affirmative defense is aimed at encouraging plaintiffs to utilize internal complaint mechanisms, why not protect employees from retaliation when they do what the affirmative defense essentially requires them to do? This argument was made to the Eleventh Circuit by the EEOC and rejected. *EEOC v. Total Sys. Servs., Inc.*, 221 F.3d 1171 (11th Cir. 2000).

Is *Breeden* inconsistent with *Ellerth* in yet a more fundamental way? If a purpose of the affirmative defense is to encourage victims to report offensive conduct before it becomes severe or pervasive, thereby allowing employers to promptly correct the conduct, *see Casiano v. AT&T*, 213 F.3d 278 (5th Cir. 2000), why should retaliation against employees who do what *Ellerth* encourages plaintiffs to do *not* be protected? In *Crawford v. Metro Gov't of Nashville & Davidson County*, 211 Fed. Appx. 373 (6th Cir. 2006), the Sixth Circuit held that an employee's report of sexual harassment during an internal investigation was not protected under Section 704 because no charge of harassment had been filed. The Supreme Court has agreed to hear the *Crawford case*, 2008 U.S. LEXIS 1102 (2008). *Cf. Jordan v. Alternative Res. Corp.*, 458 F.3d 332, 343 (4th Cir. 2006) ("Only at an impermissibly high level of generality, where meaningful distinctions can no longer be observed, can it be argued that the law inconsistently encourages employees to report and at the same time not to report violations [and the argument that the] rule creates a perverse incentive for employers to 'fire workers quickly before they have [Title VII] claims' is hyperbolic"). For discussion of the interaction between §704 and internal complaint procedures, *see* Edward Marshall, *Excluding Participation in Internal Complaint Mechanisms from Absolute Retaliation Protection: Why Everyone, Including the Employer, Loses*, 5 EMP. RTS. & EMPLOY. POL'Y J. 549 (2001); Dorothy E. Larkin, Note, *Participation Anxiety: Should Title VII's Participation Clause Protect Employees Participating in Internal Investigations*, 33 GA. L. REV. 1181 (1999).

4. *Reasonable, Good Faith Belief.* The *Breeden* Court questioned, although it did not decide, whether the opposition clause's protections attach if the challenged practice is not in fact unlawful. In other words, will a reasonable, good faith belief that the employer has acted unlawfully suffice under the opposition clause? While the statutory language certainly supports limiting the statute's protections only to opposition to conduct that is in fact unlawful, would such an interpretation be

consistent with the policy objectives of §704? *See Robinson v. Shell Oil* , 519 U.S. 337 (1997) (since policy of §704 furthered by including former employees within the protections of the statute, they are within the protected class). Even prior to *Robinson*, courts generally agreed that a reasonable, good faith belief is sufficient; the challenged conduct need not actually be unlawful.

Although the lower courts have held that a reasonable, good faith belief is both necessary and sufficient, it is clear that reasonableness is not to be determined by the ultimate success of the underlying claim. While the conduct of which Breeden complained is a far cry from the "severe or pervasive" conduct envisioned by the Court in *Meritor* and its progeny, how much of a difference is there between conduct that will support a claim of hostile work environment and that which will support a reasonable, good faith belief that the workplace is hostile? Russell Robinson, *Perceptual Segregation*, 108 COLUM. L. REV. (forthcoming 2008), documents that African Americans, for example, perceive far more discrimination against themselves than whites perceive against African Americans. Without taking a position as to which perception is more accurate, he argues that one implication of this ought to be a wider scope of protection when blacks complain of adverse employment actions. *See also* Lawrence D. Rosenthal, *To Report or Not to Report: The Case for Eliminating the Objectively Reasonable Requirement for Opposition Activities Under Title VII's Anti-Retaliation Provision*, ARIZ. ST. L. J. (2007).

5. *Determining Causation.* In analyzing the participation claim, the *Breeden* Court thought it "immaterial" that the transfer was finalized a month after suit was filed, reasoning that the transfer was contemplated earlier. Should the trier of fact have been allowed to determine the decision-maker's motivation in "finalizing" the transfer? Would a contrary ruling in practice have required employers to "suspend previously planned transfers upon discovering that a Title VII suit has been filed"? Must a plaintiff now present evidence regarding the proximity between the decision-maker's knowledge of the protected activity and its initial contemplation of the adverse employment action?

Does *Breeden* mean that the plaintiff always loses on a summary judgment motion where the employer has denied retaliation and the plaintiff's only evidence of causation is that the adverse employment action occurred three months or more after the decision-maker learned of the protected activity? See *Strong v. University Health Care Sys.*, 482 F.3d 802 (5th Cir. 2007) (temporal proximity alone not enough to prove "but for" causation). What if the decision-maker began "contemplating" such action within three months of learning of the protected activity? *See Franzoni v. Hartmarx Corp.*, 300 F.3d 767 (7th Cir. 2002) (six-month time lapse between charge of discrimination and termination, standing alone, insufficient proof of causation). *Meiners v. University of Kansas*, 359 F.3d 1222 (10th Cir. 2004) (a six-week period between protected activity and adverse action may be sufficient, standing alone, to show causation, but a three-month period, standing alone, is insufficient"). *But see EEOC v. Kohler, Inc.*, 335 F.3d 766 (8th Cir. 2003) (termination less than one month after employee complained of racial discrimination, together with evidence of supervisor's reaction to complaint and inconsistent enforcement of attendance policy, sufficed); *Lampley v. Onyx Acceptance Corp.*, 340 F.3d 478 (7th Cir. 2003) (employee was terminated three days after going to EEOC; evidence that the company covered up the retaliatory reason for the termination supported award of compensatory and punitive damages).

6. *Retaliation Claims and Mixed Motives Analysis.* Does the mixed-motives approach in the 1991 Civil Rights Act, §§703(m), 706(g)(2)(B), apply in a Title VII retaliation case? The Fifth Circuit has held that, when a retaliation case is a pretext-

based, as opposed to a mixed motive case, it is plain error for the court to instruct that a plaintiff need only show retaliation was a motivating factor for an adverse action. *Septimus v. Univ. of Houston*, 399 F.3d 601 (5th Cir. 2005). Most circuits have now stated that *Price Waterhouse* but for causation, not §703(m), is controlling in Title VII retaliation actions involving mixed-motives. *E.g., Pennington v. City of Huntsville*, 261 F.3d 1262 (11th Cir. 2001); *Speedy v. Rexnord Corp.*, 243 F.3d 397 (7th Cir. 2001); *Matima v. Celli*, 228 F.3d 68 (2d Cir. 2000).

7. *Eleventh Amendment Immunity*. In *Crumpacker v. Kansas Dep't of Resources*, 338 F.3d 1163 (10th Cir. 2003), the court held the 11th Amendment does not bar a claim of retaliation because Title VII's antiretaliation provision is within Congress' power under §5 of the 14th Amendment. See Chapter 7, p. 648.

1. Protected Conduct

As we saw in *Breeden*, participation conduct has received greater protection than opposition conduct. While opposition conduct must be supported by a reasonable, good faith belief that the employer has acted unlawfully (if not a finding that the employer's action was in fact unlawful), no such determination appears to be required for participation conduct.

The clauses differ in another important way. The form of participation activities generally will not take the plaintiff outside the protection of the Act. Courts have found employers liable for unlawful retaliation when they act on *any* ground related to filing a discrimination charge. *See, e.g., EEOC v. Bd. of Governors of State Colls. and Univs.*, 957 F.2d 424 (7th Cir. 1992) (invalidating a collective bargaining agreement provision terminating grievance proceedings when a lawsuit is filed; the policy constitutes retaliation, although not motivated by malice). That the employer is invoking a neutral rule that would have been applied to employees engaging in other forms of litigation does not mean those rules may be applied to persons who have engaged in participation activities under employment discrimination statutes. *See, e.g., EEOC v. Bd. of Governors of State Colls. and Univs.*, 957 F.2d 424 (7th Cir. 1992) (invalidating a collective bargaining agreement provision terminating grievance proceedings when a lawsuit is filed; the policy constitutes retaliation, although not motivated by malice). In a sense, §704's participation clause entitles plaintiffs to special treatment.

The extent to which this protection can be carried is illustrated by *Womack v. Munson*, 619 F.2d 1292 (8th Cir. 1980), in which the black plaintiff, after being hired by the county prosecutor, filed a Title VII suit against his former employer, the county sheriff. The prosecutor immediately questioned the plaintiff about the suit, investigated his responses, and shortly thereafter discharged him. In the course of the investigation, the plaintiff first admitted physically abusing black suspects while working for the sheriff, but subsequently denied it. Although the Eighth Circuit did not seem to doubt that either lying or physical abuse of prisoners would be grounds for dismissing a law enforcement officer, the opinion stressed that the physical abuse of black suspects was a focus of the plaintiff's suit against the sheriff. The court concluded that "the admission and denial of abuse by Womack are so inextricably related to the allegation in the complaint that they cannot be considered independently of one another." *Id.* at 1297. It was, therefore, clear that the prosecutor fired the plaintiff because of allegations in his complaint, that is, because he "made a charge . . . or participated in any manner in a . . . proceeding" under Title VII.

But what about the opposition clause? Can the *form* the employee's opposition takes remove her from the protections of the Act? As should be obvious from

McDonnell Douglas Corp. v. Green, reproduced at p. 50, the answer is yes. Recall that Green had engaged in a "stall in" to protest alleged discrimination by the company, and the company had asserted his participation in those activities as the explanation for why Green was not rehired. Although the *McDonnell Douglas* Court did not directly rule on §704(a), as that claim was not before it, the Court, in language broad enough to embrace §704(a), wrote: "Nothing in Title VII compels an employer to absolve and rehire one who has engaged in such deliberate, unlawful activity against it." *Id.* at 803.

How far does *McDonnell Douglas* go in allowing an employer to discriminate because of an employee's "opposition"? Is it merely a "law and order" decision in that it permits retaliation where the opposition violates criminal statutes, or can it be read more broadly? In justifying its ruling, the Court looked to the "disloyalty doctrine" under the National Labor Relations Act. The opinion quoted from *NLRB v. Fansteel Metallurgical Corp.*, 306 U.S. 240 (1939) (sitdown strikers' discharge upheld), which set out the core concept: some acts of protest by employees, even if done for a protected purpose, are sufficiently disloyal to justify discharge. *See also NLRB v. Electrical Workers Local 1229*, 346 U.S. 464 (1953) (upholding the discharge of engineers who distributed handbills that disparaged the employer's product but did not mention a labor dispute). Should the *Fansteel* approach be transplanted to Title VII and the ADEA?

The Supreme Court again addressed the issue in *Emporium Capwell Co. v. Western Addition Community Org.*, 420 U.S. 50 (1975), holding that the NLRA does not protect concerted action by minority employees who seek to bargain directly with their employer about employment discrimination when the employees are represented by a union. Although *Emporium Capwell* is not dispositive of any Title VII question, the Court suggested that the employees' call for a consumer boycott of their employer, with handbills referring to the employer as a "20th Century colonial plantation," a "racist pig" and a "racist store," *might* fall outside the protections of the statute.

What does it take for opposition to what the employee reasonably and in good faith believes is unlawful discrimination to fall outside the protection of the statute? Is it plaintiff's burden to persuade, as part of her prima facie case, that the form the opposition takes is protected by the statute? Or is it enough for prima facie purposes to find that the action was taken in opposition to what was or what plaintiff reasonably and in good faith believed to be an unlawful employment practice? Once a prima facie case is stated, need the employer only articulate the form the opposition conduct took as a legitimate, nondiscriminatory reason for its retaliatory action, thereby distinguishing the conduct from the expression? Or should the employer be required to prove that any retaliation for the form of opposition conduct was justified? The following case may assist you in thinking about and answering these questions.

LAUGHLIN v. METROPOLITAN WASHINGTON AIRPORTS AUTHORITY
149 F.3d 253 (4th Cir. 1998)

WILLIAMS, Circuit Judge.

[Plaintiff sued for retaliation, claiming her conduct was protected under both the participation and opposition clauses of Title VII. The district court granted summary judgment to the employer, concluding that plaintiff was not engaged in participation conduct and that conduct that is "surreptitious, dishonest and disloyal" is presumptively unprotected by the opposition clause, a presumption plaintiff had not overcome].

I . . .

Essential to understanding the incident that directly led to Laughlin's termination are the events related to another MWAA [Metropolitan Washington Airports Authority] employee. Kathy LaSauce, an operations officer at the MWAA, filed an informal complaint with the EEO officer at the MWAA against William Rankin, LaSauce's supervisor. In her complaint, she alleged that Rankin had retaliated against her for providing testimony in another operations officer's EEO action. Initially LaSauce took her complaint to the Washington National Airport manager, Augustus Melton, Jr., in April 1994. Melton took steps to settle the complaint informally. Those steps failed, and LaSauce filed a formal complaint with the MWAA EEO officer and tendered her resignation. In the process of investigating and attempting to settle the LaSauce/Rankin dispute, in September 1994, Melton drafted a written warning to Rankin regarding the inappropriate retaliatory actions that he had taken against LaSauce. The written warning, however, was never formalized; it was neither signed by Melton nor seen by Rankin, it was simply prepared and left on Melton's desk. At about the same time that LaSauce's resignation became effective and Melton had drafted the written warning, Rankin was selected for the job of El Paso Airport manager and tendered his resignation to the MWAA officials.

Meanwhile, Laughlin, a secretary to Melton, reported directly to the airport manager's staff assistant. During the course of her regular duties, on or about September 29, 1994, she discovered a copy of the unsigned written warning on Melton's desk addressed to Rankin. She noticed immediately that the written warning discussed the LaSauce dispute. The written warning was date-stamped September 8, 1994. Laughlin believed that the existence of the dated warning on the desk was highly irregular because correspondence was not generally date-stamped at the MWAA until it was in final form awaiting signature. Alongside the written warning she found Rankin's resignation letter explaining that he had been offered the position in El Paso, and a news clipping, predating the resignation letter, from an El Paso newspaper mentioning that Rankin was the front runner for the position in El Paso. Laughlin was so surprised to see the unsigned correspondence on her boss's desk that she immediately concluded that he was engaging in a coverup to prevent LaSauce from having adequate access to relevant documents for a future lawsuit. As a result of these suspicions, Laughlin removed the documents, photocopied them, and replaced the originals on her boss's desk. She sent the copies to LaSauce with a note stating that she thought LaSauce might find them interesting.

Laughlin's removal and copying of the documents was discovered in 1996 during a deposition in a civil suit filed by LaSauce. Laughlin was terminated as a result of removing the documents. Her termination notice stated in pertinent part that:

> 1) you are a confidential employee in that you are an employee who acts in a confidential capacity with respect to me, the Airport Manager, who effectuates management policies in labor-management relations; 2) you released a draft letter of reprimand, a personnel related document which is confidential by nature; 3) you released personal documents of Mr. William Rankin's, without his or my consent, that had been sent to me for my information; 4) you sent these documents to Ms. Kathy LaSauce on your own accord, without my consent; and 5) according to Ms. LaSauce's sworn deposition, she never asked you for these documents.

III . . .

On appeal, Laughlin contends that she forecasted sufficient evidence to establish a prima facie case of retaliation under Title VII and that the district court erred when it granted summary judgment to MWAA. To establish a prima facie case of retaliation, a plaintiff must prove three elements: (1) that she engaged in protected activity, (2) that an adverse employment action was taken against her, and (3) that there was a causal link between the protected activity and the adverse employment action. It is undisputed that Laughlin suffered an adverse employment action and therefore satisfies the second requirement of a prima facie case: She was terminated. Moreover, it is undisputed that Laughlin was terminated as a result of removing the documents in question. To survive summary judgment, therefore, Laughlin must have evidence that removing the documents was a protected activity.

Laughlin urges us to conclude that the district court erred when it did not characterize her removal of documents as participation in LaSauce's EEO claim. She argues that her actions were taken to assist LaSauce in her investigation. The evidence, however, does not support Laughlin's assertion. First, at the time the documents were removed from the desk, LaSauce was not involved in any ongoing investigation under Title VII. LaSauce had recently resigned from her position at the MWAA and had not yet filed suit. Second, LaSauce herself testified that she had not requested Laughlin's assistance and that she was surprised to receive the documents in the mail. There was quite simply no ongoing "investigation, proceeding or hearing" in which Laughlin could participate at the time she discovered the documents on her boss's desk. On that basis, we disagree with Laughlin's contention that her case should have been analyzed under the participation clause.[4]

Because Laughlin's actions are not cognizable as participation, they must be oppositional or her case fails as a matter of law. To qualify as opposition activity an employee need not engage in the formal process of adjudicating a discrimination claim. *See Armstrong v. Index Journal Co.*, 647 F.2d 441, 448 (4th Cir. 1981). Opposition activity encompasses utilizing informal grievance procedures as well as staging informal protests and voicing one's opinions in order to bring attention to an employer's discriminatory activities. *See id.* To determine whether an employee has engaged in legitimate opposition activity we employ a balancing test. *See id.* We " 'balance the purpose of the Act to protect persons engaging reasonably in activities opposing . . . discrimination, against Congress' equally manifest desire not to tie the hands of employers in the objective selection and control of personnel.' " *Id.* (quoting *Hochstadt v. Worcester Found. for Experimental Biology*, 545 F.2d 222, 231 (1st Cir. 1976)).

The district court initially did not use this test, but rather determined that the circumstances of this case, in which an employee committed an egregious breach of confidentiality, mandated a rebuttable presumption that the activity was not protected under Title VII. Laughlin asserts that the district court erred by analyzing her case utilizing this rebuttable presumption that activity that constitutes a "breach of the employee's obligations of honest and faithful service" is not protected under the

---

4. The distinction between participation clause protection and opposition clause protection is significant because the scope of protection is different. Activities under the participation clause are essential to " 'the machinery set up by Title VII.' " *Hashimoto v. Dalton*, 118 F.3d 671, 680 (9th Cir. 1997). As such, the scope of protection for activity falling under the participation clause is broader than for activity falling under the opposition clause. *See Booker v. Brown & Williamson Tobacco Co.*, 879 F.2d 1304, 1312 (6th Cir. 1989).

opposition clause. We believe that this Circuit's well-established balancing test provides an adequate, workable framework for assessing opposition clause claims and, thus, decline to adopt the district court's rationale. . . .

When we apply the balancing test to the facts of this case, we easily conclude that the employer's interest in maintaining security and confidentiality of sensitive personnel documents outweighs Laughlin's interest in providing those documents to LaSauce. Laughlin's reaction to the situation was disproportionate and unreasonable under the circumstances. This court has recognized that complaining to the employer, *see Hopkins v. Baltimore Gas & Elec., Co.*, 77 F.3d 745, 754 (1996); *Armstrong*, and participating in an employer's informal grievance procedures, *see Armstrong*, when done in a manner that is "not disruptive or disorderly," *id.*, constitute opposition activities that merit protection under Title VII. Laughlin's drastic actions are not akin to the measured responses to employer discrimination that we have approved in the past.

In contrast, the MWAA's decision to terminate Laughlin was sound. The MWAA had a reasonable and significant interest in preventing the dissemination of confidential personnel documents. *See Jefferies v. Harris County Community Action Ass'n*, 615 F.2d 1025, 1036-37 (5th Cir. 1980) ("[Employer] clearly had a legitimate and substantial interest in keeping its personnel records and agency documents confidential"). Laughlin had breached her employer's trust by copying confidential material and sending it to an outside party. Title VII was "not intended to immunize insubordinate, disruptive, or nonproductive behavior at work." *Armstrong*. Because the MWAA's strong interest in protecting sensitive records outweighs Laughlin's interest in this instance, the district court was correct in holding that Laughlin, as a matter of law, did not engage in protected oppositional activity and, therefore, did not establish a prima facie case of retaliatory discharge. . . .

NOTES

1. *Retaliation Claims and the* McDonnell Douglas *Proof Scheme. Laughlin* follows the approach adopted by the circuit courts in relying on the *McDonnell Douglas* method of drawing inferences to determine an employer's motivation when there is no direct evidence. This includes three stages: the plaintiff establishes a prima facie case, the employer articulates a nondiscriminatory reason for its actions, and the plaintiff rebuts by proving pretext.

2. *The Prima Facie Case.* The court's statement of the three elements of the prima facie case is generally recognized: (1) plaintiff engaged in protected expression, (2) she suffered an adverse employment action, and (3) there was a causal link between the former and the latter. Some courts also add a fourth requirement: employer knowledge of the employee's expression. *See, e.g., Gordon v. New York City Bd. of Educ.*, 232 F.3d 111 (2d Cir. 2002). Others consider employer knowledge as embraced within the causation element. Either way, knowledge is necessary, a point that *Breeden* made clear.

3. *"Prima Facie Unprotected"?* The Fourth Circuit found that plaintiff had no prima facie case because the conduct was unprotected under the opposition clause. In so doing, the court acknowledges the broader protection Laughlin would have received had she been able to convince the court she was engaged in participation clause activities. Had the investigation of her co-worker's claim been ongoing, presumably this court would have found that Laughlin's copying the documents and

sending them to her co-worker was protected activity. Do you agree that likely outcome is what Congress intended?

But, as we've seen earlier and as *Laughlin* confirms, the protections of the opposition clause are far less sweeping. *McDonnell Douglas*, reproduced at p. 50, establishes that some conduct is too unreasonable to be protected. And in a footnote omitted from your text, *Laughlin* asserts it is "black letter law" that illegal actions are not protected by Title VII. As is clear from the case, even legal actions that are deemed sufficiently unreasonable can be unprotected as well. At the same time, the mere fact that the employer perceives the conduct to be disloyal does not, of itself, deprive the conduct of protection. *Scarbrough v. Board of Trustees of Florida A&M Univ.*, 504 F.3d 1220 (11th Cir. 2007) (contacting police for protection from supervisor's sexual harassment was protected activity, not unprotected "unprofessional" conduct). *Laughlin* uses a balancing test to determine, at the prima facie case stage, whether the opposition conduct is protected. Essentially, this approach concludes that some *forms* of opposition so beyond the pale as to prevent plaintiff from establishing a prima facie case.

4. *Or Legitimate, Nondiscriminatory Reason?* Alternatively, so long as the opposition is directed toward unlawful discrimination, should the first element of the prima facie case be considered met, leaving it to the employer to articulate the form of opposition as a legitimate, nondiscriminatory reason for its action? There is some confusion with terminology here: it is "discrimination" to retaliate against individuals for opposing discrimination, but perhaps it is clearer to speak of legitimate nonretaliatory reason when an employer is responding to a plaintiff's inferential case. In any event, will a similar "balancing test" apply to determine whether the proffered reason is a retaliatory, as opposed to a nonretaliatory, reason? *Compare Jennings v. Tinley Park Community Consolidated School District No. 146*, 864 F.2d 1368 (7th Cir. 1988) (supervisor's loss of confidence in his assistant for going over his head to complain of discrimination was a legitimate reason to fire her), *with EEOC v. Crown Zellerbach Corp.*, 720 F.2d 1008 (9th Cir. 1983) (warehouse employees' protests to employer's major customer regarding employer's receipt of civil rights award were protected and could not be a legitimate basis for termination).

5. *Applying the Balancing Test.* Whether analyzed at the prima facie stage or in determining whether the proffered reason is a legitimate, nondiscriminatory one, the courts are balancing employer and employee interests. But what goes on the scales? The "reasonableness" of the employee's conduct is one factor, but is the situation to which the employee is responding relevant? *See Cruz v. Coach Stores, Inc.*, 202 F.3d 560 (2d Cir. 2000) (slapping co-worker in response to sexual harassment not protected activity); *Douglas v. DynMcDermott Petro. Oper. Co.*, 144 F.3d 364 (5th Cir. 1998) (unethical disclosure by attorney unprotected); *O'Day v. McDonnell Douglas Helicopter Co.*, 79 F.3d 756 (9th Cir. 1996) (conduct unprotected when employee searched his supervisor's desk and showed the discovered documents to other employees). What if the employee is a high-level affirmative action official? *See Johnson v. Univ. of Cincinnati*, 215 F.3d 561 (6th Cir. 2000) (Title VII protects VP for Human Resources advocating on behalf of women and minorities). What about the extent of any resulting disruption? Could even substantial disruption be outweighed by employer provocation? Should the court consider whether the plaintiff was more disruptive than necessary or whether the plaintiff had ulterior motivations? *See generally* Terry Smith, *Everyday Indignities: Race, Retaliation, and the Promise of Title VII*, 34 COLUM. HUM. RTS. L. REV. 529 (2003) (criticizing the courts' reactions to opposition to "subtle discrimination").

Reread *Slack v. Havens*, reproduced at p. 2. The employees there refused to work because of their belief that discrimination had motivated their job assignment. If they had been wrong in their allegations of discrimination, would the refusal to work have been a protected or unprotected form of opposition? *See Hazel v. Postmaster Gen.*, 7 F.3d 1 (1st Cir. 1993) (refusal to work not protected).

What if an employer believes an employee lied during an investigation of sexual harassment? Will the employer's reasonable, good faith belief that the employee was not telling the truth constitute a legitimate, nondiscriminatory reason for firing her? Or is protection lost only if the employee in fact lied? *See EEOC v. Total Sys. Servs., Inc.*, 221 F.3d 1171 (11th Cir. 2000) (reasonable, good faith belief that employee lied entitles employer to terminate employee).

Suppose an employee did not engage in protected activity, but the employer mistakenly believes that he did and fires him for that reason. Would the employee have a retaliation claim? *Fogleman v. Mercy Hosp., Inc.*, 283 F.3d 561 (3d Cir. 2002) (yes). The *Fogelman* court also found, however, that retaliation against an individual because his father engaged in protected activity was not within the reach of the ADEA's antiretaliation provision, although it was actionable under the ADA. See p. 585.

6. *Who Is Protected?* Title VII's antiretaliation provision may protect only employees who assist another employee, not those who participate in investigations on the side of the employer. *See Twisdale v. Snow*, 325 F.3d 950 (7th Cir. 2003) (employee who participated in investigation of Title VII claim on behalf of an employer was not protected). Does this make sense?

2. Adverse Action

As we saw in Chapter 1, the courts have required that discrimination be sufficiently "adverse" to be actionable. Even when an intent to discriminate is unquestionably present, courts nonetheless have required that there be an "adverse action" before a claim may be stated. Is this "adverse action" a requirement of a retaliation claim as well? The Supreme Court addressed that question in the following case.

**BURLINGTON NORTHERN AND SANTA FE
RAILWAY CO. v. WHITE**
126 S. Ct. 2405 (2006)

BREYER, J.

Title VII of the Civil Rights Act of 1964 forbids employment discrimination against "any individual" based on that individual's "race, color, religion, sex, or national origin." A separate section of the Act — its anti-retaliation provision — forbids an employer from "discriminating against" an employee or job applicant because that individual "opposed any practice" made unlawful by Title VII or "made a charge, testified, assisted, or participated in" a Title VII proceeding or investigation.

The Courts of Appeals have come to different conclusions about the scope of the Act's anti-retaliation provision, particularly the reach of its phrase "discriminate against." Does that provision confine actionable retaliation to activity that affects the terms and conditions of employment? And how harmful must the adverse actions be to fall within its scope?

We conclude that the anti-retaliation provision does not confine the actions and harms it forbids to those that are related to employment or occur at the workplace. We also conclude that the provision covers those (and only those) employer actions that would have been materially adverse to a reasonable employee or job applicant. In the present context that means that the employer's actions must be harmful to the point that they could well dissuade a reasonable worker from making or supporting a charge of discrimination.

[Shortly after Sheila White, the only woman working in her department at the Railroad's Tennessee yard, complained of harassment by her supervisor, she was reassigned from her position operating a forklift to a track laborer job, a more physically demanding and dirtier job. The pay and benefits, however, were the same. After White filed a charge of discrimination with the EEOC, she was suspended without pay for 37 days, a suspension that would have become a termination had she not filed a grievance. The company contended White had been suspended because she was insubordinate. White did grieve her suspension, and the hearing officer found she had not been insubordinate and ordered her reinstated with backpay. Despite having suffered no economic harm, White filed suit, alleging that the change in her job responsibilities and her suspension constituted actionable retaliation under Title VII. A jury agreed with White. The Sixth Circuit, en banc, affirmed the judgment in White's favor.]

II

Title VII's anti-retaliation provision forbids employer actions that "discriminate against" an employee (or job applicant) because he has "opposed" a practice that Title VII forbids or has "made a charge, testified, assisted, or participated in" a Title VII "investigation, proceeding, or hearing." No one doubts that the term "discriminate against" refers to distinctions or differences in treatment that injure protected individuals. See *Jackson v. Birmingham Bd. of Ed.*, 544 U.S. 167, 174 (2005); *Price Waterhouse v. Hopkins* (plurality opinion); see also 4 Oxford English Dictionary 758 (2d ed. 1989) (def. 3b). But different Circuits have come to different conclusions about whether the challenged action has to be employment or workplace related and about how harmful that action must be to constitute retaliation.

[The Court trifurcated the approaches taken by the circuits. Some insist on a close relationship between the retaliatory action and employment. The Sixth Circuit majority in this case, for example, said that a plaintiff must show an "adverse employment action," which it defined as a "materially adverse change in the terms and conditions" of employment. Other circuits have adopted a more restrictive approach, requiring an "ultimate employment decision," which limits actionable retaliation to acts such as hiring, granting leave, discharging, promoting, and compensating. Still other circuits have said that the plaintiff must show that the "employer's challenged action would have been "material to a reasonable employee."] which in contexts like the present one means that it would likely have "dissuaded a reasonable worker from making or supporting a charge of discrimination." *Washington v. Ill. Dep't of Revenue*, 420 F.3d 658, 662 (CA7 2005); see *Rochon v. Gonzales*, 438 F.3d 1211, 1217-1218 (CADC 2006). And the Ninth Circuit, following EEOC guidance, has said that the plaintiff must simply establish "'adverse treatment that is based on a retaliatory motive and is reasonably likely to deter the charging party or others from engaging in protected activity.'" *Ray v. Henderson*, 217 F.3d 1234, 1242-1243 (CA9 2000). The concurring judges below would have applied this last mentioned standard.

We granted certiorari to resolve this disagreement. To do so requires us to decide whether Title VII's anti-retaliation provision forbids only those employer actions and resulting harms that are related to employment or the workplace. And we must characterize how harmful an act of retaliatory discrimination must be in order to fall within the provision's scope.

A

Petitioner and the Solicitor General both argue that the Sixth Circuit is correct to require a link between the challenged retaliatory action and the terms, conditions, or status of employment. They note that Title VII's substantive anti-discrimination provision protects an individual only from employment-related discrimination. They add that the anti-retaliation provision should be read *in pari materia* with the anti-discrimination provision. And they conclude that the employer actions prohibited by the anti-retaliation provision should similarly be limited to conduct that "affects the employee's 'compensation, terms, conditions, or privileges of employment.'" . . .

We cannot agree. The language of the substantive provision differs from that of the anti-retaliation provision in important ways. . . .

Section 704(a) sets forth Title VII's anti-retaliation provision in the following terms:

> It shall be an unlawful employment practice for an employer *to discriminate against* any of his employees or applicants for employment . . . because he has opposed any practice made an unlawful employment practice by this subchapter, or because he has made a charge, testified, assisted, or participated in any manner in an investigation, proceeding, or hearing under this subchapter.

(Emphasis added.)

[In contrast, the substantive provisions of §703 use words such as] "hire," "discharge," "compensation, terms, conditions, or privileges of employment," "employment opportunities," and "status as an employee" [which] explicitly limit the scope of that provision to actions that affect employment or alter the conditions of the workplace. No such limiting words appear in the anti-retaliation provision. Given these linguistic differences, the question here is not whether identical or similar words should be read *in pari materia* to mean the same thing. Rather, the question is whether Congress intended its different words to make a legal difference. We normally presume that, where words differ as they differ here, "'Congress acts intentionally and purposely in the disparate inclusion or exclusion.'" *Russello v. United States*, 464 U.S. 16, 23 (1983).

There is strong reason to believe that Congress intended the differences that its language suggests, for the two provisions differ not only in language but in purpose as well. The anti-discrimination provision seeks a workplace where individuals are not discriminated against because of their racial, ethnic, religious, or gender-based status. See *McDonnell Douglas Corp. v. Green*, [reproduced at p. 50]. The anti-retaliation provision seeks to secure that primary objective by preventing an employer from interfering (through retaliation) with an employee's efforts to secure or advance enforcement of the Act's basic guarantees. The substantive provision seeks to prevent injury to individuals based on who they are, *i.e.*, their status. The anti-retaliation provision seeks to prevent harm to individuals based on what they do, *i.e.*, their conduct.

To secure the first objective, Congress did not need to prohibit anything other than employment-related discrimination. The substantive provision's basic objective of "equality of employment opportunities" and the elimination of practices that tend to bring about "stratified job environments," would be achieved were all employment-related discrimination miraculously eliminated.

But one cannot secure the second objective by focusing only upon employer actions and harm that concern employment and the workplace. Were all such actions and harms eliminated, the anti-retaliation provision's objective would *not* be achieved. An employer can effectively retaliate against an employee by taking actions not directly related to his employment or by causing him harm *outside* the workplace. See, *e.g., Rochon v. Gonzales* , 438 F.3d [1211, 1213 (CADC 2006) (FBI retaliation against employee "took the form of the FBI's refusal, contrary to policy, to investigate death threats a federal prisoner made against [the agent] and his wife"); *Berry v. Stevinson Chevrolet*, 74 F.3d 980, 984, 986 (CA10 1996) (finding actionable retaliation where employer filed false criminal charges against former employee who complained about discrimination). A provision limited to employment-related actions would not deter the many forms that effective retaliation can take. Hence, such a limited construction would fail to fully achieve the anti-retaliation provision's "primary purpose," namely, "maintaining unfettered access to statutory remedial mechanisms." *Robinson v. Shell Oil Co.*, 519 U.S. 337 (1997).

Thus, purpose reinforces what language already indicates, namely, that the anti-retaliation provision, unlike the substantive provision, is not limited to discriminatory actions that affect the terms and conditions of employment. . . .

Our precedent does not compel a contrary conclusion. [Indeed, we have found no case in this Court that offers petitioner or the United States significant support. *Burlington Industries, Inc. v. Ellerth*, [reproduced at p. 384] as petitioner notes, speaks of a Title VII requirement that violations involve "tangible employment action" such as "hiring, firing, failing to promote, reassignment with significantly different responsibilities, or a decision causing a significant change in benefits." But *Ellerth* does so only to "identify a class of [hostile work environment] cases" in which an employer should be held vicariously liable (without an affirmative defense) for the acts of supervisors. . . . *Ellerth* did not discuss the scope of the general anti-discrimination provision. . . . And *Ellerth* did not mention Title VII's anti-retaliation provision at all. At most, *Ellerth* sets forth a standard that petitioner and the Solicitor General believe the anti-retaliation provision ought to contain. But it does not compel acceptance of their view. . . .

Finally, we do not accept the petitioner's and Solicitor General's view that it is "anomalous" to read the statute to provide broader protection for victims of retaliation than for those whom Title VII primarily seeks to protect, namely, victims of race-based, ethnic-based, religion-based, or gender-based discrimination. Congress has provided similar kinds of protection from retaliation in comparable statutes without any judicial suggestion that those provisions are limited to the conduct prohibited by the primary substantive provisions. [The Court cited the National Labor Relations Act, "to which this Court has drawn analogies . . . in other Title VII contexts"; *Hishon v. King & Spalding*, reproduced at p. 16, provides an illustrative example. *Compare* 29 U.S.C. § 158(a)(3) (substantive provision prohibiting employer "discrimination in regard to . . . any term or condition of employment to encourage or discourage membership in any labor organization") with § 158(a)(4) (retaliation provision making it unlawful for an employer to "discharge or otherwise discriminate against an employee because he has filed charges or given testimony under this subchapter"); see also *Bill Johnson's Restaurants, Inc. v. NLRB*, 461 U.S. 731, 740 (1983) (construing that statute's anti-retaliation provision to go far beyond work-related retaliation to bar even "'prohibit a wide variety of employer conduct that is intended to restrain, or that has the likely effect of restraining, employees in the exercise of protected activities,' including the retaliatory filing of a lawsuit against an employee"); *NLRB v. Scrivener*, 405 U.S. 117 (1972) (purpose of the anti-retaliation provision is to ensure that employees are "'completely free from coercion against reporting'" unlawful practices).]

In any event, as we have explained, differences in the purpose of the two provisions remove any perceived "anomaly," for they justify this difference of interpretation. Title VII depends for its enforcement upon the cooperation of employees who are willing to file complaints and act as witnesses. "Plainly, effective enforcement could thus only be expected if employees felt free to approach officials with their grievances." *Mitchell v. Robert DeMario Jewelry, Inc.*, 361 U.S. 288 (1960). Interpreting the anti-retaliation provision to provide broad protection from retaliation helps assure the cooperation upon which accomplishment of the Act's primary objective depends.

For these reasons, we conclude that Title VII's substantive provision and its anti-retaliation provision are not coterminous. The scope of the anti-retaliation provision extends beyond workplace-related or employment-related retaliatory acts and harm. We therefore reject the standards applied in the Courts of Appeals that have treated the anti-retaliation provision as forbidding the same conduct prohibited by the anti-discrimination provision and that have limited actionable retaliation to so-called "ultimate employment decisions."

B

The anti-retaliation provision protects an individual not from all retaliation, but from retaliation that produces an injury or harm. As we have explained, the Courts of Appeals have used differing language to describe the level of seriousness to which this harm must rise before it becomes actionable retaliation. We agree with the formulation set forth by the Seventh and the District of Columbia Circuits. In our view, a plaintiff must show that a reasonable employee would have found the challenged action materially adverse, "which in this context means it well might have 'dissuaded a reasonable worker from making or supporting a charge of discrimination.'" *Rochon.*

We speak of *material* adversity because we believe it is important to separate significant from trivial harms. Title VII, we have said, does not set forth "a general civility code for the American workplace." Oncale v. Sundowner Offshore Services, Inc., [reproduced at p. 332]; see *Faragher* (judicial standards for sexual harassment must "filter out complaints attacking 'the ordinary tribulations of the workplace, such as the sporadic use of abusive language, gender-related jokes, and occasional teasing'"). An employee's decision to report discriminatory behavior cannot immunize that employee from those petty slights or minor annoyances that often take place at work and that all employees experience. See 1 B. Lindemann & P. Grossman, Employment Discrimination Law 669 (3d ed. 1996) (noting that "courts have held that personality conflicts at work that generate antipathy" and "'snubbing' by supervisors and co-workers" are not actionable under §704(a)). The anti-retaliation provision seeks to prevent employer interference with "unfettered access" to Title VII's remedial mechanisms. *Robinson.* It does so by prohibiting employer actions that are likely "to deter victims of discrimination from complaining to the EEOC," the courts, and their employers. *Ibid.* And normally petty slights, minor annoyances, and simple lack of good manners will not create such deterrence. See 2 EEOC 1998 Manual §8, p. 8-13.

We refer to reactions of a *reasonable* employee because we believe that the provision's standard for judging harm must be objective. An objective standard is judicially administrable. It avoids the uncertainties and unfair discrepancies that can plague a judicial effort to determine a plaintiff's unusual subjective feelings. We have emphasized the need for objective standards in other Title VII contexts, and those same concerns animate our decision here. See, *e.g.*, *Suders*, [reproduced at p. 394] (constructive discharge doctrine); *Harris v. Forklift Systems, Inc.*, [reproduced at p. 376] (hostile work environment doctrine).

We phrase the standard in general terms because the significance of any given act of retaliation will often depend upon the particular circumstances. Context matters. "The real social impact of workplace behavior often depends on a constellation of surrounding circumstances, expectations, and relationships which are not fully captured by a simple recitation of the words used or the physical acts performed." *Oncale.* A schedule change in an employee's work schedule may make little difference to many workers, but may matter enormously to a young mother with school age children. Cf., *e.g.*, *Washington* (finding flex-time schedule critical to employee with disabled child). A supervisor's refusal to invite an employee to lunch is normally trivial, a nonactionable petty slight. But to retaliate by excluding an employee from a weekly training lunch that contributes significantly to the employee's professional advancement might well deter a reasonable employee from complaining about discrimination. See 2 EEOC 1998 Manual §8, p. 8-14. Hence, a legal standard that speaks in general terms rather than specific prohibited acts is preferable, for an "act that would be immaterial in some situations is material in others." *Washington.*

Finally, we note that contrary to the claim of the concurrence, this standard does *not* require a reviewing court or jury to consider "the nature of the discrimination that led to the filing of the charge." Rather, the standard is tied to the challenged retaliatory act, not the underlying conduct that forms the basis of the Title VII complaint. By focusing on the materiality of the challenged action and the perspective of a reasonable person in the plaintiff's position, we believe this standard will screen out trivial conduct while effectively capturing those acts that are likely to dissuade employees from complaining or assisting in complaints about discrimination.

III

Applying this standard to the facts of this case, we believe that there was a sufficient evidentiary basis to support the jury's verdict on White's retaliation claim. . . . Burlington does not question the jury's determination that the motivation for these acts was retaliatory. But it does question the statutory significance of the harm these acts caused. The District Court instructed the jury to determine whether respondent "suffered a materially adverse change in the terms or conditions of her employment," and the Sixth Circuit upheld the jury's finding based on that same stringent interpretation of the anti-retaliation provision (the interpretation that limits §704 to the same employment-related conduct forbidden by §703). Our holding today makes clear that the jury was not required to find that the challenged actions were related to the terms or conditions of employment. And insofar as the jury also found that the actions were "materially adverse," its findings are adequately supported.

First, Burlington argues that a reassignment of duties cannot constitute retaliatory discrimination where, as here, both the former and present duties fall within the same job description. We do not see why that is so. Almost every job category involves some responsibilities and duties that are less desirable than others. Common sense suggests that one good way to discourage an employee such as White from bringing discrimination charges would be to insist that she spend more time performing the more arduous duties and less time performing those that are easier or more agreeable. That is presumably why the EEOC has consistently found "retaliatory work assignments" to be a classic and "widely recognized" example of "forbidden retaliation." 2 EEOC 1991 Manual §614.7, pp. 614-31 to 614-32. . . .

To be sure, reassignment of job duties is not automatically actionable. Whether a particular reassignment is materially adverse depends upon the circumstances of the particular case, and "should be judged from the perspective of a reasonable person in the plaintiff's position, considering 'all the circumstances.'" *Oncale*. But here, the jury had before it considerable evidence that the track labor duties were "by all accounts more arduous and dirtier"; that the "forklift operator position required more qualifications, which is an indication of prestige"; and that "the forklift operator position was objectively considered a better job and the male employees resented White for occupying it." Based on this record, a jury could reasonably conclude that the reassignment of responsibilities would have been materially adverse to a reasonable employee.

Second, Burlington argues that the 37-day suspension without pay lacked statutory significance because Burlington ultimately reinstated White with backpay. Burlington says that "it defies reason to believe that Congress would have considered a rescinded investigatory suspension with full back pay" to be unlawful, particularly because Title VII, throughout much of its history, provided no relief in an equitable action for victims in White's position.

We do not find Burlington's last mentioned reference to the nature of Title VII's remedies convincing. After all, throughout its history, Title VII has provided for injunctions to "bar like discrimination in the future," *Albemarle Paper Co.* v. *Moody*, [reproduced at p. 276], an important form of relief. And we have no reason to believe that a court could not have issued an injunction where an employer suspended an employee for retaliatory purposes, even if that employer later provided backpay. In any event, Congress amended Title VII in 1991 to permit victims of intentional discrimination to recover compensatory (as White received here) and punitive damages, concluding that the additional remedies were necessary to "'help make victims whole.'" *West* v. *Gibson*, 527 U.S. 212 (1999). We would undermine the significance of that congressional judgment were we to conclude that employers could avoid liability in these circumstances.

Neither do we find convincing any claim of insufficient evidence. White did receive backpay. But White and her family had to live for 37 days without income. They did not know during that time whether or when White could return to work. Many reasonable employees would find a month without a paycheck to be a serious hardship. And White described to the jury the physical and emotional hardship that 37 days of having "no income, no money" in fact caused. ("That was the worst Christmas I had out of my life. No income, no money, and that made all of us feel bad. . . . I got very depressed"). Indeed, she obtained medical treatment for her emotional distress. A reasonable employee facing the choice between retaining her job (and paycheck) and filing a discrimination complaint might well choose the former. That is to say, an indefinite suspension without pay could well act as a deterrent, even if the suspended employee eventually received backpay. . . . Thus, the jury's conclusion that the 37-day suspension without pay was materially adverse was a reasonable one.

[Justice Alito's concurring opinion omitted].

NOTES

1. *Section 703 vs. Section 704.* The Court holds that, while §703 reaches only actions that affect employment or that alter the conditions of the workplace, §704 is *not* limited to discriminatory acts that affect the terms and conditions of employment. Given that the actions White complained did affect her employment, why do you think the Court felt it necessary to decide whether §704 applied to actions that did not affect the terms and conditions of employment?

Could the Court be reaching out to decide this question because it did not believe the actions White complained of, even though arising from the workplace, would have been sufficient to state a claim under §703? Obviously, this would have important implications for the concept of "adverse employment action" we discussed in Chapter 1. In his concurring opinion, Justice Alito disagreed with the majority's analysis, believing that the scope of §§703 and 704 are the same and both reach only materially adverse employment actions. But he finds the actions White complained of were materially adverse within the meaning of either section.

2. *Why Not Defer to the EEOC?* In embracing the test adopted by the Seventh and the D.C. Circuits, the *Burlington* Court rejected the reading favored by the Ninth Circuit and the EEOC, which found "that the plaintiff must simply establish 'adverse treatment that is based on a retaliatory motive and is reasonably likely to deter the charging party or others from engaging in protected activity.'" How does the Court's standard differ?

3. *The Limits of Language.* Having looked to the text of §704 to distinguish its scope from that of §703, the Court then declines to apply the language of §704 literally. That is, instead of recognizing a cause of action for any discrimination based on protected conduct, it requires the discrimination to be sufficiently severe to deter a reasonable employee from engaging in that conduct. Why? And if the literal language is not to be followed, isn't that another reason to defer to the agency's interpretation?

4. *Employer Liability.* Does the Court's opinion mean that employers are strictly liable for supervisory retaliation when a reasonable employee would have found the challenged action materially adverse? To borrow language from the sexual harassment area, is any conduct that would be actionable under *Burlington* a tangible employment action when done by a supervisor? Isn't that the logical reading of *Burlington*? But if not, would the affirmative defense outlined in *Ellerth* apply to retaliation claims if the supervisor's action is not deemed tangible but *is* sufficiently severe or pervasive? What about actions taken by co-workers? Recall *Matvia v. Bald Head Island Mgmt.*, reproduced at p. 403. Assuming that the shunning conduct of Matvia's co-workers would satisfy the *Burlington* standard, is the employer liable — at least under a negligence standard?

5. *What Counts as "Materially Adverse"?* Would denying an employee the opportunity to have her work reviewed by a different supervisor with more authority be viewed by a reasonable employee as materially adverse? In a decision preceding *White*, the D.C. Circuit said no. *See Broderick v. Donaldson*, 437 F.3d 1226 (D.C. Cir. 2006). More generally, what would deter a reasonable employee from opposing discrimination or participating in proceedings? Some post-*Burlington* cases have viewed employees as being made of pretty stern stuff. *E.g., Dehart v. Baker Hughes Oilfield Operations, Inc.*, 214 Fed. Appx. 437 (5th Cir. 2007) (written disciplinary warning not an adverse action); *Carpenter v. Con-Way Cent. Express, Inc.*, 481 F.3d 611 (8th Cir. 2007) (failure to stop co-worker's slurs and placement of garbage in plaintiff's truck not materially adverse). *But see Ridley v. Costco Wholesale Corp.*,

217 Fed. Appx. 130 (3d Cir. 2007) (transfer that required several hours of commuting each day could have been found likely to deter); *Kessler v. Westchester County Dep't of Soc. Servs.*, 461 F/.3d 199 (2d Cir. 2006) (transfer to an outlying office, resulting in plaintiff's going from supervising 100 employees to none with other reductions in responsibilities created a disputed issue of material fact issue as on the question of whether an adverse action had occurred).

6. *Threats Just Fine?* One consequence of the Court's definition of actionable retaliation in *White* is that threats to retaliate are not necessarily actionable. Suppose White's boss threatened to fire her, but didn't; or suppose he just threatened to "get even," without being more specific? In *EEOC v. Sundance Rehab. Corp.*, 466 F.3d 490 (6th Cir. 2006), the court found no facial violation of anti-retaliation provisions in severance pay agreement conditioned on not filing charges with the EEOC. Although the threat was implicit that suit might be brought to recover the payments should a charge be filed, that wasn't enough for the court. The agreement might have been unenforceable, which would have made the threat not meaningful. Or is that true? Might a reasonable employee, who didn't want to risk her severance or retain an attorney to defend a suit, forbear from filing a charge? *See Williams v. W.D. Sports N.M., Inc.*, 497 F.3d 1079 (10th Cir. 2007) (threatening to publicize rumors of an employee's sexual activities and opposing her unemployment benefits was sufficiently adverse).

7. A recent article by a business school professor, Anne Marie Knott, advocates that employers, in order to determine whether a prospective employee is likely to sue, should present prospective workers with an "anti-discrimination bond." Employees would make contributions to the "ADB" that would be forfeited if the employee sued. The article asserts that the bond is a screening tool because an employee who buys the bond is not likely to sue. See www.newswise.com/articles/view/530879/. Having read through the materials in this chapter, as well as the relevant statutory provisions, do you think Professor Knott's approach is viable under Title VII and other anti-discrimination statutes?

H. AGE DISCRIMINATION

Treatment of the Age Discrimination in Employment Act has been largely integrated into the discussion of the theories of discrimination analyzed in earlier chapters, with difference between discrimination on account of age and discrimination on the grounds prohibited by Title VII noted throughout. For example, we saw in Chapter 1 that the *McDonnell Douglas* framework for individual disparate treatment cases has frequently been adapted to age cases, but that the courts have retained the *Price Waterhouse* "direct evidence" approach under the ADEA since that statute was not amended in 1991 to make liability turn on the plaintiff showing that age was a motivating factor for an adverse employment action. We saw in Chapter 2 that the ADEA has a bona fide occupational qualification defense much like that of Title VII but that there is no need for a defense for "reverse discrimination" since *General Dynamics Land Systems, Inc. v. Cline*, pp. 77-78, held that favoring older members of the protected class over younger members is not prohibited by the ADEA. Finally, in Chapter 3, we learned that disparate impact, while actionable in the age context, is subject to a much looser scrutiny than would be true under Title VII. *Smith v. City of Jackson*, reproduced at p. 223. This is in part because the ADEA declares that it is not unlawful "to take any action otherwise prohibited . . . where the differentiation is based on reasonable factors other than age." §4(f)(1), 29 U.S.C. §623(f)(1) (2007).

This section considers several additional differences between the ADEA and other antidiscrimination statutes, most notably with respect to exceptions from the statute's prohibitions.

1. Bona Fide Executive Exception

Although mandatory retirement is generally prohibited by the ADEA, "bona fide executives" can be mandatorily retired at age 65 under certain circumstances:

> [A]ny employee who has attained 65 years of age, and who, for the 2-year period immediately before retirement, is employed in a bona fide executive or high policy-making position, if such employee is entitled to an immediate nonforfeitable annual retirement benefit from a pension, profit-sharing, savings or deferred compensation plan, or any combination of such plans, of the employer of such employee, which equals, in the aggregate, at least $44,000.

§12(c)(1), 29 U.S.C. §631(c)(1). See also 29 C.F.R. §1625.12 (2007). The exception obviously is highly qualified. First, a "bona fide executive" remains fully protected by the ADEA until age 65. Even thereafter, such an executive may not be discriminated against on age grounds except for mandatory retirement. Second, the statute's requirements for the exception are conjunctive: to be subject to the provision, the employee must both (1) be in a "bona fide executive" or "high policymaking position" and (2) receive the defined benefits of $44,000 a year. See Morrissey v. Boston Five Cents Sav. Bank, 54 F.3d 27 (1st Cir. 1995).

2. Exception for Police and Firefighters

The only major sector of the economy exempted from the ADEA's prohibition of age discrimination, including mandatory retirement, is state and municipal law enforcement and firefighting. The ADEA permits states or political subdivisions to set age limitations both for hire and for discharge after age 55 for individuals employed "as a firefighter or as a law enforcement officer." See Jones v. City of Cortland Police Dep't, 448 F.3d 369 (6th Cir. 2006) (no ADEA claim by 54 year old applicant for police position since Ohio law requires police to be under age 35 at hiring and city was thereby protected by ADEA exemption). Both "firefighter" and "law enforcement officer" are defined broadly. See EEOC v. State of Ill., 986 F.2d 187 (7th Cir. 1993) (special agents of Division of Criminal Investigation counted as state police and, therefore, were law enforcement officers). This is somewhat limited by the proviso that the action must be taken "pursuant to a bona fide hiring or retirement plan that is not a subterfuge to evade the purposes of this Act." 29 U.S.C. §623(j) (2007), but the courts have been very permissive on this criterion. See Minch v. City of Chi., 363 F.3d 615, 623 (7th Cir. 2004) ("proof that local officials exercised this right for impure motives will not in and of itself suffice to establish subterfuge"; rather, to establish subterfuge, plaintiff must adduce "that the employer is using the exemption as a way to evade another substantive provision of the act").

3. *Bona Fide Employee Benefit Plans*

With respect to fringe benefits, perhaps the ADEA's most sweeping "exception" is the Supreme Court's decision in *General Dynamics Land Systems, Inc. v. Cline*, 540 U.S. 581 (2004), which held that favoring older workers over younger workers in the protected class is not prohibited by the statute. See p. 77. This decision permits skewing of fringe benefits (as well as other employment decisions) towards the older end of the workforce spectrum with no liability.

However, even beyond *Cline*, the ADEA has a "bona fide employee benefit plan" provision that acts as a significant exception to the statute's general prohibition of age discrimination and permits discrimination against older workers in some circumstances. While benefits law is a specialty unto itself, the ADEA's exemption permits age to be taken into account in a limited fashion despite the statute's general prohibition on discrimination in "compensation, terms, conditions, or privileges of employment." §623(a)(1). Where a "bona fide employee benefit plan" is involved, an employer will not violate the statute if it either (1) provides its workers equal benefits (in which case there is no discrimination) or (2) provides age-differentiated benefits but incurs equal costs in doing so. 29 U.S.C. §623(f)(2) (2007). This provision recognizes that the costs of some fringe benefits (typically life and health insurance) rise with the age of the worker and permits employers to take that into account. For example, suppose the cost of $100,000 of employer-provided life insurance is $1,000 for workers aged 40. If the same $1,000 will buy only $70,000 of insurance for workers aged 60, the employer may provide them that lesser benefit without violating the law.

The ADEA also defers to employer economic interests by allowing employers to avoid "double dipping." Thus, defined benefit plans may be "coordinated" with Social Security and Medicare to reduce employer costs. §4(*l*)(1)(B), 29 U.S.C. §623(*l*)(1)(B). *See also AARP v. EEOC*, 489 F.3d 558 (3d Cir. 2007) (upholding proposed EEOC regulation on coordination of benefits). Similarly, employers may reduce any severance pay "made available as a result of a contingent event unrelated to age" by the value of retiree health benefits and the value of "additional" pension benefits stemming from such a contingency. §4(*l*)(2)(A), 29 U.S.C. §623(*l*)(2)(A). *See Stokes v. Westinghouse Savannah River Co.*, 206 F.3d 420 (4th Cir. 2000). Finally, a bona fide benefit plan may reduce long-term disability benefits by the amount of pension benefits that the employee will receive at the later of age 62 or normal retirement age. §4(*l*)(3), 29 U.S.C. §623(*l*)(3). *But see Kalvinskas v. Cal. Inst. of Tech.*, 96 F.3d 1305 (9th Cir. 1996) (employer violated the ADEA when it offset disability benefits by benefits that an employee could receive only by retiring; the offset essentially forced the employee to retire, and was not within §623(*l*)(3)'s "safe harbor" because the employee was not eligible for benefits until he retired).

These provisions have become less important as defined benefit plans (those in which the employer guarantees a benefit upon retirement) have been increasingly replaced by defined contribution plans. The latter, as the name suggests, do not guarantee any particular level of benefits at retirement but rather provide for employer (and usually employee) contributions that can be invested in various ways to, hopefully, provide sufficient funds on retirement. A 401(k) is the most common kind of defined contribution plan. The ADEA explicitly provides that an ERISA pension benefit plan may specify "a minimum age as a condition for normal or early retirement benefits." §4(*l*)(1)(A), 29 U.S.C. §623(*l*)(1)(A). However, it prohibits any age-based reduction in allocations to the employee's account. As a result, benefit plans may specify a "normal retirement age" for benefits but may not force individuals to retire at that age or cut off the accrual of benefits.

4. Early Retirement Incentive Plans

Early retirement incentive plans play a critical role in corporate downsizing, and the ADEA permits such plans subject to certain limitations. These plans often involve both carrots and sticks. As for the carrot, the employer creates a "window of opportunity" during which employees can obtain greater retirement benefits if they elect early retirement. When the window shuts, the enhanced benefits disappear. As for the stick, early retirement incentive plans usually do not explicitly threaten termination of those who do not accept, but these plans are typically offered by companies in the process of downsizing. There often is, therefore, an implicit threat that layoffs will follow if enough workers do not accept the early retirement incentive. *See generally* Michael C. Harper, *Age-Based Exit Incentives, Coercion, and the Prospective Waiver of ADEA Rights: The Failure of the Older Workers Benefit Protection Act*, 79 VA. L. REV. 1271 (1993).

In the past, employees challenged retirement incentive plans, claiming that they had accepted early retirement only because of the implicit threat of discharge, *e.g.*, *Henn v. National. Geographic Society*, 819 F.2d 824 (7th Cir. 1987). However, such challenges are not likely to be successful today, *e.g.*, *Rowell v. Bellsouth Corp.*, 433 F.3d 794 (11th Cir. 2005) (no constructive discharge where older worker accepted early retirement package as part of a RIF when he believed, but was not formally told, he would be terminated if he did not accept package). Ironically, in the past other plaintiffs sometimes sued because they were not offered an opportunity to participate. *E.g.*, *Cipriano v. Bd. of Educ.*, 785 F.2d 51 (2d Cir. 1986).

The Older Workers Benefit Protection Act amended the ADEA to address both these problems while striking a balance between employer and employee interests. First, the ADEA permits a benefit plan "that is a voluntary early retirement incentive plan" consistent with the purposes of the Act. §4(f)(2)(B)(ii), 29 U.S.C. §623(f)(2)(B)(ii) (2007). To qualify, any such plan "must make retirement a relatively more attractive option than continuing to work." *Abrahamson v. Bd. of Educ. of the Wappingers Falls Cent. Sch. Dist.*, 374 F.3d 66, 74 (2d Cir. 2004) ("Option #2 provides no real incentive to retire because it does not make retirement a relatively more attractive financial option than continuing to teach"). The requirement that the plan be "consistent with the purposes of the Act" tends to invalidate retirement incentive plans that exclude older workers, as in *Cipriano*, although the statute does not expressly forbid them. *See Jankovitz v. Des Moines Indep. Cmty.*, 421 F.3d 649, 655 (8th Cir. 2005) (school district's early retirement incentive plan not within the statutory safe harbor because it was inconsistent with the purposes of the ADEA in providing that "available early retirement benefits drop to zero upon an employee's attainment of the age of 65. That adverse change in benefits is based solely upon age"). The statute also provides that a pension plan will not violate the statute by providing a minimum age of eligibility," §4(l)(1)(a), 29 U.S.C. §623(l)(1)(a), but this provision is surplusage after *General Dynamics Land Systems, Inc. v. Cline*, 540 U.S. 581 (2004), which holds that it is not discriminatory to favor older workers.

Most significantly, employees who do not accept the incentive plan will rarely have standing to challenge it, and those who do sign may find themselves unable to attack even a plan that is, in some sense, illegal because OWBPA also authorizes "knowing and voluntary" waivers of ADEA rights, and specifies a rigorous laundry list of substantive and procedural requirements before a waiver of ADEA rights will be deemed "knowing and voluntary." The topic of OWBPA releases, as well as releases of rights under other antidiscrimination statutes, is taken up in Chapter 9.

NOTE ON INTERNATIONAL AND COMPARATIVE ANTIDISCRIMINATION LAW

Sex Discrimination   The question whether pregnancy discrimination in hiring was prohibited by Mexican labor law arose in a NAALC proceeding before the U.S. N.A.O. Public Report of Review of NAO Submission No. 9701, U.S. National Administrative Office, Bureau of International Labor Affairs, U.S. Department of Labor, January 12, 1998. Mexican Federal Labor Law was structured so that the government paid maternity leave benefits to workers who had been employed for more than six months. But the employer had to pay benefits to workers with less than six months service. That created a tremendous incentive for employers, particularly in the maquilladora industries that focused on low labor cost work for the export market, to discriminate in hiring through pregnancy screening. In response to the submission that Mexico had failed to enforce its law prohibiting sex discrimination, the Mexican government claimed that "pregnancy screening is not widely practiced, and that to the extent that it is, it is legal in Mexico." But, another entity within the Mexican government, the Alliance for Equality, took the position that pregnancy screening was common and, along with post-hire protection against discharge, should be viewed as discrimination. While that case led to ministerial consultations between labor secretaries of the two countries, it also led to action by the Mexican government. In the 2003 Federal Law to Prevent and Eliminate Discrimination, all pregnancy discrimination is prohibited.

The EU in Directive 2000/78/EC requires the member states to prohibit harassment, which is defined in Article 2 as:

> 3. Harassment shall be deemed to be a form of discrimination within the meaning of paragraph 1, when unwanted conduct related to any of the grounds referred to in Article 1 takes place with the purpose or effect of violating the dignity of a person and of creating an intimidating, hostile, degrading, humiliating or offensive environment. In this context, the concept of harassment may be defined in accordance with the national laws and practice of the Member States.

Further, the EU, in Directive 2000/73/EC, added a specific definition of sexual harassment: "where any form of unwanted verbal, non-verbal or physical conduct of a sexual nature occurs, with the purpose or effect of violating the dignity of the person, in particular when creating an intimidating, hostile, degrading, humiliating or offensive environment."

Religion   The equal treatment directive, Directive 2000/78/EC allows the member states to make exceptions from the proscription of religious discrimination for certain religious organizations. Article 4(2) provides:

> . . . in the case of occupational activities within churches and other public or private organisations the ethos of which is based on religion or belief, a difference of treatment

based on a person's religion or belief shall not constitute discrimination where, by reason of the nature of these activities or of the context in which they are carried out, a person's religion or belief constitute a genuine, legitimate and justified occupational requirement, having regard to the organisation's ethos. . . .

Similarly, churches and other religiously-oriented organisations may "require individuals working for them to act in good faith and with loyalty to the organisation's ethos." How does this exception comport with the exceptions provided in Title VII to religious organizations in the United States?

Age   EU Directive 2000/78/EC also provides some defenses to discrimination because of age. Article 6 provides:

1. Notwithstanding Article 2(2), Member States may provide that differences of treatment on grounds of age shall not constitute discrimination, if, within the context of national law, they are objectively and reasonably justified by a legitimate aim, including legitimate employment policy, labour market and vocational training objectives, and if the means of achieving that aim are appropriate and necessary.
Such differences of treatment may include, among others:
    (a) the setting of special conditions on access to employment and vocational training, employment and occupation, including dismissal and remuneration conditions, for young people, older workers and persons with caring responsibilities in order to promote their vocational integration or ensure their protection;
    (b) the fixing of minimum conditions of age, professional experience or seniority in service for access to employment or to certain advantages linked to employment;
    (c) the fixing of a maximum age for recruitment which is based on the training requirements of the post in question or the need for a reasonable period of employment before retirement.

It also permits age distinctions in "occupational social security schemes."

The EU Commission declared that Germany had failed to harmonize its national laws with the equal treatment directive, Directive 2000/78/EC, by failing to prohibit age discrimination. Thereafter, Germany enacted a new General Equal Treatment Act that now prohibits age discrimination in employment. In two cases decided under the new law, however, defendants have successfully used statutory defenses. In *Arbeitsgericht Frankfurt, Urteil vom 14.03.2007*, Az. 6 Ca 740/06, the Frankfort Labor Court upheld Lufthansa's mandatory retirement age of 60, even though other German airlines allowed pilots to fly until age 65. The age limit, which the pilot's union had agreed to in a collective bargaining agreement, was justified by the legitimate purposes of safety and protection of air travelers. Similarly, in *Verwaltungsgericht Mainz, Urteil vom 17.04.2007*, Az. 6 L 149/07.MZ, the Administrative Court in Mainz upheld a rule of the local Chamber of Commerce limiting setting an age 70 cap on appointment of expert witnesses, indicating that "a person's abilities generally decline in the seventh decade of his life." *See* Global Employment Law Update at http://www.faegre.com/articles/downloadfrom2.asp?doc_num = 2&aid = 2224.

In the U.S., the FAA sets age 60 as the mandatory retirement for pilots of commercial airlines. But, what if the FAA rescinded the rule, but an airline persisted in requiring its pilots to retire at age 60? Would a U.S. court agree with the German court that, essentially, there was a BFOQ for requiring pilots to retire at age 60?

Chapter 6

Disability Discrimination

A. INTRODUCTION

The Americans with Disabilities Act of 1990 (ADA) prohibits employment dis-crimination against persons with disabilities. Title I, 42 U.S.C. §§ 12111-12117 (2007), covers most employment agencies, labor organizations, and employers, including state and local governments. Title II, 42 U.S.C. §§ 12131-12134, which generally prohibits disability discrimination by state and local governments, may also prohibit such entities from discriminating in employment. Thus, private employers are subject only to Title I, but state and local public employers *may* be subject to both Title I and Title II. The circuits are split, however, on whether Title II encompasses employment discrimination claims by government employees. Before Congress enacted the ADA, the most comprehensive federal legislation prohibiting disability discrimination was the Rehabilitation Act of 1973, 29 U.S.C. §§ 701-795(I) (2007), which barred disability discrimination in most federal employment and by those doing business with the federal government or receiving federal financial assistance from it.

The statutory scheme for protecting individuals with disabilities from discrimination in employment is somewhat more complicated than the other antidiscrimination statutes. Prohibiting discrimination on account of disability poses difficult practical and legal problems. The primary practical difficulty is the scope and severity of such discrimination. The following excerpt from the legislative history of the ADA suggests the dimensions of the problem:

Individuals with disabilities experience staggering levels of unemployment and poverty. . . . Two-thirds of all disabled Americans between the age of 16 and 64 are not working at all; yet, a large majority of those not working say that they want to work. . . .

Despite the enactment of Federal legislation such as the Education for All Handicapped Children Act of 1975 and the Rehabilitation Act of 1973, a U.S. Census Bureau Report issued in July, 1989 reported the following findings:

(A) The percentage of men with a work disability working full time fell 7 percent from 30 percent in 1981 to 23 percent in 1988.

(B) The income of workers with disabilities dropped sharply compared to other workers. In 1980, men with disabilities earned 23 percent less than men with no work disability, and by 1988 this had dropped to 36 percent less than their counterparts. In 1980, women with disabilities earned 30 percent less than women with no disabilities, and by 1988 this had dropped to 38 percent less than their counterparts.

. . . In 1984, fifty percent of all adults with disabilities had household incomes of $15,000 or less. Among non-disabled persons, only twenty-five percent had household incomes in this wage bracket.

H.R. Rep. No. 101-485, pt. 2, at 32 (1990), *reprinted in* 1990 U.S.C.C.A.N. 303, 314. *See generally* Ruth Colker, *The ADA's Journey Through Congress,* 39 WAKE FOREST L. REV. 1 (2004).

In addition, an earlier report of the United States Commission on Civil Rights provides further insight into the problem:

[S]tudies indicate that only in a tiny percentage of cases is inability to perform a regular, full-time job the reason a handicapped person is not employed.

Frequently, employer prejudices exclude handicapped persons from jobs. Biases operate subtly, sometimes unconsciously, to eliminate handicapped job applicants in the application, screening, testing, interviewing, and medical examination process:

> Often, the employer makes erroneous assumptions regarding the effect of a person's disability on his or her ability to perform on the job. In most cases the disabled person is never given an opportunity to disprove those assumptions; in some cases, the disabled person never knows why he or she didn't get the job.

Deborah Kaplan, *Employment Rights: History, Trends and Status,* in LAW REFORM IN DISABILITY RIGHTS, VOL. 2 (Berkeley: Disability Rights Education and Defense Fund, 1981), p. E-4. . . .

The majority of unemployed handicapped people, if given the chance, are quite capable of taking their places in the job market. Numerous studies indicate that handicapped workers, when assigned appropriate positions, perform as well as or better than their nonhandicapped fellow workers. . . .

. . . Studies have demonstrated that, for every educational level, the average wage rate of disabled people is below that of the nondisabled population. . . .

Such differences in wage levels cannot be explained by any differential in productivity. Studies dating back to a massive 1948 Department of Labor study of disabled and nondisabled workers have consistently concluded that handicapped and nonhandicapped workers are equally productive. A recent survey of such research studies concluded: "the existing literature appears to show both that the disabled who are working are as productive in their jobs as their co-workers and that employers perceive the handicapped as being comparably productive."

UNITED STATES COMMISSION ON CIVIL RIGHTS, ACCOMMODATING THE SPECTRUM OF INDIVIDUAL ABILITIES 13, 29-31 (1983).

In short, Congress, in enacting the ADA, found that discrimination against individuals with disabilities is pervasive, takes a variety of forms, and costs the

United States billions of dollars in unnecessary expenses, which result from the dependency and non-productivity of those with disabilities. See ADA § 2(a)(1)-(9).

While the scope and severity of disability discrimination are daunting, the difficult legal problems associated with ending disability discrimination result primarily from the fact that disabilities are sometimes relevant to an individual's ability to work. Some disabilities deprive people of the physical and/or mental prerequisites to perform essential job functions. Prohibiting "discrimination" against such individuals would unduly interfere with employers' ability to select a qualified workforce. Other disabled individuals may be qualified to work but only if the employer accommodates their disability in some way. These individuals, unlike most other statutorily protected groups, require some form of accommodation or different treatment in order to enjoy equal access to employment opportunities and benefits. Guaranteeing equal treatment for similarly situated individuals is an inadequate legal response to the problem of promoting employment for individuals who may require different treatment or accommodation.

The ADA seeks to deal with these problems in two separate ways. First, the statute protects only a "qualified individual with a disability," which means that employers are permitted to engage in disparate treatment when the disabled employee is unable to perform the essential functions of the job. In addition, employers are free to use qualification standards that screen out disabled individuals if those qualifications are job related and consistent with business necessity.

Counterbalancing this, disabled individuals have rights beyond those guaranteed to most other groups protected by antidiscrimination legislation. The centerpiece of disability discrimination law is the employer's affirmative duty to provide reasonable accommodation to ensure that individuals with disabilities secure equal employment opportunities and benefits. The focus of the duty to accommodate is on equal employment opportunity, rather than on equal treatment.

As a result, employers are legally obligated to treat covered employees equally or differently depending on the circumstances — employers *must treat individuals with disabilities equally* if they are qualified and their disabilities do not require accommodation; employers are *permitted to treat such individuals differently* if their disabilities cannot be accommodated; and employers *are required to treat such individuals differently* if reasonable accommodations are necessary to ensure equal employment opportunity and benefits.

Further, accommodation providing equal opportunity for individuals with disabilities can be costly for employers. The ADA, therefore, includes an "undue hardship" defense, which makes cost, usually irrelevant under other antidiscrimination statutes, an expressly enumerated statutory defense to discrimination based on the duty to accommodate.

The success of the Americans with Disabilities Act in achieving its goals is unclear. Certainly, some data suggest little or no impact, but the question is complicated. As measured by success in litigation, Title I plaintiffs overall have fared quite poorly. *See, e.g.,* Melanie D. Winegar, Note, *Big Talk, Broken Promises: How Title I of the Americans with Disabilities Act Failed Disabled Workers,* 34 HOFSTRA L. REV. 1267 (2006). And there have been scholarly suggestions that the ADA has actually hurt employment of the disabled. *See* Samuel R. Bagenstos, *Has the Americans with Disabilities Act Reduced Employment for People with Disabilities?,* 25 BERKELEY J. EMP. & LAB. L. 527, 555-58 (2004), *reviewing* DAVID C. STAPLETON & RICHARD V. BURKHAUSER, THE DECLINE IN EMPLOYMENT OF PEOPLE WITH DISABILITIES: A POLICY PUZZLE (2003) (Empirical evidence is broadly consistent with theoretical reasons to expect that mandated accommodations negatively effect the employment of people with disabilities, and the empirical evidence seems to support the theory. But alternative explanations are possible, including "the real prospect that any disemployment effect of the ADA is a short-term phenomenon," in part because of the falling costs of accommodation).

The focus of this chapter will be Title I of the ADA. Statutory interpretation, however, has leaned heavily on ADA regulations and Interpretive Guidance promulgated by the Equal Employment Opportunity Commission, which in turn borrow from the Rehabilitation Act and its regulations. As we will see, however, the courts do not always defer to the EEOC's regulations and interpretation of the statute, and the ADA differs in important respects from the Rehabilitation Act.

This chapter will proceed as follows: Section B focuses on what constitutes a "disability" under the ADA, a threshold question that has generated considerable litigation; Section C then turns to what makes a disabled individual "qualified," in the process exploring the concepts of "essential function," "reasonable accommodation," and "undue hardship;" Section D examines discriminatory qualification standards, including the provision that employers may discriminate against employees who pose a "direct threat" to health or safety; and Section E addresses special problems under the ADA, including coverage for individuals addicted to drugs or alcohol, medical examinations and inquiries, retaliation, harassment, relationships with covered individuals, health and disability insurance plans, and rights under the Family and Medical Leave Act.

B. THE MEANING OF "DISABILITY"

In contrast to other statutes prohibiting discrimination in employment, establishing membership in the ADA's protected classification often requires extensive legal analysis. Generally speaking, to claim protection under the ADA, a plaintiff must be "a qualified individual with a disability"; that is, the plaintiff must be an individual with a disability who can perform essential job functions with or without reasonable accommodation.

Section 3(2) defines "disability" as

  (A) a physical or mental impairment that substantially limits one or more of the major life activities of . . . [an] individual;
  (B) a record of such an impairment; or
  (C) being regarded as having such an impairment.

However, §§ 508 and 511 expressly exclude certain practices or conditions from this definition. Many of these are sex related, such as homosexuality, bisexuality, transvestism, pedophilia, transexualism, and exhibitionism. Also excluded are compulsive gambling, kleptomania, pyromania, and disorders resulting from the current illegal use of psychoactive drugs.

The EEOC's ADA regulations broadly define the terms "physical or mental impairment" and "major life activities." Moreover, the regulations provide that an individual is substantially limited if totally or significantly restricted in her ability to perform major life activities in comparison with "the average person in the general population." 29 C.F.R. § 1630.2(j)(1)(i)(ii) (2002). Factors to be considered in determining whether an individual is substantially limited include:

(i) The nature and severity of the impairment;
(ii) The duration or expected duration of the impairment; and
(iii) The permanent or long term impact, or the expected permanent or long term impact of or resulting from the impairment.

29 C.F.R. § 1630.2(j)(2).

ADA coverage does not depend on establishing an actual, present disability. An individual who has a "record" of a physical or mental impairment that substantially limits a major life activity is within the definition of disability. Even if a person does not currently have such an impairment or was previously misclassified as having such an impairment, he is within the definition if he has a record of such an impairment. 29 C.F.R. § 1630.2(k).

A final method of establishing a "disability" is to show that an employer regarded the individual as having a disability. The ADA regulations define "regarded as having such an impairment" to mean:

(1) Has a physical or mental impairment that does not substantially limit major life activities but is treated by a covered entity as constituting such limitation;
(2) Has a physical or mental impairment that substantially limits major life activities only as a result of the attitudes of others toward such impairment; or
(3) Has none of the impairments [discussed above] but is treated by a covered entity as having a substantially limiting impairment.

29 C.F.R. § 1630.2(l).

Thus, a person can be disabled within the meaning of the statute not only if he has an "actual disability" but also if he is "regarded as" disabled or has a "record" of a disability. Employers are among the ADA's "covered entities" and the focus of Title I.

The Supreme Court considered the meaning of this three-pronged definition of disability for the first time in *School Board of Nassau County v. Arline*, 480 U.S. 273 (1987). Although *Arline* was a Rehabilitation Act case, the definition of "handicapped" individual (the term used at the time in the Rehabilitation Act) is identical to the definition of individual with a disability under the ADA. In *Arline*, the school board had fired plaintiff, an elementary school teacher, because it believed her active tuberculosis posed a threat to the health of others. Essentially, the school board contended that a person with a contagious disease was not within the protections of the Rehabilitation Act if the adverse employment action was based on the employee's contagiousness and not on the condition itself. In finding Arline to be a handicapped individual, the Supreme Court refused to allow the school board to disassociate the contagious effects of the teacher's impairment from the impairment itself. As the Court stated, "Arline's contagiousness and her physical impairment each resulted from the same underlying condition, tuberculosis. It would be unfair to allow an employer to seize upon the distinction between the effects of a disease on others and the effects of a disease on a patient and use that distinction to justify discriminatory intent." *Id.* at 282.

In light of *Arline*'s holding that a contagious disease can be a "disability," a person who has developed acquired immune deficiency syndrome (AIDS) is undoubtedly an "individual with a disability" under both the Rehabilitation Act and the ADA. Active AIDS clearly qualifies as a physical impairment and also substantially limits major life activities. But *Arline* left open the question of whether a person can be considered "handicapped" purely on the basis of contagiousness alone. Is a person who tests positively for the antibodies produced in reaction to HIV, the virus that causes AIDS, an "individual with a disability"? The Supreme Court addressed this issue in its first ADA case confronting the definition of disability. Although *Bragdon v. Abbot* was a Title III case involving public accommodation discrimination, the at-issue definition of disability applies to Titles I and II as well.

1. Actual Disability

BRAGDON v. ABBOTT
524 U.S. 624 (1998)

Justice KENNEDY delivered the opinion of the Court in which Justices STEVENS, SOUTER, GINSBURG, and BREYER, joined.

We address in this case the application of the Americans with Disabilities Act of 1990 (ADA) to persons infected with the human immunodeficiency virus (HIV). We granted certiorari to review, first, whether HIV infection is a disability under the ADA when the infection has not yet progressed to the so-called symptomatic phase. . . .

I

Respondent Sidney Abbott has been infected with HIV since 1986. When the incidents we recite occurred, her infection had not manifested its most serious symptoms. On September 16, 1994, she went to the office of petitioner Randon Bragdon in Bangor, Maine, for a dental appointment. She disclosed her HIV infection on the patient registration form. Petitioner completed a dental examination, discovered a cavity, and informed respondent of his policy against filling cavities of HIV-infected patients. He offered to perform the work at a hospital with no added fee for his services, though respondent would be responsible for the cost of using the hospital's facilities. Respondent declined.

Respondent sued petitioner under . . . § 302 of the ADA, alleging discrimination on the basis of her disability. . . . [Section 302 of Title III of the ADA prohibits discrimination on the basis of disability "by any person who . . . operates a place of public accommodation." The term "public accommodation" is defined to include the "professional office of a health care provider." § 12181(7)(F).]

II

We first review the ruling that respondent's HIV infection constituted a disability under the ADA. The statute defines disability as:

(A) a physical or mental impairment that substantially limits one or more of the major life activities of such individual;

(B) a record of such an impairment; or

(C) being regarded as having such impairment.

§12102(2). We hold respondent's HIV infection was a disability under subsection (A) of the definitional section of the statute. In light of this conclusion, we need not consider the applicability of subsections (B) or (C).

Our consideration of subsection (A) of the definition proceeds in three steps. First, we consider whether respondent's HIV infection was a physical impairment. Second, we identify the life activity upon which respondent relies (reproduction and child bearing) and determine whether it constitutes a major life activity under the ADA. Third, tying the two statutory phrases together, we ask whether the impairment substantially limited the major life activity. In construing the statute, we are informed by interpretations of parallel definitions in previous statutes and the views of various administrative agencies which have faced this interpretive question.

A

The ADA's definition of disability is drawn almost verbatim from the definition of "handicapped individual" included in the Rehabilitation Act of 1973. . . . Congress' repetition of a well-established term carries the implication that Congress intended the term to be construed in accordance with pre-existing regulatory interpretations. In this case, Congress did more than suggest this construction; it adopted a specific statutory provision in the ADA directing as follows:

> Except as otherwise provided in this chapter, nothing in this chapter shall be construed to apply a lesser standard than the standards applied under title V of the Rehabilitation Act of 1973 or the regulations issued by Federal agencies pursuant to such title.

42 U.S.C. §12201(a). The directive requires us to construe the ADA to grant at least as much protection as provided by the regulations implementing the Rehabilitation Act.

1

The first step in the inquiry under subsection (A) requires us to determine whether respondent's condition constituted a physical impairment. [The governing regulations were first issued by the Department of Health, Education and Welfare (HEW) under the Rehabilitation Act in 1977. They continue to govern without change although enforcement responsibility for §504 has been transferred to the Department of Justice. They define "physical or mental impairment" to mean:

(A) any physiological disorder or condition, cosmetic disfigurement, or anatomical loss affecting one or more of the following body systems: neurological; musculoskeletal; special sense organs; respiratory, including speech organs; cardiovascular; reproductive, digestive, genito-urinary; hemic and lymphatic; skin; and endocrine; or
(B) any mental or psychological disorder, such as mental retardation, organic brain syndrome, emotional or mental illness, and specific learning disabilities.

45 CFR §84.3(j)(2)(i) (1997). In issuing these regulations, HEW decided against including a list of disorders constituting physical or mental impairments, out of concern that any specific enumeration might not be comprehensive. 42 Fed. Reg. 22685 (1977), reprinted in 45 CFR pt. 84, App. A, p. 334 (1997). The commentary accompanying the regulations, however, contains a representative list of disorders

and conditions constituting physical impairments, including "such diseases and conditions as orthopedic, visual, speech, and hearing impairments, cerebral palsy, epilepsy, muscular dystrophy, multiple sclerosis, cancer, heart disease, diabetes, mental retardation, emotional illness, and . . . drug addiction and alcoholism." Id. . . .

HIV infection is not included in the list of specific disorders constituting physical impairments, in part because HIV was not identified as the cause of AIDS until 1983. HIV infection does fall well within the general definition set forth by the regulations, however.

The disease follows a predictable and, as of today, an unalterable course. Once a person is infected with HIV, the virus invades different cells in the blood and in body tissues. Certain white blood cells, known as helper T-lymphocytes or CD4+ cells, are particularly vulnerable to HIV. The virus attaches to the CD4 receptor site of the target cell and fuses its membrane to the cell's membrane. HIV is a retrovirus, which means it uses an enzyme to convert its own genetic material into a form indistinguishable from the genetic material of the target cell. The virus' genetic material migrates to the cell's nucleus and becomes integrated with the cell's chromosomes. Once integrated, the virus can use the cell's own genetic machinery to replicate itself. Additional copies of the virus are released into the body and infect other cells in turn.

The virus eventually kills the infected host cell. CD4+ cells play a critical role in coordinating the body's immune response system, and the decline in their number causes corresponding deterioration of the body's ability to fight infections from many sources. Tracking the infected individual's CD4+ cell count is one of the most accurate measures of the course of the disease.

The initial stage of HIV infection is known as acute or primary HIV infection. In a typical case, this stage lasts three months. The virus concentrates in the blood. The assault on the immune system is immediate. The victim suffers from a sudden and serious decline in the number of white blood cells. There is no latency period. Mononucleosis-like symptoms often emerge between six days and six weeks after infection, at times accompanied by fever, headache, enlargement of the lymph nodes (lymphadenopathy), muscle pain (myalgia), rash, lethargy, gastrointestinal disorders, and neurological disorders. Usually these symptoms abate within 14 to 21 days. HIV antibodies appear in the bloodstream within 3 weeks; circulating HIV can be detected within 10 weeks.

After the symptoms associated with the initial stage subside, the disease enters what is referred to sometimes as its asymptomatic phase. The term is a misnomer, in some respects, for clinical features persist throughout, including lymphadenopathy, dermatological disorders, oral lesions, and bacterial infections. Although it varies with each individual, in most instances this stage lasts from 7 to 11 years. The virus now tends to concentrate in the lymph nodes, though low levels of the virus continue to appear in the blood. It was once thought the virus became inactive during this period, but it is now known that the relative lack of symptoms is attributable to the virus' migration from the circulatory system into the lymph nodes. The migration reduces the viral presence in other parts of the body, with a corresponding diminution in physical manifestations of the disease. The virus, however, thrives in the lymph nodes, which, as a vital point of the body's immune response system, represents an ideal environment for the infection of other CD4+ cells.

A person is regarded as having AIDS when his or her CD4+ count drops below 200 cells/mm3 of blood or when CD4+ cells comprise less than 14% of his or her total lymphocytes. During this stage, the clinical conditions most often associated with HIV, such as pneumocystis carninii pneumonia, Kaposi's sarcoma, and non-Hodgkin's lymphoma, tend to appear. In addition, the general systemic disorders present during all stages of the disease, such as fever, weight loss, fatigue, lesions, nausea, and diarrhea, tend to worsen. In most cases, once the patient's CD4+ count drops below 10 cells/mm3, death soon follows.

In light of the immediacy with which the virus begins to damage the infected person's white blood cells and the severity of the disease, we hold it is an impairment from the moment of infection. As noted earlier, infection with HIV causes immediate abnormalities in a person's blood, and the infected person's white cell count continues to drop throughout the course of the disease, even when the attack is concentrated in the lymph nodes. In light of these facts, HIV infection must be regarded as a physiological disorder with a constant and detrimental effect on the infected person's hemic and lymphatic systems from the moment of infection. HIV infection satisfies the statutory and regulatory definition of a physical impairment during every stage of the disease.

2

The statute is not operative, and the definition not satisfied, unless the impairment affects a major life activity. Respondent's claim throughout this case has been that the HIV infection placed a substantial limitation on her ability to reproduce and to bear children. Given the pervasive, and invariably fatal, course of the disease, its effect on major life activities of many sorts might have been relevant to our inquiry. Respondent and a number of amici make arguments about HIV's profound impact on almost every phase of the infected person's life. In light of these submissions, it may seem legalistic to circumscribe our discussion to the activity of reproduction. We have little doubt that had different parties brought the suit they would have maintained that an HIV infection imposes substantial limitations on other major life activities. . . .

We have little difficulty concluding that [reproduction is a major life activity]. As the Court of Appeals held, "the plain meaning of the word 'major' denotes comparative importance" and "suggests that the touchstone for determining an activity's inclusion under the statutory rubric is its significance." Reproduction falls well within the phrase "major life activity." Reproduction and the sexual dynamics surrounding it are central to the life process itself.

While petitioner concedes the importance of reproduction, he claims that Congress intended the ADA only to cover those aspects of a person's life which have a public, economic, or daily character. The argument flounders on the statutory language. Nothing in the definition suggests that activities without a public, economic, or daily dimension may somehow be regarded as so unimportant or insignificant as to fall outside the meaning of the word "major." The breadth of the term confounds the attempt to limit its construction in this manner.

As we have noted, the ADA must be construed to be consistent with regulations issued to implement the Rehabilitation Act. Rather than enunciating a general principle for determining what is and is not a major life activity, the Rehabilitation Act regulations instead provide a representative list, defining the term to include "functions such as caring for one's self, performing manual tasks, walking, seeing, hearing, speaking, breathing, learning, and working." 45 CFR § 84.3(j)(2)(ii) (1997); 28 CFR § 41.31(b)(2) (1997). As the use of the term "such as" confirms, the list is illustrative, not exhaustive.

These regulations are contrary to petitioner's attempt to limit the meaning of the term "major" to public activities. The inclusion of activities such as caring for one's self and performing manual tasks belies the suggestion that a task must have a public or economic character in order to be a major life activity for purposes of the ADA. On the contrary, the Rehabilitation Act regulations support the inclusion of reproduction as a major life activity, since reproduction could not be regarded as any less important than working and learning. Petitioner advances no credible basis for confining major life activities to those with a public, economic, or daily aspect. . . . [R]eproduction is a major life activity for the purposes of the ADA.

3

The final element of the disability definition in subsection (A) is whether respondent's physical impairment was a substantial limit on the major life activity she asserts. The Rehabilitation Act regulations provide no additional guidance.

Our evaluation of the medical evidence leads us to conclude that respondent's infection substantially limited her ability to reproduce in two independent ways. First, a woman infected with HIV who tries to conceive a child imposes on the man a significant risk of becoming infected. The cumulative results of 13 studies collected in a 1994 textbook on AIDS indicates that 20% of male partners of women with HIV became HIV-positive themselves, with a majority of the studies finding a statistically significant risk of infection.

Second, an infected woman risks infecting her child during gestation and child-birth, i.e., perinatal transmission. Petitioner concedes that women infected with HIV face about a 25% risk of transmitting the virus to their children. Published reports available in 1994 confirm the accuracy of this statistic.

Petitioner points to evidence in the record suggesting that antiretroviral therapy can lower the risk of perinatal transmission to about 8%. . . . It cannot be said as a matter of law that an 8% risk of transmitting a dread and fatal disease to one's child does not represent a substantial limitation on reproduction.

The Act addresses substantial limitations on major life activities, not utter inabilities. Conception and childbirth are not impossible for an HIV victim but, without doubt, are dangerous to the public health. This meets the definition of a substantial limitation. The decision to reproduce carries economic and legal consequences as well. There are added costs for antiretroviral therapy, supplemental insurance, and long-term health care for the child who must be examined and, tragic to think, treated for the infection. The laws of some States, moreover, forbid persons infected with HIV from having sex with others, regardless of consent.

In the end, the disability definition does not turn on personal choice. When significant limitations result from the impairment, the definition is met even if the difficulties are not insurmountable. For the statistical and other reasons we have cited, of course, the limitations on reproduction may be insurmountable here. . . . Respondent's HIV infection is a physical impairment which substantially limits a major life activity, as the ADA defines it. In view of our holding, we need not address the second question presented, i.e., whether HIV infection is a per se disability under the ADA.

B

Our holding is confirmed by a consistent course of agency interpretation before and after enactment of the ADA. Every agency to consider the issue under the

Rehabilitation Act found statutory coverage for persons with asymptomatic HIV. Responsibility for administering the Rehabilitation Act was not delegated to a single agency, but we need not pause to inquire whether this causes us to withhold deference to agency interpretations under *Chevron U.S.A. Inc. v. Natural Resources Defense Council, Inc.*, 467 U.S. 837, 844 (1984). It is enough to observe that the well-reasoned views of the agencies implementing a statute "constitute a body of experience and informed judgment to which courts and litigants may properly resort for guidance." *Skidmore v. Swift & Co.*, 323 U.S. 134, 139-140 (1944).

[The Court cited a 1988 opinion of the Office of Legal Counsel of the Department of Justice (OLC) concluding that the Rehabilitation Act "protects symptomatic and asymptomatic HIV-infected individuals against discrimination in any covered program", and it noted that every court decision before the enactment of the ADA agreed.] We are aware of no instance prior to the enactment of the ADA in which a court or agency ruled that HIV infection was not a handicap under the Rehabilitation Act.

Had Congress done nothing more than copy the Rehabilitation Act definition into the ADA, its action would indicate the new statute should be construed in light of this unwavering line of administrative and judicial interpretation. All indications are that Congress was well aware of the position taken by OLC when enacting the ADA and intended to give that position its active endorsement. [See, e.g.], H.R. Rep. No. 101-485, pt. 2, p. 52 (1990) (endorsing the analysis and conclusion of the OLC Opinion). . . .

We find the uniformity of the administrative and judicial precedent construing the definition significant. When administrative and judicial interpretations have settled the meaning of an existing statutory provision, repetition of the same language in a new statute indicates, as a general matter, the intent to incorporate its administrative and judicial interpretations as well. The uniform body of administrative and judicial precedent confirms the conclusion we reach today as the most faithful way to effect the congressional design.

c

Our conclusion is further reinforced by the administrative guidance issued by the Justice Department to implement the public accommodation provisions of Title III of the ADA. As the agency directed by Congress to issue implementing regulations, see 42 U.S.C. §12186(b), to render technical assistance explaining the responsibilities of covered individuals and institutions, §12206(c), and to enforce Title III in court, §12188(b), the Department's views are entitled to deference. See *Chevron*.

[The Justice Department not only incorporated verbatim the HEW language but went further to add "HIV infection (symptomatic and asymptomatic)" to the list of disorders constituting a physical impairment. §36.104(1)(iii). Other agencies authorized to administer other sections of the ADA, including the EEOC, agreed.] Most categorical of all is EEOC's conclusion that "an individual who has HIV infection (including asymptomatic HIV infection) is an individual with a disability." EEOC Interpretive Manual §902.4(c)(1), p. 902-21; accord, id., §902.2(d), p. 902-14, n. 18. In the EEOC's view, "impairments . . . such as HIV infection, are inherently substantially limiting." 29 CFR pt. 1630, App., p. 350 (1997); EEOC Technical Assistance Manual II-4; EEOC Interpretive Manual §902.4(c)(1), p. 902-21.

The regulatory authorities we cite are consistent with our holding that HIV infection, even in the so-called asymptomatic phase, is an impairment which substantially limits the major life activity of reproduction.

NOTES

1. *A Three-Step Inquiry.* As *Bragdon* makes clear, determining whether an actual disability exists requires examination of three separate elements: whether there is a (1) physical or mental impairment that (2) substantially limits (3) one or more major life activities. Moreover, analysis of each of these elements must occur, regardless of which of the three routes to disability status is at issue — actual, "record of," or "regarded as."

2. *Is There an Impairment?* As in *Bragdon*, whether an impairment exists is often not difficult to determine. But sometimes it is. The EEOC has stated that the term "physical or mental impairment" does not include physical characteristics, such as weight, height, and eye color that are in the "normal range" and are not the result of a physiological disorder. The Interpretive Guidance also excludes common personality traits, illiteracy, economic disadvantages, and temporary physical conditions. Advanced age also is excluded, although physical and mental impairments associated with aging are not. *See* 29 C.F.R. pt. 1630, app. § 1630.2(h), (j). Is any physical characteristic outside the normal range an "impairment"? Consider unusual strength or high intelligence. Are these impairments (because they are out of the normal range), but not disabilities (because they do not substantially impair life activities)? Or are they not impairments at all because they are out of the normal range on the "positive," rather than the "negative," side?

(a) *Pregnancy.* Pregnancy shares many of the characteristics of a disability as defined by the ADA. Nonetheless, the EEOC's ADA Guidance suggests that pregnancy is not a disability covered by the statute because pregnancy is not an impairment. *See* 29 C.F.R. pt. 1630, app. § 1630.2(h). *But see* Melissa Cole, *Beyond Sex Discrimination: Why Employers Discriminate against Women with Disabilities when Their Employee Health Plans Exclude Contraceptives from Prescription Coverage,* 42 Ariz. L. Rev. 501 (2001).

(b) *Voluntary Conditions.* Can a physical condition that is caused at least in part by voluntary conduct constitute an impairment? In *Cook v. Rhode Island Dept. of Mental Health*, 10 F.3d 17 (1st Cir. 1993), the First Circuit held, in a claim under the Rehabilitation Act, that morbid obesity could be an impairment, rejecting the defendant's argument that "mutable" conditions or those "caused, or at least exacerbated, by voluntary conduct," were not impairments. As the court stated,

> The Rehabilitation Act contains no language suggesting that its protection is linked to how an individual became impaired, or whether an individual contributed to his or her impairment. On the contrary, the Act indisputably applies to numerous conditions that may be caused or exacerbated by voluntary conduct, such as alcoholism, AIDS, diabetes, cancer resulting from cigarette smoking, heart disease resulting from excesses of various types, and the like. Consequently, voluntariness, like mutability, is relevant only in determining whether a condition has a substantially limiting effect.

Id. at 24. *Cf. EEOC v. Watkins Motor Lines, Inc.*, 463 F.3d 436 (6th Cir. 2006) (morbid obesity, not related to any physiological cause, was not an impairment). The

EEOC does not regard "common obesity" as an impairment. 29 C.F.R. pt. 1630, app. §1630.2(j).

(c) *Temporary Impairments*. Another question is whether temporary impairments are covered by the Rehabilitation Act or the ADA. The answer is no. In *Toyota Motor Mfg. Co. v. Williams*, reproduced at p. 50, the Supreme Court stated that to substantially limit performance of manual tasks, "the impairment's impact must also be permanent or long-term." Subsequent to *Toyota*, the Fourth Circuit concluded that a medical condition necessitating surgery and a recovery period requiring a nine-month leave of absence was temporary and thus not substantially limiting. *See Pollard v. High's of Baltimore, Inc.*, 281 F.3d 462 (4th Cir. 2002). Even if not permanent, isn't this "long-term"?

In *Vande Zande v. Wisconsin Dept. of Admin.*, reproduced at p. 552, Vande Zande, who is paralyzed from the waist down, sought ADA accommodations relating to pressure ulcers caused by her paralysis. Her employer argued that, because her ulcers were intermittent and episodic impairments, they did not fit the definition of a disability. The Seventh Circuit disagreed:

> [A]n intermittent impairment that is a characteristic manifestation of an admitted disability is, we believe, a part of the underlying disability. . . . Often the disabling aspect of a disability is, precisely, an intermittent manifestation of the disability, rather than the underlying impairment. The AIDS virus progressively destroys the infected person's immune system. The consequence is a series of opportunistic diseases which . . . often prevent the individual from working. If they are not part of the disability, then people with AIDS do not have a disability which seems to us a very odd interpretation of the law, and one expressly rejected by the regulations. We hold that Vande Zande's pressure ulcers are a part of her disability.

Id. at 544. *Vande Zande*'s treatment of the symptom of a disability is consistent with the Supreme Court's treatment of contagiousness in *Arline*.

(d) *Genetic Conditions as Impairments*. Is an individual with a genetic propensity to disease impaired? If so, does this impairment substantially limit any major life activity? A few diseases, like Huntington's disease, are inevitable for those with the allele, although they may not manifest the symptoms until late in life. Most "genetic diseases," however, simply make individuals more susceptible to the condition (although sometimes increasing the risk factor enormously). Is someone with the Huntington's allele but no symptoms impaired? If so, does this impairment substantially limit any major life activity? Even if the answer is yes, what about those genetic diseases whose appearance is not inevitable? *See* John V. Jacobi, *Genetic Discrimination in a Time of False Hopes* 30 FLA. ST. U.L. REV. 363, 362 (2003).

3. *Major Life Activities*. The Court's holding in *Bragdon* that reproduction is a major life activity has significance beyond the question of whether HIV infection is a disability within the meaning of the ADA, given that *Bragdon* acknowledges that the §1630.2(i) list of major life activities is not exclusive. After *Bragdon*, what other activities are major life activities under the ADA? In *Toyota Motor Mfg. Co. v. Williams*, reproduced at p. 50, the Supreme Court held that performing manual tasks is a major life activity. What about the ability to eat, drink, sleep, drive a car, think, or get along with people? Are these major life activities under the ADA? *See Littleton v. Wal-Mart*, 231 Fed. Appx. 874 (11th Cir. 2007) (learning is a major life activity; unclear whether thinking, communicating or social interaction are major life activities); *Carlson v. Liberty Mut. Ins. Co.*, 237 Fed. Appx. 446 (11th Cir. 2007)

(driving not a major life activity); *Head v. Glacier Northwest, Inc.*, 413 F.3d 1053, 1058 (9th Cir. 2005) (thinking, reading, interacting with others, sleeping were all major life activities); *Fraser v. Goodale*, 342 F.3d 1032 (9th Cir. 2003) (eating is a major life activity); *Heiko v. Colombo Sav. Bank*, 434 F.3d 249, 255 (4th Cir. 2006) (waste elimination is a major life activity); *Fiscus v. Wal-Mart Stores, Inc.*, 385 F.3d 378 (3d Cir. 2004) (same); *Jacques v. DiMarzio, Inc.*, 386 F.3d 192, 203-04 (2d Cir. 2004) (interacting with others is a major life activity, but to be substantially limited in this respect, "the impairment [must] severely limit the plaintiff's ability to connect with others, i.e., to initiate contact with other people and respond to them, or to go among other people — at the most basic level of these activities"); *Rohan v. Networks Presentation LLC*, 375 F.3d 266 (4th Cir. 2004) (questioning whether interacting with others is a major life activity and collecting cases). For a discussion of cases before and after *Bragdon* confronting the question of what constitutes a major life activity, *see* Curtis D. Edmonds, *Snakes and Ladders: Expanding the Definition of "Major Life Activity" in the Americans with Disabilities Act*, 33 TEX. TECH. L. REV. 321 (2002); Wendy F. Hensel, *Interacting with Others: A Major Life Activity under the Americans with Disabilities Act?*, 2002 WIS. L. REV. 1139; Ann Hubbard, *Meaningful Lives and Major Life Activities*, 55 ALA. L. REV. 997 (2004); Ann Hubbard, *The Major Life Activity of Belonging*, 39 WAKE FOREST L. REV. 217 (2004); Ann Hubbard, *The Myth of Independence and the Major Life Activity of Caring*, 8 J. Gender Race & Just. 327 (2004).

Must a *particular* major life activity be identified in determining disability status? Justice Ginsburg's concurrence in *Bragdon* addressed ADA coverage for HIV-infected individuals:

> HIV infection, as the description set out in the Court's opinion documents, has been regarded as a disease limiting life itself. The disease inevitably pervades life's choices: education, employment, family and financial undertakings. It affects the need for and, as this case shows, the ability to obtain health care because of the reaction of others to the impairment. No rational legislator, it seems to me apparent, would require nondiscrimination once symptoms become visible but permit discrimination when the disease, though present, is not yet visible. I am therefore satisfied that the statutory and regulatory definitions are well met. HIV infection is "a physical . . . impairment that substantially limits . . . major life activities," or is so perceived, 42 U.S.C. §§ 12102(2)(A),(C), including the afflicted individual's family relations, employment potential, and ability to care for herself, see 45 CFR § 84.3(j)(2)(ii) (1997); 28 CFR § 41.31(b)(2) (1997).

524 U.S. at 624. Justice Ginsburg suggests that HIV infection is substantially limiting in part because it will later develop into a seriously debilitating illness. If this is so, what about multiple sclerosis, which in its early stages can be relatively asymptomatic, but which is likely to ultimately be seriously disabling? Consider the impact of the EEOC Interpretive Guidance:

> Some impairments may be disabling for particular individuals but not for others, depending on the stage of the disease or disorder, the presence of other impairments that combine to make the impairment disabling or any number of other factors.

29 C.F.R. pt. 1630, app. § 1630.2(j).

An issue that has caused considerable controversy is whether working is a major life activity and what it means to be substantially limited in the ability to work.

Consideration of this question is deferred to the notes after *Sutton v. United Air Lines, Inc.*, 527 U.S. 471 (1999), reproduced at p. 509.

4. *Substantially Limits. Bragdon* resolves the issue of ADA coverage for *most* individuals who are infected with HIV. Does the decision provide any assistance to HIV-infected plaintiffs who are unable to bear children for reasons other than their HIV infection? What about an HIV-infected woman who had her fallopian tubes tied prior to her infection? Is such an individual "substantially limited" for other reasons? In *Blanks v. Southwestern Bell Corp.*, 310 F.3d 398 (5th Cir. 2002), the court held that an HIV-positive worker who did not intend to have more children failed to establish a disability under the ADA. But doesn't the *Bragdon* opinion support an argument that HIV infection is substantially limiting because it restricts an individual's freedom to engage in sexual intercourse? Don't you think the Court would regard sexual intercourse as a major life activity?

The Court further explored what it means for an impairment to substantially limit a major life activity in the following case.

TOYOTA MOTOR MANUFACTURING, KENTUCKY, INC. v. WILLIAMS
534 U.S. 184 (2002)

Justice O'CONNOR delivered the opinion of the Court.

Under the Americans with Disabilities Act of 1990 (ADA or Act), a physical impairment that "substantially limits one or more . . . major life activities" is a "disability." 42 U.S.C. §12102(2)(A). Respondent, claiming to be disabled because of her carpal tunnel syndrome and other related impairments, sued petitioner, her former employer, for failing to provide her with a reasonable accommodation as required by the ADA. See §12112(b) (5)(A). The District Court granted summary judgment to petitioner, finding that respondent's impairments did not substantially limit any of her major life activities. The Court of Appeals for the Sixth Circuit reversed, finding that the impairments substantially limited respondent in the major life activity of performing manual tasks, and therefore granting partial summary judgment to respondent on the issue of whether she was disabled under the ADA. We conclude that the Court of Appeals did not apply the proper standard in making this determination because it analyzed only a limited class of manual tasks and failed to ask whether respondent's impairments prevented or restricted her from performing tasks that are of central importance to most people's daily lives.

I

Respondent began working at petitioner's automobile manufacturing plant in Georgetown, Kentucky, in August 1990. She was soon placed on an engine fabrication assembly line, where her duties included work with pneumatic tools. Use of these tools eventually caused pain in respondent's hands, wrists, and arms. . . . Respondent consulted a personal physician who placed her on permanent work restrictions that precluded her from lifting more than 20 pounds or from "frequently lifting or carrying of objects weighing up to 10 pounds," engaging in "constant repetitive . . . flexion or extension of [her] wrists or elbows," performing "overhead work," or using "vibratory or pneumatic tools."

In light of these restrictions, for the next two years petitioner assigned respondent to various modified duty jobs. . . . [P]etitioner placed respondent on a team in Quality Control Inspection Operations (QCIO). QCIO is responsible for four tasks: (1) "assembly paint"; (2) "paint second inspection"; (3) "shell body audit"; and (4) "ED surface repair." Respondent was initially placed on a team that performed only the first two of these tasks, and for a couple of years, she rotated on a weekly basis between them. . . . The parties agree that respondent was physically capable of performing both of these jobs and that her performance was satisfactory.

During the fall of 1996, petitioner announced that it wanted QCIO employees to be able to rotate through all four of the QCIO processes. . . . A short while after the shell body audit job was added to respondent's rotations, she began to experience pain in her neck and shoulders. . . . Respondent requested that petitioner accommodate her medical conditions by allowing her to return to doing only her original two jobs in QCIO, which respondent claimed she could still perform without difficulty.

The parties disagree about what happened next. According to respondent, petitioner refused her request and forced her to continue working in the shell body audit job, which caused her even greater physical injury. According to petitioner, respondent simply began missing work on a regular basis. Regardless, it is clear that on December 6, 1996, the last day respondent worked at petitioner's plant, she was placed under a no-work-of-any-kind restriction by her treating physicians. On January 27, 1997, respondent received a letter from petitioner that terminated her employment, citing her poor attendance record. . . .

[The District Court granted summary judgment for defendant, finding that at the time respondent requested accommodation, she was not disabled within the meaning of the statute because her impairment did not substantially limit any major life activity. It further found that at the time of her termination she was not a qualified individual with a disability because her doctor had precluded her from performing any work whatsoever.]

The Court of Appeals for the Sixth Circuit reversed the District Court's ruling on whether respondent was disabled at the time she sought an accommodation. . . . The Court of Appeals held that in order for respondent to demonstrate that she was disabled due to a substantial limitation in the ability to perform manual tasks at the time of her accommodation request, she had to "show that her manual disability involved a 'class' of manual activities affecting the ability to perform tasks at work." Respondent satisfied this test, according to the Court of Appeals, because her ailments "prevented her from doing the tasks associated with certain types of manual assembly line jobs, manual product handling jobs and manual building trade jobs (painting, plumbing, roofing, etc.) that require the gripping of tools and repetitive work with hands and arms extended at or above shoulder levels for extended periods of time." In reaching this conclusion, the court disregarded evidence that respondent could "tend to her personal hygiene [and] carry out personal or household chores," finding that such evidence "does not affect a determination that her impairment substantially limited her ability to perform the range of manual tasks associated with an assembly line job." Because the Court of Appeals concluded that respondent had been substantially limited in performing manual tasks and, for that reason, was entitled to partial summary judgment on the issue of whether she was disabled under the Act, it found that it did not need to determine whether respondent had been substantially limited in the major life activities of lifting or working, or whether she had had a "record of" a disability or had been "regarded as" disabled. . . .

III

The question presented by this case is whether the Sixth Circuit properly determined that respondent was disabled under subsection (A) of the ADA's disability definition [an actual disability, that is, "a physical or mental impairment that substantially limits one or more of the major life activities of such individual"] at the time that she sought an accommodation from petitioner. 42 U.S.C. §12102(2)(A). The parties do not dispute that respondent's medical conditions, which include carpal tunnel syndrome, myotendinitis, and thoracic outlet compression, amount to physical impairments. The relevant question, therefore, is whether the Sixth Circuit correctly analyzed whether these impairments substantially limited respondent in the major life activity of performing manual tasks. Answering this requires us to address an issue about which the EEOC regulations are silent: what a plaintiff must demonstrate to establish a substantial limitation in the specific major life activity of performing manual tasks.

Our consideration of this issue is guided first and foremost by the words of the disability definition itself. "Substantially" in the phrase "substantially limits" suggests "considerable" or "to a large degree." See Webster's Third New International Dictionary 2280 (1976) (defining "substantially" as "in a substantial manner" and "substantial" as "considerable in amount, value, or worth" and "being that specified to a large degree or in the main"); see also 17 Oxford English Dictionary 66-67 (2d ed. 1989) ("substantial": "relating to or proceeding from the essence of a thing; essential"; "of ample or considerable amount, quantity, or dimensions"). The word "substantial" thus clearly precludes impairments that interfere in only a minor way with the performance of manual tasks from qualifying as disabilities. Cf. *Albertson's, Inc. v. Kirkingburg* 527 U.S. 555 (1999) [reproduced at p. 576] (explaining that a "mere difference" does not amount to a "significant restriction" and therefore does not satisfy the EEOC's interpretation of "substantially limits").

"Major" in the phrase "major life activities" means important. See Webster's, supra, at 1363 (defining "major" as "greater in dignity, rank, importance, or interest"). "Major life activities" thus refers to those activities that are of central importance to daily life. In order for performing manual tasks to fit into this category — a category that includes such basic abilities as walking, seeing, and hearing — the manual tasks in question must be central to daily life. If each of the tasks included in the major life activity of performing manual tasks does not independently qualify as a major life activity, then together they must do so.

That these terms need to be interpreted strictly to create a demanding standard for qualifying as disabled is confirmed by the first section of the ADA, which lays out the legislative findings and purposes that motivate the Act. See 42 U.S.C. §12101. When it enacted the ADA in 1990, Congress found that "some 43,000,000 Americans have one or more physical or mental disabilities." §12101(a)(1). If Congress intended everyone with a physical impairment that precluded the performance of some isolated, unimportant, or particularly difficult manual task to qualify as disabled, the number of disabled Americans would surely have been much higher. Cf. *Sutton v. United Air Lines, Inc.*, 527 U.S. 471 (1999) [reproduced at p. 509] (finding that because more than 100 million people need corrective lenses to see properly, "had Congress intended to include all persons with corrected physical limitations among those covered by the Act, it undoubtedly would have cited a much higher number [than 43 million disabled persons] in the findings").

We therefore hold that to be substantially limited in performing manual tasks, an individual must have an impairment that prevents or severely restricts the individual from doing activities that are of central importance to most people's daily lives. The impairment's impact must also be permanent or long-term. See 29 CFR §§ 1630.2(j)(2)(ii)-(iii) (2001).

It is insufficient for individuals attempting to prove disability status under this test to merely submit evidence of a medical diagnosis of an impairment. Instead, the ADA requires those "claiming the Act's protection . . . to prove a disability by offering evidence that the extent of the limitation [caused by their impairment] in terms of their own experience . . . is substantial." *Albertson's, Inc. v. Kirkingburg* (holding that monocular vision is not invariably a disability, but must be analyzed on an individual basis, taking into account the individual's ability to compensate for the impairment). That the Act defines "disability" "with respect to an individual," 42 U.S.C. § 12102(2), makes clear that Congress intended the existence of a disability to be determined in such a case-by-case manner. See *Sutton v. United Air Lines, Inc.*; *Albertson's, Inc. v. Kirkingburg*; cf. *Bragdon v. Abbott* (relying on unchallenged testimony that the respondent's HIV infection controlled her decision not to have a child, and declining to consider whether HIV infection is a *per se* disability under the ADA); 29 CFR pt. 1630, App. § 1630.2(j) (2001).

An individualized assessment of the effect of an impairment is particularly necessary when the impairment is one whose symptoms vary widely from person to person. Carpal tunnel syndrome, one of respondent's impairments, is just such a condition. While cases of severe carpal tunnel syndrome are characterized by muscle atrophy and extreme sensory deficits, mild cases generally do not have either of these effects and create only intermittent symptoms of numbness and tingling. Carniero, Carpal Tunnel Syndrome: The Cause Dictates the Treatment, 66 Cleveland Clinic J. Medicine 159, 161-162 (1999). Studies have further shown that, even without surgical treatment, one quarter of carpal tunnel cases resolve in one month, but that in 22 percent of cases, symptoms last for eight years or longer. See DeStefano, Nordstrom, & Uierkant, Long-term Symptom Outcomes of Carpal Tunnel Syndrome and its Treatment, 22A J. Hand Surgery 200, 204-205 (1997). When pregnancy is the cause of carpal tunnel syndrome, in contrast, the symptoms normally resolve within two weeks of delivery. See Ouellette, Nerve Compression Syndromes of the Upper Extremity in Women, 17 Journal of Musculoskeletal Medicine 536 (2000). Given these large potential differences in the severity and duration of the effects of carpal tunnel syndrome, an individual's carpal tunnel syndrome diagnosis, on its own, does not indicate whether the individual has a disability within the meaning of the ADA.

IV

The Court of Appeals' analysis of respondent's claimed disability suggested that in order to prove a substantial limitation in the major life activity of performing manual tasks, a "plaintiff must show that her manual disability involves a 'class' of manual activities," and that those activities "affect the ability to perform tasks at work." Both of these ideas lack support.

The Court of Appeals relied on our opinion in *Sutton v. United Air Lines, Inc.*, for the idea that a "class" of manual activities must be implicated for an impairment to substantially limit the major life activity of performing manual tasks. But *Sutton* said only that *"when the major life activity under consideration is that of working,* the statutory phrase 'substantially limits' requires . . . that plaintiffs allege that they are unable to work in a broad class of jobs." (emphasis added). Because of the conceptual difficulties inherent in the argument that working could be a major life activity, we have been hesitant to hold as much, and we need not decide this difficult question today. In *Sutton*, we noted that even assuming that working is a major life activity, a claimant would be required to show an inability to work in a "broad range of jobs," rather than a specific job. But *Sutton* did not suggest that a class-based analysis should be applied to any major life activity other than working. Nor do the EEOC regulations. In defining "substantially limits," the EEOC regulations only mention the "class" concept in the context of the major life activity of working. 29 CFR § 1630.2(j)(3) (2001) ("With respect to the major life activity of *working*[,] the term *substantially limits* means significantly restricted in the ability to perform either a class of jobs or a broad range of jobs in various classes as compared to the average person having comparable training, skills and abilities"). Nothing in the text of the Act, our previous opinions, or the regulations suggests that a class-based framework should apply outside the context of the major life activity of working.

While the Court of Appeals in this case addressed the different major life activity of performing manual tasks, its analysis circumvented *Sutton* by focusing on respondent's inability to perform manual tasks associated only with her job. This was error. When addressing the major life activity of performing manual tasks, the central inquiry must be whether the claimant is unable to perform the variety of tasks central to most people's daily lives, not whether the claimant is unable to perform the tasks associated with her specific job. Otherwise, *Sutton*'s restriction on claims of disability based on a substantial limitation in working will be rendered meaningless because an inability to perform a specific job always can be recast as an inability to perform a "class" of tasks associated with that specific job.

There is also no support in the Act, our previous opinions, or the regulations for the Court of Appeals' idea that the question of whether an impairment constitutes a disability is to be answered only by analyzing the effect of the impairment in the workplace. Indeed, the fact that the Act's definition of "disability" applies not only to Title I of the Act, 42 U.S.C. §§ 12111-12117, which deals with employment, but also to the other portions of the Act, which deal with subjects such as public transportation, §§ 12141-12150, 42 U.S.C. §§ 12161-12165, and privately provided public accommodations, §§ 12181-12189, demonstrates that the definition is intended to cover individuals with disabling impairments regardless of whether the individuals have any connection to a workplace.

Even more critically, the manual tasks unique to any particular job are not necessarily important parts of most people's lives. As a result, occupation-specific tasks may have only limited relevance to the manual task inquiry. In this case, "repetitive work with hands and arms extended at or above shoulder levels for extended periods of time," the manual task on which the Court of Appeals relied, is not an important part of most people's daily lives. The court, therefore, should not have considered respondent's inability to do such manual work in her specialized assembly line job as sufficient proof that she was substantially limited in performing manual tasks.

At the same time, the Court of Appeals appears to have disregarded the very type of evidence that it should have focused upon. It treated as irrelevant "the fact that [respondent] can . . . tend to her personal hygiene [and] carry out personal or household chores." Yet household chores, bathing, and brushing one's teeth are among the types of manual tasks of central importance to people's daily lives, and should have been part of the assessment of whether respondent was substantially limited in performing manual tasks.

The District Court noted that at the time respondent sought an accommodation from petitioner, she admitted that she was able to do the manual tasks required by her original two jobs in QCIO. In addition, according to respondent's deposition testimony, even after her condition worsened, she could still brush her teeth, wash her face, bathe, tend her flower garden, fix breakfast, do laundry, and pick up around the house. The record also indicates that her medical conditions caused her to avoid sweeping, to quit dancing, to occasionally seek help dressing, and to reduce how often she plays with her children, gardens, and drives long distances. But these changes in her life did not amount to such severe restrictions in the activities that are of central importance to most people's daily lives that they establish a manual-task disability as a matter of law. On this record, it was therefore inappropriate for the Court of Appeals to grant partial summary judgment to respondent on the issue whether she was substantially limited in performing manual tasks, and its decision to do so must be reversed. . . .

NOTES

1. *A Narrow Holding.* The decision in *Toyota* was unanimous, presumably because of the very narrow holding of the case. The Court did not determine whether Williams's impairment substantially limited her ability to perform manual tasks. Nor did it determine whether Williams's impairment substantially limited her ability to perform any other major life activity. Williams also had contended that lifting and working were major life activities and that her impairment substantially limited those activities as well. The appeals court did not rule on those contentions, and neither did the Supreme Court. Is lifting a major life activity? Is working? On the latter question, see the Court's decision in *Sutton*, reproduced at p. 509.

At the district court level, Williams also had alleged that housework, gardening, and playing with her children were major life activities, but she did not appeal the district court's rejection of those contentions. In light of the Court's language in *Toyota*, do you agree with her decision to abandon those contentions?

Although the *Toyota* holding is narrow, its language is very broad, insisting that the definition of disability be "interpreted strictly to create a demanding standard for qualifying as disabled." Why? Given that disability status is but a threshold step toward protected status under Title I, does the Court's interpretation of "disability" raise the bar too high?

2. *Performing Manual Tasks as a Major Life Activity.* Importantly, the Court agreed with the Sixth Circuit that performing manual tasks *is* a major life activity. But it held that the manual tasks, either singly or together, must be "central to daily life." If a particular manual task is central to daily life, is it a major life activity, standing alone? When would one need a combination of tasks central to daily life for their performance to be a major life activity? What are the manual tasks "central to daily life"? Is using one's arms and hands to communicate with others a manual task? *See Thornton v. McClatchy Newspapers, Inc.*, 292 F.3d 1045, 1046 (9th Cir. 2002) ("While most lawyers or law office personnel would undoubtedly consider continuous keyboarding and handwriting to be activities of central importance to their lives, we cannot say that is so for 'most people's daily lives,' as *Williams* requires").

The Sixth Circuit had focused only on a "class" of manual tasks that were work related. The appeals court had not determined that Williams was substantially limited in her ability to work, and yet the only limitations it had considered were those that were work related. Was the Court concerned that the Sixth Circuit may have been trying to circumvent the rigors of establishing that an individual is substantially limited in her ability to work? See *Sutton*, reproduced at p. 509. On remand, would Williams be better served by emphasizing her contention that working is a major life activity and the impairment's impact on her ability to work? See *McKay v. Toyota Motor Mfg., U.S.A., Inc.*, 110 F.3d 369 (6th Cir. 1997) (plaintiff whose carpal tunnel syndrome precluded repetitive factory work not substantially limited in the major life activity of working).

3. *Substantially Limits.* The primary question before the *Toyota* Court was whether Williams's impairment *substantially limited* her major life activity of performing manual tasks. The Court answered that question by stating that only if the impairment "prevents or severely restricts the individual from doing activities that are of central importance to most people's daily lives" will it be substantially limiting. Moreover, the impairment's impact must also be permanent or long-term. Is the Court's approach to "substantially limits" in *Toyota* consistent with its approach to that term in *Bragdon v. Abbott*? See *Taylor v. Fed. Express Corp.*, 429 F.3d 461, 464 (4th Cir. 2005) (assuming working was a major life activity, plaintiff's evidence established only that his inability to lift more than 30 pounds barred him from a number of jobs; it did not create a jury question as to whether he was substantially limited in working when "even with the impairment he qualified for over 1,400 different types of jobs and over 130,000 actual jobs in the Baltimore-Washington region").

The EEOC has promulgated regulations that define "substantially limited" to mean "unable to perform a major life activity that the average person in the general population can perform" or "significantly restricted as to the condition, manner or duration under which an individual can perform a particular major life activity as compared to the condition, manner, or duration under which the average person in the general population can perform that same major life activity." 29 C.F.R. § 1630.2(j). The regulations state that the following factors should be considered: "the nature and severity of the impairment; the duration or expected duration of the impairment; and the permanent or long-term impact, or the expected permanent or long-term impact of or resulting from the impairment." §§ 1630.2(j)(2)(i)-(iii). Although the *Toyota* Court quoted these regulations (and assumed their reasonableness) in a portion of the opinion not reproduced, it pointedly declined to decide whether the EEOC's regulations were entitled to any deference. The Court noted, however, that the regulations did not address the precise issue confronting the Court, that is, what constitutes a substantial limitation on the performance of manual tasks? In *EEOC v. Sears, Roebuck & Co.*, 417 F.3d 789, 797 (7th Cir. 2005), the court reversed summary judgment in defendant's favor, finding the trial court incorrectly determined that *Toyota* rejected the EEOC's interpretation of "substantially limits."

4. *Is Comparative Evidence Needed?* To prove that a limitation is substantial as compared with the average person, must the plaintiff come forward with some sort of comparative evidence of his limitations vis-à-vis the general population? *In Hayes v. United Parcel Serv., Inc.*, 17 Fed. Appx. 317, 321 (6th Cir. 2001), the court answered no, when plaintiff could sit only 20 to 25 minutes. "Common sense and life experiences will permit finders of fact to determine whether someone who cannot sit for more than this period of time is significantly restricted as compared to the average

person." *Id.* at 321. However, when the major life activity is working, some courts have required plaintiffs to present specific evidence about the relevant labor market and the jobs the impairments preclude them from performing. *See, e.g., Gelabert-Ladenheim v. Am. Airlines, Inc.*, 252 F.3d 54 (1st Cir. 2001).

5. *A Question of Fact or a Question of Law? Bristol v. Bd. of County Comm'rs of Clear Creek*, 281 F.3d 1148, 1156 (10th Cir.), *vacated in part on other grounds*, 312 F.3d 1213 (10th Cir. 2002), stated that determining whether a condition constitutes an impairment or a major life activity is a question for the court, but whether the impairment *substantially limits* the major life activity is a question of fact for the jury. Would the *Toyota* Court agree?

6. *Catch-22.* Understand the catch-22 the Court's construction of "disability" poses for persons such as Williams. One who can perform basic life functions despite her impairment may have a difficult time establishing she is disabled. However, once Williams's condition worsened to the point where she was placed on a "no work of any kind" restriction, her termination was held by both lower courts to be lawful. She was no longer a "qualified" individual, whether or not she had a disability.

7. *Applying the Substantially Limits Test.* In *Muller v. Costello*, 187 F.3d 298 (2d Cir. 1999), a corrections officer suffered from bronchitis and asthma that made it difficult for him to breathe in smoky environments. Exposure to smoke at work caused him to suffer sufficiently serious breathing problems that he was required to leave work for one to ten days at a time, visit his doctor, and on some occasions report to a hospital emergency room. Muller's medical evidence indicated that his lung function diminished 45 percent when exposed to irritants. Nevertheless, the court found that Muller was not substantially limited with respect to breathing: "Other than Muller's difficulties while at work at Midstate, what we are left with is testimony that Muller was physically active outside of work, that he could potentially have severe reactions to environmental irritants, and that, on one occasion, he did have such a reaction." *Id.* at 314. Doesn't *Toyota* suggest *Muller* was correctly decided? *See also Mack v. Great Dane, Inc.*, 308 F.3d 776 (7th Cir. 2002) (impairment's impact on ability to lift at work insufficient to establish disability because no evidence of impact on lifting outside the workplace); *Williams v. Excel Foundry & Machine, Inc.*, 489 F.3d 227 (7th Cir. 2007) (foundry worker with fractured spine unable to stand for more than 30-40 minutes not substantially limited in major life activity of standing); *McWilliams v. Jefferson County*, 463 F.3d 1113, 1117 (10th Cir. 2006) (although intermittent depressive episodes caused plaintiff difficulty in sleeping and getting along with co-workers, "she has not shown how these limitations prevented her from performing her job 'or that she is unable to perform any of the life activities completely'"); *Holt v. Grand Lake Mental Health Ctr., Inc.*, 443 F.3d 762 (10th Cir. 2006) (plaintiff with cerebral palsy, who could not cut her own nails, slice food, and buttoning her clothes without assistance, not substantially limited in performing manual tasks). *But see Albert v. Smith's Food & Drug Centers, Inc.*, 356 F.3d 1242, 1250-51 (10th Cir. 2004) (whether asthma substantially limited plaintiff's breathing was a question for the jury when asthma was triggered by long list of irritants); *Capobianco v. City of New York*, 422 F.3d 47 (2d Cir. 2005) (plaintiff's night blindness could be found to substantially limit the major life activity of seeing where his condition prevented him from driving at night, or even from safely walking, running, or riding a bicycle outdoors at night).

8. *Differently Abled?* In *Albertson's v. Kirkingburg*, reproduced at p. 576, the Supreme Court held that the fact that an impairment requires an individual to perform

a major life activity differently does not mean it is substantially limiting. As the Court stated,

> [T]he Ninth Circuit . . . conclud[ed] that because Kirkingburg had presented "uncontroverted evidence" that his vision was effectively monocular, he had demonstrated that "the manner in which he sees differs significantly from the manner in which most people see." That difference in manner, the court held, was sufficient to establish disability. . . . But in several respects the Ninth Circuit was too quick to find a disability. First, although the EEOC definition of "substantially limits" cited by the Ninth Circuit requires a "significant restriction" in an individual's manner of performing a major life activity, the court appeared willing to settle for a mere difference. By transforming "significant restriction" into "difference," the court undercut the fundamental statutory requirement that only impairments causing "substantial limitations" in individuals' ability to perform major life activities constitute disabilities. While the Act "addresses substantial limitations on major life activities, not utter inabilities," *Bragdon v. Abbott*, it concerns itself only with limitations that are in fact substantial.

527 U.S. at 461. This does not mean, however, that just because someone with a disability has been able to overcome that disability in many aspects of his life that he is no longer disabled. *See Emory v. AstraZeneca Pharms. LP*, 401 F.3d 174, 181 (3d Cir. 2005) ("'That [a plaintiff], through sheer force of will, learned accommodations, and careful planning, is able to perform a wide variety of activities despite his physical impairments does not mean that those activities are not substantially more difficult for him than they would be for an unimpaired individual.' . . . What a plaintiff confronts, not overcomes, is the measure of substantial limitation under the ADA").

One issue concerning "substantial limitation" arose in many disability cases. Individuals with impairments that can be controlled or corrected asserted that whether their impairments are substantially limiting should be assessed without considering the medication or devices that ameliorate the impact of their impairments. The Supreme Court resolved this issue in the following case.

SUTTON v. UNITED AIR LINES, INC.
527 U.S. 471 (1999)

Justice O'CONNOR delivered the opinion of the Court. . . .

I

. . . Petitioners are twin sisters, both of whom have severe myopia. Each petitioner's uncorrected visual acuity is 20/200 or worse in her right eye and 20/400 or worse in her left eye, but "with the use of corrective lenses, each . . . has vision that is 20/20 or better." Consequently, without corrective lenses, each "effectively cannot see to conduct numerous activities such as driving a vehicle, watching television or shopping in public stores," but with corrective measures, such as glasses or contact lenses, both "function identically to individuals without a similar impairment."

In 1992, petitioners applied to respondent for employment as commercial airline pilots. They met respondent's basic age, education, experience, and FAA certification qualifications. After submitting their applications for employment, both petitioners were invited by respondent to an interview and to flight simulator tests.

Both were told during their interviews, however, that a mistake had been made in inviting them to interview because petitioners did not meet respondent's minimum vision requirement, which was uncorrected visual acuity of 20/100 or better. Due to their failure to meet this requirement, petitioners' interviews were terminated, and neither was offered a pilot position.

In light of respondent's proffered reason for rejecting them, petitioners [filed suit] alleging that respondent had discriminated against them "on the basis of their disability, or because [respondent] regarded [petitioners] as having a disability" in violation of the ADA.

The District Court dismissed petitioners' complaint for failure to state a claim upon which relief could be granted. Because petitioners could fully correct their visual impairments, the court held that they were not actually substantially limited in any major life activity and thus had not stated a claim that they were disabled within the meaning of the ADA. . . . [T]he Court of Appeals for the Tenth Circuit affirmed the District Court's judgment. . . .

II . . .

[To fall within the definition of "disability" of § 12102(2)] one must have an actual disability (subsection (A)), have a record of a disability (subsection (B)), or be regarded as having one (subsection (C)).

The parties agree that the authority to issue regulations to implement the Act is split primarily among three Government agencies. According to the parties, the EEOC has authority to issue regulations to carry out the employment provisions in Title I of the ADA, §§ 12111-12117, pursuant to § 12116. . . . The Attorney General is granted authority to issue regulations with respect to Title II, subtitle A, §§ 12131-12134, which relates to public services. See § 12134. . . . Finally, the Secretary of Transportation has authority to issue regulations pertaining to the transportation provisions of Titles II and III. See § 12149(a); § 12164; § 12186(a)(1); § 12143(b). . . . Moreover, each of these agencies is authorized to offer technical assistance regarding the provisions they administer. See § 12206(c)(1).

No agency, however, has been given authority to issue regulations implementing the generally applicable provisions of the ADA, see §§ 12101-12102, which fall outside Titles I-V. Most notably, no agency has been delegated authority to interpret the term "disability." § 12102(2). Justice Breyer's contrary, imaginative interpretation of the Act's delegation provisions is belied by the terms and structure of the ADA. The EEOC has, nonetheless, issued regulations to provide additional guidance regarding the proper interpretation of this term. After restating the definition of disability given in the statute, see 29 CFR § 1630.2(g) (1998), the EEOC regulations define the three elements of disability: (1) "physical or mental impairment," (2) "substantially limits," and (3) "major life activities." See id. at §§ 1630.2(h)-(j). Under the regulations, a "physical impairment" includes

> any physiological disorder, or condition, cosmetic disfigurement, or anatomical loss affecting one or more of the following body systems: neurological, musculoskeletal, special sense organs, respiratory (including speech organs), cardiovascular, reproductive, digestive, genito-urinary, hemic and lymphatic, skin, and endocrine.

§ 1630.2(h)(1). The term "substantially limits" means, among other things, "unable to perform a major life activity that the average person in the general population can perform;" or significantly restricted as to the condition, manner or duration under which an individual can perform a particular major life activity as compared to the condition, manner, or duration under which the average person in the general population can perform that same major life activity.

§ 1630.2(j). Finally, "major life activities means functions such as caring for oneself, performing manual tasks, walking, seeing, hearing, speaking, breathing, learning, and working." § 1630.2(i). Because both parties accept these regulations as valid, and determining their validity is not necessary to decide this case, we have no occasion to consider what deference they are due, if any.

The agencies have also issued interpretive guidelines to aid in the implementation of their regulations. For instance, at the time that it promulgated the above regulations, the EEOC issued an "Interpretive Guidance," which provides that "the determination of whether an individual is substantially limited in a major life activity must be made on a case by case basis, without regard to mitigating measures such as medicines, or assistive or prosthetic devices." 29 CFR pt. 1630, App. § 1630.2(j) (1998) (describing § 1630.2(j)). The Department of Justice has issued a similar guideline. See 28 CFR pt. 35, App. A, § 35.104 ("The question of whether a person has a disability should be assessed without regard to the availability of mitigating measures, such as reasonable modification or auxiliary aids and services"); pt. 36, App. B, § 36.104 (same). Although the parties dispute the persuasive force of these interpretive guidelines, we have no need in this case to decide what deference is due.

III

With this statutory and regulatory framework in mind, we turn first to the question whether petitioners have stated a claim under subsection (A) of the disability definition, that is, whether they have alleged that they possess a physical impairment that substantially limits them in one or more major life activities. Because petitioners allege that with corrective measures their vision "is 20/20 or better," they are not actually disabled within the meaning of the Act if the "disability" determination is made with reference to these measures. Consequently, with respect to subsection (A) of the disability definition, our decision turns on whether disability is to be determined with or without reference to corrective measures.

Petitioners maintain that whether impairment is substantially limiting should be determined without regard to corrective measures. They argue that, because the ADA does not directly address the question at hand, the Court should defer to the agency interpretations of the statute, which are embodied in the agency guidelines issued by the EEOC and the Department of Justice. These guidelines specifically direct that the determination of whether an individual is substantially limited in a major life activity be made without regard to mitigating measures. See 29 CFR pt. 1630, App. § 1630.2(j); 28 CFR pt. 35, App. A, § 35.104 (1998); 28 CFR pt. 36, App. B, § 36.104.

Respondent, in turn, maintains that an impairment does not substantially limit a major life activity if it is corrected. It argues that the Court should not defer to the agency guidelines cited by petitioners because the guidelines conflict with the plain meaning of the ADA. The phrase "substantially limits one or more major life activities," it explains, requires that the substantial limitations actually and presently exist. Moreover, respondent argues, disregarding mitigating measures taken by an individual defies the statutory command to examine the effect of the impairment on the major life activities "of such individual." And even if the statute is ambiguous, respondent claims, the guidelines' directive to ignore mitigating measures is not reasonable, and thus this Court should not defer to it.

We conclude that respondent is correct that the approach adopted by the agency guidelines — that persons are to be evaluated in their hypothetical uncorrected state — is an impermissible interpretation of the ADA. Looking at the Act as a whole, it is apparent that if a person is taking measures to correct for, or mitigate, a physical or mental impairment, the effects of those measures — both positive and negative — must be taken into account when judging whether that person is "substantially limited" in a major life activity and thus "disabled" under the Act. The dissent relies on the legislative history of the ADA for the contrary proposition that individuals should be examined in their uncorrected state (opinion of Stevens, J.). Because we decide that, by its terms, the ADA cannot be read in this manner, we have no reason to consider the ADA's legislative history.

Three separate provisions of the ADA, read in concert, lead us to this conclusion. The Act defines a "disability" as "a physical or mental impairment that *substantially limits* one or more of the major life activities" of an individual. § 12102(2)(A) (emphasis added). Because the phrase "substantially limits" appears in the Act in the present indicative verb form, we think the language is properly read as requiring that a person be presently — not potentially or hypothetically — substantially limited in order to demonstrate a disability. A "disability" exists only where an impairment "substantially limits" a major life activity, not where it "might," "could," or "would" be substantially limiting if mitigating measures were not taken. A person whose physical or mental impairment is corrected by medication or other measures does not have an impairment that presently "substantially limits" a major life activity. To be sure, a person whose physical or mental impairment is corrected by mitigating measures still has an impairment, but if the impairment is corrected it does not "substantially limit" a major life activity.

The definition of disability also requires that disabilities be evaluated "with respect to an individual" and be determined based on whether an impairment substantially limits the "major life activities of such individual." § 12102(2). Thus, whether a person has a disability under the ADA is an individualized inquiry. See Bragdon v. Abbott (declining to consider whether HIV infection is a per se disability under the ADA); 29 CFR pt. 1630, App. § 1630.2(j) ("The determination of whether an individual has a disability is not necessarily based on the name or diagnosis of the impairment the person has, but rather on the effect of that impairment on the life of the individual").

The agency guidelines' directive that persons be judged in their uncorrected or unmitigated state runs directly counter to the individualized inquiry mandated by the ADA. The agency approach would often require courts and employers to speculate about a person's condition and would, in many cases, force them to make a disability determination based on general information about how an uncorrected impairment usually affects individuals, rather than on the individual's actual condition. For instance, under this view, courts would almost certainly find all diabetics to be disabled, because if they failed to monitor their blood sugar levels and administer insulin, they would almost certainly be substantially limited in one or more major life activities. A diabetic whose illness does not impair his or her daily activities would therefore be considered disabled simply because he or she has diabetes. Thus, the guidelines approach would create a system in which persons often must be treated as members of a group of people with similar impairments, rather than as individuals. This is contrary to both the letter and the spirit of the ADA.

The guidelines approach could also lead to the anomalous result that in determining whether an individual is disabled, courts and employers could not consider any negative side effects suffered by an individual resulting from the use of mitigating measures, even when those side effects are very severe. This result is also inconsistent with the individualized approach of the ADA.

Finally, and critically, findings enacted as part of the ADA require the conclusion that Congress did not intend to bring under the statute's protection all those whose uncorrected conditions amount to disabilities. Congress found that "some 43,000,000 Americans have one or more physical or mental disabilities, and this number is increasing as the population as a whole is growing older." § 12101(a)(1). This figure is inconsistent with the definition of disability pressed by petitioners.

[While there was dispute as to the "likely source" of the 43,000,000 number, the probable source was a National Council on Disability titled "On the Threshold of Independence" (1988). That report "took an explicitly functional approach to evaluating disabilities." In any event, "the 43 million figure reflects an understanding that those whose impairments are largely corrected by medication or other devices are not 'disabled' within the meaning of the ADA." In contrast, "nonfunctional approaches to defining disability produce significantly larger numbers."]

Because it is included in the ADA's text, the finding that 43 million individuals are disabled gives content to the ADA's terms, specifically the term "disability." Had Congress intended to include all persons with corrected physical limitations among those covered by the Act, it undoubtedly would have cited a much higher number of disabled persons in the findings. That it did not is evidence that the ADA's coverage is restricted to only those whose impairments are not mitigated by corrective measures.

The dissents suggest that viewing individuals in their corrected state will exclude from the definition of "disabled" those who use prosthetic limbs or take medicine for epilepsy or high blood pressure. This suggestion is incorrect. The use of a corrective device does not, by itself, relieve one's disability. Rather, one has a disability under subsection A if, notwithstanding the use of a corrective device, that individual is substantially limited in a major life activity. For example, individuals who use prosthetic limbs or wheelchairs may be mobile and capable of functioning in society but still be disabled because of a substantial limitation on their ability to walk or run. The same may be true of individuals who take medicine to lessen the symptoms of an impairment so that they can function but nevertheless remain substantially limited. Alternatively, one whose high blood pressure is "cured" by medication may be regarded as disabled by a covered entity, and thus disabled under subsection C of the definition. The use or non-use of a corrective device does not determine whether an individual is disabled; that determination depends on whether the limitations an individual with an impairment actually faces are in fact substantially limiting.

Applying this reading of the Act to the case at hand, we conclude that the Court of Appeals correctly resolved the issue of disability in respondent's favor. As noted above, petitioners allege that with corrective measures, their visual acuity is 20/20 and that they "function identically to individuals without a similar impairment." In addition, petitioners concede that they "do not argue that the use of corrective lenses in itself demonstrates a substantially limiting impairment." Accordingly, because we decide that disability under the Act is to be determined with reference to corrective measures, we agree with the courts below that petitioners have not stated a claim that they are substantially limited in any major life activity.

[The Court's discussion of whether the plaintiffs were "regarded as having a disability" is reproduced at p. 509.]

Justice STEVENS, with whom Justice BREYER joins, dissenting.

When it enacted the Americans with Disabilities Act in 1990, Congress certainly did not intend to require United Air Lines to hire unsafe or unqualified pilots. Nor, in all likelihood, did it view every person who wears glasses as a member of a "discrete and insular minority." Indeed, by reason of legislative myopia it may not have foreseen that its definition of "disability" might theoretically encompass, not just "some 43,000,000 Americans," 42 U.S.C. §12101(a)(1), but perhaps two or three times that number. Nevertheless, if we apply customary tools of statutory construction, it is quite clear that the threshold question whether an individual is "disabled" within the meaning of the Act — and, therefore, is entitled to the basic assurances that the Act affords — focuses on her past or present physical condition without regard to mitigation that has resulted from rehabilitation, self-improvement, prosthetic devices, or medication. One might reasonably argue that the general rule should not apply to an impairment that merely requires a nearsighted person to wear glasses. But I believe that, in order to be faithful to the remedial purpose of the Act, we should give it a generous, rather than a miserly, construction.

There are really two parts to the question of statutory construction presented by this case. The first question is whether the determination of disability for people that Congress unquestionably intended to cover should focus on their unmitigated or their mitigated condition. If the correct answer to that question is the one provided by eight of the nine Federal Courts of Appeals to address the issue, and by all three of the Executive agencies that have issued regulations or interpretive bulletins construing the statute — namely, that the statute defines "disability" without regard to ameliorative measures — it would still be necessary to decide whether that general rule should be applied to what might be characterized as a "minor, trivial impairment." *Arnold v. United Parcel Service, Inc.,* 136 F.3d 854, 866, n. 10 (CA1 1998) (holding that unmitigated state is determinative but suggesting that it "might reach a different result" in a case in which "a simple, inexpensive remedy," such as eyeglasses, is available "that can provide total and relatively permanent control of all symptoms"). I shall therefore first consider impairments that Congress surely had in mind before turning to the special facts of this case.

I

. . . The three parts of [the definition of disability] do not identify mutually exclusive, discrete categories. On the contrary, they furnish three overlapping formulas aimed at ensuring that individuals who now have, or ever had, a substantially limiting impairment are covered by the Act.

An example of a rather common condition illustrates this point: There are many individuals who have lost one or more limbs in industrial accidents, or perhaps in the service of their country in places like Iwo Jima. With the aid of prostheses, coupled with courageous determination and physical therapy, many of these hardy individuals can perform all of their major life activities just as efficiently as an average couch potato. If the Act were just concerned with their present ability to participate in society, many of these individuals' physical impairments would not be viewed as disabilities. Similarly, if the statute were solely concerned with whether these individuals viewed themselves as disabled — or with whether a majority of employers regarded them as unable to perform most jobs — many of these individuals would lack statutory protection from discrimination based on their prostheses.

The sweep of the statute's three-pronged definition, however, makes it pellucidly clear that Congress intended the Act to cover such persons. The fact that a prosthetic device, such as an artificial leg, has restored one's ability to perform major life activities surely cannot mean that subsection (A) of the definition is inapplicable. Nor should the fact that the individual considers himself (or actually is) "cured," or that a prospective employer considers him generally employable, mean that sub-sections (B) or (C) are inapplicable. But under the Court's emphasis on "the present indicative verb form" used in subsection (A), that subsection presumably would not apply. And under the Court's focus on the individual's "present — not potential or hypothetical" — condition and on whether a person is "precluded from a broad range of jobs," subsections (B) and (C) presumably would not apply.

In my view, when an employer refuses to hire the individual "because of" his prosthesis, and the prosthesis in no way affects his ability to do the job, that employer has unquestionably discriminated against the individual in violation of the Act. Sub-section (B) of the definition, in fact, sheds a revelatory light on the question whether Congress was concerned only about the corrected or mitigated status of a person's impairment. If the Court is correct that "[a] 'disability' exists only where" a person's "present" or "actual" condition is substantially impaired, there would be no reason to include in the protected class those who were once disabled but who are now fully recovered. Subsection (B) of the Act's definition, however, plainly covers a person who previously had a serious hearing impairment that has since been completely cured. See *School Bd. of Nassau Cty. v. Arline.* Still, if I correctly under-stand the Court's opinion, it holds that one who continues to wear a hearing aid that she has worn all her life might not be covered — fully cured impairments are covered, but merely treatable ones are not. The text of the Act surely does not require such a bizarre result.

The three prongs of the statute, rather, are most plausibly read together not to inquire into whether a person is currently "functionally" limited in a major life activity, but only into the existence of an impairment — present or past — that substantially limits, or did so limit, the individual before amelioration. This reading avoids the counter-intuitive conclusion that the ADA's safeguards vanish when individuals make them-selves more employable by ascertaining ways to overcome their physical or mental limitations. To the extent that there may be doubt concerning the meaning of the statutory text, ambiguity is easily removed by looking at the legislative history. . . .

The ADA originated in the Senate. The Senate Report states that "whether a person has a disability should be assessed without regard to the availability of mitigating measures, such as reasonable accommodations or auxiliary aids." S. Rep. No. 101-116, p. 23 (1989). The Report further explained, in discussing the "regarded as" prong:

> [An] important goal of the third prong of the [disability] definition is to ensure that persons with medical conditions that are under control, and that therefore do not currently limit major life activities, are not discriminated against on the basis of their medical conditions. For example, individuals with controlled diabetes or epilepsy are often denied jobs for which they are qualified. Such denials are the result of negative attitudes and misinformation.

When the legislation was considered in the House of Representatives, its Commit-tees reiterated the Senate's basic understanding of the Act's coverage, with one minor modification: They clarified that "correctable" or "controllable" disabilities were covered in the first definitional prong as well. The Report of the House Committee on the Judiciary states, in discussing the first prong, that, when determining whether an individual's impairment substantially limits a major life activity, "the impairment should be assessed without considering whether mitigating measures, such as auxiliary aids or reasonable accommodations, would result in a less-than-substantial limitation." H. R. Rep. No. 101-485, pt. III, p. 28 (1990). The Report continues that "a person with epilepsy, an impairment which substantially limits a major life activity, is covered under this test," as is a person with poor hearing, "even if the hearing loss is corrected by the use of a hearing aid."

The Report of the House Committee on Education and Labor likewise states that "whether a person has a disability should be assessed without regard to the availability of mitigating measures, such as reasonable accommodations or auxiliary aids." To make matters perfectly plain, the Report adds:

> For example, a person who is hard of hearing is substantially limited in the major life activity of hearing, *even though the loss may be corrected through the use of a hearing aid.* Likewise, persons with impairments, such as epilepsy or diabetes, which substantially limit a major life activity are covered under the first prong of the definition of disability, *even if the effects of the impairment are controlled by medication.*

(Emphasis added.)

All of the Reports, indeed, are replete with references to the understanding that the Act's protected class includes individuals with various medical conditions that ordinarily are perfectly "correctable" with medication or treatment.

In addition, each of the three Executive agencies charged with implementing the Act has consistently interpreted the Act as mandating that the presence of disability turns on an individual's uncorrected state. . . . At the very least, these interpretations "constitute a body of experience and informed judgment to which [we] may properly resort" for additional guidance. *Skidmore v. Swift & Co.,* 323 U.S. 134, 139-140 (1944). See also *Bragdon.* . . .

In my judgment, the Committee Reports and the uniform agency regulations merely confirm the message conveyed by the text of the Act — at least insofar as it applies to impairments such as the loss of a limb, the inability to hear, or any condition such as diabetes that is substantially limiting without medication. The Act generally protects individuals who have "correctable" substantially limiting impairments from unjustified employment discrimination on the basis of those impairments. The question, then, is whether the fact that Congress was specifically concerned about protecting a class that included persons characterized as a "discrete and insular minority" and that it estimated that class to include "some 43,000,000 Americans" means that we should construe the term "disability" to exclude individuals with impairments that Congress probably did not have in mind.

II

. . . If a narrow reading of the term "disability" were necessary in order to avoid the danger that the Act might otherwise force United to hire pilots who might endanger the lives of their passengers, it would make good sense to use the "43,000,000 Americans" finding to confine its coverage. There is, however, no such danger in this case. If a person is "disabled" within the meaning of the Act, she still cannot prevail on a claim of discrimination unless she can prove that the employer took action "because of" that impairment, 42 U.S.C. §12112(a), and that she can, "with or without reasonable accommodation, . . . perform the essential functions" of the job of a commercial airline pilot. See §12111(8). Even then, an employer may avoid liability if it shows that the criteria of having uncorrected visual acuity of at least 20/100 is "job-related and consistent with business necessity" or if such vision (even if correctable to 20/20) would pose a health or safety hazard. §§12113(a) and (b).

This case, in other words, is not about whether petitioners are genuinely qualified or whether they can perform the job of an airline pilot without posing an undue safety risk. The case just raises the threshold question whether petitioners are members of the ADA's protected class. It simply asks whether the ADA lets petitioners in the door. . . . Inside that door lies nothing more than basic protection from irrational and unjustified discrimination because of a characteristic that is beyond a person's control. Hence, this particular case, at its core, is about whether, assuming that petitioners can prove that they are "qualified," the airline has any duty to come forward with some legitimate explanation for refusing to hire them because of their uncorrected eyesight, or whether the ADA leaves the airline free to decline to hire petitioners on this basis even if it is acting purely on the basis of irrational fear and stereotype.

I think it quite wrong for the Court to confine the coverage of the Act simply because an interpretation of "disability" that adheres to Congress' method of defining the class it intended to benefit may also provide protection for "significantly larger numbers" of individuals than estimated in the Act's findings. . . .

Accordingly, although I express no opinion on the ultimate merits of petitioners' claim, I am persuaded that they have a disability covered by the ADA. I therefore respectfully dissent.

Justice BREYER, dissenting.

We must draw a statutory line that either (1) will include within the category of persons authorized to bring suit under the Americans with Disabilities Act of 1990 some whom Congress may not have wanted to protect (those who wear ordinary eyeglasses), or (2) will exclude from the threshold category those whom Congress certainly did want to protect (those who successfully use corrective devices or medicines, such as hearing aids or prostheses or medicine for epilepsy). Faced with this dilemma, the statute's language, structure, basic purposes, and history require us to choose the former statutory line, as Justice Stevens (whose opinion I join) well explains. I would add that, if the more generous choice of threshold led to too many lawsuits that ultimately proved without merit or otherwise drew too much time and attention away from those whom Congress clearly sought to protect, there is a remedy. The Equal Employment Opportunity Commission (EEOC), through regulation, might draw finer definitional lines, excluding some of those who wear eyeglasses (say, those with certain vision impairments who readily can find corrective lenses), thereby cabining the overly broad extension of the statute that the majority fears.

The majority questions whether the EEOC could do so, for the majority is uncertain whether the EEOC possesses typical agency regulation-writing authority with respect to the statute's definitions. The majority poses this question because the section of the statute, 42 U.S.C. §12116, that says the EEOC "shall issue regulations" also says these regulations are "to carry out *this subchapter*" (namely, §12111 to §12117, the employment subchapter); and the section of the statute that contains the three-pronged definition of "disability" precedes "this subchapter," the employment subchapter, to which §12116 specifically refers. (Emphasis added.)

Nonetheless, the employment subchapter, i.e., *"this* subchapter," includes other provisions that use the defined terms, for example a provision that forbids "discriminating against a qualified individual with a disability because of the disability." §12112(a). The EEOC might elaborate through regulations the meaning of "disability" in this last-mentioned provision, if elaboration is needed in order to "carry out" the substantive provisions of "this subchapter." An EEOC regulation that elaborated the meaning of this use of the word "disability" would fall within the scope both of the basic definitional provision and also the substantive provisions of "this" later subchapter, for the word "disability" appears in both places.

There is no reason to believe that Congress would have wanted to deny the EEOC the power to issue such a regulation, at least if the regulation is consistent with the earlier statutory definition and with the relevant interpretations by other enforcement agencies. The physical location of the definitional section seems to reflect only drafting or stylistic, not substantive, objectives. And to pick and choose among which of "this subchapter['s]" words the EEOC has the power to explain would inhibit the development of law that coherently interprets this important statute.

NOTES

1. *Unambiguous Statute?* On the question of whether Congress intended to cover individuals whose impairments would be substantially limiting without treatment, who has the better argument, the majority or the dissent? Is the statute unambiguous on this issue? Is the EEOC's interpretation of the statute unreasonable? In footnote 3 of his dissent, Justice Stevens reminds the Court that in *General Elec. Co. v. Gilbert*, "the majority rejected an EEOC guideline and the heavy weight of authority in the federal courts of appeals in order to hold that Title VII did not prohibit discrimination on the basis of pregnancy-related conditions" only to be "swiftly 'overruled'" by Congress in the Pregnancy Discrimination Act of 1978. Has the Court misread congressional intent in *Sutton?* Remember the question in this case is not whether the petitioners were qualified to fly airplanes but whether they have a disability within the meaning of the ADA.

2. *Legislative Purpose.* Putting aside such interpretive devices as the present indicative verb tense and the meaning of the 43,000,000 number, what would Congress have likely said had it explicitly addressed the question of mitigating measures? In *The Americans with Disabilities Act as Welfare Reform*, 44 WM. & MARY L. REV. 921, 927 (2003), Professor Samuel Bagenstos suggests a rationale for cases like *Sutton:*

> If the "basic premise" of the ADA is seen as the imperative to reduce the cost of dependency of people with disabilities, then many of the restrictive decisions attacked by ADA supporters begin to make sense. Roughly put, those decisions limit the statute's protections to individuals who would be largely unable to work without them, and they limit required accommodations to those that are necessary to move those individuals into the workforce in a reasonably cost-effective manner. In short, on at least one plausible account of the statute's "basic premises," the restrictive interpretations offered by many courts reflect a vindication rather than a betrayal of those premises.

Cf. Sharona Hoffman, *Corrective Justice and Title I of the ADA*, 52 AM. U. L. REV. 1213, 1214 (2003) (urging a new definition of disability to "reshape the ADA's protected class so that it more closely resembles a discrete and insular minority, such as those traditionally protected by the civil rights laws").

3. *"Presently" Substantially Limited.* Does the Court's requirement that "a person be presently — not potentially or hypothetically — substantially limited in order to demonstrate a disability" resolve the question whether individuals with genetic predisposition for a disease are covered by the ADA? What about an individual stricken by multiple sclerosis in the early stages of the disease? What would you argue on behalf of such individuals? *See Sorensen v. Univ. of Utah Hosp.*, 194 F.3d 1084 (10th Cir. 1999) (nurse diagnosed with multiple sclerosis not disabled because not currently substantially limited).

4. *The Effect of Medication and Other Mitigating Measures. Murphy v. United Parcel* Serv., 527 U.S. 516 (1999), decided the same day as *Sutton*, considered the claim of a mechanic dismissed from his job because of high blood pressure. The plaintiff asserted that the disability determination should be made without reference to the medication he took to control his blood pressure, a claim the Court rejected in light of its resolution of this issue in *Sutton*. Murphy, however, did not seek review of the lower court's conclusion that, when medicated, Murphy's high blood pressure did not substantially limit him in any major life activity. The Court therefore, did not consider "whether petitioner is 'disabled' due to limitations that persist despite his medication or the negative side effects of his medication." After *Sutton*, plaintiffs like Murphy must develop factual records to support a claim that their impairment is substantially limiting even when controlled by medication.

If the effects of mitigating measures must be taken into account in assessing disability status, what happens if it is the medication for one impairment causes a second impairment to substantially limit a major life activity? Remember that the court in *Bragdon* stated that "[r]eproduction and the sexual dynamics surrounding it are central to the life process itself." Many medications, including antidepressants such as Prozac, substantially impair sexual function. Are individuals who take such medications "disabled" under the ADA? Does it matter if the condition that they are medicating would not itself have been disabling?

5. *"Voluntary" Disabilities Again.* Should an individual be covered by the ADA if his impairment is substantially limiting only because he fails to control an otherwise controllable illness such as diabetes or a psychiatric disorder? *Sutton's* focus on the actual condition of the individual, not his hypothetical condition, suggests yes, but Professor Bagenstos's rationale for the case (encouragement for disabled people to be self-sufficient) suggests no. Authority on the point is sparse. *See Tangires v. Johns Hopkins Hosp.*, 79 F. Supp. 2d 587 (D. Md. 2000), *aff'd*, 2000 U.S. App. LEXIS 23555 (4th Cir. 2000) (an alternate holding that, since plaintiff had not availed herself of proper medical treatment to deal with her condition, she was not protected by the ADA). *See generally* Jill Elaine Hasday, *Mitigation and the Americans with Disabilities Act*, 103 MICH. L. REV. 217 (2004); Lawrence D. Rosenthal, *Requiring Individuals To Use Mitigating Measures in Reasonable Accommodation Cases After the* Sutton *Trilogy: Putting the Brakes on a Potential Runaway Train*, 54 S.C. L. REV. 421 (2002).

6. *What Counts as a Mitigating Measure?* In *Albertson's, Inc. v. Kirkingburg*, reproduced at p. 576, also decided the same day as *Sutton*, the plaintiff had monocular vision, but his brain had subconsciously adjusted to the impairment. Although the Ninth Circuit had ignored the impact of those adjustments, the Supreme Court held that a body's coping mechanisms that mitigate an impairment must be considered in assessing disability status. "We see no principled basis for distinguishing

between measures undertaken with artificial aids, like medications and devices, and measures undertaken, whether consciously or not, with the body's own systems." 527 U.S. at 565. The *Kirkingburg* Court also criticized the Ninth Circuit's determination that monocular vision was a per se disability, emphasizing, as it had in *Sutton*, the need for a case-by-case determination of whether a disability exists. *Kirkingburg* makes clear that even impairments that seem obviously disabling must be examined on a case-by-case basis to determine if they are, in fact, substantially limiting. The Court also indicated that this decision must be based on detailed medical evidence, specific to the individual, demonstrating the precise way in which an impairment substantially limits major life activities.

Kirkingburg states, on the other hand, that individuals with monocular vision do not have "an onerous burden" to show that they are disabled. Is the Court saying that some impairments obviously are substantially limiting and therefore require little evidence to support a finding of disability?

NOTE ON DEFERENCE TO THE EEOC

The EEOC is a federal administrative agency charged with the administration and enforcement of Title VII, the ADEA, and the ADA. Importantly, each of these statutes requires a complaining party to file charges with the EEOC prior to filing suit. The EEOC enforcement process is explored in Chapter 7. Additionally, we have seen in a number of cases that the EEOC may be a plaintiff in Title VII litigation, bringing suit on behalf of workers it contends are victims of discrimination.

To what extent, however, is the EEOC entitled to meaningful deference from the courts in its *interpretation* of the statutes it administers? As we have seen in earlier chapters, the Court's willingness to defer to EEOC interpretations of Title VII's substantive provisions has been limited. Although Congress gave the EEOC the power to issue procedural regulations under Title VII, it withheld from the agency the power to issue substantive regulations under that statute. *See General Elec. Co. v. Gilbert*, 429 U.S. 125, 140-42 (1976) (Because "Congress . . . did not confer upon the EEOC authority to promulgate rules or regulations," the level of deference afforded depends on "the thoroughness evident in its consideration, the validity of its reasoning, its consistency with earlier and later pronouncements, and all those factors which give it power to persuade, if lacking power to control").

But there is good reason to believe that deference to the EEOC should be greater under the Americans with Disabilities Act. This question was presented to, but not answered by, the Court in *Sutton*. The question is complicated by the fact that the EEOC has issued not only regulations but also Interpretive Guidances, and other materials, and that, as we saw in *Bragdon*, other agencies are also charged with administration and enforcement of the ADA. Congress was aware when it enacted the ADA that considerable uncertainty over the rights and obligations conferred by the statute would exist, and it charged various agencies with authority to promulgate regulations to carry out particular subchapters.

Title I of the ADA confers substantive rule-making authority on the EEOC. The statute directs that "Not later than one year after July 26, 1990, the Commission shall issue regulations in an accessible format to carry out this subchapter in accordance with [the Administrative Procedure Act.]" 42 U.S.C. § 12116 (2007). The EEOC carried out that mandate, issuing regulations promulgated after notice and comment. The regulations contained as an appendix an Interpretive Guidance.

The Supreme Court's decision in *Bragdon v. Abbott*, reproduced at p. 492, suggested the Court not only was willing to adopt an expansive approach to the definition of disability but also was willing to allow agencies a leading role in interpreting the statute. However, the Court's deference to the HEW regulations in *Bragdon* was a product of Congress's directive that the ADA be interpreted in accordance with those regulations. The Court has been more equivocal when it came to deferring to agency pronouncements issued under the ADA, declining to decide what level of deference such pronouncements were due.

Sutton v. United Air Lines, Inc., presented the question of what deference was due the EEOC's Interpretive Guidance, arguably agency action entitled to less deference than its regulations. The Interpretive Guidance provided that an impairment was to be assessed in its unmitigated state in determining whether a disability was present. The EEOC, backed by the Justice Department, urged the Court to defer to its interpretation.

The basis of that argument was *Chevron U.S.A., Inc. v. Natural Res. Def. Council, Inc.*, 467 U.S. 837 (1984), in which the Supreme Court recognized that agency interpretations of silent or ambiguous statutes are due deference from the courts when Congress has delegated law-interpreting power to the agency. More recently, in *United States v. Mead Corp.*, 533 U.S. 218 (2001), the Court explained when such an implied delegation would be found. A delegation of rule-making or adjudicative authority to an agency will support an implied delegation of interpretive authority. Other comparable indicia may also support an implied delegation of interpretive authority. *Chevron* review will attach to such an agency's statutory interpretations, if the agency was exercising that authority when it promulgated the interpretation for which deference is claimed. Even when an agency has not been delegated interpretive authority, however, its interpretations of the statutes it administers still will merit attention from the courts. Such interpretations may be persuasive, depending on "the thoroughness evident in its consideration, the validity of its reasoning, its consistency with earlier and later pronouncements, and all [other] factors which give it power to persuade, if lacking power to control." *Skidmore v. Swift & Co.*, 323 U.S. 134 (1944). This level of deference is referred to as *Skidmore* deference.

In *Sutton*, the EEOC contended its position on the mitigating measures question was deserving of heightened deference under *Chevron*. But the Supreme Court refused to defer to the agency's view as expressed in its Interpretive Guidance. It found the EEOC's reading was an impermissible interpretation of the statute because it was inconsistent with the statutory text. Under *Chevron*, a reviewing court will *not* defer to an agency's construction of a statute if it finds that Congress itself has spoken to the precise question at issue. In such cases, no implied delegation has occurred since Congress itself has made the policy choice. The *Sutton* Court, through its textualist approach, appeared to find that Congress had determined impairments are to be assessed in their mitigated state.

In rejecting the EEOC's Interpretive Guidance as an impermissible interpretation of the ADA, the Court was able to sidestep difficult, but important, questions concerning the EEOC's role in interpreting the ADA. However, even if the *Sutton* Court had conceded ambiguity in the statutory definition, it is not clear it would have deferred to the EEOC's interpretation. That is because the Court noted that the definition of disability is not contained within Title I but instead is in the generally applicable provisions of the Act. Although the EEOC was given authority to issue regulations carrying out Title I, "no agency has been delegated authority to interpret the term 'disability.'" Thus, the Court questioned, although it did not decide, whether the

EEOC's extensive regulations and Interpretive Guidance addressing what constitutes a disability were entitled to any deference at all. The suggestion of Justice Breyer's dissent that the EEOC's authority to interpret the term "qualified individual with a disability" necessarily carried with it the authority to determine what constitutes a disability was dismissed as "an imaginative interpretation of the Act's delegation provisions."

Another complicating factor in *Sutton* was that the EEOC's position on mitigating measures was found not in the text of the regulation itself but in the Interpretive Guidance, which was issued as an appendix accompanying the regulations. That appendix, however, had also been subject to notice and comment proceedings. The Court noted, but did not resolve, the format issue. *See Christensen v. Harris County*, 529 U.S. 576 (2000) (*Chevron* deference not due Labor Department opinion letter). In other words, the Court may be willing to extend *Chevron* deference to the EEOC's disability regulations but not to its Interpretive Guidance. Accordingly, *Sutton* throws up in the air the question of whether courts need pay any attention at all to the EEOC's interpretation of "disability." But *Mead* suggests that, even if such interpretations are not deserving of *Chevron* deference, they should at least be entitled to deference under *Skidmore*.

It is important, however, to distinguish the interpretive issue presented in *Sutton* from interpretive questions arising from provisions of Title I itself. Issues concerning what constitutes an essential job function, a reasonable accommodation, an undue hardship, or a direct threat, for example, would implicate the terms of Title I, where Congress has clearly delegated interpretive authority to the EEOC. Even if the EEOC has not been delegated interpretive authority over the definition of disability, it has been delegated authority to interpret the provisions of Title I itself. Accordingly, its regulations, and perhaps the appendix to those regulations, interpreting that sub-chapter are entitled to analysis under *Chevron*. Recognizing this point, the Supreme Court deferred, under *Chevron*, to an EEOC regulation interpreting "direct threat" in *Chevron U.S.A., Inc. v. Echazabal*, 536 U.S. 73 (2002), reproduced at p. 568.

The EEOC also has issued various other interpretations in even more informal forms. Its Compliance Manual sets forth Enforcement Guidances, and it also has promulgated a Technical Assistance Manual. Although the failure to follow notice and comment procedures presumably deprives these interpretations of deference under *Chevron*, they still are entitled to deference under a *Skidmore* review standard. *See National Railroad Passenger Corp. v. Morgan*, 536 U.S. 101 (2002). *See generally* Rebecca Hanner White, *Deference and Disability Discrimination*, 99 MICH. L. REV. 532 (2000); Lisa Eichhorn, *The* Chevron *Two-Step and the* Toyota *Sidestep: Dancing Around The EEOC's "Disability" Regulations Under the ADA*, 39 WAKE FOREST L. REV. 177, 202-03 (2004); Melissa Hart, *Skepticism and Expertise: The Supreme Court and the EEOC*, 74 FORDHAM L. REV. 1937, 1938 (2006); Rebecca Hanner White, *The EEOC, the Courts, and Employment Discrimination Policy: Recognizing the Agency's Leading Role in Statutory Interpretation*, 1995 UTAH L. REV. 51.

PROBLEM 6.1

Sarah Smith is an assembly line worker who is diabetic and dependant on insulin injections to maintain her glucose level. She must inject up to four times a day to maintain ideal glucose levels. If her glucose level drops too low, she will become hypoglycemic and go into a coma. If her glucose level is too high, it will cause long-term physical deterioration of numerous body systems. Eating increases glucose levels, so Sarah needs to inject one half-hour before eating larger meals. Her doctor has recommended that she eat smaller and more frequent meals to help her modulate variations in her glucose levels. Outside of work, Sarah leads an active life and exercises regularly. She must be careful to time her injections depending on her exercise and eating patterns. Exercise reduces glucose levels on a short-term basis and can upset the balance of insulin and glucose in the body, possibly resulting in a hypoglycemic reaction. Because Sarah is careful about her eating, exercise, and treatment regimen, her diabetes is reasonably well controlled. She does not yet exhibit any physical damage related to excess glucose levels. She carries small amounts of sugar with her to minimize the incidence of hypoglycemic reactions. Assembly line workers operate on a very rigid schedule. Sarah wants to seek accommodations from her employer to make it easier for her to maintain her glucose levels while at work. Is Sarah an individual with a disability under the ADA? *See, e.g., Nawrot v. CPC Intl.,* 277 F.3d 896 (7th Cir. 2002) (finding diabetic plaintiff to be a qualified individual with a disability where even with medication his ability to think and to care for himself was substantially limited and raising but not resolving whether not permitting plaintiff to take short breaks to monitor and adjust his blood sugar violated the duty of reasonable accommodation).

PROBLEM 6.2

Serum alpha-1 antitrypsin (SAT) is a serum protein that protects the lungs from proteolytic enzymes. Approximately 80 percent of individuals who inherit an SAT deficiency from both parents develop chronic obstructive pulmonary disease (COPD). Individuals who inherit the deficiency from only one parent have a much lower risk but nevertheless higher than the general population of developing COPD (1 in 10), especially if they smoke or work in dusty environments. Tuan, who inherited SAT deficiency from both of his parents, does not yet suffer from any symptoms of COPD. Is Tuan impaired? Is he substantially limited with respect to a major life activity and, therefore, disabled under the ADA?

2. Record of Such an Impairment

Section 3(2) of the ADA defines disability to include having a "record" of an impairment that substantially limits a major life activity. A variety of records contain such information, including employment records, medical records, and education records. In light of *Sutton,* individuals with impairments that, as a result of successful treatment, are not currently substantially limiting may seek to establish that they are protected by the ADA based on a "record" of an impairment. However, "[t]he impairment indicated in the record must be an impairment that would substantially limit one or more of the individual's major life activities." 29 C.F.R. pt. 1630, app. § 1630.2(k).

What evidence is necessary to meet this requirement? Numerous courts have held that impairments resulting in hospitalization and subsequent extended recuperation do not constitute substantially limiting impairments (or records of such impairments) in the absence of some chronic long-term impact.

Are these decisions consistent with *Arline?* In *Arline,* the Court stated that Arline's tuberculosis "was serious enough to require hospitalization, a fact more than sufficient to establish that one or more of her major life activities were substantially limited." Consider the following analysis from the Fifth Circuit:

> [Arline] cannot be construed to obviate the requirement, explicit in the ADA and its implementing regulations, that purported conditions be examined to ascertain whether a specific condition substantially limited a major life activity. The ADA requires an individualized inquiry beyond the mere existence of a hospital stay. Although the Court in Arline noted that the plaintiff's hospitalization established a record of impairment, the defendant had conceded that her acute tuberculosis had been substantially limiting. . . . [The contrary reading of Arline] would work a presumption that any condition requiring temporary hospitalization is disabling — a presumption that runs counter to the very goal of the ADA.

Burch v. Coca-Cola Co., 119 F.3d 305, 317 (5th Cir. 1997).

The EEOC has taken the position that the ADA "protects former cancer patients from discrimination on the basis of their prior medical history." 29 C.F.R. pt. 1630, app. §1630.2(k). Is this interpretation consistent with *Sutton's* and *Kirkingburg's* emphasis on individualized inquiry into substantial limitations? For a discussion of how the ADA's definition of "disability" treats cancer survivors, with a particular focus on breast cancer survivors, see Jane Byeff Korn, *Cancer and the ADA: Rethinking Disability*, 74 S. CAL. L. REV. 399 (2001).

Are individuals who establish coverage under the ADA by demonstrating a record of a substantially limiting impairment entitled to reasonable accommodations relating to continuing nonsubstantial limitations associated with their impairment? And, for liability to exist, must the employer discriminate based on the record of disability rather than on the basis of continuing nonsubstantial limitations? In thinking about how best to answer these questions, reconsider *Arline*. *See generally* Alex B. Long, (*Whatever Happened to*) *The ADA's "Record of" Prong(?)*, 81 WASH. L. REV. 669 (2006) (analyzing the puzzling disappearance of the record of disability prong).

PROBLEM 6.3

Reconsider Problems 6.1 and 6.2. Could you make a "record of impairment" argument on behalf of Sarah or Tuan?

3. *Regarded as Having Such an Impairment*

SUTTON v. UNITED AIR LINES, INC.
527 U.S. 471 (1999)

[The facts of this case are found at p. 509.]

IV

Our conclusion that petitioners have failed to state a claim that they are actually disabled under subsection (A) of the disability definition does not end our inquiry. Under subsection (C), individuals who are "regarded as" having a disability are disabled within the meaning of the ADA. See §12102(2)(C). Subsection (C) provides that having a disability includes "being regarded as having," §12102(2)(C), "a physical or mental impairment that substantially limits one or more of the major life activities of such individual," §12102(2)(A). There are two apparent ways in which individuals may fall within this statutory definition: (1) a covered entity mistakenly believes that a person has a physical impairment that substantially limits one or more major life activities, or (2) a covered entity mistakenly believes that an actual, nonlimiting impairment substantially limits one or more major life activities. In both cases, it is necessary that a covered entity entertain misperceptions about the individual — it must believe either that one has a substantially limiting impairment that one does not have or that one has a substantially limiting impairment when, in fact, the impairment is not so limiting. These misperceptions often "result from stereotypic assumptions not truly indicative of . . . individual ability." See 42 U.S.C. §12101(7).

There is no dispute that petitioners are physically impaired. Petitioners do not make the obvious argument that they are regarded due to their impairments as substantially limited in the major life activity of seeing. They contend only that respondent mistakenly believes their physical impairments substantially limit them in the major life activity of working. To support this claim, petitioners allege that respondent has a vision requirement, which is allegedly based on myth and stereotype. Further, this requirement substantially limits their ability to engage in the major life activity of working by precluding them from obtaining the job of global airline pilot, which they argue is a "class of employment." In reply, respondent argues that the position of global airline pilot is not a class of jobs and therefore petitioners have not stated a claim that they are regarded as substantially limited in the major life activity of working.

Standing alone, the allegation that respondent has a vision requirement in place does not establish a claim that respondent regards petitioners as substantially limited in the major life activity of working. By its terms, the ADA allows employers to prefer some physical attributes over others and to establish physical criteria. An employer runs afoul of the ADA when it makes an employment decision based on a physical or mental impairment, real or imagined, that is regarded as substantially limiting a major life activity. Accordingly, an employer is free to decide that physical characteristics or medical conditions that do not rise to the level of an impairment — such as one's height, build, or singing voice — are preferable to others, just as it is free to decide that some limiting, but not substantially limiting, impairments make individuals less than ideally suited for a job.

Considering the allegations of the amended complaint in tandem, petitioners have not stated a claim that respondent regards their impairment as substantially limiting their ability to work. The ADA does not define "substantially limits," but "substantially" suggests "considerable" or "specified to a large degree." See Webster's Third New International Dictionary 2280 (1976) (defining "substantially" as "in a substantial manner" and "substantial" as "considerable in amount, value, or worth" and "being that specified to a large degree or in the main"). The EEOC has codified regulations interpreting the term "substantially limits" in this manner, defining the term to mean "unable to perform" or "significantly restricted." See 29 CFR §§1630.2(j)(1)(i),(ii) (1998).

When the major life activity under consideration is that of working, the statutory phrase "substantially limits" requires, at a minimum, that plaintiffs allege they are unable to work in a broad class of jobs. Reflecting this requirement, the EEOC uses a specialized definition of the term "substantially limits" when referring to the major life activity of working:

> significantly restricted in the ability to perform either a class of jobs or a broad range of jobs in various classes as compared to the average person having comparable training, skills and abilities. The inability to perform a single, particular job does not constitute a substantial limitation in the major life activity of working.

§ 1630.2(j)(3)(i). The EEOC further identifies several factors that courts should consider when determining whether an individual is substantially limited in the major life activity of working, including the geographical area to which the individual has reasonable access, and "the number and types of jobs utilizing similar training, knowledge, skills or abilities, within the geographical area, from which the individual is also disqualified." §§ 1630.2(j)(3)(ii)(A), (B). To be substantially limited in the major life activity of working, then, one must be precluded from more than one type of job, a specialized job, or a particular job of choice. If jobs utilizing an individual's skills (but perhaps not his or her unique talents) are available, one is not precluded from a substantial class of jobs. Similarly, if a host of different types of jobs are available, one is not precluded from a broad range of jobs.

Because the parties accept that the term "major life activities" includes working, we do not determine the validity of the cited regulations. We note, however, that there may be some conceptual difficulty in defining "major life activities" to include work, for it seems "to argue in a circle to say that if one is excluded, for instance, by reason of [an impairment, from working with others] . . . then that exclusion constitutes an impairment, when the question you're asking is, whether the exclusion itself is by reason of handicap." Tr. of Oral Argument in [*Arline*] (argument of Solicitor General). Indeed, even the EEOC has expressed reluctance to define "major life activities" to include working and has suggested that working be viewed as a residual life activity, considered, as a last resort, *only* "if an individual is not substantially limited with respect to *any other* major life activity." 29 CFR pt. 1630, App. § 1630.2(j) (1998) (emphasis added).

Assuming without deciding that working is a major life activity and that the EEOC regulations interpreting the term "substantially limits" are reasonable, petitioners have failed to allege adequately that their poor eyesight is regarded as an impairment that substantially limits them in the major life activity of working. They allege only that respondent regards their poor vision as precluding them from holding positions as a "global airline pilot." Because the position of global airline pilot is a single job, this allegation does not support the claim that respondent regards petitioners as having a substantially limiting impairment. See 29 CFR § 1630.2(j)(3)(i) ("The inability to perform a single, particular job does not constitute a substantial limitation in the major life activity of working"). Indeed, there are a number of other positions utilizing petitioners' skills, such as regional pilot and pilot instructor to name a few, that are available to them. Even under the EEOC's Interpretive Guidance, to which petitioners ask us to defer, "an individual who cannot be a commercial airline pilot because of a minor vision impairment, but who can be a commercial airline co-pilot or a pilot for a courier service, would not be substantially limited in the major life activity of working." 29 CFR pt. 1630, App. § 1630.2.

Petitioners also argue that if one were to assume that a substantial number of airline carriers have similar vision requirements, they would be substantially limited in the major life activity of working. Even assuming for the sake of argument that the adoption of similar vision requirements by other carriers would represent a sub-stantial limitation on the major life activity of working, the argument is nevertheless flawed. It is not enough to say that if the physical criteria of a single employer were *imputed* to all similar employers one would be regarded as substantially limited in the major life activity of working *only as a result of this imputation.* An otherwise valid job requirement, such as a height requirement, does not become invalid simply because it would limit a person's employment opportunities in a substantial way if it were adopted by a substantial number of employers. Because petitioners have not alleged, and cannot demonstrate, that respondent's vision requirement reflects a belief that petitioners' vision substantially limits them, we agree with the decision of the Court of Appeals affirming the dismissal of petitioners' claim that they are regarded as disabled.

EEOC v. SCHNEIDER NAT'L, INC.
481 F.3d 507 (7th Cir. 2007)

POSNER, Circuit Judge.

In 2002, shortly after receiving an award from his employer, the Schneider trucking company, for having driven a million miles for the company without an avoidable accident, Jerome Hoefner had a fainting spell and was diagnosed with a condition called "neurocardiogenic syncope." This is a disorder of the nervous system that can produce a sudden drop in blood pressure that in turn reduces the amount of blood reaching the brain, causing the person with the disorder to faint. Schneider's policy is (with a possible exception discussed later in this opinion) not to employ a truck driver who has the disorder, although it is treatable with medicines such as Florinef and does not prevent a person from satisfying the safety standards required by federal law of anyone who drives, on a public highway, a truck that weighs (with its load) at least 26,001 pounds or is used to transport hazardous materials or at least 16 passengers. 49 U.S.C. §31136(a)(3); 49 C.F.R. §§383.5, 391.11(a).

After being dismissed by Schneider, Hoefner obtained a similar job with another trucking company. Nevertheless the EEOC brought suit on Hoefner's behalf against Schneider, contending that the company had fired him because it mistakenly believes that neurocardiogenic syncope is a disabling condition within the meaning of the Americans with Disabilities Act, which among other things forbids discrimi-nation in employment against persons mistakenly believed to be disabled. 42 U.S.C. §12102(2)(C). The district court granted summary judgment for Schneider, pre-cipitating this appeal.

There usually and here are two issues to resolve in such a case. The first is whether the employer's decision to terminate or take some other adverse employment action against the employee was motivated by a mistaken belief that the condition pre-cludes him from engaging in some activity. If so, the second question is whether the activity that the employer mistakenly believes the employee to be disabled from engaging in is a "major life activit[y]." *Id.,* §§12102(2)(A), (C). Suppose an employer mistakenly thinks that a person who has a hernia cannot lift 150 pounds and therefore is disabled from working for a moving company that specializes in moving refrigerators and grand pianos. The lifting of 150 pounds is not a major life activity. So unless the employer thought that a hernia that prevented such lifting substantially limited a life activity that is major — maybe the employer thinks that anyone who can't lift 150 pounds is incapable of *any* type of gainful employment — the employee would not be "regarded [by the employer] as having such an impairment," *§ 12102(2)(C)*, and so the employer would not have violated the Act.

The Commission's case relies primarily on statements by a nurse who heads Schneider's occupational health unit and believes that anyone with Hoefner's condition should be disqualified from driving Schneider's trucks as "a matter of safety and direct threat." But the reason for this belief, as she further explained and the Commission does not question, is that two years before Hoefner's fainting spell another driver for Schneider, Michael Kupsky, whom Schneider had hired shortly after Kupsky had been diagnosed with neurocardiogenic syncope while driving for another trucking company, had driven a Schneider truck off a bridge and been killed. Schneider was "advised that it appeared that [Kupsky] may have fallen asleep" at the wheel. The incident precipitated the company's adoption of a "zero tolerance" policy for drivers with neurocardiogenic syncope. The nurse stated that "Schneider made the right decision after the Kupsky accident. . . . [W]e don't know what caused that accident. We'll never know. And Schneider is not going to take the chance that . . . that horrible accident happens to anybody else." The executive who fired Hoefner echoed what the nurse had said: "we simply cannot take the risk that while driving, you would lose consciousness."

There is nothing to suggest that Schneider has a mistaken understanding of neurocardiogenic syncope. It simply is unwilling to risk a repetition (a possible repetition, since Kupsky's autopsy could not determine whether he had fainted and if so whether that was why he had veered off the road) of the Kupsky calamity. The risk is not zero, as the EEOC suggests, even if Florinef is totally efficacious, because Hoefner could forget to take his medicine. Anyway the drug is not totally efficacious. It merely reduces the risk of dehydration, and that is only one risk factor for neurocardiogenic syncope.

No doubt the risk that a person afflicted with this disorder will faint while driving is small, as otherwise Hoefner wouldn't be allowed to drive big trucks, as he is, for the trucking company that with full knowledge of his medical history hired him after Schneider fired him. But Schneider is entitled to determine how much risk is too great for *it* to be willing to take. "[A]n employer is free to decide that physical characteristics or medical conditions that do not rise to the level of an impairment — such as one's height, build, or singing voice — are preferable to others, just as it is free to decide that some limiting, but not substantially limiting, impairments make individuals less than ideally suited for a job." *Sutton v. United Air Lines, Inc.*. The fact that another employer and, as in all such cases, the worker himself are willing to assume a risk does not compel the worker's current employer to do likewise. *Chevron U.S.A. Inc. v. Echazabal* [reproduced at p. 568].

Schneider is the nation's largest truck company, employing 13,000 drivers. . . . Suppose 2 percent of Schneider's drivers had [neurocardiogenic syncope]; that would be 260. The risk that at least one of them would have a Kupsky-type accident could not be thought wholly negligible, and the liability implications for Schneider (should there be an accident that killed or injured someone other than the driver, whose rights against Schneider would be limited to workers' compensation) could be calamitous. The victims' lawyers would wave the Kupsky accident in front of the jury, asking it to award punitive damages because the company had continued to employ drivers with neurocardiogenic syncope after having been warned by Kupsky's accident. The argument for punitive damages would be that employing Hoefner in the wake of Kupsky's accident showed that Schneider had acted in the face of a known risk and was therefore reckless.

The argument might not succeed; the risk might be deemed insufficiently large to make Schneider reckless for not eliminating it by barring drivers who have neuro-cardiogenic syncope. But once burned, twice shy. Because of Kupsky's unfortunate accident, Schneider may be excessively risk averse, as United Air Lines and other airlines (*Sutton v. United Air Lines, Inc.*) may be in refusing to hire pilots who do not have at least 20-100 uncorrected vision. But as there is no evidence that Schneider exaggerates the severity of Hoefner's condition and the risk he poses as a driver, there is no violation of the Americans with Disabilities Act.

The EEOC has confused risk with risk aversion. Two companies might each correctly believe that the risk of a particular type of accident was 1 in 10,000, yet one company, perhaps because it was small, financially fragile, owned by a trust, or as in this case had had an experience of the risk materializing, might be unwilling to assume the risk. That would be a decision irrelevant to liability under the Americans with Disabilities Act, even if that company's degree of risk aversion was "unique" in its industry. *EEOC v. J.B. Hunt Transport, Inc.*, 321 F.3d 69, 76 (2d Cir. 2003).

But if this is wrong, the EEOC still must lose because there is no evidence that Schneider considers neurocardiogenic syncope to impair any "life activity" other than driving a truck for Schneider, and perhaps for some other truck companies (we do not know whether there are any) that like Schneider have safety standards higher than the minimum required by the federal government. That is too esoteric a capability to be judged a "major" life activity. If being able to drive a huge truck or a truck filled with hazardous chemicals safely, or being able to fly a plane or guide climbers to the summit of Mt. Everest, is a major life activity, then virtually the entire population of the United States is disabled, which would be a ridiculous construction to place on the Americans with Disabilities Act. "[E]ven assuming that working is a major life activity" — as the EEOC believes, 29 C.F.R. § 1630.2(j)(3), but the Supreme Court doubts, *Sutton v. United Air Lines, Inc.* — "a claimant would be required to show an inability to work in a 'broad range of jobs,' rather than a specific job." *Toyota Motor Mfg. Inc. v. Williams*; see also *Sutton v. United Air Lines, Inc.*; *Kupstas v. City of Greenwood*, 398 F.3d 609, 612-13 (7th Cir. 2005). In a "regarded as" case, such as this, the claimant (here the EEOC on the claimant's behalf) would have to show that the employer believed that the claimant had a condition that would disable him from working in a broad range of jobs. Otherwise, minor physical defects would count as impairments of major life activities. . . .

[The court also noted that, even if Schneider believed Hoefner incapable of driving any trucks at all, there would still be no "regarded as" claim, because the company simply would be acting "consistent with its having decided to set a higher safety standard than law or custom requires, as United Air Lines had done. As we know from *Sutton*, that is a decision the Act does not touch"].

NOTES

1. *Substantially Limited in Ability to Work.* The *Sutton* Court's analysis of the plaintiffs' claim that they were regarded as substantially limited with respect to working is consistent with the EEOC regulations insofar as the Court requires the plaintiffs to establish that they were regarded as excluded from "either a class of jobs or a broad range of jobs" as compared to persons with "comparable training, skills and abilities." The opinion also rests comfortably within the EEOC's Interpretive

Guidance in concluding that the plaintiffs were not substantially limited with respect to working because other airline positions were open to them.

But how does *Sutton* conclude that the plaintiffs were not *regarded as* substantially limited with respect to working? Reread the last paragraph of the opinion. What evidence would be necessary to satisfy the Court? The Seventh Circuit's decision in *Schneider* drives home (so to speak) the difficulties of establishing a "regarded as" claim. Even when federal law would not find an impairment to preclude working in the at-issue job, an employer may choose to take a more stringent approach to avoid any "risk." Is this what Congress had in mind when it included "regarded as" within the definition of disability?

2. *Broad Class of Jobs?* What is a broad class or range of jobs? In *Murphy v. United Parcel Serv.*, 527 U.S. 516 (1999), the plaintiff was denied DOT certification to drive a commercial truck because of his high blood pressure. UPS dismissed Murphy from his job because he could not obtain the certification. The Court held that the defendant did not regard Murphy as substantially limited in the activity of working but only regarded Murphy as unable to perform mechanics' jobs that required driving a commercial motor vehicle (defined as a vehicle weighing over 10,000 pounds, designed to carry 16 or more passengers, or used in the transportation of hazardous materials).

In *Giordano v. City of New York*, 274 F.3d 740 (2d Cir. 2001), the court held plaintiff had not shown he was regarded as being substantially limited in his ability to work. His employer regarded him as unable to perform police or other investigative work that involved a risk of physical confrontation, and he thus had no evidence he was regarded as being unable to work in a broad class of jobs. Do you agree? Is fire fighting a class of jobs? *See Bridges v. City of Bossier*, 92 F.3d 329 (5th Cir. 1996) (no). Is law enforcement generally? *See McKenzie v. Dovola*, 242 F.3d 967 (10th Cir. 2001) (yes). *But see Rossbach v. City of Miami*, 371 F.3d 1354 (11th Cir. 2004) (even assuming the city perceived officers as being precluded by their impairments from working as police officers, "police officer" was not a "class of jobs" or "broad range of jobs" for ADA purposes). In *Gasser v. District of Columbia*, 442 F.3d 758 (D.C. Cir. 2006), a jury verdict in plaintiff's favor was reversed where plaintiff failed to introduce evidence of the jobs he was regarded as unable to perform because of the risk of bleeding.

3. *Working as a Major Life Activity.* The analysis of how broad a class of jobs needs to be arises only if "working" is a major life activity under the ADA. Note that the *Sutton* Court reserves the question, and *Toyota* did as well. The Court's comments in *Sutton* suggest that the Court may not accept as "major" *all* of the activities, including working, listed in the regulations. Other activities defined as major in the EEOC's regulations include "caring for oneself, performing manual tasks, walking, seeing, hearing, speaking, breathing, [and] learning." 29 C.F.R. § 1630.2(i). Could it be argued that any of these listed activities are *not* "major life activities"? Could a holding that working is not a major life activity be squared with Congress's directive that the ADA standards be no less protective than regulations adopted under the Rehabilitation Act. 42 U.S.C. § 12201(a)(2007). See *Bragdon*, reproduced at p. 492. Those regulations include working as a major life activity. 45 C.F.R. 84.3(j)(2)(ii)) *See* Mark C. Rahdert, Arline's *Ghost: Some Notes on Working as a Major Life Activity Under the ADA*, 9 TEMP. POL. & CIV. RTS. L. REV. 303 (2000).

4. *Must There Be an Impairment?* Is ADA coverage dependent on the perceived disability at least meeting the statutory definition of impairment? The First Circuit in *Cook v. Rhode Island Dept. of Mental Health*, 10 F.3d 17, 25 (1st Cir. 1993),

suggested that an individual with turquoise eyes would be covered under the "regarded as" provision if an employer regarded people with blue eyes as incapable of lifting heavy weights. Is this correct? Addressing allegations of discrimination on the basis of weight, both the Second and the Sixth Circuits have held that plaintiffs claiming perceived disability must establish that the defendant perceived an impairment as defined by the statute. *See Andrews v. Ohio*, 104 F.3d 803 (6th Cir. 1997); *Francis v. City of Meriden*, 129 F.3d 281 (2d Cir. 1997).

5. *Genetic Information.* Reconsider ADA coverage for individuals with a genetic propensity for disease. The EEOC's Compliance Manual, §902: Definition of the Term "Disability," states:

> Covered entities that discriminate against individuals on the basis of . . . genetic information are regarding the individuals as having impairments that substantially limit a major life activity. Those individuals, therefore, are covered by the third part of the definition of "disability." See 136 Cong. Rec. H4623 (daily ed. July 12, 1990) (statement of Rep. Owens); *id.* at H4624-25 (statement of Rep. Edwards); *id.* at H4627 (statement of Rep. Waxman).

Is the EEOC's position consistent with *Sutton?*

6. *The Perceptions of Others as "Disabling."* Part (2) of the ADA regulations defining "regarded as impaired" allows a plaintiff with a physical or mental impairment to argue that the impairment is substantially limiting "as a result of the attitudes of others toward such impairment." The Interpretive Guidance further explains this provision:

> For example, an individual may have a prominent facial scar or disfigurement, or may have a condition that periodically causes an involuntary jerk of the head but does not limit the individual's major life activities. If an employer discriminates against such an individual because of the negative reactions of customers, the employer would be regarding the individual as disabled and acting on the basis of that perceived disability.

29 C.F.R. pt. 1630, app. §1630.2(*l*). Is this regulation consistent with *Sutton?* Reconsider discrimination based on obesity. Could Cook have established her case under part (2) of the "regarded as" provisions? *See* Jane B. Korn, *Fat*, 77 B.U. L. Rev. 25 (1997).

7. *Applying the "Regarded as" Test.* Lower courts have varied in their approaches to the ADA's "regarded as" provision. For example, *Stewart v. County of Brown*, 86 F.3d 107 (7th Cir. 1996), declined to find that a deputy sheriff was regarded as having a substantially limiting mental illness despite evidence that the deputy sheriff's employer referred to him as "excitable," ordered psychological evaluations for him, and told third parties that he considered him to be emotionally or psychologically imbalanced. How would you prove that an employer regarded an employee as psychologically disabled? *See also Cassimy v. Bd. of Educ.*, 461 F.3d 932, 937 (7th Cir. 2006) (while plaintiff told members of the board of education that he was being treated for depression and anxiety, and the Board received medical records so indicating, the record "does not show . . . that the Board held exaggerated views about the seriousness of his illness."); *Tockes v. Air-Land Transp. Serv. Inc.*, 343 F.3d 895 (7th Cir. 2003) (plaintiff failed to establish regarded as status even though he was told by his manager, when he was fired, that it had been

a "mistake" to hire someone who was "handicapped" and manager called him crippled and disabled; while plaintiff had established his employer regarded him as disabled, he did not establish the employer regarded him as disabled within the meaning of the ADA). On the other hand, in *Levelle v. Penske Logistics*, 197 Fed. Appx. 729 (10th Cir. 2006), the court found a delivery driver with lifting restrictions to have been regarded as unable to perform a broad range of jobs where he was not considered for other positions and a clerk job was filled shortly after his discharge and he was not hired for other delivery positions.

8. *"Regarded as" Claims and Stereotyping.* When plaintiffs prevail in "regarded as" claims, it is usually when there is evidence that an employer is acting on the basis of bias, prejudice, or stereotypes. For example, in *Josephs v. Pacific Bell*, 443 F.3d 1050 (9th Cir. 2006), the Ninth Circuit upheld a jury verdict in favor of a service technician. Years before being hired by PacBell, plaintiff had been found not guilty of attempted murder by reason of insanity and had been institutionalized. There was evidence PacBell employees had considered Josephs unemployable because he had spent time in a "mental ward" and might "go off" on a customer. Since PacBell considered Josephs unfit for any job with the company, the jury could find that it viewed him as having a mental disability that "substantially limited" him in the "major life activity" of working. And in *EEOC v. Heartway Corp.*, 466 F.3d 1156 (10th Cir. 2006), a nursing home cook with hepatitis C was regarded as disabled in the major life activity of working where an administrator's remarks indicated that he did not believe that she could work in any food-related position.

However, animus, in the sense of bad faith or ill will, is not necessary for a violation. A good faith, or "innocent misperception," can still result in liability under the regarded as prong. *See Taylor v. Pathmark Stores, Inc.*, 177 F.3d 180 (3d Cir. 1999) ("the law in this circuit is that a 'regarded as' plaintiff can make out a case if the employer is innocently wrong about the extent of his or her impairment"); *See also Arline v. School Bd. of Nassau County*, 480 U.S. 273 (1987). *See generally* Michelle A. Travis, *Perceived Disabilities, Social Cognition, and "Innocent Mistakes,"* 55 VAND. L. REV. 481 (2002).

9. *"Regarded as" Plaintiffs and Reasonable Accommodation.* Is an employee who is "regarded as" disabled entitled to reasonable accommodation? In *D'Angelo v. Conagra Foods*, 422 F.3d 1220, 1235 (11th Cir. 2005), the Eleventh Circuit said yes, reasoning that "the plain language of the ADA yields no statutory basis for distinguishing among individuals who are disabled in the actual-impairment sense and those who are disabled only in the regarded-as sense; both are entitled to reasonable accommodations." *Accord Williams v. Phila. Hous. Auth. Police Dep't*, 380 F.3d 751 (3d Cir. 2004); *Kelly v. Metallics West, Inc.*, 410 F.3d 670 (10th Cir. 2005). The courts that go the other way view the plain meaning as insufficient to overcome the oddity of accommodating individuals who do not require an accommodation. *Weber v. Strippit, Inc.*, 186 F.3d 907 (8th Cir. 1999); *Newbery v. East Tex. State Univ.*, 161 F. 3d 276 (5th Cir. 1998). *See generally* Michelle A. Travis, *Leveling the Playing Field or Stacking the Deck? The "Unfair Advantage" Critique of Perceived Disability Claims*, 78 N.C. L. REV. 901 (2000); Lawrence D. Rosenthal, *Reasonable Accommodations for Individuals Regarded as Having Disabilities Under the Americans with Disabilities Act? Why "No" Should Not Be the Answer*, 36 SETON HALL L. REV. 895 (2006).

C. THE MEANING OF "QUALIFIED INDIVIDUAL WITH A DISABILITY"

Establishing the existence of a disability is alone insufficient to bring an individual within Title I's protected class. Title I, the ADA's employment subchapter, contains the following prohibition:

> No covered entity shall discriminate against a *qualified individual with a disability* because of the disability of such individual in regard to job application procedures, the hiring, advancement, or discharge of employees, employee compensation, job training and other terms, conditions and privileges of employment.

42 U.S.C. § 12112(a) (emphasis added). The concept of protecting only qualified individuals from disability discrimination is borrowed from § 504 of the Rehabilitation Act of 1973, which protects only those disabled persons who are "otherwise qualified." 29 U.S.C. § 794(a) (2003). In *Southeast Community College v. Davis*, 442 U.S. 397 (1979), a case decided under § 504, the Supreme Court rejected a reading of "otherwise qualified" that would protect individuals who were qualified apart from their disability. Instead, the Court interpreted the term to mean an individual who can meet the demands of the job or program *despite* the disability. The Court went on to hold, however, that an entity may be required to make changes in its program to accommodate the need of the disabled individual. As *Davis* was later described by the Court:

> *Davis* thus struck a balance between the statutory rights of the handicapped to be integrated into society and the legitimate interests of federal grantees in preserving the integrity of their programs: while a grantee need not be required to make "fundamental" or "substantial" modifications to accommodate the handicapped, it may be required to make reasonable ones.

Alexander v. Choate, 469 U.S. 287, 301 (1985).

This structure is carried over into Title I of the ADA. Title I defines a "qualified individual with a disability" as:

> an individual with a disability who, with or without reasonable accommodation, can perform the essential functions of the employment position that such individual holds or desires. For the purposes of this title, consideration shall be given to the employer's judgment as to what functions of a job are essential, and if an employer has prepared a written description before advertising or interviewing applicants for the job, this description shall be considered evidence of the essential functions of the job.

42 U.S.C. § 12111(8).

While Title I extends its protections to disabled individuals who can perform the essential tasks of their jobs, it will not permit employers to deny employment because a disability precludes the performance of nonessential or relatively unimportant aspects of the job. On the other hand, denying employment to someone who cannot perform the essential functions of the job with or without reasonable accommodation is not a statutory violation. Accordingly, it is necessary to distinguish the essential functions of the job from those that are not.

1. Essential Job Functions

REHRS v. THE IAMS COMPANY
486 F.3d 353 (8th Cir. 2007)

RILEY, Circuit Judge.

I. BACKGROUND

Rehrs, who suffers from Type I diabetes, worked as a warehouse technician for the Iams Company (Iams) in Aurora, Nebraska, from 1997 until 2003. Iams operated the facility on a 24-hour basis using a straight-shift schedule, i.e., three daily shifts. From 1997 until 1999, Rehrs worked a fixed schedule from 4 p.m. to midnight.

In August 1999, P&G [Procter & Gamble] acquired Iams, and in January 2000, P&G implemented a rotating-shift schedule for all warehouse technicians. The rotating-shift schedule consisted of two daily twelve hour shifts, one from 6:00 a.m. to 6:00 p.m. and the other from 6:00 p.m. to 6:00 a.m. Employees on this schedule worked two days, were off two days, and worked alternating weekends. Every two weeks the first and second shift workers rotated.

Rehrs worked the rotating shift from January 2000 to February 2002 when he suffered a heart attack. Rehrs underwent bypass surgery and had a defibrillator and pacemaker implanted. Due to his medical condition, and at Rehrs's request, P&G placed Rehrs on short-term disability leave.

Rehrs returned to work by early August 2003. However, in September 2003, Rehrs's doctor submitted a letter to P&G, requesting Rehrs be placed on a fixed daytime schedule because his diabetes had become difficult to control. Rehrs's doctor believed a routine or fixed schedule would enhance the efforts to control Rehrs's blood sugar level. Rehrs was granted this accommodation and worked a straight eight-hour shift for sixty days. When P&G learned Rehrs's doctor intended for the requested accommodation to be permanent, P&G informed Rehrs that his accommodation would not continue because shift rotation was an essential part of his job. . . .

[The district court granted summary judgment to P&G, concluding that] even assuming Rehrs's diabetes was a disability within the meaning of the ADA, Rehrs was not a qualified individual under the ADA because Rehrs could not perform an essential function of the job, specifically, shift rotation at the Aurora facility.

II. DISCUSSION. . . .

An individual is qualified if he satisfies the requisite skill, experience, education, and other job-related requirements, and "can perform the essential job functions, with or without reasonable accommodation." *Cravens* [*v. Blue Cross & Blue Shield of Kan. City*, 214 F.3d 1011, 1016 (8th Cir. 2000)]. Essential functions are the fundamental job duties but not the marginal functions of a particular job. *Canny v. Dr Pepper/Seven-Up Bottling Group*, 439 F.3d 894, 900 (8th Cir. 2006) (citing 29 C.F.R. § 1630.2(n)(1)). An employer has the burden of showing a particular job function is an essential function of the job. *Benson v. Nw. Airlines, Inc.*, 62 F.3d 1108, 1113 (8th Cir. 1995). Evidence of whether a particular function is essential includes, but is not limited to, (1) the employer's judgment as to which functions are essential; (2) written job descriptions prepared before advertising or interviewing applicants for the job; (3) the amount of time spent on the job performing the function; (4) the consequences of not requiring the incumbent to perform the function; (5) the terms of a collective bargaining agreement; (6) the work experience of past incumbents in the job; and (7) the current work experience of incumbents in similar jobs. 29 C.F.R. § 1630.2(n)(3); *Heaser v. Toro Co.*, 247 F.3d 826, 831 (8th Cir. 2001).

For summary judgment purposes, it is undisputed that, aside from his inability to work a rotating shift schedule, Rehrs satisfactorily discharged the responsibilities of his warehouse technician position. Thus, the only question is whether the rotating shift implemented by P&G is an essential function of Rehrs's technician job. . . .

P&G claims shift rotation was an essential function of the positions at the Aurora facility during the relevant period because all P&G subsidiaries operated under a High Performance Work System (HPWS), and shift rotation was a component of this system. According to P&G, it had employed shift rotation since the 1960s in its new production facilities, and in the 1980s began transitioning its existing production facilities from traditional work systems to HPWS. P&G contends shift rotation exposes employees to management, and to more resources, suppliers, and outside customers with whom the company only interfaces during the day shift. P&G believes this type of exposure provides all employees with additional opportunities for training and development to further their career opportunities in the company and, in turn, increases productivity. P&G asserts that not implementing shift rotation for all warehouse technicians would harm the company from a production stand-point and allowing an employee to work a straight shift would undermine the team concept. P&G further claims not enforcing shift rotation would adversely affect other technicians, creating inequities, because these other technicians would be forced to work the night shift exclusively or for longer periods and lose the benefits of shift rotation, thereby decreasing their opportunities for promotion and development.

All of these factors weigh heavily in favor of finding shift rotation in the P&G work culture is an essential function of working as a warehouse technician. Com-mencing in January 2000, the facility did not have a straight day-shift technician position-all technician positions were on rotating shifts. Allowing Rehrs to work a straight day-shift schedule would have placed a heavier or unfavorable burden on other technicians at the facility. Under the ADA, an accommodation that would cause other employees to work harder, longer, or be deprived of opportunities is not mandated. *Turco v. Hoechst Celanese Corp.*, 101 F.3d 1090, 1094 (5th Cir. 1996) (citing *Milton v. Scrivner, Inc.*, 53 F.3d 1118, 1125 (10th Cir. 1995), and 29 C.F.R. § 1630.2(p)(2)(v)).

Based on the affidavits of two co-workers, Rehrs claims shift rotation is not an essential function of his warehouse technician job. Rehrs argues the plant operated on a straight-shift schedule before P&G's acquisition of the plant and again after P&G outsourced the facility to Excel, while all other functions of the facility, with the exception of the shift rotation, remained the same. However, as the district court noted, the fact that straight shifts were in effect at the Aurora facility before and after P&G ran the facility has little relevance. P&G does not have to exercise the same business judgment as other employers who may believe a straight shift is more productive. It is not the province of the court to question the legitimate operation of a production facility or determine what is the most productive or efficient shift schedule for a facility. See *Milton*.

Rehrs also contends the duties performed at the facility on the day shift were the same duties performed on the night shift. He contends essential functions are duties

to be *performed* and a rotating shift is not *performed*. See 29 C.F.R. §1630.2(n)(1).
Thus, Rehrs asserts, shift rotation is not an essential part of the job. However, the
term essential function encompasses more than core job requirements; indeed, it
also may include scheduling flexibility. *Laurin v. Providence Hosp.*, 150 F.3d 52, 59
n. 6 (1st Cir. 1998).

Rehrs also argues P&G allowed him a temporary exception from shift rotation,
which demonstrates shift rotation is not essential. However, "[a]n employer does not
concede that a job function is 'non-essential' simply by voluntarily assuming the
limited burden associated with a temporary accommodation, nor thereby acknowledge that the burden associated with a permanent accommodation would not be
unduly onerous." *Id.* (citing *Shiring v. Runyon*, 90 F.3d 827, 831 (3d Cir. 1996)).
"To find otherwise would unacceptably punish employers from doing more than the
ADA requires, and might discourage such an undertaking on the part of employers."
Phelps v. Optima Health, Inc., 251 F.3d 21, 26 (1st Cir. 2001) (citations omitted).

Here, P&G required all employees in Rehrs's position to rotate shifts. Such a generally applicable requirement was not discriminatory. The ADA does not require P&G
to create a new straight shift position for Rehrs. *Fjellestad v. Pizza Hut of Am., Inc.*, 188
F.3d 944, 950 (8th Cir. 1999) (holding an employer is not obligated to create a new
position, or to transform a temporary position into a permanent position as an accommodation, or to eliminate or reallocate the essential functions of a job to accommodate its disabled employees); *Malabarba v. Chi. Tribune Co.*, 149 F.3d 690, 696
(7th Cir. 1998) ("[T]he ADA does not require that employers transform temporary
work assignments into permanent positions."); *Dalton v. Subaru-Isuzu Auto., Inc.*, 141
F.3d 667, 680 (7th Cir. 1998) (stating the ADA does not require employers to create
full-time positions to accommodate disabled employees). "The [ADA] does not require
affirmative action in favor of individuals with disabilities. It merely prohibits employment discrimination against qualified individuals with disabilities, no more and no
less." *Turco* (citing *Daugherty v. City of El Paso*, 56 F.3d 695, 700 (5th Cir. 1995)). . . .

Viewing the facts in the light most favorable to Rehrs, we conclude shift rotation
was a non-discriminatory essential function of Rehrs's technician job at P&G and
Rehrs's restrictions to work only a straight shift rendered him unqualified to carry out
all the essential functions of his P&G technician job. Thus, summary judgment was
appropriate.

NOTES

1. *The Employer's Judgment.* Recall that §101(8), 42 U.S.C. §12111(8) (2007),
states that "consideration shall be given to the employer's judgment as to what
functions of a job are essential" and that written job descriptions prepared prior to
advertising or interviewing applicants "shall be considered evidence of the essential
functions of the job." Does this allow employers too often to dictate the outcome of
ADA claims by labeling tasks as "essential" ones? The *Rehrs* court gives consideration to the employer's judgment but claims not to view it as dispositive. At the same
time, it declares it "not the province of the court to question the legitimate operation
of a production facility or determine what is the most productive or efficient shift
schedule for a facility." *See also Branham v. Snow*, 392 F.3d 896 (7th Cir. 2005)
(while acknowledging it was not limited to employer's judgment, "[w]e shall not
second-guess an employer's judgment as to the essential functions of the job").

2. *Burden of Proof.* The Eighth Circuit in *Rehrs* states it is the employer's burden to prove a job function is an essential one. Is that correct? Or is it the employee's burden to prove he can perform the essential functions of the job, with or without reasonable accommodation?

3. *Defining the Term.* The EEOC's regulations, promulgated under Title I, define essential job function to mean the "fundamental job duties," as opposed to the "marginal functions" of the job. Factors to consider in making that distinction are whether the position exists to perform the function, the number of employees available to perform the function, and/or whether the function is highly specialized, thus requiring special expertise. In addition to the employer's job description, other evidence to consider includes, although it is not limited to, the employer's judgment, the amount of time spent performing the function, the work experience of people previously or currently in the job or similar jobs, and the terms of any collective bargaining agreement. 29 C.F.R. § 1630.2(n). Applying this standard, do you think the *Rehrs* court made the right call? *Cf. Turner v. Hershey Chocolate USA*, 440 F.3d 604 (3d Cir. 2006) (jury should decide whether rotation among three production lines was essential job function despite employer's contentions that it was essential to reduce repetitive stress injuries, where neither job description nor cba mentioned rotation, little time was spent rotating, and inspectors had not rotated in past). *See generally* Michelle A. Travis, *Recapturing the Transformative Potential of Employment Discrimination Law*, 62 WASH & LEE L. REV. 3, 6 (2005) ("For either the ADA or Title VII to restructure the workplace successfully . . . judges must be able — and willing — to parse out the malleable ways that job tasks are organized from the actual tasks that comprise the essence of the job.").

4. *Attendance as an Essential Job Function.* Numerous courts have held that regular and timely attendance at work is an essential job function, and, therefore, a disabled individual who cannot meet that requirement is not "qualified" within the meaning of the ADA or the Rehabilitation Act. *See, e.g., Mulloy v. Acushnet Co.*, 460 F.3d 141, 153-54 (1st Cir. 2006) (since physical presence was an essential function, working remotely was not reasonable; it was not an accommodation but a redefinition of the job); *Schierhoff v. Glaxosmithkline Consumer Healthcare, L.P.*, 444 F.3d 961 (8th Cir. 2006) (excessive absenteeism made employee unqualified since regular attendance was essential job function); *Brenneman v. Medcentral Health Sys.*, 366 F.3d 412 (6th Cir. 2004) (a large number of absences rendered plaintiff not qualified since regular attendance is an essential function of Pharmacy Technician position, which entails preparing and delivering medications to hospital patients, ordering, receiving, and stocking medications, and posting charges to patients' accounts). *See also Mason v. Avaya Communs., Inc.*, 357 F.3d 1114 (10th Cir. 2004) (employee did not create fact issue by her self-serving testimony that presence in the workplace was not an essential function). The Sixth Circuit has cautioned, however, that a presumption that uninterrupted attendance is an essential job requirement improperly avoids the individualized assessment of accommodations required by the ADA. *See Cehrs v. Northeast Ohio Alzheimer's Research Ctr.*, 155 F.3d 775 (6th Cir. 1998). Is there a difference between an employee whose disability results in sporadic absences and one whose disability requires a medical leave? And while regular attendance may be an essential job function, "strict punctuality" may or may not be, depending upon the demands of the particular job. *See Holly v. Clairson Indus.*, 492 F.3d 1247 (11th Cir. 2007) (reversing summary judgment for employer when a question of fact existed on whether strict punctuality was an essential job function). Leave as a reasonable accommodation is discussed further in Subsection C.2.

5. *Essential Job Functions and the Duty of Reasonable Accommodation.* If being able to work rotating shifts is an essential job function for a warehouse technician, then the employer need not relieve the employee from the rotation schedule. And there is no accommodation available that would allow Rehrs to permanently work a rotating shift. But if the essential job functions are the duties themselves, and not the time of day they are performed, then being able to work a rotating shift would be nonessential. An employer may not deny employment to a disabled individual because she is unable to perform nonessential job functions.

But if plaintiff works only day shifts, then other employees necessarily will need to work more night and evening shifts. Is it appropriate to take this burden on other employees into account in determining whether or not a job function is essential? Or should that instead be considered a question of undue hardship? Since the *Rehrs* court holds that the employer had the burden of proving the job function was essential, does it matter?

6. *Quality and Quantity of Work.* Can the quantity or quality of work produced be an essential function of the job? The Interpretive Guidance provides:

> [T]he inquiry into essential functions is not intended to second guess an employer's business judgment with regard to production standards, whether qualitative or quantitative, nor to require employers to lower such standards. . . . If an employer requires its typists to be able to accurately type 75 words per minute, it will not be called upon to explain why an inaccurate work product, or a typing speed of 65 words per minute, would not be adequate. . . . However, if an employer does require accurate 75 word per minute typing . . . , it will have to show that it actually imposes such requirements on its employees in fact, and not simply on paper.

29 C.F.R. pt. 1630, app. § 1630.2(n). *See Milton v. Scrivner, Inc.*, 53 F.3d 1118 (10th Cir. 1995) (employer's new production standard constituted an essential function of the selector job). What arguments would you make on the issue of essential functions on behalf of a dyslexic lawyer who produces a good product but is denied partnership on the basis of low productivity? Is she a qualified individual with a disability? Note that the statute prohibits discriminatory qualification standards unless job-related for the position in question and consistent with business necessity and the duty of reasonable accommodation. 42 U.S.C. § 12112(b)(6). Is the Interpretive Guidance consistent with this statutory provision?

PROBLEM 6.4

Sam is hearing impaired. He has applied for a secretarial job that includes answering phones. He asserts that he can perform all aspects of the job, except for answering the phone, without any accommodation. With respect to answering the phone, he has proposed two alternative accommodations: (1) eliminating the phone responsibilities or (2) providing a telecommunications device (TDD) that would allow him to answer the phone. Is he qualified for this job? What arguments can he make? What arguments can the employer make? Do you need any additional information to answer these questions?

PROBLEM 6.5

Jan works as a supervisor for Acme Products, a small manufacturing company. Jan suffers from Tourette's syndrome, a disorder that causes some individuals to uncontrollably burst out with obscene or extremely insulting remarks. Jan's outbursts usually take the form of racial epithets. Fifty percent of Acme Products' employees are African Americans. Several of these employees have complained to the EEO officer at Acme about Jan's outbursts. Acme has consulted you for advice. What advice would you give?

2. The Duty of Reasonable Accommodation

A qualified individual with a disability is one who can perform the essential functions of the job she holds or desires *with or without reasonable accommodation.* The concept of reasonable accommodation distinguishes the ADA from other antidiscrimination statutes. Under the ADA, it is *not* enough for an employer to treat its disabled employees the same — no better and no worse — than it treats its non-disabled employees. In appropriate circumstances, the employer must take affirmative steps that will allow disabled employees to perform their jobs. *See Holly v. Clairson Industries,* 492 F.3d 1247, 1262 (11th Cir. 2007) (Defendant "is not insulated from liability under the ADA by treating its non-disabled employees exactly the same as its disabled employees . . . the very purpose of reasonable accommodation laws is to *require* employers to treat disabled individuals differently in some circumstances"). It is often the accommodation that will allow the disabled employee who otherwise would be unable to work at all to perform the essential functions of the job. *See Cleveland v. Policy Management Systems Corp.,* 526 U.S. 795 (1999) (recognizing this point in holding that a social security claim of total and permanent disability is not necessarily inconsistent with a Title I claim under the ADA alleging failure to accommodate).

Failing to provide reasonable accommodations constitutes one form of discrimination under the statute. Section 102(b)(5) of the ADA defines discrimination to include:

(A) not making reasonable accommodations to the known physical or mental limitations of an otherwise qualified individual with a disability who is an applicant or employee, unless such covered entity can demonstrate that the accommodation would impose an undue hardship on the operation of the business of such covered entity; or

(B) denying employment opportunities to a job applicant or employee who is an otherwise qualified individual with a disability, if such denial is based on the need of such covered entity to make reasonable accommodation to the physical or mental impairments of the employee or applicant.

Section 102(b)(5) makes reasonable accommodation relevant both to establishing and defending against a discrimination claim based on the failure to accommodate. If a disabled individual can perform essential functions with reasonable accommodation, the employer has a duty to provide those accommodations. If the disabled individual requires accommodations that are not reasonable or that impose an undue hardship, disparate treatment on the basis of disability is permitted and accommodating the disability is not required.

This section considers "reasonable accommodation" in the context of proving a disability discrimination claim of "not making reasonable accommodations." Reasonable accommodation goes beyond providing accommodations required to perform essential job functions. Employers also have a duty to provide accommodations that permit disabled individuals to enjoy equal access to the benefits and privileges of employment. The ADA also requires employers to make "accommodations that are required to ensure equal opportunity in the application process." *See* 29 C.F.R. pt. 1630, App. § 1630.2(o). Section 101(9) identifies some of the areas in which accommodation may be required:

The term "reasonable accommodation" may include —

   (A) making existing facilities used by employees readily accessible to and usable by individuals with disabilities; and
   (B) job restructuring, part-time or modified work schedules, reassignment to a vacant position, acquisition or modification of equipment or devices, appropriate adjustment or modifications of examinations, training materials or policies, the provision of qualified readers or interpreters, and other similar accommodations for individuals with disabilities.

Note that the issue in a "failure to accommodate" case is not whether the employer has treated the disabled individual differently. Nor is the question whether the employer has legitimate reasons for treating a disabled individual differently. In a reasonable accommodation case, the disabled individual is *requesting* different treatment. The question is not whether the disability was considered but rather whether the disability entitled the employee or applicant to accommodation (different treatment).

US AIRWAYS, INC. v. BARNETT
535 U.S. 391 (2002)

BREYER, J., delivered the opinion of the Court, in which REHNQUIST, C. J., and STEVENS, O'CONNOR, and KENNEDY, JJ., joined. STEVENS, J., and O'CONNOR, J., filed concurring opinions. SCALIA, J., filed a dissenting opinion, in which THOMAS, J., joined. SOUTER, J., filed a dissenting opinion, in which GINSBURG, J., joined.

The Americans with Disabilities Act of 1990 prohibits an employer from discriminating against an "individual with a disability" who, with "reasonable accommodation," can perform the essential functions of the job. This case, arising in the context of summary judgment, asks us how the Act resolves a potential conflict between: (1) the interests of a disabled worker who seeks assignment to a particular position as a "reasonable accommodation," and (2) the interests of other workers with superior rights to bid for the job under an employer's seniority system. In such a case, does the accommodation demand trump the seniority system?

In our view, the seniority system will prevail in the run of cases. As we interpret the statute, to show that a requested accommodation conflicts with the rules of a seniority system is ordinarily to show that the accommodation is not "reasonable." Hence such a showing will entitle an employer/defendant to summary judgment on the question — unless there is more. The plaintiff remains free to present evidence of special circumstances that make "reasonable" a seniority rule exception in the particular case. And such a showing will defeat the employer's demand for summary judgment.

I

In 1990, Robert Barnett, the plaintiff and respondent here, injured his back while working in a cargo-handling position at petitioner US Airways, Inc. He invoked seniority rights and transferred to a less physically demanding mailroom position. Under US Airways' seniority system, that position, like others, periodically became open to seniority-based employee bidding. In 1992, Barnett learned that at least two employees senior to him intended to bid for the mailroom job. He asked US Airways to accommodate his disability-imposed limitations by making an exception that would allow him to remain in the mailroom. After permitting Barnett to continue his mailroom work for five months while it considered the matter, US Airways eventually decided not to make an exception. And Barnett lost his job.

Barnett then brought this ADA suit claiming, among other things, that he was an "individual with a disability" capable of performing the essential functions of the mailroom job, that the mailroom job amounted to a "reasonable accommodation" of his disability, and that US Airways, in refusing to assign him the job, unlawfully discriminated against him. . . .

The District Court found that the undisputed facts about seniority warranted summary judgment in US Airways' favor. The Act says that an employer who fails to make "reasonable accommodations to the known physical or mental limitations of an [employee] with a disability" discriminates *"unless"* the employer "can demonstrate that the accommodation would impose an *undue hardship* on the operation of [its] business." 42 U.S.C. §12112(b)(5)(A) (emphasis added). The court said:

> The uncontroverted evidence shows that the USAir seniority system has been in place for "decades" and governs over 14,000 USAir Agents. Moreover, seniority policies such as the one at issue in this case are common to the airline industry. Given this context, it seems clear that the USAir employees were justified in relying upon the policy. As such, any significant alteration of that policy would result in undue hardship to both the company and its nondisabled employees.

An en banc panel of the United States Court of Appeals for the Ninth Circuit reversed. It said that the presence of a seniority system is merely "a factor in the undue hardship analysis." And it held that "[a] case-by-case fact intensive analysis is required to determine whether any particular reassignment would constitute an undue hardship to the employer."

US Airways petitioned for certiorari, asking us to decide whether "the [ADA] requires an employer to reassign a disabled employee to a position as a 'reasonable accommodation' even though another employee is entitled to hold the position under the employer's bona fide and established seniority system." . . .

II

In answering the question presented, we must consider the following statutory provisions. First, the ADA says that an employer may not "discriminate against a qualified individual with a disability." 42 U.S.C. §12112(a). Second, the ADA says that a "qualified" individual includes "an individual with a disability who, *with* or without *reasonable accommodation,* can perform the essential functions of" the relevant "employment position." §12111(8) (emphasis added). Third, the ADA says that "discrimination" includes an employer's *"not making reasonable accommodations* to the known physical or mental limitations of an otherwise qualified . . . employee, *unless* [the employer] can demonstrate that the accommodation would impose an *undue hardship* on the operation of [its] business." §12112(b)(5)(A) (emphasis added). Fourth, the ADA says that the term " 'reasonable accommodation' may include . . . reassignment to a vacant position." §12111(9)(B).

The parties interpret this statutory language as applied to seniority systems in radically different ways. In US Airways' view, the fact that an accommodation would violate the rules of a seniority system always shows that the accommodation is not a "reasonable" one. In Barnett's polar opposite view, a seniority system violation never shows that an accommodation sought is not a "reasonable" one. Barnett concedes that a violation of seniority rules might help to show that the accommodation will work "undue" employer "hardship," but that is a matter for an employer to demonstrate case by case. We shall initially consider the parties' main legal arguments in support of these conflicting positions.

A

US Airways' claim that a seniority system virtually always trumps a conflicting accommodation demand rests primarily upon its view of how the Act treats workplace "preferences." Insofar as a requested accommodation violates a disability-neutral workplace rule, such as a seniority rule, it grants the employee with a disability treatment that other workers could not receive. Yet the Act, US Airways says, seeks only "equal" treatment for those with disabilities. See, e.g., 42 U.S.C. § 12101(a)(9). It does not, it contends, require an employer to grant preferential treatment. Cf. H. R. Rep. No. 101-485, pt. 2, p. 66 (1990); S. Rep. No. 101-116, pp. 26-27 (1989) (employer has no "obligation to prefer *applicants* with disabilities over other *applicants*" (emphasis added)). Hence it does not require the employer to grant a request that, in violating a disability-neutral rule, would provide a preference.

While linguistically logical, this argument fails to recognize what the Act specifies, namely, that preferences will sometimes prove necessary to achieve the Act's basic equal opportunity goal. The Act requires preferences in the form of "reasonable accommodations" that are needed for those with disabilities to obtain the *same* workplace opportunities that those without disabilities automatically enjoy. By definition any special "accommodation" requires the employer to treat an employee with a disability differently, *i.e.*, preferentially. And the fact that the difference in treatment violates an employer's disability-neutral rule cannot by itself place the accommodation beyond the Act's potential reach.

Were that not so, the "reasonable accommodation" provision could not accomplish its intended objective. Neutral office assignment rules would automatically prevent the accommodation of an employee whose disability-imposed limitations require him to work on the ground floor. Neutral "break-from-work" rules would automatically prevent the accommodation of an individual who needs additional breaks from work, perhaps to permit medical visits. Neutral furniture budget rules would automatically prevent the accommodation of an individual who needs a different kind of chair or desk. Many employers will have neutral rules governing the kinds of actions most needed to reasonably accommodate a worker with a disability. See 42 U.S.C. § 12111(9)(b) (setting forth examples such as "job restructuring," "part-time or modified work schedules," "acquisition or modification of equipment or devices," "and other similar accommodations"). Yet Congress, while providing such examples, said nothing suggesting that the presence of such neutral rules would create an automatic exemption. . . .

In sum, the nature of the "reasonable accommodation" requirement, the statutory examples, and the Act's silence about the exempting effect of neutral rules together convince us that the Act does not create any such automatic exemption. The simple fact that an accommodation would provide a "preference" — in the sense that it would permit the worker with a disability to violate a rule that others must obey — cannot, *in and of itself,* automatically show that the accommodation is not "reasonable." As a result, we reject the position taken by US Airways and Justice Scalia to the contrary. . . .

B

Barnett argues that the statutory words "reasonable accommodation" mean only "effective accommodation," authorizing a court to consider the requested accommodation's ability to meet an individual's disability-related needs, and nothing more. On this view, a seniority rule violation, having nothing to do with the accommodation's effectiveness, has nothing to do with its "reasonableness." It might, at most, help to prove an "undue hardship on the operation of the business." . . . Barnett adds that any other view would make the words "reasonable accommodation" and "undue hardship" virtual mirror images — creating redundancy in the statute. And he says that any such other view would create a practical burden of proof dilemma.

The practical burden of proof dilemma arises, Barnett argues, because the statute imposes the burden of demonstrating an "undue hardship" upon the employer, while the burden of proving "reasonable accommodation" remains with the plaintiff, here the employee. This allocation seems sensible in that an employer can more frequently and easily prove the presence of business hardship than an employee can prove its absence. But suppose that an employee must counter a claim of "seniority rule violation" in order to prove that an "accommodation" request is "reasonable." Would that not force the employee to prove what is in effect an absence, *i.e.,* an absence of hardship, despite the statute's insistence that the employer "demonstrate" hardship's presence?

These arguments do not persuade us that Barnett's legal interpretation of "reasonable" is correct. For one thing, in ordinary English the word "reasonable" does not mean "effective." It is the word "accommodation," not the word "reasonable," that conveys the need for effectiveness. An *ineffective* "modification" or "adjustment" will not *accommodate* a disabled individual's limitations. Nor does an ordinary English meaning of the term "reasonable accommodation" make of it a simple, redundant mirror image of the term "undue hardship." The statute refers to an "undue hardship on the operation of the business." 42 U.S.C. § 12112 (b)(5)(A). Yet a demand for an effective accommodation could prove unreasonable because of its impact, not on business operations, but on fellow employees — say because it will lead to dismissals, relocations, or modification of employee benefits to which an employer, looking at the matter from the perspective of the business itself, may be relatively indifferent.

Neither does the statute's primary purpose require Barnett's special reading. The statute seeks to diminish or to eliminate the stereotypical thought processes, the thoughtless actions, and the hostile reactions that far too often bar those with disabilities from participating fully in the Nation's life, including the workplace. See generally §§ 12101(a) and (b). These objectives demand unprejudiced thought and reasonable responsive reaction on the part of employers and fellow workers alike. They will sometimes require affirmative conduct to promote entry of disabled people into the workforce. They do not, however, demand action beyond the realm of the reasonable. . . .

Finally, an ordinary language interpretation of the word "reasonable" does not create the "burden of proof" dilemma to which Barnett points. Many of the lower courts, while rejecting both US Airways' and Barnett's more absolute views, have reconciled the phrases "reasonable accommodation" and "undue hardship" in a practical way.

They have held that a plaintiff/employee (to defeat a defendant/employer's motion for summary judgment) need only show that an "accommodation" seems reasonable on its face, *i.e.*, ordinarily or in the run of cases. See, *e.g.*, *Reed v. LePage Bakeries, Inc.*, 244 F.3d 254, 259 (CA1 2001) (plaintiff meets burden on reasonableness by showing that, "at least on the face of things," the accommodation will be feasible for the employer); *Borkowski v. Valley Central School Dist.*, 63 F.3d 131, 138 (CA2 1995) (plaintiff satisfies "burden of production" by showing "plausible accommodation"); *Barth v. Gelb*, 2 F.3d 1180, 1187 (CADC 1993) (interpreting parallel language in Rehabilitation Act, stating that plaintiff need only show he seeks a *"method of accommodation* that is reasonable in the run of cases") (emphasis in original).

Once the plaintiff has made this showing, the defendant/employer then must show special (typically case-specific) circumstances that demonstrate undue hardship in the particular circumstances. See *Reed* ("'undue hardship inquiry focuses on the hardships imposed . . . in the context of the particular [employer's] operations'") (quoting *Barth*); *Borkowski* (after plaintiff makes initial showing, burden falls on employer to show that particular accommodation "would cause it to suffer an undue hardship"); *Barth* ("undue hardship inquiry focuses on the hardships imposed . . . in the context of the particular agency's operations").

Not every court has used the same language, but their results are functionally similar. In our opinion, that practical view of the statute, applied consistently with ordinary summary judgment principles, see Fed. Rule Civ. Proc. 56, avoids Barnett's burden of proof dilemma, while reconciling the two statutory phrases ("reasonable accommodation" and "undue hardship").

III

The question in the present case focuses on the relationship between seniority systems and the plaintiff's need to show that an "accommodation" seems reasonable on its face, *i.e.*, ordinarily or in the run of cases. We must assume that the plaintiff, an employee, is an "individual with a disability." He has requested assignment to a mailroom position as a "reasonable accommodation." We also assume that normally such a request would be reasonable within the meaning of the statute, were it not for one circumstance, namely, that the assignment would violate the rules of a seniority system. See §12111(9) ("reasonable accommodation" may include "reassignment to a vacant position"). Does that circumstance mean that the proposed accommodation is not a "reasonable" one?

In our view, the answer to this question ordinarily is "yes." The statute does not require proof on a case-by-case basis that a seniority system should prevail. That is because it would not be reasonable in the run of cases that the assignment in question trump the rules of a seniority system. To the contrary, it will ordinarily be unreasonable for the assignment to prevail.

A

Several factors support our conclusion that a proposed accommodation will not be reasonable in the run of cases. Analogous case law supports this conclusion, for it has recognized the importance of seniority to employee-management relations. [The Court cited numerous decisions issued under Title VII, the Rehabilitation Act, and the ADA holding that seniority systems found in collective bargaining agreements trump requested accommodations. It then noted that disadvantages posed by violating seniority systems did not belong to collectively bargained systems alone.]

For one thing, the typical seniority system provides important employee benefits by creating, and fulfilling, employee expectations of fair, uniform treatment. These benefits include "job security and an opportunity for steady and predictable advancement based on objective standards." They include "an element of due process," limiting "unfairness in personnel decisions." And they consequently encourage employees to invest in the employing company, accepting "less than their value to the firm early in their careers" in return for greater benefits in later years.

Most important for present purposes, to require the typical employer to show more than the existence of a seniority system might well undermine the employees' expectations of consistent, uniform treatment — expectations upon which the seniority system's benefits depend. That is because such a rule would substitute a complex case-specific "accommodation" decision made by management for the more uniform, impersonal operation of seniority rules. Such management decision making, with its inevitable discretionary elements, would involve a matter of the greatest importance to employees, namely, layoffs; it would take place outside, as well as inside, the confines of a court case; and it might well take place fairly often. Cf. ADA, 42 U.S.C. §12101(a)(1), (estimating that some 43 million Americans suffer from physical or mental disabilities). We can find nothing in the statute that suggests Congress intended to undermine seniority systems in this way. And we consequently conclude that the employer's showing of violation of the rules of a seniority system is by itself ordinarily sufficient.

B

The plaintiff (here the employee) nonetheless remains free to show that special circumstances warrant a finding that, despite the presence of a seniority system (which the ADA may not trump in the run of cases), the requested "accommodation" is "reasonable" on the particular facts. That is because special circumstances might alter the important expectations described above. The plaintiff might show, for example, that the employer, having retained the right to change the seniority system unilaterally, exercises that right fairly frequently, reducing employee expectations that the system will be followed — to the point where one more departure, needed to accommodate an individual with a disability, will not likely make a difference. The plaintiff might show that the system already contains exceptions such that, in the circumstances, one further exception is unlikely to matter. We do not mean these examples to exhaust the kinds of showings that a plaintiff might make. But we do mean to say that the plaintiff must bear the burden of showing special circumstances that make an exception from the seniority system reasonable in the particular case. And to do so, the plaintiff must explain why, in the particular case, an exception to the employer's seniority policy can constitute a "reasonable accommodation" even though in the ordinary case it cannot.

IV

In its question presented, US Airways asked us whether the ADA requires an employer to assign a disabled employee to a particular position even though another employee is entitled to that position under the employer's "established seniority system." We answer that *ordinarily* the ADA does not require that assignment. Hence, a showing that the assignment would violate the rules of a seniority system warrants summary judgment for the employer — unless there is more. The plaintiff must present evidence of that "more," namely, special circumstances surrounding the particular case that demonstrate the assignment is nonetheless reasonable. . . .

[Justice O'CONNOR's concurring opinion omitted].

Justice SCALIA, with whom Justice THOMAS joins, dissenting.

The principal defect of today's opinion . . . goes well beyond the uncertainty it produces regarding the relationship between the ADA and the infinite variety of seniority systems. The conclusion that any seniority system can ever be overridden is merely one consequence of a mistaken interpretation of the ADA that makes all employment rules and practices — even those which (like a seniority system) pose no *distinctive* obstacle to the disabled — subject to suspension when that is (in a court's view) a "reasonable" means of enabling a disabled employee to keep his job. That is a far cry from what I believe the accommodation provision of the ADA requires: the suspension (within reason) of those employment rules and practices *that the employee's disability prevents him from observing.*

I

The Court begins its analysis by describing the ADA as declaring that an employer may not "discriminate against a qualified individual with a disability." In fact the Act says more: an employer may not "discriminate against a qualified individual with a disability *because of the disability* of such individual." 42 U.S.C. § 12112(a) (1994 ed.) (emphasis added). It further provides that discrimination includes "not making reasonable accommodations *to the known physical or mental limitations* of an otherwise qualified individual with a disability." § 12112(b)(5)(A) (emphasis added).

Read together, these provisions order employers to modify or remove (within reason) policies and practices that burden a disabled person "because of [his] disability." In other words, the ADA eliminates workplace barriers only if a disability prevents an employee from overcoming them — those barriers that would not be barriers *but for* the employee's disability. These include, for example, work stations that cannot accept the employee's wheelchair, or an assembly-line practice that requires long periods of standing. But they do not include rules and practices that bear no more heavily upon the disabled employee than upon others — even though an exemption from such a rule or practice might in a sense "make up for" the employee's disability. It is not a required accommodation, for example, to pay a disabled employee more than others at his grade level — even if that increment is earmarked for massage or physical therapy that would enable the employee to work with as little physical discomfort as his co-workers. That would be "accommodating" the disabled employee, but it would not be "making . . . accommodation *to the known physical or mental limitations*" of the employee, § 12112(b)(5)(A), because it would not eliminate any workplace practice that constitutes an obstacle because of his disability.

So also with exemption from a seniority system, which burdens the disabled and non-disabled alike. In particular cases, seniority rules may have a harsher effect upon the disabled employee than upon his co-workers. If the disabled employee is physically capable of performing only one task in the workplace, seniority rules may be, for him, the difference between employment and unemployment. But that does not make the seniority system a disability-related obstacle, any more than harsher impact upon the more needy disabled employee renders the salary system a disability-related obstacle. When one departs from this understanding, the ADA's accommodation provision becomes a standardless grab bag — leaving it to the courts to decide which workplace preferences (higher salary, longer vacations, reassignment to positions to which others are entitled) can be deemed "reasonable" to "make up for" the particular employee's disability. . . .

II

[Beyond this fundamental misunderstanding of the statute, the majority's] "rebuttable presumption does not merely give disabled employees the opportunity to unmask sham seniority systems; it gives them a vague and unspecified power (whenever they can show "special circumstances") to undercut *bona fide* systems. The Court claims that its new test will not require exceptions to seniority systems "in the run of cases," but that is belied by the disposition of this case. The Court remands to give respondent an opportunity to show that an exception to petitioner's seniority system "will not likely make a difference" to employee expectations, despite the following finding by the District Court:

> The uncontroverted evidence shows that [petitioner's] seniority system has been in place for "decades" and governs over 14,000 . . . Agents. Moreover, seniority policies such as the one at issue in this case are common to the airline industry. Given this context, it seems clear that [petitioner's] employees were justified in relying upon the policy. As such, any significant alteration of that policy would result in undue hardship to both the company and its non-disabled employees. . . .

Justice SOUTER, with whom Justice GINSBURG joins, dissenting.

"Reassignment to a vacant position," 42 U.S.C. § 12111(9) is one way an employer may "reasonably accommodate" disabled employees under the Americans with Disabilities Act of 1990.

Nothing in the ADA insulates seniority rules from the "reasonable accommodation" requirement, in marked contrast to Title VII of the Civil Rights Act of 1964 and the Age Discrimination in Employment Act of 1967, each of which has an explicit protection for seniority.

Because a unilaterally-imposed seniority system enjoys no special protection under the ADA, a consideration of facts peculiar to this very case is needed to gauge whether Barnett has carried the burden of showing his proposed accommodation to be a "reasonable" one despite the policy in force at US Airways. . . .

He held the mailroom job for two years before learning that employees with greater seniority planned to bid for the position, given US Airways' decision to declare the job "vacant." Thus, perhaps unlike ADA claimants who request accommodation through reassignment, Barnett was seeking not a change but a continuation of the status quo. All he asked was that US Airways refrain from declaring the position "vacant"; he did not ask to bump any other employee and no one would have lost a job on his account. There was no evidence in the District Court of any unmanageable ripple effects from Barnett's request, or showing that he would have overstepped an inordinate number of seniority levels by remaining where he was.

In fact, it is hard to see the seniority scheme here as any match for Barnett's ADA requests, since US Airways apparently took pains to ensure that its seniority rules raised no great expectations. . . .

With US Airways itself insisting that its seniority system was noncontractual and modifiable at will, there is no reason to think that Barnett's accommodation would have resulted in anything more than minimal disruption to US Airways' operations, if that. Barnett has shown his requested accommodation to be "reasonable," and the burden ought to shift to US Airways if it wishes to claim that, in spite of surface appearances, violation of the seniority scheme would have worked an undue hardship. I would therefore affirm the Ninth Circuit.

NOTES

1. *Is There a Vacancy?* US Air contended that a position that would be allocated under a seniority system's bumping or bidding provisions was not a "vacancy" within the meaning of the statute. The majority rejected that argument out of hand. But notice the predicate of the argument — an accommodation can't require bumping of a co-worker out of a position he or she already holds. *Barnett* strongly implies that is correct, and that may be true regardless of whether there is a seniority system.

2. *Enforceability.* A seniority system contained in a collective bargaining agreement is contractually enforceable. The lower courts, including the Ninth Circuit, had agreed that a collectively bargained for seniority system would trump a disabled employee's request for reassignment to a vacant position under the ADA. *See, e.g., Willis v. Pacific Maritime Assn.*, 244 F.3d 675 (9th Cir. 2001). But the Ninth Circuit had refused to extend the same deference to a seniority system that was not the product of collective bargaining. Was the Supreme Court correct in its assumption that a unilaterally imposed system generally confers the same advantages on workers as do those that are the result of collective bargaining?

Justice O'Connor, in her concurring opinion, was willing to accept that a unilaterally imposed system could grant such advantages *if* it were legally enforceable; thus, she would have preferred to limit the presumption in favor of seniority systems to those the employer was contractually obligated to follow. She joins the Court's opinion, however, in order to make a majority, observing that the majority's rule and her preferred one will generally reach the same result. Is she saying that if a plaintiff can demonstrate the unilaterally imposed system is not legally enforceable, then "special circumstances" will have been shown?

3. *Reasonable Accommodation as Special Treatment.* The *Barnett* Court expressly acknowledged that the ADA will sometimes require that the disabled worker receive a preference. "By definition any special 'accommodation' requires the employer to treat an employee with a disability differently, i.e., preferentially. And the fact that the difference in treatment violates an employer's disability-neutral rule cannot by itself place the accommodation beyond the Act's potential reach." 535 U.S. at 397. The majority's conclusion that the duty of reasonable accommodation can require preferential treatment was foreshadowed by its opinion in *Board of Trustees of Univ. of Ala. v. Garrett*, 531 U.S. 356 (2001), in which the Court viewed the ADA's accommodation mandate as going beyond that demanded by the constitution. Is Justice Scalia's dissent in *Barnett* consistent with the Court's position (which he joined) in *Garrett*?

Although *Barnett* arose and was decided in the context of a seniority system dispute, the issue raised by the case in fact is much broader. Consider the following:

HUBER v. WAL-MART
486 F.3d 480 (8th Cir.), *cert. dismissed*, 2008 U.S. LEXIS 1095 (2008)

RILEY, Circuit Judge.

We are faced with an unanswered question: whether an employer who has an established policy to fill vacant job positions with the most qualified applicant is required to reassign a qualified disabled employee to a vacant position, although the disabled employee is not the most qualified applicant for the position. . . .

I. BACKGROUND

Huber worked for Wal-Mart as a dry grocery order filler earning $13.00 per hour, including a $0.50 shift differential. While working for Wal-Mart, Huber sustained a permanent injury to her right arm and hand. As a result, she could no longer perform the essential functions of the order filler job. The parties stipulated Huber's injury is a disability under the ADA.

Because of her disability, Huber sought, as a reasonable accommodation, reassignment to a router position, which the parties stipulated was a vacant and equivalent position under the ADA. Wal-Mart, however, did not agree to reassign Huber automatically to the router position. Instead, pursuant to its policy of hiring the most qualified applicant for the position, Wal-Mart required Huber to apply and compete for the router position with other applicants. Ultimately, Wal-Mart filled the job with a non-disabled applicant and denied Huber the router position. Wal-Mart indicated, although Huber was qualified with or without an accommodation to perform the duties of the router position, she was not the most qualified candidate. The parties stipulated the individual hired for the router position was the most qualified candidate.

Wal-Mart later placed Huber at another facility in a maintenance associate position (janitorial position), which paid $6.20 per hour. Huber continues to work in that position and now earns $7.97 per hour. . . .

II. DISCUSSION. . . .

Here, the parties do not dispute Huber (1) has a disability under the ADA, (2) suffered an adverse employment action, or (3) possessed the requisite skills for the router position. The parties' only dispute is whether the ADA requires an employer, as a reasonable accommodation, to give a current disabled employee preference in filling a vacant position when the employee is able to perform the job duties, but is not the most qualified candidate. . . .

Huber contends Wal-Mart, as a reasonable accommodation, should have automatically reassigned her to the vacant router position without requiring her to compete with other applicants for that position. Wal-Mart disagrees, citing its non-discriminatory policy to hire the most qualified applicant. Wal-Mart argues that, under the ADA, Huber was not entitled to be reassigned automatically to the router position without first competing with other applicants. This is a question of first impression in our circuit. As the district court noted, other circuits differ with respect to the meaning of the reassignment language under the ADA.

The Tenth Circuit in *Smith v. Midland Brake, Inc.*, 180 F.3d 1154, 1164-65 (10th Cir. 1999) (en banc), stated:

> [I]f the reassignment language merely requires employers to consider on an equal basis with all other applicants an otherwise qualified existing employee with a disability for reassignment to a vacant position, that language would add nothing to the obligation not to discriminate, and would thereby be redundant. . . .
>
> Thus, the reassignment obligation must mean something more than merely allowing a disabled person to compete equally with the rest of the world for a vacant position.

In the Tenth Circuit, reassignment under the ADA results in automatically awarding a position to a qualified disabled employee regardless whether other better qualified applicants are available, and despite an employer's policy to hire the best applicant.[2]

On the other hand, the Seventh Circuit in *EEOC v. Humiston-Keeling, Inc.*, 227 F.3d 1024, 1027-28 (7th Cir. 2000), explained:

> The reassignment provision makes clear that the employer must also consider the feasibility of assigning the worker to a different job in which his disability will not be an impediment to full performance, and if the reassignment is feasible and does not require the employer to turn away a superior applicant, the reassignment is mandatory.

In the Seventh Circuit, ADA reassignment does not require an employer to reassign a qualified disabled employee to a job for which there is a more qualified applicant, if the employer has a policy to hire the most qualified applicant.

Wal-Mart urges this court to adopt the Seventh Circuit's approach and to conclude (1) Huber was not entitled, as a reasonable accommodation, to be reassigned automatically to the router position, and (2) the ADA only requires Wal-Mart to allow Huber to compete for the job, but does not require Wal-Mart to turn away a superior applicant. We find this approach persuasive and in accordance with the purposes of the ADA. As the Seventh Circuit noted in *Humiston-Keeling*:

> The contrary rule would convert a nondiscrimination statute into a mandatory preference statute, a result which would be both inconsistent with the nondiscriminatory aims of the ADA and an unreasonable imposition on the employers and coworkers of disabled employees. A policy of giving the job to the best applicant is legitimate and nondiscriminatory. Decisions on the merits are not discriminatory.

(Internal quotation omitted.) "[T]he [ADA] is not a mandatory preference act." Id.

We agree and conclude the ADA is not an affirmative action statute[3] and does not require an employer to reassign a qualified disabled employee to a vacant position when such a reassignment would violate a legitimate nondiscriminatory policy of the employer to hire the most qualified candidate. This conclusion is bolstered by the Supreme Court's decision in *US Airways, Inc. v. Barnett* [reproduced at p. 540], holding that an employer ordinarily is not required to give a disabled employee a higher seniority status to enable the disabled employee to retain his or her job when another qualified employee invokes an entitlement to that position conferred by the employer's seniority system. We previously have stated in dicta that "an employer is not required to make accommodations that would subvert other, more qualified applicants for the job." *Kellogg v. Union Pac. R.R. Co.*, 233 F.3d 1083, 1089 (8th Cir. 2000) (per curiam).

---

2. Contrary to Huber's assertion, *Aka v. Washington Hospital Center*, 156 F.3d 1284 (D.C. Cir. 1998), does not hold the ADA requires an employer to place a disabled employee in a position while passing over more qualified applicants. Rather, *Aka* only rejects an "interpretation of the reassignment provision as mandating nothing more than that the employer allow the disabled employee to submit his application along with all of the other candidates."

3. See *Turco v. Hoechst Celanese Corp.*, 101 F.3d 1090, 1094 (5th Cir. 1996) ("The [ADA] does not require affirmative action in favor of individuals with disabilities. It merely prohibits employment discrimination against qualified individuals with disabilities, no more and no less.").

3

Thus, the ADA does not require Wal-Mart to turn away a superior applicant for the router position in order to give the position to Huber. To conclude otherwise is "affirmative action with a vengeance. That is giving a job to someone solely on the basis of his status as a member of a statutorily protected group." *Humiston-Keeling.*

Here, Wal-Mart did not violate its duty, under the ADA, to provide a reasonable accommodation to Huber. Wal-Mart reasonably accommodated Huber's disability by placing Huber in a maintenance associate position. The maintenance position may not have been a perfect substitute job, or the employee's most preferred alternative job, but an employer is not required to provide a disabled employee with an accommodation that is ideal from the employee's perspective, only an accommodation that is reasonable. See *Cravens v. Blue Cross & Blue Shield of Kan. City,* 214 F.3d 1011, 1019 (8th Cir. 2000). In assigning the vacant router position to the most qualified applicant, Wal-Mart did not discriminate against Huber. On the contrary, Huber was treated exactly as all other candidates were treated for the Wal-Mart job opening, no worse and no better.

NOTES

1. *Special Treatment and Affirmative Action.* The Eighth Circuit asserts the ADA is not an affirmative action statute, and it relies on *Barnett* in so holding. But *Barnett,* as noted above, flatly states that the statute *will* sometimes require preferential treatment and that observation of a neutral rule will not always satisfy the statute. The District Court in *Huber* had relied in part on *Barnett* in granting summary judgment to the plaintiff. *See also Holly v. Clairson,* 492 F.3d 1247 (11th Cir. 2007) (employer cannot avoid ADA liability by claiming it treated the disabled employee the same as nondisabled workers). But acknowledging, as *Barnett* does, that special treatment will sometimes be required, how far does the preferential treatment requirement extend?

Certainly, an employer could not point to a neutral rule prohibiting reassignment of employees as a successful defense to a claim that a disabled employee had been denied reassignment. What do you think the Eighth Circuit would have said if the employer's neutral rule were one allocating job openings by date of birth rather than by qualifications? Would it still have held Huber was not entitled to any "special treatment"? *Shapiro v. Township of Lakewood,* 292 F.3d 356 (3d Cir. 2002), in the wake of *Barnett,* overturned a district court's grant of summary judgment in favor of the employer in a failure to reassign case. The trial court reasoned that the disabled worker's failure to follow interdepartmental transfer procedures when seeking reassignment to a vacant position precluded his claim. The Third Circuit held this result could not be squared with *Barnett.*

How does a neutral rule of filling vacancies with the best qualified applicant compare to a seniority system? Do the attributes of a seniority system, particularly the reliance interests of other workers, make it *sui generis* when it comes to special treatment of disabled workers? But shouldn't workers be entitled to rely on an employer's assurances that it will pick the most qualified applicant?

2. *Best Qualified.* In *Huber,* we don't know whether Huber was less qualified than the person awarded the job because of the effects of her disability or for some other reason. Should that matter? *See* Cheryl L. Anderson, *"Neutral" Employer Policies*

and the ADA: *The Implications of* U.S. Airways Inc. v. Barnett *Beyond Seniority Systems,* 51 DRAKE L. REV. 1 (2002); Stephen F. Befort, *Reasonable Accommodation and Reassignment Under the Americans with Disabilities Act: Answers, Questions and Suggested Solutions After* U.S. Airways, Inc. v. Barnett, 45 ARIZ. L. REV. 931, 979-81 (2003); *Cf.* Alex B. Long, *The ADA's Reasonable Accommodation Requirement and "Innocent Third Parties,"* 68 MO. L. REV. 863, 905 (2003).

VANDE ZANDE V. STATE OF WISCONSIN
DEPARTMENT OF ADMINISTRATION
44 F.3d 538 (7th Cir. 1995)

POSNER, Chief Judge.

In 1990, Congress passed the Americans with Disabilities Act. The stated purpose is "to provide a clear and comprehensive national mandate for the elimination of discrimination against individuals with disabilities." . . . [Many] impairments are not in fact disabling but are believed to be so, and the people having them may be denied employment or otherwise shunned as a consequence. Such people, objectively capable of performing as well as the unimpaired, are analogous to capable workers discriminated against because of their skin color or some other vocationally irrelevant characteristic.

The more problematic case is that of an individual who has a vocationally relevant disability — an impairment such as blindness or paralysis that limits a major human capability, such as seeing or walking. In the common case in which such an impairment interferes with the individual's ability to perform up to the standards of the workplace, or increases the cost of employing him, hiring and firing decisions based on the impairment are not "discriminatory" in a sense closely analogous to employment discrimination on racial grounds. The draftsmen of the Act knew this. But they were unwilling to confine the concept of disability discrimination to cases in which the disability is irrelevant to the performance of the disabled person's job. Instead, they defined "discrimination" to include an employer's "not making reasonable accommodations to the known physical or mental limitations of an otherwise qualified individual with a disability who is an applicant or employee, unless . . . [the employer] can demonstrate that the accommodation would impose an undue hardship on the operation of the . . . [employer's] business." . . .

Lori Vande Zande, aged 35, is paralyzed from the waist down as a result of a tumor of the spinal cord. Her paralysis makes her prone to develop pressure ulcers, treatment of which often requires that she stay at home for several weeks. The defendants and the amici curiae argue that there is no duty of reasonable accommodation of pressure ulcers because they do not fit the statutory definition of a disability. Intermittent, episodic impairments are not disabilities, the standard example being a broken leg. 29 C.F.R. pt. 1630 app., § 1630.2(j). But an intermittent impairment that is a characteristic manifestation of an admitted disability is, we believe, a part of the underlying disability and hence a condition that the employer must reasonably accommodate. Often the disabling aspect of a disability is, precisely, an intermittent manifestation of the disability, rather than the underlying impairment. The AIDS virus progressively destroys the infected person's immune system. The consequence is a series of opportunistic diseases which . . . often prevent the individual from working. If they are not part of the disability, then people with AIDS do not have a disability, which seems to us a very odd interpretation of the law, and one expressly rejected in the regulations. We hold that Vande Zande's pressure ulcers are a part of her disability, and therefore a part of what the State of Wisconsin had a duty to accommodate — reasonably.

Vande Zande worked for the housing division of the state's department of administration for three years, beginning in January 1990. . . . Her job was that of a program assistant, and involved preparing public information materials, planning meetings, interpreting regulations, typing, mailing, filing, and copying. In short, her tasks were of a clerical, secretarial, and administrative assistant character. In order to enable her to do this work, the defendants, as she acknowledges, "made numerous accommodations relating to the plaintiff's disability." As examples, in her words, "they paid the landlord to have bathrooms modified and to have a step ramped; they bought special adjustable furniture for the plaintiff; they ordered and paid for one-half of the cost of a cot that the plaintiff needed for daily personal care at work; they sometimes adjusted the plaintiff's schedule to perform backup telephone duties to accommodate the plaintiff's medical appointments; they made changes to the plans for a locker room in the new state office building; and they agreed to provide some of the specific accommodations the plaintiff requested in her October 5, 1992 Reasonable Accommodation Request."

But she complains that the defendants did not go far enough in two principal respects. One concerns a period of eight weeks when a bout of pressure ulcers forced her to stay home. She wanted to work full time at home and believed that she would be able to do so if the division would provide her with a desktop computer at home (though she already had a laptop). Her supervisor refused. . . . [S]he was able to work all but 16.5 hours in the eight-week period. She took 16.5 hours of sick leave to make up the difference. As a result, she incurred no loss of income, but did lose sick leave that she could have carried forward indefinitely. She now works for another agency of the State of Wisconsin, but any unused sick leave in her employment by the housing division would have accompanied her to her new job. Restoration of the 16.5 hours of lost sick leave is one form of relief that she seeks in this suit.

She argues that a jury might have found that a reasonable accommodation required the housing division either to give her the desktop computer or to excuse her from having to dig into her sick leave to get paid for the hours in which, in the absence of the computer, she was unable to do her work at home. No jury, however, could in our view be permitted to stretch the concept of "reasonable accommodation" so far. Most jobs in organizations public or private involve team work under supervision rather than solitary unsupervised work, and team work under supervision generally cannot be performed at home without a substantial reduction in the quality of the employee's performance. This will no doubt change as communications technology advances, but is the situation today. Generally, therefore, an employer is not required to accommodate a disability by allowing the disabled worker to work, by himself, without supervision, at home. This is the majority view, illustrated by *Tyndall v. National Education Centers, Inc.*, 31 F.3d 209, 213-14 (4th Cir. 1994), and *Law v. United States Postal Service*, 852 F.2d 1278 (Fed. Cir. 1988) (per curiam). The District of Columbia Circuit disagrees. *Langon v. Dept. of Health & Human Services*, 959 F.2d 1053, 1060-61 (D.C. Cir. 1992); *Carr v. Reno*, 23 F.3d 525, 530 (D.C. Cir. 1994). But we think the majority view is correct. An employer is not required to allow disabled workers to work at home, where their productivity inevitably would be greatly reduced. No doubt to this as to any generalization about so complex and varied an activity as employment there are exceptions, but it would take a very extraordinary case for the employee to be able to create a triable issue of the employer's failure to allow the employee to work at home.

And if the employer, because it is a government agency and therefore is not under intense competitive pressure to minimize its labor costs or maximize the value of its output, or for some other reason, bends over backwards to accommodate a disabled worker — goes further than the law requires — by allowing the worker to work at home, it must not be punished for its generosity by being deemed to have conceded the reasonableness of so far-reaching an accommodation. That would hurt rather than help disabled workers. Wisconsin's housing division was not required by the Americans with Disabilities Act to allow Vande Zande to work at home; even more clearly it was not required to install a computer in her home so that she could avoid using up 16.5 hours of sick leave. It is conjectural that she will ever need those 16.5 hours; the expected cost of the loss must, therefore, surely be slight. An accommodation that allows a disabled worker to work at home, at full pay, subject only to a slight loss of sick leave that may never be needed, hence never missed, is, we hold, reasonable as a matter of law.

Her second complaint has to do with the kitchenettes in the housing division's building, which are for the use of employees during lunch and coffee breaks. Both the sink and the counter in each of the kitchenettes were 36 inches high, which is too high for a person in a wheelchair. The building was under construction, and the kitchenettes not yet built, when the plaintiff complained about this feature of the design. But the defendants refused to alter the design to lower the sink and counter to 34 inches, the height convenient for a person in a wheelchair. . . . [S]he argues that once she brought the problem to the attention of her supervisors, they were obliged to lower the sink and counter, at least on the floor on which her office was located but possibly on the other floors in the building as well, since she might be moved to another floor. All that the defendants were willing to do was to install a shelf 34 inches high in the kitchenette area on Vande Zande's floor. That took care of the counter problem. As for the sink, the defendants took the position that since the plumbing was already in place it would be too costly to lower the sink and that the plaintiff could use the bathroom sink, which is 34 inches high.

Apparently it would have cost only about $150 to lower the sink on Vande Zande's floor; to lower it on all the floors might have cost as much as $2,000, though possibly less. Given the proximity of the bathroom sink, Vande Zande can hardly complain that the inaccessibility of the kitchenette sink interfered with her ability to work or with her physical comfort. Her argument rather is that forcing her to use the bathroom sink for activities (such as washing out her coffee cup) for which the other employees could use the kitchenette sink stigmatized her as different and inferior; she seeks an award of compensatory damages for the resulting emotional distress. We may assume without having to decide that emotional as well as physical barriers to the integration of disabled persons into the workforce are relevant in determining the reasonableness of an accommodation. But we do not think an employer has a duty to expend even modest amounts of money to bring about an absolute identity in working conditions between disabled and nondisabled workers. The creation of such a duty would be the inevitable consequence of deeming a failure to achieve identical conditions "stigmatizing." That is merely an epithet. We conclude that access to a particular sink, when access to an equivalent sink, conveniently located, is provided, is not a legal duty of an employer. The duty of reasonable accommodation is satisfied when the employer does what is necessary to enable the disabled worker to work in reasonable comfort. . . .

NOTES

1. *The Essential Job Function Inquiry.* What would have been the result in *Vande Zande* if Wisconsin had argued convincingly that working at the office was an essential function of Vande Zande's job? Would Vande Zande no longer meet the definition of a qualified individual with a disability? See *Rehrs*, reproduced at p. 534. Remember that § 108(a) requires the individual with a disability to be able to perform the job's "essential functions" with or without reasonable accommodation in order to be "qualified." Reasonable accommodation and essential functions thus are often interrelated. Whether a function is essential or not determines whether reallocating that job function is a reasonable accommodation.

2. *Analogizing to Title VII.* Improving employment opportunities for disabled individuals required Congress to devise an antidiscrimination statute for individuals who are different from other employees in job-related ways. This problem is analogous to the problem of guaranteeing equal employment opportunities for pregnant women. Recall Title VII's approach. Pregnant women must be treated like others similar in their ability or inability to work. Title VII permits different treatment of pregnant women if pregnancy alters their ability to perform job functions; thus, Title VII does *not* require that pregnancy be accommodated to allow equal employment opportunity although we saw in *California Federal Sav. & Loan Ass'n v. Guerra*, reproduced at p. 362, that it permits at least limited accommodations. In contrast, the ADA *requires* employers to accommodate individuals with disabilities to ensure equal employment opportunity. Which approach is the better policy?

How does the duty to accommodate differ from Title VII's prohibition against employment criteria that have a disparate impact? Could Vande Zande have argued, for example, that requiring employees to work at the office has a disparate impact on individuals with disabilities or, more particularly, individuals suffering from pressure ulcers? Is working under a supervisor a business necessity? What would be the remedy for an impact claim? Would a successful disparate impact claim require the employer to allow *all* employees to work at home? *See* Christine Jolls, *Antidiscrimination and Accommodation*, 115 HARV. L. REV. 642 (2001) (analogizing Title VII's disparate impact theory to the ADA's duty to reasonably accommodate the disabled). *But see* Samuel Issacharoff & Justin Nelson, *Discrimination with a Difference: Can Employment Discrimination Law Accommodate the Americans with Disabilities Act?*, 79 N.C. L. REV. 307 (2001) (describing the ADA as very different from Title VII because of the ADA's redistributive obligation absent any discrimination simpliciter).

A number of recent articles take issue with the notion that the duty of reasonable accommodation is fundamentally different from discrimination, at least disparate impact discrimination. *See, e.g.,* Samuel R. Bagenstos, *"Rational Discrimination," Accommodation, and the Politics of (Disability) Civil Rights*, 89 VA. L. REV. 825, 828 (2003); Stewart J. Schwab & Steven L. Willborn, *Reasonable Accommodation of Workplace Disabilities*, 44 WM. & MARY L. REV. 1197, 1283-84 (2003); Seth D. Harris, *Re-thinking the Economics of Discrimination*: US Airways v. Barnett, *the ADA, and the Application of Internal Labor Markets Theory*, 89 IOWA L. REV. 123, 126-127 (2003); Michael Ashley Stein, *The Law and Economics of Disability Accommodations*, 53 DUKE L.J. 79 (2003); Michael Ashley Stein, *Same Struggle, Different Difference: ADA Accommodations as Antidiscrimination*, 153 U. PA. L. REV. 579 (2004); J. H. Verkerke, *Disaggregating Antidiscrimination and Accommodation*, 44 WM. & MARY L. REV. 1385 (2003).

3. *Forms of Reasonable Accommodation.* In addition to the accommodations mentioned in the statutory definition, the ADA Interpretive Guidance suggests other accommodations that might be relevant to assisting an individual in performing essential job functions, including "making employer provided transportation accessible and providing reserved parking spaces," permitting "an individual who is blind to use a guide dog at work," and permitting "an employee with a disability that inhibits the ability to write . . . to computerize records that were customarily maintained manually." 29 C.F.R. pt. 1630, App. § 1630.2(o).

ADA § 101(9) suggests that providing qualified readers or interpreters may be a reasonable accommodation. The Interpretive Guidance suggests additional accommodations that involve providing personal assistants such as a page turner for an employee with no hands or a travel attendant for an employee who is blind. Again, the concept of essential functions is critical: "[S]uppose a security guard position requires the individual who holds the job to inspect identification cards. An employer would not have to provide an individual who is legally blind with an assistant to look at the identification cards for the legally blind employee. In this situation the assistant would be performing the job for the individual with a disability rather than assisting the individual to perform the job." 29 C.F.R. pt. 1630, app. § 1630.2(o). These provisions do not make it clear under what circumstances providing a reader, interpreter, page turner, or travel attendant would constitute "assisting the individual [with a disability] to perform the job" rather than "performing the job for the individual."

4. *Attendance Policies and the Duty of Reasonable Accommodation.* As noted previously, courts have ruled that timely and regular attendance is an essential job function for most jobs. See Note 4 on p. 537. If attending work regularly or starting work at a particular time of day or working full-time is an essential function, the employer need not offer part-time or modified work schedules as a reasonable accommodation. But when working time is flexible, a modified work schedule will be seen as a reasonable accommodation. *See EEOC v. Convergys Mgt. Group, Inc.*, 491 F.3d 790 (8th Cir. 2007) (not allowing wheel chair-bound plaintiff a 15 minute extension on lunch and starting time violated employer's duty of reasonable accommodation). Moreover, a short-term leave of absence often will be viewed as a reasonable accommodation, particularly when the employer's own policies provide for paid or unpaid leave as great as that requested by the disabled employee. *See* Stephen F. Befort, *The Most Difficult Reasonable Accommodation Issues: Reassignment and Leave of Absence*, 37 WAKE FOREST L. REV. 439 (2002).

Eligible employees who are covered by the Family and Medical Leave Act are entitled to up to 12 weeks of unpaid leave per year for a serious health condition and may be permitted to take intermittent leave without pay in blocks as small as an hour at a time and without prior notice if the need for leave is unforeseeable. See p. 591. If the employee's absences are protected by FMLA, wouldn't providing that leave under the ADA necessarily be viewed as a reasonable accommodation? In other words, how could an employer contend that doing what federal laws requires is unreasonable?

5. *Disability-Related Misconduct.* What happens when an employee engages in misconduct that is the product of the disability? Is the employer entitled to take action based on the misconduct, or is that in essence discrimination on the basis of the disability? Alternatively, does the duty of reasonable accommodation require the employer to excuse work rule violations by disabled workers that would result in discipline if engaged in by nondisabled employees?

In *Raytheon Company v. Hernandez*, 540 U.S. 44 (2003), plaintiff was forced to resign from defendant's employ after testing positive for cocaine. Two years later, he reapplied for employment, but his application was denied. The company contended it had a policy of refusing to rehire anyone who had been terminated for violation of workplace conduct rules. The Supreme Court granted certiorari to decide whether "the ADA confers preferential rehire rights on disabled employees lawfully terminated for violation of workplace conduct rules." It did not reach that question, however. Instead, the Court ruled the Ninth Circuit had mistakenly applied disparate impact analysis to a disparate treatment claim. And it pointed out that if the employer in fact did not know about the addiction-related misconduct, it could not have intentionally discriminated on the basis of disability.

The Ninth Circuit faced the question of employee misconduct in a case arising under Washington state's disability law, but in so doing, made clear its analysis was based on the ADA.

GAMBINI v. TOTAL RENAL CARE, INC.
486 F.3d 1087 (9th Cir. 2007)

SHADUR, Senior District Judge:

... BACKGROUND

In November 2000 Gambini began working as a contracts clerk at DaVita, a company that provides dialysis to renal patients. It is undisputed that Gambini had a history of health problems that predated her employment at DaVita. After several months at DaVita she began to experience depression and anxiety, and in April 2001 she experienced an emotional breakdown at work. Gambini eventually met with a mental health provider at the community health clinic and was told that her symptoms were consistent with bipolar disorder.

Upon returning to work several days later, Gambini informed her supervisor Robin Warren ("Warren") that she was seeking medical treatment for bipolar disorder. When Warren was promoted in May 2001, DaVita replaced her with Carrie Bratlie ("Bratlie"), who became Gambini's new direct supervisor. Gambini also told Bratlie that she was suffering from bipolar disorder and requested several accommodations. In addition, Gambini told her co-workers that she was experiencing mood swings, which she was addressing with medications, and asked that they not be personally offended if she was irritable or short with them. Gambini privately divulged to Bratlie that she was seeing a therapist and struggling with some medication issues.

Gambini's bipolar symptoms grew more severe in April 2002 — she found herself increasingly irritable and easily distracted and began to have a hard time concentrating or assigning priorities as between her tasks. Gambini admitted to a fellow co-worker, who also suffered from bipolar disorder, that she was struggling to perform her job because of her symptoms. That co-worker recommended that Gambini seek treatment from psychiatric nurse practitioner Bobbie Fletcher ("Fletcher"), who confirmed Gambini's bipolar disorder based on Gambini's "short fuse," high energy, and propensity to exhibit anger and irritability.

During that period Gambini's current and former supervisors, Warren and Bratlie, convened to discuss Gambini's attitude and what they perceived as her poor job performance. Their meeting culminated in a decision to deliver a written performance improvement plan to Gambini at a later meeting that would include Bratlie, Gambini, and Gina Lovell ("Lovell"), the Supervisor of Payor Contracting. Accordingly, on July 11, 2002 Bratlie emailed Gambini, requesting that she come to Bratlie's office without indicating any specific purpose for the meeting.

Upon arriving at Bratlie's office Gambini was already agitated because she did not know the purpose of the meeting or why Lovell was in attendance. When Bratlie presented Gambini with the improvement plan, the first sentence of which stated, "[Gambini's] attitude and general disposition are no longer acceptable in the SPA department," Gambini began to cry. Reading the remainder of the document did not alleviate Gambini's symptoms — instead she found her face growing hot and felt a tightening feeling in her chest, as well as shortness of breath and shaking. When she had finished reading the performance plan, Gambini threw it across the desk and in a flourish of several profanities expressed her opinion that it was both unfair and unwarranted. Before slamming the door on her way out, Gambini hurled several choice profanities at Bratlie. There is a dispute about whether during her dramatic exit Gambini warned Lovell and Bratlie that they "will regret this," but Bratlie did observe Gambini kicking and throwing things at her cubicle after the meeting. Back at her cubicle, Gambini tried unsuccessfully to call Fletcher to tell her about how upset the meeting made her feel and about her ensuing suicidal thoughts. . . .

[Several days later], McLemore and Bratlie called Gambini on her cell phone to tell her that her employment was being terminated. Three days later Gambini sent DaVita a letter stating that her behavior during the July 11 meeting was a consequence of her bipolar disorder and asking DaVita to reconsider its decision to terminate her. When DaVita refused to reconsider, Gambini filed this action, which proceeded to trial in December 2004. [The jury returned a verdict in favor of DaVita on all claims.]

. . . INSTRUCTION AS TO CONDUCT RESULTING FROM DISABILITY

Gambini submitted and the trial court denied Prop. Instr. 26:

> Conduct resulting from a disability is part of the disability and not a separate basis for termination.

We conclude (1) that the district court abused its discretion when it declined to give that instruction and (2) that such exclusion was not harmless error.

Most significantly, the Washington Supreme Court has itself enunciated the rule embodied in that instruction. On that score *Riehl v. Foodmaker, Inc.*, 94 P.3d 930, 938 (Wash. 2004) (en banc) has stated explicitly [precisely the instruction Gambini sought].

In so doing *Riehl* drew on our own holding in *Humphrey v. Memorial Hospitals Ass'n*, 239 F.3d 1128, 1139-40 (9th Cir. 2001), which in the context of the Americans With Disabilities Act ("ADA") similarly articulated that "conduct resulting from a disability is considered part of the disability, rather than a separate basis for termination." As a practical result of that rule, where an employee demonstrates a causal link between the disability-produced conduct and the termination, a jury must be instructed that it may find that the employee was terminated on the impermissible basis of her disability.

Because of the Washington Supreme Court's express reliance on *Humphrey*, we may properly look to that decision in applying the Washington Law. Indeed, the facts in *Humphrey* are substantially analogous to Gambini's situation, and we held there that a jury could reasonably find the "requisite causal link between" the symptoms of obsessive compulsive disorder and Humphrey's inability to conform her behavior to her employer's expectations of punctuality and attendance, so that she was fired because of her disability.

. . . . Failure to have instructed the jury on that score plainly requires reversal. At trial Gambini presented evidence that DaVita signed an interrogatory response, which stated that one of the reasons it terminated Gambini was because she had "frightened her co-workers with her violent outbursts," as "documented by emails to the People Services Department." Her "violent outbursts," . . . were arguably symptomatic of her bipolar disorder. Gambini had informed her supervisors about her condition and kept them apprised of her medication issues and the various accommodations she thought might reduce the chances of an outburst at work. When her temper erupted during the July 11 meeting, Gambini was in the throes of a medication change, which heightened the volatility of the mood swings that she and her health care providers were trying to get under control.

Under all the circumstances it was surely permissible for a properly instructed jury to review the events culminating in the July 11 meeting and Gambini's eventual termination and to conclude that it was her personality and not her work product that motivated DaVita. In fact, the very first sentence of the written performance improvement plan that Bratlie presented to Gambini on July 11 stated, "[Gambini's] attitude and general disposition are no longer acceptable in the SPA department." It is undisputed that people who suffer from bipolar disorder struggle to control their moods, which may vacillate wildly from deep depressions to wild frenzies of hypomania. Hence the record is replete with examples of how Gambini's bipolar disorder manifested itself through her irritability, her "short fuse" and her sometimes erratic emotions.

Accordingly the jury was entitled to infer reasonably that her "violent outburst" on July 11 was a consequence of her bipolar disorder, which the law protects as part and parcel of her disability. In those terms, if the law fails to protect the manifestations of her disability, there is no real protection in the law because it would protect the disabled in name only. As *School Board of Nassau County, Florida v. Arline* instructs, the disability discrimination laws are necessary because Congress acknowledged that "the American people are simply unfamiliar with and insensitive to the difficulties confront[ing] individuals with handicaps." . . .

In its petition for rehearing, which has been joined by an amicus brief, DaVita argues that "[n]either the *Riehl* nor *Humphrey* Courts state or imply that arguably disabled employees are entitled to absolute protection regardless of their transgressions against the employer, let alone *more* protection than would be afforded a nondisabled employee for the same misconduct." But the law often does provide more protection for individuals with disabilities. Unlike other types of discrimination where identical treatment is the gold standard, identical treatment is often not equal treatment with respect to disability discrimination — *see, e.g., Holland v. Boeing Co,* 583 P.2d 621, 623 (Wash. 1978) (en banc) ("Identical treatment may be a source of discrimination in the case of the handicapped, whereas *different* treatment may eliminate discrimination against the handicapped and open the door to employment opportunities"). That's why the ADA and Washington Law require employers to make reasonable accommodations for disabilities.

That said, requiring Prop. Instr. 26 in no way provides employees with *absolute* protection from adverse employment actions based on disability-related conduct. Under the ADA a plaintiff must still establish that she is "an individual with a disability who, with or without reasonable accommodation, can perform the essential functions of the employment position that such individual holds or desires". Even if a plaintiff were to establish that she's qualified, under the ADA the defendant would still be entitled to raise a "business necessity" or "direct threat" defense against the discrimination claim (*see 42 U.S.C. §12113(a)-(b)*). Defendant may also raise the defense that the proposed reasonable accommodation poses an undue burden (*see id. §12111(10)*). . . .

NOTES

1. *Facially Discriminatory?* The Ninth Circuit holds that taking action based on misconduct that is a product of the underlying disability is the same as acting on the basis of the disability itself. Remember the Seventh Circuit's treatment of symptoms of a disability in *Vande Zande*, reproduced at p. 552, and the Supreme Court's treatment of the same issue in *Arline*, discussed at p. 491. Is the Ninth Circuit correct in viewing misconduct as comparable to the contagiousness in *Arline* or the pressure ulcers in *Vande Zande?*

In cases with similar facts, the Sixth and Second Circuits reached a different result from the Ninth. In *Macy v. Hopkins County*, 484 F.3d 357 (6th Cir. 2007), the court upheld summary judgment for the employer who fired a teacher for making threats and inappropriate remarks, even though the conduct was a product of a head injury. It viewed the misconduct as a legitimate, nondiscriminatory reason for termination, not disability discrimination. It noted, "this court has repeatedly stated that an employer may legitimately fire an employee for conduct, even conduct that occurs as a result of a disability, if that conduct disqualifies the employee from his or her job." *See also Sista v. CDC Ixis North America, Inc.*, 445 F. 3d 161 (2d Cir. 2006) (making threats is a legitimate, nondiscriminatory reason for termination, even if the threats were caused by disability). Which is the better view of the statute?

2. *Reasonable Accommodation and Employee Misconduct.* In its Enforcement Guidance on Reasonable Accommodation, the EEOC takes the position that an employer never need excuse employee misconduct, even when it is the product of a disability, so long as the conduct rule is job related for the position in question and consistent with business necessity and it would impose the same discipline on a nondisabled worker. Which is the better rule: the EEOC's or the Ninth Circuit's?

Or are the two positions that far apart? After all, the Ninth Circuit recognized the employer would be entitled to rely on a business necessity defense. Wouldn't it be a business necessity in almost every workplace for an employee to refrain from the conduct Gambini engaged in? And is the EEOC, through its Guidance, insisting that, if misconduct is caused by a disability, then it will be the employer's burden to justify the conduct rule, even if it is a conduct rule applied uniformly? Perhaps the problem is that an occasional outburst might be tolerated by workers whom the employer did not view as suffering from a condition that would make them recur. *See generally* Kelly Cahill Timmons, *Accommodating Misconduct under the Americans with Disabilities Act*, 57 FLA. L. REV. 187 (2005) ("Courts should not assume that plaintiffs who engaged in misconduct cannot prove disparate treatment. . . . Rather, courts should scrutinize the record for evidence of pretext, keeping in mind that employers may view misconduct committed by employees with mental disabilities more severely because of the stigma and stereotypes associated with such disabilities"). *See also* Deirdre M. Smith,

The Paradox of Personality: Mental Illness, Employment Discrimination and the Americans with Disabilities Act, 17 GEO. MASON U. CIV. RTS. L.J. 79 (2006) (exploring the leeway the courts have accorded employers dealing with "difficult" or "unpleasant" employees whose conduct can be traced to "personality disoders" or more serious mental conditions); Elizabeth F. Emens, *The Sympathetic Discriminator: Mental Illness, Hedonic Costs and the ADA*, 94 Geo. L.J. 399 (2006) (understanding emotional contagion and hedonic costs is important for deciding claims brought by plaintiffs with mental illness).

3. *Essential Job Functions.* Alternatively, some courts have reasoned that individuals who pose a threat of violence to others are not "otherwise qualified" individuals. *See Williams v. Motorola, Inc.*, 303 F.3d 1284, 1290-91 (11th Cir. 2002) (employee's "inability to work with others . . . insubordination, and threats of violence" rendered her not "otherwise qualified" within the meaning of the ADA); *Palmer v. Circuit Court of Cook County*, 117 F.3d 351(7th Cir. 1997) (employee's threats of physical violence rendered her not "otherwise qualified" under the ADA). Or should that approach work only if the employer establishes the employee is a "direct threat"? See Section D1, p. 567, for discussion of the direct threat defense.

NOTE ON ACCOMMODATIONS NECESSARY TO ENJOY BENEFITS AND PRIVILEGES OF EMPLOYMENT

Beyond accommodations enabling employees to perform essential functions is the question of accommodations enabling disabled employees "to enjoy equal benefits and privileges of employment as are enjoyed by employees without disabilities." 29 C.F.R. pt. 1630, App. §1630.2(o). This includes, for example, accommodations designed to permit equal access to cafeterias, lounges, and restrooms. Is an individual with a disability entitled to access to all unrestricted areas of the employer's business, even areas that relate neither to essential functions nor to specific job benefits? Is it a "privilege of employment" to have access to all unrestricted areas? What if a deaf employee requests an interpreter at workplace social events? Should he be entitled to this accommodation?

Vande Zande discussed the degree of equality of access to benefits required by the ADA. While acknowledging that emotional barriers to equal employment of disabled individuals are relevant to determining the reasonableness of an accommodation, the court ruled that the employer need not spend "even modest amounts of money to bring about an absolute identity in working conditions." Why not?

Cases involving accommodations relating to the privileges and benefits of employment may also raise questions about the distinction between personal and work-related accommodations. Consider the EEOC's Interpretive Guidance:

> The obligation to make reasonable accommodation . . . does not extend to the provision of adjustments or modifications that are primarily for the personal benefit of the individual with a disability. Thus, if an adjustment or modification is job-related, e.g., specifically assists the individual in performing the duties of a particular job, it will be considered a type of reasonable accommodation. On the other hand, if an adjustment or modification assists the individual throughout his or her daily activities, on and off the job, it will be considered a personal item that the employer is not required to provide. Accordingly, an employer would generally not be required to provide an employee with a disability with a prosthetic limb, wheelchair, or eyeglasses.

29 C.F.R. pt. 1630, app. § 1630.9. *See Nelson v. Ryan*, 860 F. Supp. 76 (W.D.N.Y. 1994) (while an employer may be required to permit a blind employee to use a guide dog at work, an employer is not required to provide a guide dog or paid leave to train a guide dog because guide dogs are personal items even if the employee uses the dog for work purposes). *See generally* Samuel R. Bagenstos, *The Future of Disability Law* 114 YALE L.J. 1, 3-4 (2004) (increasing employment of the disabled requires "more than simply mandating that individual employers cease discriminating and provide accommodations; they require more direct and sustained government interventions such as the public funding and provision of benefits").

In Lyons v. Legal Aid Socy., 68 F.3d 1512 (2d Cir. 1995), a disabled attorney sought financial assistance to park her car near her office because injuries limited her mobility. Legal Aid, in defending its refusal to pay for parking, argued that the requested accommodation was merely "a matter of personal convenience" and therefore not within its obligation to provide accommodation. The Second Circuit ruled that a parking place was a work-related need, not merely a personal need. Lyons could not do her job without parking near the office, reaching the office and the courts was an essential function of her job, and there was no evidence on the record that she planned to use the space for any other purpose. *Id.* at 1517. *See also Wood v. Crown Redi-Mix*, 339 F.3d 682, 687 (8th Cir. 2003) (substantial limitation on ability to procreate did not trigger duty to accommodate. "There must be a causal connection between the major life activity that is limited and the accommodation sought"). *See generally* Kelly Cahill Timmons, *Limiting "Limitations": The Scope of the Duty of Reasonable Accommodation under the Americans with Disabilities Act*, 57 S.C. L. REV. 313 (2005). Was Vande Zande's request for accessible kitchen sinks a request for a personal benefit or was it job related?

NOTE ON KNOWING THAT ACCOMMODATION IS NEEDED

The ADA provides that employers must make "reasonable accommodations to the *known* physical and mental limitations of an otherwise qualified individual with a disability. . . ." ADA § 102(b)(5)(A) (emphasis added). The Interpretive Guidance provides:

> Employers are obligated to make reasonable accommodation only to the physical or mental limitations resulting from the disability of a qualified individual with a disability that is known to the employer. . . . If an employee with a known disability is having difficulty performing his or her job, an employer may inquire whether the employee is in need of a reasonable accommodation. In general, however, it is the responsibility of the individual with a disability to inform the employer that an accommodation is needed.

29 C.F.R. pt. 1630, app. § 1630.9. What if the employer is aware of the disability but not of the need for accommodation? Does the ADA require or merely *permit* an employer to ask an employee with a disability if he needs accommodation? Or must the employee specifically request accommodation? *See EEOC v. Convergys Customer Management Group, Inc.*, 491 F.3d 790 (8th Cir. 2007) (wheelchair-bound employee not required to request specific accommodations to trigger employer duty). *See generally* EEOC Enforcement Guidance: Reasonable Accommodation and Undue Hardship Under the Americans with Disabilities Act (October 17, 2002), available at http://www.eeoc.gov/docs/accommodation.html ("To request accommodation, an

individual may use 'plain English' and need not mention the ADA or use the phrase 'reasonable accommodation'").

The Interpretive Guidance clearly contemplates that reasonable accommodation will be achieved through an "interactive process" by which disabled individuals and their employers meet and negotiate accommodations that satisfy the needs of both parties. *See Tobin v. Liberty Mut. Ins. Co.*, 433 F.3d 100, 109-10 (1st Cir. 2005) (great deal of discussion and significant action by the employer in providing multiple accommodations satisfied the "interactive process" duty even if the employer ultimately failed to provide a reasonable accommodation). Is failing to discuss accommodation a violation of the ADA even if a court ultimately concludes that no reasonable accommodation is possible? Despite language in some cases suggesting otherwise, the lower courts generally have been unwilling to impose liability on an employer *solely* for failure to engage in the interactive process. There must also be a showing that a reasonable accommodation could have been found had the process been pursued. *See Lucas v. W. W. Grainger, Inc.*, 257 F.3d 1249, 1255 n. 2 (11th Cir. 2001); *Kvorjak v. Maine*, 259 F.3d 48 (1st Cir. 2001). *See generally* John R. Autry, *Reasonable Accommodation under the ADA: Are Employers Required to Participate in the Interactive Process? The Courts Say "Yes" but the Law Says No*, 79 CHI.-KENT. L. REV. 665, 669 (2004) (while failure to engage in an interactive process is not independently actionable, it can influence the decision of other issues).

The duty to engage in an interactive process is not a one-way street. An employee who fails to participate in discussions about accommodation may forfeit protection against disability discrimination. See *Whelan v. Teledyne Metalworking Prods.*, 226 Fed. Appx. 141 (3d Cir. 2007). *See also Templeton v. Neodata Servs., Inc.*, 162 F.3d 617 (10th Cir. 1998) (terminating employee for refusing to provide reasonably requested medical information does not violate the ADA); *Hennenfent v. Mid Dakota Clinic*, 164 F.3d 419 (8th Cir. 1998) (same).

3.   *Undue Hardship*

Relatively few cases have examined closely the question of undue hardship; instead, as in *Barnett*, reproduced at p. 540, they have determined the proposed accommodation is unreasonable. However, a claimed failure to accommodate can be defended on the ground that the plaintiff rejected a reasonable accommodation, *see* 29 C.F.R. § 1630.9(d), or that the necessary or proposed accommodation would pose an "undue hardship" on the operation of the employer's business, ADA § 102(b)(5)(A); 29 C.F.R. § 1630.15(d). The ADA provides in § 101(10) that an "undue hardship" is an accommodation requiring "significant difficulty or expense," which must be determined by considering all relevant factors, including the size and financial resources of the covered entity. *See* 29 C.F.R. § 1630.2(p). Section 102(b)(5)(A) expressly states that the covered entity must "demonstrate" the existence of an "undue hardship." *See Woodruff v. Peters*, 482 F.3d 521 (D.C. Cir. 2007) (accommodations of plaintiff and telecommuting policy precluded summary judgment in favor of defendant on undue hardship defense) (Rehabilitation Act claim).

The concepts of reasonable accommodation and undue hardship, as has been observed, go somewhat "hand in hand." *Riel v. Electronic Data Sys. Corp.*, 99 F.3d 678, 681 (5th Cir. 1996). But they are analytically distinct. Reasonable accommodation involves an assessment not only of whether the accommodation would enable the employee to do the job but also whether it is facially reasonable. If this showing is made, the employer has the opportunity to prove that under the facts and circumstances of the particular situation, the accommodation would pose an undue hardship. Reasonable accommodation is thus a more "generalized inquiry," while undue hardship focuses on the particular employer. *See Barnett*. Thus, while the plaintiff bears the burden of proving a reasonable accommodation exists, the burden of proving that an accommodation would pose an undue hardship is on the employer.

The Second Circuit in *Borkowski v. Valley Cent. Sch. Dist.*, 63 F.3d 131 (2d Cir. 1995), discussed the elements of "undue hardship," citing ADA provisions that define "undue hardship" to mean "an action requiring significant difficulty or expense, when considered in light of" the following factors:

(i) the nature and cost of the accommodation needed under this Act;

(ii) the overall financial resources of the facility or facilities involved in the provision of the reasonable accommodation; the number of persons employed at such facility; the effect on expenses and resources, or the impact otherwise of such accommodation upon the operation of the facility;

(iii) the overall financial resources of the covered entity; the overall size of the business of a covered entity with respect to the number of its employees; the number, type, and location of its facilities; and

(iv) the type of operation or operations of the covered entity, including the composition, structure, and functions of the workforce of such entity; the geographic separateness, administrative, or fiscal relationship of the facility or facilities in question to the covered entity.

42 U.S.C. §12111(10) (2003). The issue, according to *Borkowski*, is one of degree: "[E]ven this list of factors says little about how great a hardship an employer must bear before the hardship becomes undue." The court held that employers are not required to show that they would be driven to the brink of insolvency. It relied on ADA legislative history rejecting a provision that would have defined an undue hardship as one that threatened the continued existence of the employer. *Borkowski*, 63 F.3d at 139. "Where the employer is a government entity, Congress could not have intended the only limit on the employer's duty to make reasonable accommodation to be the full extent of the tax base on which the government entity could draw." *Id.*

The court concluded that, in order to demonstrate both that the proposed accommodation is unreasonable and that the hardship it would impose is undue, the employer must "undertake a refined analysis" of the relative costs and benefits of the accommodation, considering both "the industry to which the employer belongs as well as the individual characteristics of the particular defendant-employer." *Id.* The court further noted that "mathematical precision" and "complex economic formulae" are not required. Rather "a common-sense balancing of the costs and benefits in light of the factors listed in the regulations is all that is expected." *Id.* at 140. Is a cost-benefit analysis appropriate under the ADA? The House of Representatives rejected an amendment that would have presumed undue hardship if a reasonable accommodation cost more than 10 percent of the employee's annual salary. *See* 136 Cong. Rec. H1475 (1990).

Is it an undue hardship if accommodations for one employee will have a negative effect on the morale of other employees? Should *Rehrs*, reproduced at p. 534, have been analyzed as an undue hardship case? What about *Barnett*?

Can undue hardship be raised as an affirmative defense if plaintiff has not requested, or does not need, an accommodation? Doesn't the statutory structure suggest the answer is no?

NOTE ON BURDENS OF PRODUCTION AND PROOF

By now, it is obvious that disability discrimination claims often differ in significant ways from disparate treatment claims brought under Title VII, Section 1981 and the ADEA.

For example, the ADA expressly permits employers to act on the basis of an employee's disability. Thus, for example, if an individual's disability precludes him from performing the essential functions of a job, with or without reasonable accommodation, then the employer may disqualify him on that basis without incurring liability. Under Title VII, however, an employer could disqualify an employee because of her sex or age only in the rare instances where a bona fide occupational qualification can be established. See p. 171.

At the same time, as the statutory language makes clear and *Barnett* confirms, the ADA at times requires more than equal treatment; it expressly requires employers to treat individuals differently because of the disability by providing a reasonable accommodation. Given these differences, how do, or should, the burden of proof schemes devised under Title VII, the ADEA and Section 1981 apply, if at all, to ADA claims?

It is clear that the plaintiff bears the burden of proving he is an individual with a disability within the meaning of the ADA. But placement of the burdens of production and proof are more complicated when considering whether the plaintiff is a *qualified* individual with a disability. In those cases, that the plaintiff's disability is causally related to the challenged decision is rarely in dispute; instead the question is who has the burden of proving that job functions are essential or that an accommodation is reasonable or is instead an undue hardship.

But sometimes, whether the plaintiff's disability is causally related to the challenged action *is* the issue to be resolved. In those cases, courts have frequently borrowed the *McDonnell Douglas* proof structure with its three stages — prima facie case, articulation of a legitimate, nondiscriminatory reason, and proof of pretext for discrimination — for ADA claims. *See, e.g., Simpson v. Des Moines Water Works*, 425 F.3d 538 (8th Cir. 2005); *Kiel v. Select Artificials, Inc.*, 169 F.3d 1131 (8th Cir. 1998). Of course, as we've seen earlier, courts disagree on whether acting on the basis of misconduct caused by a plaintiff's disability is the articulation of a legitimate, nondiscriminatory reason or a discriminatory one. See *Gambini*, reproduced at p. 557. The ADA does not expressly address mixed motives, and §703(m) does not expressly apply to the ADA. The ADA, however, is "linked" to Title VII, in the sense that it incorporates the "powers, remedies, and procedures set forth in sections 2000e-4, 2000e-5, 2000e-6, 2000e-8, and 2000e-9" of Title VII. Some courts have thus found §703(m) applicable to claims under the ADA.

Many ADA cases, however, do not involve motive based inquiries at all. Instead they raise the question of whether the disabled individual is "qualified" within the meaning of the ADA. A frequent question, as we have seen, is whether a job function is essential. In *Rehrs*, reproduced at p. 534, the Eighth Circuit placed the burden of proof on the employer to prove a job function was essential, but this issue is far from settled. Another and often related question is whether an accommodation is a reasonable one, and questions arose over whether it was the plaintiff's burden to prove the accommodation reasonable or the defendant's burden to prove it was not. In *U.S. Airways v. Barnett*, reproduced at p. 540, the Court approached the burden of proof issues in reasonable accommodation cases as follows: it is the plaintiff's burden to show that an accommodation "is reasonable on its face, i.e., ordinarily or in the run of cases." Once the plaintiff has made that showing, the burden shifts to the employer to prove that, while the accommodation may generally be reasonable, there are case specific circumstances that prove the accommodation would pose an undue hardship on the employer. It is clear that the burden of proving undue hardship belongs to the employer.

As we will see in the next section, the ADA also provides a "direct threat" defense to employers, and the statute also permits the use of other standards or selection criteria that screen out or tend to screen out individuals with disabilities so long as the standard is job related for the position in question and consistent with business necessity. As the cases below demonstrate, the Supreme Court appears to place the burden of persuasion on the employer in these cases.

D. DISCRIMINATORY QUALIFICATION STANDARDS

ADA § 102(b) provides that "discriminate" includes

> (3) utilizing standards, criteria, or methods of administration . . . that have the effect of discrimination on the basis of disability, . . .
>
> (6) using employment tests or other selection criteria that screen out or tend to screen out an individual with a disability or a class of individuals with disabilities unless the standard, test or other selection criteria, as used by the covered entity, is shown to be job-related for the position in question and is consistent with business necessity. . . .

ADA regulations indicate that both § 102(b)(3) and § 102(b)(6) are subject to a job-relatedness and business necessity defense. *See* 29 C.F.R. §§ 1630.7, 1630.10. Further, § 103(a), which sets forth defenses, provides that the use of criteria with a disparate impact on the basis of disability must also be consistent with the employer's duty to provide reasonable accommodation. *See* § 1630.15(b)(1), (c). Standards or selection criterion may also be defended on the basis that they are permitted or required by another federal statute or regulation. *See* 29 § 1630.15(e). Finally, ADA § 103(b) provides that "[t]he term 'qualification standards' may include a requirement that an individual shall not pose a direct threat to the health or safety of other individuals in the workplace."

In its Interpretive Guidance, the EEOC further explains that selection criteria with a disparate impact that "do not concern an essential function of the job would not be consistent with business necessity." *See* 29 C.F.R. pt. 1630, App. § 1630.10. The Interpretive Guidance goes on to suggest that most challenges to selection criteria can be resolved by reasonable accommodation. Finally, the EEOC interprets these provisions as "applicable to all types of selection criteria, including safety requirements, vision or hearing requirements, walking requirements, and employment tests. . . . As previously noted, however, it is not the intent of this part to second guess an employer's business judgment with regard to production standards. . . . Consequently, production standards will generally not be subject to a challenge under this provision." *Id.*

In short, qualification standards that are either facially discriminatory or that have a disparate impact on disabled individuals can violate the ADA, but all discriminatory qualification standards are subject to the same defenses — they may be defended on the basis that they are job related and consistent with business necessity, permitted or required by another federal statute or regulation, or necessary to prevent a direct threat to health and safety.

Most challenges to qualification standards do not raise significant issues about whether the challenged standard or criteria screens out disabled individuals. Challenged standards or selection criteria frequently are facially discriminatory, such as vision requirements for drivers. Even standards or criteria that do not expressly concern a disabling impairment generally are challenged on the ground that a disabled individual cannot meet the standard because of his or her disability. Thus, the fact that the standard or criterion screens out an individual with a disability is obvious. The primary issue in these cases, therefore, is whether the discriminatory standard or criterion can be defended.

This section first examines the direct threat defense. Second, we will consider the job-relatedness and business necessity defense as it applies to qualification standards that screen out disabled individuals, including qualification standards promulgated by the federal government. Finally, we address the application of disparate impact theory in disability discrimination cases.

1. Direct Threat

ADA § 103(b) provides that "[t]he term 'qualification standards' may include a requirement that an individual shall not pose a direct threat to the health or safety of other individuals in the workplace." Direct threat is defined by § 101(3) as a "significant risk to the health or safety of others" that cannot be eliminated by a reasonable accommodation. The EEOC requires the "direct threat" determination to be based on a reasonable medical judgment that considers such factors as the duration of the risk, the nature and severity of the potential harm, the likelihood of the potential harm, and the imminence of the potential harm. *See* 29 C.F.R. § 1630.2(r). Direct threat is simultaneously relevant to whether the individual with a disability is "qualified" to perform essential functions, whether the employer is justified in basing an employment decision on the individual's disability, and whether the employer has a duty to accommodate the individual's disability.

The ADA's "direct threat" provision is derived from the Supreme Court's decision in *Sch. Bd. of Nassau County v. Arline*, 480 U.S. 273 (1987). In *Arline*, a case decided under Section 504 of the Rehabilitation Act, the Court confronted the question of whether an individual with tuberculosis was otherwise qualified to be an elementary school teacher. The Court concluded the answer is no, if she poses a significant risk of transmitting the disease to others, and that risk cannot be eliminated through reasonable accommodation. In determining whether a significant risk exists, the Court explained that the inquiry:

> should include [findings of] facts, based on reasonable medical judgments given the state of medical knowledge, about (a) the nature of the risk (how the disease is transmitted), (b) the duration of the risk (how long is the carrier infectious), (c) the severity of the risk (what is the potential harm to third parties) and (d) the probabilities the disease will be transmitted and will cause varying degrees of harm.

Id. at 288.

In making this determination, courts were directed to defer to the "reasonable medical judgments of public health officials," with the Court reserving judgment on whether or not courts should defer to the judgment of private physicians.

In *Bragdon v. Abbott*, reproduced at p. 492, the defendant, a dentist, asserted that whether a risk is significant is to be assessed from the point of view of the person denying the service. The Court, however, confirmed that such assessments are to be made on the basis of medical or other objective evidence available at the time that the allegedly discriminatory action occurred. A good faith belief that a significant risk exists is not enough, nor would any special deference be afforded a defendant who is himself a medical professional.

The EEOC's regulation interpreting "direct threat" defines the term to include "a significant risk of substantial harm to the health or safety of *the individual* or others that cannot be eliminated or reduced by reasonable accommodation." 29 C.F.R. §1630.2(r) (emphasis added). The validity of that regulation was at issue in the following case.

CHEVRON U.S.A. INC. v. ECHAZABAL
536 U.S. 73 (2002)

Justice SOUTER delivered the opinion of the Court.

A regulation of the Equal Employment Opportunity Commission authorizes refusal to hire an individual because his performance on the job would endanger his own health, owing to a disability. The question in this case is whether the Americans with Disabilities Act of 1990 permits the regulation. We hold that it does.

I

Beginning in 1972, respondent Mario Echazabal worked for independent contractors at an oil refinery owned by petitioner Chevron U.S.A. Inc. Twice he applied for a job directly with Chevron, which offered to hire him if he could pass the company's physical examination. Each time, the exam showed liver abnormality or damage, the cause eventually being identified as Hepatitis C, which Chevron's doctors said would be aggravated by continued exposure to toxins at Chevron's refinery. In each instance, the company withdrew the offer, and the second time it asked the contractor employing Echazabal either to reassign him to a job without exposure to harmful chemicals or to remove him from the refinery altogether. The contractor laid him off in early 1996.

Echazabal filed suit, ultimately removed to federal court, claiming, among other things, that Chevron violated the Americans With Disabilities Act in refusing to hire him, or even to let him continue working in the plant, because of a disability, his liver condition. Chevron defended under a regulation of the Equal Employment Opportunity Commission permitting the defense that a worker's disability on the job would pose a "direct threat" to his health, see 29 CFR §1630.15(b)(2) (2001). Although two medical witnesses disputed Chevron's judgment that Echazabal's liver function was impaired and subject to further damage under the job conditions in the refinery, the District Court granted summary judgment for Chevron. It held that Echazabal raised no genuine issue of material fact as to whether the company acted reasonably in relying on its own doctors' medical advice, regardless of its accuracy.

On appeal, the Ninth Circuit asked for briefs on a threshold question not raised before, whether the EEOC's regulation recognizing a threat-to-self defense, exceeded the scope of permissible rulemaking under the ADA. The Circuit held that it did and reversed the summary judgment. The court rested its position on the text of the ADA itself in explicitly recognizing an employer's right to adopt an employment qualification barring anyone whose disability would place others in the workplace at risk, while saying nothing about threats to the disabled employee himself. The majority opinion reasoned that "by specifying only threats to 'other individuals in the workplace,' the statute makes it clear that threats to other persons — including the disabled individual himself — are not included within the scope of the [direct threat] defense," and it indicated that any such regulation would unreasonably conflict with congressional policy against paternalism in the workplace. The court went on to reject Chevron's further argument that Echazabal was not "'otherwise qualified'" to perform the job, holding that the ability to perform a job without risk to one's health or safety is not an "'essential function'" of the job. . . .

II

Section 102 of the Americans with Disabilities Act of 1990 prohibits "discrimination against a qualified individual with a disability because of the disability . . . in regard to" a number of actions by an employer, including "hiring." 42 U.S.C. §12112(a). The statutory definition of "discrimination" covers a number of things an employer might do to block a disabled person from advancing in the workplace, such as "using qualification standards . . . that screen out or tend to screen out an individual with a disability." §12112(b)(6). By that same definition, as well as by separate provision, §12113(a), the Act creates an affirmative defense for action under a qualification standard "shown to be job-related for the position in question and . . . consistent with business necessity." Such a standard may include "a requirement that an individual shall not pose a direct threat to the health or safety of other individuals in the workplace," §12113(b), if the individual cannot perform the job safely with reasonable accommodation, §12113(a). By regulation, the EEOC carries the defense one step further, in allowing an employer to screen out a potential worker with a disability not only for risks that he would pose to others in the workplace but for risks on the job to his own health or safety as well: "The term 'qualification standard' may include a requirement that an individual shall not pose a direct threat to the health or safety of the individual or others in the workplace." 29 CFR §1630.15(b)(2) (2001).

Chevron relies on the regulation here, since it says a job in the refinery would pose a "direct threat" to Echazabal's health. In seeking deference to the agency, it argues that nothing in the statute unambiguously precludes such a defense, while the regulation was adopted under authority explicitly delegated by Congress, 42 U.S.C. §12116, and after notice-and-comment rulemaking. See *United States v. Mead Corp.*, 533 U.S. 218, 227 (2001); *Chevron U.S.A. Inc. v. Natural Resources Defense Council, Inc.*, 467 U.S. 837, 842-844 (1984). Echazabal, on the contrary, argues that as a matter of law the statute precludes the regulation, which he claims would be an unreasonable interpretation even if the agency had leeway to go beyond the literal text.

A

As for the textual bar to any agency action as a matter of law, Echazabal says that Chevron loses on the threshold question whether the statute leaves a gap for the

EEOC to fill. Echazabal recognizes the generality of the language providing for a defense when a plaintiff is screened out by "qualification standards" that are "job-related and consistent with business necessity" (and reasonable accommodation would not cure the difficulty posed by employment). 42 U.S.C. §12113(a). Without more, those provisions would allow an employer to turn away someone whose work would pose a serious risk to himself. That possibility is said to be eliminated, however, by the further specification that "'qualification standards' may include a requirement that an individual shall not pose a direct threat to the health or safety of other individuals in the workplace." §12113(b); see also §12111(3) (defining "direct threat" in terms of risk to others). Echazabal contrasts this provision with an EEOC regulation under the Rehabilitation Act of 1973, as amended, 29 U.S.C. §701 *et seq.*, antedating the ADA, which recognized an employer's right to consider threats both to other workers and to the threatening employee himself. Because the ADA defense provision recognizes threats only if they extend to another, Echazabal reads the statute to imply as a matter of law that threats to the worker himself cannot count.

The argument follows the reliance of the Ninth Circuit majority on the interpretive canon, *expressio unius exclusio alterius,* "expressing one item of [an] associated group or series excludes another left unmentioned." *United States v. Vonn,* 535 U.S. 55, 65 (2002). The rule is fine when it applies, but this case joins some others in showing when it does not. See, *e.g., id.; United Dominion Industries, Inc. v. United States,* 532 U.S. 822, 836 (2001); *Pauley v. Beth Energy Mines, Inc.,* 501 U.S. 680, 703 (1991).

The first strike against the expression-exclusion rule here is right in the text that Echazabal quotes. Congress included the harm-to-others provision as an example of legitimate qualifications that are "job-related and consistent with business necessity." These are spacious defensive categories, which seem to give an agency (or in the absence of agency action, a court) a good deal of discretion in setting the limits of permissible qualification standards. That discretion is confirmed, if not magnified, by the provision that "qualification standards" falling within the limits of job relation and business necessity "may include" a veto on those who would directly threaten others in the workplace. Far from supporting Echazabal's position, the expansive phrasing of "may include" points directly away from the sort of exclusive specification he claims. . . .

Just as statutory language suggesting exclusiveness is missing, so is that essential extrastatutory ingredient of an expression-exclusion demonstration, the series of terms from which an omission bespeaks a negative implication. The canon depends on identifying a series of two or more terms or things that should be understood to go hand in hand, which are abridged in circumstances supporting a sensible inference that the term left out must have been meant to be excluded. E. Crawford, Construction of Statutes 337 (1940) (*expressio unius* "'properly applies only when in the natural association of ideas in the mind of the reader that which is expressed is so set over by way of strong contrast to that which is omitted that the contrast enforces the affirmative inference,'" *United States v. Vonn, supra.*

Strike two in this case is the failure to identify any such established series, including both threats to others and threats to self, from which Congress appears to have made a deliberate choice to omit the latter item as a signal of the affirmative defense's scope. [The Rehabilitation Act tracked the current text of the ADA, excluding only threats to self. Under the Rehabilitation Act, however, the EEOC had adopted a regulation, like the one at issue here, which reached threat-to-self employment. Against this backdrop,] Echazabal argues that Congress's adoption only of the threat-to-others exception in the

ADA must have been a deliberate omission of the Rehabilitation Act regulation's tandem term of threat-to-self, with intent to exclude it. . . .

Even if we . . . look no further than the EEOC's Rehabilitation Act regulation pairing self and others, the congressional choice to speak only of threats to others would still be equivocal. . . . Instead of making the ADA different from the Rehabilitation Act on the point at issue, Congress used identical language, knowing full well what the EEOC had made of that language under the earlier statute. Did Congress mean to imply that the agency had been wrong in reading the earlier language to allow it to recognize threats to self, or did Congress just assume that the agency was free to do under the ADA what it had already done under the earlier Act's identical language? There is no way to tell. Omitting the EEOC's reference to self-harm while using the very language that the EEOC had read as consistent with recognizing self-harm is equivocal at best. No negative inference is possible.

There is even a third strike against applying the expression-exclusion rule here. It is simply that there is no apparent stopping point to the argument that by specifying a threat-to-others defense Congress intended a negative implication about those whose safety could be considered. When Congress specified threats to others in the workplace, for example, could it possibly have meant that an employer could not defend a refusal to hire when a worker's disability would threaten others outside the workplace? If Typhoid Mary had come under the ADA, would a meat packer have been defenseless if Mary had sued after being turned away? See 42 U.S.C. §12113(d). *Expressio unius* just fails to work here.

B

Since Congress has not spoken exhaustively on threats to a worker's own health, the agency regulation can claim adherence under the rule in *Chevron*, so long as it makes sense of the statutory defense for qualification standards that are "job-related and consistent with business necessity." 42 U.S.C. §12113(a). Chevron's reasons for calling the regulation reasonable are unsurprising: moral concerns aside, it wishes to avoid time lost to sickness, excessive turnover from medical retirement or death, litigation under state tort law, and the risk of violating the national Occupational Safety and Health Act of 1970. Although Echazabal claims that none of these reasons is legitimate, focusing on the concern with OSHA will be enough to show that the regulation is entitled to survive.

Echazabal points out that there is no known instance of OSHA enforcement, or even threatened enforcement, against an employer who relied on the ADA to hire a worker willing to accept a risk to himself from his disability on the job. In Echazabal's mind, this shows that invoking OSHA policy and possible OSHA liability is just a red herring to excuse covert discrimination. But there is another side to this. The text of OSHA itself says its point is "to assure so far as possible every working man and woman in the Nation safe and healthful working conditions," §651(b), and Congress specifically obligated an employer to "furnish to each of his employees employment and a place of employment which are free from recognized hazards that are causing or are likely to cause death or serious physical harm to his employees," §654(a)(1). Although there may be an open question whether an employer would actually be liable under OSHA for hiring an individual who knowingly consented to the particular dangers the job would pose to him, there is no denying that the employer would be asking for trouble: his decision to hire would put Congress's policy in the ADA, a disabled individual's right to operate on equal terms within the workplace, at loggerheads with the competing policy of OSHA, to ensure the safety of "each" and "every" worker. Courts would, of course, resolve the tension if there were no agency action, but the EEOC's resolution exemplifies the substantive choices that agencies are expected to make when Congress leaves the intersection of competing objectives both imprecisely marked but subject to the administrative leeway found in 42 U.S.C. § 12113(a).

Nor can the EEOC's resolution be fairly called unreasonable as allowing the kind of workplace paternalism the ADA was meant to outlaw. It is true that Congress had paternalism in its sights when it passed the ADA, see § 12101(a)(5) (recognizing "overprotective rules and policies" as a form of discrimination). But the EEOC has taken this to mean that Congress was not aiming at an employer's refusal to place disabled workers at a specifically demonstrated risk, but was trying to get at refusals to give an even break to classes of disabled people, while claiming to act for their own good in reliance on untested and pretextual stereotypes.[5] Its regulation disallows just this sort of sham protection, through demands for a particularized enquiry into the harms the employee would probably face. The direct threat defense must be "based on a reasonable medical judgment that relies on the most current medical knowledge and/or the best available objective evidence," and upon an expressly "individualized assessment of the individual's present ability to safely perform the essential functions of the job," reached after considering, among other things, the imminence of the risk and the severity of the harm portended. 29 CFR § 1630.2(r) (2001). The EEOC was certainly acting within the reasonable zone when it saw a difference between rejecting workplace paternalism and ignoring specific and documented risks to the employee himself, even if the employee would take his chances for the sake of getting a job.[6]

Finally, our conclusions that some regulation is permissible and this one is reasonable are not open to Echazabal's objection that they reduce the direct threat

---

5. Echazabal's contention that the Act's legislative history is to the contrary is unpersuasive. Although some of the comments within the legislative history decry paternalism in general terms, see, e.g., H. R. Rep. No. 101-485, pt. 2, p. 72 (1990) ("It is critical that paternalistic concerns for the disabled person's own safety not be used to disqualify an otherwise qualified applicant"); ADA Conf. Rep., 136 Cong. Rec. 17377 (1990) (statement of Sen. Kennedy) ("An employer could not use as an excuse for not hiring a person with HIV disease the claim that the employer was simply 'protecting the individual' from opportunistic diseases to which the individual might be exposed"), those comments that elaborate actually express the more pointed concern that such justifications are usually pretextual, rooted in generalities and misperceptions about disabilities. See, e.g., H. R. Rep. No. 101-485, at 74 ("Generalized fear about risks from the employment environment, such as exacerbation of the disability caused by stress, cannot be used by an employer to disqualify a person with a disability"); S. Rep. No. 101-116, p. 28 (1989) ("It would also be a violation to deny employment to an applicant based on generalized fears about the safety of the applicant. . . . By definition, such fears are based on averages and group-based predictions. This legislation requires individualized assessments").

Similarly, Echazabal points to several of our decisions expressing concern under Title VII, which like the ADA allows employers to defend otherwise discriminatory practices that are "consistent with business necessity," 42 U.S.C. § 2000e-2(k), with employers adopting rules that exclude women from jobs that are seen as too risky. See, e.g., *Dothard v. Rawlinson* [reproduced at p. 246]; *Automobile Workers v. Johnson Controls, Inc.* [reproduced at p. 173]. Those cases, however, are beside the point, as they, like Title VII generally, were concerned with paternalistic judgments based on the broad category of gender, while the EEOC has required that judgments based on the direct threat provision be made on the basis of individualized risk assessments.

6. Respect for this distinction does not entail the requirement, as Echazabal claims, that qualification standards be "neutral," stating what the job requires, as distinct from a worker's disqualifying characteristics. It is just as much business necessity for skyscraper contractors to have steelworkers without vertigo as to have well-balanced ones. Reasonableness does not turn on formalism. We have no occasion, however, to try to describe how acutely an employee must exhibit a disqualifying condition before an employer may exclude him from the class of the generally qualified. This is a job for the trial courts in the first instance.

provision to "surplusage," see *Babbitt v. Sweet Home Chapter, Communities for Great Ore.*, 515 U.S. 687, 698 (1995). The mere fact that a threat-to-self defense reasonably falls within the general "job related" and "business necessity" standard does not mean that Congress accomplished nothing with its explicit provision for a defense based on threats to others. The provision made a conclusion clear that might otherwise have been fought over in litigation or administrative rulemaking. It did not lack a job to do merely because the EEOC might have adopted the same rule later in applying the general defense provisions, nor was its job any less responsible simply because the agency was left with the option to go a step further. A provision can be useful even without congressional attention being indispensable . . .

NOTES

1. *Individualized Medical Inquiry.* The Court did not decide whether Chevron had made the requisite individualized inquiry into Echazabal's medical condition that the EEOC's regulation required. That issue was left for the lower court on remand, and the Ninth Circuit then found a genuine issue of material fact as to whether the defendant had performed the medical assessment required by the EEOC's regulation, reversing summary judgment in favor of defendant, *Echazabal v. Chevron U.S.A., Inc.,* 336 F.3d 1023 (9th Cir. 2003). *See also Ollie v. Titan Tire Corp.,* 336 F.3d 680 (8th Cir. 2003) (doctor's report that individual "may have trouble working near dust or fumes" was insufficient basis to exclude him from employment; jury verdict on plaintiff's "regarded as" claim upheld).

2. *To Defer or Not to Defer?* The central question before the Court was whether the EEOC's regulation, which expanded the "direct threat" defense to include threats to an individual's own health and safety, was entitled to judicial deference. Is the Court's decision to defer to the EEOC in *Echazabal* consistent with its refusal to do so in *Sutton?* In *Echazabal,* the Court found the statute itself left room for agency interpretation, whereas it found no such room available in *Sutton.* Do you agree with the Court's view that the statutory language in *Sutton* was clear, while the statutory language in *Echazabal* was sufficiently ambiguous to open the door to the agency?

Note that in *Echazabal,* the EEOC was interpreting a provision of Title I, the chapter on which the EEOC has been expressly delegated rule-making authority. Also, the EEOC's definition in *Echazabal* was found in the regulation itself, not in an Interpretive Guidance. Thus, the *Echazabal* Court did not question whether *Chevron's* two-step review standard applied to the EEOC's interpretation; it unquestionably did. But this question was left open in *Sutton* vis à vis EEOC regulations interpreting the statutory definition of "disability" and the agency's Interpretive Guidance generally.

For criticism of the inclusion of the threat-to-self in the ADA's direct threat defense, see, e.g., Samuel R. Bagenstos, *The Supreme Court, The Americans with Disabilities Act, and Rational Discrimination,* 55 ALA. L. REV. 923 (2004); D. Aaron Lacy, *Am I My Brother's Keeper: Disabilities, Paternalism, and Threats to Self,* 44 SANTA CLARA L. REV. 55 (2003).

3. *Extent of the Defense. Echazabal* involved a potentially life threatening condition. Suppose the disability is less potentially fatal. Could Toyota have avoided the whole disability question by claiming that Mrs. Williams's employment posed a direct threat to her carpel tunnel condition?

4. *Special Treatment of Food Handlers.* After *Arline*, the Rehabilitation Act's definition of an "individual with a disability" was amended to exclude carriers of currently contagious disease or infection who pose a "direct threat" to the health or safety of others. *See* 29 U.S.C. §705(20)(D) (2007). ADA §103(d)(1)-(3) provides that a food-handling position may be denied to a person who has an infectious or communicable disease that is transmittable to others through food handling if the risk to others cannot be "eliminated" by a reasonable accommodation. This defense, however, is available only for a person with a disease that the Secretary of Health and Human Services has identified as infectious and communicable and transmittable through the handling of the food. Why was it necessary to include this as a separate defense? Wouldn't a contagious individual be a "direct threat" in a food-handling job? The EEOC recently has issued a guide for the food service industry, How to Comply with the Americans with Disabilities Act: A Guide for Restaurants and Other Food Service Employers, at www.eeoc.gov.

5. *Direct Threat Examples.* In *Den Hartog v. Wasatch Academy*, 129 F.3d 1076 (10th Cir. 1997), held that an employee's association with a disabled individual was a direct threat and therefore provided a defense to associational discrimination. In *Hartog*, the plaintiff was a boarding school teacher whose son suffered from psychiatric disorders that caused him to engage in threatening behavior toward other boarding school personnel and their families. *See also Darnell v. Thermafiber, Inc.*, 417 F.3d 657, 659 (7th Cir. 2005) ("uncontrolled" diabetes made plaintiff a direct threat to safety at a plant that melted and processed material at high temperatures when there was testimony that he would eventually pass out and therefore pose a risk to himself and others).

A number of courts have considered the "direct threat" defense in cases involving persons infected with HIV, and most have found the defense satisfied. *See, e.g., Waddell v. Valley Forge Dental Assocs.*, 276 F.3d 1275 (11th Cir. 2001) (HIV-positive dental hygienist posed a direct threat to the health and safety of others); *Estate of Mauro v. Borgess Med. Ctr.*, 137 F.3d 398 (6th Cir. 1998) (surgical technician with HIV was a direct threat to the health and safety of others because his job required that he place his hands in patients' body cavities in the presence of sharp instruments). *But see Chalk v. United States Dist. Court*, 840 F.2d 701 (9th Cir. 1988) (teacher with AIDS did not pose a "significant risk" in the workplace); *Taylor v. Rice*, 451 F.3d 898 (D.C. Cir. 2006) (summary judgment overturned with regard to HIV-positive State Department employee on direct threat to oneself defense because it was not clear that the job necessarily entailed assignments that would put the individual at risk). For an article arguing that courts have used their own fears about HIV to strip many individuals of ADA protection when making direct threat determinations, *see* Katrina Atkins & Richard Bales, *HIV and the Direct Threat Defense*, 91 KY. L.J. 859 (2002-2003).

6. *Direct Threat and Mental Illness.* Recall *Gambini*, reproduced at p. 557. If the case had been brought under the ADA and had a "direct threat" defense been asserted, what result? In *The ADA, The Workplace, and the Myth of the "Dangerous Mentally Ill,"* 34 U.C. DAVIS L. REV. 849, 850-51 (2001), Professor Ann Hubbard addresses the question of the direct threat defense in the context of mental disabilities. She notes that public fears concerning persons with mental disabilities are out of proportion to the risk of violence actually posed. In another article, *Understanding and Implementing the ADA's Direct Threat Defense*, 95 NW. U. L. REV. 1279 (2001), Professor Hubbard elaborates on the direct threat defense more generally. She contends that lower courts

and employers tend to overestimate risk that is unfamiliar or uncontrollable or more publicized over risks that are known or within our control or less in the media spotlight. Do you agree? *See also* Jane Byeff Korn, *Crazy (Mental Illness Under the ADA)*, 36 U. MICH. J.L. REF. 585, 589 (2003); Wendy F. Hensel & Gregory Todd Jones, *Bridging the Physical-Mental Gap: An Empirical Look at the Impact of Mental Illness Stigma on ADA Outcomes*, 73 TENN. L. REV. 47 (2005).

PROBLEM 6.6

On remand, the district court made the following findings of fact in *Arline:*

[Tuberculosis] infection begins with the inhalation by one person of "droplet nuclei" expelled by another. Droplet nuclei are tuberculosis germs suspended in moisture. . . . [W]hen droplet nuclei are expelled . . . 99.9% of the nuclei die within a second of contacting room air. The droplet nuclei that survive must reach the distal portion, which is the microscopic air space, of the lungs of the person inhaling the germs. . . . If any germ does reach the distal portion of the lungs, the body's immunological defenses are capable of rendering it harmless. . . . If a tuberculosis germ successfully implants itself into the distal portion of the lungs, and the immunological defenses of the body do not destroy it, the germ can then multiply. If this occurs, the person is infected. If the germs continue to multiply, at some point the number of tuberculosis cells becomes so great as to cause disease. . . .

The . . . test for tuberculosis is the sputum culture. A patient's sputum is placed on a laboratory dish and allowed to "grow" for a number of weeks. The organism grown on culture indicates that the person from whom the specimen came is, at present, infected with tuberculosis. . . . If growth is detected during the eight week period, the culture is allowed to continue to grow until there is a large enough culture to test. Usually growth is detected by the sixth week. . . . Communicability is determined by the actual number of colonies detected. . . . A culture can grow just one colony, but a person is not considered to be able to communicate the infection unless a vastly larger number of organisms are present. The test that will quickly determine a large number of organisms is known as the sputum smear test. This test is considered the threshold indicator of a person's communicability because the sputum smear test is not very sensitive, and thus, many organisms need to be present before the test is positive. . . .

[O]nce a person begins medical treatment for tuberculosis, the risk of communicability becomes very small. Within two weeks of drug therapy, 99% of sputum organisms are killed. In addition, the medication quickly stops the patient's cough. . . . Communicability also depends upon environmental factors. The people at the highest risk of infection are [those] in close proximity to the actively communicable person. . . .

In the summer of 1977, [Arline] suffered a relapse of tuberculosis. She was hospitalized, and treated. . . . In March of 1978 a culture tested positive with over one hundred colonies of tuberculosis. Additional drugs were added to the regimen that [Arline] was taking, and testing was continued. In November, 1978 another culture tested positive with only one colony of tuberculosis. This particular culture was grown for thirteen weeks. . . . No subsequent cultures tested positive [and Arline] did not have a positive smear test after August, 1977.

On these facts, should the court find Arline "qualified"? *See Arline v. School Board of Nassau County*, 692 F. Supp. 1286 (M.D. Fla. 1988). Is Arline "disabled" under current ADA law?

2. *Job-Related and Consistent with Business Necessity*

ALBERTSON'S, INC. v. KIRKINGBURG
527 U.S. 555 (1999)

Justice SOUTER, delivered the opinion for a unanimous Court with respect to Parts I and III, and the opinion of the Court with respect to Part II, in which Chief Justice REHNQUIST, and Justices O'CONNOR, SCALIA, KENNEDY, THOMAS, and GINSBURG, joined.

The question posed is whether, under the Americans with Disabilities Act of 1990 an employer who requires as a job qualification that an employee meet an otherwise applicable federal safety regulation must justify enforcing the regulation solely because its standard may be waived in an individual case. We answer no.

I

In August 1990, petitioner, Albertson's, Inc., a grocery-store chain with super-markets in several States, hired respondent, Hallie Kirkingburg, as a truck driver based at its Portland, Oregon, warehouse. Kirkingburg had more than a decade's driving experience and performed well when Albertson's transportation manager took him on a road test.

Before starting work, Kirkingburg was examined to see if he met federal vision standards for commercial truck drivers. For many decades the Department of Transportation or its predecessors has been responsible for devising these standards for individuals who drive commercial vehicles in interstate commerce. Since 1971, the basic vision regulation has required corrected distant visual acuity of at least 20/40 in each eye and distant binocular acuity of at least 20/40. See 49 CFR § 391.41(b)(10) (1998). Kirkingburg, however, suffers from amblyopia, an uncorrectable condition that leaves him with 20/200 vision in his left eye and monocular vision in effect. Despite Kirkingburg's weak left eye, the doctor erroneously certified that he met the DOT's basic vision standard, and Albertson's hired him.

In December 1991, Kirkingburg injured himself on the job and took a leave of absence. Before returning to work in November 1992, Kirkingburg went for a further physical as required by the company. This time, the examining physician correctly assessed Kirkingburg's vision and explained that his eyesight did not meet the basic DOT standards. The physician, or his nurse, told Kirkingburg that in order to be legally qualified to drive, he would have to obtain a waiver of its basic vision standards from the DOT. The doctor was alluding to a scheme begun in July 1992 for giving DOT certification to applicants with deficient vision who had three years of recent experience driving a commercial vehicle without a license suspension or revocation, involvement in a reportable accident in which the applicant was cited for a moving violation, conviction for certain driving-related offenses, citation for certain serious traffic violations, or more than two convictions for any other moving viola-tions. A waiver applicant had to agree to have his vision checked annually for deterioration, and to report certain information about his driving experience to the Federal Highway Administration, the agency within the DOT responsible for overseeing the motor carrier safety regulations. Kirkingburg applied for a waiver, but because he could not meet the basic DOT vision standard Albertson's fired him from his job as a truck driver. In early 1993, after he had left Albertson's, Kirkingburg received a DOT waiver, but Albertson's refused to rehire him.

Kirkingburg sued Albertson's, claiming that firing him violated the ADA. . . .

III

Albertson's primary contention is that even if Kirkingburg was disabled, he was not a "qualified" individual with a disability because Albertson's merely insisted on the minimum level of visual acuity set forth in the DOT's Motor Carrier Safety Regulations, 49 CFR §391.41(b)(10) (1998). If Albertson's was entitled to enforce that standard as defining an "essential job function of the employment position," see 42 U.S.C. §12111(8), that is the end of the case, for Kirkingburg concededly could not satisfy it.

Under Title I of the ADA, employers may justify their use of "qualification standards . . . that screen out or tend to screen out or otherwise deny a job or benefit to an individual with a disability," so long as such standards are "job-related and consistent with business necessity, and . . . performance cannot be accomplished by reasonable accommodation. . . ." 42 U.S.C. §12113(a).

Kirkingburg and the Government argue that these provisions do not authorize an employer to follow even a facially applicable regulatory standard subject to waiver without making some enquiry beyond determining whether the applicant or employee meets that standard, yes or no. Before an employer may insist on compliance, they say, the employer must make a showing with reference to the particular job that the waivable regulatory standard is "job-related . . . and . . . consistent with business necessity," see §12112(b)(6), and that after consideration of the capabilities of the individual a reasonable accommodation could not fairly resolve the competing interests when an applicant or employee cannot wholly satisfy an otherwise justifiable job qualification.

The Government extends this argument by reference to a further section of the statute, which at first blush appears to be a permissive provision for the employer's and the public's benefit. An employer may impose as a qualification standard "a requirement that an individual shall not pose a direct threat to the health or safety of other individuals in the workplace," §12113(b), with "direct threat" being defined by the Act as "a significant risk to the health or safety of others, which cannot be eliminated by reasonable accommodation," §12111(3). The Government urges us to read subsections (a) and (b) together to mean that when an employer would impose any safety qualification standard, however specific, tending to screen out individuals with disabilities, the application of the requirement must satisfy the ADA's "direct threat" criterion. That criterion ordinarily requires "an individualized assessment of the individual's present ability to safely perform the essential functions of the job," 29 CFR §1630.2(r) (1998), "based on medical or other objective evidence," *Bragdon*, see 29 CFR §1630.2(r) (1998) (assessment of direct threat "shall be based on a reasonable medical judgment that relies on the most current medical knowledge and/or on the best available objective evidence.").[15]

---

15. This appears to be the position taken by the EEOC in the Interpretive Guidance promulgated under its authority to issue regulations to carry out Title I of the ADA, 42 U.S.C. §12116, see 29 CFR pt. 1630, App., §§1630.15(b) and (c) (1998) (requiring safety-related standards to be evaluated under the ADA's direct threat standard); see also App. §1630.10 (noting that selection criteria that screen out individuals with disabilities, including "safety requirements, vision or hearing requirements," must be job-related, consistent with business necessity, and not amenable to reasonable accommodation). Although it might be questioned whether the Government's interpretation, which might impose a higher burden on employers to justify safety-related qualification standards than other job requirements, is a sound one, we have no need to confront the validity of the reading in this case.

Albertson's answers essentially that even assuming the Government has proposed a sound reading of the statute for the general run of cases, this case is not in the general run. It is crucial to its position that Albertson's here was not insisting upon a job qualification merely of its own devising, subject to possible questions about genuine appropriateness and justifiable application to an individual for whom some accommodation may be reasonable. The job qualification it was applying was the distant visual acuity standard of the Federal Motor Carrier Safety Regulations, 49 CFR §391.41(b)(10) (1998), which is made binding on Albertson's by §391.11: "a motor carrier shall not . . . permit a person to drive a commercial motor vehicle unless that person is qualified to drive," by, among other things, meeting the physical qualification standards set forth in §391.41. The validity of these regulations is unchallenged, they have the force of law, and they contain no qualifying language about individualized determinations.

If we looked no further, there would be no basis to question Albertson's' unconditional obligation to follow the regulation and its consequent right to do so. This, indeed, was the understanding of Congress when it enacted the ADA.[16] But there is more: the waiver program.

The Court of Appeals majority . . . assumed that the regulatory provisions for the waiver program had to be treated as being on par with the basic visual acuity regulation, as if the general rule had been modified by some different safety standard made applicable by grant of a waiver. On this reading, an individualized determination under a different substantive safety rule was an element of the regulatory regime, which would easily fit with any requirement of 42 U.S.C. §§ 12113(a) and (b) to consider reasonable accommodation. An employer resting solely on the federal standard for its visual acuity qualification would be required to accept a waiver once obtained, and probably to provide an applicant some opportunity to obtain a waiver whenever that was reasonably possible. . . .

But the reasoning underlying the Court of Appeal's decision was unsound, for we think it was error to read the regulations establishing the waiver program as modifying the content of the basic visual acuity standard in a way that disentitled an employer like Albertson's to insist on it. . . .

Nothing in the waiver regulation, of course, required an employer of commercial drivers to accept the hypothesis and participate in the Government's experiment. The only question, then, is whether the ADA should be read to require such an employer to defend a decision to decline the experiment. Is it reasonable, that is, to read the ADA as requiring an employer like Albertson's to shoulder the general statutory burden to justify a job qualification that would tend to exclude the disabled, whenever the employer chooses to abide by the otherwise clearly applicable, unamended substantive regulatory standard despite the Government's willingness to waive it experimentally and without any finding of its being inappropriate? If the answer were yes, an employer would in fact have an obligation of which we can think of no comparable example in our law. The employer would be required in effect to justify de novo an existing and otherwise applicable safety regulation issued by the Government itself. The employer would be required on a case-by-case basis to reinvent the Government's own wheel when the Government had merely begun an experiment to provide data to consider changing the underlying specifications. And

---

16. The implementing regulations of Title I also recognize a defense to liability under the ADA that "a challenged action is required or necessitated by another Federal law or regulation," 29 CFR § 1630.15(e) (1998). As the parties do not invoke this specific regulation, we have no occasion to consider its effect.

what is even more, the employer would be required to do so when the Government had made an affirmative record indicating that contemporary empirical evidence was hard to come by. It is simply not credible that Congress enacted the ADA (before there was any waiver program) with the understanding that employers choosing to respect the Government's sole substantive visual acuity regulation in the face of an experimental waiver might be burdened with an obligation to defend the regulation's application according to its own terms.

Justice THOMAS, concurring . . .

As the Court points out, though, DOT's visual acuity standards might also be relevant to the question whether respondent was a "qualified individual with a disability" under 42 U.S.C. § 12112(a). That section provides that no covered entity "shall discriminate against a qualified individual with a disability because of the disability of such individual." § 12112(a). Presumably, then, a plaintiff claiming a cause of action under the ADA bears the burden of proving, inter alia, that he is a qualified individual. The phrase "qualified individual with a disability" is defined to mean:

> an individual with a disability who, *with or without reasonable accommodation,* can perform the *essential functions* of the employment position that such individual holds or desires. For the purposes of this subchapter, consideration shall be given to the employer's judgment as to what functions of a job are essential, and if an employer has prepared a written description before advertising or interviewing applicants for the job, this description shall be considered evidence of the essential functions of the job.

§ 12111(8) (emphasis added).

In this case, respondent sought a job driving trucks in interstate commerce. The quintessential function of that job, it seems to me, is to be able to drive a commercial truck in interstate commerce, and it was respondent's burden to prove that he could do so.

As the Court explains, DOT's Motor Carrier Safety Regulations have the force of law and bind petitioner — it may not, by law, "permit a person to drive a commercial motor vehicle unless that person is qualified to drive." 49 CFR § 391.11 (1999). But by the same token, DOT's regulations bind respondent who "shall not drive a commercial motor vehicle unless he/she is qualified to drive a commercial motor vehicle." Given that DOT's regulation equally binds petitioner and respondent, and that it is conceded in this case that respondent could not meet the federal requirements, respondent surely was not "qualified" to perform the essential functions of petitioner's truck driver job without a reasonable accommodation. The waiver program might be thought of as a way to reasonably accommodate respondent, but for the fact, as the Court explains, that the program did nothing to modify the regulation's unconditional requirements. For that reason, requiring petitioner to make such an accommodation most certainly would have been unreasonable.

. . . I would prefer to hold that respondent, as a matter of law, was not qualified to perform the job he sought within the meaning of the ADA. I nevertheless join the Court's opinion. . . . I join the Court's opinion, however, only on the understanding that it leaves open the argument that federal laws such as DOT's visual acuity standards might be critical in determining whether a plaintiff is a "qualified individual with a disability."

NOTES

1. *Analogizing to Title VII's BFOQ.* Under the ADA, evaluating qualification standards, such as the DOT visual acuity standard in *Kirkingburg*, that expressly screen out disabled individuals to determine whether they are justified is somewhat analogous to establishing a bona fide occupational qualification defense in a gender discrimination case under Title VII. What differences do you see? Why is disability discrimination treated differently than gender discrimination? *See Morton v. United Parcel Serv., Inc.*, 272 F.3d 1249,1260 (9th Cir. 2001) (business necessity defense under the ADA may apply to standards that are facially discriminatory as well as to those having a disparate impact, but "Congress must have intended to permit across-the-board exclusion of employees based upon disability-related safety criterion only on a showing somewhat similar to the one used for safety qualifications under the Title VII and the ADEA BFOQ standard").

2. *A Higher Threshold for Safety Standards?* The Court notes that the regulations require an individualized determination when an employer asserts that an individual's disability constitutes a direct threat. Neither the statute nor the regulations mention individualized determinations in the context of job qualifications that are not based on the direct threat defense. Is the standard for establishing a safety qualification more stringent than the standard for establishing other qualifications that screen out those with disabilities? The Court questioned this interpretation. See footnote 15. *See also Morton v. United Parcel Serv., Inc.*, 272 F.3d 1249, 1258 (9th Cir. 2001) (rejecting plaintiff's argument that a safety-related qualification standard must be defended under the "direct threat" provision of the statute); *Kapche v. San Antonio*, 304 F.3d 493 (5th Cir. 2002) (rejecting per se rule that persons with insulin-treated diabetes cannot perform essential job function of driving; individualized assessment of plaintiff required); *EEOC v. Exxon Corp.*, 203 F.3d 871 (5th Cir. 2000) (qualification standard involving safety to be tested under business necessity, not direct threat, provision).

3. *Job Related to the Position in Question and Consistent with Business Necessity.* Is the ADA more or less burdensome on employers than Title VII in terms of the job-related and business necessity defense? On the one hand, under the ADA, employers may use the defense to justify facially discriminatory policies — a defense that is not available under Title VII. On the other hand, does the ADA impose a more stringent evidentiary standard to establish the defense? *See Morton v. United Parcel Serv., Inc.*, 272 F.3d 1249 (9th Cir. 2001) (employer rule that all applicants for "package car driver" positions have DOT certification challenged as discriminatory qualification standard as applied to driving non-DOT vehicles; court drew on both BFOQ and business necessity standards under Title VII to find that UPS not entitled to summary judgment).

4. *Burdens of Proof.* Is it appropriate to refer to the proof of job relationship and business necessity as a "defense" when the statute defines covered individuals in terms of whether they are "qualified" to perform essential functions of the job? This is the point of Justice Thomas's concurrence in *Kirkingburg* — that it is the *plaintiff's* burden to prove that he is a qualified individual with a disability, which includes proof that he can perform the essential functions of driving trucks in interstate commerce; Thomas would hold it not the defendant's burden to prove he cannot. But the Court in *Echazabal*, reproduced at p. 568, repeatedly refers to the showing

that a qualification standard that screens out a disabled person be job related for the position in question and consistent with business necessity as an affirmative defense. Don't *Echazabal* and *Kirkingburg* clearly contemplate placing the burden of proof on this issue on the employer?

3. *Disparate Impact*

Many disparate impact claims under the ADA can be recast as reasonable accommodation claims and vice versa. Which approach is more advantageous to plaintiffs? Do you think inability to accommodate, undue hardship, and direct threat are harder defenses for the employer to prove than job-relatedness and business necessity? How do the remedies differ?

Some reasonable accommodation claims, however, are more difficult to frame as disparate impact claims. Consider, for example, the request of a covered individual for extra sick leave to deal with medical problems. Restricting sick leave may not exclude the person from work, but it may make it more difficult for her to schedule doctor's appointments or more expensive because she must take unpaid personal days to see the doctor. This policy would "impact" individuals with disabilities because their needs differ from those of other individuals.

Is disparate impact designed to deal with claims like this? ADA § 102(b)(3) provides that "discriminate" includes "utilizing standards, criteria, or methods of administration . . . that have the effect of discrimination on the basis of disability. . . . " The EEOC Guidance relating to disparate impact defenses seems to contemplate disparate impact claims based on a variety of employer policies: "there may be uniformly applied standards, criteria and policies not relating to selection that may also screen out or tend to screen out an individual with a disability or a class of individuals with disabilities. Like selection criteria that have a disparate impact, non-selection criteria having such an impact may also have to be job-related and consistent with business necessity, subject to consideration of reasonable accommodation." 29 C.F.R. pt. 1630, App. § 1630.15(c) (1998).

Does the leave policy violate this section? In *Alexander v. Choate*, 469 U.S. 287 (1985), a case decided under the Rehabilitation Act, the Supreme Court rejected the claim that the Tennessee Medicaid Program's 14-day limitation on inpatient coverage would have an unlawful disparate impact on the disabled. *Choate* seems most directly relevant to a claim by an individual with a disability for more sick leave than other individuals receive. Under the ADA, can such an employee attack a sick leave policy that restricts paid leave to 14 days on the ground that the policy has a disparate impact on employees with disabilities? The EEOC suggests that such a claim is not viable but that an employee affected by such a policy may be entitled to leave as a reasonable accommodation:

> "No-leave" policies (e.g., no leave during the first six months of employment) are . . . not subject to challenge under the adverse impact theory. However, an employer, in spite of its "no-leave" policy, may, in appropriate circumstances, have to consider the provision of leave to an employee with a disability as a reasonable accommodation, unless the provision of leave would impose an undue hardship.

29 C.F.R. pt. 1630, App. § 1630.15(c). What does this mean?

E. SPECIAL PROBLEMS OF DISABILITY DISCRIMINATION

The ADA contains detailed provisions relating to applicants and employees who use illegal drugs or alcohol and to employers who use medical examinations or inquiries. In addition, the ADA prohibits retaliation and interference and discrimination against someone who has a relationship with a person with a disability, and it has been interpreted to prohibit disability-based harassment. Also, the impact of the ADA on health and disability insurance plans warrants special consideration. Finally, rights granted under the Family and Medical Leave Act may be a useful alternative to the ADA for individuals whose health problems make regular attendance at work difficult.

1. Drug or Alcohol Users

Section 104(a) provides that the term "qualified individual with a disability" shall not include a person "who is currently engaging in the illegal use of drugs" when the covered entity acts on the basis of such use. Such individuals simply are not covered by the statute. In contrast, the plain language of §104(a) states that an alcoholic who is currently using alcohol may be disabled under the ADA. In any event, alcoholics and drug addicts are protected from discrimination on the basis of their alcoholism or drug *addiction*. Section 104(b) provides that nothing in §104(a) shall exclude from the definition of qualified individual with a disability an individual who:

(1) has successfully completed a supervised drug rehabilitation program and is no longer engaging in the illegal use of drugs, or has otherwise been rehabilitated successfully and is no longer engaging in such use;
(2) is participating in a supervised rehabilitation program and is no longer engaging in such use;
(3) is erroneously regarded as engaging in such use, but is not engaging in such use.

However, §104(c) provides employers with a number of potential defenses against a person claiming disability discrimination because of drug or alcohol addiction or use. For example, §104(c)(1)-(2) permits a covered entity to prohibit the use of illegal drugs and alcohol, or being under the influence of alcohol, at the workplace, and §104(c)(4) permits covered entities to "hold an employee who engages in the illegal use of drugs or who is an alcoholic to the same qualification standards for employment or job performance and behavior that such entity holds other employees, even if any unsatisfactory performance or behavior is related to the drug use or alcoholism of such employee."

In *Zenor v. El Paso Health Care*, 176 F.3d 847 (5th Cir. 1999), the Fifth Circuit considered the meaning of the exclusion and the safe harbor. The court found that, in determining whether an individual is "currently" engaged in the illegal use of drugs, the operative moment is the time the employment decision is made, not when it goes into effect. In that case, at the time the company made the decision to fire a pharmacist, his illegal drug use had occurred roughly one month previously, which was "current" enough to deprive him of protection under the ADA. The court read "currently" to mean "sufficiently recent" to justify the employer's belief that the drug use was a continuing problem, and no doubt the fact that plaintiff was a pharmacist made his employer's concerns about his drug use particularly credible.

2.   *Medical Examinations and Inquiries*

Section 102(c)(1)-(4) contains a number of provisions restricting the use of medical examinations and inquiries.

a.   Pre-Employment Medical Examinations and Inquiries

An employer is prohibited from using a medical examination or inquiry to determine whether a job applicant has a disability or the nature and severity of such a disability. But the employer (1) may inquire into the applicant's ability to do the job before making a job offer and (2) may condition an offer of employment on the results of a medical examination if certain conditions are met. These conditions include subjecting all entering employees to a medical examination and keeping the results confidential. Such medical examinations given *after* an offer of employment has been made but prior to the commencement of employment need not be job related or consistent with business necessity. Thus, there is no restriction on the *scope* of such examinations — only on the *use* to which they are put. Of course, if they are used to exclude an individual because of disability, then the exclusionary criteria must be job related and consistent with business necessity. Presumably, Congress thought this somewhat cumbersome structure would force disability-related decisions out in the open and make employers think twice about whether their physical requirements were justified.

In contrast to these provisions, § 104(d)(1) provides that testing for the illegal use of drugs shall not be considered a "medical examination." Further, § 104(d)(2) provides that the ADA shall not be construed to "encourage, prohibit, or authorize" testing for the illegal use of drugs or making employment decisions based on the results of such tests. As you would expect, the ADA regulations contain lengthy and detailed interpretations of these provisions. *See* 29 C.F.R. §§ 1630.13, 1630.14, 1630.16(c).

The EEOC has issued detailed guidance to agency personnel explaining its position on pre-employment questions. EEOC Notice 915.002 (Oct. 10, 1995). The document identifies as illegal any questions that seek information about whether the applicant is disabled including:

Do you have AIDS?
Have you ever filed for workers' compensation?
What prescription drugs are you currently taking?
Have you ever been treated for mental health problems?
How much alcohol do you drink each week?

On the other hand, the following questions are identified as lawful:

Can you perform the functions of this job with or without reasonable accommodation?
Please describe or demonstrate how you would perform these functions.
Can you meet the attendance requirements of the job?
Do you have the required licenses to perform these jobs?

Since pre-offer tests are prohibited if they are "medical," the definition of that term is critical. For the EEOC, prohibited "medical" tests are those that seek to reveal the existence of an impairment rather than measure an individual's performance of a task. Physical fitness tests, for example, are not medical examinations and are permitted but, since they will tend to screen out disabled applicants, they must be job related for the position in question and consistent with business necessity. Under the EEOC's Enforcement Guidance, psychological tests that are "designed to identify a mental disorder or impairment" qualify as medical examinations, but psychological tests "that measure personality traits such as honesty, preferences, and habits" do not. In *Karracker v. Rent-A-Center, Inc.*, 411 F.3d 831 (7th Cir. 2005), the Seventh Circuit held that the Minnesota Multiphasic Personality Inventory (MMPI) was a medical examination within the meaning of the ADA and not a test designed merely to identify personality traits as the employer had claimed. Thus, it could not be administered in a pre-offer setting.

In *Grenier v. Cyanamid Plastics, Inc.*, 70 F.3d 667 (1st Cir. 1995), an employee on disability leave due to psychological problems, including paranoia, sought reinstatement as an electrician. The employer asked whether his mental state might interfere with his ability to get along with co-workers and asked for medical documentation as to his limitations and his need for accommodation. The First Circuit ruled that the ADA does not preclude an employer, during the pre-offer stage, from asking an individual with a known disability whether he can perform the job. In addition, requests for medical documentation to confirm the existence of a claimed disability or to determine ability to perform are permissible. The court reasoned that the ban on pre-offer inquiries is designed to ensure that a hidden disability stays hidden. Because the employer already was familiar with the former employee's disability, the employer had a right to assess his recovery and his ability to perform.

If an employer asks an applicant questions that are *lawful* under the ADA and the applicant lies, the employer is justified in discharging the employee when the lie is discovered. *See Smith v. Chrysler Corp.*, 155 F.3d 799 (6th Cir. 1998). But what if the employer asks questions that are *unlawful* under the ADA and the applicant lies? Should she be permitted to sue under the ADA, or is she no longer qualified because she lied on the application? *See Leonel v. Am. Airlines, Inc.*, 400 F.3d 702 (9th Cir. 2005) (HIV-positive applicants for flight attendant positions whose job offers were rescinded for their failure to disclose that status raised factual issue as to whether airline violated ADA in requiring applicants to disclose medical information and undergo medical examinations before background checks had been completed).

Suppose an employer asks an applicant questions that are unlawful under the ADA and the applicant is not hired, allegedly because of his or her response to those questions. Must the applicant be a "qualified" disabled individual in order to sue the employer? The Ninth and Tenth Circuits have ruled that non-disabled applicants and employees can sue for medical inquiry violations of this section. *See Fredenburg v. Contra Costa County Dept. of Health Servs.*, 172 F.3d 1176 (9th Cir. 1999) (employees) (ADA provisions governing permissible examinations refer to "employees" and "job applicants" not "qualified individual with a disability"); *Griffin v. Steeltek Inc.*, 160 F.3d 591 (10th Cir. 1998) (applicants). What remedy is appropriate?

b. Medical Examinations and Inquiries of Current Employees

Employers are prohibited from requiring medical examinations and inquiries of current employees, unless such examination or inquiry is job related and consistent with a business necessity. *See Thomas v. Corwin*, 483 F.3d 516 (8th Cir. 2007) (employer's request that employee submit to fitness-for-duty examination was job-related and consistent with business necessity when employer had reason to doubt employee's ability to perform duties due to stress and anxiety); *Gajda v. Manhattan & Bronx Surface Transit Operating Auth.*, 396 F.3d 187, 189 (2d Cir. 2005) (requiring an employee to disclose the results of HIV tests was permissible in order for the employer to determine whether plaintiff could safely perform his duties in light of representations by plaintiff and his doctor that he was unable to perform his job and needed "intermittent leave at undetermined times for lifetime"). Again, however, the results of such examinations or inquiries are confidential.

See Enforcement Guidance on Disability-Related Inquiries and Medical Examinations of Employees under the Americans with Disabilities Act No. 915.002 (July 26, 2000) ("Enforcement Guidance on Employees"). *See generally* Jarod Spencer González, *A Matter of Life and Death — Why the ADA Permits Mandatory Periodic Medical Examinations of "Remote-Location" Employees*, 66 LA. L. REV. 681 (2006) (challenging EEOC enforcement guidance prohibiting remote-location employers from demonstrating that their mandatory periodic medical examination policies are job-related and consistent with business necessity).

3.   *Retaliation and Interference*

Section 12203 prohibits certain acts of retaliation and interference. Section 12203(a) provides that "no person" shall discriminate against "any individual" because that person has opposed an act made unlawful by the ADA or because such person has participated in an investigation or a proceeding under the ADA. See Chapter 5, section G, dealing with similar language under Title VII and the ADEA. Similarly, § 12203(b) prohibits coercion of, or interference with, a person who exercises or asserts ADA rights for himself or another. ADA § 12203(c). The Third Circuit, in *Krouse v. American Sterilizer Co.*, 126 F.3d 494 (3d Cir. 1997), held that, because the language of the ADA retaliation provision protects "any individual," a plaintiff asserting a retaliation claim under the ADA need not establish that he or she is a qualified individual with a disability. *Accord Muller v. Costello*, 187 F.3d 298 (2d Cir. 1999).

As noted above, the ADA's antiretaliation provision is broader than that contained in Title VII or the ADEA. While § 12203(a) parallels the antiretaliation provisions of Title VII and the ADEA, § 12203(b) has been analogized to § 8(a)(1) of the National Labor Relations Act. In *Fogelman v. Mercy Hosp., Inc.*, 283 F.3d 561 (3d Cir. 2002), a son and father worked for the same employer. The son claimed he had been fired because his father had sued the employer, alleging violations of the antiretaliation provisions of the ADA and ADEA. The Third Circuit held that the ADEA did not reach the son's claim, reasoning that it protects only persons who themselves have engaged in protected activity. But the court found a third-party retaliation claim actionable under the ADA, pointing to the broader language of § 12203(b). Moreover, the court also upheld the son's alternative claim that he had been fired because his employer believed, albeit mistakenly, that he had been assisting his father with his suit. The court found this "perception theory" viable as well. "That [plaintiff] was fired because Mercy thought he was engaged in protected activity, even if he actually was not, presents a valid legal claim." *Id.* at 565. It is the employer's intent, not the employee's actions, that are determinative, said the court.

In analyzing claims under § 12203(a), courts, consistent with their practice under Title VII and the ADEA, have insisted that the plaintiff identify an adverse action in order to state a retaliation claim. Presumably, however, the Supreme Court's decision in *Burlington Northern*, reproduced at p. 473 will govern analysis of the "adverse action" element in ADA §12203(a)'s retaliation claims as well. *See, e.g., Stewart v. Indep. Sch. Dist. No. 196*, 481 F.3d 1034 (8th Cir. 2007).

4. *Harassment*

The lower courts have either assumed or have expressly acknowledged that a claim for hostile work environment may be brought under the ADA. *See, e.g., Arrieta-Colon v. Wal-Mart P.R., Inc.*, 434 F.3d 75, 79 (1st Cir. 2006) (upholding a jury verdict finding harassment of plaintiff stemming from supervisors' and co-workers' reactions to a penile implant used to correct a sexual dysfunction that left plaintiff with the appearance of a constant semi-erection); *Quiles-Quiles v. Henderson*, 439 F.3d 1, 3 (1st Cir. 2006) (upholding jury verdict under Rehabilitation Act for employee who suffered a hostile work environment on account of his depression when he was subjected to such constant ridicule that he was hospitalized and eventually forced to resign). *But see Mason v. Wyeth, Inc.*, 183 Fed. Appx. 353, 361-62 (4th Cir. 2006) (no disability harassment when plaintiff was only one of several individuals subjected to pranks, even if the pranks were often more startling and disruptive for him due to his hearing impairment); *Shaver v. Indep. Stave Co.*, 350 F.3d 716 (8th Cir., 2003) (while disability harassment is actionable, two years of calling plaintiff "platehead" because of a metal appliance implanted his skull to treat epilepsy not severe enough to qualify).

A hostile work environment claim may arise when plaintiff can show he was targeted for harassment either because of his disability or because of his request for an accommodation. When the hostile work environment claim is based on a request for accommodation, the line between a retaliation claim and a hostile work environment claim becomes murky. Courts have sometimes divided the allegations into two separate claims, looking to see whether there is a materially adverse job action to support a retaliation claim and then looking at taunts, threats, cartoons, and jokes to see if the conduct is sufficiently severe or pervasive to constitute harassment. *See Silk v. City of Chicago*, 194 F.3d 788 (7th Cir. 1999). Is this a correct approach? What about §12203(b)? *See Brown v. City of Tucson*, 336 F.3d 1181 (9th Cir. 2003). For a discussion of disability-based harassment claims and criticism of courts' importation of Title VII standards, *see* Lisa Eichhorn, *Hostile Environment Actions, Title VII, and the ADA: The Limits of the Copy-and-Paste Function*, 77 WASH. L. REV. 575 (2002). *See also* Mark C. Weber, *Exile and the Kingdom: Integration, Harassment, and the Americans with Disabilities Act*, 63 MD. L. REV. 162, 189-90 (2004) ("Verbal threats, which are commonly found in cases that courts throw out as inadequate to sustain a harassment claim, are specific violations of 12203(b)").

5. *Protected Relationships*

Section 12112(b)(4), prohibits a covered entity from discriminating against a qualified individual "because of the known disability of an individual with whom the qualified individual is known to have a relationship or association." Section 504 of the Rehabilitation Act was amended to provide the same protection. The EEOC, however, believes that this prohibition does not entitle such an individual to reasonable accommodation so that he or she can attend to the needs of his or her relative or associate. *See* 29 C.F.R. pt. 1630, app. § 1630.8.

The Fourth Circuit, in *Tyndall v. National Educ. Ctrs.*, 31 F.3d 209 (4th Cir. 1994), held, consistent with the EEOC view, that a business school was not required to restructure an employee's work schedule to enable her to care for her disabled son. The court found further that the school had not discharged the plaintiff because of her association with her disabled son and unfounded fears that this would lead to increased costs or absences. Rather, the school discharged her because of her excessive absenteeism. *Id.* at 211.

In order to make out a case of discrimination based on association with a disabled individual, the plaintiff must show that the individual with whom she has a relationship is disabled and that the employer was aware of the third party's disability. *Ennis v. National Assn. of Bus. & Educ. Radio, Inc.*, 53 F.3d 55 (4th Cir. 1995). Even if these minimum requirements are satisfied, the employee must be fired *because of* the relationship. In *Ennis*, the court concluded that plaintiff was discharged for inadequate performance, not because of her relationship with her disabled son. Cases of discrimination based on association are subject to ADA defenses, including the direct threat defense. *See Den Hartog v. Wasatch Academy*, 129 F.3d 1076 (10th Cir. 1997) (boarding school teacher lawfully discharged based on relationship with son who suffered from psychiatric disorder that caused the son to engage in threatening behavior toward other boarding school personnel and their families). *See generally* Lawrence D. Rosenthal, *Association Discrimination Under the Americans with Disabilities Act: Another Uphill Battle for Potential ADA Plaintiffs*, 22 HOFSTRA LAB. & EMP. L.J. 132 (2004).

6.   Health and Disability Insurance

EEOC INTERIM GUIDANCE ON APPLICATION OF
ADA TO HEALTH INSURANCE
EEOC Compliance Manual 915.002; 6902 (CCH) (June 8, 1993)

II.   BACKGROUND AND LEGAL FRAMEWORK

The ADA provides that it is unlawful for an employer to discriminate on the basis of disability against a qualified individual with a disability in regard to ". . . terms, conditions, and privileges of employment.". . . Section 1630.4 of the Commission's regulations implementing the employment provisions of the ADA further provides, in pertinent part, that it is unlawful for an employer to discriminate on the basis of disability against a qualified individual with a disability in regard to "[f]ringe benefits available by virtue of employment, whether or not administered by the [employer]." 29 C.F.R. § 1630.4(f). Employee benefit plans, including health insurance plans provided by an employer to its employees, are a fringe benefit available by virtue of employment. Generally speaking, therefore, the ADA prohibits employers from discriminating on the basis of disability in the provision of health insurance to their employees. . . .

Several consequences result from the application of these statutory provisions. First, disability-based insurance plan distinctions are permitted only if they are within the protective ambit of section 501(c) of the ADA. Second, decisions about the employment of an individual with a disability cannot be motivated by concerns about the impact of the individual's disability on the employer's health insurance plan. Third, employees with disabilities must be accorded "equal access" to whatever health insurance the employer provides to employees without disabilities. . . . Fourth, in view of the statute's "association provision," it would violate the ADA for an employer to make an employment decision about any person, whether or not that person has a disability, because of concerns about the impact on the health insurance plan of the disability of someone else with whom that person has a relationship. . . .

III.   DISABILITY-BASED DISTINCTIONS

A.   FRAMEWORK OF ANALYSIS

Whenever it is alleged that a health-related term or provision of an employer provided health insurance plan violates the ADA, the first issue is whether the challenged term or provision is, in fact, a disability-based distinction. If the Commission determines that a challenged health insurance plan term or provision is a disability-based distinction, the respondent will be required to prove that that disability-based distinction is within the protective ambit of section 501(c) of the ADA.

In pertinent part, section 501(c) permits employers, insurers, and plan administrators to establish and/or observe the terms of an insured health insurance plan that is "bona fide," based on "underwriting risks, classifying risks, or administering such risks that are based on or not inconsistent with State law," and that is not being used as a "subterfuge" to evade the purposes of the ADA. Section 501(c) likewise permits employers, insurers, and plan administrators to establish and/or observe the terms of a "bona fide" self-insured plan that is not used as a "subterfuge." . . .

B.   WHAT IS A DISABILITY-BASED DISTINCTION?

It is important to note that not all health-related plan distinctions discriminate on the basis of disability. Insurance distinctions that are not based on disability, and that are applied equally to all insured employees, do not discriminate on the basis of disability and so do not violate the ADA.[7]

For example, a feature of some employer provided health insurance plans is a distinction between the benefits provided for the treatment of physical conditions on the one hand, and the benefits provided for the treatment of "mental/nervous" conditions on the other. Typically, a lower level of benefits is provided for the treatment of mental/nervous conditions than is provided for the treatment of physical conditions. Similarly, some health insurance plans provide fewer benefits for "eye care" than for other physical conditions. Such broad distinctions, which apply to the treatment of a multitude of dissimilar conditions and which constrain individuals both with and without disabilities, are not distinctions based on disability. Consequently, although such distinctions may have a greater impact on certain individuals

---

7. The term "discriminates" refers only to disparate treatment. The adverse impact theory of discrimination is unavailable in this context. See *Alexander v. Choate*, 469 U.S. 287 (1985). . . .

with disabilities, they do not intentionally discriminate on the basis of disability[8] and do not violate the ADA.

Blanket pre-existing condition clauses that exclude from the coverage of a health insurance plan the treatment of conditions that pre-date an individual's eligibility for benefits under that plan also are not distinctions based on disability, and do not violate the ADA. Universal limits or exclusions from coverage of all experimental drugs and/or treatments, or of all "elective surgery," are likewise not insurance distinctions based on disability. Similarly, coverage limits on medical procedures that are not exclusively, or nearly exclusively utilized for the treatment of a particular disability are not distinctions based on disability. Thus, for example, it would not violate the ADA for an employer to limit the number of blood transfusions or X-rays that it will pay for, even though this may have an adverse effect on individuals with certain disabilities. . . .

In contrast, however, health-related insurance distinctions that are based on disability may violate the ADA. A term or provision is "disability-based" if it singles out a particular disability (e.g., deafness, AIDS, schizophrenia), a discrete group of disabilities (e.g., cancers, muscular dystrophies, kidney diseases), or disability in general (e.g., non-coverage of all conditions that substantially limit a major life activity).

As previously noted, employers may establish and/or observe the terms and provisions of a bona fide benefit plan, including terms or provisions based on disability, that are not a "subterfuge to evade the purposes" of the ADA. Such terms and provisions do not violate the ADA. However, disability-based insurance distinctions that are a "subterfuge" do intentionally discriminate on the basis of disability and so violate the ADA.

Example 2. R Company's new self-insured health insurance plan caps benefits for the treatment of all physical conditions, except AIDS, at $100,000 per year. The treatment of AIDS is capped at $5,000 per year. CP, an employee with AIDS enrolled in the health insurance plan, files a charge alleging that the lower AIDS cap violates the ADA. The lower AIDS cap is a disability-based distinction. Accordingly, if R is unable to demonstrate that its health insurance plan is bona fide and that the AIDS cap is not a subterfuge, a violation of the ADA will be found. . . .

C. THE RESPONDENT'S BURDEN OF PROOF

Once the Commission has determined that a challenged health insurance term or provision constitutes a disability-based distinction, the respondent must prove that the health insurance plan is either a bona fide insured plan that is not inconsistent with state law, or a bona fide self-insured plan. The respondent must also prove that the challenged disability-based distinction is not being used as a subterfuge. . . . [The Commission justified this allocation of burden of proof on the ground that employers control the relevant data.]

---

8. However, it would violate the ADA for an employer to selectively apply a universal or "neutral" non-disability based insurance distinction only to individuals with disabilities. Thus, for example, it would violate the ADA for an employer to apply a "neutral" health insurance plan limitation on "eye care" only to an employee seeking treatment for a vision disability, but not to other employees who do not have vision disabilities. Charges alleging that a universal or "neutral" non-disability based insurance distinction has been selectively applied to individuals with disabilities should be processed using traditional disparate treatment theory and analysis.

1. The Health Insurance Plan Is "Bona Fide" and Consistent with Applicable Law

... If the health insurance plan is an insured plan, the respondent will be able to satisfy this requirement by proving that: (1) the health insurance plan is bona fide in that it exists and pays benefits, and its terms have been accurately communicated to eligible employees; and (2) the health insurance plan's terms are not inconsistent with applicable state law as interpreted by the appropriate state authorities. If the health insurance plan is a self-insured plan, the respondent will only be required to prove that the health insurance plan is bona fide in that it exists and pays benefits, and that its terms have been accurately communicated to covered employees.

2. The Disability-Based Distinction Is Not a Subterfuge

... "Subterfuge" refers to disability-based disparate treatment that is not justified by the risks or costs associated with the disability. Whether a particular challenged disability-based insurance distinction is being used as a subterfuge will be determined on a case by case basis, considering the totality of the circumstances.

The respondent can prove that a challenged disability-based insurance distinction is not a subterfuge in several ways. A non-exclusive list of potential business/insurance justifications follows.

a. The respondent may prove that it has not engaged in the disability-based disparate treatment alleged. For example, where a charging party has alleged that a benefit cap of a particular catastrophic disability is discriminatory, the respondent may prove that its health insurance plan actually treats all similarly catastrophic conditions in the same way.

b. The respondent may prove that the disparate treatment is justified by legitimate actuarial data, or by actual or reasonable anticipated experience, and that conditions with comparable actuarial data and/or experience are treated in the same fashion. In other words, the respondent may prove that the disability-based disparate treatment is attributable to the application of legitimate risk classification and underwriting procedures to the increased risks (and thus increased cost to the health insurance plan) of the disability, and not to the disability per se.

c. The respondent may prove that the disparate treatment is necessary (i.e., that there is no nondisability-based health insurance plan change that could be made) to ensure that the challenged health insurance plan satisfies the commonly accepted or legally required standards for the fiscal soundness of such an insurance plan. The respondent, for example, may prove that it limited coverage for the treatment of a discrete group of disabilities because continued unlimited coverage would have been so expensive as to cause the health insurance plan to become financially insolvent, and there was no nondisability-based health insurance plan alteration that would have avoided insolvency.

d. The respondent may prove that the challenged insurance practice or activity is necessary (i.e., that there is no nondisability-based change that could be made to prevent the occurrence of an unacceptable change either in the coverage of the health insurance plan, or in the premiums charged for the health insurance plan). An "unacceptable" change is a drastic increase in premium payments (or in co-payments or deductibles), or a drastic alteration to the scope of coverage or level of benefits provided, that would: (1) make the health insurance plan effectively unavailable to a significant number of other employees, (2) make the health insurance plan so unattractive as to result in significant adverse selection, or (3) make the health insurance plan so unattractive that the employer cannot compete in recruiting and maintaining qualified workers due to the superiority of health insurance plans offered by other employers in the community.

e. Where the charging party is challenging the respondent's denial of coverage for disability-specific treatment, the respondent may prove that this treatment does not provide any benefit (i.e., has no medical value). . . .

NOTES

1. *Status of the Guidelines.* Although it is now more than a decade later, these guidelines are still "interim," to be used until final guidelines are promulgated after publication for notice and comment. What deference should courts give them?

2. *Undue Hardship?* Failure to provide individuals with disabilities with equal access to benefit plans is discrimination under the ADA. Can an employer defend against such a claim by proving that to provide equal access constitutes an undue hardship?

3. *Excluding or Capping Benefits.* If an employer excludes or caps benefits for AIDS treatment, would this violate the ADA? What arguments could you make on behalf of the employee? What arguments could you make for the employer? Would it be permissible under the ADA for an employer's health plan to limit coverage for specific drugs used only to prevent the recurrence of breast cancer or used only to treat schizophrenia? Does the answer to this question depend on other circumstances?

7. Family and Medical Leave Act

The Family and Medical Leave Act of 1993, 29 U.S.C. §§ 2601 et seq. (2007) requires covered employers to provide "eligible" employees with up to 12 weeks of unpaid leave per year when the employee is unable to work because of a "serious health problem." Other aspects of the FMLA are discussed in Chapter 5 at p. 369, including limitations on coverage. Employers also are required to maintain pre-existing health insurance while the employee is on leave and to reinstate the employee to the same or an equivalent job when the leave period is over. An employer may require an employee to provide medical certification from a health care provider to demonstrate that the employee is suffering from a serious health condition that makes the employee unable to perform job functions and is, therefore, eligible for leave. *See generally* Jane Rigler, *Analysis and Understanding of the Family and Medical Leave Act of 1993*, 45 CASE W. RES. L. REV. 457 (1995).

FMLA regulations define "serious health condition":

"[S]*erious health condition*" entitling an employee to FMLA leave means an illness, injury, impairment, or physical or mental condition that involves —
(1) Inpatient care (i.e., an overnight stay) in a hospital, hospice, or residential medical care facility, including any period of incapacity . . . or any subsequent treatment in connection with such inpatient care; or
(2) Continuing treatment by a health care provider.

29 C.F.R. §825.114(a).

The regulations define "incapacity" for purposes of this section to mean inability to work or to perform other regular daily activities. *Id.* The definition of "continuing treatment by a health care provider" in the regulations provides for five different types of continuing treatment: (1) a period of incapacity of more than three consecutive calendar days; (2) a period of incapacity due to pregnancy or prenatal care; (3) a period of incapacity due to a chronic serious health condition (e.g., asthma, diabetes, epilepsy); (4) a period of incapacity that is permanent or long term due to a condition for which treatment may not be effective (e.g., Alzheimer's, stroke, terminal illness); and (5) a period of absence to receive multiple treatments for necessary restorative surgery or for conditions such as cancer, arthritis, or kidney disease that, without treatment, would result in absences of more than three days. In order to qualify for FMLA leave, each of these situations must involve specified levels of active treatment or supervision by health care professionals. *See* 29 C.F.R. §825.114(a)(2)(i)-(v).

The regulations provide specific examples of conditions and treatments that are, and are not, eligible for FMLA leave. Routine physical, dental, or eye examinations are not covered. Cosmetic treatments not medically required do not constitute "serious health conditions," unless inpatient hospital care is required or complications arise. A variety of common short-term illnesses, such as colds and flu, do not qualify for FMLA leave, absent complications. On the other hand, restorative dental surgery following an accident; surgery to remove cancerous growths; and treatments for allergies, stress, or substance abuse are included if the other conditions of the regulation are met. Absence resulting from drug use without treatment clearly does not qualify for leave. *See* 29 C.F.R. §825.114(b)-(d). Treating substance abuse as a "serious health condition" should not prevent an employer from taking action against an employee whose abuse interferes with job performance as long as the employer complies with the ADA and does not take action against the employee because the employee has exercised his or her right to take FMLA leave for treatment of that condition.

According to FMLA regulations, being "unable to perform the functions of the position of the employee" means: "where the health care provider finds that the employee is unable to work at all or is unable to perform any one of the essential functions of the employee's position" as defined by the ADA. *See* 29 C.F.R. §825.115. The FMLA regulations expressly provide that the FMLA does not modify the ADA in any way and that employers are obligated to comply with both statutes. *See* 29 C.F.R. §825.702. *See Berry v. T-Mobile USA Inc.*, 490 F.3d 1211 (10th Cir. 2007) (approval of FMLA leave for employee with multiple sclerosis insufficient evidence that employer regarded employee as disabled).

With respect to the notice that employees must give in order to be eligible for FMLA leave, the statute provides that, when the need for leave is foreseeable, an employee must provide her employer with no less than 30 days' advance notice. *See* 29 U.S.C. §2612(e)(1) & (2)(B); *see also* 29 C.F.R. §825.302. The statute does not address notice requirements when the need for leave is unforeseeable. FMLA regulations, however, provide that "an employee should give notice to the employer of the need for FMLA leave as soon as practicable under the facts and circumstances of the particular case. It is expected that an employee will give notice to the employer within no more than one or two working days of learning of the need for leave, except in extraordinary circumstances where such notice is not feasible." *See* 29 C.F.R. §825.303.

Although these notice provisions are very generous to employees, employees will not be entitled to FMLA leave unless they provide their employer with information "sufficient to reasonably apprise it of the employee's request to take time off for a serious health condition." *See Spangler v. Federal Home Loan Bank*, 278 F.3d 847 (8th Cir. 2002) (requesting time off for "depression again" possibly valid request when employer knew employee suffered from depression); *Collins v. NTN-Bower Corp.*, 272 F.3d 1006 (7th Cir. 2001) (telling employer that employee was "sick" not sufficient);

The Supreme Court's first decision under FMLA concerned *employers'* notification requirements. Under regulations promulgated by the Department of Labor, an employer may not count leave against an employee's FMLA entitlement unless the employer has promptly notified the employee that the leave has been designated as FMLA leave. In *Ragsdale v. Wolverine World Wide*, 535 U.S. 81 (2002), an employer's policy provided eligible employees with up to seven months of unpaid leave for illness. Tracey Ragsdale, who had cancer, requested and received the seven months of leave, although her employer did not tell Ragsdale the leave was being counted as FMLA leave. When she was unable to return to work at the leave's conclusion, Ragsdale was fired. She then asked for twelve additional weeks of leave under FMLA, but her employer refused to provide the additional leave. Although Ragsdale was entitled to the additional leave under the Labor Department regulations, the Supreme Court affirmed the grant of summary judgment to the employer. It viewed the regulation as inconsistent with the statutory requirements, which guarantee an employee only up to twelve weeks of leave a year. Importantly, Ragsdale could not show she had been prejudiced or harmed by the employer's failure to give notice. The Court did not decide what would happen in a case when an employee could show harm flowing from the employer's failure to provide notice.

What are the similarities and differences between the ADA and the FMLA in terms of coverage and substantive rights? Individuals who are covered by both statutes should be aware that, if they suffer from an impairment that necessitates frequent absence, they have more than one option for dealing with this issue. Even if accommodations with respect to leave are not reasonable given their employer's needs, leave without pay under the FMLA is a statutory right with no business necessity defense as long as the employer is provided with adequate notice. In addition, employees with attendance problems that are health related, but who do not meet the ADA definition of "disabled," will not be covered by the ADA. They will, however, be entitled to leave without pay if their health problem is a "serious health condition" under the FMLA.

Chapter 7

Procedures for Enforcing Antidiscrimination Laws

A. INTRODUCTION

Title VII, 42 U.S.C. §§ 2000e et seq. (2007), the Age Discrimination in Employment Act, 29 U.S.C. §§ 621 et seq. (2007), and the Americans with Disabilities Act, 42 U.S.C. §§ 12101 et seq. (2007) all have complicated procedural requirements as a prerequisite to filing suit. The paradigm is Title VII, which Title I of the ADA incorporates by reference. § 12117(a).* The ADEA, although originally somewhat different in its provisions, has been amended several times to bring its procedures largely but not completely in line with those of Title VII. Because of the substantial identity of all three statutes, the following discussion will be framed in terms of Title VII, although relevant differences between it and the ADEA are noted.

Essentially, Title VII creates a unique amalgam of methods — administrative and judicial — for enforcement of its substantive proscriptions. *See generally* Roy L. Brooks, *A Roadmap through Title VII's Procedural and Remedial Labyrinth*, 24 Sw. U. L. REV. 511 (1995). Title VII procedures for enforcing its substantive rights are found in § 706, 42 U.S.C. § 2000e-5. A person claiming to be aggrieved by an alleged act of discrimination may file a charge with the EEOC within a specified time from the occurrence of the unfair employment practice. A charge must also be filed with any existing state antidiscrimination agency.

---

* Title II of the ADA prohibits disability discrimination by a "public entity," which includes any state or local governmental agency. 42 U.S.C. §§ 12132, 12131. *See also* 28 C.F.R. § 35.140(a) (2007). Title II enforcement procedures and remedies differ from those of Title I. *See generally* Michael Waterstone, *The Untold Story of the Rest of the Americans with Disabilities Act*, 58 VAND. L. REV. 1807 (2005).

The EEOC is directed by Title VII to serve notice of the charge on the respondent and then to conduct an investigation, culminating in a determination of whether there is reasonable cause to believe that the charge is true. If the EEOC finds no reasonable cause, it must dismiss the charge and notify the charging party, who may then bring a private action within 90 days. If, however, the EEOC does find reasonable cause, it is directed first to attempt conciliation. If that fails to eliminate the alleged unlawful employment practice, the EEOC may bring a civil suit against the respondent in district court or send a "right to sue" letter to the charging party, who may then file her own suit within 90 days.

If the EEOC does not sue within 180 days from the filing of the charge, the charging party may request a right-to-sue letter (receipt of which will start the 90 days running) to bring an action; or the charging party may permit EEOC processes to proceed to their conclusion and bring suit within 90 days of that point. If the EEOC does commence suit, the charging party loses the right to bring suit, but has a statutory right to intervene to protect his or her interests against governmental delay or inadequate representation.

B.   THE ADMINISTRATIVE PHASE: CHARGE FILING

1. Introduction

Although Title VII establishes elaborate prescriptions for EEOC processing of individual charges, the only preconditions for private suit are timely resort to the EEOC and seasonable filing of a court suit thereafter. Even an EEOC finding that there is no reasonable cause to believe discrimination occurred does not bar suit. *McDonnell Douglas Corp. v. Green*, 411 U.S. 792, 798-99 (1972). Thus, defects in EEOC proceedings — such as failing to notify the defendant of a filed charge or failing to conduct conciliation efforts prior to private suit — do not prejudice the private plaintiff. There is, however, some authority that requires the charging party to cooperate with the EEOC's investigation as a precondition to suit. *E.g., Shikles v. Sprint/United Mgmt. Co.*, 426 F.3d 1304 (10th Cir. 2005) (under both Title VII and the ADA, an employee must cooperate with the EEOC in order to exhaust his or her administrative remedies under the ADEA); *contra Doe v. Oberweis Dairy*, 456 F.3d 704 (7th Cir. 2006), *cert. denied* 127 S. Ct. 1828 (2007). Further, the EEOC determination may be admitted as evidence in any subsequent trial. *See DeCorte v. Jordan*, 497 F.3d 433 (5th Cir. 2007); *but see Coleman v. Home Depot, Inc.*, 306 F.3d 1333 (3d Cir. 2002) (while EEOC determinations are presumably trustworthy, they may be excluded under Rule 403 if their probative value is outweighed by the danger of prejudice).

The following subsections undertake a more detailed examination of the two procedural prerequisites to private suit that the Supreme Court has identified: (1) timely filing of an appropriate charge with the EEOC and (2) timely filing of a court suit after receipt of an EEOC right-to-sue letter (or notice of dismissal). In looking at these two prerequisites, it is necessary to distinguish between procedures in states that have antidiscrimination agencies (deferral states) and procedures in those that do not (nondeferral states).

2. *Filing a Timely Charge*

Every private Title VII suit must begin with a charge under oath filed with the Equal Employment Opportunity Commission. §706(b), 42 U.S.C. §20003-5(b). Title VII requires that the charge comply with EEOC requirements as to form and content, but the EEOC regulations specifically provide that, notwithstanding the absence of preferred information, "a charge is sufficient when the Commission receives from the person making the charge a written statement sufficiently precise to identify the parties and to describe generally the action or practice complained of." 29 C.F.R. §1601.12(b) (2007).

Consistent with the regulations, the courts have been generally permissive as to what will be deemed a charge for purposes of satisfying this requirement. For example, §1601.12(b) provides that the absence of an oath at the time of filing can be remedied later. *Edelman v. Lynchburg College*, 535 U.S. 106, 115 (2002), upheld this regulation: "Construing §706 to permit the relation back of an oath omitted from an original filing ensures that the lay complainant, who may not know enough to verify on filing, will not risk forfeiting his rights inadvertently. At the same time, the Commission looks out for the employer's interest by refusing to call for any response to an otherwise sufficient complaint until the verification has been supplied."

Prior to *Edelman*, the preliminary intake questionnaire used by the EEOC in its filing procedure had been held by some courts to constitute a valid charge at the time it was completed even though it was unsigned and unverified and the formal charge was not executed until later. *E.g., Wilkerson v. Grinnell Corp.*, 270 F.3d 1314 (11th Cir. 2001). *Edelman*, however, suggested that it may be important whether the charging party and/or the EEOC treated an unverified document as a "charge." The Court remanded for determination of this issue.

On remand, the Fourth Circuit held that the plaintiff's intent that the letter function as a charge sufficed, even if the EEOC failed to treat it as one. *Edelman v. Lynchburg College*, 300 F.3d 400 (4th Cir. 2002). *Accord Holowecki v. Fed. Express Corp.*, 440 F.3d 558 (2d Cir. 2006), *cert. granted*, 127 S. Ct. 2914 (2007) (intake questionnaire and affidavit satisfied ADEA's charge requirement where the tone and content of affidavit communicated plaintiff's intent to activate the EEOC procedures); *but see Bost v. Fed. Express Corp.*, 372 F.3d 1233, 1241 (11th Cir. 2004) ("plaintiff's conduct showed he did not intend to activate the administrative process" before filing a formal charge). *See also Buck v. Hampton Twp. Sch. Dist.*, 452 F.3d 256 (3d Cir. 2006) (employer's detailed response to charge without raising lack of verification before issuance of right to sue letter waived such a challenge).

This liberality as to what constitutes a charge is not, however, reflected in the law that has developed as to when a charge is deemed timely. Title VII provides two applicable periods of limitations. The "rule" is that a charge must be filed within 180 days "after the alleged unlawful employment practice occurred." §706(e), 42 U.S.C. §2000e-5(e); *see also* ADEA, §7(d)(1), 29 U.S.C. §626(d)(1). The "exception" applies when a state or local antidiscrimination agency exists; in such cases, the charge must be filed with both the state agency and the EEOC within 300 days of the alleged violation or within thirty days after notice that the state proceedings are terminated, whichever is earlier. §706(e), 42 U.S.C. §2000e-5(e). With the spread of fair employment practices laws at the state and local levels, the 300/30-day period is more the rule than the exception.

For either the 180 or the 300 day period, it is critical to know when the alleged violation occurred and whether any factors will toll the running of the period.

LEDBETTER v. THE GOODYEAR TIRE &
RUBBER COMPANY, INC.
127 S. Ct. 2162 (2007)

ALITO, J., delivered the opinion of the Court.

This case calls upon us to apply established precedent in a slightly different context. We have previously held that the time for filing a charge of employment discrimination with the Equal Employment Opportunity Commission (EEOC) begins when the discriminatory act occurs. We have explained that this rule applies to any "discrete act" of discrimination, including discrimination in "termination, failure to promote, denial of transfer, [and] refusal to hire." *National Railroad Passenger Corporation* v. *Morgan*, 536 U.S. 101 (2002). Because a pay-setting decision is a "discrete act," it follows that the period for filing an EEOC charge begins when the act occurs. Petitioner . . . asks us to deviate from our prior decisions in order to permit her to assert her claim under Title VII. Petitioner also contends that discrimination in pay is different from other types of employment discrimination and thus should be governed by a different rule. But because a pay-setting decision is a discrete act that occurs at a particular point in time, these arguments must be rejected. We therefore affirm the judgment of the Court of Appeals.

I

Petitioner Lilly Ledbetter (Ledbetter) worked for respondent Goodyear Tire and Rubber Company (Goodyear) at its Gadsden, Alabama, plant from 1979 until 1998. During much of this time, salaried employees at the plant were given or denied raises based on their supervisors' evaluation of their performance. In March 1998, Ledbetter submitted a questionnaire to the EEOC alleging certain acts of sex discrimination, and in July of that year she filed a formal EEOC charge. . . .

[At trial on her claim of pay discrimination under Title VII] Ledbetter introduced evidence that during the course of her employment several supervisors had given her poor evaluations because of her sex, that as a result of these evaluations her pay was not increased as much as it would have been if she had been evaluated fairly, and that these past pay decisions continued to affect the amount of her pay throughout her employment. Toward the end of her time with Goodyear, she was being paid significantly less than any of her male colleagues. Goodyear maintained that the evaluations had been nondiscriminatory, but the jury found for Ledbetter and awarded her backpay and damages.

On appeal, Goodyear contended that Ledbetter's pay discrimination claim was time barred with respect to all pay decisions made prior to September 26, 1997 — that is, 180 days before the filing of her EEOC questionnaire.[1] And Goodyear argued that no discriminatory act relating to Ledbetter's pay occurred after that date.

[The Eleventh Circuit reversed. It refused to allow plaintiff to challenge decisions prior to September 26, 1997 and, as to the two pay decisions that occurred within that time span, found insufficient evidence that Goodyear had acted with discriminatory

---

1. The parties assume that the EEOC charging period runs backwards from the date of the questionnaire, even though Ledbetter's discriminatory pay claim was not added until the July 1998 formal charge. We likewise assume for the sake of argument that the filing of the questionnaire, rather than the formal charge, is the appropriate date.

intent. Ledbetter did not seek certiorari with respect to the insufficient evidence holding.]. . . .

II

Title VII of the Civil Rights Act of 1964 makes it an "unlawful employment practice" to discriminate "against any individual with respect to his compensation . . . because of such individual's . . . sex." 42 U.S.C. § 2000e-2(a)(1). An individual wishing to challenge an employment practice under this provision must first file a charge with the EEOC. § 2000e-5(e)(1). Such a charge must be filed within a specified period (either 180 or 300 days, depending on the State) "after the alleged unlawful employment practice occurred," *ibid.*, and if the employee does not submit a timely EEOC charge, the employee may not challenge that practice in court, § 2000e-5(f)(1).

In addressing the issue whether an EEOC charge was filed on time, we have stressed the need to identify with care the specific employment practice that is at issue. *Morgan.* Ledbetter points to two different employment practices as possible candidates. Primarily, she urges us to focus on the paychecks that were issued to her during the EEOC charging period (the 180-day period preceding the filing of her EEOC questionnaire), each of which, she contends, was a separate act of discrimination. Alternatively, Ledbetter directs us to the 1998 decision denying her a raise, and she argues that this decision was "unlawful because it carried forward intentionally discriminatory disparities from prior years." Both of these arguments fail because they would require us in effect to jettison the defining element of the legal claim on which her Title VII recovery was based.

Ledbetter asserted disparate treatment, the central element of which is discriminatory intent. However, Ledbetter does not assert that the relevant Goodyear decisionmakers acted with actual discriminatory intent either when they issued her checks during the EEOC charging period or when they denied her a raise in 1998. Rather, she argues that the paychecks were unlawful because they would have been larger if she had been evaluated in a nondiscriminatory manner *prior to* the EEOC charging period. Similarly, she maintains that the 1998 decision was unlawful because it "carried forward" the effects of prior, uncharged discrimination decisions. In essence, she suggests that it is sufficient that discriminatory acts that occurred prior to the charging period had continuing effects during that period. This argument is squarely foreclosed by our precedents.

In *United Air Lines, Inc. v. Evans*, 431 U.S. 553 (1977), we rejected an argument that is basically the same as Ledbetter's. Evans was forced to resign because the airline refused to employ married flight attendants, but she did not file an EEOC charge regarding her termination. Some years later, the airline rehired her but treated her as a new employee for seniority purposes. Evans then sued, arguing that, while any suit based on the original discrimination was time barred, the airline's refusal to give her credit for her prior service gave "present effect to [its] past illegal act and thereby perpetuated the consequences of forbidden discrimination."

We agreed with Evans that the airline's "seniority system [did] indeed have a continuing impact on her pay and fringe benefits," but we noted that "the critical question [was] whether any present *violation* existed." (Emphasis in original.) We concluded that the continuing effects of the precharging period discrimination did not make out a present violation. As Justice Stevens wrote for the Court:

> United was entitled to treat [Evans' termination] as lawful after respondent failed to file a charge of discrimination within the 90 days then allowed by § 706(d). A discriminatory

act which is not made the basis for a timely charge . . . is merely an unfortunate event in history which has no present legal consequences.

It would be difficult to speak to the point more directly.

Equally instructive is *Delaware State College* v. *Ricks*, 449 U.S. 250 (1980), which concerned a college librarian, Ricks, who alleged that he had been discharged because of race. In March 1974, Ricks was denied tenure, but he was given a final, nonrenewable one-year contract that expired on June 30, 1975. Ricks delayed filing a charge with the EEOC until April 1975, but he argued that the EEOC charging period ran from the date of his actual termination rather than from the date when tenure was denied. In rejecting this argument, we recognized that "one of the *effects* of the denial of tenure," namely, his ultimate termination, "did not occur until later." (emphasis in original). But because Ricks failed to identify any specific discriminatory act "that continued until, or occurred at the time of, the actual termination of his employment," we held that the EEOC charging period ran from "the time the tenure decision was made and communicated to Ricks."

This same approach dictated the outcome in *Lorance* v. *AT&T Technologies, Inc.*, 490 U.S. 900 (1989), which grew out of a change in the way in which seniority was calculated under a collective-bargaining agreement. Before 1979, all employees at the plant in question accrued seniority based simply on years of employment at the plant. In 1979, a new agreement made seniority for workers in the more highly paid (and traditionally male) position of "tester" depend on time spent in that position alone and not in other positions in the plant. Several years later, when female testers were laid off due to low seniority as calculated under the new provision, they filed an EEOC charge alleging that the 1979 scheme had been adopted with discriminatory intent, namely, to protect incumbent male testers when women with substantial plant seniority began to move into the traditionally male tester positions.

We held that the plaintiffs' EEOC charge was not timely because it was not filed within the specified period after the adoption in 1979 of the new seniority rule. We noted that the plaintiffs had not alleged that the new seniority rule treated men and women differently or that the rule had been applied in a discriminatory manner. Rather, their complaint was that the rule was adopted originally with discriminatory intent. And as in *Evans* and *Ricks*, we held that the EEOC charging period ran from the time when the discrete act of alleged intentional discrimination occurred, not from the date when the effects of this practice were felt. We stated:

> Because the claimed invalidity of the facially nondiscriminatory and neutrally applied tester seniority system is wholly dependent on the alleged illegality of signing the underlying agreement, it is the date of that signing which governs the limitations period.[2]

---

2. After *Lorance*, Congress amended Title VII to cover the specific situation involved in that case. See 42 U.S.C. § 2000e-5(e)(2) (allowing for Title VII liability arising from an intentionally discriminatory seniority system both at the time of its adoption and at the time of its application). The dissent attaches great significance to this amendment, suggesting that it shows that *Lorance* was wrongly reasoned as an initial matter. However, the very legislative history cited by the dissent explains that this amendment and the other 1991 Title VII amendments "'*expanded* the scope of relevant civil rights statutes in order to provide adequate protection to victims of discrimination'" (emphasis added). For present purposes, what is most important about the amendment in question is that it applied only to the adoption of a discriminatory seniority system, not to other types of employment discrimination. *Evans* and *Ricks*, upon which *Lorance* relied, and which employed identical reasoning, were left in place, and these decisions are more than sufficient to support our holding today.

Our most recent decision in this area confirms this understanding. In *Morgan*, we explained that the statutory term "employment practice" generally refers to "a discrete act or single 'occurrence'" that takes place at a particular point in time. We pointed to "termination, failure to promote, denial of transfer, [and] refusal to hire" as examples of such "discrete" acts, and we held that a Title VII plaintiff "can only file a charge to cover discrete acts that 'occurred' within the appropriate time period."

The instruction provided by *Evans, Ricks, Lorance,* and *Morgan* is clear. The EEOC charging period is triggered when a discrete unlawful practice takes place. A new violation does not occur, and a new charging period does not commence, upon the occurrence of subsequent nondiscriminatory acts that entail adverse effects resulting from the past discrimination. But of course, if an employer engages in a series of acts each of which is intentionally discriminatory, then a fresh violation takes place when each act is committed. See *Morgan*.

Ledbetter's arguments here — that the paychecks that she received during the charging period and the 1998 raise denial each violated Title VII and triggered a new EEOC charging period — cannot be reconciled with *Evans, Ricks, Lorance,* and *Morgan*. Ledbetter, as noted, makes no claim that intentionally discriminatory conduct occurred during the charging period or that discriminatory decisions that occurred prior to that period were not communicated to her. Instead, she argues simply that Goodyear's conduct during the charging period gave present effect to discriminatory conduct outside of that period. But current effects alone cannot breathe life into prior, uncharged discrimination; as we held in *Evans*, such effects in themselves have "no present legal consequences." Ledbetter should have filed an EEOC charge within 180 days after each allegedly discriminatory pay decision was made and communicated to her. She did not do so, and the paychecks that were issued to her during the 180 days prior to the filing of her EEOC charge do not provide a basis for overcoming that prior failure.

In an effort to circumvent the need to prove discriminatory intent during the charging period, Ledbetter relies on the intent associated with other decisions made by other persons at other times. . . .

Ledbetter's attempt to take the intent associated with the prior pay decisions and shift it to the 1998 pay decision is unsound. It would shift intent from one act (the act that consummates the discriminatory employment practice) to a later act that was not performed with bias or discriminatory motive. The effect of this shift would be to impose liability in the absence of the requisite intent.

Our cases recognize this point. In *Evans*, for example, we did not take the airline's discriminatory intent in 1968, when it discharged the plaintiff because of her sex, and attach that intent to its later act of neutrally applying its seniority rules. Similarly, in *Ricks*, we did not take the discriminatory intent that the college allegedly possessed when it denied Ricks tenure and attach that intent to its subsequent act of terminating his employment when his nonrenewable contract ran out. On the contrary, we held that "the only alleged discrimination occurred — and the filing limitations periods therefore commenced — at the time the tenure decision was made and communicated to Ricks."

[The majority justified its approach as faithful to the "integrated, multistep enforcement procedure" *Occidental Life Ins. Co. of Cal.* v. *EEOC*, 432 U.S. 355 (1977), and the compromises that led to the enactment of Title VII. Further, it stressed that statutes of limitations serve a legislative judgment favoring repose.]

The EEOC filing deadline "protects employers from the burden of defending claims arising from employment decisions that are long past." *Ricks*. Certainly, the

180-day EEOC charging deadline, is short by any measure, but "by choosing what are obviously quite short deadlines, Congress clearly intended to encourage the prompt processing of all charges of employment discrimination." *Mohasco* [*v. Silver*, 447 U.S. 807, 825 (1988)]. This short deadline reflects Congress' strong preference for the prompt resolution of employment discrimination allegations through voluntary conciliation and cooperation.

A disparate-treatment claim comprises two elements: an employment practice, and discriminatory intent. Nothing in Title VII supports treating the intent element of Ledbetter's claim any differently from the employment practice element.[3] If anything, concerns regarding stale claims weigh more heavily with respect to proof of the intent associated with employment practices than with the practices themselves. For example, in a case such as this in which the plaintiff's claim concerns the denial of raises, the employer's challenged acts (the decisions not to increase the employee's pay at the times in question) will almost always be documented and will typically not even be in dispute. By contrast, the employer's intent is almost always disputed, and evidence relating to intent may fade quickly with time. In most disparate-treatment cases, much if not all of the evidence of intent is circumstantial. Thus, the critical issue in a case involving a long-past performance evaluation will often be whether the evaluation was so far off the mark that a sufficient inference of discriminatory intent can be drawn. See *Watson* [*v. Fort Worth Bank & Trust*, 487 U.S. 977, 1004 (1998)] (Blackmun, J., joined by Brennan and Marshall, JJ., concurring in part and concurring in judgment) (noting that in a disparate-treatment claim, the *McDonnell Douglas* factors establish discrimination by inference). See also, *e.g., Zhuang* v. *Datacard Corp.*, 414 F.3d 849 (CA8 2005) (rejecting inference of discrimination from performance evaluations); *Cooper* v. *Southern Co.*, 390 F.3d 695, 732-733 (CA11 2004) (same). This can be a subtle determination, and the passage of time may seriously diminish the ability of the parties and the factfinder to reconstruct what actually happened.[4] Ledbetter contends that employers would be protected by the equitable doctrine of laches, but Congress plainly did not think that laches was sufficient in this context. Indeed, Congress took a diametrically different approach, including in Title VII a provision allowing only a few months in most cases to file a charge with the EEOC.

Ultimately, "experience teaches that strict adherence to the procedural requirements specified by the legislature is the best guarantee of evenhanded administration of the law." *Mohasco*. By operation of §§ 2000e-5(e)(1) and 2000e-5(f)(1), a Title VII "claim is time barred if it is not filed within these time limits." *Morgan*. We therefore reject the suggestion that an employment practice committed with no improper purpose and no discriminatory intent is rendered unlawful nonetheless because it

---

3. Of course, there may be instances where the elements forming a cause of action span more than 180 days. Say, for instance, an employer forms an illegal discriminatory intent towards an employee but does not act on it until 181 days later. The charging period would not begin to run until the employment practice was executed on day 181 because until that point the employee had no cause of action. The act and intent had not yet been joined. Here, by contrast, Ledbetter's cause of action was fully formed and present at the time that the discriminatory employment actions were taken against her, at which point she could have, and should have, sued.

4. The dissent dismisses this concern, but this case illustrates the problems created by tardy lawsuits. Ledbetter's claims of sex discrimination turned principally on the misconduct of a single Goodyear supervisor, who, Ledbetter testified, retaliated against her when she rejected his sexual advances during the early 1980's, and did so again in the mid-1990's when he falsified deficiency reports about her work. His misconduct, Ledbetter argues, was "a principal basis for [her] performance evaluation in 1997." Yet, by the time of trial, this supervisor had died and therefore could not testify. A timely charge might have permitted his evidence to be weighed contemporaneously.

gives some effect to an intentional discriminatory act that occurred outside the charging period. Ledbetter's claim is, for this reason, untimely.

III

A

In advancing her two theories Ledbetter does not seriously contest the logic of *Evans, Ricks, Lorance,* and *Morgan* as set out above, but rather argues that our decision in *Bazemore* v. *Friday,* 478 U.S. 385 (1986) *(per curiam),* requires different treatment of her claim because it relates to pay. Ledbetter focuses specifically on our statement that "each week's paycheck that delivers less to a black than to a similarly situated white is a wrong actionable under Title VII." She argues that in *Bazemore* we adopted a "paycheck accrual rule" under which each paycheck, even if not accompanied by discriminatory intent, triggers a new EEOC charging period during which the complainant may properly challenge any prior discriminatory conduct that impacted the amount of that paycheck, no matter how long ago the discrimination occurred. On this reading, *Bazemore* dispensed with the need to prove actual discriminatory intent in pay cases and, without giving any hint that it was doing so, repudiated the very different approach taken previously in *Evans* and *Ricks.* Ledbetter's interpretation is unsound.

Bazemore concerned a disparate-treatment pay claim brought against the North Carolina Agricultural Extension Service (Service). Service employees were originally segregated into "a white branch" and "a 'Negro branch,'" with the latter receiving less pay, but in 1965 the two branches were merged. After Title VII was extended to public employees in 1972, black employees brought suit claiming that pay disparities attributable to the old dual pay scale persisted. The Court of Appeals rejected this claim, which it interpreted to be that the "'discriminatory difference in salaries should have been affirmatively eliminated.'"

This Court reversed in a *per curiam* opinion, but all of the Members of the Court joined Justice Brennan's separate opinion. Justice Brennan wrote:

> The error of the Court of Appeals with respect to salary disparities created prior to 1972 and perpetuated thereafter is too obvious to warrant extended discussion: that the Extension Service discriminated with respect to salaries *prior* to the time it was covered by Title VII does not excuse perpetuating that discrimination *after* the Extension Service became covered by Title VII. To hold otherwise would have the effect of exempting from liability those employers who were historically the greatest offenders of the rights of blacks. A pattern or practice that would have constituted a violation of Title VII, but for the fact that the statute had not yet become effective, became a violation upon Title VII's effective date, and to the extent an employer continued to engage in that act or practice, it is liable under that statute. While recovery may not be permitted for pre-1972 acts of discrimination, to the extent that this discrimination was perpetuated after 1972, liability may be imposed.

(Emphasis in original.)

Far from adopting the approach that Ledbetter advances here, this passage made a point that was "too obvious to warrant extended discussion," namely, that when an employer adopts a facially discriminatory pay structure that puts some employees on a lower scale because of race, the employer engages in intentional discrimination whenever it issues a check to one of these disfavored employees. An employer that adopts and intentionally retains such a pay structure can surely be regarded as intending to discriminate on the basis of race as long as the structure is used.

Bazemore thus is entirely consistent with our prior precedents, as Justice Brennan's opinion took care to point out. Noting that *Evans* turned on whether "'any *present violation* existed,'" Justice Brennan stated that the *Bazemore* plaintiffs were alleging that the defendants "had *not* from the date of the Act forward made all their employment decisions in a wholly nondiscriminatory way," (emphasis in original; internal quotation marks and brackets omitted) — which is to say that they had engaged in fresh discrimination. Justice Brennan added that the Court's "holding in no sense gave legal effect to the pre-1972 actions, but, consistent with *Evans* . . . focused on the present salary structure, which is illegal if it *is a mere continuation of the pre-1965 discriminatory pay structure.*" (Emphasis added.)

The sentence in Justice Brennan's opinion on which Ledbetter chiefly relies comes directly after the passage quoted above, and makes a similarly obvious point:

> Each week's paycheck that delivers less to a black than to a similarly situated white is a wrong actionable under Title VII, regardless of the fact that this pattern was begun prior to the effective date of Title VII.

In other words, a freestanding violation may always be charged within its own charging period regardless of its connection to other violations. We repeated this same point more recently in *Morgan*: "The existence of past acts and the employee's prior knowledge of their occurrence . . . does not bar employees from filing charges about related discrete acts so long as the acts are independently discriminatory and charges addressing those acts are themselves timely filed." Neither of these opinions stands for the proposition that an action not comprising an employment practice and alleged discriminatory intent is separately chargeable, just because it is related to some past act of discrimination.

Ledbetter attempts to eliminate the obvious inconsistencies between her interpretation of *Bazemore* and the *Evans/Ricks/Lorance/Morgan* line of cases on the ground that none of the latter cases involved pay raises, but the logic of our prior cases is fully applicable to pay cases. To take *Evans* as an example, the employee there was unlawfully terminated; this caused her to lose seniority; and the loss of seniority affected her wages, among other things. The relationship between past discrimination and adverse present effects was the same in *Evans* as it is here. Thus, the argument that Ledbetter urges us to accept here would necessarily have commanded a different outcome in *Evans*.

Bazemore stands for the proposition that an employer violates Title VII and triggers a new EEOC charging period whenever the employer issues paychecks using a discriminatory pay structure. But a new Title VII violation does not occur and a new charging period is not triggered when an employer issues paychecks pursuant to a system that is "facially nondiscriminatory and neutrally applied." *Lorance*. The fact that precharging period discrimination adversely affects the calculation of a neutral factor (like seniority) that is used in determining future pay does not mean that each new paycheck constitutes a new violation and restarts the EEOC charging period.

Because Ledbetter has not adduced evidence that Goodyear initially adopted its performance-based pay system in order to discriminate on the basis of sex or that it later applied this system to her within the charging period with any discriminatory animus, *Bazemore* is of no help to her. Rather, all Ledbetter has alleged is that Goodyear's agents discriminated against her individually in the past and that this discrimination reduced the amount of later paychecks. Because Ledbetter did not file timely EEOC charges relating to her employer's discriminatory pay decisions in the past, she cannot maintain a suit based on that past discrimination at this time.

B

The dissent also argues that pay claims are different. Its principal argument is that a pay discrimination claim is like a hostile work environment claim because both types of claims are "'based on the cumulative effect of individual acts,'" but this analogy overlooks the critical conceptual distinction between these two types of claims. And although the dissent relies heavily on *Morgan*, the dissent's argument is fundamentally inconsistent with *Morgan*'s reasoning.

Morgan distinguished between "discrete" acts of discrimination and a hostile work environment. A discrete act of discrimination is an act that in itself "constitutes a separate actionable 'unlawful employment practice'" and that is temporally distinct. *Morgan.* As examples we identified "termination, failure to promote, denial of transfer, or refusal to hire." A hostile work environment, on the other hand, typically comprises a succession of harassing acts, each of which "may not be actionable on its own." In addition, a hostile work environment claim "cannot be said to occur on any particular day." In other words, the actionable wrong is the environment, not the individual acts that, taken together, create the environment.[7]

Contrary to the dissent's assertion, what Ledbetter alleged was not a single wrong consisting of a succession of acts. Instead, she alleged a series of discrete discriminatory acts, each of which *was* independently identifiable and actionable, and *Morgan* is perfectly clear that when an employee alleges "serial violations," *i.e.,* a series of actionable wrongs, a timely EEOC charge must be filed with respect to each discrete alleged violation.

While this fundamental misinterpretation of *Morgan* is alone sufficient to show that the dissent's approach must be rejected, it should also be noted that the dissent is coy as to whether it would apply the same rule to all pay discrimination claims or whether it would limit the rule to cases like Ledbetter's, in which multiple discriminatory pay decisions are alleged. The dissent relies on the fact that Ledbetter was allegedly subjected to a series of discriminatory pay decisions over a period of time, and the dissent suggests that she did not realize for some time that she had been victimized. But not all pay cases share these characteristics.

If, as seems likely, the dissent would apply the same rule in all pay cases, then, if a single discriminatory pay decision made 20 years ago continued to affect an employee's pay today, the dissent would presumably hold that the employee could file a timely EEOC charge today. And the dissent would presumably allow this even if the employee had full knowledge of all the circumstances relating to the 20-year-old decision at the time it was made.[8] The dissent, it appears, proposes that we adopt

---

7. Moreover, the proposed hostile salary environment claim would go far beyond *Morgan*'s limits. *Morgan* still required at least some of the discriminatorily-motivated acts predicate to a hostile work environment claim to occur within the charging period. ("Provided that *an act contributing to the claim occurs within the filing period*, the entire time period of the hostile environment may be considered by a court" (emphasis added)). But the dissent would permit claims where no one acted in any way with an improper motive during the charging period.

8. The dissent admits as much, responding only that an employer could resort to equitable doctrines such as laches. But first, as we have noted, Congress has already determined that defense to be insufficient. Second, it is far from clear that a suit filed under the dissent's theory, alleging that a paycheck paid recently within the charging period was itself a freestanding violation of Title VII because it reflected the effects of 20-year-old discrimination, would even be barred by laches.

a special rule for pay cases based on the particular characteristics of one case that is certainly not representative of all pay cases and may not even be typical. We refuse to take that approach.

IV

In addition to the arguments previously discussed, Ledbetter relies largely on analogies to other statutory regimes and on extrastatutory policy arguments to support her "paycheck accrual rule."

A

Ledbetter places significant weight on the [Equal Pay Act], which was enacted contemporaneously with Title VII and prohibits paying unequal wages for equal work because of sex. 29 U.S.C. §206(d). Stating that "the lower courts routinely hear [EPA] claims challenging pay disparities that first arose outside the limitations period," Ledbetter suggests that we should hold that Title VII is violated each time an employee receives a paycheck that reflects past discrimination.

The simple answer to this argument is that the EPA and Title VII are not the same. In particular, the EPA does not require the filing of a charge with the EEOC or proof of intentional discrimination. Ledbetter originally asserted an EPA claim, but that claim was dismissed by the District Court and is not before us. If Ledbetter had pursued her EPA claim, she would not face the Title VII obstacles that she now confronts.

[The majority also rejected Ledbetter's analogy to the Fair Labor Standards Act of 1938 because "an FLSA minimum wage or overtime claim does not require proof of a specific intent to discriminate." Her appeal to the National Labor Relations Act was "on firmer ground . . . since the NLRA provided a model for Title VII's remedial provisions and, like Title VII, requires the filing of a timely administrative charge (with the National Labor Relations Board) before suit may be maintained." But the Court read its authority under than statute as consistent with its precedent under Title VII. *Machinists* v. *NLRB*, 362 U.S. 411 (1960).]

B

Ledbetter, finally, makes a variety of policy arguments in favor of giving the alleged victims of pay discrimination more time before they are required to file a charge with the EEOC. Among other things, she claims that pay discrimination is harder to detect than other forms of employment discrimination.[10]

We are not in a position to evaluate Ledbetter's policy arguments, and it is not our prerogative to change the way in which Title VII balances the interests of aggrieved employees against the interest in encouraging the "prompt processing of all charges of employment discrimination," *Mohasco*, and the interest in repose.

Ledbetter's policy arguments for giving special treatment to pay claims find no support in the statute and are inconsistent with our precedents.[11] We apply the statute

10. We have previously declined to address whether Title VII suits are amenable to a discovery rule. *Morgan*. Because Ledbetter does not argue that such a rule would change the outcome in her case, we have no occasion to address this issue.

11. Ledbetter argues that the EEOC's endorsement of her approach in its Compliance Manual and in administrative adjudications merits deference. But we have previously declined to extend *Chevron* deference to the Compliance Manual, *Morgan*, and similarly decline to defer to the EEOC's adjudicatory

as written, and this means that any unlawful employment practice, including those involving compensation, must be presented to the EEOC within the period prescribed by statute. . . .

Justice GINSBURG, with whom Justice STEVENS, Justice SOUTER, and Justice BREYER join, dissenting.

Lilly Ledbetter was a supervisor at Goodyear Tire and Rubber's plant in Gadsden, Alabama, from 1979 until her retirement in 1998. For most of those years, she worked as an area manager, a position largely occupied by men. Initially, Ledbetter's salary was in line with the salaries of men performing substantially similar work. Over time, however, her pay slipped in comparison to the pay of male area managers with equal or less seniority. By the end of 1997, Ledbetter was the only woman working as an area manager and the pay discrepancy between Ledbetter and her 15 male counterparts was stark: Ledbetter was paid $3,727 per month; the lowest paid male area manager received $4,286 per month, the highest paid, $5,236.

[Ledbetter filed with the EEOC and, when her case was tried, the jury found that Goodyear paid Ledbetter an unequal salary because of her sex. The district court entered judgment for Ledbetter for backpay and damages, plus counsel fees and costs, but the Eleventh Circuit reversed] because it was incumbent on Ledbetter to file charges year-by-year, each time Goodyear failed to increase her salary commensurate with the salaries of male peers. Any annual pay decision not contested immediately (within 180 days), the Court affirms, becomes grandfathered, a *fait accompli* beyond the province of Title VII ever to repair.

The Court's insistence on immediate contest overlooks common characteristics of pay discrimination. Pay disparities often occur, as they did in Ledbetter's case, in small increments; cause to suspect that discrimination is at work develops only over time. Comparative pay information, moreover, is often hidden from the employee's view. Employers may keep under wraps the pay differentials maintained among supervisors, no less the reasons for those differentials. Small initial discrepancies may not be seen as meet for a federal case, particularly when the employee, trying to succeed in a nontraditional environment, is averse to making waves.

Pay disparities are thus significantly different from adverse actions "such as termination, failure to promote, . . . or refusal to hire," all involving fully communicated discrete acts, "easy to identify" as discriminatory. See *National Railroad Passenger Corporation v. Morgan*, 536 U.S. 101 (2002). It is only when the disparity becomes apparent and sizable, *e.g.*, through future raises calculated as a percentage of current salaries, that an employee in Ledbetter's situation is likely to comprehend her plight and, therefore, to complain. Her initial readiness to give her employer the benefit of the doubt should not preclude her from later challenging the then current and continuing payment of a wage depressed on account of her sex.

. . . Our precedent suggests, and lower courts have overwhelmingly held, that the unlawful practice is the *current payment* of salaries infected by gender-based (or race-based) discrimination — a practice that occurs whenever a paycheck delivers

---

positions. The EEOC's views in question are based on its misreading of *Bazemore*. Agencies have no special claim to deference in their interpretation of our decisions. *Reno v. Bossier Parish School Bd.*, 528 U.S. 320 (2000). Nor do we see reasonable ambiguity in the statute itself, which makes no distinction between compensation and other sorts of claims and which clearly requires that discrete employment actions alleged to be unlawful be motivated "because of such individual's . . . sex." 42 U.S.C. § 2000e-2(a)(1).

less to a woman than to a similarly situated man. See *Bazemore* v. *Friday*, 478 U.S. 385 (1986).

I . . .

A

[The dissent first recounted *Bazemore*, stressing the language, "each week's paycheck that delivers less to a black than to a similarly situated white is a wrong actionable under Title VII."] Paychecks perpetuating past discrimination, we thus recognized, are actionable not simply because they are "related" to a decision made outside the charge-filing period, but because they discriminate anew each time they issue.

Subsequently, in *Morgan*, we set apart, for purposes of Title VII's timely filing requirement, unlawful employment actions of two kinds: "discrete acts" that are "easy to identify" as discriminatory, and acts that recur and are cumulative in impact. "[A] discrete act such as termination, failure to promote, denial of transfer, or refusal to hire," we explained, "'occurs' on the day that it 'happens.' A party, therefore, must file a charge within . . . 180 . . . days of the date of the act or lose the ability to recover for it."

"Different in kind from discrete acts," we made clear, are "claims . . . based on the cumulative effect of individual acts." The *Morgan* decision placed hostile work environment claims in that category. "Their very nature involves repeated conduct." "The unlawful employment practice" in hostile work environment claims, "cannot be said to occur on any particular day. It occurs over a series of days or perhaps years and, in direct contrast to discrete acts, a single act of harassment may not be actionable on its own." (Internal quotation marks omitted.) The persistence of the discriminatory conduct both indicates that management should have known of its existence and produces a cognizable harm. Because the very nature of the hostile work environment claim involves repeated conduct,

> it does not matter, for purposes of the statute, that some of the component acts of the hostile work environment fall outside the statutory time period. Provided that an act contributing to the claim occurs within the filing period, the entire time period of the hostile environment may be considered by a court for the purposes of determining liability.

Consequently, although the unlawful conduct began in the past, "a charge may be filed at a later date and still encompass the whole."

Pay disparities, of the kind Ledbetter experienced, have a closer kinship to hostile work environment claims than to charges of a single episode of discrimination. Ledbetter's claim, resembling Morgan's, rested not on one particular paycheck, but on "the cumulative effect of individual acts." She charged insidious discrimination building up slowly but steadily. Initially in line with the salaries of men performing substantially the same work, Ledbetter's salary fell 15 to 40 percent behind her male counterparts only after successive evaluations and percentage-based pay adjustments. Over time, she alleged and proved, the repetition of pay decisions undervaluing her work gave rise to the current discrimination of which she complained. Though component acts fell outside the charge-filing period, with each new paycheck, Goodyear contributed incrementally to the accumulating harm.[2]

---

2. [*Morgan*], the Court emphasizes, required that "an act contributing to the claim occur within the [charge-] filing period." (emphasis deleted; internal quotation marks omitted). Here, each paycheck

B

The realities of the workplace reveal why the discrimination with respect to compensation that Ledbetter suffered does not fit within the category of singular discrete acts "easy to identify." A worker knows immediately if she is denied a promotion or transfer, if she is fired or refused employment. And promotions, transfers, hirings, and firings are generally public events, known to co-workers. When an employer makes a decision of such open and definitive character, an employee can immediately seek out an explanation and evaluate it for pretext. Compensation disparities, in contrast, are often hidden from sight. It is not unusual, decisions in point illustrate, for management to decline to publish employee pay levels, or for employees to keep private their own salaries.[3] Tellingly, as the record in this case bears out, Goodyear kept salaries confidential; employees had only limited access to information regarding their colleagues' earnings.

The problem of concealed pay discrimination is particularly acute where the disparity arises not because the female employee is flatly denied a raise but because male counterparts are given larger raises. Having received a pay increase, the female employee is unlikely to discern at once that she has experienced an adverse employment decision. She may have little reason even to suspect discrimination until a pattern develops incrementally and she ultimately becomes aware of the disparity. Even if an employee suspects that the reason for a comparatively low raise is not performance but sex (or another protected ground), the amount involved may seem too small, or the employer's intent too ambiguous, to make the issue immediately actionable — or winnable.

Further separating pay claims from the discrete employment actions identified in *Morgan*, an employer gains from sex-based pay disparities in a way it does not from a discriminatory denial of promotion, hiring, or transfer. When a male employee is selected over a female for a higher level position, someone still gets the promotion and is paid a higher salary; the employer is not enriched. But when a woman is paid less than a similarly situated man, the employer reduces its costs each time the pay differential is implemented. . . .

C

In light of the significant differences between pay disparities and discrete employment decisions of the type identified in *Morgan*, the cases on which the Court relies [*Evans, Ricks,* and *Lorance*] hold no sway. . . .

[The dissent viewed the majority's reliance on *Lorance* as perplexing since "that decision is no longer effective, having been superseded" by a provision added by the 1991 Civil Rights Act, 42 U.S.C. §2000e-5(e)(2). The statutory amendment "repudiated the Court's decision." It provides that an unlawful employment practice occurs "when the seniority system is adopted, when an individual becomes subject to the seniority system, or when a person aggrieved is injured by the application of the

---

within the filing period compounded the discrimination Ledbetter encountered, and thus contributed to the "actionable wrong," *i.e.,* the succession of acts composing the pattern of discriminatory pay, of which she complained.

3. See also Bierman & Gely, "Love, Sex and Politics? Sure. Salary? No Way": Workplace Social Norms and the Law, 25 Berkeley J. Emp. & Lab. L. 167, 168, 171 (2004) (one-third of private sector employers have adopted specific rules prohibiting employees from discussing their wages with co-workers; only one in ten employers has adopted a pay openness policy).

seniority system." While the dissent agreed that this amendment directly addressed only seniority systems, Congress had more generally disapproved of the Court's contraction of Title VII, and the Senate Report accompanying the precursor to the 1991 Act expressly approved of *Bazemore*.]

A clue to congressional intent can be found in Title VII's backpay provision. The statute expressly provides that backpay may be awarded for a period of up to two years before the discrimination charge is filed. 42 U.S.C. § 2000e-5(g)(1) ("Back pay liability shall not accrue from a date more than two years prior to the filing of a charge with the Commission."). This prescription indicates that Congress contemplated challenges to pay discrimination commencing before, but continuing into, the 180-day filing period. See *Morgan* ("If Congress intended to limit liability to conduct occurring in the period within which the party must file the charge, it seems unlikely that Congress would have allowed recovery for two years of backpay"). As we recognized in *Morgan*, "the fact that Congress expressly limited the amount of recoverable damages elsewhere to a particular time period [*i.e.*, two years] indicates that the [180-day] timely filing provision was not meant to serve as a specific limitation . . . [on] the conduct that may be considered."

II

The Court asserts that treating pay discrimination as a discrete act, limited to each particular pay-setting decision, is necessary to "protect employers from the burden of defending claims arising from employment decisions that are long past." But the discrimination of which Ledbetter complained is *not* long past. As she alleged, and as the jury found, Goodyear continued to treat Ledbetter differently because of sex each pay period, with mounting harm. [Further, *Morgan* protected employers from unreasonable or prejudicial delay by recognizing defenses such as waiver, estoppel, and equitable tolling.]

In a last-ditch argument, the Court asserts that this dissent would allow a plaintiff to sue on a single decision made 20 years ago "even if the employee had full knowledge of all the circumstances relating to the . . . decision at the time it was made." It suffices to point out that the defenses just noted would make such a suit foolhardy. No sensible judge would tolerate such inexcusable neglect.

Ledbetter, the Court observes, dropped an alternative remedy she could have pursued: Had she persisted in pressing her claim under the Equal Pay Act of 1963 (EPA), she would not have encountered a time bar [because that statute has a two/three year statute of limitations]; cf. *Corning Glass Works* v. *Brennan*, 417 U.S. 188 (1974). Notably, the EPA provides no relief when the pay discrimination charged is based on race, religion, national origin, age, or disability. Thus, in truncating the Title VII rule this Court announced in *Bazemore*, the Court does not disarm female workers from achieving redress for unequal pay, but it does impede racial and other minorities from gaining similar relief.

Furthermore, the difference between the EPA's prohibition against paying unequal wages and Title VII's ban on discrimination with regard to compensation is not as large as the Court's opinion might suggest. The key distinction is that Title VII requires a showing of intent. In practical effect, "if the trier of fact is in equipoise about whether the wage differential is motivated by gender discrimination," Title VII compels a verdict for the employer, while the EPA compels a verdict for the plaintiff. 2 C. Sullivan, M. Zimmer, & R. White, Employment Discrimination: Law and Practice § 7.08[F][3], p. 532 (3d ed. 2002). In this case, Ledbetter carried the burden of persuading the jury that the pay disparity she suffered was attributable to intentional sex discrimination.

III

[Justice Ginsberg then recounted the evidence Ledbetter presented at trial, including (1) an admission by a supervisor that her pay at one point was below Goodyear's minimum threshold for her position; (2) she received a "Top Performance Award" in 1996; (3) another supervisor whose evaluation of Ledbetter in 1997 led to her most recent raise denial was openly biased against women; (4) testimony by two female co-workers of pervasive discrimination and lower pay, one of whom was paid less than the men she supervised; (5) Ledbetter being told by a plant manager that the "plant did not need women, that [women] didn't help it, [and] caused problems."[10]]

Yet, under the Court's decision, the discrimination Ledbetter proved is not redressable under Title VII. Each and every pay decision she did not immediately challenge wiped the slate clean. Consideration may not be given to the cumulative effect of a series of decisions that, together, set her pay well below that of every male area manager. Knowingly carrying past pay discrimination forward must be treated as lawful conduct. . . .

This is not the first time the Court has ordered a cramped interpretation of Title VII, incompatible with the statute's broad remedial purpose. Once again, the ball is in Congress' court. As in 1991, the Legislature may act to correct this Court's parsimonious reading of Title VII. . . .

NOTES

1. *Notice of Decision of Adverse Employment Action.* The Court begins by saying that "We have previously held that the time for filing a charge of employment discrimination . . . begins when the discriminatory act occurs." This isn't quite accurate. Rather, the charge filing period begins to run when the employee receives *notice* of a discriminatory employment action. *Ricks*, 449 U.S. at 259. ("We conclude . . . that the limitations periods commenced to run when the tenure decision was made and Ricks was notified.") At another point in the majority opinion, Justice Alito confirms this: "Ledbetter, as noted, makes no claim that . . . discriminatory decisions that occurred prior to that period were not communicated to her."

A "notice of decision" rule can effectively truncate an already short limitations period. Professor Ricks' time for filing a charge for his discharge expired before he actually left his employment at Delaware State. *See also Curby v. Solutia, Inc.*, 351 F.3d 868 (8th Cir. 2003) (discrimination occurred when white male was chosen over plaintiff for a position in a prospective joint venture even though the venture was not yet operative). It is possible, however, that the notice requirement will extend the time. If an applicant is turned down for employment but is not sent a rejection letter for several months, the time period will presumably run from her receipt of the letter. *See Vadie v. Miss. State Univ.*, 218 F.3d 365 (5th Cir. 2000) (plaintiff could have held a legitimate expectation of being hired until he learned that the last vacancy was filled). *See also Wright v. AmSouth Bancorporation*, 320 F.3d 1198, 1203 (11th Cir. 2003) (no adverse action has yet occurred "when an employee is left simply to infer and deduce his employment status from the surrounding events").

---

10. Given this abundant evidence, the Court cannot tenably maintain that Ledbetter's case "turned principally on the misconduct of a single Goodyear supervisor." See n. 4.

2. *When Does a "Decision" Occur?* Typically, it is clear when a decision "occurs" — an individual is fired or is denied a promotion. But some employment decisions are more complicated. Consider *Ricks*, which involved a multi-stage tenure process at each step of which Ricks lost. The question, however, was when the actual *decision* to deny tenure occurred. Certain negative actions were not decisions because they were merely recommendations of the tenure committee or faculty senate. The College Board of Trustees then voted against Ricks, which seemed to be a decision, but the Board simultaneously provided him with a grievance procedure, which he pursued. Nevertheless, the Court found that a grievance or appeal process did not prevent the Board's formal action from constituting the relevant decision; therefore, Ricks' time to file a charge began to run from that point. While academic institutions may have unusually Byzantine procedures, the problem of whether one person's action is a "recommendation" or a "decision" or an "appeal" can arise in all hierarchical structures.

3. *No Tolling for Grievances.* Further, *Ricks* refused to even toll that period during the pendency of Ricks' grievance. It relied on *Int'l Union of Elec. Workers v. Robbins & Myers, Inc.*, 429 U.S. 229 (1976), where an employee filed a grievance under the governing collective bargaining agreement two days after he was terminated. After pursuing the multi-step grievance procedure, he filed a charge with the EEOC beyond the statutory period. The Court rejected the argument that the termination was "tentative" and "nonfinal" until completion of the grievance procedure. While the parties could have agreed to such a contract, the Court interpreted the governing collective bargaining agreement as making the at-issue action a "decision," despite the concomitant right to grieve.

The Supreme Court has rejected any formal doctrine of election of remedies in a Title VII suit, *Alexander v. Gardner-Denver Co.*, 415 U.S. 36 (1974). Indeed, this was one factor underlying *Robbins & Myers:* because the rights under the collective bargaining agreement and under Title VII are independent, plaintiff's pursuit of the grievance procedure should not toll the time to file an EEOC charge. Nevertheless, the practical effect of cases such as *Ricks* and *Robbins & Myers* may be to require such election: an employee cannot safely await completion of internal procedures before filing with the EEOC. Note, however, that filing a charge could itself prejudice an employee's rights by generating antagonism by his employer. Is the statutory prohibition of retaliation for filing (see Chapter 5) sufficient to prevent this problem? *See* Deborah L. Brake & Joanna Grossman, The *Failure of Title VII as a Rights Claiming System*, 86 N.C. L. REV. (forthcoming 2008) (Title VII's strict requirements on employees to promptly report and assert claims of discrimination on the front end leave little room for gaps in knowledge, hesitation in responding, or fears of retaliation to delay rights-claiming, and thus conflicts with extensive social science research on how people perceive and respond to discrimination in the real world; further, employees make out poorly at the back end because of grossly inadequate protection from retaliation); Scott Moss, *Fighting Discrimination while Fighting Litigation: A Tale of Two Supreme Courts*, 76 FORDHAM L. REV 981 (2008) (arguing that the Court is pursuing two inconsistent policies: encouraging internal resolution of claims while also requiring suit to be brought quickly; "These policies are plausible independently but incoherent together.").

4. *Filing a "Charge."* We saw earlier that the courts have been relatively permissive as to what constitutes a charge, and *Ledbetter* is consistent with that approach. Recall that plaintiff did not file a formal charge originally but rather answered an EEOC "questionnaire." The Court assumed that the filing of this

questionnaire with the EEOC sufficed to protect plaintiff's rights, *see* n. 1. Shortly after deciding *Ledbetter*, however, the Court granted certiorari in *Holowecki v. Fed. Express Corp.*, 440 F.3d 558 (2d Cir. 2006), *cert. granted*, 127 S. Ct. 2914 (2007), raising that issue.

5. *Does a Discovery Rule Toll the Period?* In a footnote, the *Ledbetter* majority noted that "We have previously declined to address whether Title VII suits are amenable to a discovery rule [citing *Morgan*]. Because Ledbetter does not argue that such a rule would change the outcome in her case, we have no occasion to address this issue." While Justices O'Connor, Rehnquist, and Breyer stated in a separate opinion in *Morgan* that "some version of the discovery rule applies to discrete-act claims," two of those justices are no longer on the Court.

Two issues would have to be addressed in developing "some version" of such a rule. First, does the plaintiff know (or should she have known) that she has been treated differently than other employees? While most employment benefits and burdens are highly visible, Justice Ginsburg is surely right that compensation decisions are often secret. Ms. Ledbetter knew what her compensation and raises were but might or might not have known that she was paid less than others. Second, even if the plaintiff knows about a disparity, does she have reason to know any difference is the result of discrimination? *See Beamon v. Marshall & Ilsley Trust Co.*, 411 F.3d 854 (7th Cir. 2005) (no equitable tolling for black employee since a reasonable person would have been aware that discrimination could be one possible basis for the employer's actions when he was replaced by a white with no explanation); *Wastak v. Lehigh Valley Health Network*, 342 F.3d 281 (3d Cir. 2003) (age discrimination claim accrued on date employee was fired although he had little reason to believe he had been the victim of age discrimination until he learned that he had been replaced by a younger employee nine months later). A robust discovery rule would alleviate many, though not all, of the concerns that Justice Ginsburg expressed. Is it significant that the majority did not provide any comfort in that regard?

6. *180 or 300 Days?* Don't let the Court's repeated references to 180 days fool you. That period governs only in states without a state (or local) fair employment practices agency. In states with such agencies, the period is extended to "ensure[ ] that employees are neither time barred from later filing their charges with the EEOC nor dissuaded from first filing with a state agency." *Morgan* 536 U.S. at 120. *Ledbetter* arose in Alabama, one of the few remaining states without an antidiscrimination law. In all other states (known as "deferral states" because the EEOC must defer to the state agency), a plaintiff has 300 days to file with the EEOC, although there is also a requirement of filing with the relevant state agency, which can raise complications. See Note 12, p. 616.

7. *Contaminated Environment as a Continuing Violation.* For much of the history of Title VII, the "continuing violation" question confounded the courts. The argument was that some violations of the statute were continuing such that a plaintiff could sue for harm stretching out over several years so long as the violation continued into the charge filing period. One statutory basis for the argument was Title VII's limit on backpay for two years prior to filing a charge, § 706(g), 42 U.S.C. § 2000e-5(g). Since this provision would have been largely unnecessary if no violations were continuing, Congress must have envisioned continuing remediable violations that existed prior to the running of the period. *Ledbetter* confirms what *Morgan* had previously held: the vast majority of discrimination consists of "discrete" acts that are actionable only if a charge is filed within 180/300 days of the act.

Morgan, however, recognized one exception: "We also hold that consideration of the entire scope of a hostile work environment claim, including behavior alleged outside the statutory time period, is permissible for the purposes of assessing liability, so long as any act contributing to that hostile environment takes place within the statutory time period." *Id.* at 105. Outside of the contaminated environment setting, the *Morgan* Court explicitly rejected the "serial violation argument," which would have allowed for recovery for acts outside of the statutory period when there was a series of related acts, at least one of which was within the limitations period. In this context, *Ledbetter's* rejection of the pay discrimination as a kind of serial violation is hardly groundbreaking.

But what of *Morgan's* holding that a contaminated work environment is a continuing violation? The Court reconciled its exception for hostile work environment claims with its rule for discrete violations by positing that a hostile environment "is comprised of a series of separate acts that collectively constitute one 'unlawful employment practice.'" While a charge must be timely filed

> after the unlawful practice happened, [i]t does not matter, for purposes of the statute, that some of the component acts of the hostile work environment fall outside the statutory time period. Provided that an act contributing to the claim occurs within the filing period, the entire time period of the hostile environment may be considered by a court for the purposes of determining liability.
>
> That act need not, however, be the last act. As long as the employer has engaged in enough activity to make out an actionable hostile environment claim, an unlawful employment practice has "occurred," even if it is still occurring. Subsequent events, however, may still be part of the one hostile work environment claim and a charge may be filed at a later date and still encompass the whole.

Id. at 117. *See also Jensen v. Henderson*, 315 F.3d 854, 859 (8th Cir. 2002) ("Only the smallest portion of that 'practice' needs to occur within the limitations period for the claim to be timely"); *Shields v. Fort James Corp.*, 305 F.3d 1280 (11th Cir. 2002) (same). However, a precondition for *Morgan's* "series of acts" rule is that all acts be connected so that they can be viewed as part of a single unlawful practice. *See Porter v. Cal. Dep't of Corr.*, 383 F.3d 1018, 1028-29 (9th Cir. 2004) (finding a sufficient linkage); *Rowe v. Hussmann Corp.*, 381 F.3d 775, 781 (8th Cir. 2004) (same).

8. *Pay Discrimination Not Continuing. Ledbetter* did not retreat from *Morgan's* approach to contaminated environment cases, but it refused to apply the "series of acts constituting on unlawful practice" reasoning to pay discrimination. Justice Ginsburg's dissent argued forcefully that pay discrimination was more like contaminated environment harassment than, say, a discharge. Which paradigm is more persuasive? Justice Ginsberg's dissent in *Ledbetter* leaned heavily on Title VII's two-year limitation on backpay liability to contend that Congress intended some continuing violations to be remediable. The *Morgan* majority had also looked to this provision to justify its rule for contaminated work environments. Do you understand why the Court would have deployed this argument only for harassment when Congress obviously did not have harassment (which emerged as a theory years after Title VII was enacted) in mind when it enacted the two-year limitation?

9. *Continuing Effects Don't Do It.* Both *Ledbetter* and *Morgan* relied heavily on *United Air Lines, Inc. v. Evans*, 431 U.S. 553 (1977), where plaintiff had been forced to resign in 1968 because she got married. United's no marriage policy was later invalidated in a suit in which Ms. Evans was not a party, and she applied and was rehired in 1972. United, however, refused to credit her with seniority she had

accrued before being discharged. The plaintiff's charge was not filed until more than a year after she was rehired as a new employee.

The Court found no actionable violation. Plaintiff's original discharge had not been timely challenged, nor had United's action in rehiring her without seniority credit. As for the seniority system, there was no claim that it, as such, was discriminatory. All employees — male and female — hired between 1968 and 1972 had the same advantage over plaintiff, and the failure to credit prior service was applied even-handedly. Thus, as *Ledbetter* quotes *Evans*, "A discriminatory act which is not made the basis for a timely charge is the legal equivalent of a discriminatory act which occurred before the statute was passed." In short, as to the conduct that was a violation, Evans had not filed a timely charge. As to the conduct that still affected her, there was no violation.

10. *Problems with the Paradigm.* It's not so clear how the *Morgan/Ledbetter* analytic scheme would treat some common problems. Perhaps the easiest case is the proper filing period for a hiring list compiled on the basis of results of a test alleged to have been discriminatory. It seems likely that the promulgation of the list, not each hire from it, is the cognizable violation under *Morgan, see Bishop v. New Jersey*, 84 Fed. Appx. 220, 225 (3d Cir. 2004) (when no allegation of discrimination in the selection of names from the eligibility list, a charge was time-barred when it was not filed within 300 days of the promulgation of the list), but, of course, it may not be possible to determine whether a list has a discriminatory impact until the employer has completed its hiring.

A more difficult problem is the negative evaluation that has no tangible effects when it is given but results in a discharge several years later. Consider *Thomas v. Eastman Kodak*, 183 F.3d 38 (1st Cir. 1999), which held that a discriminatory evaluation more than 300 days in the past could be challenged when it was the basis for a later layoff that was itself nondiscriminatory. Such cases predated *Ledbetter*, and so may no longer be good law. After all, Ms. Ledbetter claimed that one raise was denied because of a prior discriminatory evaluation. While the decision to deny the raise was, considered alone, nondiscriminatory, it resulted from a past discriminatory act. We have seen that some courts view an unfavorable evaluation as not, by itself, an actionable adverse employment action. See Note 2 on p. 20. Under such a rule, application of the *Morgan/Ledbetter* paradigm would make it possible to discriminate without the employer's conduct ever being actionable! Is the clear implication of *Ledbetter* that such cases are wrong? Justice Alito opposes imputed intent and wants to focus on actions driven by discriminatory intent at that moment. Or does his footnote 3 suggest a solution: "Say, for instance, an employer forms an illegal discriminatory intent towards an employee but does not act on it until 181 days later. The charging period would not begin to run until the employment practice was executed on day 181 because until that point the employee had no cause of action. The act and intent had not yet been joined." Or is this too optimistic? Alito elsewhere requires the discriminatory intent to occur during the filing period. Another possibility is that *Ledbetter* offers plaintiffs the hope of expanding the notion of what constitutes an "adverse employment action." Recall that Justice Alito's concurrence in *Burlington Northern RR v. White*, reproduced at p. 473, seemed to suggest a broad view of actionable conduct under §703(a) as well as under §704.

11. *Evidence.* The fact that a past violation is no longer actionable does not mean it is irrelevant. Assuming that some violation is timely challenged, *Morgan* made clear that "prior acts [may be used] as background evidence in support of a timely claim." 536 U.S. at 113. *See Wedow v. City of Kan. City*, 442 F.3d 661, 671 (8th Cir.

2006) ("The district court correctly permitted acts occurring outside the 300-day window to be admitted as relevant to discriminatory intent and correctly limited recovery to acts occurring within the limitations period"); *West v. Ortho-McNeil Pharm. Corp.*, 405 F.3d 578, 581 (7th Cir. 2005) (district court's exclusion of evidence on timeliness grounds was an abuse of discretion since a timely claim may be supported by proof of acts outside of the statutory timeframe).

12. The administrative enforcement scheme for private suit is somewhat different when the violation occurs in jurisdictions that have state or local antidiscrimination agencies, which now include the vast majority of states. In such states, plaintiffs have a longer period to file with the EEOC — 300 days instead of the 180 applicable in nondeferral states. However, this extension comes at a price: Title VII and the ADA (which incorporates Title VII procedures by reference) require a filing with the state agency prior to filing with the EEOC, 42 U.S.C. §2000e-5(c), §706(c). Further, the state agency must be accorded 60 days to act before the EEOC can commence its processes. This scheme creates complications. While a charge lodged with the EEOC may be held by it in "suspended animation" during the required period of state deferral, *Love v. Pullman*, 404 U.S. 522 (1972), the EEOC filing becomes effective only when the required period for state deferral has expired. *Mohasco Corp. v. Silver*, 447 U.S. 807 (1980). This means that charges must be filed with the EEOC within 240 days of the violation (in order to ensure compliance with both the 60-day period for state deferral and the 300-day period for EEOC filing). The ADEA is more relaxed than Title VII since a charge of age discrimination may be filed simultaneously with the state and the federal agencies. *See Oscar Mayer & Co. v. Evans*, 441 U.S. 750, 765 (1979).

The difficulties these rules have generated are often ameliorated by worksharing agreements between the EEOC and state agencies which typically divide charge-processing responsibility between the federal and state agencies, as by providing that the agency with which the charge was first filed will process it. The agreements often speak in terms of each agency "waiving" its right to process a charge, or authorize each agency to process a charge on behalf of the other. *See EEOC v. Commercial Office Products Co.*, 486 U.S. 107 (1988) (state waiver of its exclusive period of charge processing in worksharing agreement terminated the deferral period, thereby allowing the EEOC to begin its processes immediately). A filing need not be timely under state law to satisfy the federal statute.

13. *Statutory Change.* Justice Ginsberg's appeal to Congress generated a bill, the Lilly Ledbetter Fair Pay Act, H.R. 2831, 110th Cong. (2007), which passed the House on July 31, 2007 but faces an uncertain fate in the Senate and the threat of a presidential veto. It would amend Title VII, the ADEA and the ADA to declare that an unlawful employment practice occurs when: (1) a discriminatory compensation decision or other practice is adopted; (2) an individual becomes subject to the decision or practice; or (3) an individual is affected by application of the decision or practice, including each time compensation is paid. This would address some of the timeliness problems we have encountered, but not respond to others. Professor Tristin K. Green, in *Insular Individualism: Employment Discrimination Law after Ledbetter v. Goodyear*, 42 HARV. C.R.-C.L. L. REV. (forthcoming 2008), argues that the problem with *Ledbetter* is not merely the result but more broadly the "insular individualism" it reflects, that is, the belief that discrimination can be reduced to the action of an individual decisionmaker isolated from the work environment and the employer. She believes this mind-set has tremendous potential to reshape individual disparate treatment law in ways adverse to employees. *See also* Scott A. Moss, *Fighting Discrimination While Fighting Litigation: A Tale of Two Supreme Courts*, 76 FORDHAM L. REV. 981 (2007).

NOTE ON TIMELINESS IN PATTERN AND PRACTICE CASES

If one takes *Ledbetter* at face value, *Bazemore* remains good law for at least some kinds of "pattern or practice" cases:

> when an employer adopts a facially discriminatory pay structure that puts some employees on a lower scale because of race, the employer engages in intentional discrimination whenever it issues a check to one of these disfavored employees. An employer that adopts and intentionally retains such a pay structure can surely be regarded as intending to discriminate on the basis of race as long as the structure is used.

But this description requires a "facially discriminatory pay structure." *Lorance v. AT&T Technologies, Inc.*, 490 U.S. 900 (1989), also recognized this kind of continuing violation. In that case, plaintiffs challenged a 1979 collective bargaining agreement that altered a prior method of calculating seniority. As *Lorance* stressed: "There is no doubt, of course, that a facially discriminatory seniority system (one that treats similarly situated employees differently) can be challenged at any time." *Id.* at 911-12.

In short, continuing *facial policies* of discrimination can, presumably, be challenged at any time they adversely affect an individual. *See Courtney v. La Salle Univ.*, 124 F.3d 499 (3d Cir. 1997) (long-established facially discriminatory mandatory retirement policy could be challenged by a charge filed within 300 days of the policy's application to a particular professor). And, as the *Ledbetter* Court noted, Congress amended Title VII in 1991 to overrule *Lorance* and permit challenges to seniority systems "when the seniority system is adopted, when an individual becomes subject to the seniority system, or when a person aggrieved is injured by the application of the seniority system."

But, assuming no seniority system, when is a policy or practice "facially" discriminatory? This is not as easy a question as it appears since the pay policy in *Bazemore* did not, expressly, treat blacks and whites differently: it merely continued the salary system of prior segregated units. Indeed, *Bazemore* is more often cited for its approval of the use of multiple regression analysis to establish discrimination in salaries, an unnecessary exercise if the discrimination was "facial." And what about systemic *practices* of discrimination as in *Teamsters* and *Hazelwood*? Such policies can be viewed from two different lenses. One is that they reflect a series of continuing acts, each of which is discrete and each of which, therefore, could be properly charged. Under this view, *Ledbetter* would control and (except perhaps where the EEOC is the plaintiff), suit will be limited to acts within 180/300 days of the charge. *See Williams v. Giant Food, Inc.*, 370 F.3d 423, 429 (4th Cir. 2004) ("even if failures to promote plaintiff were part of a broader pattern or practice of discrimination, they remain discrete acts of discrimination").

A second view is that the various acts of discrimination reflect an underlying policy, and that policy can be attacked as long as it continues. This, of course, could be a description of *Bazemore*, without the "facial" discrimination language. Lower court decisions support such a view, *e.g.*, *Alexander v. Local 496, Laborer's Intl. Union*, 177 F.3d 394 (6th Cir. 1999), but they predate *Ledbetter*.

Another possible way to explain *Bazemore* is that it was a disparate impact case. While the original low salaries for blacks were intentional, their continuation may constitute a facially neutral practice with a disparate impact, rather than intentional discrimination. In such cases, perhaps the violation occurs whenever the impact is felt. *See Lorance*, 490 U.S. at 908-09 (stating that the "most natural" reading of the statute is that a "discriminatory impact under §703(a)(2), *caus[es] the statute of limitations to run from the time that impact is felt*," at least outside the seniority area where proof of discriminatory intent is necessary) (emphasis added). Suppose a female applied for a job in 1998 and was denied it on the grounds that she was shorter than the employer's height minimum, which would not survive disparate impact attack; she then waited until 2008 and filed a charge with the EEOC upon which she now sues. At first glance, the charge is untimely. But suppose further that plaintiff can prove that during the entire ten years the defendant continued to use the same minimum. Had plaintiff applied to fill a vacancy during that period, she would have been again excluded on the basis of the continuing policy of utilizing the discriminatory requirement. She would then have been able to timely file with the Commission within 180 (300) days of the second denial. In such a context, requiring a plaintiff to apply again is an exercise in futility: what is at stake is a continuing policy that would render timely any charge filed by plaintiff no more than 180 (300) days after its discontinuance. *E.g.*, *Harris v. City of New York*, 186 F.3d 243, 250 (2d Cir. 1999) (to bring a timely continuing violation claim, "claimant must allege both the existence of an ongoing policy of discrimination and some non-time-barred acts taken in furtherance of that policy"). The time of the filing, however, will influence the relief available to the plaintiff, both in terms of computing the two-year limitation on backpay and perhaps even prevent the award of any monetary relief if, say, the absence of job openings means that the policy was not causally related to plaintiff's harm during a particular time period.

NOTE ON WAIVER, TOLLING, AND ESTOPPEL

Morgan made clear "the filing period is not a jurisdictional prerequisite to filing a Title VII suit. Rather, it is a requirement subject to waiver, estoppel, and equitable tolling 'when equity so requires.'" 536 U.S. at 121 (citing *Zipes v. Trans World Airlines, Inc.*, 455 U.S. 385 (1982)). It stressed, however, that such doctrines were "to be applied sparingly," *see Baldwin County Welcome Center v. Brown*, 466 U.S. 147, 152 (1984) (per curiam). Further, such doctrines may be a double-edged sword: "The application of equitable doctrines, however, may either limit or toll the time period within which an employee must file a charge." *Morgan*, 536 U.S. at 105. In short, while such doctrines may operate to expand the time for filing, they may also contract it when plaintiff's failure to timely act prejudices the defendant.

Prior Supreme Court cases, however, provide little guidance, and the lower courts have not been very receptive, although they have provided some relief in limited situations.

Waiver. In *Zipes* itself, the issue was whether defendants had waived the timely filing requirement by failing to assert it, and the Court merely remanded for a decision once it had decided that waiver might operate. A few cases have found objections to procedural requirements waived. *See Buck v. Hampton Twp. Sch. Dist.*, 452 F.3d 256 (3d Cir. 2006) (defendant's failure to raise plaintiff's omission of a verification of her charge waived its right to dismissal for failure to verify).

Tolling. The only situation in which the Supreme Court has actually held tolling appropriate is when a class action is filed. *Crown, Cork & Seal Co. v. Parker*, 462 U.S. 345 (1983), held that the filing of a class action tolls the "applicable statute of limitations" for putative class members; thus, class members may use whatever still remains of the statutory time period after class certification is denied. Although *Parker* dealt with tolling the 90-day period for filing suit after receipt of an EEOC dismissal, its logic is broad enough to encompass tolling the time period for filing a charge with the EEOC. In a class action, a worker who is a proper member of the class need not file a separate charge of discrimination because the charge filed by the named plaintiff can embrace the claims of nonfiling class members as long as they are within its scope. Thus, even if the action is not certified (or is later decertified), one filing should toll the time for filing a charge with the EEOC. *See Yang v. Odom*, 392 F.3d 97, 111 (3d Cir. 2004) ("where class certification has been denied solely on the basis of the lead plaintiffs' deficiencies as class representatives, and not because of the suitability of the claims for class treatment," tolling applies not only to individual claims but to subsequent class actions). The Court has, however, rejected tolling in one situation: the time for filing with the EEOC is not tolled during the pendency of a grievance proceeding. See Note 3 on p. 612.

Even prior to *Morgan*, the lower courts sometimes mitigated the rigors of strict adherence to time limits, *e.g.*, *Bennett v. Quark, Inc.*, 258 F.3d 1220, 1226 (10th Cir. 2001) ("To warrant tolling, the circumstances must rise to the level of active deception."), although they used a variety of different nomenclatures and tests, sometimes speaking of tolling, sometimes of equitable estoppel, and sometimes of fraudulent concealment. For example, the period has been tolled when the employer failed to post antidiscrimination notices required by the statutes. *E.g.*, *Hammer v. Cardio*, 131 Fed. Appx. 829, 831-32 (3d Cir. 2005) (equitable tolling "if the plaintiff can demonstrate 'excusable ignorance' of her statutory rights, where, for instance, her employer has failed to post the required notices"). The time period was also tolled for reasons having nothing to do with defendant's fault, as when the EEOC improperly refused to accept a charge or otherwise misled the plaintiff. *Lawrence v. Cooper Communities, Inc.*, 132 F.3d 447 (8th Cir. 1998). One case even tolled the time period when the plaintiff was misled by her own attorney. *Seitzinger v. Reading Hosp. & Med. Ctr.*, 165 F.3d 236 (3d Cir. 1999).

Equitable tolling also has been found for plaintiff's mental incapacity. *Stoll v. Runyon*, 165 F.3d 1238 (9th Cir. 1999) (time to file charge tolled even when plaintiff retained counsel because wrongful conduct including severe physical abuse by defendant and extraordinary circumstances of plaintiff proven). *But see Boos v. Runyon*, 201 F.3d 178 (2d Cir. 2000) (no equitable tolling where plaintiff's claims of paranoia, panic attacks, and depression were vague and insufficient). However, courts have often rejected seemingly appealing bases for tolling. For example, the Seventh Circuit concluded that threatened employer retaliation for filing a charge would not be a basis for equitable estoppel. *Beckel v. Wal-Mart Assocs.*, 301 F.3d 621, 624 (7th Cir. 2002).

Laches. The *Morgan* opinion stated that

> an employer may raise a laches defense, which bars a plaintiff from maintaining a suit if he unreasonably delays in filing a suit and as a result harms the defendant. This defense "requires proof of (1) lack of diligence by the party against whom the defense is asserted, and (2) prejudice to the party asserting the defense."

536 U.S. at 121-22. Laches would has its greatest potential application in contaminated work environment cases, which are the only cases where a plaintiff could otherwise long delay filing a charge and still bring a timely suit. *See Pruitt v. City of Chi.*, 472 F.3d 925, 927 (7th Cir. 2006) (laches barred sexual harassment suit where

plaintiffs alleged a hostile work environment dating back twenty years and the delay prejudiced the defendant's access to relevant documents and witnesses).

But laches can also bar suit or limit recovery when a plaintiff files a timely charge with the EEOC but delays too long in bringing suits. *Compare Brown-Mitchell v. Kan. City Power & Light Co.*, 267 F.3d 825 (8th Cir. 2001) (a six-year delay in bringing suit is "unreasonable" and justifies dismissal) *with EEOC v. Watkins Motor Lines, Inc.*, 463 F.3d 436 (6th Cir. 2006) (defendants could not demonstrate prejudice from two-year delay when no showing of memory fading or lost documents, other than those lost due to defendants' own negligence).

C. FILING SUIT

As we have seen, timely resort to the EEOC is a prerequisite to any court suit under Title VII, the ADA and the ADEA. Under all three statutes, a timely charge of discrimination must be filed with the Commission before suit can be brought to vindicate statutory rights. Contrary to normal administrative law principles, however, exhaustion of agency remedies is not required, reflecting a congressional decision not to subject private plaintiffs to the long delays that have always plagued the Commission's charge processing. Nevertheless, it is still desirable that charging parties who are willing to tolerate delay be permitted to exhaust EEOC processes because a court action might be thereby avoided through the agency's conciliation efforts.

Three principles have evolved that give the Commission the opportunity to act while safeguarding the rights of discriminatees to prompt judicial relief. First, a charging party must usually wait 180 days from filing with the Commission before bringing suit unless EEOC procedures are terminated earlier. §706(b), 42 USCS §2000e-5(b). Mechanically, this is achieved by requiring a "right-to-sue" letter from the Commission as a condition for maintaining an action; the charging party may demand the suit letter from the EEOC once 180 days have passed. Upon receipt of the letter, the charging party has 90 days to file a court suit, in default of which she is barred from bringing an action based on that charge.* Should the charging party wish to go to court more quickly, EEOC regulations allow the agency to terminate its proceedings early upon the charging party's request, 29 C.F.R. 91601.28(a)(2) (2007), thus permitting suit to be brought immediately. Most courts have upheld the regulation, *e.g., Walker v. UPS*, 240 F.3d 1268 (10th Cir. 2001); *contra Martini v. Fed. Nat'l Mortgage Assn.*, 178 F.3d 1336 (D.C. Cir. 1999).

Second, the charging party may elect to permit the EEOC's procedures to continue after the 180-day period, but she retains the power to demand a right-to-sue letter at any time. There is no specific time limit within which the EEOC must act, and the agency sometimes takes years to finish its proceedings. The charging party can generally allow the Commission to continue to process the charge indefinitely while retaining the power to demand a right-to-sue letter at any time. As we have seen, however, some cases hold a charging party's decision to permit the EEOC to complete its charge processing may result in laches barring the suit or at least limiting defendant's back pay liability. See p. 619.

---

* Under the ADEA, while a charge must be filed with the EEOC, a right-to-sue letter from the EEOC is not a prerequisite for suit. *Julian v. City of Houston*, 314 F.3d 721 (5th Cir. 2002), although the 90-day period for suit governs when the EEOC in fact sends such a letter. 29 U.S.C. §626 (2003).

Third, if the charging party permits the agency to process the charge to conclusion, the EEOC will either (1) find no reasonable cause to believe a violation has
occurred and issue a notice of dismissal; or (2) find reasonable cause, attempt
conciliation, and, if that fails to resolve the matter and the Commission does not file
suit itself, ultimately issue a right-to-sue letter. In either case, the charging party must
file suit within 90 days or forfeit all power to sue on the basis of the subject charge.

Several issues have arisen under these three principles. Most obviously, the statute
requires suit within 90 days after EEOC gives its notice, 42 U.S.C. § 2000e-5, which
has been interpreted to mean the actual "receipt" of the right-to-sue letter by the
charging party, *Threadgill v. Moore U.S.A. Inc.*, 269 F.3d 848 (7th Cir. 2001) (actual
receipt of right-to-sue letter by plaintiff starts 90-day period regardless of whether
attorney has notice), or constructive receipt by her attorney of record. *Irwin v.
Veterans Admin.*, 498 U.S. 89 (1990). But other kinds of constructive receipt are also
possible, *see Bobbitt v. Freeman Cos.*, 268 F.3d 535 (7th Cir. 2001) (an employee's
failure to pick up certified mail from the EEOC is "patently irresponsible"), and a
number of courts have, absent proof of actual receipt, "presumed" the date of receipt
to be anywhere from three to seven days from the date of mailing. *See Baldwin
County Welcome Center v. Brown*, 466 U.S. 147, 148 (1984); *Payan v. Aramark
Mgmt. Serv.*, 495 F.3d 1119 (9th Cir. 2007) (3 days); *Morgan v. Potter*, 489 F.3d 195
(5th Cir. 2007) (5 days).

Once the starting point is established, filing a complaint is normally necessary to
satisfy the 90-day rule. *See Baldwin County*, 466 U.S. 147. However, the Federal
Rules are relatively permissive, and something less than a formal complaint may
satisfy them as long as the filing gives notice of the factual basis of the discrimination
claim. *Page v. Ark. Dep't of Corr.*, 222 F.3d 453 (8th Cir. 2000) (letter and attach-
ment sufficient).

Filing suit within 90 days is, however, not always required. *Zipes v. Trans World
Airlines*, 455 U.S. 385 (1984), held the time limit for filing a charge with the EEOC
not to be "jurisdictional," but "a requirement that, like a statute of limitations, is
subject to waiver, estoppel, and equitable tolling." 455 U.S. at 393. *Zipes* has been
carried over by several lower courts to the 90-day suit-filing provision, and the Supreme
Court strongly suggested in *Baldwin County* that this was correct. In *Baldwin County*,
however, the Court held that the mere filing of the right-to-sue letter did not constitute
timely filing of suit and listed a number of possible bases for tolling the suit-filing
period, including the pendency of a motion for court appointment of counsel.

One final question concerning the timeliness of Title VII suits is whether state
statutes of limitations have any applicability to private suits. The answer is no. Lower
courts have built on *Occidental Life Ins. Co. v. EEOC*, 432 U.S. 355 (1977), which
held that such state laws did not apply to suits by the EEOC, to find them also
irrelevant to private suits. *E.g., Burgh v. Borough Council of Montrose*, 251 F.3d 465
(3d Cir. 2001).

PROBLEM 7.1

Susan Russo, 21 years old, completed secretarial school in June 2006. Shortly after
graduating and before looking for employment, she was in a serious car accident.
Although she has otherwise fully recovered, she lost the effective use of her legs and
now relies on a wheelchair to get around. In early January 2007, she sent a letter and
résumé in response to a help-wanted advertisement placed in the *Gazette* by Firm

Bodies Health Spa. She received a phone call scheduling an interview, and on January 15, 2007, she went to the spa to meet with the personnel director. The director seemed awkward during the interview, which Russo attributed to her being in a wheelchair. The interview ended with the director telling Russo that there were "many, many applicants for this job, but we'll get back to you." Russo heard nothing further until December 15, 2007, when she received a letter thanking her for "your interest in Firm Bodies," but informing her that "your interests and ours do not coincide at this time."

Russo, however, noticed that the help-wanted ad to which she had responded was republished every Sunday in the *Gazette* throughout January and February, last appearing on March 13, 2007. Russo was upset about this, but did not want to be paranoid. About April 15, she discovered that one of her friends was a member of Firm Bodies and asked her to "nose around." The friend reported back to Russo on May 15 the following information: a secretary was employed who had begun work around April 4. The new secretary had found out about the position through an ad in March. Firm Bodies must know about the Americans with Disabilities Act because there is a poster in the cafeteria listing individuals' rights under the ADA. The cafeteria, however, is upstairs from the business offices (including the office of the personnel director), and there is no elevator or ramp leading to the second floor.

Russo had first learned about the ADA from the physical therapist who had worked with her during her convalescence in the second half of 2006. At that time, however, she had not thought much about employment discrimination against individuals with disabilities. In the wake of her turndown from Firm Bodies, and unable to find another suitable job, Russo joined a support group. Over the next few months, she became more and more upset about what had happened. On August 16, 2007, Russo visited the office of the state fair employment practices agency. The intake officer there told her she could file a charge of discrimination if she wished, but they were overworked, and it would make more sense if she filed with the federal Equal Employment Opportunity Commission. Russo did not then file a charge with the state agency. On October 17, 2007 she went to the offices of the EEOC, where an investigator completed an intake questionnaire, informed her that "you have a good case," and promised to fill out a charge form for her signature. On December 16, not having heard anything further, Russo went to the EEOC office again. The investigator she had first met had, it turned out, been transferred. The new investigator reviewed the intake questionnaire in the file and helped Russo complete a charge, which she signed and he notarized on that date.

If the EEOC does not pursue this matter, may Russo bring a private suit under the Americans with Disabilities Act? Does 42 U.S.C. § 12115 bear on the question? You may assume that the state fair employment practices agency in question has jurisdiction over disability claims and that it has a six-month statute of limitations for filing a state charge.

D. RELATIONSHIP OF THE EEOC CHARGE TO PRIVATE SUIT

Since any Title VII action must be properly predicated on a charge filed with the EEOC, questions of the relationship between the charge and the suit have arisen along three axes: first, who may sue on the basis of a charge filed with the EEOC; second, what defendants may be sued on the basis of a particular charge; and, third, to what extent is the scope of the suit circumscribed by the content of the charge?

1. Proper Plaintiffs

To bring a Title VII suit, like any suit in federal court, the plaintiff must have both constitutional and statutory standing. Standing under the Constitution has not, however, been a serious obstacle in the discrimination arena because the Supreme Court has been very generous in recognizing "dignitary" standing to attack racial discrimination. Thus, *Northeastern Fla. Chapter of Associated Gen. Contractors of Am. v. City of Jacksonville*, 508 U.S. 656 (1993), permitted an attack on a city's affirmative action program even though there was no showing that the plaintiff or any of its member contractors would have won an award absent the alleged discrimination. *But see Texas v. Lesage*, 528 U.S. 18 (1999) (any dignitary harm ends when a challenged program was terminated, and a suit can survive only if the plaintiff must show concrete harm, such as a loss of income).

Assuming constitutional standing, however, the plaintiff must also have standing under the relevant statute, that is, she must be what Title VII describes as a "person aggrieved." 42 U.S.C. §2000e-5(b) (2007). This is rarely a serious issue, but interesting questions have been posed when plaintiffs can be viewed as seeking to redress discrimination against other individuals. Even then, standing is often recognized. For example, plaintiffs have been permitted to sue for discrimination against others if they claim resultant harm to themselves, as for example, "the loss of important benefits from interracial associations," *Trafficante v. Metropolitan Life Ins. Co.*, 409 U.S. 205 (1972) (Fair Housing Act). Further, some plaintiffs have been successful in arguing standing by a kind of domino effect analysis. *See Anjelino v. New York Times Co.*, 200 F.3d 73, 92 (3d Cir. 1999) (employer's refusal to hire women from a list allegedly resulted in the male plaintiffs, who were lower down on the list, also not being hired). *But see Childress v. City of Richmond, Virginia*, 134 F.3d 1205, 1209 (4th Cir. 1998) (en banc) (since plaintiff has standing under the statue only if a direct victim of prohibited conduct, white male police officers could not challenge their supervisor's derogatory remarks to and about female and African-American police officers). *See generally* Noah Zatz, *Beyond the Zero-Sum Game: Toward Title VII Protection for Intergroup Solidarity*, 77 IND. L.J. 63, 66-67 (2002).

The most serious "proper plaintiff" question, however, is whether a particular plaintiff must file his own charge or whether he can rely on a charge filed by someone else. In the class action context, persons who have not filed a charge with the EEOC may nevertheless be class members. See p. 628. But even where no class action is involved, some courts have adopted a "single filing" or "piggybacking" rule to allow persons who did not file charges to be named plaintiffs, either by joining originally with charging parties or by intervention in actions brought by charging parties. *E.g., Holowecki v. Fed. Express Corp.*, 440 F.3d 558 (2d Cir. 2006), *cert. granted on another question*, 127 S. Ct. 2914 (2007) (piggybacking permits any individual who has not filed her own charge to rely on the charge by another so long as there is some indication that the grievance affects a group of individuals including those who seek to piggyback); *contra Communications Workers of Am., Local 1033 v. New Jersey Dept. of Pers.*, 282 F.3d 213 (3d Cir. 2002) (unless asserting a claim in a class action, each individual plaintiff must file a timely charge).

2. Proper Defendants

Even when a plaintiff's suit is based on a charge filed with the EEOC, a question may arise about what parties may be named as defendants in the complaint. Title VII authorizes the bringing of a civil action only "against the respondent named in the charge," §706(f)(1), 42 U.S.C. §2000e-5(f)(1), but the courts have been more liberal than the statutory language might suggest. E.g., *Hafez v. Avis Rent-A-Car Sys.*, 2000 U.S. App. LEXIS 31032 (2d Cir. 2000) (allowing a Title VII action to proceed against an uncharged party where there is a "clear identity of interests" between it and the named party). *But see Vital v. Interfaith Medical*, 168 F.3d 615 (2d Cir. 1999) (no identity of interest between union local and employer). This includes successors of charged parties who have also been found proper defendants. E.g., *EEOC v. MacMillan Bloedel Containers, Inc.*, 503 F.2d 1086 (6th Cir. 1974).

3. Scope of the Suit

Because every private Title VII, ADA, and ADEA suit must be predicated on a charge properly filed with the EEOC, a significant issue is the extent to which the subsequent court complaint will be limited to the contents of the EEOC charge. In resolving this question, the courts have tried to reconcile competing considerations by giving effect to the statutory filing requirement without encroaching any more than necessary on the remedial purposes of the statutes. Because many charges are filed by unsophisticated, perhaps undereducated, workers, limiting the scope of the suit to the face of the charge would be a major blow to effective statutory enforcement.

The test the courts have selected to balance these factors was first articulated by the Fifth Circuit in *Sanchez v. Standard Brands, Inc.*, 431 F.2d 455, 466 (5th Cir. 1970), which laid down a liberal standard to govern the proper scope of a charge-based complaint:

> [T]he allegations in a judicial complaint filed pursuant to Title VII "may encompass any kind of discrimination like or related to allegations contained in the charge and growing out of such allegations during the pendency of the case before the Commission.". . . In other words, the "scope" of the judicial complaint is limited to the "scope" of the EEOC investigation which can reasonably be expected to grow out of the charge of discrimination.

The court saw this rule as being rooted in the statutory scheme: the charge is filed not to trigger a lawsuit, but rather to invoke EEOC processes. Because suit is necessary only if the Commission fails to resolve the problems, the civil action is "much more intimately related to the EEOC investigation than to the words of the charge." *Id.* Further, a stricter rule would impede the EEOC's ability to obtain voluntary compliance because employers' incentives to settle would be reduced if no issue unspecified in the charge could be sued on.

Most courts claim to follow *Sanchez*. E.g., *Williams v. N.Y. City Hous. Auth.*, 458 F.3d 67 (2d Cir. 2006) (sex discrimination charges were reasonably related to "retaliation" formally charged in the EEOC charge, where plaintiff's charge alleged facts that made clear that sex bias underlay her claim); *Wallace v. DTG Operations, Inc.*, 442 F.3d 1112, 1123 (8th Cir. 2006) ("EEOC charge must be sufficient to give the employer notice of the subject matter of the charge and identify generally the basis for a claim, but it need not specifically articulate the precise claim or set forth all the evidence an employee may choose to later present in court"). However, there are numerous opinions evincing a clear reluctance to permit suits to go beyond a plain reading of the charge. Such courts tend to mechanically compare the charge to the complaint rather than look to the purposes of the charge in triggering an EEOC investigation. *Duncan v. Delta Consol. Indus.*, 371 F.3d 1020 (8th Cir. 2004) (checking wrong box on charge form bars subsequent suit on that type of discrimination); *Freeman v. Oakland Unified Sch. Dist.*, 291 F.3d 632, 637 (9th Cir. 2002) (plaintiff's Title VII allegations in his EEOC charge, concerning race and sex discrimination in the Faculty Council Election, were not like or reasonably related to those in his complaint, concerning discrimination in teaching assignments and class size); *Dorsey v. Pinnacle Automation Co.*, 278 F.3d 830 (8th Cir. 2002) (claims for age discrimination based on the failure to promote at a discrete time not sufficient to encompass hostile work environment claims that occurred throughout the plaintiff's employment).

NOTE ON AVOIDING THE TITLE VII PROCEDURAL MAZE VIA § 1981

Unlike the other antidiscrimination laws we have encountered, no federal agency is charged with enforcing 42 U.S.C. § 1981 (or its companion, § 1983). Thus a plaintiff may prosecute such suits in either federal or state court without concern for the procedural niceties we have just studied. This alternative, however, has its downsides. Most obviously, § 1981 does not reach many of the types of discrimination barred by the more modern antidiscrimination statutes, and there are limitations as to its reach where state agencies are involved. *See Pittman v. Oregon*, 2007 U.S. App. LEXIS 28028 (9th Cir.) (no § 1981 cause of action against the states).

Further, § 1981 has its own complications in terms of the applicable statute of limitations. For most of its history, state limitations periods were "borrowed" in such suits. *Goodman v. Lukens Steel Co.*, 482 U.S. 656 (1987) (§ 1981 suits subject to the state statute applicable to "personal injury" actions), including state rules concerning the accrual of the cause of action, continuing violation, and tolling, *Johnson v. Railway Express Agency, Inc.*, 421 U.S. 454, 463-64 (1975), although "considerations of state law may be displaced where their application would be inconsistent with the federal policy underlying the cause of action under consideration." *Id.* at 465.

This authority was dramatically altered by the Supreme Court's decision in *Jones v. R. R. Donnelley & Sons Co.*, 541 U.S. 369 (2004), construing 28 U.S.C. § 1658, which creates a four-year federal statute of limitations for federal claims that do not otherwise have a limitations period specified. However, § 1658 is limited to "civil actions arising under an Act of Congress enacted after" December 1, 1990. Section 1981, of course, originated more than a century earlier, but it was significantly amended in the 1991 Civil Rights Act. The question for *R. R. Donnelley*, therefore, was whether the courts should look to the original enactment, the subsequent amendment, or split the difference. It chose the latter course and held that § 1658 governed claims that would not have existed before the statutory amendments but not claims that could have been stated under the original statute. The latter remain subject to borrowed state laws.

The effect of this ruling is to revive questions about the meaning of *Patterson v. McLean Credit Union*, 491 U.S. 164 (1989), whose restrictive interpretation of § 1981 had in part generated the 1991 Amendments. After *R. R. Donnelley*, it will be necessary, for statute of limitations purposes, to determine whether a claim would have arisen under *Patterson's* interpretation of § 1981 (in which case, state statutes of limitations control) or under the statute as amended (in which case § 1658 governs). *See generally* Harold S. Lewis, Jr., *Walking the Walk of Plain Text: The Supreme Court's Markedly More Solicitous Treatment of Title VII Following the Civil Rights Act of 1991*, 41 St. Louis L.J. 1081, 1092 (2005). Since four years is a longer period than most state tort statutes, this distinction will often determine whether a suit is timely. *E.g., Dandy v. UPS*, 388 F.3d 263, 269 (7th Cir. 2004) (claims of hostile work environment, failure to promote, disparate treatment in terms of compensation, and retaliation were all subject to § 1658 because they would not have been actionable before the 1991 Amendments).

E.   THE INTERRELATIONSHIP OF VARIOUS RIGHTS AND REMEDIES

We have encountered separate federal remedies that address the same wrong. For example, Title VII and § 1981 overlap when race discrimination is involved. In addition, most states have state laws prohibiting race, sex, age, and disability discrimination. Finally, discrimination may be prohibited by collective bargaining agreements. The interrelationship of these remedies has raised difficult questions.

Coordinating Federal Remedies. With respect to federal remedies, the Supreme Court has generally treated them as separate and independent, *Johnson v. Railway Express Agency*, 421 U.S. 454, 462 (1975), thus leaving coordination of separate suits to the normal doctrines of res judicata (or claim preclusion) and collateral estoppel (or issue preclusion). *See, e.g., Moody v. Kraft Foods Global, Inc.*, 212 Fed. Appx. 285 (5th Cir. 2006) (plaintiff's age discrimination claim was barred by res judicata by the final judgment rendered in plaintiff's earlier suit for race and national origin discrimination against the same defendant under the same facts). Preclusion typically operates to foreclose a plaintiff from bringing a second suit, but it sometimes assists plaintiffs. In *Meredith v. Beech Aircraft Corp.*, 18 F.3d 890 (10th Cir. 1994), the court held that plaintiff B in the second suit could rely on a finding in the first suit that defendant's promotion decision was based on sex, but that the defendant could not rely on a finding in the first suit that plaintiff A was the best-qualified applicant. Plaintiff B, while allowed to use estoppel offensively, was not bound by the first suit because she was not a party, or in privity with a party, to that suit and thus had no opportunity to litigate the "best-qualified" issue.

Coordinating State and Federal Remedies. State remedies for employment discrimination typically parallel federal prohibitions but may in fact go further than the federal law (in substantive protections and in remedies). The general rule is that federal law does not preempt the "field" of discrimination, meaning that state laws are valid so long as they do not actually conflict with federal law. Further, the courts are slow to find a conflict. For example, *California Fed. Sav. & Loan Assn. v. Guerra*, 479 U.S. 272 (1987), reproduced at p. 362, concluded that a state statute requiring unpaid maternity leave did not conflict with Title VII's prohibition of sex discrimination.

One exception to the rule against field preemption arises from the Employee Retirement Income Security Act of 1974 (ERISA), 29 U.S.C. §§ 1001 et seq. (2007), which was enacted to curb a variety of abuses associated with pension and other employee benefit plans. *See Shaw v. Delta Air Lines, Inc.*, 463 U.S. 85 (1983) (state antidiscrimination law was preempted insofar as it prohibits practices that are lawful under Title VII). *See also Hawaiian Airlines, Inc. v. Norris,* 512 U.S. 246 (1994) (state law suit foreclosed by National Labor Relations Act when an action between an employee and an employer or union would require interpretation of a collective bargaining agreement).

Assuming an employee has available both state and federal remedies for the same basic wrong, there still remain coordination questions. Further, because, as we have seen, Title VII requires deferral to state agencies, an attack on discrimination will, in most states, set in motion two separate proceedings against discriminatory employment practices. These proceedings may converge in a single suit in either state court or federal court asserting all claims. Thus, state courts have concurrent jurisdiction with federal courts over Title VII claims, *e.g., Yellow Freight Sys., Inc. v. Donnelly,* 494 U.S. 820 (1990), so state and federal claims can be joined in state court. Similarly, supplemental jurisdiction will normally allow a plaintiff filing Title VII suit in federal court to join state law claims. 28 U.S.C. § 1367 (2007). *See generally* Denis F. McLaughlin, *The Federal Supplemental Jurisdiction Statute — A Constitutional and Statutory Analysis,* 24 ARIZ. ST. L.J. 849 (1992).

If a plaintiff chooses to file suit in one forum, normal preclusion principles will apply should she later file a second suit in another forum. Thus, *Kremer v. Chem. Const. Corp.,* 456 U.S. 461 (1982), held that a state *court judgment* precludes a subsequent Title VII suit in federal district court. However, state *administrative determinations,* even those made upon a full hearing with a panoply of procedural safeguards, are not entitled to full faith and credit with respect to a Title VII claim unless they have been reviewed by a state court. *Univ. of Tenn. v. Elliott,* 478 U.S. 788 (1986) (Title VII); *Astoria Fed. Sav. & Loan Assn. v. Solimino,* 501 U.S. 104 (1991) (ADEA). Such state administrative determination may, however, preclude federal suits under §§ 1981 and 1983. *Elliott,* at 793.

Collective Bargaining Agreements. Collective bargaining agreements typically contain both job security protections and nondiscrimination clauses, and a worker in a unionized setting is likely to seek relief under the CBA's grievance procedure, typically culminating in binding arbitration. Should that be unsuccessful, the employee might well seek to vindicate her statutory antidiscrimination rights in court. The Supreme Court has held both that pursuit of a grievance procedure does not toll the requirement of filing a charge with the EEOC, *Int'l Union of Elec. Workers v. Robbins & Myers, Inc.,* 429 U.S. 229 (1976), and that a final arbitration decision on the CBA claims does not foreclose a court suit directly under the antidiscrimination laws. *Alexander v. Gardner-Denver Co.,* 415 U.S. 36 (1974).

These decisions, however, do not consider the effects of the *employee's* (as opposed to the union's) agreement to arbitrate statutory claims. Where such an agreement exists and is valid, the decision of the arbitrator will foreclose any separate proceedings in either state or federal court. See Chapter 9.

F.   CLASS ACTIONS

1.   *Introduction*

Employment discrimination suits frequently pose an attorney with the threshold question of whether to proceed solely on behalf of a particular plaintiff or rather to also initiate a class action "on behalf of those similarly situated." The class action possibility is implicit in most Title VII litigation simply because a "suit for violation of Title VII is necessarily a class action as the evil sought to be ended is discrimination on the basis of a class characteristic, i.e., race, sex, religion or national origin." *Bowe v. Colgate-Palmolive Co.*, 416 F.2d 711, 719 (7th Cir. 1969). As in other areas of the law, employment discrimination class actions, have generated considerable criticism, *see, e.g.*, Michael Selmi, *The Price of Discrimination: The Nature of Class Action Employment Discrimination Litigation and Its Effects*, 81 TEX. L. REV. 1249 (2003) (class actions and settlements have relatively little effect on shareholder value and frequently produce little to no substantive change), but some scholars argue that they have, or will, produce meaningful reform, Tristin K. Green, *Targeting Workplace Context: Title VII as a Tool for Institutional Reform*, 72 FORDHAM L. REV. 659 (2003); Susan Sturm, *Second Generation Employment Discrimination: A Structural Approach*, 101 COLUM. L. REV. 458, 512-13 (2001). *See also* Nancy Levit, *Mega-Cases, Diversity, and the Elusive Goal of Workplace Reform*, 49 B.C.L. REV. (forthcoming 2008).

While discrimination is necessarily a class evil, that does not mean that every suit attacking such discrimination qualifies as a class action. Class actions under Title VII, §1981, or the ADA suit must satisfy Rule 23 of the Federal Rules of Civil Procedure, although ADA class actions have been rare. *See* Michael Ashley Stein & Michael Evan Waterstone, *Disability, Disparate Impact, and Class Actions*, 56 DUKE L.J. 861 (2006). Suits under the ADEA, while technically not governed by Rule 23, have nevertheless largely borrowed Title VII principles, although there remain important differences between the two approaches.*

Before considering whether Rule 23 permits a class action in a particular case, however, the plaintiff's attorney should consider whether he or she wants to bring a class action. This decision involves both strategic questions and professional responsibility issues, making the choice complex. On the one hand, a class action may well increase the leverage of the case because the defendant may be more likely to settle favorably as the stakes in losing rise. Escalating an individual's suit to a class action may multiply by a factor of hundreds or even thousands the potential monetary liability as well as threaten restructuring of employment practices. On the other hand, it is possible that the class action may stiffen the defendant's resolve, thus making settlement more difficult and triggering a tougher defense. Further, the costs of litigation may soar, both in terms of the out-of-pocket costs that will have to be paid somehow and in terms of the lawyer's time, which, in most Title VII cases, is not compensated until the litigation is terminated. See Chapter 8 for discussion of attorneys' fee awards. Overarching these concerns are the professional responsibility questions of the lawyer's obligations to his or her client. *See generally* Nancy Morawetz, *Bargaining, Class Representation, and Fairness*, 54 OHIO ST. L.J. 1 (1993); Mary Kay Kane, *Of Carrots and Sticks: Evaluating the Role of the Class Action Lawyer*, 66 TEX. L. REV. 385 (1987).

---

* The Age Discrimination in Employment Act expressly incorporates the enforcement provisions of the Fair Labor Standards Act, including 29 U.S.C. §216 (2007), which requires each member of a "collective," or "representative," action to provide written consent. Functionally, this means that the ADEA action is "opt-in," while we will see that Rule 23 class actions are typically "opt-out." *Mooney v. Aramco Servs. Co.*, 54 F.3d 1207, 1212 (5th Cir. 1995). *See generally* Douglas D. Scherer & Robert Belton, *Handling Class Actions Under the ADEA*, 10 EMPL. RTS. & EMPLOY. POL'Y J. 553 (2006). *See also Hoffman-La Roche, Inc. v. Sperling*, 493 U.S. 165, 169 (1989) (upholding district court's notice to potential class members under §216(b)).

If the plaintiff's attorney decides that a class suit is desirable, it is then necessary to determine whether such a suit is permissible. Although Title VII does not provide explicitly for class actions, they are available in appropriate circumstances. E.g., *Albemarle Paper Co. v. Moody*, 422 U.S. 405 (1975). Further, each class member need not file a charge with the EEOC in order to be a member of the class, *id.* at 414 n. 8, because an otherwise proper Title VII class action may be brought attacking any discrimination implicated by the charge filed with the EEOC by the representative plaintiff. The purposes of the filing requirement are achieved by one charge because "[i]t would be wasteful, if not vain, for numerous employees, all with the same grievance, to have to process many identical complaints with the EEOC." *Oatis v. Crown Zellerbach Corp.*, 398 F.2d 496, 498 (5th Cir. 1968).

However, membership in Title VII and ADA class actions is restricted by the time limitations on filing a charge with the EEOC. The charge on which the suit is predicated must be timely, just as in an individual action, but timeliness considerations are also applicable to other class members. While filing a charge tolls the time period for class members, persons whose claims are already time barred at that point cannot be class members. E.g., *Wetzel v. Liberty Mut. Ins. Co.*, 508 F.2d 239 (3d Cir. 1975). These questions do not affect suits under §1981.

2.   *Requirements of Rule 23(a)*

Suits under Title VII, §1981 and the ADA, are governed by Rule 23 of the Federal Rules of Civil Procedure, which establishes two sets of requirements that class actions must meet; the party seeking to maintain the suit as a class action has the burden of persuasion with respect to them. The first set is found in Rule 23(a), which sets forth four factors, all of which must be met:

(1) the class is so numerous that joinder of all members is impracticable,
(2) there are questions of law or fact common to the class,
(3) the claims or defenses of the representative parties are typical of the claims or defenses of the class, and
(4) the representative parties will fairly and adequately protect the interests of the class.

While each of these requirements must be satisfied, a mechanical analysis of the four categories risks overlooking the underlying concept of Rule 23(a): because class actions necessarily commit the rights of unnamed class members into the hands of the named plaintiff and her attorneys, the courts must ensure that a class action is both appropriate to the claims alleged and structured to maximize the quality of the representation of the interests of the unnamed class members.

To this end, Rule 23(a)(1), "*numerosity*," focuses on whether the case is appropriate for class action treatment or whether traditional multiparty litigation is preferable. The remaining three parts of paragraph (a) examine facets of the adequacy of the named plaintiff (or her counsel) as a representative of the class. Thus, Rule 23(a)(2), "*commonality*," and (3), "*typicality*," attempt to ensure that the named plaintiff will, in the course of representing her own interests, necessarily represent the other class members because her claims are identical or very similar to theirs. However, Rule 23(a)(2) requires only the existence of *some* common questions. The existence of non-common questions does not preclude commonality. Typicality requires a closer fit between the representative plaintiff's claims and the unnamed class members. Finally, Rule 23(a)(4) considers the *adequacy of representation* in two senses: first, possible conflicts of interest between the named plaintiff and other class members and, second, the adequacy of counsel.

Although the lower courts were originally receptive to employment discrimination class actions, the Supreme Court was far more restrictive in two encounters with employment discrimination class actions. In *East Tex. Motor Freight Sys., Inc. v. Rodriguez*, 431 U.S. 395 (1977), three Mexican Americans initiated suit, challenging the company's "no-transfer" policy to better-paid line-driver jobs. Although the named plaintiffs stipulated that they had not been discriminated against in their hiring as city drivers, the suit sought to represent all Negroes and Mexican Americans denied all employment opportunities, including hiring. The district court held against the three plaintiffs on their individual claims, finding that none of them was qualified to be a road driver. Although the plaintiffs never moved for class certification, the Fifth Circuit itself certified a sweeping class and simultaneously found class liability.

The Supreme Court found plain error in this certification: "[I]t was evident by the time the case reached that court that the named plaintiffs were not proper class representatives" under Rule 23(a). *Id.* at 403. A class representative must be part of the class and possess the same interest and suffer the same injury as the class members. Since the named plaintiffs lacked the qualifications to be line drivers, "they could have suffered no injury as a result of the alleged discriminatory [transfer] practices, and they were, therefore, simply not eligible to represent a class of persons who did allegedly suffer injury." *Id.* at 403-04. Since each had stipulated that he had not been discriminated against in his initial hire, "they were hardly in a position to mount a classwide attack on the no-transfer rule and seniority system on the ground that these practices perpetuated past discrimination and locked minorities into the less desirable jobs to which they had been discriminatorily assigned." *Id.* at 404.

East Texas Motor Freight stressed that "a different case would be presented if the District Court had certified a class and only later had it appeared that the named plaintiffs were not class members." *Id.* at 406 n. 12. A proper class certification would protect the claims of the class members even if "subsequent events or the proof at trial . . . undermined the named plaintiffs' individual claims." *Id. See Franks v. Bowman Transp. Co.*, 424 U.S. 747 (1976) (after a class is properly certified, a finding that the named plaintiff had been legally discharged did not bar relief to the class members).

While "the named plaintiffs' evident lack of class membership" was enough to preclude certification in *East Texas Motor Freight*, the Court noted two other strong indicators of inadequate representation. The first was the individual plaintiffs' failure to move for certification as a class action in the district court; that "surely bears strongly on the adequacy of the representation that those class members might expect to receive." 431 U.S. at 405.

The second factor that *East Texas Motor Freight* found strongly indicated inadequate representation "was the conflict between the vote by members of the class rejecting a merger of the city- and line-driver collective-bargaining units, and the demand in the plaintiffs' complaint for just such a merger." 431 U.S. at 405. This conflict obviously implicated Rule 23(a)(4). But does it follow that such a conflict is fatal to a class action? Won't the question of remedy for a violation *always* divide members of the class? After all, class members will typically compete with each other generally and in terms of the benefits of the lawsuit. One example of such a conflict arose in a case involving pregnancy leave. Although the class of female employees had a general interest in striking down restrictive rules, the remedy aspect could divide class members. Present employees, for example, would not want former employees reinstated with retroactive seniority because that would make present employees more vulnerable to layoff. *Air Line Stewards & Stewardesses Ass'n, Local 550 v. Am. Airlines, Inc.*, 490 F.2d 636 (7th Cir. 1973).

In the Court's next encounter with certifying an employment discrimination class action, *Gen. Tel. Co. of the Southwest v. Falcon*, 457 U.S. 147 (1982), the named plaintiff had been denied a promotion. He then brought suit pursuant to Rule 23(b)(2) seeking to represent a class composed of Mexican Americans who were, or might be, employed by the defendant at its Irving, Texas, facility and who were adversely affected by the challenged practices. The district court certified a class including Mexican-American employees and unsuccessful Mexican-American applicants for employment. It ultimately found that the employer had not discriminated against Falcon in hiring, but that it did discriminate against him in its promotion practices. "The court reached converse conclusions about the class, finding no discrimination in promotion practices, but concluding that petitioner had discriminated against Mexican-Americans at its Irving facility in its hiring practices." 457 U.S. at 152.

Noting the efficiency of the class action device when issues involved are "common to the class as a whole" and when they "turn on a question of law applicable in the same manner to each member of the class," the Court stressed that the requirements of Rule 23 must be met even though a discrimination suit in a sense always focuses on a "class claim":

> We cannot disagree with the proposition underlying the across-the-board rule [which broadly permitted discrimination class actions] — that racial discrimination is by definition class discrimination. But the allegation that such discrimination has occurred neither determines whether a class action may be maintained in accordance with Rule 23 nor defines the class that may be certified. Conceptually, there is a wide gap between (a) an individual's claim that he has been denied a promotion on discriminatory grounds, and his otherwise unsupported allegation that the company has a policy of discrimination, and (b) the existence of a class of persons who have suffered the same injury as that individual, such that the individual's claim and the class claims will share common questions of law or fact and that the individual's claim will be typical of the class claim. For respondent to bridge that gap, he must prove much more than the validity of his own claim. Even though evidence that he was passed over for promotion when several less deserving whites were advanced may support the conclusion that respondent was denied the promotion because of his national origin, such evidence would not necessarily justify the additional inferences (1) that this discriminatory treatment is typical of petitioner's promotion practices, (2) that petitioner's promotion practices are motivated by a policy of ethnic discrimination that pervades petitioner's Irving division, or (3) that this policy of ethnic discrimination is reflected in petitioner's other employment practices, such as hiring, in the same way it is manifested in the promotion practices. . . .

Id. at 157-58.

The Court thus found it error to "presume" that Falcon's individual claim was typical of claims by other Mexican-American employees and applicants. The Court noted that, "As the District Court's bifurcated findings on liability demonstrate, the individual and class claims might as well have been tried separately." *Id.* at 159. And it sounded a strong caution about employment discrimination class actions: "If one allegation of specific discriminatory treatment were sufficient to support an across-the-board attack, every Title VII case would be a potential companywide class action. We find nothing in the statute to indicate that Congress intended to authorize such a wholesale expansion of class-action litigation." *Id.*

The Court did indicate when a class suit might be appropriate:

> If petitioner used a biased testing procedure to evaluate both applicants for employment and incumbent employees, a class action on behalf of every applicant or employee who might have been prejudiced by the test clearly would satisfy the commonality and typicality requirements of Rule 23(a). Significant proof that an employer operated under a general policy of discrimination conceivably could justify a class of both applicants and employees if the discrimination manifested itself in hiring and promotion practices in the same general fashion, such as through entirely subjective decisionmaking processes.

457 U.S. at 159, n. 15.

In *Gratz v. Bollinger*, 539 U.S. 244 (2003), the Court returned to the question of the relationship between the named plaintiff's claims and those of the class members, suggesting a more permissive view. *Gratz* was a class action brought by white students denied admission to the University of Michigan undergraduate program; these students had been permitted by the district court to represent the class of whites who would seek freshman admission in the future. The individual plaintiffs would not be affected by any changes to the admissions policy for freshmen, which arguably made them not appropriate representatives of the class. Over a dissent, the Court held that the named plaintiffs could represent the class in seeking injunctive relief. Whether framed as an Article III standing problem or as a challenge to class certification, the suit was appropriate: "the University's use of race in undergraduate transfer admissions does not implicate a significantly different set of concerns than does its use of race in undergraduate freshman admissions." *Id.* at 265. The majority found "particularly instructive" the passage quoted in the text from *Falcon*, to the effect that a biased testing procedure for both applicants for employment and incumbent employees would permit a class action on behalf of every member of either group who was prejudiced. *Id* at 267. In a footnote, it also stressed the savings in time and resources of permitting this unified challenge to undergraduate affirmative action. Unlike *Falcon*, the issues facing the named plaintiff and the class did not rely on different "evidentiary approaches." *Id.* at n. 17.

These doctrines have played out in a variety of ways, but perhaps none is more interesting than the Ninth Circuit's recent affirmance of class certification in the largest employment discrimination class action ever brought.

DUKES v. WAL-MART, INC.
2007 U.S. App. LEXIS 28558 (9th Cir. 2007)

PREGERSON, Circuit Judge: . . .

Plaintiffs' Third Amended Complaint, brought on behalf of six named plaintiffs and all others similarly situated, asserts claims against Wal-Mart for sex discrimination under Title VII of the 1964 Civil Rights Act. Plaintiffs alleged that women employed in Wal-Mart stores: (1) are paid less than men in comparable positions, despite having higher performance ratings and greater seniority, and (2) receive fewer — and wait longer for — promotions to in-store management positions than men. Plaintiffs contend that Wal-Mart's strong, centralized structure fosters or facilitates gender stereotyping and discrimination, that the policies and practices underlying this discriminatory treatment are consistent throughout Wal-Mart stores, and that this discrimination is common to all women who work or have worked in Wal-Mart stores.

On April 28, 2003, Plaintiffs filed a motion to certify a nationwide class of women who have been subjected to Wal-Mart's allegedly discriminatory pay and promotions policies. The proposed class consists of women employed in a range of Wal-Mart positions — from part-time entry-level hourly employees to salaried managers — and is estimated to include more than 1.5 million women. The class seeks injunctive and declaratory relief, back pay, and punitive damages, but does not seek traditional "compensatory" damages.

Plaintiffs proposed that the district court certify the following class pursuant to Federal Rule of Civil Procedure 23:

> All women employed at any Wal-Mart domestic retail store at any time since December 26, 1998, who have been or may be subjected to Wal-Mart's challenged pay and management track promotions policies and practices.

On September 23, 2003, after the parties had conducted extensive discovery and filed copious briefs, the district court heard oral argument. At the hearing, Wal-Mart emphasized the "historic" nature of Plaintiffs' motion, inasmuch as it concerns a class of approximately 1.5 million women who work or worked in one or more of Wal-Mart's 3,400 stores in 41 regions at any time since 1998. The court acknowledged Wal-Mart's concerns but noted that, while the class size was large, the issues were not unusual.

[The court certified the proposed class regarding equal pay; as for promotion, it certified the class with regard to most relief, including punitive damages, but denied certification as to backpay because data relating to challenged promotions were not available for all class members. Both parties appealed. The court of appeals reviewed under an abuse of discretion standard.]

II.   CLASS CERTIFICATION AND RULE 23

A district court may certify a class only if: "(1) the class is so numerous that joinder of all members is impracticable; (2) there are questions of law and fact common to the class; (3) the claims or defenses of the representative parties are typical of the claims or defenses of the class; and (4) the representative parties will fairly and adequately protect the interests of the class." *Fed. R. Civ. P. 23(a)*.

[The district court must also find that one of the three alternative requirements of *Rule 23(b)* is satisfied.]

The party seeking certification bears the burden of showing that each of the four requirements of *Rule 23(a)* and at least one requirement of *Rule 23(b)* have been met.

A.   RULE 23(A)

The class in this case is broad and diverse. It encompasses approximately 1.5 million employees, both salaried and hourly, with a range of positions, who are or were employed at one or more of Wal-Mart's 3,400 stores across the country.

Plaintiffs contend, and the district court found, that the large class is united by a complex of company-wide discriminatory practices against women.

1. Numerosity

Rule 23(a)(1) requires that the class be "so numerous that joinder of all members is impracticable." Wal-Mart does not contest that numerosity is satisfied here, given that both parties estimate that the proposed class includes approximately 1.5 million women.

2. Commonality

Rule 23(a)(2) requires that "there are questions of law or fact common to the class." *Fed. R. Civ. P. 23(a)(2)*. Commonality focuses on the relationship of common facts and legal issues among class members. See, e.g., 1 Herbert B. Newberg & Alba Conte, Newberg on Class Actions § 3:10 at 271 (4th ed. 2002). We noted in *Hanlon v. Chrysler Corp.*, 150 F.3d 1011 (9th Cir. 1998):

> *Rule 23(a)(2)* has been construed permissively. All questions of fact and law need not be common to satisfy the rule. The existence of shared legal issues with divergent factual predicates is sufficient, as is a common core of salient facts coupled with disparate legal remedies within the class.

Id. at 1019.

The commonality test is qualitative rather than quantitative — one significant issue common to the class may be sufficient to warrant certification. As the district court properly noted, "plaintiffs may demonstrate commonality by showing that class members have shared legal issues by divergent facts or that they share a common core of facts but base their claims for relief on different legal theories." . . .

a. "Significant Proof" of a Corporate Policy of Discrimination

Plaintiffs presented four categories of evidence: (1) facts supporting the existence of company-wide policies and practices; (2) expert opinions supporting the existence of company-wide policies and practices; and (3) expert statistical evidence of class-wide gender disparities attributable to discrimination; and (4) anecdotal evidence from class members around the country of discriminatory attitudes held or tolerated by management. Wal-Mart contends that this evidence is not sufficient to raise an inference of discrimination.

(1) Factual Evidence Plaintiffs presented evidence of: (1) uniform personnel and management structure across stores; (2) Wal-Mart headquarter's extensive oversight of store operations, company-wide policies governing pay and promotion decisions, and a strong, centralized corporate culture; (3) consistent gender-related disparities in every domestic region of the company; and (4) gender stereotyping. Such evidence supports Plaintiffs' contention that Wal-Mart operates a highly centralized company that promotes policies common to all stores and maintains a single system of oversight. Wal-Mart does not challenge this evidence.

(2) Expert Opinion Plaintiffs presented evidence from Dr. William Bielby, a sociologist, to interpret and explain the facts that suggest that Wal-Mart has and promotes a strong corporate culture — a culture that may include gender stereotyping.

Dr. Bielby based his opinion on, among other things, Wal-Mart managers' deposition testimony; organizational charts; correspondence, memos, reports, and presentations relating to personnel policy and practice, diversity, and equal employment opportunity issues; documents describing the culture and history of the company; and a large body of social science research on organizational policy and practice and on workplace bias.

Dr. Bielby testified that by employing a "social framework analysis,"[3] he examined the distinctive features of Wal-Mart's policies and practices and evaluated them "against what social science shows to be factors that create and sustain bias and those that minimize bias." In Dr. Bielby's opinion, "social science research demonstrates that gender stereotypes are especially likely to influence personnel decisions when they are based on subjective factors, because substantial decision-maker discretion tends to allow people to 'seek out and retain stereotyping-confirming information and ignore or minimize information that defies stereotypes.'" Dr. Bielby concluded: (1) that Wal-Mart's centralized coordination, reinforced by a strong organizational culture, sustains uniformity in personnel policy and practice; (2) that there are significant deficiencies in Wal-Mart's equal employment policies and practices; and (3) that Wal-Mart's personnel policies and practices make pay and promotion decisions vulnerable to gender bias.

Wal-Mart challenges Dr. Bielby's third conclusion as vague and imprecise because he concluded that Wal-Mart is "vulnerable" to bias or gender stereotyping but failed to identify a specific discriminatory policy at Wal-Mart. Specifically, Wal-Mart contends that Dr. Bielby's testimony does not meet the standards for expert testimony set forth in *Federal Rule of Evidence 702* and *Daubert v. Merrell Dow Pharm., Inc.*, 509 U.S. 579 (1993), which held that a trial court must act as a "gatekeeper" in determining whether to admit or exclude evidence.

Wal-Mart made an identical argument to the district court and the district court properly rejected it. Wal-Mart did not (and does not) challenge Dr. Bielby's methodology or contend that his findings lack relevance because they "do[ ] not relate to any issue in the case," *Daubert*, but challenges *only* whether certain inferences can be persuasively drawn from his data. Because *Daubert* does not require a court to admit or exclude evidence based on its persuasiveness, but rather, requires a court to admit or exclude evidence based on its scientific reliability and relevance (evidence is relevant if it has "'any tendency to make the existence of any fact that is of consequence to the determination of the action more probable or less probable than it would be without the evidence'" (citing Fed. R. Evid. 401), and relevance standard "is a liberal one"), testing Dr. Bielby's testimony for "*Daubert* reliability" would not have addressed Wal-Mart's objections. It would have simply revealed what Wal-Mart itself has admitted and courts have long accepted: that properly analyzed social science data, like that offered by Dr. Bielby, may add probative value to plaintiffs' class action claims. *See Price Waterhouse v. Hopkins* (considering similar evidence offered by expert social psychologist).

Accordingly, Wal-Mart's contention that the district court was required to subject Dr. Bielby's testimony to the *Daubert* test, simply because the conclusion he reached seemed unpersuasive absent certain corroborating evidence, is misplaced. *See Daubert* ("The focus, of course, must be solely on principles and methodology, not

---

3. For a description of the "social framework analysis," see John Monahan and Larry Walker, *Social Science in the Law: Cases and Materials* (4th ed. 1998).

on the conclusions that they generate."). While a *jury* may ultimately agree with Wal-Mart that, in the absence of a specific discriminatory policy promulgated by Wal-Mart, it is hard to believe, based solely on Dr. Bielby's social science analysis, that Wal-Mart engaged in actual gender discrimination, that question must be left to the merits stage of the litigation. At the class certification stage, it is enough that Dr. Bielby presented properly-analyzed, scientifically reliable evidence tending to show that a common question of fact — i.e., "Does Wal-Mart's policy of decentralized, subjective employment decision making operate to discriminate against female employees?" — exists with respect to all members of the class. This he did and, thus, we find no error in the district court's acceptance of Dr. Bielby's evidence to support its finding of commonality.

(3) Statistical Evidence   It is well-established that commonality may be established by raising an inference of class-wide discrimination through the use of statistical analysis. See *Caridad* [*v. Metro-North Commuter R.R.*, 191 F.3d 283, 292 (2d Cir. 1999)]; *see also Stastny v. S. Bell Tel. & Tel. Co.*, 628 F.2d 267, 278 (4th Cir. 1980) (recognizing that statistical data showing comparable disparities experienced by protected employees may raise an inference of a policy or practice of discrimination).

Dr. Richard Drogin, Plaintiffs' statistician, analyzed data at a regional level. He ran separate regression analyses for each of the forty-one regions containing Wal-Mart stores. He concluded that "there are statistically significant disparities between men and women at Wal-Mart in terms of compensation and promotions, that these disparities are wide-spread across regions, and that they can be explained only by gender discrimination." Dr. Marc Bendick Plaintiffs' labor economics expert, conducted a "benchmarking" study comparing Wal-Mart with twenty of its competitors and concluded that Wal-Mart promotes a smaller percentage of women than its competitors.

Wal-Mart challenges Dr. Drogin's findings and faults his decision to conduct his research on the regional level, rather than analyze the data store-by-store. However, the proper test of whether workforce statistics should be viewed at the macro (regional) or micro (store or sub-store) level depends largely on the similarity of the employment practices and the interchange of employees at the various facilities.

Here, Dr. Drogin explained that a store-by-store analysis would not capture: (1) the effect of district, regional, and company-wide control over Wal-Mart's uniform compensation policies and procedures; (2) the dissemination of Wal-Mart's uniform compensation policies and procedures resulting from the frequent movement of store managers; or (3) Wal-Mart's strong corporate culture. Because Dr. Drogin provided a reasonable explanation for conducting his research at the regional level, the district court did not abuse its discretion when it credited Dr. Drogin's analysis and concluded that his analysis supported Plaintiffs' contention that Wal-Mart's corporate structure and policies led to a "pattern or practice" of discrimination.

Wal-Mart also contends that the district court erred by not finding Wal-Mart's statistical evidence *more* probative than Plaintiffs' evidence because, according to Wal-Mart, its analysis was conducted store-by-store. However, contrary to Wal-Mart's characterization of its analysis, its research was not conducted at the individual store level. Dr. Joan Haworth, Wal-Mart's expert, did not conduct a store-by-store analysis; instead she reviewed data at the sub-store level by comparing departments to analyze the pay differential between male and female hourly employees. Moreover, our job on this appeal is to determine whether the district court *abused its discretion* in finding that, based on all the evidence, there existed common questions of fact. . . .

Because the district court reasonably concluded that Dr. Drogin's regional analysis was probative and based on well-established scientific principles, and because Wal-Mart provided little or no proper legal or factual challenge to it, and because the district court was within its discretion when it found that Dr. Haworth's evidence — which was stricken for failure to satisfy the standards of Federal Rules of Evidence 702 and 703 — did not undermine Dr. Drogin's evidence (as Wal-Mart insists), the district court did not abuse its discretion when it relied on Dr. Drogin's use and interpretation of statistical data as a valid component of its commonality analysis.

(4) Anecdotal Evidence Circumstantial and anecdotal evidence of discrimination is commonly used in Title VII "pattern and practice" cases to bolster statistical proof by bringing "the cold numbers convincingly to life." *Int'l Bhd. of Teamsters v. United States*. Wal-Mart contends that the district court erred by concluding that the anecdotal evidence, presented by Plaintiffs in the form of 120 declarations, supported a finding of commonality. Wal-Mart maintains that the declarations depict a handful of "widely divergent" events that cannot be deemed probative or representative of discrimination in pay or management-track promotions.

In their declarations, the potential class members testified to being paid less than similarly situated men, being denied or delayed in receiving promotions in a disproportionate manner when compared with similarly situated men, working in an atmosphere with a strong corporate culture of discrimination, and being subjected to various individual sexist acts. The district court credited this evidence.

Wal-Mart contends that the district court erred because the 120 declarations cannot sufficiently represent a class of 1.5 million. However, we find no authority requiring or even suggesting that a plaintiff class submit a statistically significant number of declarations for such evidence to have any value. Further, the district court did not state that this anecdotal evidence provided sufficient proof to *establish* commonality by itself, but rather noted that such evidence provides *support* for Plaintiffs' contention that commonality is present. Because the declarations raise an inference of common discriminatory experiences and are consistent with Plaintiffs' statistical evidence, the district court did not abuse its discretion when it credited Plaintiffs' anecdotal evidence.

b.   Subjective Decision-Making

As discussed above, the district court found substantial evidence suggesting common pay and promotion policies among Wal-Mart's many stores. The court also reasoned that Wal-Mart's decision to permit its managers to utilize subjectivity in interpreting those policies offers additional support for a commonality finding. [Wal-Mart challenged this conclusion because decentralized, discretionary decision-making was not inherently discriminatory. The court agreed with that proposition, but held that such discretion may be a factor supporting commonality.]

Plaintiffs produced substantial evidence of Wal-Mart's centralized company culture and policies, which provides a nexus between the subjective decision-making and the considerable statistical evidence demonstrating a pattern of discriminatory pay and promotions for female employees. Therefore, for the reasons stated above, we find that the district court did not abuse its discretion when it held that

Wal-Mart's subjective decision-making policy raises an inference of discrimination, and provides support for Plaintiffs' contention that commonality exists among possible class members.

c. Conclusion

Plaintiffs' factual evidence, expert opinions, statistical evidence, and anecdotal evidence demonstrate that Wal-Mart's female employees nationwide were subjected to a *single set of corporate policies* (not merely a number of independent discriminatory acts) that may have worked to unlawfully discriminate against them in violation of Title VII. Evidence of Wal-Mart's subjective decision making policies provide further evidence of a common practice of discrimination. Many other courts have reached the same conclusion based on similar evidence. Accordingly, we conclude that the district court did not abuse its discretion in holding that the "commonality" prerequisite to class certification was satisfied.

3. Typicality

[The court considered the defendant's typicality argument, although plaintiff claimed it had been waived, in large part because typicality and commonality are similar and tend to merge, citing *Falcon*; nevertheless, it stressed that "each factor serves a discrete purpose. Commonality examines the relationship of facts and legal issues common to class members, while typicality focuses on the relationship of facts and issues between the class and its representatives. See I Newberg on Class Actions, §3:13 at 317."]

a. Plaintiffs' Claims Are Sufficiently Typical

Rule 23(a)(3) requires that "the claims or defenses of the representative parties are typical of the claims or defenses of the class." We stated in *Hanlon* that "[u]nder the rule's permissive standards, representative claims are 'typical' if they are reasonably coextensive with those of absent class members; they need not be substantially identical." Some degree of individuality is to be expected in all cases, but that specificity does not necessarily defeat typicality.

Thus, we must consider whether the injury allegedly suffered by the named plaintiffs and the rest of the class resulted from the same allegedly discriminatory practice. We agree with the district court that it did. Even though individual employees in different stores with different managers may have received different levels of pay or may have been denied promotion or promoted at different rates, because the discrimination they allegedly suffered occurred through an alleged common practice — e.g., excessively subjective decision-making in a corporate culture of uniformity and gender stereotyping — their claims are sufficiently typical to satisfy Rule 23(a)(3).

b. Plaintiffs' Representatives Are Sufficiently Typical of the Class

Typicality requires that the named plaintiffs be members of the class they represent. *See Falcon.* There is no dispute that the class representatives are "typical" of the hourly class members, because almost all of the class representatives hold hourly positions. Instead, Wal-Mart contends that the class representatives are not typical of all female in-store managers because only one of six class representatives holds a salaried management position, and she holds a somewhat low-level position.

However, because all female employees faced the same alleged discrimination, the lack of a class representative for each management category does not undermine Plaintiffs' certification goal. *See Hartman v. Duffey,* 19 F.3d 1459 (D.C. Cir. 1994) (recognizing that an employee can challenge discrimination in "different job categories where the primary practices used to discriminate in the different categories are themselves similar. While it may be prudent to have the class divided into sub-classes represented by a named plaintiff from each of the differing job categories, it would not be necessary to the validity of the class certification to do so.").

In addition, because the range of managers in the proposed class is limited to those working in Wal-Mart's stores, it is not a very broad class, and a named plaintiff occupying a lower-level, salaried, in-store management position is sufficient to satisfy the "permissive" typicality requirement.

Because Plaintiffs' claims and Plaintiffs' representatives are sufficiently typical of the class, the district court acted within its discretion when it found that Plaintiffs satisfied the typicality prerequisite.

4. Adequate Representation

Rule 23(a)(4) permits certification of a class action only if "the representative parties will fairly and adequately protect the interests of the class." This factor requires: (1) that the proposed representative Plaintiffs do not have conflicts of interest with the proposed class, and (2) that Plaintiffs are represented by qualified and competent counsel.

Before the district court, Wal-Mart argued that Plaintiffs cannot satisfy this factor because of a conflict of interest between female in-store managers who are both plaintiff class members and decision-making agents of Wal-Mart. [T]he district court recognized that courts need not deny certification of an employment class simply because the class includes both supervisory and non-supervisory employees. We agree. Finally, because Wal-Mart does not challenge the district court's finding that Plaintiffs' class representatives and counsel are adequate, we need not analyze this factor.

5. Conclusion

[W]e conclude that the district court did not abuse its discretion when it found that Plaintiffs offered evidence sufficient to satisfy *Rule 23(a)*.

[Several portions of the opinion, including those upholding the district court's finding of compliance with Rule 23(b) and that a class of 1.5 million individuals was "manageable," are omitted.]

KLEINFELD, Circuit Judge, dissenting. . . .

In this case, the only one of the four Rule 23 requirements that is satisfied is "numerosity." In seeking to represent as large a class as imaginable, plaintiffs have destroyed their commonality, typicality, and adequacy of representation, as in many other attempted class certifications that have overreached.

This class lacks "commonality" because the questions "common to the class" are insubstantial. The only common question plaintiffs identify with any precision is whether Wal-Mart's promotion criteria are "excessively subjective." This is not a commonality with any clear relationship to sex discrimination in pay, promotions or terminations. Plaintiffs' sociologist claims merely that a subjective system is "vulnerable" to sex discrimination. But the Supreme Court recognized in *Watson v. Fort Worth Bank & Trust* [reproduced at p. 232] that, although disparate impact analysis may be usable in subjective criteria cases, "leaving promotion decisions to the unchecked discretion of lower level supervisors should itself raise no inference of discriminatory conduct" because "[i]t is self-evident that many jobs . . . require personal qualities that have never been considered amenable to standardized testing." "Vulnerability" to sex discrimination is not sex discrimination.

Plaintiffs' only evidence of sex discrimination is that around 2/3 of Wal-Mart employees are female, but only about 1/3 of its managers are female. But as the Supreme Court recognized in *Watson*, "[i]t is entirely unrealistic to assume that unlawful discrimination is the sole cause of people failing to gravitate to jobs and employers in accord with the laws of chance." Not everybody wants to be a Wal-Mart manager. Those women who want to be managers may find better opportunities elsewhere. Plaintiffs' statistics do not purport to compare women who want to be managers at Wal-Mart with men who want to be managers at Wal-Mart, just female and male employees, whether they want management jobs or not.

This class lacks "typicality" because "the claims or defenses of the representative parties" are not "typical of the claims or defenses of the class." Plaintiffs must show "the existence of a class of persons who have suffered the same injury" as themselves. . . .

"Typicality" exists only if [the claims of seven named plaintiffs] are "typical of the claims or defenses of the class." They are not even typical with respect to each other, let alone with respect to the class of "[a]ll women employed at any Wal-Mart domestic retail store at any time since December 26, 1998 who have been or may be subjected to Wal-Mart's challenged pay and management track promotions policies and practices." Some of the seven named plaintiffs and members of the putative class work for Wal-Mart, some have quit, some have been fired. Some claim sex discrimination, some claim mixed motive race and sex discrimination, some appear to claim only race discrimination. Some claim retaliation, and some appear to claim unfairness but not discrimination. Some of the seven plead a prima facie case, some do not.

Nor are the defenses to the claims likely to be common even as to these seven, let alone all female employees. Some are likely to be vulnerable to defenses such as misconduct, some are not. . . .

The fourth requirement under Rule 23 is that the seven named plaintiffs "will fairly and adequately protect the interests of the class." The majority opinion and the district court give this little attention, no doubt because everyone knows that the lawyers, being without real clients who can instruct them if a class is certified, will run the case as they choose. Based on their own descriptions of the wrongs done to them in the complaint, the interests of the seven named plaintiffs diverge from each other, as will the interests of other members of the class. Women who still work at Wal-Mart and who want promotions have an interest in the terms of an injunction. But an injunction and declaratory judgment cannot benefit women who have quit or been fired and do not want to return. For them, compensatory and punitive damages are what matter. Those who are managers, and many Wal-Marts have female store managers, have interests in preserving their own managerial flexibility under whatever injunction may issue, while those who are not and do not want to be managers may not share this concern. Those who face strong defenses, such as if they did indeed steal time or money, have a considerable interest in a fast, mass settlement, while those who have impressive performance records have an interest in pushing their individual cases to trial.

[Portions of the dissent dealing with 23(b)(2) and due process arguments are omitted.]

NOTES

1. *Procedure and Substance.* It should be instantly apparent from reading the *Dukes* opinion that the class action certification question is intimately bound up with the merits determination. Judge Kleinfeld's dissent sees the named plaintiffs as asserting cases of individual disparate treatment, essentially unconnected to other class members' claims. In contrast, the majority views the case as presenting systemic claims, probably systemic disparate treatment, as in *EEOC v. Sears, Roebuck*, reproduced at p. 157. One appellate court noted that, under the systemic theories, the class action and merit inquiries tend to coincide: to answer the procedural question of whether there is a class sufficiently homogeneous to challenge a pattern of discrimination, in effect, requires answering the substantive question of whether, under either of the available theories, there exists the requisite policy or practice of discrimination affecting an identifiable class of protected employees. Because of this, a "fair determination of the propriety of a class action may be exceedingly difficult without conducting an inquiry roughly comparable to that required to resolve the 'pattern or practice' issue on the merits." *Stastny v. Southern Bell Tel. & Tel. Co.*, 628 F.2d 267, 274 (4th Cir. 1980). Melissa Hart, *Learning From Wal-Mart*, 10 EMPL. RTS. & EMPLOY. POL'Y J. 355, 382-84 (2006), writes:

> the question of whether the employees are affected by a common policy — the certi-
> fication question — can look very similar to the question whether the employer has a
> discriminatory policy — the merits question. And the question of whether geographic
> dispersion should defeat certification is fundamentally tied to a judgment about the
> appropriateness of suits challenging the aggregate effects of decisions made through the
> exercise of unguided discretion. Indeed, given that most class actions that are certified
> settle before they go to trial, arguments about geographic dispersion and the charac-
> terization of a policy of delegation as either centralized and uniform or not may be the
> closest that the courts get to truly addressing the particular claims of discrimination
> made in these suits.

2. *Discretion.* The majority applies an abuse of discretion standard and finds none in the certification. Does that mean that it would also have affirmed had the district court denied certification? The court did affirm the lower court's refusal to certify a class as to backpay liability. The dissent does not focus on the standard of review, but its language suggests that it thought both the district court and the majority were out in left field — which may be what abuse of discretion means in more common parlance.

3. *Source and Reach of At-Issue Policies.* The Wal-Mart ethos, maintained by a very centralized regime, may have been critical to the majority's decision. Prior cases have narrowed class actions when it became clear that challenged practices were established locally and not centrally, *e.g., Cooper v. Southern Co.*, 390 F.3d 695, 714-715 (11th Cir. 2004) (no commonality, since "the hiring, compensation, and pro-motion decisions at issue were made by different managers in different companies implementing different policies"); *Stastny v. Southern Bell Tel. & Tel. Co.*, 628 F.2d 267, 280 (4th Cir. 1980) (statewide statistics unrelated to any separate local facilities do not establish commonality because discrimination could have been limited to only a few facilities). Similarly, some policies may apply to some kinds of employees and not others, limiting the certification. *Cooper v. Fed. Reserve Bank of Richmond*, 467 U.S. 867 (1984) (named plaintiffs did not have claims typical of members of the putative class who were denied senior management positions).

The battle over "commonality" is preliminarily set by the scope of plaintiffs' claim. Here the claim was that Wal-Mart generally controlled every aspect of its operation everywhere in a highly centralized way but nevertheless granted supervisors unstructured discretion to evaluate employees reporting to them for purposes of pay and promotions. Plaintiffs' experts, therefore, used statistical analyses to establish that across all of the organization women earned less than men and were less well represented in manager positions. In other words, the statistical showing of plaintiffs was based on that aggregation of all women workers at Wal-Mart. Defendant's expert tried to defeat commonality by claiming that the decisionmaking was local and so only local, department-by-department statistical evidence was relevant. That evidence showed a random pattern of pay and promotions across those individual departments. Plaintiff's expert, Dr. William T. Beilby, rebutted by arguing that disaggregation often works basically to reduce the sample sizes (from regions or stores to departments), which may destroy the statistical significance of the resulting findings without affecting their showing of disparities. William T. Bielby & Pamela Coukos, *"Statistical Dueling" with Unconventional Weapons: What Courts Should Know about Experts in Employment Discrimination Class Actions*, 56 EMORY L. J. 1563 (2007).

4. *The Real Dispute*. The majority's doctrinal approach to class actions is a "by the numbers" checking off of the four factors of Rule 23(a) (and corresponding analysis under 23(b)), but there is obviously more going on under the surface. In the original version of the opinion, 474 F.3d 1214, the dissent manifested an intense skepticism about class actions in general. Such skepticism is likely to result in a very grudging reading of the four factors. Why the hostility? It's possible to discern at least three separate bases for hostility in Judge Kleinfeld's original opinion: unfairness to class members; unfairness to defendants; and distortion of the attorney-client relationship.

5. *Unfairness to Class Members*. Class actions may be unfair to class members, who may find their claims lost by virtue of preclusion if they are not adequately represented in the litigation. Note that *Dukes* did *not* certify a class as to backpay liability, which limited class members' risk (while also limiting their recovery). But it remains true that some members of the class might be foreclosed by a judgment in the *Dukes* class action. Recall, however, that the Supreme Court has made clear that the preclusive effects of class actions are much more limited than might first appear. In *Cooper v. Fed. Reserve Bank of Richmond*, 467 U.S. 867, 869 (1984), the Court held "a judgment in a class action determining that an employer did not engage in a general pattern or practice of racial discrimination against the certified class of employees [does not preclude] a class member from maintaining a subsequent civil action alleging an individual claim of racial discrimination against the employer."

The *Cooper* litigation resolved two kinds of claims in the bank's favor: the individual claims of each of the four named plaintiffs and the class claim of discriminatory "policies and practices." But that did not logically mean that the bank had never engaged in individual acts of discrimination against other employees:

> That judgment (1) bars the class members from bringing another class action against the Bank alleging a pattern or practice of discrimination for the relevant time period and (2) precludes the class members in any other litigation with the Bank from relitigating the question whether the Bank engaged in a pattern and practice of discrimination against black employees during the relevant time period. The judgment is not, however, dispositive of the individual claims the Baxter petitioners have alleged in their separate action.

467 U.S. at 880.

6. *Unfairness to Defendants*. The dissent's original opinion was also concerned that actions are unfair to defendants, who may be forced to settle regardless of the merits by the sheer magnitude of potential liability and costs of defense. The straightforward economic calculation Judge Kleinfeld proffered was that, as the amount of exposure rises, even a very small risk of liability will push an economically rational defendant to settle. Are you convinced? Given Wal-Mart's success in obtaining price concessions from its vendors because of its huge buying power, do you find it odd that the dissent should worry about the potential liability generated by its very size?

7. *Distorting the Attorney-Client Relationship*. The original dissent also thought that class actions may be inimical because they effectively divorce the attorney from her client. This is a standard objection to class actions, and there are certainly many instances where the major beneficiaries of a class action are not the class members but rather the attorneys. This risk, however, has not been sufficient to end class actions generally, and there is no hint of any particular problem with the *Dukes* attorneys. *See* Deborah R. Hensler, *Revisiting the Monster: New Myths and Realities of Class Action and Other Large Scale Litigation*, 11 DUKE J. COMP. & INT'L L. 179, 190 (2001) ("Many plaintiffs with conflicting interests may be represented by a single lawyer, who may find it attractive to compromise one client's claim in order to obtain payment for another's . . . [and] find it attractive to settle a large block of claims for less than full value and with a substantial fee, thereby freeing themselves to move on to the next set of cases"); Lisa Litwiller, *Why Amendments to Rule 23 Are Not Enough: A Case for the Federalization of Class Actions*, 7 CHAP. L. REV. 201 (2004) (proposing federalization of class actions to safeguard against attorneys who use them as a "mechanism to enrich themselves at the expense of the clients whom they represent").

8. *Shaping the Class to Justify Certification*. To a large extent, the plaintiff can influence the certification question by defining the class she seeks to represent. For example, an African American denied employment as a welder might seek to represent (1) the class of black applicants denied employment as welders; (2) the class of black applicants denied employment for any job by the defendant; (3) the class of blacks, both applicants and employees, within the welding category; (4) the class of blacks, applicants, and employees, within every job category of the defendant; or (5) the class of "minority" applicants (African Americans and other minorities) for the welder's job. One can confidently predict that the prospects of class action certification will vary depending on which class is urged and that the courts will be more likely to find plaintiff an adequate representative of a narrower, rather than a broader, class.

While class definitions may be manipulated to some extent to satisfy Rule 23 requirements, it may be difficult to thread a way among all the requirements. For example, joinder will obviously be impracticable in an action that seeks injunctive relief to protect the rights of potential future employees simply because they are not ordinarily identifiable. But such manipulation itself may cause problems under other requirements of the rule. In one case, the class claim failed because the class defined one way was too small (falling afoul of the numerosity requirement); yet defined another way, it was too large (hence unmanageable). *Hill v. Am. Airlines, Inc.*, 479 F.2d 1057 (5th Cir. 1973). The difficulties of certifying entire suits as class actions have led one commentator to urge courts to use issue certification in classes with "a common core of issues related to defendant's conduct, but with significant individual variability," Jon Romberg, *Half a Loaf is Predominant and Superior to None: Class Certification of Particular Issues Under Rule 23(c)(4)(A)*, 2002 UTAH L. REV. 249, 265 (2002). Would this be a preferable solution for *Dukes?*

3.   Requirements of Rule 23(b)

Even if a particular suit meets all the requirements of Rule 23(a), it still may not be brought as a class action unless it meets a second set of requirements: it must fall within one of the three categories in paragraph (b) of Rule 23. In employment discrimination cases, the dispute is whether the suit is certified under (b)(2) or (b)(3). Rule 23(b)(2) requires that "the party opposing the class . . . act[ ] or refuse[ ] to act on grounds generally applicable to the class, thereby making appropriate final injunctive relief or corresponding declaratory relief with respect to the class as a whole." In contrast, Rule 23(b)(3) requires that

> the court find that the questions of law or fact common to the members of the class predominate over any questions affecting only individual members, and that a class action [be] superior to other available methods for the fair and efficient adjudication of the controversy.

The most important difference between (b)(2) and (b)(3) classes is that (b)(3) class members must be given both notice and the opportunity to "opt out" of the class action. In classes as large as *Dukes*, the requirement to provide 1.5 million former and present employees with notice, at the expense of the named plaintiffs or the class attorneys, would have doomed the suit.

The portions of *Dukes* dealing with this issue have been omitted, but they replay a dispute that has roiled the circuit courts. The most basic question is whether, in view of (b)(2)'s language about injunctive and declaratory relief, (b)(2) certification is ever appropriate in employment discrimination suits where monetary relief is sought.

When backpay was the basic monetary award available, the courts of appeals generally approved (b)(2) certification. Some courts stated that the provision in Rule 23(b)(2) relating to injunctive and declaratory relief is not a limitation on the type of relief available, but a specification of the kind of conduct by a defendant that permits a class action to be brought under Rule 23(b)(2). Other courts held that the provision did not bar suits seeking a backpay award because such relief is equitable and not legal. A court taking either of these positions would award backpay even if it were the only relief granted. Still other courts, noting that the comments of the Advisory Committee on the Federal Rules state that Rule 23(b)(2) "does not extend to cases in which the appropriate final relief relates exclusively or *predominately* to money damages," Advisory Committee's Notes, 1966 F.R.D. 62, 102 (emphasis added), seemed to require for a (b)(2) case that traditional injunctive relief be the "predominate" remedy and that the backpay award be merely "incidental."

The availability of compensatory damages in the wake of the Civil Rights Act of 1991, however, changed the landscape. *Dukes*, like a number of other decisions, continued to certify class actions seeking damages by finding that such relief was not the primary thrust of the case. *See also Robinson v. Metro-North Commuter R.R.*, 267 F.3d 147, 164 (2d Cir. 2001) ("a district court may allow (b)(2) certification if it finds that the value to the plaintiffs of the injunctive or declaratory relief sought is predominant even though compensatory or punitive damages are also claimed").

However, other circuits take the view that such recoveries "necessarily predominate over requested declaratory or injunctive relief." *Reeb v. Ohio Dep't of Rehab. & Corr., Belmont Corr. Inst.*, 435 F.3d 639, 651 (6th Cir. 2006) (2-1); *Allison v. Citgo Petroleum Corp.*, 151 F.3d 402 (5th Cir. 1998) (2-1) (suit seeking compensatory and punitive damages could not be certified under (b)(2) because such relief was not incidental to the declarative and injunctive relief sought). *See generally* Suzette Malveaux, *Fighting to Keep Employment Discrimination Class Actions Alive: How Allison v. Citgo's Predomination Requirement Threatens to Undermine Title VII Enforcement*, 26 BERKELEY J. EMP. & LAB. L. 405 (2005) ("it is imperative that the predomination approach — taken by the majority of circuits that have ruled on this issue — be abandoned in favor of the more equitable ad hoc balancing approach established by the Second Circuit in *Robinson*"); Melissa Hart, *Will Employment Discrimination Class Actions Survive?*, 37 AKRON L. REV. 813, 814-15 (2004) ("neither the new remedies nor the jury trial right that Congress added to Title VII provides sufficient justification to deny certification in most employment discrimination class actions").

Some courts have split the difference. The Seventh Circuit, which had rejected certification of Title VII suits seeking damages, nevertheless approved of certifying a class for injunctive purposes while handling damages claims individually. *See Allen v. Int'l Truck & Engine Corp.*, 358 F.3d 469, 471-72 (7th Cir. 2004); *but see Cooper v. Southern Co.*, 390 F.3d 695, 721 (11th Cir. 2004) (refusing to certify a class action for only injunctive and declaratory relief because the named plaintiffs' willingness to forego class certification on damages raised questions about adequate representation and determining damages).

Even if (b)(2) certification is not available, employment discrimination suits may typically be certified under (b)(3). Indeed, if (b)(2) certification is appropriate, (b)(3) will normally also be satisfied. *Wetzel v. Liberty Mut. Ins. Co.*, 508 F.2d 239 (3d Cir. 1975). However, where (b)(2) certification is appropriate, (b)(3) may be unavailable because the wider res judicata effects of (b)(2) are preferable. *See Thomas v. Albright*, 139 F.3d 227 (D.C. Cir. 1998) (permitting class members to opt out was an abuse of discretion since the right to opt out of a non-(b)(3) action is not expressly provided in Rule 23(c)(2) and there was not tenable ground for permitting it); *but see Eubanks v. Billington*, 110 F.3d 87 (D.C. Cir. 1997) (while class members do not have an unqualified right to opt out, district courts may accord such rights). And at least one appellate court has held that res judicata is not permissible where there is no right to opt out. *Johnson v. General Motors Corp.*, 598 F.2d 432 (5th Cir. 1979). *See also Marshall v. Kirkland*, 602 F.2d 1282 (8th Cir. 1979); *Contra Wetzel v. Liberty Mut. Ins. Co.*, 508 F.2d 239, 256-57 (1977).

4. Settling Class Actions

While some class actions are prosecuted to judgment, *see Falcon* and *Cooper*, other problems arise when the two sides consider settlement. Because a representative class member may not properly represent other members' interests in settling the action, Rule 23(e) provides: "A class action shall not be dismissed or compromised without the approval of the court, and notice of the proposed dismissal or compromise shall be given to all members of the class in such manner as the court directs." Although Rule 23(e) does not specify the procedure that follows the notice, the district court should accord a hearing to any class members making serious objections to the settlement. Judge Kleinfeld notes this protection but seems dubious about its effectiveness. Perhaps this is because, assuming proper procedures are followed, the discretion accorded the district court in approving the settlement is great. Further, while there is widespread agreement on the factors to be considered, these factors are so diverse that it is difficult to predict how they will be balanced. Recently, however, courts have shown heightened concern where class counsel attorney fees negotiations may have distorted the proposed settlement. *E.g. Staton v. Boeing Co.*, 313 F.3d 447 (9th Cir. 2002).

Some class actions are "settlement only," that is, there is no class certification prior to the settlement, and the court is presented with simultaneous motions for class certification and approval of the settlement. *Amchem Prods. v. Windsor*, 521 U.S. 591 (1997), rejected a "settlement only" (b)(3) class action because of conflicts of interests among members of the proposed class. *See also Ortiz v. Fireboard Corp.*, 527 U.S. 815 (1999) (certification of a settlement class needs at least a showing that the fund is limited by more than the agreement of the parties and that it has been allocated among class members by a process that addresses their conflicting interests). An employment discrimination class action could often pose analogous problems.

G. FEDERAL GOVERNMENT ENFORCEMENT

Title VII and the Americans with Disabilities Act enforcement by the federal government is largely committed to the Equal Employment Opportunity Commission, although the Attorney General retains a role with respect to suits against state and local governments. § 706(f)(1), 42 U.S.C. § 2000e-5(f)(1). The Age Discrimination in Employment Act has a somewhat different enforcement scheme, and no government agency is charged with enforcing § 1981.

The enforcement scheme we have examined means that the EEOC is the recipient of a huge number of charges of discrimination, recently exceeding 75,000 a year. The ability of the Commission to effectively process these charges has been a subject of continued dispute. *See generally* Julie Chi-hye Suk, *Antidiscrimination Law in the Administrative State*, 2006 U. ILL. L. REV. 405, 467-73 (2006) (recommending a lesser role for EEOC charge processing and congressional conferral on the Commission of rule-making power in implementing Title VII); Michael Selmi, *The Value of the EEOC: The Agency's Role in Employment Discrimination Law*, 57 OHIO ST. L.J. 1 (1996). Recently, the EEOC has moved to formal mediation, with mixed reviews. See p. 723.

Earlier sections exploring the relationship of this administrative procedure to private suits concluded that defects in EEOC charge processing do not affect the right of charging parties to sue employees; partly for that reason, charging parties do not have a cause of action against the EEOC for failure to properly process a charge. *E.g., Baba v. Japan Travel Bureau Int'l*, 111 F.3d 2, 5-6 (2d Cir. 1997). Such defects, however, may limit the EEOC when it attempts to sue the employer. While a court will not review an EEOC reasonable cause determination before the Commission files suit, *EEOC v. Caterpillar*, 409 F.3d 831 (7th Cir. 2005), some cases have barred

Commission suit when the agency has failed to conduct an investigation and find reasonable cause before suing. *E.g., EEOC v. Asplundh Tree Expert Co.*, 340 F.3d 1256, 1261 (11th Cir. 2003) (affirming lower court's ruling that the EEOC did not act in good faith in conciliating a race discrimination charge). A continuing question is whether the Commission suit can exceed the scope of the predicate charge. *See EEOC v. Harvey L. Walner & Assocs.*, 91 F.3d 963 (7th Cir. 1996) (EEOC could not sue for sex harassment when there were no active, timely individual charges and it did not file a Commissioner's charge).

There has also been some question as to the extent of the EEOC's power to investigate charges of discrimination. The EEOC has extensive investigatory powers, and the courts are likely to uphold EEOC subpoenas. *See EEOC v. Shell Oil Co.*, 466 U.S. 54 (1984) (liberal approach to what constitutes a sufficient charge); *United States EEOC v. Technocrest Sys.*, 448 F.3d 1035, 1040 (8th Cir. 2006) (given the allegations of the charging parties, the personnel files of all employees were relevant to whether Technocrest discriminated on the basis of national origin and the district court abused its discretion in quashing the requests for DOL and INS documents and personnel files for all employees); *but see EEOC v. United Air Lines, Inc.*, 287 F.3d 643, 655 (7th Cir. 2002) (EEOC could not use its subpoena power because "in light of the tangential need for the information," the request unduly burdened UAL); *EEOC v. Southern Farm Bureau Cas. Ins. Co.*, 271 F.3d 209 (5th Cir. 2001) (EEOC could not use its subpoena power in investigating race discrimination to obtain gender information).

Since an EEOC suit seeks, in some sense, to vindicate employee rights, there have also been efforts to limit EEOC suits on behalf of individual employees. In *EEOC v. Waffle House, Inc.*, 534 U.S. 279 (2002), the Court permitted the EEOC to obtain relief in Commission lawsuits on behalf of employees even if these employees had agreed to arbitrate any claims against their employers. While recoveries by such employees, either after litigation or by arbitration, would presumably bar duplicate recovery in the EEOC action, the Commission cannot be foreclosed from suing by virtue of an arbitration agreement to which it is not a party. *See EEOC v. Sidley Austin LLP*, 437 F.3d 695, 696 (7th Cir. 2006) (EEOC can seek damages on behalf of individuals who had agreed to arbitrate any claims against the firm so long as there is no double recovery). *See also EEOC v. Pemco Aeroplex*, 383 F.3d 1280, 1294 (11th Cir. 2004) (EEOC not bound by previous action brought by 22 plaintiffs claiming hostile work environment where EEOC was not party to earlier action, and it did not sit at counsel table, attend every day of trial, examine any witnesses, or exert any control over plaintiffs' decisions).

A final question concerning EEOC suits relates to the governing time limitations. *Occidental Life Ins. Co. v. EEOC*, 432 U.S. 355 (1977), effectively settled most such issues, holding that there was no statute of limitations for EEOC suits. However, the Court did suggest that laches, or some related doctrine, may limit such suits. *Id.* at 373. Efforts to use laches against the EEOC have had mixed results. *See EEOC v. Navy Fed. Credit Union*, 424 F.3d 397, 410 (4th Cir. 2005) (refusing to apply laches when any delay was not the responsibility of the EEOC); *but see EEOC v. Alioto Fish Co.*, 623 F.2d 86 (9th Cir. 1980) (19-month delay period before EEOC reasonable cause determination, subsequent ten-month delay before beginning conciliation, and 20-month delay after before bringing suit justified district court's finding of unreasonableness).

H. SUIT AGAINST GOVERNMENTAL EMPLOYERS

1. *State and Local Government Employment*

a. Tenth and Eleventh Amendment Challenges

The application of Title VII, as well as the Age Discrimination in Employment Act and the Americans with Disabilities Act, to state and local governments has survived constitutional challenge on Tenth Amendment grounds. *Garcia v. San Antonio Metro. Trans. Auth.*, 469 U.S. 528 (1985) overruled contrary precedent and upheld federal authority under the Commerce Clause to regulate state employment. However, the ADEA and ADA have not been as fortunate with regard to the Eleventh Amendment, which bars private suit against the state or its instrumentalities. Despite Congress's unequivocally expressed intent to override that immunity with respect to both laws, neither statute survived scrutiny. *Kimel v. Florida Bd. of Regents*, 528 U.S. 62 (1999) (ADEA); *Board of Trustees v. Garrett*, 531 U.S. 356 (2001) (Title I of the ADA); *see also Latham v. Office of the Attorney Gen. of Ohio*, 395 F.3d 261 (6th Cir. 2005) (ADEA retaliation claim did not abrogate Eleventh Amendment immunity despite claim that this provision safeguarded First Amendment rights of free speech); *but see Tennessee v. Lane*, 541 U.S. 509 (2004) (upholding abrogation of state immunity in an ADA Title II suit for at least some applications). *See generally* Timothy J. Cahill & Betsy Malloy, *Overcoming the Obstacles of Garrett: An "As Applied" Saving Construction for the ADA's Title II*, 39 WAKE FOREST L. REV. 133 (2004).

The significance of *Kimel* and *Garrett* is substantial but should not be exaggerated. They do not hold that the ADA and ADEA inapplicable to the states; rather, they hold only that *private* suits against the states are not permitted. Accordingly, federal government enforcement is still allowed. *E.g.*, *State Police for Automatic Ret. Ass'n v. DiFava*, 317 F.3d 6, 12 (1st Cir. 2003) (Eleventh Amendment did not preclude the EEOC from enforcing ADEA claims for money damages and injunctive relief against the state); *EEOC v. Bd. of Regents of the Univ. of Wis. Sys.*, 288 F.3d 296 (7th Cir. 2002) (even when the EEOC is proceeding on behalf of private individuals, it is not subject to Eleventh Amendment immunity in suits against the state). Secondly, *Kimel* and *Garrett* do not bar suits against local governmental entities. They merely prohibit private suits against an employer that counts as the state, and most public sector employment will remain actionable by private suit because the employers involved are local governmental units. *E.g.*, *Mt. Healthy City Sch. Dist. Bd. of Ed. v. Doyle*, 429 U.S. 274, 280 (1977) (Eleventh Amendment immunity does not reach to counties and similar municipal corporations); *Woods v. Rondout Valley Cent. Sch. Dist. Bd. of Educ.*, 466 F.3d 232 (2d Cir. 2006) (local board of education not entitled to immunity as arm of New York).

Third, Eleventh Amendment immunity is not absolute: it may be waived by the state. *Lapides v. Bd. of Regents*, 535 U.S. 613 (2002) (a state can waive its Eleventh Amendment immunity by removing a state lawsuit from state court to federal court). Ironically, on remand in *Garrett* itself, the Eleventh Circuit found that Alabama had waived its immunity to suit under the Rehabilitation Act. *Garret v. Univ. of Al. at Birmingham Bd. of Trs.*, 344 F.3d 1288, (11th Cir. 2003). To this effect, a number of circuits have held that state receipt of federal funds expressly conditioned on waiver of immunity does indeed waive that immunity. *E.g.*, *Barbour v. Wash. Metro. Area Transit Auth.*, 374 F.3d 1161 (D.C. Cir. 2004) (acceptance of federal funds waived Eleventh Amendment immunity); *Miller v. Tex. Tech Univ. Health Scis. Ctr.*, 421 F.3d 342 (5th Cir. 2005) (en banc) (a state waives its Eleventh Amendment immunity from suit in federal court under § 504 of the Rehabilitation Act of 1973 when it accepts federal funds expressly conditioned on waiver of immunity). *See generally* Ann Carey Juliano, *The More You Spend, the More You Save: Can the Spending Clause Save Federal Anti-Discrimination Laws?*, 46 VILLANOVA L. REV. 1111 (2001).

Fourth, injunctive relief may be available against state officials under *Ex Parte Young*, 209 U.S. 123 (1980), the theory of which is that state officials who are violating federal law are acting ultra vires and may be enjoined to follow governing law; the official, not the state, is the defendant. This theory has been employed to permit antidiscrimination suits. *E.g.*, *Henrietta D. v. Bloomberg*, 331 F.3d 261 (2d Cir. 2003). Fifth, the Court stressed in *Garrett* that most states had state remedies against disability discrimination that provided adequate redress for victims. *But see* Ruth Colker & Adam Milani, *The Post-*Garrett *World: Insufficient State Protection Against Disability Discrimination*, 53 ALA. L. REV. 1075 (2002).

In contrast to the ADEA and ADA, Title VII was held to trump state Eleventh Amendment immunity in *Fitzpatrick v. Bitzer*, 427 U.S. 445 (1976), although the court dropped a footnote indicating that there was no dispute in the case before it that Title VII was an exercise of Congress's power under § 5 of the Fourteenth Amendment. Lower courts have generally viewed *Fitzpatrick* as good law despite substantial subsequent development of Eleventh Amendment doctrine. *E.g.*, *Crumpacker v. Kan. Dep't of Human Res.*, 338 F.3d 1163 (10th Cir. 2003) (Congress properly abrogated states' immunity under Eleventh Amendment for retaliation claims based on reasonable good-faith belief that underlying conduct violated Title VII). This authority was reinforced by *Nev. Dep't of Human Res. v. Hibbs*, 538 U.S. 721 (2003) (permitting private suit against the state under the Family & Medical Leave Act). The effect of the Eleventh Amendment on other sex- and race-based statutes is mixed. *See Kovacevich v. Kent State Univ.*, 224 F.3d 806 (6th Cir. 2000) (Equal Pay Act validly abrogated state Eleventh Amendment immunity); *Ellis v. Univ. of Kan. Med. Ctr.*, 163 F.3d 1186, 1196 (10th Cir. 1998) (Congress did not abrogate state immunity under § 1981).

The rationale for *Fitzpatrick* and its progeny is that Title VII is partially based on § 5 of the Fourteenth Amendment, which accords Congress the power "to enforce, by appropriate legislation, the provisions of this article." In the proper exercise of this power, Congress may abrogate what would otherwise be state immunity to private suit. The Court, however, had held Congress can *enforce* Fourteenth Amendment rights, not define them. *City of Boerne v. Flores*, 521 U.S. 507, 517 (1997). It is possible, then, that some applications of Title VII suits are not sufficiently linked to the Fourteenth Amendment to be valid. While Congress is not limited to parroting the provisions of the Fourteenth Amendment, to be "appropriate" under § 5 "there must be a congruence and proportionality between the injury to be prevented or remedied and the means adopted to that end." *Id.* at 520. That is why *Kimel* and *Garrett* held against abrogation: while age and disability classifications are subject to only rational basis review under the Equal Protection Clause, the two statutes apply something more like strict scrutiny analysis and therefore go too far beyond the Equal Protection Clause. This would be permissible only by a satisfactory showing of the need for prophylactic action, which the Court found lacking in both the ADEA and ADA.

As applied to Title VII, disparate treatment race and gender discrimination by states would support the 1972 extension of that statute to the states. *See Downing v. Bd. of Trustees of the Univ. of Ala.*, 321 F.3d 1017 (11th Cir. 2003) (dismissing Eleventh Amendment defense in a same sex-harassment suit); *Nanda v. Bd. of Trs. of the Univ. of Ill.*, 303 F.3d 817 (7th Cir. 2002) (disparate treatment theory valid as applied to the states). But some of the broader reaches of Title VII, such as disparate impact, may be more questionable, although the Court has, without noting any problem, enforced disparate impact claims against a state. *Connecticut. v. Teal*, 457 U.S. 440 (1982).

Thus far, only one circuit has rejected a private Title VII suit on Eleventh Amendment grounds. *See Holmes v. Marion County Office of Family & Children*, 349 F.3d 914, 921 (7th Cir. 2003) (private suits seeking to enforce a state employer duty to reasonably accommodate religious beliefs not permitted under the Eleventh Amendment). *See generally* James M. Oleske, Jr., *Federalism, Free Exercise and Title VII: Reconsidering Reasonable Accommodations*, 6 U. PA. J. CONST. L. 525 (2004). It is possible, of course, that the appropriate test is not whether any particular provision of Title VII is justified by §5 but rather whether the statute as a whole is, in which case *Holmes* is incorrect.

b. Exemptions

Remaining federalism concerns in the antidiscrimination statutes are reflected mainly in special statutory provisions and in judicial approaches to interpreting laws such as exceptions for elected officials and their appointees found in Title VII, the ADEA, and the ADA. For example, Title VII excludes from the definition of "employee"

> any person elected to public office in any State or political subdivision of any State by the qualified voters thereof, or any person chosen by such officer to be on such officer's personal staff, or an appointee on the policy making level or an immediate adviser with respect to the exercise of the constitutional or legal power of the office.

§701(f), 42 U.S.C. §200e(f) (2007). There is a comparable provision in the ADEA. 29 U.S.C. §630(f).

The Supreme Court construed the ADEA version of this exception in *Gregory v. Ashcroft*, 501 U.S. 452 (1991), and held that appointed state judges are within it, in part because Congress had not clearly enough included them in the statute, After *Ashcroft*, Congress passed the Government Employee Rights Act as part of the Civil Rights Act of 1991, to provide a "plain statement" of its intent to intrude into state operations that the Court had required. *See* 42 U.S.C. §2000e-16c (2007). GERA also changed the ground rules somewhat. It left the original statutory exemption technically intact but created a new statutory protection for appointed officials by which the EEOC adjudicates disputes through a formal agency hearing. The EEOC's decision is then subject to limited judicial review, rather than the trial de novo that exists in the private sector. *See Bd. of County Comm'rs v. EEOC*, 405 F.3d 840 (10th Cir. 2005) (affirming EEOC decision that Title VII bars retaliation against previously exempt state employees); *Brazoria County v. EEOC*, 391 F.3d 685 (5th Cir. 2004) (same). *But see State of Alaska v. EEOC*, 2007 U.S. App. LEXIS 25989 (9th Cir. 2007) (the Eleventh Amendment bars GERA's application to members of a governor's staff).

2. *Federal Employment*

While neither Title VII nor the ADEA originally included the federal government, amendments to both statutes extended their reach to most federal workers. However, rather than merely adding federal employment to the statutes' coverage, Congress added a separate provision to each law, §717 of Title VII, 42 U.S.C. §2000e-16 (2007), and §15, 29 U.S.C. §633a (2007), to the ADEA. Some remaining pockets of employment were later covered by other laws, including employees of the House of Representatives, the Senate, and instrumentalities of Congress, and many "presidential appointees." *See Fields v. Office of Eddie Bernice Johnson*, 459 F.3d 1 (D.C. Cir. 2006), *appeal dismissed sub nom Office of Senator Dayton v. Hanson*, 127 S. Ct. 2018 (2007). While the substantive coverage of these provisions has been generally construed to parallel normal statutory analysis, there are some marginal differences. *See Gómez-Pérez v. Potter*, 476 F.3d 54 (1st Cir.), *cert. granted*, 168 L. Ed. 2d 806 (2007) (ADEA's provision prohibiting discrimination in federal employment did not reach retaliation). The Americans with Disabilities Act does not generally reach federal employees, but these employees receive comparable protection under the Rehabilitation Act, which specifically adopts the "remedies, procedures, and rights" of §717. 29 U.S.C. §794(a). These procedures are the exclusive avenue for redress for federal employees for harms within their scope. *Brown v. Gen. Servs. Admin.*, 425 U.S. 820 (1976).

The normal provisions of the federal laws were not, however, simply applied to federal employees. Each statute created a different scheme, which basically entrusts enforcement to an administrative process, and the procedures differ somewhat between Title VII and the ADEA. Employees file an administrative complaint with the agency responsible for the discrimination, and, after final agency action on that complaint, the charging party may either appeal to the EEOC or file suit in district court. If appeal to the EEOC does not resolve the matter, suit may then be brought in federal court, where trial is de novo. *Chandler v. Roudebush*, 425 U.S. 840 (1976). Requirements, such as time limitations, that are analogous, but not identical, to those governing private sector suit, apply. *See Irwin v. Dept. of Veterans Affairs*, 498 U.S. 89, 95-96 (1990).

Chapter 8

Judicial Relief

A. INTRODUCTION

This chapter explores the judicial relief available once a violation of Title VII, § 1981, the ADEA, or the ADA has been proven. These statutes have similar, but distinct, remedial schemes. As a result, the availability of, and limitations on, relief vary from statute to statute. Two examples will illustrate: (1) compensatory (traditional tort) damages are available under Title VII, § 1981, Title I, and probably Title II of the ADA, but not under the ADEA; (2) a statutory maximum is placed on compensatory damages in Title VII and Title I actions, but not in § 1981 and Title II actions.

When Title VII was originally enacted, its proponents did not want it to include compensatory damages because the grant of those damages would likely trigger a right to a jury trial. At the time, there was rampant discrimination in jury selection, often linked to discrimination in voting rights. *See Castenada v. Partida*, 430 U.S. 482 (1977) (systematic exclusion of Latinos from juries). Accordingly, equitable relief administered by a federal judge was believed to be a surer way of vindicating the rights Title VII created. Compensatory and punitive damages, as well as a jury trial right for such claims, were added to Title VII by the Civil Rights Act of 1991, but only for disparate treatment discrimination; thus, there is neither a jury trial right nor compensatory or punitive damages available for disparate impact claims.

We begin with a discussion of the policies that are served by the remedial schemes provided under the antidiscrimination statutes.

ALBEMARLE PAPER CO. v. MOODY
422 U.S. 405 (1975)

Justice STEWART delivered the opinion of the Court.

I

[The district court found that the employer's seniority system violated Title VII by locking black employees into low-level jobs under the now-discredited theory that practices giving "present effects of past discrimination" were illegal. It ordered the employer to implement a system of "plant-wide" seniority, but refused to award backpay in part because the respondents had assured the court that the suit involved no claim for any monetary awards on a class basis until, after several years of discovery, they moved to add a class demand for backpay.]

II . . .

Though at least some of the members of the plaintiff class obviously suffered a loss of wage opportunities on account of Albemarle's unlawfully discriminatory system of job seniority, the District Court decided that *no* backpay should be awarded to *anyone* in the class. The court declined to make such an award on two stated grounds: the lack of "evidence of bad faith non-compliance with the Act," and the fact that "the defendants would be substantially prejudiced" by an award of backpay that was demanded contrary to an earlier representation and late in the progress of the litigation. . . . [T]he Court of Appeals reversed, holding that backpay could be denied only in "special circumstances." The petitioners argue that the Court of Appeals was in error — that a district court has virtually unfettered discretion to award or deny backpay. . . .

. . . It is true that backpay is not an automatic or mandatory remedy; like all other remedies under the Act, it is one which the courts "may" invoke. The scheme implicitly recognizes that there may be cases calling for one remedy but not another, and — owing to the structure of the federal judiciary — these choices are, of course, left in the first instance to the district courts. However, such discretionary choices are not left to a court's "inclination, but to its judgment; and its judgment is to be guided by sound legal principles." The power to award backpay was bestowed by Congress, as part of a complex legislative design directed at a historic evil of national proportions. A court must exercise this power "in light of the large objectives of the Act." That the court's discretion is equitable in nature hardly means that it is unfettered by meaningful standards or shielded from thorough appellate review. . . .

It is true that "[e]quity eschews mechanical rules . . . [and] depends on flexibility." But when Congress invokes the Chancellor's conscience to further transcendent legislative purposes, what is required is the principled application of standards consistent with those purposes and not "equity [which] varies like the Chancellor's foot." Important national goals would be frustrated by a regime of discretion that "produce[d] different results for breaches of duty in situations that cannot be differentiated in policy."

The District Court's decision must therefore be measured against the purposes which inform Title VII. As the Court observed in *Griggs* [*v. Duke Power Co.*] reproduced at p. 207, the primary objective was a prophylactic one: "It was to achieve equality of employment opportunities and remove barriers that have operated in the past to favor an identifiable group of white employees over other employees." Backpay has an obvious connection with this purpose. If employers faced only the prospect of an injunctive order, they would have little incentive to shun practices of dubious legality. It is the reasonably certain prospect of a backpay award that "provide[s] the spur or catalyst which causes employers and unions to self-examine and to self-evaluate their employment practices and to endeavor to eliminate, so far as possible, the last vestiges of an unfortunate and ignominious page in this country's history."

It is also the purpose of Title VII to make persons whole for injuries suffered on account of unlawful employment discrimination. This is shown by the very fact that Congress took care to arm the courts with full equitable powers. For it is the historic purpose of equity to "secur[e] complete justice." "[W]here federally protected rights have been invaded, it has been the rule from the beginning that courts will be alert to adjust their remedies so as to grant the necessary relief." Title VII deals with legal injuries of an economic character occasioned by racial or other antiminority discrimination. The terms "complete justice" and "necessary relief" have acquired a clear meaning in such circumstances. Where racial discrimination is concerned, "the [district] court has not merely the power but the duty to render a decree which will so far as possible eliminate the discriminatory effects of the past as well as bar like discrimination in the future."

And where a legal injury is of an economic character, "[t]he general rule is, that when a wrong has been done, and the law gives a remedy, the compensation shall be equal to the injury. The latter is the standard by which the former is to be measured. The injured party is to be placed, as near as may be, in the situation he would have occupied if the wrong had not been committed." . . .

The District Court's stated grounds for denying backpay in this case must be tested against these standards. The first ground was that Albemarle's breach of Title VII had not been in "bad faith." This is not a sufficient reason for denying backpay. Where an employer *has* shown bad faith — by maintaining a practice which he knew to be illegal or of highly questionable legality — he can make no claims whatsoever on the Chancellor's conscience. But, under Title VII, the mere absence of bad faith simply opens the door to equity; it does not depress the scales in the employer's favor. If backpay were awardable only upon a showing of bad faith, the remedy would become a punishment for moral turpitude, rather than a compensation for workers' injuries. This would read the "make whole" purpose right out of Title VII, for a worker's injury is no less real simply because his employer did not inflict it in "bad faith." Title VII is not concerned with the employer's "good intent or absence of discriminatory intent" for "Congress directed the thrust of the Act to the *consequences* of employment practices, not simply the motivation." *Griggs.* To condition the awarding of backpay on a showing of "bad faith" would be to open an enormous chasm between injunctive and backpay relief under Title VII. There is nothing on the face of the statute or in its legislative history that justifies the creation of drastic and categorical distinctions between those two remedies.

The District Court also grounded its denial of backpay on the fact that the respondents initially disclaimed any interest in backpay, first asserting their claim five years after the complaint was filed. The court concluded that the petitioners had been "prejudiced" by this conduct. . . .

. . . Title VII contains no legal bar to raising backpay claims after the complaint for injunctive relief has been filed, or indeed after a trial on that complaint has been had. Furthermore, Fed. Rule Civ. Proc. 54(c) directs that "every final judgment shall grant the relief to which the party in whose favor it is rendered is entitled, even if the party has not demanded such relief in his pleadings." But a party may not be "entitled" to relief if its conduct of the cause has improperly and substantially prejudiced the other party. The respondents here were not merely tardy, but also inconsistent, in demanding backpay. To deny backpay because a *particular* cause has been prosecuted in an eccentric fashion, prejudicial to the other party, does not offend the broad purposes of Title VII. This is not to say, however, that the District Court's ruling was necessarily correct. Whether the petitioners were in fact prejudiced, and whether the respondents' trial conduct was excusable, are questions that will be open to review by the Court of Appeals, if the District Court, on remand, decides again to decline to make any award of backpay. But the standard of review will be the familiar one of whether the District Court was "clearly erroneous" in its factual findings and whether it "abused" its traditional discretion to locate "a just result" in light of the circumstances peculiar to the case. . . .

[The concurring opinions of Justices MARSHALL and BLACKMUN have been omitted.]

Justice REHNQUIST, concurring. . . .

To the extent that an award of backpay were to be analogized to an award of damages, such an award upon proper proof would follow virtually as a matter of course from a finding that an employer had unlawfully discriminated contrary to the provisions of Title VII. . . .

But precisely to the extent that an award of backpay is thought to flow as a matter of course from a finding of wrongdoing, and thereby becomes virtually indistinguishable from an award for damages, the question (not raised by any of the parties, and therefore quite properly not discussed in the Court's opinion), of whether either side may demand a jury trial under the Seventh Amendment becomes critical. We said in *Curtis v. Loether*, 415 U.S. 189, 197 (1974), in explaining the difference between the provision for damages under §812 of the Civil Rights Act of 1968 and the authorization for the award of backpay which we treat here: "In Title VII cases, also, the courts have relied on the fact that the decision whether to award backpay is committed to the discretion of the trial judge. There is no comparable discretion here: if a plaintiff proves unlawful discrimination and actual damages, he is entitled to judgment for that amount. . . . Whatever may be the merit of the 'equitable' characterization in Title VII cases, there is surely no basis for characterizing the award of compensatory and punitive damages here as equitable relief." . . .

To the extent, then, that the District Court retains substantial discretion as to whether or not to award backpay notwithstanding a finding of unlawful discrimination, the nature of the jurisdiction which the Court exercises is equitable, and under our cases neither party may demand a jury trial. To the extent that discretion is replaced by awards which follow as a matter of course from a finding of wrongdoing, the action of the Court in making such awards could not be fairly characterized as equitable in character, and would quite arguably be subject to the provisions of the Seventh Amendment. . . .

NOTES

1. *The Statutory Objectives.* Based on what it said were the twin statutory objectives of Title VII — eliminating discrimination and making its victims whole — the Court created a presumption of full, make whole relief: "[G]iven a finding of unlawful

discrimination, backpay should be denied only for reasons which, if applied generally, would not frustrate the central statutory purposes of eradicating discrimination throughout the economy and making persons whole for injuries suffered through past discrimination." Notice, however, that "make-whole" was an inaccurate statement of the Title VII remedial scheme when *Albemarle* was decided since no damages other than backpay were available. The 1991 Civil Rights Act's addition of compensatory damages to Title VII, perfected the make-whole goal for disparate treatment, and its addition of punitive added a deterrent component that had previously been lacking.

2. *Limiting the Twin Objectives.* The Court cut back on *Albemarle* in *Los Angeles Dept. of Water & Power v. Manhart*, 435 U.S. 702, 719-21 (1978), reproduced in part at p. 116, which held the employer had violated Title VII when, pursuant to sex-based actuarial tables, female employees were required to contribute more than male employees to its retirement program; this amounted to discrimination in compensation against the women. However, the Court also held that the district court erred in ordering a refund of the excess contributions. After noting that "conscientious and intelligent administrators of pension funds" might have thought the program was legal and that there was no reason to think that they would not amend their practices without the threat of backpay liability, the Court went on:

> . . . These plans, like other forms of insurance, depend on the accumulation of large sums to cover contingencies. The amounts set aside are determined by a painstaking assessment of the insurer's likely liability. Risks that the insurer foresees will be included in the calculation of liability, and the rates or contributions charged will reflect that calculation. The occurrence of major unforeseen contingencies, however, jeopardizes the insurer's solvency and, ultimately, the insureds' benefits. Drastic changes in the legal rules governing pension and insurance funds, like other unforeseen events, can have this effect. Consequently, the rules that apply to these funds should not be applied retroactively unless the legislature has plainly commanded that result. . . .
>
> . . . . Retroactive liability could be devastating for a pension fund. The harm would fall in large part on innocent third parties. If, as the courts below apparently contemplated, the plaintiffs' contributions are recovered from the pension fund, the administrators of the fund will be forced to meet unchanged obligations with diminished assets. If the reserve proves inadequate, either the expectations of all retired employees will be disappointed or current employees will be forced to pay not only for their own future security but also for the unanticipated reduction in the contributions of past employees.
>
> Without qualifying the force of the *Albemarle* presumption in favor of retroactive relief, we conclude that it was error to grant such relief in this case.

Is *Manhart* consistent with *Albemarle*'s emphasis on the make-whole and prophylactic purposes of Title VII? With *Albemarle*'s analysis of the role of good faith in awarding backpay? Has "the *Albemarle* presumption" been limited, or were there overriding factors that caused the *Manhart* Court to deny backpay? The "refunds" should come from the employer since it was the entity that discriminated and not out of the corpus of funds held in a separate trust set up to fund retirement. How could that put the retirement plan at risk and how would that cause the harm to "fall in large part on innocent third parties?" Did it just not understand who would be liable, or was the Court fearful that liability rectifying the discrimination would bankrupt the employer?

3. *Prejudice to the Defendant.* With respect to Albemarle Paper's claim of prejudice from the plaintiffs' tardy and inconsistent backpay claims, the trial court said that, if backpay had been claimed from the start, the company "might have chosen to

exercise unusual zeal" to resolve the case. *Moody v. Albemarle Paper Co.*, 4 FEP (BNA) 561, 570 (E.D.N.C. 1971). Is this what the Supreme Court meant by "prejudice," or does "prejudice" mean being hindered in presenting a defense on the merits? *See Occidental Life Ins. Co. v. EEOC*, 432 U.S. 355 (1977).

4. *Equitable vs. Legal Remedies.* Section 706(g)(1), as interpreted by *Albemarle*, establishes that Title VII backpay is in some sense discretionary and thus an equitable remedy. Justice Rehnquist explained the importance of this characterization for the right to a jury trial on a Title VII backpay claim: The Seventh Amendment gives a right to trial by jury to "suits at common law" but not to claims brought in equity. While there is now a right to jury trial for intentional discrimination claims under Title VII, the backpay remedy under that statute (and therefore under Title I of the ADA) remains equitable. Thus, both judge and jury are involved in deciding remedies under these statutes. However, the backpay award is considered legal in certain ADEA and other actions (where it is called "unpaid wages"), which gives rise to the right to a jury trial.

B.   EQUITABLE RELIEF TO THE VICTIMS OF DISCRIMINATION

1.   Reinstatement, Retroactive Seniority, and Injunctive Relief

Section 703(g) sets forth the broad array of equitable remedies available in Title VII actions. When a violation is established, "the court may enjoin the respondent from engaging in such unlawful employment practice, and order such affirmative action as may be appropriate, which may include, but is not limited to, reinstatement or hiring of employees, with or without back pay . . . or any other equitable relief as the court deems appropriate." Both prohibitory and restorative equitable relief is available, and both types of equitable relief can take a variety of forms. The most common prohibitory relief is an injunction against the discriminatory practice, and a common form of restorative relief is an award of instatement or reinstatement — making the employer hire or rehire the victim of discrimination. Another form of restorative equitable relief is an award of retroactive seniority — the seniority lost due to the discrimination.

In *Franks v. Bowman Transp. Co.*, which follows, the plaintiffs sought to enjoin discriminatory practices and to obtain instatement and retroactive seniority. The trial court granted the first two forms of relief but refused to award lost seniority.

FRANKS v. BOWMAN TRANSPORTATION CO.
424 U.S. 747 (1976)

Justice BRENNAN delivered the opinion of the Court. . . .

[Black applicants who had sought over-the-road (OTR) driving positions brought a Title VII class action, alleging racially discriminatory hiring and discharge policies in these positions. The trial court enjoined the discriminatory practices and ordered that priority consideration be given to members of the class in filling OTR positions. The trial court declined, however, to award seniority relief. Certiorari was granted on this last aspect of the judgment.]

In affirming the District Court's denial of seniority relief . . . , the Court of Appeals held that the relief was barred by §703(h) [which permits an employer to have a bona fide seniority system]. We disagree. . . .

The black applicants for OTR positions . . . are limited to those whose applications were put in evidence at the trial. The underlying legal wrong affecting them is not the alleged operation of a racially discriminatory seniority system but of a racially discriminatory hiring system. Petitioners do not ask for modification or elimination of the existing seniority system, but only for an award of the seniority status they would have individually enjoyed under the present system but for the illegal discriminatory refusal to hire. It is this context that must shape our determination as to the meaning and effect of §703(h).

On its face, §703(h) appears to be only a definitional provision; as with the other provisions of §703, subsection (h) delineates which employment practices are illegal and thereby prohibited and which are not. Section 703(h) certainly does not expressly purport to qualify or proscribe relief otherwise appropriate under the remedial provisions of Title VII, §706(g), in circumstances where an illegal discriminatory act or practice is found. . . . We therefore hold that the Court of Appeals erred in concluding that, as a matter of law, §703(h) barred the award of seniority relief to the [class].

III

There remains the question whether an award of seniority relief is appropriate under the remedial provisions of Title VII, specifically, §706(g).

. . . Last Term's *Albemarle Paper* [reproduced at p. 654], consistently with the congressional plan, held that one of the central purposes of Title VII is "to make persons whole for injuries suffered on account of unlawful employment discrimination." To effectuate this "make-whole" objective, Congress in §706(g) vested broad equitable discretion in the federal courts . . . This is emphatic confirmation that federal courts are empowered to fashion such relief as the particular circumstances of a case may require to effect restitution, making whole insofar as possible the victims of racial discrimination in hiring. Adequate relief may well be denied in the absence of a seniority remedy slotting the victim in that position in the seniority system that would have been his had he been hired at the time of his application. It can hardly be questioned that ordinarily such relief will be necessary to achieve the "make-whole" purposes of the Act. . . .

Seniority standing in employment with respondent Bowman, computed from the departmental date of hire, determines the order of layoff and recall of employees. Further, job assignments for OTR drivers are posted for competitive bidding and seniority is used to determine the highest bidder. As OTR drivers are paid on a per-mile basis, earnings are therefore to some extent a function of seniority. Additionally, seniority computed from the company date of hire determines the length of an employee's vacation and pension benefits. Obviously merely to require Bowman to hire the . . . victim of discrimination falls far short of a "make-whole" remedy. A concomitant award of the seniority credit he presumptively would have earned but for the wrongful treatment would also seem necessary in the absence of justification for denying that relief. Without an award of seniority dating from the time when he was discriminatorily refused employment, an individual who applies for and obtains employment as an OTR driver pursuant to the District Court's order will never obtain his rightful place in the hierarchy of seniority according to which these various employment benefits are distributed. He will perpetually remain subordinate to persons who, but for the illegal discrimination, would have been in respect to entitlement to these benefits his inferiors. . . .

IV

We are not to be understood as holding that an award of seniority status is requisite in all circumstances. The fashioning of appropriate remedies invokes the sound equitable discretion of the district courts. . . . [But] no less than with the denial of the remedy of backpay, the denial of seniority relief to victims of illegal racial discrimination in hiring is permissible "only for reasons which, if applied generally, would not frustrate the central statutory purposes of eradicating discrimination throughout the economy and making persons whole for injuries suffered through past discrimination.". . .

Respondent Bowman raises an alternative theory of justification. Bowman argues that an award of retroactive seniority to the class of discriminatees will conflict with the economic interests of other Bowman employees. Accordingly, it is argued, the District Court acted within its discretion in denying this form of relief as an attempt to accommodate the competing interests of the various groups of employees.

We reject this argument. . . . [I]t is apparent that denial of seniority relief to identifiable victims of racial discrimination on the sole ground that such relief diminishes the expectations of other, arguably innocent, employees would if applied generally frustrate the central "make-whole" objective of Title VII. These conflicting interests of other employees will, of course, always be present in instances where some scarce employment benefit is distributed among employees on the basis of their status in the seniority hierarchy. But, as we have said, there is nothing in the language of Title VII, or in its legislative history, to show that Congress intended generally to bar this form of relief to victims of illegal discrimination, and the experience under its remedial model in the National Labor Relations Act points to the contrary. Accordingly, we find untenable the conclusion that this form of relief may be denied merely because the interests of other employees may thereby be affected. "If relief under Title VII can be denied merely because the majority group of employees, who have not suffered discrimination, will be unhappy about it, there will be little hope of correcting the wrongs to which the Act is directed."

With reference to the problems of fairness or equity respecting the conflicting interests of the various groups of employees, the relief which petitioners seek is only seniority status retroactive to the date of individual application, rather than some form of arguably more complete relief. No claim is asserted that nondiscriminatee employees holding OTR positions they would not have obtained but for the illegal discrimination should be deprived of the seniority status they have earned. It is therefore clear that even if the seniority relief petitioners seek is awarded, most if not all discriminatees who actually obtain OTR jobs under the court order will not truly be restored to the actual seniority that would have existed in the absence of the illegal discrimination. Rather, most discriminatees even under an award of retroactive seniority status will still remain subordinated in the hierarchy to a position inferior to that of a greater total number of employees than would have been the case in the absence of discrimination. Therefore, the relief which petitioners seek . . . in no sense constitutes "complete relief." Rather, the burden of the past discrimination in hiring is with respect to competitive status benefits divided among discriminatee and nondiscriminatee employees under the form of relief sought. . . .

[Dissent of Chief Justice BURGER omitted.]

Justice POWELL, with whom Justice REHNQUIST joins, concurring in part and dissenting in part. . . .

[T]o the extent that the Court today finds a . . . presumption in favor of granting *benefit-type* seniority, it is recognizing that normally this relief . . . will be equitable. As the Court notes, this type of seniority, which determines pension rights, length of vacations, size of insurance coverage and unemployment benefits, and the like, is analogous to backpay in that its retroactive grant serves "the mutually reinforcing effect of the dual purposes of Title VII." Benefit-type seniority, like backpay, serves to work complete equity by penalizing the wrongdoer economically at the same time that it tends to make whole the one who was wronged.

But the Court fails to recognize that a retroactive grant of *competitive-type* seniority invokes wholly different considerations. This is the type of seniority that determines an employee's preferential rights to various economic advantages at the expense of other employees. These normally include the order of layoff and recall of employees, job and trip assignments, and consideration for promotion.

It is true, of course, that the retroactive grant of competitive-type seniority does go a step further in "making whole" the discrimination victim, and therefore arguably furthers one of the objectives of Title VII. But apart from extending the make-whole concept to its outer limits, there is no similarity between this drastic relief and the granting of backpay and benefit-type seniority. First, a retroactive grant of competitive-type seniority usually does not directly affect the employer at all. It causes only a rearrangement of employees along the seniority ladder without any resulting increase in cost. Thus, Title VII's "primary objective" of eradicating discrimination is not served at all, for the employer is not deterred from the practice.

The second, and in my view controlling, distinction between these types of relief is the impact on other workers. As noted above, the granting of backpay and of benefit-type seniority furthers the prophylactic and make-whole objectives of the statute without penalizing other workers. But competitive seniority benefits, as the term implies, directly implicate the rights and expectations of perfectly innocent employees. The economic benefits awarded discrimination victims would be derived not at the expense of the employer but at the expense of other workers. Putting it differently, those disadvantaged — sometimes to the extent of losing their jobs entirely — are not the wrongdoers who have no claim to the Chancellor's conscience, but rather are innocent third parties. . . .

NOTES

1. *The Equitable Relief Granted.* The package of relief granted in *Franks* shows how broad equitable relief is available in Title VII actions.

(a) *Mandatory Injunction against Further Discrimination.* The trial court in *Franks* enjoined the discriminatory practices at issue. The Fifth Circuit has said that "absent clear and convincing proof of no reasonable probability of further noncompliance with the law a grant of injunctive relief is mandatory." *James v. Stockham Valves & Fittings Co.*, 559 F.2d 310, 354 (5th Cir. 1977). *See also Karraker v. Rent-a-Center*, 492 F.3d 896 (7th Cir. 2007) (injunction requiring defendant to find and destroy all of the test scores of a test plaintiff's challenged as a medical exam under the ADA and ordered the defendant to not utilize any of the results of its prior administrations of the test).

(b) *Priority Hiring as Jobs Open.* The trial court also awarded qualified discriminatees priority in filling vacant line-driver positions. This is something short of an order of immediate instatement, but, if there has been disparate treatment discrimination, such relief is granted in the absence of special circumstances. *Tadlock v. Powell*, 291 F.3d 541 (8th Cir. 2002); *Local 97, IBEW v. Niagra Mohawk Power Corp.*, 196 F.3d 117 (2d Cir. 1999). Cases finding special circumstances include: *Palasota v. Haggar Clothing Co.*, 499 F.3d 474 (5th Cir. 2007) (absence of a comparable sales position without terminating another employee or shrinking others' sales territories together with other factors including lingering animosity between the parties justified reversal of order of reinstatement); *Ellis v. Ringgold Sch. Dist.*, 832 F.2d 27 (3d Cir. 1987) (effective employment relationship now impossible); and *Overstreet v. El Paso Elec. Co.*, 176 F. Appx. 607 (5th Cir, 2006) (employer's publication of reasons for discharge created hostility at the workplace making reinstatement inappropriate). If hiring practices have been invalidated for having a disparate impact, however, the court may not know the proper job qualifications. In such a case, the court may order the employer to develop job-related standards and then to reconsider the discriminatees. *Young v. Edgcomb Steel Co.*, 499 F.2d 97 (4th Cir. 1974). To compensate a discriminatee for losses while awaiting employment, the court can also award "front pay." See p. 680.

(c) *Bumping Discouraged.* Notice that the "first available vacancy" rule effectively means that incumbent workers will not be bumped, or displaced, by a successful plaintiff. Indeed, the concern of the dissent in *Bowman* for the rights of "innocent bystanders" has been reflected at least to the extent that bumping, while permissible, has often been avoided by the courts. *See Doll v. Brown*, 75 F.3d 1200, 1205 (7th Cir. 1996) (while no one has a right to occupy a position that he obtained as a result of unlawful discrimination, even if he himself was not complicit, the effects on innocent parties may be taken into account in deciding whether to bump or instead to award front pay until a vacancy arises). Does the burden-sharing philosophy of *Franks* support a preference for nondisplacement?

2. *Grant of Seniority Relief. Franks* established a presumption in favor of seniority relief. Thus, the victims of defendant's discriminatory failure to hire them as over-the-road truck drivers were, once hired to fill a job opening, granted seniority under the collective bargaining agreement for the purpose of various benefits, like length of vacation, as well as to protect them from layoff. Their date of seniority was the date they would have been hired but for defendant's discrimination.

The *Franks* Court's remedial philosophy differs markedly from that expressed in *Albemarle Paper Co.* The latter opinion grandly spoke of granting "complete justice" and said that courts have "the duty to render a decree which will so far as possible eliminate the discriminatory effects of the past. . . . " *Franks*, on the other hand, emphasized that the seniority relief sought in that case "in no sense constitutes 'complete relief'" because it did not grant the class members the seniority positions they would have had in the absence of discrimination. The seniority that was awarded was not complete relief because the individuals hired instead of these victims maintained their original date of hire as their date of seniority. Thus, in a future layoff, a victim of prior discrimination and the person hired instead of her would have equal seniority protection because they shared the same date of hire. Further, in a systemic case, any given victim of discrimination could be pushed well down the seniority ladder because those actually hired retained their seniority.

3. *Innocence. Franks* thought the discriminatees and the white employees should share the burden of past discrimination. The dissent characterizes the white workers as "innocent." While they are innocent in the sense that they themselves did not perpetrate the discrimination against these plaintiffs, aren't they something like third party beneficiaries of their employers' discrimination since they would not have been hired if plaintiffs had been hired in the first instance? Seth D. Harris, *Innocence and The Sopranos*, 46 N.Y.L. SCH. L. REV. 577, 580 (2004), argues that the Supreme Court "has repeatedly relied on the innocence of white and male workers to deprive African-American and female discrimination victims of complete relief from discrimination." He explains:

[T]he Supreme Court's "innocence" jurisprudence, at least in the workplace discrimination cases, amounts to nothing more than a subtle bait-and-switch of one definition of "innocence" for the other. The white and male co-workers of the victims of discrimination are "innocents" only in the sense that they satisfy the narrow definition: "freedom from specific guilt" or, in the words of one Supreme Court justice, "not the wrongdoers." Even though these workers satisfy only the narrow definition of "innocence," however, the Supreme Court has afforded them almost parental care and protection appropriate only for the sleeping infant who exemplifies the broader, moral definition of "innocence." Further, by casting their co-workers as "innocents," the Supreme Court re-casts the victims of discrimination in the role of perpetrators — in this metaphor, baby-bottle thieves or, worse, child abusers — who would harm "innocents." In this morality play, a neutral and beneficent judiciary restrains the perpetrators and thereby fulfills its obligation to care for and protect the "innocent." "Innocence" thereby alchemizes cases about discrimination against disadvantaged groups into narratives in which African-Americans and women seek to deprive white and male workers of their rightful interests. In this way, the debate over workplace discrimination minimizes discrimination and its victims, while emphasizing the purported plight of "innocent" co-workers.

4. *"Seniority" Outside the Collective Bargaining Context.* In 2006, only 12% of American workers were union members, as were only 7.4% of private sector workers. Union Members Summary, United States Department of Labor, http://www.bls.gov/news.release/union2.nr0.htm (last visited Aug. 31, 2007). But, employers sometimes use seniority outside of collective bargaining. *US Airways v. Barnett*, reproduced at p. 540, was an instance where an employer unilaterally adopted a seniority system, although that system was not legally enforceable by the employees. Presumably, *Franks*-type relief would be available to a victim of discrimination in such a system. If, instead of some official policy of seniority, length of service is merely a factor an employer uses in making various employment decisions, such as promotion and layoff, how can a victim of discrimination be made whole? Must that loss be calculated as part of backpay?

5. *Is Tenure or a Partnership Like Seniority?* Can a court award tenure to a successful plaintiff in an academic setting? This is rare but not unknown, *See Brown v. Trs. of Boston Univ.*, 891 F.2d 337, 360 (1st Cir. 1989) (tenure awarded after court found university had "impermissibly discriminated in making a tenure decision"); *Kunda v. Muhlenberg Coll.*, 621 F.2d 532 (3d Cir. 1980) (tenure award appropriate, at least where district court did not have to evaluate plaintiff's teaching, scholarship, and service). *But see Gurmankin v. Costanzo*, 626 F.2d 1115 (3d Cir. 1980) (affirming the denial of a tenure in a § 1983 suit when the school district had not evaluated plaintiff's qualifications and performance). *See generally* Scott Moss, *Against "Academic Deference": How Recent Developments in Employment Discrimination Law Undercut an Already Dubious Doctrine*, 27 BERKELEY J. EMP. & LAB. L. 1 (2006). What about

ordering an employer to make an employee a partner? Remember that the trial court granted Ann Hopkins partnership on remand in *Price Waterhouse*, 737 F. Supp. 1202 (D.D.C. 1990).

2.   Who Gets Retroactive Seniority and Backpay?

Awarding retroactive seniority and backpay can pose especially difficult problems in systemic cases where a large number of individuals have been the victims of various acts of discrimination extending over a long period of time and involving numerous employment decisions. Must the court determine the precise injuries suffered by each class member when a simpler and less burdensome alternative would provide substantial justice? What if individual determinations are highly impractical because of the factual complexities of the case?

TEAMSTERS v. UNITED STATES
431 U.S. 324 (1977)

Justice STEWART delivered the opinion of the Court. . . .

I

[After finding that the defendant had a standard operating procedure of discriminating against blacks and Latinos by not hiring them for line driver jobs, the question was what relief was appropriate and to whom. The] Court of Appeals held that all Negro and Spanish-surnamed incumbent employees were entitled to bid for future line-driver jobs on the basis of their company seniority, and that once a class member had filled a job, he could use his full company seniority — even if it predated the effective date of Title VII — for all purposes, including bidding and layoff. . . .

III

[The Supreme Court held that individual post-Act discriminatees "may obtain full 'make-whole' relief, including retroactive seniority, but such seniority may not begin before the effective date of Title VII." The Court then turned to the relief awarded below.]

The petitioners argue generally that the . . . Court of Appeals' [seniority relief] sweeps with too broad a brush by granting a remedy to employees who were not shown to be actual victims of unlawful discrimination. Specifically, the petitioners assert that no employee should be entitled to relief until the Government demonstrates that he was an actual victim of the company's discriminatory practices; [and] that no employee who did not apply for a line-driver job should be granted retroactive competitive seniority. . . .

A

The petitioners' first contention is in substance that the Government's burden of proof in a pattern or practice case must be equivalent to that outlined in *McDonnell Douglas v. Green* [reproduced at p. 50]. Since the Government introduced specific evidence of company discrimination against only some 40 employees, they argue that the District Court properly refused to award retroactive seniority to the remainder of the class of minority incumbent employees. . . .

In *Franks v. Bowman Transportation Co.* [reproduced at p. 658], we held that the trial court had erred in placing this burden on the individual plaintiffs [to show they were qualified and a vacancy had been available]. By "demonstrating the existence of a discriminatory hiring pattern and practice," the plaintiffs had made out a prima facie case of discrimination against individual class members; the burden therefore shifted to the employer "to prove that individuals who reapply were not in fact victims of previous hiring discrimination." The *Franks* case thus illustrates another means by which a Title VII plaintiff's initial burden of proof can be met. The class there alleged a broad-based policy of employment discrimination; upon proof of that allegation there were reasonable grounds to infer that individual hiring decisions were made in pursuit of the discriminatory policy and to require the employer to come forth with evidence dispelling that inference.[45]

Although not all class actions will necessarily follow the *Franks* model, the nature of a pattern-or-practice suit brings it squarely within our holding in *Franks*. . . .

. . . Without any further evidence from the Government, a court's finding of a pattern or practice justifies an award of prospective relief. Such relief might take the form of an injunctive order against continuation of the discriminatory practice, an order that the employer keep records of its future employment decisions and file periodic reports with the court, or any other order "necessary to ensure the full enjoyment of the rights" protected by Title VII.

When the Government seeks individual relief for the victims of the discriminatory practice, a district court must usually conduct additional proceedings after the liability phase of the trial to determine the scope of individual relief. The petitioners' contention in this case is that if the Government has not, in the course of proving a pattern or practice, already brought forth specific evidence that each individual was discriminatorily denied an employment opportunity, it must carry that burden at the second, "remedial" stage of trial. That basic contention was rejected in the *Franks* case. As was true of the particular facts in *Franks*, and as is typical of Title VII pattern-or-practice suits, the question of individual relief does not arise until it has been proved that the employer has followed an employment policy of unlawful discrimination. The force of that proof does not dissipate at the remedial stage of the trial. The employer cannot, therefore, claim that there is no reason to believe that its individual employment decisions were discriminatorily based; it has already been shown to have maintained a policy of discriminatory decisionmaking.

The proof of the pattern or practice supports an inference that any particular employment decision, during the period in which the discriminatory policy was in force, was made in pursuit of that policy. The Government need only show that an

---

45. The holding in *Franks* that proof of a discriminatory pattern and practice creates a rebuttable presumption in favor of individual relief is consistent with the manner in which presumptions are created generally. Presumptions shifting the burden of proof are often created to reflect judicial evaluations of probabilities and to conform with a party's superior access to the proof. These factors were present in *Franks*. Although the prima facie case did not conclusively demonstrate that all of the employer's decisions were part of the proved discriminatory pattern and practice, it did create a greater likelihood that any single decision was a component of the overall pattern. Moreover, the finding of a pattern or practice changed the position of the employer to that of a proved wrongdoer. Finally, the employer was in the best position to show why any individual employee was denied an employment opportunity. Insofar as the reasons related to available vacancies or the employer's evaluation of the applicant's qualifications, the company's records were the most relevant items of proof. If the refusal to hire was based on other factors, the employer and its agents knew best what those factors were and the extent to which they influenced the decision making process.

alleged individual discriminatee unsuccessfully applied for a job and therefore was a potential victim of the proved discrimination. As in *Franks*, the burden then rests on the employer to demonstrate that the individual applicant was denied an employment opportunity for lawful reasons. . . .

On remand, therefore, every post-Act minority group applicant for a line-driver position will be presumptively entitled to relief, subject to a showing by the company that its earlier refusal to place the applicant in a line-driver job was not based on its policy of discrimination.

B

. . . We now decide that an incumbent employee's failure to apply for a job is not an inexorable bar to an award of retroactive seniority. Individual nonapplicants must be given an opportunity to undertake their difficult task of proving that they should be treated as applicants and therefore are presumptively entitled to relief accordingly.

(1)

[I]n *Albemarle Paper v. Moody* [reproduced at p. 654], the Court noted that a primary objective of Title VII is prophylactic: to achieve equal employment opportunity and to remove the barriers that have operated to favor white male employees over other employees. The prospect of retroactive relief for victims of discrimination serves this purpose by providing the " 'spur or catalyst which causes employers and unions to self-examine and to self-evaluate their employment practices and to endeavor to eliminate, so far as possible, the last vestiges' " of their discriminatory practices. An equally important purpose of the Act is "to make persons whole for injuries suffered on account of unlawful employment discrimination." . . .

Thus, . . . the purpose of Congress in vesting broad equitable powers in Title VII courts was "to make possible the 'fashion[ing] [of] the most complete relief possible,' " and . . . the district courts have " 'not merely the power but the duty to render a decree which will so far as possible eliminate the discriminatory effects of the past as well as bar like discrimination in the future.' " More specifically, in *Franks* we decided that a court must ordinarily award a seniority remedy unless there exist reasons for denying relief " 'which, if applied generally, would not frustrate the central statutory purposes of eradicating discrimination . . . and making persons whole for injuries suffered.' "

Measured against these standards, the company's assertion that a person who has not actually applied for a job can never be awarded seniority relief cannot prevail. The effects of and the injuries suffered from discriminatory employment practices are not always confined to those who were expressly denied a requested employment opportunity. A consistently enforced discriminatory policy can surely deter job applications from those who are aware of it and are unwilling to subject themselves to the humiliation of explicit and certain rejection.

If an employer should announce his policy of discrimination by a sign reading "Whites Only" on the hiring-office door, his victims would not be limited to the few who ignored the sign and subjected themselves to personal rebuffs. The same message can be communicated to potential applicants more subtly but just as clearly by an employer's actual practices — by his consistent discriminatory treatment of actual applicants, by the manner in which he publicizes vacancies, his recruitment techniques, his responses to casual or tentative inquiries, and even by the racial or ethnic composition of that part of his workforce from which he has discriminatorily excluded members of minority groups. When a person's desire for a job is not translated into a formal application solely because of his unwillingness to engage in a futile gesture he is as much a victim of discrimination as is he who goes through the motions of submitting an application. . . .

(2)

To conclude that a person's failure to submit an application for a job does not inevitably and forever foreclose his entitlement to seniority relief under Title VII is a far cry, however, from holding that nonapplicants are always entitled to such relief. A nonapplicant must show that he was a potential victim of unlawful discrimination. Because he is necessarily claiming that he was deterred from applying for the job by the employer's discriminatory practices, his is the not always easy burden of proving that he would have applied for the job had it not been for those practices. When this burden is met, the nonapplicant is in a position analogous to that of an applicant and is entitled to the presumption discussed in Part III-A, supra.

The Government contends that the evidence it presented in this case at the liability stage of the trial identified all nonapplicants as victims of unlawful discrimination "with a fair degree of specificity." . . . It further argues that since the class of nonapplicant discriminatees is limited to incumbent employees, it is likely that every class member was aware of the futility of seeking a line-driver job and was therefore deterred from filing both an initial and a follow-up application.

We cannot agree. While the scope and duration of the company's discriminatory policy can leave little doubt that the futility of seeking line-driver jobs was communicated to the company's minority employees, that in itself is insufficient. The known prospect of discriminatory rejection shows only that employees who wanted line-driving jobs may have been deterred from applying for them. It does not show which of the nonapplicants actually wanted such jobs, or which possessed the requisite qualifications.[53]

There are differences between city- and line-driving jobs, for example, but the desirability of the latter is not so self-evident as to warrant a conclusion that all employees would prefer to be line drivers if given a free choice. Indeed, a substantial number of white city drivers who were not subjected to the company's discriminatory practices were apparently content to retain their city jobs.

In order to fill this evidentiary gap, the Government argues that a nonapplicant's current willingness to transfer into a line-driver position confirms his past desire for the job. An employee's response to the court-ordered notice of his entitlement to relief demonstrates, according to this argument, that the employee would have sought a line-driver job when he first became qualified to fill one, but for his knowledge of the company's discriminatory policy.

This assumption falls short of satisfying the appropriate burden of proof. An employee who transfers into a line-driver unit is normally placed at the bottom of the seniority "board." He is thus in jeopardy of being laid off and must, at best, suffer

53. Inasmuch as the purpose of the nonapplicant's burden of proof will be to establish that his status is similar to that of the applicant, he must bear the burden of coming forward with the basic information about his qualifications that he would have presented in the application. As in *Franks*, and in accord with Part III-A, supra, the burden then will be on the employer to show that the nonapplicant was nonetheless not a victim of discrimination. For example, the employer might show that there were other, more qualified persons who would have been chosen for a particular vacancy, or that the nonapplicant's stated qualifications were insufficient.

through an initial period of bidding on only the least desirable runs. Nonapplicants who chose to accept the appellate court's post hoc invitation, however, would enter the line-driving unit with retroactive seniority dating from the time they were first qualified. A willingness to accept the job security and bidding power afforded by retroactive seniority says little about what choice an employee would have made had he previously been given the opportunity freely to choose a starting line-driver job. While it may be true that many of the nonapplicant employees desired and would have applied for line-driver jobs but for their knowledge of the company's policy of discrimination, the Government must carry its burden of proof, with respect to each specific individual, at the remedial hearings to be conducted by the District Court on remand.[58] . . .

NOTES

1. *Bifurcation of Class-Wide Litigation*. The Court envisions that systemic cases in which relief is sought for a group of victims should be tried in two stages: The first focuses on establishing liability and, if liability is established, the second stage determines the appropriate remedies. Systemic cases include both EEOC suits and class actions. One great advantages of a systemic case for plaintiffs is that, once liability is established, the defendant carries the burden of proving that the presumptive victims of that discrimination were, in fact, not discriminated against. May the plaintiff in an individual case utilize a systemic theory to establish liability, with the burden then shifting to the defendant to prove that she was not entitled to relief? *Williams v. Giant Food, Inc.*, 370 F.3d 423 (4th Cir. 2004) (no); *contra Cox v. Am. Cast Iron Pipe Co.*, 784 F.2d 1546, 1559 (11th Cir. 1986).

2. *Identifying the Beneficiaries of the Presumption*. Who are the presumptive victims? In *Teamsters*, those African Americans and Latinos who applied for line driver jobs were clearly victims. The Court also allows nonapplicants to try to establish that they too were victims of defendant's practice to not hire minority group members for the over-the-road jobs. But *Teamsters* held that a non-applicant's present desire to become a line driver was not sufficient to establish that he would have sought the position earlier. Is the Court too tough on minority employees of the defendant, who were city drivers or otherwise were qualified to drive trucks, but who nevertheless never actually applied for the better-paid white-only line driver positions?

3. *Rebutting the Presumption*. To escape liability to a presumptive victim, it seems likely that the employer will have to establish the "same decision anyway" defense. While the systemic cases we have examined precede the adoption of the same-decision defense in §706(g)(2)(B) for "motivating factor" cases, see p. 23, the current statute seems to reflect what the Court held in the earlier systemic cases. The preponderance of the evidence standard applies. *Berger v. Iron Workers, Local 201*, 170 F.3d 1111 (D.C. Cir. 1999).

---

58. While the most convincing proof would be some overt act such as a pre-Act application for a line-driver job, the District Court may find evidence of an employee's informal inquiry, expression of interest, or even unexpressed desire credible and convincing. The question is a factual one for determination by the trial judge.

4. *Disparate Impact.* Is the *Teamsters* burden-shifting procedure applicable in disparate impact cases? It would seem likely, with the twist that determining whether the presumptive victim is qualified can itself be problematic. Suppose the individual had been denied a position because she had failed a written examination with a disparate impact. Could the employer satisfy its burden by showing that she had later failed a written test that was job-related? *Cf. Cohen v. West Haven Bd.*, 638 F.2d 496 (2d Cir. 1980) (failure of applicants to pass the nondiscriminatory agility test in 1978 did not demonstrate that they were disqualified after failing a discriminatory test in 1977).

5. *Is Each Victim Entitled to Full Relief?* The courts think the employer's liability cannot exceed the amount of backpay that was lost, that is, there is "one backpay award." *E.g., United States v. City of Miami*, 195 F.3d 1292 (11th Cir. 1999); *Dougherty v. Barry*, 869 F.2d 605 (D.C. Cir. 1989). That means that a court must either decide which of several competitors for a single position would have gotten the job absent discrimination or it must split the award money among each presumptive victim on some basis. Suppose two employees were discriminatorily denied transfer to a vacant position that was filled by a third employee, but the court cannot determine who would have received the position in the absence of discrimination. *Doll v. Brown*, 75 F.3d 1200 (7th Cir. 1996), raised, but did not decide, that in such cases each victim should receive the percentage of a backpay award that corresponds to the chance he had to obtain the position (say, 33 percent). *See also Dukes v. Wal-Mart, Inc.*, 474 F.3d 1214, 1239 (9th Cir. 2007) ("individualized hearings may be inappropriate where the employer's conduct would reduce efforts to reconstruct individually what would have happened in the absence of discrimination to a 'quagmire of hypothetical judgments'"). *See generally* Paul M. Secunda, *A Public Interest Model for Applying Lost Chance Theory to Probabilistic Injuries in Employment Discrimination Cases*, 2005 WIS. L. REV. 747. The need for probabilistic determinations stems from the "one backpay award" principle. Is that principle consistent with *Albemarle Paper* and *Teamsters?*

6. *Equal Protection and Remedying Discrimination.* Courts ordering remedies against defendants in discrimination cases obviously are governmental actors for purpose of equal protection principles. Since the beneficiaries of hiring orders, awards of backpay and grants of retroactive seniority are usually women and minority men — actions based on race or sex — how do those awards of remedies comport with equal protection? The problem arises largely because of the impossibility of identifying each victim of discrimination. Were each actual victim to be identified and instated with appropriate seniority, the employer's workforce would then mirror what would have occurred had there never been any discrimination. Further, the Court has been clear that remedying discrimination against actual victims is a compelling state interest; thus, there is no equal protection violation. *Wygant v. Jackson Bd. of Educ.*, 476 U.S. 267, 274 (1986) ("the Court has insisted upon some showing of prior discrimination by the governmental unit involved before allowing limited use of racial classifications in order to remedy such discrimination"). *See also Parents Involved in Cmty. Schs. v. Seattle Sch. Dist. No.* 127 S. Ct. 2738 (2007) (all members of the Court appeared to accept the use of race to provide a remedy for the actual victims of the past intentional discrimination of the defendant).

In the real world, however, providing relief to identifiable victims will rarely, if ever, leave the employer's workforce reflective of the race or sex composition that it would have had absent discrimination. Courts have thought that the purposes of Title VII often require further action, and the question is, what further relief is permissible. In *Local 28, Sheet Metal Workers' Intl. Assn. v. EEOC*, 478 U.S. 421 (1986), the Court limited, but did not bar, the use of race by courts in remedying employment discrimination in such situations. Since the case involved a union that had long persisted in excluding African Americans from membership, such a remedy was appropriate only in light of (1) the pervasive and egregious discrimination of the defendant and (2) its history of discouraging nonwhites from applying for membership. Even then, the remedy could not seek to *maintain* racial balancing, although using race as a benchmark for progress was permissible; thus, the court order to admit nonwhite applicants ended when the goal of minority membership matched the goal that had been established. Finally, the remedy must not trammel the rights of innocent third parties. The highwater mark of race-based class remedies (often opposed as "quotas," even when they are remedies for proven intentional discrimination) is *United States v. Paradise*, 480 U.S. 149 (1987), which approved the use of race to order the one-for-one promotion of black and white state police officers to the position of sergeant, even though some of the African-American beneficiaries of that relief had themselves not been shown to be victims of discrimination. *Paradise* was based not only on the proven disparate treatment by the defendant but also its repeated flouting of earlier, less drastic orders.

3. Limits on Backpay

Each antidiscrimination statute permits the recovery of income lost due to the employer's discrimination. The backpay award includes all the compensation the successful plaintiff would have received in the absence of discrimination — lost wages, raises, overtime compensation, bonuses, vacation pay, and retirement benefits. *E.g., United States v. Burke*, 504 U.S. 229 (1992); *Smith v. World Ins. Co.*, 38 F.3d 1456 (8th Cir. 1994) (refusing to reduce backpay award by pension benefits). At least one court has rejecting "grossing up" the award to reflect adverse tax consequences from receiving the award as a lump sum rather than as normal compensation over several year. *Fogg v. Gonzales*, 492 F.3d 447, 456 (D.C. Cir. 2007). The award is reduced by amounts that were, and reasonably could have been, earned and is limited to a defined period of time. *See Arneson v. Callahan*, 128 F.3d 1243, 1248 (8th Cir. 1997) (refusing to deduct disability benefits from backpay award because they were from a collateral source and should not be considered interim earnings).

The statutory provision governing the recovery of backpay under Title VII is § 706(g)(1), which also applies to ADA Title I actions. 42 U.S.C. § 12117(a). The statute, however, provides little guidance on how the amount of a backpay award is to be calculated. The ADEA, ADA Title II, and § 1981 contain no similar provision, although the ADEA authorizes "such legal or equitable relief as will effectuate the purposes of this Act," 29 U.S.C. § 626.

Section 706(g)(1), however, has two provisions that limit backpay awards in Title VII and Title I actions. One provides that "[b]ack pay liability shall not accrue from a date more than two years prior to the filing of a charge with the Commission." The other states that "[i]nterim earnings or amounts earnable with reasonable diligence . . . shall operate to reduce the backpay otherwise allowable." As suggested by these provisions, the calculation of backpay frequently presents problems concerning the beginning or ending date of the backpay period and the discriminatee's duty to mitigate damages.

a.   The Backpay Period

The beginning date of the backpay period is normally the date the plaintiff first lost wages due to the discrimination in issue. *E.g., Welborn v. Reynolds Metals Co.,* 868 F.2d 389 (11th Cir. 1989). This may or may not be the same date the discriminatory act occurred for purposes of the EEOC filing period. In fact, the backpay period frequently begins *after* the date of the discriminatory act. For example, in *Del. State Coll. v. Ricks,* 449 U.S. 250 (1980), the Court found that the act of discrimination occurred when plaintiff was notified in the spring of one academic year that his job would be terminated at the end of the following academic year. Therefore, had plaintiff filed a timely charge, the beginning period for any backpay relief would have been at the end of the following academic year, more than a year after the act of discrimination.

Although § 1981 and Title II do not contain an express limitation on the beginning of the backpay period, the applicable statute of limitations operates to limit recovery. As explained in Chapter 7, see pp. 624-25, § 1981 suits may be governed by either the most analogous state statute of limitations or the federal catch-all statute, either of which would preclude recovery of wages lost prior to the statutory period. Title II is probably also subject to the most analogous state limitation period. *See Andrews v. Consolidated Rail Corp.,* 831 F.2d 678 (7th Cir. 1987). These limitations periods are measured from the date suit was filed in court, as opposed to the date when an EEOC charge was filed, as in Title VII and Title I actions.

A more difficult problem is presented, however, by claims under the ADEA. Prior to the 1991 Amendments, § 7(e), 29 U.S.C. § 626(e) contained a provision that incorporated the statute of limitations in § 6(a) of the Portal-to-Portal Act, 29 U.S.C. § 255(a) (2007). The repeal of this provision leaves no obvious limitation period on ADEA lost wages claims. There are five possible solutions. The courts are most likely to apply either the two-year provision in § 706(g)(1) as the best indication of congressional intent, *cf. DelCostello v. International Bhd. of Teamsters,* 462 U.S. 151 (1983), or the most analogous state statute of limitations, as in § 1981 actions. Two other possible solutions — enforcing no limitations period on backpay claims and limiting such claims to the EEOC filing period — seem too extreme to be adopted. The final possibility — the federal catch-all statute, 28 U.S.C. § 1658 — seems inapplicable by its terms but might be stretched to reach this situation.

The backpay period normally ends on the date of judgment. *E.g., Walsdorf v. Bd. of Comm'rs.,* 857 F.2d 1047 (5th Cir. 1988). But the backpay period can end before this date. If, for example, the plaintiff has died or would have been permanently laid off prior to the date of judgment, the backpay period ends on the date his employment would have ceased. *Berger v. Iron Workers, Local 201,* 170 F.3d 1111 (D.C. Cir. 1999). More controversially, the backpay period may also end on the date the discriminatee either resigned his or her position with the defendant or rejected the defendant's offer of employment.

FORD MOTOR CO. v. EEOC
458 U.S. 219 (1982)

Justice O'CONNOR delivered the opinion of the Court.

This case presents the question whether an employer charged with discrimination in hiring can toll the continuing accrual of backpay liability under § 706(g) of Title VII simply by unconditionally offering the claimant the job previously denied, or whether the employer also must offer seniority retroactive to the date of the alleged discrimination. . . .

I

In June and July 1971, Judy Gaddis, Rebecca Starr, and Zettie Smith applied at a Ford Motor Company (Ford) parts warehouse located in Charlotte, North Carolina, for jobs as "picker-packers." . . . Gaddis and Starr recently had been laid off from equivalent jobs at a nearby General Motors (GM) warehouse, and Smith had comparable prior experience. . . . Ford, however, [discriminatorily] filled the three vacant positions with men. . . .

In January 1973, [GM] recalled Gaddis and Starr to their former positions at its warehouse. The following July, while they were still working at GM, a single vacancy opened up at Ford. Ford offered the job to Gaddis, without seniority retroactive to her 1971 application. Ford's offer, however, did not require Gaddis to abandon or compromise her Title VII claim against Ford. Gaddis did not accept the job, in part because she did not want to be the only woman working at the warehouse, and in part because she did not want to lose the seniority she had earned at [GM]. Ford then made the same unconditional offer to Starr, who declined for the same reasons. . . . [In 1974, Gaddis and Starr were again laid off by GM.]

[The Court of Appeals concluded that Ford's 1973 offer was "incomplete and unacceptable" without retroactive seniority and that Gaddis and Starr were entitled to backpay from 1971 through the 1977 trial.]

III

[T]he legal rules fashioned to implement Title VII should be designed, consistent with other Title VII policies, to encourage Title VII defendants promptly to make curative, unconditional job offers to Title VII claimants, thereby bringing defendants into "voluntary compliance" and ending discrimination far more quickly than could litigation proceeding at its often ponderous pace. Delays in litigation unfortunately are now commonplace, forcing the victims of discrimination to suffer years of underemployment or unemployment before they can obtain a court order awarding them the jobs unlawfully denied them. . . .

The rule tolling the further accrual of backpay liability if the defendant offers the claimant the job originally sought well serves the objective of ending discrimination through voluntary compliance, for it gives an employer a strong incentive to hire the Title VII claimant. While the claimant may be no more attractive than the other job applicants, a job offer to the claimant will free the employer of the threat of liability for further backpay damages. Since paying backpay damages is like paying an extra worker who never came to work, Ford's proposed rule gives the Title VII claimant a decided edge over other competitors for the job he seeks.

The rule adopted by the court below, on the other hand, fails to provide the same incentive, because it makes hiring the Title VII claimant more costly than hiring one of the other applicants for the same job. To give the claimant retroactive seniority before an adjudication of liability, the employer must be willing to pay the additional costs of the fringe benefits that come with the seniority that newly hired workers usually do not receive. More important, the employer must also be prepared to cope with the deterioration in morale, labor unrest, and reduced productivity that may be engendered by inserting the claimant into the seniority ladder over the heads of the incumbents who have earned their places through their work on the job. In many cases, moreover, disruption of the existing seniority system will violate a collective bargaining agreement, with all that such a violation entails for the employer's labor relations. . . .

IV

Title VII's primary goal, of course, is to end discrimination; the victims of job discrimination want jobs, not lawsuits. But when unlawful discrimination does occur, Title VII's secondary, fallback purpose is to compensate the victims for their injuries. To this end, §706(g) aims "'to make the victims of unlawful discrimination whole'" by restoring them, "'so far as possible . . . to a position where they would have been were it not for the unlawful discrimination.'" We now turn to consider whether the rule urged by Ford not only better serves the goal of ending discrimination, but also properly compensates injured Title VII claimants.

A

If Gaddis and Starr had rejected an unconditional offer from Ford before they were recalled to their jobs at GM, tolling Ford's backpay liability from the time of Ford's offer plainly would be consistent with providing Gaddis and Starr full compensation for their injuries. An unemployed or underemployed claimant, like all other Title VII claimants, is subject to the statutory duty to minimize damages set out in §706(g). This duty, rooted in an ancient principle of law, requires the claimant to use reasonable diligence in finding other suitable employment. Although the un- or underemployed claimant need not go into another line of work, accept a demotion, or take a demeaning position, he forfeits his right to backpay if he refuses a job substantially equivalent to the one he was denied. Consequently, an employer charged with unlawful discrimination often can toll the accrual of backpay liability by unconditionally offering the claimant the job he sought, and thereby providing him with an opportunity to minimize damages.[18]

An employer's unconditional offer of the job originally sought to an un- or underemployed claimant, moreover, need not be supplemented by an offer of retroactive seniority to be effective, lest a defendant's offer be irrationally disfavored relative to other employers' offers of substantially similar jobs. The claimant, after all, plainly would be required to minimize his damages by accepting another employer's offer even though it failed to grant the benefits of seniority not yet earned.[19] Of course, if the claimant fulfills the requirement that he minimize damages by accepting the defendant's unconditional offer, he remains entitled to full compensation if he wins his case. A court may grant him backpay accrued prior to the effective date of the offer, retroactive seniority, and compensation for any losses suffered as a result of his lesser seniority before the court's judgment.

---

18. The claimant's obligation to minimize damages in order to retain his right to compensation does not require him to settle his claim against the employer, in whole or in part. Thus, an applicant or discharged employee is not required to accept a job offered by the employer on the condition that his claims against the employer be compromised.

19. For the same reasons, a defendant's job offer is effective to force minimization of damages by an un- or underemployed claimant even without a supplemental offer of backpay. . . .

In short, the un- or underemployed claimant's statutory obligation to minimize damages requires him to accept an unconditional offer of the job originally sought, even without retroactive seniority. Acceptance of the offer preserves, rather than jeopardizes, the claimant's right to be made whole; in the case of an un- or under-employed claimant, Ford's suggested rule merely embodies the existing require-ment of §706(g) that the claimant minimize damages, without affecting his right to compensation. . . .

C

Therefore, we conclude that, when a claimant rejects the offer of the job he originally sought, as supplemented by a right to full court-ordered compensation, his choice can be taken as establishing that he considers the ongoing injury he has suffered at the hands of the defendant to have been ended by the availability of better opportunities elsewhere. For this reason, we find that, absent special circum-stances,[27] the simple rule that the ongoing accrual of backpay liability is tolled when a Title VII claimant rejects the job he originally sought comports with Title VII's policy of making discrimination victims whole. . . .

Justice BLACKMUN, with whom Justice BRENNAN and Justice MARSHALL join, dissenting. . . .
. . . The Court's approach authorizes employers to . . . terminate their backpay liability unilaterally by extending to their discrimination victims offers they cannot reasonably accept. Once an employer has refused to hire a job applicant, and that applicant has mitigated damages by obtaining and accumulating seniority in another job, the employer may offer the applicant the same job that she was denied un-lawfully several years earlier. In this very case, for example, Ford offered Gaddis and Starr jobs only after they had obtained employment elsewhere and only because they had filed charges with the EEOC. If, as here, the applicant declines the offer to preserve existing job security, the employer has successfully cut off all future backpay liability to the applicant. . . .
The Court's rule also violates Title VII's second objective — making victims of discrimination whole. . . . [I]f Gaddis and Starr had accepted those offers, they would not have been made whole. . . .

NOTES

1. *Why Was the Backpay Period Terminated?* Were Gaddis's and Starr's backpay periods terminated on the dates they rejected Ford's offers because they failed to mitigate damages or because such termination furthered the purposes of Title VII? Wouldn't a violation of the duty to mitigate simply have required a *reduction* of their backpay awards by the amounts they earned at GM and any additional amounts they could have earned with reasonable diligence? If their pay at GM was equal to what they would have earned at Ford but for the alleged discrimination, their claim for

---

27. If, for example, the claimant has been forced to move a great distance to find a replacement job, a rejection of the employer's offer might reflect the costs of relocation more than a judgment that the replacement job was superior, all things considered, to the defendant's job. In exceptional circum-stances, the trial court, in the exercise of its sound discretion, could give weight to such factors when deciding whether backpay damages accrued after the rejection of an employer's offer should be awarded to the claimant. . . .

backpay would have been suspended during the period they worked for GM. In short, *Ford Motor* seems to be mostly about what happens if GM also lays plaintiffs off again, and the decision leaves plaintiffs with neither jobs nor a backpay award. Why?

2. *Probing* Ford *More Deeply.* To understand this case, it is essential to appreciate the cyclical fluctuations in employment in the automobile industry, at least at the time. Newer workers often went through a cycle of layoffs and recalls until they obtained sufficient seniority to have some meaningful job security. Accepting the offer Ford made to plaintiffs would have actually put them in a worse position than they had at GM in the sense that they would have no seniority at Ford while they had at least some at GM. Nevertheless, rejecting Ford's offer cuts off the plaintiffs' backpay claim. Notice, however, the requirements for such a cut-off. First, Ford did not require them to release their claims; second, Ford offered them work at their prior pay. Presumably, had Ford offered something less, the question of whether plaintiffs would have been reasonable in staying at GM would have been more complicated and might turn on whether the GM or Ford compensation was higher. Had plaintiffs accepted the offer, they could have continued to litigate their claims, seeking accrued seniority and perhaps wage increases they would have received if they had not been laid off.

3. *Does* Ford Motor *Undermine* Albemarle Paper? If a plaintiff declines a defendant's offer, her backpay claim terminates as of the date of that offer. This complete cutoff means that these plaintiffs are unlikely to receive "make whole" relief. How can *Ford Motor* be reconciled with the "make whole" purpose articulated in *Albemarle Paper?* Is the Court simply diminishing the value of Title VII claims in order to make them less attractive and less feasible?

4. *Making an Offer Plaintiffs Will Refuse.* Once Ford knew the plaintiffs had accepted jobs at GM, it decided to offer to rehire plaintiffs. Do you think this was a strategic ploy designed to achieve exactly what happened — cutting off the plaintiff's right to backpay? As Justice O'Connor's opinion suggests, this is essentially costless to the employer, whether or not accepted. The majority wants to encourage such conduct by employers. Why? Mitigation kicked in when the plaintiffs started working at equivalent jobs at GM, so plaintiffs lost backpay once they started working for GM (except for any difference in pay between the two jobs)? Doesn't the duty to mitigate serve any appropriate policy interest here?

5. *Extending* Ford. Does *Ford* imply that an acceptance of a higher-paying job with another employer completely terminates the accrual of backpay from the old employer? Some courts think so. *E.g., Stephens v. C.I.T. Group, Inc.,* 955 F.2d 1023 (5th Cir. 1992). Is this fair to a discriminatee who loses that new job prior to trial, considering that he was required to seek and accept such other employment? One decision applied this rule at the urging of the plaintiff: if the backpay period was so terminated, her higher earnings would not retroactively offset the defendant's backpay liability. *Matthews v. A-1, Inc.,* 748 F.2d 975 (5th Cir. 1984). Was this fair to the defendant?

6. *Special Circumstances Exception.* The Court recognized that the rule terminating backpay does not apply when there are "special circumstances," but provided little further guidance. The Eighth Circuit interprets this as meaning only that the rejection must have been reasonable. *Smith v. World Ins. Co.,* 38 F.3d 1456 (8th Cir. 1994) (rejection reasonable where plaintiff thought that the higher pay offered was not worth the risk of being subjected to discrimination since he had no guarantees of how long he would be kept and his poor performance record would not be expunged). Was Gaddis reasonable in not accepting Ford's offer because "she did not

want to be the only woman working in the warehouse"? Apparently, the exception is most commonly invoked when there is "excessive hostility" between the parties. *See Lewis v. Fed. Prison Indus.*, 953 F.2d 1277 (11th Cir. 1992); *Thorne v. City of El Segundo*, 802 F.2d 1131 (9th Cir. 1986).

McKENNON v. NASHVILLE BANNER PUBLISHING CO.
513 U.S. 352 (1995)

Justice KENNEDY delivered the opinion of the Court.

The question before us is whether an employee discharged in violation of the [ADEA] is barred from all relief when, after her discharge, the employer discovers evidence of wrongdoing that, in any event, would have led to the employee's termination on lawful and legitimate grounds. . . .

I

For some 30 years, petitioner Christine McKennon worked for respondent Nashville Banner Publishing Company. She was discharged, the Banner claimed, as part of a work force reduction plan necessitated by cost considerations. McKennon, who was 62 years old when she lost her job, thought another reason explained her dismissal: her age. She filed suit [seeking] a variety of legal and equitable remedies available under the ADEA, including backpay.

In preparation of the case, the Banner took McKennon's deposition. She testified that, during her final year of employment, she had copied several confidential documents bearing upon the company's financial condition. . . . McKennon took the copies home and showed them to her husband. Her motivation, she averred, was an apprehension she was about to be fired because of her age. When she became concerned about her job, she removed and copied the documents for "insurance" and "protection." A few days after these deposition disclosures, the Banner sent McKennon a letter declaring that removal and copying of the records was in violation of her job responsibilities and advising her (again) that she was terminated. . . .

II

We shall assume [for purposes of summary judgment] . . . that the misconduct revealed by the deposition was so grave that McKennon's immediate discharge would have followed its disclosure in any event. The District Court and the Court of Appeals found no basis for contesting that proposition, and for purposes of our review we need not question it here. We do question the legal conclusion reached by those courts that after-acquired evidence of wrongdoing which would have resulted in discharge bars employees from any relief under the ADEA. That ruling is incorrect. . . .

The ADEA and Title VII share common substantive features and also a common purpose: "the elimination of discrimination in the workplace." Congress designed the remedial measures in these statutes to serve as a "spur or catalyst" to cause employers "to self-examine and to self-evaluate their employment practices and to endeavor to eliminate, so far as possible, the last vestiges" of discrimination. Deterrence is one object of these statutes. Compensation for injuries caused by the prohibited discrimination is another. . . . The private litigant who seeks redress for his or her injuries vindicates both the deterrence and the compensation objectives of the ADEA. It would not accord with this scheme if after-acquired evidence of wrongdoing that would have resulted in termination operates, in every instance, to bar all relief for an earlier violation of the Act.

The objectives of the ADEA are furthered when even a single employee establishes that an employer has discriminated against him or her. The disclosure through litigation of incidents or practices which violate national policies respecting non-discrimination in the work force is itself important, for the occurrence of violations may disclose patterns of noncompliance resulting from a misappreciation of the Act's operation or entrenched resistance to its commands, either of which can be of industry-wide significance. The efficacy of its enforcement mechanisms becomes one measure of the success of the Act. . . .

[T]he case comes to us on the express assumption that an unlawful motive was the sole basis for the firing. McKennon's misconduct was not discovered until after she had been fired. The employer could not have been motivated by knowledge it did not have and it cannot now claim that the employee was fired for the nondiscriminatory reason. Mixed motive cases are inapposite here, except to the important extent they underscore the necessity of determining the employer's motives in ordering the discharge, an essential element in determining whether the employer violated the federal antidiscrimination law. As we have observed, "proving that the same decision would have been justified . . . is not the same as proving that the same decision would have been made."

Our inquiry is not at an end, however, for even though [for purposes of summary judgment we assume] the employer has violated the Act, we must consider how the after-acquired evidence of the employee's wrongdoing bears on the specific remedy to be ordered. [The Court rejected the equitable "unclean hands" doctrine as inapplicable "where Congress authorizes broad equitable relief to serve important national policies."] That does not mean, however, the employee's own misconduct is irrelevant to all the remedies otherwise available under the statute. . . . In giving effect to the ADEA, we must recognize the duality between the legitimate interests of the employer and the important claims of the employee who invokes the national employment policy mandated by the Act. The employee's wrongdoing must be taken into account, we conclude, lest the employer's legitimate concerns be ignored. The ADEA, like Title VII, is not a general regulation of the workplace but a law which prohibits discrimination. The statute does not constrain employers from exercising significant other prerogatives and discretion in the course of the hiring, promoting, and discharging of their employees. In determining appropriate remedial action, the employee's wrongdoing becomes relevant not to punish the employee, or out of concern "for the relative moral worth of the parties," but to take due account of the lawful prerogatives of the employer in the usual course of its business and the corresponding equities that it has arising from the employee's wrongdoing.

The proper boundaries of remedial relief in the general class of cases where, after termination, it is discovered that the employee has engaged in wrongdoing . . . will vary from case to case. We do conclude that here, and as a general rule in cases of this type, neither reinstatement nor front pay is an appropriate remedy. It would be both inequitable and pointless to order the reinstatement of someone the employer would have terminated, and will terminate, in any event and upon lawful grounds.

The proper measure of backpay presents a more difficult problem. Resolution of this question must give proper recognition to the fact that an ADEA violation has occurred which must be deterred and compensated without undue infringement upon the employer's rights and prerogatives. The object of compensation is to restore the employee to the position he or she would have been in absent the discrimination, but that principle is difficult to apply with precision where there is after-acquired evidence of wrongdoing that would have led to termination on legitimate grounds had the employer known about it. Once an employer learns about employee wrongdoing that would lead to a legitimate discharge, we cannot require the employer to ignore the information, even if it is acquired during the course of discovery in a suit against the employer and even if the information might have gone undiscovered absent the suit. The beginning point in the trial court's formulation of a remedy should be calculation of backpay from the date of the unlawful discharge to the date the new information was discovered. In determining the appropriate order for relief, the court can consider taking into further account extraordinary equitable circumstances that affect the legitimate interests of either party. An absolute rule barring any recovery of backpay, however, would undermine the ADEA's objective of forcing employers to consider and examine their motivations, and of penalizing them for employment decisions that spring from age discrimination.

Where an employer seeks to rely upon after-acquired evidence of wrongdoing, it must first establish that the wrongdoing was of such severity that the employee in fact would have been terminated on those grounds alone if the employer had known of it at the time of the discharge. The concern that employers might as a routine matter undertake extensive discovery into an employee's background or performance on the job to resist claims under the Act is not an insubstantial one, but we think the authority of the courts to award attorney's fees, mandated under the statute, and in appropriate cases to invoke the provisions of Rule 11 of the Federal Rules of Civil Procedure will deter most abuses. . . .

NOTES

1. *ADEA Backpay Is Legal, Not Equitable Relief.* In a private ADEA action like *McKennon*, the unpaid wages (i.e., backpay) award is a legal remedy, *Lorillard v. Pons*, 434 U.S. 575 (1978), so the plaintiff has a right to trial by jury on her backpay claim. Yet *McKennon* seems to treat the award as equitable, suggesting that "[i]n determining the appropriate order for relief, the *court* can consider taking into further account equitable circumstances." (Emphasis added.) If in fact this is a question for the jury, how should a jury in an ADEA after-acquired evidence case after *McKennon*, be instructed on the availability and amount of backpay?

2. *After-Acquired Evidence Rule.* Finding evidence that would have resulted in an employee's discharge at some earlier date cuts off backpay as of the date of discovery. *McKennon* is also applicable to backpay awards in Title VII actions. *Wallace v. Dunn Constr. Co.*, 62 F.3d 374 (11th Cir. 1995); *Wehr v. Ryan's Family Steak Houses, Inc.*, 49 F.3d 1150 (6th Cir. 1995).

Suppose the employer, during the investigation of her claim of age discrimination, had discovered that McKennon obtained her job in the first instance by a fraudulent resume or job application. Should the "would have been terminated" standard or a "would not have been hired" standard be used to calculate backpay? *Shatluck v. Kinetic Concepts*, 49 F.3d 1106 (5th Cir. 1995) (first standard). *See also Harris v. Chand*, 506 F.3d 1135 (8th Cir. 2007) (no error to admit evidence of resume fraud when employer proved policy and practice of terminating hires who engaged in such fraud).

McKennon has also been applied to limit the front pay award for loss of income after the date of judgment of a successful plaintiff on the ground that her misconduct made her unsuitable for re-employment in her former field. *Sellers v. Mineta*, 358 F.3d 1058 (8th Cir. 2004). Can compensatory and punitive damages nevertheless be recovered in an after-acquired evidence case for the defendant's discrimination?

3. *After-Acquired Evidence vs. Mixed-Motive Case.* The Court carefully distinguished between the factual situation before it and a mixed-motives case. Change the facts a bit. If McKennon had been discharged because of both her sex and her misconduct, but she would have been discharged even if her sex had not been considered, would she have been eligible for backpay under Title VII? Would there be eligibility at all under the ADEA if she were discharged both for her age and her misconduct? The answer seems almost certainly no, whether or not the court applies the *Desert Palace* rule, based on Title VII's §703(m) and §706(g)(2)(B), in ADEA cases. See *Rachid v. Jack in the Box*, reproduced at p. 95.

4. *Chilling Effects?* Regardless of the abstract merits of the after-acquired evidence rule, it arguably creates undesirable litigation incentives for employers to turn every discrimination case into an inquiry into the employee's character and past acts. *See* Melissa Hart, *Retaliatory Litigation Tactics: The Chilling Effect of After-Acquired Evidence* http://papers.ssrn.com/sol3/papers.cfm?abstract_id=1013587 (arguing that it should be illegal retaliation to misuse the doctrine by asserting it frivolously).

b.   The Duty to Mitigate Damages

Section 706(g)(1), 42 U.S.C. §2000e-5(g)(1) (2007), which is applicable in Title VII and Title I actions, requires the backpay award to be reduced by amounts that were earned and could have been earned with reasonable diligence. The same principle is applied in ADEA and §1981 actions, even without explicit statutory authorization. *E.g., Hansard v. Pepsi-Cola Metro. Bottling Co.*, 865 F.2d 1461 (5th Cir. 1989) (ADEA); *Murphy v. City of Flagler Beach*, 846 F.2d 1306 (11th Cir. 1988) (§1981). Undoubtedly, the principle would also be applied in Title II actions. *See generally* Howard C. Eglit, *Damages Mitigation Doctrine in the Statutory Anti-Discrimination Context: Mitigating Its Negative Impact*, 69 U. Cinc. L. Rev. 71 (2000).

The courts are not entirely consistent in allocating the evidentiary burdens on these issues. Most hold that the plaintiff must establish "damages by measuring the difference between her actual earnings and those which she would have earned absent the discrimination." *E.g., Kamberos v. GTE Automatic Elec., Inc.*, 603 F.2d 598, 602 (7th Cir. 1979). For example, a discriminatee who was denied employment or was discharged must show the amount — or lack — of any interim earnings and the amount she would have earned from the defendant. The defendant, however, must show the amount the plaintiff could have earned with reasonable diligence, and this requires proof of jobs that were substantially equivalent that plaintiff could have obtained with reasonable diligence. *E.g., Caufield v. Ctr. Area Sch. Dist.*, 133 Fed. Appx. 4, 11 (3d Cir. 2005) (defendant had burden of demonstrating the existence of substantially equivalent employment at other school districts); *Vaughn v. Sabine County*, 104 Fed. Appx. 980, 984 (5th Cir. 2004) ("although a Title VII claimant has a duty to mitigate her damages, she has no obligation to accept employment that is not substantially equivalent to her prior employment"). One court carried this principle as far as to find no abuse of discretion for holding that a plaintiff, who was fired from his subsequent job for misconduct, was no longer mitigating his damages, although this did not mean that his award of backpay was permanently cut off. *Johnson v. Spencer Press of Me., Inc.*, 364 F.3d 368 (1st Cir 2004).

Several recent decisions, however, shift this traditional allocation by allowing an employer to carry its burden merely by showing that the plaintiff made no effort to find comparable employment, thus presuming that a reasonably diligent plaintiff would have obtained equivalent employment. In *Le v. Univ. of Pa.*, 321 F.3d 403 (3d Cir. 2003), the court upheld a finding that plaintiff failed to mitigate, even though the defendant did not show equivalent jobs were available had plaintiff looked for them. *See also Broadnax v. City of New Haven*, 415 F.3d 265, 270 (2d Cir. 2005) ("an employer, when arguing that a Title VII plaintiff failed to mitigate damages but seeking to avoid the requirement of showing that comparable employment is available, bears the burden on the issue of whether the plaintiff made no reasonable efforts to seek alternative employment"). Can it be true that a qualified person can always find a suitable job? Or is it likely to be so only in a booming economy? And even if the person is objectively qualified, what about the prospect that the market will view him as "damaged goods," precisely because he was fired? *See generally* J. Hoult Verkerke, *Legal Regulation of Employment Reference Practices*, 65 U. CHI. L. REV. 115, 118 (1998) ("scarring" occurs when employers rely on labor market signals to refuse to hire productive workers). See Note 4, p. 686, dealing with lost earning capacity.

The intended effect of these decisions is to put pressure on plaintiff to look for, and perhaps accept, alternative employment. But even that course of action is not risk free. In *West v. Nabors Drilling USA, Inc.*, 330 F.3d 379 (5th Cir. 2003), the court held that plaintiff, who had taken a different type of job at lower pay with less responsibility in order to support his family, had failed to mitigate. Thus, his backpay was cut off from the date he took the new job. This decision is inconsistent with the make whole objective of antidiscrimination law. It punishes the plaintiff who is forced to seek an inferior job because of economic necessity, thereby relieving defendant of its obligation to provide a remedy to a victim of its discrimination.

4. Front Pay

Backpay ends on the date of the court's judgment. Sometimes, however, the plaintiff has yet to receive full make whole relief. For example, the court may have ordered defendant to hire or to reinstate plaintiff, but, at the time of the judgment, no job for which plaintiff is qualified has an opening. Therefore, front pay continues backpay until that opening occurs. While it is generally stated that the preferred remedy is to order the instatement or reinstatement of the plaintiff, in practice neither the plaintiff nor the defendant may want that relief for a variety of reasons, including the mutual hostility that often develops during litigation. Therefore, the discriminatee may be awarded front pay in the form of "damages in lieu of reinstatement" — a lump sum award. In calculating that amount, it is necessary to determine the (1) appropriate time front pay should extend into the future and (2) the amount of pay for, say, each year, (3) taking into account projected future earnings but (4) reduced by projected mitigation; and (5), where a lump sum is awarded, reducing the award by appropriate present value calculations. The amount of future pay must include the value of fringe benefits the plaintiff is not receiving but would have received if she were working for the defendant.

CASSINO v. REICHHOLD CHEMICALS, INC.
817 F.2d 1338 (9th Cir. 1987)

SCHROEDER, Circuit Judge.

... Cassino filed this suit in federal court alleging that his termination was based on age in violation of the ADEA.... A jury verdict in Cassino's favor awarded him $81,000 in backpay [and] $150,000 in front pay....

The ADEA provides that "[i]n any action brought to enforce this chapter the court shall have jurisdiction to grant such legal or equitable relief as may be appropriate ... including without limitation judgments compelling employment, reinstatement or promotion. ... " 29 U.S.C. §626(b). In discriminatory discharge cases, the decision whether to order reinstatement is within the discretion of the trial court. Although reinstatement is the preferred remedy in these cases, it may not be feasible where the relationship is hostile or no position is available due to a reduction in force. Under such circumstances, an award of future damages or "front pay" in lieu of reinstatement furthers the remedial goals of the ADEA by returning the aggrieved party to the economic situation he would have enjoyed but for the defendant's illegal conduct. Thus, front pay is an award of future lost earnings to make a victim of discrimination whole.

The jury in this case was instructed on the measure of damages for front pay. The district court explained that "Front pay is compensation for the loss of future salary and benefits." Aside from this cursory definition, however, the jury was merely told that "If you find age discrimination ... , you may award front pay."

It is clear that front pay awards, like backpay awards, must be reduced by the amount plaintiff could earn using reasonable mitigation efforts. ... [T]he plaintiff's duty to mitigate must serve as a control on front pay damage awards. Thus, front pay is intended to be temporary in nature. An award of front pay "does not contemplate that a plaintiff will sit idly by and be compensated for doing nothing." The jury in this case, in effect, without instruction on mitigation, found that Cassino was entitled to front pay from the time of trial until the time he would have retired. Because of this defect, the front pay award ... is reversed.

We do not find persuasive Reichhold's remaining challenges to the front pay award. First, Reichhold contends that the district court erred in failing to instruct the jury that a finding of hostility was a prerequisite to a front pay award. The court's failure to instruct on hostility was not error because the decision whether to order the equitable remedy of reinstatement or, in the alternative, to award front pay, is a decision for the trial court. If the court concludes that reinstatement is not feasible, the jury then decides the amount of the front pay award. ...

Second, Reichhold argues that Cassino failed to present competent evidence establishing future damages. Specifically, Reichhold maintains that Cassino's lay opinion testimony about future earnings and benefits, and the application of inflation and discount rates to those figures, was inadmissible because Cassino was unqualified to make such calculations.

Although the Ninth Circuit has not addressed the issue of what constitutes adequate inflation and discount rate evidence, several circuits have adopted the view that as long as the jury is properly instructed, expert testimony is not an absolute prerequisite to submitting to the jury the issue of future lost earnings and their reduction to present value. Courts that do not require expert testimony reason that the effect of inflation and interest rates on the value of money is within the common knowledge of jurors and that jurors are sufficiently intelligent to reduce an award to present value if properly instructed. Here, Reichhold does not dispute the adequacy of the jury instruction on present value. . . .

Moreover, expert testimony is not required to prove what the plaintiff would receive in future earnings and raises. Here, Cassino testified about his projected earnings based primarily on his own periodic pay increases during more than twenty years of employment at Reichhold. Therefore, Cassino's evidence was sufficient to establish the loss of future earnings and benefits. . . .

NOTES

1. *Front Pay as Alternative to Reinstatement.* Although a front pay award is discretionary, a strong presumption favors the award when reinstatement is inappropriate but plaintiff is able to work. *E.g., Farber v. Massillon Bd. of Educ.*, 917 F.2d 1391 (6th Cir. 1990); *King v. Staley*, 849 F.2d 1143 (8th Cir. 1988). The converse of this is that front pay should not be awarded when reinstatement is possible. *Kucia v. Southeast Ark. Cmty. Action Corp.* 284 F.3d 944, 949 (8th Cir. 2002) ("front pay is an exceptional award" and that "[r]einstatement should be the norm" unless it proves to be impractical or impossible).

2. *"Liquidated Damages" and Front Pay.* The ADEA (but not the other statutes) permits successful plaintiffs to recover "liquidated damages" over and above back-pay. See p. 700. Where such damages are awarded, front pay should not be included in the award. *Farley v. Nationwide Mut. Ins. Co.*, 197 F.3d 1322, 1340 (11th Cir. 1999) ("All eight federal circuits that have interpreted the 'amounts owing' provision in the context of front pay recovery under ADEA have concluded that front pay should not be included in liquidated damages awards").

3. *Determining the Length of the Front Pay Period.* What did the *Cassino* court mean when it stated that "front pay is intended to be temporary in nature"? One possibility is that the front pay period should end at the time when a reasonable discriminatee would be able to obtain comparable employment? *See Dominic v. Consolidated Edison Co.*, 822 F.2d 1249, 1258 (2d Cir. 1987) (front pay award not necessarily a lifetime award and calculation must reflect "plaintiff's ability to mitigate damages in the future").

What if a successful plaintiff could not be expected to ever obtain comparable employment? In *Padilla v. Metro-North Commuter R.R.*, 92 F.3d 117 (2d Cir. 1996), an employee demoted in violation of the ADEA was denied reinstatement but was awarded continuing front pay for his reduced future salary (about $20,000 per year) until he either left the company or retired (in about 25 years). The appellate court upheld the award, noting that reinstatement was infeasible due to animosity and the employee had no reasonable prospect of obtaining comparable employment. Nevertheless, courts are reluctant to find that a victim of discrimination will remain unemployable. *Peyton v. DiMario*, 287 F.3d 1121, 1030 (D.C. Cir. 2002) (disapproving future lost earnings award as an abuse of discretion when plaintiff was only 34 years old and not incapacitated).

Did the court in *Cassino* determine that plaintiff would be able to find comparable work at some point before retirement and is that why it reversed the award of front pay?

The front pay period will end no later than the projected retirement date for the employer, but in a world without mandatory retirement, that date is itself problematic. It may depend on when most workers in that position retire. Plaintiff's life expectancy is also relevant, and his health may affect that decision radically. In *Price v. Marshall Erdman & Assocs., Inc.*, 966 F.2d 320 (7th Cir. 1992), the court said that each year's projected earnings had the plaintiff been employed by the defendant should be discounted by the probability that he would not have lived that long.

4. *Determining the Amount of Front Pay.* The *Cassino* court indicated some of the problems with calculating future lost earnings, problems that become graver as the front pay period extends further into the future. The complexities of such calculations more properly belong in a Remedies course, but the core issues are straightforward. First, the court must calculate what raises and bonuses (and increases in benefits) the plaintiff would have received had he been working; inflation obviously plays a role, but the plaintiff might also have received raises related to her individual performance. Past raises might be a good predictor for the future or might not. *Cassino*'s testimony about her compensation history was obviously very important for the court. Second, if, as usual, the court awards a lump sum (rather than some per year amount that can be adjusted), the amount has to be reduced to present value — that's the "discount rate" the court refers to. The calculations can be complex but the concept is simple: plaintiff should be awarded a sufficient amount of money now that will, if prudently invested, produce the amount she is projected to have been paid in the future. More concretely, if the plaintiff is projected to earn $100,000 in Year 10, the amount awarded now must be reduced to reflect the interest she could earn on the sum for the next 9 years. Only then will the plaintiff have the "correct" amount, rather than a windfall, when Year 10 arrives.

5. *Experts.* The plaintiff in *Cassino* got away with proving front pay by his "lay" testimony. This is not advisable! An expert on such aspects of the award as working life expectancy is desirable if not essential. Such an expert can also project inflation and provide calculations as to present value as well as opine on the appropriate discount rate.

Some courts have allowed the front pay calculation to be simplified by taking neither the discount rate nor the increasing cost of living into account. *See Jackson v. City of Cookeville*, 31 F.3d 1354 (6th Cir. 1994). *But see Ramirez v. New York City Off-Track Betting Corp.*, 112 F.3d 38 (2d Cir. 1997). It is hard to determine whether this "wash" approach tends to benefit one side or the other in an era in which, generally speaking, wages are barely keeping pace with inflation.

6. *Who Decides Entitlement to Front Pay?* The *Cassino* jury was instructed that it "may" award front pay. Based on the court's discussion of allocation of functions between judge and jury, shouldn't the jury have been instructed that the judge had determined that the plaintiff was entitled to front pay, but that the jury had to determine the appropriate amount? What if the jury concludes that the plaintiff's future earnings capacity was not impaired? The ADEA unpaid wages award is a form of legal relief that gives rise to the constitutional right to a jury trial, at least where the federal government is not the defendant. The Ninth Circuit is among the few circuits that hold there is also the right to a jury trial on the amount of an ADEA front pay award. *McLean v. Runyon*, 222 F.3d 1150 (9th Cir. 2000). Most courts hold that this is for the judge to decide. *E.g., Farley v. Nationwide Mut. Ins. Co.*, 197 F.3d 1322 (11th Cir. 1999); *Nelson v. Boatmen's Bancshares*, 26 F.3d 796 (8th Cir, 1994). Certainly, this issue is for the judge under other antidiscrimination statutes.

7. *Risk of Trammeling Rights of Incumbents.* The potential of a substantial front pay award creates an incentive for the defendant to create a job opening for the plaintiff by discharging an incumbent worker. This may be offset by the employer's desire not to take back the plaintiff for morale and other reasons. While the law

rarely requires an employer to "bump" an incumbent to make room for a prevailing plaintiff, there are few legal obstacles to doing so.

C.   LEGAL REMEDIES TO THE VICTIMS OF DISCRIMINATION

Prior to November 1991, compensatory and punitive damages were not available under Title VII and Title I. However, the Civil Rights Act of 1991 enacted 42 U.S.C. § 1981a (2007), which authorizes such damages in certain Title VII and Title I actions and grants the right to a jury trial when either compensatory or punitive damages are sought. The statutory scheme includes six important provisions:

(1) § 1981(a)(1) provides for "compensatory and punitive damages . . . in addition to any [equitable] relief authorized by section 706(g)" subject to two conditions: the respondent must have "engaged in unlawful intentional discrimination" (not an employment practice that is unlawful because of its disparate impact); and "the complaining party cannot recover" under § 1981.

(2) § 1981a(b)(2) excludes from compensatory damages "backpay, interest on backpay, or any other type of relief authorized under section 706(g) of the Civil Rights Act of 1964."

(3) § 1981a(b)(1) provides that punitive damages are available when plaintiff proves defendant "engaged in a discriminatory practice or discriminatory practices with malice or with reckless indifference to the federally protected rights of an aggrieved individual."

(4) § 1981a(b)(3) acts as a definition of what constitutes compensatory damages and then sets caps on compensatory and punitive damages:

> The sum of the amount of compensatory damages awarded under this section for future pecuniary losses, emotional pain, suffering, inconvenience, mental anguish, loss of enjoyment of life, and other nonpecuniary losses, and the amount of punitive damages awarded under the section, shall not exceed, for each complaining party [amounts that depend on the size of employers, with minimum of $50,000 and a maximum of $300,000 for employers with more than 500 employees].

(5) § 1981a(b)(4) provides that the caps do not apply to cases of race and alienage discrimination brought under 43 U.S.C. § 1981: "Nothing in this section shall be construed to limit the scope of, or the relief available under [§ 1981]."

(6) § 1981a(b)(c) provides a right to trial by jury:

> If a complaining party seeks compensatory or punitive damages under this section —
>
> (1)   any party may demand a trial by jury; and
> (2)   the court shall not inform the jury of the limitations [in § 1981a(b)(3)].

The availability of common-law-type legal remedies, such as compensatory and punitive damages, varies from statute to statute. Both compensatory and punitive damages awards are available under § 1981, *Johnson v. Railroad Express Agency*, 421

U.S. 454 (1975), but are subject to several restrictions when sought from a public official or governmental entity. At the other extreme, the ADEA does not authorize either type of damages for age discrimination, although it does allow the recovery of "liquidated damages." See p. 700.

1. Compensatory Damages

TURIC v. HOLLAND HOSPITALITY, INC.
85 F.3d 1211 (6th Cir. 1996)

KRUPANSKY, Circuit Judge.

[Holland Hospitality violated Title VII by discharging Turic, who was pregnant, because she contemplated having an abortion. The district court granted various relief, including $50,000 for emotional distress.]

To be eligible for compensatory damages, Turic was required to prove that Holland Hospitality's unlawful actions caused her emotional distress. A plaintiff's own testimony, along with the circumstances of a particular case, can suffice to sustain the plaintiff's burden in this regard. . . .

The court . . . found that as a young, unwed mother who was walking an "economic tightrope" and who had just discovered she was pregnant for a second time, Turic was in a particularly vulnerable position and was highly dependent upon her job. Vulnerability is relevant in determining damages. See *Williamson v. Handy Button Mach. Co.*, 817 F.2d 1290 (7th Cir. 1987) ("Perhaps [plaintiff] was unusually sensitive, but a tortfeasor takes its victims as it finds them. . . . In some cases unusual sensitivity will enhance the loss; in others unusual hardiness will reduce it; payment of the actual damage in each case will both compensate the victim and lead the injurer to take account of the full consequences of its acts"). Turic's vulnerability is particularly relevant in this case, because her supervisors had direct knowledge of her vulnerability before they discharged her. The trial judge did not err, therefore, in considering the unusual economic and emotional sensitivity of this plaintiff.

It is well settled that Title VII plaintiffs can prove emotional injury by testimony without medical support. However, damages for mental and emotional distress will not be presumed, and must be proven by "competent evidence." . . . Witnesses testified that Turic was extremely upset and frightened after being discharged, and that she ran from the meeting in tears. The Supreme Court in *Carey* [*v. Piphus*, 435 U.S. 247 (1978),] instructed that such witness testimony bolsters a finding of emotional distress: "Although essentially subjective, genuine injury in this respect may be evidenced by one's conduct and observed by others." Further, Turic testified that she continued to suffer nightmares, weight loss during her pregnancy (an undesirable occurrence often leading to low birth weight of the baby), and excessive nervousness. This testimony distinguishes the instant case from *Rodgers* [*v. Fisher Body Div., General Motors Corp.*, 739 F.2d 1102 (6th Cir. 1984)], in which the plaintiff failed to testify that he suffered any manifestations of his alleged mental distress, and from *Erebia v. Chrysler Plastic Prods. Corp.*, 772 F.2d 1250 (6th Cir. 1985), wherein the plaintiff testified merely that he was "highly upset" about racial slurs made at his workplace. See also *DeNieva v. Reyes*, 966 F.2d 480 (9th Cir. 1992) (plaintiff testified to suffering emotional distress manifested by insomnia, dizziness and vomiting and received $50,000 compensatory damages); *Secretary of HUD v. Blackwell*, 908 F.2d 864 (11th Cir. 1990) ($40,000 award upheld on basis of testimony regarding humiliation, insomnia and headaches); *Moody v. Pepsi-Cola Metro. Bottling Co.*, 915 F.2d 201 (6th Cir. 1990) ($150,000 award upheld on basis of testimony that plaintiff was shocked and humiliated and forced to live apart from family because of termination). For the above reasons, the amount awarded as compensatory damages is not grossly excessive, and the decision of the court below as to compensatory damages is affirmed. . . .

NOTES

1. *Proving Mental Distress.* Damages for mental distress can be recovered only when actual injury is proved; such injury cannot be presumed or inferred merely from a civil rights violation. *Carey v. Piphus*, 435 U.S. 247 (1978). As in *Turic*, many decisions have upheld awards for distress, humiliation, or anxiety based only on the testimony of the plaintiff and other lay persons. *E.g., Farfaras v. Citizens Bank & Trust*, 433 F.3d 558, 566 (7th Cir. 2006) (upholding $100,000 pain and suffering award since medical testimony not necessary to prove emotional injury in a Title VII case); *Migis v. Pearle Vision, Inc.*, 135 F.3d 1041 (5th Cir. 1998); *Walz v. Town of Smithtown*, 46 F.3d 162 (2d Cir. 1995). *But see Peña Crespo v. Puerto Rico*, 408 F.3d 10 (1st Cir. 2005) (district court did not err in limiting to $12,000 damages for emotional suffering for hostile-work environment because she presented no psychiatric expert testimony). *Cf. Akouri v. Fla. DOT*, 408 F.3d 1338, 1345-1346 (11th Cir. 2005) ($552,000 compensatory damages award overturned when plaintiff presented no evidence of emotional distress except for being turned down three times for promotions he believed he deserved). But at least one court seems to think that expert testimony of a medically cognizable injury is necessary. *Price v. City of Charlotte*, 93 F.3d 1241 (4th Cir. 1996). *See also Brady v. Fort Bend County*, 145 F.3d 691, 720 (5th Cir. 1998). *See generally* Zachary A. Kramer, *After Work*, 95 CAL. L. REV. 627, 629 (2007) (while employment discrimination plaintiffs may recover compensatory damages for emotional distress manifested in familial relationships, such as harm causing a strain on a relationship with partner or child, this compensation scheme is underutilized).

2. *"Hypersensitive" Plaintiffs Manifesting Distress.* Should damages for mental distress be limited to the amount necessary to compensate an ordinarily sensitive person or should a "thin skulled" plaintiff get full recovery? Recall that the Supreme Court has said that an unreasonably offended person has no claim at all for a sexually hostile work environment. See *Harris v. Forklift Sys., Inc.*, reproduced at p. 376. Would such a standard have produced a lower award in *Turic?*

3. *Other Compensatory Damages.* Of course, compensatory damages can be recovered for injuries other than mental distress. For example, plaintiff can recover the expenses incurred in seeking other employment. *E.g., Knapp v. Whitaker*, 757 F.2d 827 (7th Cir. 1985); *Woods-Drake v. Lundy*, 667 F.2d 1198 (5th Cir. 1982). In theory consequential damages could be recovered for harms caused by, say, a discharge, but there are few such cases. In any event, plaintiff cannot recover damages merely for being deprived of a civil right. *Memphis Cmty. Sch. Dist. v. Stachura*, 477 U.S. 299 (1986).

4. *Lost Earning Capacity vs. Front Pay.* What about lost earning capacity? In *Williams v. Pharmacia, Inc.*, 137 F.3d 944 (7th Cir. 1998), the court held that a Title VII plaintiff can recover both damages for lost future earning capacity and front pay. The jury had awarded the discharged plaintiff $300,000 in compensatory damages, including $250,000 for lost future earnings. The judge then added

$180,000 for lost backpay and, after denying reinstatement, another $115,530 for one year's front pay. The appellate court said that the plaintiff's discriminatory job evaluations and termination justified the damages for lost future earning capacity with other employers. The front pay award compensated a different injury — the loss plaintiff suffered from the failure to regain her old job. Is this correct? Would a different result have been reached if the front pay award had been based on losses to the date of retirement?

5. *Mitigation and Other Causation Rules.* Compensatory damages claims are subject to the usual causation rules. A familiar rule precludes liability for injuries that the plaintiff could have avoided by reasonable effort or expense. *See generally* 1, 2 DAN B. DOBBS, LAW OF REMEDIES §§3.9, 8.7(2) (2d ed. 1993). If your client has an employee who has been sexually harassed, would you advise your client to offer her professional counseling? Another rule precludes recovery for pre-existing injuries. *See McKinnon v. Kwong Wah Restaurant*, 83 F.3d 498 (1st Cir. 1996), a sexual harassment action in which plaintiff's emotional distress was partially caused by unrelated sexual encounters.

6. *Court Review of Jury Awards.* Many courts have reduced jury compensatory or punitive damages awards that are "grossly excessive" or "shock the conscience." *E.g., Walz v. Town of Smithtown*, 46 F.3d 162 (2d Cir. 1995); *Sheets v. Salt Lake County*, 45 F.3d 1383 (6th Cir. 1995). Can a court set aside a damages award under §1981a as "grossly excessive or shocking" even though it is within the statutory limit? *Hennessy v. Penril Datacomm Networks, Inc.*, 69 F.3d 1344 (7th Cir. 1995) (yes). Should courts look to the §1981a caps to determine whether an award is excessive in a §1981 action? Section 1981a(b)(4) provides that §1981a does not "limit" the relief available in §1981 actions.

7. *Special ADA Rules.* ADA §12112(d) contains a number of specific prohibitions regarding medical examinations and inquiries, and the maintenance of employee medical records. To date, three circuits have rejected attempts to recover compensatory or punitive damages for violations of these provisions, insisting that no actual injury had been shown. *E.g. Griffin v. Steeltek, Inc.*, 261 F.3d 1026 (10th Cir. 2001).

POLLARD v. E. I. DU PONT DE NEMOURS & CO.
532 U.S. 843 (2001)

Justice THOMAS delivered the opinion of the Court.

This case presents the question whether a front pay award is an element of compensatory damages under the Civil Rights Act of 1991. We conclude that it is not.

I

Petitioner Sharon Pollard sued her former employer, alleging that she had been subjected to a hostile work environment based on her sex, in violation of Title VII. . . . The District Court further found that the harassment resulted in a medical leave of absence from her job for psychological assistance and her eventual dismissal for refusing to return to the same hostile work environment. The court awarded Pollard $107,364 in backpay and benefits, $252,997 in attorney's fees, and, as relevant here, $300,000 in compensatory damages — the maximum permitted under the statutory cap for such damages in 42 U.S.C. §1981a(b)(3). . . .

The issue presented for review here is whether front pay constitutes an element of "compensatory damages" under 42 U.S.C. §1981a and thus is subject to the statutory damages cap imposed by that section. Although courts have defined "front pay" in numerous ways, front pay is simply money awarded for lost compensation during the period between judgment and reinstatement or in lieu of reinstatement. For instance, when an appropriate position for the plaintiff is not immediately available without displacing an incumbent employee, courts have ordered reinstatement upon the opening of such a position and have ordered front pay to be paid until reinstatement occurs. In cases in which reinstatement is not viable because of continuing hostility between the plaintiff and the employer or its workers, or because of psychological injuries suffered by the plaintiff as a result of the discrimination, courts have ordered front pay as a substitute for reinstatement. . . .

II

Plaintiffs who allege employment discrimination on the basis of sex traditionally have been entitled to such remedies as injunctions, reinstatement, backpay, lost benefits, and attorney's fees under §706(g). . . . In the Civil Rights Act of 1991, Congress expanded the remedies available to these plaintiffs by permitting, for the first time, the recovery of compensatory and punitive damages. The amount of compensatory damages awarded under §1981a for "future pecuniary losses, emotional pain, suffering, inconvenience, mental anguish, loss of enjoyment of life, and other nonpecuniary losses," and the amount of punitive damages awarded under §1981a, however, may not exceed the statutory cap set forth in §1981a(b)(3). The statutory cap is based on the number of people employed by the respondent. In this case, the cap is $300,000 because DuPont has more than 500 employees.

. . . For the reasons discussed below, we conclude that front pay is not an element of compensatory damages within the meaning of §1981a, and, therefore, we hold that the statutory cap of §1981a(b)(3) is inapplicable to front pay.

A

[As originally enacted, §706(g) authorized the award of backpay, modeling it on a comparable provision in the National Labor Relations Act. Consistent with NLRB practice] courts finding unlawful intentional discrimination in Title VII actions awarded this same type of backpay under §706(g). In the Title VII context, this form of "backpay" occurring after the date of judgment is known today as "front pay."

In 1972, Congress expanded §706(g) to specify that a court could, in addition to awarding those remedies previously listed in the provision, award "any other equitable relief as the court deems appropriate." After this amendment to §706(g), courts endorsed a broad view of front pay. See, e.g., *Patterson v. American Tobacco Co.*, 535 F.2d 257, 269 (CA4 1976) (stating that where reinstatement is not immediately feasible, backpay "should be supplemented by an award equal to the estimated present value of lost earnings that are reasonably likely to occur between the date of judgment and the time when the employee can assume his new position"). Courts recognized that reinstatement was not always a viable option, and that an award of front pay as a substitute for reinstatement in such cases was a necessary part of the "make whole" relief mandated by Congress and by this Court in *Albemarle* [reproduced at p. 654]. . . .

In 1991, without amending §706(g), Congress further expanded the remedies available in cases of intentional employment discrimination to include compensatory and punitive damages. At that time, §1981 permitted the recovery of unlimited compensatory and punitive damages in cases of intentional race and ethnic discrimination, but no similar remedy existed in cases of intentional sex, religious, or disability discrimination. Thus, §1981a brought all forms of intentional employment discrimination into alignment, at least with respect to the forms of relief available to successful plaintiffs. However, compensatory and punitive damages awarded under §1981a may not exceed the statutory limitations set forth in §1981a(b)(3), while such damages awarded under §1981 are not limited by statute.

B

In the abstract, front pay could be considered compensation for "future pecuniary losses," in which case it would be subject to the statutory cap. §1981a(b)(3). . . . However, we must not analyze one term of §1981a in isolation. When §1981a is read as a whole, the better interpretation is that front pay is not within the meaning of compensatory damages in §1981a(b)(3), and thus front pay is excluded from the statutory cap.

In the Civil Rights Act of 1991, Congress determined that victims of employment discrimination were entitled to *additional* remedies. . . . Congress therefore made clear through the plain language of the statute that the remedies newly authorized under §1981a were *in addition to* the relief authorized by §706(g). Section 1981a(a)(1) provides that, in intentional discrimination cases brought under Title VII, "the complaining party may recover compensatory and punitive damages as allowed in subsection (b) of [§1981a], *in addition to any relief authorized by section 706(g) of the Civil Rights Act of 1964*, from the respondent." (Emphasis added.) And §1981a(b)(2) states that "[c]ompensatory damages awarded under [§1981a] shall not include backpay, interest on backpay, *or any other type of relief authorized under section 706(g) of the Civil Rights Act of 1964*." (Emphasis added.) According to these statutory provisions, if front pay was a type of relief authorized under §706(g), it is excluded from the meaning of compensatory damages under §1981a.

As discussed above, the original language of §706(g) authorizing backpay awards was modeled after the same language in the NLRA. This provision in the NLRA had been construed to allow awards of backpay up to the date of reinstatement, even if reinstatement occurred after judgment. Accordingly, backpay awards made for the period between the date of judgment and the date of reinstatement, which today are called front pay awards under Title VII, were authorized under §706(g).

As to front pay awards that are made in lieu of reinstatement, we construe §706(g) as authorizing these awards as well. We see no logical difference between front pay awards made when there eventually is reinstatement and those made when there is not. Moreover, to distinguish between the two cases would lead to the strange result that employees could receive front pay when reinstatement eventually is available but not when reinstatement is not an option — whether because of continuing hostility between the plaintiff and the employer or its workers, or because of psychological injuries that the discrimination has caused the plaintiff. Thus, the most egregious offenders could be subject to the least sanctions. . . . We conclude that front pay awards in lieu of reinstatement fit within this statutory term.

Because front pay is a remedy authorized under §706(g), Congress did not limit the availability of such awards in §1981a. . . .

NOTES

1. *Front Pay as Equitable Relief.* The *Pollard* Court recognizes that front pay, like backpay, is available in Title VII and Title I actions and is not subject to the statutory caps in §1981a(b)(3). Thus, even though "front pay" is not included in the list of uncapped equitable remedies, it is treated the same as "back pay," which is listed.

2. *The Trial Judge Decides Front Pay.* The second consequence of finding that front pay is not "compensatory" is that such awards will be determined by the judge not the jury. Thus, the protocol in a case that goes to the jury and involves both claims for equitable relief, such as backpay and front pay, as well as compensatory and punitive damages is for the jury to decide the compensatory and punitive damage issues, subject to limited review by the court, but to also give an advisory opinion on backpay and front pay, which the trial judge may accept or reject in favor of what she considers the appropriate amounts.

2. Punitive Damages

KOLSTAD v. AMERICAN DENTAL ASSOCIATION
527 U.S. 526 (1999)

Justice O'CONNOR delivered the opinion of the Court.

Under the terms of the Civil Rights Act of 1991 (1991 Act) punitive damages are available in claims under Title VII [and Title I]. Punitive damages are limited, however, to cases in which the employer has engaged in intentional discrimination and has done so "with malice or with reckless indifference to the federally protected rights of an aggrieved individual." 42 U.S.C. §1981a(b)(1). . . .

I

In September 1992, Jack O'Donnell announced that he would be retiring as the Director of Legislation and Legislative Policy . . . for respondent, American Dental Association (respondent or Association). Petitioner, Carole Kolstad, was . . . serving as respondent's Director of Federal Agency Relations. When she learned of O'Donnell's retirement, she expressed an interest in filling his position. Also interested in replacing O'Donnell was Tom Spangler, [who] was serving as the Association's Legislative Counsel. . . . Both petitioner and Spangler . . . had received "distinguished" performance ratings by the acting head of the Washington office, Leonard Wheat.

. . . Wheat requested that Dr. William Allen, then serving as respondent's Executive Director in the Association's Chicago office, make the ultimate promotion decision. After interviewing both petitioner and Spangler, Wheat recommended that Allen select Spangler for O'Donnell's post. Allen notified petitioner in December 1992 that he had, in fact, selected Spangler. . . .

. . . In petitioner's view, the entire selection process was a sham. Counsel for petitioner urged the jury to conclude that Allen's stated reasons for selecting Spangler were pretext for gender discrimination, and that Spangler had been chosen for the position before the formal selection process began. Among the evidence offered in support of this view, there was testimony to the effect that Allen modified the description of O'Donnell's post to track aspects of the job description used to hire Spangler. In petitioner's view, this "preselection" procedure suggested an intent by the Association to discriminate on the basis of sex. Petitioner also introduced testimony at trial that Wheat told sexually offensive jokes and that he had referred to certain prominent professional women in derogatory terms. . . .

The District Court denied petitioner's request for a jury instruction on punitive damages. The jury concluded that respondent had discriminated against petitioner on the basis of sex and awarded her backpay totaling $52,718. . . .

The Court of Appeals . . . concluded that, "before the question of punitive damages can go to the jury, the evidence of the defendant's culpability must exceed what is needed to show intentional discrimination." [T]he court determined, specifically, that a defendant must be shown to have engaged in some "egregious" misconduct. . . .

II

A

. . . The 1991 Act limits compensatory and punitive damages awards, however, to cases of "intentional discrimination" — that is, cases that do not rely on the "disparate impact" theory of discrimination. §1981a(a)(1). Section 1981a(b)(1) further qualifies the availability of punitive awards:

> A complaining party may recover punitive damages . . . if the complaining party demonstrates that the respondent engaged in a discriminatory practice or discriminatory practices *with malice or with reckless indifference to the federally protected rights of an aggrieved individual.*

(Emphasis added.) The very structure of §1981a suggests a congressional intent to authorize punitive awards in only a subset of cases involving intentional discrimination. Section 1981a(a)(1) limits compensatory and punitive awards to instances of intentional discrimination, while §1981a(b)(1) requires plaintiffs to make an additional "demonstrat[ion]" of their eligibility for punitive damages. Congress plainly sought to impose two standards of liability — one for establishing a right to compensatory damages and another, higher standard that a plaintiff must satisfy to qualify for a punitive award.

. . . The terms "malice" and "reckless" [in §1981a(b)(1)] ultimately focus on the actor's state of mind. While egregious misconduct is evidence of the requisite mental state, §1981a does not limit plaintiffs to this form of evidence, and the section does not require a showing of egregious or outrageous discrimination independent of the employer's state of mind. Nor does the statute's structure imply an independent role for "egregiousness" in the face of congressional silence. On the contrary, the view that §1981a provides for punitive awards based solely on an employer's state of mind is consistent with the 1991 Act's distinction between equitable and compensatory relief. Intent determines which remedies are open to a plaintiff here as well; compensatory awards are available only where the employer has engaged in *"intentional discrimination."* (Emphasis added.)

Moreover, §1981a's focus on the employer's state of mind gives some effect to Congress' apparent intent to narrow the class of cases for which punitive awards are available to a subset of those involving intentional discrimination. The employer must act with "malice or with reckless indifference (*to [the plaintiff's] federally protected rights.*") (Emphasis added). The terms "malice" or "reckless indifference" pertain to the employer's knowledge that it may be acting in violation of federal law, not its awareness that it is engaging in discrimination. . . .

We gain an understanding of the meaning of the terms "malice" and "reckless indifference," as used in § 1981a, from this Court's decision in *Smith v. Wade*, 461 U.S. 30 (1983). . . . Employing language similar to what later appeared in § 1981a, the Court concluded in *Smith* that "a jury may be permitted to assess punitive damages in an action under § 1983 when the defendant's conduct is shown to be motivated by evil motive or intent, or when it involves reckless or callous indifference to the federally protected rights of others." While the *Smith* Court determined that it was unnecessary to show actual malice to qualify for a punitive award, its intent standard, at a minimum, required recklessness in its subjective form. The Court referred to a "subjective consciousness" of a risk of injury or illegality and a "'criminal indifference to civil obligations.'" . . . Applying this standard in the context of § 1981a, an employer must at least discriminate in the face of a perceived risk that its actions will violate federal law to be liable in punitive damages.

There will be circumstances where intentional discrimination does not give rise to punitive damages liability under this standard. In some instances, the employer may simply be unaware of the relevant federal prohibition. There will be cases, moreover, in which the employer discriminates with the distinct belief that its discrimination is lawful. The underlying theory of discrimination may be novel or otherwise poorly recognized, or an employer may reasonably believe that its discrimination satisfies a bona fide occupational qualification defense or other statutory exception to liability. . . .

To be sure, egregious or outrageous acts may serve as evidence supporting an inference of the requisite "evil motive." "The allowance of exemplary damages depends upon the bad motive of the wrong-doer *as exhibited by his acts.*" Sedgwick [Measure of Damages, p. 529 (8th ed. 1891)] (emphasis added). Likewise, under § 1981a(b)(1), pointing to evidence of an employer's egregious behavior would provide one means of satisfying the plaintiff's burden to "demonstrat[e]" that the employer acted with the requisite "malice or . . . reckless indifference." Again, however, respondent has not shown that the terms "reckless indifference" and "malice," in the punitive damages context, have taken on a consistent definition including an independent, "egregiousness" requirement.

B

The inquiry does not end with a showing of the requisite "malice or . . . reckless indifference" on the part of certain individuals, however. The plaintiff must impute liability for punitive damages to respondent. . . . While we decline to engage in any definitive application of the agency standards to the facts of this case, it is important that we address the proper legal standards for imputing liability to an employer in the punitive damages context. . . .

Although jurisdictions disagree over whether and how to limit vicarious liability for punitive damages, our interpretation of Title VII is informed by "the general common law of agency, rather than . . . the law of any particular State." The common law as codified in the Restatement (Second) of Agency (1957), provides a useful starting point for defining this general common law. The Restatement of Agency places strict limits on the extent to which an agent's misconduct may be imputed to the principal for purposes of awarding punitive damages:

> Punitive damages can properly be awarded against a master or other principal because of an act by an agent if, but only if:
>   (a) the principal authorized the doing and the manner of the act, or
>   (b) the agent was unfit and the principal was reckless in employing him, or

(c) the agent was employed in a managerial capacity and was acting in the scope of employment, or

(d) the principal or a managerial agent of the principal ratified or approved punitive damages if it authorizes or ratifies the agent's tortious act, or if it acts recklessly in employing the malfeasing agent.

See also Restatement (Second) of Torts §909 (same).

The Restatement, for example, provides that the principal may be liable for punitive damages if it authorizes or ratifies the agent's tortuous act, or if it acts recklessly in employing the malfeasing agent. The Restatement also contemplates liability for punitive awards where an employee serving in a "managerial capacity" committed the wrong while "acting in the scope of employment." "Unfortunately, no good definition of what constitutes a 'managerial capacity' has been found," and determining whether an employee meets this description requires a fact-intensive inquiry. "In making this determination, the court should review the type of authority that the employer has given to the employee, the amount of discretion that the employee has in what is done and how it is accomplished." Suffice it to say here that the examples provided in the Restatement of Torts suggest that an employee must be "important," but perhaps need not be the employer's "top management, officers, or directors," to be acting "in a managerial capacity."

Additional questions arise from the meaning of the "scope of employment" requirement. The Restatement of Agency provides that even intentional torts are within the scope of an agent's employment if the conduct is "the kind [the employee] is employed to perform," "occurs substantially within the authorized time and space limits," and "is actuated, at least in part, by a purpose to serve the" employer. According to the Restatement, so long as these rules are satisfied, an employee may be said to act within the scope of employment even if the employee engages in acts "specifically forbidden" by the employer and uses "forbidden means of accomplishing results." On this view, even an employer who makes every effort to comply with Title VII would be held liable for the discriminatory acts of agents acting in a "managerial capacity."

Holding employers liable for punitive damages when they engage in good faith efforts to comply with Title VII, however, is in some tension with the very principles underlying common law limitations on vicarious liability for punitive damage — that it is "improper ordinarily to award punitive damages against one who himself is personally innocent and therefore liable only vicariously." Where an employer has undertaken such good faith efforts at Title VII compliance, it "demonstrat[es] that it never acted in reckless disregard of federally protected rights."

Applying the Restatement of Agency's "scope of employment" rule in the Title VII punitive damages context, moreover, would reduce the incentive for employers to implement antidiscrimination programs. In fact, such a rule would likely exacerbate concerns among employers that §1981a's "malice" and "reckless indifference" standard penalizes those employers who educate themselves and their employees on Title VII's prohibitions. Dissuading employers from implementing programs or policies to prevent discrimination in the workplace is directly contrary to the purposes underlying Title VII. The statute's "primary objective" is "a prophylactic one"; it aims, chiefly, "not to provide redress but to avoid harm.". . . The purposes underlying Title VII are similarly advanced where employers are encouraged to adopt antidiscrimination policies and to educate their personnel on Title VII's prohibitions.

In light of the perverse incentives that the Restatement's "scope of employment" rules create, we are compelled to modify these principles to avoid undermining the objectives underlying Title VII. Recognizing Title VII as an effort to promote prevention as well as remediation, and observing the very principles underlying the Restatement's strict limits on vicarious liability for punitive damages, we agree that, in the punitive damages context, an employer may not be vicariously liable for the discriminatory employment decisions of managerial agents where these decisions are contrary to the employer's "good-faith efforts to comply with Title VII." As [Judge Tatel] recognized, "[g]iving punitive damages protection to employers who make good-faith efforts to prevent discrimination in the workplace accomplishes" Title VII's objective of "motivat[ing] employers to detect and deter Title VII violations."

. . . We leave for remand the question whether petitioner can identify facts sufficient to support an inference that the requisite mental state can be imputed to respondent. . . .

[Chief Justice REHNQUIST and Justice THOMAS joined concurred in Part II-B of the Court's opinion. The partial dissent and partial concurrence of Justice STEVENS, with whom Justice SOUTER, Justice GINSBURG, and Justice BREYER joined, is omitted.]

NOTES

1. *Is* Kolstad *a Retreat from* Albemarle? The Court viewed restricting the scope of an employer's liability for punitive damages in ADA and Title VII actions as consistent with a "primary objective" of antidiscrimination statute, the prophylactic purpose "not to provide redress but to avoid harm." *Id.* at 545. Thus, *Kolstad* limited the liability of employers based on agency principles so that punitive damages would turn on what the corporate employer did (or didn't do) rather than on the conduct of a "rogue" supervisor. The result is to encourage voluntary employer policies prohibiting discrimination. But is *Kolstad* at odds with the rationale in *Albemarle* that backpay was necessary to further the objective of giving employers an "incentive to shun practices of dubious legality?" Or does the fact that backpay, even if not punitive damages, remains available sufficient incentive? Since *punitive* damages are at stake, there is no need to worry about the compensatory objective that *Albemarle* announced.

2. *Two Elements of a Punitive Damage Award.* There are two hurdles to the recovery of § 1981a punitive damages — first, the malice or reckless indifference requirement and, second, satisfaction of the agency principles.

3. *Defendant's State of Mind.* As to the first, how can the plaintiff show that the employer subjectively knew that it was or might be violating Title I or Title VII? Where the employer does not rely on a statutory defense or exception, would the intent requirement be satisfied by showing the employer knew that its action was subject to federal antidiscrimination law? Such a low threshold would make defendants in most disparate treatment cases susceptible to punitive damages. If the employer relies on a statutory defense or exception, is it enough to show the employer failed to seek legal advice? An example of a case where defendant was liable for discriminating but not with malice is *Allen v. Tobacco Superstore, Inc.,* 475 F.3d 931 (8th Cir. 2007), where plaintiff's insubordination was not a sufficient, legitimate nondiscriminatory reason for her employer to fail to promote her but nevertheless disproved that the employer acted with malice or reckless indifference.

Does *Smith v. Wade,* discussed in the Court's opinion, suggest that the malice or reckless indifference requirement also applies in § 1981 cases? *See, e.g., Rowlett v.*

Anheuser-Busch, Inc., 832 F.2d 194 (1st Cir. 1987) (yes). The reckless indifference requirement has proved to be an especially serious obstacle in ADA cases. *See, e.g., Webner v. Titan Distribution, Inc.*, 267 F.3d 828 (8th Cir. 2001) (employer feared employee would reinjure his back and miss work); *Gile v. United Airlines, Inc.*, 213 F.3d 365 (7th Cir. 2000) (employer negligently failed to realize that condition was a disability under the ADA).

4. *The Agency Element.* Aside from the hostile work environment cases like *Ellerth*, p. 384, agency principles have not been applied to limit backpay or compensatory damages for a Title I or Title VII violation. Why do agency principles have more bite in actions seeking punitive damages? Is it because the Court fears that the low threshold for showing malice would otherwise make punitive damages available in almost all disparate treatment cases? Are you satisfied with the Court's policy reasons for not imputing a lower level manager's malicious discrimination to the corporate employer? Recall that individuals are not personally liable under Title VII, see p. 699, so a failure to impute liability will leave such conduct unpunished by the law.

5. *The Two Step Agency Issue.* The agency determination requires two steps. First, there must be a determination of whether liability would be appropriate — whether the actor was in a managerial capacity and acting within the scope of the actor's employment. Second, there must be a determination of whether the employer used good faith efforts to comply with the law.

(a) *Who Is a Manager?* Consider who is a "manager" and what is the meaning of "scope of employment." Is the manager of a Wal-Mart store a "manager"? *EEOC v. Wal-Mart Stores, Inc.*, 187 F.3d 1241 (10th Cir. 1999) (yes); *contra, Dudley v. Wal-Mart Stores, Inc.*, 166 F.3d 1317 (11th Cir. 1999). If a "manager" creates a sexually hostile environment for which the employer is liable, might the scope of employment requirement nevertheless preclude recovery of punitive damages? The Fourth Circuit has held that a supervisor who created a hostile environment and who had authority over the victimized employee acted in the scope of his employment. *Anderson v. G.D.C., Inc.*, 281 F.3d 452 (4th Cir. 2002). The court also held that the "manager" requirement is satisfied by an employee who has the power to hire, fire, and discipline other employees. The Tenth Circuit has gone even further, holding that an employee who can make hiring and firing *recommendations* is a "manager." *EEOC v. Wal-Mart Stores, Inc.*, 187 F.3d 1241 (10th Cir. 1999).

(b) *Employer's Good Faith Compliance.* Even if a manager acting within the scope of his employment discriminates maliciously, the employer is still not liable for punitive damages if it made a good faith effort to prevent discrimination. Why? Would employers be more vigilant with or without this exception? *Romano v. U-Haul Int'l*, 233 F.3d 655 (1st Cir. 2000), held this to be an affirmative defense on which the employer had the burden of proof. A nondiscrimination policy is not by itself sufficient. *Id.* at 670 ("A defendant must also show that efforts have been made to implement its anti-discrimination policy, through education of its employees and actual enforcement of its mandate"). *See also McInnis v. Fairfield Cmtys., Inc.*, 458 F.3d 1129 (10th Cir. 2006) (upholding punitive damages despite contention that employer made good-faith efforts to educate its employees about its written policies against discrimination and retaliation).

Note the Supreme Court's reference in *Kolstad* to "good faith efforts to *enforce* an antidiscrimination policy" (emphasis added). *See Parker v. Gen. Extrusions, Inc.*, 491 F.3d 596, 604 (6th Cir. 2007) ("a rational fact-finder could plausibly [find that] any investigation into those complaints was, at best, half-hearted and, at worst, a sham"). Nevertheless, a number of employers have successfully invoked the defense. *See*

Dominic v. DeVilbiss Air Power Co., 493 F.3d 968 (8th Cir. 2007) (punitive damages award overturned when defendant neither terminated supervisor nor transferred employee when employer's response was otherwise proper and transferring the victim was impossible due to employer's small size while terminating the supervisor would have subjected employer to suit); *Hatley v. Hilton Hotels Corp.*, 308 F.3d 473 (5th Cir. 2002) (employer who had a policy forbidding sexual harassment, trained new employees on sexual harassment, had grievance procedure for complaints, and initiated investigation of complaints had a good faith defense to punitive damages although its agent failed to respond to employee's complaints and acted with reckless indifference); *Bryant v. Aiken Reg'l Med. Ctrs., Inc.*, 333 F.3d 536, 548-49 (4th Cir. 2003) (equal employment opportunity policy, grievance policy, assurance that employees would not be retaliated against, diversity training program, and voluntary monitoring of departmental demographics "to keep the employee base reflective of the pool of potential employees in the area" were "widespread anti-discrimination efforts" that barred the award of punitive damages).

6. *No Affirmative Defense for Direct Liability.* Two circuits have agreed that the good faith defense is available only where the employer has derivative liability, as opposed to direct liability, for the discrimination. Accordingly, the defense is unavailable where the discriminator was by such a high level person who was acting as a proxy for the corporation. *Passentino v. Johnson & Johnson Consumer Prods.*, 212 F.3d 493 (9th Cir. 2000). Similarly, the defense is unavailable where the employees charged with enforcing the company's antidiscrimination policies knew or should have known of the discrimination but failed to act. *Deters v. Equifax Credit Info. Servs.*, 202 F.3d 1262 (10th Cir. 2000).

7. *Kolstad on Remand.* On remand, if no additional facts surface, should Kolstad's claim for punitive damages go to a jury? Did she present sufficient evidence that the Association discriminated "in the face of a perceived risk that its actions will violate federal law"? Did she present sufficient evidence that Allen and Wheat were "managers"? *See also Carter v. Kan. City S. Ry. Co.*, 456 F.3d 841 (8th Cir. 2006) (even egregious racial harassment did not warrant punitive damages where employer investigated complaints, discharged primary offender, established compliance policy, and offensive conduct did not continue after complaints).

8. *Punitive Damages under § 1981.* The Fourth Circuit has held that *Kolstad's* agency principles are applicable in § 1981 actions. *Lowery v. Circuit City Stores, Inc.*, 206 F.3d 431 (4th Cir. 2000).

9. *Jury Discretion.* If the jury finds that the two *Kolstad* requirements have been satisfied, it has discretion to award punitive damages. This discretion is exercised in light of the need for punishment and deterrence. *See Smith v. Wade*, 461 U.S. 30 (1983). The jury determines the amount of the award by considering "such factors as the grievousness of the conduct, the solvency of the guilty party, and the potential for deterrence of the verdict." *Rowlett v. Anheuser-Busch, Inc.*, 832 F.2d 194, 207 (1st Cir. 1987). *See also Patterson v. Balsamico*, 440 F.3d 104, 122 (2d Cir. 2006) (reducing $20,000 punitive damages award against individual in § 1983 case in light of his personal financial situation). *See generally* Judith J. Johnson, A *Standard for Punitive Damages under Title VII*, 46 FLA. L. REV. 521 (1995).

10. *Are Compensatory and Punitive Damages Linked?* Some circuits have added an additional threshold to the grant of punitive damages — that punitive damages may be recovered only where compensatory damages or backpay has also been awarded. *E.g., Provencher v. CVS Pharmacy*, 145 F.3d 5 (1st Cir. 1998); *contra Tisdale v. Fed. Express Corp.*, 415 F.3d 516, 535 (6th Cir. 2005) ("we agree with the reasoning of our sister

circuits and conclude that there is no reason to condition punitive damages on the award of actual or nominal compensatory damages"); *EEOC v. W&O, Inc.*, 213 F.3d 600, 615 (11th Cir. 2000) ("punitive damages may be appropriate where a plaintiff has received back pay but no compensatory damages").

11. *Substantive Due Process Limits on Punitive Damages.* In several recent cases over the last decade, the Supreme Court has held that punitive damage awards may violate due process even if they satisfy state law standards. Jury awards are to be reviewed by both trial and appellate courts de novo to assure compliance with due process. As to what due process requires, *BMW of N. Am., Inc. v. Gore*, 517 U.S. 559 (1996), held that a punitive damages award that is "grossly excessive" violates due process. An award is "grossly excessive" when either the amount of the award exceeds the state's legitimate interests in punishment and deterrence or the controlling legal principles fail to provide fair notice of the conduct subject to punishment and the severity of the punishment. More recently, *State Farm Mut. Auto. Ins. Co. v. Campbell*, 538 U.S. 408 (2003), set a presumptive constitutional cap on punitive damages by limiting them to a single-digit ratio to compensatory damages. While not establishing a bright-line ratio, the Court wrote "in practice, few awards exceeding a single-digit ratio between punitive and compensatory damages, to a significant degree, will satisfy due process." *Id.* at 424. The Court then went further to suggest that a limit of quadruple punitive damages while not binding was "instructive." *Id.* Does *State Farm* link punitive damages to some multiple of compensatory damages? If plaintiff proves only $100 in compensatory damages, does that limit her punitive damages to a maximum of $1,000? If plaintiff proves no compensatory damages or backpay, can she get any punitives? See Note 10 for cases so holding without constitutional compulsion. Most recently, *Philip Morris USA v. Williams*, 127 S. Ct. 1057 (2007), held that while "evidence of actual harm to nonparties can help to show that the conduct that harmed the plaintiff also posed a substantial risk to the general public, and so was particularly reprehensible, a jury may not go further and use a punitive damages verdict to punish a defendant directly for harms to those nonparties." *See generally* Stacy A. Hickox, *Reduction of Punitive Damages for Employment Discrimination: Are Courts Ignoring Our Juries?* 54 MERCER L. REV. 1081, 1121 (2003).

These cases clearly apply in a §1981 action, which has no statutory ceiling on punitive damages awards. *Zhang v. Am. Gem Seafoods Inc.*, 339 F.3d 1020 (9th Cir. 2003) (upholding jury award of $2.6 million in punitive damages to former executive of Chinese national origin who was discharged in violation of §1981). But several courts have indicated that statutory damage caps in Title VII and Title I actions obviate any need to apply them in that context. *E.g., Lust v. Sealy, Inc.*, 383 F.3d 580, 590-591 (7th Cir. 2004) (no need to review punitive damages awards for constitutionality where Congress has placed a tight cap on total, including punitive, damages); *Schexnayder v. Bonfiglio*, 167 Fed. Appx. 364, 368 (5th Cir. 2006) (dictum that challenge to award of punitive damages would fail, in part because "the punitive damages award here was controlled by a relatively modest federal statutory cap"). *See generally* Colleen P. Murphy, *Statutory Caps and Judicial Review of Damages*, 39 AKRON L. REV. 1001 (2006) (caps should not alter normal judicial review of jury awards; when awards based on more than one claim exceed a total cap, judicial review for excessiveness should be combined with plaintiff choice as to how to allocate the awards).

12. *Compensatory and Punitive Damages in ADA Actions.* Section 1981a(a)(2) authorizes compensatory and punitive damages in Title I ADA actions for disparate

treatment discrimination. *But see Kramer v. Banc of Am. Sec., LLC,* 355 F.3d 961 (7th Cir. 2004) (the section does not authorize compensatory or punitive damages for retaliation claims). *See generally* Katie M. Mueting, Note, *A Case for Allowing Victims of ADA Retaliation and Coercion in Employment to Recover Legal Damages,* 92 IOWA L. REV. 1493 (2007). This relief is in addition to the backpay, front pay, and interest permitted by §706(g). However, compensatory and punitive damage awards are subject to the same limitations and conditions as in Title VII actions, including the immunity of governmental entities from punitive damage awards. *See Cook County v. U.S. ex rel. Chandler,* 538 U.S. 119, 129 (2003). In addition §1981a(a)(3) provides that damages may not be awarded for the failure to make a reasonable accommodation in an ADA case where the defendant demonstrates good faith efforts, in consultation with the discriminatee, to make such an accommodation.

NOTE ON OPERATION OF THE STATUTORY CAPS

As we have seen, the sum of compensatory plus punitive damages available to one claimant under this provision is capped. You may be surprised to discover that the existence of the caps is not revealed to the jury, which explains why courts so often reduce jury awards to comply with the caps. *See generally* Rebecca Hollander-Blumoff & Matthew T. Bodie, *The Effects of Jury Ignorance About Damage Caps: The Case of the 1991 Civil Rights Act,* 90 IOWA L. REV. 1361 (2005). What does this tell you about the differing perceptions of the wrongfulness of discrimination in the eyes of the courts and juries?

The operation of the caps can be more complicated than would first appear. The employer's size is computed as of the time of the violation, *e.g., Depaoli v. Vacation Sales Assocs., LLC,* 489 F.3d 615 (4th Cir. 2007), and the award is capped separately for each plaintiff, *see EEOC v. W&O Inc.,* 213 F.3d 600, 613 (11th Cir. 2000) ("each aggrieved employee may receive up to the full amount permitted by the applicable statutory cap," even when the EEOC sues on behalf of several plaintiff). The caps apply to the entire amount recoverable by any one claimant on all of her Title VII claims and not to each Title VII claim of any plaintiff. *See Hudson v. Reno,* 130 F.3d 1193 (6th Cir. 1997) (recovery limited to capped amount even though plaintiff recovered for both sex discrimination and retaliation); *Baty v. Willamette Indus.,* 172 F.3d 1232, 1246 (10th Cir. 1999) (caps apply to each party in an action, not to each claim).

Despite these limitations, there have been questions how the caps operate when different statutory claims intersect. The most basic question, the interrelationship of Title VII claims with claims brought under §1981, is addressed in the statute: in Title VII actions under §1981a(a)(1) (but not as to ADA actions under §1981a(a)(2)) plaintiff is eligible for compensatory damages as long as she "cannot recover under 42 U.S.C. 1981 . . . " The intent of this section was to avoid double recovery for the same harm, with the §1981 claim taking priority because it is not capped. Where, therefore, the plaintiff alleges a single harm, such as race discrimination but brings both a Title VII and a §1981 cause of action, there can only be one recovery, but that recovery for compensatory damages will be under §1981, which is not subject to the Title VII caps. The priority of uncapped §1981 claims is further confirmed by §1981a(c)(4), which provides that "[n]othing in this section shall be construed to limit the scope of, or the relief available under, section 1981. . . . " A single plaintiff, however, can make separate claims of, say, sex discrimination and race discrimination under Title VII, and these are subject to the caps. Suppose such a plaintiff claimed sex discrimination under Title VII and race discrimination under §1981. She is entitled to a separate recovery not limited by the caps on her race claim, although the court must guard against compensation for the same injury twice in the award should it also compensate her on the sex claim, which is capped.

A second interrelationship question arises when a jury finds the same discrimination violates both federal and state employment statutes and awards compensatory damages without apportioning the award between the two claims. When the award exceeds the §1981a(b)(3) cap, the courts have tended to treat the amount in excess of the cap as having been awarded under state law, thus allowing the entire award to stand. *E.g. Rodriguez-Torres v. Caribbean Forms Mfr., Inc.*, 399 F.3d 52, 66 (1st Cir. 2005) (an unspecified award may be considered as fungible between the state and federal claims and allocated so as to maximize the plaintiff's recovery while adhering to the Title VII cap); *Gagliardo v. Connaught Labs*, 311 F.3d 565 (3d Cir. 2002) (ADA) (court properly applied §1981 cap only to punitive damages part of award, apportioning the compensatory damages to the state claim). Would your answer change if the state statute contained the same cap? *See Giles v. GE*, 245 F.3d 474 (5th Cir. 2001) (caps are coextensive, not cumulative); *Bradshaw v. Sch. Bd. of Broward County*, 486 F.3d 1205 (11th Cir. 2007) (federal cap could not be avoided by attributing some recovery to state claims where state had its own, lower, cap).

NOTE ON PERSONAL LIABILITY OF EMPLOYEES

One issue that frequently arises is whether the person who committed the discriminatory act has personal liability or whether liability is limited to the employer. *See generally* Rebecca Hanner White, *Vicarious and Personal Liability for Employment Discrimination*, 30 GA. L. REV. 509 (1996). A seminal case is *Miller v. Maxwell's Int'l, Inc.*, 991 F.2d 583 (9th Cir. 1993), which held that neither Title VII nor the ADEA imposes personal liability. The court reasoned that these statutes are addressed to "employers" and, even though this term is defined to include "agents" of the employer, this inclusion was intended to incorporate the doctrine of respondeat superior. Moreover, because both statutes exempt small employers from coverage, the court thought it "inconceivable" that Congress would have intended to impose liability on individual employees. A dissenting judge agreed as to Title VII but reasoned that the personal liability of employees was established under the Fair Labor Standards Act, and, because the ADEA adopted that statute's enforcement procedures, employees also have personal liability under the ADEA.

Other appellate decisions generally agree that employees do not have personal liability to the discriminatee under Title VII. *E.g., Dearth v. Collins*, 441 F.3d 931 (11th Cir. 2006) (reaffirming no individual liability, even in a sexual harassment suit where the employer is not liable because of the affirmative defense); *Lissau v. Southern Food Serv., Inc.*, 159 F.3d 177 (4th Cir. 1998). The same result has also been reached in ADEA litigation. *E.g., Stults v. Conoco, Inc.*, 76 F.3d 651 (5th Cir. 1996); *Smith v. Lomax*, 45 F.3d 402 (11th Cir. 1995). And the appellate decisions under Title I, which contains coverage provisions like those in the ADEA and Title VII, have also reached the same conclusion. *E.g., Albra v. Advan, Inc.*, 490 F.3d 826 (11th Cir. 2007) (individuals are not amenable to private suit for violating the ADA's anti-retaliation provision for employment); *Butler v. City of Prairie Village*, 172 F.3d 736 (10th Cir. 1999).

In contrast to the ADA, Title VII, and ADEA, individuals do have personal liability to the discriminatee under § 1981. *E.g., Gierlinger v. New York State Police,* 15 F.3d 32 (2d Cir. 1994); *Jones v. Continental Corp.,* 789 F.2d 308 (6th Cir. 1986). *Contra, Oden v. Oktibbeha County,* 246 F.3d 458 (5th Cir. 2001). While a public official may have qualified immunity from § 1981 (and § 1983) suits, such immunity can usually be overcome in a race discrimination case. *See generally* Alan K. Chen, *The Facts about Qualified Immunity,* 55 EMORY L.J. 229 (2006).

3. Liquidated Damages

The ADEA (but not Title VII, the ADA, or § 1981) allows the recovery of "liquidated damages" (which in effect double the amount of the claim for unpaid wages) where the defendant's statutory violation was willful. Section 7(b), 29 U.S.C. § 626(b) (2007), incorporates the enforcement procedures and remedies contained in § 16 of the Fair Labor Standards Act (FLSA), 29 U.S.C. § 216. Section 16, in turn, allows the EEOC or a private plaintiff to recover (1) unpaid wages and (2) liquidated damages in an amount equal to the amount of unpaid wages recovered. Section 7(b), however, imposes a condition on the recovery of liquidated damages: "*Provided,* That liquidated damages shall be payable only in cases of willful violations of this chapter."

After an initial attempt to delineate the meaning of the phrase "willful violations," the Supreme Court found it necessary to revisit the issue.

HAZEN PAPER CO. v. BIGGINS
507 U.S. 604 (1993)

Justice O'CONNOR delivered the opinion of the Court.

[The case was tried before a jury, which specifically found that the employer "willfully" violated the ADEA by discharging him because of his age.]

As to the issue of "willfulness" under § 7(b) of the ADEA, the Court of Appeals adopted and applied the definition set out in *Trans World Airlines, Inc. v. Thurston,* 469 U.S. 111 (1985). In *Thurston,* we held that the airline's facially discriminatory job-transfer policy was not a "willful" ADEA violation because the airline neither "knew [nor] showed reckless disregard for the matter of whether" the policy contravened the statute. The Court of Appeals found sufficient evidence to satisfy the *Thurston* standard, and ordered that respondent be awarded liquidated damages equal to and in addition to the underlying damages of $419,454.38.

We granted certiorari to decide [whether] the *Thurston* standard for liquidated damages appl[ies] to the case where the predicate ADEA violation is not a formal, facially discriminatory policy, as in *Thurston,* but rather an informal decision by the employer that was motivated by the employee's age. . . .

In *Thurston,* we thoroughly analyzed § 7(b) and concluded that "a violation of the Act [would be] 'willful' if the employer knew or showed reckless disregard for the matter of whether its conduct was prohibited by the ADEA." We sifted through the legislative history of § 7(b), which had derived from § 16(a) of the [FLSA], and determined that the accepted judicial interpretation of § 16(a) at the time of the passage of the ADEA supported the "knowledge or reckless disregard" standard. We found that this standard was consistent with the meaning of "willful" in other criminal and civil statutes.

Finally, we observed that Congress aimed to create a "two-tiered liability scheme," under which some but not all ADEA violations would give rise to liquidated damages. We therefore rejected a broader definition of "willful" providing for liquidated damages whenever the employer knew that the ADEA was "in the picture." . . .

Surprisingly, the courts of appeals continue to be confused about the meaning of the term "willful" in §7(b) of the ADEA. A number of circuits have declined to apply *Thurston* to what might be called an informal disparate treatment case — where age has entered into the employment decision on an ad hoc, informal basis rather than through a formal policy. At least one circuit refuses to impose liquidated damages in such a case unless the employer's conduct was "outrageous." Another requires that the underlying evidence of liability be direct rather than circumstantial. Still others have insisted that age be the "predominant" rather than simply a determinative factor. The chief concern of these circuits has been that the application of *Thurston* would defeat the two-tiered system of liability intended by Congress, because every employer that engages in informal age discrimination knows or recklessly disregards the illegality of its conduct.

We believe that this concern is misplaced. The ADEA does not provide for liquidated damages "where consistent with the principle of a two-tiered liability scheme." It provides for liquidated damages where the violation was "willful." That definition must be applied here unless we overrule *Thurston*, or unless there is some inherent difference between this case and *Thurston* to cause a shift in the meaning of the word "willful."

As for the first possibility, petitioners have not persuaded us that *Thurston* was wrongly decided, let alone that we should depart from the rule of stare decisis. The two-tiered liability principle was simply one interpretive tool among several that we used in *Thurston* to decide what Congress meant by the word "willful," and in any event we continue to believe that the "knowledge or reckless disregard" standard will create two tiers of liability across the range of ADEA cases. It is not true that an employer who knowingly relies on age in reaching its decision invariably commits a knowing or reckless violation of the ADEA. The ADEA is not an unqualified prohibition on the use of age in employment decisions, but affords the employer a "bona fide occupational qualification" defense, and exempts certain subject matters and persons, see, e.g., §623(f)(2) (exemption for bona fide seniority systems and employee benefit plans); §631(c) (exemption for bona fide executives and high policymakers). If an employer incorrectly but in good faith and nonrecklessly believes that the statute permits a particular age-based decision, then liquidated damages should not be imposed. Indeed, in *Thurston* itself we upheld liability but *reversed* an award of liquidated damages because the employer "acted [nonrecklessly] and in good faith in attempting to determine whether [its] plan would violate the ADEA."

Nor do we see how the instant case can be distinguished from *Thurston*, assuming that petitioners did indeed fire respondent because of his age. The only distinction between *Thurston* and the case before us is the existence of formal discrimination. Age entered into the employment decision there through a formal and publicized policy, and not as an undisclosed factor motivating the employer on an ad hoc basis, which is what respondent alleges occurred here. But surely an employer's reluctance to acknowledge its reliance on the forbidden factor should not cut against imposing a penalty. It would be a wholly circular and self-defeating interpretation of the ADEA to hold that, in cases where an employer more likely knows its conduct to be illegal, knowledge alone does not suffice for liquidated damages. We therefore reaffirm that the *Thurston* definition of "willful" — that the employer either knew or showed reckless disregard for the matter of whether its conduct was prohibited by the statute — applies to all disparate treatment cases under the ADEA. Once a "willful" violation has been shown, the employee need not additionally demonstrate that the employer's conduct was outrageous, or provide direct evidence of the employer's motivation, or prove that age was the predominant rather than a determinative factor in the employment decision. . . .

[The concurring opinion of Justice KENNEDY, with whom The Chief Justice and Justice THOMAS joined, is omitted.]

NOTES

1. *What Is a "Willful" Violation?* If the employer is asked, during discovery or at trial, whether he knew that federal law prohibited age discrimination, what happens if he testifies that he didn't? Can plaintiff use that to claim both that ignorance of the law is no excuse and that, if true, it just demonstrates how insensitive the defendant was to discrimination? If the employer acknowledges that he knows of the law, is that sufficient to find his discrimination "willful?" To avoid the "willful" finding, must the employer assert that, while knowing of the law, he believed he was not discriminating because his actions were sheltered by the BFOQ or another defense?

2. *Comparing* Biggins *with* Kolstad. Is the Supreme Court's interpretation of "willful" in the ADEA the same as its interpretation of "malice or reckless indifference" in §1981a? It seems difficult to draw a distinction between the two standards and even more difficult to get a jury to understand any such distinction. On the other hand, a defendant would probably prefer to have to be found malicious or recklessly indifferent in order to be held liable. *See Kight v. AutoZone, Inc.*, 494 F.3d 727, 732 (8th Cir. 2007) (finding no "plain error" in jury instruction to find defendant's conduct "willful if you find by the greater weight of the evidence that when defendant discharged plaintiff, defendant knew the discharge was in violation of the federal law prohibiting age discrimination or acted with reckless disregard of that law.") As for agency questions, *Biggins* does not mention any limitation based on the position of the decisionmaker in the organization or the reasonableness of the employer's antidiscrimination efforts. Do the *Kolstad* agency principles limit liability for the ADEA award? It is arguable that the ADEA's liquidated damages provision reflects Congress' judgment that it is fair to impose double liability (but not more open-ended punitive damages) whenever the conditions are met, regardless of the moral culpability of the employer. *See generally* Judith J. Johnson, A *Uniform Standard for Exemplary Damages in Employment Discrimination Cases*, 33 U. RICH. L. REV. 41 (1999).

3. *More about* Thurston. The decision *Biggins* elaborates on, *Trans World Airlines, Inc. v. Thurston*, clarified two further aspects of the liquidated damages award. First, liquidated damages *must* be awarded to a plaintiff who proves a "willful violation." *See also Loveless v. John's Ford, Inc.*, 232 Fed. Appx. 229 (4th Cir. 2007) (award affirmed despite claim that plaintiff would receive a windfall). But, if a "willful violation" is not proved, the plaintiff cannot be awarded any liquidated damages. Second, the liquidated damages award has a punitive purpose. *See also Comm'r v. Schleier*, 515 U.S. 323 (1995) (legislative history suggests Congress intended ADEA liquidated damages to be punitive in nature and not compensatory). If the liquidated damages award is punitive, can a plaintiff recover both liquidated damages and state

law punitive damages for the same misconduct? *See Denesha v. Farmers Ins. Exch.*, 161 F.3d 491 (8th Cir. 1998) (even though plaintiff was awarded liquidated damages, court held on appeal that employer's discriminatory conduct justified a punitive damages award).

4. *Calculating Liquidated Damages.* Several courts have stated that the liquidated damages award should equal the amount awarded for unpaid wages and lost fringe benefits, *e.g., Blim v. Western Elec. Co.*, 731 F.2d 1473 (10th Cir. 1984), although we have seen that it should not include front pay. See Note 2 at p. 682. But the Tenth Circuit held that a $4.4 million award for future lost gains on stock options was properly excluded from the liquidated damages calculation. Although the court acknowledged that the stock options "were a component of [the plaintiff's] compensation package" and the dates used to calculate the award were in the past, the court reasoned that the speculative nature of the award made it more like front pay than backpay. *Greene v. Safeway Stores, Inc.*, 210 F.3d 1237 (10th Cir. 2000).

5. *Liquidated Damages and Government Employees.* The liquidated damages award is not available in federal employee ADEA actions. *See Lehman v. Nakshian*, 453 U.S. 156 (1981), and we have seen that state governments are not subject to private suit under the ADEA (or the ADA). See p. 648. However local government employers can be liable for liquidated damages under the ADEA even if they are not normally held liable for punitive damages under other federal statutes. *Cross v. N.Y. City Transit Auth.*, 417 F.3d 241, 257 (2d Cir. 2005) ("the ADEA authorizes the imposition of liquidated damages against government employers who engage in willful age discrimination").

D. ATTORNEYS' FEES

The general "American" rule as to attorneys' fees is that each side pays its own. The Civil Rights Act of 1964, however, created an exception. Section 706(k) of Title VII provides for the grant of attorneys fees:

> In any action or proceeding under this title the court, in its discretion, may allow the prevailing party, other than the Commission or the United States, a reasonable attorney's fee (including expert fees) as part of the costs, and the Commission and the United States shall be liable for costs the same as a private person.

The fee provisions for § 1981 actions, 42 U.S.C. § 1988(b), (c), and ADA actions, 42 U.S.C. § 12205, generally follow the Title VII pattern. However, the ADA provision permits the recovery of "litigation expenses" rather than "expert fees." Most surprisingly, the ADA provision permits the EEOC, as well as a court, to make a fee award. Presumably, this agency power applies in federal employee proceedings.

CHRISTIANSBURG GARMENT CO. v. EEOC
434 U.S. 412 (1978)

Justice STEWART delivered the opinion of the Court.

... The question in this case is under what circumstances an attorney's fee should be allowed when the defendant is the prevailing party in a Title VII action — a question about which the federal courts have expressed divergent views.

[In 1972, Title VII was amended to allow the EEOC to sue on behalf of complainants, including those who had a charge "pending" on the amendment's effective date. The EEOC then filed suit on behalf of a person who had received a right-to-sue letter two years earlier. The district court granted summary judgment to the employer, but refused its request for attorneys' fees against the EEOC.]

II

It is the general rule in the United States that in the absence of legislation providing otherwise, litigants must pay their own attorney's fees. Congress has provided only limited exceptions to this rule "under selected statutes granting or protecting various federal rights." Some of these statutes make fee awards mandatory for prevailing plaintiffs [citing 29 U.S.C. §216(b), governing awards in ADEA suits]; others make awards permissive but limit them to certain parties, usually prevailing plaintiffs. But many of the statutes are more flexible, authorizing the award of attorney's fees to either plaintiffs or defendants, and entrusting the effectuation of the statutory policy to the discretion of the district courts. Section 706(k) of Title VII of the Civil Rights Act of 1964 falls into this last category, providing as it does that a district court may in its discretion allow an attorney's fee to the prevailing party.

In *Newman v. Piggie Park Enterprises*, 390 U.S. 400 (1968), the Court considered a substantially identical statute authorizing the award of attorney's fees under Title II of the Civil Rights Act of 1964. In that case the plaintiffs had prevailed, and the Court of Appeals had held that they should be awarded their attorney's fees "only to the extent that the respondents' defenses had been advanced 'for purposes of delay and not in good faith.'" We ruled that this "subjective standard" did not properly effectuate the purposes of the counsel-fee provision of Title II. Relying primarily on the intent of Congress to cast a Title II plaintiff in the role of "a 'private attorney general,' vindicating a policy that Congress considered of the highest priority," we held that a prevailing plaintiff under Title II "should ordinarily recover an attorney's fee unless special circumstances would render such an award unjust." We noted in passing that if the objective of Congress had been to permit the award of attorney's fees only against defendants who had acted in bad faith, "no new statutory provision would have been necessary," since even the American common-law rule allows the award of attorney's fees in those exceptional circumstances.

In *Albemarle Paper Co. v. Moody* [reproduced at p. 654], the Court made clear that the *Piggie Park* standard of awarding attorney's fees to a successful plaintiff is equally applicable in an action under Title VII of the Civil Rights Act. It can thus be taken as established, as the parties in this case both acknowledge, that under §706(k) of Title VII a prevailing *plaintiff* ordinarily is to be awarded attorney's fees in all but special circumstances.

III

The question in the case before us is what standard should inform a district court's discretion in deciding whether to award attorney's fees to a successful *defendant* in a Title VII action. . . .

. . . The terms of §706(k) provide no indication whatever of the circumstances under which either a plaintiff or a defendant should be entitled to attorney's fees.

And a moment's reflection reveals that there are at least two strong equitable considerations counseling an attorney's fee award to a prevailing Title VII plaintiff that are wholly absent in the case of a prevailing Title VII defendant.

First, as emphasized so forcefully in *Piggie Park*, the plaintiff is the chosen instrument of Congress to vindicate "a policy that Congress considered of the highest priority." Second, when a district court awards counsel fees to a prevailing plaintiff, it is awarding them against a violator of federal law. As the Court of Appeals clearly perceived, "these policy considerations which support the award of fees to a prevailing plaintiff are not present in the case of a prevailing defendant." A successful defendant seeking counsel fees under § 706(k) must rely on quite different equitable considerations.

But if the company's position is untenable, the Commission's argument also misses the mark. It seems clear, in short, that in enacting § 706(k) Congress did not intend to permit the award of attorney's fees to a prevailing defendant only in a situation where the plaintiff was motivated by bad faith in bringing the action. As pointed out in *Piggie Park*, if that had been the intent of Congress, no statutory provision would have been necessary, for it has long been established that even under the American common-law rule attorney's fees may be awarded against a party who has proceeded in bad faith. . . .

. . . The first federal appellate court to consider what criteria should govern the award of attorney's fees to a prevailing Title VII defendant was the Court of Appeals for the Third Circuit in *United States Steel Corp. v. United States*, 519 F.2d 359. There a District Court had denied a fee award to a defendant that had successfully resisted a Commission demand for documents, the court finding that the Commission's action had not been "'unfounded, meritless, frivolous or vexatiously brought.'" The Court of Appeals concluded that the District Court had not abused its discretion in denying the award. A similar standard was adopted by the Court of Appeals for the Second Circuit in *Carrion v. Yeshiva University*, 535 F.2d 722. In upholding an attorney's fee award to a successful defendant, that court stated that such awards should be permitted "not routinely, not simply because he succeeds, but only where the action brought is found to be unreasonable, frivolous, meritless or vexatious."

To the extent that abstract words can deal with concrete cases, we think that the concept embodied in the language adopted by these two Courts of Appeals is correct. We would qualify their words only by pointing out that the term "meritless" is to be understood as meaning groundless or without foundation, rather than simply that the plaintiff has ultimately lost his case, and that the term "vexatious" in no way implies that the plaintiff's subjective bad faith is a necessary prerequisite to a fee award against him. In sum, a district court may in its discretion award attorney's fees to a prevailing defendant in a Title VII case upon a finding that the plaintiff's action was frivolous, unreasonable, or without foundation, even though not brought in subjective bad faith.

In applying these criteria, it is important that a district court resist the understandable temptation to engage in post hoc reasoning by concluding that, because a plaintiff did not ultimately prevail, his action must have been unreasonable or without foundation. This kind of hindsight logic could discourage all but the most airtight claims, for seldom can a prospective plaintiff be sure of ultimate success. No matter how honest one's belief that he has been the victim of discrimination, no matter how meritorious one's claim may appear at the outset, the course of litigation is rarely predictable. Decisive facts may not emerge until discovery or trial. The law may change or clarify in the midst of litigation. Even when the law or the facts appear questionable or unfavorable at the outset, a party may have an entirely reasonable ground for bringing suit.

That §706(k) allows fee awards only to *prevailing* private plaintiffs should assure that this statutory provision will not in itself operate as an incentive to the bringing of claims that have little chance of success. To take the further step of assessing attorney's fees against plaintiffs simply because they do not finally prevail would substantially add to the risks inhering in most litigation and would undercut the efforts of Congress to promote the vigorous enforcement of the provisions of Title VII. Hence, a plaintiff should not be assessed his opponent's attorney's fees unless a court finds that his claim was frivolous, unreasonable, or groundless, or that the plaintiff continued to litigate after it clearly became so. And, needless to say, if a plaintiff is found to have brought or continued such a claim in *bad faith*, there will be an even stronger basis for charging him with the attorney's fees incurred by the defense.

IV

In denying attorney's fees to the company in this case, the District Court focused on the standards we have discussed. The court found that "the Commission's action in bringing the suit cannot be characterized as unreasonable or meritless" because "the basis upon which petitioner prevailed was an issue of first impression requiring judicial resolution" and because the "Commission's statutory interpretation of . . . the 1972 amendments was not frivolous." The court thus exercised its discretion squarely within the permissible bounds of §706(k). . . .

NOTES

1. *Different Standards for "Prevailing" Parties.* The Court says that attorney's fees should be awarded to a prevailing defendant in a Title VII case only upon a finding that the plaintiff's action was "frivolous, unreasonable, or without foundation, even though not brought in subjective bad faith." This standard is not appreciably different from the general rules of civil litigation in the federal courts. See Rule 11, FRCP. Is the Court failing to give the plain meaning to §706(k)'s use of the words "prevailing party?" Do you agree with the Court that plaintiffs, as "private attorneys general" with a special role in protecting civil rights against violators of federal law, is a sufficient justification for differentiating between the standards for attorneys fees for prevailing plaintiffs versus prevailing defendants?

2. *When Is a Prevailing Defendant Entitled to Attorneys Fees?* Several factors determine whether a prevailing defendant is entitled to a fee award under the frivolous, unreasonable, or groundless standard: while stressing the fact-intensive nature of the inquiry, one court thought that factors to be considered included at least "(1) whether the plaintiff established a prima facie case; (2) whether the defendant offered to settle; and (3) whether the trial court dismissed the case prior to trial or held a full-blown trial on the merits." *EEOC v. L.B. Foster Co.*, 123 F.3d 746, 751 (3d Cir. 1997) (quoting *Sullivan v. School Bd.*, 773 F.2d 1182, 1189 (11th Cir. 1985)). However, awarding fees because of the failure of a plaintiff to prove pretext

was an abuse of discretion. *Quintana v. Jenne*, 414 F.3d 1306, 1311 (11th Cir. 2005) *See also Balmer v. HCA, Inc.*, 423 F.3d 606 (6th Cir. 2005) (attorneys' fees may not be awarded to defendant where plaintiff has asserted at least one non-frivolous claim).

3. *When Does a Party Prevail?* Under the fee provisions, only a "prevailing party" is eligible for a fee award. After the meaning of this term had produced conflicting views, the Supreme Court attempted to clarify the matter in *Farrar v. Hobby*, 506 U.S. 103 (1992). The precise issue was whether a plaintiff who had recovered only nominal damages in a §1983 action was the "prevailing party." After reviewing its previous decisions, the Court said:

> [T]o qualify as a prevailing party, a civil rights plaintiff must obtain at least some relief on the merits of his claim. The plaintiff must obtain an enforceable judgment against the defendant from whom fees are sought, or comparable relief through a consent decree or settlement. Whatever relief the plaintiff secures must directly benefit him at the time of the judgment or settlement. . . . Only under these circumstances can civil rights litigation effect "the material alteration of the legal relationship of the parties" and thereby transform the plaintiff into a prevailing party. In short, a plaintiff "prevails" when actual relief on the merits of his claim materially alters the legal relationship between the parties by modifying the defendant's behavior in a way that directly benefits the plaintiff.

Id. at 111. Later in the opinion, the Court commented, "No material alteration of the legal relationship . . . occurs until the plaintiff becomes entitled to enforce a judgment, consent decree, or settlement against the defendant." *Id.* at 114. The Court then held that the instant plaintiff was the "prevailing party" because he could enforce the nominal damages award. In a recent case, the Seventh Circuit held that a court order requiring defendant to destroy the test results of an illegally administered test made plaintiff a prevailing party: "It is a close question, but we are convinced that the value of the destruction of the test results is at least as great as the $1 in nominal damages which made the plaintiff in *Farrar* a prevailing party." *Karraker v. Rent-A-Center, Inc.*, 492 F.3d 896, 898 (7th Cir. 2007)

4. *Rule 68.* The prevailing party question can be influenced by the operation of Rule 68, under which a defendant may make an offer of judgment. If that offer is not accepted and the plaintiff does not ultimately recover a "more favorable" judgment, the plaintiff is liable for any further costs of the defendant, *Pittari v. Am. Eagle Airlines, Inc.*, 468 F.3d 1056 (8th Cir. 2006), and, of course, cannot recover attorneys fees or other costs incurred after the offer of judgment. Application of Rule 68, however, sometimes requires valuing ·nonmonetary relief obtained in the final judgment in order to determine whether it is "more favorable than the offer." *Reiter v. MTA N.Y. City Transit Auth.*, 457 F.3d 224 (2d Cir. 2006) (equitable relief had substantial value). *See generally* Harold S. Lewis, Jr. & Thomas A. Eaton, *Revitalizing FRCP 68: Can Offers of Judgment Provide Adequate Incentives for Fair, Early Settlement of Fee-Recovery Cases?*, 57 MERCER L. REV. 791 (2006). In any event, a defendant who makes an offer of judgment does not become a "prevailing party" for purposes of the award of attorneys' fees merely because plaintiff ultimately obtains a lower judgment. *See Payne v. Milwaukee County*, 288 F.3d 1021 (7th Cir. 2002).

BUCKHANNON BOARD & CARE HOME, INC. v. WEST
VIRGINIA DEPARTMENT OF HEALTH &
HUMAN RESOURCES
532 U.S. 598 (2001)

Chief Justice REHNQUIST delivered the opinion of the Court.

Numerous federal statutes allow courts to award attorney's fees and costs to the "prevailing party." The question presented here is whether this term includes a party that has failed to secure a judgment on the merits or a court-ordered consent decree, but has nonetheless achieved the desired result because the lawsuit brought about a voluntary change in the defendant's conduct. We hold that it does not.

Buckhannon Board and Care Home, Inc., which operates care homes that provide assisted living to their residents, failed an inspection by the West Virginia Office of the State Fire Marshal because some of the residents were incapable of "self-preservation" as defined under state law. [Buckhannon and other petitioners brought suit], seeking declaratory and injunctive relief that the "self-preservation" requirement violated the Fair Housing Amendments Act of 1988 (FHAA) and the Americans with Disabilities Act of 1990 (ADA).

. . . In 1998, the West Virginia Legislature enacted two bills eliminating the "self-preservation" requirement, and respondents moved to dismiss the case as moot. The District Court granted the motion. . . .

Petitioners requested attorney's fees as the "prevailing party" under the FHAA, 42 U.S.C. § 3613(c)(2) ("[T]he court, in its discretion, may allow the prevailing party . . . a reasonable attorney's fee and costs"), and ADA, 42 U.S.C. § 12205 ("[T]he court . . . , in its discretion, may allow the prevailing party . . . a reasonable attorney's fee, including litigation expenses, and costs"). Petitioners argued that they were entitled to attorney's fees under the "catalyst theory," which posits that a plaintiff is a "prevailing party" if it achieves the desired result because the lawsuit brought about a voluntary change in the defendant's conduct. Although most Courts of Appeals recognize the "catalyst theory," the Court of Appeals for the Fourth Circuit [has] rejected it. . . . The District Court accordingly denied the motion. . . .

In the United States, parties are ordinarily required to bear their own attorney's fees — the prevailing party is not entitled to collect from the loser. Under this "American Rule," we follow "a general practice of not awarding fees to a prevailing party absent explicit statutory authority." Congress, however, has authorized the award of attorney's fees to the "prevailing party" in numerous statutes in addition to those at issue here, such as the Civil Rights Act of 1964, the Voting Rights Act Amendments of 1975, and the Civil Rights Attorney's Fees Awards Act of 1976.[4]

In designating those parties eligible for an award of litigation costs, Congress employed the term "prevailing party," a legal term of art. Black's Law Dictionary 1145 (7th ed. 1999) defines "prevailing party" as "[a] party in whose favor a judgment is rendered, regardless of the amount of damages awarded. — Also termed successful party." This view that a "prevailing party" is one who has been awarded some relief by the court can be distilled from our prior cases.

In *Hanrahan v. Hampton*, 446 U.S. 754, 758 (1980) (per curiam), we reviewed the legislative history of § 1988 and found that "Congress intended to permit the interim award of counsel fees only when a party has prevailed on the merits of at least some

---

4. We have interpreted these fee-shifting provisions consistently, and so approach the nearly identical provisions at issue here.

of his claims." . . . We have held that even an award of nominal damages suffices under this test.

In addition to judgments on the merits, we have held that settlement agreements enforced through a consent decree may serve as the basis for an award of attorney's fees. Although a consent decree does not always include an admission of liability by the defendant, it nonetheless is a court-ordered "chang[e] [in] the legal relationship between [the plaintiff] and the defendant."[7]

These decisions, taken together, establish that enforceable judgments on the merits and court-ordered consent decrees create the "material alteration of the legal relationship of the parties" necessary to permit an award of attorney's fees.

We think, however, the "catalyst theory" falls on the other side of the line from these examples. It allows an award where there is no judicially sanctioned change in the legal relationship of the parties. Even under a limited form of the "catalyst theory," a plaintiff could recover attorney's fees if it established that the "complaint had sufficient merit to withstand a motion to dismiss for lack of jurisdiction or failure to state a claim on which relief may be granted." This is not the type of legal merit that our prior decisions, based upon plain language and congressional intent, have found necessary. . . . A defendant's voluntary change in conduct, although perhaps accomplishing what the plaintiff sought to achieve by the lawsuit, lacks the necessary judicial imprimatur on the change. Our precedents thus counsel against holding that the term "prevailing party" authorizes an award of attorney's fees without a corresponding alteration in the legal relationship of the parties. . . .

Petitioners finally assert that the "catalyst theory" is necessary to prevent defendants from unilaterally mooting an action before judgment in an effort to avoid an award of attorney's fees. They also claim that the rejection of the "catalyst theory" will deter plaintiffs with meritorious but expensive cases from bringing suit. We are skeptical of these assertions, which are entirely speculative and unsupported by any empirical evidence.

Petitioners discount the disincentive that the "catalyst theory" may have upon a defendant's decision to voluntarily change its conduct, conduct that may not be illegal. "The defendants' potential liability for fees in this kind of litigation can be as significant as, and sometimes even more significant than, their potential liability on the merits," and the possibility of being assessed attorney's fees may well deter a defendant from altering its conduct.

And petitioners' fear of mischievous defendants only materializes in claims for equitable relief, for so long as the plaintiff has a cause of action for damages, a defendant's change in conduct will not moot the case. Even then, it is not clear how often courts will find a case mooted: "It is well settled that a defendant's voluntary cessation of a challenged practice does not deprive a federal court of its power to determine the legality of the practice" unless it is "absolutely clear that the allegedly wrongful behavior could not reasonably be expected to recur." If a case is not found to be moot, and the plaintiff later procures an enforceable judgment, the court may of course award attorney's fees. Given this possibility, a defendant has a strong incentive to enter a settlement agreement, where it can negotiate attorney's fees and costs.

---

7. . . . Private settlements do not entail the judicial approval and oversight involved in consent decrees. And federal jurisdiction to enforce a private contractual settlement will often be lacking unless the terms of the agreement are incorporated into the order of dismissal.

We have also stated that "[a] request for attorney's fees should not result in a second major litigation," and have accordingly avoided an interpretation of the fee-shifting statutes that would have "spawn[ed] a second litigation of significant dimension." Among other things, a "catalyst theory" hearing would require analysis of the defendant's subjective motivations in changing its conduct, an analysis that "will likely depend on a highly factbound inquiry and may turn on reasonable inferences from the nature and timing of the defendant's change in conduct." Although we do not doubt the ability of district courts to perform the nuanced "three thresholds" test required by the "catalyst theory" — whether the claim was colorable rather than groundless; whether the lawsuit was a substantial rather than an insubstantial cause of the defendant's change in conduct; whether the defendant's change in conduct was motivated by the plaintiff's threat of victory rather than threat of expense, it is clearly not a formula for "ready administrability."

Given the clear meaning of "prevailing party" in the fee-shifting statutes, we need not determine which way these various policy arguments cut. . . .

Justice SCALIA, with whom Justice THOMAS joins, concurring.

. . . As the dissent would have it, by giving the term its normal meaning the Court today approves the practice of denying attorney's fees to a plaintiff with a proven claim of discrimination, simply because the very merit of his claim led the defendant to capitulate before judgment. That is not the case. To the contrary, the Court approves the result in *Parham v. Southwestern Bell Tel. Co.*, 433 F.2d 421 (8th Cir. 1970), where attorney's fees were awarded "after [a] finding that the defendant had acted unlawfully." What the dissent's stretching of the term produces is something more, and something far less reasonable: an award of attorney's fees when the merits of plaintiff's case remain unresolved — when, for all one knows, the defendant only "abandon[ed] the fray" because the cost of litigation — either financial or in terms of public relations — would be too great. . . .

It could be argued, perhaps, that insofar as abstract justice is concerned, there is little to choose between the dissent's outcome and the Court's: If the former sometimes rewards the plaintiff with a phony claim (there is no way of knowing), the latter sometimes denies fees to the plaintiff with a solid case whose adversary slinks away on the eve of judgment. But it seems to me the evil of the former far outweighs the evil of the latter. There is all the difference in the world between a rule that denies the extraordinary boon of attorney's fees to some plaintiffs who are no less "deserving" of them than others who receive them, and a rule that causes the law to be the very instrument of wrong — exacting the payment of attorney's fees to the extortionist. . . .

Justice GINSBURG, with whom Justice STEVENS, Justice SOUTER, and Justice BREYER join, dissenting.

The Court today holds that a plaintiff whose suit prompts the precise relief she seeks does not "prevail," and hence cannot obtain an award of attorney's fees, unless she also secures a court entry memorializing her victory. The entry need not be a judgment on the merits. Nor need there be any finding of wrongdoing. A court-approved settlement will do.

The Court's insistence that there be a document filed in court — a litigated judgment or court-endorsed settlement — upsets long-prevailing Circuit precedent applicable to scores of federal fee-shifting statutes. The decision allows a defendant to escape a statutory obligation to pay a plaintiff's counsel fees, even though the suit's merit led the defendant to abandon the fray, to switch rather than fight on, to accord plaintiff sooner rather than later the principal redress sought in the complaint. Concomitantly, the Court's constricted definition of "prevailing party," and consequent rejection of the "catalyst theory," impede access to court for the less well-heeled, and shrink the incentive Congress created for the enforcement of federal law by private attorneys general. . . .

A lawsuit's ultimate purpose is to achieve actual relief from an opponent. Favorable judgment may be instrumental in gaining that relief. Generally, however, "the judicial decree is not the end but the means. At the end of the rainbow lies not a judgment, but some action (or cessation of action) by the defendant. . . . " On this common understanding, if a party reaches the "sought-after destination," then the party "prevails" regardless of the "route taken."

Under a fair reading of the FHAA and ADA provisions in point, I would hold that a party "prevails" in "a true and proper sense" when she achieves, by instituting litigation, the practical relief sought in her complaint. The Court misreads Congress, as I see it, by insisting that, invariably, relief must be displayed in a judgment, and correspondingly that a defendant's voluntary action never suffices. In this case, Buckhannon's purpose in suing West Virginia officials was not narrowly to obtain a judge's approbation. The plaintiffs' objective was to stop enforcement of a rule requiring Buckhannon to evict residents like centenarian Dorsey Pierce as the price of remaining in business. If Buckhannon achieved that objective on account of the strength of its case — if it succeeded in keeping its doors open while housing and caring for Ms. Pierce and others similarly situated — then Buckhannon is properly judged a party who prevailed. . . .

[The dissent then cited Senate and House Reports for the 1976 Civil Rights Attorney's Fees Awards Act, which contemplated attorney fee awards even when no formal relief was obtained.]

NOTES

1. *What's a "Material" Alteration of the Parties' "Legal Relationship"?* The Court held that "prevailing party" status is established where a party obtains an "enforceable judgment on the merits" or a "court-ordered consent decree" that results in a "material alteration of the legal relationship of the parties." This can be seen as imposing two separate requirements. The first is formal, but the second is substantive. Oddly enough, the formal aspect may be less difficult to establish. Justices Scalia and Thomas seem to indicate that prevailing party status can be established by a finding that the defendant discriminated. Is a plaintiff who obtains a declaratory judgment a "prevailing party?" But the district court dismissed plaintiffs' case as moot even though they asked for declaratory relief. Could plaintiffs have avoided the problem by seeking damages, even nominal damages? *See also Richard v. Dep't of Developmental Servs.*, 317 F.3d 1080 (9th Cir. 2003) (legally enforceable settlement agreement sufficient to make plaintiffs prevailing parties).

As for a material alteration, the Supreme Court has held that a plaintiff who obtains a preliminary injunction but is denied a permanent injunction, has not materially altered the legal relationship: it has won the battle but lost the war. *Sole v. Wyner*, 127 S. Ct. 2188, 2197 (2007). Note, however, that in *Wyner* the court had ultimately denied a permanent injunction. In many, perhaps most, cases, the grant of a preliminary injunction is the functional end of the proceedings, and it seems likely that its award in such cases makes plaintiff a prevailing party. *See Watson v.*

County of Riverside, 300 F.3d 1092 (9th Cir. 2002). (holding that a plaintiff who wins a preliminary injunction can be qualified as a "prevailing party"). *But see John T. v. Del. County Intermediate Unit,* 318 F.3d 545 (3d Cir. 2003) (IDEA suit).

2. *Will the "Bright Line" Rule Have Much Impact?* Will rejection of the "catalyst theory" have much impact on the availability of fee awards in private employment discrimination litigation? An employer's change in conduct will not moot a case in which the plaintiff has a viable claim for injunctive relief, backpay, compensatory damages, punitive damages, or nominal damages. Perhaps the greatest potential impact will be in those actions against a state in which the Eleventh Amendment precludes relief other than a prohibitory injunction.

3. *Which Incentive Works Best to Advance Civil Rights?* On one hand, giving the employer the incentive of avoiding an attorneys' fee award by giving the plaintiff what she wants might increase the chances that the employer would make the changes voluntarily. On the other hand, the prospect of full remedies, including an award of attorneys' fees, is also a strong incentive to employers to take action. Does the "catalyst" theory make employers more or less likely to improve their practices? *See* Catherine R. Albiston & Laura Beth Nielsen, *The Procedural Attack on Civil Rights: The Empirical Reality of* Buckhannon fo*r the Private Attorney General,* 54 UCLA L. REV. 1087, 1088 (2007) (survey evidence shows that "*Buckhannon* encourages 'strategic capitulation,' makes settlement more difficult, and discourages both public interest organizations and private counsel from taking on enforcement actions").

ARBOR HILL CONCERNED CITIZENS NEIGHBORHOOD ASS'N v. COUNTY OF ALBANY
484 F.3d 162 (2d Cir. 2007)

WALKER, Circuit Judge.

In this appeal from the district court's disposition of their motion for an award of attorney's fees, plaintiffs-appellants ("plaintiffs"), who prevailed in a suit brought under the Voting Rights Act of 1965 ("VRA"), seek a recalculation of the amount that they may recoup. The fee-historically known as the "lodestar" — to which their attorneys are presumptively entitled is the product of hours worked and an hourly rate. Plaintiffs argue that the district court applied an unnecessarily strict "forum rule": The district court, they contend, required them to show extraordinary special circumstances before it would use in its "lodestar" calculation an hourly rate greater than the hourly rate charged by attorneys in the district where the district court sits.

We agree that the district court may have applied the forum rule in too unyielding a fashion. We therefore clarify its proper application in this circuit: While the district court should generally use the prevailing hourly rate in the district where it sits to calculate what has been called the "lodestar" — what we think is more aptly termed the "presumptively reasonable fee" — the district court may adjust this base hourly rate to account for a plaintiff's reasonable decision to retain out-of-district counsel, just as it may adjust the base hourly rate to account for other case-specific variables.

Moreover, this dispute concerning the "forum rule" is but a symptom of a more serious illness: Our fee-setting jurisprudence has become needlessly confused — it has come untethered from the free market it is meant to approximate. We therefore suggest that the district court consider, in setting the reasonable hourly rate it uses to calculate the "lodestar," what a reasonable, paying client would be willing to pay, not just in deciding whether to use an out-of-district hourly rate in its fee calculation. A plaintiff bringing suit under the Voting Rights Act, pursuant to which fees can be recovered from the other side, has little incentive to negotiate a rate structure with his attorney prior to the litigation; the district court must act later to ensure that the attorney does not recoup fees that the market would not otherwise bear. Indeed, the district court (unfortunately) bears the burden of disciplining the market, stepping into the shoes of the reasonable, paying client, who wishes to pay the least amount necessary to litigate the case effectively.

Bearing these background principles in mind, the district court should, in determining what a reasonable, paying client would be willing to pay, consider factors including, but not limited to, the complexity and difficulty of the case, the available expertise and capacity of the client's other counsel (if any), the resources required to prosecute the case effectively (taking account of the resources being marshaled on the other side but not endorsing scorched earth tactics), the timing demands of the case, whether the attorney had an interest (independent of that of his client) in achieving the ends of the litigation or initiated the representation himself, whether the attorney was initially acting *pro bono* (such that a client might be aware that the attorney expected low or non-existent remuneration), and other returns (such as reputation, etc.) the attorney expected from the representation.

Although we clarify the application of the forum rule, we affirm the judgment of the district court in this case. It is clear that the district court would adhere to its fee award were we to vacate the district court's judgment and remand for reconsideration. Indeed, we believe that a reasonable, paying resident of Albany would have made a greater effort to retain an attorney practicing in the Northern District of New York, whether in Syracuse, Binghamton, Utica, or Kingston, than did plaintiffs. The rates charged by attorneys practicing in the Southern District of New York would simply have been too high for a thrifty, hypothetical client — at least in comparison to the rates charged by local attorneys, with which he would have been familiar. . . .

During the course of this litigation, three entities have rendered legal services to the plaintiffs: (1) the Albany law firm of DerOhannesian & DerOhannesian ("D&D"), as local counsel; (2) the Washington, D.C.-based non-profit Lawyer's Committee for Civil Rights Under Law ("LCCRUL"), selected for its voting rights expertise; and (3) the Manhattan law firm of Gibson, Dunn & Crutcher ("Gibson Dunn"), chosen because of the firm's practice before the Second Circuit and the firm's "muscle," specifically, its ability to quickly prepare the appeal on an abbreviated briefing schedule.

Gibson Dunn sought in the district court to recoup attorney's fees calculated on the basis of the hourly rate charged by most attorneys in the Southern District of New York (and the hourly rate usually charged by Gibson Dunn).

[The court traced the history of methodologies for calculating reasonable attorney's fees after the 1976 Civil Rights Attorney's Fees Awards Act. One method, devised by Third Circuit in *Lindy Bros., Builders, Inc. v. Am. Radiator & Standard Sanitary Corp.*, 487 F.2d 161 (3d Cir. 1973), was to compute a "lodestar," which was the product of the attorney's usual hourly rate and the number of hours worked, and then adjust that lodestar based on case-specific considerations. *See Hensley v. Eckerhart*, 461 U.S. 424, 429-30 & n. 3 (1983). The second method was announced in *Johnson v. Ga. Highway Express, Inc.*, 488 F.2d 714 (5th Cir. 1974), and required a twelve factor analysis ranging over almost any conceivable factor that might influence fees. In theory,] a district court that adopted the lodestar method was expected to consider fewer variables than a district court utilizing the *Johnson* method. In practice, however, both considered substantially the same set of variables — just at a different point in the fee-calculation process. A district court using the lodestar method would set the lodestar *and then* consider whether, in light of variables such as the difficulty of the case, it should adjust the lodestar before settling on the reasonable fee it was ultimately inclined to award. By contrast, a district court employing the *Johnson* method would consider factors, such as the difficulty of the case, earlier in the fee-calculation process by weighing them in setting its tentative reasonable fee, from which there would seldom be a need to depart.

The Supreme Court adopted the lodestar method in principle, *see Hensley*; *Blum v. Stenson*, 465 U.S. 886 (1984), without, however, fully abandoning the *Johnson* method. Rather than using the attorney's own billing rate to calculate the lodestar and then examining the lodestar in light of case-specific variables to ensure that it was in fact a reasonable fee, . . . the Supreme Court instructed district courts to use a *reasonable hourly rate* — which it directed that district courts set in light of the *Johnson* factors — in calculating what it continued to refer to as the lodestar. The Supreme Court collapsed what had once been a two-step inquiry into a single-step inquiry; it shifted district courts' focus from the reasonableness of the lodestar to the reasonableness of the hourly rate used in calculating the lodestar, which in turn became the *de facto* reasonable fee.

But the Supreme Court's emphasis on the Third Circuit's economic model, and its simultaneous invocation of the equitable *Johnson* factors at an early stage of the fee-calculation process, proved to be in tension, *see Blum* ("We recognize, of course, that determining an appropriate 'market rate' for the services of a lawyer is inherently difficult . . . [since m]arket prices . . . are determined by supply and demand"). While the Third Circuit had expected district courts to correct for market dysfunction, the Supreme Court now asked district court judges to *hypothesize* that market on the basis of their experience as lawyers within their districts and on the basis of affidavits provided by the parties. Generally speaking, the rates an attorney routinely charges are those that the market will bear; yet the Supreme Court required that the district courts conjure a different, "reasonable" hourly rate.

The net result of the fee-setting jurisprudence here and in the Supreme Court is that the district courts must engage in an equitable inquiry of varying methodology while making a pretense of mathematical precision. The "lodestar" is no longer a lodestar in the true sense of the word — "a star that leads," *Webster's Third International Dictionary* 1329 (1981). Nor do courts use it in the way the term was first used by the Third Circuit as a base amount that is susceptible of ready adjustment; rather, circuit court deference to the district court's estimate of a "reasonable" hourly rate is a "lodestar" only in the sense that it is a guiding jurisprudential principle. What the district courts in this circuit produce is in effect not a lodestar as originally conceived, but rather a "presumptively reasonable fee." The focus of the district courts is no longer on calculating a reasonable *fee*, but rather on setting a reasonable *hourly rate*, taking account of all case-specific variables. . . .

The meaning of the term "lodestar" has shifted over time, and its value as a metaphor has deteriorated to the point of unhelpfulness. This opinion abandons its use. We think the better course — and the one most consistent with attorney's fees jurisprudence — is for the district court, in exercising its considerable discretion, to bear in mind *all* of the case-specific variables that we and other courts have identified as relevant to the reasonableness of attorney's fees in setting a reasonable hourly rate. The reasonable hourly rate is the rate a paying client would be willing to pay. In determining what rate a paying client would be willing to pay, the district court should consider, among others, the *Johnson* factors[1]; it should also bear in mind that a reasonable, paying client wishes to spend the minimum necessary to litigate the case effectively. The district court should also consider that such an individual might be able to negotiate with his or her attorneys, using their desire to obtain the reputational benefits that might accrue from being associated with the case. The district court should then use that reasonable hourly rate to calculate what can properly be termed the "presumptively reasonable fee." . . .

We now clarify that a district court may use an out-of-district hourly rate — or some rate in between the out-of-district rate sought and the rates charged by local attorneys — in calculating the presumptively reasonable fee if it is clear that a reasonable, paying client would have paid those higher rates. We presume, however, that a reasonable, paying client would in most cases hire counsel from within his district, or at least counsel whose rates are consistent with those charged locally. This presumption may be rebutted — albeit only in the unusual case — if the party wishing the district court to use a higher rate demonstrates that his or her retention of an out-of-district attorney was reasonable under the circumstances as they would be reckoned by a client paying the attorney's bill. . . .

[Although the district court applied the local forum rule too strictly, the resulting fee was not erroneous.] We are confident that a reasonable, paying client would have known that law firms undertaking representation such as that of plaintiffs often obtain considerable non-monetary returns — in experience, reputation, or achievement of the attorneys' own interests and agendas — and would have insisted on paying his attorneys at a rate no higher than that charged by Albany attorneys. . . .

NOTES

1. *The Reasonable Client Standard.* The *Arbor Hills* court does an excellent job of reviewing the somewhat tangled history of methodologies of calculating attorneys' fees in civil rights cases, which include the employment discrimination laws. But its ultimate synthesis is a dramatic departure from prior methods, at least in theory. For *Arbor Hills*, the critical factor is what a paying client would pay, and the other methods were merely different ways of coming at that ultimate issue. This principle has a deceptive appeal, but there is a fundamental flaw. Certainly when discounted by the possibility of losing, the monetary claims of employment discrimination plaintiffs — backpay, front pay, compensatory and punitive damages — are often too low to induce an attorney to take a case on a contingency fee arrangement. That can't mean that attorneys' fees are not available if a reasonable client would forego the claim absent the prospect of an attorneys' fees award.

But if it doesn't mean that, does the *Arbor Hills* touchstone make any sense? One possibility is that the court was trying to focus on what a cost-conscious client would do if she had decided to bring suit. But even that formulation is problematic. After

---

1. The twelve *Johnson* factors are: (1) the time and labor required; (2) the novelty and difficulty of the questions; (3) the level of skill required to perform the legal service properly; (4) the preclusion of employment by the attorney due to acceptance of the case; (5) the attorney's customary hourly rate; (6) whether the fee is fixed or contingent; (7) the time limitations imposed by the client or the circumstances; (8) the amount involved in the case and the results obtained; (9) the experience, reputation, and ability of the attorneys; (10) the "undesirability" of the case; (11) the nature and length of the professional relationship with the client; and (12) awards in similar cases. *Johnson*.

all, even a cost-conscious client might spend more to enhance her chances of winning. Isn't that what Gibson Dunn's "muscle" meant?

2. *Balance Billing.* Even before *Arbor Hills*, the prospect of the recovery of an attorneys' fee award was often insufficient to attract lawyers to take employment discrimination cases. In *Venegas v. Mitchell*, 495 U.S. 82 (1990), the Supreme Court held that a fee award did not invalidate a contingent-fee contract that entitled the attorney to a larger amount. The Court found nothing in the text or legislative history of §1988 that suggested otherwise. Moreover, "depriving plaintiffs of the option of promising to pay more than the statutory fee if that is necessary to secure counsel of their choice would not further §1988's general purpose of enabling such plaintiffs in civil rights cases to secure competent counsel." *Id.* at 89. *See also Gobert v. Williams*, 323 F.3d 1099, 1100 (5th Cir. 2003) (Title VII does not "regulate what plaintiffs may or may not promise to pay their attorneys if they lose or if they win").

3. *Why Did Congress Create a Right to Attorneys Fees?* In providing that the prevailing party could recover attorneys' fees, Congress wanted to make private enforcement of the Civil Rights Act possible. Remember the language in *Christianburg Garment* quoting the landmark *Newman v. Piggie Park* decision that broad recovery of attorneys fees was based "primarily on the intent of Congress to cast a Title II plaintiff in the role of a 'private attorney general' vindicat[ing] a policy that Congress considered of the highest priority." To say it another way, Congress decided that virtue being its own reward was insufficient motivation to trigger real enforcement of the Civil Rights Act. Judge Walker seems to agree, although he frames the issue in more economic terms: Congress wanted to overcome a market deficiency by providing a right to attorneys' fees because otherwise attorneys would not bring these kinds of cases. Is there any difference between these two perspectives.

4. *Glory Its Own Reward?* Perhaps the most disturbing aspect of *Arbor Hills* is not its enshrining of the reasonable client standard but its suggestion that the reasonable client would trade on attorney incentives to take civil rights cases. By definition, this will not often operate in commercial litigation, although even there an occasional case might be viewed as a "loss leader" by a firm. Nevertheless, the effect of throwing this consideration onto the scales is to tend to depress attorney fee awards in civil rights cases. Does using the court to bring discipline to the market undermine the intent of Congress? Does *Arbor Hills* take us back to having virtue (or maybe glory) be its own reward? Is the court taking advantage of the expansion of pro bono work to reduce the compensation lawyers can expect to recover for work that is not taken on a pro bono basis?

5. *Few "Special Circumstances."* The good news for plaintiff is that courts have rejected most arguments that "special circumstances" require the denial of a fee award to a prevailing plaintiff. *E.g., Saski v. Class*, 92 F.3d 232 (4th Cir. 1996) (generous damages recovered); *Love v. Mayor of Cheyenne*, 620 F.2d 235 (10th Cir. 1980) (defendant's good faith); *Int'l Soc'y for Krishna Consciousness, Inc. v. Collins*, 609 F.2d 151 (5th Cir. 1980) (plaintiff's ability to pay). In *New York Gaslight Club, Inc. v. Carey*, 447 U.S. 54 (1980), the Supreme Court found no special circumstances where the plaintiff had been represented by a "public interest group" and was eligible for limited assistance by a state attorney. Where special circumstances have been found, several factors were usually present, such as the defendant's extraordinary good faith, the adverse effect of the award on innocent third persons, and the questionable conduct of the plaintiff. *E.g., Walker v. NationsBank of Fla., N.A.*, 53 F.3d 1548 (11th Cir. 1995). *See also Lewis v. Kendrick*, 944 F.2d 949 (1st Cir. 1991) (fee award denied because plaintiff had greatly exaggerated her injuries and had

failed to reduce the amount of her fee request to reflect her very limited recovery ($1,000) at trial).

6. *The Legal Work That Counts.* A fee award includes the attorney's services for every stage in the enforcement scheme. In a Title VII action, for example, these stages may include: arbitration, *Keenan v. City of Phila.*, 983 F.2d 459 (3d Cir. 1992); the proceeding before a state agency, *New York Gaslight Club, Inc. v. Carey*, 447 U.S. 54 (1980); the taking of a successful appeal, *Morrow v. Dillard*, 580 F.2d 1284 (5th Cir. 1978); postjudgment monitoring of the decree, *Pennsylvania v. Delaware Valley Citizens' Council for Clean Air*, 478 U.S. 546 (1986); *Johnson v. City of Tulsa*, 489 F.3d 1089 (10th Cir. 2007) (prevailing party in a class-action may be entitled to attorney fees for post-consent-decree monitoring even if no court order resulted); and even the hearing to establish the propriety and amount of the fee award, *Davis v. City and County of San Francisco*, 976 F.2d 1536 (9th Cir. 1992).

7. *Attorneys Fees in §703(m) Cases.* As we saw in Chapter 1, when a plaintiff demonstrates that race, sex, etc. was "a motivating factor" in an employer's action, liability is established and plaintiff is entitled to attorneys fees, even if the defendant is successful in proving it would have made the same decision "in the absence of the impermissible motivating factor." Section 706(g)(2)(B)(i) provides that the court "may grant declaratory relief, injunctive relief . . . and attorney's fees and costs demonstrated to be directly attributable only to the pursuit of a claim under section 703(m)" but "(ii) shall not award damages or issue an order requiring any admission, reinstatement, hiring, promotion, or payment [of compensatory or punitive damages]." A fee award under this provision turns on such factors as whether the plaintiff obtained injunctive or declaratory relief, the public interest in the litigation, and the conduct of the parties. *Canup v. Chipman-Union, Inc.*, 123 F.3d 1440 (11th Cir. 1997); *Sheppard v. Riverview Nursing Ctr., Inc.*, 88 F.3d 1332 (4th Cir. 1996). *But see Gudenkauf v. Stauffer Commc'n, Inc.*, 158 F.3d 1074 (10th Cir. 1998) (attorneys' fees awarded at discretion of court, even when plaintiff did not recover damages). Thus, the standards for making a fee award under §706(k) are inapplicable, although the amount of the award should be calculated in the same way.

8. *Advisory Jury Determination.* When a case involving compensatory or punitive damages is tried to a jury, the jury frequently plays an advisory role in determining equitable relief such as backpay and front pay. Since attorneys fees are part of that package of equitable remedies provided in §706, should the jury be asked its advice as to that? *Cf. Collins v. Alco Parking Corp.*, 448 F.3d 652 (3d Cir. 2006) (not deciding whether it was error to instruct the jury that attorneys fees would be awarded above and beyond any damages the jury gave but determining it was not "plain error" warranting correction without an objection).

9. *The Take-Away.* Many believe that the crisis in employment discrimination law is not that plaintiffs' attorneys are getting rich at the expense of more or less innocent defendants. Instead, the crisis is that, even with the right to recover attorney's fees if a plaintiff prevails, all too many employment discrimination cases are not brought at all or proceed on a *pro se* basis. Even with the prospect of an attorney's fee award, these cases are still not that attractive to lawyers in comparison to other kinds of legal work they can be doing. You should keep this in mind when you consider whether and when arbitration might be a good alternative to traditional litigation. See Chapter 9. You should also realize that, at least in the class action context, attorneys' fees pose different problems. Most such cases are resolved by settlement, and the argument in that context is that plaintiffs' class attorneys are overcompensated, not undercompensated. *See generally* Myriam Gilles & Gary B. Friedman *Exploding the*

Class Action Agency Costs Myth: The Social Utility of Entrepreneurial Lawyers 2006, 155 U. PA. L. REV. 103 (2006). See p. 627.

NOTE ON TAXATION, INSURANCE, AND BANKRUPTCY

Three issues not normally considered part of the study of "remedies" can nevertheless have important implications for employment discrimination litigation and settlement. They are the taxation of recoveries, the extent of insurance coverage, and the effect of bankruptcy of the employer.

Taxation. Prior to 1996, the Internal Revenue Code, 26 U.S.C § 104(a)(2) excluded from gross income "the amount of any damages received (whether by suit or agreement . . .) on account of personal injuries or sickness." In 1996 the statute was amended to exclude only damages received on account of physical injuries or physical sickness. As a result, most employment discrimination recoveries became taxable. *See Murphy v. IRS*, 493 F.3d 170 (D.C. Cir. 2007) (upholding constitutionality of taxability of emotional distress damages). When these recoveries included attorneys' fees, which were then paid by the plaintiff to her attorney, serious problems arose for some taxpayers. If, as the Supreme Court held, the full amount of the recovery is income, some taxpayers were not able to take full advantage of deducting the payment to their attorneys because of the alternative minimum tax. *See Comm'r v. Banks*, 543 U.S. 426 (2005). This problem and other tax rules sometimes resulted in plaintiffs owing more in taxes than they recovered from the defendant! *See generally* Gregg D. Polsky, *The Contingent Attorney's Fee Tax Trap: Ethical, Fiduciary Duty, and Malpractice Implications*, 23 VA. TAX REV. 615 (2004) (discussing ethical, fiduciary duty, and malpractice implications for lawyers representing plaintiffs who may be affected by the alternative minimum tax trap).

Congress addressed this problem in the American Jobs Creation Act of 2004, Pub. L. 108-357, 118 Stat. 1418 (2004), by a provision ending the double taxation of lawyer fees. The Act amends section 62 of the Internal Revenue Code, defining adjusted gross income, to add new subsection (19), which allows successful discrimination litigants to deduct from their income taxes the attorneys' fees and court costs associated with monetary awards they receive as a result of the litigation or settlement of the claim. That means that the taxpayer does not pay taxes on attorneys' fees or court costs she wins in a discrimination case. Her attorney, however, continues to have to report the amount she receives as income. Of course, if proceeds of a settlement are taxable, the employer may legally withhold taxes from any payment. *See Rivera v. Baker West, Inc.*, 430 F.3d 1253 (9th Cir. 2005) (when the settlement proceeds were reasonably classified as backpay, they were subject to income tax withholding, even though claimant was not currently employed by company).

Insurance. Individuals and businesses shift the risk for financial losses they may incur by paying premiums to insurance carriers. Since a large discrimination claim could result in a severe financial loss for an employer, several carriers offer coverage for Title VII violations. Richard A. Bales & Julie McGhghy, *Insuring Title VII Violations*, 27 S. ILL. U.L.J. 71 (2002), outline various policies. Many insurance carriers have developed Employment Practices Liability Insurance (EPLI) policies specifically geared to employment-related practices. These policies typically cover liability arising out of the insured's employment-related offenses against its employees, *id.* at 82, including court costs. However, EPLI policies usually exclude intentional acts from coverage as against public policy. *But see Mo. Pub. Entity Risk Mgmt. Fund v. Investors Ins. Co. of Am.*, 451 F.3d 925 (8th Cir. 2006) (upholding indemnification for cost of settlement of sex harassment charges and holding that payment does not violate state public policy); *GNFH, Inc. v. W. Am. Ins. Co.*, 873 N.W.2d 345 (Ohio Ct. App. 2007) (duty to defend for sexual harassment claim not negated by public policy when some of the conduct at issue was merely negligent and even the assault charges did not implicate a specific intent crime). Under that same rationale, punitive damages are also usually excluded. Other Title VII forms of relief such as equitable or injunctive relief may be excluded because they are not deemed to be "damages." The result can be very limited coverage. Further, EPLI policies are costly, making them not common among employers. Instead employers hope that if discrimination claims do arise, courts will find coverage under the traditional general insurance policies they have purchased.

The typical General Liability policy obligates the insurer to pay damages arising from property damage or personal injury caused by a covered occurrence. *See* Francis J. Mootz III, *Insurance Coverage of Employment Discrimination Claims*, 52 U. MIAMI L. REV. 1, 10-11 (1997). However, these policies often include specific exclusions of coverage for employment discrimination claims. For example, a policy may create an obligation to pay for only "damages," as opposed to any form of equitable relief. Bales & McGhghy at 80. Employment discrimination awards often include backpay or reinstatement, which are not sums payable as damages. This provision limits the insurer's obligation to compensate employers for such equitable relief awards. A second provision, limiting coverage to "bodily injury," is intended to exclude claims of mental or reputational injury. Finally, most policies contain an exclusion for any injuries "expected or intended from the standpoint of the insured," which is aimed at excluding coverage for intentional discrimination claims. *Id.*

However, many courts have found at least some discrimination claims to be covered under these General Liability policies. Some courts protect the insured's reasonable expectations by using a broad interpretation of "bodily injury" to include emotional distress. *Id.* at 83; *Griffin v. Cameron Coll.*, 1997 U.S. Dist. LEXIS 14218, *5 (E.D. La. 1997). A broader question is whether insurance policies should cover intentional discrimination. Holding insurance companies responsible for intentional acts of their insureds would reduce the incentives for employers not to engage in those acts. However, not to require insurance carriers to cover these discrimination claims might deny compensation to the victims of discrimination when the employer went bankrupt or was otherwise unable to pay valid claims. *See* Bales & McGhghy and Mootz for a more in-depth analysis of these questions. *See also* Catherine M. Sharkey, *Revisiting the Noninsurable Costs of Accidents*, 64 Md. L. Rev. (2005) (the traditional public-policy driven debate, which focuses on whether damages are compensatory or punitive, should give way to the market-driven intentionality line, which focuses on the nature of the underlying conduct).

Bankruptcy. The question of what happens to employment discrimination claims against employers that go into bankruptcy has, surprisingly, not been much litigated. Joanne Gelfand, *The Treatment of Employment Discrimination Claims in Bankruptcy: Priority Status, Stay Relief, Dischargeability, and Exemptions*, 56 MIAMI L. REV. 601 (2002), lays out the issues that would likely arise. The first question is the priority of employment discrimination claims vis-à-vis other unsecured claims by creditors. Ms. Gelfand argues that claims that arise after the commencement of bankruptcy, as well as claims incurred during the bankruptcy case, should be treated as administrative expenses, which have the highest priority among unsecured claims. In contrast, "Back pay, front pay, and damages stemming from pre-petition acts may be eligible for priority as wages in amounts up to $4,650"; they are entitled to third priority status as long as the claims arose within ninety days of the date that the bankruptcy petition was filed. *Id.* at 621. Claims for earlier periods are paid only after all the priority claims are satisfied. Employees, however, must not sleep on their rights. *See Jaurdon v. Cricket Commc'n*, 412 F.3d 1156 (10th Cir. 2005) (appeal dismissed for Title VII claimants who failed to file proof of claim after they received formal notice from employer that it had filed for Chapter 11 protection under U.S. Bankruptcy Code).

With the filing of a bankruptcy petition, an automatic stay is imposed on all other judicial proceeding unless relief is granted for cause. "Cause" generally means that the bankruptcy court lacks jurisdiction to decide the case. Since bankruptcy courts lack jurisdiction to determine personal injury torts, the question arises whether employment discrimination claims will be treated as personal injury torts. There is a split of authority based on analogous claims as to what constitutes a personal injury tort claim. Gelfand, at 624-27.

At least as to individual debtors in bankruptcy, it is possible to except employment discrimination claims for the debtor's discharge "for willful and malicious injury by the debtor to another entity or to the property of another entity." 11 U.S.C. § 523(a)(6). The question is whether disparate treatment claims and claims of sexual and racial harassment are within the willful and malicious exception to discharge. Gelfand, at 635-38. *See Jones v. Svreck (In re Jones)*, 300 B.R. 133 (B.A.P. 1st Cir. 2003) (state agency decision that Chapter 7 debtor's sexual harassment was "willful and malicious injury" was sufficient under Bankruptcy Code for nondischarge of $125,829 in damages owed to sexual-harassment victim).

Finally, a plaintiff may be judicially estopped from pursuing a discrimination claim because of failure to reveal it as an asset in a bankruptcy filing. *See Barger v. City of Cartersville*, 348 F.3d 1289 (11th Cir. 2003) (plaintiff estopped from seeking monetary damages (although not reinstatement) from her employer because she did not fully disclose her assets to the bankruptcy court by properly notifying the court of that suit). *Cannon-Stokes v. Potter*, 453 F.3d 446 (7th Cir. 2006) (judicial estoppel foreclosed ADA claims by employee who failed to disclose pending EEOC charge in bankruptcy petition, even though her omission allegedly resulted from good-faith reliance on bankruptcy attorney's advice. *See generally* Theresa M. Beiner & Robert B. Chapman, *Take What You Can, Give Nothing Back: Judicial Estoppel, Employment Discrimination, Bankruptcy, and Piracy in the Courts*, 60 U. MIAMI L. REV. 1 (2005) (district courts should deny motions to dismiss employment discrimination actions that were not listed as assets by a plaintiff who has filed bankruptcy).

Chapter 9

MANAGING RISKS IN EMPLOYMENT
DISCRIMINATION DISPUTES

A. INTRODUCTION

The antidiscrimination laws, like other employment regulations, create enormous incentives for employers to manage the risks of liability and the costs of defending lawsuits. Perhaps the most obvious example we have seen is the Supreme Court's effort to structure sexual harassment liability for employers in order to encourage them to take steps to prevent and correct violations. See p. 384. But we have also seen more general efforts by employers to "bullet proof" the workplace in various ways, including diversity training. See p. 409.

The antidiscrimination laws confer non-waivable rights on employees, at least rights that are not waivable prospectively. Thus, discrimination claims provide less room to engage in the kind of "private ordering" that typifies other areas of employment law. Nevertheless, there is some room for maneuver. For example, in Chapter 5 we explored the definition of "employee," distinguishing the employment relationship from other legal relationships such as independent contractor or partner. A firm, therefore, can avoid the antidiscrimination laws by not having employees, or not having enough employees to satisfy the statutory minimums. (Of course, there are also state laws, many of which reach smaller employers.) In addition, firms can sometimes shift the risks of employment by "leasing" workers or by outsourcing. One kind of private ordering, then, is the decision not to become a statutory employer at all. Even this strategy, however, will not always avoid risks under § 1981 because that covers all contractual relationships.

Although it is the employer who has the most control over the employment relationship, and thus more room to manage risk in the structuring of that relationship, employees also have a significant role to play. In the first instance, the employee decides whether the terms offered are ones he is willing to accept, or to continue working under, and thus the employer's need to attract and retain good workers serves as a practical limit on how the workplace is structured. Additionally, there are some risks an employer cannot avoid. For example, a victim of harassment often can avoid the affirmative defense by promptly invoking internal mechanisms for relief. Further, employee complaints of discrimination create difficult problems for employers because of the statutory proscriptions on retaliation.

But there are some strategies statutory employers can take to avoid or minimize risks. Such techniques include efforts to ensure compliance with the law (such as promulgating harassment policies and undertaking investigations of grievances), to prevent disputes, and to reduce the costs associated with legal disputes when they inevitably arise. Larger employers frequently consult with attorneys and human resource experts in advance of making personnel decisions to ensure compliance with the law and even to avoid even the appearance of a violation. And where an employee contests a decision, employers frequently seek cost-effective ways of dealing with the dispute short of litigation, such as private resolution or settlement.

There are an enormous number of such risk management techniques, which are explored in more detail in TIMOTHY GLYNN, RACHEL ARNOW-RICHMAN & CHARLES A. SULLIVAN, EMPLOYMENT LAW: PRIVATE ORDERING AND ITS LIMITATIONS (Aspen 2007). For example, employers have attempted to reduce risks in litigation by using forum selection clauses and choice-of-law clauses to channel litigation to the employer's benefit. Stipulated damages clauses safeguard employer interests by providing a monetary remedy in the event that an employee breaches its obligations to the employer. And noncompetition clauses can, effectively, bind an employee to an employer and discourage suit. As we saw in Chapter 8, employer liability insurance is increasingly common, see p. 718, and employers sometimes use the ultimate risk management technique — bankruptcy — to avoid liabilities to their workers, especially in the collective bargaining context. See p. 719.

This chapter, however, focuses on two of the more common risk management techniques used by employers and, therefore, ones that must be faced by employees. The first is the use of severance and release agreements in employment terminations to avoid possible litigation. Particularly in large layoff situations, employers typically promise post-termination pay, and perhaps other benefits, in exchange for the employee's promise not to sue the employer.

The second is the increasingly common practice of requiring employees to sign pre-dispute arbitration agreements. Under such agreements, parties do not waive or settle the merits of claims but rather agree that, should a dispute arise, they will resolve it through a private arbitration process rather than through traditional litigation.

As you read the following materials, you will understand that study of risk management begins with techniques employers implement, but the focus quickly shifts to the responses of employees and the policy choices implicated in deciding the extent to which the law permits private ordering in the employment setting.

A. SETTLEMENTS AND RELEASES

From a litigation perspective, the settlement of a plaintiff's claim offers both sides valuable opportunities, although it obviously requires each side to trade-off the bird in the bush for the one in the hand. Settlements of disputes can occur at any stage during the employment discrimination dispute process, from the time of charge filing to eve of trial or even post-judgment. *See Powell v. Omnicom*, 497 F.3d 124 (2d Cir. 2007) (oral settlement reached on the record in court enforceable); *Dillard v. Starcon Int'l, Inc.*, 483 F.3d 502 (7th Cir. 2007) (oral settlement agreement enforceable). It is a truism of litigation that most filed cases settle before trial, and settlement is even more pervasive when the timeframe is pushed further back to the charge-filing period. Indeed, Title VII is predicated on the notion that the EEOC will "conciliate" claims, and new EEOC mediation procedures emphasize more than ever the desirability of the parties reaching an amicable resolution. *See generally*, Michael Z. Green, *Tackling Employment Discrimination With ADR: Does Mediation Offer a Shield for the Haves or Real Opportunity for the Have-Nots?*, 26 Berkeley J. Emp. & Lab. L. 321 (2005); Emily M. Calhoun, *Workplace Mediation: The First-Phase, Private Caucus in Individual Discrimination Disputes*, 9 Harv. Neg. L. Rev. 187 (2004); Michael Z. Green, *Proposing a New Paradigm for EEOC Enforcement After 35 Years: Outsourcing Charge Processing by Mandatory Mediation*, 105 Dick. L. Rev. 305 (2001); Michael J. Yelnosky, *Title VII, Mediation, and Collective Action*, 1999 U. Ill. L. Rev. 583.

From a risk management perspective, however, it is preferable to avoid a dispute entirely rather than to settle it once it has arisen. Thus, an important risk management technique for employers is obtaining contractual releases of liability from employees as part of the termination process. Such "buyouts" occur frequently in cases of individual discharges. A common technique is for the employer to condition severance pay on the employee's execution of a release. Further, buyouts are standard in the context of large scale reductions in force, or "RIFs." As we saw in Chapters 2 and 3, RIFs pose many legal and practical challenges for employers since companies must ensure they do not select employees for layoff based on an impermissible criterion, such as age. This is true whether the potential liability arises under a systematic disparate treatment or a disparate impact theory. In addition, employers must comply with certain statutory requirements, such as providing advance notice of "mass layoffs" in compliance with the federal Workers Adjustment and Retraining Act, 29 U.S.C. §2101 et seq. (2007), or WARN's state analogs.

The validity of employee releases is often at issue in both individual and RIF settings. Employees cannot *prospectively* waive substantive claims under any of the antidiscrimination statutes: such legislation would be rendered wholly inoperative if employees could be required to waive, or to release, rights as a condition of employment. *See Alexander v. Gardner-Denver Co.*, 415 U.S. 36, 51 (1974) ("[W]e think it clear that there can be no prospective waiver of an employee's rights under Title VII"). However, once a cause of action arises, the employee may release (or waive) any claims he or she may have under certain conditions. Releases, like all contracts, require consideration, and effective release agreements are typically obtained by providing terminated employees with severance pay contingent upon signing a waiver of rights. What other requirements exist for a valid release?

The answer varies among the antidiscrimination statutes. We saw in Chapter 5 that employers may create retirement incentive plans without violating the ADEA. See p. 484. This provision was added in 1990 by the Older Workers Benefit Protection Act, codified at 29 U.S.C. §626(f) (2007). Perhaps more importantly for present purposes, OWBPA also authorized waivers of ADEA rights while simultaneously providing some safeguards: "an individual may not waive any right or claim under this Act unless the waiver is knowing and voluntary." The combination of the two provisions means that early retirement incentive plans will rarely be subject to judicial scrutiny. Employees who do not accept the incentive plan will usually lack standing to challenge it, and those who do sign may find themselves unable to attack even a plan that is, in some sense, illegal because they will have signed a "knowing and voluntary" waiver.

OWBPA's authorization of releases, however, has implications far beyond the retirement incentive context. The provision governs any waiver of ADEA rights, even after an ADEA suit is filed. The validity of the release, therefore, becomes the key question. Although OWBPA borrowed its "voluntary and knowing" standard from the Supreme Court's decision in *Alexander v. Gardner-Denver Co.*, 415 U.S. at 52 n. 15, *Gardner-Denver* did not elaborate on what was necessary for a waiver to be knowing and voluntary. The innovation of OWBPA was to make clear that the employer has the burden of establishing that a waiver qualifies, §7(f)(3), 29 U.S.C. §626(f)(3), by proving compliance with a laundry list of substantive and procedural requirements. To satisfy the statute, an agreement is knowing and voluntary, if it *at least*

(A) is "written in a manner calculated to be understood";
(B) makes specific reference to ADEA claims;
(C) does not waive rights arising after its execution;
(D) is supported by "consideration in addition to anything of value to which the individual already is entitled";
(E) advises the individual in writing to consult an attorney;
(F) provides at least 21 days for the employee to consider her decision; and
(G) provides a seven-day period during which the waiver may be revoked.

§7(f)(1), 29 U.S.C. §626(f)(1). *But see Powell v. Omnicom*, 497 F.3d 124 (2d Cir. 2007) (OWBPA timing requirements do not apply to actions filed in court; instead, §626(f)(2) requires only "'a reasonable period of time within which to consider the settlement agreement.'"). There are additional requirements when the waiver is sought as part of a program offered to a group of workers, such as an early retirement incentive plan. §7(f)(1)(H), 29 U.S.C. §626(f)(1)(H). First, the notice period is expanded from 21 days to 45 days. Second, the employer must provide the group being offered the plan with detailed information concerning it, including job titles and ages of those selected for the program. Obviously, this kind of information can help recipients assess the legality of the plan from the perspective of a systemic violation. *See Adams v. Ameritech Servs., Inc.*, 231 F.3d 414 (7th Cir. 2000); *Adams v. Moore Bus. Forms, Inc.*, 224 F.3d 324, 328 (4th Cir. 2000). *Cf. Burlison v. McDonald's Corp.*, 455 F.3d 1242 (11th Cir. 2006) (no violation of OWBPA when employer failed to provide nationwide data on reduction in force where EEOC regulations limit required information for decisional unit encompassing affected employees).

The courts have tended to strictly enforce the requirements of OWBPA for a valid release.

OUBRE v. ENTERGY OPERATIONS, INC.
522 U.S. 422 (1998)

Justice KENNEDY delivered the opinion of the Court.

An employee, as part of a termination agreement, signed a release of all claims against her employer. In consideration, she received severance pay in installments. The release, however, did not comply with specific federal statutory requirements for a release of claims under the Age Discrimination in Employment Act of 1967. After receiving the last payment, the employee brought suit under the ADEA. The employer claims the employee ratified and validated the nonconforming release by retaining the monies paid to secure it. The employer also insists the release bars the action unless, as a precondition to filing suit, the employee tenders back the monies received. We disagree and rule that, as the release did not comply with the statute, it cannot bar the ADEA claim. . . .

[Dolores Oubre received a poor performance rating. Her supervisor gave her the option of either improving her performance or accepting a severance package. She had 14 days to consider her options, during which she consulted with attorneys. Oubre decided to accept, and she signed a release], in which she "agree [d] to waive, settle, release, and discharge any and all claims, demands, damages, actions, or causes of action . . . that I may have against Entergy. . . . " In exchange, she received six installment payments over the next four months, totaling $6,258.

The Older Workers Benefits Protection Act (OWBPA) imposes specific requirements for releases covering ADEA claims. 29 U.S.C. §§626(f)(1)(B), (F), (G). In procuring the release, Entergy did not comply with the OWBPA in at least three respects: (1) Entergy did not give Oubre enough time to consider her options. (2) Entergy did not give Oubre seven days after she signed the release to change her mind. And (3) the release made no specific reference to claims under the ADEA.

Oubre filed [suit] alleging constructive discharge on the basis of her age in violation of the ADEA and state law. Oubre has not offered or tried to return the $6,258 to Entergy, nor is it clear she has the means to do so. [Entergy was awarded summary judgment on the basis that] Oubre had ratified the defective release by failing to return or offer to return the monies she had received. . . .

II

The employer rests its case upon general principles of state contract jurisprudence. As the employer recites the rule, contracts tainted by mistake, duress, or even fraud are voidable at the option of the innocent party. *See* 1 Restatement (Second) of Contracts §7, and Comment b (1979). The employer maintains, however, that before the innocent party can elect avoidance, she must first tender back any benefits received under the contract. See, e.g., *Dreiling v. Home State Life Ins. Co.*, 515 P.2d 757, 766-767 (Kan. 1973). If she fails to do so within a reasonable time after learning of her rights, the employer contends, she ratifies the contract and so makes it binding. Restatement (Second) of Contracts, supra, §7, Comments d, e. The employer also invokes the doctrine of equitable estoppel. As a rule, equitable estoppel bars a party from shirking the burdens of a voidable transaction for as long as she retains the benefits received under it. See, e.g., *Buffum v. Peter Barceloux Co.*, 289 U.S. 227, 234 (1933) (citing state case law from Indiana and New York). Applying these principles, the employer claims the employee ratified the ineffective release (or faces estoppel) by retaining all the sums paid in consideration of it. The employer, then, relies not upon the execution of the release but upon a later, distinct ratification of its terms.

These general rules may not be as unified as the employer asserts. And in equity, a person suing to rescind a contract, as a rule, is not required to restore the consideration at the very outset of the litigation. *See* 3 Restatement (Second) of Contracts, supra, §384, and Comment b; Restatement of Restitution §65, Comment d (1936); D. Dobbs, Law of Remedies §4.8, p. 294 (1973). Even if the employer's statement of the general rule requiring tender back before one files suit were correct, it would be unavailing. The rule cited is based simply on the course of negotiation of the parties and the alleged later ratification. The authorities cited do not consider the question raised by statutory standards for releases and a statutory declaration making non-conforming releases ineffective. It is the latter question we confront here.

In 1990, Congress amended the ADEA by passing the OWBPA. The OWBPA provides: "An individual may not waive any right or claim under [the ADEA] unless the waiver is knowing and voluntary. . . . [A] waiver may not be considered knowing and voluntary unless at a minimum" it satisfies certain enumerated requirements, including the three listed above. 29 U.S.C. §626(f)(1).

The statutory command is clear: An employee "may not waive" an ADEA claim unless the waiver or release satisfies the OWBPA's requirements. The policy of the Older Workers Benefit Protection Act is likewise clear from its title: It is designed to protect the rights and benefits of older workers. The OWBPA implements Congress' policy via a strict, unqualified statutory stricture on waivers, and we are bound to take Congress at its word. Congress imposed specific duties on employers who seek releases of certain claims created by statute. Congress delineated these duties with precision and without qualification: An employee "may not waive" an ADEA claim unless the employer complies with the statute. Courts cannot with ease presume ratification of that which Congress forbids.

The OWBPA sets up its own regime for assessing the effect of ADEA waivers, separate and apart from contract law. The statute creates a series of prerequisites for knowing and voluntary waivers and imposes affirmative duties of disclosure and waiting periods. The OWBPA governs the effect under federal law of waivers or releases on ADEA claims and incorporates no exceptions or qualifications. The text of the OWBPA forecloses the employer's defense, notwithstanding how general contract principles would apply to non-ADEA claims.

The rule proposed by the employer would frustrate the statute's practical operation as well as its formal command. In many instances a discharged employee likely will have spent the monies received and will lack the means to tender their return. These realities might tempt employers to risk noncompliance with the OWBPA's waiver provisions, knowing it will be difficult to repay the monies and relying on ratification. We ought not to open the door to an evasion of the statute by this device.

Oubre's cause of action arises under the ADEA, and the release can have no effect on her ADEA claim unless it complies with the OWBPA. In this case, both sides concede the release the employee signed did not comply with the requirements of the OWBPA. Since Oubre's release did not comply with the OWBPA's stringent safeguards, it is unenforceable against her insofar as it purports to waive or release her ADEA claim. As a statutory matter, the release cannot bar her ADEA suit, irrespective of the validity of the contract as to other claims.

In further proceedings in this or other cases, courts may need to inquire whether the employer has claims for restitution, recoupment, or setoff against the employee, and these questions may be complex where a release is effective as to some claims but not as to ADEA claims. We need not decide those issues here, however. It suffices to hold that the release cannot bar the ADEA claim because it does not conform to the statute. Nor did the employee's mere retention of monies amount to a ratification equivalent to a valid release of her ADEA claims, since the retention did not comply with the OWBPA any more than the original release did. The statute governs the effect of the release on ADEA claims, and the employer cannot invoke the employee's failure to tender back as a way of excusing its own failure to comply. . . .

Justice BREYER, with whom Justice O'CONNOR joins, concurring.

... I write these additional words because I believe it important to specify that the statute need not, and does not, thereby make the worker's procedurally invalid promise totally void, i.e., without any legal effect, say, like a contract the terms of which themselves are contrary to public policy. *See* 1 Restatement (Second) of Contracts, §7, Comment a; 2 id., §178. Rather, the statute makes the contract that the employer and worker tried to create voidable, like a contract made with an infant, or a contract created through fraud, mistake or duress, which contract the worker may elect either to avoid or to ratify. See 1 id., §7 and Comment b. . . .

That the contract is voidable rather than void may prove important. For example, an absolutely void contract, it is said, "is void as to everybody whose rights would be affected by it if valid." 17A Am. Jur. 2d, Contracts §7, p. 31 (1991). Were a former worker's procedurally invalid promise not to sue absolutely void, might it not become legally possible for an employer to decide to cancel its own reciprocal obligation, say, to pay the worker, or to provide ongoing health benefits — whether or not the worker in question ever intended to bring a lawsuit? It seems most unlikely that Congress, enacting a statute meant to protect workers, would have wanted to create — as a result of an employer's failure to follow the law — any such legal threat to all workers, whether or not they intend to bring suit. To find the contract voidable, rather than void, would offer legal protection against such threats.

At the same time, treating the contract as voidable could permit an employer to recover his own reciprocal payment (or to avoid his reciprocal promise) where doing so seems most fair, namely, where that recovery would not bar the worker from bringing suit. Once the worker (who has made the procedurally invalid promise not to sue) brings an age-discrimination suit, he has clearly rejected (avoided) his promise not to sue. As long as there is no "tender-back" precondition, his (invalid) promise will not have barred his suit in conflict with the statute. Once he has sued, however, nothing in the statute prevents his employer from asking for restitution of his reciprocal payment or relief from any ongoing reciprocal obligation. *See* Restatement of Restitution §47, Comment b (1936) ("A person who transfers something to another believing that the other thereby comes under a duty to perform the terms of a contract . . . is ordinarily entitled to restitution for what he has given if the obligation intended does not arise and if the other does not perform"); Dobbs, supra, at 994 (restitution is often allowed where benefits are conferred under voidable contract). A number of older state cases indicate, for example, that the amount of consideration paid for an invalid release can be deducted from a successful plaintiff's damages award. . . .

[Justice THOMAS, joined by Chief Justice REHNQUIST, dissented, as did Justice SCALIA. The Thomas opinion critiqued the majority for not "so much as acknowledging the long-established principle that a statute 'must "speak directly"' to the question addressed by the common law" in order to abrogate it. Since OWBPA did not address either common-law ratification or the doctrine that a party must "tender back" consideration received under a release before bringing suit, it should not be held to have abrogated them.]

NOTES

1. *Reading OWBPA Act Strictly.* As *Oubre* makes clear, releases of ADEA claims are subject to strict requirements. *See also Ruehl v. Viacom, Inc.*, 500 F.3d 375 (3d

Cir. 2007) (waiver invalid even though it acknowledged employee's receipt of required information when such information was not actually provided the employee); *Syverson v. IBM*, 472 F.3d 1072 (9th Cir. 2006) (direction to consult an attorney did not cure ambiguous waiver language used by IBM since waiver was not written in a manner calculated to be understood by the intended participants); *Kruchowski v. Weyerhaeuser Co.*, 446 F.3d 1090 (10th Cir. 2006) (waiver invalid under OWBPA when employer notified plaintiffs of an incorrect "decisional unit" and provided other inaccurate information); *American Airlines, Inc. v. Cordoza-Rodriguez*, 133 F.3d 111 (1st Cir. 1998) (release invalidated for failure to explicitly advise employees to consult an attorney).

2. *Releases under Other Discrimination Statutes.* OWBPA on its face reaches only ADEA claims, not claims under other antidiscrimination statutes. Since releases that satisfy OWBPA are the "gold standard," employers should structure their forms to ensure that they meet the OWBPA and to use such forms for the release of all kinds of discrimination claims. However, when they fail to do so, the law governing releases under other federal laws is less clear. Some courts have applied the policies underlying OWBPA to statutes such as Title VII, the ADA, or § 1981. *See Richardson v. Sugg*, 448 F.3d 1046, 1054 (8th Cir. 2006) (the policy concerns that led *Oubre* to reject the tender back requirement for the ADEA also apply to Title VII).

The dominant approach, however, is more amorphous: the courts look to the "totality of the circumstances" to determine whether the release was "knowing and voluntary." *E.g.*, *Melanson v. Browning-Ferris Indus.*, 281 F.3d 272 (1st Cir. 2002); *See generally* Daniel Gorman, *A State of Disarray: The "Knowing and Voluntary" Standard for Releasing Claims Under Title VII of the Civil Rights Act of 1964*, 8 U. PA. J. LAB. & EMP. L. 73 (2005); Craig Robert Senn, *Knowing and Voluntary Waivers of Federal Employment Claims: Replacing the Totality of Circumstances Test With a "Waiver Certainty" Test*, 58 FLA. L. REV. 305 (2006). At the very least, this approach allows courts to enforce releases that would not be valid under OWBPA. However, it is a more demanding standard than would govern under normal contract law, which would validate a release that met the minimal requirements for a contract so long as the employee did not establish an invalidating defense, like fraud, duress, undue influence, or unconscionability.

3. *Beyond Minimum Conditions.* As *Oubre* indicates, OWBPA provides certain minimum conditions for the validity of waivers. But its overarching requirement is that any waiver be "knowing and voluntary." This suggests that even a waiver that satisfies the specific requirements of the statute may still not be valid. Presumably, the kinds of defenses that would invalidate any contract, such as undue influence, duress, or fraud would also invalidate a waiver. *See Bennett v. Coors Brewing Co.*, 189 F.3d 1221, 1228 (10th Cir. 1999) (OWBPA "factors are not exclusive and other circumstances, outside the express statutory requirements, may impact whether a waiver under the OWBPA is knowing and voluntary"). *See also Littrell v. City of Kan. City*, 459 F.3d 918 (8th Cir. 2006) (release valid despite claim that it was signed under duress where the only threatening comments were that plaintiff could be discharged if he did not sign the agreement). *Cf. Odorizzi v. Bloomfield School Dist.*, 54 Cal. Rptr. 533 (Cal. Ct. App. 1966) (invalidating teacher's resignation for undue influence under state law).

4. *Employer Rights after* Oubre. The *Oubre* majority did not wholly deprive employers of remedies for breach of a release that does not satisfy OWBPA but said the employer may be able to recover back the money paid by a claim for "restitution, recoupment or setoff." What did the Court mean? Does Justice Breyer's concurrence

help? EEOC regulations provide that the employee cannot be liable for more than the lesser of "the amount recovered by the employee, or the consideration the employee received for signing the waiver." 29 C.F.R. § 1625.23(c)(1) (2007).

5. *Good or Bad Policy Under the ADEA?* Professor Michael C. Harper, in *Age-Based Exit Incentives, Coercion, and the Prospective Waiver of ADEA Rights: The Failure of the Older Workers Benefit Protection Act*, 79 VA. L. REV. 1271, 1277-79 (1993), argues that the incentive plan and release scheme, in effect, encourages age discrimination:

> To understand how conditional exit incentive offers can be used to induce retirement from employees who would prefer continued employment, consider how a typical offer of this type would be weighed by an offeree. Assume that an employer announces to its workforce that because of general recessionary conditions or deep cuts in the demand for its particular product, employment will have to be cut by thirty percent over the next four months. The employer also announces at the same time that in order to avoid as many involuntary layoffs as possible, it will offer retirement incentives to all employees over the age of fifty-five. . . . The offer is conditional, however, because the benefits will only be granted to those who voluntarily retire within the next two months. Those offerees who are involuntarily laid off, or those offerees who decide to retire after the expiration of the two month period, will not obtain the benefits. Finally, assume that the employer does not specify how it will determine who will be laid off to achieve the necessary residual amount of reductions in staff after the closure of the voluntary retirement window.
>
> A post-fifty-five-year-old offeree in this typical exit window scenario might well rationally accept early retirement even though she prefers continuing employment. The reason is that the offeree must include in her calculations the chance that she will be terminated without the extra benefits offered for voluntary retirement. Thus, an offeree who prefers employment to retirement with increased benefits might prefer the latter to the perceived chance of continued employment plus the perceived chance of termination without enhanced benefits. Clearly it is the conditional nature of the retirement incentive that makes the two preferences consistent, that, in other words, makes it rational for an offeree to accept the incentive even though she prefers continued employment. This is highly significant for an employer wanting to rid itself of more older workers than could be justified by individualized comparisons of the productivity of all its workers. . . .

The waiver provisions of OWBPA only enhance this result. Indeed, Professor Harper argues that the statute functionally approves a prospective waiver of ADEA rights, *id.* at 1294, although OWBPA expressly bars such waivers. Harper argues that "[t]he only practical way to prevent employers from using retirement incentives to effect the termination of particular workers selected on the basis of age who would prefer continued employment is to prohibit age-based incentives from being temporally or otherwise conditioned." *Id.* at 1329. Do you agree? Would there be other consequences? Will employers cease offering such incentives? *See also* Judith A. McMorrow, *Retirement Incentives in the Twenty-First Century: The Move toward Employer Control of the ADEA*, 31 U. RICH. L. REV. 795 (1997) (arguing that a combination of OWBPA and the increasing use of arbitration largely removes the operation of the retirement incentive system from public scrutiny).

6. *Good or Bad Policy Generally?* Releases pose difficult choices for employees in any setting. They are least problematic for employees settling law suits after significant discovery and with the advice of the attorney litigating that suit. In such settings, the employee is likely to have adequate information to assess the trade-offs. At the other extreme, an individual employee faced with an imminent termination

and the offer of relatively little severance must decide whether to waive rights (often for a sum that ranges between one week's and one month's pay for every year worked) with little opportunity to assess the worth of any claims he or she may have.

7. *Prospective Waivers.* Waivers of prospective rights are explicitly barred by OWBPA, which requires that a valid release "not waive rights arising after its execution." We have seen, however, that this rule originated in a Title VII case, *Alexander v. Gardner-Denver Co.*, 415 U.S. 36, 51 (1974): "we think it clear that there can be no prospective waiver of an employee's rights under Title VII." The courts, therefore, have generally refused to enforce agreements that purport to waive discrimination claims that may arise in the future. A good illustration is *Richardson v. Sugg*, 448 F.3d 1046, 1057 (8th Cir. 2006), where a former Arkansas Razorbacks basketball coach, Nolan Richardson, was held not bound by a clause in his employment contract. That clause specified that, should Richardson be terminated by the university for any reason, he would accept a guaranty by the Razorback Foundation, Inc. of the remaining years on his contract "as full and complete satisfaction of any obligations of the University," and he "release[s] and discharge[s] the University, its officers, trustees and employees from and against any liability of any nature whatsoever." *Id.* at 1053. The Eighth Circuit held the release ineffective (although the coach lost on the merits of his claim). *See also Adams v. Philip Morris, Inc.*, 67 F.3d 580, 585 (6th Cir. 1995) ("An employer cannot purchase a license to discriminate"). *But see Nilsson v. City of Mesa*, (9th Cir, 2007) (upholding waiver of discrimination claims relating to employer's pre-hire background investigation). However, the courts have been unclear about the validity of releases that explicitly absolve the employer of any duty to rehire the releasing employee. *Kellogg Co. v. Sabhlok*, 471 F.3d 629 (6th Cir. 2006).

8. *Gag Clauses.* One advantage of settlement, usually for the employer but sometimes for the employee, is the ability to avoid the publicity inherent in any lawsuit. Releases, therefore, typically have "confidentiality" clauses that bar the employee from voluntarily providing information about her claim to others (although they typically provide that the former employee can respond to legal process). Such releases sometimes go further and have very broad "nondisparagement" clauses, which limit the former employee's ability to "bad mouth" the employer at all. There is a lively debate about the systemic effects of these kinds of clauses. *See generally* Scott A. Moss *Illuminating Secrecy: A New Economic Analysis Of Confidential Settlements*, 105 MICH. L. REV. 867 (2007); Minna J. Kotkin, *Invisible Settlements, Invisible Discrimination*, 84 N. CAR. L. REV. 927, 927 (2006). Employees often require the employer to similarly not publicize the settlement or otherwise disparage them.

9. *Enforcing Settlements.* Most settlements finally resolve the dispute, but questions sometimes arise regarding their enforcement. We saw one kind of issue in *Oubre* — whether a tender-back requirement was applicable should a plaintiff seek to sue despite having signed a release. Another issue is whether federal courts have jurisdiction to enforce settlement agreements. *See Kokkonen v. Guardian Life Ins. Co. of Am.*, 511 U.S. 375 (1994) (after a district court has dismissed the case, it needs ancillary jurisdiction to enforce any underlying settlement agreement unless it specifically retained jurisdiction for that purpose or incorporated the agreement in the order for dismissal). As for applicable law, the circuits have split as to whether state or federal law governs the question of whether two private parties have reached a settlement. *Compare Makins v. District of Columbia*, 277 F.3d 544 (D.C. Cir. 2002) (state law governs), with *Fennell v. TLB Kent Co.*, 865 F.2d 498, 501 (2d Cir. 1986) (federal law). Finally, the threshold question in suits concerning such agreements is

whether the suit can be brought without resort to the charge filing procedure. Some courts have held these procedures to be irrelevant because the suit is not to enforce statutory rights but rather to enforce the settlement agreement; a defense that the employer had not violated the statute would be irrelevant. *Cisneros v. ABC Rail Corp.*, 217 F.3d 1299 (10th Cir. 2000).

10. *Waivers and the EEOC.* It seems clear that a waiver by an individual employee of her right to file a charge of discrimination would be unenforceable, *see EEOC v. Cosmair*, 821 F.2d 1085 (5th Cir. 1987) (waiver of right to file administrative charges, if covered by employee's release, would be void against public policy), although the courts have been unwilling to find the inclusion of such a provision sufficient to either invalidate the waiver, *see Wastak v. Lehigh Valley Health Network*, 342 F.3d 281 (3d Cir. 2003), or to be actionable retaliation. *EEOC v. Sundance Rehab. Corp.*, 466 F.3d 490 (6th Cir. 2006). However, any incentive to file a charge will be blunted since the EEOC may not be able to recover monetary relief on behalf of any employee who has validly waived his rights. That result applies in the analogous area of arbitration. See p. 647. Of course, the EEOC may settle its own suits, and the principles for such settlement have generated some questions. *See generally* Michael J. Zimmer & Charles A. Sullivan, *Consent Decree Settlements by Administrative Agencies in Antitrust and Employment Discrimination: Optimizing Public and Private Interest*, 1976 DUKE L.J. 163.

11. *Consent Decrees.* Most settlements providing for basically monetary relief pose few special problems, but other questions can arise when the parties wish to settle if the defendant will agree to change its conduct in some way. For example, the employer could promise to reinstate the plaintiff, to modify its seniority system, or to alter work rules. Such changes in conduct may affect not only the parties to the suit but also nonparties. The form of the settlement may bear on this issue. Two basic approaches are possible. The first is a purely contractual one, and the second is incorporation of any settlement into a court order, often called a "consent decree." The consent decree is a hybrid creature with aspects of both a contract and a judgment, subject to special rules for both interpretation and modification. *See Firefighters Local Union No. 1784 v. Stotts*, 467 U.S. 561 (1984) (court decision that decree trumped collective bargaining agreement's seniority system was not appropriate either as an interpretation or modification). *But see Local No. 93, Intl. Assn. of Firefighters v. Cleveland*, 478 U.S. 501 (1986) (true agreements of the parties could override a valid seniority system); *Local 28, Sheet Metal Workers' Intl. Assn. v. EEOC*, 478 U.S. 421, 426 (1986) (seniority system may be modified after a finding of discrimination).

In either case, the rights of non-parties cannot normally be affected. *See Martin v. Wilks*, 490 U.S. 755 (1989); *see also W. R. Grace & Co. v. Local Union 759, Intl. Union of the United Rubber Workers*, 461 U.S. 757 (1983). The Civil Rights Act of 1991, however, amended Title VII to allow decrees to bind non-parties in certain circumstances. Pub. L. No. 102-166, 105 Stat. 1071 (1991). It allows nonparties to be bound by either consent or litigated decrees when (1) they are adequately represented by a party or (2) they have actual notice of the threat to their interest and an opportunity to protect themselves. *See generally* Andrea Catania & Charles A. Sullivan, *Judging Judgments: The 1991 Civil Rights Act and the Lingering Ghost of* Martin v. Wilks, 57 BROOK. L. REV. 995 (1992); Susan Grover, *The Silenced Majority:* Martin v. Wilks *and the Legislative Response*, 1992 U. ILL. L. REV. 43 (1992); Marjorie A. Silver, *Fairness and Finality: Third-Party Challenges to Employment Discrimination Consent Decrees After the 1991 Civil Rights Act*, 62 FORDHAM L. REV. 321 (1993).

B. ARBITRATING DISCRIMINATION CLAIMS

Another important risk management technique in employment discrimination is arbitration. While parties can agree to arbitrate (or use other alternate dispute resolution techniques) at any point in the dispute resolution process, the most controversial use of this device is "mandatory arbitration," that is, an employer requiring all of its employees to agree to arbitrate any employment-related disputes as a condition of hiring or continued employment. While the pervasiveness of this practice is unclear, some research indicates that 15% to 25% of employers require their employees to arbitrate all claims. Alexander J.S. Colvin, *Empirical Research on Employment Arbitration: Clarity Amidst the Sound and Fury?*, EMP. RTS & EMPL. POL'Y J. (forthcoming 2008).

Arbitration has a long and respectable history in labor relations, and the first Title VII arbitration case arose in that context. *Alexander v. Gardner-Denver Co.*, 415 U.S. 36 (1974) involved a plaintiff who sued his employer after his union had unsuccessfully claimed discrimination by the employer in violation of the governing collective bargaining agreement in an arbitration the union had pursued on his behalf. The Court viewed Title VII and collective bargaining agreement remedies as independent remedies, which meant that the failure of the arbitration did not prejudice plaintiff's right to a federal court action to vindicate his Title VII rights. *See also Elec. Workers v. Robbins & Myers*, 429 U.S. 229 (1976) (since the remedies were independent, resort to grievance arbitration does not toll Title VII time limits).

Gardner-Denver not only held that submission of a dispute to arbitration does not preclude a subsequent Title VII suit but also ruled improper any judicial deference to prior arbitral awards. Thus, an employee could pursue a grievance procedure established by a collective bargaining agreement without fear of prejudicing his or her Title VII rights. *Gardner-Denver* noted that enforcing Title VII compliance was entrusted to federal courts, not to arbitrators; that the elaborate suit prerequisites did not refer to arbitration; and that Congress had evinced an intent to provide parallel or overlapping remedies. The Court stressed the inappropriateness of deference to collective bargaining arbitration because arbitrators are selected for their knowledge and judgment concerning industrial relations, not public law concepts; further, arbitrators are bound to effectuate the intent of the parties as embodied in the contract, even though that intent may be in conflict with the law. In addition, unions control the process, which may prejudice individual rights. Finally, the Court also noted defects in the arbitral procedure, which are independent of the collective bargaining context, and may affect the quality of the decisions rendered:

> Moreover, the factfinding process in arbitration usually is not equivalent to judicial factfinding. The record of the arbitration proceedings is not as complete; the usual rules of evidence do not apply; and rights and procedures common to civil trials, such as discovery, compulsory process, cross-examination, and testimony under oath, are often severely limited or unavailable. And as this Court has recognized, "arbitrators have no obligation to the court to give their reasons for an award." Indeed, it is the informality of arbitral procedure that enables it to function as an efficient, inexpensive, and expeditious means for dispute resolution. This same characteristic, however, makes arbitration a less appropriate forum for final resolution of Title VII issues than the federal courts.

451 U.S. 57-58. The Court did state that, while an arbitration award was in no sense preclusive in a subsequent court suit, courts might admit arbitral decisions as evidence, *id* at 60 n. 21, and some courts have given evidentiary effect to arbitration awards that

seems to border on preclusion. *See Collins v. N.Y.C. Transit Auth.*, 305 F.3d 113, 119 (2d Cir. 2002) ("Where, as here, that decision follows an evidentiary hearing and is based on substantial evidence, the Title VII plaintiff, to survive a motion for summary judgment, must present strong evidence that the decision was wrong as a matter of fact — e.g., new evidence not before the tribunal — or that the impartiality of the proceeding was somehow compromised").

Gardner-Denver seemed to render useless pre-dispute agreements to arbitrate employment discrimination claims. However, a series of later Supreme Court decisions outside the employment context reinvigorated the use of arbitration as part of the ADR movement that developed so strongly in the 1980s and 1990s. For an excellent review and critique of that jurisprudence about arbitration generally, see Margaret L. Moses, *Statutory Misconstruction: How the Supreme Court Created a Federal Arbitration Law Never Enacted by Congress*, 34 FLA. ST. U. L. REV. 99 (2006). The Supreme Court revisited the issue of the relationship of arbitration to litigation in the discrimination context in the next case, which arose outside of the collective bargaining setting, taking a markedly different approach than in *Gardner-Denver*.

GILMER v. INTERSTATE/JOHNSON LANE CORP.
500 U.S. 20 (1991)

Justice WHITE delivered the opinion of the Court.

The question presented in this case is whether a claim under the Age Discrimination in Employment Act of 1967 can be subjected to compulsory arbitration pursuant to an arbitration agreement in a securities registration application. The Court of Appeals held that it could, and we affirm.

I

Respondent Interstate/Johnson Lane Corporation (Interstate) hired petitioner Robert Gilmer as a Manager of Financial Services in May 1981. As required by his employment, Gilmer registered as a securities representative with several stock exchanges, including the New York Stock Exchange (NYSE). His registration application, entitled "Uniform Application for Securities Industry Registration or Transfer," provided, among other things, that Gilmer "agreed to arbitrate any dispute, claim or controversy" arising between him and Interstate "that is required to be arbitrated under the rules, constitutions or by-laws of the organizations with which I register." Of relevance to this case, NYSE Rule 347 provides for arbitration of "any controversy between a registered representative and any member or member organization arising out of the employment or termination of employment of such registered representative."

Interstate terminated Gilmer's employment in 1987, at which time Gilmer was 62 years of age. [Gilmer filed a charge with the EEOC and then sued in federal district court for age discrimination in violation of the ADEA. Interstate moved to compel arbitration, relying on the arbitration agreement in Gilmer's registration application and the Federal Arbitration Act (FAA). 9 U.S.C. §1 *et seq.* (2003).]

II

The FAA was originally enacted in 1925, and then reenacted and codified in 1947 as Title 9 of the United States Code. Its purpose was to reverse the longstanding judicial hostility to arbitration agreements that had existed at English common law and had been adopted by American courts, and to place arbitration agreements upon the same footing as other contracts. Its primary substantive provision states that "[a] written provision in any maritime transaction or a contract evidencing a transaction involving commerce to settle by arbitration a controversy thereafter arising out of such contract or transaction . . . shall be valid, irrevocable, and enforceable, save upon such grounds as exist at law or in equity for the revocation of any contract." 9 U.S.C. §2. The FAA also provides for stays of proceedings in federal district courts when an issue in the proceeding is referable to arbitration, §3, and for orders compelling arbitration when one party has failed, neglected, or refused to comply with an arbitration agreement, §4. These provisions manifest a "liberal federal policy favoring arbitration agreements." *Moses H. Cone Memorial Hospital v. Mercury Construction Corp.*, 460 U.S. 1, 24 (1983).[2]

It is by now clear that statutory claims may be the subject of an arbitration agreement, enforceable pursuant to the FAA. Indeed, in recent years we have held enforceable arbitration agreements relating to claims arising under the Sherman Act; §10(b) of the Securities Exchange Act of 1934; the civil provisions of the Racketeer Influenced and Corrupt Organizations Act (RICO); and §12(2) of the Securities Act of 1933. See *Mitsubishi Motors Corp. v. Soler Chrysler-Plymouth, Inc.*, 473 U.S. 614 (1985); *Shearson/American Express Inc. v. McMahon*, 482 U.S. 220 (1987); *Rodriguez de Quijas v. Shearson/American Express, Inc.*, 490 U.S. 477 (1989). In these cases we recognized that "by agreeing to arbitrate a statutory claim, a party does not forgo the substantive rights afforded by the statute; it only submits to their resolution in an arbitral, rather than a judicial, forum." *Mitsubishi.*

Although all statutory claims may not be appropriate for arbitration, "having made the bargain to arbitrate, the party should be held to it unless Congress itself has evinced an intention to preclude a waiver of judicial remedies for the statutory rights at issue." Ibid. In this regard, we note that the burden is on Gilmer to show that Congress intended to preclude a waiver of a judicial forum for ADEA claims. See *McMahon.* If such an intention exists, it will be discoverable in the text of the ADEA, its legislative history, or an "inherent conflict" between arbitration and the ADEA's underlying purposes. See ibid. Throughout such an inquiry, it should be kept in mind that "questions of arbitrability must be addressed with a healthy regard for the federal policy favoring arbitration." *Moses H. Cone.*

---

2. Section 1 of the FAA provides that "nothing herein contained shall apply to contracts of employment of seamen, railroad employees, or any other class of workers engaged in foreign or interstate commerce." 9 U.S.C. §1. Several *amici curiae* in support of Gilmer argue that that section excludes from the coverage of the FAA *all* "contracts of employment." Gilmer, however, did not raise the issue in the courts below; it was not addressed there; and it was not among the questions presented in the petition for certiorari. In any event, it would be inappropriate to address the scope of the §1 exclusion because the arbitration clause being enforced here is not contained in a contract of employment. . . . Rather, the arbitration clause at issue is in Gilmer's securities registration application, which is a contract with the securities exchanges, not with Interstate. The lower courts addressing the issue uniformly have concluded that the exclusionary clause in §1 of the FAA is inapplicable to arbitration clauses contained in such registration applications. We implicitly assumed as much *in Perry v. Thomas*, 482 U.S. 483 (1987), where we held that the FAA required a former employee of a securities firm to arbitrate his statutory wage claim against his former employer, pursuant to an arbitration clause in his registration application. Unlike the dissent, we choose to follow the plain language of the FAA and the weight of authority, and we therefore hold that §1's exclusionary clause does not apply to Gilmer's arbitration agreement. Consequently, we leave for another day the issue raised by *amici curiae.*

III

Gilmer concedes that nothing in the text of the ADEA or its legislative history explicitly precludes arbitration. He argues, however, that compulsory arbitration of ADEA claims pursuant to arbitration agreements would be inconsistent with the statutory framework and purposes of the ADEA. Like the Court of Appeals, we disagree.

A

Congress enacted the ADEA in 1967 "to promote employment of older persons based on their ability rather than age; to prohibit arbitrary age discrimination in employment; [and] to help employers and workers find ways of meeting problems arising from the impact of age on employment." 29 U.S.C. §621 (b). To achieve those goals, the ADEA, among other things, makes it unlawful for an employer "to fail or refuse to hire or to discharge any individual or otherwise discriminate against any individual with respect to his compensation, terms, conditions, or privileges of employment, because of such individual's age." §623(a)(1). This proscription is enforced both by private suits and by the EEOC. In order for an aggrieved individual to bring suit under the ADEA, he or she must first file a charge with the EEOC and then wait at least 60 days. §626(d). An individual's right to sue is extinguished, however, if the EEOC institutes an action against the employer. §626(c)(1). Before the EEOC can bring such an action, though, it must "attempt to eliminate the discriminatory practice or practices alleged, and to effect voluntary compliance with the requirements of this chapter through informal methods of conciliation, conference, and persuasion." §626(b); see also 29 CFR §1626.15 (1990).

As Gilmer contends, the ADEA is designed not only to address individual grievances, but also to further important social policies. We do not perceive any inherent inconsistency between those policies, however, and enforcing agreements to arbitrate age discrimination claims. It is true that arbitration focuses on specific disputes between the parties involved. The same can be said, however, of judicial resolution of claims. Both of these dispute resolution mechanisms nevertheless also can further broader social purposes. The Sherman Act, the Securities Exchange Act of 1934, RICO, and the Securities Act of 1933 all are designed to advance important public policies, but, as noted above, claims under those statutes are appropriate for arbitration. "So long as the prospective litigant effectively may vindicate [his or her] statutory cause of action in the arbitral forum, the statute will continue to serve both its remedial and deterrent function." *Mitsubishi.*

We also are unpersuaded by the argument that arbitration will undermine the role of the EEOC in enforcing the ADEA. An individual ADEA claimant subject to an arbitration agreement will still be free to file a charge with the EEOC, even though the claimant is not able to institute a private judicial action. Indeed, Gilmer filed a charge with the EEOC in this case. In any event, the EEOC's role in combating age discrimination is not dependent on the filing of a charge; the agency may receive information concerning alleged violations of the ADEA "from any source," and it has independent authority to investigate age discrimination. See 29 CFR §§1626.4, 1626.13 (1990). Moreover, nothing in the ADEA indicates that Congress intended that the EEOC be involved in all employment disputes. Such disputes can be settled, for example, without any EEOC involvement.[3] Finally, the mere involvement of an administrative agency in the enforcement of a statute is not sufficient to preclude arbitration. For example, the Securities Exchange Commission is heavily involved in the enforcement of the Securities Exchange Act of 1934 and the Securities Act of 1933, but we have held that claims under both of those statutes may be subject to compulsory arbitration.

Gilmer also argues that compulsory arbitration is improper because it deprives claimants of the judicial forum provided for by the ADEA. Congress, however, did not explicitly preclude arbitration or other nonjudicial resolution of claims, even in its recent amendments to the ADEA. "If Congress intended the substantive protection afforded [by the ADEA] to include protection against waiver of the right to a judicial forum, that intention will be deducible from text or legislative history." *Mitsubishi*. Moreover, Gilmer's argument ignores the ADEA's flexible approach to resolution of claims. The EEOC, for example, is directed to pursue "informal methods of conciliation, conference, and persuasion," 29 U.S.C. §626(b), which suggests that out-of-court dispute resolution, such as arbitration, is consistent with the statutory scheme established by Congress. In addition, arbitration is consistent with Congress' grant of concurrent jurisdiction over ADEA claims to state and federal courts, see 29 U.S.C. §626 (c)(1) (allowing suits to be brought "in any court of competent jurisdiction"), because arbitration agreements, "like the provision for concurrent jurisdiction, serve to advance the objective of allowing [claimants] a broader right to select the forum for resolving disputes, whether it be judicial or otherwise." *Rodriguez de Quijas*.

B

In arguing that arbitration is inconsistent with the ADEA, Gilmer also raises a host of challenges to the adequacy of arbitration procedures. Initially, we note that in our recent arbitration cases we have already rejected most of these arguments as insufficient to preclude arbitration of statutory claims. Such generalized attacks on arbitration "rest on suspicion of arbitration as a method of weakening the protections afforded in the substantive law to would-be complainants," and as such, they are "far out of step with our current strong endorsement of the federal statutes favoring this method of resolving disputes." *Rodriguez de Quijas*. Consequently, we address these arguments only briefly.

Gilmer first speculates that arbitration panels will be biased. However, "we decline to indulge the presumption that the parties and arbitral body conducting a proceeding will be unable or unwilling to retain competent, conscientious and impartial arbitrators." *Mitsubishi*. In any event, we note that the NYSE arbitration rules, which are applicable to the dispute in this case, provide protections against biased panels. The rules require, for example, that the parties be informed of the employment histories of the arbitrators, and that they be allowed to make further inquiries into the arbitrators' backgrounds. See 2 CCH New York Stock Exchange Guide ¶2608, p. 4314 (Rule 608) (1991) (hereinafter 2 N.Y.S.E. Guide). In addition, each party is allowed one peremptory challenge and unlimited challenges for cause.

---

3. In the recently enacted Older Workers Benefit Protection Act, Congress amended the ADEA to provide that "an individual may not waive any right or claim under this Act unless the waiver is knowing and voluntary." See §201. Congress also specified certain conditions that must be met in order for a waiver to be knowing and voluntary. Ibid.

Id., ¶2609, at 4315 (Rule 609). Moreover, the arbitrators are required to disclose "any circumstances which might preclude [them] from rendering an objective and impartial determination." Id., ¶2610, at 4315 (Rule 610). The FAA also protects against bias, by providing that courts may overturn arbitration decisions "where there was evident partiality or corruption in the arbitrators." 9 U.S.C. § 10 (b). There has been no showing in this case that those provisions are inadequate to guard against potential bias.

Gilmer also complains that the discovery allowed in arbitration is more limited than in the federal courts, which he contends will make it difficult to prove discrimination. It is unlikely, however, that age discrimination claims require more extensive discovery than other claims that we have found to be arbitrable, such as RICO and antitrust claims. Moreover, there has been no showing in this case that the NYSE discovery provisions, which allow for document production, information requests, depositions, and subpoenas, see 2 N.Y.S.E. Guide ¶2619, pp. 4318 – 4320 (Rule 619); Securities and Exchange Commission Order Approving Proposed Rule Changes by New York Stock Exchange, Inc., Nat. Assn. of Securities Dealers, Inc., and the American Stock Exchange, Inc., Relating to the Arbitration Process and the Use of Predispute Arbitration Clauses, 54 Fed. Reg. 21144, 21149-21151 (1989), will prove insufficient to allow ADEA claimants such as Gilmer a fair opportunity to present their claims. Although those procedures might not be as extensive as in the federal courts, by agreeing to arbitrate, a party "trades the procedures and opportunity for review of the courtroom for the simplicity, informality, and expedition of arbitration." *Mitsubishi.* Indeed, an important counterweight to the reduced discovery in NYSE arbitration is that arbitrators are not bound by the rules of evidence. See 2 N.Y.S.E. Guide ¶2620, p. 4320 (Rule 620).

A further alleged deficiency of arbitration is that arbitrators often will not issue written opinions, resulting, Gilmer contends, in a lack of public knowledge of employers' discriminatory policies, an inability to obtain effective appellate review, and a stifling of the development of the law. The NYSE rules, however, do require that all arbitration awards be in writing, and that the awards contain the names of the parties, a summary of the issues in controversy, and a description of the award issued. See id., ¶¶2627(a), (e), at 4321 (Rules 627(a), (e)). In addition, the award decisions are made available to the public. See id., ¶2627(f), at 4322 (Rule 627(f)). Furthermore, judicial decisions addressing ADEA claims will continue to be issued because it is unlikely that all or even most ADEA claimants will be subject to arbitration agreements. Finally, Gilmer's concerns apply equally to settlements of ADEA claims, which, as noted above, are clearly allowed.[4]

It is also argued that arbitration procedures cannot adequately further the purposes of the ADEA because they do not provide for broad equitable relief and class actions. [H]owever, arbitrators do have the power to fashion equitable relief. Indeed, the NYSE rules applicable here do not restrict the types of relief an arbitrator may award, but merely refer to "damages and/or other relief." 2 N.Y.S.E. Guide ¶2627(e), p. 4321 (Rule 627(e)). The NYSE rules also provide for collective proceedings. Id., ¶2612(d), at 4317 (Rule 612(d)). But "even if the arbitration could not go forward as a class action or class relief could not be granted by the arbitrator, the fact that the

---

4. Gilmer also contends that judicial review of arbitration decisions is too limited. We have stated, however, that "although judicial scrutiny of arbitration awards necessarily is limited, such review is sufficient to ensure that arbitrators comply with the requirements of the statute" at issue. *Shearson/American Express Inc. v. McMahon,* 482 U.S. 220, 232 (1987).

[ADEA] provides for the possibility of bringing a collective action does not mean that individual attempts at conciliation were intended to be barred." *Nicholson v. CPC Int'l Inc.*, 877 F.2d 221, 241 (CA3 1989) (Becker, J., dissenting). Finally, it should be remembered that arbitration agreements will not preclude the *EEOC* from bringing actions seeking class-wide and equitable relief.

C

An additional reason advanced by Gilmer for refusing to enforce arbitration agreements relating to ADEA claims is his contention that there often will be unequal bargaining power between employers and employees. Mere inequality in bargaining power, however, is not a sufficient reason to hold that arbitration agreements are never enforceable in the employment context. Relationships between securities dealers and investors, for example, may involve unequal bargaining power, but we nevertheless held in *Rodriguez de Quijas* and *McMahon* that agreements to arbitrate in that context are enforceable. As discussed above, the FAA's purpose was to place arbitration agreements on the same footing as other contracts. Thus, arbitration agreements are enforceable "save upon such grounds as exist at law or in equity for the revocation of any contract." 9 U.S.C. §2. "Of course, courts should remain attuned to well-supported claims that the agreement to arbitrate resulted from the sort of fraud or overwhelming economic power that would provide grounds 'for the revocation of any contract.'" *Mitsubishi*. There is no indication in this case, however, that Gilmer, an experienced businessman, was coerced or defrauded into agreeing to the arbitration clause in his registration application. As with the claimed procedural inadequacies discussed above, this claim of unequal bargaining power is best left for resolution in specific cases.

IV

In addition to the arguments discussed above, Gilmer vigorously asserts that our decision in Alexander v. Gardner-Denver Co. and its progeny — Barrentine *v. Arkansas-Best Freight System, Inc.*, 450 U.S. 728 (1981), and *McDonald v. West Branch*, 466 U.S. 284 (1984) — preclude arbitration of employment discrimination claims. Gilmer's reliance on these cases, however, is misplaced.

In *Gardner-Denver*, the issue was whether a discharged employee whose grievance had been arbitrated pursuant to an arbitration clause in a collective-bargaining agreement was precluded from subsequently bringing a Title VII action based upon the conduct that was the subject of the grievance. In holding that the employee was not foreclosed from bringing the Title VII claim, we stressed that an employee's contractual rights under a collective-bargaining agreement are distinct from the employee's statutory Title VII rights:

> In submitting his grievance to arbitration, an employee seeks to vindicate his contractual right under a collective-bargaining agreement. By contrast, in filing a lawsuit under Title VII, an employee asserts independent statutory rights accorded by Congress. The distinctly separate nature of these contractual and statutory rights is not vitiated merely because both were violated as a result of the same factual occurrence.

We also noted that a labor arbitrator has authority only to resolve questions of contractual rights. The arbitrator's "task is to effectuate the intent of the parties" and he or she does not have the "general authority to invoke public laws that conflict with the bargain between the parties." By contrast, "in instituting an action under Title VII, the employee is not seeking review of the arbitrator's decision. Rather, he is asserting a statutory right independent of the arbitration process." We further expressed concern that in collective-bargaining arbitration "the interests of the individual employee may be subordinated to the collective interests of all employees in the bargaining unit."[5]

Barrentine and *McDonald* similarly involved the issue whether arbitration under a collective-bargaining agreement precluded a subsequent statutory claim. In holding that the statutory claims there were not precluded, we noted, as in *Gardner-Denver*, the difference between contractual rights under a collective-bargaining agreement and individual statutory rights, the potential disparity in interests between a union and an employee, and the limited authority and power of labor arbitrators.

There are several important distinctions between the *Gardner-Denver* line of cases and the case before us. First, those cases did not involve the issue of the enforceability of an agreement to arbitrate statutory claims. Rather, they involved the quite different issue whether arbitration of contract-based claims precluded subsequent judicial resolution of statutory claims. Since the employees there had not agreed to arbitrate their statutory claims, and the labor arbitrators were not authorized to resolve such claims, the arbitration in those cases understandably was held not to preclude subsequent statutory actions. Second, because the arbitration in those cases occurred in the context of a collective-bargaining agreement, the claimants there were represented by their unions in the arbitration proceedings. An important concern therefore was the tension between collective representation and individual statutory rights, a concern not applicable to the present case. Finally, those cases were not decided under the FAA, which, as discussed above, reflects a "liberal federal policy favoring arbitration agreements." *Mitsubishi*. Therefore, those cases provide no basis for refusing to enforce Gilmer's agreement to arbitrate his ADEA claim. . . .

Justice STEVENS, with whom Justice MARSHALL joins, dissenting.
Section 1 of the Federal Arbitration Act (FAA) states:

> [N]othing herein contained shall apply to contracts of employment of seamen, railroad employees, or any other class of workers engaged in foreign or interstate commerce. 9 U.S.C. § 1.

The Court today, in holding that the FAA compels enforcement of arbitration clauses even when claims of age discrimination are at issue, skirts the antecedent question whether the coverage of the Act even extends to arbitration clauses contained in employment contracts, regardless of the subject matter of the claim at issue. In my opinion, arbitration clauses contained in employment agreements are specifically exempt from coverage of the FAA, and for that reason respondent Interstate/Johnson

---

5. The Court in *Alexander v. Gardner-Denver Co.* also expressed the view that arbitration was inferior to the judicial process for resolving statutory claims. That "mistrust of the arbitral process," however, has been undermined by our recent arbitration decisions. *McMahon.* "We are well past the time when judicial suspicion of the desirability of arbitration and of the competence of arbitral tribunals inhibited the development of arbitration as an alternative means of dispute resolution." *Mitsubishi Motors Corp. v. Soler Chrysler-Plymouth, Inc.*

Lane Corporation cannot, pursuant to the FAA, compel petitioner to submit his claims arising under the [ADEA]. . . .

Not only would I find that the FAA does not apply to employment-related disputes between employers and employees in general, but also I would hold that compulsory arbitration conflicts with the congressional purpose animating the ADEA, in particular. As this Court previously has noted, authorizing the courts to issue broad injunctive relief is the cornerstone to eliminating discrimination in society. *Albemarle Paper Co. v. Moody* [reproduced at p. 654]. The ADEA, like Title VII of the Civil Rights Act of 1964, authorizes courts to award broad, class-based injunctive relief to achieve the purposes of the Act. Because commercial arbitration is typically limited to a specific dispute between the particular parties and because the available remedies in arbitral forums generally do not provide for class-wide injunctive relief, see Shell, ERISA and Other Federal Employment Statutes: When is Commercial Arbitration an "Adequate Substitute" for the Courts?, 68 Texas L. Rev. 509, 568 (1990), I would conclude that an essential purpose of the ADEA is frustrated by compulsory arbitration of employment discrimination claims.

. . . The Court's holding today clearly eviscerates the important role played by an independent judiciary in eradicating employment discrimination.

NOTES

1. *Collective Bargaining Agreements Untouched?* The most obvious difference between *Gardner-Denver* and *Gilmer* was that the latter did not arise in the context of a collective bargaining agreement. This had two important implications, one factual and the other legal. From a factual perspective, the union controls the individual employee's claim when arbitration is conducted under a collective bargaining agreement, and *Gardner-Denver* was obviously unwilling to trust individual Title VII or ADEA rights to a union. From a legal perspective, *Gilmer* arose under the Federal Arbitration Act, not the National Labor Relations Act.

The first question, therefore, was whether *Gilmer* overruled *Gardner-Denver* entirely or left *Gardner-Denver* to govern collective bargaining arbitration. The overwhelming majority of circuits read *Gilmer* as not overruling *Gardner-Denver* in the unionized workplace, limiting *Gilmer* to arbitration where the employee herself, not her union, agrees to arbitrate her statutory claims. E.g., *Pyett v. Pennsylvania Bldg. Co.*, 498 F.3d 88 (2d Cir. 2007); *Johnson v. Bodine Elec. Co.*, 142 F.3d 363, 367 (7th Cir. 1998).

One circuit, however, held to the contrary: arbitration clauses, even when contained in collective bargaining agreements, may bar suit by individual employees. *Austin v. Owens-Broadway Glass Container, Inc.*, 78 F.3d 875 (4th Cir. 1996). The Supreme Court granted certiorari to resolve the circuit split in *Wright v. Universal Maritime Serv. Corp.*, 525 U.S. 70 (1998), but ultimately punted, deciding only that the collective bargaining agreement's general arbitration clause was not a sufficiently clear waiver on the facts before it. *Wright*, therefore, left open the underlying question of whether a properly drafted collective bargaining agreement could terminate a union member's right to sue in federal court on her statutory antidiscrimination claims. *See also Safrit v. Cone Mills Corp.*, 248 F.3d 306 (4th Cir. 2001) (finding explicit waiver).

2. *Arbitration as a Viable Alternative to Litigation.* The *Gilmer* majority swept aside the concerns *Gardner-Denver* had raised about the inherent limitations of the arbitral forums as compared to court proceedings. *Gilmer* also rejected several frontal

attacks on arbitration as a means of deciding ADEA cases. It first dismissed as speculative plaintiff's claim that the arbitral process, governed by the New York Stock Exchange rules, would be biased toward the employer. It then noted that there was no showing that discovery would be inadequate for an ADEA claim under those rules. Additionally, awards would be public so that objections to hidden decisions were inapplicable. Finally, the Court stressed that arbitrators have the power to award broad equitable relief, and, to the extent their remedial powers are deficient, the EEOC remains able to sue the employer. *Gilmer* obviously marked a sea change in the Court's attitude toward arbitration of employment disputes, but its actual effect depended upon several developments.

Given the significance of *Gilmer* for antidiscrimination laws, you might be interested in the backstory of the case. *See generally* Charles A. Sullivan, *Gilmering Antidiscrimination Law* in EMPLOYMENT DISCRIMINATION STORIES (Friedman, ed. 2006, Foundation Press). An interesting, some would say revealing, epilogue is that Mr. Gilmer won in the arbitration that followed the Supreme Court's decision, but the award appeared to be substantially less than he would have received had a court found in his favor. *Id.* Another development is that the U-4 Form in the securities industry, which resulted in *Gilmer* and many of the other cases involving arbitration, has been eliminated by changes in rules by the NYSE, NASD, and similar organizations. Nevertheless, individual employers, in and outside of the securities industry, continue to use arbitration clauses on their own initiative.

3. *Application to Other Antidiscrimination Statutes.* One issue was whether *Gilmer* applied to the ADEA only or to other discrimination statutes. The lower courts have uniformly applied the holding across the board. *E.g., Seus v. Nuveen,* 146 F.3d 175 (3d Cir. 1998) (Title VII); *McWilliams v. Logicon, Inc.,* 143 F.3d 573 (10th Cir. 1998) (ADA).

4. *Application to Individual Contracts with Employers.* A more serious question was whether the *Gilmer* rule applied only to the somewhat unusual setting in which the case arose. The arbitration agreement in that case was a part of plaintiff's registration with the New York Stock Exchange, not directly a contract with the brokerage firm that employed him. For that reason, the *Gilmer* Court did not address the argument that the Federal Arbitration Act did not apply. Section 1 of the FAA provides that "nothing herein contained shall apply to contracts of employment of seamen, railroad employees, or any other class of workers engaged in foreign or interstate commerce." If this were read to exclude coverage of all employment contracts, *Gilmer* would have had little practical effect. The dissenters in *Gilmer* had argued that the Court should have reached the question and decided that employment contracts were exempt, and a lively literature emerged on the question.

However, when the Court encountered the question in *Circuit City Stores, Inc. v. Adams,* 532 U.S. 105 (2001), it held that "Section 1 exempts from the FAA only contracts of employment of transportation workers." *Id.* at 119. The Court, therefore, concluded that the employment discrimination claims made by plaintiff must be submitted to arbitration. For a critique of this holding, see, Margaret L. Moses, *Statutory Misconstruction: How the Supreme Court Created a Federal Arbitration Law Never Enacted by Congress,* 34 FLA. ST. U. L. REV. 99 (2006).

While *Circuit City* involved state law discrimination claims, it clearly applies to federal claims as well. *Circuit City* is also important for its holding that the adhesive nature of the agreement to arbitrate was irrelevant to whether §1 applied, as were state decisions related to whether arbitration was an appropriate forum to decide matters of state law.

5. *Potential Limitations on Arbitration by OWBPA?* We encountered OWBPA in section A, where we saw that that statute prohibits waiver of rights under the ADEA unless the release meets certain conditions. These conditions are much more stringent than the formalities that typically attend agreements to arbitrate employment disputes. Accordingly, there is a plausible textual argument that such arbitration agreements, which necessarily waive the employee's right to a jury trial, are invalid under the ADEA. Despite this, the courts have interpreted OWBPA to apply only "to substantive rights, or, at any rate, not to the right to proceed in court rather than in arbitration." *Rosenberg v. Merrill Lynch,* 170 F.3d 1 (1st Cir. 1999). *Accord Seus v. Nuveen,* 146 F.3d 175 (3d Cir. 1998). *Oubre v. Entergy Operations, Inc.,* reproduced at p. 724, which stressed giving effect to the plain language of OWBPA, was dismissed as "not particularly relevant"; indeed, "[t]o the degree that *Oubre* has any relevance here, the reference to "claim" suggests that the waiver provisions refer to substantive claims. A substantive ADEA claim may be presented in an arbitral or a judicial forum." *Rosenberg* at 13.

6. *Potential Limitations on Arbitration by the Civil Rights Act of 1991?* Since *Gilmer* was decided before the enactment of the Civil Rights Act of 1991, that statute could conceivably supersede *Gilmer.* Section 118 provides that "[w]here appropriate and to the extent authorized by law, the use of alternative means of dispute resolution, including . . . arbitration, is encouraged to resolve disputes arising under the Acts or provisions of Federal law amended by this title." Pub. L. No. 102-166, § 118, 105 Stat. 1071, 1081 (1991).

The word "appropriate" might be thought ambiguous, which would support resort to the statute's legislative history. That history, in turn, had statements opposing mandatory arbitration. Further, the House rejected an amendment that would have explicitly permitted pre-dispute mandatory arbitration agreements, *see also* H.R.Rep. No. 102- 40(I), at 104 (1991), *reprinted in* 1991 U.S.C.C.A.N. 549, 642, although there was some contrary legislative history. Despite this, the lower courts have required a more explicit statement to overcome the FAA's presumption of arbitrability. *See, e.g., EEOC v. Luce, Forward, Hamilton & Scripps,* 345 F.3d 742, 752-53 (9th Cir. 2003) (en banc). *See generally* Mara Kent, *"Forced" vs. Compulsory Arbitration of Civil Rights Claims,* 23 LAW & INEQ. J. 95, 115 (2005) (while courts have recognized that Congress did not intend to permit employers to force employees to choose between their civil rights and their jobs, they have refused to implement this intent); Mark L. Adams, *Compulsory Arbitration of Discrimination Claims and the Civil Rights Act of 1991: Encouraged or Prescribed?,* 44 WAYNE L. REV. 619 (1999) (Congress intended in the 1991 Act to encourage only voluntary, not compulsory, arbitration). However, while not reading § 118 to bar mandatory arbitration, some courts have looked to it as a basis for requiring a somewhat more searching review of the arbitration agreement than they might otherwise undertake. See Note 9.

7. *Waiver of the Right to Jury Trial?* Restrictive doctrines govern the waiver of a jury trial in federal court once a jury has been demanded. Some have argued that these rules should be carried over to the arbitration context and, irrespective of § 118 or OWBPA, require more rigorous conditions than currently obtain. *See* Stephen J. Ware, *Arbitration Clauses, Jury Waiver Clauses and Other Contractual Waivers of Constitutional Rights,* 67 L. & CONTEMP. PROBS. 167 (2004). Thus far, such arguments have not been accepted by the courts. *See Caley v. Gulfstream Aero. Corp.,* 428 F.3d 1359 (11th Cir. 2005) (normal contract principles applied to an employer policy requiring employees to arbitrate disputes; it was not subject to the heightened knowing and voluntary standard usually used when a jury trial is waived).

8. *Antiretaliation.* Courts have also rejected arguments that discharge for failure to sign an agreement to arbitrate disputes is proscribed by antiretaliation provisions. *Weeks v. Harden Mfg. Corp.*, 291 F.3d 1307 (11th Cir. 2002) (employee could not reasonably believe that arbitration system was unlawful employment practice).

9. *The FAA as a "Super-Statute."* The preceding Notes can be summed up simply: the FAA trumps all other statutes, even those that were enacted years after it and reflect very important policy choices. While the Supreme Court has indicated that the presumption in favor of arbitration can be overcome when "Congress has evinced an intention to preclude a waiver of judicial remedies for the statutory rights at issue," it has yet to find one. And, while it has indicated that Congress' "intention will be deducible from text or legislative history," *Mitsubishi Motors Corp. v. Soler Chrysler-Plymouth, Inc.*, 473 U.S. 614, 628 (1985), the lower courts have failed to give effect to congressional statements opposing mandatory arbitration.

A good example of the strength of the presumption in favor of arbitration is *Rosenberg v. Merrill Lynch*, 170 F.3d 1 (1st Cir. 1999), which rejected both § 118 and OWBPA as limitations on pre-dispute agreements to arbitrate. To do so, the court had to deploy contradictory interpretive methodologies in the same opinion. Thus, in dealing with the 1991 Civil Rights Act, *Rosenberg* found the word "appropriate" so clear as to obviate any need to look to legislative history, which would have cut the other way. But in dealing with OWBPA, which expressly limits the waiver of any "right," the court interpolated the qualifying adjective "substantive" to narrow the prohibition, again despite legislative history going the other way. Similarly, we saw in Note 7 that courts that have refused to apply the heightened standard normally governing waiver of a jury trial in federal court.

These and other decisions suggest that the courts are viewing the Federal Arbitration Act as a kind of "super statute," one that is of higher status than other statutes and which, therefore, can be avoided only by legislation with some sort of "clear statement." *See* William N. Eskridge, Jr. & John Ferejohn, *Super-Statutes*, 50 DUKE L.J. 1215 (2001) (viewing the FAA as a super-statute). Assuming that's a fair characterization, do you understand why the FAA is so viewed? Might it have something to do with being a mechanism for reducing court dockets?

10. *Who Decides Whether an Agreement Is Valid?* The preceding discussion might suggest that courts decide whether an agreement to arbitrate is valid and then arbitrators decide the underlying dispute. Things are not that simple. The presumption is that the question is one for the court but that the parties may commit the question to the arbitrator. *AT&T Techs., Inc. v. Communications Workers of Am.*, 475 U.S. 643, 656 (1986) ("[T]he question of arbitrability — whether a collective-bargaining agreement creates a duty for the parties to arbitrate the particular grievance — is undeniably an issue for judicial determination. Unless the parties clearly and unmistakably provide otherwise, the question of whether the parties agreed to arbitrate is to be decided by the court, not the arbitrator"). In *Howsam v. Dean Witter Reynolds, Inc.*, 537 U.S. 79 (2002), however, the Court cut back on this principle by narrowly reading "the question of arbitrability." According to *Howsam*, the phrase is applicable "in the kind of narrow circumstance where contracting parties would likely have expected a court to have decided the gateway matter." *Id.* at 83. Applying this approach, the question whether a six-year time limit on arbitration precluded arbitration of the dispute in question was one for the arbitrator, not the court.

11. *EEOC Enforcement and Arbitration. Gilmer* stressed that, even though private suit might be foreclosed by an arbitration agreement, the EEOC remained free to bring an action. Despite this language, there were efforts to limit EEOC suits on

behalf of individual employees who had agreed to arbitrate claims. In *EEOC v. Waffle House, Inc.*, 534 U.S. 279 (2002), the Court rejected such arguments and permitted the EEOC to obtain relief in Commission lawsuits on behalf of employees even if these employees had agreed to arbitration with their employers. *See also EEOC v. Circuit City*, 285 F.3d 404 (6th Cir. 2002) (holding that an arbitration agreement between an employer and an employee did not bar a non-party to the agreement, such as the EEOC, from filing its own suit against the employer). While recoveries by such employees, either after litigation or by arbitration, would presumably bar duplicate recovery in the EEOC action, the agency is not foreclosed from suing by virtue of an arbitration agreement to which it is not a party.

NOTE ON THE POLICY IMPLICATIONS OF ARBITRATION

Gilmer is written as if it is a straightforward application of the 1925 Federal Arbitration Act, which provides that a written arbitration clause in any "contract evidencing a transaction involving commerce . . . shall be valid, irrevocable, and enforceable, save upon such grounds as exist at law or in equity for the revocation of any contract." 9 U.S.C.A. §2. Under such a view, the policy decisions were made by Congress, not the courts. But this seems unlikely. Commentators have documented various departures from the statutory language and its legislative history, *e.g.*, Margaret L. Moses, *Statutory Misconstruction: How the Supreme Court Created a Federal Arbitration Law Never Enacted by Congress*, 34 FLA. ST. U. L. REV. 99 (2006); David S. Schwartz, *Correcting Federalism Mistakes in Statutory Interpretation: The Supreme Court and the Federal Arbitration Act* 67 L. & CONTEMP. PROBS. 5 (2004). Indeed, we have seen that the FAA has become a superstatute, one which presumes arbitration to be the preferred method of dispute resolution and which downplays any possibly conflicting statutory enactments. In *Gilmer* itself, the Court saw no conflict between the commands of the ADEA and the FAA's preference for arbitration; the lower courts' refusal to restrict arbitration through reference to the 1991 Civil Rights Act or OWBPA confirms that view.

But even if the courts are not imposing their own policy preferences, perhaps influenced largely by the benefits of arbitration for court dockets, there still remain significant policy concerns. After all, Congress enacted the FAA in 1925, and the American economy and workforce have changed enormously since then. Is arbitration a good idea in such settings? Or, more precisely, is mandatory arbitration as a condition of employment a good idea?

There is a consensus that employers and employees ought to be free to agree to arbitration after a dispute has arisen. In this setting, the parties can make an informed trade-off between the likely lower costs and greater speed of arbitration and the greater procedural protections of traditional court proceedings. The controversy arises, as in *Gilmer* and *Circuit City*, when arbitration agreements are required as a condition of employment, or (in the case of Mr. Gilmer) as a condition for working in a particular industry. In theory, opting for arbitration does not increase the risk of being on the losing end of a dispute but merely reduces the costs of resolving it by substituting a cheaper and speedier alternative mechanism. Such features could make arbitration a more accessible and, hence, more effective form of dispute resolution for employees who lack the time, financial resources, and access to counsel necessary to pursue litigation in court. *See* Samuel Estreicher, *Saturns for Rickshaws: The Stakes in the Debate Over Predispute Employment Arbitration Agreements*, 16

OHIO ST. J. ON DISP. RESOL. 559 (2001). *But see* David S. Schwartz, *If You Love Arbitration, Set It Free: How "Mandatory" Undermines "Arbitration,"* http://papers .ssrn.com/sol3/papers.cfm?abstract_id = 1006826 (arguing that forcing employer and consumer cases into arbitration has resulted in judicialization of the process).

However, arbitration is quicker and less costly precisely because certain procedures and safeguards associated with court litigation are abandoned. Further, since employers generally select the particular forum and its procedures, it is possible that arbitration will favor employers in both substantive outcomes and generosity of remedies. Even assuming an objectively neutral forum, some commentators believe systemic factors will incline arbitrators toward employers, in part because of the "repeat player" phenomenon, that is, the tendency of arbitrators to favor those with whom they will be interacting in the future. *See generally* Lisa B. Bingham, *On Repeat Players, Adhesive Contracts, and the Use of Statistics in Judicial Review of Employment Arbitration Awards,* 29 MCGEORGE L. REV. 223 (1998). Further, there are those who fear that employers, with greater experience in these mechanisms, will have a substantial edge in gaming the system. *See* Sarah Rudolph Cole, *Arbitration and the Batson Principle,* 38 GA. L. REV. 1145, 1239 (2004) (employers "may use their greater knowledge and experience with the arbitral process to gain control over the arbitrator selection process through the use of invidious peremptory strikes, discriminatory peremptory strikes"); Michael Z. Green, *An Essay Challenging the Racially Biased Selection of Arbitrators for Employment Discrimination Suits,* 4 J. AM. ARB. 1 (2005). The EEOC maintains that mandatory arbitration has a built-in bias favoring employers who tend to be "repeat players." Policy Statement on Mandatory Binding Arbitration of Employment Disputes as a Condition of Employment, No. 915.002 (July 10, 1997) *http://www.eeoc.gov/docs/mandarb. html* (last visited Sept. 13, 2007).

Such concerns are heightened by the common employer practice of requiring employees to sign contracts to arbitrate upon applying for or commencing a job, that is, well before a dispute actually arises. In contrast to the decision to arbitrate an existing dispute, an employee faced with a pre-dispute arbitration agreement may be less likely to appreciate the importance of choice of forum or to have had the opportunity to consult counsel. *See* Matthew T. Bodie, *Questions About the Efficiency of Employment Arbitration Agreements,* 39 GA. L. REV. 1, 41 (2004) (employee assent to pre-dispute arbitration agreements is "more likely to be based on primitive guesswork, or less," while employers are likely to have a significant informational advantages that they may use "to construct inefficient agreements that employees would not agree to if they had perfect information"). Moreover, such agreements are generally boilerplate documents that individual employees are generally not in a position to refuse. If employees are unable to negotiate the terms or arbitration agreements or even to weigh the trade offs involved, such agreements could effectively serve as waivers of substantive employment rights. *See also* Katherine Van Wezel Stone, *Mandatory Arbitration of Individual Employment Rights: The Yellow Dog Contract of the 1990s,* 73 DENV. U. L. REV. 1017 (1996).

Yet another set of objections to arbitration stems from the fact that, as a private dispute resolution mechanism, arbitration may not serve the wider goals of the antidiscrimination laws, even if it achieves justice in individual cases. Chief among the concerns are the confidentiality of the process, which arguably inhibits public education about discrimination and limits the development of the law by removing a large source of potential precedential cases. *See* Geraldine Szott Moohr, *Arbitration and the Goals of Employment Discrimination Law,* 56 WASH. & LEE L. REV. 395, 426-39 (1999).

Intermingled with the policy objections to mandatory arbitration per se are arguments about how arbitration works in practice. This has two thrusts, both of which we will explore in more detail. First, the structure of the particular arbitral forum may be problematic. Because it is private, the nature of the arbitration process varies depending on the particular forum and rules the parties select. *Gilmer*, for example, involved a particular arbitral system; while the Court found no reason to believe the N.Y.S.E. regime would be inadequate to vindicate ADEA rights, that may not be true of other systems.

In many instances, parties opt for an established arbitration service, such as the American Arbitration Association, which has an extensive set of rules and procedures for resolving employment disputes. *See AAA National Rules for the Resolution of Employment Disputes* (2005) *available at* http://www.adr.org/sp.asp?id = 22075. But an employer might choose a less formal venue or develop its own set of rules and procedures. The non-standard nature of arbitration systems has two implications. First, arbitrators can vary significantly in terms of their expertise and background. Second, the rules governing arbitration can vary dramatically from those the Supreme Court blessed in *Gilmer*. An ADR Protocol, endorsed by organizations such as the AAA, suggests procedures for arbitrating workplace disputes, and urges arbitrators to refuse cases that do not provide appropriate safeguards. See http:www.naarb.org/protocol.html. The National Employment Law Association, which represents the plaintiff's bar, has subscribed to the Protocol but urged that the profession go further and refuse to arbitrate when the arbitration agreement is a condition of employment. Richard A. Bales, *The Employment Due Process Protocol at Ten: Twenty Unresolved Issues, and a Focus on Conflicts of Interest*, 21 OHIO ST. J. DISPUTE RES. 165 (2005); Leona Green, *Mandatory Arbitration of Statutory Employment Disputes: A Public Policy Issue in Need of a Legislation Solution*, 12 NOTRE DAME J.L. ETHICS & PUB. POLY. 173 (1998).

In addition, arbitration agreements typically specify who pays the costs of arbitration, and this can itself be an obstacle to the vindication of rights under the antidiscrimination statutes. See Note on the Elephant in the Room, p. 755. Such agreements may also attempt to go beyond merely substituting an arbitral forum for a court by narrowing the remedial rights of the employee, as by capping damages or excluding punitive damages. Further, while arbitration necessarily changes the procedural rights of employees by eliminating the judicial forum and its concomitant protections, particular arbitration agreements might go further down this road. For example, they might contract the time within which a claim is filed. Again, these issues are not objections to arbitration as such but rather problems with particular arbitration regimes. *See generally* Richard A. Bales, *A Normative Consideration of Employment Arbitration at* Gilmer's *Quinceañera*, 81 TUL. L. REV. 331 (2006) (a clear set of "due process rules" should be developed and penalties, perhaps in the form of awarding attorneys' fees to employees who successfully challenge lopsided agreements, should be imposed); Martin A. Malin, *Privatizing Justice — But By How Much? Questions* Gilmer *Did Not Answer*, 16 OHIO ST. J. ON DISP. RESOL. 589, 631 (2001) ("In policing mandatory arbitration systems courts should insist on certain basic due process safeguards."); *but see* Kenneth R. Davis, *A Model for Arbitration: Autonomy, Cooperation, and Curtailment of State Power*, 26 FORDHAM URB. L.J. 167 (1999) (arguing for a very restrictive judicial approach to arbitration).

All this theorizing leaves unanswered the underlying question: is arbitration an inferior alternative to litigation for employees? This is essentially an empirical question and one complicated by both the secrecy of arbitral regimes and their variance. Some argue that arbitration is more effective than litigation for lower level workers who can not afford legal representation or at least cannot afford the more costly representation that a court suit might require. It is, for them, the only game in town. Others claim that arbitration discourages claims that would be brought if the employee were free to file suit. Finally, many argue that, even if arbitration achieves desirable results, it is not clear that *mandatory* arbitration is necessary for those benefits. If both sides wish to arbitrate after a dispute arises, there are no legal obstacles.

Although there is disagreement about the appropriate metrics for assessing the results of available arbitration, the evidence using available data so far is mixed, *See* Alexander J.S. Colvin, *Empirical Research on Employment Arbitration: Clarity Amidst the Sound and Fury?* EMP. RTS & EMPL. POL'Y J. (forthcoming 2008) (more recent data show employee win rates and damages lower than those in litigation); Theodore Eisenberg & Elizabeth Hill, *Employment Arbitration and Litigation: An Empirical Comparison,* http://papers.ssrn.com/sol3/papers.cfm?abstract_id = 389780 ("For higher paid employees, we find little evidence that arbitrated outcomes materially differ from trial outcomes. . . . These results are consistent with the belief that lower pay employees lack systematic, realistic access to court"). *See also* Michael Z. Green, *Debunking the Myth of Employer Advantage from Using Mandatory Arbitration for Discrimination Claims,* 31 RUTGERS L.J. 399, 401-05 (2000) (arguing that mandatory arbitration presents a significant number of disadvantages for employers).

CIRCUIT CITY STORES, INC. v. ADAMS
279 F.3d 889 (9th Cir. 2002)

NELSON, Circuit Judge.

The Supreme Court granted certiorari, reversed this court's prior decision, and remanded for proceedings in accordance with its opinion in Circuit City Stores, Inc. v. Adams, 532 U.S. 105 (2001). Now that the Federal Arbitration Act ("FAA"), 9 U.S.C. § 1 et seq., applies to the arbitration agreement in this case, we must decide whether the district court erred in exercising its authority under the Act to compel arbitration.

I. FACTUAL AND PROCEDURAL BACKGROUND

On October 23, 1995, Saint Clair Adams completed an application to work as a sales person at Circuit City. As part of the application, Adams signed the "Circuit City Dispute Resolution Agreement" ("DRA"). The DRA requires employees to submit all claims and disputes to binding arbitration.[1] Incorporated into the DRA are a set of "Dispute Resolution Rules and Procedures". . . . that define the claims subject to arbitration, discovery rules, allocation of fees, and available remedies. Under these rules, the amount of damages is restricted: back pay is limited to one year, front pay to two years, and punitive damages to the greater of the amount of front and back pay awarded or $5000. In addition, the employee is required to split the costs of the

---

1. The DRA specifies that job applicants agree to settle "all previously unasserted claims, disputes or controversies arising out of or relating to my application or candidacy for employment, employment and/ or cessation of employment with Circuit City, *exclusively* by final and binding *arbitration* before a neutral Arbitrator. By way of example only, such claims include claims under federal, state, and local statutory or common law, such as Age Discrimination in Employment Act, Title VII of the Civil Rights Act of 1964, as amended, including the amendments to the Civil Rights Act of 1991, the Americans with Disabilities Act, the law of contract and law of tort." (emphasis in original).

arbitration, including the daily fees of the arbitrator, the cost of a reporter to transcribe the proceedings, and the expense of renting the room in which the arbitration is held, unless the employee prevails and the arbitrator decides to order Circuit City to pay the employee's share of the costs. Notably, Circuit City is not required under the agreement to arbitrate any claims against the employee.

An employee cannot work at Circuit City without signing the DRA. If an applicant refuses to sign the DRA (or withdraws consent within three days), Circuit City will not even consider his application.

[Adams filed a state court lawsuit against Circuit City and three co-workers alleging sexual harassment. Circuit City responded by filing a petition in federal district court to stay the state court proceedings and compel arbitration. The Supreme Court held that the FAA applied to the contract between Adams and Circuit City and remanded for an assessment of the legality of the arbitration agreement under California law.]

II. DISCUSSION

Circuit City has devised an arbitration agreement that functions as a thumb on Circuit City's side of the scale should an employment dispute ever arise between the company and one of its employees. We conclude that such an arrangement is unconscionable under California law.

A. APPLICABLE LAW

The FAA was enacted to overcome courts' reluctance to enforce arbitration agreements. The Act not only placed arbitration agreements on equal footing with other contracts, but established a federal policy in favor of arbitration, and a federal common law of arbitrability which preempts state law disfavoring arbitration. Section 2 of the FAA provides that arbitration agreements "shall be valid, irrevocable, and enforceable, *save upon such grounds that exist at law or in equity for the revocation of any contract.*" 9 U.S.C. §2 (emphasis added). Thus, although "courts may not invalidate arbitration agreements under state laws applicable only to arbitration provisions," general contract defenses such as fraud, duress, or unconscionability, grounded in state contract law, may operate to invalidate arbitration agreements. *Doctor's Assocs., Inc. v. Casarotto*, 517 U.S. 681, 687 (1996).

Adams argues that the DRA is an unconscionable contract of adhesion. Because Adams was employed in California, we look to California contract law to determine whether the agreement is valid.

Under California law, a contract is unenforceable if it is both procedurally and substantively unconscionable. *Armendariz v. Found. Health Psychcare Svcs., Inc.*, 6 P.3d 669, 690 (2000). When assessing procedural unconscionability, we consider the equilibrium of bargaining power between the parties and the extent to which the contract clearly discloses its terms. A determination of substantive unconscionability, on the other hand, involves whether the terms of the contract are unduly harsh or oppressive.

B. THE DRA AND UNCONSCIONABILITY

The DRA is procedurally unconscionable because it is a contract of adhesion: a standard-form contract, drafted by the party with superior bargaining power, which relegates to the other party the option of either adhering to its terms without modification or rejecting the contract entirely. Circuit City, which possesses considerably more bargaining power than nearly all of its employees or applicants, drafted the contract and uses it as its standard arbitration agreement for all of its new employees. The agreement is a prerequisite to employment, and job applicants are not permitted to modify the agreement's terms — they must take the contract or leave it. *See Armendariz*, (noting that few applicants are in a position to refuse a job because of an arbitration agreement).

The California Supreme Court's recent decision in *Armendariz* counsels in favor of finding that the Circuit City arbitration agreement is substantively unconscionable as well. In *Armendariz*, the California court reversed an order compelling arbitration of a FEHA [Fair Employment and Housing Act] discrimination claim because the arbitration agreement at issue required arbitration only of employees' claims and excluded damages that would otherwise be available under the FEHA. The agreement in *Armendariz* required employees, as a condition of employment, to submit all claims relating to termination of that employment — including any claim that the termination violated the employee's rights — to binding arbitration. The employer, however, was free to bring suit in court or arbitrate any dispute with its employees. In analyzing this asymmetrical arrangement, the court concluded that in order for a mandatory arbitration agreement to be valid, some "modicum of bilaterality" is required. Since the employer was not bound to arbitrate its claims and there was no apparent justification for the lack of mutual obligations, the court reasoned that arbitration appeared to be functioning "less as a forum for neutral dispute resolution and more as a means of maximizing employer advantage."

The substantive one-sidedness of the *Armendariz* agreement was compounded by the fact that it did not allow full recovery of damages for which the employees would be eligible under the FEHA. The exclusive remedy was back pay from the date of discharge until the date of the arbitration award, whereas plaintiffs in FEHA suits would be entitled to punitive damages, injunctive relief, front pay, emotional distress damages, and attorneys' fees.

We find the arbitration agreement at issue here virtually indistinguishable from the agreement the California Supreme Court found unconscionable in *Armendariz*. Like the agreement in *Armendariz*, the DRA unilaterally forces employees to arbitrate claims against the employer. The claims subject to arbitration under the DRA include "any and all employment-related legal disputes, controversies or claims *of an Associate* arising out of, or relating to, an Associate's application or candidacy for employment, employment or cessation of employment with Circuit City." (Emphasis added.) The provision does not require Circuit City to arbitrate its claims against employees. Circuit City has offered no justification for this asymmetry, nor is there any indication that "business realities" warrant the one-sided obligation. This unjustified one-sidedness deprives the DRA of the "modicum of bilaterality" that the California Supreme Court requires for contracts to be enforceable under California law.

And again as in *Armendariz*, the asymmetry is compounded by the fact that the agreement limits the relief available to employees. Under the DRA, the remedies are limited to injunctive relief, up to one year of back pay and up to two years of front pay, compensatory damages, and punitive damages in an amount up to the greater of the amount of back pay and front pay awarded or $5,000. By contrast, a plaintiff in a civil suit for sexual harassment under the FEHA is eligible for all forms of relief that are generally available to civil litigants — including appropriate punitive damages and damages for emotional distress. The DRA also requires the employee to split the arbitrator's fees with Circuit City. This fee allocation scheme alone would render an arbitration agreement unenforceable. But the DRA goes even further: it also imposes a strict one year statute of limitations on arbitrating claims that would deprive Adams of the benefit of the continuing violation doctrine available in FEHA suits. In short, and just like the agreement invalidated by the California Supreme Court in *Armendariz*, the DRA forces Adams to arbitrate his statutory claims without affording him the benefit of the full range of statutory remedies. . . .

NOTES

1. *Not Really Arbitration?* Some agreements to arbitrate may provide a process that is so one-sided that it is not fairly described as arbitration. *Gilmer* left open the possibility that an arbitral system might be so deficient as to not be enforceable, and a few cases have refused to enforce agreements on that ground. *See McMullen v. Meijer Inc.*, 355 F.3d 485 (6th Cir. 2004) (mandatory arbitration agreement did not preclude suit because it gave employer unilateral control over the pool of arbitrators); *Hooters of Am., Inc. v. Phillips*, 173 F.3d 933, 938 (4th Cir. 1999) ("The Hooters rules when taken as a whole, however, are so one-sided that their only possible purpose is to undermine the neutrality of the proceeding").

2. *Just Plain Contracts?* Assuming that the arbitration in question is not fundamentally flawed, what is the test for whether an agreement is enforceable? *See generally* Rachel Arnow-Richman, *Cubewrap Contracts: The Rise of Delayed Term, Standard Form Employment Agreements*, 49 ARIZ. L. REV. 637 (2007). Unlike the "knowing and voluntary" standard for releases (much less how releases need to be structured to comply with OWBPA where ADEA claims are concerned), *Circuit City II* does not seem to require that agreements to arbitrate satisfy any heightened test for validity. In other words, it applies normal contract analysis (including invalidating causes such as unconscionability). Other courts have applied plain vanilla contracts law and held general language about arbitration to include discrimination claims. *E.g., Seus v. Nuveen*, 146 F.3d 175 (3d Cir. 1998) (rejecting a heightened knowing and voluntary standard that considers such factors as specificity of language in agreement, plaintiff's education and experience, plaintiff's opportunity for deliberation and negotiation, and whether plaintiff was encouraged to consult counsel); *Patterson v. Tenet Healthcare*, 113 F.3d 832 (8th Cir. 1997) (general language of arbitration clause in employee handbook encompassed federal statutory claims even though other portions of handbook disclaimed contractual obligation).

Other courts, however, seem to require something more. For example, *Rosenberg v. Merrill Lynch, Pierce, Fenner & Smith, Inc.*, 170 F.3d 1 (1st Cir. 1999) looked to § 118 of the Civil Rights Act of 1991. See Note 9 on p. 743. That provision did not bar mandatory arbitration entirely, but the court read it to make arbitration "appropriate" only when there is "some minimal level of notice to the employee that statutory claims are subject to arbitration." *Id.* at 21. In so holding, the court looked to the Supreme Court's decision in *Wright v. Universal Maritime Serv. Corp*, 525 U.S. 70, 79-80 (1998), which held that, assuming arguendo a union could waive individual employees' rights to a federal judicial forum for statutory antidiscrimination claims, its agreement to arbitrate such claims must be "clear and unmistakable."

Still other courts also seem to apply a heightened consent requirement to enforcing employment-related arbitration agreements without looking to § 118 as the basis.

For example, they require that the employee must have "knowingly" agreed to arbitrate such claims, either by reference to the standard for releases or by reference to standards for waiving the right to jury trial. This requirement is not satisfied unless the agreement clearly refers to employment discrimination claims. *E.g., Paladino v. Avnet Computer*, 134 F.3d 1054 (11th Cir. 1998) (to fall within the FAA, an arbitration agreement must contain terms that generally and fairly inform the signatories that it covers statutory claims although it need not list every statute); *Renteria v. Prudential Ins. Co.*, 113 F.3d 1104 (9th Cir. 1997) (a U-4 form, stating that arbitrable disputes encompass those "as amended from time to time," was ineffective as a waiver since a knowing waiver of a right must be determined at the time the agreement is made). *See generally* Eileen Silverstein, *From Statute to Contract: The Law of the Employment Relationship Reconsidered*, 18 HOFSTRA LAB. & EMP. L.J. 479 (2001).

One thing that is clear is that, in deciding whether an agreement to arbitrate is valid, the court cannot give effect to state laws that would require something more rigorous for arbitration agreements than for other contracts. *E.g., Doctor's Assocs. v. Casarotto*, 517 U.S. 681 (1996) (striking down state law prescribing special procedural requirements for arbitration agreements). In other words, the FAA preempts state law to the extent it treats arbitration agreements differently. *But see* David S. Schwartz, *Correcting Federalism Mistakes in Statutory Interpretation: The Supreme Court and the Federal Arbitration Act* 67 L. & CONTEMP. PROBS. 5 (2004) (arguing that FAA preemption is inconsistent with congressional intent and contrary to the purported support for federalism of the Court's conservative majority). As you work through these notes, ask yourself whether this principle is being honored or whether some courts are not more hostile to arbitration than to other agreements, at least where the arbitration agreement is slanted towards the employer.

3. *Contract Formation: Finding an Agreement.* Regardless of the standard, employers seeking to enforce an arbitration agreement must at least establish offer, acceptance, and consideration. The employer in *Circuit City* seemed to have covered these bases by requiring applicants to sign and return written documents (manifesting their assent) in return for being considered for employment. Not all employers have planned as well. For example, some have attempted to impose arbitration on current workers merely by unilaterally amending an employee handbook or providing an e-mail notification. The results have been mixed. *Compare Campbell v. Gen. Dynamics Gov't Sys. Corp.*, 407 F.3d 546, 556-58 (1st Cir. 2005) (no enforceable arbitration agreement where policy distributed via hyperlink in e-mail notification and employee did not reply to message); *Salazar v. Citadel Communs. Corp.*, 90 P.3d 466, 469-70 (N.M. 2004) (no enforceable arbitration agreement where policy was annexed to employee manual containing disclaimer permitting employer to modify manual at will); *with Hardin v. First Cash Fin. Servs.*, 465 F.3d 470 (10th Cir. 2006) (employee's continuing to work constituted agreement to employer's dispute resolution program that required arbitration despite her expressly rejecting program and stating that her continued employment would not serve as consent); *Berkley v. Dillard's Inc.*, 450 F.3d 775 (8th Cir. 2006) (employee bound to arbitrate when she continued to work after being presented an agreement that she refused to sign). Should the manner in which the employer establishes and communicates its arbitration policy matter in assessing contract enforceability? If most employees simply sign whatever documents the employer places before them in the application process, why is it any more objectionable to bind them to a handbook or e-mail arbitration policy?

4. *Contract Formation: Consideration.* Like all contracts, agreements to arbitrate require consideration or a consideration substitute. *See, e.g., Saylor v. Ryan's Family Steak Houses,* 613 S.E.2d 914, 924 (W. Va. 2005) ("meager" promise to review employment application insufficient consideration to support applicant's promise to submit all disputes to arbitration). *Floss v. Ryan's Family Steak Houses Inc.,* 211 F.3d 306 (6th Cir. 2000) (pre-hire arbitration agreements unenforceable for lack of consideration); *cf. Hill v. PeopleSoft USA, Inc.,* 412 F.3d 540, 543-44 (4th Cir. 2005) (arbitration agreement not illusory due to lack of consideration because employer reserved right to change without notice). *See generally* Richard A. Bales, *Contract Formation Issues in Employment Arbitration,* 44 BRANDEIS L. J. 415 (2006) (examining how courts have applied state contract formation law to employment arbitration agreements, including: notice, consent, the employer's retention of a right unilaterally to modify the agreement, non-reciprocal obligations to arbitrate, and consideration).

5. *Contract Formation: Statute of Frauds.* Normal contract analysis often hinges enforceability on a writing signed by the party to be charged. While this is not the place for a detailed analysis of the statute of frauds, the FAA itself requires the agreement to arbitrate to be in writing in order to be enforceable under that law. 9 U.S.C. §2. However, unlike normal statutes of frauds, it has been held that the writing need not be signed by the party to be charged to satisfy the FAA. *Caley v. Gulfstream Aero. Corp.,* 428 F.3d 1359, 1369 (11th Cir. 2005) ("no signature is needed to satisfy the FAA's written agreement requirement").

6. *Invalidating Doctrines.* If assent and consideration are established, an employee's only means of defeating an arbitration agreement is to invoke one of the traditional defenses to contract such as fraud, duress, mistake, or unconscionability. Each of these doctrines, and some others, has been deployed to resist arbitration, but the only one to have gained much traction is unconscionability, as we saw in *Circuit City.* You may recall unconscionability from your first-year Contracts class; it is often defined as a lack of meaningful choice coupled with terms unreasonably favorable to one side. *See, e.g., Williams v. Walker-Thomas,* 350 F.2d 445 (D.C. Cir. 1965). This description embraces the ideas of "procedural" and "substantive" unconscionability, the former concept dealing with the manner in which agreement is reached while the latter refers to the fairness of the terms themselves. In which respect is the *Circuit City* arbitration agreement unconscionable?

Given the limited role unconscionability plays in other areas of contract law, there are a surprising number of cases striking arbitration clauses as unconscionable. Indeed, arbitration may be the only area of American law where unconscionability doctrine is alive and well. *See, e.g., Parilla v. IAP Worldwide Servs. VI, Inc.,* 368 F.3d 269 (3d Cir. 2004) (arbitration agreement imposing thirty-day statute of limitations and requiring each party is to bear its own expenses was substantively unconscionable); *Murray v. United Food & Commercial Workers Intl. Union,* 289 F.3d 297, 302-04 (4th Cir. 2002) (arbitration agreement giving employer discretion in naming possible arbitrators and constraining arbitrators' ability to rule on authority of employer's president was unconscionable and unenforceable); *Saylor v. Ryan's Family Steak Houses,* 613 S.E.2d 914, 922 (W. Va.) (arbitration agreement was an unenforceable contract of adhesion where plaintiff had a tenth-grade education, was applying for low-skill server position, and employer was a multi-state restaurant chain). *But see Circuit City v. Ahmed,* 283 F.3d 1198 (9th Cir. 2002) (arbitration agreement not unconscionable where employee given opportunity to opt out within 30 days of receiving written materials and video presentation of terms); *Howell v.*

Rivergate Toyota, Inc., 441 F.3d 230 (6th Cir. 2005) (agreement to arbitrate not invalid despite (1) 180-day limitations period; (2) unilateral right of the employer to amend the procedures; (3) limits on discovery; and (4) the "peculiar" requirement to apply to a Bexar County, Texas, court for appointment of an arbitrator). *See generally* Jeffrey W. Stempel, *Arbitration, Unconscionability, and Equilibrium: The Return of Unconscionability Analysis as a Counterweight to Arbitration Formalism*, 19 OHIO ST. J. DISP. RESOL. 757, 766-67 (2004) (uneven application of unconscionability doctrine suggests "that the judiciary has been unduly cowed by the critics of unconscionability, [who have] been too strident in criticizing the concept"). *But see* Stephen J. Ware, *The Case for Enforcing Adhesive Arbitration Agreements — with Particular Consideration of Class Actions and Arbitration Fees*, 5 J. AM. ARB. 251 (2006) (general enforcement of adhesive arbitration clauses is socially desirable and benefits most employees).

7. *Fixing Overreaching?* One way to think about the result in *Circuit City* is to recognize that the agreement did far more than merely substitute an arbitral tribunal for a judicial forum. It also limited the employees' substantive rights by providing for far lesser remedies than would be available in a court suit. Should this part of the agreement (as opposed merely to the agreement to arbitrate) be subject to some sort of more rigorous test or simply be invalid as a prospective waiver of a substantive right? To understand this, suppose that, instead of requiring employees to agree to arbitrate, Circuit City had required as a condition of employment that all applicants and employees waive their rights to more than one year of backpay under Title VII. Such an agreement would not be within the FAA. If viewed as a prospective waiver of substantive rights, it would almost certainly be invalid. If viewed as a release of past claims, it would at least be subject to the knowing and voluntary test. Why should the employer escape the more searching standards associated with waivers and releases merely because it places the offending clause in an arbitration agreement?

While courts have not generally framed the issue in terms of bifurcating agreements into arbitration and non-arbitration components, they sometimes "sever" bad clauses, striking down only the objectionable provisions while still enforcing the agreement to arbitrate. A few courts find that the entire agreement tainted; however, most courts enforce arbitration agreements after invalidating the objectionable terms. *Compare Ingle v. Circuit City Stores, Inc.*, 328 F.3d 1165 (9th Cir. 2003) (procedurally and substantively unconscionable provisions of pre-employment arbitration agreement not severable because they overwhelmingly and unconscionably favored employer), *with Morrison v. Circuit City Stores*, 317 F.3d 646 (6th Cir. 2003) (en banc) (limitations of remedies provisions severable); *Spinetti v. Service Corp. Intern.*, 324 F.3d 212 (3d Cir. 2003) (agreement to arbitrate enforceable after severing attorney fee and costs provision); *Booker v. Robert Half Int'l, Inc.*, 413 F.3d 77, 85 (D.C. Cir. 2005) (severing the punitive damages bar and otherwise enforcing the arbitration clause was proper when the agreement contained a severability clause and it contained only one discrete illegal provision).

Is this an appropriate response to the problem of unconscionable arbitration agreements? Severance encourages overreaching by assuring employers that they will get arbitration no matter how outrageously they draft their agreements. *See* Cynthia Estlund, *Rebuilding the Law of the Workplace in an Era of Self-Regulation*, 105 COLUM. L. REV. 319 (2005). What are the ethics of attorney participation in such drafting? *See* Martin H. Malin, *Ethical Concerns in Drafting Employment Arbitration Agreements after* Circuit City *and* Green Tree, 41 BRANDEIS L.J. 779 (2003). A final twist is the Supreme Court's decision in *PacifiCare Health Sys. v. Book*, 538

U.S. 401 (2003), which suggests that any ambiguity about the limitations imposed by an agreement is, in the first instance, for the arbitrator to decide. In that case, the Court held that a prohibition on "punitive" damages would not necessarily bar award of treble damages. Thus, the district court should compel arbitration and leave that question to the arbitrator. *See also Scovill v. WSYX/ABC, Sinclair Broad Group, Inc.,* 425 F.3d 1012 (6th Cir. 2005) (while district court properly nullified invalid cost-shifting provision, it should have left to the arbitrator an evidentiary clause that might have been interpreted as consistent with the law).

8. A *"Modicum of Bilaterality."* In refusing to compel arbitration, *Circuit City* points out that the agreement does not subject *employer* claims to arbitration. Why is "bilaterality" important? One possibility is that the term refers to "mutuality of obligation," one way of expressing a consideration requirement. A few courts have held that an arbitration agreement is "illusory" and consequently lacking consideration where the agreement does not treat employer and employee claims equally or where the employer retains significant discretion over the arbitration policy. *E.g., Goins v. Ryan's Family Steakhouses, Inc.,* 181 Fed. Appx. 435 (5th Cir. 2006) (refusing to compel arbitration because "It is plain from the face of the employee/EDSI contract that Ryan's is not bound by its terms and that the contract merely requires the employee to bring claims in a particular forum"); *Cheek v. United Healthcare of Mid-Atlantic, Inc.,* 835 A.2d 656, 661 (Md. 2003) (refusing to enforce arbitration clause in employment manual that reserved to employer right to alter agreement "at its sole and absolute discretion . . . with or without notice"). Most courts, however, have rejected this theory, pointing out that contract law does not require equivalency of obligation with respect to specific terms, but merely that "the contract as a whole is otherwise supported by consideration on both sides" *Walters v. AAA Waterproofing,* 85 P.3d 389, 392 (Wash. App. 2004); *see also Oblix v. Winiecki,* 374 F.3d 488, 491 (7th Cir. 2004) (That the employer "did not promise to arbitrate all of its potential claims is neither here nor there. [Plaintiff] does not deny that the arbitration clause is supported by consideration — her salary").

But there is another possible justification for a bilaterality requirement — it provides incentives to the employer to ensure that the arbitral process is fair. After all, if the employer's claims are to be entrusted to the process, not merely the employees', the employer may be interested in at least minimal due process. *See* Cynthia Estlund, *Rebuilding the Law of the Workplace in an Era of Self-Regulation,* 105 COLUM. L. REV. 319, 436 (2005).

If a bilateral commitment is important, it seems easy for employers to address in the drafting and planning stage. Why, then, would Circuit City exclude its claims against its workers from its arbitration clause? Employer suits against their employees are relatively rare, the employee is frequently judgment-proof, and juries tend not be sympathetic to employers as plaintiffs. At first blush, it would seem that employers have little to lose and perhaps much to gain by committing themselves to the same dispute resolution procedure that they impose on their employees. Can you think of reasons why an employer might be reluctant to allow some claims, perhaps non-compete or trade secret claims, to be settled through arbitration?

9. *Class Actions and Arbitration.* One hidden advantage of arbitration for employers is the ability to avoid class actions. While the question of whether there can be a class arbitration is one in the first instance for the arbitrator, *Green Tree Fin. Corp. v. Bazzle,* 539 U.S. 444 (2003), arbitration agreements are increasingly barring class arbitration. Further, to the extent that class members have agreed to arbitrate instead of litigate, a court class action cannot include those members. *But see Gentry v.*

Superior Court, 165 P.3d 556 (Cal. 2007) (class action waiver in arbitration agreement may be contrary to public policy). *See generally*, Cynthia Estlund, Note 8. She states that "for many employers, the perceived ability to foreclose class actions is the single greatest advantage to mandatory arbitration. . . . [A] ban on aggregate actions may doom some otherwise viable claims." She goes on to argue that this seriously undercuts the ability of employees to vindicate their substantive rights and therefore should be invalid. *See also* Maureen A. Weston, *Universes Colliding: The Constitutional Implications of Arbitral Class Actions*, 47 WM. & MARY L. REV. 1711 (2006).

NOTE ON THE ELEPHANT IN THE ROOM: ALLOCATING THE COSTS OF ARBITRATION

A continuing conundrum of arbitration agreements is who pays. In *Circuit City II*, the court noted that the fee allocation scheme alone would render an arbitration agreement unenforceable. But how should arbitration be financed? Unlike judges, arbitrators are private individuals rather than civil servants; the parties must pay for their services, which can cost thousands of dollars. In contrast, a party need only pay a onetime filing fee to initiate a suit in federal court, and this may be waived on a demonstration of indigency.

Before you conclude that courts are more financially accessible than arbitration, however, consider the time and money that attorneys invest in preparing cases for trial. Many plaintiffs in employment cases cannot pay out-of-pocket for legal representation (or can only pay considerably less than the per-hour value of the services obtained). As a consequence, lawyers are extremely cautious about the cases they will pursue on contingency. It has been suggested that lawyers in private practice whose fees are largely, or wholly, contingent will not take on cases without a minimum of $75,000 in provable economic damages. Think about what types of employees are likely to have claims with this much money at stake. Would it surprise you to learn that an estimated 95% of employees who seek legal help are turned away? Does this change how you feel about arbitration? *See* Christopher R. Drahozal, *Arbitration Costs and Contingent Fee Contracts*, 59 VAND. L. REV. 729, 2006, (arguing that the contingent fee contract provides "a mechanism by which arbitration can enhance, rather than restrict, claimants' access to justice"). Of course, if arbitration is such a good idea, the employer and employee can always agree to arbitrate after a dispute has arisen — there is no need for an arbitration agreement as a condition of employment. And even if mandatory arbitration is beneficial to some, or most, employees, that doesn't answer the question about who pays for it. If shifting part of the cost to the employee is prohibited, that must mean that the employer pays the full freight. Is this a good idea? Won't arbitrators tend to be influenced by who is paying their fees?

In *Green Tree Fin. Corp. v. Randolph*, 531 U.S. 79 (2000), the Court held an arbitration agreement valid even though it "was silent with respect to payment of filing fees, arbitrators' costs, and other arbitration expenses." *Id.* at 84. The Supreme Court found that the "risk [of plaintiff being] saddled with prohibitive costs is too speculative to justify the invalidation of an arbitration agreement." *Id.* at 91. But *Green Tree* did not address an agreement that specifically allocated costs to the employee, and, before the decision, the circuits had frequently refused to enforce arbitration agreements which so allocated costs. *E.g., Shankle v. B-G Maint.*, 163 F.3d 1230 (10th Cir. 1999) (mandatory arbitration agreement requiring the employee to pay a portion of the arbitrator's fees is unenforceable; to supplant a judicial forum, arbitration must provide an effective and accessible forum, and the prohibitive cost the employee would have been required to pay meant that the arbitral forum was not accessible). *See generally* Michael H. LeRoy & Peter Feuille, *When Is Cost an Unlawful Barrier to Alternative Dispute Resolution? The Ever* Green Tree *of Mandatory Employment Arbitration*, 50 UCLA L. REV. 143 (2002).

Even after *Green Tree*, some circuits continued to hold that some allocations of arbitration costs invalidate the agreement to arbitrate, but they typically did so when the allocation could be said to infringe upon a plaintiff's substantive right to a remedy. For example, in *McCaskill v. SCI Mgmt. Corp.*, 298 F.3d 677 (7th Cir. 2002), the court held that a provision in an arbitration agreement requiring each party to bear its own attorneys fees, regardless of the outcome, was unenforceable. *Contra Summers v. Dillards, Inc.*, 351 F.3d 1100, 1101 (11th Cir. 2003) (district court's concerns that fee-shifting clause *might* harm the employee were too speculative since plaintiff might prevail at arbitration and could "seek judicial review of an award if . . . her available remedies were hindered"); *Bradford v. Rockwell Semiconductor Sys.*, 238 F.3d 549 (4th Cir. 2001) (fee-splitting does not automatically render an arbitration agreement unenforceable). In *Blair v. Scott Specialty Gases*, 283 F.3d 595 (3d Cir. 2002), the Third Circuit allowed a former employee, who claimed that the cost of arbitrating her employment discrimination claims would be prohibitive, to conduct discovery to determine what it would cost to arbitrate her claims. Professor Estlund suggests capping arbitral fees for an employee at what she would have to pay to file a complaint in court. *See* Estlund, p. 754, Note 8 at 430.

NOTE ON ENFORCING THE ARBITRAL AWARD

Parties typically commence arbitration pursuant to the rules of the arbitral association that will conduct the proceeding. But, as you will have gathered from *Circuit City*, employees sometimes simply file court suit. If the defendant prefers the arbitral forum, it will then move in federal court to "stay" the court proceedings pending arbitration. But don't be fooled by the word "stay": the suit is effectively ended, and the plaintiff's only recourse is arbitration. Should the arbitration go forward, the arbitrator will ultimately issue an award. That award, by itself, has no legal effect, but the prevailing party can move to enforce it in federal district court or the losing party can seek to vacate it.

Students tend to think that these post-arbitration court proceedings are like an appeal, with the court able to correct arbitrator errors in the same way that an appeals court can reverse a district court. That is *not* true. A court may not overturn an arbitrator's decision even if it believes that the arbitrator is wrong on the facts and the law. The FAA provides an award may be vacated only in extreme circumstances — where it was procured by corruption, fraud, or undue means, there was evident partiality or corruption in the arbitrators' decision, the arbitrators were guilty of misconduct, or they exceeded their powers. 9 U.S.C. § 10(a). It is true that the courts have added a somewhat broader basis for review — an award may be vacated when there has been a "manifest disregard" for the law. *Wilko v. Swan*, 346 U.S. 427 (1953); *Porzig v. Dresdner, Kleinwort, Benson, N. Am. LLC*, 497 F.3d 133 (2d Cir. 2007) (arbitrators acted in manifest disregard by denying attorneys' fees and assessing arbitration costs against prevailing employee); *Patten v. Signator Ins. Agency*, 441 F.3d 230 (4th Cir.), *cert. denied* 127 S. Ct. 434 (2006) (arbitrator acted in manifest disregard when he ignored the plain and unambiguous language of the governing arbitration agreement and concluded that it included an implied one-year limitations period). But an arbitrator must be truly extreme to fall afoul of this rule. *See Vu Luong v. Circuit City Stores, Inc.*, 368 F.3d 1109 (9th Cir. 2004) (ADA claimant could not establish that arbitrator's award was rendered in manifest disregard of federal law, where the arbitrator discussed federal law and therefore did not ignore it).

What exactly this manifest disregard means is uncertain. *See* Rebecca Hanner White, *Arbitration And The Administrative State*, 38 WAKE FOREST L. REV. 1283, 1303 (2003) ("If a court hearing the statutory claim were required to apply a particular statutory meaning, so too must the arbitrator. But if the court were free to supply its own interpretation of the statute, an arbitrator may do so as well"). *See also* Christopher R. Drahozal, *Codifying Manifest Disregard*, NEVADA L. J. (forthcoming 2008); Nicholas Weiskopf, *Arbitral Injustice: Rethinking the Manifest Disregard Standard for Judicial Review of Awards*, http://ssrn.com. One case, *Cole v. Burns*, 105 F.3d 1465 (D.C. Cir. 1997), suggested that arbitral legal determinations, as opposed to fact finding, should be fully reviewable in court. However, application of that principle would require the arbitrator to write an opinion and, in doing so, to draw a distinction between his findings of fact and conclusions of law. Arbitrators do not necessarily write opinions, much less ones that are sufficiently detailed to provide a basis for review. *See generally* Calvin William Sharpe, *Integrity Review of Statutory Arbitration Awards*, 54 HASTINGS L.J. 311 (2003); Stephen L. Hayford, *A New Paradigm for Commercial Arbitration: Rethinking the Relationship Between Reasoned Awards and the Judicial Standards for Vacatur*, 66 GEO. WASH. L. REV. 443 (1998).

Addressing these concerns, some arbitration agreements have provided for more robust judicial review, a provision that has raised questions as to whether private ordering can trump statutory restrictions on court jurisdiction. The Supreme Court recently granted certiorari in a case that raises this issue. *Hall St. Assocs., L.L.C. v. Mattel, Inc.*, 196 Fed. Appx. 476 (9th Cir. 2006), *cert. granted*, 127 S. Ct. 2875 (2007). *See generally* Margaret Moses, *Can Parties Tell Courts What to Do? Expanded Judicial Review of Arbitral Awards*. 52 KAN. L. REV. 429, 431-32 (2004) (the FAA is better interpreted to permit expanded judicial review).

PROBLEM 9.1

You are in-house employment counsel for My-Tube.Com, an Internet start-up company. Although it has relatively few employees at this point, it expects to expand rapidly and to have employees in a number of different states. You are looking down the road regarding potential liability and know that many employers require all employees to sign arbitration agreements. Is this a good strategy for My-Tube to pursue, and, if so, what kind of arbitration would you recommend? How would you get employees (both existing and prospective) to agree to arbitration?

NOTE ON INTERNATIONAL AND COMPARATIVE ANTIDISCRIMINATION LAW

Professor Jean R. Sternlight, in *In Search of the Best Procedures for Enforcing Employment Discrimination Laws: A Comparative Analysis*, 78 TULANE L. REV. 1401, 1498 (2004), looked at how the United States, Britain, and Australia set up systems of dispute resolution for employment discrimination, including litigation, conciliation, mediation, arbitration, and administrative processes. She concludes that:

The comparison of multiple jurisdictions' approaches to employment discrimination claims does not provide us with a single "best" way to resolve such disputes, but the comparison does yield three key insights as to the existing processes. First, the comparison shows numerous similarities in the types of issues that arise as jurisdictions attempt to devise a process for resolving such disputes. Second, the comparison shows a tendency, in all three jurisdictions, to oscillate among a series of formal and informal disputes resolution mechanisms. Third, upon analysis we have seen that the variety of processes and the vacillation among these processes can be attributed to societies' and disputants' multiple and sometimes conflicting goals.

Professor Sternlight finds that, at the broadest level, the three sets of interests — societal interests in eliminating discrimination, individual interests in personal well-being, and interests in procedural justice (perceived fairness in the process) — create tensions between public and private goals. Thus, no single process will satisfy all three interests. The challenge, in setting up multiple processes is to allow for all these interests to be served.

1. *Some National Dispute Systems.* Different national legal systems have developed different ways to resolve employment disputes. For example, Canadian law requires that all collective bargaining agreements between unions and employers include provisions for arbitration. This means that all disputes between the parties arising from the collective agreement, whether or not raising statutory or common law claims, are subject to collective agreement arbitration. *Weber v. Ontario Hydro,* [1995] 2 S.C.R. 928. Outside of collective bargaining, the common law courts have jurisdiction to hear individual employment cases, federal and provincial human rights boards have jurisdiction over human rights claims, and labor law disputes are decided by labor boards. Some of these boards are tripartite tribunals, with the presiding officer, a neutral, and equal representatives of union and management. Judicial review is quite limited. *See* ROGER BLANPAIN, SUSAN BISOM-RAPP, WILLIAM R. CORBETT, HILARY K. JOSEPHS & MICHAEL J. ZIMMER, THE GLOBAL WORKPLACE: INTERNATIONAL AND COMPARATIVE EMPLOYMENT LAW — CASES AND MATERIALS (2007).

In Mexico, the Federal Labor Law is applicable to all employment, but most enforcement is by state Conciliation and Arbitration Boards (CAB). These tripartite boards, made up of equal representatives of the government, employers and unions, are quite controversial. Employers complain that the CABs are too employee friendly in individual employment disputes, *id.* at 235, and the emerging independent union movement complains that many of the CABs are controlled by the older, established unions that are more closely identified with the interests of the government and the PRI political party that dominated Mexican politics until 2000, *id.* at 237-40. *See Public Report of Review of NAO Submission No. 9702 (Han Young),* U.S. National Administrative Office, Bureau of International Labor Affairs, U.S. Department of Labor, April 28, 1998 (Tijuana CAB interfered with independent union attempting to replace a "ghost" union that employees never even knew had been granted representation rights on their behalf).

There is no direct judicial review of the actions of CABs. However, the Mexican Constitution provides a procedure — an "amparo suit" — that can be brought under the original jurisdiction of the Mexican Supreme Court against a government agency, such as a CAB, for violating constitutional rights. Since the Mexican Supreme Court was reformed in 1996, the Court has decided a series of important "amparo" suits involving labor law issues but, so far, not questions of discrimination law. *See* BLANPAIN, THE GLOBAL WORKPLACE, at 240-48.

In the United Kingdom, statutory employment claims go to Employment Tribunals and contract claims go to common law courts (although tribunals can hear contract claims up to a cap amount of £25,000). Each panel of the tribunal is made up of a chairperson, who is an experienced barrister or solicitor, a representative from a trade union or consulting organization for employees, and a representative of one of the federations of employers, *id.* at 324. Appeals from tribunals go to the Employment Appeal Tribunal and then, with leave, to the courts. *Id.*

In France, labor disputes are heard by the Conseils de Prud'hommes, or labor courts. Each court has four members, none of whom is a judge. Two are appointed by pro-employer organizations and two by pro-employee groups. *Id.* at 435. Depending on the value of the case, the case may be appealed from the labor court to the Cour d'Appel or the Cour de Cassation. *Id.* at 436.

In China, labor disputes are decided by what is called "arbitration," but the arbitration tribunals more clearly resemble specialized labor courts. Arbitration committees are established on the county or municipal level, with committee members made up of representatives of the government's labor department, labor union representatives, and representatives of employers. 1 INTERNATIONAL LABOR AND EMPLOYMENT LAWS (William L. Keller & Timothy J. Darby, 2d ed. 2003) 31-14 to 31-16. The committees establish and assign individual tribunals to hear labor disputes. In 2002, arbitration committees heard 184,000 cases, involving 610,000 employees. *Id.* at 31-14. Parties who lose in arbitration may bring a lawsuit in the local court, with that court exercising broad judicial review of the arbitration award. *Id.* at 31-16.

The most obvious difference between these various schemes and the American approach we have studied is the presence of employee or union (or at least "public") representatives on the deciding body. Would American law be less controversial if arbitration tribunals included such representation? If so, how would you ensure that the employee representative in fact represented employee interests? And wouldn't increasing the number of decisionmakers necessarily increase costs?

2. *"Soft Law."* Under international law, the violation of a labor standard by a private employer is not subject to redress by the victim. Some countries, such as Mexico, but not others, like the United States, provide that international treaties that have been ratified are directly enforceable as would be any violation of domestic law.

The basic enforcement approach of the ILO is through a series of procedures that essentially operate to shame the defaulting member nation into bringing its actions into compliance with the Conventions it has ratified. Article 33 of the ILO Constitution, however, provides that in egregious situations the other Member states can be asked to undertake trade sanctions against a defaulting Member. So far, that has been used only with regard to Myanmar, but the imposition of trade sanctions has failed so far to moderate the conduct of that government in violating the fundamental principle against forced labor. *See* BLANPAIN, THE GLOBAL WORKPLACE, at 75.

Each of the three NAFTA countries has established offices — National Administrative Offices (NAO) — that hear complaints that one of the other countries has violated the North American Agreement on Labor Cooperation by failing to enforce its own labor laws. As of July 2006, 34 submissions have been made to the three NAOs. So far, the most extensive sanction has been to recommend consultations between the labor secretaries of the two countries. While it is hard to establish that NAALC has made very much difference in how the three countries enforce their respective labor laws, an unintended effect has been to build ties across borders among unions and NGOs interested in advancing workers rights. *Id.* at 292.

In contrast to NAALC and NAFTA, the European Court of Justice, which is the judicial branch of the EU, does exercise enforcement power over the member states; EU members can be subject to court orders to bring their actions into compliance with the EU Treaties and the Directives that the EU has promulgated. See BLANPAIN, THE GLOBAL WORKPLACE at 279.

Even "softer law" approaches involve voluntary codes of conduct that some brand name companies, such as Nike, have adopted that commit them to require that all of the products they sell are produced under high labor standards. *See* Michael Posner & Justine Nolan, *Can Codes of Conduct Play a Role in Promoting Workers' Rights?*, in INTERNATIONAL LABOR STANDARDS: GLOBALIZATION, TRADE, AND PUBLIC POLICY (Robert J. Flanagan & William B. Gould IV, eds., 2003) 207. These codes have dealt with a variety of structures, with the early ones being unilaterally adopted without much, if any, monitoring of subcontractors. Another variant is for codes to be created and monitored by industry or trade associations, such as the World-Wide Responsible Apparel Production Initiative (WRAP) initiative, which was launched by the American Apparel Manufacturing Association. A third category involves third-party (labor unions and other NGOs) consultation and monitoring, with transparency as a part of the process. See, BLANPAIN, THE GLOBAL WORKPLACE at 602-06.

A final category involves the involvement of the United Nations and includes the United Nations Global Compact, which is a voluntary initiative that brings together corporations, U.N. agencies, labor unions, other NGOs, and governments to advance universal principles such as the elimination of discrimination. *Id.* at 604-05.

The question underlying all of these soft law approaches is whether they make a real difference. In a way, that is the same question that arises in the discussion of the "new structuralism" views of how to combat discrimination that were discussed at p. 167 in Chapter 2.

Chapter 10

The Policy Bases for Antidiscrimination Law

A. INTRODUCTION

It is, quite literally, impossible to have completed this book without having encountered the themes we will develop in this chapter. Indeed, your professor may well have assigned some of this material in connection with earlier chapters. Nevertheless, it seems appropriate to close this book by stepping away from the demands of antidiscrimination laws on the ground and by trying to assess the phenomenon of discrimination from the 30,000 foot level. Accordingly, Section B begins by asking how discrimination survives in a free market. Section C then turns to a more normative question: should we try to eliminate discrimination and, if so, to what extent? Finally, Section D turns to the costs and benefits of the antidiscrimination project.

As you work through this chapter, you will notice that most of the discussion in this chapter is framed in terms of race discrimination. That is appropriate historically because federal antidiscrimination policy has its roots in the African-American civil rights movement. Further, there is no doubt that race relations remain a critical problem for the United States both for African Americans and for other racial and ethnic minorities. The materials, however, will often ask you to consider whether the policy issues addressed in the context of race discrimination are equally applicable to other forms of discrimination.

B. DISCRIMINATION AND THE FREE MARKET

It may seem an odd question to ask — why discrimination exists — at the end of a long book in which we've encountered literally hundreds of instances of employment discrimination. For theorists, however, it is not an easy question. The problem for economists is not why there are impulses to discriminate — that is the domain of psychologists or maybe evolutionary biologists, *see* Nancy Wartik, *Hard-Wired for Prejudice? Experts Examine Human Response to Outsiders*, N.Y. Times, Apr. 20, 2004, at F5. In any event, economists usually take individual preferences as given. Rather, the hard theoretical question is why the free market allows discrimination to continue to exist. An employer that discriminates, after all, must pay a price: artificially contracting the supply of available labor tends to raise the price of the labor purchased. If many employers discriminate, the price (wages) of their workforce will climb. Competitors will be free to exploit the pool of excluded black workers at lower wages, thus gaining a competitive advantage. As more employers seek lower-cost black workers, their value will rise. Thus, discrimination will be corrected by the market, without the need for legal intervention.

While no one believes the competitive model perfectly reflects the real world, noted economists have argued that in the long run the market will in fact eliminate discrimination if government action does not intervene. Professor John J. Donohue III, in *Advocacy Versus Analysis in Assessing Employment Discrimination Law*, 44 STAN. L. REV. 1583, 1591 (1992), recounts Chicago School opposition to Title VII's passage:

> Thirty years ago, powerful intellectual voices at the University of Chicago registered their strong opposition to the passage of federal civil rights legislation on theoretical grounds. For example, in 1962, Milton Friedman [in CAPITALISM AND FREEDOM] emphasized that fair employment practice laws were unnecessary because the existing free markets were generating great progress for blacks: "The maintenance of the general rules of private property and of capitalism have [sic] been a major source of opportunity for Negroes and have [sic] permitted them to make greater progress than they otherwise could have made."
>
> Friedman's view became the established orthodoxy for many within the Chicago School tradition who believed that antidiscrimination laws were both unnecessary and unsuccessful at providing economic benefits for blacks. . . .
>
> Implicit in this view is the suggestion that (at least absent government compulsion, as in the pre-1964 South) discrimination does not exist; the poor economic status of statutorily protected groups must, therefore, result from their own choices or their lack of the qualifications necessary to compete.

The market forces argument has reappeared periodically, in work by Judge Richard Posner, *e.g.*, *An Economic Analysis of Sex Discrimination Laws*, 56 U. CHI. L. REV. 1311, 1312 (1989) ("I believe it is a plausible hypothesis — no stronger statement is possible — that sex discrimination law has not increased, and it may even have reduced, the aggregate welfare of women"), and, most forcefully in a book by Professor Richard A. Epstein, which glossed its economic argument with a strong libertarian thrust against government intervention. As its title indicates, FORBIDDEN GROUNDS: THE CASE AGAINST EMPLOYMENT DISCRIMINATION LAWS (1992) was an assault on the whole concept of antidiscrimination statutes. Professor Epstein's book triggered an avalanche of criticism defending the antidiscrimination project.

JACOB E. GERSEN, MARKETS AND DISCRIMINATION
82 N.Y.U.L. Rev. 689, 690-702 (2007)

In 2004, the Equal Employment Opportunity Commission (EEOC) received 27,696 charges of racial employment discrimination and 24,249 charges of sex discrimination. Whether these figures represent the nagging persistence of employment discrimination in the United States or a remarkable decline in such discrimination is the subject of significant debate.[2] Empirical evidence about the gap between the hiring, wages, and firing of workers of different races and sexes abounds,[3] but the significance of that evidence is hotly contested. Equally important, widespread conflict remains about the accuracy of different positive explanations for discrimination[5] and the implications for the efficiency and efficacy of employment antidiscrimination law.[6] Despite decades of scholarship in law and economics, then, significant disagreement remains about the extent of employment discrimination in the United States, the correct explanation for such discrimination, and the normative implications of the various pieces of the discrimination puzzle. . . .

The law and economics literature contains no shortage of theories about employment discrimination [but there are four main] approaches in the law and economics literature generally understood to be the dominant schools of thought: the taste, statistical discrimination, sorting and search, and status-production theories.

The first general economic approach to employment discrimination was Gary Becker's taste model, presented in his 1955 doctoral dissertation. According to this theory, discrimination is just another exogenously given taste or preference of

2. *See* Laura Beth Nielsen & Robert L. Nelson, *Rights Realized? An Empirical Analysis of Employment Discrimination Litigation as a Claiming System*, 2005 WIS. L. REV. 663, 666-69 (summarizing current debates about extent of employment discrimination). *Compare* William A. Darity Jr. & Patrick L. Mason, *Evidence on Discrimination in Employment: Codes of Color, Codes of Gender*, 12 J. ECON. PERSP. 63, 65, 68-81 (1998) (concluding race and sex employment discrimination have declined but are still prevalent), *with* RICHARD A. EPSTEIN, FORBIDDEN GROUNDS: THE CASE AGAINST EMPLOYMENT DISCRIMINATION LAWS 47-58 (1992) (questioning evidence of continuing employment discrimination), and James J. Heckman, *Detecting Discrimination*, 12 J. ECON. PERSP. 101, 102, 104 (1998) (arguing Darity and Mason overstate strength of evidence for widespread discrimination).

3. *See, e.g.*, Francine D. Blau & Lawrence M. Kahn, *Swimming Upstream: Trends in the Gender Wage Differential in the 1980s*, 15 J. LAB. ECON. 1, 12-13, 13 tbl.1 (1997) (providing empirical evidence of continuing wage differences between sexes).

5. For an overview of economic theories of employment discrimination, *see generally* Stewart J. Schwab, *Employment Discrimination*, in 3 ENCYCLOPEDIA OF LAW AND ECONOMICS: THE REGULATION OF CONTRACTS 572 (Boudewijn Bouckaert & Gerrit De Geest eds., 2000). For detailed presentations of the specific theories of employment discrimination tested in this Article, *see generally* GARY S. BECKER, THE ECONOMICS OF DISCRIMINATION (2d ed. 1971), for an introduction to the taste model; Epstein, *supra* note 2, for his proposal of the sorting and search model; Dennis J. Aigner & Glen G. Cain, *Statistical Theories of Discrimination in Labor Markets*, 30 INDUS. & LAB. REL. REV. 175 (1977), for a comparison of several versions of the statistical discrimination model; Richard H. McAdams, *Cooperation and Conflict: The Economics of Group Status Production and Race Discrimination*, 108 HARV. L. REV. 1003 (1995), for an introduction to the status-production model; Edmund S. Phelps, *The Statistical Theory of Racism and Sexism*, 62 AM. ECON. REV. 656 (1972), for a presentation of the statistical discrimination model.

6. *Compare* John J. Donohue III, *Is Title VII Efficient?*, 134 U.PA. L. REV. 1411, 1426-30 (1986) (specifying conditions under which Title VII will increase efficiency), *with* Richard A. Posner, *The Efficiency and the Efficacy of Title VII*, 136 U. PA. L. REV. 513, 516 (1987) (arguing Title VII is likely inefficient). *See also* Mayer G. Freed & Daniel D. Polsby, *Privacy, Efficiency, and the Equality of Men and Women: A Revisionist View of Sex Discrimination in Employment*, 1981 AM. B. FOUND. RES. J. 583, 602-12 (discussing relevance of efficiency considerations in characterizing bona fide occupational qualifications); Edward J. McCaffery, *Slouching Towards Equality: Gender Discrimination, Market Efficiency, and Social Change*, 103 YALE L.J. 595, 648-51 (1993) (arguing efficiency considerations alone do not justify either retaining or repealing Title VII).

employers, employees, or customers that they are willing to pay to indulge. Becker's thinking dominated early work but soon came under attack in the 1970s by advocates of statistical models of discrimination, in which employers use group characteristics to make rational inferences about individual employee productivity. More recently, Richard Epstein and other scholars have presented a mixed sorting and search model that incorporates aspects of both the taste and statistical models. Finally, Richard McAdams has proposed a status-production model of employment discrimination. According to this theory, groups of workers discriminate against others to elevate their own status, a model that is part sociological and part economic. . . .

1. TASTES

The modern economic analysis of employment discrimination is generally traced to Becker's doctoral thesis, a microeconomic account rooted in individual tastes for discrimination either by employers, employees, or consumers. The employer version of the theory posits that some employers have a taste for discrimination which they are willing to pay to indulge. If employers enjoy positive utility from discriminating, they may be willing to trade profits for discrimination. In the context of race discrimination, the employer taste model suggests that although employers with such tastes will be willing to pay whites more than nonwhites, those discriminating firms will also earn lower profits than nondiscriminating firms because of their labor costs. Firms are, therefore, less profitable in the long run when they indulge their discriminatory tastes. In the consumer and employee taste models, consumers or workers demand lower prices or higher wages, respectively, to associate with members of other racial groups. Over time, this produces occupational segregation.

Because discriminating firms in Becker's model are less profitable than nondiscriminating ones, many scholars suggest that the taste model predicts that there will be no employment discrimination in equilibrium, because the discriminating, less-profitable firms will be driven from the marketplace by those with lower labor costs.[40] The dual critique consistently advanced against this model is that "it predicts the absence of the phenomenon it was designed to explain"[41] and requires employers to behave irrationally rather than as profit-maximizers. However, these critiques are only appropriately advanced against the employer taste model, rather than the employee or consumer model.

2. STATISTICAL DISCRIMINATION

[E]arly on, economists developed a series of statistical (or informational) models to respond to the alleged weaknesses of the taste model. These models suggest that with imperfect information about potential employees, employers rely on group characteristics to predict individual characteristics (e.g., productivity). In contrast to taste models (which assume that employers have invidious preferences), statistical models assume that employers differentiate among individuals from different groups for

---

40. *See, e.g.,* John J. Donohue III, *Discrimination in Employment, in* 1 THE NEW PALGRAVE DICTIONARY OF ECONOMICS AND THE LAW 615, 617 (Peter Newman ed., 1998) (claiming Becker's model implies market would "discipline discriminators"); Posner, *supra* note 6, at 514 (citing Becker's model to support finding that competition should ameliorate effects of discrimination in the long run by rewarding firms that are not constrained by an "aversion to associating with blacks").

41. Kenneth J. Arrow, *Some Mathematical Models of Race Discrimination in the Labor Market, in* RACIAL DISCRIMINATION IN ECONOMIC LIFE 187, 192 (Anthony H. Pascal ed., 1972).

"benign" profit-maximizing motives. Employers make inferences about individual-level worker characteristics based on an employee's membership in a group.

The initial accuracy of such group-based inferences or stereotypes can vary widely. Over time, however, inaccurate inferences should be driven out of the market. That is, because employers who make accurate inferences about worker productivity have a competitive advantage over firms that consistently make errors, in equilibrium, only accurate inferences should remain. Thus, statistical discrimination may persist in equilibrium if the stereotypes used by employers are accurate.[50]

Of course, from a policy perspective, the lack of animus need not justify government inaction. Average group characteristics may reflect prior invidious discrimination or be endogenously determined by different incentives for investment in human capital.[51] For example, if women or nonwhites are paid lower wages and promoted less often than a favored group, the returns on investment in education or skills training for them may be lower than for members of the favored group. Given the diminished returns, it is rational for members of these disfavored groups to underinvest in education or skills training, which in turn produces group characteristics that mirror employers' stereotypes. In this case, the statistical inference is accurate but only because of historical discrimination. If this occurs, the welfare consequences of statistical discrimination are far from benign, even if there is no underlying invidious discrimination in the current inference.

3. SORTING AND SEARCH

In his own analysis of employment discrimination [in FORBIDDEN GROUNDS], Richard Epstein combined elements of both the taste and statistical models. Epstein argued that some portion of employment discrimination is an efficient response by firms to sorting problems. If employee tastes are tied to group characteristics, then employers may prefer homogenous workforces, seeing them as a way to minimize the chance of conflict among employees of the firm.

Thus, while Epstein acknowledges that employment antidiscrimination laws did reduce much invidious discrimination, he suggests that a significant portion of the remaining discrimination is a rational means of avoiding employee conflict, the result of which is sorting or occupational segregation by demographic characteristics. As with the statistical model, discrimination does not result from employers' invidious preferences. Rather, discrimination is a rational response by employers to the discriminatory preferences of their employees. In this sense, the sorting model shares elements of both Becker's employee taste model and the statistical discrimination model.

---

50. *See* Stewart Schwab, *Is Statistical Discrimination Efficient?*, 76 AM. ECON. REV. 228, 231-32 (1986) (deriving necessary and sufficient conditions for efficiency of statistical discrimination given truth of stereotype).

51. *See* Shelly J. Lundberg & Richard Startz, *Private Discrimination and Social Intervention in Competitive Labor Markets*, 73 AM. ECON. REV. 340, 342 (1983) (recognizing that decisions regarding investment in human capital are affected by labor-market discrimination); Cass R. Sunstein, *Why Markets Don't Stop Discrimination*, 8 SOC. PHIL. & POL. 22, 29-30 (1991) (highlighting effects of discrimination on investment in human capital).

4.   STATUS PRODUCTION

McAdams's status-production theory of employment discrimination has much in common with what is sometimes termed a cartel theory of discrimination. McAdams argues that the notions of tastes or associational preferences that dominate the economics literature give inadequate consideration to group status. In the status-production model, members of one group invest in elevating the status of their own group by subordinating other groups. Discrimination allows members of one group to raise their self-esteem by lowering the status of the group against whom they discriminate.

Whereas the taste model focuses on the individual discriminator, the status-production model emphasizes the importance of groups and social norms in producing and maintaining discriminatory practices. For example, whites might enforce a norm against hiring or promoting nonwhites. Because employers who fail to adhere to the norm may lose status within their own group and simultaneously risk punishment for violating the discrimination norm, both primary and secondary norms operate to maintain discrimination.[60]

Thus, even though an employer could theoretically obtain cheaper labor and maximize profits by not discriminating, the employer might also face sanctions from other firms or customers, negating the competitive advantage. If those sanctions outweigh potential profit gains, employers who would otherwise hire nonwhites (in the race context) or women (in the sex context) may refrain from doing so.

Not surprisingly, the status-production theory has also drawn criticism.[62] For example, John Donohue has suggested that although the status-production model captured important elements of pre-1960s discrimination, Becker's model may now provide more insight into current racial discrimination.[63] Be that as it may, the status-production model remains relatively untested, at least compared to various other economic theories of discrimination.

NOTES

1. *Testing the Models.* After describing the four models, Professor Gersen attempts to test them using data comprised of employment discrimination claims, market conditions, and labor force characteristics. Although he recognizes the limitations of his data and stresses that his conclusions are preliminary, Professor Gersen finds that "the status-production theory has genuine legs" for race discrimination. He notes, however, different findings for race and sex discrimination. *See also* Major G. Coleman, *Racial Discrimination in the Workplace: Does Market Structure Make a Difference?*, 43 IND. REL. 660 (2004) ("increased competition has no impact on the

---

60. See Schwab, *supra* note 5, at 582 (noting role of group solidarity among whites as means of enforcing discriminatory norm). The role of social norms in perpetuating discrimination has also been recognized by John J. Donohue III & James J. Heckman, *Re-evaluating Federal Civil Rights Policy*, 79 GEO. L.J. 1713, 1728-29 (1991), and J. Hoult Verkerke, *Free to Search*, 105 HARV. L. REV. 2080, 2091-94 (1992) (reviewing Epstein, *supra* note 2).

62. *See generally* Richard A. Epstein, *The Status-Production Sideshow: Why the Antidiscrimination Laws Are Still a Mistake*, 108 HARV. L. REV. 1085 (1995) (offering comprehensive critique of McAdams's status-production model of discrimination).

63. *Cf.* Donohue, [*The Law and Economics of Antidiscrimination Law* 35-38 (Nat'l Bureau of Econ. Research, Working Paper No. 11631, 2006), available at http://www.nber.org/papers/w11631 at 22] (suggesting profit-seeking U.S. companies' practice of establishing foreign call centers is inconsistent with self-enforcing discriminatory norms).

number of discrimination reports, racial wage discrimination, or the racial demo-graphics of the workforce"; thus "competition cannot be relied on to reduce racial discrimination").

2. *A Taste for Discrimination?* Professor Gersen refers to the Becker theory that significant discrimination may persist despite free markets because employers have a "taste for discrimination" that they are willing to indulge. The basic idea is that individuals are willing to pay a price to indulge their taste for discrimination (or distaste for associating with certain groups). They will, therefore, forgo the gains to be made by dealing with members of those groups. Such out-groups, precisely because they are less desired in market terms, command a lower price. Refusing to hire or do business with them means passing up desirable opportunities. *See* Richard A. Posner, ECONOMIC ANALYSIS OF LAW § 27.1, at 525-26 (2d ed. 1977). Presumably, over time, such firms will lose business to firms who are not passing up such opportunities. *But see* Michael Selmi, *The Price of Discrimination: The Nature of Class Action Employment Discrimination Litigation and Its Effects*, 81 TEX. L. REV. 1249 (2003) (questioning whether the market is having much of an effect on the basis of market reactions to class action settlements).

As Gersen notes, the "taste" may be that of the employer itself or of someone whose tastes the employer has to consider — other employees or customers. It is easier to understand the persistence of discrimination in terms of customer tastes than it is in terms of employer tastes since employers may cater to those tastes without losing much business. In any event, depending on the strength of the taste, an African American may not be employed at all or may be employed at a wage that is low enough to compensate for the "distaste" of employing her. *See* David A. Strauss, *The Law and Economics of Racial Discrimination in Employment: The Case for Numerical Standards*, 79 GEO. L.J. 1619 (1991).

3. *Statistical Discrimination.* The second model seeks to explain the persistence of discrimination in free markets on the grounds that some types of discrimination are "rational" because race (or sex or some other prohibited ground) is correlated with ability. This theory is sometimes called "statistical discrimination." A rational employer will discriminate, even if no relevant actor has any discriminatory animus, if the employer concludes that race is a useful proxy for job qualifications.

> Discrimination of this form occurs because information about an employee's qualifi-cations is often costly to obtain. An employee's race, however, is cheaply ascertained. Therefore, if a firm concludes that an employee's race correlates with his or her qual-ifications, and if better information about the qualifications is too costly to discover, it will be rational, profit-maximizing behavior for the firm to offer lower wages to a minority employee than it would offer to a nonminority employee.
>
> A firm might rationally discriminate in this way even if, so far as the firm has determined, the two employees are identical except for race. In a world of cost-free information, the employer could ascertain each employee's qualifications perfectly. If two employees were found to be identical in every relevant respect, it would not be rational to offer them different wages. In the real world, however, information is costly, and the employer will therefore stop trying to ascertain qualifications at some point. At that point, it may be rational for the employer to rely on a surrogate that it knows to be imperfect but that is cheaply ascertained.

Strauss, Note 2 at 1622.

The logic of statistical discrimination does not require any assertion that racial or gender differences are inherent — the correlation between race or gender and productivity could be the result of factors such as past employer discrimination or societal discrimination. Particular groups may in fact be different if, due to the diminishing expected returns for them, they disproportionately chose not to invest in human capital. The term "statistical discrimination" does not, however, mean that the employer acts only on the basis of scientifically ascertained differences. Indeed, such discrimination will be more or less "rational" depending on the relationship between the stereotype used and statistical reality. Professor Strauss concludes that, if racial generalizations reflect actual differences among groups, they are more likely to persist than if they do not: "If an employer is using an inaccurate generalization about minority employees in making employment decisions, it has an incentive to correct its assumptions. If it does not, there is an opportunity for an employer who is not using such a generalization to seize a competitive advantage." Strauss, at 1640. *See also* David Charny & G. Mitu Gulati, *Efficiency — Wages, Tournaments, and Discrimination: A Theory of Employment Discrimination Law for High-Level Jobs*, 33 HARV. C.R.-C.L. L. REV. 57, 77 (1998) ("statistical discrimination will sustain itself vis-à-vis job applicants in high-wage sectors of the labor market. Members of minority groups who plan to enter this sector — e.g., those who have begun training to enter a profession — will be induced to make smaller investments in human capital than 'typical' applicants because they expect to make lower returns from their investment in training").

4. *Sorting and Search.* As Professor Gersen explains, Richard Epstein's theory is a variant on both of the Becker and statistical discrimination models, but it does not require any animus or dislike. Rather, Epstein argues that, while diversity might be a good business model for many employers, other firms are better off with homogeneity in their workforces:

> [A]ssume for the moment that all workers have identical preferences on all matters relevant to the employment relation. If the question is whether or not they wish to have music piped into a common work area, they all want music. If the question is what kind of music they wish to hear, the answer is classical — indeed, mostly Mozart. If the question is how loud, the agreement is perfect down to the exact decibel. In this employment utopia, decisions of collective governance are easy to make. The employer who satisfies preferences of any single worker knows that he or she has satisfied the preferences of the entire work force. It takes little effort and little money to achieve the highest level of group satisfaction. The nonwage terms of collective importance can be set in ways that unambiguously promote firm harmony.
>
> The situation is quite different once it is assumed that there is no employee homogeneity in taste within the workplace. . . . The general proposition is clear: as the tastes within the group start to diverge, it becomes harder to reach a decision that works for the common good. If half the workers crave classical music but loathe rock, and half like rock but disdain classical music, it is very difficult to decide whether music shall be played in the workplace at all, and if so what kind. The wider the variation in taste, the more troublesome these collective decisions are. . . . If the level of dissatisfaction increases exponentially as the gap between private choice and collective decision increases, then the people at either tail of the distribution have additional incentives to leave the group when the decision goes against them.

FORBIDDEN GROUNDS at 61-2. Where Epstein's theory intersects with the statistical discrimination model is the notion that race (or national origin or sex) is a good predictor for the homogeneity that such employers seek:

> The increase in the harmony of tastes and preferences thus works in the long-run interest of all members. To the extent, therefore, that individual tastes are grouped by

race, by sex, by age, by national origin — and to some extent they are — then there is a necessary conflict between the commands of any antidiscrimination law and the smooth operation of the firm. Firms whose members have diverse and clashing views may well find it more difficult to make collective decisions than firms with a closer agreement over tastes.

Id. at 66-7.

5. *Status Production Model*. In some ways, Professor McAdams model is both the most sophisticated and the most obvious. It views discrimination as a means for a group to gain status by distinguishing themselves from other groups in society. Such status seeking is endemic, whether in the purchase of cars or homes or in association with popular groups. In a sense, we all learned about gaining status in middle school. Professor McAdams, however, adds both the racial and gender component and a sophisticated explanation of how discrimination works to achieve these goals:

> [A] material view of human motivation underestimates both the level of cooperation that groups elicit from their members and the level of conflict that groups elicit from each other. A single group dynamic connects these added increments of cooperation and conflict: groups achieve solidarity and elicit loyalty beyond what economic analysis conventionally predicts, but solidarity and loyalty within groups lead predictably, if not inevitably, to competition and conflict between groups. The connection is the desire for esteem or status. Groups use intra-group status rewards as a non-material means of gaining material sacrifice from members, but the attendant desire for inter-group status causes inter-group conflict. . . .
>
> This two-fold importance of status is essential to a genuine understanding of race discrimination, which has eluded economics. Discrimination is a means by which social groups produce status for their members, but pivotal to understanding this form of inter-group conflict is the role that status plays in generating the intra-group cooperation necessary to make discrimination effective. Absent the desire for intra-group status, selfish individuals would not make the material sacrifices that discrimination requires.

108 HARV. L. REV. at 1007-08.

6. *The Reality Critique*. Both the Becker taste theory and the statistical discrimination theory suggest that, as Milton Friedman argued, the market should eliminate most discrimination over time. Even Professor Epstein would expect most discrimination to dissipate, although it would continue where it was efficient through "voluntary" market segregation.

But if these theories are correct, how did race and gender segregation exist so pervasively in our country before 1964? There were very few laws requiring segregation in employment by either race or sex. *See* J. Hoult Verkerke, *Free to Search*, 105 HARV. L. REV. 2080, 2080 (1992) ("With the exception of the South Carolina textile employment segregation law, all of the statutes to which Epstein refers involved areas of economic and social life other than labor markets"). Nevertheless, the mostly-free market left most employment in the South racially segregated. In *Griggs*, for example, Duke Power's policy limiting blacks to the Labor Department was not mandated by any law. Similarly, there were relatively few laws segregating occupations by sex; nevertheless, the free market left most employment throughout the nation sexually segregated.

Professor Epstein recognized that discrimination in the South prior to the Civil Rights Act of 1964 may have been influenced by state and local governments condoning private violence to keep the black population "in its place." *See* Gregory

S. Crespi, *Market Magic: Can the Invisible Hand Strangle Bigotry?*, 72 B.U. L. REV.
991, 1002 (1992). Because of this, Professor Donohue notes that, despite philosophical similarities to Friedman, "Epstein departs from the Chicago School
orthodoxy by acknowledging the initial economic gains for blacks that [Title VII]
generated." John J. Donohue III, *Advocacy Versus Analysis in Assessing Employment
Discrimination Law*, 44 STAN. L. REV. 1583, 1593 (1992). It is not so clear under
Professor Epstein's analysis, however, why Title VII was necessary to trigger the
massive integration of women into fields that had had few if any females prior to
1964. In any event, for him the fact that a dramatic intervention like Title VII was
necessary to shift norms does not mean that the antidiscrimination laws continue to
be necessary.

7. *The Bad Old Days?* A pervasive theme in this course has been the question of
whether discrimination (however defined) continues to be a major problem along
any of the axes of interest. We have seen conflicting views on this throughout the
book. Do you think that remaining discrimination is simply a few bad racist or sexist
apples; or, conversely, that such actors are numerous and will continue to cause
enormous harm unless constrained by the law? Or perhaps you take some middle
ground: discrimination continues to be pervasive, but it is of the softer, unconscious
bias kind. If the latter, how do the theories Professor Gersen canvasses apply?

8. *Where Do We Go from Here?* If market forces may reduce discrimination but
not eliminate it, the question whether government regulation prohibiting discrimination is necessary, therefore, cannot rest solely on the argument that discrimination
does not exist in a free market system. Given that economists acknowledge that
discrimination — employment decisions based on membership in a statutorily protected group — exists even when the market is unregulated, the issue becomes the
extent to which discrimination is harmful. Even if discrimination is wrong, government prohibition might not be the appropriate solution, but government regulation certainly makes no sense unless discrimination causes meaningful harm.

C.   WHY PROHIBIT DISCRIMINATION?

Opponents of the Civil Rights Act argued that prohibiting discrimination infringes
on the freedom to associate. In this view, discrimination is not wrongful because it is
merely a form of the right to associate with whomever one pleases. Echoes of this
debate were heard in connection with the 1987 nomination of Judge Robert Bork as
a justice of the United States Supreme Court. In 1963, Judge Bork had written an
article attacking proposed civil rights legislation:

> Of the ugliness of racial discrimination there need be no argument (though there
> may be some presumption in identifying one's own hotly controverted aims with the
> objective of the nation). But it is one thing when stubborn people express their racial
> antipathies in laws which prevent individuals, whether white or Negro, from dealing
> with those who are willing to deal with them, and quite another to tell them that even
> as individuals they may not act on their racial preferences in particular areas of life. The
> principle of such legislation is that if I find your behavior ugly by my standards, law or
> aesthetic, and if you prove stubborn about adopting my view of the situation, I am
> justified in having the state coerce you into more righteous paths. That is itself a
> principle of unsurpassed ugliness.

Robert Bork, *Civil Rights — A Challenge*, The New Republic, Aug. 31, 1963, at 22. While Bork's position contributed to the defeat of his nomination in 1987, the notion that discrimination is not necessarily wrongful and that prohibiting it is bad policy have reappeared in a different form in Professor Epstein's FORBIDDEN GROUNDS:

> The [law's] standard prohibition against force and fraud does not depend on a simple assertion that killing or murder is just illegitimate. Rather, it rests on the powerful, albeit empirical, judgment that all people value their right to be free from coercion far more than they value their right to coerce others in a Hobbesian war of all against all. . . . But there are no similar universal gains from a rule that says people who have distinct and distasteful preferences cannot go their own way by working and associating only with people of similar views. We may find their tastes offensive, just as they find our tastes offensive and our actions meddlesome. But we do not have to determine the relative intensity of clashing preferences in order to make powerful social judgments. . . . [T]here is good evidence that the preferences are so strong on both sides that no mutually acceptable gains are to be made from long-term forced amalgamation. The fallback position when the antidiscrimination norm is eliminated is not violence and anarchy; it is voluntary separation and competition.

Id. at 75.

But what of the other side of the coin? The four economic theories all depend upon explaining discrimination without necessarily justifying it. Professor Epstein comes closest to approving of discrimination (as a legal, not necessarily moral, matter). He has three reasons. First, from the libertarian perspective the government should not interfere with private conduct absent "force or fraud," and discrimination is neither. Second, there are heavy costs in making discrimination illegal. And third, discrimination can be efficient.

This is not the place to debate the libertarian philosophy although it might not be amiss to note that Professor George Rutherglen, in *Abolition in a Different Voice*, 78 VA. L. REV. 1463, 1469 (1992), critiques Professor Epstein's consistency. While Epstein has struck a strong libertarian theme in TAKINGS: PRIVATE PROPERTY AND THE POWER OF EMINENT DOMAIN (1985), that government appropriations of property should be compensated, FORBIDDEN GROUNDS dismisses any need for government efforts to deal with historic injustices like slavery, perhaps the most complete of "takings." He rejects all questions of rectification at the outset with the assertion that "there is no adequate remedy" for such historical injustices. *See also* J. Hoult Verkerke, in *Free to Search*, 105 HARV. L. REV. 2080, 2085 (1992) (even assuming a libertarian perspective, antidiscrimination laws are "justified as necessary to remedy an unjust distribution of resources").

As for costs, it would be foolish to deny that enforcing discrimination law is costly. But whether the cost is justified turns on an assessment of the benefits, which includes an analysis of whether it is efficient. That, in turn, requires focusing not only on individual instances but also on more general costs.

Relying on generalizations (perhaps better called stereotypes), whether or not "rational" as some economists use that term, excludes entire groups from full participation in our economy without any assessment of individual abilities. This is particularly problematic if the generalization is itself rooted in prior discrimination. All of the antidiscrimination laws were predicated at least in part on this perception. This economic thrust emerges most clearly with respect to the Age Discrimination in Employment Act and the Americans with Disabilities Act, in both of which Congress stressed the waste of human resources caused by discrimination against older workers and workers with disabilities. Employer discrimination results not only in individual harm but also in the loss to society of the contributions of those whose abilities are not fully utilized. Similarly, the economic consequences of discrimination were also prominent in the enactment of Title VII, although the economic goal was often subordinated to the powerful moral imperative of the statute. Congress clearly hoped to facilitate full participation by African Americans in the U.S. economy and to end a vicious cycle by which minorities who anticipated discrimination failed to make the human capital investments necessary to success in a competitive economy.

Discrimination, even "rational" discrimination, can be devastating to the individual victims and to the groups to which they belong; indeed, discrimination does not merely affect the immediate victims. Professor Mary Becker, in *The Law and Economics of Racial Discrimination in Employment: Needed in the Nineties: Improved Individual and Structural Remedies for Racial and Sexual Disadvantages in Employment*, 79 GEO. L.J. 1659, 1664 (1991), writes:

> [A]s a historical matter, current preferences are in part the result of past forms of regulation which are not exogenous to the legal system. Slavery and Jim Crow are closely connected to the refusal of many whites today to interact with African Americans as equals. Past legal limitations on women's ability to function as autonomous human beings are closely connected to the refusal of many men today to interact with women as equals.

Professor Becker uses "exogenous" to mean preferences arising outside the legal system. A number of scholars, most notably those writing from a feminist perspective, have argued that racial and gender differences are "socially constructed" in part by the legal system, but also by other powerful societal forces. *See also* Nancy E. Dowd, *Liberty vs. Equality: In Defense of Privileged White Males*, 34 WM. & MARY L. REV. 429 (1993) (criticizing Epstein for ignoring the rich literature on the social construction of gender differences and Critical Race Studies scholarship).

Even if the perceived productivity differences are real at this point in time, i.e., that discrimination would truly be rational for any given employer, is it necessarily efficient in the long run for an employer to rely on them? Professor Samuel Issacharoff, in *Contractual Liberties in Discriminatory Markets*, 70 TEX. L. REV. 1219, 1222 (1992), criticizes Epstein's "fundamental assumption that each individual is delivered to the labor market as a more or less intact bundle of skills and abilities." This is "a shockingly static view" of what is, in fact, a dynamic process. Indeed, it is the very "disincentives for optimal acquisition of human capital" brought about by discrimination that justify intervention in the market. *See also* Strauss, *supra*; Cass Sunstein, *Why Markets Don't Stop Discrimination*, in REASSESSING CIVIL RIGHTS 23 (Ellen F. Paul et al. eds., 1991). *But see* John J. Donohue III & James J. Heckman, *The Law and Economics of Racial Discrimination in Employment: Re-Evaluating Federal Civil Rights Policy*, 79 Geo. L.J. 1713, 1725 (1991) ("Since 1980, however, young blacks (those with less than sixteen years of labor market experience) have actually earned somewhat greater returns than their white counterparts from each additional year of schooling.").

Professor Nancy E. Dowd views Epstein as a relatively frank apologist for racism and sexism. She quotes Epstein to the effect that individual tastes are grouped to some extent by race and sex and that these tastes necessarily conflict with the smooth operation of at least some firms:

> These are outrageous statements, filled with stereotypes and race and gender essentialism reduced to implicit biological "natural" preference, amounting to an outright

justification for skin and gender privilege. Epstein is saying that the costs of diversity make discrimination reasonable and logical. He assumes that the characteristics he names are related to differences that affect governing the workplace with no other authority than his own perception that "[i]t is harder to do business as social distance between persons increases." What we also know, and what Epstein ignores, is that in most firms of any size women and minorities are present, but in positions of inferiority. That evidence suggests that it is not that privileged white males do not like to associate with women or minorities; rather, they like to associate with them, but only as long as it is in unequal ways. Group stereotyping replaces individual characteristics in Epstein's scheme. Furthermore, group-identified differences (stereotypes with a basis in fact, he would call these) are presumed to have employment consequences. There is little consideration of the possibility that other characteristics — such as education, class background, socioeconomic status, marital or parental status — may be more predictive of workplace-related governance costs than those he cites. There also is little examination of whether diversity has any benefits — after all, aren't we looking at both costs and benefits?

Dowd at 442. *See also* Andrew Koppelman, *Feminism & Libertarianism: A Response to Richard Epstein*, 1999 U. CHI. LEGAL F. 115 (1999); Marion Crain, *Rationalizing Inequality: An Antifeminist Defense of the "Free" Market*, 61 GEO. WASH. L. REV. 556 (1993); Kathryn Abrams, *Social Construction, Roving Biologism, and Reasonable Women: A Response to Professor Epstein*, 41 DEPAUL L. REV. 1021 (1992).

In more temperate language, Professor J. Hoult Verkerke, in *Free to Search*, 105 HARV. L. REV. 2080, 2088 (1992), doubts "the usefulness of racial and ethnic affiliations as a proxy for job-related preferences of workers. The potential for intragroup heterogeneity of preferences seems to me every bit as great as the potential for disagreement between members of different racial or ethnic groups."

Professor Mary Becker criticizes economic models for ignoring the human dimension. She begins by stressing that much discrimination is not rational. Indeed, "discrimination" is a poorly chosen word because it also means the ability to make fine distinctions.

> Racism and misogyny — the belief that people of color and women are less than fully human — are not "discrimination" in this sense. One does not believe that African Americans and women are less than fully human because of an analytically rigorous delineation of subtle differences between them and white men. To the contrary, racism and misogyny are deeply irrational emotions, based on hatred or a lack of empathy for "the other," often accompanied by the need to establish one's own importance by denying others' humanity. . . .
>
> The failure to include the desire to subordinate is a major gap in [the taste for discrimination and the statistical discrimination] economic models of discrimination. Some people discriminate, not because of a desire to work with those like themselves, but because they desire to dominate certain people from other groups.
>
> Another form of discrimination not addressed by the economic models is a lessened ability to empathize and identify with women and people of color and to put oneself in their shoes, incorporating their hurts and needs into one's perceptions. We all empathize best with those most like ourselves, but we live in a society in which white men disproportionately hold positions of power. . . .
>
> Again, the economic models fail to describe this form of discrimination. It is based neither on an aversion to contact with members of certain groups nor on a perception that groups differ with respect to productivity, the two forms of discrimination encompassed by the economic models. If lessened ability to empathize with women and people of color is widespread, the market will not drive out this unconscious emotional failing. It certainly has not eliminated it yet. . . .

Becker at 1664. While Professor Becker's argument is designed to identify forms of discrimination that are not accounted for by economic analysis, doesn't her approach also suggest that, whether or not discrimination is otherwise efficient, it causes psychic harms that the government has an interest in preventing? *See also* Verkerke at 2086 (Epstein's "account ignores the denigration, frustration and anger that the victim of discrimination experiences").

Devon Carbado & Mitu Galati, in *The Law and Economics of Critical Race Theory: Crossroads, Directions, and a New Critical Race Theory*, 112 YALE L.J. 1757 (2003), agree with Professor Epstein that employers favor homogeneity of their workforces, at least in positions where teamwork is critical. "In order to increase efficiency, employers have incentives to screen prospective employees for homogeneity, and, in order to counter racial stereotypes, employees have incentives to demonstrate a willingness and capacity to assimilate." *Id.* at 1762. Employers, then, may not discriminate on the basis of skin color per se but on the basis of characteristics related to race and culture.

> A black person's vulnerability to discrimination is shaped in part by her racial position on this spectrum. The less stereotypical she is, the more palatable her identity is. The more palatable her identify is, the less vulnerable she is to discrimination. [This] creates an incentive for black people to signal — though identity performance — that they are not conventionally black. These signals convey the idea that the sender is black in a phenotype but not a social sense.

Id. at 1772. This theory applies not only to African Americans but also to other racial minorities. In short, while the authors decry the reality, "Epstein need not worry." *Id.* at 1791.

PATRICIA J. WILLIAMS, THE ALCHEMY OF RACE AND RIGHTS
44-49 (1991)

Buzzers are big in New York City. Favored particularly by smaller stores and boutiques, merchants throughout the city have installed them as screening devices to reduce the incidence of robbery: if the face at the door looks desirable, the buzzer is pressed and the door is unlocked. If the face is that of an undesirable, the door stays locked. Predictably, the issue of undesirability has revealed itself to be a racial determination. While controversial enough at first, even civil-rights organizations backed down eventually in the face of arguments that the buzzer system is a "necessary evil," that it is a "mere inconvenience" in comparison to the risks of being murdered, that suffering discrimination is not as bad as being assaulted, and that in any event it is not all blacks who are barred, just "17-year-old black males wearing running shoes and hooded sweatshirts."

The installation of these buzzers happened swiftly in New York; stores that had always had their doors wide open suddenly became exclusive or received people by appointment only. I discovered them and their meaning on a Saturday in 1986. I was shopping in Soho and saw in a store window a sweater that I wanted to buy for my mother. I pressed my round brown face to the window and my finger to the buzzer, seeking admittance. A narrow-eyed, white teenager wearing running shoes and feasting on bubble gum glared out, evaluating me for signs that would pit me against the limits of his social understanding. After about five seconds, he mouthed "We're closed," and blew pink rubber at me. It was two Saturdays before Christmas, at one o'clock in the afternoon; there were several white people in the store who appeared to be shopping for things for their mothers.

I was enraged. At that moment I literally wanted to break all the windows of the store and take lots of sweaters for my mother. In the flicker of his judgmental gray eyes, that saleschild had transformed my brightly sentimental, joy-to-the-world, pre-Christmas spree to a shambles. He snuffed my sense of humanitarian catholicity, and there was nothing I could do to snuff his, without making a spectacle of myself.

I am still struck by the structure of power that drove me into such a blizzard of rage. There was almost nothing I could do, short of physically intruding upon him, that would humiliate him the way he humiliated me. No words, no gestures, no prejudices of my own would make a bit of difference to him; his refusal to let me into the store — it was Benetton's, whose colorfully punnish ad campaign is premised on wrapping every one of the world's peoples in its cottons and woolens — was an outward manifestation of his never having let someone like me into the realm of his reality. He had no compassion, no remorse, no reference to me; and no desire to acknowledge me even at the estranged level of arm's-length transactor. He saw me only as one who would take his money and therefore could not conceive that I was there to give him money.

In this weird ontological imbalance, I realized that buying something in that store was like bestowing a gift, the gift of my commerce, the lucre of my patronage. In the wake of my outrage, I wanted to take back the gift of appreciation that my peering in the window must have appeared to be. I wanted to take it back in the form of unap-preciation, disrespect, defilement. I wanted to work so hard at wishing he could feel what I felt that he would never again mistake my hatred for some sort of plaintive wish to be included. I was quite willing to disenfranchise myself, in the heat of my need to revoke the flattery of my purchasing power. I was willing to boycott Benetton's, random white-owned businesses, and anyone who ever blew bubble gum in my face again.

My rage was admittedly diffuse, even self-destructive, but it was symmetrical. The perhaps loose-ended but utter propriety of that rage is no doubt lost not just to the young man who actually barred me, but to those who would appreciate my being barred only as an abstract precaution, who approve of those who would bar even as they deny that they would bar me.

The violence of my desire to burst into Benetton's is probably quite apparent. I often wonder if the violence, the exclusionary hatred, is equally apparent in the repeated public urgings that blacks understand the buzzer system by putting themselves in the shoes of white storeowners — that, in effect, blacks look into the mirror of frightened white faces for the reality of their undesirability; and that then blacks would "just as surely conclude that [they] would not let [themselves] in under similar circumstances." (That some blacks might agree merely shows that some of us have learned too well the lessons of privatized intimacies of self-hatred and ratio-nalized away the fullness of our public, participatory selves.)

On the same day I was barred from Benetton's, I went home and wrote the above impassioned account in my journal. On the day after that, I found I was still brooding, so I turned to a form of catharsis I have always found healing. I typed up as much of the story as I have just told, made a big poster of it, put a nice colorful border around it, and, after Benetton's was truly closed, stuck it to their big sweater-filled window. I exercised my first-amendment right to place my business with them right out in the street.

So that was the first telling of this story. The second telling came a few months later, for a symposium on Excluded Voices sponsored by a law review. I wrote an essay summing up my feelings about being excluded from Benetton's and analyzing "how the rhetoric of increased privatization, in response to racial issues, functions as the rationalizing agent of public unaccountability and, ultimately, irresponsibility." Weeks later, I received the first edit. From the first page to the last, my fury had been carefully cut out. My rushing, run-on-rage had been reduced to simple declarative sentences. The active personal had been inverted in favor of the passive impersonal. My words were different; they spoke to me upside down. I was afraid to read too much of it at a time — meanings rose up at me oddly, stolen and strange.

A week and a half later, I received the second edit. All reference to Benetton's had been deleted because, according to the editors and the faculty adviser, it was defamatory; they feared harassment and liability; they said printing it would be irresponsible. I called them and offered to supply a footnote attesting to this as my personal experience at one particular location and of a buzzer system not limited to Benetton's; the editors told me that they were not in the habit of publishing things that were unverifiable. I could not but wonder, in this refusal even to let me file an affidavit, what it would take to make my experience verifiable. The testimony of an independent white bystander? (a requirement in fact imposed in the U.S. Supreme Court holdings through the first part of the century).

Two days after the piece was sent to press, I received copies of the final page proofs. All reference to my race had been eliminated because it was against "editorial policy" to permit descriptions of "physiognomy." . . .

Ultimately I did convince the editors that mention of my race was central to the whole sense of the subsequent text; that my story became one of extreme paranoia without the information that I am black; or that it became one in which the reader had to fill in the gap by assumption, presumption, prejudgment, or prejudice. What was most interesting to me in this experience was how the blind application of principles of neutrality, through the device of omission, acted either to make me look crazy or to make the reader participate in old habits of cultural bias.

That was the second telling of my story. The third telling came last April, when I was invited to participate in a law-school conference on equality and difference. . . . I opined:

> Law and legal writing aspire to formalized color-blind, liberal ideals. Neutrality is the standard for assuring these ideals; yet the adherence to it is often determined by reference to an aesthetic of uniformity, in which difference is simply omitted. For example, when segregation was eradicated from the American lexicon, its omission led many to actually believe that racism therefore no longer existed. Race-neutrality in law has become the presumed antidote for race bias in real life. With the entrenchment of the notion of race-neutrality came attacks on the concept of affirmative action and the rise of reverse discrimination suits. Blacks for so many generations deprived of jobs based on the color of our skin, are now told that we ought to find it demeaning to be hired, based on the color of our skin. Such is the silliness of simplistic either-or inversions as remedies to complex problems.
>
> What is truly demeaning in this era of double-speak-no-evil is going to interviews and not getting hired because someone doesn't think we'll be comfortable. It is demeaning not to get promoted because we're judged "too weak," then putting in a lot of energy the next time and getting fired because we're "too strong." It is demeaning to be told what we find demeaning. It is very demeaning to stand on street corners unemployed and begging. It is downright demeaning to have to explain why we haven't been

employed for months and then watch the job go to someone who is "more experi-enced." It is outrageously demeaning that none of this can be called racism, even if it happens only to, or to large numbers of, black people; as long as it's done with a smile, a handshake and a shrug; as long as the phantom-word "race" is never used.

NOTES

1. *Narrative Scholarship.* Professor Williams's book, THE ALCHEMY OF RACE AND RIGHTS, was a pathbreaking effort in a school described as narrative scholarship. Much narrative scholarship tries to bring an outsider's views into the legal mainstream, often a Critical Race Studies, Lat Crit, or feminist perspective. Williams's Benetton story critiques not only the retailer's buzzer system but also the resistance of traditional legal forums, i.e., law reviews, to publish writing discussing such realities from a personal perspective. Some defended the reviews' resistance to work such as this. The debate, often focusing on Williams and the Benetton story in particular, roiled the legal academy. *E.g.,* DANIEL A. FARBER & SUZANNA SHERRY, BEYOND ALL REASON: THE RADICAL ASSAULT ON TRUTH IN AMERICAN LAW 50 (1997); Marc A. Fajer, *Authority, Credibility, and Pre-Understanding: A Defense of Outsider Narratives in Legal Schol-arship,* 82 GEO. L.J. 1845 (1994).

One obvious criticism of storytelling is the difficulty of determining the truth, or at least the pervasiveness, of the experiences revealed by the narratives. But does that mean that such stories are irrelevant to law? Even if not, there can be competing narratives. A similar story is told about Condoleezza Rice, although with a consid-erably different ending. As recounted in the NEW YORKER of Oct. 14, 2002, p. 164, Dr. Rice was shopping at a store and the clerk tried to show her costume jewelry. There followed an exchange of words capped by Dr. Rice saying, "Let's get one thing straight. You're behind the counter because you have to work for six dollars an hour. I'm on this side asking to see the good jewelry because I make considerably more."

2. *The Psychological Literature.* Professor Williams's intense reaction to perceived discrimination is not unique to her. Professor Richard Delgado reviewed the psycho-logical literature on the impact of prejudice and discrimination in *Words That Wound: A Tort Action for Racial Insults, Epithets, and Name-Calling,* 17 HARV. C.R.-C.L. L. REV. 133 (1982):

> The psychological harms caused by racial stigmatization are often much more severe than those created by other stereotyping actions. Unlike many characteristics upon which stigmatization may be based, membership in a racial minority can be considered neither self-induced, like alcoholism or prostitution, nor alterable. Race-based stig-matization is, therefore, "one of the most fruitful causes of human misery. Poverty can be eliminated — but skin color cannot." . . .
>
> . . . Kenneth Clark has observed, "Human beings . . . whose daily experience tells them that almost nowhere in society are they respected and granted the ordinary dignity and courtesy accorded to others will, as a matter of course, begin to doubt their own worth." Minorities may come to believe the frequent accusations that they are lazy, ignorant, dirty, and superstitious. "The accumulation of negative images . . . present[s] them with one massive and destructive choice: either to hate one's self, as culture so systematically demand[s], or to have no self at all, to be nothing."
>
> The psychological responses to such stigmatization consist of feelings of humiliation, isolation, and self-hatred. Consequently, it is neither unusual nor abnormal for stigmatized

individuals to feel ambivalent about their self-worth and identity. This ambivalence arises from the stigmatized individual's awareness that others perceive him or her as falling short of societal standards, standards which the individual has adopted. Stigmatized individuals thus often are hypersensitive and anticipate pain at the prospect of contact with "normals." . . .

The psychological effects of racism may also result in mental illness and psychosomatic disease. The affected person may react by seeking escape through alcohol, drugs, or other kinds of antisocial behavior. The rates of narcotic use and admission to public psychiatric hospitals are much higher in minority communities than in society as a whole.

The achievement of high socioeconomic status does not diminish the psychological harms caused by prejudice. The effort to achieve success in business and managerial careers exacts a psychological toll even among exceptionally ambitious and upwardly mobile members of minority groups. . . . As a result, the incidence of severe psychological impairment caused by the environmental stress of prejudice and discrimination is not lower among minority group members of high socioeconomic status. . . .

In addition to such emotional and physical consequences, racial stigmatization may damage a victim's pecuniary interests. The psychological injuries severely handicap the victim's pursuit of a career. The person who is timid, withdrawn, bitter, hypertense, or psychotic will almost certainly fare poorly in employment settings. An experiment in which blacks and whites of similar aptitudes and capacities were put into a competitive situation found that the blacks exhibited defeatism, halfhearted competitiveness, and "high expectancies of failures." . . .

Id. at 136-40. *See also* Martha Chamallas, *Discrimination and Outrage: The Migration from Civil Rights to Tort Law*, 48 WM. & MARY L. REV. 2115 (2007).

3. *Self-Help?* Should the harm described by Professors Williams and Delgado be a matter of legal concern? Professor Williams resorted to self-help, hanging a damning sign in the window of the offending shop and publishing books and articles exposing her unfair treatment. She also contemplated an economic attack — boycotting Benetton or perhaps all white-owned businesses. Secretary Rice resorted to a more direct put-down. Why aren't these kinds of responses sufficient to control discrimination? Is legal regulation more effective? Is law capable of changing deeply ingrained social attitudes?

4. *Racial Profiling.* Professor Williams viewed the buzzer system as a kind of "racial profiling." Outside the employment context, racial profiling by police has been the subject of considerable news interest and scholarship. *See generally* Bernard E. Harcourt, *Rethinking Racial Profiling: A Critique of the Economics, Civil Liberties, and Constitutional Literature, and of Criminal Profiling More Generally*, 71 U. CHI. L. REV. 1275 (2004). What started out as a focus on police stops of African Americans and Latinos became more complicated in the wake of 9/11 as profiling in airports was extended to persons perceived to be Arabs or Muslims. *See* R. Richard Banks, *Racial Profiling and Antiterrorism Efforts*, 89 CORNELL L. REV. 1201 (2004).

5. *Psychological Costs and Economics.* Consider Professor John J. Donohue III's criticism of Professor Epstein in *Advocacy Versus Analysis in Assessing Employment Discrimination Law*, 44 STAN. L. REV. 1583, 1587 (1992), which stresses the economic nature of such harms:

To support his contention that governmental efforts to inhibit discrimination in labor markets are misguided, Epstein enlists the standard microeconomic argument that wealth will be maximized if competitive markets can operate without restraint. This conclusion only follows, however, if either all costs are internalized or the transaction costs of the affected parties are low. For example, free markets do not maximize wealth in settings where pollution costs and bargaining costs are high. Because of free rider problems and other transaction costs, the victims of widespread pollution will generally be unable to induce the polluters to stop polluting, even when the social benefits from such a contract would exceed the social costs. Once it is recognized that discrimination in labor markets imposes external costs that are quite analogous to the costs of pollution, the case for laissez-faire evaporates at a theoretical level and can only be sustained through a proper assessment of the costs and benefits of an antidiscrimination regime. Private discrimination is a form of psychological pollution that corrodes the well-being of both victims and [those who have not personally suffered discrimination but are morally offended by it], and excluding these costs from the social calculus — as Epstein does — would be as illogical as excluding the costs of chemical pollution in assessing environmental programs.

Professor J. Hoult Verkerke agrees that that the psychic harm associated with discrimination is relevant because it creates inefficiencies in the market:

> Once black workers learn that they will experience discrimination in the labor market, this dignitary harm operates as a tax on their efforts to search for employment opportunities. Blacks would react rationally to this tax by decreasing their search efforts. [This reduction in search activity is an economic inefficiency of discrimination and if it produces] inefficiencies that private transactions cannot remedy, regulatory intervention would be justified even in Epstein's libertarian regime.

Free to Search, 105 HARV. L. REV. 2080, 2086 (1992).

D.   THE COSTS AND BENEFITS OF PROHIBITING DISCRIMINATION

Whether the psychic harm associated with discrimination is weighed in the balance as an economic factor or weighed against efficiency as a matter of fairness, the question remains whether laws prohibiting discrimination generate more benefits than costs. Prohibiting discrimination clearly has costs for society. There are possible losses in efficiency, and, even without considering the theoretical losses that might be associated with regulating the free market, prohibiting discrimination imposes administrative costs on society. But before addressing these issues, it is important to understand the economic dimensions of the problems faced by the groups protected by antidiscrimination statutes and the impact of antidiscrimination laws on the economic condition of protected groups.

1.   Weighing Economic Costs and Benefits

There is no doubt about African-American progress, whether or not attributable to Title VII, since 1965. *E.g.*, John J. Donohue III & James J. Heckman, *The Law and Economics of Racial Discrimination in Employment: Re-Evaluating Federal Civil Rights Policy*, 79 GEO. L.J. 1713 (1991); John J. Donohue III & James Heckman, *Continuous versus Episodic Change: The Impact of Civil Rights Policy on the Economic Status of Blacks*, 29 J. ECON. LITERATURE 1603 (1991). Nor is there much doubt about the progress of women in many sectors of the economy. But these and other groups remain at risk in the American economy. In a book published in 1980, THE ZERO SUM SOCIETY, Professor Lester C. Thurow wrote:

> The essence of any minority group's position can be captured with the answer to three questions: (1) Relative to the majority group, what is the probability of the minority's finding employment? (2) For those who are employed, what are the earnings opportunities relative to the majority? (3) Are minority group members making a breakthrough into the high-income jobs of the economy?

Id. at 184. He reported some sobering facts, including persistent, heavy black unemployment (twice the rate of whites). *Id.* at 185. Similarly, "Using the top 5 percent of all jobs (based on earnings) as the definition of a 'good job,' blacks hold 2 percent of these jobs while whites hold 98 percent. Since blacks constitute 12 percent of the labor force they are obviously underrepresented in this category." *Id.* at 186. Hispanics were doing slightly better than African Americans, although various subgroups showed differing success. Native Americans were the poorest ethnic/racial group. As for women, in 1980, Thurow wrote: "Female workers hold the dubious distinction of having made the least progress in the labor market. In 1939 full-time, full-year women earned 61 percent of what men earned. In 1977 they earned 57 percent as much." *Id.* at 187. Female unemployment also rose relative to male unemployment, and this group held only 4 percent of the top jobs in the country.

Professor Thurow drew many of his statistics from the 1970 census. If the economic conditions of protected groups improved substantially over time, his data would be of historical interest only. After the 1990 census, however, Professor David Benjamin Oppenheimer, *in Understanding Affirmative Action*, 23 HASTINGS CONST. L.Q. 921 (1996), updated Thurow's findings. He found improvement to be both spotty and limited:

> Blacks, Hispanics and Asian Americans earn substantially less than do whites, and in some respects things are getting worse. In 1980, the average black male worker earned $751 for every $1,000 earned by a white male worker. By 1990 it had dropped to $731. . . .
>
> Women of all races continue to earn substantially less than men. In the 1960s women earned 60% of what men earned on average; by 1993, it had risen only to 72%. The average woman with a masters degree earns the same amount as the average man with an associate (junior college) degree. Hispanic women earn less than 65% of the wages earned by white men at the same education level.

Id. at 965. In terms of occupational stratification, "white men make up only 43% of the workforce, [but] they constitute 97% of the top executives (vice-presidents and above) at the 1,500 largest American corporations." *Id.* at 967. Unemployment had also climbed for African Americans, increasing from twice the white rate to 2.76 times higher than the white rate by 1990. *Id. See also* Nancy E. Dowd, *Liberty vs. Equality: In Defense of Privileged White Males*, 34 WM. & MARY L. REV. 429, 476 (1993) (analyzing the economic progress of women).

The 2000 census provided more information, but introduced a complication by for the first time allowing individuals to identify themselves as of more than one race. This makes it hard to be confident about comparisons against prior censuses. Nevertheless, black and Hispanic labor force participation rates, both at about 61%, continued to trail whites (74.3%) and Asians (68%). EMPLOYMENT STATUS: 2000,

Census 2000 Brief, tbl. at 5. Asian and white unemployment rates were about the same (3%), but African Americans and Hispanics were about double (6.9% and 5.5%, respectively). Earnings followed this pattern with one notable exception. In 2005, Asian men had the highest median income among men, ($48,693), with white men at $46,807; black men's median was $34,433, and Hispanic males trailed at $27,380. Women's earnings were always lower within a race, but varied considerable among races: Hispanic females were at 85% of Hispanic males while white women had only 73% of the median earnings of white men. Bruce H. Webster, Jr. & Alemayehu Bishaw, U.S. Census Bureau, *American Community Census Reports, ACS-02, Data from the 2005 American Community Survey* (2006), http://www.census .gov/prod/2006pubs/acs-02.pdf. *See also* Judith Hellerstein & David Neumark, *Workplace Segregation in the United States: Race, Ethnicity, and Skill*, http://papers .ssrn.com.

As this data indicates, while most minorities have made limited progress since the passage of Title VII, Asian Americans have done better. For example, we saw that Asian men had the highest median income among men, ($48,693), almost $2000 higher than white men. Subgroups of Asians, however, do not fare nearly so well, and there has been a spirited debate about the significance of Asian Americans being the "model minority." *See* Professors Miranda Oshige McGowan & James Lindgren, *Testing the "Model Minority" Myth*, 100 Nw. U.L. Rev. 331, 333 (2006) ("we found that the model minority stereotype is not correlated with hostility to Asians, immigrants, African Americans, or government programs to increase opportunities for minorities. . . . However, the data do strongly support one important part of the Asian critical scholars' critique. Those who hold positive views of Asians as hard working or intelligent are indeed more likely to believe that there is little or no discrimination against Asian Americans in jobs and housing"). *But see* Robert Chang & Rose Villazor, *Testing the 'Model Minority Myth': A Case of Weak Empiricism*, 101 Nw. U. L. Rev. 101 (2007) (critiquing the methodology undergirding these findings).

As for gender, there are more hopeful indicators. The most obvious is with respect to women, whose labor force participation rate is closer to that of men — a 13 point difference, 58% to 71% — than at any time in history. *Census 2000 Brief* at 4 (in 1990, the gap was 17 points, 57% for women and 74% for men). Yet women's earnings, even among full-time workers, continued to lag: median earnings of men in 2005 were $41,965, while the women's median was $32,168, or 76.7 percent of men's earnings. Webster & Bishaw. In some states, however, the gap was much less, and in some cities, younger women actually earn more than their age cohort of men. Sam Roberts, *For Young Earners in Big City, a Gap in Women's Favor*, NY Times, Aug. 3, 2007 ("Young women in New York and several of the nation's other largest cities who work full time have forged ahead of men in wages").

The status of two other groups in society of concern to the antidiscrimination laws is more complicated. For example, older Americans are wealthier than the average American, but many subgroups — particularly minority women — are among the poorest in our society. The participation of older individuals in the workforce drops off relatively early. In Census 2000, for example, almost 60% of the age 62-64 cohort was *not* in the workforce, although, of course, some significant portion of this group voluntarily retired. *Census 2000 Brief*. at 4. However, many older workers "retire" or accept Social Security involuntarily, and for them there are often inadequate benefits to maintain even minimally decent living standards. Similarly, while older workers who remain employed are often very well paid, those who lose their positions frequently find themselves unable to obtain comparable employment.

Scholarship has considered whether the differences between age discrimination and race/gender discrimination require reconsidering of the rules. Professor George Rutherglen, *From Race to Age: The Expanding Scope of Employment Discrimination Laws*, 24 J. LEG. STUD. 491 (1995), questioned the underlying basis of the ADEA. Taking up this theme, Samuel Issacharoff and Erica Worth Harris, *Is Age Discrimination Really Age Discrimination?: The ADEA's Unnatural Solution*, 72 N.Y.U. L. REV. 780 (1997), argued that older individuals do not fit into the usual antidiscrimination model because "far from being discrete and insular, the elderly represent the normal unfolding of life's processes for all persons. As a group, older Americans do not suffer from poverty or face the disabling social stigma characteristically borne by black Americans. . . . " *Id.* at 781. Their article does not recommend repeal of the ADEA but rather proposes modifying it to recognize that "the dramatic shift in wealth towards older Americans and the diminished job prospects of the young provoke grave concern that a misguided antidiscrimination model has allowed a concerted and politically powerful group of Americans to engage in a textbook example of what economists would term 'rent-seeking.'" *Id.* at 783. *See also* Rhonda M. Reaves, *One of These Things Is Not Like the Other: Analogizing Ageism to Racism in Employment Discrimination Cases*, 38 U. RICH. L. REV. 839 (2004) (treating older workers "like" blacks fails to fully address older workers' unique problems and tends to marginalize the experiences of black workers).

Professor Christine Jolls, *Hands-Tying and the Age Discrimination in Employment Act*, 74 TEX. L. REV. 1813 (1996), agrees that the traditional justifications for antidiscrimination legislation may not apply to the ADEA. However, she argues that the statute may prevent employer opportunism. The empirical observation that older workers are often paid more for doing the same work as younger employees may simply reflect a preference by both workers and employers for wages to rise over time. Such a preference, however, can only be achieved if employers can tie their own hands, that is, avoid the temptations of opportunistically replacing expensive, older workers with cheaper, younger ones. The ADEA, by providing legal protection for older workers, permits this "hands-tying."

Another group whose economic condition is hard to capture statistically is the disabled. We encountered some of the data concerning individuals with disabilities in Chapter 6, pp. 487-88, but we also saw there that the statutory definition of disability may not match up with the data collected for other purposes, including the census. That does not mean that the disabled do not face profound economic challenges, but it does mean that the ADA addresses only a small part of them.

More alarming, some scholars have suggested that the ADA has actually hurt employment of the disabled. *See* Samuel R. Bagenstos, *Has the Americans with Disabilities Act Reduced Employment for People with Disabilities?*, 25 BERKELEY J. EMP. & LAB. L. 527, 555-58 (2004), *reviewing* DAVID C. STAPLETON & RICHARD V. BURKHAUSER, THE DECLINE IN EMPLOYMENT OF PEOPLE WITH DISABILITIES: A POLICY PUZZLE (2003) ("Empirical evidence is broadly consistent with theoretical reasons to expect that mandated accommodations negatively effect the employment of people with disabilities"; but "alternative explanations are possible, including 'the real prospect that any disemployment effect of the ADA is a short-term phenomenon,' in part because of the falling costs of accommodation.").

Even assuming the ADA is effective, there is the normative question of whether it is efficient. Professor J. H. Verkerke, *Is the ADA Efficient?*, 50 UCLA L. REV. 903 (2003), views the duty of reasonable accommodation as implying that some employers will have to hire workers "whose disabilities make them less productive than other workers," which means that the costs of accommodation can be viewed "as a mandated benefit funded by an implicit payroll tax on employers. Predictable objections follow from this characterization . . . " including that "the costs of such benefits are shifted to workers." *Id.* at 907. Nevertheless, Verkerke thinks the ADA may be justified on economic grounds in terms of reducing some inefficiencies, including the avoidance of "employee churning" caused by repetitive hiring and discharge of workers with hidden disabilities and "the risk of severe mismatching in comparatively high-risk jobs and the possibility of scarring when repeated discharges make someone unemployable." *Id.* at 957. Amy Wax, *Disability, Reciprocity, and "Real Efficiency": A Unified Approach*, 44 WM. & MARY L. REV. 1421, 1450 (2003), takes a more conventional distributionist approach to the same question: "[T]he ADA is not necessarily inefficient overall, given the basic safety net and regulatory programs to which our society is committed. Rather, its principal design flaw is that it forces employers to pay costs that should arguably be borne by everyone."

All this economic data, of course, raises a critical question for this course and our society: to what extent is discrimination by employers responsible for the economic problems of these groups? No one believes that the sole cause of disadvantage of various groups is present-day discrimination by employers or, more generally, by today's society at large. The economic condition of African Americans, for example, can be traced in large part to slavery and its legacy. *See* Owen Fiss, in *A Theory of Fair Employment Laws*, 38 U. CHI. L. REV. 235, 238-39 (1971). Similar points can be made about women. Centuries of pigeonholing women into primary roles as wives and mothers, with employment limited to strictly defined kinds of "women's work," are reflected in today's persistent occupational segregation. Nevertheless, some believe that one substantial explanation for this data is discrimination against women and minority group members. *See, e.g.,* Oppenheimer, at 969-73. However, even if discrimination is largely responsible, the perpetrators may frequently not be employers: Professor Oppenheimer documents other barriers to minority advancement, including education and housing. Nevertheless, he claims that discrimination in employment against women and minorities is "pervasive," *id.* at 969, and recurrent manifestations we have seen in this course lend weight to this view. However, others disagree, and the degree to which these problems are the result of continuing discrimination by employers is, to a large extent, the subject of this entire book.

An illustration of the complexity of the problem of ascertaining whether employer discrimination contributes to poor economic outcomes may be drawn from the statistical discrepancy between male and female wages. Factors other than intentional discrimination are clearly at work. Some part of the "gender gap" is undoubtedly due to lower female education rates and less sustained participation in the labor market by women as a group. However, a large part of this gap is due to occupational segregation. Vicki Schultz, in *Telling Stories About Women and Work: Judicial Interpretations of Sex Segregation in the Workplace in Title VII Cases Raising the Lack of Interest Argument*, 103 HARV. L. REV. 1749, 1749 n. 1 (1990), reports that "[a]s recently as 1985, over two-thirds of working women were employed in occupations in which at least 70% of the workers were female." Although the origins of most occupational segregation can be traced to societal and employer discrimination in earlier times, the extent to which it is perpetuated, or at least capitalized on, by current employer practices is much debated. Such practices can range from blatantly discriminatory assignments to channeling of workers through unthinking stereotyping to neutral practices that tend to maintain the earlier segregated occupations. *But see* Joni Hersch, *The New Labor Market for Lawyers: Will Female Lawyers Still Earn*

Less?, 10 CARDOZO WOMEN'S L.J. 1, 3 (2003) ("female lawyers who earned their J.
D. before 1990 earn substantially less than their male counterparts, even after
controlling for gender differences in work-related characteristics," but female lawyers
earning their J.D. between 1990 and 1993 "earn more than their male counterparts").

Even if there are positive trends in the economic conditions of various groups, and
these can be traced to the enactment of Title VII and other antidiscrimination laws,
are any such gains outweighed by losses of efficiency that negatively impact on the
economic welfare of society as a whole? This debate can be analyzed in economically oriented terms by considering the application of two different types of "efficiency" — Pareto optimality and Kaldor-Hicks efficiency. A reallocation of resources
is Pareto-optimal when someone is better off and no one is worse off. Antidiscrimination laws, like all other sorts of governmental regulation, are unlikely to be Pareto-
optimal because, while, say, blacks and women may be better off, others (employers,
employee competitors, and white racists) are worse off. That is, of course, one
argument against affirmative action.

The competing test for efficiency is "the broader, more controversial Kaldor-Hicks
wealth-maximization criterion — which endorses all measures whose total benefits
exceed their total costs, as measured by willingness-to-pay, without regard to the
incidence of costs and benefits across the affected population." Gregory S. Crespi,
Market Magic: Can the Invisible Hand Strangle Bigotry?, 72 B.U. L. REV. 991, 994
(1992). Put otherwise, Kaldor-Hicks "requires only that government action produce
sufficient gains for its beneficiaries to allow them hypothetically to compensate those
who are injured by the regulation, not that those who are injured in fact are compensated." J. Hoult Verkerke, *Free to Search*, 105 HARV. L. REV. 2080, 2088 (1992).
The antidiscrimination laws have been defended as efficient in the Kaldor-Hicks
sense of increasing total societal output. The basic argument is that these laws bring
about a more efficient economy by encouraging more efficient use of human
resources. Discrimination can underutilize millions of disfavored individuals. In
other words, endemic discrimination against certain groups not only prevents
members of those groups from fully developing their opportunities but also deprives
society of the fruits of that development. By eliminating discrimination, society, not
merely the immediate victims, will be better off. Subjecting this belief to a cost-
benefit analysis can, however, be daunting. *See* John J. Donohue III, *Is Title VII
Efficient?*, 134 U. PA. L. REV. 1411 (1986) (Title VII may produce allocative benefits
by accelerating the processes by which discriminatory employers will be driven out
of the market).

Some have argued that some of the benefits flowing to African Americans from
Title VII are offset by concomitant harms to blacks. Professor Epstein, for example,
suggests that there are costs to blacks from antidiscrimination laws, including a
preference for high-skilled black labor at the expense of low-skilled black labor. *Id.* at
261-66. Further, he argues that the antidiscrimination laws have benefited middle-
class blacks at the expense of poorer blacks. Professor Samuel Issacharoff, in *Contractual Liberties in Discriminatory Markets*, 70 TEX. L. REV. 1219, 1241 (1992),
responds:

> Epstein takes as his premise numerous observations, including those of sociologist
> William Julius Wilson, that Title VII has been a tremendous boon to skilled blacks,
> particularly in the professions, but has produced no discernible improvement in the life
> station of the increasing black underclass. Epstein attempts to argue that just as the

minimum wage is thought to raise the cost of marginal labor and actually decrease opportunity for teenage and other marginal laborers, so too must Title VII be responsible for shutting out the low-skilled layers of the black work force: "The chief effect of Title VII is to make highly skilled black labor more desirable relative to low-skilled black labor. As with the minimum wage, Title VII works a redistribution from worse-off to better-off blacks, which is surely far from what its principled supporters intended."

The logic here is startling. Epstein's best evidence to support his thesis is that the black lower classes have grown more desperate, more atomized, and more forlorn since the 1960s, when Title VII went into effect. . . . None of this evidence leads to the causation analysis that Epstein reaches for. It is nothing less than stunning that there is no mention in this section of the beginning of the deindustrialization of the United States during the period in question and the long cyclical decline in manufacturing and other industrial jobs that had long provided the primary avenue of advancement for ethnic groups arriving into the work force.

Issacharoff goes on to ask why opening up advancement to the black middle class should not "stand as a real, though partial, gain[.] Epstein argues that whatever gains blacks accomplished under Title VII must have been at the expense of the lower layers of the black community. The evidence for this is tenuous and unpersuasive." *Id.* at 1243.

Christine Jolls, *Accommodation Mandates*, 53 STAN. L. REV. 223, 225-30 (2000), takes a more theoretic and nuanced approach to Epstein's point that antidiscrimination laws may not help their intended beneficiaries, or at least not all of them. Speaking to laws requiring employers to provide specified benefits, such as accommodation of the disabled and of family leave, she writes:

> In broad terms, my framework predicts that accommodation mandates targeted to disabled workers will increase or leave unchanged the wages of these workers relative to the wages of nondisabled workers while simultaneously reducing disabled workers' relative employment levels; the framework also predicts that accommodation mandates targeted to female workers will reduce the relative wages of these workers (contrary to the case of disabled workers) and will have ambiguous effects on their relative employment levels. . . .

See also John J. Donohue III, *Understanding the Reasons for and Impact of Legislatively Mandated Benefits for Selected Workers*, 53 STAN. L. REV. 897, 904 (2001) ("the Jolls framework indicates that women will pay for the anti-sex harassment mandate with lower wages. Uncertainty remains, however, as to whether the lower relative wages of women are offset by increases in the employment of women (which would be my hunch, as this would be consistent with the observed large increases in female labor force participation in the United States), or whether women suffer the double whammy of lower wages and lower employment (in this case where they value the mandate less than its cost of provision)").

2. Weighing Noneconomic Costs and Benefits

Whether or not antidiscrimination laws improve the economic condition of protected groups and whether or not they improve or impair the efficiency of the economy in general, antidiscrimination laws provide protected groups with a remedy for the loss of dignity and associated psychic harm caused by discrimination. These harms exist even if Professor Epstein's benign "voluntary sorting" occurs. Consider the similarities between Epstein's viewpoint and the following extract from *Plessy v. Ferguson*, 163 U.S. 537, 550-52 (1896), the case that held segregation by the "separate but equal" standard did not violate the Fourteenth Amendment's equal protection clause:

> We consider the underlying fallacy of the plaintiff's argument to consist in the assumption that the enforced separation of the two races stamps the colored race with a badge of inferiority. If this be so, it is not by reason of anything found in the act, but solely because the colored race chooses to put that construction upon it. . . . Legislation is powerless to eradicate racial instincts or to abolish distinctions based upon physical differences, and the attempt to do so can only result in accentuating the difficulties of the present situation. If the civil and political rights of both races be equal one cannot be inferior to the other civilly or politically. If one race be inferior to the other socially, the Constitution of the United States cannot put them upon the same plane.

Professor George Schatzki, in United Steelworkers of America v. Weber: *An Exercise in Understandable Indecision*, 56 WASH. L. REV. 51, 56-57 (1980), recognized the advantages of voluntary separation, but nonetheless reached a very different conclusion:

> It is not clear we would want to outlaw racial employment discrimination, however irrational we believed it to be, if all persons were sometimes the discriminators and sometimes the discriminatees; if all ethnic groups had equal, statistical access to jobs; if all ethnic groups were equally affluent, prestigious, and influential. At least I am not sure we should want to outlaw a pluralism that allowed random ethnic discrimination. Although, on balance, I might prefer the "melting pot," or I might prefer some integration as well as some identifiable pluralism, it is not clear to me that we, as a society, desire to destroy ethnic pride, consciousness, and behavior. Destruction of that pluralistic attitude and behavior would be difficult; quick destruction might be possible, but only with involvement of the law.
>   [But] the burden of discrimination (in employment and elsewhere) has fallen on the members of certain ethnic groups. Racial discrimination is not random. Most of us do not suffer the burdens and barbs of ethnic discrimination; more importantly, whether or not we do suffer this irrationality sometimes, most of us have been treated most of the time by dominant persons or institutions without our race being a handicap. Saying that about blacks or chicanos, for example, would be an outright lie. These are people in our society — as a whole — who suffer in a vastly disproportionate way because of their ethnicity. The degrees of suffering and disparity are probably immeasurable, but few — if any — would deny their existence.

Is the benefit of providing a remedy for the "tort" of discrimination outweighed by the economic and social costs of antidiscrimination laws? Are there other benefits associated with antidiscrimination laws? Professor John J. Donohue III, in *Advocacy Versus Analysis in Assessing Employment Discrimination Law*, 44 STAN. L. REV. 1583, 1606 (1992), sounds a chilling note:

> In considering the value of antidiscrimination law, one should at least consider that the repeal of Title VII holds the remote possibility of cataclysmic racial conflict. The lessons of slavery, Jim Crow, and Nazi Germany all serve to remind us that racial prejudice can be a dangerous force. Just as efforts to push affirmative action too

forcefully may ignite dangerous passions, the injustices of private sector employment discrimination, at a time when black incomes and wealth are far below those of whites, also has a potential for explosive consequences. . . . Therefore, society may tolerate a law that seems socially costly, based on a purely contemporary assessment of costs and benefits, in order to diminish the (albeit small) likelihood that the repeal of Title VII would breach the bigotry threshold and lead to catastrophic social costs [which is the argument economists use regarding the need to restrain inflation given the small risk but . devastating consequences of hyperinflation.] [S]ociety may not be willing to gamble with the risk of suffering a near infinite burden — such as the holocaust in Nazi Germany — even if the chance of such a burden is minuscule.

TABLE OF CASES

Bold indicates principal cases.

TABLE OF SELECTED SECONDARY
AUTHORITIES

Befort, Stephen F., Reasonable Accommodation and Reassignment Under the Americans with Disabilities Act: Answers, Questions and Suggested Solutions After *U.S. Airways, Inc. v. Barnett*, 45 Ariz. L. Rev. 931 (2003), 552

Befort, Stephen F., The Most Difficult Reasonable Accommodation Issues: Reassignment and Leave of Absence, 37 Wake Forest L. Rev. 439 (2002), 556

Befort, Stephen F. & Sarah J. Gorajski, When Quitting is Fitting: The Need for a Reformulated Sexual Harassment/Constructive Discharge Standard in the Wake of *Pennsylvania State Police v. Suders*, 67 Ohio St. L.J. 595 (2006), 402

Beiner, Theresa M., Do Reindeer Games Count as Terms, Conditions or Privileges of Employment Under Title VII?, 37 B.C. L. Rev. 643 (1996), 23

Beiner, Theresa M., Let the Jury Decide: The Gap Between What Judges and Reasonable People Believe Is Sexually Harassing, 75 S. Cal. L. Rev. 791 (2002), 380

Beiner, Theresa M., Sex, Science and Social Knowledge: The Implications of Social Science Research on Imputing Liability to Employers for Sexual Harassment, 7 Wm. & Mary J. Women & L. 273 (2001), 412

Beiner, Theresa M., Sexy Dressing Revisited: Does Target Dress Play a Part in Sexual Harassment Cases?, 14 Duke J. Gender L. & Pol'y 125, 127 (2007), 375

Beiner, Theresa M., Using Evidence of Women's Stories in Sexual Harassment Cases, 24 U. Ark. Little Rock L. Rev. 117 (2001), 412

Beiner, Theresa M. & Robert B. Chapman, Take What You Can, Give Nothing Back: Judicial Estoppel, Employment Discrimination, Bankruptcy, and Piracy in the Courts, 60 U. Miami L. Rev. 1 (2005), 720

Beiner, Theresa M. & John M.A. DiPappa, Hostile Environments and the Religious Employee, 19 U. Ark. Little Rock L.J. 577 (1977), 434

Berg, Thomas C., Religious Speech in the Workplace: Harassment or Protected Speech?, 22 Harv. L.J. & Pub. Pol'y 954, 959 (1999), 434

Bertrand, Marianne & Sendhil Mullainathan, Are Emily and Greg More Employable than Lakisha and Jamal?, 94 Am. Econ. Rev. 991 (2004), 7

Bielby, William T. & Pamela Coukos, "Statistical Dueling" with Unconventional Weapons: What Courts Should Know about Experts in Employment Discrimination Class Actions, 56 Emory L.J. 1563 (2007), 642

Bierman, Leonard & Rafael Gely, So, You Want to Be a Partner at Sidley & Austin?, 40 Hous. L. Rev. 969, 991 (2003), 325

Bingham, Lisa B., On Repeat Players, Adhesive Contracts, and the Use of Statistics in Judicial Review of Employment Arbitration Awards, 29 McGeorge L. Rev. 223 (1998), 745

Bisom-Rapp, Susan, How Well Do Internal EEO Alternative Dispute Resolution and Litigation Prevention Measures Advance the Traditional Goal of Anti-Discrimination Law?, 11 Employee Rts. & Emp. Pol'y J. 139 (2007), 168

Bisom-Rapp, Susan, An Ounce of Prevention Is a Poor Substitute for a Pound of Cure: Confronting the Developing Jurisprudence of Education and Prevention in Employment Discrimination Law, 22 Berkeley J. Emp. & Lab. L. 1 (2001), 168, 409

Bisom-Rapp, Susan, Fixing Watches with Sledgehammers: The Questionable Embrace of Employee Sexual Harassment Training by the Legal Profession, 24 U. Ark. Little Rock L. Rev. 147 (2001), 409

Blanpain, Roger, et. al., The Global Workplace: International and Comparative Employment Law — Cases and Materials (2007), 112, 114

Blumrosen, Alfred W. & Ruth G. Blumrosen, Intentional Job Discrimination — New Tools for Our Oldest Problem, 37 U. Mich. J.L. Ref. 681 (2004), 140

Blumrosen, Alfred W. & Ruth G. Blumrosen, The Reality of Intentional Discrimination in Metropolitan America — 1999 (2002), 140

Bodie, Matthew T., Questions About the Efficiency of Employment Arbitration Agreements, 39 Ga. L. Rev. 1, 41 (2004), 745

Booth, Dean & James L. Mackay, Legal Constraints on Employment Testing and Evolving Trends in the Law, 29 Emory L.J. 121, 125 (1980), 279

Bork, Robert, Civil Rights — A Challenge, The New Republic, Aug. 31, 1963, 771

Brake, Deborah L. & Joanna Grossman, The Failure of Title VII as a Rights Claiming System, 86 N.C. L. Rev. (forthcoming 2008), 612

Brooks, Roy L., A Roadmap through Title VII's Procedural and Remedial Labyrinth, 24 Sw. U. L. Rev. 511 (1995), 595

Browne, Kingsley R., Statistical Proof of Discrimination: Beyond "Damned Lies," 68 Wash. L. Rev. 477 (1993), 141, 143-144

Bryant, Anna Laurie & Richard A. Bales, Using the Same Actor "Inference" in Employment Discrimination Cases, 1999 Utah L. Rev. 225, 107

Bublick, Ellen M., Summers' Personal as Political: Reasoning Without Effort from Stereotypes, 11 Cardozo Women's L.J. 529 (2005), 164

Buchanan, Kim Shayo, Beyond Modesty: Privacy in Prison and the Risk of Sexual Abuse, 88 Marq. L. Rev. 751 (2005), 183

Buchanan, Paul & Courtney W. Wisall, The Evolving Understanding of Workplace Harassment and Employer Liability: Implications of Recent Supreme Court Decisions Under Title VII, 34 Wake Forest L. Rev. 55 (1999), 409

Mueting, Katie M., A Case for Allowing Victims of ADA Retaliation and Coercion in Employment to Recover Legal Damages, 92 Iowa L. Rev. 1493 (2007), 698

Murphy, Colleen P., Statutory Caps and Judicial Review of Damages, 39 Akron L. Rev. 1001 (2006), 697

Murr, Heather S., The Continuing Expansive Pressure to Hold Employers Strictly Liable for Supervisory Sexual Extortion: An Alternative Approach Based on Reasonableness, 39 U.C. Davis L. Rev. 529 (2006), 393, 412

Nance, Cynthia E., The Continuing Significance of Color under Title VII Forty Years after Its Passage, 26 Berkeley J. Emp. & Lab. L. 435, 473 (2005), 75

Nessel, Lori, Undocumented Immigrants in the Workplace: The Fallacy of Labor Protection and the Need for Reform, 36 Harv. C.R.-C.L. L. Rev. 345 (2001), 459

Neumark, David, Sex Discrimination in Restaurant Hiring: An Audit Study, 111 Q.J. Econ. 915 (1996), 310

Nosek, Brian A., Harvesting Implicit Group Attitudes and Beliefs from a Demonstration Web Site, 6 Group Dynamics 101, 101-02 (2002), 7

Oleske, James M., Jr., Federalism, Free Exercise and Title VII: Reconsidering Reasonable Accommodations, 6 U. Pa. J. Const. L. 525 (2004), 650

Onwuachi-Willig, Angela & Mario L. Barnes, By Any Other Name?: On Being "Regarded As" Black, and Why Title VII Should Apply Even if Lakisha and Jamal Are White, 2005 Wisc. L. Rev. 1283, 75

Oppenheimer, David Benjamin, Negligent Discrimination, 141 U. Pa. L. Rev. 899 (1993), 8, 221

Oppenheimer, David Benjamin, The Story of Green v. McDonnell Douglas, Employment Discrimination Stories, Joel Wm. Friedman ed. 2006, 54

Oppenheimer, David Benjamin, Understanding Affirmative Action, 23 Hastings Const. L.Q. 921 (1996), 780

Oppenheimer, David Benjamin, Verdicts Matter: An Empirical Study of California Employment Discrimination and Wrongful Discharge Jury Verdicts Reveals Low Success Rates for Women and Minorities, 37 U.C. Davis L. Rev. 511, 516-17 (2003), 110

Oyer, Paul E. & Scott Schaeffer, Sorting, Quotas, and the Civil Rights Act of 1991: Who Hires When It's Hard to Fire?, 45 J.L. & Econ. 41 (2002), 223

Oyer, Paul E. & Scott Schaeffer, The Unintended Consequences of the '91 Civil Rights Act, 26 Regulation 42 (2003), 223

Paetzold, Ramona L. & Steven L. Willborn, Deconstructing Disparate Impact: A View of the Model Through New Lenses, 74 N.C. L. Rev. 325, 356 (1995), 230

Parker, Wendy, Lessons in Losing: Race and National Origin Employment Discrimination Litigation in Federal District Court, 81 Notre Dame L. Rev. 889 (2006), 111

Pearce, John A., II, The Dangerous Intersection of Independent Contractor Law and the Immigration Reform and Control Act: The Impact of the Wal-Mart Settlement, 10 Lewis & Clark L. Rev. 597 (2006), 454

Perea, Juan F., Buscando America: Why Integration and Equal Protection Fail to Protect Latinos, 117 Harv. L. Rev. 1420 (2004), 457

Petterson, Stephen, Race, Gender, and Choice: An Empirical Study of the Lack of Interest Defense in Title VII Cases Challenging Job Segregation, 59 U. Chi. L. Rev. 1073 (1992), 165

Polsky, Gregg. D., The Contingent Attorney's Fee Tax Trap: Ethical, Fiduciary Duty, and Malpractice Implications, 23 Va. Tax Rev. 615 (2004), 718

Posner, Michael & Justine Nolan, Can Codes of Conduct Play a Role in Promoting Workers' Rights? International Labor Standards: Globalization, Trade, and Public Policy (Robert J. Flanagan & William B. Gould IV, eds., 2003), 760

Posner, Richard, An Economic Analysis of Sex Discrimination Laws, 56 U. Chi. L. Rev. 1311, 1312 (1989), 762

Post, Robert, Prejudicial Appearances: The Logic of American Antidiscrimination Law, 88 Cal. L. Rev. 1, 30-34 (2000), 352

Prescott, Natalie, Immigration Reform Fuels Employment Discrimination, 55 Drake L. Rev. 1 (2006), 452

Price, Joseph & Justin Wolfers, Racial Discrimination Among NBA Referees, http://ssrn.com, 7

Primus, Richard A., Equal Protection and Disparate Impact: Round Three, 117 Harv. L. Rev. 493 (2003), 201

Radford, Mary F., By Invitation Only: The Proof of Welcomeness in Sexual Harassment Cases, 72 N.C. L. Rev. 499 (1994), 384

Radford, Mary F., Sex Stereotyping and the Promotion of Women to Positions of Power, 41 Hastings L.J. 471 (1990), 8

Rahdert, Mark C., Arline's Ghost: Some Notes on Working as a Major Life Activity Under the ADA, 9 Temp. Pol. & Civ. Rts. L. Rev. 303 (2000), 530

Ramachandran, Gowri, Freedom of Dress: State and Private Regulation of Clothing, Hairstyle, Jewelry, Makeup, Tatooes, and Piercing, 66 Md. L. Rev. 11 (2006), 353

Ramachandran, Gowri, Intersectionality as "Catch 22": Why Identity Performance Demands Are Neither Harmless Nor Reasonable, 69 Alb. L. Rev. 299 (2005), 353

Reaves, Rhonda M., One of These Things Is Not Like the Other: Analogizing Ageism to Racism in Employment Discrimination Cases, 38 Rich. L. Rev. 839 (2004), 782

INDEX